Butterworths
Employment Law Guide

Butterworths Employment Law Guide

Second Edition

General editor
Christopher Osman, LLB
Solicitor; Partner and Head of the Employment Unit, Clifford Chance

Contributors
John McMullen, MA, PhD (Cantab), FIPD, FRSA
Solicitor; Partner and National Head of Employment Law, Pinsent Curtis
Professor of Labour Law, University of Leeds

Barry Mordsley, LLM (London), FIPD
Solicitor; Partner and Head of Employment Law, Harris Rosenblatt and Kramer
Formerly Principal Lecturer in Law, London Guildhall University
A Chairman of Industrial Tribunals (England and Wales)

Brian Napier
Advocate and Barrister of Middle Temple and Gray's Inn
Visiting Professor of Law, Centre for Commercial Law Studies,
Queen Mary and Westfield College

Ian Smith, MA, LLB (Cantab)
of Gray's Inn, Barrister
Chairman of Social Security Appeal Tribunals
Member of the ACAS Panel of Industrial Arbitrators

Butterworths
London, Edinburgh, Dublin
1996

United Kingdom	Butterworths, a Division of Reed Elsevier (UK) Ltd, Halsbury House, 35 Chancery Lane, LONDON WC2A 1EL and 4 Hill Street, EDINBURGH EH2 3JZ
Australia	Butterworths, SYDNEY, MELBOURNE, BRISBANE, ADELAIDE, PERTH, CANBERRA and HOBART
Canada	Butterworths Canada Ltd, TORONTO and VANCOUVER
Ireland	Butterworth (Ireland) Ltd, DUBLIN
Malaysia	Malayan Law Journal Sdn Bhd, KUALA LUMPUR
New Zealand	Butterworths of New Zealand Ltd, WELLINGTON and AUCKLAND
Singapore	Reed Elsevier (Singapore) Pte Ltd, SINGAPORE
South Africa	Butterworths Publishers (Pty) Ltd, DURBAN
USA	Michie, CHARLOTTESVILLE, Virginia

A CIP Catalogue record for this book is available from the British Library.

ISBN 0 406 01652 6

Typeset by Columns Design Ltd, Reading, UK
Printed by Clays Ltd, St Ives plc

Preface

The aim of the second edition of the *Employment Law Guide* remains unaltered from the first. This is to occupy the middle ground between those works which deal in great detail with relatively narrow aspects of employment law and those at the other end of the spectrum which, like *Harvey on Industrial Relations and Employment Law*, are intended to cover the whole topic and also include materials such as statutes, statutory instruments, codes of practice etc. The objective of the *Guide* remains the succinct coverage, in a readily accessible way, of individual employment rights and in this to serve also as a companion to *Harvey*.

The structure of the book remains unchanged, dealing with the contractual relationship between the employer and the employee first; second, the consequences of the termination of employment; third, the various statutory rights of an employee and finally discrimination. The *Guide* retains the appendices which contain reproductions of some of the more important forms which those engaged in employment work may require from time to time together with check lists and notes which may be of assistance in practice.

The statutory and case law developments over the four years since the first edition have been considerable, particularly in the areas of discrimination and the Transfer of Undertakings Regulations; but even the quieter contractual back waters have seen ripples on their surface as well. Keeping up with these developments during the preparation of the second edition (which was delayed several times, first whilst we awaited news of the proposed consolidation legislation and then to allow necessarily detailed references to the Employment Rights Act 1996 and the Industrial Tribunals Act 1996 to be incorporated) has not been particularly easy for those who have contributed to the book and merits particular thanks to them on this occasion as it does to our publishers, whose typical forbearance and patience has been tested to a greater extent than usual.

The forms in the appendices are Crown copyright and reproduced with the kind permission of the Controller of Her Majesty's Stationery Office.

The law is stated as at August 1996.

Christopher Osman

Contents

Table of statutes

References in this Table to *Statutes* are to Halsbury's Statutes of England (Fourth Edition) showing the volume and page at which the annotated text of the Act will be found.

Table of cases

B

C

PARA

PARA

Coates v Modern Methods and Materials Ltd [1983] QB 192, [1982] 3 All ER 946, [1982] 3 WLR 764, [1982] ICR 763, [1982] IRLR 318, 126 Sol Jo 577, CA . . . 19.214
Cofone v Spaghetti House Ltd [1980] ICR 155, EAT 5.10
Cold Drawn Tubes Ltd v Middleton [1992] ICR 318, [1992] IRLR 160, EAT 19.498
Cole v Fred Stacey Ltd [1974] IRLR 73, 9 ITR 11 . . . . 7.02, 16.06
Coleman v S and W Baldwin [1977] IRLR 342 . . . . 19.105
Coleman and Stephenson v Magnet Joinery Ltd [1975] ICR 46, [1974] IRLR 343, [1975] KILR 139, CA 19.499
Colley v Corkindale [1995] ICR 965, EAT 7.04, 7.13
Collier v Sunday Referee Publishing Co Ltd [1940] 2 KB 647, [1940] 4 All ER 234, 109 LJKB 974, 84 Sol Jo 538, 164 LT 10, 57 TLR 2 . . . . . . 1.38, 3.62, 4.60
Collin v Flexiform Ltd (1966) 1 KIR 109, 1 ITR 253 . . . . 20.93
Colwyn Borough Council v Dutton [1980] IRLR 420, EAT 13.61
Commercial Plastics Ltd v Vincent [1965] 1 QB 623, [1964] 3 All ER 546, [1964] 3 WLR 820, 108 Sol Jo 599, CA 4.34
Commission for Racial Equality v Amari Plastics Ltd [1982] QB 1194, [1982] 2 All ER 499, [1982] 2 WLR 972, [1982] ICR 304, [1982] IRLR 252, 126 Sol Jo 227, CA . 22.09
Commission for Racial Equality v Dutton [1989] QB 783, [1989] 1 All ER 306, [1989] 2 WLR 17, [1989] IRLR 8, 133 Sol Jo 19, [1989] 1 LS Gaz R 38, CA 24.49
Community Task Force v Rimmer [1986] ICR 491, [1986] IRLR 203, EAT 10.48
Company's Application, A, Re [1989] Ch 477, [1989] 2 All ER 248, [1989] 3 WLR 265, [1989] ICR 449, [1989] IRLR 477, [1989] BCLC 462, 133 Sol Jo 917 . . . . 4.12
Conlin v United Distillers [1994] IRLR 169, Ct of Sess 19.417, 19.418
Construction Industry Training Board v Labour Force Ltd [1970] 3 All ER 220, 114 Sol Jo 704 . . . . 1.18
Construction Industry Training Board v Leighton [1978] 2 All ER 723, [1978] IRLR 60, sub nom Leighton v Construction Industry Training Board [1978] ICR 577, EAT . . 5.08
Continental Tyre and Rubber (Great Britain) Co Ltd v Heath (1913) 29 TLR 308 . . . 4.27
Cook (James W) & Co (Wivenhoe) Ltd (in liquidation) v Tipper [1990] ICR 716, [1990] IRLR 386, CA 19.44
Cook v Thomas Linnell & Sons Ltd [1977] ICR 770, [1977] IRLR 132 . . . . 19.280, 19.437
Cooper v Firth Brown Ltd [1963] 2 All ER 31, [1963] 1 WLR 418, 107 Sol Jo 295 . . 3.45
Coopind (UK) Ltd v Buckland 403/89, unreported, EAT 20.59
Copson and Trahearn v Eversure Accessories Ltd [1974] ICR 636, [1974] IRLR 247, [1975] KILR 61, 9 ITR 406, NIRC 19.531, 19.550
Coral Leisure Group Ltd v Barnett [1981] ICR 503, [1981] IRLR 204, 125 Sol Jo 374, EAT 7.02, 19.13
Corby v Morrison [1980] ICR 564, [1980] IRLR 218 . . . . 7.02
Corkhill v North Sea Ferries (11 February 1994, unreported), CA 7.26
Cormack v TNT Sealion 1825/126, unreported 19.399
Cornelius v University College of Swansea [1987] IRLR 141, 131 Sol Jo 359, [1987] LS Gaz R 1141, CA 24.54
Corner v Buckinghamshire County Council (1978) 77 LGR 268, [1978] ICR 836, [1978] IRLR 320, 13 ITR 421, EAT 14.54
Cort (Robert) & Son Ltd v Charman [1981] ICR 816, [1981] IRLR 437, EAT . . 3.24, 3.30, 19.55
Coulson v City of London Polytechnic [1976] 3 All ER 234, [1976] 1 WLR 834, [1976] ICR 433, [1976] IRLR 212, [1976] ITR 121, 120 Sol Jo 471, EAT 7.07
Council of Civil Service Unions v Minister for the Civil Service [1985] AC 374, [1984] 3 All ER 935, [1984] 3 WLR 1174, [1985] ICR 14, 128 Sol Jo 837, [1985] LS Gaz R 437, sub nom R v Secretary of State for Foreign and Commonwealth Affairs, ex p Council of Civil Service Unions [1985] IRLR 28, HL 19.197
Council of Engineering Institutions v Maddison [1977] ICR 30, [1976] IRLR 389, 11 ITR 272, EAT 19.61, 19.605
Courage Take Home Trade Ltd v Keys [1986] ICR 874, [1986] IRLR 427, EAT . 19.59, 19.605
Courtaulds Northern Spinning Ltd v Moosa [1984] ICR 218, [1984] IRLR 43, EAT . . 19.537
Courtaulds Northern Spinning Ltd v Sibson [1988] ICR 451, [1988] IRLR 305, 132 Sol Jo 1033, CA 1.30, 1.33, 10.32, 19.106, 20.26
Courtaulds Northern Textiles Ltd v Andrew [1979] IRLR 84, EAT 19.108
Cowell v Quilter Goodison & Co Ltd and Q G Management Services Ltd [1989] IRLR 392, CA 8.11

D

E

PARA

F

G

H

I

J

PARA

L

PARA

M

PARA

Martin v Yeoman Aggregates Ltd [1983] ICR 314, [1983] IRLR 49, EAT 2.17, 19.84
Mason v Provident Clothing and Supply Co Ltd [1913] AC 724, 82 LJKB 1153, [1911–13] All ER Rep 400, 57 Sol Jo 739, 109 LT 449, 29 TLR 727, HL . . 4.33, 4.46, 4.47, 4.48
Mason v Wimpey Waste Management Ltd [1982] IRLR 454 . . . . . . 19.584
Massey v Crown Life Insurance Co [1978] 2 All ER 576, [1978] 1 WLR 676, [1978] ICR 590, [1978] IRLR 31, 13 ITR 5, 121 Sol Jo 791, CA 1.06
Mathewson v R B Wilson Dental Laboratory Ltd [1988] IRLR 512, EAT . . 19.329, 19.434
Mathieson v W J Noble [1972] IRLR 76 . . . . 19.371
Mathieson v United News Shops Ltd (25 January 1995, unreported), EAT 8.39
Matthews v Kuwait Bechtel Corpn [1959] 2 QB 57, [1959] 2 All ER 345, [1959] 2 WLR 702, 103 Sol Jo 393, CA 1.44
Mauldon v British Telecommunications plc [1987] ICR 450, EAT 19.25
Maund v Penwith District Council [1984] ICR 143, [1984] IRLR 24, 134 NLJ 147, CA . 19.149, 19.267
Mayne v AB Electronic Components Ltd 1/80, unreported, EAT 20.42
Meacham v Amalgamated Engineering and Electrical Union [1994] IRLR 218 . . . 3.72
Meade-Hill and National Union of Civil and Public Servants v British Council [1996] 1 All ER 79, [1995] ICR 847, [1995] IRLR 478, CA 20.24, 24.15
Meadows v Faithful Overalls Ltd [1977] IRLR 330, IT 11.17
Mears v Safecar Security Ltd [1983] QB 54, [1982] 2 All ER 865, [1982] 3 WLR 366, [1982] ICR 626, [1982] IRLR 183, 126 Sol Jo 496, [1982] LS Gaz R 921, CA . . 1.30, 1.40, 5.07, 9.01
Measures Bros Ltd v Measures [1910] 2 Ch 248, 79 LJ Ch 707, 18 Mans 40, 54 Sol Jo 521, 102 LT 794, 26 TLR 488, [1908–10] All ER Rep Ext 1188, CA. 4.60
Mediguard Services Ltd v Thame [1994] ICR 751, [1994] IRLR 504, EAT . . . 19.72A, 21.13, 23.09A
Meer v London Borough of Tower Hamlets [1988] IRLR 399, CA 24.16
Meikle v McPhail (Charleston Arms) [1983] IRLR 351 . . . . 8.70
Melon v Hector Powe Ltd [1981] 1 All ER 313, [1981] ICR 43, [1980] IRLR 477, 124 Sol Jo 827, HL 7.47, 8.14
Menzies v Smith and McLaurin [1980] IRLR 180, EAT 14.17, 14.18
Merckx and Patrick Neuhuys v Ford Motors Co Belgium SA: C-171, 172/94 [1996] All ER (EC) 667, [1996] IRLR 467, ECJ 8.27, 8.39, 8.49
Meridian Ltd v Gomersall [1977] ICR 597, [1977] IRLR 425, 12 ITR 323, EAT . . 19.499
Merseyside and North Wales Electricity Board v Taylor [1975] ICR 185, [1975] IRLR 60, 10 ITR 52, 119 Sol Jo 272 . . . . 19.301, 19.410
Merton London Borough Council v Gardiner [1981] QB 269, [1981] 2 WLR 232, 79 LGR 374, [1981] ICR 186, sub nom Gardiner v London Borough of Merton [1980] IRLR 472, 125 Sol Jo 97, CA 1.12, 7.61
Methilhill Bowling Club v Hunter [1995] ICR 793, [1995] IRLR 232, EAT . 19.72A, 23.09A
Metro Rod Services Ltd v Waugh (5 June 1991, unreported) 182/90, EAT 8.27
Meyer Dunmore International v Rogers [1978] IRLR 167, EAT 19.313
Michael (John) Design plc v Cooke [1987] 2 All ER 332, [1987] ICR 445, 131 Sol Jo 595, [1987] LS Gaz R 1492, CA 4.68
Micklefield v SAC Technology Ltd [1991] 1 All ER 275, [1990] 1 WLR 1002, [1990] IRLR 218, [1990] 28 LS Gaz R 43 . . . . 3.26
Midland Foot Comfort Centre Ltd v Richmond [1973] 2 All ER 294, [1973] IRLR 141, sub nom Midland Foot Comfort Centre Ltd v Moppett [1973] ICR 219, 117 Sol Jo 340, NIRC 20.21
Midland Plastics v Till [1983] ICR 118, [1983] IRLR 9, 126 Sol Jo 707, EAT . . 13.27, 19.210
Mikkelsen v Danmols Inventar A/S: 105/84 [1985] ECR 2639, [1986] 1 CMLR 316, ECJ: 8.11, 8.55
Miles v Wakefield Metropolitan District Council [1987] AC 539, [1987] 1 All ER 1089, [1987] 2 WLR 795, 85 LGR 649, [1987] ICR 368, [1987] IRLR 193, 131 Sol Jo 408, [1987] LS Gaz R 1239, [1987] NLJ Rep 266, HL 1.42, 3.20
Milestone School of English v Leakey [1982] IRLR 3, EAT 19.613
Millbrook Furnishing Industries Ltd v McIntosh [1981] IRLR 309, EAT 19.105
Miller v Hamworthy Engineering Ltd [1986] ICR 846, [1986] IRLR 461, [1986] LS Gaz R 1901, CA 1.41, 3.06, 20.69
Miller v Karlinski (1945) 62 TLR 85, CA 7.02
Miller v Nettle Accessories Ltd (1966) 1 ITR 328 . . . . 20.62

O

P

PARA

Post Office v Union of Post Office Workers and Crouch [1974] 1 All ER 229, [1974] 1 WLR 89, [1974] ICR 378, [1974] IRLR 22, 9 ITR 136, 118 Sol Jo 182, HL. . 13.31, 19.140
Potter v Hunt Contracts Ltd [1992] ICR 337, [1992] IRLR 108, EAT . 6.08
Powdrill v Watson [1995] 2 AC 394, [1995] 2 All ER 65, [1995] 2 WLR 312, [1995] ICR 1100, [1995] IRLR 269, [1995] 1 BCLC 386, [1995] 17 LS Gaz R 47, [1995] NLJR 449, HL 15.31, 15.32
Powell v Braun [1954] 1 All ER 484, [1954] 1 WLR 401, 98 Sol Jo 144, CA . . 1.27
Powell v Brent London Borough Council [1988] ICR 176, [1987] IRLR 466, CA . 3.67
Powell v Hubbard Group Services Ltd [1995] IRLR 195 . . . . . . 19.363
Power Packing Casemakers v Faust [1983] QB 471, [1983] 2 All ER 166, [1983] 2 WLR 439, [1983] ICR 292, 127 Sol Jo 187, sub nom Faust v Power Packing Casemakers [1983] IRLR 117, CA 11.15, 19.210
Powers v A Clarke & Co (Smethwick) Ltd [1981] IRLR 483 . . . . . 19.191
Presho v Insurance Officer [1984] AC 310, [1984] 1 All ER 97, [1984] 2 WLR 29, [1984] ICR 463, [1984] IRLR 74, 128 Sol Jo 18, HL 9.08, 19.219
Presley v Llanelli Borough Council [1979] ICR 419, [1979] IRLR 381, EAT . . 19.48
Prestcold Ltd v Irvine [1981] ICR 777, [1981] IRLR 281, CA 24.33
Prestwick Circuits Ltd v McAndrew. See McAndrew v Prestwick Circuits Ltd
Price v Civil Service Commission [1978] 1 All ER 1228, [1977] 1 WLR 1417, [1978] ICR 27, [1977] IRLR 291, 12 ITR 482, 121 Sol Jo 558, EAT 24.15, 24.18
Priddle v Dibble [1978] 1 All ER 1058, [1978] 1 WLR 895, [1978] ICR 149, 122 Sol Jo 486 . . . . 19.402
Pritchard-Rhodes Ltd v Boon and Milton [1979] IRLR 19, EAT 20.12, 20.14
Procter v British Gypsum Ltd [1992] IRLR 7, EAT 19.423, 19.456
Property Guards Ltd v Taylor and Kershaw [1982] IRLR 175, EAT . . . 19.196, 19.574
Provident Financial Group plc and Whitegates Estate Agency Ltd v Hayward [1989] 3 All ER 298, [1989] ICR 160, [1989] IRLR 84, CA 3. 56, 3.61, 4.53, 4.65
Pruden v Cunard Ellerman Ltd [1993] IRLR 317, EAT 19.40
Puglia v James & Sons [1996] ICR 301, [1996] IRLR 70, EAT. 19.531
Putsman v Taylor [1927] 1 KB 637, 96 LJKB 315, 136 LT 285, 43 TLR 153; affd [1927] 1 KB 741, 96 LJKB 726, [1927] All ER Rep 356, 137 LT 291, 43 TLR 392, CA . . 4.48

Q

Qualcast (Wolverhampton) Ltd v Ross [1979] ICR 386, [1979] IRLR 98, EAT . . . 19.504
Quinnen v Hovells [1984] ICR 525, [1984] IRLR 227, 128 Sol Jo 431, EAT . . . 1.19

R

R v BBC, ex p Lavelle [1983] 1 All ER 241, [1983] 1 WLR 23, [1983] ICR 99, [1982] IRLR 404, 126 Sol Jo 836 . . . . 3.84, 3.88
R v British Coal Corpn, ex p Vardy [1993] 1 CMLR 721, [1993] ICR 720, sub nom R v British Coal Corpn and Secretary of State for Trade and Industry, ex p Vardy [1993] IRLR 104 . . . . 20.102
R v British Coal Corpn and Secretary of State for Trade and Industry, ex p Price [1994] IRLR 72 . . . . 20.103
R v Chief Constable of the Thames Valley Police, ex p Cotton [1990] IRLR 344, CA . . 3.89
R v Civil Service Appeal Board, ex p Bruce [1988] 3 All ER 686, [1988] ICR 649; affd sub nom R v Civil Service Appeal Board, ex p Bruce (A-G intervening) [1989] 2 All ER 907, [1989] ICR 171, CA 1.17
R v Derbyshire County Council, ex p Noble [1990] ICR 808, [1990] IRLR 332, 4 BMLR 103, CA 3.87
R v East Berkshire Health Authority, ex p Walsh [1985] QB 152, [1984] 3 All ER 425, [1984] 3 WLR 818, [1984] ICR 743, [1984] IRLR 278, 128 Sol Jo 664, [1984] LS Gaz R 2223, CA 3.24, 3.85
R v Gwent County Council, ex p Bryant [1988] COD 19 . . . . 20.103
R v Liverpool City Corpn, ex p Ferguson and Ferguson [1985] IRLR 501 . . . . 3.89
R v London Borough of Hammersmith and Fulham, ex p NALGO [1991] IRLR 249, [1991] COD 397 . . . . 3.87

PARA

PARA

Reading v A-G [1951] AC 507, [1951] 1 All ER 617, 95 Sol Jo 155, [1951] 1 TLR 480, HL: 1.52, 4.03
Ready Case Ltd v Jackson [1981] IRLR 312, EAT 20.15
Ready Mixed Concrete (South East) Ltd v Minister of Pensions and National Insurance [1968] 2 QB 497, [1968] 1 All ER 433, [1968] 2 WLR 775, 112 Sol Jo 14 . . . 1.07
Red Bank Manufacturing Co Ltd v Meadows [1992] ICR 204, [1992] IRLR 209, EAT . 19.542
Redland Roof Tiles Ltd v Eveleigh [1979] IRLR 11, EAT 19.355
Redmond (Dr Sophie) Stichting v Bartol. C-29/91 [1992] ECR I-3189, [1992] IRLR 366, ECJ 8.05, 8.11, 8.15, 8.17, 8.19, 8.28, 20.34
Reed Packaging Ltd v Boozer [1988] ICR 391, [1988] IRLR 333, EAT . . . 23.19, 23.31
Regal (Hastings) Ltd v Gulliver (1942) [1967] 2 AC 134n, [1942] 1 All ER 378, HL . 4.03, 4.70
Reid v Rush & Tompkins Group plc [1989] 3 All ER 228, [1990] 1 WLR 212, [1990] RTR 144, [1989] 2 Lloyd's Rep 167, [1990] ICR 61, [1989] IRLR 265, CA. . . 1.47
Rencoule (H A) (Joiners and Shopfitters) Ltd v Hunt (1967) 2 ITR 475, 1967 SC 131, 1967 SLT 218 . . . . 7.47, 8.14
Renfrew District Council v Lornie (23 June 1995, unreported) 20.18
Rennie v Grampian Regional Council 475/90, unreported, EAT 19.367
Rentokil Ltd v Mackin [1989] IRLR 286, EAT 19.418
Retarded Children's Aid Society Ltd v Day [1978] 1 WLR 763, [1978] ICR 437, [1978] IRLR 128, 122 Sol Jo 385, CA 19.426, 19.458
Rewe-Zentralfinanz GmbH v Landwirtschaftskammer für Saarland: 33/76 [1976] ECR 1989, [1977] 1 CMLR 533, CMR 8382, ECJ 24.23
Richmond Precision Engineering Ltd v Pearce [1985] IRLR 179, EAT 19.386
Rickard v PB Glass Supplies Ltd [1990] ICR 150, CA 6.08
Ridge v Baldwin [1964] AC 40, [1963] 2 All ER 66, [1963] 2 WLR 935, 61 LGR 369, 127 JP 295, 107 Sol Jo 313, HL 3.85
Ridgway v Hungerford Market Co (1835) 3 Ad & El 171, 4 LJKB 157, 1 Har & W 244, 4 Nev & MKB 797 . . . . 17.01
Rigby v Ferodo Ltd [1988] ICR 29, [1987] IRLR 516, HL . 1.43, 3.09, 3.11, 3.24, 5.05, 19.383
Riley (Lifting Equipment) Ltd v Shorrock (1989) IRLIB 21 . . . . . . 3.36
Riley v Tesco Stores Ltd [1980] ICR 323, [1980] IRLR 103, CA 19.45
Rinner-Kühn v FWW Spezial-Gebäudereinigung GmbH & Co KG: 171/88 [1989] ECR 2743, [1993] 2 CMLR 932, [1989] IRLR 493, ECJ 21.06, 21.14, 23.18
Riordan v War Office [1959] 3 All ER 552, [1959] 1 WLR 1046, 103 Sol Jo 921; affd [1960] 3 All ER 774n, [1961] 1 WLR 210, CA. 18.12
Roach v CSB (Moulds) Ltd [1991] ICR 349, [1991] IRLR 200, EAT 7.08
Roadchef Ltd v Hastings [1988] IRLR 142, EAT 19.536
Robb v Green [1895] 2 QB 315, 59 JP 695, 64 LJQB 593, 14 R 580, 44 WR 25, [1895–9] All ER Rep 1053, 39 Sol Jo 653, 73 LT 15, 11 TLR 517, CA 1.52, 4.16
Robb v Hammersmith and Fulham London Borough Council [1991] ICR 514, [1991] IRLR 72 . . . . 3.73
Robb v Leon Motor Services Ltd [1978] ICR 506, [1978] IRLR 26, EAT 13.36, 19.141
Roberts v Essoldo Circuit (Control) Ltd (1967) 2 ITR 351 . . . . . . 20.62
Roberts v Northwest Fixings [1993] FSR 281, CA 4.23
Robertson (Charles) (Developments) Ltd v White [1995] ICR 349, EAT 19.528
Robertson v British Gas Corpn [1983] ICR 351, [1983] IRLR 302, CA 1.25, 5.05
Robinson v British Island Airways Ltd [1978] ICR 304, [1977] IRLR 477, 13 ITR 111, EAT 20.37
Robinson v Crompton Parkinson Ltd [1978] ICR 401, [1978] IRLR 61, EAT . . . 19.109
Robinson v Harman (1848) 18 LJ Ex 202, 1 Exch 850, [1843–60] All ER Rep 383, 13 LTOS 141 . . . . 3.04
Robinson v Ulster Carpet Mills Ltd [1991] IRLR 348, NICA 19.480
Rockall Ltd v Murray (1 March 1988, unreported), CA 4.68
Rockfon A/S v Specialarbejderforbundet i Danmark: C-449/93 [1995] ECR I-4291, [1996] IRLR 168, ECJ 20.113
Rogers v Bodfari (Transport) Ltd [1973] ICR 325, [1973] IRLR 172, 14 KIR 532, NIRC . 19.40
Rogers v Chloride Systems Ltd [1992] ICR 198, EAT 19.217
Rolls Royce Ltd v Walpole [1980] IRLR 343 . . . . 19.416
Rose v Plenty [1976] 1 All ER 97, [1976] 1 WLR 141, [1976] 1 Lloyd's Rep 263, [1975] ICR 430, [1976] IRLR 60, 119 Sol Jo 592, CA. 1.49
Rose v Shelley & Partners (1966) 1 ITR 169 . . . . 20.62

S

PARA

T

U

V

Decisions of the European Court of Justice are listed below numerically. These decisions are also included in the preceeding alphabetical list.

PARA

PART I
THE RELATIONSHIP AND CONTRACT OF EMPLOYMENT

1 The creation of the contract of employment

Ian Smith

1 THE RELATIONSHIP OF EMPLOYER AND EMPLOYEE

The background

1.01 Since the late nineteenth century, the corner-stone of the law relating to employment has been the contract of employment. This is so in relation not only to longstanding common law rights and obligations but also in relation to the modern statutory rights which can normally only be exercised by an 'employee'. Thus, a person whose employment has been terminated may be able to claim unfair dismissal or a redundancy payment, and a pregnant employee may be able to insist on returning to her employment after childbirth. The legislation gives such rights to employees, and then defines an employee quite simply as someone 'under a contract of employment' (which is not then further defined).

1.02 The corollary of this is that if a person is not an employee, but is instead self-employed (usually referred to in law by the more archaic term 'an independent contractor'), he or she will not have the protection of modern employment law.[1] This is traded away in the decision to be self employed. For example, if such a person's engagement is terminated that is *not* a 'dismissal' and so there can be no claim for unfair dismissal.

[1] Except where a wider definition is specifically adopted (eg in the discrimination legislation), where *some* independent contractors may be included; see para 1.19, below.

1.03 There are of course other legal differences between an employee and an independent contractor. The obvious example is in the area of taxation, where the self-employed person enjoys the advantages of Schedule D taxation (with its payment in arrears, higher deductions and, it must be said, the possibility of under declaration of earnings), whereas the employee is subject to the stricter regime of Schedule E, and also has the tax deducted at source under PAYE. A similar distinction can be seen in liability for National Insurance Contributions (with the added complication that if the employer takes on a person as an employee, the employer too is liable for NI contributions). In addition, there are disadvantages in being self-employed—there is no entitlement to unemployment benefit for workless periods, the statutory sick pay and statutory maternity pay schemes do not apply and if the self-employed person is injured at work he is not eligible for disablement benefit in respect of any lasting injury. Basically, therefore, the self-employed person may enjoy financial advantages while the going is good, but if he is 'fired' or falls off a ladder he may discover the longer term disadvantages.

1.04 The other principal legal significance of the employment/self-employment divide is of course the law of tort. Except in the restricted category of certain non-delegable duties, an employer is *not* liable for the torts of an independent contractor, whereas he is vicariously liable for the torts of his employee (provided that the latter was acting in the course of his employment). This could of course be highly material to a third party (eg a member of the public passing by a building site and being injured), or even to another employee injured while at work—if the person to blame for the injury was an employee (or, in the latter case, a fellow employee) then the employer can be sued; if, however, the injury was caused by an independent contractor working in the pursuance of his calling on the employer's premises, the injured person must look primarily to that independent contractor for damages (and pray that he was insured).

1.05 The divide between employment and self-employment is thus of major importance in several areas of law, not just employment law itself. We must now turn to the question as to how that divide is defined.

Tests for a contract of employment

1.06 In the last century, the test for whether a person was or was not an employee was the 'control' test, ie whether the putative employer had the right to control not just what the person was to do, but also the way in which he was to do it; if so, that person was an employee. While control may still be a factor, it is not enough now, given the increased sophistication of many forms of employment (eg could a hospital authority be said to 'control' one of its surgeons in this manner?). Other tests have had to be devised. This has the advantage of flexibility, but the disadvantage of not having one single, sufficient test. In a case of doubt, a court or tribunal may take one of the following approaches:[1]

—The 'organisational' test: was the person an integral part of the employer's organisation?

—The 'economic reality' test: who bears the risk of loss and the chance of profit? If it is the person in question, then he is probably an independent contractor. Another way of posing much the same question is to ask whether the facts show that the person was really in business on his own account. Working for several 'employers' could be important evidence here.

—The 'multiple' test: looking at *all* the relevant factors, do the scales come down in favour of employment or self-employment? This is now the most widely used test,[2] and may involve consideration of the following factors:

(i) method of payment (invoice and lump sum normally indicating an independent contractor);[3]
(ii) method of selection and termination of the relationship;
(iii) organisation of the work—the extent to which the person may choose his hours and methods of working; whether he can delegate;
(iv) provision of tools and equipment (though there can still be labour-only subcontracting);
(v) whether PAYE and NI contributions are deducted;[4]
(vi) how the parties themselves see their relationship (though this must be treated with caution—it may be evidence, but by itself certainly is *not*

sufficient if the other factors point to the opposite conclusion; you cannot simply call it self-employment and expect to get away with it).

—'Mutuality of obligations': in some cases (especially of less typical employment, eg homeworking) it may be relevant to consider the extent to which the parties expect to be called upon to work and to provide/pay for work. A loose arrangement whereby work is provided and done on a fairly ad hoc basis may point towards self-employment; if, however, there is a genuine expectation of work being provided fairly consistently, that may induce a court or tribunal to find an employment relationship.

—The 'global contract' notion: in certain cases of sporadic 'employment' over a period of time,[5] there may be two problems for the person in question—

(a) it may be viewed simply as self-employment (as above), *or*

(b) even if an employment relationship is found, the court or tribunal may find that there were in fact *separate* employment contracts covering each job. This latter can be as disadvantageous for the person as the former, since his problem then becomes that he does not have continuity of employment (vital for most statutory rights)[6] *unless* he can further show that on the facts these individual jobs were covered by one, overall 'global' or 'umbrella' contract. This may be difficult to show, but if it can be it will be of immense importance in allowing the person to establish employed status *and* to qualify for statutory rights.

---

1 *Harvey* Div A. For the extensive case law and further discussion, see Smith & Wood, *Industrial Law* (6th edn, 1996) ch 1.

2 For its application by the tax authorities, see the leaflet 'Tax: Employed or Self-Employed', IR 56 (August 1989).

3 Terms and conditions other than pay could also be important; an independent contractor would not normally expect holiday or sick pay, or to be included in a firm's pension scheme.

4 This is only a factor, and is not conclusive. Even if the Inland Revenue have accepted the person as self-employed, they may still change their mind later and reassess retrospectively under Schedule E (on the basis that they cannot be estopped in the exercise of their duty), for example if a tribunal in an unfair dismissal case finds that the person was in fact an employee all along. This could be particularly important in a case where the person has been happy to be self-employed until he is dismissed and then wants to claim that he was in fact an employee all along, in order to claim unfair dismissal (see *Massey v Crown Life Assurance Co* [1978] ICR 590, [1978] IRLR 31, CA; *Young & Woods Ltd v West* [1980] IRLR 201, CA). Even if successful, the 'employee' may find that his unfair dismissal compensation is exceeded by his reassessed tax liability.

5 See particularly the long series of individual voyage contracts on trawlers in *McLeod v Hellyer Bros Ltd* [1987] ICR 526, [1987] IRLR 232, CA.

6 Continuity of employment is considered in Chapter 7, below.

1.07 At the end of the day, some cases will involve a very fine balance between these factors. In one case,[1] the judge posed three questions:

(1) Did the worker undertake to provide his own work and skill in return for remuneration?

(2) Was there a sufficient degree of control to enable the worker fairly to be called an employee?

(3) Were there any other factors inconsistent with the existence of a contract of employment?

---

1 *Ready Mixed Concrete (South East) Ltd v Minister of Pensions and National Insurance* [1968] 2 QB 497, [1968] 1 All ER 433; the case is a good example of the problems that can arise when the relevant factors are equally balanced.

1.08 However, another judge was driven to this conclusion:

> 'One perhaps cannot get much beyond this, "was the contract a contract of employment within the meaning which an ordinary person would give under the words?"'[1]

[1] *Cassidy v Ministry of Health* [1951] 2 KB 343, [1951] 1 All ER 574, CA, per Somervell LJ. This is a legal version of the elephant phenomenon — you know one when you see one, but try to define it!

1.09 This may be analytically unsatisfactory, but at least in tribunal proceedings where such a question arises there are two lay members who may be expected to apply their industrial experience to its resolution. Finally, it should be noted in this context that in such tribunal proceedings the application of the above tests is ultimately a question of fact, which means that the tribunal's decision will be paramount, and difficult to challenge on appeal.[1]

[1] *O'Kelly v Trusthouse Forte plc* [1983] ICR 728, [1983] IRLR 369, CA; *Nethermere (St Neots) Ltd v Taverna* [1984] ICR 612, [1984] IRLR 240, CA. Doubt appeared to be cast on this by a dictum of Lord Templeman in *Davies v Presbyterian Church of Wales* [1986] ICR 280, [1986] IRLR 194, HL, but subsequently the Court of Appeal in *McLeod v Hellyer Bros*, above and *Clifford v Union of Democratic Mineworkers* [1991] IRLR 518, CA and the Privy Council in *Lee v Chung* [1990] ICR 409, [1990] IRLR 236 'explained' the dictum and re-established orthodoxy.

Treatment of atypical employments

1.10 Not so many years ago, employment legislation could be drafted by bearing in mind 'typical' employment, where the employee would normally be male, work 9 am to 5 pm, five days per week on manual work and be paid on an hourly rate plus overtime. However, with the decline of heavy industry and manufacturing and the rise of service and high-tech industries, such assumptions may now be less valid. Many of the jobs created recently have not conformed to the old stereotype and 'flexibility' is a modern axiom of personnel management. The definition of 'employment' has had to keep pace with these changes; up to a point, it has been successful in doing so. The fact that a person is part-time, casual, seasonal or some form of homeworker or outworker will not mean that he or she cannot be accorded the employment status so vital if they are to benefit from the employment protection legislation. Equally, however, it must be accepted that that status must still be established on the facts,[1] and the more casual, etc, the relationship is, the more difficult it may be to establish it, even with the aid of more modern devices such as 'mutuality of obligations' (see the preceding paragraphs).

[1] Compare the facts and decisions in *Nethermere (St Neots) Ltd v Taverna* [1984] ICR 612, [1984] IRLR 240, CA and *O'Kelly v Trusthouse Forte plc* [1983] ICR 728, [1983] IRLR 369, CA.

1.11 Overall, therefore, the time may be coming when it is not appropriate to talk of 'atypical employments' given the far more diverse and flexible nature of the workforce. However, it must be remembered that in some such employments the establishment of employed status may be only the first hurdle. Even if it is surmounted there is still the second hurdle that in order to claim most statutory rights the employee must serve a qualifying period (eg two years for unfair dismissal) of continuous employment.[1] This can materially prejudice the rights of temporary, seasonal or casual workers. It is this factor (as much as the need to demonstrate employed status) that leads to the argument that we are seeing a transition to a two-tier workforce, of those in more traditional employment who can claim statutory rights and those in newer, non-traditional employment who may remain permanently unprotected.

[1] Continuity of employment is considered in Chapter 7, below.

1.12 One class of atypical employee that merits special mention is company directors. An ordinary director, remunerated only by fees, is not an employee of the company. However, an executive director with a service contract may qualify as an employee.[1] There are two principal effects of this. The first is that such a director may be able to claim unfair dismissal if the company dispenses with his services. The second is that, when doing a head-count in order to decide whether a company qualifies as a 'small firm' under a particular piece of legislation, such a director must be counted in, along with other (more usual) employees.

[1] *Parsons v Albert J Parsons & Sons Ltd* [1979] ICR 271, [1979] IRLR 117, CA; *Eaton v Robert Eaton Ltd* [1988] ICR 302, [1988] IRLR 83, EAT.

Associated employers

1.13 It is important that modern employment rights should not be prejudiced by the structure (particularly the corporate structure) of the employing concern; that structure could be of some complexity (usually for financial reasons with little or nothing to do with employment law), and a strict approach to the nature of the employer (especially when allied to the doctrine of corporate personality) could be highly disadvantageous to an employee. To take an example, an employee working within a group of companies could swap from Company A to Company B (eg by way of promotion); to him that might be a technical matter only, but prima facie his continuity of employment would be broken, so that if he was dismissed by Company B within two years he would not be able to claim unfair dismissal or a redundancy payment, no matter how long he had worked for Company A, or indeed for the group as a whole. Such a result is avoided by the concept of 'associated employers'. These are defined as follows:

> '... any two employers are to be treated as associated if (a) one is a company of which the other (directly or indirectly) has control, or (b) if both are companies of which a third person (directly or indirectly) has control ...'.[1]

[1] ERA, s 224; associated employers are considered in *Harvey* Div C.

1.14 The most important application of this concept is in the area of continuity of employment. Thus, if in the above example Company A and Company B are in common control (either by a natural person or by another company), then merely by moving between them (or any other company under similar control) the employee does *not* break his continuity of employment.[1] If he is dismissed by Company B after one year but had served Company A for nine years, he will be able to claim unfair dismissal, and a redundancy payment (if payable) will be calculated on ten years' employment. References to associated employers are found elsewhere in employment law (eg in the law on maternity leave, and in relation to small firms, where in counting the number of employees, one must count in any employed by an associated employer so that a larger firm cannot be artificially subdivided into a number of 'small firms' in order to avoid certain employment rights).

1 ERA, s 218(6).

1.15 In one way, the above definition is limited, in that only companies or natural persons can be associated employers; partnerships (which in English law lack legal personality) are not covered and neither, more significantly, are public sector bodies such as local government bodies or health authorities. The Court of Appeal have held that the definition is exhaustive, so that *only* those bodies covered by the definition can in law be associated.[1] In the field of local government, this position has been mitigated (at least in relation to the redundancy rights of a person who has moved between different local government bodies in the course of a career) by specific regulations,[2] but outside these there may still be difficulties, especially with continuity of employment.

1 *Gardiner v London Borough of Merton* [1981] ICR 186, [1980] IRLR 472, CA.

2 Redundancy Payments (Local Government) (Modification) Order 1983, SI 1983/1160, *Harvey* Div R; for the position of employees (particularly teachers) moving between schools run by the same LEA, see the ERA, s 218(7).

1.16 The crucial factor in the definition is 'control'. This will normally mean voting control of the company in question. De facto control is unlikely to be enough[1] neither is a 50% shareholding since that only gives 'negative control', in the sense of being able to veto someone else's proposals.[2] In one case the EAT held that control can mean control by a *group* of people, provided that they in fact act as one.[3] That was doubted obiter by the Court of Appeal,[4] though the EAT subsequently declined to follow those remarks and applied the earlier case[5] (on the basis that it had been relied on frequently in the past). If this doctrine of group control were to continue to apply, one limitation would be that the control must be exercised by the same group of people in the case of each employer claimed to be associated (ie you could not have A, B and C exercising control over Company X and A, B and D exercising control over Company Y).[6] However, in their latest pronouncement[7] (at the date of writing) the EAT have expressed approval of the Court of Appeal's doubts and although their remarks are again obiter, it is now likely that the whole idea of group control will soon be officially disapproved.

1 *Secretary of State for Employment v Newbold* [1981] IRLR 305, EAT.

2 *Hair Colour Consultants Ltd v Mena* [1984] ICR 671, [1984] IRLR 386, EAT; *South West Launderettes Ltd v Laidler* [1986] ICR 455, [1986] IRLR 305, CA; cf, however, where there is evidence of nominee shareholding: *Payne v Secretary of State for Employment* [1989] IRLR 352, CA.

3 *Zarb and Samuels v British and Brazilian Produce Co (Sales) Ltd* [1978] IRLR 78, EAT.

4 *South West Launderettes v Laidler*, above, per Mustill LJ.

5 *Harford v Swiftrim Ltd* [1987] ICR 439, [1987] IRLR 360, EAT.
6 *Poparm Ltd v Weekes* [1984] IRLR 388.
7 *Strudwick v Iszatt Bros Ltd* (or IBL) [1988] ICR 796, [1988] IRLR 457, EAT.

2 OTHER FORMS OF ENGAGEMENT

1.17 So far, the divide has been viewed as being between employment and self-employment. It is true that this is the most important distinction, but at the same time there are certain other forms of engagement that could be an alternative to employment. Partners, agents and non-executive directors do not normally qualify as employees. In addition, the following categories are worth a mention:

(i) Office holders. This concept is of more immediate significance in tax law than in employment law where it has little importance as such—an office holder may or may not be an employee, depending on the circumstances. However, if he is an employee, it is possible that his office-holding status may give him certain legal advantages if he is dismissed and wishes to challenge the dismissal as contrary to natural justice.

(ii) Apprentices. Apprenticeship is now much more unusual than previously. Where it exists, it is a separate relationship, apart from employment. However, statutory definitions frequently include it under the general heading of employment for statutory purposes.[1]

(iii) Crown servants. Technically, a Crown servant is employed at the Crown's pleasure and may be dismissed at will (though in practice most have considerable job security). At one point, it was thought that a Crown servant had no contract with the Crown at all, and later it was thought that there is such a contract (though not of employment); in more recent cases, the view has been taken that, in modern circumstances, there is nothing to *prevent* the Crown from entering into contracts of employment (if that is the intent of the parties), and there have been instances where the decision has been that such a relationship has indeed been created.[2] The theoretical position (whatever it may be) is however materially supplemented by the ERA, s 184 which specifically applies most of the employment protection provisions of the legislation to Crown servants,[3] thus rendering the common law position to a large extent irrelevant.

(iv) YTS and ET trainees. Such trainees are not under contracts of employment. Instead, training contracts have to contain terms giving a measure of protection akin to normal employment rights. In addition, the protection of the Health and Safety at Work etc Act 1974 and the sex and race discrimination legislation has been specifically extended to them by orders.

1 ERA, s 230(2): '"contract of employment" means a contract of service or apprenticeship . . .'.
2 *R v Civil Service Appeal Board, ex p Bruce* [1988] 3 All ER 686, [1988] ICR 649, Div Ct; *MaClaren v Home Office* [1990] ICR 824, [1990] IRLR 338, CA; *R v Lord Chancellor's Department, ex p Nangle* [1991] ICR 743, [1991] IRLR 343, Div Ct.
3 Crown servants are also expressly covered by the discrimination legislation and covered by the TULR(C)A 1992 definition of 'worker' (below).

1.18 In addition to these categories, there occur every so often cases where the person in question falls into no recognised category, where in fact he or she is in limbo. In such a case, all that one may be able to say is that, whatever the person may be, he or she is not an employee—ie that decision may if necessary have to be taken (to dispose of the case) even though it is difficult to see what he or she *is*.[1]

[1] See, eg, *Wiltshire Police Authority v Wynn* [1981] QB 95, [1980] ICR 649, CA (police cadet); *Construction Industry Training Board v Labour Force Ltd* [1970] 3 All ER 220 (A contracting with B to work for C); *Wadi v Cornwall and Isles of Scilly Family Practitioner Committee* [1985] ICR 492, EAT (doctor and local committee); *Ironmonger v Movefield Ltd* [1988] IRLR 461, EAT ('contract appointment' through an agency). Ministers of religion are not employees *(Davies v Presbyterian Church of Wales* [1986] ICR 280, [1986] IRLR 194, HL), though they could be considered to be office holders. Parliamentary staff are in an uncertain theoretical position, but are covered specifically by the ERA, ss 194 and 195 and the TULR(C)A 1992, ss 277, 278.

1.19 So far, these 'other forms of engagement' have been such that they do not usually fall within employment. However, it should be noticed that sometimes a statutory definition may have the opposite effect of *extending* the scope of the employment relationship. Normally, 'employee' is defined as a person under a contract of employment (or apprenticeship). However, two extensions can be seen:

(1) Some statutes use the term 'worker' (especially in relation to collective trade union law), and this may be wider than 'employee'. Under the TULR(C)A 1992, s 296, 'worker' includes not only someone under a contract of employment, but also someone under 'any other contract . . . whereby he undertakes to do or perform personally any work or services for another party to the contract who is not a professional client of his'.[1] This is wide enough to cover certain independent contractors who perform work personally.

(2) The discrimination legislation (the Sex Discrimination Act 1975, the Race Relations Act 1976 and the Equal Pay Act 1970) uses the concepts of 'employment' and 'employee', *but* defines them more widely (in a way akin to 'worker' above)—'"employment" means employment under a contract of service or apprenticeship, or a contract personally to execute any work or labour . . .'. Again, this is capable of including certain independent contractors.[2]

[1] There is a similar definition in the ERA, s 230(2).

[2] *Quinnen v Hovells* [1984] ICR 525, [1984] IRLR 227, EAT; *Tanna v Post Office* [1981] ICR 374, EAT; *Mirror Group Newspapers Ltd v Gunning* [1986] ICR 145, [1986] IRLR 27, CA.

3 CONSTRUCTING A CONTRACT OF EMPLOYMENT

Express terms

1.20 What goes into a contract of employment is largely a matter between the parties; in any later dispute, a court's only function is to interpret and apply what was agreed—it has no wider supervisory jurisdiction based on ideas of fairness or equity.[1] Thus, it is essential that both sides ensure that the contract says what it means and means what it says. There is no legal obligation of writing for a contract of employment, which may therefore come into being quite informally;[2] indeed, until the last quarter of a century such informal, 'factory gate' employments were common. Now, however, with the increased formalism of the employment relationship due to the enactment of employment protection laws (especially unfair dismissal) there is more inclination to have written contracts with express terms governing the relationship. Some matters may validly be *added* by implied terms[3] if necessary, but it must be recognised that express terms may be a double-edged sword—they are highly desirable *provided* they are properly thought out and accurate; if they are inaccurate, it will be difficult for a party to convince a court not to apply them, since normally oral evidence cannot override a written term. That apart, however, the advantages in modern employment law of clear express terms normally outweigh any disadvantages (of loss of 'flexibility'); this is particularly so, given that the implication of terms can be an unreliable matter. A good cautionary tale is provided by the case of *Stubbes v Trower, Still & Keeling*[4] where solicitors offered articles to a mature applicant who (having failed the Bar finals) was enrolled for the solicitors' finals; when the articles came to be taken up, the solicitors found that the applicant had failed the finals comprehensively and declared his intention not to resit them. In the light of this, the solicitors refused to accept him as an articled clerk and he sued them for breach of contract. The whole problem arose because the solicitors had not *expressly* made it a condition of the contract that he should have passed the finals. Naturally, they relied on an implied term to that effect; this succeeded at first instance, but the Court of Appeal allowed the appeal—there was no such implied term (as it was not necessary in order to make sense of the contract), the solicitors could easily have made the condition express but had failed to do so, and the court would not repair the damage done by that omission. The applicant was awarded damages of £14,351, plus interest. Caveat contractor!

1 Unless the courts develop further the idea of overriding implied terms, placing certain restrictions on the employer's ability to exercise his contractual rights; see para 1.33, below.

2 One sometimes hears such phrases as 'I have been working for him for a year but still do not have a contract'; legally, this is nonsense—a contract began at the latest once the work was commenced, but all that is meant is that it remains an implied contract.

3 See, eg, *Tayside Regional Council v McIntosh* [1982] IRLR 272, EAT where both in the job advert and at the interview a clean driving licence was stated to be essential, but this was not actually incorporated into the written terms of employment; *held* it was still a term of the contract.

4 [1987] IRLR 321, CA.

1.21 Many of the problems that arise in relation to contracts (of any sort, but particularly employment contracts) are attributable to insufficient attention to detail or forethought. A lawyer can advise on the form and drafting of contractual terms, but ultimately it is for the parties to ensure that those terms reflect their actual agreement and the way that the employment is to work in practice. To take a couple of examples, a term relating to holidays should be clear as to the method for fixing them, the computation of holiday pay and what is to happen if the employee leaves part way through the holiday year; a sick pay term should be clear as to the relationship between contractual sick pay and SSP; if the contract refers to and incorporates any provisions of a collective agreement, it should be unambiguous as to which agreement is meant (especially if there are both national and local agreements) and how changes in the agreement are to be dealt with. Moreover (and particularly from the employer's point of view), a little advance thought when drafting a contract can avoid or minimise future conflict; for example, (a) questions of continued confidentiality after the employee leaves the employment could be covered by a restraint of trade clause[1] (usually preferable to reliance on the vague implied duty of confidence), and (b) an express term empowering the employer to require the employee to undergo a medical examination could be of great practical importance if the employee is later off work ill for such a period of time that (depending on the prognosis obtainable from such an examination) the employer may have to consider a dismissal for incapability. From the above brief discussion and examples it can be seen that the traditional approach of many contracting parties (especially employers) that the less said the better, and that it is preferable to avoid a formal contract if possible, has little to commend it under modern employment law.

[1] Restraint of trade clauses are considered in Chapter 4, below.

1.22 Even if an employer does not wish to go as far as a formal written contract, it must still be remembered that he is under a statutory duty to give a written statement of the major terms of employment to each new employee within two months of taking him on.[1] This is considered below,[2] as are the potential pitfalls of ignoring this obligation. Its existence reinforces the point that a little advance thought and an intelligent approach to the drafting of express terms can be of considerable use later. One point to notice in relation to such written statement is that if the parties sign such a statement as more than just receiving it, ie they sign it as the contract, that may in law transform it into a formal written contract[3] in which case it is especially important that the terms are accurately drafted.

[1] ERA, s 1.
[2] Chapter 5(1).
[3] *Gascol Conversions Ltd v Mercer* [1974] ICR 420, [1974] IRLR 155, CA.

Incorporation of terms

1.23 Terms may be incorporated into a contract of employment from some other source. The most obvious is an applicable collective bargain. This might be done expressly, with the contract referring to the bargain on some particular point or points (eg 'Holidays—these shall be laid down in . . .'). This has the advantage of certainty, *provided* that it is made clear *which* bargain is the relevant one (and, possibly, what is to happen if there are any changes to it); any ambiguity here would be highly undesirable, giving rise to a dispute as to which bargain was actually incorporated.[1] There could, for example, be a dispute as to whether the contract was referring to a national or a local bargain; even in these times of the declining importance of national bargaining, there could be more than one possibly applicable local agreement, or more than one set of terms within one agreement. Express incorporation must therefore be carried out with care.

[1] See, for example, the problems arising in this context in *Gascol Conversions Ltd v Mercer* [1974] ICR 420, [1974] IRLR 155, CA.

1.24 Alternatively, a term may be incorporated from a collective agreement *impliedly*, possibly by reliance on custom and practice as evidence. Three points are to be noticed which show that such an exercise must be treated delicately. The first is that of course an implied term cannot replace an express term; thus, one cannot incorporate what appears to be a 'better' term if the matter is already covered by an express term.[1] The second is that the incorporation of one term from a collective bargain is not in itself evidence that other terms are to be incorporated too; each term claimed for incorporation must be considered on its own merits in all the circumstances of the case.[2] The third is that not all terms of a collective bargain are *appropriate* for incorporation into a contract of employment. A collective bargain may serve two distinct functions: (a) the setting of basic terms and conditions of employment for individuals, and (b) the 'industrial peace treaty' function of laying down procedures governing the collective relations between the union and the employer. Matters falling within the latter category (such as disputes procedures, recognition, redundancy consultation, pension funds) may well be thought by a tribunal or court to be inappropriate for incorporation into an individual employee's contract.[3]

---

[1] There is, however, a difficult borderline here, for a term may be implied if it merely expands upon or interprets an express term.

[2] *Alexander v Standard Telephones and Cables Ltd (No 2)* [1991] IRLR 286.

[3] For example, see *National Coal Board v National Union of Mineworkers* [1986] ICR 736, [1986] IRLR 439 and *Alexander v Standard Telephones and Cables Ltd (No 2)*, above.

1.25 If a term is incorporated into a contract of employment from a collective bargain (either expressly or impliedly), it becomes legally enforceable at the suit of the individual employee. This is significant because as a mere clause in the bargain it is *not* legally enforceable.[1] This could be most material in a case where the employer decided to withdraw unilaterally from a collective bargain (eg as part of a strategy of derecognition). The collective bargain itself being unenforceable, the union itself would have no legal redress. However, *if* a particular term has been incorporated into contracts of employment, that term continues to have independent contractual effect (even after the demise of the bargain itself) unless and until varied with the employees' consent. Thus, one tactic for the union might be to back a common law action by an individual employee to enforce continued respect for at least that term (and any others that have been incorporated) on the part of the employer.[2] Thus, while the legal unenforceability of collective bargains would suggest that an employer may at any time rip up such a bargain (if that appears to him to be feasible in the prevailing economic conditions), such a view may be simplistic, for the employer must also take into account the extent to which terms of the bargain may have contractual effect in individuals' contracts of employment; such terms do *not* lapse with the bargain.

---

[1] TULR(C)A 1992, s 236.

[2] *Robertson v British Gas Corpn* [1983] ICR 351, [1983] IRLR 302, CA; *National Coal Board v National Union of Mineworkers*, para 1.24, above.

1.26 One other source of incorporated terms in modern conditions is a company handbook. These have become relatively common[1] and may serve a useful function in fleshing out the bare bones of the employment relationship in a practical and readable way, available to each new employee on joining the company. Express incorporation can work well (eg 'Disciplinary procedures—these are set out in Part 4 of the Company Handbook') but care may be needed with implied incorporation. The point is that a company handbook can be quite a substantial document containing some matters which are quite arguably intended to be contractual terms (even if not expressly incorporated), but also many matters which are more in the nature of what used to be called 'works rules', ie procedures and requirements for the smooth running of the business which remain within the managerial prerogative and discretion; matters within the latter category are not appropriate for incorporation and, moreover, being non-contractual may be subject to unilateral alteration by the employer.[2]

[1] ACAS Advisory Handbook No 9, 'The Company Handbook'.

[2] A particularly good recent example is *Dryden v Greater Glasgow Health Board* [1992] IRLR 469, EAT where it was held that there was no contractual term allowing smoking at work, so that the introduction of a 'no smoking' policy was effectively a matter within the employer's prerogative.

Implied terms

1.27 In the days before at least a written statement of terms and conditions of employment became a statutory requirement and so relatively common, most contracts of employment had few written terms, and so the implication of terms was of particular importance, more so probably than in any other type of contract. With more in writing now, there is correspondingly less need for implied terms, but they can still be contended for. Where such a term is still relevant, it can be essential in order to complete a contract and as a result a rather wider view has been taken in relation to the implication of terms into a contract of employment than in relation to other contracts. For example, if there is a major gap in express terms, it may be that in ordinary contract law the contract could be void for uncertainty; however, to hold so in the case of a contract of employment (under which the employee may have been working for some time) would be such an obvious nonsense[1] that there will be considerable pressure on a court or tribunal to find the necessary implied terms in order to make legal sense of a subsisting employment relationship. The effects of this can be seen in the bases on which an implied term may be found in a contract of employment.

[1] The contractual doctrine of uncertainty has received short shrift in employment law, necessarily: *Powell v Braun* [1954] 1 All ER 484, [1954] 1 WLR 401, CA; *National Coal Board v Galley* [1958] 1 All ER 91, [1958] 1 WLR 16, CA.

(i) The presumed intention of the parties

1.28 In classic contract law, the courts apply either the 'officious bystander' test[1] or the 'business efficiency' test.[2] Under these, the essence is still to look at what the parties themselves would probably have agreed, had they put their minds to the matter at the time of contracting—it is a subjective test and does not, in theory at least, involve the court in imposing its own views. Such tests may of course be relied upon in a case concerning a contract of employment. However, the point is that in such a case reliance can also be placed on two *wider* concepts which involve departing from ordinary contract principles.

[1] Ie that if an officious bystander has suggested the term to the parties at the time of contracting, they would have 'testily suppressed him with a common "Oh, of course"': *Shirlaw v Southern Foundries (1926) Ltd* [1939] 2 KB 206, 227, [1939] 2 All ER 113, CA, per MacKinnon LJ.

[2] That is the implementation of the presumed intent of the parties in order to give business efficiency to the whole contract: *The Moorcock* (1889) 14 PD 64, CA.

(ii) Conduct and custom

1.29 'Custom and practice' is a term frequently resorted to in practical industrial relations. In this context, it could provide important evidence for or against the implication of a particular term. To the extent that an employee may be said to have taken employment subject to existing customs, this may not be too much of a strain on ordinary contract principles, since it can still be said that there is an implied agreement to that effect at the time of entering the contract. However, it goes wider than that, in that the conduct of the parties subsequently may well be taken into account, for or against the proposed implied term; this is a step away from the presumed intention of the parties at the time of contracting.

(iii) Reasonableness

1.30 The major step away from normal contract principles, however, comes in those cases where courts or tribunals find implied terms simply on the ground that they are reasonable in the circumstances,[1] ie an objective test. Such a result may be forced on the court or tribunal because of a substantial lack of evidence as to any presumed intent of the parties; the court or tribunal, still finding it essential to complete the contract and make legal sense of it, may then have to resort to their own notion of what would be a reasonable term in all the circumstances. While a suggestion in one case before the Court of Appeal[2] that ultimately a court or tribunal may have to 'invent' a missing term was later disapproved by that court as being too extreme a statement,[3] it remains the case that one is a long way from orthodox contract theory here, a point well made in the following passage from a further decision of the Court of Appeal:

> 'Thus in cases such as the present where it is essential to imply some term into the contract of employment as to place of work, the court does not have to be satisfied that the parties, if asked, would in fact have agreed the term before entering into the contract. The court merely has to be satisfied that the implied term is one which the parties would probably have agreed *if they were being reasonable*.'[4]

[1] A longstanding example is *Lister v Romford Ice and Cold Storage Co Ltd* [1957] AC 555, [1957] 1 All ER 125, HL.

[2] *Mears v Safecar Security Ltd* [1982] 2 All ER 865, [1982] IRLR 183, CA.

[3] *Eagland v British Telecommunications plc* [1992] IRLR 323, CA.

[4] *Courtaulds Northern Spinning Ltd v Sibson* [1988] ICR 451 at 460, [1988] IRLR 305 at 309, CA, per Slade LJ (emphasis added); the court adopted judgments to similar effect by Browne-Wilkinson P in the EAT in *Jones v Associated Tunnelling Co Ltd* [1981] IRLR 477, EAT and *Howman & Son v Blyth* [1983] ICR 416, [1983] IRLR 139, EAT.

Characteristic, or 'imposed', terms

1.31 One important aspect of the wide, reasonableness-based test for implied terms (discussed in the previous paragraph) is that it can be used by a court or tribunal for a purpose other than that of given effect to what may (or may not) have been the basis of the agreement between that particular employer and that particular employee. It may be used instead as a device to regulate contracts of employment by the imposition of implied terms based on the nature of the employment itself. Such terms might be considered to be 'characteristic' or 'imposed' terms, which will normally be implied into employment contracts (either generally, or into contracts of a particular type) unless there is clear evidence that the parties do not intend them to apply. Such terms have little or nothing to do with any supposed intention of the parties themselves. The implied term is here simply being used as a device with which to apply what are really just free-standing rules and concepts of the law of employment. Much of the law relating to confidentiality in the employment relationship (both during employment and after it has terminated) falls into this category—duties of fidelity and confidentiality are ensured by the imposition of the relevant implied terms.[1] The point is well made in the following passage from *Lister v Romford Ice and Cold Storage Co Ltd*[2] (where the employee was arguing, unsuccessfully, for an implied term that in modern employment conditions an employer should look after all matters of insurance covering the employee's work):

> 'Just as the duty of care . . . is imposed on the servant . . . just so that question must be asked and answered whether, in the world in which we live today, it is a necessary condition of the relationship of master and man that the master should . . . look after the whole matter of insurance. If I were to try to apply the familiar tests where the question is whether a term should be implied in a particular contract in order to give it what is called business efficiency, I should lose myself in the attempt to formulate it with the necessary precision . . . for . . . the solution of the problem rests, not on the implication of a term in a particular contract of service, but on more general considerations.'

[1] See under 'Characteristics of the relationship', para 1.35 ff, below.

[2] [1957] AC 555, at 576, [1957] 1 All ER 125 at 132, HL, per Lord Simonds. For a more recent example of this process in a different context (of landlord and tenant) see *Liverpool City Council v Irwin* [1977] AC 239, [1976] 2 All ER 39, HL.

1.32 Such 'general considerations' in effect require the court to consider whether to impose a particular term, as being reasonable in the circumstances. Much of what is considered below as the generally applicable duties of the employer and duties of the employee fall into this category. In addition, courts have sometimes used the 'imposed' term as a device to reach a desired result in a one-off case.[1] Either way, the position is summed up in the following passage from *Sterling Engineering Co Ltd v Patchett*:[2]

> 'There are cases in which it has been said that the employer's rights to inventions made by an employee in the course of his employment arises from an implied term in the contract of employment. Strictly speaking, I think that an implied term is something which, in the circumstances of a particular case, the law may read into the contract if the parties are silent, and it would be reasonable to do so; it is something over and above the ordinary incidents of the particular type of contract. If it were necessary in this case to find an implied term in that sense I should be in some difficulty. But the phrase "implied term" can be used to denote a term

inherent in the nature of the contract which the law will imply in every case unless the parties agree to vary or exclude it.'

[1] See, eg, *Morgan v Fry* [1968] 2 QB 710, [1968] 3 All ER 452, CA (strike notice); *Morris v Ford Motor Co Ltd* [1973] QB 792, [1973] 2 All ER 1084, CA (subrogation rights). See also the more recent case law on the implied duty of the employer to treat the employee with respect, etc, which can be so important in a constructive dismissal case (see 'Characteristics of the relationship', para 1.35 ff, below).

[2] [1955] AC 534 at 547, [1955] 1 All ER 369 at 376, HL, per Lord Reid. Note that the question of employee inventions is now covered by a statutory code: Patents Act 1977, ss 39–43.

Overriding terms?

1.33 There have been signs recently of the courts perhaps being prepared to go further even than the above, and to imply certain terms of an *overriding* nature, due to the nature of the employment and the term itself. While this may be highly desirable as a matter of policy, it has to be accepted that it involves a major departure from orthodox contract law, since it may involve an express term of the contract being overridden by an implied term. Essentially it poses this question—can an employer always insist on his strict rights under a contract of employment, or will a tribunal or court limit his right to do so if the end result is unconscionable? To take one example of particular importance, if there is a mobility clause in the contract expressly giving the employer carte blanche to move the employee, can he do so at will, or may a court deem that express clause to be subject to an overriding implied term, eg, of reasonable notice?

In *Prestwick Circuits Ltd v McAndrew*[1] the Court of Session upheld the implication of a mobility clause into a contract that was silent on the matter, and further held of necessity that the clause was subject to implied restrictions of reasonable distance[2] *and reasonable notice*. In a sense this was not too drastic, as the court was finding an implied term in the first place and so found it relatively easy to construct and add on such a limitation. However, the case that showed a more fundamental approach was *United Bank Ltd v Akhtar*[3] where the EAT held that an apparently watertight mobility clause which the employer sought to exercise at short notice was in fact subject to a requirement of reasonable notice, partly as a matter of necessary implication, but also because of the 'overriding obligation' of trust and respect[4] 'which is independent of, and in addition to, the literal interpretation of the actions which are permitted to the employer under the terms of the contract'. This meant that the employee could show the breach of contract necessary for constructive dismissal. The EAT later appeared to resile from an extreme version of this in *White v Reflecting Roadstuds Ltd*[5] where the opposite result was reached, *but* when the case is read carefully it becomes clear that what the EAT were disapproving was a wider argument that (quite simply) an express term must always be exercised reasonably. That would be too heretical. However, at the end of the judgment the point is made that reliance in such a case could be placed instead on the 'overriding implied term' of trust and respect, to reach much the same conclusion. In a different context, that term was applied by Browne-Wilkinson VC in *Imperial Group Pension Trust Ltd v Imperial Tobacco Ltd*[6] to limit the application of powers under pension trusts to those which do not infringe the implied obligation of trust and respect towards the employees subject to the pension scheme.

The idea of an overriding term can also be seen in *Johnstone v Bloomsbury*

Health Authority,[7] the newsworthy case involving a legal challenge to the contracts of junior doctors which permitted (or appeared to do so) the hospital to require them to work for 88 hours per week or more. The majority of the Court of Appeal held that to exercise such a contractual right might be in breach of a fundamental implied term of the contract of employment, namely that the employer must exercise reasonable care to safeguard the health and safety of the employee.[8]

If this development continues, and is eventually approved by the higher courts, it could lead to common law protection for employees greater than that existing before—it was seen in the previous paragraph that some protection has come from 'imposed' terms, *but* the weakness of that concept can be seen from the final phrase of the quotation in that paragraph from *Sterling Engineering Co Ltd v Patchett*, namely that such a term will apply '*unless the parties agree to vary or exclude it*'. The advantage of an overriding term is that it could be used to attack unconscionable conduct by the employer even where he has sought to enshrine his right to act in precisely that way in the black and white of the contract itself. Developments in this area will be watched with interest.

[1] [1990] IRLR 191, Ct Sess.

[2] Such a limitation has usually been added to an implied mobility clause in the past; see eg, *O'Brien v Associated Fire Alarms Ltd* [1969] 1 All ER 93, [1968] 1 WLR 1916, CA.

[3] [1989] IRLR 507, EAT.

[4] See para 1.44, below. There was previous authority *against* any ideas of restricting the exercise of express contractual rights. In *Courtaulds Northern Spinning Ltd v Sibson* [1988] ICR 451, [1988] IRLR 305, CA, the court refused to make the exercise of an implied mobility clause subject to a requirement of reasonableness (see also *Rank Xerox Ltd v Churchill* [1988] IRLR 280, EAT), and in *Kenneth MacRae & Co Ltd v Dawson* [1984] IRLR 5 the EAT would not subject an express lay-off clause to an implied restriction that it should only apply for a reasonable period. On the other hand, an implied requirement of reasonableness and proportionality *has* in the past been read into the exercise by an employer of his discretion under a firm's disciplinary procedure (*BBC v Beckett* [1983] IRLR 43, EAT; *Cawley v South Wales Electricity Board* [1985] IRLR 89, EAT).

[5] [1991] ICR 733, [1991] IRLR 331, EAT.

[6] [1991] ICR 524, [1991] IRLR 66.

[7] [1991] ICR 269, [1991] IRLR 118, CA.

[8] There was a similar, much-publicised industrial tribunal decision in Cambridge in 1991 that an agricultural employee (in an unusual and important job) whose contract stipulated that he was on call seven days a week with no provision for holidays was justified in leaving and claiming constructive dismissal.

1.34 Finally, it may be noted that the drafters of legislation may also use the contract of employment (and the imposition of terms upon it) as a device for achieving a certain result. Thus, to take two examples:

(1) the equal pay legislation states that an 'equality clause' is deemed to be included in any contract of employment that does not already include one;[1] this notional clause is then the peg upon which the substantive rights to equality are hung;

(2) where an employer refuses to disclose to a recognised trade union bargaining information to which the CAC has held it to be entitled under the legislation,[2] the union may complain to the CAC and part of the remedy is to attach to the complaint a substantive claim for improved terms and conditions for the employees in question; if the CAC find the complaint well founded, they may grant some or all of the substantive claim, which then takes effect 'as part of the contract of employment of any such employee'.[3]

[1] Equal Pay Act 1970, s 1(1).
[3] TULR(C)A 1992, ss 181–185.
[4] Ibid, s 185(5).

4 CHARACTERISTICS OF THE RELATIONSHIP

Duties of the employer (1): financial

1.35 Employment has been characterised as a 'work-wages bargain'; we shall see later that this is an oversimplification in at least one way, in that the employee's consideration is not necessarily the actual performance of work, but rather the readiness and willingness to work. However, it remains true that on the other side the employer's obligation to pay the wages due under the contract is one of the most fundamental terms. If they are not paid, the employee may sue for them in the ordinary courts and, in most cases, would be entitled to leave and claim constructive dismissal.[1] Likewise, any unwarranted deductions from wages could be recovered by an action in the ordinary courts; in addition now, any deductions made in contravention of the ERA, s 13 can be recovered by a complaint to an industrial tribunal.[2]

[1] ERA, s 95; *Industrial Rubber Products v Gillon* [1977] IRLR 389, EAT; *Stokes v Hampstead Wine Co Ltd* [1979] IRLR 298, EAT. This is not an absolute rule, but must depend on the facts as to how serious the employer's breach was: *Adams v Charles Zub Associates Ltd* [1978] IRLR 551, EAT; *Gillies v Richard Daniels & Co Ltd* [1979] IRLR 457, EAT. On constructive dismissal generally, see Chapter 19, below.
[2] See Chapter 6, below.

1.36 The amount of wages (and the method of payment) will usually be a matter which depends entirely on the terms of the contract of employment; there is little 'law' on the point and in cases of doubt the outcome will depend on the construction of the relevant term (whether individually agreed or incorporated from some governing collective agreement). By virtue of the ERA, s 1(4)(a) the employee should have been given a written statement of terms of employment within two months of commencing employment, and this should have included particulars of 'the scale or rate of remuneration, or the method of calculating remuneration'.[1] Provided that it has been kept up to date (as is legally required), this statement should be the starting point in resolving any dispute, in the absence of a formal, written contract of employment. 'Scale or rate' of pay will be appropriate for ordinary time workers or salaried workers, whereas 'method' of calculation may be more appropriate for piece workers or those remunerated partly or wholly by commission or bonus.

[1] Section 1 statements are considered in Chapter 5(1), below.

1.37 The present government are not in favour of statutory intervention in the fixing of wages and in the early 1980s took several steps towards a more free market in labour.[1] There remained an area where minimum wages *were* fixed by law, and that was where the employment was covered by a Wages Council. The powers of these bodies were restricted by the Wages Act 1986, and eventually the decision was taken to abolish them altogether. This was effected by the Trade Union Reform and Employment Rights Act 1993. Needless to say, the government are strongly against any EC-led ideas of a national minimum wage.

[1] See particularly the repeal of Sch 11 of the EPA and the abrogation of the Fair Wages Resolution. The Teachers' Pay and Conditions Act 1987 was exceptional.

1.38 Provided that due wages are paid, in most cases the employer will have discharged his side of the bargain; in particular, this means that in law there is not normally any obligation on the employer to provide work for the employee actually to do.[1] There are certain exceptional categories such as those paid on a piece work basis,[2] or a commission basis,[3] or employees such as actors who rely on publicity, etc, through actual performances as well as on wages.[4] However, they remain exceptional, and one well known attempt by Lord Denning MR to erect a wider principle based on a legal 'right to work'[5] has not been further developed. Outside these particular categories, there is thus no general right to be given work to do; two practical aspects of this are that the employer will normally be acting lawfully by (a) suspending an employee with pay,[6] or (b) dismissing an employee by giving wages in lieu of notice.[7]

[1] *Collier v Sunday Referee Publishing Co Ltd* [1940] 2 KB 647, [1940] 4 All ER 234; *Turner v Sawdon & Co* [1901] 2 KB 653, CA.
[2] *Devonald v Rosser & Sons* [1906] 2 KB 728, CA; *Langston v Amalgamated Union of Engineering Workers (No 2)* [1974] ICR 510, [1974] IRLR 182, NIRC.
[3] *Turner v Goldsmith* [1891] 1 QB 544, CA.
[4] *Marbé v George Edwardes (Daly's Theatre)* [1928] 1 KB 269, CA; *Herbert Clayton and Jack Waller Ltd v Oliver* [1930] AC 209, HL. This exception may also apply to the holder of a particular office of a professional nature; *Collier v Sunday Referee Publishing Co Ltd*, above.
[5] *Langston v Amalgamated Union of Engineering Workers* [1974] 1 All ER 980, [1974] ICR 180, CA.
[6] As indeed is suggested in the ACAS Code of Practice No 1, para 11, when a serious allegation against the employee has to be investigated. Note, however, that there is *no* inherent right to suspend *without* pay—any power to do so must arise clearly under the contract (usually by being written into a disciplinary procedure expressly).
[7] Dismissal by notice generally is considered in Chapter 6(2), below.

1.39 In addition to these general principles on the obligation to pay wages, three particular applications should be noted.

(i) Payment of wages during sickness

1.40 An employer of any size is now obliged by law to operate the Statutory Sick Pay (SSP) scheme, whereby he administers on behalf of the government what used to be state sickness benefit; this is considered below.[1] In addition, however, nearly all employments will be covered by some contractual scheme whereby the employer also pays 'sick pay' of sorts.[2] Usually of course this will be expressly set out in the contract of employment, and will take the form of 'topping-up' SSP to a certain level for a certain period of time (eg basic wages for a period of three months, followed by half basic wages for a further three months). Thus, in most cases, the question of what is payable during sickness is a matter of construing and applying the contractual term.[3] However, an untypical case may arise where there is no express term. In such a case, the courts have to decide whether a sick pay term is to be implied. There is no rule that such a term must be implied[4] and matters of custom and practice may be important. If such a term is implied, its quantification is a matter for the court, but in reality it is likely to be set as a topping up of SSP (rather than full wages) and to be limited to a reasonable period (as most express terms are), rather than being open-ended.[5]

---

1 Chapter 9.

2 Sick pay (and lay-offs, below) are considered in *Harvey* Div B.

3 Written particulars of sick pay entitlement should be included in the section 1 statement: ERA, s 1(4)(d)(ii).

4 *Mears v Safecar Security Ltd* [1982] ICR 626, [1982] IRLR 183, CA, disapproving the suggestion of a presumption in favour of sick pay made in *Orman v Saville Sportswear Ltd* [1960] 3 All ER 105, [1960] 1 WLR 1055.

5 *Howman & Son v Blyth* [1983] ICR 416, [1983] IRLR 139, EAT.

(ii) Payment of wages during lay-off or short-time

1.41 Once again, the question of lay-off or short-time is likely to be covered by some form of express agreement (either generally in a collective agreement, or on an ad hoc basis covering a particular downturn in the employer's business). If it is not, the legality or otherwise of a reduction of wages by the employer will depend on whether a lay-off term can be implied in the contract of employment; in deciding that, questions such as custom and practice (within the company or the industry) and whether there had been previous accepted lay-offs might be important. If, however, no term can be implied then, provided that the employee remains ready and willing to serve, the reduction in (or non-payment of) wages during the lay-off or short-time will be a breach of contract by the employer (since there is no inherent power to do so),[1] and the employee may bring an action for wages. This has been reaffirmed by the Court of Appeal.[2] In practice, however, it is likely that most lay-offs will be covered by an express or implied contractual term which may, for example, provide for a guaranteed minimum wage. If there is no such provision, the employee's recourse may be either to the statutory guarantee payment scheme[3] (though this is set at fairly minimum levels) or to the state for unemployment benefit for the period of lay-off or short-time.[4]

---

1 *Hanley v Pease & Partners Ltd* [1915] 1 KB 698; *Marshall v English Electric Co Ltd* [1945] 1 All ER 653, CA; *Gorse v Durham County Council* [1971] 2 All ER 666, [1971] 1 WLR 775; *Neads v CAV Ltd* [1983] IRLR 360.

2 *Miller v Hamworthy Engineering Ltd* [1986] ICR 846, [1986] IRLR 461, CA.

3 ERA, s 28; see Chapter 11, below.

4 See Smith & Wood, *Industrial Law* (6th edn, 1996), ch 9, part 3. This is due to change in October with the inception of jobseeker's allowance, much of which is based on means testing.

(iii) Refusal to work

1.42 If an employee refuses to perform work that he is contractually obliged to perform (eg as part of industrial action), the simple principle of 'no work, no wages' applies.[1] This is easy where there is a complete refusal (as in a strike) or where because of a partial refusal the employer declines to accept any work from the employee. In the latter case, the employer may suspend the employee or may (provided he makes clear his position from the outset) refuse to pay anything, even if the employee has in fact carried out part of his duties (a point of some importance, for example, where the employer cannot physically prevent the employee from attending work; it may also be important where the employer wishes to issue an ultimatum to work fully or not at all).[2] Short of that drastic approach, however, an employer faced with partial performance of work by the employee may wish to accept that part but only pay for that work actually done. In the light of the case law, the employer is within his legal rights to deduct[3] from wages an amount representing the value of the service refused. In *Sim v Rotherham Metropolitan Borough Council*[4] (refusal of teachers to cover for absent colleagues) Scott J put this on the basis that full wages were payable but subject to the employer's right of equitable set-off in respect of the duties not performed. However, in the later decision of the House of Lords in *Miles v Wakefield Metropolitan District Council*[5] (registrar refusing to conduct ceremonies during his normal three hours on a Saturday morning having $^{3}/_{37}$ths of his pay for a 37-hour week lawfully deducted) the issue was put on the simpler ground that in respect of the refused duties there was a failure of consideration on the part of the employee and so no wages were due in respect of that part in the first place. Either way, the important point is that the employer may deduct fair amounts from wages; he does not have to adopt the more cumbersome procedure (as argued by the employees in these cases) of paying out wages in full and then suing the employees for damages.

---

1 *Cresswell v Board of Inland Revenue* [1984] ICR 508, [1984] IRLR 190. This of course may beg the question as to *what* the contract actually does require, a point very much in issue in this case.

2 *Wiluszynski v Tower Hamlets London Borough Council* [1989] ICR 493, [1989] IRLR 259, CA; *Ticehurst v British Telecommunications plc* [1992] IRLR 219, CA.

3 A deduction for this purpose does not infringe the normal procedural requirements of Part II of the ERA, s 14(5).

4 [1986] ICR 897, [1986] IRLR 391. See also *Royle v Trafford Borough Council* [1984] IRLR 184.

5 [1987] ICR 368, [1987] IRLR 193, HL.

1.43 One final point to note is that the employer's duty to pay the wages required by the contract may be used to advantage by an employee in a case where the employer tries to force through a change in the contractual terms to which the employee objects strongly (especially if the net result is a decrease in wages). It may be possible for the employee to maintain that objection, hold himself ready and willing to work to the original contractual terms (arguing that there has been no consensual variation) and then sue for the wages that were due under those old terms. As a tactic to force the employer's hand, this has proved to be effective.[1]

---

1 *Rigby v Ferodo Ltd* [1988] ICR 29, [1987] IRLR 516, HL; see also *Burdett-Coutts v Hertfordshire County Council* [1984] IRLR 91.

Duties of the employer (2): reasonable behaviour

1.44 The duty of an employer to behave reasonably towards an employee has its original, and perhaps most obvious, application in the case of industrial safety. In terms of the law of tort, it is trite law to say that an employer owes to his employee a duty of care.[1] This general duty has evolved over many years into four particular duties, ie to take reasonable care to provide (i) a safe workplace, (ii) safe plant and equipment,[2] (iii) competent and safe fellow employees, and (iv) a safe system of work in all the circumstances.[3] Depending on what types of premises, these general common law duties will probably be supplemented by more specific statutory duties on the employer, breach of which will enable the injured employee to sue for damages.[4] The obligation to take reasonable care of the employee's safety arises not just as a matter of tort law, but also as an implied term of the contract of employment.[5] Normally, this contractual aspect is of little importance; however, it has been held that one manifestation of it is that a blatant refusal by an employer to listen to an employee's genuine complaints on health and safety matters may be a sufficiently grave breach of contract to justify the employee leaving and claiming constructive dismissal.[6] In addition to the purely tortious aspects of the duty of care, there are statutory duties on an employer under the Health and Safety at Work etc Act 1974, enforceable by administrative means (such as prohibition or improvement notices) or by criminal prosecution; in particular, s 2 provides that 'It shall be the duty of every employer to ensure, so far as is reasonably practicable, the health, safety and welfare at work of all his employees'.[7]

---

1 See generally Munkman, *Employer's Liability* (12th edn, 1995).

2 This particular duty is expanded by the Employer's Liability (Defective Equipment) Act 1969.

3 *Wilsons and Clyde Coal Co Ltd v English* [1938] AC 57, HL; for a recent affirmation of the personal and non-delegable nature of these duties, see *McDermid v Nash Dredging and Reclamation Co Ltd* [1987] ICR 917, [1987] IRLR 334, HL.

4 Historically these important provisions were contained in the factories legislation, particularly the Factories Act 1961, the Offices, Shops and Railway Premises Act 1963 and the Mines and Quarries Act 1954. However, from 1 January 1993 most of this legislation was repealed and replaced by radically up-dated Health and Safety Regulations, enacting a series of EC directives. See Smith & Wood, *Industrial Law* (6th edn, 1996) chs 12, 13 and Smith, Goddard & Randall, *Health and Safety, the New Legal Framework* (1993).

5 *Matthews v Kuwait Bechtel Corpn* [1959] 2 QB 57, [1959] 2 All ER 345, CA.

6 *British Aircraft Corpn v Austin* [1978] IRLR 332, EAT.

7 Note also s 3 which imposes a duty of care to those not in the employer's employment but who may nevertheless be exposed to risks to their health and safety; *R v Mara* [1987] ICR 165 [1987] IRLR 154, CA; Smith & Wood, op cit, ch 13.

1.45 The duty of reasonable behaviour has, however, been extended outside the area of health and safety. There is said to be a general, implied duty to treat the employee with respect and not to act in a manner likely to destroy the relationship of trust and confidence between employer and employee.[1] This may be seen as an element of the increased legal protection for employees, particularly under the law of unfair dismissal. At that generalised level it could also be seen as a meaningless platitude. However, in one context the evolution of this implied term has been of major practical importance. That context is the law on constructive dismissal.[2] By virtue of the ERA, s 95(1)(c), an employee may resign but still claim to have been dismissed if the employer's behaviour towards him was such that he was entitled to walk out. The question arose as to what was meant by 'entitled', and two constructions were possible—the narrow view that it meant 'contractually entitled' (ie that the employer had committed a definable, repudiatory breach of contract) or the wide view that it simply meant that the employer had behaved sufficiently unreasonably (whether or not actually in breach of contract) to justify the employee leaving. When the matter went to the Court of Appeal[3] it was held that the former was the law. At first sight, this was capable of narrowing the law of constructive dismissal considerably. However, that was avoided by the evolution of an implied contractual term of reasonable behaviour by the employer.[4] Thus, if the employer now treats the employee manifestly unreasonably (or in such a manner as to destroy mutual confidence, etc), and the employee walks out, that may be a constructive dismissal—not because it is unreasonable per se, but because it constitutes a sufficiently serious breach of this implied contractual term to justify the employee terminating the contract. This development has been important in retaining flexibility in the law of unfair dismissal. As seen above,[5] the implied term has also been used recently to place limits on unconscionable attempts by employers to exercise their black and white express contractual rights, for example in relation to mobility clauses.

1 *Secretary of State for Employment v Associated Society of Locomotive Engineers and Firemen (No 2)* [1972] 2 QB 455, [1972] 2 All ER 949, CA (a case concerning provisions of the Industrial Relations Act 1971, under which this point assumed important, incidental significance).

2 See Chapter 19, below.

3 *Western Excavating (ECC) Ltd v Sharp* [1978] ICR 221, [1978] IRLR 27, CA.

4 There is a particularly useful explanation of the role of this implied term in the judgment of Browne-Wilkinson P in the EAT in *Woods v WM Car Services (Peterborough) Ltd* [1981] ICR 666, [1981] IRLR 347, EAT (upheld on appeal by the CA). See also the same learned judge's application of the implied term in the topical context of occupational pension scheme rights for employees in *Imperial Group Pension Trust Ltd v Imperial Tobacco Ltd* [1991] ICR 524, [1991] IRLR 66.

5 Para 1.33, above.

1.46 The duty of reasonable care has recently been canvassed in another specialised area, namely a duty of care towards an employee (or ex-employee) when writing a reference. There is no legal obligation to provide a reference. If one is provided, it is clear that the writer may assume a duty of care to the new prospective employer (unless liability is expressly and effectively disclaimed by the writer) under the normal principle in *Hedley Bryne & Co Ltd v Heller & Partners Ltd*.[1] However, liability has recently been extended to cover the *subject* of the reference, ie the employee or ex-employee, who may sue the reference writer for damages if he can prove that the reference was *negligently* bad (eg because the writer had not checked the facts properly).[2] Although this may be difficult in many cases, this liability is potentially wider than what was traditionally the subject's only cause of action, namely the law of defamation.

1 [1964] AC 465, [1963] 2 All ER 575, HL.

2 *Spring v Guardian Assurance plc* [1994] 3 All ER 129, HL.

Duties of the employer (3): further developments

1.47 There have been two recent developments which may show a more expansive approach by the courts to the overall duties of employers towards their employees. The first is the interesting decision of the House of Lords in *Scally v Southern Health and Social Services Board*.[1] In this case, a pension scheme gave valuable extra rights to young doctors on taking up employment but only if they were claimed within 12 months of employment, a fact not made known to the plaintiff doctors, who succeeded in an action for breach of contract, in that the employers were in breach of an implied term to notify them. It is true that this was a very complicated scheme, which had been negotiated at a higher, collective level (not with the doctors themselves) and this no doubt had a bearing on the decision, *but* the case may show a generally more pro-active approach by the courts to an employer's responsibilities, especially in relation to informing employees of matters not reasonably within their own knowledge.[2] The second development is the decision of the Court of Session in *Dalgleish v Lothian and Borders Police Board*[3] granting an injunction to employees preventing their employer from divulging their names and addresses to the local council who were trying to identify community charge defaulters. This approach could possibly form the basis of an implied duty of confidentiality owed *to* (not just *by*) an employee, ie not to misuse information relating to the employee which is held by the employer only for the purposes of the employer-employee relationship.

1 [1991] ICR 771, [1991] IRLR 522, HL.

2 The traditional, more negative approach (that it is up to a party to the contract to look after his own interests and know his own rights) can perhaps be seen in the earlier decision of *Reid v Rush & Tompkins Group plc* [1990] ICR 61, [1989] IRLR 265 where the Court of Appeal held that an employer was not in breach of contract by failing to insure the employee or warn him to take out insurance while working abroad for the company.

3 [1991] IRLR 422, Ct Sess.

Duties of the employee (1): care and obedience

1.48 It is normally said that the employee's consideration for the contract of employment is his being ready and willing to work,[1] rather than his actually performing work. It may be that in some contracts wages are only payable for work actually done (as in the case of hourly paid or piece workers), but that is because of the particular payment method and does not necessarily contradict the general principle. That principle gives rise to certain duties of loyalty, as we shall see in the next paragraph. First, however, it is necessary to look at the employee's duties of care and obedience.

1 *Warburton v Co-operative Wholesale Society Ltd* [1917] 1 KB 663, CA; *Henthorn and Taylor v Central Electricity Generating Board* [1980] IRLR 361, CA.

1.49 An employee taking up employment impliedly warrants that he has any competence necessary for the job;[1] this is, however, a matter which many employers would wish to cover expressly in the contract, eg by making it a condition that the employee has or will gain certain qualifications[2] or that the employee has and will keep a valid driving licence. However, the duty goes beyond competence and extends to an implied duty to exercise reasonable care while in the employer's employment. This is obviously important when the employee is in charge of valuable equipment while working,[3] and failure to exercise due care leading to substantial loss to the employer could constitute a serious disciplinary matter. Moreover, the duty of care is of equal importance when the employee is dealing with third parties (such as customers or passers-by), for it is a fundamental principle of the law of tort that if the employee injures a third party (or, indeed, a fellow employee) while acting in the course of his employment the injured person may sue the *employer* who is vicariously liable for the acts of the employee.[4] Negligence by the employee may thus incur liability on his employer. Technically, the employer could then sue the employee for an indemnity[5] (ie for some or all of the damages that he has had to pay to the injured party) or the employer's insurance company (who will most likely have paid the damages) could so do by virtue of the doctrine of subrogation. While this is technically possible,[6] it is in practice most unlikely to happen since insurance companies have a 'gentlemen's agreement' not to exercise such rights against employees (in personal injury cases where there is no wilful misconduct or collusion).

[1] *Harmer v Cornelius* (1858) 5 CBNS 236.

[2] See the problems that arose from failure to stipulate expressly the requirement of passing the solicitors' exams in *Stubbes v Trower, Still & Keeling* [1987] IRLR 321, CA.

[3] If an employer wished to oblige the employee to pay for any damage from his wages, he would have to obtain prior agreement in writing to any deductions for the purpose: ERA, s 14 (and note the special rules applying to stock and till deficiencies in retail employment); see Chapter 6, below.

[4] Vicarious liability is dealt with in the standard tort texts; for recent case law, see *Rose v Plenty* [1976] 1 All ER 97, [1976] 1 WLR 141, CA; *Heasmans v Clarity Cleaning Co Ltd* [1987] ICR 949, [1987] IRLR 286, CA; *Aldred v Nacanco* [1987] IRLR 292, CA; *Smith v Stages* [1989] 1 All ER 833, [1989] ICR 272, HL.

[5] The employer's action for an indemnity could arise either under the contract for breach of the implied duty of care, or independently under the Civil Liability (Contribution) Act 1978.

[6] It happened in the well-known case of *Lister v Romford Ice and Cold Storage Co Ltd* [1957] AC 555, [1957] 1 All ER 215, HL (where there was an element of collusion, in that the plaintiff had been run over by his own son, and was suing the son's employer). For the details of such an action, see Smith & Wood, *Industrial Law* (6th edn, 1996), ch 3, part 5.

1.50 Obedience to lawful orders is an implied obligation in the contract of employment (which could, of course, in an appropriate case, be expanded upon expressly in the contract which could, for example, set out the chain of command on serious matters). The word 'lawful' here has a double meaning. Its first meaning is that any order must not be illegal under the general law; thus, if the employer orders the employee to commit an illegal act (eg to defraud a customer or to tamper with a tachograph) the employee may refuse—if summarily dismissed for such a refusal, that dismissal would be wrongful at common law and also highly likely to be unfair under statute.[1] The second meaning of 'lawful' is 'within the proper ambit of the contract'. Thus the employer may not order the employee to do something that he is not contractually obliged to do (eg to work elsewhere than his normal workplace if the contract does not, expressly or impliedly, require him to be mobile, or to work overtime if there is not contractual power to require it). Moreover, 'personal' orders ('Get you hair cut') will only be lawful if they are within the scope of the employment (eg because long hair is a safety risk or is relevant to presentability of employees dealing with the public). If an order is lawful, it will be a disciplinary offence to disobey it. Whether such disobedience is serious enough to warrant dismissal (especially summary dismissal), or only a formal warning, will depend on all the circumstances of the case.

[1] *Gregory v Ford* [1951] 1 All ER 121; *Morrish v Henlys (Folkestone) Ltd* [1973] 2 All ER 137, [1973] ICR 482.

1.51 It should be clear from the above paragraph, with its emphasis on the need for contractual authority for an order, that the employer has no general power to order the employee to accept any alteration to the contract. Variation of contract remains a consensual matter.[1] However, a case could arise where the employer argues that he is not requiring the employee to change his contractual duties, but only the means of carrying them out (especially where the employer is wishing to introduce more modern methods, eg word processors in place of typewriters). In such a case, the employee may argue that even the means are a matter of contractual entitlement and so can only be changed by agreement.[2] However, in *Cresswell v Board of Inland Revenue*[3] there are suggestions that if necessary a court might evolve an implied term of adaptation to new methods and techniques, reasonably within the scope of the overall contractual duties. While it would be important to ensure that any such implied duty was not cast so widely as to enable the employer to force through changes which in reality altered the very nature of the contract (hence the importance of a 'reasonableness' requirement), it can be argued that such a duty would be of use in resolving one of the longstanding tensions in the law on contracts of employment—that contracts are basically static, whereas jobs and methods of performing them change (sometimes remarkably rapidly in modern conditions).

1 See paras 1.35–1.43, above.
2 Which he may be withholding as part of a collective dispute.
3 [1984] ICR 508, [1984] IRLR 190. The case concerned the refusal of Inland Revenue staff to operate a new computerised PAYE system as part of a dispute. They argued that computerisation changed the nature of their jobs and so could not be ordered by the employer, but Walton J held that it was merely a different means of performing their existing job, and so the employer was entitled to expect them to adapt to it.

Duties of the employee (2): loyalty

1.52 There will generally be implied into a contract of employment a term requiring loyalty and/or good faith on the part of the employee. This is a rather generalised concept but it has recently been reaffirmed by the Court of Appeal in terms of an obligation to serve the employer faithfully within the requirements of the contract. It is potentially of importance in the law on industrial action, for it provides the argument that a 'work to rule' or 'withdrawal of good will' which appears to be strictly within the terms of the contract may in fact be a breach of this overall implied term of loyalty and will, in any event, normally constitute 'other industrial action' within the statutory definitions. However, its principal importance has been in the area of confidentiality and good faith,[1] where it can be used by an employer to prevent acts by the employee (or sometimes an ex-employee and his new employer) which are fundamentally inconsistent with his position as employee. Four particular areas have been important in the case law:

(i) Secret profits. If an employee misuses his position to make secret profits (including the acceptance of bribes), that may of course be a good ground for dismissal, but also there is a common law right for the employer to recover the profit.[2]

(ii) Competition. An employee is under a duty not to compete with his employer in a way that is inconsistent with his employment. Normally a court will not restrict an employee's free time, but if activities during that time (either by working for a competitor or by operating on his own) can be shown to be harming the employer, those activities may be restrained.[3] Unlawful competition may also be a ground for dismissal, but some care is needed here for it has been held that merely preparing to set up in competition while still employed may not (in the absence of any definable breach of confidence) be a fair ground for a 'pre-emptive dismissal'.[4] This is because generally the law will *not* suppress bona fide competition, and so a fine line has to be drawn here. One clear aspect of that is that the implied duty of loyalty will *not* prevent competition by an ex-employee. If the employer wishes to achieve that result (eg in a small and sensitive market) he can only do so by the use of an express restraint of trade clause.[5]

(iii) Misuse of confidential information.[6] There is a general duty not to misuse the employer's confidential information while in employment; usually, this will be tied in with the rules on employee competition (above). However, unlike those rules, this general duty may continue to apply *after* the employment has terminated. Thus, if an employee leaves and takes with him material such as customer lists or details of scientific processes (especially if he unlawfully removes it in written form), the employer may be able to restrain use of it if the ex-employee sets up in competition.[7] However, line-drawing is again important here for the courts will be careful not to restrain ordinary competition and it is clear that the ex-employer may not restrain the use of ordinary 'know-how' by the ex-employer, even where it was acquired during the previous employment. In what is now the leading case,[8] the Court of Appeal made it clear that the implied duty of confidence after employment is *narrower* than the equivalent duty during employment, and is confined to the protection of material that is so confidential that it can reasonably be said to fall within the generalised heading of 'trade secrets'. Neill LJ put the matter thus:

> 'The implied term which imposes an obligation on the employee as to his conduct after the termination of the employment is more restricted in its scope than that which imposes a general duty of good faith. It is clear that the obligation not to use or disclose information may cover secret processes of manufacture such as chemical formulae or designs or special methods of construction and other information which is of a sufficiently high degree of confidentiality as to amount to a trade secret. The obligation does not extend, however, to cover all information which is given to or acquired by the employee while in his employment, and in particular may not cover information which is only "confidential" in the sense that an unauthorised disclosure of such information to a third party while the employment subsisted would be a clear breach of the duty of good faith.'

---

1 *Ticehurst v British Telecommunications plc* [1992] IRLR 219, CA. A contract of employment is not a contract uberrimae fidei requiring voluntary and total disclosure; however, fraud in obtaining a job may be a good ground for dismissal (*City of Birmingham District Council v Beyer* [1978] 1 All ER 910, [1977] IRLR 211, EAT) and an employee may be under a duty to disclose wrongdoing by others in the organisation, even if strictly he is not under a duty to disclose his own (*Sybron Corpn v Rochem Ltd* [1983] 2 All ER 707, [1983] IRLR 253, CA).

2 *Boston Deep Sea Fishing and Ice Co v Ansell* (1888) 39 Ch D 339, CA; *Reading v A-G* [1951] AC 507, [1951] 1 All ER 617, HL.

3 *Hivac Ltd v Park Royal Scientific Instruments Ltd* [1946] Ch 169, [1946] 1 All ER 350, CA.

4 *Harris and Russell Ltd v Slingsby* [1973] ICR 454, [1973] IRLR 221; *Laughton and Hawley v Bapp Industrial Supplies Ltd* [1986] ICR 634, [1986] IRLR 245, EAT.

5 Restraint of trade clauses are considered in Chapter 4, below.

6 *Harvey* Div A.

[7] *Robb v Green* [1895] 2 QB 315, CA; *Roger Bullivant Ltd v Ellis* [1987] ICR 464, [1987] IRLR 491, CA.

[8] *Faccenda Chicken Ltd v Fowler* [1986] ICR 297, [1986] IRLR 69, CA; see also *Johnson & Bloy (Holdings) Ltd v Wolstenholme Rink plc and Fallon* [1987] IRLR 499, CA.

1.53 The overall point is quite simply that if the employer wishes to protect all confidential material from misuse by an ex-employee, he must do so by the use of an express restraint of trade clause; this has two advantages over reliance only on the implied duty of confidence:

(i) it is capable of covering a wider range of material; and

(ii) the implied duty does not prevent the ex-employee from entering other similar employment or setting up in competition (and when he does so, the ex-employer then has to *prove* misuse of confidential information when the competition suddenly starts to produce similar goods), whereas a restraint of trade clause (if valid) prevents the ex-employee from doing so, and so prevents him taking up a position in which he *may* misuse confidential information.

Finally, there is one exception to the duty of confidentiality (either during or after employment) which is where disclosure by the employee or ex-employee would be in the public interest; this is an ill-defined category, but would arise principally where the employer was being exposed as involved in criminal offences or other forms of 'iniquity'.[1]

(iv) Employee inventions. These used to be covered by implied terms, but are now governed by a statutory code in the Patents Act 1977, ss 39–43 which (a) lays down when an invention made in the course of employment belongs to the employee and when to the employer, and (b) provides a statutory scheme for rewarding the employee where the employer has obtained 'outstanding benefit' from the invention.[2]

[1] *Initial Services Ltd v Putterill* [1968] 1 QB 396, [1967] 3 All ER 145, CA; *Lion Laboratories Ltd v Evans* [1985] QB 526, [1984] 2 All ER 417, CA.

[2] See Smith & Wood, *Industrial Law* (6th edn, 1996), ch 3, part 5.

1.54 Where there has been a breach of the duty of confidence by an existing employee, there could theoretically be an action for damages by the employer, though dismissal would probably be a more realistic possible remedy. However, in the case of an ex-employee, an action for damages (or an account of profits) would be more realistic against the ex-employee *and* any new employer who has taken advantage of the breach. In addition, of course, the immediate remedy sought may well be an injunction to prevent further breach or to restrain the use of any existing breaches. These remedies (and those for breach of a restraint of trade clause) are considered below.[1]

[1] Chapter 4.

2 The termination of the contract of employment

Ian Smith

1 TERMINATION WITHOUT A DISMISSAL

Termination by agreement

2.01 In ordinary contract law, if parties agree to enter into a contract they are normally free to agree to terminate it. This is so in theory with contracts of employments. However, as elsewhere in modern employment law, it is important here to ensure that an over-strict adherence to classical contract notions does not have the effect of reducing (or negativing altogether) statutory employment rights. In this context, that means being wary of arguments that employment has simply been terminated by agreement in some way, since the effect of such a finding would be that there was *no dismissal*, which would be fatal to any claim for, inter alia, unfair dismissal. It is worth noting here three areas where this problem has arisen.

2.02 The first concerns *fixed term contracts*. If a contract of employment is expressed to be for a fixed period only,[1] in ordinary contract law the contract ends automatically at the end of that period without the need for a dismissal by the employer. Such a contract may be an attractive option, for example, if it is unsure whether the funding for the post is going to continue; moreover, under the statutes[2] an employee on a fixed term contract may lawfully sign away his unfair dismissal rights (if the fixed term is for a year or more) and his redundancy payment rights (if the fixed term is for two years or more). However, in any case where there is no such agreed exclusion of rights, the employee is given some statutory protection in that the expiry of a fixed term contract without renewal is deemed to be a dismissal for the purposes of unfair dismissal and redundancy payments.[3]

---

[1] Such a contract may have a notice provision and still qualify as fixed term: *Dixon v BBC* [1979] ICR 281, [1979] IRLR 114, CA. In order to be a fixed term contract, the date of termination must be ascertainable: *Wiltshire County Council v National Association of Teachers in Further and Higher Education* [1980] ICR 455, [1980] IRLR 198, CA. In *McLeod v Hellyer Bros Ltd* [1987] ICR 526, [1987] IRLR 232, CA, separate crew arrangements for trawlermen were held to terminate automatically at the end of each voyage. For fixed term contracts generally, see *Harvey* Div A.

[2] ERA, s 197(1), (3).

[3] Ibid, ss 95(1)(b) and 136(1)(b) respectively. In an unfair dismissal action, this may mean that the employer has to prove that the reason for not renewing the contract was fair; note, however, that the normal two year qualifying period continues to apply.

2.03 The second area concerns *consensual termination*. An employer may seek to avoid an unfair dismissal action by arguing that in some way the employee agreed to a parting of the ways, so that there was no actual dismissal. If the facts are strong enough, such an argument may succeed—one example was where an employee, faced with loss of employment and looking for a new job, asked to be released from his contract (in order to avoid the six months' notice that he was obliged to give, and a restraint of trade clause), and this was held to be consensual termination, so that he could not later claim unfair dismissal.[1] However, in less extreme cases (for example, where an employee under notice asks to leave a week or two before the expiry of the notice in order to take up a new job) courts and tribunals will hopefully look at the matter realistically and hold that at the end of the day there was still a dismissal by the employer. In *McAlwane v Boughton Estates Ltd*[2] (a redundancy payments case) Sir John Donaldson said:

> 'We would further suggest that it would be a very rare case indeed in which it could properly be found that the employer and the employee had got together and, notwithstanding that there was a current notice of termination of the employment, agreed mutually to terminate the contract, particularly when one realises the financial consequences to the employee involved in such an agreement. We do not say that such an agreement cannot arise; we merely say that, viewed in a real life situation, it would seem to be a possibility which might appeal to a lawyer more than to a personnel manager.'

1 *Lipton Ltd v Marlborough* [1979] IRLR 179, EAT.
2 [1973] 2 All ER 299, [1973] ICR 470; cf, in the specialised context of a voluntary early retirement scheme, *Scott v Coalite Fuels and Chemicals Ltd* [1988] ICR 355, [1988] IRLR 131, EAT.

2.04 Moreover, it has recently been reaffirmed that ultimately the tribunal may have to look past the form of the dealings to see who 'really' terminated the employment; normally, it will be the employer.[1] There is, however, one exceptional category where mutual termination *has* been found more readily—although it seems clear that merely volunteering for redundancy does not affect statutory rights (the volunteering being then followed by actual dismissal by the employer),[2] if the employee in fact voluntarily takes early retirement (in lieu of being made redundant), that *will* be viewed as a consensual termination and the employee will be treated as losing his statutory rights.[3] There is a clear ground of policy behind such a holding of no dismissal since, for example, to hold that there was a dismissal so that the employee could turn round and claim a redundancy payment *as well* would probably be inconsistent with the bargain struck for the early retirement (especially if that bargain already included the payment of an ex gratia lump sum). It is probably the case therefore that early retirement cases should be treated separately and viewed as sui generis; they should not be seen as authority for a wider, more pro-employer, view of consensual termination generally.

1 *Caledonian Mining Co Ltd v Bassett and Steel* [1987] ICR 425, [1987] IRLR 165, EAT (employee inveigled into resigning; held still to constitute a dismissal by the employer in all the circumstances), applying *Martin v MBS Fastenings (Glynwed) Distributions Ltd* [1983] ICR 511, [1983] IRLR 198, CA. Moreover, where an employee's resignation is hot-headed or ambiguous, there may be an onus on the employer to ensure that it is meant before accepting it: *Kwik-Fit (GB) Ltd v Lineham* [1992] IRLR 156, EAT.
2 *Burton, Allton and Johnson Ltd v Peck* [1975] ICR 193, [1975] IRLR 87; *Morley v C T Morley Ltd* [1985] ICR 499, EAT.

3 *Birch and Humber v University of Liverpool* [1985] ICR 470, [1985] IRLR 165, CA; this was extended in *Scott v Coalite Fuels and Chemicals Ltd* [1988] ICR 355, [1988] IRLR 131, EAT to a case where the employee was already under notice of redundancy when he volunteered for early retirement instead.

2.05 The third area concerns *automatic termination* (sometimes called 'self-dismissal'). An employer could try to avoid a dismissal (and hence avoid an unfair dismissal claim) by setting up a consensual termination, eg by phrasing a final warning in terms that 'if you do this again, you agree that your contract will terminate automatically' or 'you will be deemed to have dismissed yourself'. In ordinary contract law, any such agreement between the parties could well be effective; however, it constituted such an obvious coach and horses through the employee's statutory rights that the courts have fairly clearly disapproved such arguments and held such agreements to be invalid for statutory purposes, as will be seen below.[1]

1 See paras 2.25–2.28, below.

Termination by performance or operation of law

2.06 We have seen in a previous paragraph that if a contract of employment is expressed to last for a certain period of time (or until a particular date, either by stating that date or linking it to a particular event such as the end of a course in a school which can be dated accurately in advance), that is termed a 'fixed term contract'. In contract law, the contract simply terminates without the need for a dismissal at the end of the relevant period; however, for statutory purposes the end of such a fixed term contract without renewal is deemed to be a dismissal. However, if a contract of employment is expressed to last only until a particular event which cannot be dated or until a particular piece or amount of work is completed (eg a contract to fell an area of trees), then that is *not* a fixed term contract.[1] The result is that at the end of the contract it terminates by performance, and in such a case there is *no* special statutory provision deeming it to be a dismissal. This would mean that the employee would not be able to claim unfair dismissal or a redundancy payment; realistically, however, it must be remembered that in order to claim either of these the employee must have been employed for at least two years, and presumably most such 'purpose contracts' will be for periods less than this anyway.

1 *Wiltshire County Council v National Association of Teachers in Further and Higher Education* [1980] ICR 455, [1980] IRLR 198, CA.

2.07 Termination by performance has thus not figured largely in reported cases, though it remains a possibility. Indeed, one extension of it was seen in the decision of the EAT in *Brown v Knowsley Borough Council*;[1] in that case, a teacher's contract for the academic year was expressed to be subject to continued MSC or other outside funding for the course; when the contract was not renewed for the next academic year because of the lack of such funding she claimed a redundancy payment, but the EAT upheld the tribunal decision that there was no dismissal (and so no payment)—the contract had terminated automatically by performance, on the happening of the contingency to which it was subject, ie the lack of outside funding.

[1] [1986] IRLR 102, EAT.

2.08 Potentially more of a threat to an employee's statutory rights is the other principal head of termination by operation of law—the doctrine of frustration.[1] A contract is frustrated if there is a change in circumstances which means either that the contract becomes impossible to perform or that its performance would produce a radically different result from that intended. If a contract is frustrated, it terminates automatically. In the context of a contract of employment, that means that there is no need for a dismissal by the employer;[2] once again, if there is no dismissal, the employee cannot claim unfair dismissal (or a redundancy payment if appropriate). If the employee tries to bring an unfair dismissal action and the employer raises and establishes frustration as his primary defence, that is an end to the hearing—the tribunal then has no jurisdiction to consider the fairness or otherwise of the employer's actions. Termination in such a case comes about purely by operation of law. The two cases most likely to arise in the employment context are frustration through illness or imprisonment.

[1] The frustration of contracts of employment is considered in *Harvey* Div D2.
[2] Any wages due up to the date of frustration could, if necessary, be recovered under the Law Reform (Frustrated Contracts) Act 1943.

2.09 Normally, a dismissal because of illness will, in the law of unfair dismissal, come under the heading of a dismissal for 'incapability', to be considered by a tribunal in the normal way.[1] Indeed, it is arguable that preferably the doctrine of frustration should not apply here, since it short-circuits such a tribunal action and prevents the tribunal from investigating the merits of the case. However, that is not the law, and it has been reaffirmed recently that the doctrine can apply in a suitable case.[2] In the early case of *Marshall v Harland and Wolff Ltd*,[3] Sir John Donaldson set out factors to be considered when deciding whether a contract of employment has been frustrated through illness; these are:

(i) the terms of the contract, especially on sick pay;
(ii) how long the contract was to have lasted;
(iii) the nature of the employment, especially whether the employee was in a 'key post' and had to be replaced;
(iv) the nature of the illness and prospects of recovery;
(v) the period of past employment.

[1] See Chapter 19, below.
[2] *Notcutt v Universal Equipment Co (London) Ltd* [1986] ICR 414, [1986] IRLR 218, CA disapproving *Harman v Flexible Lamps Ltd* [1980] IRLR 418 where the EAT had declined to apply the doctrine at all. *Notcutt* was in fact a common law, contractual action, but the decision also applies to a statutory action for unfair dismissal.
[3] [1972] ICR 101, [1972] IRLR 90, NIRC.

2.10 It was later pointed out in *Egg Stores (Stamford Hill) Ltd v Leibovici*[1] that the doctrine of frustration, though possibly essential in a case of serious illness part of the way through a fixed term contract, raises greater problems in ordinary employments with relatively short notice periods—should not the tribunal or court expect the employer to dismiss on notice in the normal way (and take his chances with an unfair dismissal action)? In such a case, for there to be frustration the EAT suggested the following additional factors:

- (vi) the risk to the employer of a replacement qualifying for unfair dismissal or redundancy rights against the employer;
- (vii) whether wages have continued to be paid;
- (viii) the acts and statements of the employer, in particular whether there has been a dismissal of sorts and if not, why not;
- (ix) whether in all the circumstances a reasonable employer could be expected to wait any longer.

[1] [1977] ICR 260, [1976] IRLR 376, EAT, applied in *Williams v Watsons Luxury Coaches Ltd* [1990] ICR 536, [1990] IRLR 164, EAT.

2.11 The matter is thus a difficult one; given the drastic effects on statutory rights, it is suggested that a tribunal should only find frustration through illness in exceptional cases.

2.12 Frustration through imprisonment of the employee is more straightforward and less likely to cause injustice; after all, even if frustration was not found and an unfair dismissal action was allowed to proceed, there must be a high probability that the employer would succeed in showing that the dismissal was fair.[1] However (as with illness), after some recent controversy in the case law it has now been reaffirmed by the Court of Appeal that a contract of employment may well be frustrated by the imposition of an immediate term of imprisonment on the employee.[2] One theoretical problem here has been the normal rule of contract law against the use of 'self-induced frustration', the point being that the employee himself was responsible for his imprisonment. However, the Court of Appeal laid this point to rest by holding that that rule only prevents a party from relying on his own acts as frustration; in such a case as this, it is the employer who is relying on the doctrine and so the employee's fault is not relevant. As with illness, a tribunal will have to consider all the circumstances (especially the length of the sentence and how important it was to replace the employee), but it seems likely that any substantial term of imprisonment will give rise to a strong argument by the employer based on frustration.

[1] *Kingston v British Railways Board* [1982] ICR 392, [1982] IRLR 274, EAT.
[2] *F C Shepherd & Co Ltd v Jerrom* [1986] ICR 802, [1986] IRLR 358, CA.

2 TERMINATION BY DISMISSAL

The importance of dismissal and the dangers of resignation

2.13 Dismissal has always been important, with the possibility at common law of an action in the courts for wrongful dismissal. However, with the advent over the last quarter of a century of the present statutory rights for employees, 'dismissal' has become a key *jurisdictional* factor. Putting it simply, for example you cannot be unfairly dismissed unless you have been dismissed;[1] if for some reason there is no dismissal in law, then a tribunal has no jurisdiction to hear an unfair dismissal action—hence the importance of legal doctrines such as frustration (above), which can terminate a contract without dismissal. However, the point goes further—it means that a normal *resignation* will materially jeopardise any statutory rights which depend on there being a dismissal in law.[2] It is true that if the employee feels that he has in some sense been 'squeezed out', he may (for redundancy or unfair dismissal purposes) claim to have been 'constructively dismissed',[3] *or* that if he has been presented with an ultimatum ('resign or be sacked') he may be able to argue before a tribunal or court that he was in reality dismissed;[4] likewise, an ambiguous or hot-headed 'resignation' may be considered later not to have been an actual resignation, but instead a dismissal (if the employer did not take reasonable steps to investigate the true position).[5] However, even where any such arguments can be maintained, the employee remains at a disadvantage in that in any tribunal proceedings the initial burden of proof will (untypically) be on *him*, not on the employer, to establish 'dismissal' before the case can proceed. Resignation is therefore a potentially perilous step legally.

1 The other areas in which it is vital are the law relating to redundancy payments and maternity leave (failure to allow which is treated as dismissal).

2 This can be particularly so if an employee resigns from job A in order to take up job B. Unless continuity of employment is specifically protected (eg because employer A and employer B are 'associated employers') it will be broken; this means that accrued statutory rights will have to start from scratch with the new employer (having, for example, to serve two years before being able to claim unfair dismissal if dismissed by that new employer).

3 *Harvey* Div D.

4 *Sheffield v Oxford Controls Co Ltd* [1979] ICR 396, [1979] IRLR 133, EAT; *Martin v MBS Fastenings (Glynwed) Distribution Ltd* [1983] ICR 511, [1983] IRLR 198, CA; *Caledonian Mining Co Ltd v Bassett* [1987] ICR 425, [1987] IRLR 165, EAT.

5 *Kwik-Fit (GB) Ltd v Lineham* [1992] IRLR 156, EAT.

2.14 For statutory purposes, dismissal is defined[1] as:

(a) where 'the contract under which he is employed by the employer is terminated by the employer, whether with or without notice';
(b) the expiry of a fixed term contract;
(c) constructive dismissal.

1 ERA, s 95(1) (unfair dismissal) and s 136(1) (redundancy payments).

2.15 Heads (b) and (c) are statutory extensions; head (a) will cover most normal dismissals, and it is notable that although this is a statutory definition it largely adopts the common law meaning of dismissal, and so it is still necessary to consider that meaning, under three headings—dismissal by notice, summary dismissal and whether there can be 'automatic' dismissal. It is then necessary to consider the meaning of wrongful dismissal, partly because it still exists as a possible common law remedy and partly in order to contrast it with the modern statutory remedy of unfair dismissal.

Dismissal by notice

2.16 Contracts of employment have always been unusual (from the standpoint of normal contract law) in that they are almost invariably terminable unilaterally at the option of either party by the giving of notice. Traditionally, the length of that notice depended primarily on the status of the employee, so that an employee in low status employment could well be subject to fairly short notice (a matter of days, if not hours), no matter how long he worked for that particular employer. A major departure came by statute in the Contracts of Employment Act 1963, which for the first time linked minimum notice periods to be given by the employer to the length of service, so that notice became in fact an *accruing* right; the relevant provisions are now contained in the ERA, s 86[1] and require an employer to give one week's notice for each year of employment, up to a maximum of 12 weeks.[2] This is frequently expressly incorporated into contracts of employment as the contractual term of notice, but it must be remembered that it is only the legal minimum and so it is entirely open to the parties to improve upon it by agreeing to a more generous provision in the contract.[3] Likewise, the minimum notice to be given by an employee under s 86 is one week, but the parties may agree to more (though in practice notice on the employee's part may be difficult to enforce).

---

1 See Chapter 17, below and *Harvey* Div A.

2 One week's notice becomes due after the employee has been in employment for a month, except in the case of a temporary job expected to last (and actually lasting) for less than three months: ERA, s 86(5).

3 Further, if the contract is silent on notice, there will be implied into it a term of 'reasonable notice' at common law, which might well exceed this statutory minimum (depending on the status of the employee); see, for example, the six month notice provision implied into an engineer's contract in *Hill v C A Parsons & Co Ltd* [1972] Ch 305, [1971] 3 All ER 1345, CA.

2.17 The giving of notice is a relatively formal matter; it must be given personally so that, for example, notice given collectively to a union but not individually was held not to be sufficient,[1] and likewise a mere warning of impending dismissals (eg for redundancy) is unlikely to be construed as notice.[2] Moreover, once effective notice has been given, the party giving it may not withdraw it unilaterally–any such withdrawal needs mutual consent.[3]

---

1 *Morris v Bailey* [1969] 2 Lloyds Rep 215, CA.

2 *Morton Sundour Fabrics Ltd v Shaw* (1966) 2 ITR 84; *Doble v Firestone Tyre and Rubber Co Ltd* [1981] IRLR 300, EAT.

3 There is a possible exception in the case of a hot-tempered resignation by an employee followed fairly quickly by repentance and retraction; it has been said that a tribunal should take a broad, common-sense approach to the matter and may expect the employer to investigate the true position rather than just seizing on the opportunity; *Sothern v Franks Charlesly & Co* [1981] IRLR 278, CA; *Barclay v City of Glasgow District Council* [1983] IRLR 313, EAT; *Kwik-Fit (GB) Ltd v Lineham* [1992] IRLR 156, EAT; this may also apply to a hot-headed dismissal quickly retracted: *Martin v Yeoman Aggregates Ltd* [1983] ICR 314, [1983] IRLR 49, EAT.

2.18 Where an employee is working out his notice period, ss 87–91 of the ERA protect certain basic employee rights in relation to continued payment through lay-off, sickness or holidays.[1] Section 91(5) then provides that if the employer fails to give the notice required by s 86 (above), those protected rights are to be taken into account in any action for damages for breach of contract.

[1]*Harvey* Div A. Note that the rights in ERA, ss 87–91 do not apply if the contractual notice due from the employer under the contract of employment is one week or more longer than the statutory minimum under s 87: s 87(4). This is a curious exception.

2.19 In many cases, however, an employer will *not* want the employee to work out his notice. Thus, dismissal 'with wages in lieu of notice' is common. Unless the contract had exceptional characteristics, this will normally be perfectly lawful, for three reasons: first, the employer's consideration for the contract will usually be the payment of wages, *not* the provision of work to do;[1] secondly, this means that by paying in full the wages for what should have been the notice period, the employer is discharging the contract lawfully; thirdly, this is approved in s 81(3) which states that '. . . this section does not prevent either party from waiving his right to notice on any occasion or from accepting a payment in lieu of notice'.[2] One practical point to notice is that if an employee leaves employment with money in lieu he will not be able to claim unemployment benefit during the period covered by the payment[3] (even though he may have had to work a week or two in hand at the beginning of the employment before receiving his first wages).

[1] See Chapter 1(4), above.

[2] The acceptance of wages in lieu may bring forward the date of dismissal (for contractual, if not necessarily statutory, purposes): *Staffordshire County Council v Secretary of State for Employment* [1989] IRLR 117, CA.

[3] Social Security (Unemployment, Sickness and Invalidity Benefit) Regulations 1983, SI 1983/1598, reg 7(1)(d); a similar rule applies in relation to Income Support: Income Support (General) Regulations 1987, SI 1987/1967, regs 29 and 31. Similar rules will apply under jobseeker's allowance after October 1996.

Summary dismissal; gross misconduct

2.20 Summary dismissal means the termination of the contract of employment by the employer without the giving of the notice normally required by the contract. Since employment is rationalised legally in such contractual terms, the theoretical basis for it is that the employee has behaved in such a manner that he has committed a *repudiatory breach of contract*; the employer then 'accepts the repudiation' by terminating the contract immediately, ie by treating the contract as discharged by the breach.[1] This common law right of summary dismissal (where the facts support it) is *not* abolished by the modern laws on employment protection and unfair dismissal. This can be seen from (a) ERA, s 86(6) which states that the normal right to minimum notice based on length of service (see the previous paragraph) 'does not affect any right of either party to a contract of employment to treat the contract as terminable without notice by reason of such conduct of the other party', and (b) the ACAS Code of Practice No 1 'Disciplinary Practice and Procedures in Employment', para 10(h), which states that a disciplinary procedure should 'ensure that *except for gross misconduct*, no employees are dismissed for a first breach of discipline'.

[1] *Laws v London Chronicle Ltd* [1959] 2 All ER 285, [1959] 1 WLR 698, CA; *Denmark Productions Ltd v Boscobel Productions Ltd* [1969] 1 QB 699, [1968] 3 All ER 513, CA; for a rather colourful example, see *Pepper v Webb* [1969] 2 All ER 216, [1969] 1 WLR 514, CA.

2.21 Not only is the old law on summary dismissal retained, but it is also the case that a summary dismissal is *not* of itself unfair—as at common law, a major question is whether such a drastic remedy was warranted on the facts. However, the existence today of unfair dismissal law may have the indirect effect of making an employer more wary of dismissing summarily (hence the prevalence in practice of dismissal with wages in lieu, as a generally safer option). If he decides to do so, he should make certain that he has the facts straight and adheres to any applicable procedure under the contract. This is because, quite simply, a summary dismissal does *not* mean a *hasty* dismissal; the existence of possible grounds for summary dismissal does not absolve the employer from the normal procedural requirements of (a) making such investigations as are reasonable in the circumstances, and (b) following any procedures laid down as to, in particular, affording the employee a reasonable chance to be heard and to pursue any existing appeal procedure.[1] Thus, to be lawful at common law there must be a good reason for summary dismissal, and to be fair under the statute there must such a good reason *and* the procedure adopted must have been fair in all the circumstances.[2]

[1] Of course, in a blatant case of obvious misconduct (the hand found in the till, or the homicidal assault) there may be little need for further investigation in order to act reasonably. However, even here care is needed on the part of the employer since it is not possible for him to argue later that, looked at objectively, the lack of a proper procedure actually made no difference (this defence, the so-called 'rule in *British Labour Pump v Bryne*', was disapproved by the House of Lords in *Polkey v A E Dayton Services Ltd* [1988] ICR 142, [1987] IRLR 503, HL). In this context, it may be important to notice para 10(e) of the Code of Practice which suggests that disciplinary procedure should ensure that 'immediate superiors do not normally have the power to dismiss without reference to senior management', which should provide at least *some* cooling-off period and detached reflection rather than the foreman summarily dismissing the employee at the height of a heated personal argument.

[2] Misconduct dismissals in the law of unfair dismissal are considered in Chapter 19, below.

2.22 The terminology usually adopted in practice is that summary dismissal is warranted by 'gross misconduct' on the part of the employee. It is impossible to lay down and categorise what will and will not constitute gross misconduct in every case, and indeed any attempt to do so is, as a matter of law, ill conceived. The question is one of fact in all the circumstances, given the contractual test—was this a repudiatory breach of contract?[1] However, it may well be in the interests of both parties for a firm's disciplinary procedure to indicate the sort of conduct that will put an employee in danger of summary dismissal. This is stated in the ACAS Code of Practice para 8:

> 'Employees should be made aware of the likely consequences of breaking rules and in particular they should be given a clear indication of the type of conduct which may warrant summary dismissal.'

[1] '... [T]he true question is whether the acts and conduct of the party evince an intention no longer to be bound by the contract' per Lord Coleridge CJ in *Freeth v Burr* (1874) LR 9 CP 208. See also *Wilson v Racher* [1974] ICR 428, [1974] IRLR 114, CA, where the point was also made that views as to what merits instant dismissal may well change over time.

2.23 Certain forms of misconduct will clearly put an employee at risk of summary dismissal in almost any kind of employment (eg theft from the employer)[1] but it is still worth covering such matters expressly. The ACAS advisory handbook 'Discipline at Work' gives in Appendix 3 a precedent for a disciplinary procedure,[2] which includes the following paragraph:

> '(4) *Gross misconduct*
> The following list provides examples of offences which are normally regarded as gross misconduct:
> —theft, fraud, deliberate falsification of records;
> —fighting, assault on another person;
> —deliberate damage to company property;
> —serious incapability through alcohol or being under the influence of illegal drugs;
> —serious acts of insubordination.
> If you are accused of an act of gross misconduct, you may be suspended from work on full pay, normally for no more than five working days, while the company investigates the alleged offence. If, on completion of the investigation and the full disciplinary procedure, the company is satisfied that gross misconduct has occurred, the result will normally be summary dismissal without notice or payment in lieu of notice.'

1 Note, however, that theft outside employment (or even theft from a fellow employee) might not be so clear cut—see para 15(c) of the Code of Practice on criminal offences outside employment.
2 Appendix 4 contains a simplified precedent for use by small firms.

2.24 Two points should be noticed about this guidance. The first is that the matters listed are fairly immutable and, up to a point, obvious.[1] In addition, however, when drafting a clause to cover his own particular enterprise the employer should think hard as to whether there are *other* matters which, though normally not drastic in most employments, are absolutely unacceptable in *his* business (such as the proverbial smoking in an armaments factory!); if so, these could well be listed specifically,[2] but still using the above rubric that these are 'examples' of gross misconduct (it being important not to present such a list as exhaustive, ie the *only* grounds on which someone may be summarily dismissed). The second point is that the clear references to the exhaustion of normal procedures reinforce the fundamental point made above that a summary dismissal does not mean a hasty dismissal.

1 There may still be occasions, however, when the law has to catch up with new developments, as in the fascinating case of *Denco Ltd v Joinson* [1991] ICR 172, [1991] IRLR 63, where the EAT held that usually any computer misuse will merit instant dismissal, even if no actual harm can be shown.
2 In *Denco Ltd v Joinson*, above, the EAT suggested that, wherever relevant, rules relating to the use of computers should be made express.

Automatic termination

2.25 Given that dismissal is such an important jurisdictional factor, the courts have been faced with occasional attempts by employers to short-circuit an unfair dismissal case by arguing that the contract of employment in question terminated *automatically* (so that there was no 'dismissal', so no jurisdiction for a tribunal to hear the case). Such arguments usually seek to establish that in some way the employee is deemed to have resigned. While it is true that there must in exceptional cases be a concept of resignation by conduct (eg where the employee walks out and is never heard from again), such arguments could, if pushed further, drive the proverbial coach and pair through the law on unfair dismissal. Fortunately, two decisions of the Court of Appeal have disapproved these arguments in the two areas in which they tended to appear:

(i) Resignation by prior agreement

2.26 In this type of case, the employer would rely on an agreement with the employee that if a certain event occurred (or not), the employment would terminate by mutual agreement. It tended to occur in cases where the employee was given leave of absence, but subject to a condition that 'if you do not return on the due date, your employment will terminate'. The argument that there was then no dismissal was accepted in one notorious earlier case,[1] but that case was distinguished in later cases and was finally overruled by the Court of Appeal in *Igbo v Johnson Matthey Chemicals Ltd*[2] on the ground that any such prior agreement is void under the ERA, s 203 which renders void any attempt to contract out of the protection of the statute (including the protection of the law of unfair dismissal). This particular avenue has thus been effectively closed off.

1 *British Leyland (UK) Ltd v Ashraf* [1978] ICR 979, [1978] IRLR 330, *Harvey* Div D.

2 [1986] ICR 505, [1986] IRLR 215, CA. A similar argument based on the EP(C)A, s 140 failed before the EAT in *Scott v Coalite Fuels and Chemicals Ltd* [1988] ICR 355, [1988] IRLR 131, EAT, but that was in the specialised context of an agreement for voluntary early retirement.

(ii) 'Self-dismissal' or 'constructive resignation'

2.27 The idea behind this potential horror was that in some cases an employee could behave *so* badly that he must be considered to have resigned or 'sacked himself' by his conduct. In an early case,[1] the employees (in pursuit of a dispute) walked out without informing the management and left machinery in a dangerous state; the EAT were persuaded that this constituted such repudiatory conduct that it terminated their employment by itself;[2] as there was therefore no need for the employer to dismiss them they could not claim unfair dismissal. Not only was this approach a threat generally to the law of unfair dismissal, it could also be used by an employer to try to 'set up' a self dismissal, eg by giving a final warning written in terms that 'if you do this again, you will be considered as having dismissed yourself'. This case was followed in two later reported decisions of the EAT, but was finally overruled by the Court of Appeal in *London Transport Executive v Clarke*[3] where, applying normal notions of contract law, it was held that even if the employee commits a grossly repudiatory act, the contract can still only end if the employee takes the further step of *accepting* that repudiation. By doing so, the employer in law dismisses the employee.[4] Self dismissal has thus been disapproved.

1 *Gannon v Firth* [1976] IRLR 415, EAT.

2 The theoretical justification for this view was the adoption of the 'automatic' theory that (in the exceptional case of contracts of employment) such a contract is terminated automatically merely by repudiation of it by one party; the contrary theory (the 'acceptance' theory) is now more prevalent, ie that a contract of employment is like any other contract, so that 'an unaccepted repudiation is a thing writ in water'.

[3] [1981] ICR 355, [1981] IRLR 166, CA.

[4] There is presumably also the further ground now (in the light of *Igbo*, above) that any attempt by the employer to set up a self dismissal by some form of agreement could be attacked as void under s 203.

2.28 It should not be necessary for employers to throw up their hands in despair at these developments. After all, if the employee is materially late back from agreed leave or commits a grossly repudiatory act and is sacked in consequence, it is quite likely that that dismissal will at the end of the day be found to have been fair anyway.[1] However, from the point of view of the application of unfair dismissal law these two Court of Appeal decisions are of major importance in ensuring that an employer cannot avoid an unfair dismissal action completely on spurious grounds of automatic termination.

[1] This was the eventual result in *London Transport Executive v Clarke* itself.

Wrongful dismissal

2.29 At common law, 'wrongful dismissal' is an ordinary action for breach of contract, the contract in question being a contract of employment. As we have seen, such a contract can normally be terminated either (a) summarily, for good cause, or (b) by giving the notice laid down in the contract; this means that normally wrongful dismissal will mean either:

(a) a purported summary dismissal for cause where the facts do not support such a dismissal; or
(b) a dismissal (other than for cause) where the employer has not given the notice required by the contract (either in full or not at all).

2.30 It may be that on the facts of a particular case there is some other way in which the dismissal can be said to be in breach of the contract,[1] but normally a wrongful dismissal will be one of these two; in fact normally it will mean (b). This emphasis at common law on the right to terminate by notice (for whatever reason) has meant that normally the common law remedy looks at form and procedure, rather than at the substance of the dismissal. Moreover, it tended to render ineffective other theoretical rights of an employee at common law—after all, what use was a right to disobey an illegal order[2] if, having refused it, you could then be lawfully dismissed simply by giving your proper contractual notice (which may only have been a week or two)?

[1] If, for example, a fixed term contract (subject to no notice provision) is terminated prematurely; or in the (unusual) case of a contract stating that it is only terminable on grounds A–C, and the employer purports to terminate on ground D: *McClelland v Northern Ireland General Health Services Board* [1957] 2 All ER 129, [1957] 1 WLR 594, HL. There has recently been interest in using a breach of contract action in order to enforce compliance with a (contractually binding) disciplinary procedure before an employee is dismissed—eg *Dietman v Brent London Borough Council* [1988] ICR 842, [1988] IRLR 299, CA.

[2] *Gregory v Ford* [1951] 1 All ER 121; *Morrish v Henlys (Folkestone) Ltd* [1973] 2 All ER 137, [1973] ICR 482, NIRC.

2.31 It is for this reason that the introduction of the statutory right of action for *unfair* dismissal was such a radical change; such an action looks at the reason behind the dismissal, ie at the *substance* of the matter, not just at whether proper notice has been given. Even where dismissal was purportedly for cause (ie head (a) above, where even at common law the court could look at the reason behind the dismissal), there is a significant difference in a case concerning 'after-acquired evidence'; this could arise, for example, if the employee was dismissed hastily and without notice on weak grounds of bad timekeeping, but it later comes to light that the employee had been embezzling the company. Such evidence will *not* render the (otherwise unfair) dismissal fair, because in unfair dismissal law the tribunal may only consider the facts as known to the employer at the date of dismissal.[1] However, at common law the evidence *can* be considered and may well mean that the dismissal was not wrongful, since the relevant question in a wrongful dismissal action is whether *in fact* there were good grounds to dismiss.[2]

1 *W Devis & Sons Ltd v Atkins* [1977] ICR 662, [1977] IRLR 314, HL; however, the law relating to compensation for unfair dismissal is so flexible that such an 'undisclosed rogue' may end up with a finding of unfairness in his favour, but an award of nil compensation.

2 *Boston Deep Sea Fishing and Ice Co v Ansell* (1888) 39 Ch D 339, CA.

2.32 The words 'unfair' and 'wrongful' should *never* be used interchangeably. A dismissal could be both unfair and wrongful, or could be one but not the other,[1] or neither. Each action must be considered separately. In particular, of course, it must be remembered that an unfair dismissal action goes to an industrial tribunal, whereas traditionally a wrongful action had to go to the county court or the High Court.[2] This was because an industrial tribunal had no jurisdiction over breach of contract actions. An inroad into this very unfortunate split jurisdiction was finally made by the Industrial Tribunals Extension of Jurisdiction Order 1994 (as from July 1994) which allowed tribunals to hear such breach of contract actions (up to a maximum of £25,000), provided they arise or are outstanding on termination of employment.

1 A dismissal for a good reason but without notice could be fair but wrongful; a dismissal for a poor or unsubstantiated reason but with the payment of wages in lieu could be unfair but not wrongful.

2 *Treganowan v Robert Knee & Co Ltd* [1975] ICR 405, [1975] IRLR 247; *BSC Sports and Social Club v Morgan* [1987] IRLR 391, EAT.

2.33 Remedies for wrongful dismissal are considered below,[1] where it will be seen that any form of reinstatement is unlikely to occur, and that in many cases (especially where the notice period is short) the damages awardable are fairly limited. For many people, therefore, an action for wrongful dismissal is a theoretical possibility only. However, such an action could still be of some residual importance, in at least two instances: (i) where the employee had not served the required two years' qualifying period in order to bring an action for unfair dismissal,[2] so that an action on the contract is the *only* possibility; (ii) where a highly paid employee on long notice (or a fixed term contract) is wrongfully dismissed, and damages for the notice period (or for the remainder of the fixed term contract) are likely to be significantly in excess of the statutory maximum for unfair dismissal.[3]

---

1 Chapter 3, below.
2 ERA, s 108(1); Chapter 19, below.
3 Currently £17,600 in most cases.

---

3 Remedies for breach of the contract of employment

John McMullen and Christopher Osman

3.01 In this chapter we examine, first, monetary claims for breach of contract respectively available to an employee and an employer, secondly, the employee's action for wrongful dismissal and, thirdly, injunctive relief available to employers and employees to restrain termination of employment.

1 MONETARY CLAIMS BY AN EMPLOYEE FOR BREACH OF CONTRACT SHORT OF DISMISSAL

3.02 A breach of contract by an employer gives rise to a potential monetary claim by an employee. Even if the breach is very serious, entitling the employee to repudiate the contract, he does not have to end the contract. He may keep the contract alive and sue in debt or for damages.[1]

[1] As to the distinction between damages and a claim for an agreed sum in debt see B W Napier 'Aspects of the Wage-Work Bargain' [1984] CLJ 337.

3.03 Whether an employee should in legal theory pursue his claim for breach of contract for an agreed sum in debt or in damages, depends, it may be argued, on whether he has provided the consideration to his employer necessary to earn remuneration or other benefits under the contract of employment which have been denied to him as a result of the breach. And the consideration for such remuneration or benefits is usually thought of as provision of labour. If he has provided consideration, he should be able to present a claim for the lost remuneration or benefits in debt.[1] Thus, suppose an employee who is faced with a unilateral change in terms or conditions such as a pay cut or withdrawal of fringe benefit resists the change and insists that his employer honours the existing contract terms. If he is able to carry on performing his work (indicating, while doing so, that this does not connote acceptance of the new terms[2]) he is entitled to be paid at the original, unvaried, rate. He can sue in debt for any monies not paid to him because he has been able to provide the consideration for them.

[1] See comments in *Gunton v Richmond-upon-Thames London Borough Council* [1981] Ch 448, [1980] ICR 755, CA. It could also follow that consideration is provided where there has also been *substantial* performance (*Hoenig v Isaacs* [1952] 2 All ER 176, CA: see Freedland *The Contract of Employment*, p 135). But the Court of Appeal has more recently doubted whether the doctrine of substantial performance applies to anything other than entire contracts: *Wiluszynski v Tower Hamlets Borough Council* [1989] IRLR 259, CA. *Cf*, however, Staughton LJ in *Boyo v Lambeth London Borough Council* [1994] ICR 727.

2 It is important that the employee indicates his resistance to the change—otherwise he may be deemed to have waived the breach and consensually varied the contract. Inactivity for too long will also prejudice any right to rescind the contract for breach where the breach is fundamental: *Marriott v Oxford and District Co-operative Society (No 2)* [1970] 1 QB 186, CA; *Western Excavating (ECC) Ltd v Sharp* [1978] 1 All ER 713, CA.

3.04 However, on some occasions, the employer's breach of contract may have effectively prevented the employee from providing the consideration for all of the sums due to him. This may happen, for example, where he is unlawfully laid off or is put on short-time working in breach of contract. In such a situation, theoretically, the employee's claim for remuneration is converted into a claim for damages for loss of chance to earn such remuneration. In many cases it will come down to the same thing. For the basic test of damages in contract law is to ask the question what would have happened had the contract been properly performed by the employer. And in our examples, if it had, the employee would of course have been paid his full wages and fringe benefits by the employer. As Oliver J said in *Radford v De Froberville*:[1]

> 'As to principle, I take my starting point on what I think is the universal starting point in any inquiry of this nature—that is to say, the well known statement of Parke B in *Robinson v Harman* (1848) 1 Exch 850 at 855 which is in these terms: "the rule of common law is, that where a party sustains a loss by reason of breach of contract, he is, so far as money can do it, to be placed in the same situation with respect to damages, as if the contract had been performed".'

1 [1977] 1 WLR 1262 at 1268.

3.05 The case law examples below illustrate that the employee who is the victim of a breach of contract may recover compensation from the employer. Most of them, however, fail to deal with or, alternatively, blur, the distinction between the action in debt or damages.

3.06 In *Miller v Hamworthy Engineering Ltd*[1] the company reduced the employee's working week to three days without the agreement of the employee or his trade union. His contract did not provide for him being put on to a three day week. He continued his employment after the short-time working had been introduced, after which he was, in due course, made redundant and he then left the company. He then put in a claim for loss of wages which he suffered during periods when short-time working was not agreed to by him or his union. The Court of Appeal held that the company was liable to the employee for the net loss of pay which he suffered as a result of being put on to short-time without his agreement.

1 [1986] ICR 846, [1986] IRLR 461, CA.

3.07 There are also reported instances where an employer has unilaterally reduced remuneration or withdrawn benefits. In many cases, claims by employees to recover the lost benefits have succeeded. Thus, in *Burdett-Coutts v Hertfordshire County Council*[1] six dinner ladies employed by the County Council received a letter purporting to be a letter of amendment to their contracts. The net effect of this letter was to unilaterally reduce the pay of the employees concerned. They continued to work, thereby performing their contracts in full, but they reserved their rights, and made it clear that they did not accept the change to their remuneration. It was held that they were entitled to recover arrears of remuneration of which the employer had unilaterally attempted to deprive them. The head note in the *Industrial Relations Law Reports* indicates that the employees were awarded 'damages' in the form of arrears of wages. In *Gibbons v Associated British Ports*[2] the employers purported to reduce a dock worker's weekly minimum basic wage on the ground that his union had terminated a local agreement applicable to the port in which he worked. But the employers were wrong, of course, to conclude that termination of the collective agreement of itself altered a term of the individual contract of employment which originated from the collective agreement.[3] Thus, the employee was entitled to refuse to go along with the employer's decision, and a declaration was made that payment of wages at a rate lower than the minimum basic wage would be in breach of contract. Arrears were therefore ordered to be paid.[4]

1 [1984] IRLR 91.

2 [1985] IRLR 376.

3 *Gibbons v Associated British Ports* [1985] IRLR 376; *Morris v CH Bailey Ltd* [1969] 2 Lloyd's Rep 215, CA.

4 See also Chapter 6 on the provisions of Part II of the ERA which provide an alternative means of recovery in circumstances such as these. See eg *Bruce v Wiggins Teape (Stationery) Ltd* [1994] IRLR 536, EAT; *Davies v Hotpoint Ltd* [1994] IRLR 538, EAT.

3.08 In *Keir and Williams v County Council of Hereford and Worcester*[1] the employer decided to review motor car allowances payable to employees under their contracts of employment and decided, unilaterally, that these allowances were no longer necessary. The affected employees brought an action claiming that the withdrawal of these allowances was in breach of the contract of employment. The High Court held that this was a breach of contract and therefore the employees were entitled to a declaration to that effect. The case, as reported, is mainly concerned with the issue of whether there was liability for a breach of contract. But it would certainly follow that the case had the practical effect of preventing the employer from withdrawing the allowances and the employees would have been able to recover any arrears of allowances denied to them after the breach.

1 [1985] IRLR 505, CA.

3.09 The unlawfulness of a unilateral reduction in wages or other benefits has been stoutly confirmed by the House of Lords in *Rigby v Ferodo Ltd.*[1] In this case Mr Rigby was employed as a lathe operator. Due to financial problems in 1982 the employer attempted to agree a wage reduction with the CSEU, the union representing Mr Rigby. No agreement was reached but the employer unilaterally reduced wage rates, in Mr Rigby's case by about £30 per week. Mr Rigby continued to work but issued proceedings claiming damages for breach of contract. It was held that the employer's action was a repudiatory breach of contract. But this did not of itself bring the contract to an end, as it needed acceptance by the employee for this to happen. The employee was entitled to carry on working and insist upon his rights under his contract as they stood. In this case he had not impliedly agreed to a change in his working conditions by carrying on working. He had protested about the change and had indicated that he was relying upon rights under his original contract. Accordingly he was entitled to judgment in his favour. The employer had advanced the argument that the claim for damages for breach of contract should be limited to the 12 week period of notice by which Mr Rigby, under his contract, could have been lawfully dismissed. The House of Lords rejected this proposition. The employers had not purported to issue any notice to terminate employment on the old terms and the House of Lords refused to construe the employer's repudiation as a valid notice. Accordingly, the employee's claim for damages extended to the entire period over which he had been underpaid.

[1] [1988] ICR 29, [1987] IRLR 516.

3.10 After this decision it would therefore seem that an employer who wants effectively to vary a term about payment or benefits or such like will have to issue a valid and genuine notice of termination of the contract of employment as a whole and therefore effectively dismiss employees, coupling that notice of termination with an offer to re-engage under a wholly new contract containing the new terms, to take effect from the expiry of the employer's notice. This would not entitle an employee to claim his benefits and conditions under this original contract for any longer than the notice period. But although it limits the risk of a contractual claim, it is a policy which has other risks for an employer. Since the employer will have expressly dismissed employees, that may give rise to eligibility to claim unfair dismissal and the employer will then be required to put forward a reason for the dismissal (presumably some other substantial reason) and the industrial tribunal must be satisfied as to its fairness (see Chapter 19).[1]

[1] See *Gilham v Kent County Council (No 2)* [1985] ICR 233, CA where such a dismissal was unfair, principally because the changes involved breach of collective agreements.

A controversial example of such an exercise was when, in 1991, Rolls Royce decided to terminate contracts of employment of individuals will refused to go along with contractual change. Whilst such action of course removes the risk of breach of contract (if termination is with full notice) there are other possible problems. The potential unfair dismissal risks associated with such a situation were discussed in the legal press at the time (see McGlyne [1990] New Law Journal 705). Another dimension, is the duty to inform and consult the worker representatives pursuant to s 188 of TULR(C)A. Section 188 of TULR(C)A (formerly s 99 of the Employment Protection Act 1975) dealt, until the enactment of TURERA, with consultation over multiple redundancies as defined in s 139 of the ERA 1995 (see Chapter 20). However, by virtue of s 34 of TURERA, s 188 of TULR(C)A was enlarged to cover the requirement of information and consultation with representatives over a wider range of dismissals. Information and consultation under s 188 now relates to dismissals 'for a reason not related to the individual concerned or for a number of reasons all of which are not so related' (s 195(1)). It is submitted that a dismissal for a reason not related to the individual concerned, etc. relates not only to a redundancy dismissal as traditionally defined (in the ERA) but also to a re-organisational dismissal. In other words, if multiple dismissal notices are issued in a case where this is a response to objections by employees to a change in their contracts of employment, information and consultation obligations under s 188 in favour of worker representatives will be triggered. It is important to note too that TURERA strengthened TULR(C)A in other respects concerning the duty to inform and consult, and furthermore the decision in *EC Commission v United Kingdom* [1994] IRLR 412, ECJ has, by virtue of the Collective Redundancies and Transfer of Undertakings (Protection of Employment) (Amendment) Regulations 1995 (SI 1995/2587), meant extension of the right to worker representatives other than (previously solely) recognised trade union representatives, and the duty therefore is not to be lightly disregarded. (See, in detail, Chapter 20).

3.11 Finally, returning to *Rigby v Ferodo*, it was agreed by the parties that Mr Rigby's claim, if well founded, sounded in damages rather than debt. Was this the only way of framing the claim? Could the claim have been brought equally successfully in debt? Lord Oliver said the question was 'whether the action is in truth one for damages rather than for debt and whether if the latter the same principles should apply'. But he then said: 'for my part I derive no assistance from the distinction between the action for debt and damages for it seems to me entirely immaterial whether Mr Rigby's claim be treated as one for his agreed remuneration for services rendered or as one for damages for breach of an agreement to pay it'.[1]

---

1 [1987] IRLR 516 at 519, HL.

3.12 It is respectfully submitted that this was correct in Mr Rigby's case, for not only had he been the victim of a breach of contract, thus entitling him to damages for that breach, but he could also, as suggested above, have equally well sued in debt. This was because he had continued working and been allowed to provide the consideration required to be given for the wages as fixed by his original contract. Having provided the consideration he was entitled to sue in debt for the entire amount of wages that had originally been promised to him. Thus, as Lord Oliver rightly said, it made no difference in that case whether the claim was brought in damages or debt.

3.13 Nonetheless, there can be situations where the distinction between the two claims is important. If the employee has a claim for damages for breach of contract, this claim involves a duty to take reasonable steps to mitigate loss. But no such duty applies to a person claiming in debt. However, in cases of unilateral variation of terms while the employment is continuing, the employee can do relatively little to mitigate loss as, in the majority of cases, it is entirely reasonable for him to stay in employment with the contract breaker. So, in practice, any damages claim will be met in full and will, in practice, be the same in quantum as if the claim were brought in debt. The distinction is however more relevant in relation to claims for wrongful dismissal, for example, where the employment has ended and where the employee is claiming sums (such as a payment in lieu of notice) which relate to a period following the termination of the employment rather than to a period prior to the ending of the employment. In those circumstances the duty to mitigate is a real issue. Claims for wrongful dismissal are discussed later in this chapter.

3.14 It remains to be considered whether, as an alternative to claiming wages in debt or damages for non-payment of wages, a mandatory injunction may be applied for requiring the employer to pay wages over. Generally, however, this will be a non-starter. In *Jakeman v South West Thames Regional Health Authority and London Ambulance Service*[1] the court held that where mandatory interlocutory relief is sought a more onerous test applies than that applicable to negative injunctions where the issue is whether the plaintiffs have a good arguable claim that there is a serious question to be tried.[2] The court followed the decision of the Court of Appeal in *Locabail International Finance Ltd v Agroexport*[3] to the effect that unless there are special circumstances a mandatory interlocutory injunction which, if granted, would amount to a major part of the relief claimed, should only be granted in 'a clear case'. In this case ambulance workers undertook industrial action in a pay dispute. As a result the health authority declined to pay overtime. The ambulance workers sought mandatory interlocutory relief against the authority in the form of an injunction and a supporting declaration of entitlement requiring the authority to pay them their full monthly salaries. It was held, however, that whilst there was undoubtedly a serious question to be tried the workers' case could not be said to be a 'clear' one, and the balance of convenience also lay in favour of refusing the interlocutory relief. If the workers were to succeed at trial in establishing their right to the deducted wages they would be adequately compensated by an award of damages. No authority was cited to the court in which the court had regarded temporary hardship as a ground for granting interlocutory relief in a claim for payment of wages. The court held that mandatory interlocutory relief was generally not appropriate even in a clear case of entitlement to unpaid wages. That would be effectively to by-pass the machinery provided for early recovery by the rules of the Supreme Court such as under Order 14 (summary judgment) and interim payments (Order 29, rr 10 and 11). Finally, another reason for not giving the relief asked for was that the court would not, save in exceptional circumstances, grant mandatory injunctions, as distinct from prohibitory injunctions, in cases arising out of industrial disputes. The court was of the view that it should not take any positive step by way of the grant of mandatory relief which might give to either side a greater bargaining position in the dispute than it would otherwise have.[4]

---

1 [1990] IRLR 62.

2 *American Cyanamid Co v Ethicon Ltd* [1975] AC 396, HL.

3 [1986] 1 WLR 657.

4 See also *MacPherson v London Borough of Lambeth* [1988] IRLR 470, where the High Court also refused an application for a mandatory injunction for payment of wages, again in an industrial dispute.

2 CLAIMS BY AN EMPLOYER FOR BREACH OF CONTRACT

3.15 Employees also break contracts of employment. Commonly, claims arise when an employee resigns from his employment and fails to give proper notice to the employer. An employee could even be sued for breaking his contract in not performing it properly although claims of that nature are very rarely brought in practice.

3.16 An employer who is the victim of a breach of contract has, if he claims damages for the breach from the employee, to show that he can quantify his claim and that he has mitigated his loss, and, on the whole, the general principles of contract law apply to the calculation of damages claimed by an employer in the same way as they apply to damages claimed by an employee. For example, what is the yardstick of damages in the case of an employee who resigns without giving due notice? The employer has to ask a court to consider what would have happened had the contract been performed. Had the contract been performed the employer would have enjoyed the services of the employee at the rate contractually agreed between them for the period of the notice concerned. Thus, if an individual leaves prematurely and a more expensive replacement has to be found for the period of the departing employee's notice, an employer should at least be able to recover the difference between the replacement employee's wages and the departing employee's wages (at least if it were reasonable to engage the replacement at the wage concerned). He has been put to that extra expense during the period of notice which he had not contractually bargained for.

3.17 If an employee leaves prematurely it is also possible for more indirect or consequential loss (eg loss of production, loss of profit and the like) to arise, and, in theory, if this was or ought to have been in the contemplation of the parties as a possibility if the employee broke his contract, damages under this head can also be recovered. However, the courts will think carefully before making an employee liable to an employer for large claims for consequential loss. In *National Coal Board v Galley*[1] the defendant was employed as a deputy by the National Coal Board and was contractually required to work on Saturdays if directed by the Coal Board. His trade union banned working on Saturday shifts. As a result, no productive work was possible in the mines on Saturdays. After two months had elapsed the Coal Board engaged substitute deputies at £3 18s 2d per shift; but the Coal Board's loss of production was over £3,000, a considerable sum in those days. The Coal Board brought an action for damages for breach of contract. The court declined to make the deputy liable for a proportion of the loss of production arising from the industrial action in breach of contract. As the deputy was one individual out of a number and was also a supervisor, as opposed to a face worker, the court was not satisfied that the breach of contract contributed to the loss of production. Accordingly, judgment was given only for the cost of employing a substitute.[2]

1 [1958] 1 All ER 91, [1958] 1 WLR 16, CA.

2 See also *Ebbw Vale Steel, Iron & Coal Co v Tew* (1935) 79 Sol Jo 593, 1 Law Journal Notes County Court Appeals 284 (damages limited to loss of individual output less salary saved).

3.18 It is possible also for an employer to attempt to fix the amount of damages arising from breach of contract in advance. This will be enforceable so long as it does not amount to a penalty. A common situation these days is for employers to agree in advance with an employee in respect of whom training is given or paid for the amount of the cost of training to be refunded if the employee leaves the employment of the employer within a certain period, say two or three years, after the training has been given and paid for. Such agreements may be struck down as penalties but only where they are not an attempt by the parties genuinely to pre-estimate the employer's loss and fix damages for breach of contract in advance.[1] Recent experience in the courts suggests that if it can be shown that the period over which there is a risk of repayment or reimbursement is reasonably short and that if the employee resigned his employment within that period there would be substantial inconvenience and expense on the part of the employer thrown away, such a clause will be enforceable. The clause will no doubt appear even more reasonable to the court if there is some reducing basis scheme of reimbursement, for example, if the parties agree that the amount of the sum liable to be reimbursed will reduce pro rata over the period concerned. The issue came up for consideration in the case of *Neil v Strathclyde Borough Council*.[2] In this case an employer claimed to recover from an employee a proportion of training expenses incurred in relation to the contract of employment. The contract of employment provided that in consideration of the employee being granted two years' paid leave of absence and being paid course fees for training as a social worker the employee would undertake to remain in the service of the employer for a minimum period of two years after completion of the course or repay a proportion of the cost of putting her through the course.

[1] *Dunlop Pneumatic Tyre Co Ltd v New Garage and Motor Co Ltd* [1915] AC 79, HL; Treitel *The Law of Contract* (7th edn), p 669.

[2] [1984] IRLR 14. At one stage it was proposed to introduce measures to allow employers to recover training costs thrown away in the event of premature departure by employees (see *People, Jobs and Opportunity* (CM 1810, 1992)) but this has so far come to nothing.

3.19 In the court the employee attempted to say that the clause was unenforceable and void as a penalty. It was held that the stipulation was valid and was a genuine pre-estimate of damages rather than a penalty. As the loss of the benefit of the training expenses was something that might reasonably be supposed to have been in the contemplation of both parties at the time they made the contract as a probable result of the breach of it, a claim for reimbursement of part of those expenses was well founded. The employee attempted to rely upon the case of *National Coal Board v Galley* (above) to suggest that the damages that the employer was entitled to were limited to the cost of finding a replacement and therefore, as the repayment clause went further than this, the clause was a penalty. However, the facts of the present case were quite different from those in *National Coal Board v Galley* because of the specific agreement to give two years' leave and the costs of training that had been borne by the employer.

3.20 It is to be noted that employers may occasionally revert to self-help as a remedy for an employee's breach of contract, the most common form of which being a deduction from pay. However, deductions from pay are prohibited by the ERA unless the deduction is authorised to be made by virtue of any statutory provision, or any relevant provision of a worker's contract, or the worker has previously signified in writing his agreement or consent to the making of the deduction.[1] Further, in relation to deductions from wages of workers in retail employment on account of cash shortages, the deduction has to be made within 12 months beginning with the date when the employer established the existence of the shortage or deficiency and cannot exceed 1/10th of the gross amount of wages payable to the worker on the day in question.[2] The provisions of the ERA do not, however, apply to deductions on account of a worker's participation in strike or other industrial action and, in this area, courts frequently allow deductions from pay.[3] The ERA provisions in respect of wages are dealt with in more detail in Chapter 6 and the subject of deductions from pay on account of strike or industrial action in Chapter 1.

[1] ERA, s 13.

[2] ERA, s 18.

[3] ERA, s 16(3); *Miles v Wakefield Metropolitan District Council* [1987] ICR 368, [1987] IRLR 193, HL; *Wiluszynski v Tower Hamlets Borough Council* [1989] IRLR 259, CA; *MacPherson v London Borough of Lambeth* [1988] IRLR 470. In *Sunderland Polytechnic v Evans* [1993] ICR 392; [1993] IRLR 196, EAT it was also held that for the purposes of what is now s 16 of the Wages Act 1986 whether a deduction was excluded from the operation of the Part II of the ERA was not dependent upon the lawfulness or otherwise of the deduction. In *Evans* the employee went on strike for half a day and the employer deducted a whole day's pay. The employee complained to the effect that the employer was not entitled to deduct more than half a day's pay. However, it was held that the deduction was made on account of the employee's partaking in industrial action and, as a result, the industrial tribunal had no jurisdiction to entertain the complaint, irrespective of the lawfulness of the amount of the deduction concerned. Although the case was concerned with a deduction on account of industrial action under what is now s 16(5) the principle holds good in respect of other deductions under s 16: *SIP (Industrial Products) Ltd v Swinn* [1994] IRLR 323, EAT.

3 THE EMPLOYEE'S ACTION FOR DAMAGES FOR WRONGFUL DISMISSAL

3.21 Part 1 dealt with employee claims for breach of contract *short of dismissal* and this part deals with employee claims arising from *dismissals* that are in breach of contract.

3.22 A wrongfully dismissed employee is an employee who has been dismissed in breach of contract. This usually means a dimissal with no or short notice in circumstances where this is not justified by the employee's conduct.[1] The wrongful dismissal claim can also include other breaches by the employer such as dismissal in breach of a disciplinary procedure.

[1] What type of conduct on the part of an employee will justify a summary dismissal is essentially a question of fact and is well documented and discussed elsewhere (see *Encyclopaedia of Employment Law*, Sweet and Maxwell, para 1.3.2). The most common examples include misconduct (*Sinclair v Neighbour* [1967] 2 QB 279), disobedience to a lawful order (*Laws v London Chronicle (Indicator Newspapers) Ltd* [1959] 1 WLR 698 and *Pepper v Webb* [1969] 1 WLR 514) and negligence (*Jupiter General Insurance Co Ltd v Shroff* [1937] 3 All ER 67). As far as negligence is concerned however, *Jackson v Invicta Plastics Ltd* [1987] BCLC 329 makes salutary reading for employers seeking to justify a summary dismissal on the grounds of alleged poor performance that did not on the facts amount to a case so serious as to justify summary termination.

3.23 A wrongfully dismissed employee who seeks a financial remedy will, in practice, have to seek damages for breach of contract. This contrasts with the position of an employee in continuing employment who is the victim of some other type of breach of contract which nonetheless allows him to continue performing work for the employer. As can be seen from the discussion above this will often enable him to claim arrears of wages in debt rather than in damages, thus releasing him from the duty to mitigate his loss (see below) as he has provided the consideration to enable him to earn the wages due under his contract (even though, in practice, as has been seen, the distinction between the two types of claim outside a context of wrongful dismissal is often blurred).

3.24 May a wrongfully dismissed employee claim wages in debt, for example, in relation to the notice period denied to him? To do this he must at the very least keep the contract alive. But will this serve any purpose? It has been held that a wrongfully dismissed employee may keep the contract alive even in the face of this most repudiatory of breaches.[1] However, in *Gunton v Richmond-upon-Thames London Borough Council*[2] it was also held that the consideration for wages under the contract was the provision of actual work. The court declined to hold that an employee provided consideration for his wages simply by being ready and willing to perform his work under the contract when prevented from actually doing so by the employer. So, on the basis of this authority, even if the employee keeps the contract alive in the face of a wrongful dismissal, this will serve no practical purpose in relation to a financial claim since the claim must convert itself into an action for damages for breach of contract, ie loss of chance to earn remuneration due to the employer's wrongdoing. As the action is converted into one for damages it is subject to the principles of mitigation of loss (see below). Keeping a contract alive without mitigating loss (for example, by seeking employment elsewhere) may prejudice the right to damages and therefore an employee would be unwise to keep the contract alive in this way. On the other hand, keeping the contract alive in the face of a wrongful dismissal may be important and indeed vital if the employee seeks some sort of injunctive relief (see below) (or perhaps to continue to enjoy some other right which depends on the existence of an employment contract). The wrongfully dismissed employee is therefore somewhat on the horns of a dilemma and must choose at that stage whether to keep the contract alive for the purposes of seeking injunctive relief or whether to accept the breach as terminating the employment and seek damages forthwith. And the Court of Appeal said in *Gunton* that acceptance would be readily inferred from the actions of the employee. As, in most cases (see below), injunctive relief is not available, the employee will have no practical choice other than to accept the wrongful dismissal as ending the employment contract.

---

1 *Gunton v Richmond-upon-Thames London Borough Council* [1980] ICR 755, [1980] IRLR 321, CA (majority view – see the dissenting judgment of Shaw LJ). See also comments in *Dietman v Brent London Borough Council* [1987] IRLR 259, [1988] IRLR 299, CA; see also Lord Oliver in *Rigby v Ferodo* [1988] ICR 29 at 34, HL; *Automatic Fire Sprinklers Ltd v Watson* (1946) 72 CLR 435; *Turner v Australian Coal and Shale Employees' Federation* (1984) 55 ALR 635; *Thomas Marshall (Exports) Ltd v Guinle* [1978] 3 All ER 193. There has always been a contrary argument, however, that a wrongful dismissal will put an end to the contract automatically: see eg *Sanders v Ernest A Neale Ltd* [1974] 3 All ER 327; *R v East Berkshire Health Authority, ex p Walsh* [1984] ICR 743, [1984] IRLR 278, CA. For further debate, see *Delaney v Staples* [1992] ICR 483, HL, [1992] IRLR 191 and *Boyo v Lambeth Borough Council* [1994] ICR 72; *Marsh v National Autistic Society* [1993] ICR 453. Contrast the position under statute for the purposes of unfair dismissal law where it has been held that automatic termination is the rule: *Robert Cort & Son Ltd v Charman* [1981] ICR 816, [1981] IRLR 437, EAT; *Stapp v Shaftesbury Society* [1982] IRLR 326, CA.

2 [1980] ICR 755.

3.25 What then are the general principles relative to the calculation for wrongful dismissal? As with the case of breach of contract short of dismissal (discussed) above the exercise is to ask what would have happened had the contract been performed in accordance with its terms. The court limits loss to the minimum period over which the contract would have run if terminated lawfully, ie by proper notice by the employer or until the end of a fixed term as the case may be. The court assumes that the employer, the guilty party, would have performed the contract in the manner least disadvantageous to it.[1] This will mean that the employee is entitled to recover compensation for loss of chance to earn all remuneration and other benefits receivable by the employee during the period over which the contract could have continued had the employer performed it lawfully, ie over its due term or notice period as the case may be.

[1] *Hartley v Harman* (1840) 11 Ad & El 798; *British Guiana Credit Corpn v Da Silva* [1965] 1 WLR 248; M R Freedland *The Contract of Employment* p 244, 250 et seq.

3.26 The heads of loss recoverable include salary,[1] bonuses and commissions (but only if these are contractual, as opposed to discretionary)[2] loss of use of company vehicle,[3] loss of free accommodation or board and lodgings,[4] loss of free medical insurance (such as BUPA)[5] and tips and gratuities (if there was a contractual right to receive them) from customers.[6] Other types of benefit to which the employee was contractually entitled under his employment should also be recoverable such as loss of the benefit of membership of the employer's pension scheme, loss of preferential loans or mortgages, luncheon vouchers, life assurance and any other concessions or privileges of a contractual nature.

[1] *Shove v Downs Surgical plc* [1984] 1 All ER 7, [1984] ICR 532.

[2] *Lavarack v Woods of Colchester Ltd* [1967] 1 QB 278, [1966] 3 All ER 683, CA.

[3] *Shove v Downs Surgical plc* [1984] 1 All ER 7, [1984] ICR 532.

[4] *Lindsay v Queen's Hotel Co* [1919] 1 KB 212; *British Guiana Credit Corpn v Da Silva* [1965] 1 WLR 248.

[5] *Shove v Downs Surgical plc* [1984] 1 All ER 7, [1984] ICR 532 [1984] IRLR 1.

[6] *Manubens v Leon* [1919] 1 KB 208. Another possible head is loss of opportunity to exercise share option rights (if the rights to exercise would have fallen in during the contract period). But often the scheme will be drafted in such a way that the right lapses on termination of employment for any reason. This will mean that compensation may not be available (see *Micklefield v SAC Technology Ltd* [1990] IRLR 218); cf *Chapman v Aberdeen Construction Group plc* [1991] IRLR 505 where the Court of Session in Scotland avoided such an exclusion under the Unfair Contract Terms Act 1977 for the purposes of Scottish law (using the argument that s 23 of the Act could be employed to avoid the exclusion of the employee's rights). However, some care needs to be exercised in this area as the courts are keen to avoid a contract breaker profiting from his own wrong save where the exclusion is clear, the position in each case must be examined (see *Alghussein Establishment v Eton College* [1988] 1 WLR 587, HL).

3.27 An employee who is dismissed in breach of a contractual disciplinary procedure may also be entitled to additional damages. Again, the court will look at what would have happened had the contract been followed by the employer. In two cases the courts have held that an employee dismissed in breach of a disciplinary procedure was entitled to damages equivalent to loss of wages over a period during which the disciplinary procedure would have been estimated to take place, in one case assessed at eight weeks.[1] In both of these cases the aspect of the disciplinary procedure broken was the employer's failure to hold a disciplinary procedure prior to implementing dismissal. Awards in practice are most likely to be of this order, ie a number of weeks' wages. But it is arguable that an employee entitled to the benefit of a contractual disciplinary procedure which (as recommended by the ACAS Code of Practice) contains a procedure for warnings before dismissal and who is dismissed early into his employment in circumstances where ordinarily he would be entitled to further warnings before the dismissal was implemented, may be entitled to damages for a much longer period. That would be, for example, for the period over which the whole range of warnings would have been given combined with the period given to the employee for him to meet the standards imposed in the warnings. Further, if the procedural omission is failure to hold a disciplinary hearing, is it strictly correct simply to limit damages to the period over which the disciplinary hearing would have taken place? Should the court also consider the possibility of an employee's success at the disciplinary hearing thus giving him damages for a period of employment that would have continued after the successful outcome of the disciplinary hearing? This is at least arguable under contract law.[2] Most practitioners would consider such claims ambitious, however, and the courts might instinctively refrain from awarding damages on this rather speculative basis. For to do so implies restraint on the basic right of the employer to dismiss at any time upon notice. On the other hand, what is the point, critics say, of a disciplinary procedure if it is not to be followed and if not followed, full compensation paid? This is likely to be a developing area and further cases are to be expected.

[1] *Gunton v Richmond-upon-Thames London Borough Council* [1980] ICR 755 [1980] IRLR 321, CA; *Dietman v Brent London Borough Council* [1988] IRLR 299, CA (eight weeks' loss) See also *Boyo v Lambeth London Borough Council* [1994] ICR 727 (five months loss).

[2] That damages for loss of chance may be awarded in contract law is supported by the case of *Chaplin v Hicks* [1911] 2 KB 786, CA.

3.28 The idea, however, that an employee dismissed in breach of contract might be able to claim damages at large until it is estimated he might subsequently lawfully be dismissed was dealt somewhat of a blow by the court in *Alexander v Standard Telephones and Cables Ltd (No 2)*.[1] In this case, subsequently discussed in relation to injunctions (see para 3.70), employees were employed subject to provisions of a collective agreement which provided for last in, first out in the event of compulsory redundancy. The employers ignored the provisions of last in, first out in selecting people for redundancy, substituting therefore, a balance of skills. In a preliminary action the court held that it was likely that the provisions of the redundancy procedure in the collective agreement were incorporated into the individual contract of employment and therefore there was an arguable case that those selected contrary to last in, first out had a claim for breach of contract. But on the facts, an injunction was refused.[2] At the later hearing[3] it was held by a different High Court Judge that the seniority provisions in the redundancy procedure contained in the collective agreement were not expressly or impliedly incorporated into the individual contracts of employment so as to entitle employees to claim that they had a contractual right not to be made redundant without last in, first out being applied. In any event, even if there *had* been a breach of contract in not applying last in, first out the defendants would not be entitled to damages, as claimed, covering a period down to their respective retirement ages. The notice provisions in their contracts were the relevant criterion for the assessment of their damages and since the defendant had already paid the plaintiffs a sum sufficient to cover their entitlement during the notice period they had been fully compensated and had, according to the court, suffered no damage.

[1] [1991] IRLR 286.

[2] *Alexander (No 1)* [1990] ICR 291.

[3] *Alexander (No 2)* [1991] IRLR 286.

3.29 The court therefore would not accept the argument that the employer's right to terminate the contract was qualified by the employee's right not to be selected for redundancy save upon application of the principle of seniority. With respect, this reasoning may be criticised. But it reflects the inherent conservatism of judges in refusing to award contract damages beyond the notice entitlement, save in exceptional circumstances.[1]

[1] See also *Marsh v National Autistic Society* [1993] ICR 453. An interesting contrast, however, is *Barber v Manchester Regional Hospital Board* [1958] 1 WLR 181 and also the Australian cases of *Gregory v Philip Morris Ltd* (1988) 80 ALR 455; *Wheller v Philip Morris Ltd* (1989) 97 ALR 282 and *Nicolson v Heaven & Earth Gallery Pty Ltd* (1994) 126 ALR 233 (although the Australian line of authority may dry up somewhat following the ruling of the High Court of Australia in *Byrne and Frew v Australian Airlines* (1995) 131 ALR 422 that industrial awards (containing disciplinary procedures) are not incorporated into contracts under Australian law. See McMullen (1996) ILJ 140. See also the discussion by Deakin and Morris, *Labour Law*, chapter 5, including *R v Lord President of the Privy Council, ex p Page* [1993] ICR 114, HL. See the valuable discussion by K D Ewing in 'Remedies for Breach of the Contract of Employment' [1993] CLJ 405. See also McMullen, 'Enforcing Contracts of Employment – Going Back to Basics' in the Resolution of Employment Rights Disputes (1995) ILJ 353.

3.30 Sometimes an employee is summarily and wrongfully dismissed immediately prior to the attainment of the qualifying period for claiming unfair dismissal or redundancy or some other statutory right. Even if the employee is given a payment in lieu of notice, unless the contract of employment *provides* for dismissal with a payment in lieu of notice this will be a breach of contract and therefore wrongful dismissal.[1] Indeed the employer may have wrongfully dismissed specifically to bring about an effective date of termination of employment prior to the employee's attainment of the qualifying period. Although at common law an employee might seek to reject a payment in lieu of notice and purport to keep the contract alive this will not work for statutory purposes and the statutory definition of termination of employment. For the purposes of the 'effective date of termination' under unfair dismissal law, employment terminates on dismissal irrespective of whether that dismissal is wrongful at common law.[2] It has been held, however, that in these circumstances an employee may recover damages for loss of chance to enjoy statutory employment rights such as unfair dismissal, of which he was deprived due to the employer's wrongful action.[3]

[1] *Dixon v Stenor Ltd* [1973] ICR 157, [1973] IRLR 28; M R Freedland *The Contract of Employment*, pp 183–184. Compare *Konski v Peet* [1915] 1 Ch 530. Lord Browne-Wilkinson in *Delaney v Staples* [1992] IRLR 191, HL, succinctly summarised the law as follows:

> 'The phrase "payment in lieu of notice" is not a term of art. It is commonly used to describe many types of payment, the legal analysis of which differs. Without attempting to give an exhaustive list, the following are the principal categories:
>
> (1) an employer gives proper notice of termination to his employee, tells the employee that he need not work until the termination date and gives him the wages attributable to the notice period in a lump sum. In this case (commonly called "garden leave") there is no breach of contract by the employer. The employment continues until the expiry of notice; the lump sum payment is simply advance payment of wages;
> (2) the contract of employment provides expressly that the employment may be terminated either by notice or, on payment of a sum in lieu of notice, summarily. In such a case if the employer summarily dismisses the employee he is not in breach of contract provided that he makes the payment in lieu. But the payment in lieu is not a payment of wages in the ordinary sense since it is not a payment for work to be done under the contract of employment;
> (3) at the end of the employment the employer and the employee agree that the employment is to terminate forthwith on payment of a sum in lieu of notice. Again, the employer is

not in breach of contract by dismissing summarily and the payment in lieu is not strictly wages since it is not remuneration for work done during the continuance of employment;

(4) without the agreement of the employee the employer summarily dismisses the employee and tenders a payment in lieu of proper notice. This is by far the most common type of payment in lieu and the present case falls into this category. The employer is in breach of contract by dismissing the employee without proper notice. However the summary dismissal is effective to put an end to the employment relationship, whether or not it unilaterally discharges the contract of employment. Since the employment relationship has ended, no further services are to be rendered by the employee under the contract. It follows that the payment in lieu is not a payment of wages in the ordinary sense since it is not a payment for work done under the contract of employment.'

In relation to (3) see also *Marshall (Cambridge) Ltd v Hamblin* [1994] IRLR 260, EAT. Employers should be aware of the case of *Abrahams v Performing Right Society Ltd* [1995] ICR 1028 where, as matter of construction of the contract concerned, a payment in lieu of notice clause drafted by the employer was treated as giving rise to an entitlement to a liquidated sum equivalent to two years notice monies without a duty to mitigate. It is important for employers who are seeking to reserve the right to terminate on giving a payment in lieu of notice to ensure that this is discretionary on the employer's part.

2 *Robert Cort & Son Ltd v Charman* [1981] ICR 816, [1981] IRLR 437, EAT.

3 Ibid.

3.31 It is not possible to claim damages for injured feelings or distress or for the manner of the dismissal or for the fact that the mode or manner of the dismissal has made it more difficult for the employee to obtain future employment. This rule comes from the long-standing authority of *Addis v Gramophone Co Ltd.*[1] In *Cox v Philips Industries Ltd*[2] the court held, however, that the principle did not apply for breach of contract which was *independent* of a wrongful dismissal (there the breach of a term under which the employee was promised promotion), thus enabling the court in that case to award damages for disappointment and distress. But this was not followed in *Shove v Downs Surgical plc*[3] which distinguished *Cox*. In *Shove* the employee's contract was repudiated by a wrongful dismissal upon a visit to the employee's home where he was convalescing after an illness thus causing him considerable distress. But damages could not be awarded for this fact alone.[4] The Court of Appeal in *Bliss v South East Thames Regional Health Authority*[5] refused to award damages for vexation and distress to a consultant orthopaedic surgeon whose contract was repudiated by conduct by the employer which broke the relationship of trust and confidence between the parties. The court followed *Addis* and took the view that *Cox* was simply wrong and should be considered overruled. Finally, in *Malik v BCCI SA*[6] the court followed *Addis* in holding that 'stigma damages' arising from association with an employer involved in fraudulent activities and said to reflect the increased difficulty those concerned would experience in trying to obtain alternative employment were not recoverable.

---

1 [1909] AC 488, HL, described by M R Freedland *The Contract of Employment*, p 244 as '[an] outstanding example of the restrictive approach . . .'. In unfair dismissal law (Chapter 20) too, compensation cannot be awarded for the manner of dismissal itself. But in unfair dismissal law, compensation may be payable if the circumstances of the dismissal have made it harder for the employee to get another job: *Norton Tool Co Ltd v Tewson* [1972] ICR 501, [1972] IRLR 86. An apprentice, however, may be able to sue for damages for loss of prospects if his contract of apprenticeship is prematurely terminated: *Dunk v George Waller & Son Ltd* [1970] 2 QB 163, CA.

2 [1976] 3 All ER 161, [1976] ICR 138.

3 [1984] ICR 532, [1984] IRLR 17.

4 Ibid.

[5] [1987] ICR 700, [1985] IRLR 308, CA. At the time of writing the case is due to be heard by the House of Lords.
[6] [1995] IRLR 375, CA.

3.32 An employee is under a duty to mitigate his loss. This means he must take reasonable steps to find alternative employment. However, the employee is only obliged to act reasonably and may not have to take a job which is substantially lower in status than the one he has lost.[1] It may also not be unreasonable for an employee to decline an offer of re-employment which would have the effect of mitigating loss when made by the contract breaker himself especially where confidence has been lost between employer and employee.[2]

[1] *Yetton v Eastwoods Froy Ltd* [1966] 3 All ER 353, [1967] 1 WLR 104; *Edwards v Society of Graphical and Allied Trades* [1971] Ch 354.
[2] *Shindler v Northern Raincoat Co Ltd* [1960] 2 All ER 239, [1960] 1 WLR 1038.

3.33 If an employee receives earnings in fresh employment during a period to which his wrongful dismissal claim relates these will be taken into account and deducted from his wrongful dismissal claim. Similarly if it is held that the employee has acted unreasonably during the period to which his claim relates and has failed to mitigate his loss properly a deduction will be made from the claim that the employee has brought on that ground. The amount of the deduction will depend on when the court considers it was appropriate for the employee to have mitigated his loss in response to an opportunity that arose and if so to what extent. If at trial the contract period to which the claim relates has still not run its course then a deduction from damages may be made to allow for the contingency that the employee will be able to mitigate at some stage in the near future.[1] Other contingencies can also be taken into account. Thus in *Salt v Power Plant Co Ltd*[2] a deduction was made on account of the possibility that had the contract continued there might have arisen grounds for the employer lawfully to have terminated the contract before its expiry on the ground of the employee's conduct. And in *Bold v Brough, Nicholson and Hall Ltd*[3] a deduction was made on account of the possibility of illness of the employee at some time in the future which would have given the employer the opportunity lawfully to terminate the contract prematurely.

[1] *Edwards v Society of Graphical and Allied Trades* [1971] Ch 354, [1970] 1 WLR 379; *Slingsby v News of the World Organisation Ltd* (1980) Times, 2 May.
[2] [1936] 3 All ER 322, CA.
[3] [1963] 3 All ER 849, [1964] 1 WLR 201. See the helpful discussion of this area in Freedland, *The Contract of Employment* pp 269–271.

3.34 Unemployment benefit received following a dismissal has to be deducted in calculating the amount of damages due to an employee for wrongful dismissal.[1] Also deducted will be income support (formerly supplementary benefit) and a sum equivalent to the Social Security contributions which the employee has been relieved from paying during a period of an employment following the wrongful dismissal.[2] However, in *Hopkins v Norcros plc*[3] it was held that monies received by way of pension arising out of a termination of employment could not be set off against damages to which a former employee was entitled where the termination of the contract was wrongful. Accordingly payments made under the scheme were not deductible from damages recoverable from the plaintiff for wrongful dismissal.

---

1 *Parson v BNM Laboratories Ltd* [1964] 1 QB 95, [1963] 2 All ER 658, CA. Explained in more detail in *Westwood v Secretary of State for Employment* [1984] IRLR 209.

2 *Plummer v PW Wilkins & Son Ltd* [1981] 1 All ER 91; *Cooper v Firth Brown Limited* [1963] 2 All ER 31, [1963] 1 WLR 418; *Shove v Downs Surgical plc* [1984] ICR 532.

3 [1993] ICR 338, [1994] IRLR 18, CA.

3.35 It is also important to look at the interaction between the claim for wrongful dismissal and any statutory sums received by way of compensation for dismissal. A redundancy payment will not be deducted from the sums arrived at in calculating damages for wrongful dismissal since it is an award based on previous service and not loss following dismissal.[1] However, if the employee has also brought an unfair dismissal claim sums awarded under the unfair dismissal compensatory award (but not the basic award) will be set off and deducted from the claim for damages for breach of contract in so far as the compensatory award relates to the same period of loss as the wrongful dismissal claim, for there can be no double recovery.[2] The unfair and wrongful dismissal claims do not always overlap and cancel each other out though. It is often advisable therefore to file claims for unfair dismissal and wrongful dismissal in tandem. For example, the unfair dismissal claim is not confined to the period of notice to which the employee would be entitled and can therefore take in loss suffered by an employee after the expiry of his notice period. Conversely, though, the standard unfair dismissal compensatory award is limited to £11,300 at present (from 27 September 1995) and, in the case of a highly paid employee with a fairly generous period of notice, a wrongful dismissal claim may be necessary to recover loss which is in excess of £11,300, and which still arise within the notice period. Also, certain heads of claim are recoverable in unfair dismissal law but not in a wrongful dismissal claim. For example, an unfair dismissal claim may include a payment for loss of statutory rights and, in contrast with the common law, may include an award for the fact that the manner of dismissal has made it more difficult to obtain fresh employment. An interesting case on the interaction between wrongful dismissal damages and unfair dismissal compensation arose in *O'Laoire v Jackel International Ltd (No 2)*.[3] In this case Mr Jackel had succeeded in his claim for unfair dismissal and an industrial tribunal had awarded the then maximum sum of £8,000 by way of compensation (his actual loss was much higher but the tribunal was obliged to cut this down to the statutory maximum then operating). In the claim in the High Court for damages for wrongful dismissal it was argued that the £8,000 maximum award made by the tribunal had to be set off against the damages recoverable at common law for loss of earnings during the six month notice period. It was held that since the industrial tribunal had not attributed the £8,000 maximum award to any one of the particular elements making up the total loss which they found the plaintiff to have suffered, the defendants were unable to establish double recovery by the plaintiff for the same loss and that, accordingly, no part of that award could be deducted from the damages assessed.

---

1 *Yorkshire Engineering and Welding Co Ltd v Burnham* [1973] 3 All ER 1176, [1974] ICR 77. However, in *Baldwin v British Coal Corpn* [1995] IRLR 139 it was held that an employee given less than full notice (thereby breaking the contract) in order to qualify for a supplementary or 'special'

redundancy payment had to give credit for the payment received against wrongful dismissal damages. The argument was that the employee would not have received the payment but for the employer's failure to give full notice. So this was an exception to the rule that a redundancy payment does not have to be deducted.

[2] *Berry v Ainsley Trust Ltd* (1976) 127 NLJ 1052.

[3] [1991] ICR 718, CA.

3.36 Putting in an unfair dismissal claim in addition to suing for wrongful dismissal also has a tactical advantage. As will be seen from Chapter 19, ACAS are involved at an early stage, the unfair dismissal claim will be listed for hearing quite soon and these two factors might promote settlement earlier than would otherwise be the case.[1]

---

[1] On the other hand it is always open for one party or another for technical reasons to apply for an adjournment of the industrial tribunal proceedings pending the outcome of High Court proceedings especially where the issues are the same, but perhaps very complex; see Industrial Tribunals (Constitution and Rules of Procedure) Regulations 1993 (SI 1993/16), Sch 1, r 13(7). As the case of *Carter v Credit Change Ltd* [1980] 1 All ER 252, [1979] ICR 908, CA shows, the industrial tribunal Chairman hearing the application has a wide discretion and such postponements are commonly granted. If so the employer will be able to take the heat out of the progress of the litigation: see *Riley (Lifting Equipment) Ltd v Shorrock* (1989) IRLIB 21 March 1989 p 12.

3.37 This area is affected by the long-awaited conferment on industrial tribunals of breach of contract jurisdiction. From 12 July 1994 it has been possible to pursue a common law claim in the industrial tribunal, alongside an unfair dismissal claim. However, there is a jurisdictional limit of £25,000 for a common law claim in the industrial tribunal and a limitation period of three months, neither of which apply in the ordinary courts. Naturally, then, many dismissal complaints will continue to be handled by the split jurisdictions. But although limited, this is a welcome and overdue reform.[1]

---

[1] SI 1994/1623, made pursuant to what was formerly EP(C)A 1978, s 131, as amended by TURERA.

3.38 A deduction from wrongful dismissal compensation will also be made for accelerated receipt of a sum of compensation. It is advantageous for an employee to receive compensation relating to a future period immediately in one lump sum and he may profit out of this by investing such sum until such time that he needs to use it. Accordingly, a deduction will generally be made for accelerated payment, the amount of the deduction depending on how much of the award relates to the future and indeed how far in the future. In *Shove v Downs Surgical plc*[1] an employee was awarded damages with reference to a 2½ year period of notice and a deduction of 7 per cent was made by way of a discount for accelerated payment. What the appropriate rate is of course depends upon the extent of the acceleration and the current bank rate.

---

[1] [1984] 1 All ER 7, [1984] ICR 532.

3.39 Lastly, it will be necessary to take into account the effect of taxation in relation to damages for wrongful dismissal.

3.40 Having regard to Parke B's statement quoted by Oliver J[1] to the effect that the wrongfully dismissed employee is to be placed, as far as money can do it, in the same position as if the contract had been validly terminated the necessity to ensure that the employee should be no better and no worse off requires the court, in assessing damages, to have regard to the distorting effect of tax on the payment of damages, and adjust for it.

[1] *Radford v De Froberville* [1977] 1 WLR 1262 at 1268.

3.41 The difficulty is that awards of damages for wrongful dismissal fall to be dealt with under the provisions of ss 148 and 188 of the Income and Corporation Taxes Act 1988. To the extent that damages do not exceed £30,000 they are free of tax and, in order to keep to the 'no better no worse' approach, it is necessary to adjust damages to ensure that after payment of tax (if any) on the amount of damages awarded the dismissed employee receives only the same net of tax he or she would have received had the contract been honoured (subject of course to any adjustments in respect of mitigation and accelerated payment). Additionally care must be taken where damages exceed £30,000, before adjustment for tax, to ensure that the balance over and above the tax free limit is 'grossed up' with the consequence that, after payments of tax, the amount left equates to the net loss suffered by the dismissed employee as found by the court.

3.42 The calculation exercise is somewhat complex, a state of affairs compounded historically by a fair degree of indecision, first as to whether an adjustment should be made at all, and second, as to how it should be made. The principle that an adjustment is necessary can be traced back to a personal injury case, *British Transport Commission v Gourley*,[1] which gave rise to 'the rule in *Gourley's* case'. Lord Goddard recognised in *Gourley* that the rule which was established in it to the effect that in personal injury cases tax must be taken into account and damages adjusted to ensure no benefit or detriment to the employee by virtue of receiving damages instead of salary or wages was equally applicable to wrongful dismissal cases. However, it took a number of wrongful dismissal cases to reach the point where there could be said to be a consensus as to how the rule in *Gourley's* case should be applied.[2] It was the approach followed in *Stewart v Glentaggart*[3] which got the nod of approval in the most recent case on the subject (*Shove v Downs Surgical plc*).[4] In *Stewart* the damages (before applying *Gourley*) exceeded the (then) tax-free limit and the court held that the whole 'gross amount' of the damages should be reduced applying the rule in *Gourley's* case before being grossed up by the amount of tax the employee would pay receiving the payment by way of damages. In contrast the approach in *Bold v Brough, Nicholson and Hall Ltd*[5] was to deduct the tax-free element from the 'gross' damages, apply *Gourley* to it and award the balance of the damages gross to be taxed in the hands of the dismissed employee. The court in *Shove* preferred *Stewart* which in truth appeared (though more complicated) to get close to Parke B's principle at a time when the treatment of damages (with top slicing relief) was more complex than it is now. On balance, notwithstanding the recent simplification of the tax treatment of such payments, this approach is still to be preferred.

[1] [1956] AC 185, [1955] 3 All ER 796, HL.
[2] *Parsons v BNM Laboratories Ltd* [1964] 1 QB 95, [1963] 2 All ER 658, CA; *Stewart v Glentaggart* 1963 SLT 119, [1963] TR 345; *Bold v Brough, Nicholson and Hall Ltd* [1963] 3 All ER 849, [1964] 1 WLR 201.

[3] 1963 SLT 119, [1963] TR 345.
[4] [1984] ICR 532, [1984] IRLR 17.
[5] [1963] 3 All ER 849, [1964] 1 WLR 201.

3.43 *Shove* provides a useful guide to the way in which it may be anticipated the courts will calculate damages for wrongful dismissal although without the benefit of the detailed calculations of the parties which resulted in some of the figures quoted in the judgment of Sheen J. Mr Shove's contractual benefits comprised:

(a) a gross salary of £36,000 per annum;
(b) private use of a fully expensed Daimler car;
(c) membership of the company pension scheme;
(d) private medical cover for himself and his wife;
(e) disability insurance.

3.44 His contract provided for 30 months' notice. For this period his net salary (applying *Gourley*) came to £53,000 (note the tax rates applicable are those prevailing at the date of dismissal); the private use of his company car was valued at £10,000 (the court being guided not by the artificially low value placed on such a benefit by the Inland Revenue at the time but by the running cost figures published by the Automobile Association assuming 5,000 private miles a year); the loss of life insurance cover (part of the pension scheme) was valued at £6,600 and private health cover at £700. From the resultant total (£70,300), £5,000 was deducted (being the court's assessment of likely earnings in mitigation) and 7 per cent discount to adjust for accelerated payment applied giving a running total of £60,729 which was then grossed up by the amount of tax Mr Shove would have to pay on the award to arrive at a figure of £83,477. Loss of pension rights was dealt with separately and in cases like that of Mr Shove it will usually be necessary to employ actuarial assistance to calculate the dismissed employee's loss. Shortly stated it will be the value to the employee of a further period of membership of the scheme to which he or she belonged (excluding any contribution by the employee to the scheme in question). In practice this will not generally be calculated by reference to the employer's contributions to the scheme in respect of the employee as many modern 'final salary' schemes are funded by the employer paying a contribution in respect of all staff who are members of the scheme in question expressed as a percentage of the patrol. This percentage will be fixed by the scheme's actuaries having regard to the actual and contingent liabilities in respect of the members of the scheme. This 'across the board' calculated contribution is no real guide (or at best a crude one) as to what the dismissed employee will have lost as a consequence of being forced to cease membership of the relevant scheme prematurely. The true loss may be a much larger figure in the case of a long-serving employee nearing retirement and a much smaller one where the employee is young and has only recently joined the scheme.

3.45 What the report of *Shove* did not reveal was the precise method of calculation used in the course of arriving at the final award of damages and the following calculation attempts to replicate the approach that the parties' accountants are likely to follow in a typical wrongful dismissal case. It should be noted that:

(1) the *Gourley* calculation begins by working out the applicable tax rates as far as the damages payment is concerned at the time of dismissal and

having regard to tax already paid (and personal allowances exhausted) during the relevant tax year in which the dismissal takes place;

(2) the calculation ensures that the true non-taxable element of any fringe benefits such as a company car or life insurance cover (often part of a pension scheme) is included;

(3) that in order to arrive at net salary, not only the employee's tax but also pension and NI contributions are deducted;[1]

(4) the rates of tax in calculating the dismissed employee's net loss and then grossing up so that after payment of tax the employee will receive the correct amount of damages equal to his net loss, are those applicable at the date of dismissal not the date of the judgment (or calculation).

1 *Cooper v Firth Brown Ltd* [1963] 2 All ER 31, [1963] 1 WLR 418.

3.46 Ironically, there is a slight benefit to the employer as a consequence of the application of *Gourley*, in that the tax on the first £30,000 of the payment of damages is saved. It is deducted from the dismissed employee's payment but it is not, of course, paid to the Inland Revenue. However, the amount saved is much less than it used to be under the old top slicing provisions, and seldom represents a true 'saving' once all the other costs (eg professional fees associated with a wrongful dismissal—even one which is settled amicably before the commencement of proceedings) are taken into account.

3.47 The Inland Revenue have said that 'termination of employment in circumstances which amount to unfair dismissal, whether that comes about because the employee is sacked or forced to resign, will not constitute "retirement" for taxation purposes'. However, employers should take care that the dismissed employee will not be considered by the Inland Revenue to have 'retired' rather than to have been dismissed. This would have the effect of making the entire termination payment fully taxable as a payment under retirement benefit and therefore the £30,000 exemption is lost.

3.48 Classifying such payments as retirement benefits sometimes happens when the dismissed employee is in his or her 50s or older, and 'retires' for the purposes of receiving an early pension through the company pension scheme (often where it is unlikely that that employee will find new employment) albeit that that employee is below normal retirement age and looking for other full-time employment. The Revenue have said that an *ex gratia* payment to an employee of older years who has no other full-time employment in prospect should be treated as fully taxable, although conversely age and availability to work can be put forward when arguing that the payment be treated as a 'golden handshake' for tax purposes.

3.49 Where there is a risk that the payment may become fully taxable employers should seek Revenue clearance from their local tax inspector prior to making the termination payment (or withhold tax until that clearance is given). Furthermore, to avoid this risk, in correspondence the employer should state specifically what the termination payment relates to, ie compensation for loss of office, unfair dismissal rights, statutory redundancy etc., and not merely express the payment as '*ex gratia*'.

A typical calculation of damages for wrongful dismissal

The facts

3.50 The calculation in Table 3.51 assumes that the dismissed employee was employed by a company under a contract which required two years' notice of termination and that none was given. The employee's annual salary was £55,000; the employee received a contractual bonus of £20,000 (which it is reasonable to assume would have continued to be paid at this level during the notice period having regard to the company's past and prospective performance), and had the use of a 2.5 litre car less than four years old costing less than £25,000 when new which the employee drove for more than 2,500 miles on business but less than 18,000 each year, but in respect of which petrol consumed during private use was also paid for by the company that employed him. The annual value of the use of the car is considered to be £6,500 for the purposes of the calculation. The dismissed employee is assumed to be married and to have a mortgage of £30,000 on which the rate of interest is 8 per cent per annum. Additionally the company made pension contributions in respect of the employee (which in fact equate to the loss suffered as a consequence of the dismissed employee ceasing to be a member of the company's pension scheme) as did the employee himself, and the company also paid for private health cover. It is further assumed that the dismissed employee will be successful in mitigating his loss at least to the extent of £10,000 per annum net for the two years the contract would have continued had proper notice been given. The discount for accelerated payment is based on a rate of interest of 6 per cent net of tax.

3.51 First stage—applying *Gourley*:

Salary and taxable benefits for 12 months		
Salary	£55,000	
Contractual bonus	20,000	
Inland Revenue value of company car	5,833	
Petrol (including private use)	1,320	
Health Insurance premiums	500	
	£82,653	£82,653
Less:		
Personal allowance (say, married man's)	£5,555	
Personal pension contributions	2,750	
Mortgage interest relief (at 8%)	2,400	
Taxable salary	£10,705	£10,705
Taxable salary		£71,948
Tax thereon:		
20% £1–£3,900	£780	
24% £3,901–£25,500	5,184	
40% £25,501–£71,948	18,579	
Tax on 12 months salary and taxable benefits	£24,543	£24,543
Salary and taxable benefits net of tax		£47,405
Add value of benefits not liable to tax		
Car (£6,500–£5,833)	£667	
Health insurance (£1,000–£500)	500	
Company pension contributions	5,500	
	£6,667	£6,667
		£54,072

Less:		
National Insurance contributions	£2,112	
Mitigation (not after reliefs and allowances)	10,000	
	£12,112	£12,112
After tax loss for 12 months		£41,960
After tax loss for 24 months		£83,920
Less:		
Discount for accelerated payment at, say 6%		£5,035
Amount to be grossed up		£78,887
Less:		
Tax free relief		£30,000
Total to be grossed up		£48,887

[1] For any period of less than 12 months a separate calculation should be done, using the appropriate proportion of salary, benefits and reliefs.

3.52 Second stage—Grossing up:

Calculation to gross up £48,887

Taxable salary received from 5 April to date of termination (calculated proportionately after deduction of full reliefs) £14,800

Gross	*Rate*	*Amount*	*Tax*	*Net*	*Net total*
14,801–25,500	24%	14,077	3,378	10,699	10,699
25,501 and above	40%	63,646	25,458	38,188	48,887

Summary

Tax free amount	£30,000
Net of tax amount	£48,887
Tax payable	£28,836
TOTAL AWARD OF DAMAGES:	£107,723

3.53 Typically, many potential wrongful dismissal claims are settled before they reach the court (or at least before a hearing). Unlike unfair dismissal, the parties can freely conclude a settlement agreement without the intervention of ACAS and the completion of form COT3 or following the procedure introduced by TURERA.[1] Subject to checking with the employer's relevant Inspector of Taxes, it is usual (where the amount being paid exceeds £30,000 being the tax-free amount) for the employer to be allowed, following the issue of a P45 upon the termination of employment, to pay the first £30,000 without deduction of tax, and to deduct and account to the Inland Revenue for tax at the basic rate on the balance of the payment in excess of £30,000 leaving further adjustments to be subsequently sorted out between the Inland Revenue and the former employee.

[1] See Chapter 19.

4 INJUNCTIVE RELIEF

(A) Introduction

3.54 The courts have for long set themselves against ordering specific performance of contracts of employment, either to order an employer to take back an employee who has been wrongfully dismissed, or to order an employee to return to work.[1] There are various reasons for this, for example that the contract of employment is a contract for personal services which the courts should not be asked specifically to enforce on the ground of inability of the court to supervise any order granted. And also courts would not wish to turn the contract into one, in effect, of slavery.[2] However, there are instances, albeit in limited circumstances, when the courts will depart from this stance.

[1] *Chitty on Contracts*, vol 2, para 3527.
[2] *Chitty on Contracts*, vol 1, para 1771.

(B) Injunctive relief in favour of an employer

3.55 As stated, the courts will not order specific performance of a contract of employment and order an employee to return to work. This common law position is underpinned by statute, for in s 236 of TULR(C)A it is provided that:

> 'no court shall, whether by way of (a) an order for specific performance or specific implement of a contract of employment or (b) an injunction or interdict restraining a breach or threatened breach of such a contract, compel an employee to do any work or attend at any place for the doing of any work'.

3.56 Subject to TULR(C)A, s 236, it is, however, possible for an employer to seek an injunction against an employee. The rule is, though, that the injunction must not indirectly have the effect of an order for specific performance. The area in which this possibility most commonly arises is where an employer wishes to stop an employee breaking his contract by working for a competitor. Here, though an employer cannot compel performance due to him, he may seek an order restraining the employee from working for another. This does not offend against the rule against specific performance provided two conditions are met. First, there must (on the traditional view, see below) be an express negative covenant in the contract, ie a promise by an employee not to work for another. The authorities say that the court will not enforce a positive covenant and the court will not imply a negative covenant.[1] (On the other hand, the Court of Appeal in *Provident Financial Group plc and Whitegates Estate Agency Ltd v Hayward*[2] considered that it could enforce a negative obligation not to work for another employer during any period of notice based on the implied duty of good faith.)

[1] *Mortimer v Beckett* [1920] 1 Ch 571; *Whitwood Chemical Co v Hardman* [1891] 2 Ch 416.
[2] [1989] IRLR 84, CA.

3.57 Second, the principles of restraint of trade (see Chapter 4) must be borne in mind. The form of injunction sought must not be so wide as to stop the employee working for anyone at all and therefore amounting to a 'work or starve' order. To ensure success the application must be made for an order preventing the employee working for another employer doing the type of work for which he was employed by the first employer.

3.58 Thus in *Warner Bros Pictures Inc v Nelson*[1] the actress Bette Davis undertook to work exclusively for the plaintiff but then broke the agreement and sought to work for another film company. An injunction was sought to restrain her from working for any other film company therefore enforcing the express negative covenant to that effect in her contract of employment. It was held the injunction should be granted. An argument was raised on her behalf that the injunction would amount to a 'work or starve' order because she was an actress who starred in films. But this was countered by the finding that there were other means by which Miss Davis might earn her living apart from appearing in films.

1 [1937] 1 KB 209, [1936] 3 All ER 160. See too *Lumley v Wagner* (1852) 1 De GM & G 604.

3.59 A more enlightened attitude as to whether the enforcement of a negative covenant would amount to a 'work or starve' order can be found in *Page One Records Ltd v Britton*.[1] In this case the 'Troggs' pop group had contracted with their manager not to employ any other manager or agent during the life of their contract with their present manager. This contract was broken and the manager sought an injunction to restrain the group from engaging another manager. The case has obvious similariites with the *Warner Bros* case. In theory, the Troggs could continue as a group and earn their living without employing any manager or agent at all, thus complying with an injunction. But judicial notice was taken of the fact that pop groups need to have managers to be successful and therefore, in effect, this would amount to a 'work or starve' order and thus an order for specific performance by the back door. An injunction was therefore not granted. Likewise, in *Warren v Mendy*[2] the plaintiff boxer's manager claimed that a third party had, by taking over management of the boxer, induced breach of the contract of management between the plaintiff and the boxer, Mr Nigel Benn. But the injunction claimed against the third party was refused because it would, in effect, have compelled Mr Benn to perform his obligation to be managed by the plaintiff.

1 [1967] 3 All ER 822, [1968] 1 WLR 157.
2 [1989] IRLR 210, CA.

3.60 The courts may, in a suitable case, take a different view where an employer, faced with a situation where an employee is about to leave in breach of contract to join a competitor, affirms the contract and continues to perform his side of the bargain by continuing payment of wages or salary to the employee. In such circumstances he may be able to obtain an injunction to restrain the employee from working for the competitor or rival. In *Evening Standard Co Ltd v Henderson*,[1] Henderson was employed by the *London Evening Standard* as production manager. His contract of employment provided for one year's notice to be given by either party to terminate the contract and contained a negative stipulation preventing the employee from working for anybody else during the life of the contract. Mr Henderson then purported to join the staff of a rival paper but declined to give the one year's notice of termination due under his contract. It was held that the employers were entitled to an injunction restraining the employee from working for a rival newspaper during the currency of the contract. The employers were entitled to this injunction because they had declined to accept the repudiation as terminating the contract and they had offered to continue to perform their side of the contract by paying wages to the employee as if he were still employed. Although the court was mindful of the fact that an injunction to restrain breach of a negative covenant can, in many cases, have the effect of an order for specific performance and therefore a 'work or starve' order, this was mitigated in the present circumstances by the fact that the employer had undertaken to continue paying salary and contractual benefits throughout the remainder of the contractual notice period irrespective of whether the employee was willing to perform his work.

---

[1] [1987] ICR 588, [1987] IRLR 64, CA. A recent example is *GFI Group Inc v Eaglestone* [1994] IRLR 119. In this case a highly paid, highly skilled options broker whose customer connections had been expensively fostered at his employer's expense terminated his employment at short notice. He intended to enter into competition with his employer. The employer obtained an ex parte order restraining the employee. At an interlocutory hearing, the employee sought to have the order set aside to allow him to work for the competitor before the 20 week contractual period of notice had expired. The employer resisted this, undertaking to pay the employee his salary and bonuses to the end of the period covered by any order and not to claim such sums as damages for breach of contract. It was accepted that the employee was exceptionally highly paid, of great experience and standing, and had close personal relationships with the employer's customers carefully and expensively fostered at the employer's expense. Were he to move directly to a commercial rival he would enable such rival to have some substantial benefit from the customer connections built up through the employer's employment of an investment in him. It was proved that there was an interim period between employments during which the employer would suffer damage reflected in loss of goodwill which would not be readily quantifiable in terms of damages. However, looking at the balance of convenience, the Judge held that relief should not be granted otherwise than where was absolutely necessary. Other employees who were to leave with the employee, the defendant in the case, were under a four week notice period, which had expired, and were now working for the competitor. Given that, the question was whether it was really necessary in order to protect the interests of the employer for the remainder of the 20 weeks to pass before the employee could join them. Accordingly, the application for an order covering the full 20 weeks was refused, and a period of 13 weeks substituted. However, this was the only factor against the employer's application. Had it not been for the position of the fellow employees already being in employment with a competitor the Judge would have been strongly motivated to hold the employee to his word: 'if there was a current impression that the periods in contracts negotiated with highly paid, highly skilled employees did not have the meaning that they purported to have, then the sooner that was corrected the better'.

3.61 But a subsequent case illustrates the need for the court to have in mind the principles of restraint of trade in considering the terms of the injunction. In *Provident Financial Group plc and Whitegates Estate Agency Ltd v Hayward*[1] Mr Hayward was employed by Provident as a financial director of Whitegates Estate Agency Ltd. His contract of employment stipulated that he would not undertake any other business or profession or become an employee or agent of any other person, or have any financial interest in any other business or profession during the life of his contract. In July of 1988 he resigned, and although his notice period was 12 months, it was agreed that this could be reduced by six months so that he would leave in December 1988. In September, however, Provident decided that it did not want Mr Hayward to work out his notice and required him to stay at home and receive his full pay until December until his contract would terminate. He was therefore put on what is known as 'garden leave'. In response, Mr Hayward then handed his notice in with a view to leaving and joining a competitor. The employer sought an injunction restraining him from joining a competitor. At trial, the employer was refused the injunction applied for. In the Court of Appeal the decision was upheld; in the very short time that the agreed period of notice had yet to run there was no serious prospect of any damage to the employer's business from the employee's new activity. His job was an administrative one and any confidential information that he had would not be relevant to the new employer. However, the Court of Appeal firmly stated the court was empowered to grant an injunction in such circumstances given appropriate facts.

[1] [1989] ICR 160, [1989] IRLR 84, CA.

3.62 Although the employee won, two key points argued by him for refusal of an injunction were rejected by the Court of Appeal. First, it will be noted that the express negative stipulation in the contract was extremely wide and did not relate solely to work with a competitor. The employee argued that for a negative stipulation to be enforced it must be specific and the terms of the injunction applied for have to follow the words in the contract. If this would mean the injunction, if granted, would be too far-ranging then an injunction should not be granted. However, the court held that it had discretion to narrow the term of the restraint and grant a lesser form of relief if applied for by the employer, thus enforcing the implied duty of good faith in the contract.[1] Secondly, the employer argued that when he was put on 'garden leave', he was prejudiced by not being able to work. But it was held there was no good reason in principle why an injunction should not be granted on the grounds solely that the employee's skills would allegedly atrophy over a period of three months; over such a short period it was unlikely that any damage of this nature would ensue. It might be different in a case where the period of restraint was longer, but not in the present situation. Interestingly, it was not argued that by sending the employee home the employers were in breach of contract because of an implied right in certain contracts of employment that an employee must be given work to do.[2] Had this been the case the employee would, arguably, have been entitled to repudiate the contract on the grounds of the employer's breach of contract under the principle in *General Billposting Co Ltd v Atkinson* thereby releasing him from the restraint altogether (see Chapter 4).[3]

[1] The traditional rule is that there is no right to work: *Collier v Sunday Referee Publishing Co Ltd* [1940] 2 KB 647, [1940] 4 All ER 234. But there are some exceptions to that these days: *Langston v Amalgamated Union of Engineering Workers* [1974] 1 All ER 980, [1974] ICR 180, CA; *Breach v Epsylon Industries Ltd* [1976] ICR 316, (1976) IRLR 180, EAT; *Bosworth v Angus Jowett & Co Ltd* [1977] IRLR 374, IT; McMullen [1978] NLJ 848.

[2] The discretion a court has to be more flexible and award injunctions for shorter periods than the full notice period was confirmed by Neil LJ in *Credit Suisse Asset Management Ltd v Armstrong and others* [1996] IRLR 450, CA when he said that the court had 'a wide discretion both to the period of the injunction and as to its scope'. This contrasts with the treatment of restrictive covenants where the court is supposed not, in general terms, to modify the scope of the period of the restraint lest it falls foul of the rule that it should not be re-writing the covenant for the parties.

[3] [1909] AC 118, HL. The answer for the employer is to include an express 'garden leave' clause in the employment contract. But if drafted it should not seek to be too ambitious for the reasons explained in this discussion.

3.62A The conditions to be inferred from *Provident Financial* for a garden leave type injunction were synthesised by Mehigan and Griffiths in *Restraint of Trade and Business Secrets: Law and Practice*,[1] as follows:

'(a) that the employer has not accepted the employee's repudiatory breach;
(b) that the employer has not agreed to provide the employee with any particular type of work. If there is such an agreement and the employee is required to be on "garden leave" he can argue that the employer has repudiated the agreement;
(c) that the employee will receive the same salary and benefits whilst on garden leave as he did whilst at work;
(d) that the employer can demonstrate existing or likely detriments. In *Provident* it was said that fostering the profitability of a trade rival can constitute detriment . . .;
(e) that the period for which garden leave is sought is not excessive;
(f) that the employee is not engaged in an activity where to grant a garden leave injunction might deprive him of future work or if his skills might atrophy during the relevant period.'

---

[1] 2nd edn, p 213.

3.62B It therefore seems useful when drafting garden leave clauses and when looking at the service agreement generally:

(1) to provide an express negative stipulation that work should not be carried out for others;
(2) that no particular work is assignable to the employee by the employer;
(3) that the employer has the right to require an employee specifically to be on garden leave during a period of notice (and where the period of notice concerned is long, thought should be given to allowing the employer at its discretion to impose a period of garden leave shorter than the period of notice concerned).

3.62C It has been doubted whether all of these conditions are strictly necessary (for example as explained above it has been doubted whether an express negative stipulation is required for a garden leave injunction on the view that the implied duty of good faith would suffice to require an employee not to work for another during his notice period) but out of an abundance of caution the above should be considered.

3.62D In the latest case on garden leave, the court took a robust view notwithstanding that, arguably, the drafting of the garden leave clause did not entirely meet the above points.

3.62E In *Euro Brokers Ltd v Rabey*[1] Rabey was employed by Euro Brokers as a money broker. Success in the job depended on establishing good relations with customers and he was given generous expenses to foster customer relations. He had very close working relationships with five customers in particular. He was given a new contract in February 1994 and he was given the opportunity to have legal advice on it. The contract was for one year to be determined by either party giving to the other six months notice. The contract provided that in the event of the employee giving inadequate or no notice of termination 'the company may elect to waive your breach of contract and hold you to the terms of this agreement for the notice period or a maximum period of six months whichever is the lesser period in circumstances where it is reasonable to believe that you will be interested or concerned in any business, company or firm carrying on the business of money broking'.

[1] [1995] IRLR 206.

3.62F In June Rabey purported to resign forthwith. The employer rejected this and required him to give six months notice and stated that he would be bound under the terms of the contract until December. When they discovered that he intended to join a rival firm, they told him he would be placed on garden leave in that he would not be required to attend the company's offices during the notice period but would continue to receive his salary and all other benefits.

3.62G It was held that an interlocutory injunction should be given. A lavish and expensive customer connection which has been furthered at the employer's expense forms part of the goodwill of the business and is something that the employer is entitled to protect. Six months was not unnecessarily long in view of the customer connection concerned on the facts and there was no evidence that he would be damaged himself in any way if he was kept out of the market for six months rather than some lesser period. A factor, too, was that no objection was made to the term requiring six months notice when the new contract was signed. Also, it was not accepted that a pre-requisite for granting an injunction to enforce a garden leave provision was that the employee should be offered to work of a similar type rather than remaining idle.

3.63 Finally, employers are frequently granted injunctions to restrain breach of duty of fidelity under the contract of employment, principally where the employee has taken with him and used for his own benefit the trade secrets of his former employer and to enforce restrictive covenants. These cases are discussed separately in Chapter 4, including the issue of the interrelationship between garden leave injunctions and the enforcement of post termination restrictive covenants.

(C) Injunctions to restrain dismissals and other breaches of contract of employment

3.64 Section 236 of TULR(C)A does not prevent an employee applying for an order for specific performance against an employer but there is a reluctance at common law to grant orders in favour of employees for continuation of contracts.[1] The basic rule is that an order will not be made. However, the policy considerations against awarding specific performance in favour of employees are not as compelling, it is submitted, as the arguments restraining an employer seeking specific performance against an employee. Such considerations, which include the personal element of the employment relationship and the difficulty of supervising injunctive relief are, these days, somewhat unsatisfactory in the context of the appropriateness of orders in favour of employees. Many employers are now large statutory authorities or public or private corporations where the personal nature of the relationship is not so pronounced. And the question of difficulty of supervising an order for continuation of the contract did not deter the legislator from providing for reinstatement of an employee as a remedy for unfair dismissal in the statutory context. It may well be that the considerations which caused the courts to decline specifically to enforce a contract in Victorian times are no longer apposite today. Some trenchant criticisms against the arguments for refusing specific performance can be found in the judgment of Megarry J in *CH Giles & Co Ltd v Morris*[2] when he said:

> '. . . one day perhaps the courts will look again at the so-called rule that contracts for personal services or involving the continuous performance of services will not be specifically enforced. Such a rule is plainly not absolute and without exception, nor do I think that it can be based on any narrow consideration such as difficulties of constant superintendence by the courts. I do not think that it should be assumed that as soon as any element of personal service or continuous services can be discerned in a contract the court will without more refuse specific performance.'

1 *De Francesco v Barnum* (1890) 45 Ch D 430.
2 [1972] 1 All ER 960, [1972] 1 WLR 307.

3.65 The case which first seemed to break the mould is *Hill v C A Parsons & Co Ltd.*[1] In this case a chartered engineer was wrongfully dismissed by his employers as a result of pressure applied upon the employers by a trade union. An injunction was granted restraining the employers from treating the employment as at an end until the expiry of the period of notice to which the employee was entitled. Lord Denning MR said 'it may be said that by granting an injunction in such a case the court is indirectly enforcing specifically a contract for personal services. So be it.' However, the case has been explained as being an exception to the general rule and having three special features which will not be present in many cases.[2] First, confidence between the employer and employee was still existing. The employer only reluctantly dismissed at the behest of the trade union. Confidence in the employment relationship and the willingness of the employer to continue the relationship will be absent in most cases of wrongful dismissal. Secondly, the effect of Mr Hill's wrongful dismissal would otherwise have been to terminate his employment effectively before the commencement date of the new unfair dismissal law contained in the Industrial Relations Act 1971. The court was anxious to extend his employment so that his period of employment straddled the commencement date of the Act thus enabling him to exercise his new statutory right to claim unfair dismissal. Thirdly, in all the circumstances, damages would not have been an adequate remedy.

1 [1972] Ch 305, [1971] 3 All ER 1345, CA. Mutuality is another argument raised against specific performance from time to time. That is that unless the contract is mutually enforceable by both parties, the court will not grant specific performance to one of them. Counsel in *MacPherson v London Borough of Lambeth* [1988] IRLR 470 submitted that because employers were restricted by TULR(C)A, s 236 (formerly TULRA, s 16), no order could be granted to an employee. The point was not decided. But it is submitted that this should be rejected. Even if the principle of mutuality is applicable in this area, s 236 only restricts an employer obtaining an order to compel work—it does not prevent him getting an order for the contract to be continued.
2 By Megarry J in *Chappell v Times Newspapers Ltd* [1975] 2 All ER 233, [1975] ICR 145, CA.

3.66 For a long time *Hill v C A Parsons* stood alone and looked like a case depending on its own, very special, facts. But, later, injunctions to stop dismissal re-emerged as a possibility. In *Irani v Southampton and South West*

Hampshire Health Authority[1] the plaintiff was an ophthalmologist employed by the authority. A difference of opinion arose between the plaintiff and the consultant in charge of the clinic where he worked. As a result of this clash the authority set up an inquiry and concluded that the differences were irreconcilable and that, to resolve the situation, the plaintiff (who was more junior and part time) should be dismissed. In doing so it failed to follow the disputes procedure laid down by the Whiteley Council for the Health Services incorporated into the contract of employment. An injunction was sought to restrain the employers from acting upon the dismissal until the procedures had been applied. It was held that the injunction should be given. In granting the injunction the High Court stressed the similarity with some of the features in *Hill v C A Parsons*, principally, that confidence in the employee's abilities was intact. However, there is one fundamental difference between *Irani* and *Hill*. In the former, the dismissal was voluntary. The authority *wanted* to dismiss Mr Irani, whereas in *Hill* the employer did not want to dismiss Mr Hill. In that sense it could be argued that *Irani* broke new ground.

1 [1985] ICR 590, [1985] IRLR 203,

3.67 In *Powell v Brent London Borough Council*[1] the plaintiff was already employed by the Council as a senior benefits officer and applied for promotion to the post of principal benefits officer (policy and training). She was interviewed and informed that she had been selected. She reported to her new place of employment but, in the meantime, one of the other unsuccessful candidates raised a query about the selection process, alleging that the selection might have been in breach of the Authority's equal opportunity code of practice. Accordingly the plaintiff was informed that it was not possible to carry out the appointment and that the position had to be re-advertised. She contended that this was a breach of contract and applied for an injunction to restrain the Council from advertising the post and to require the Council to treat her as if she were appointed to the position to which she had been promoted. The Court of Appeal held that the plaintiff was entitled to the injunction until it was determined at the trial of the action whether she had been validly and effectively appointed to the post in question. New evidence was let in at the appeal to the effect that there had been no complaints about the way in which she had undertaken her new duties, confidence was still subsisting in the employment relationship and there was no friction in the workplace. Damages were not adequate if the employee were excluded from the post as she would have lost job satisfaction and would be distressed and embarrassed at having to return to her former position.

1 [1988] ICR 176, [1987] IRLR 466, CA.

3.68 In *Hughes v London Borough of Southwark*[1] the plaintiff, along with others, was employed as a social worker at Maudsley Hospital. Due to staffing difficulties, the Council asked the employees to go and work in a different area for three days a week without their consent. This was held to be a breach of contract. The employee applied for an injunction to restrain the Council from implementing its instruction. The injunction was granted. It was held that the most important criterion for the order was whether there was mutual confidence.

It was clear in this case that there was full confidence between the employer and the employee. And damages were not adequate as, if the instruction were implemented, the plaintiff would lose job satisfaction which could not be compensated for by damages. As any detriment suffered by the Council could be compensated by damages, the balance of convenience was in favour of granting the injunction to the plaintiff.

[1] [1988] IRLR 55.

3.69 Finally, though, in *Ali v Southwark London Borough*[1] an injunction was not granted. In this case, the plaintiff was employed as a care assistant at an old people's home run by the Council. There was some report of mistreatment of residents and it was suggested by the Council that the plaintiff was among those to blame. Disciplinary action was brought against the plaintiff and she was invited to a disciplinary hearing. The Council proposed to call no further evidence apart from a report that had been commissioned. The employee therefore asserted that the disciplinary hearing would be in breach of contract as it required the hearing to hear evidence before deciding on the charge. She applied for an injunction restraining the Council from hearing the disciplinary allegations without producing evidence. Some doubt was expressed as to whether the proposed mode of conduct of the investigation would be in breach of contract in any event, but even if it were, no injunction should be granted because there was no confidence subsisting now between the employer and the employee. The Council had lost all confidence in the ability of the employee to carry out the work of caring for others. Even though, if the charges were dismissed at the disciplinary hearing confidence might return, for the moment it was absent and this was fatal to the injunction applied for.

[1] [1988] ICR 567, [1988] IRLR 100.

3.70 Further illustrations of refusals by the court to entertain injunctions in a case where confidence has been lost are *Alexander v Standard Telephones and Cables plc*[1] and *Wishart v National Associaton of Citizens Advice Bureaux Ltd.*[2] In *Alexander*, the interesting point raised in the case was whether the terms of a collective agreement about redundancy procedures providing for, basically, last in, first out, were incorporated into individual contract (see also para 3.29 above in a different context). For if they were, there was a departure therefrom by the company which in this case decided that it needed to retain workers whose skills and flexibility were best suited in the circumstances. Following unsuccessful negotiations to resolve the dispute dismissal notices were issued to certain workers selected under the employers' crieria. They obtained an ex parte injunction restraining the employers from implementing the dismissal notices until last in, first out had been complied with. On hearing the application for an interlocutory injunction the Judge, however, dismissed the application . The first point he made was that the workers had an arguable case for saying that the redundancy procedure in the collective agreement had become part of the individual contract of employment (although this was disagreed with by Mr Justice Hobhouse in *Alexander v Standard Telephone and Cables Ltd (No 2)*).[3] Assuming that were the case, would an injunction lie to restrain the employers from dismissing the workers or giving effect to their purported dismissals pending trial? It was held that once an employer had lost confidence in an employee an injunction should not be granted. And other cases such as *Irani v Southampton and South West Hampshire Health Authority* and *Powell v Brent London Borough Council* differed from the present case in that in the present case there was no work left for the workers. And it could not be said that the employers had complete confidence in the workers in that they had less confidence that they could do the work than other members of the workforce who were retained. As a result the relationship with employer and employee had broken down in that the employer believed it did not have any work for the employees to do. Accordingly, the plaintiffs' remedy would be in damages rather than by way of injunction.

1 [1990] IRLR 55.
2 [1990] ICR 794, [1990] IRLR 393, CA.
3 [1991] IRLR 286.

3.71 In *Wishart*, the plaintiff, who had been a Citizens Advice Bureau employee with various bureaux since 1986, applied for the post of information officer with the defendant, the National Association of Citizens Advice Bureaux Ltd. After he had been interviewed the company wrote to him in January 1990 offering him employment in the post 'subject to receipt of satisfactory written references'. One of the references taken up by the company was unsatisfactory to the company in terms of the plaintiff's sick record. This was because the post was a demanding one which required constant attendance. Accordingly the offer was withdrawn. The plaintiff applied for an interlocutory order restraining he company from re-advertising the post or appointing any other person to the post.

3.72 Although the trial judge granted the order, this was reversed by the Court of Appeal. It was held that since there was no established employment relationship between the parties and it was evident that the company did not have trust and confidence in the plaintiff the first instance Judge was wrong to order an injunction. As Mustill LJ said:

> 'The question was not whether it would be reasonable for the defendants to employ him, but whether it would be reasonable for the court to enforce them to employ someone whom they assert that they have never employed and do not wish to employ in the future. All that the plaintiff can give by way of reasons for taking the case out of the general rule is that his qualifications and experience were impressive enough to cause the defendants to select him, and that if he prevails at the trial damages may not furnish a complete remedy. This seems to me a situation far distant from that of *Powell v Brent London Borough Council*. There is here no established comfortable relationship in the old post and in the new which all concerned with the practicalities rather than the legalities were very happy to continue in *Powell v Brent London Borough Council*. Instead, there is a still born relationship to which one party strongly objects.'

Ralph Gibson LJ said:

> 'The facts upon which *Powell* was held by this court to be most unusual and exceptional are fully set out in the detailed statement of facts in the report of that case. In this case there is a dispute as to whether any effective contract of employment was made. The plaintiff has never worked for the

defendants. They do not wish to employ him. Their good faith is not questioned. It is conceded that, on the terms of employment which are applicable if the contract was made, the defendants can lawfully terminate the employment by a four week notice. There is no evidence that the defendants have, or have expressed, confidence in the plaintiff or in the potential relationship between the plaintiff and the defendants under a contract of employment, other than by the act of making the conditional offer of employment subject to satisfactory references which, as explained, they found to be unsatisfactory'.[1]

[1] In any event, Mustill and Ralph Gibson LJ doubted whether there was an enforceable contract of employment between the plaintiff and the defendants and they doubted whether there was an objective test for the approval of references, involving a notional reasonable prospective employer. They thought it was more likely that it would be considered that the test was subjective and that all that was required of the defendants was to consider the references in good faith. Good faith was not challenged in the case and undoubtedly the defendants genuinely considered that the references were unsatisfacory. If no breach of contract thereby arose, *ex hypothesi* no remedy for breach of contract such as an injunction could possibly lie. See also *Meacham v Amalgamated Engineering and Electrical Union* [1994] IRLR 218 where the plaintiff who had been elected a full-time officer of the Union was not employed for financial reasons and sought a declaration that the decision not to employ him was void and of no effect. The Court held that his remedy was limited to damages for breach of contract.

3.73 In other cases, however, the courts have shifted their approach from any requirement of the existence of trust and confidence. In *Robb v Hammersmith and Fulham London Borough Council*[1] Mr Robb was employed as the Borough's director of finance. He held that position when certain capital market transactions and interest rate swaps carried out by the Council were declared unlawful. As a result, disciplinary procedures were invoked against him. He was put on special leave with pay pending their conclusion. However, negotiations began about possible terms for termination of his contract. As a result the chief executive wrote to Mr Robb informing him that 'in view of your impending termination of service' there was no useful purpose in carrying out the preliminary investigation and disciplinary procedure. However, the negotiations for amicable termination were not successful and Mr Robb was then summarily dismissed on grounds of alleged lack of capability. He sought an injunction restraining the employers from giving effect to the purported dismissal until the contractual disciplinary procedures had been complied with. At the hearing before the High Court it was conceded by the employers that the dismissal had been in breach of the procedures and therefore in breach of contract. It was made clear, in applying for an injunction to restrain the employers from relying upon the dismissal that the employee was not requiring the employers actually to reinstate Mr Robb so that he could come back to work and perform his duties but rather that he be treated as suspended on full pay pending the completion of the due contractual procedures.

[1] [1991] IRLR 72.

3.74 The High Court granted the injunction notwithstanding that the employers had expressly lost trust and confidence in the employee's ability to perform his job, coining a new test, to the effect that whether injunctive relief would be granted was subject to the important criterion whether the order sought was 'workable'. Normally of course if an injunction is sought to reinstate an employee dismissed for breach of contract so that when reinstated he can perform his job, trust and confidence are highly relevant since without trust and confidence the employee cannot perform his job in practice. As such his position as an employee would be 'unworkable'. But, all importantly, in the present case, the plaintiff did not seek reinstatement so that he could perform his duties and responsbilities. He simply sought an order restoring the position as it was before the disciplinary procedure was aborted. He was then on leave and he sought to remain on leave under his contract pending the completion of the procedures. In such circumstances, lack of trust and confidence in his ability to do his job had no relevance to the workability of the disciplinary procedure if, in the present case, the balance of convenience required that the relief sought be granted. There was an admitted breach of contract in not following the disciplinary procedure and in the summary dismissal in breach of such procedure. An injunction would restore him to his previous position. Such disciplinary procedure was still workable but could become impracticable if delayed until the conclusion of the trial. And without the injunction the plaintiff would lose the opportunity of airing his case and justifying himself at the hearings and enquiries under the procedure. Although damages would be an adequate remedy for the breach of contract in one sense in that the plaintiff would be entitled to damages representing loss of salary during notice and a time extended for the probable length of the disciplinary procedure to completion, such damages would not be an adequate remedy for the manner of the dismissal and his loss of enjoyment of the disciplinary procedure. Therefore the balance of convenience required the Judge to give the relief sought otherwise the defendants would be 'snapping their fingers' at the legal rights of the plaintiff.

3.75 In *Wadcock v London Borough of Brent*[1] Mr Wadcock had been employed as a social worker since 1975. Brent social workers were employed to work on an area basis. However, a reorganisation took place under which social workers were allocated to one of three specialist teams. In 1989 staff were asked which specialist team they wanted to join. Mr Wadcock and about 30 others failed to indicate a preference. He was therefore allocated to the special needs division. But he said that this was not acceptable to him. He refused to go along with the reorganisation. However, he stated that he would continue to make himself available for his usual work.

1 [1990] IRLR 223.

3.76 The employers tried to persuade him to go along with the reorganisation and join the new team but he was still dissatisfied and he grieved under the agreed procedure. In December he reported to his new team leader but he was unco-operative and refused to accept mental health cases. He was dismissed with 12 weeks' notice on ground of his refusal to work in the department in its restructured form. The letter did not require him to work during his notice period.

3.77 He applied for a declaration that the instruction to work with the special needs division was unreasonable and that the purported termination of his employment was unlawful. He applied for an injunction to restrain the Council from acting on its decision. During the course of interlocutory hearings before the High Court Mr Wadcock's counsel indicated that, subject to certain terms, Mr Wadcock was willing to work in the special needs division pending trial. In defence, the Council pleaded that there was a breakdown of confidence and it was unrealistic to expect the employer/employee relationship to be re-established. The High Court allowed the application and granted an interlocutory order requiring the employers pending trial to allow Mr Wadcock to work for the employer in the special needs division at the usual rate of pay upon his undertaking to work in accordance with the orders, instructions and wishes expressed by his team leader or any other member of the Social Services Department having authority over him. It was held that there was a serious question to be tried as to whether or not dismissal was justified having regard to the terms of the contract of employment. Furthermore, there was a disciplinary procedure laid down in the case of serious offences including the right to a formal disciplinary hearing.

3.78 These procedures had not taken place in this case. It was at least arguable that they should have been followed. Damages were not an adequate remedy and the balance of convenience dictated that an order should be made in the employee's favour. Mutual confidence between the employer and the employee had to exist but only in the sense that if an injunction were granted there would arise a situation that was 'workable'.

3.79 As the employee was a competent social worker and would be able to work in the special needs division if he were willing to obey the orders of his team leader and other supervisors the situation was 'workable' and an injunction granted.

3.80 The requirement of maintenance of trust and confidence was similarly eschewed in *Jones v Gwent County Council*.[1] In this case, Jones was employed as a lecturer who unsuccessfully applied for a promotion given to a male colleague. She claimed that her unsuccessful application was due to sex discrimination. Subsequently, she was suspended and disciplinary proceedings brought against her on the ground that in pursuit of her grievance she had provided false information regarding her qualifications. The college claimed that, as a result, mutual confidence had been destroyed. In accordance with the contractual disciplinary procedure the complaint was heard by a disciplinary sub-committee established by the college governors. It reported that there was no misconduct. However, because of the publicity surrounding the case and the bad feelings it had generated it recommended that Mrs Jones should not return to the college and that she should be redeployed. A further sub-committee considered the matter afresh after the Council informed the governors that no alternative employment was available. It recommended that a further effort should be made to redeploy her but that if this was unsuccessful she should be reinstated at the college. The governors rejected this decision and asked the council to take steps to terminate Mrs Jones's employment. The council took no action and therefore the governors unilaterally wrote to Mrs Jones asking her to attend a third disciplinary hearing which 'may result in serious disciplinary action being taken against you'. The hearing was to consider the charge against her that her return to the college would cause 'an irrevocable breakdown in relationships between managment and staff based on your past behaviour'.

---

1 [1992] IRLR 521.

3.81 An objection was made by Mr Jones on her behalf that there were no grounds for further disciplinary action but the hearing went ahead without her attendance and it was decided that she should be dismissed. A letter of dismissal was issued. She sought an injunction restraining the council from dismissing her pending trial unless, in accordance with her contract of employment, grounds existed, and a proper procedure was carried out. The High Court granted an injunction. It was held that she had been cleared of misconduct by two disciplinary hearings and therefore the letter from the Council purporting to dismiss her was invalid because it did not comply with her contract. She had not received sufficient notice of the dismissal hearing and nor did the letter received by the plaintiff asking her to attend inform her (as was required) that dismissal was to be considered. Nor did the charge against her satisfy the requirement that full particulars be given. The governors' belief that the plaintiff's return to the college would cause an irrevocable breakdown in relationships could not justify dismissal for misconduct since a belief that some future event might cause an irrevocable breakdown in relationships could not be misconduct. In any event, the elements on which the governors' expression of belief was said to be based were either charges which had been adjudicated by an earlier disciplinary committee and could not be revived or else were wholly unparticularised.

3.82 A declaration that the letter of dismissal was not a valid and effective dismissal was made under Order 14A, r 1 of the Rules of the Supreme Court which provides that:

> 'the court may . . . determine any question of law or construction of any document arising in any cause or matter at any stage of the proceedings where it appears to the court that:
> (a) such question is suitable for determination without a full trial of the action; and
> (b) such determination will finally determine (subject only to any possible appeal) the entire cause or matter or any claim or issue therein.'

The use of Order 14A was appropriate since the question of law about whether the notice of dismissal was valid could adequately be determined at this interlocutory stage. The question of trust and confidence was irrelevant to the exercise by the court of the power under Order 14A which was to determine questions of law or construction. Whether the letter was a valid notice of dismissal did not depend upon any question of trust or confidence. A declaration was also made that the suspension of the plaintiff was invalid. The suspension could only be justified on the basis that the decision to dismiss the plaintiff was itself justified. A permanent injunction was therefore issued restraining the council from dismissing the plaintiff pursuant to its dismissal letter and from dismissing the plaintiff at all unless grounds existed and after carrying out a proper procedure in accordance with her contract of employment.

3.83 The case is interesting, albeit adventurous, in that it completely ignores any requirement of trust and confidence *or* a 'workable' relationship.

3.84 In conclusion, specific performance is not generally available. But the rule that an injunction cannot be granted to an employee in relation to his contract of employment is no longer immutable. In all the circumstances, particularly if there is confidence subsisting between the employer and employee, an injunction might be granted in an appropriate case. It is to be noted, however, that in many (if not most) cases, particularly of wrongful dismissal, that element of confidence will be absent.[1] But it may be there is a sea-change in principle at least. Only time will tell if the alternative approaches in *Powell*, *Wadcock* and *Jones* will encourage more flexible approaches to the rules about orders stopping dismissals or breaches of contract. This may be an emerging area of labour law.

---

1 See eg *Kearney v NSPCC IDS Brief 385*, November 1988, p 2. On the other hand, the question of policing an employer's application of disciplinary procedures is very much a live and potential issue; see the discussion about *R v BBC, ex p Lavelle* [1983] ICR 99 (although, on the facts, an injunction was refused) at para 3.88. See also *Dietman v Brent London Borough Council* [1988] IRLR 299, CA; an injunction might have been given but for the delay in bringing proceedings and possible acceptance of breach. There the court applied a robust interpretation of a disciplinary procedure, implying under the construction thereof, a right to be heard. In different circumstances this might have led to injunctive relief.

(D) Public law remedies

3.85 Public law remedies for dismissal or other administrative action is too involved a subject to be fully dealt with here.[1] At the end of our discussions on injunctions and specific performance, it is, however, important to take note of an area in which it is possible to challenge dismissals and other decisions by employers on grounds of illegality, irrationality or procedural impropriety. Historically, the beneficiaries of this set of controls have been office holders, those whose employment has been supported by statute or others whose employment has a public or statutory flavour.[2] A traditional analysis of this area, differentiating the rights of employees in public law from those having purely private law rights, derives from the judgment of Lord Reid in *Ridge v Baldwin*.[3] In that case he suggested that there was a threefold analysis of workers' rights in this area, that is to say there were three categories of individuals, the rights of which differed according to their status. These were:

(1) those employed under a master and servant relationship (ie a simple contract of employment);
(2) those dismissable from office at pleasure; and
(3) office holders, the dismissal of whom was constrained by procedures and who could not be dismissed without cause and who were entitled to the benefit of natural justice before termination of employment.

'Public law' rights as traditionally perceived applied to those workers in category (3) but not otherwise. A number of challenges can be seen in the cases based on grounds that dismissals of such workers were, for example, *ultra vires* the dismissing body or were in breach of natural justice.[4] Applications for judicial review are nowadays made under RSC Order 53. But this now more clearly than before highlights the difference between public law and private law remedies. To make an application under Order 53, employment must be underpinned by statute and the case must raise issues of public law.[5] It follows therefore that the mere holding of an office or employment by a public body will not suffice *per se*. For example, a nursing officer who had a contract of employment with a local authority was not entitled to proceed by way of judicial review,[6] whereas a prison officer appointed by the Home Secretary, the procedures for the dismissal of whom were in statute and not in the contract of employment, could.[7] Further, in *McClaren v Home Office*[8] Mr McLaren brought an action to complain that the Home Office was in breach of an agreement between it and the Prison Officers' Association in a local collective agreement and that as the terms of the local agreement had been incorporated into his contract of employment there had therefore been a breach of his contract of employment. He sought relief by way of declarations to that effect and payment of salary withheld from him. At first instance, the High Court struck out his claim holding that no cause of action in private law was disclosed. Hoffman J took the view that there was no contract of employment between a prison officer and the Home Office and therefore its claim was misconceived: it should have been brought in public law and not private law and therefore if he had any claim against the Home Office it had to be raised by way of an application for judicial review.

1 See the discussion in Smith and Wood *Industrial Law* (4th edn) pp 219–226; Ewing and Grubb 'The Emergence of a New Labour Injunction?' (1987) ILJ 145.

2 *Ridge v Baldwin* [1964] AC 40, HL; *Malloch v Aberdeen Corpn* [1971] 2 All ER 1278, HL; *McClelland v Northern Ireland General Health Services Board* [1957] 2 All ER 129, HL.

3 [1964] AC 40.

4 See n 2 above.

5 *R v East Berkshire Health Authority, ex p Walsh* [1984] ICR 743, [1984] IRLR 278, CA.

6 Ibid.

7 *R v Secretary of State for the Home Office, ex p Benwell* [1985] QB 554.

8 [1990] IRLR 338, CA.

3.86 The Court of Appeal overturned the ruling of the High Court. The cause of action was in private law rather than public law. The Home Office had power to enter into a contractual relationship with prison officers and the question whether a public body had the power to enter into a contract of service with a particular individual in a particular case must necessarily be a question of private and not public law.

3.87 Woolf LJ set out the following principles that should be borne in mind in determining whether an employee of a public body is required to bring proceedings by way of judicial review:

(1) In relation to his personal claims against an employer, an employee of a public body is normally in exactly the same position as other employees and can bring proceedings in the ordinary way for damages, and a declaration or an injunction (except in relation to the Crown).
(2) An employee of a public body can seek judicial review and obtain a remedy which would not be available to an employee in the private sector where there exists some disciplinary or other body established under the prerogative or by statute to which the employer or employee is entitled or required to refer disputes affecting their relationships.
(3) In addition if an employee of a public body is adversely affected by a decision of general application by his employer he can be entitled to challenge that decision by way of judicial review on grounds that it is flawed.
(4) Judicial review will not be available where disciplinary procedures are of a purely domestic nature albeit that their decisions might affect the public.[1]

1 See, for example, *R v Derbyshire County Council, ex p Noble* [1990] IRLR 332 where the Court of Appeal approved the Divisional Court ruling that there was insufficient public element in a

police surgeon's claim that his contract had been terminated unfairly to allow him to proceed by way of judicial review. The Court of Appeal held that there was no universal test as to when judicial review was or was not available. The approach which the courts adopted was to look at the subject matter of the decision which it is suggested should be subject to judicial review and then come to a decision as to whether judicial review was appropriate. See, in Scotland, *Blair v Lochaber District Council* [1995] IRLR 135.

Contrast *R v London Borough of Hammersmith and Fulham, ex p NALGO* [1991] IRLR 249 where the Council adopted a policy of redeployment and redundancy. The union and the employees in the Council's housing benefit department, affected by the redundancies, applied for judicial review seeking an order of certiorari to quash the decision to adopt the policy. The ground for the application was that the criteria for redundancy were discriminatory being contrary to the Sex Discrimination Act, Race Relations Act and the EC Equal Treatment Directive. On the facts, an order was not granted. On the evidence available the applicants had not established that the Council's policy was contrary to the discrimination statutes or was in some other way unlawful. However, the court operated on the assumption that if a public authority proposes to embark on an employment or redeployment policy which is in breach of the Sex Discrimination Act or Race Relations Act or is otherwise unlawful public remedies *should* be available to the unions and employees affected.

3.88 If an application for judicial review is commenced under Order 53 but found not to concern an issue of public law, it means of course that the action should have been brought under private law, by writ, eg to claim an injunction against dismissal (see above). But, in such a case, the courts hearing the action can allow the matter to proceed, even if wrongly brought under Order 53, by way of an action begun by a writ (Order 53, r 9(5)). One case where this occurred continued to cause controversy in relation to its suggestion that most employees in the private sector are impliedly entitled to the benefit of natural justice before dismissal (whereas, as stated above in relation to *Ridge v Baldwin*, this has been traditionally regarded as the province of public sector employees). In *R v BBC, ex p Lavelle*[1] an employee employed by the BBC sought to challenge a dismissal on the ground of procedural impropriety. It was decided that the action was wrongly brought under Order 53 as it concerned a private dispute between employer and employee. But discretion was exercised under Order 53, r 9(5) and the action continued as if begun by writ. At the end of the day, Woolf J declined to grant an injunction on the facts. But the case has attracted considerable attention because of Woolf J's *obiter* remarks that because of modern employment law legislation, such as the right not to be unfairly dismissed, the employee in the private sector has some of the attributes of the holder of an office envisaged by Lord Reid in *Ridge v Baldwin* and so may restrain a dismissal in breach of natural justice where there are procedural limitations on dismissal. This has been heralded as a significant development in labour law[2] but the impact of Woolf J's views has not yet been felt, if indeed they are to be followed in future cases.[3]

---

1 [1983] ICR 99.

2 Ewing and Grubb (1987) ILJ 145.

3 See earlier cases of *Jones v Lee* [1980] ICR 310, CA and *Stevenson v United Road Transport Union* [1977] ICR 893, CA, where an employer's procedure was challenged, apparently in a purely contractual context. In *Dietman v Brent London Borough Council* [1988] IRLR 299, CA an employee dismissed in breach of procedure before summary dismissal claimed an injunction. On the facts this was refused but the right to be heard before summary dismissal was implied into the procedures (on the facts, and on the construction of a particular contract concerned) thus indicating that the courts are increasingly aware of the desirability of hearings before dismissal. However, when counsel for the plaintff in *Molyneux v Liverpool City Council* (12 November 1987, unreported), CA

(LEXIS) argued that there should be implied into this client's contract (which contained a disciplinary procedure) a term that the employee would not be dismissed without a hearing even outside the context of disciplinary proceedings, this was rejected by the court.

3.89 Returning to judicial review, there are, as has been stated, three situations where adminstrative action might be subject to judicial review, that is to say, illegality, irrationality and procedural impropriety. In the employment context it is the third which most frequently arises, particularly in relation to breach of natural justice. In *Calveley v Merseyside Police*[1] the defendant failed to inform police officers about complaints about them for 2½ years which prejudiced their ability to defend the disciplinary charges they faced. In *R v Secretary of State for the Home Department, ex p Benwell*[2] a prison officer was dismissed on evidence of which he was not made aware and was not able to answer. In both cases the applications succeeded. In *R v Liverpool City Corpn, ex p Ferguson*,[3] however, the High Court granted an order of certiorari on an application for judicial review to quash a decision of a council not to pay any employee who had failed to work during a strike on a 'day of action'. The decision covered some 2,000 teachers who reported for work and were willing and able to do so but were prevented by the fact that the schools were closed because the caretakers were on strike. This was the type of decision that could be attacked under the 'irrationality' heading mentioned above. Remedies for judicial review are certiorari, mandamus or prohibition. It may also be possible to obtain a declaration, injunction or damages.

1 [1986] IRLR 177, CA.
2 [1985] QB 554, [1986] IRLR 6; cf *R v Chief Constable of the Thames Valley Police, ex p Cotton* [1990] IRLR 344, CA.
3 [1985] IRLR 501.

4 Obligations which survive the termination of the contract of employment: confidentiality, trade secrets and competition

John McMullen

1 INTRODUCTION

4.01 The knowledge and contacts that an employee can acquire during his period of employment can be extremely valuable to him and to competitors of his employer. Thus, most employers will be concerned, if they can, to protect themselves against the activities of former employees after the termination of the employment relationship. Balanced against this consideration, however, is the policy argument in favour of control of restrictions which are in restraint of trade and which fetter an employee's availability on the labour market and his ability to earn a living.[1]

[1] The two leading works in this area are Brearley and Bloch, *Employment Covenants and Confidential Information* (1993) and Mehigan and Griffiths, *Restraint of Trade and Business Secrets: Law and Practice* (2nd ed, 1991). See, also, Gurry, *Breach of Confidence* (1984) and, in the context of directors of companies, Shepherd, *The Law of Fiduciaries* (1981); Finn, *Fiduciary Obligations* (1977).

4.02 As will be seen below, an employer may give himself some protection by express undertakings agreed to by an employee. But if he has failed to do that he can rely only on what the general law is prepared to imply into the relationship. In the absence of express restrictions there is an implied term as to good faith and fidelity which exists during the contract of employment which *inter alia* obliges an employee to respect confidentiality and trade secrets. This may extend also beyond the ending of the employment in so far as it is necessary to protect the employer's trade secrets. But an employer cannot stop an employee using his skill and know-how to earn a living, even if this was acquired during his employment with the former employer.[1] And there is nothing in the general law to stop an employee competing with his former employer, or from contacting and canvassing customers and clients, or from soliciting employees of his former employer (as long as the employee's activities do not involve inducements to break existing contracts) provided these activities take place after the ending of the employment. Such post-employment activities can only be restricted by express covenants.[2] Although such covenants will be subject to the restraint of trade doctrine and must survive scrutiny by the courts as to enforceability, it can be seen that a prudent employer who wishes to protect himself against the activities of a former employee must consider seeking express covenants from his staff. First, though, we examine what is implied by the law about faithfulness, confidentiality and trade secrets.

[1] See eg, *Sir W C Leng & Co Ltd v Andrews* [1909] 1 Ch 763, CA; *Cantor Fitzgerald (UK) Ltd v Wallace* [1992] IRLR 215.
[2] Although see para 4.43 on the validity of covenants against the poaching of staff.

2 CONFIDENTIALITY, TRADE SECRETS AND THE IMPLIED DUTY OF FIDELITY

4.03 Every employee owes a duty of fidelity that applies during the contract of employment and which may, to an extent, continue thereafter.[1] For example, during the employment the employee must not take up competing employment with another nor solicit the employer's customers for himself.[2] Generally, though, the contract is only broken here if there is *actual* competition or solicitation during employment. It has been held that discovery by an employer of an employee's mere intention to set himself up in competition with the employer in the future does not of itself justify summary dismissal on the ground of breach of the implied duty of fidelity. Only if there was evidence that the employee was breaking confidentiality or using his employer's time to set up a competing business or soliciting custom for himself would there be any breach of the implied duty of fidelity.[3] The case of *Balston Ltd v Headline Filters Ltd*,[4] both at the interlocutory stage and at trial, provides a recent discussion of the extent to which preparatory acts may be undertaken by employees whilst the duty of fidelity subsists. The facts in *Balston* were that the company manufactured and sold glass microfibre filter tubes. Mr Head, who was an employee and director of the company, gave notice of termination of his employment, which was agreed to expire on 11 July 1986. Prior thereto, on 16 April he resigned his directorship. It was agreed that he did not have to attend for work during his notice period. But on 25 April Mr Head bought a company off the shelf and thereafter prepared it to commence business manufacturing microfibre filter tubes with effect from 11 July. Mr Head mentioned to one of Balston's customers that he was leaving and that after 11 July would be able to supply filter tubes to that customer at the price which Balston had charged prior to 1 May. On 11 July that customer placed an order with Mr Head's new company. Balston applied for an injunction to stop Mr Head using confidential information about the blend of microfibres employed in the manufacturing process and certain other technical data. The question was to what extent (if any) Mr Head had breached his duty of fidelity under his contract of employment in the above actions. It was held, first, that there was no reason why he should not during the period between 16 April and 11 July, whilst he was still an employee, have established his new company, arranged premises for it and ordered the materials preparatory to the intended commencement of business on 11 July.

[1] *Sinclair v Neighbour* [1967] 2 QB 279, CA; *Reading v A-G* [1951] AC 507, HL; *Sybron Corpn v Rochem Ltd* [1983] 2 All ER 707, CA. It is also important to remember that some employees may also be directors of companies. Directors also owe a fiduciary duty to their company which duty includes fidelity and an obligation not to let one's own interest and duty to the company conflict. This is highly relevant in this area: see eg *Regal (Hastings) Ltd v Gulliver* [1942] 1 All ER 378, HL; *Horcal Ltd v Gatland* [1984] IRLR 288, CA; *Industrial Development Consultants Ltd v Cooley*

[1972] 2 All ER 162, [1972] 1 WLR 443; *Canadian Aero Service Ltd v O'Malley* (1973) 40 DLR (3d) 371; cf *Island Export Finance Ltd v Umunna* [1986] BCLC 460 (discussed at para 4.09); Farrar, *Company Law* (2nd edn) p 422ff. The remedy for a breach of fiduciary duty is not damages, but an account of profits (see para 4.70).

2 *Sanders v Parry* [1987] IRLR 753; *Wessex Dairies Ltd v Smith* [1935] 2 KB 80, CA; *Cranleigh Precision Engineering Ltd v Bryant* [1964] 3 All ER 289, [1965] 1 WLR 1293; *Marshall v Industrial Systems and Control Ltd* [1992] IRLR 294, EAT.

3 *Laughton and Hawley v Bapp Industrial Supplies Ltd* [1986] ICR 634, [1986] IRLR 245, EAT; *Harris and Russell Ltd v Slingsby* [1973] 3 All ER 31, [1973] ICR 454; *GD Searle & Co Ltd v Celltech Ltd* [1982] FSR 92, CA. Likewise there is of course nothing to stop an employee applying for another job. See also *Tithebarn v Hubbard* EAT 532/89 LEXIS transcript.

4 [1987] FSR 330 (Scott J); [1990] FSR 385 (Falconer J).

4.04 At the interlocutory hearing it was held that it was certainly arguable, though, that it was in breach of contract to solicit an order for custom from one of his employer's customers. This applied even if Mr Head had been relieved from normal duties.

4.05 It was also arguable that Balston's specific fibre blends were trade secrets and therefore Mr Head was prevented from using or disclosing them. However, Balston could not get an injunction to restrain Mr Head from using blends that were only similar to the specific blends. For this would not be a claim to protect a trade secret but a claim to prevent Mr Head from using his knowledge and experience of mixing grades of fibres in order to produce similar products. Mr Head could not, as a matter of principle, be prevented from using his skill and knowledge as long as this did not infringe a trade secret. (See para 4.12 for a fuller discussion on the nature of confidential information and trade secrets.)

4.06 When the matter came to trial, three years later, before Falconer J, the same arguments were run by the employer as at the interlocutory stage, together with the additional argument that the employee's activities during the remainder of his period of notice amounted to a breach of fiduciary duty as company director.

4.07 The learned judge confirmed that there was no breach of the duty of fidelity as an employee in forming the intention to set up a business in competition and carrying out preparatory acts for that purpose. However, in so far as he had been in active competition for the custom of one of his employer's customers, Mr Head was clearly in breach of his duty of good faith as an employee and he was also in breach of that duty in approaching one of his former employer's employees and offering her employment.

4.08 As to the claim concerning misuse of confidential information, it was held that the fibre-mix recipes were confidential information which the employer would not wish to have made public or disclosed to a competitor; but it had not been suggested that the employee had made any written record of the recipes and it was highly unlikely that he had deliberately memorised them especially when, from his own expertise, he knew the general area in which a recipe must arise in order to produce a particular result. Accordingly this claim failed.

4.09 Finally, there was the allegation that the employee had been in breach of his fiduciary duty as director. By analogy with the reasoning on the claim for breach of duty of fidelity under the contract it was held, applying *Island Export Finance Ltd* *v Umunna*,[1] that an intention by a director of a company to set up business in competition with the company after his directorship had ceased was not an activity which conflicted with his fiduciary duty to the company, nor was the taking of any preliminary steps to further this aim so long as there was no actual competition whilst he was still a director. Thus the employee was not in breach of duty as a director in not disclosing his intention to set up in competition; nor had he been in breach of fiduciary duty by diverting a maturing business opportunity to himself as he had not resigned to take advantage of any such opportunity.

---

[1] [1986] BCLC 460. In this case Umunna was previously the managing director of a company which pursued business in West Africa. In 1976 Mr Umunna secured a contract from the Cameroons Postal Authorities for postal call boxes. No further contracts ensued however. In 1977 Mr Umunna resigned due to dissatisfaction with the company rather, it was held, than a desire to appropriate any postal call box business for his own company. At the time of the resignation his former company was not actively seeking repeat business or further orders. Subsequently Mr Umunna obtained for his own company an order for postal call boxes from the Cameroons Postal Authorities. It was claimed that he had breached his fiduciary duty to the company notwithstanding his resignation and that he had made improper use of his former company's confidential information. It was accepted that a director's fiduciary duty did not come to an end when he ceased to be a director (see *Industrial Development Consultants Ltd v Cooley* [1972] 2 All ER 162). But on the facts, the resignation was not influenced by a desire to acquire any maturing business opportunity which his former company was actively pursuing. Nor had he improperly exploited any confidential information. Knowledge acquired as director of the existence of a particular market could not amount to confidential information which a director was prohibited from using after the termination of his directorship. To say otherwise would conflict with the public policy arguments about restraint of trade.

See also the facts in *Ixora Trading Inc v Jones* [1990] FSR 251 where again, on the facts, the plaintiffs found it difficult to establish that the defendants had been guilty of diverting a maturing business opportunity, thereby breaching fiduciary duties.

4.10 However, there can be a fine line between legitimate and illegitimate activities and the facts are all important.

4.11 On the other hand, in the absence of an express covenant against spare time employment, and in the absence of any breach of an express term as to hours of work to be performed for the employer, there is nothing to stop an employee taking up part-time employment for another employer during his employment with the first employer.[1] However, exceptionally, an employee might have a duty not to work for a competitor employer in his spare time. In *Hivac Ltd v Park Royal Scientific Instruments Ltd*[2] employees who were skilled assemblers of hearing aids and who worked for a rival company on their day off were held to have broken their implied duty of fidelity. But it seems that for this principle to apply, the employee must occupy a position whereby he has access to confidential information or trade secrets so that work for another would involve the risk of such information being passed to a competitor. Thus, in *Nova Plastics Ltd v Frogatt*[3] it was held that an odd-job man who did work for a rival concern in his spare time was not in breach of contract.

---

[1] *Nova Plastics Ltd v Frogatt* [1982] IRLR 146, EAT.

[2] [1946] Ch 169, [1946] 1 All ER 350, CA. See also *United Sterling Corpn Ltd v Felton and Mannion* [1974] RPC 162.

[3] [1982] IRLR 146, EAT. See also *Philip Kunick Ltd v Smyth* 15.11.73 NIRC, IRLIB 483, October 1993, p 2.

4.12 As is implicit from the discussion of *Balston* (para 4.03) it will also be a breach of the duty of fidelity to give away or make personal use of confidential information and trade secrets belonging to the employer, but it seems there is a vital distinction between the extent of the duty owed by an employee during the life of the contract and the extent of the duty thereafter.[1] The emphasis shifts after termination of employment, following which the duty is less stringent. The leading case is *Faccenda Chicken Ltd v Fowler*[2] which laid down a distinction between confidential information on the one hand, and trade secrets on the other. Both are protected during the course of the employment but only the latter after the employment has ended. In *Faccenda* itself, Mr Fowler was one of nine former employees of a company which sold chickens for consumption by the public. Mr Fowler was a sales manager and had built up a large van sales operation. The van salesmen possessed very detailed information about customers, customers' requirements, prices and other matters. Mr Fowler then left the company and set up on his own. Shortly thereafter the company alleged that Mr Fowler was in breach of his contract of employment by using confidential sales information belonging to the company. There was no express term in the contract restricting use of confidential information or trade secrets gained during employment and the case turned on the extent of the implied duty. It was held that the action should fail because, although the sales information was of such a nature as to make it confidential and therefore it could not be used or disclosed during the employment (otherwise than for the employer's benefit), on leaving the employment the employee was entitled to use the information for his own benefit as it became part of his skill and knowledge. In the absence of an express covenant not to compete, the employee could only be restrained if the information amounted to a trade secret, which was not the case here.

[1] Although an injunction to restrain disclosure will be refused where the information, even if secret, relates to employer misconduct which it is in the public interest to disclose: *Initial Services Ltd v Putterill* [1968] 1 QB 396, [1967] 3 All ER 145, CA (existence of restrictive practice under the Restrictive Trade Practices Acts); in *Re A Company's Application* [1989] ICR 449, [1989] IRLR 477 (breach of FIMBRA's regulatory requirements). See also *Fraser v Evans* [1969] 1 QB 349, [1969] 1 All ER 8, CA; *Hubbard v Vosper* [1972] 2 QB 84, [1972] 1 All ER 1023, CA; *Lion Laboratories Ltd v Evans* [1985] QB 526, [1984] 2 All ER 417, CA; *A-G v Guardian Newspapers Ltd* (No 2) [1988] 3 All ER 545, HL; and the valuable discussion in Smith and Wood, *Industrial Law* (5th edn) pp 120–124. A private member's bill, the Whistleblowers Protective Bill 1995 recently sought to confer statutory protection on employees who disclose more practice in the public interest. See also Vickers 'Whistleblowing and Freedom of Speech in the NHS' (1995) NLJ 1257; Vickers, *Protecting Whistleblowers at Work* (Institute of Employment Rights, 1995); Lewis, 'Whistleblowers and Job Security' (1995) MLR 208. Cripps, *The Legal Implications of Disclosure in the Public Interest: An Analysis of Prohibitions and Prosecutions with Particular Reference to Employers and Employees* (2nd edn, 1994).

[2] [1987] Ch 117, [1986] ICR 297, CA.

4.13 From the judgment of Neill LJ[1] the following principles can be established:

(1) Where there is a contract of employment the obligations between the employer and employee are determined by that contract.
(2) In the absence of an express term the law about use and disclosure of information is the subject of an implied term.
(3) During the employment the employee is subject to an implied term

imposing a duty of good faith or fidelity. This duty of good faith varies according to the nature of the contract. The duty is certainly broken if an employee makes or copies a list of customers of the employer for use after his employment ends or deliberately memorises such a list even though there is no general restriction on him canvassing or doing business with customers of his former employer.

(4) The implied term imposing the duty of good faith is more restricted after the termination of employment than during. The information, use or disclosure of which is restricted after the ending of the employment, must amount to more than simply confidential information. It must amount to a trade secret, such as, for example, a secret process of manufacture, chemical formulae, designs, or special methods of construction. Misuse of confidential information *per se* may be actionable during the life of the contract but trade secrets must be abused for action to follow after it has ended.

(5) In order to determine whether any particular item of information amounts to a trade secret, and therefore may be prohibited from use or disclosure after the end of the employment, it is necessary to consider all of the circumstances of the case.

---

1 [1987] Ch 117, [1986] ICR 297, CA.

4.14 The court then proceeded to indicate which factors were of particular relevance in determining whether information amounted to a trade secret. First, regard must be had to the nature of the employment. The more sensitive the area or capacity in which the employee is employed the stricter the obligation of confidentiality. Secondly, regard must be had to the nature of the information itself. The information must amount to a trade secret or be of such a highly confidential nature as to require the same protection as a trade secret.

4.15 The court wisely declined to provide a list of matters which would amount to a trade secret or its equivalent but, in the opinion of Neill LJ, secret processes or methods of manufacture and other similar information are capable of being trade secrets although, depending on the facts, the secrecy of some types of information may be relatively short lived. Also, the fact that circulation of certain information is restricted to a limited number of individuals may give an insight as to whether it is simply confidential or highly confidential. Third, it is relevant whether the employer emphasised to the employee the confidentiality of the information. Although, according to the court, labelling by the employer of information as confidential cannot of itself turn non-confidential information into confidential information, if measures are taken by the employer to impress the confidentiality of the information upon the employee, this may be relevant.[1] Fourth, it is also relevant whether the information can be isolated easily from other information which the employee is free to use or disclose. If, for example, the alleged confidential information is part of a wider collection of information and know-how which is not confidential, that may be some indication of the degree of confidentiality attached to the information under scrutiny. The distinction between confidential information and highly confidential information (hereafter 'trade secrets') has now been employed in a number of subsequent cases to determine the extent of a former employee's duty and whether it has been broken.

[1] It is to be noted, however, that Harman J in *Systems Reliability Holdings plc v Smith* [1990] IRLR 377 did not feel bound by a view expressed in the Court of Appeal in *Faccenda* that an express covenant cannot impose a restriction on information held by an ex-employee which is not a trade secret or its equivalent, at least in the case of a covenant between a vendor and a purchaser in a business or share sale agreement (see also *Balston Ltd v Headline Filters Ltd* [1987] FSR 330 (per Scott J)).

4.16 For example, in *Roger Bullivant Ltd v Ellis*[1] Mr Ellis left his employer and began working in competition. The employer obtained an *Anton Piller* order[2] and discovered a large number of documents belonging to the company in Mr Ellis's possession, including a card index listing customers. It was held that the information on the card index was not a trade secret, but merely confidential information, at least to the extent that the information (not being a trade secret or the like) was inevitably carried away in the employee's head (although this should not be taken to mean that an employee is entitled as a general principle to use anything that may be carried away in the head). This might, to employers, seem a rather inequitable conclusion, without more, since no doubt the former employee was considerably advantaged by continuing possession of the information. But Neill LJ's point 3 discussed at para 4.13 came into play. It was a breach of the contract of employment to make or copy a list of the employer's customers with the intention of using it after the termination of his employment or deliberately to memorise the list for that purpose. Therefore, an injunction was granted (although on appeal it was limited in time (see para 4.69)). So, too, in *Robb v Green*[3] a manager who deliberately copied a list of customers during his employment for use afterwards in a competing employment was in breach of the duty of fidelity.[4]

[1] [1987] ICR 464, [1987] IRLR 491, CA.

[2] An order deriving from the case of *Anton Piller KG v Manufacturing Processes Ltd* [1976] Ch 55, CA which is an extremely useful tool to investigate alleged misconduct; see Mehigan and Griffiths, op cit, ch 22 for an account. See also the very practical guidance in Brearley and Bloch, op cit, pp 219-233. See, recently, *Lock International plc v Beswick* [1989] IRLR 481; *Universal Thermosensors Ltd v Hibben* [1992] 3 All ER 257.

[3] [1895] 2 QB 315, CA.

[4] A decision confirmed and clarified in *Wessex Dairies Ltd v Smith* [1935] 2 KB 80, CA. See also Mehigan and Griffiths, op cit, p 66ff for a useful discussion of the extent to which an employee is permitted to make preparations for future employment.

4.17 In *Johnson & Bloy (Holdings) Ltd and Johnson & Bloy Ltd v Wolstenholme Rink plc and Fallon*[1] an employer discovered (again through the use of an *Anton Piller* order) that a former employee had taken with him certain formulations for printing inks used in the employer's business. It was held that there had been an infringement of the duty of fidelity as the formulations in this case were trade secrets belonging to the first employer.

[1] [1987] IRLR 499, CA.

4.18 On the other hand, the courts have been less willing (see above) to classify business information such as customer names and other non-technical information as trade secrets. The layman often finds this curious. However, in *Lansing Linde Ltd v Kerr*[1] two Judges in the Court of Appeal were prepared to broaden the definition of trade secret to include such matters. Staughton LJ said as follows:

> '[Counsel] suggested that a trade secret is information which, if disclosed to a competitor, would be liable to cause real (or significant) harm to the owner of the secret. I would add first, that it must be information used in a trade or business and secondly that the owner must limit the dissemination of it or at least not encourage or permit widespread publication.
>
> That is my preferred view of the meaning of trade secret in this context. It can thus include not only secret formulae for the manufacture of products but also, in an appropriate case, the names of customers and the goods which they buy.'

And Butler-Sloss LJ stated:

> '. . . we have moved into the age of multi-national businesses and worldwide business interests. Information may be held by very senior executives which, in the hands of competitors, might cause significant harm to the companies employing them. "Trade secrets" has, in my view, to be interpreted in the wider context of highly confidential information of a non-technical or non-scientific nature, which may come within the ambit of information the employer is entitled to have protected, albeit for a limited period.'

Thus Staughton LJ thought that protection could be given to plans for the development of new products and for the discontinuance of existing products.

A further example of this approach may be seen in *Poly Lina Ltd v Finch*[2] where detailed information on costing, customer accounts, profit margins, actual and hoped for sales and development plans were regarded as being in the nature of a trade secret, and *Faccenda Chicken* distinguished on its facts.

---

1 [1991] IRLR 80, CA.
2 [1995] FSR 751.

4.19 On the other hand, misuse of trade secrets is not so easy to prove in practice.[1] One highly important matter to bear in mind is that the courts are vigilant to stop plaintiffs using a complaint of misuse of information to stifle competition *per se*. In *Ixora Trading Inc v Jones*[2] the employer was a group of companies operating Bureaux de Change. The employees were executives. They had received training including familiarisation with the contents of two manuals. They had also during the course of their employment visited Paris to assess the feasibility of opening Bureaux de Change in France. They produced a document called an 'initial feasibility study'. The plaintiffs subsequently opened up a number of Bureaux de Change in Paris. But the employees left the company and themselves opened Bureaux de Change in Paris. The employer alleged misuse of confidential information and that the employees had breached their duties of good faith during the course of employment by planning and preparing to acquire an interest in a Bureau de Change business in Paris and that they had similarly breached fiduciary duties (see para 4.03) owed to the company by diverting to themselves a maturing business opportunity. The confidential information relied upon was a collection of technical knowledge and experience and, in particular, the contents of the two manuals and contents of the initial feasibility study. It was held, however, that none of the documents relied upon by the company amounted to confidential information so as to entitle an employer to prevent an ex-employee from using it after the termination of employment. The information, instead, was the kind of knowledge of the organisation and day-to-day management of a business which it was *not* a breach of confidence for an ex-employee to reveal.[3]

[1] See, eg *Malden Timber Ltd v Leitch* (1992) IRLIB, May 1992, p 18 (Court of Session).
[2] [1990] FSR 251.
[3] See para 4.02. See also *Lock v International plc v Beswick* [1989] IRLR 481.

4.20 Finally, it was considered that the initial feasibility study was both too obvious and unspecific to amount to a maturing business opportunity (see para 4.09) and no claim for breach of fiduciary duty as director could lie either.

4.21 In a case in the same area, *Berkeley Administration Inc v McClelland*,[1] the employer was again part of a group of companies operating Bureaux de Change. Certain employees had been employed in senior positions before being dismissed. After their dismissal they drafted a business plan for the purposes of raising finance to set up a Bureaux de Change business in competition with the former employer. They also invited other executives to join them. It was alleged that in preparing the business plan they had used five specific items of information derived from financial projections contained in an appendix to their employer's business plan, namely:

(1) the average operating profit per Bureau de Change;
(2) the average profit in the first year of operation as a percentage of a full year's profit;
(3) the average capital cost per bureau;
(4) the average number of annual transactions per bureau;
(5) the average value of each transaction.

It was held that the figures in the appendix were not genuine historical or forecast figures but were assumptions for the purpose of supporting a proposal to raise money; and in any event the information it contained was not sufficiently confidential to be protectable after the termination of employment.[2]

[1] [1990] 2 QB 407, [1990] 1 All ER 958, CA.
[2] Wright J said in relation to this action:

> 'I have come to the . . . conclusion that . . . the true motivation behind the plaintiffs' conduct was an attempt and a determined attempt at that, to strangle this infant competitor at or shortly after birth. It is unnecessary for me to point out that this is not an aim to which the court will lend its aid.'

4.22 Another example where the employer got into difficulty is *Mainmet Holdings v Austin*.[1] There, on fairly unusual facts, it was alleged that two reports, one concerning alleged problems with equipment installed by an employer, had been anonymously sent out to the employer's customers by an employee after he had left their employment. It was held that there was no serious question to be tried whether the material constituted confidential information because there was no evidence of abuse of specific identifiable trade secrets. Neither the contents of the reports nor their description as confidential nor their restricted distribution amounted to evidence that they contained trade secrets. The employer had not been able to identify any specific information which was not public information or which the employee might not have taken away with him as part of his own skill and knowledge.

[1] [1991] FSR 538. See also *Lock International plc v Beswick* [1989] IRLR 481.

4.23 In *Roberts v Northwest Fixings*[1] a number of employees had been employed as salesmen in which capacity they had received a list of customers together with a list of customer particulars (called customer management cards). Later they left the company and started up another firm in competition with it. They took with them the list of customers but not, they said, the customer management cards. An *Anton Piller* order was obtained to secure the return of the list of customers and an injunction against use of any confidential information was also granted.

1 [1993] FSR 281, CA.

4.24 The order was lifted on appeal, it being accepted that once the documents had been handed over the employees would in the future have to rely upon their memory as to who had been the firm's customers. In such circumstances the court could not restrain the employees. According to Lawton LJ:

> 'This is one of the cases where the law and the courts are being used by the plaintiffs to stop competition. If the plaintiff firm had taken the trouble to have a valid restraint of trade clause in the second and third defendant's contracts of employment they might have been able to get relief from the court. There were no such clauses in the contracts. In my judgment they should not now be allowed by means of an interlocutory injunction to get that which they did not take the trouble by contract to get . . . .'

4.25 So, notwithstanding the comments in the *Lansing Linde* case, the distinction drawn between confidential information and trade secrets illustrates that an employer may often not be able to prevent an employee competing solely because he is using certain information which, during the life of his contract, he was prevented from using or disclosing (subject to the *Robb v Green* principle). The difficulty that an employer may face in establishing that the information the employee is using to compete after the ending of the employment is a trade secret (and, also, the problems of proving use) emphasises the desirability of a restrictive covenant. This may stop the employee setting up or being employed in competition with his former employer, or prevent him from soliciting customers (which may sometimes be equally effective). This important topic is dealt with in the next section.

3 RESTRICTIVE COVENANTS

General

4.26 As will have been seen from the discussion above, it is not entirely satisfactory for an employer to rely solely upon the implied duty of fidelity to control the activities of an employee after the employment has ended.[1] An express restrictive covenant has many advantages for the employer. Once employment has ended an employer cannot, for example, at common law, stop an employee canvassing or soliciting former customers, or generally setting up in competition with the employer or joining a competitor. Only an express covenant can do this.

[1] See *Attwood v Lamont* [1920] 3 KB 571, CA; *Diamond Stylus Co Ltd v Bauden Precision Diamonds Ltd* [1973] RPC 675 and Mehigan and Griffiths, *Restraint of Trade and Business Secrets: Law and Practice* p 75.

4.27 A restrictive covenant may take many forms. Commonly, it is a clause in an agreement (usually, in the present context, in a contract of employment, but not necessarily), which restrains an employee from soliciting or canvassing an employer's former employees or customers or in some way impedes him from taking up employment or earning a living in a field which competes with the employer. The doctrine of restraint of trade applies to such covenants and holds that the covenants are invalid unless justifiable.[1] For a restrictive covenant to be justifiable, and not an unlawful restraint of trade, it has to be shown that the clause is necessary to protect the legitimate interests of the employer and that the protection taken is no more than is reasonably necessary to protect those interests. These interests include protection of trade secrets and trade connections.[2] It is also theoretically the position that a restrictive covenant must, in addition, be justifiable in the public interest. But this consideration features relatively rarely in cases of covenants between employers and employees and may, in practice, not be as major an issue in employment law as in other contexts. It is, however, available as an additional argument.[3]

[1] *Nordenfelt v Maxim Nordenfelt Guns and Ammunition Co Ltd* [1894] AC 535, HL; *Esso Petroleum Co Ltd v Harper's Garage (Stourport) Ltd* [1968] AC 269, [1967] 1 All ER 99, HL.

[2] *Allied Dunbar (Frank Weisinger) Ltd v Weisinger* [1988] IRLR 60. Whether an employee has access to trade secrets and trade connections (eg customers or suppliers) depends on the facts and the nature of the employment. Some employments inevitably put the employee in contact with customers and therefore raise a prima facie legitimate interest for an employer to protect, eg salesmen (*Continental Tyre and Rubber (Great Britain) Co Ltd v Heath* (1913) 29 TLR 308; *Gledhow Autoparts Ltd v Delaney* [1965] 3 All ER 288, [1965] 1 WLR 1366, CA), hairdressers (*Marion White Ltd v Francis* [1972] 3 All ER 857, [1972] 1 WLR 1423, CA) and milkmen (*Home Counties Dairies Ltd v Skilton* [1970] 1 All ER 1227, CA) (and there are many other examples).

[3] See, in more detail, *Harvey* Div A 3(2)(b). Cf *Wyatt v Kreglinger and Fernau* [1933] 1 KB 793, CA (employee liable to lose pension if he entered a competing employment – public interest relevant on enforceability). The decline of this element in the construction of employer/employee covenants is noted by Brearley and Bloch, op cit, p 111. See also the comments of Jenkins LJ in *Kores Manufacturing Co Ltd v Kolok Manufacturing Co Ltd* [1958] 2 All ER 65, CA at 75. Cf *Marshall v NM Financial Management Ltd* [1996] IRLR 20.

4.28 The doctrine applies not only to an express provision prohibiting a certain activity but also to a clause which does not actually prohibit such activity but imposes a financial penalty when an employee engages in such activity, and thereby tends to have the same effect. Thus, in *Sadler v Imperial Life Assurance Co of Canada Ltd*[1] an employee was an insurance agent remunerated on a commission basis. He was entitled to commission on policies effected during the period of his employment. When he left the employment of his company there were a number of policies in existence which were effected during the period of his employment in respect of which commission would have been paid in future years had this employment continued. His contract, however, provided that his entitlement to post-termination commission ended if he became employed by any other company involved in selling insurance. The question was whether this financial penalty was subject to the restraint of trade doctrine. It was held that it was, having regard to the earlier decisions of *Wyatt v Kreglinger and Fernau*[2] and *Bull v Pitney-Bowes Ltd.*[3] And on the facts of the case itself the provision was held to be an unlawful restraint of trade.

---

[1] [1988] IRLR 388.

[2] [1933] 1 KB 793, CA (where a pension stood to be forfeited if competition took place).

[3] [1966] 3 All ER 384, [1967] 1 WLR 273 (where entitlement to a pension was at stake). See also *Stenhouse Australia Ltd v Phillips* [1974] AC 391 (clause providing that if former client dealt with, fees to be paid to former employer – held: in reality, a restrictive covenant). Finally, in *Marshall v NM Financial Management Ltd* [1996] IRLR 20, a contractual provision that commission was payable to an employee after the termination of his employment provided that he did not compete with the former employee was held to be a restraint of trade and unlawful.

Business v employment agreements

4.29 Restrictive covenants appear of course not only in employment contracts but also, for example, in contracts for the sale of businesses, sales of shares in companies, agency and distribution agreements, franchise agreements, consultancy agreements and joint venture agreements. In non-employment agreements the courts will take a more lenient view of a restriction and be less prepared to strike it down. This is particularly so in the context of sales of businesses and share capital of companies where the sale involves a transfer of goodwill which the restrictive covenant is there to protect for the purchaser. In *Allied Dunbar (Frank Weisinger) Ltd v Weisinger*[1] Mr Weisinger had previously been a self-employed associate of Allied Dunbar and had an independent practice with a great deal of personal goodwill. In 1985 Allied Dunbar put forward proposals whereby sales associates could sell their practices to the company for a capital sum. Mr Weisinger was bought out for nearly £400,000 which included the goodwill and connections. In return he accepted a restriction over a period of two years which barred him from competing with the company. In effect, this meant that he would have to retire from the financial services industry for two years. It was held that the restriction was valid. Here the covenant was taken primarily for the protection of the goodwill of the practice acquired by the company. As it was a business sale, the validity of the covenant was to be determined in accordance with the less stringent approach adopted by the courts where a covenant is taken for the protection of goodwill of a business sold by a covenantor to a covenantee, as opposed to the way in which pure employment cases are looked at. So it is legitimate in order to protect the goodwill sold by the vendor of a business for a purchaser to take a covenant for a time which is necessary to protect the extent of the goodwill transferred. Another good example is *Systems Reliability Holdings plc v Smith.*[2] In this case Mr Smith was a computer engineer and a key employee. During his employment he had purchased shares totalling 1.6% of the issued share capital. After his dismissal the plaintiffs acquired all of the shares in the company and Mr Smith received £247,000 for his holding. The share sale agreement contained a restrictive covenant preventing him competing with the company. The period of restriction was 17 months. Shortly afterwards Mr Smith set up his own business supplying computer services. An injunction was granted. The court confirmed that there was a distinction between a business or *quasi* business agreement and a simple contract of employment. Harman J said:

> 'There are undoubtedly two streams of authority and two processes of thought in reaching a conclusion as to what restrictions are reasonable so

> that the court will enforce a covenant in restraint of trade. Those streams of authority apply on the one hand to covenants between master and servant, where the courts have imposed a very stringent limit on what restraints upon competition will be enforced, and, on the other, to covenants between vendors and purchasers where the courts have been much more liberal. In vendor and purchaser cases the courts have held that if a man is selling something he is entitled to get the best price for it that he can and if a purchaser is buying something a purchaser is entitled to have the full benefit of what he buys and that the public interest in permitting a man to exercise his trade so that the community as a whole has the benefit of his services and skill provided in the course of trade are overridden by the proper interests in both sides – the purchaser and the vendor – in making a deal which is effective to give both the full advantages of what they are dealing with.'

Interestingly, the learned judge felt that this principle could not be confined to a case where a purchaser bought the whole of the business from a number of proprietors who have substantial and controlling interests. Employees are increasingly encouraged, he noted, to have shareholding stakes in companies and there was, in his view, no reason why such employees should not be bound as vendors of the goodwill of a business. In particular, this case was a true vendor and purchaser situation because the defendant employee received £247,000 for his shareholding.

1 [1988] IRLR 60.
2 [1990] IRLR 377. See also, recently, *Alliance Paper Group plc v Prestwich* [1996] IRLR 25.

4.30 It is for this reason that it is worth considering, when advising a company acquiring the shares or business of another company or individuals and which also proposes to employ the former proprietors of the business under service agreements, that the usual restrictive covenants might be included in the sale agreement itself as opposed to in the contract of employment. Arguably (in a genuine case, of course), if inserted in the business or share sale agreement covenants will be subject to the less stringent approach referred to in the *Allied Dunbar* case.

Construction and enforceability

4.31 In examining covenants in contracts of employment, the courts will generally look at the nature of the employer's business and the employee's position therein. The higher the status of the individual, and the more access to or influence over customers or suppliers and the more access to confidential information, the more likely it will be that the covenant is enforceable. Likewise, the radius, duration and subject matter of the covenant must be closely geared to the status and position of the employee, his contact with customers and the nature and geography of the employer's business. The higher the status or greater the involvement of the individual in the business, the more comprehensive the clause may be.[1]

1 *Herbert Morris Ltd v Saxelby* [1916] 1 AC 688, HL; *Littlewoods Organisation Ltd v Harris* [1978] 1 All ER 1026, [1977] 1 WLR 1272, CA.

4.32 However, clauses are commonly attacked on the basis that they extend over too wide a radius, cover activities that go beyond the legitimate interest of the employer which it is necessary to protect, and endure for too long a time. There is certainly no merit in drafting a clause which is extreme: for it may not be enforceable. It is better to have a milder restriction that is enforceable than one which is fiercer and is not. All cases depend on their own circumstances but some examples of the courts' approach now follow.

4.33 In *Spencer v Marchington*[1] the employee was employed to manage an employment agency in Banbury. Subsequently, she also became manager of another agency in Leamington Spa. She agreed to a restriction on taking competing employment for a period of two years after termination within a radius of 25 miles of both the Banbury and Leamington offices. After termination the employee set up her own employment agency in Banbury in apparent breach of the clause. It was held that the restriction preventing competing employment within 25 miles of the employer's offices could not be enforced. The area concerned was wider than was necessary to protect the employer's legitimate interests. All but one of the employer's existing customers were within 20 miles not 25 miles of the offices concerned. The employer's interests could have been just as adequately protected by a non-solicitation clause but, instead, the employer had gone too far and so no restraint applied. The employer (who was not asking for an injunction) was not entitled to damages for breach of the covenant. In *Greer v Sketchley Ltd*[2] the employers were dry cleaners based in the Midlands and the South East. The employee was a director based in the Midlands. But he was subject to a UK-wide covenant. It was held that this was unenforceable as its width went beyond the legitimate interests of the employer that needed protecting. In *Mason v Provident Clothing and Supply Co Ltd*[3] the employers were clothing suppliers and the employee was employed as a canvasser based in Islington. He was subject to a restriction against competing employment after the termination of his employment within 25 miles of London as a whole. It was held that this was unreasonable. It was not necessary to protect the employer's legitimate interests to that degree.

1 [1988] IRLR 392.

2 [1979] IRLR 445, CA.

3 [1913] AC 724, HL. At the end of the day, the permissible scope of a restrictive covenant depends upon the facts of each case and the extent of the employer's interests which it is legitimate to protect. In one extreme example, the Court of Appeal upheld a restrictive covenant preventing work for a competitor anywhere in the world for one year due to the exceptional circumstances that obtained (*Norbrook Laboratories Ltd v Smyth* [1986] 15 NIJB 9, NICA, discussed on another point by Brearley and Bloch, op cit, p 123). Only on appropriate facts, of course, would such a wide restriction be upheld.

4.34 As to the subject matter of the covenant concerned, it is generally understood that the employer may only seek to restrict activities in the field in which the employer has traded during the employment of the employee. And it has been held in other cases that the employer cannot use a restrictive covenant to stop competition per se.[1] It must be shown that due to the employee's position and status the employer requires protection because of the potential use of trade secrets and trade connections and the like. Thus, in *Commercial Plastics Ltd v Vincent*[2] an employee worked in pvc calendered sheeting used to make adhesive tape. A restrictive covenant obliged him not to work for any competitor in the pvc calendered sheeting field for one year after the termination of employment. It was held that this was too wide. The employer had a legitimate interest to protect in the area of pvc calendered sheeting for adhesive tape, but not further, as the employee did not work in the wider field sought to be protected.[3]

[1] See Mehigan and Griffiths, op cit, p 79. This is sometimes called a 'covenant in gross' and will not be enforced. See also the attitude of the courts in actions ostensibly to protect confidential information (para 4.18) which may amount to an attempt, in essence, to stop competition.

[2] [1965] 1 QB 623, CA.

[3] See also *Henry Leetham & Sons Ltd v Johnstone-White* [1907] 1 Ch 322, CA. See, too, *Fitch v Dewes* [1921] 2 AC 158, HL: solicitor's agreement not to set up within seven miles of Tamworth: valid because clients were in that catchment area.

4.35 Finally, an employer must be wary of extracting a non-competition obligation where a simple non-solicitation clause would have protected his interests just as well. In such a case the non-competition clause may be unreasonable.[1]

[1] For an interesting discussion of when contact with customers will or will not amount to solicitation, see *Austin Knight (UK) Ltd v Hinds* [1994] FSR 52.

4.36 A good example is *Office Angels Ltd v Rainer-Thomas and O'Connor*.[1] In this case the defendant employees were employed at an employment agency in Bow Lane in the City of London. One employee was the manager of the branch and the other was temporaries' consultant. The company had 34 branches mainly in the south and west of England. Four of them were in the City. The employees' work consisted of the introduction of permanent staff to employer clients and the supply of temporary workers. The latter provided the greatest volume of business. Most of the business with the client firms was done over the telephone but temporary workers tended to visit the office. Many temporaries registered with other employment agencies and some of the client firms used more than one agency. In the employees' contracts of employment there were a number of restrictions. One in particular, however, prevented the employees from engaging in the business of an employment agency within a specified area for a period of six months. *Inter alia* the company sought to enforce this restriction when the employees became directors and shareholders of a competing employment agency based in Fenchurch Street, within the area covered by the restriction.

[1] [1991] IRLR 214, CA.

4.37 The Court of Appeal held that the employers, as an employment agency, did have a legitimate interest to protect in imposing an appropriate covenant to preserve its connection with client firms and the pool of workers available for temporary workers. However, it was not reasonable to impose a restriction on engaging in the business of an employment agency over a specified area for a period of six months. A covenant which prohibits wholly the carrying on of a business by a former employee in a specified area for a specified period would be approached with caution by the court since it amounted to a covenant against competition. It was important to establish that the restriction was no greater than was necessary for protecting the employer's legitimate interest. In this case the employer could not satisfy that test. The employees were in effect restricted from opening up an employment agency over most of the City of London. An area restriction was not an appropriate covenant because it would in practice do little to protect the connection with client firms and temporary workers. Clients' orders were placed over the telephone and it was largely immaterial where the employment agency's offices were located. Accordingly, a narrower covenant would have sufficed, such as, for example, a suitably worded covenant precluding soliciting or dealing with clients with whom the employees had dealt during their employment. Any more was unnecessary and therefore unreasonable. Nor was the covenant appropriate for the purposes of protecting the connection with temporary workers. A stated interest of the employer was, as expressed in the clause, dealings with *clients* of the company. It was not now open, said the court, for the plaintiff employer to go behind the stated purpose by arguing that it would have been apparent to any employee who knew the working of the organisation that the covenant was also intended to protect the plaintiff's connection with *temporary workers*. Where the wording of a restriction does not specifically state the interest of the employer which it is intended to protect the court held it was entitled to look at both the wording and the surrounding circumstances. But where the employer chose specifically to state the interest which the covenant was intended to protect, the employer was not entitled thereafter to seek to justify the covenant by reference to some separate and additional interest which had not been specified.

4.38 It is therefore necessary for any employer considering the imposition of restrictive covenants to determine exactly what interest needs protecting and how it can be protected whilst avoiding what might amount to a simple covenant against competition for the sake of it.

4.39 But the restraint of trade rules apply also to lesser restrictions, such as non-solicitation clauses. If it is legitimate, an employer may restrain an employee from soliciting customers. In an appropriate case, if those interests justify it, the solicitation clause may be in addition to the non-competition clause. On the other hand, it may not be reasonable on the facts in some cases to restrain competition and only non-solicitation may then be allowed (see above). With non-solicitation clauses, the employer may in principle, subject to the above rules, restrain soliciting of customers. In *Spafax Ltd v Harrison*[1] the employee was a branch manager of a company which wholesaled motor parts. The restriction stopped him soliciting his own customers and also any other customer which to his knowledge had been served by any member of his staff. It was held that the covenant was enforceable as this was an interest that the employer was entitled to protect as it was possible for the branch manager to have influence over such customers. Further, it may be legitimate not only to restrict solicitation of customers but also suppliers. In *Office International (London) Ltd v Palm Court Furniture Ltd*[2] the employer imported office furniture from, *inter alia*, an Italian supplier. A substantial volume of supplies that the employer obtained were from this Italian supplier. It was held that this was an interest that it was legitimate for the employer to protect via a non-solicitation clause. In these cases, the covenant was upheld. If the employee's position is not such as to amount to a risk that he may attract customers (or suppliers) away, however, the non-solicitation covenant may be void.[3]

1 [1980] IRLR 442, CA.
2 (1985) LEXIS transcript.
3 And, in terms of drafting, it should be considered whether it is really necessary to restrict the solicitation of suppliers in general or whether a narrower obligation, eg not to do anything which might interfere with supply by suppliers, may suffice.

4.40 Thus, in *Gledhow Autoparts Ltd v Delaney*[1] a sales representative in the car accessory trade was required not to solicit any customer or potential customer in the areas in which he had worked for the three years after the ending of his employment. It was held that the clause was not enforceable as it went beyond what was necessary: it extended to customers neither he nor even the company had ever dealt with.[2]

1 [1965] 3 All ER 288, [1965] 1 WLR 1366, CA.
2 See also *SW Strange Ltd v Mann* [1965] 1 All ER 1069, [1965] 1 WLR 629; *Marley Tile Co Ltd v Johnson* [1982] IRLR 75, CA; *Gilford Motor Co Ltd v Horne* [1933] Ch 935, CA. And in *Austin Knight (UK) Ltd v Hinds* [1994] FSR 52 a restrictive covenant was not enforced as it purported to prevent the ex-employee from approaching or, on one construction, dealing at all, with former customers of the plaintiff with whom the employee had had no contact during her employment with the plaintiff.

4.41 Also, if the trade connections sought to be prohibited were actually brought to the employment by the employee himself, the employer may have difficulty in enforcing the prohibition since the trade connections never really belonged to him.[1] However, this principle was restricted in *Hanover Insurance Brokers Ltd v Schapiro*.[2] In that case, a former chairman of a company was not discharged from a covenant because it prevented him from acting for those who had been his customers before entering his latest employment and whom he had introduced to his last employer. The case was distinguishable from *M and S Drapers v Reynolds*[3] (where the contrary was the case) because in *Reynolds* the employee was a salesman whose connections when he entered the employer's service could be regarded as the tools of his trade, of which he should not be deprived.

1 *M and S Drapers v Reynolds* [1956] 3 All ER 814, [1957] 1 WLR 9, CA.
2 [1994] IRLR 82, CA.
3 See n 1, above.

4.42 Sometimes it is permissible to oblige the employee not only not to solicit, but also not to *deal* with customers or suppliers.[1] If that is necessary to protect the employer's legitimate interests that will be enforceable, if reasonable, otherwise not.[2]

1 Although, in relation to suppliers see the comment at n 3, para 4.39.
2 See *London and Solent Ltd v Brooks* (1989) IRLIB 21 March 1989, p 4 (enforceable on the facts).

4.43 Not uncommonly, one also sees covenants restricting solicitation of employees (ie the departing employee's former colleagues) or even the employment of employccs. Mchigan and Griffiths doubt whether a clause preventing solicitation/enticing away of former colleagues is enforceable. They argue that such a restraint could be an indirect restraint on the remaining employees who might be open to enticement or solicitation. As such it could be in restraint of trade of their contracts of employment.[1] They argue that the matter is bound to come before the courts before long. Time has proved the authors right. In *Hanover Insurance Brokers Ltd v Schapiro*[2] an injunction restraining a departing employee from soliciting or enticing any employees of the former employer was refused by the Court of Appeal. Dillon LJ stated:

> '. . . the difficulties in law in the way of a non-poaching agreement between employers are very clearly explained in the decision of the Court in *Kores Manufacturing Co Ltd v Kolok Manufacturing Co Ltd* [1959] Ch 108. In particular, the employee has the right to work for the employer he wants to work for if that employer is willing to employ him . . . the goodwill of an insurance broker's business depends on its staff . . . as with any other company, but that does not make the staff an asset of the company like apples or pears or other stock in trade . . .'[3]

Even if covenants against solicitation of employees are valid, such covenants often fail either on the ground that the employees liable to be solicited under the clause do not possess trade secrets or confidential information (see *Kores*, above) or, for example, that employees liable to be solicited may have joined after the defendant employee has left (see *Hanover*).

The main point of principle in *Hanover* itself was treated fairly briefly and may be read in two ways. On the one hand, the judgment of Dillon LJ is sceptical about non-poaching agreements generally. On the other hand, it stresses that the covenant in *Hanover* was verging on a covenant against competition *per se* by paying no regard to seniority or juniority of employees to whom the ban applied and by applying to employees who may have joined the employer after the defendants had left. Further guidance is perhaps needed on whether non-poaching agreements are void *per se* or fail only if badly drawn.

For the moment, the debate continues. In *Ingham v ABC Contract Services Ltd*[4] Leggatt LJ, in a judgment delivered shortly after *Schapiro*, stated that an employer does have a legitimate interest in maintaining a stable trained workforce in a highly competitive business. And finally, in *Alliance Paper Group plc v Prestwich*[5] Judge Levy adopted the reasoning of Leggatt LJ in *Ingham* and upheld an employer's application to enforce a covenant not to solicit or entice away employees 'in a senior capacity'.

Mehigan and Griffiths point out that a restrictive covenant which goes further than poaching and seeks to prevent the departing employee employing former colleagues at all is likely to be even more dubiously viewed; they question whether it can be reasonable to prevent employees joining the departing employee (or his new employer) if they have not been solicited. This must be correct in principle.

---

[1] Op cit, p 102. Cf Brearley and Bloch, op cit, where the point is not so strongly taken, pp 39–140.

[2] [1994] IRLR 82, CA.

[3] The immediate question that may be asked is this: If the employees liable to be solicited are so valuable, why are they not committed personally to restrictive covenants imposed by the employer? In *Kores Manufacturing Co Ltd v Kolok Manufacturing Co Ltd* [1958] 2 All ER 65 at 74, Jenkins LJ stated:

> 'It seems to us to be open to question whether an agreement . . . directed to preventing employees of the parties from doing that which they could not by individual covenants with their respective employers validly bind themselves not to do, should be accorded any greater validity than individual covenants by the employees themselves would possess'.

[4] FC 2 93/6609/F.

[5] [1996] IRLR 25.

4.44 The duration of the covenant must also be reasonable. This depends on the facts of each case and in particular on the status of the employee, his access to customers or other information and the nature of the employer's business. In *Rex Stewart Jeffries Parker Ginsberg Ltd v Parker*,[1] Mr Parker was employed as a joint managing director of an advertising agency. He was obliged for 18 months after the termination of employment not to solicit the custom or business of any person, concern, firm or company which to his knowledge was or had been during the period of his employment a customer of the company or its associated companies so as not to harm the goodwill of or compete with the company. As will be seen below, only part of the restrictions were upheld. But the court had also to consider the duration of that part of the covenant which applied. Whether the duration of the covenant is reasonable was a matter of impression. It was held that while a shorter period of exclusion might be appropriate for a more junior employee, in this case the individual was a managing director and bearing in mind the opportunities he had to develop relationships with customers, a period of 18 months was not unreasonable.[2] Finally, it is hard in practice to separate the questions of width and subject matter of the covenant from duration. In other words, the wider the covenant the more sensitive a court may be about duration, and vice versa.

1 [1988] IRLR 483, CA.
2 See also *Empire Meat Co Ltd v Patrick* [1939] 2 All ER 85, CA; *M and S Drapers v Reynolds* [1956] 3 All ER 814, CA. See the importance attached to the period of a covenant in *D v M* [1996] IRLR 192.

4.45 The validity of the covenant is to be judged in the light of the circumstances prevailing at the date of the contract and not subsequently.[1]

1 *Gledhow Autoparts Ltd v Delaney* [1965] 1 WLR 1366, CA; *Shell UK Ltd v Lostock Garages Ltd* [1977] 1 All ER 481, [1976] 1 WLR 1187, CA, although cf the minority view of Lord Denning MR. Very difficult practical problems arise upon a transfer of a business from the original employer to a new employer. Upon the transfer of an undertaking, by virtue of the Transfer of Undertakings (Protection of Employment) Regulations 1981 the contract of employment (and all rights and obligations in relation thereto) are transferred to the new employer. Does this include a restrictive covenant? There is no reason in principle why not (McMullen, *Business Transfers and Employee Rights* (2nd edn), p 178; *Initial Supplies Ltd v McCall* 1992 SLT 67n, IDS Employment Law Cases, 8.4.5). But the covenant may refer to, say, non-solicitation of customers of the *former* employer, not the present (amongst other difficulties). A practical approach was taken to such a problem in *Morris Angel & Son Ltd v Hollande* [1993] ICR 71, CA (covenant not to do business with customers of the transferor company construed as meaning covenant not to do business with customers of the transferred *business* in which the employee was employed).

Severance

4.46 What if aspects of the restriction are not justifiable? Does the whole clause fail? Strictly speaking, the covenant must be construed as a whole and if one aspect of it is unreasonable the covenant should be invalid. However, there is an exception to this. There is a possibility of severance. It may be appropriate to sever the part of the clause which is unreasonable from that which is reasonable and to allow the reasonable part of the clause to remain so that it is separately enforceable. However, this can only be done by the successful application of the so-called 'blue pencil' test. This means that if the unreasonable part of the clause is deleted the remainder of the clause still existing must be capable of a sensible construction standing on its own without the deleted, unreasonable, part. This very often will not be the case. The question is whether the covenant is to be construed as one individual covenant, in which case the blue pencil test will not work; or, alternatively, whether the covenant can, within itself, be broken down into a number of promises, the deletion of one of which will not be fatal to the survival of the other, reasonable, promises. In short, the court is not permitted under these rules in effect to rewrite the covenant for the employer. If, after the offending parts of the clause have been deleted, the remainder does not make sense, the court cannot rewrite the clause to have it make sense.[1]

[1] See *Mason v Provident Clothing and Supply Co Ltd* [1913] AC 724, HL; *Attwood v Lamont* [1920] 3 KB 571, CA.

4.47 Thus, in *Mason v Provident Clothing and Supply Co Ltd*[1] the employee was restricted from competing within 25 miles of London. It was not possible successfully to apply the severance rules to bind the employee to a smaller radius; to do so the court would have had virtually to rewrite the clause (presumably to confine its scope to the Islington area). Similarly, too, in *Attwood v Lamont*[2] the employee was restricted from competing as a tailor and outfitter within ten miles of Kidderminster. This was an unreasonably wide area. But it was not possible to apply the severance rules, to apply the covenant more narrowly, as the covenant was a single one and to narrow the covenant and make it enforceable would have involved rewriting the covenant. In *Living Design (Home Improvements) Ltd v Davidson*[3] the Court of Session refused to enforce a clause applicable on termination of the employee's employment, however that came about, lawful or unlawful (an ineffective attempt to contract out of the rule in *General Billposting Co Ltd v Atkinson*[4] (see para 4.58)). It would not sever the offending words. Otherwise, to do so would alter the scope and intention of the agreement. Severance should only occur where the enforceable part is clearly severable, and even then only where what is struck out is of trivial importance or technical and not part of the main substance of the clause. In *NIS Fertilisers v Neville*[5] the employer was a fertiliser and grass seed company and the employee, a sales representative, was restricted from dealing with companies within his sales territory and within a further 20 mile radius of that territory. It was held that the restraint over the additional 20 miles beyond his territory was unreasonable but it was not possible to sever that part from the reasonable parts of the covenant as the covenant was a single indivisible one.

[1] [1913] AC 724, HL.
[2] [1920] 3 KB 571, CA.
[3] [1994] IRLR 89.
[4] [1909] AC 118, HL.
[5] [1986] 2 NIJB 70.

4.48 To be contrasted is the case of *Rex Stewart Jeffries Parker Ginsberg Ltd v Parker*.[1] In this case, it will be remembered, the employee was a joint managing director of an advertising agency restrained for a period of 18 months from termination from soliciting certain clients. In particular, he was prohibited from soliciting (1) customers of the employer who had been customers up to the date of termination; (2) anybody who might have been a customer thereafter; and (3) customers not only of his employer but of associated companies. It was held that all but the first restraint (about soliciting his own employer's customers who had been customers up to the point of termination) were unreasonable.

However, in accordance with the severance rules[2] the latter two restraints could be severed from the clause so as to leave intact and enforceable the most important prohibition preventing soliciting of customers who were customers up to the time of termination of employment. As such the covenant was enforceable.[3]

1 [1988] IRLR 483, CA.
2 See *Mason v Provident Clothing and Supply Co Ltd* [1913] AC 724, HL and *Attwood v Lamont* [1920] 3 KB 571, CA.
3 See, too, *Putsman v Taylor* [1927] 1 KB 637, CA; *T Lucas & Co Ltd v Mitchell* [1974] Ch 129, [1972] 3 All ER 689, CA. The High Court in *Sadler v Imperial Life Assurance Co of Canada Ltd* [1988] IRLR 388 stated the principles of severability to be subject to the following conditions: (1) The unenforceable provision is capable of being removed without the necessity of adding to or modifying the wording of what remains. (2) The remaining terms continue to be supported by adequate consideration. (3) The removal of the unenforceable provision does not so change the character of the contract that it becomes 'not the sort of contract that the parties entered into at the time'. See also *Business Seating (Renovations) Ltd v Broad* [1989] ICR 729 (restraint on competition against not only the employing company but also associated companies: the latter was unreasonable but capable of severance). For a recent application of Sadler see *Marshall v NM Financial Management Ltd* [1996] IRLR 20.

4.49 At least three drafting devices seem appropriate for consideration here. First, it seems good sense, if at all possible, for restraints to be built into separate identifiable and discrete obligations within an agreement, and, for example, for individual obligations to be given to a separate clause or sub-clause number. It is suggested that severance of unreasonable obligations is then more likely as the reasonable obligations that remain may appear to have an independent existence. Second, it may be worth considering qualifying the restraint on future activities or solicitation by including a provision whereby such activities are not to be carried on without the consent of the employer, such consent not to be unreasonably withheld. This device gains some support from the case of *Kerchiss v Colora Printing Inks Ltd*[1] although, to be fair, it did not impress the courts in earlier reported cases,[2] and its disadvantage is that it is frequently only window dressing.

1 [1960] RPC 235.
2 *Chafer Ltd v Lilley* (1947) 176 LT 22; *Technograph Printed Circuits Ltd v Chalwyn Ltd* [1967] RPC 339; Mehigan & Griffiths, op cit, pp 95-96; *Stenhouse Australia Ltd v Phillips* [1974] 1 All ER 117; see also Brearley and Bloch, op cit, p 143.

4.50 Finally, a common clause inserted into employment contracts provides that if a court finds that any of the provisions of the agreement are void or unenforceable the agreement shall take effect to the extent that the court would otherwise find it reasonable and enforceable. The effect of such a provision was, as far as is known, untested until the Court of Session case of *Hinton & Higgs (UK) Ltd v Murphy and Valentine*.[1] In this case the pursuers sought to enforce a term of the employees' contracts of employment that they should not work for any previous or present client of the Hinton & Higgs Group of Companies for 18 months. There was also a clause which provided: 'the restrictions contained in [Clause 14] are considered reasonable by the parties, but in the event that any such restriction shall be found to be void would [*sic*] be valid if some part thereof were deleted . . . such restrictions shall apply with such modifications as may be necessary to make them valid or effective'. The pursuers were faced with the immediate problem that the court felt that a restriction on working for any previous or present client of the Group for 18 months was far too wide. As read, it stopped an employee working for a client who had been a client outside the period of the employee's employment and who might have ceased to be so, say, more than ten years ago. So by seeking to cover previous as well as present clients the restriction was too wide and could not be enforced. The court did say, however, that if that were the sole basis for holding the restriction to be unreasonable the court would have accepted a deletion of the reference to previous clients in accordance with the provisions of the clause recited above. Although the court would not make contracts for the parties, in the present case the parties themselves had agreed in advance that they would accept as continuing to bind them such part of the arrangements which they had made as the court found by deletion to be reasonable. Since that involved not rewriting the contract but selecting that version of it which the parties had made with each other and enabling the bargain to be modified to stand there was no reason why the courts should refuse to perform that role.

---

1 [1989] IRLR 519.

4.51 However, the court would not perform that function on this occasion. The clause was also unreasonably wide for two reasons. First, it placed no geographical limitation on the restrictions whatsoever. The activities of the employer were limited to the UK and therefore there was no justification for protection against competition on a worldwide scale. Second, the clause was also unreasonably wide in seeking to restrict the employee from working not only for clients of the pursuer company but also those of any other company in the same group. In the absence of some special circumstances there was no ground for considering it necessary for the protection of the interests of an employer that ex-employees be restricted from working for any client of any other company in the group. In this case there were no special circumstances. So even if the reference to previous clients was deleted the clause would still be unreasonably wide and unenforceable.

4.52 The conclusions to be drawn from the above appear to be that it does no harm to include a clause of the type discussed in *Hinton & Higgs* in a contract of employment. But whether such a provision allows the court to go further than its self-imposed limitations under the blue pencil test is questionable. For it is clear that the court in *Hinton & Higgs* did not regard the clause as entitling it to rewrite the terms of the clause. This approach was mirrored by the recent decision of the Court of Session (Outer House) in *Living Design (Home Improvements) Ltd v Davidson*.[1] In this case the Court considered a saving clause in terms 'in the event that any such restriction should be found to be void but would be valid if some part thereof could be deleted or the period or area of application reduced, such restriction should apply with such modification as may be necessary to make it valid and effective'. It was held, in essence, that the clause did not allow the court to do anything other than it might do under the normal blue pencil test. Lord Coulsfield stated as follows:

> 'It seems to me . . . to be doubtful whether a clause such as [the clause in question] really enables the court to do anything which it could not do in any case. It is recognised that even in the absence of such a clause the

court can sever the unreasonable part of a restriction, where that can be done simply by deletion of the offending part, without in consequence rewriting the contract or altering its scope . . . and I do not think [that the clause] contains anything which can be construed as entitling the court to rewrite the contract.'

[1] [1994] IRLR 69. See also *D v M* [1996] IRLR 192.

4.53 There is one well-known case in which the employer succeeded notwithstanding a finding that, as drawn, the clause was unenforceable and, to appear reasonable, would have virtually to be rewritten. In *Littlewoods Organisation Ltd v Harris*[1] a director of a mail order company (Littlewoods) with substantial contacts and knowledge of the company's strategy, mail order content and planning, undertook not to work for a certain competitor (Great Universal Stores) or any of its subsidiaries for 12 months after the termination of employment. In fact, Great Universal Stores had subsidiaries which dealt in activities in which the employee's employer did not deal at all and those subsidiaries were outside the UK. The court upheld the injunction granted against the employee and framed it in terms that the restriction applied to activities competing with Littlewoods for 12 months within the UK. In effect, it rewrote the clause for the employers, as Browne LJ pointed out, dissenting from his colleagues in the Court of Appeal, saying: 'With all deference to Lord Denning MR and Megaw LJ, I think this is rewriting the clause, and rewriting it so as to make enforceable that which would otherwise be unenforceable. With all deference and respect, I think that is something which this court cannot do.'[2] However, it is submitted that reliance upon this case would be risky. In *Greer v Sketchley Ltd*[3] discussed above, it will be remembered that the restraint was invalid as being geographically too wide. The court declined an invitation to construe the clause as applying simply to a competitor of Sketchley in order that an injunction could be granted.[4] And, in *Spencer v Marchington*[5] it will be remembered (see above) that the employee was prevented from competing within 25 miles of either Banbury or Leamington. The clause was invalid because, at most, a radius of 20 miles of these offices would be reasonable. The employee had set up in competition with the employer in the town of Banbury itself. Although it is not clear whether there was an argument on the point, the court did not seem to consider it appropriate to consider modifying the effect of the clause and limiting it to restraining employees from setting up in competition in Banbury alone in order to find a breach by the employee.[6]

[1] [1978] 1 All ER 1026, [1977] 1 WLR 1472, CA.

[2] [1978] 1 All ER 1026 at 1046.

[3] [1979] IRLR 445, CA.

[4] And one member of the court in *Greer v Sketchley* was Lord Denning MR who had sat in *Littlewoods*. In *Greer* he declined to limit the covenant by reading limiting words into it!

[5] [1988] IRLR 392.

[6] The approach in *Littlewoods Organisation Ltd plc v Harris* was mirrored, however, in *Provident Financial Group plc and Whitegates Estate Agency Ltd v Hayward* [1989] ICR 160, [1989] IRLR 84, CA which concerned the application of a negative covenant applying during employment stopping the employee, whilst employed, from working for or having an interest in any other business or profession. The employee was on notice of resignation but had been put on 'garden leave' (see Chapter 3, above) during notice, ie paid in full but required to stay at home. During this notice he purported to leave and join a competitor. However, although, on the facts, an injunc-

tion to restrain this was refused to his former employer on the ground that the post with the new employer was purely administrative and did not involve access to confidential information, the Court of Appeal did say that in such a case (ie when concerned with the scope of an express negative stipulation during employment), it could grant lesser relief than was implicit from the covenant and narrow the scope of the embargo, eg limiting an injunction to preventing work for specified rivals or rivals generally. Perhaps, though, the court was influenced by the fact that it may, in any event, be a breach of an implied duty at common law to go and work for a rival in a material way while employment subsists.

4.54 The orthodox rule was reinforced by the Court of Appeal in *J A Mont (UK) Ltd v Mills*[1] where an employer tried to enforce a covenant in terms that the employee would not join another company in the tissue industry within one year of leaving employment. The employee had been employed all his working life in the paper tissue industry. It was held that the covenant was far too wide in that it had no geographical limit and it also restrained the individual from working in any capacity whatsoever and indeed in any sector of the tissue industry. It was unenforceable. Simon Brown LJ said:

> 'If a court were to construe this covenant as the plaintiff's desire, what possible reasons would employers ever have to impose restraints in appropriately limited terms? It would always be said that covenants were basically "just and honest" and designed solely to protect the employer's legitimate interests in the confidentiality of their trade secrets rather than to prevent competition as such.'

---

1 [1993] FSR 577.

4.55 Curiously, however, in *Hanover Insurance Brokers Ltd v Schapiro*[1] a more flexible approach was adopted. Mr Schapiro and three others left the employment of HIB and sought to set up in competition. In Schapiro's service agreement there was an obligation that he would not for a period of 12 months following the termination of his employment directly or indirectly 'canvass, solicit or endeavour to take away from the company the business of . . . any of its customers or clients who have been ex-customers or clients during the period of 12 months immediately preceding the termination of [his employment]'. There was also a non-solicitation of employees clause. In the first instance HIB got injunctions to restrain the solicitation of customers and clients but not to restrain solicitation of employees. In the Court of Appeal Schapiro appealed against injunctions restraining him and his colleagues from soliciting customers and clients and the company cross-appealed against the trial judge's refusal to grant the injunction for non-solicitation of employees. The court rejected the cross-appeal. The non-solicitation of employees clause was far too wide to be enforceable. It applied to all employees of HIB irrespective of their expertise or seniority and also applied to employees who had only joined HIB after Schapiro had left the company.[2] It was also arguable whether a non-solicitation of employees clause was in restraint of trade of employees' contracts of employment (see the discussion at para 4.43).[3]

---

1 [1994] IRLR 82, CA.

2 See also *Kores Manufacturing Co Ltd v Kolok Manufacturing Co Ltd* [1958] 2 All ER 65, CA where a similar approach was taken (agreement not to poach employees unreasonable because it

applied to all employees, irrespective of whether they were possessed of trade secrets or confidential information).

[3] And see *Kores Manufacturing Co Ltd v Kolok Manufacturing Co Ltd* [1958] 2 All ER 65, CA.

4.56 However, the order restraining solicitation of customers and clients was upheld. First, Schapiro had argued that the clause should not apply to customers or clients that he himself had introduced. However, the court said that there was a distinction between someone like Schapiro who was the managing director and someone like a travelling salesman. There were dicta in case law to the effect that the latter might be able to take with him his own customer connections, but not the former. Second, he argued that the non-solicitation clause was too wide because it did not only apply to those customers or clients with whom he and his colleagues had had personal dealings but also to any customers and clients of Hanover and any of its subsidiaries. However the court interpreted this as meaning the business of any of HIB's customers or clients who had been HIB's customers or clients in the preceding 12 months. In this respect it is to be noted that there is a significant difference between the approach in this case and that in *Mont v Mills* and further appellate guidance is needed.

4.57 Finally, the utmost care must be taken in the use of words in drafting. Ambiguity tends to be resolved in favour of the employee. In *WAC Ltd v Whillock*[1] the Court of Session considered a restriction in a shareholders' agreement. Mr Whillock was, at the time of the case, a shareholder in WAC Ltd and until he resigned in January 1989 was a director of the company and one of its subsidiaries. A clause in the shareholders' agreement provided that:

> 'none of the shareholders will, for as long as they remain a shareholder in the company and for a period of two years after the date of any such shareholder ceasing to hold shares in the company, carry on in competition with the company or any of the subsidiaries or any subsidiary of the subsidiaries any business involving the distribution and installation of air conditioning and refrigeration equipment or any other business which may be carried on by the company or the subsidiaries or by any subsidiary of the subsidiaries from time to time in the Republic of Ireland or the United Kingdom'.

In February 1989 the pursuers learnt that Mr Whillock had become a director of a competing company. The pursuers claimed this was in breach of the restriction and applied for an injunction. The Court of Session discharged the injunction. The phrase 'carry on in competition' prohibited a shareholder from personally carrying on a business in competition with the company but it did *not* impose any restriction on his right to be a director or employee of another company which carried on business in competition with the original employer. There was a clear distinction between an individual carrying on business and a company carrying on business. The clause therefore did not cover the situation of the employee in question since he had not set up in competition on his own account but had merely become a director of a competing company.

[1] [1990] IRLR 23.

Wrongful repudiation by employer

4.58 It is received law that an employer may not rely upon a restrictive covenant if he has wrongfully dismissed the employee. This follows from the old authority of *General Billposting Co Ltd v Atkinson*.[1] The reasoning behind this is not clear. It is argued in *Harvey on Industrial Relations and Employment Law*[2] that the effect of a repudiatory breach on the part of the employer means that the employee is entitled to elect to treat himself as discharged from further performance of his contract including any clause in the contract restraining him from competing, soliciting and such like. However, it is submitted that this reasoning is far from satisfactory. It can be argued that termination of the employment, whether lawful or unlawful, does not of itself bring to an end all provisions of the contract, at least where the provisions of the contract are intended to cover or extend to periods following the termination of employment. Thus, for example, termination of the contract, whether in breach of contract or otherwise, does not normally destroy an exclusion clause or an arbitration clause both of which are expressed to apply after the termination of employment. The orthodox reasoning which dictates the failure of a restrictive covenant following a wrongful dismissal of an employee is based on policy. It is not fair for an employer to recruit employees, obligate them to restrictive covenants, thereby tying up the labour market, and then wrongfully dismiss them, and thus by his own unlawful act, prevent them from coming back on to the labour market again and competing with him. There are those, on the other hand, who continue to argue that the issue should be one of construction of the contract rather than policy and that the terms of a restrictive covenant should be regarded in the same way as any other type of clause intended to survive termination of the contractual relationship such as, for example, the survival of an exclusion clause in a commercial contract.[3] There has been little modern discussion of the subject in case law until recently although in *Briggs v Oates*,[4] discussed later, the approach of the court seemed to support the policy, as opposed to construction, approach, holding also that it was not possible to contract out of the rule in *General Billposting Co Ltd v Atkinson* (see para 4.64).

1 [1909] AC 118, HL.
2 1.3(f).
3 See, eg *Photo Production Ltd v Securicor Transport Ltd* [1980] AC 827, HL.
4 [1990] IRLR 472. See also *Living Design (Home Improvements) Ltd v Davidson* [1994] IRLR 69.

4.59 An employee who wishes to leave an employer and who wants also to be released from a restrictive covenant of one sort or another may very often seek to find a breach of contract on the part of the employer which will have the effect of releasing him from the restrictive covenant. If there is a straight wrongful dismissal, ie a dismissal without notice or with short notice where the employee's conduct does not warrant summary dismissal at common law, it seems the principle in *General Billposting Co Ltd v Atkinson* applies and the restrictive covenant extinguishes. An interesting off-shoot of this principle is that if an employee is dismissed summarily but with a full payment in lieu of notice it is arguable, these days, that such a dismissal is also in breach of contract.[1] In such a case it might be urged that a restrictive covenant is extinguished there, too. However, even if this is correct, if it is contractually provided that dismissal may take place with a payment in lieu of notice it seems that the employee is deprived of this argument, and the dismissal will be lawful and the restrictive covenant applies. Thus, in *Rex Stewart Jeffries Parker Ginsberg Ltd v Parker*[2] an employee was given short notice and six months salary in lieu of notice. But it was expressly provided in his agreement that his employment could be determined by the giving of six months notice or a payment of six months salary in lieu thereof. It was held that this effectively made lawful a dismissal with a payment in lieu of notice that might otherwise be unlawful at common law. Therefore there was no wrongful dismissal and the covenant still, prima facie, applied.

1 *Dixon v Stenor Ltd* [1973] ICR 157; cf *Konski v Peet* [1915] 1 Ch 530.

2 [1988] IRLR 483, CA. An employer must, however, take care to avoid the problem which befell the employer in *Abrahams v Performing Right Society Ltd* [1995] ICR 1028 where as a matter of construction the payment in lieu of notice clause gave rise to the right to a liquidated sum with no duty to mitigate. Such would make a covenant very expensive to enforce!

4.60 There is no reason in principle why *General Billposting Co Ltd v Atkinson* should not also apply to a constructive dismissal or termination at the instance of the employee because of a wrongful repudiation by an employer short of dismissal.[1] So the Court of Appeal in effect held in *Measures Bros Ltd v Measures*[2] when it decided that a covenant no longer applied following a corporate employer's inability to employ due to being compulsorily wound up. One situation that can arise in this area is where an employee is dismissed, not with immediate effect, but is sent home on 'garden leave' and asked to stay at home idle until the contract expires. Although there is some authority saying that this is not a breach of contract, a more modern view is that in many employments, at least those employments where the employee seeks to maintain reputation, skills and knowledge, this may be a breach of the implied duty of the employer to provide work – not just wages – in relation to the contract of employment.[3] If such employer conduct is a breach of contract, could an employee accept it as a wrongful repudiation releasing him from his contract and the restrictive covenant thereafter? The only case on this seems to be *Spencer v Marchington*[4] where the employee was dismissed from her employment under a 12 month fixed term contract with two months still to run. She was sent home and not allowed to perform her duties. It was held that this was not a repudiation by the employer so as to amount to a fundamental breach which might invoke the principle in *General Billposting Co Ltd v Atkinson, sed quaere.*

1 Harvey Div A (3)(2)(f).

2 [1910] 2 Ch 248, CA, especially at pp 260–261.

3 *Collier v Sunday Referee Publishing Co Ltd* [1940] 2 KB 647, [1940] 4 ALL ER 234 but cf in specific cases, *Langston v Amalgamated Union of Engineering Workers* [1974] 1 All ER 980, [1974] ICR 180, CA; *Breach v Epsylon Industries Ltd* [1976] ICR 316, [1976] IRLR 180, EAT; *Bosworth v Angus Jowett* & Co Ltd [1977] IRLR 374, IT; McMullen, 'A Right to Work in the Contract of Employment' [1978] NLJ 848.

4 [1988] IRLR 392.

4.61 Being asked to stay away from work for the last two months of the contract was not important enough, it was said, even in the context of a 12 month contract, under which a share of the profits could be earned, to amount to a fundamental breach. This is respectfully to be doubted as a proposition. However, it must be noted that there may not have been a constructive dismissal at all in this case as there was no evidence that the employee had accepted the repudiation and had treated the employment as at an end. Presumably, acceptance of the breach and premature termination would be necessary to bring the case within the principle in *General Billposting Co Ltd v Atkinson* in such a case. And it must also be noted that the cases on the right to work[1] were not cited or discussed in the judgment.

1 See n 2 to para 4.60. Many employment contracts contain express garden leave clauses however. See the discussion in Chapter 3.

4.62 Finally in *Briggs v Oates*[1] the High Court held that the dissolution of a partnership employing an employee also released the employee from his restrictive covenant with the original partners. That is because following *Brace v Calder*[2] a contract of employment by two or more partners is brought to an end by the retirement from the partnership of one or more of the partners unless the terms of the contract expressed or implied provide otherwise.

1 [1990] IRLR 472.
2 [1895] 2 QB 253, CA.

4.63 One drafting device that is used with a view possibly to circumventing *General Billposting Co Ltd v Atkinson* is a clause which purports to state that the restrictive covenant applies after termination of employment 'howsoever caused' or 'howsoever caused, lawful or unlawful'.

4.64 The validity of this type of clause (which has been very common in contracts of employment) was called into question, however, in *Briggs v Oates*.[1] As discussed above, Mr Oates, who was a salaried partner, was held to have been the victim of a repudiation of his contract of employment when, upon the dissolution of the partnership, the existing partners were no longer able to employ him under the original terms. Following *Measures Bros Ltd v Measures* and *General Billposting Co Ltd v Atkinson* it was held that this meant that the employee was thus discharged from the restrictive covenant. The employer pleaded reliance upon a clause under which the restriction applied upon termination of the employment 'for whatever reason'. It was held that the terms of the restriction including its statement that it applied whether the termination was lawful or unlawful could not be separated from the other terms of the contract. Once those other terms were discharged so was the restriction. There is little discussion in the decision about whether the rule depends on policy or construction of the contract but, implicitly, the court appeared to form the view that the construction approach could not save the covenant. The reasoning of the court in *Briggs v Oates* was adopted by the Court of Session (Outer House) in *Living Design (Home Improvements) Ltd v Davidson*.[2] The Court stated:

> 'In [our view] a restrictive covenant which is phrased so as to operate on the termination of the employment of an employee, however that comes about, and whether lawfully or not, is manifestly wholly unreasonable. In that respect [we] agree with the observations in *Briggs v Oates* . . . '

In *Living Design* the Court went on to rule that such offending wording could not be severed so as to save the basic restrictions to which it was appended. The implication is that (although some doubt the decision) such wording can make unenforceable a clause which would otherwise have been enforceable (eg if the employee had lawfully been dismissed). If that *were* correct, consideration should be given to abandoning such words from contract clauses.

---

1 [1990] IRLR 472.
2 [1994] IRLR 69. See also *D v M* [1996] IRLR 192.

Wrongful repudiation by employee

4.65 The fact that an employee repudiates his contract of employment will not mean that a restrictive covenant affecting him can be evaded. So if an employee wrongfully resigns, the covenant affecting him should still apply. And if the covenant is stated to apply *during* employment an employer may enforce this by refusing to accept an employee repudiation so to keep the contract alive.[1] It has been held (see Chapter 3, above) that *if* the employer makes this election and continues to be willing to pay the employee's remuneration during the life of the contract still remaining, he may take action to maintain the restrictive covenant contained therein[2] in so far as it applies during the currency of the contract. It seems, however, that all this is subject to the doctrine of restraint of trade which applies not only to the period following the termination of employment but also to the period of employment itself in such circumstances.[3] The only reported cases deal with a breach of contract by an employee which has not been accepted by an employer, entitling the employer (subject to continued payment by him of salary to the employee) to keep alive and enforce restrictive obligations applying to the contract period.[4] Until relatively recently no ruling had been given on whether an employer may both keep the contract alive and thereafter also enforce a restrictive covenant application once the period of the contract has expired. In contractual theory there is no reason why this should not be done though possibly a court would baulk if the combined periods of contract and post-contract restraint were too long (see now *Credit Suisse*, para 4.68).

---

1 *Thomas Marshall (Exports) Ltd v Guinle* [1979] Ch 227, [1978] 3 All ER 193.
2 *Evening Standard Co Ltd v Henderson* [1987] ICR 588, [1987] IRLR 64, CA.
3 See *AC Schroeder Music Publishing Co Ltd v Macaulay* [1974] 3 All ER 616, [1974] 1 WLR 1308, HL; *Clifford Davis Management Ltd v WEA Records Ltd* [1975] 1 All ER 237, [1975] 1 WLR 61, CA. See also Treitel, *The Law of Contract* (7th edn) p 355.
4 *Evening Standard Co Ltd v Henderson* [1987] ICR 588, [1987] IRLR 64, CA. See also *Provident Financial Group plc and Whitegates Estate Agency Ltd v Hayward* [1989] ICR 160, CA where an injunction was refused, on the facts (see the discussion in Chapter 3, above). See also, recently, *GFI Group Inc v Eaglestone* [1994] IRLR 119 where an employer of a highly paid and highly skilled options broker sought to restrain the employee from engaging in competing business during his 20 week period of notice. On the facts the employee was well paid and the employee's customer connections had been expensively fostered at the employer's expense. The period of notice in the contract was simply 20 weeks and the contract also expressly provided that the employee should not without the employer's consent be engaged in any other trade or business. The employee along with two other employees gave notice of intention to join a rival broker. The employee sought not to honour the 20 week notice period. The employer undertook to pay the employee his salary and bonuses to the end of the period covered by any order and not to claim back such sums as damages for breach of contract. On the facts an injunction was limited to a 13 week period but this was on the sole ground that the two fellow employees (who had much shorter periods of notice) had completed their periods of notice and were already working for the employee's prospective new employer. Had it not been for that position the Court would have been strongly motivated to hold the employee to his word. Holland J said:

> 'If there was a current impression that the periods in contracts negotiated with highly paid, highly skilled employees did not have the meaning that they purported to have, then the sooner that was corrected the better'.

The conditions necessary for a successful 'garden leave' style injunction are set out in Mehigan and Griffiths, op cit, p 213; see also Brearley and Bloch, op cit, p 57.

4.66 It has also been held that an employer faced with a wrongful repudiation by an employee was able to refuse to accept it as terminating the contract so as to keep alive obligations of confidentiality that apply during the contract.[1]

1 *Thomas Marshall (Exports) Ltd v Guinle* [1979] Ch 227, [1978] ICR 905

4.67 These cases, which involve injunctions to enforce express negative stipulations during the life of the contract and which run close in some cases to a decree indirectly of specific performance are discussed again, in that context, in Chapter 3, above.

Injunctions

4.68 As to enforcement, the employer's primary remedy for breach of the covenant is an injunction, although of course damages will also be available (see para 4.70). The general principles about when an interlocutory injunction may be obtained are laid down by *American Cyanamid Co v Ethicon Ltd.*[1] These hold that there must first be a serious question to be tried and second, the balance of convenience must be in favour of the employer. That is to say, that damages alone are not an adequate remedy for the employer and any damage to the employee, if the outcome of the case is in his favour, will be adequately compensated by a cross-undertaking from the employer in damages to him. A number of cases have suggested that the *American Cyanamid* principles are not applicable to a restrictive covenant case in view of the fact that this is a paradigm example where the interlocutory application itself will determine the whole outcome of the litigation between the employer and the employee, particularly in view of the length of time it takes for a case to come to trial and the usually limited duration of covenants in restraint of trade.[2] In such a case it is said that the burden on the employer is higher, that is to say, he has to show he was likely to succeed at trial.[3] However, in *Lawrence David Ltd v Ashton*[4] the Court of Appeal indicated that the legal profession should be disabused of the widely held view that the *American Cyanamid* principles were not relevant where an interlocutory injunction was sought to enforce a contractual obligation in the nature of a restrictive covenant. In its view the *American Cyanamid* principles were applicable. The type of case in which an employer sought to enforce a restrictive covenant was an appropriate case for a speedy trial and it was only if a speedy trial was not possible and the action could not be tried before the period of restriction had expired, or had almost expired, that the rule in *American Cyanamid* would not apply.[5] An example of the application of this exception may be found in *Lansing Linde Ltd v Kerr*[6] where the restriction involved was 12 months in duration and a full trial could not occur within that period (or at the earliest until it had virtually expired). As such, it was necessary to look at the prospects of the plaintiff succeeding at trial. More recently, in *D v M*[7] Laws J accepted the argument that in applying the exception it was important to recognise that whether it should be applied in a particular case will not always be clear cut. In that case there was some evidence that the defendant's business would be permanently and adversely affected by an order in the plaintiff's favour so that should be taken into account and some attention at least paid to the relative merits of the parties' cases as they would have to be determined at trial. That exercise could be regarded as part and parcel of the assessment of the balance of convenience rather as lying outside it.

Finally in *Credit Suisse Asset Management Ltd v Armstrong*[8] Neil LJ also applied the exception where following the exercise of a right of appeal by a defendant there had become a very serious risk that if the injunctions remained they would expire before the case could be heard.

---

1 [1975] AC 396, [1975] 1 All ER 504, HL.

2 Under the principle in *NWL Ltd v Woods* [1979] 1 WLR 1294, HL.

3 *Millthorpe International Ltd v Mann* (1982) LEXIS transcript; *Supercut Ltd v Woods* (1986) LEXIS transcript; *Office Overload Ltd v Gunn* [1977] FSR 39, CA. This view is also implicit from the judgment of O'Connor LJ in *John Michael Design plc v Cooke* [1987] 2 All ER 332, [1987] ICR 445, CA.

4 [1989] IRLR 22, CA.

5 See also *Dairy Crest Ltd v Pigott* [1989] ICR 92, CA; *Rockall Ltd v Murray*, 1 March 1988 LEXIS transcript CA.

6 [1991] IRLR 80, CA.

7 [1996] IRLR 192.

8 [1996] IRLR 450, CA.

4.69 It has been held that an injunction to restrain use of trade secrets should not last longer than necessary to prevent the defendant from taking unfair advantage of the springboard gained by misuse of the information concerned, and in one case the injunction was limited to one year, the same length of time referred to in a restrictive covenant in the employer's standard service agreement.[1]

---

1 *Roger Bullivant Ltd v Ellis* [1987] ICR 464, [1987] IRLR 491, CA. But for a criticism of this area see Brearley and Bloch, op cit, p 207ff.

Monetary claims

4.70 Instead of or in addition to injunctive relief, in the case of breach, the injured party may wish to claim compensation. Primarily this will be for breach of contract, whether for breach of an express covenant or breach of the implied duty of fidelity (see para 4.03). Sometimes damages are difficult to assess, but this is no bar to their recovery in principle.[1] If a breach of fiduciary duty on the part of a director is in issue, the remedy is not damages but an account of profits.[2] This often has the advantage for the employer in that he does not have to prove loss.[3]

---

1 *Industrial Development Consultants Ltd v Cooley* [1972] 1 WLR 443; *Sanders v Parry* [1967] 2 All ER 803. For a recent example, see *Universal Thermosensors Ltd v Hibben* [1992] 3 All ER 257. See also *Dowson & Mason Ltd v Potter* [1986] 2 All ER 418, CA.

2 See *Regal (Hastings) Ltd v Gulliver* [1967] 2 AC 134n, HL; *Canadian Aero Service Ltd v O'Malley* (1973) 40 DLR (3d) 371; *Industrial Development Consultants Ltd v Cooley* [1972] 2 All ER 162.

3 There is also another area touching upon but beyond the scope of this chapter, namely an action for breach of confidence (where appropriate). The relevant authorities include *Saltman Engineering Co Ltd v Campbell Engineering Co Ltd* [1963] 3 All ER 413n, CA; *Seager v Copydex Ltd* [1967] 2 All ER 415, CA; *Sun Printers Ltd v Westminster Press Ltd* [1982] IRLR 292, CA. These authorities should be considered both on the basis of liability and compensation. See, generally, Gurry, op cit.

Joining in a third party

4.71 It may be appropriate to consider whether proceedings should be taken not only against the departing employee who is in breach of contract but also his new employer. The tort of inducement of breach of contract may occur if the employee is induced by another employer, with knowledge, to break his contract of employment with the first employer.[1] And it has been held that the knowledge requirement here does not require the tortfeasor to know the detail of every term of the contract as long as he knows enough about its content to appreciate that his action might bring about a breach.[2] Whether action is taken against a third party depends very much upon the tactics in a particular case. It is not uncommon, however, immediately to draw the attention of a third party to the existence of a restrictive covenant or other term that might be liable to be broken if the employee leaves, thus dealing with the above mentioned third party knowledge requirement.

---

1 *Lumley v Gye* [1843–60] All ER Rep 208.

2 *Stratford (JT) & Son Ltd v Lindley* [1965] AC 269, HL; *Harvey* V [762]. See also *Emerald Construction Co v Lothian* [1966] 1 All ER 1013, CA. In *PSM International plc v Whitehouse and Willenhave Automation Ltd* [1992] IRLR 279, CA, an injunction was granted to stop a former employee from entering into contracts with customers of the plaintiff employer. It was further held that the court has power to grant such an injunction even if it meant restraining him from fulfilling contracts *already made* with a third party. It is material to note that this order also applied to the employee's new company (a separate legal entity) although, on the facts, this was a third party controlled by him. See also *Ansell Rubber Co Pty Ltd v Allied Rubber Industries Pty Ltd* [1967] VR 37, a case cited and discussed in Smith and Wood, op cit, p 124.

PART II
STATUTORY RIGHTS ARISING DURING THE COURSE OF EMPLOYMENT

5 Particulars of terms of employment

Ian Smith and Christopher Osman

1 WRITTEN PARTICULARS OF EMPLOYMENT

The right to receive particulars

5.01 Prior to the Contracts of Employment Act 1963, there was no legal obligation in the case of most employments for any of the terms of a contract of employment to be put into writing, and indeed informal oral contracts were common. That Act, however, required the major terms of employment to be notified to the employee in writing; the relevant provisions are now contained in the ERA, Part I. The basic requirement is that, within two months of the commencement of employment, a new employee must be given by his employer a written statement identifying the parties, stating the commencement date of the employment, specifying the date (if earlier) when the period of continuous employment with that employer began,[1] and containing particulars of the following terms and conditions of employment:

- (a) scale or rate of remuneration, or method of calculation;
- (b) intervals of payment;
- (c) hours of work (including any term relating to 'normal working hours');
- (d) holidays and holiday pay (with the necessary particulars for calculating the latter, including accrued holiday pay), incapacity for work through sickness or injury (including sick pay) and pensions;
- (e) length of notice on both sides;[2]
- (f) the job title;
- (g) where the employment is not meant to be permanent, the period it is to last or its terminal date;
- (h) the place of work;
- (i) any collective agreement directly affecting terms and conditions.

In addition, there are further and specialised requirements relating to employees required to work outside the UK for more than a month.[3]

---

[1] Continuity of employment is considered in Chapter 7, below. Any extension to continuity of employment here must be under the relevant statutory provisions (eg that allowing the counting of previous employment with an associated employer); the parties may not simply agree between them that some previous period shall count and then expect, eg, a redundancy payment to be calculated on that basis alone: *Secretary of State for Employment v Globe Elastic Thread Co Ltd* [1979] ICR 706, [1979] IRLR 327, HL (overruling *Evenden v Guildford City Association Football Club Ltd* [1975] ICR 367, [1975] IRLR 213, CA). Employment commences when the contract of employment commences, not necessarily when the employee first performs work under it (which could be later): ERA, s 211(1); *General of the Salvation Army v Dewsbury* [1984] ICR 498, [1984] IRLR 222, EAT.

[2] Note the statutory minimum periods of notice in the ERA, s 86, Chapter 17, below.

[3] ERA, s 1(4)(k).

5.02 In addition, the written document (the 'Section 1 statement') should specify any disciplinary rules and grievance procedures, and state whether (in respect to any pension scheme) a contracting-out certificate is in force.[1] If there are *no* terms under any of these headings, that should be expressly stated. With regard to the form of the statement, an employer used to be able simply to refer to 'some other document' on any particular term or terms (usually a collective agreement or company handbook). However, the original EP(C)A, s 1 was significantly altered by the Trade Union Reform and Employment Rights Act 1993, partly to conform with the new EC directive, and partly to advance government policy or the promotion of individual contracting. The position now is that an employer may refer to some other document *only* in relation to terms on sickness, pensions, discipline and grievances.[2] Otherwise, the employee must be given the necessary details individually and 'in a single document'.[3]

1 ERA, s 3, *Harvey* Div Q; the right to written particulars is considered in *Harvey* Div A.
2 An employer may therefore still set out the discipline and grievance procedures in the company handbook and refer to that in the individual statements. One other exception is that, on the question of notice, the employer may refer either to the legal minimum notice requirements or to an applicable collective bargain.
3 ERA, s 2(4).

5.03 Although the employer is given the relatively generous period of two months in which to comply, many employers will have a section 1 statement ready prepared for a new employee at the very beginning of employment, possibly along with other documentation such as a company handbook, health and safety statement and disciplinary/grievance rules, which the employer wishes to ensure the employee receives and is bound by.

5.04 Subsequent changes to terms of employment must be notified in writing to the employee within a month of the change.[1] It is important to note that this provision does *not* give the employer any right of unilateral alteration of contractual terms; all it does is to say that, *once changes have been agreed*,[2] they must be notified. Major legal problems can arise if this is not done, since the parties end up some time later with an unamended section 1 statement that does not properly reflect current terms and working practices; it is in the interests of both parties to ensure that the statement is kept up-to-date.

1 ERA, s 4. One variation is that (in the case of sickness rights, pensions, notice and disciplinary or grievance rules) just as the original statement may refer to some other document, likewise changes may be made in similar fashion: s 4(3).
2 This is particularly important where the changes are agreed at a collective level by the employer and the employee's union.

The legal status of the written particulars

5.05 A section 1 statement is not, without more, a written contract; it is *merely* evidence of the terms of the contract between the employer and the employee.[1] In many cases, however, the statement will be the principal or only evidence as to the terms of employment, and so tantamount to the actual terms, particularly if not challenged by the employee. However, the legal significance of its falling short of an actual contract is that it leaves the door open for one of the parties (usually, but not always, the employee) to argue later, if a dispute arises, that the statement was inaccurate, and to seek to establish this by parol evidence (for example, evidence of what was actually agreed verbally at a job interview, but not then incorporated properly into the statement). Three particular points are worth noting at this stage:

(i) Judicial views have changed as to how persuasive the statement is as evidence; earlier decisions tended to show greater readiness to approve and incorporate the statement,[2] but later decisions have been more wary and less ready to infer the correctness of a statement from *mere* acquiescence by the employee.[3]

(ii) This is particularly the case where the dispute is over a *change* of terms. We have seen that in law a change of terms must have the assent (somehow) of the employee,[4] and one way in which an employer may seek to achieve this is to issue a written notice of 'proposed' changes (or 'reissue your statement'), leaving it up to the employee to object; if there is no actual objection after a reasonable period, the employer will then argue that there has been an implied consensual variation due to the employee's acquiescence. It has, however, been held that in such a case a court or tribunal should be particularly careful in deciding whether to apply the amended statement terms[5]—after all, there may be other reasons for lack of objection (such as wanting to keep the job), especially if the change is to a term (such as sick pay) which is not of immediate importance to the employee. On the other hand, if the change *is* of immediate importance (eg a change in working hours or shifts), then the employee may have to make his mind up quickly whether to accept the change or not—he cannot work on indefinitely under protest.[6]

(iii) There is no legal obligation that the statement be signed by the employee. Frequently this will be done, merely as an administrative convenience to show that it has actually been received. Signing such a receipt does not alter the legal nature of the statement. However, if the employer goes further in his drafting and the employee signs to say that he has received the statement *and agrees that it constitutes the terms of his contract*, then a court or tribunal may consider that that transforms it into a written contract of employment;[7] the result of this will be that the terms then become binding per se, and it will be far harder for the employee later to challenge their correctness.[8] Equally, however, the employer will be contractually bound, and so if the parties are considering formalising their relationship further in this way, it is important that *both* parties get the terms right and understand what they are signing.

---

1 *Robertson v British Gas Corpn* [1983] ICR 351, [1983] IRLR 302, CA. The status of a section 1 statement is considered in *Harvey* Division A.

2 See, eg, *Camden Exhibition and Display Ltd v Lynott* [1966] 1 QB 555, [1965] 3 All ER 28, CA.

3 '... no more than persuasive, though not conclusive, evidence': *System Floors (UK) Ltd v Daniel* [1982] ICR 54, [1981] IRLR 475, EAT, approved by the CA in *Robertson*, above.

4 If there is no such assent, the employee can stand upon his contractual rights; one way to do this is to turn up for, and be prepared to, work as under the original agreement and then, if the employer refuses to pay wages (or pays a lesser amount), to sue in the ordinary courts for wages under the (unaltered) contract: *Burdett-Coutts v Hertfordshire County Council* [1984] IRLR 91; *Rigby v Ferodo Ltd* [1988] ICR 29, [1987] IRLR 516, HL. If this succeeds, the employer (if still determined to force the changes through) will have to consider dismissing those who will not agree, and take his chances with an unfair dismissal action: *Gilham v Kent County Council (No 2)* [1985] ICR 233, [1985] IRLR 18, CA.

5 *Jones v Associated Tunnelling Co Ltd* [1981] IRLR 477, EAT.

6 There is a similar rule relating to constructive dismissal in the law of unfair dismissal.
7 *Gascol Conversions Ltd v Mercer* [1974] ICR 420, [1974] IRLR 155, CA.
8 Under the normal rule against parol evidence in the law of contract.

Failure to provide the written particulars

5.06 The requirement upon the employer to give the section 1 statement is mandatory (subject to the two month period and any applicable exceptions). The ERA itself provides a remedy for an employee.[1] Section 11 states that where an employer does not give a statement as required by s 1 (or s 4 in the case of a change of terms), the employee may refer the matter to an industrial tribunal[2] 'to determine what particulars ought to have been included or referred to in a statement so as to comply with the requirements of the relevant section'. Further, if a statement has been given, but a question arises as to what particulars ought to have been included or referred to in it, either the employee or the employer may refer the matter to the tribunal. In either case, the tribunal is given powers to declare what particulars should have been in a statement, or to confirm or amend particulars already given.

1 *Harvey* Div A.
2 There is a three month limitation period *if* the claim is brought after the employment has ended (ie three months from the date of termination): ERA s 11(4). Technically, there is no provision for ACAS conciliation in a section 11 case, since that section is not mentioned in the Industrial Tribunals Act 1996, s 18 (an oversight?).

5.07 The section covers three principal cases:

(a) where no particulars have been given;
(b) where incomplete particulars have been given;
(c) where inaccurate particulars have been given.

Because of the rather tortuous wording of the section, it appeared at one time that the tribunal had no powers over (c); this, however, would have been a major gap (since the accuracy of a statement is often likely to be the bone of contention), and the position was rectified by the Court of Appeal in *Mears v Safecar Security Ltd*[1] where it was made clear that a tribunal does have jurisdiction over case (c).

1 [1982] ICR 626, [1982] IRLR 183, CA; as a matter of detailed drafting, it was held that cases (a) and (b) are covered by the ERA s 11(1) and case (c) by s 11(2) and 12(2).

5.08 The case of *Mears* is also central on the question of *how* a tribunal is to exercise its function under section 11. First, the tribunal should consider whether a particular term had in fact been agreed orally (eg at an interview) or by necessary implication from the dealings of the parties. If not, it should go on to consider whether any term must have been agreed (looking at all the facts and circumstances, including the *subsequent* dealings of the parties). It was further suggested in the case that ultimately if all else fails, a tribunal may have to 'invent' a missing term, but this was later specifically disapproved by the Court of Appeal[1] as being too much of a departure from basic contract law, even in the case of what they referred to as one of the 'mandatory terms' in a section 1 statement, such as notice (ie one of the terms that has to be there, rather than one, such as holiday entitlement, which only has to be recorded if it exists). However, one point that is reasonably clear is that the tribunal's jurisdiction under the section is confined to discovering and declaring what terms should be in the statement; it may not go further and *interpret or apply* those terms. Thus, if an employee is in dispute over the *meaning* of a term (eg what is meant by 'reasonable overtime' or whether a particular bonus is payable), he must take his case to the ordinary courts (usually the county court) by way of an action for breach of contract, not to a tribunal under s 11.[2] It must be recognised, however, that the distinction between the declaration of a term and its interpretation may be easy to state but difficult to apply.[3]

[1] *Eagland v British Telecommunications plc* [1992] IRLR 323, CA.

[2] *Cuthbertson v AML Distributors* [1975] IRLR 228, IT; *Construction Industry Training Board v Leighton* [1978] 2 All ER 723, [1978] IRLR 60, EAT; *Mears v Safecar Security Ltd*, above.

[3] See eg *Owens v Multilux Ltd* [1974] IRLR 113, NIRC which appears to stray over the border into interpretation (the tribunal declaring what an oral agreement for '£2,500 net of deductions' actually meant on the facts, as well as incorporating it into a statement).

5.09 In addition to laying himself open to an action under s 11, an employer who fails to give a section 1 statement may also be at a disadvantage generally in any later dispute over a contractual term which he could have covered initially by the giving of a statement. Moreover, an employer should not give a statement in too cavalier a manner, for if it later transpires that one of the given terms was inaccurate, it has been said that there will be a heavy onus on the employer to show that the actual term was otherwise[1] (since any ambiguity flows from the employer's failure to exercise his statutory obligation properly). Overall, therefore, the employer has much to lose by not giving a proper statement, but also, more positively, has much to gain by intelligent use of the section 1 statement as a way of getting the terms of employment clear at the very beginning of employment, thus minimising the chances of later disagreements.[2]

[1] *Systems Floors (UK) Ltd v Daniel* [1982] ICR 54, [1981] IRLR 475, EAT, per Browne-Wilkinson P.

[2] See the model form in the Appendix.

2 ITEMISED PAY STATEMENTS

5.10 An employee has a statutory right to an itemised pay statement, showing written particulars of (a) gross pay, (b) deductions, (c) net pay, and (d) where different parts of net pay are paid in different ways, the amount and method of payment of each part.[1] There is no qualifying period attached to this right; moreover, it arises automatically and is *not* dependent on the employee having requested such a statement.[2] The most contentious issue may well be the question of deductions. Variable deductions must be properly itemised individually; in the case of fixed deductions, the employer has a choice—he may either itemise individually each time as with variable deductions, *or* he may give the employee a 'standing statement of fixed deductions' (at least annually) and then each pay day merely state the aggregate amount of such deductions.[3]

[1] ERA, s 8; *Harvey* Div B; on payment systems generally, see ACAS Advisory Booklet No 2.

[2] *Coales v John Wood & Co* [1986] ICR 71, [1986] IRLR 129, EAT. The statement must be given 'at or before' pay day. The statement only applies to payments made by the employer, not to amounts payable from some other source: *Cofone v Spaghetti House Ltd* [1980] ICR 155, EAT (tips).

[3] ERA, s 9; a standing statement must itself be in writing and state (a) the amount of each deduction; (b) the intervals for making the deductions; (c) the purpose for which it is made.

5.11 As with section 1 statements (above), the remedy for an employee who has not been given an itemised pay statement lies to an industrial tribunal under the ERA, s 11; if a statement has been given but a dispute arises over the nature of the particulars, either the employee or the employer may refer the matter to a tribunal, *but* it should be noted that the tribunal does not have the jurisdiction if the dispute is merely as to *amount*.[1] If the tribunal finds that an itemised pay statement has not been given, or has been given incorrectly, it must make a declaration to that effect. Moreover, if within the period of 13 calendar weeks before the date of application to the tribunal the employer has made unnotified deductions, the tribunal may order the employer to pay to the employee 'a sum not exceeding the aggregate of the unnotified deductions so made'. This is so even if the employer had a legal right (contractual or statutory) to deduct the amounts in question, since the penalty is for failure to notify simpliciter.[2]

[1] ERA, s 11(3)(b) such a dispute remains a common law matter of construction of the contract. If the employment has eased, the employee must bring a s 11 complaint within three months of the date of termination: s 11(9). ACAS conciliation is available in such an action: Industrial Tribunals Act 1996, s 18.

[2] Ibid, s 12(3) to (5); *Milsom v Leicestershire County Council* [1978] IRLR 433, IT; *Scott v Creager* [1979] ICR 403, [1979] IRLR 162.

5.12 It will be apparent that, with regard to the power to order repayment, there is now an overlap between these provisions and the newer provisions of the ERA, ss 13 to 27 (below) on prior notification and/or agreement as to the making of deductions. The latter do not abrogate the former and so, in effect, the employee has the choice as to which action to use; however, it is specifically provided that there cannot be double recovery of any one deduction.[1]

1 ERA, s 26.

3 SUNDAY WORKING

(a) Introduction

5.13 The Sunday Trading Act 1994 ('STA') came into force on 26 August 1994. This followed an extensive debate concerning s 47 of the Shops Act 1950 which prohibited Sunday trading except in respect of the sale of certain goods. The 'Keep Sunday Special' lobby argued strongly against changing the law but ultimately lost out to the commercial pressures from traders and consumers. The STA provides that large shops (those exceeding 280 square metres) can lawfully open between 10.00 am and 6.00 pm for six consecutive hours on a Sunday. The STA makes it a criminal offence for such shops to be open for longer than six hours on a Sunday rendering the occupier of a shop liable on summary conviction to a fine of up to £50,000. In parallel, the STA introduced new rights for the protection of employees which, together with parallel rights for betting workers are now to be found in Part IV of the ERA.

5.14 The ERA effectively creates three categories of employee: a 'protected shop or betting worker' and 'opted-out shop or betting worker' and, in effect, an 'opted-in shop or betting worker' (s 36 and s 41(1) and (2) of the ERA).

(i) Protected 'shop and betting workers'

5.15 Section 232(1) of the ERA defines a 'shop worker' as an employee who, under his contract of employment, is or may be required to do shop work. Section 233(1) defines a 'betting worker' an an employee who, under his contract of employment, is or may be required to do betting work. Both 'shop work' and 'betting work' are defined in the ERA.[1]

[1] ERA, s 232(2) and s 233(2).

5.16 A protected shop worker is an employee who is employed at the commencement date of the STA (26 August 1994) and whose contract of employment is not one under which he or she can be required to work on a Sunday. The position is the same with regard to a protected betting worker, save that the relevant commencement date at which the employee must be employed is 3 January 1995 (ERA, s 36). Under the ERA, a protected shop or betting worker will be treated as having been automatically unfairly dismissed if the principal reason for the dismissal is that the protected shop or betting worker refused to work on a Sunday (ERA, s 101). The two year qualifying period for unfair dismissal is dis-applied (ERA, s 108).

5.17 In parallel with this, selection for redundancy on grounds of refusal to work on Sunday is treated as automatically unfair (ERA, s 105) and a right not to suffer detriment (short of dismissal) for refusal to work on a Sunday is contained in the ERA, s 45. There is no power to opt-out in terms of the right to claim compensation for unfair dismissal where a fixed term contract is used, in contrast to the normal unfair dismissal right (ERA, s 197(2)). Lastly, dismissal on the grounds of asserting statutory rights in respect of Sunday working is rendered automatically unfair by virtue of ERA, s 104.

(ii) Opted-out shop and betting workers

5.18 An opted-out shop or betting worker is one whose contract entitles the employer to require the employee to work on a Sunday, and who is not employed solely to work on a Sunday. Such an employee's contract may be one which started either before or after the relevant commencement date (see above). The ERA provides that such employees may serve a written notice on their employers opting-out of Sunday working irrespective that they have agreed to work on Sundays under their contract (ERA, s 41). The ERA does not specify a particular form for an 'opting-out notice' but the notice must be in writing and must take effect three months after it is served (ERA, s 41(3)). At the end of the three month notice period, the ERA provides that the opted-out shop or betting worker will have the same protection as that afforded to a protected shop or betting worker. It should be noted that under ERA, s 41(2)(b) an employee ceases to be an opted-out shop or betting worker if at any time the employee agrees to work 'on a particular Sunday'. As a consequence, an opted-out shop or betting worker who works on a single Sunday for some reason will lose the statutory protection afforded and will find it necessary to serve another three month notice before re-acquiring protection.

(iii) Opted-in shop and betting workers

5.19 A protected shop or betting worker may in fact decide to 'opt-in' notwithstanding his or her status and may do so by giving the employer an opting-in notice and after giving that notice, expressly agree with the employer to work on a Sunday or a particular Sunday (ERA, s 36(5)). The 'opting-in notice' must be in writing, signed and dated by the worker and must contain an express statement that he or she wishes to work on Sunday or, alternatively, does not object to working on Sunday (ERA, s 36(6)).

(b) Employers' statutory statement

5.20 The ERA provides (s 42) that where a person becomes a shop or betting worker under a contract which entitles the employer to require the employee to work on a Sunday, the employer must serve a statutory statement in the form stipulated by s 36(4) within two months of the day on which the employee became a shop or betting worker. Failure to provide a written statement in the prescribed form reduces the three month period for a 'opting-out notice' under s 41 to take effect to one month (s 42(2)).

(c) The contract of employment

5.21 A protected shop or betting worker cannot have his or her status changed by any alteration to the terms of the employee's contract of employment (s 43) and any such terms are unenforceable. A protected shop or betting worker can only lose the protected status by service of an opting-in notice (see above).

6 Deductions from wages

Ian Smith

Repeal of the Truck Acts: cashless pay

6.01 The Truck Acts 1831–1940 used to provide a longstanding exception to the normal position of little legislative intervention in the law of employment, at least until the 1960s. They served two quite separate functions. First, they required employers to pay manual workers in 'current coin of the realm', thus outlawing payment in kind (subject to exceptions), or payment in tokens to be spent at the employer's own 'tommy shop'. Secondly, they contained a complicated set of restrictions on deductions from the wages of manual workers. The second function is considered in the next paragraph. It was the first function that led to the major reforms by the government in the Wages Act 1986. The rigour of the ban on payment other than in cash had already been amended by the Payment of Wages Act 1960 which allowed payment by cheque or credit transfer with the employee's consent.[1] However, the government decided to go further for two reasons: (i) in general, these restrictions were contrary to the overall policy of deregulation; (ii) in particular, they constituted a continuing disincentive to cashless pay, which the government wanted to encourage further since the UK lagged far behind other advanced economies in adopting it. To this end, Part I of the Wages Act 1986[2] repealed the Truck legislation in toto (and the payment of Wages Act 1960), so that there was *no* statutory right to be paid in cash (whether the employee is a manual worker or otherwise). Payment method was thus left to the parties as a matter of contract. It is important to notice, however, that this repeal did *not* give an employer a right of unilateral variation of an existing contractual term of payment in cash. If an existing employee had such a term in his contract, the employer could only change to cashless pay with his consent (either express or implied), which in practice may or may not involve 'buying out' the term.[3] With a new employee, however, the employer could incorporate a cashless pay term in the contract, without it being overridden by statute. The Wages Act 1986 has now been substantially repealed and replaced by the ERA.

---

[1] One problem was that even where the employee agreed to be paid by cheque or credit transfer, he could always revoke that agreement later and revert to cash pay. Thus, bank-inspired schemes to give cash inducements to change were potentially built on sand.

[2] Wages Act 1986, s 11, Sch 1.

[3] However, once the term is bought out the employee now cannot use the Truck legislation and the 1960 Act to go back on his agreement.

Deductions from wages

6.02 When the government first proposed to repeal the Truck Acts in order to promote cashless pay, it appeared that nothing would be enacted in their place. However, the government were persuaded that it was necessary to have new provisions performing (in an updated manner) the second function of the old legislation, ie imposing certain minimum requirements on deductions from wages. These provisions formerly in the Wages Act 1986 are now contained in the ERA, ss 13 to 27.[1] They are an advance on the Truck Acts in one way–they apply to *all* workers,[2] not just manual workers, thus curing one of the main defects in the old legislation.[3] However, in one other way they mark a retreat from the Truck Acts—the latter used to apply (however imperfectly) some restrictions to *inequitable* deductions, but the new provisions look only at the *procedure* for making deductions (though with, admittedly, extra protection for those in retail employment).

1 *Harvey* Div Q; for commentary, see Div B[51]ff.

2 'Worker' is defined in the ERA, s 230(3) more widely that the normal definition of an 'employee'; it includes (in addition to one under a contract of employment) an individual under a contract to do or perform personally any work or service for another person (other than in a professional or business client relationship). It could therefore include certain self-employed persons, provided they perform work personally.

3 The old Truck Acts were also partial and uncertain in their treatment of certain classes of employee, eg shop assistants; see the point at issue in *Bristow v City Petroleum Ltd* [1988] ICR 165, [1987] IRLR 340, HL (the decision came too late to affect the government's proposals for repeal).

6.03 Section 13 of the ERA provides that an employer may not make a deduction from a worker's wages unless:

(a) the deduction is authorised by statute (eg PAYE, NI contributions, attachment of earnings) or by 'any relevant provision of the worker's contract'; or

(b) the worker has previously signified in writing his agreement or consent to the deduction.

These ostensibly simple provisions in fact caused considerable litigation, for one simple reason. Given (until July 1994) our split jurisdiction between tribunals and courts, any common law claim by an employee that his employer has refused to pay him (or has underpaid him) has always had to go to a court, not a tribunal (even if, say, a tribunal was already hearing his case of unfair dismissal). The question arose—can the employee instead *call* that non-payment or underpayment a 'deduction' and seek to challenge it before a tribunal? The issue was finally settled by the House of Lords in *Delaney v Staples*.[1] The employee sought recovery under the Wages Act before a tribunal of £55.50 commission/holiday pay owing to her on her dismissal and £82 payment in lieu of notice, which the employer refused to pay. It was held (applying both the common law notion of 'wages' and the wide definition in what is now s 27 of the ERA and was formerly s 7 of the Wages Act) that the unpaid commission/holiday pay could be recovered under the Act, but that the unpaid wages in lieu could not, because the latter were in respect of a period after termination[2] and so were not 'wages', which must essentially have the character of payments relating to the rendering of services during employment. Hence the ability to claim the (already accrued) commission and holiday pay. Apart from the specific question of wages in lieu (which must still be fought over in the ordinary courts), this case shows a wide application of the Act; further, the Act should also apply to any attempt by the employer (without the necessary agreement in writing) (a) to withhold wages, etc already earned at the end of employment because of some alleged misconduct by the employee (eg not giving proper notice to leave),[3] (b) to phase out unilaterally an element of pay such as a bonus,[4] or (c) to refuse to pay a non-contractual element of pay such as a discretionary bonus or commission which, while discretionary, was reasonably anticipated as part of the overall pay package.[5]

---

[1] [1992] ICR 483, [1992] IRLR 191, HL.

[2] This is so provided the dismissal 'in lieu' is of the normal type, ie an immediate dismissal but with the contract being paid off by the giving of wages in lieu. In the less likely case of the employee being given *actual* notice (so that the contract remains in force) but being told not to work it out (eg in a 'garden leave' case), the Act *could* be used to recover any amounts of wages not paid, because they relate to a period which was still *during* the employment.

[3] This is implicit in the reasoning of the House of Lords, and is supported by the earlier decisions of the EAT in *Chiltern House Ltd v Chambers* [1990] IRLR 88, EAT and *New Centurion Trust v Welch* [1990] ICR 383, [1990] IRLR 123, EAT. An employer wishing to have a power to retain some or all of final wages (eg in the case of failure to give proper notice or to return the employer's property) is therefore strongly advised to have a clause to that effect in his contracts of employment.

[4] *McCree v Tower Hamlets London Borough Council* [1992] ICR 99, [1992] IRLR 56, EAT.

[5] *Kent Management Services Ltd v Butterfield* [1992] ICR 272, EAT; this is because the s 7 definition of wages includes 'any fee, bonus, commission, holiday pay or other emolument referable to his employment, *whether payable under his contract of service of otherwise*'. If an employer wishes to discontinue a system of discretionary payments, that should be done properly on reasonable notice, not just by an ad hoc refusal to pay in an individual case.

6.04 Section 14 of the ERA creates certain exceptions; thus, the requirements above do not apply to deductions in respect of:

- (i) any overpayment of wages;
- (ii) any overpayment of expenses;
- (iii) statutory disciplinary proceedings;
- (iv) any statutory obligation to pay over specified amounts to a statutory authority;
- (v) any contractual agreement to pay over amounts to a third party;
- (vi) participation by the worker in a strike or other industrial action;
- (vii) the satisfaction of a court or tribunal order requiring payment by the worker to the employer.

6.05 Particularly in cases (i), (ii) and (vi), it is important to note that the section does not empower the employer to make such deductions—the employer must have that power already (either by contract or under the general law). If he does not, the employee can seek to recover the amount deducted by an action in the ordinary courts. What s 14 does do is to provide that if the employer makes the deduction on one of these grounds the normal rules on prior agreement do not apply, and so the amount cannot be claimed in tribunal proceedings.[1]

---

[1] *Sunderland Polytechnic v Evans* [1993] IRLR 196, EAT (disapproving on this point *Home Office v Ayres* [1992] ICR 175, [1992] IRLR 59, EAT) and *SIP (Industrial Products) Ltd v Swinn* [1994] IRLR 323, EAT.

6.06 Thus (exceptions aside) prior agreement in writing is the principal requirement, particularly as 'relevant provision of the workers contract' is defined as *either* a written term of contract of which the worker has received a copy *before* the date of the deduction *or* a term of the contract (express or implied, oral or written), written notice of which has been given to the employee by the employer before the date of the deduction (eg by the giving of the section 1 statement of particulars of employment).[1] Similar provisions apply in relation to the making of payments by the worker to the employer[2] (which might otherwise have been a way of avoiding the rules on deductions). As already stated, these provisions relate to the procedure for making deductions; they do not govern the fairness or amount of a deduction, which remains a matter of agreement between the parties.

[1] ERA, s 13(2). Note that even where there is an express term of the contract covering a deduction for a particular reason, an employee may still claim that the *amount* deducted was excessive and so not covered by the contractual term: *Fairfield Ltd v Skinner* [1993] IRLR 4, EAT.

[2] Ibid, s 15(1) generally, and s 21 in relation to retail employment.

6.07 An exception, however, is made in the case of workers in retail employment.[1] Due to publicity in the press about widespread unconscionable deduction clauses in certain retail trade employment contracts (eg an obligation on garage attendants to refund out of their wages *all* till or stock deficiencies for their shift, whether through their fault or not), s 18 imposes the further restriction that an employer in the retail trade may only deduct (in respect of cash shortages or stock deficiencies) up to 1/10th of the gross amount of wages due on any given pay day.[2] Welcome as this is, however, it remains the case that such shortage deduction clauses are not rendered illegal,[3] that amounts may be deducted (up to 1/10th) from successive pay packets until the full amount is made up, and that the 1/10th rule does not apply to wages payable on the final day when the contract terminates,[4] at which point any outstanding amounts still owed to the employer can be recovered from the final wages.

[1] 'Retail employment' is defined in s 17(2).

[2] The deduction must be made within 12 months of the employer establishing the existence of the cash shortage or stock deficiency or (if earlier) the date when he ought reasonably to have established it: s 18(2). The employer may not evade these restrictions by expressing the deduction not as a deduction, but instead as part of the process of calculating the worker's wage in the first place, s 19.

[3] Indeed, under s 17(4) it remains lawful to draft a term requiring reimbursement of a deficiency whether or not it was due to the worker's fault.

[4] Ibid, s 22(2).

6.08 A complaint that an employer has made an unauthorised deduction (or, where applicable, that the 1/10th rule in retail employment has been broken, may be presented to an industrial tribunal by a worker within three months of the date of the deduction (unless it was not reasonably practicable for the complaint to be presented within that period).[1] If the tribunal finds the complaint well founded, it must make a declaration to that effect. In addition, the tribunal may order repayments of the amount deducted in contravention of the Act.[2] Two final points should be noticed. The first is that these provisions may overlap with the ERA, ss 8, 9, 11, 12 on deductions and itemised pay statements, though double recovery of an unauthorised deduction is not permitted.[3] The second is that although s 205(2) states that the remedy for breach of ss 13, 15, 18(4) and 21(1) 'shall be by way of a complaint under s 23 and not otherwise', that does *not* rule out an ordinary common law action for wages in order to recover a deduction not lawfully made under the contract if, for some reason, such an action is considered preferable by the worker; all that s 205(2) does is to say that if you wish to rely on the Act (as opposed to the contract) you must use the tribunal remedy set out in the Act.[4]

---

[1] ERA, s 23. ACAS conciliation is available in such a complaint. The time limit has been criticised since it may require the worker to bring his action while still in that employment (thereby perhaps jeopardising his job). However, a dismissal because of the making of a complaint under the ERA would now be automatically unfair (whether or not the normal two year period has been served) under the ERA, s 104(1).

[2] Moreover, the employer then loses any further common law right to recover that amount which he would otherwise have had: *Potter v Hunt Contracts Ltd* [1992] IRLR 108, EAT.

[3] ERA, s 26.

[4] *Rickard v PB Glass Supplies Ltd* [1990] ICR 150, CA.

7 The concept of continuity of employment

John McMullen

1 ITS RELEVANCE TO THE MAJORITY OF STATUTORY RIGHTS

7.01 Most statutory rights depend on a qualifying period composed of continuous employment. This is so, for example, with unfair dismissal,[1] redundancy payments,[2] the extended form of maternity leave under the ERA provisions as originally drawn,[3] a written statement of main terms and conditions of employment,[4] written reasons for dismissal[5] and statutory minimum periods of notice.[6] Certain other aspects of statutory rights are also affected by the length of continuous employment, such as the calculation of a redundancy payment,[7] the calculation of a basic award for unfair dismissal[8] and the length of statutory minimum notice.[9] It is equally relevant to note that a number of statutory rights do not depend on a qualifying period. Importantly these include sex and race discrimination (including dismissals in that context), trade union membership or activities dismissals, the right to a minimum period of 14 weeks maternity leave introduced by TURERA (in response to the EC Pregnant Workers Directive),[10] the right not to be unfairly dismissed in connection with pregnancy,[11] the right not to be unfairly dismissed in connection with the assertion by an employee of a statutory right,[12] and equal pay. And this list is far from exhaustive.[13] It is important to consult the relevant statute in every instance to ascertain whether there is a qualifying period and, if so, what its length is. At the time of writing, qualifying periods certainly in the case of unfair dismissal, are under scrutiny by the courts. In *R v Secretary of State for Employment, ex p Seymour-Smith and Perez*[14] employees dismissed prior to attaining the two year qualifying period for unfair dismissal succeeded in obtaining a declaration from the Court of Appeal that (at the time of their dismissals in 1991) the two year qualifying period was incompatible with the principle of equal treatment under the EC Equal Treatment Directive and could not be objectively justified. The litigation is no doubt far from concluded – but there are clear implications for the survival of (a good many) qualifying periods depending on the exact eventual outcome.

---

[1] Two years (ERA, s 108). See Chapter 19, below.

[2] Two years (ERA, s 155). See Chapter 20, below.

[3] Two years (ERA, s 79(1)). See Chapter 10, below. But no qualifying period applies to the new 14 week period of leave applicable to female workers introduced by s 23 of TURERA (see ERA, s 71).

[4] Thirteen weeks (ERA, s 1). See Chapter 5, above. But not in relation to the right to a written statement in connection with a pregnancy dismissal (ERA, s 87(4)).

[5] Six months (ERA, s 92(3)) (although the Employment Act 1989, s 15 extended this to two years). See Chapter 17, below.

[6] One month (ERA, s 86). See Chapter 18, below.

[7] ERA, s 162. See Chapter 20, below.
[8] ERA, s 118. See Chapter 19, below.
[9] ERA, s 86. See Chapter 18, below.
[10] ERA, s 71.
[11] ERA, s 99.
[12] ERA, s 104.
[13] Other statutory rights where no minimum service is required include action short of dismissal for trade union reasons, interim relief, time off for trade union duties, time off for trade union activities, time off for ante-natal care, time off for safety representatives, health and safety dismissals under the ERA, s 100, the right to an itemised pay statement, the right to payment under a protective award under the TULR(C)A 1992 or the similar award applicable under the Transfer of Undertakings (Protection of Employment) Regulations 1981.
[14] [1995] ICR 889.

7.02 Where the right requires a qualifying period, employment must be continuous under the rules contained in the ERA, ss 210–219. In other words the statutory scheme is the sole source of the rules about continuity.[1] However, common law is indirectly relevant too. For example, continuity of employment means continuity under a contract of employment that is valid and subsisting. Employment under an illegal contract will not be continuous employment.[2] And if the contract is frustrated it will terminate automatically without the need for action for either party, and continuity of employment will at that point cease.[3]

---

[1] For example, agreements between an employer and employee that employment is continuous will not be valid for *statutory* purposes (though they may create contractual rights) if the rules in ss 210–219 provide that employment is not continuous. See *Secretary of State for Employment v Globe Elastic Thread Co Ltd* [1980] AC 506, [1979] IRLR 327, HL; *Hanson v Fashion Industries (Hartlepool) Ltd* [1981] ICR 35, [1980] IRLR 393, EAT; *Altridge v Jaydees Newsagents Ltd* EAT 603/79.
[2] *Miller v Karlinski* (1945) 62 TLR 85, CA; *Tomlinson v Dick Evans U Drive Ltd* [1978] ICR 639, [1978] IRLR 77, EAT; *Corby v Morrison (t/a The Cardshop)* [1980] ICR 564, [1988] IRLR 218; *Cole v Fred Stacey Ltd* [1974] IRLR 73; *Chang Chao v Dommett* (1976) 11 ITR 93; *Hyland v JH Barker (North West) Ltd* [1985] ICR 861, [1985] IRLR 403, EAT; cf *Coral Leisure Group Ltd v Barnett* [1981] ICR 503, [1981] IRLR 204, EAT; *Newland v Simons and Willer (Hairdressers) Ltd* [1981] ICR 521, [1981] IRLR 359, EAT; *McConnell v Bolik* [1979] IRLR 422, EAT; *Davidson v Pillay* [1979] IRLR 275, EAT; *Hewcastle Catering Ltd v Ahmed and Elkamah* [1991] IRLR 473, CA; *Euro-Diam Ltd v Bathurst* [1990] 1 QB 1; *Salvesen v Simons* [1994] ICR 409, EAT 451/93; *Annandale Engineering v Samson* [1994] IRLR 59, EAT 512/93.
[3] *Marshall v Harland and Wolff Ltd* [1972] IRLR 90; *Egg Stores (Stamford Hill) Ltd v Leibovici* [1977] ICR 260, [1976] IRLR 376, EAT; *Hart v AR Marshall & Sons (Bulwell) Ltd* [1978] 2 All ER 413, [1977] 1 WLR 1067, EAT; *Notcutt v Universal Equipment Co (London) Ltd* [1986] 3 All ER 582, [1986] IRLR 218, CA; *Hare v Murphy Bros Ltd* [1974] 3 All ER 940, [1974] IRLR 342, CA; *FC Shepherd & Co Ltd v Jerrom* [1987] QB 301, [1986] IRLR 358, CA. Note however the (limited) bridging effect of s 212(3) between two contracts in the case of the first contract being frustrated and thereby terminated through ill-health. See below, para 7.21.

7.03 There is a presumption of continuity.[1] This means that there is a presumption that continuity is unbroken and any disputed period counts. One case suggests that the onus is on an employee to show at least one counting week, but this proposition is doubtful.[2] The presumption does not however apply where there is more than one employer (for example, in business transfer cases (see below)).[3] However this is mitigated slightly by comments by the EAT in a business transfer case that 'the scheme of the Act must not be made unworkable by rigid adherence to over strict standards of proof'.[4]

[1] ERA, s 210(5); *Woolcott v Edwardes* (1966) 1 ITR 333.
[2] *Nicoll v Nocorrode* [1981] ICR 348, [1981] IRLR 163, EAT. See comment in *Harvey* I [433]. See also *Cannell v Newcastle-upon-Tyne City Council* (8 October 1993, unreported), EAT C588/91.
[3] *Secretary of State for Employment v Cohen* [1987] ICR 570, [1987] IRLR 169, EAT.
[4] Ibid.

2 THE BASIS OF CALCULATION: THE COMMENCEMENT AND TERMINATION OF CONTINUOUS EMPLOYMENT

7.04 Before looking at the detailed rules about continuity, we must bear in mind the effect of the momentous House of Lords' decision in *R v Secretary of State for Employment, ex p Equal Opportunities Commission*.[1] Much of the statutory scheme under what is now the ERA is based on continuity over 'counting' weeks of employment. Insofar as this means that there must generally be successive uninterrupted weeks of employment under the contract of employment, there is no problem. But prior to 6 February 1995, the legislation (eg EP(C)A, Sch 13, para 4) was predicated on the need for a minimum hours threshold. An employee was required to work 16 hours per week (whether actual work or work required to be done under the contract). For part-timers, however, the legislation required longer periods of continuous employment. For example, those meeting the 16 hours requirement qualified for redundancy and unfair dismissal rights after two years – whereas those who did not meet the 16 hours requirement, but nonetheless met an eight hours requirement, did not qualify until five years had been served. However, in *R v Secretary of State for Employment, ex p Equal Opportunities Commission*, the 16 hours threshold was effectively dismantled because it was held that the threshold indirectly discriminated against women (who comprise the bulk of the part-time workforce) contrary to European law. The effect of this *EOC* case was to require the UK Government to amend the EP(C)A to remove the discrimination. Therefore, with effect from 6 February 1995, the Employment Protection (Part-Time Employees) Regulations 1995[2] removed those provisions of the EP(C)A[3] and the Trade Union and Labour Relations (Consolidation) Act 1992[4] which excluded part-time workers from rights under those Acts and provided that periods of part-time employment will count in the computation of periods of employment under the ERA. Consequently, for the future, continous employment under successive counting weeks will be required (the following discussion deals with this), but the concept of a qualifying threshold of working hours during those weeks has been removed from the legislation.[5]

[1] [1994] IRLR 176, HL.
[2] SI 1995/31.
[3] EP(C)A, s 5(1)(b) repealed.
EP(C)A, s 146(4)–(8) repealed.
EP(C)A, Sch 13, para 3 repealed.
EP(C)A, Sch 13, para 4 amended, now s 212(1) of the ERA.
EP(C)A, Sch 13, paras 5–8 repealed.
[4] TULR(C)A 1992, s 281 repealed.
[5] See *Colley v Corkindale* [1995] ICR 965.

7.05 To turn now, however, to the rules calculating the length of continuous employment, the basis of calculation was revised by the Employment Act 1982, s 20 and this revised scheme operates in claims arising on or after 2 January 1983.[1] Following 1983, the following rules apply for the purposes of calculating the length of employment (which is mainly relevant for seeing whether an employee has attained a qualifying period but may be needed to calculate length of notice and the size of a basic award and redundancy payment – see chapters 18, 19 and 20, above).

[1] The old rules are discussed in *Harvey* Div B 1(1).

7.06 First, the actual beginning and the end of employment should be identified. Second, it should be assumed unless disproved that employment is continuous between those dates (because of the presumption of continuity of employment discussed above). Third, and last, the total number of calendar months or years of employment (for qualifying periods) or years (for notice, basic award and redundancy) achieved are calculated for the purposes of the statutory right in question. It is important to note that continuity of employment in relation to statutory rights is, after the Employment Act 1982, calculated by reference to the completion of a number of calendar months or years as the case may be, whereas the old rules used units of weeks.

7.07 As, for these purposes, employment commences on the day the contract commences and ends on the day the contract ends (ERA, s 211), it is not possible, if employment begins or ends mid-week, to take into account parts of weeks prior to or after the end of the employment if the employee was not actually employed during those parts. This replaces a previous rule which allowed full weeks at the end of the employment to be counted even if only part was governed by employment. This former scheme operated as follows. Under ERA, s 212(1) any week during the whole or part of which the employee's relations with the employer are governed by a contract of employment counts in computing a period of employment. Thus, if an employee were employed during part of a week only in the weeks of commencement and termination of employment the entire week in each case would nonetheless count towards continuous employment thus giving an employee extra days of notional employment. So, if he were engaged on a Friday or dismissed on a Monday the entire week in each case would count towards his length of continuous employment. In other words he could, in many cases, add a considerable number of days employment to his length of continuous employment.[1]

[1] *Coulson v City of London Polytechnic* [1976] 3 All ER 234, [1976] IRLR 212, EAT; *Wynne v Hair Control* [1978] ICR 870, EAT.

7.08 This was changed, as has been described above, by the Employment Act 1982 and, to reiterate, employment now begins when the employment actually begins and ends when the employment actually ends. This is subject only to ss 97(2) and (4), and 145(5) and (6) of the ERA which, in certain cases of summary termination of employment or dismissal with a payment in lieu of notice, may notionally add to the continuous length of employment the amount of statutory minimum notice to which the employee is entitled under s 86 of the ERA even if not given by the employer.[1] Section 212(1) still exists, but now only applies, it seems, to cases of part weeks that occur *during* employment, allowing such weeks still to count as weeks of employment.[2]

[1] ERA, s 213(1) and (3). The 'effective date of termination' in unfair dismissal law (Chapter 19, below) is extended by s 97(2) and (4) for limited purposes, ie for calculating the qualifying period for unfair dismissal, written statement of reasons for dismissal, entitlement to an unfair dismissal basic award and calculating the basic award when the financial limit is raised enabling the employment to be extended into the period of the new rate (but *not* for deciding when the three month period for submitting a claim began). The 'relevant date' in redundancy law is extended by ERA, s 145 for the purposes of calculating the two year qualifying period for redundancy claims and length of service, for the amount of a redundancy payment and, finally, calculating a week's pay when the financial limit has been raised between termination date and the postponed date (but again not for deciding when the period (six months) for submitting a claim began) (see Chapter 20, below). There is a major difference between unfair dismissal and redundancy in that this extension of employment by the length of statutory notice applies to both express *and* constructive dismissals in unfair dismissals; but, in redundancy, constructive dismissals are not covered.

[2] Cases confirming that s 212(1) (or its predecessor) allows part weeks *during* employment to count notwithstanding employment in only part include *Loggie v Alexander Hall & Son (Builders) Ltd* (1969) 4 ITR 390 and *Jennings v Salford Community Service Agency* [1981] ICR 399, [1981] IRLR 76, EAT. Although these are cases arising before the Employment Act 1982 there is no reason to suppose they are no longer valid on this point: see, for example, *Leitch v Currie* (27 January 1987, unreported), EAT – resignation and re-engagement interval between employments not fatal as there was employment throughout some part of successive counting weeks (see also para 7.13). Cf *Roach v CSB (Moulds) Ltd* [1991] IRLR 200, EAT – interval between 14 and 25 November 1988 broke continuity notwithstanding employment during part of successive weeks, the ratio being (a) he had worked for a different employer for a few days during the interval and (b) on re-employment he was given a different job: *sed quaere*.

7.09 Continuous employment begins on the first day of work[1] but sometimes this does not have to be taken literally. It has been held this can mean the start of the contract of employment even if full duties do not commence until a little later. For example, in *General of the Salvation Army v Dewsbury*[2] an employee who was offered a post with work commencing on 4 May (because of an intervening bank holiday) was held to have commenced employment on 1 May.

[1] ERA, s 211.

[2] [1984] ICR 498, [1984] IRLR 222, EAT.

7.10 The rules in the Employment Act 1982 that amended the EP(C)A (now the ERA) were intended to simplify the calculation of length of employment and it is likely that this effect is achieved. But, as can be seen above, an employee whose employment commences or finishes part way through a week may now, under the new rules, lose some days of counting employment. However this negative result for employees is in some part mitigated by more favourable rules about the effect of absence from work through a strike or lock-out during employment which are discussed below.

7.11 There are transitional provisions covering the changeover from the original rules in the EP(C)A to the new rules now to be found in the ERA introduced by the Employment Act 1982 and these are discussed in more detail in *Harvey on Industrial Relations and Employment Law*.[1]

[1] Div B.

3 WEEKS WHICH COUNT

7.12 Because of the ruling in *R v Secretary of State for Employment, ex p Equal Opportunities Commission* (see above), a counting week is no longer based on a minimum hours threshold of hours actually worked during a week or a requirement that the employee works under a contract of employment normally involving a minimum number of hours per week. But successive counting weeks of employment are still required.

7.13 If there is a counting week it will count even if, for example, the individual was absent during part or all of the week due to holiday, sickness or other absence,[1] but any week which does not count breaks continuity: and the effect of this for the purposes of seniority is that the employee has to start again after the break from scratch.[2] It follows, however, that as long as there is employment during successive counting weeks, there will be continuity of employment irrespective of whether, over the period of successive weeks of employment, there are different contracts of employment. Thus, in *Tipper v Roofdec Ltd*[3] Mr Tipper had been employed since 1 December 1975 as a lorry driver. On Friday 22 May 1987 he was dismissed from that job in consequence of a 12-month driving ban imposed by the court. But the company had found him alternative employment clearing a site which he began on the following Monday. When the work came to an end in September 1987 he was dismissed. The employers alleged that he did not have the requisite two years' continuous employment for claiming a redundancy payment.[4] An industrial tribunal agreed. It held that in May 1987 his employment had come to an end by operation of law, ie by frustration, and that he could not count his previous employment as a driver with his subsequent employment when engaged clearing the site. The EAT held that the industrial tribunal was wrong. There was no gap between the two employments and the employee had been employed during successive counting weeks by the same employer. This was enough to maintain continuity and any legal analysis for the true reason for the cessation of the first employment is of no significance in deciding whether there is continuity of employment.[5] It therefore follows that as long as an employee is employed by the same employer over successive counting weeks it does not matter whether or not there are successive contracts of employment involving different duties.

[1] See *Colley v Corkindale* [1995] ICR 965 (employee worked one week on (for five and a half hours) and one week off. As there was a subsisting employment contract in the week off, continuity was preserved even though no hours worked).

[2] As was the case in *Minetti v DVK Executive Hotels Ltd,* Court of Appeal 22.11.88 *IDS Brief* 389/January 1989 p 16.

[3] [1989] IRLR 419, EAT.

[4] The question of entitlement to a redundancy payment was remitted for reconsideration by the industrial tribunal. Ultimately it was held that the dismissal in September 1987 was not by reason of redundancy.

[5] See, here, too, *Wood v York City Council* [1978] IRLR 228, CA and *Weston v Vega Space Systems Engineering Ltd* [1989] IRLR 429, EAT.

7.14–7.16 We now return to the details of the counting week. And, as we have explained, this is no longer based on an hours threshold in the EP(C)A, following the case of *R v Secretary of State for Employment, ex p Equal Opportunities' Commission*[1] and the consequent change in the legislation introduced by the Employment Protection (Part-time Employees) Regulations 1995. In *R v Secretary of State for Employment ex p Equal Opportunities Commission*, known as the 'part-timers' case, the EOC successfully challenged by way of judicial review the threshold provisions in the EP(C)A which, it was claimed, unlawfully discriminated indirectly against women (the vast majority of part-timers) and therefore breached EC discrimination law. Two examples of the discrimination were that full-time workers qualified for unfair dismissal and redundancy rights, but part-time workers did not qualify until they had served five years. The Secretary of State for Employment, against whom the proceedings were brought, accepted that the thresholds indirectly discriminated against females, but resisted the proceedings on a number of other grounds, for example that unfair dismissal compensation and redundancy pay were not covered either by Art 119 or the Equal Treatment Directive, that judicial review was not appropriate, that the EOC had no *locus standi* to bring judicial review proceedings and that the thresholds for part-timers were objectively justifiable. In the end, the House of Lords ruled that redundancy pay constituted 'pay' under Art 119 of the Treaty of Rome (equal pay) and the right not to be unfairly dismissed fell within the Equal Treatment Directive and therefore EC discrimination law was an issue. As there was indirect discrimination the Secretary of State had not justified the discrimination inherent in the statute (it also followed that the EOC was entitled to bring judicial review proceedings in respect of correspondence between the EOC and the Secretary of State and that the EOC had *locus standi* to pursue the claim).

1 [1994] IRLR 176, HL.

4 PRESERVING CONTINUITY

7.17 In some cases intervals in employment are not fatal. Sections 212 to 217 of the ERA contain some specific bridging provisions. When these apply, their effect is not always the same. Sometimes it is provided that the weeks in the interval both fail to break continuity *and* count towards it. In other cases the effect is that continuity is not broken, but the weeks do not count.

(A) Cases under the ERA, s 212

7.18 These are where an employee is incapable of work on account of sickness or injury;[1] or absent from work on account of a temporary cessation of work;[2] or absent from work so that by custom or arrangement with the employer the employment continues;[3] or absent wholly or partly because of pregnancy or childbirth.[4]

1 ERA, s 212(3)(a); *Scarlett v Godfrey Abbott Group Ltd* [1978] IRLR 456. Pregnancy is not sickness: *Whiteley v Garfield Spinning Co Ltd* (1967) 2 ITR 128 – but see now ERA, s 212(3)(d) (n 4, below).

2 ERA, s 212(3)(b).

[3] ERA, s 212(3)(c).
[4] ERA, s 212(3)(d).

7.19 Sometimes, in absences from employment in cases that might be covered by s 212, the contract still subsists by agreement. There may be an express right to pay maternity leave under the contract of employment; an employee may enjoy paid sick leave under the contract; or there may be a contractual right to study leave or secondment. If so, there will be no need for s 212. If the contract *exists* the employment should be continuous under the ERA, s 212, provided the conditions of s 212(1) are met. In fact, in *Ford v Warwickshire County Council*[1] the House of Lords expressly held that what is now ERA, s 205 does not come into play until the contract ceases.

[1] [1983] 2 AC 71, [1983] 1 All ER 753, HL.

(i) Absence from work when incapable of work in consequence of sickness or injury (ERA, s 212(3)(a))

7.20 It is rare to see cases reported beyond industrial tribunal level under this head because, as has been pointed out elsewhere,[1] instances arising are comparatively infrequent. As has been discussed, the provisions of s 212(3) only apply where there is no contract of employment and only apply where the interval between employment is 26 weeks or less. So, to apply, there must have been a dismissal (presumably) through ill health, or frustration of contract through ill health, followed by a re-engagement within 26 weeks. This will not happen very often.[2] It has been held that pregnancy is not sickness or injury[3] and in that case protection must be sought under s 212(3)(d) (below) or under Part VIII of the ERA (Chapter 10, below).

[1] *IDS Employment Law Handbook 35*, p 36.
[2] See *IDS Employment Law Handbook 35*, pp 36–38 for a useful discussion of tribunal cases in this area.
[3] *Whiteley v Garfield Spinning Co Ltd* (1967) 2 ITR 128.

7.21 Finally, the EAT in *Pearson v Kent County Council*[1] decided that an employee's absence had to be *caused* by the sickness or injury. In that case an employee who retired early on ill health grounds and who was then re-engaged ten days later in a different and less demanding job could not claim that his continuity of employment was preserved during the gap between the two jobs. The interval had been agreed by the employer and employee simply in order that he could claim a pension. The paragraph refers, after all, to a person 'incapable' of work as a consequence of sickness or injury and, as there was no reason medically why he could not immediately have taken up the new, less demanding work, the employee's condition was not the reason for the absence from work.

[1] [1992] IRLR 110.

7.22 This decision was upheld by the Court of Appeal.[1] The Court confirmed that there had to be a causal link between absence from work and the incapacity and in consequence of sickness or injury. The Court of Appeal confirmed that 'incapable of work' does not mean incapable of work generally. Nor does it refer to the particular work provided for in the contract of employment which has been terminated. But where during a particular week the work on offer by the employer differs from that for which the employee was previously employed an industrial tribunal has to consider whether the work offered was of a kind which the employee was willing to accept or, even if unwilling, was suitable for him in his particular circumstances. The industrial tribunal then has to decide whether the employee's absence from that work was due to incapacity in consequence of sickness or injury. In this case, as the incapacity related solely to work in the original post, it did not prevent him from carrying on his new position as technical assistant.[2]

---

1 [1993] IRLR 165.

2 Cf on the other hand *Donnelly v Kelvin International Services* [1992] IRLR 496 (not referred to by the Court of Appeal in *Pearson*) where the EAT in Scotland held that an interval of five weeks between resignation and re-employment did not break continuity notwithstanding the employee took up temporary employment with another employer. In such a case the test was as follows:

> 'It seems to us, therefore, that the proper approach in a case such as the present is to look at each of the weeks which have intervened between the two periods of employment, and to ask whether, in each of those weeks, the employee was incapable of his employment in consequence of sickness or injury. If the employee works for another employer during the intervening period, that is a circumstance to be taken into account, but it does not, of itself, show that he has ceased to be incapable of work in consequence of sickness or injury . . . If the employment is . . . only of a nature intended to bridge the gap in his employment with the first employer as, for example, if it is a period of light work undertaken in the hope or expectation that the employee will in time be able to return to his previous full time employment, it may not interrupt the continuity of the employment.'

The reverse might be the case if it were full-time permanent employment – this might cast doubt on incapacity for work.

(ii) Absence from work on account of a temporary cessation of work (ERA, s 212(3)(b))

7.23 This is capable of being widely construed. It can include spasmodic lay-offs or other temporary periods of lack of availability of work.[1] And for the purposes of the paragraph the employee does not have to establish that the entire business of the employer has ceased.[2] It has also been held not to matter that the employee took another job during the period of lay-off. Such temporary alternative employment was not fatal to the application of the paragraph upon return to work after the lay-off.[3] Nor is there any maximum period of time over which the temporary cessation may last. In one extreme case an absence of *years* during a shortage of work fell within the protection of the paragraph.[4] Apparently, the absence can be regular and even foreseen and still be covered by the paragraph. Thus, in *Ford v Warwickshire County Council*,[5] a teacher had eight successive contracts each for the academic year September to July only. During the summer recess in each calendar year she had no contract at all. It was held that she had been absent each summer from her employment because of a temporary cessation of work within the meaning of the paragraph and her employment was continuous throughout.[6]

[1] *Hunter v Smith's Dock Co Ltd* [1968] 2 All ER 81, [1968] 1 WLR 1865.
[2] *Fitzgerald v Hall, Russell & Co Ltd* [1970] AC 984, [1969] 3 All ER 1140, HL.
[3] *Thompson v Bristol Channel Ship Repairers and Engineers Ltd* (1969) 4 ITR 262.
[4] *Bentley Engineering Co Ltd v Crown and Miller* [1976] ICR 225, [1976] IRLR 146.
[5] [1983] 2 AC 71, [1983] 1 All ER 753, HL.
[6] Compare *Ryan v Shipboard Maintenance Ltd* [1980] ICR 88, [1980] IRLR 16, EAT.

7.24 The House of Lords in *Ford* did not strictly have to consider the meaning of 'temporary' as the employer had conceded that the intervals between contracts were temporary in nature (the issue in the case was whether the employee was absent *on account* of a temporary cessation of work). But Lord Diplock (*obiter*) considered the test was that the word temporary meant 'transient', ie lasting only for a relatively short time. In the sort of case in *Ford* (ie a number of successive fixed term contracts separated by intervals) it was necessary to take the length of an interval between two such contracts and see whether it could be characterised as 'short', relative to the combined duration of the two fixed term contracts. This was a question of fact and degree for an industrial tribunal. This became known as the so-called 'mathematical test'.

7.25 However, in *Flack v Kodak Ltd*[1] the Court of Appeal considered a different type of case, not a succession of fixed term contracts separated by intervals, but seasonal, intermittent employment over a number of years. The employee was required to show a two year qualifying period ending with dismissal in order to claim a redundancy payment. An industrial tribunal analysed each of the breaks during that last two year period as percentages of the preceding and ensuing periods of employment and concluded that the breaks were too great to amount to a temporary cessation. It thus appeared to apply the 'mathematical test'. It was held by the Court of Appeal, however, that a mathematical approach was not always the one to apply and in this case regard should have been had to all of the circumstances over the whole period of employment to ascertain whether the breaks in the two year period prior to dismissal were temporary and, further, the tribunal should not confine itself to looking only at each break in relation to adjoining periods of employment.

[1] [1985] ICR 820, [1985] IRLR 443.

7.26 The matter was considered again in *Sillars v Charrington Fuels Ltd.*[1] Here the employee was a driver employed on a seasonal basis for 15 years. His employment each year ranged from 21½ to 32 weeks and in his last two years he was employed for 30 weeks and 27½ weeks respectively. The industrial tribunal applied the 'mathematical' approach in *Ford* and compared the length of the last two periods of unemployment with the last two periods of seasonal employment, concluding that the intervals were too long to be 'relatively short' and were therefore not temporary. The Court of Appeal held it was not wrong to apply the mathematical test. The absence pattern was regular and the tribunal was entitled to focus on the last two years of employment and compare the last two intervals with the last two periods of employment. As the employee spent about half of each year unemployed the tribunal was entitled to hold such periods were not temporary. If these cases are anything to go by the 'mathematical' test tends to be thought more appropriate where the absence pattern is regular and a more flexible approach more appropriate where the absences are intermittent.

[1] [1989] IRLR 152, CA. The 'mathematical' test seems also to have been applied in *Berwick Salmon Fisheries Co Ltd v Rutherford* [1991] IRLR 203, EAT (23 weeks in work and 29 weeks out of work – period of absence could not be 'temporary'). See also *Pearson v Shorrock Guards Ltd* (industrial tribunal) COIT 2080/225. See also, more recently, *Corkhill v North Sea Ferries* (11 February 1994, unreported), CA (change of duties so previous seasonal work of no assistance in determining overall pattern of work). See also *Cannell v Newcastle-upon-Tyne City Council* (8 October 1993, unreported), EAT (588/91).

7.27 Two *obiter* comments are interesting. First, Woolf LJ did not rule out the possibility of a period in excess of six months qualifying as a temporary cessation. It depended on the facts. He gave the example of a university teacher taking a sabbatical year. This contrasts with the opinion of Lord Diplock in *Ford* that the absences have to be 'transient'.

7.28 Secondly, it had been held that the fact that seasonal workers in *Sillars* were intended to return and also accrued seniority was not decisive about the temporary nature of the absence (it only meant the absence was not permanent, and that was not the same thing). But Woolf LJ thought *obiter* that seasonal workers, especially in such circumstances, might be able to bring themselves within s 212(3)(c) (ie absence from work through arrangement or custom) (see below).

(iii) Absence from work so that by custom or arrangement with the employer the employment continues (ERA, s 212(3)(c))

7.29 This might include, for example, a request for leave of absence where the employee is required by the employer to terminate the contract during the period of leave falling between the periods of employment.

7.30 Mere re-employment after even a short break does not necessarily mean the paragraph applies.[1] There must be some custom or arrangement. Thus in *Moore v James Clarkson & Co Ltd*[2] an employee was, by prior arrangement, allowed three months off to look after a child who was ill. Here, she was by arrangement regarded as continuing in employment and her continuity was preserved for when she returned. Although in one case it has been suggested that an 'arrangement' for the employment to be regarded as continuing may be concluded after the event,[3] this must be treated with some caution and the better view, it is submitted, is that the arrangement must be concluded before the absence.[4] 'Custom' has occurred often in the shipyards where, when work has fallen off, the employee is sent home on the understanding he will be re-engaged when work picks up. Of course such cases may also be brought under s 212(3)(b) (temporary cessation of work) and often have been.[5]

[1] *Southern Electricity Board v Collins* [1970] 1 QB 83, [1969] 2 All ER 1166; *McHugh v Thoresen Car Ferries Ltd*, EAT 239/80.

[2] (1970) 5 ITR 298. See, too, *Wishart v National Coal Board* [1974] ICR 460.

[3] *Ingram v Foxon* [1984] ICR 685, [1985] IRLR 5, EAT.

[4] *Murphy v A Birrell & Sons Ltd* [1978] IRLR 458; *MSA (Britain) Ltd v Docherty*, EAT 170/82.

[5] *Gray v Burntisland Shipbuilding Co Ltd* (1967) 2 ITR 255; *Hunter v Smith's Dock Co Ltd* [1968] 2 All ER 81, [1968] 1 WLR 1865.

7.31 Finally, too, many seasonal workers could arguably bring their cases under s 212(3)(c) rather than under s 212(3)(b) and indeed, may be advised to do so, especially where the period of absence may be too significant to be temporary when compared with the periods of actual employment.[1] A prudent adviser will plead both s 212(3)(b) and s 212(3)(c) in such cases.

[1] See the *obiter* remarks of Woolf LJ in *Sillars v Charrington Fuels Ltd* [1989] IRLR 152, CA, referred to above.

(iv) Absence wholly or in part because of pregnancy or childbirth (ERA, s 212(3)(d))

7.32 As can be seen below, provided a woman complies with the (complicated) rules about exercising her right to return to work under Part VIII of the ERA and returns to work under these rules the period of maternity leave is deemed continuous employment notwithstanding there may be no contract during maternity leave. However the rules under Part VIII of the ERA are tricky (particularly in relation to the extended leave applicable after two years service (see below)) and if a woman is disentitled under Part VIII of the ERA, s 212(3)(d) is a safety net. But, as with sickness ((i) above), cases are rare. Only 26 weeks' absence is permitted and if the employee has failed to qualify to return to work and *needs* to qualify to preserve continuity under s 212(3)(d) it will be because she has no statutory right to return. So this provision depends upon an absence during which there is no contract and which is no more than 26 weeks and a voluntary re-engagement by an employer within that period.[1]

[1] See *IDS Employment Law Handbook 35*, pp 48–49 and *Stringer v Booth* COIT 1533/86 cited therein. See also *Mitchell v Royal British Legion Club* [1981] ICR 18, [1980] IRLR 425, EAT. For an example where it was held that no contract subsisted during maternity leave see *Crouch v Kidsons Inpen* [1996] IRLR 79 cf *Hilton International Hotels Ltd v Kaissi* [1994] IRLR 270.

7.33 As stated, in absence through sickness or injury or pregnancy or childbirth the maximum interval protected by s 212(3) is 26 weeks.[1] But it is important to note that in the other cases mentioned above, ie where there is a temporary cessation of work or absence through custom or arrangement, there is no limit to the length of the interval.[2]

[1] ERA, s 212(4).
[2] The period in *Bentley Engineering Co Ltd v Crown* [1976] ICR 225, [1976] IRLR 146 was two years (held: temporary cessation of work).

(B) Maternity leave

7.34 As stated, when a woman returns to work after her extended maternity leave under Part VIII of the ERA (where two years service is required),[1] then provided that she complies with the statutory provisions about such leave[2] her period of absence counts towards continuous employment even if there was no contract subsisting throughout the maternity leave.[3] As far as the new general right to 14 weeks maternity leave for all employees, introduced by TURERA, applicable irrespective of service, there is no *express* right to return thereafter, or reference to continuity during maternity leave. However, references to 'maternity *leave* period' (emphasis added)[4] and to continuation of benefits of terms and conditions of employment (remuneration excepted)[5] clearly imply this and also imply a continuation of the contract.

1 See Chapter 10, below.
2 Under ERA, s 99.
3 ERA, s 212(2).
4 ERA, s 71.
5 ERA, s 71.

(C) Strikes and lock-outs

7.35 By virtue of s 216(1), a strike will not break continuity.[1] Employment while on strike will, however, not *count*. Under the rules prior to the Employment Act 1982 the entire week during which the employee took part in a strike did not count. The Employment Act 1982 however effected a change more favourable to employees in most cases. Under s 216 of the ERA as amended by the Employment Act 1982 the effect of strike activity on length of employment is that the period of continuous employment is regarded as reduced only by the actual number of strike days. These strike days are deemed to be deducted from the period of employment by the artificial means of postponing the commencement of employment by the number of strike days in question.

1 ERA, s 216(2).

7.36 A period during which a lock-out occurs will not break continuity. This is expressly provided by para s 216(3). Section 210 of the ERA allows for the possibility that lock-out periods will not *count* (in which case the employment period is reduced in the same manner as with strike days, above). But s 216 curiously does not say that lock-out periods do not count. Thus, whether a lock-out period counts depends on the usual rules in s 212 about whether employment may be counted as continuous. As employment normally subsists during a lock-out, it is submitted that lock-out periods will usually count.[1]

1 *Harvey* IB4(2).

7.37 A 'strike' is defined by s 235(5) as meaning the 'cessation of work by a body of persons employed acting in combination or a concerted refusal or a refusal under a common understanding of any number of persons employed to continue work for an employer in consequence of a dispute, done as a means of compelling their employer or any person or body of persons employed or to aid other employees in compelling their employer or any person or body of persons employed to accept or not to accept terms or conditions of or affecting employment'. 'Lock-out' is defined in s 235(4) as 'the closing of a place of employment or the suspension of work or the refusal by an employer to continue to employ any number of persons employed by him in consequence of a dispute done with a view to compelling those persons or to aid another employer in compelling persons employed by him to accept terms or conditions of or affecting employment'.[1]

[1] It will be noted that the expressions 'strike' and 'lock-out' also appear in ss 237–238 of the TULR(C)A 1992 which relate to unfair dismissal and industrial action. But, it has been held what is now s 235, although helpful to look at for the purposes of ss 237–238, does not provide the definition for ss 237–238: *Express and Star Ltd v Bunday* [1988] ICR 379, [1987] IRLR 422, CA. See Chapter 19. It is important to note that ss 237–238 applies not only to strikes but also to 'other industrial action'. But ERA, s 216 does *not* include industrial action. So industrial action short of a strike should have *no* effect on continuity as long as weeks during which the action takes place count under the other provisions in ss 210 to 219 of the ERA.

(D) Reinstatement and re-engagement

7.38 Continuity is also preserved on reinstatement or re-engagement following (a) the settlement of dismissal claims (unfair dismissal, and dismissals involving sex and race discrimination); (b) action taken in connection with making a claim in accordance with a dismissals procedure agreement designated by an order under s 110 of the ERA; (c) any action taken by a conciliation officer under his relevant conciliation powers;[1] or (d) the making of a relevant compromise contract.[2] If an employee is re-engaged or reinstated by his employer or a successor or associated employer after such events his continuity of employment is preserved.[3]

[1] Under the ERA, s 141(3), the Sex Discrimination Act 1975, s 64(2) and the Race Relations Act 1976, s 55(2).

[2] A 'compromise contract' is the procedure for settling industrial tribunal claims otherwise than with the assistance of a conciliation officer, introduced by s 39 of TURERA. See the ERA, s 203(2)(f), the Sex Discrimination Act 1975, s 74(4)(aa), the Race Relations Act 1976, s 72(4)(aa) and the Disability Discrimination Act 1995, s 9(2)(b).

[3] The Employment Protection (Continuity of Employment) Regulations 1993 (SI 1993/2165). These replace the Labour Relations (Continuity of Employment) Regulations 1976 (SI 1976/60).

7.39 Where an employee is reinstated or re-engaged after dismissal for redundancy under the ERA, s 138 (offer of alternative employment), weeks during the interval count. But this is for redundancy purposes only.[1]

[1] ERA, s 213(2) and (3) (NB a period of four weeks from the ending of the old contract is the relevant period under s 138).

(E) Miscellaneous cases

7.40 If an employee is re-engaged by an employer after service with the armed forces under the terms of the Reserve Forces (Safeguard of Employment) Act 1985 the permitted interval between ending of employment and re-engagement does not break continuity although the period away from employment does not count. As with other such non-counting periods the beginning of employment is deemed postponed by such period.[1]

[1] ERA, s 217(1), s 215(3).

7.41 Weeks of employment overseas do not break continuity. But for redundancy purposes only (and not unfair dismissal) weeks overseas do not count.[1]

[1] ERA, s 212(1).

7.42 In the ERA, s 214 it is provided that actual payment of a redundancy payment to an employee will break continuity for redundancy purposes only (and not for unfair dismissal or other purposes). As employees who are dismissed and paid a redundancy payment do not usually continue employment the application of this provision rarely comes into play.[1]

[1] Section 214 of the ERA does not apply where there is a reinstatement or re-engagement to which the regulations apply and the terms of such reinstatement or re-engagement include provision for the employee to repay the redundancy payment or its equivalent.

5 CHANGE OF EMPLOYER

7.43 Section 218(1) of the ERA states that unless otherwise stipulated the provisions of ss 210 to 219 about continuity relate only to employment *by the one employer*. Unless there is statutory provision allowing for the safeguard of continuity rights, continuity of employment breaks on any change of employer at common law. According to the principle in *Nokes v Doncaster Amalgamated Collieries Ltd*[1] the contract of employment, being a contract for personal services, cannot automatically be transferred from one employer to another without the employee's consent. Upon each change of employer the contract of employment terminates and a fresh contract of employment forms with a new employer. However, there are a number of situations where there is a change of employer where continuity is nonetheless preserved.

[1] [1940] AC 1014, [1940] 3 All ER 549, HL.

(A) Business transfers: ERA, s 218(2)

7.44 Upon the transfer of a trade, business or undertaking from one person to another continuity of employment will be preserved in the case of employees employed in the trade, business or undertaking at the time of transfer. Obviously, there is considerable overlap between a transfer of a trade, business or undertaking under the ERA for continuity purposes and the transfer of an undertaking under the Transfer of Undertakings (Protection of Employment) Regulations 1981 (TUPE) (see Chapter 8, below). As discussed below, the question arises whether s 218(2) of the ERA is otiose in the light of TUPE. However, s 218(2) of the ERA still remains as the statutory source of calculation of continuity of employment and may legitimately be used if that is the sole issue.

7.45 The main test under the ERA as to whether there is a relevant transfer is that 'the vital consideration is whether the effect of the transaction [is] to put the transferee in possession of a going concern, the activities of which he [can] carry on without interruption'.[1]

[1] Per Widgery J in *Kenmir Ltd v Frizzell* [1968] 1 All ER 414, [1968] 1 WLR 329. See also *Belhaven Brewery Co Ltd v Berekis* (17 March 1993, unreported), (S)EAT 724/92.

7.46 It may be repetitive, however, to set out here the factors that the courts take into account in deciding whether there has been a transfer of an undertaking, since these factors are set out in Chapter 8, below, in respect of TUPE. On the other hand, TUPE is a result of the Acquired Rights Directive and therefore subject to European law and the interpretations by the European Court on the Acquired Rights Directive. The ERA provisions are derived from the EP(C)A which predates the Acquired Rights Directive. It is therefore arguable (but, we suggest, tenuous: see the discussion at para 7.48) that the traditional case law tests outside the European Court apply to the ERA as opposed to TUPE. These tests include the following.

7.47 Sales of assets only are not transfers of businesses as going concerns.[1] Something more is needed, principally goodwill. Material considerations include transfer of customers[2] (particularly where the transferor assists in the transfer), an agreement not to compete with the transferee and transfer of trading name and whether the same economic activities are carried on after the transfer as before.[3] However, as discussed in Chapter 8, below, EC law has had a considerable effect on the interpretation of TUPE and, for that purpose, the definition of an undertaking or part of an undertaking. A much broader approach applies under European law. For that reason it may be more advantageous for an individual to rely upon TUPE as opposed to s 219(2). We discuss below (para 7.48) whether it is possible to interpret s 219(2) in line with TUPE to confer upon s 219(2) a similarly wide interpretation.

[1] *Woodhouse v Peter Brotherhood Ltd* [1972] 2 QB 520, [1972] 3 All ER 91, CA; *Melon v Hector Powe Ltd* [1981] 1 All ER 313, [1980] IRLR 477, HL.

[2] *Ward v Haines Watts* [1983] ICR 231, EAT.

[3] *Kenmir Ltd v Frizzell* [1968] 1 All ER 414; *Modiwear v Wallis Fashion Group* (1980) EAT 535/80; *Ward v Haines Watts* [1983] ICR 231, EAT; *Rencoule (Joiners and Shopfitters) Ltd v Hunt* (1967) 2 ITR 475; *Ault (Isle of Wight) Ltd v Gregory* (1967) 2 ITR 301; *Bonsor v Patara Ltd* (1966) 2 KIR 23.

7.48 As stated, TUPE has to be applied in accordance with the Acquired Rights Directive and European Court cases thereon because of the House of Lords interpretation of European law in *Litster*, ie that domestic law giving effect to European law has to be construed purposively, in line with European law. It seems, however, that the comments of the ECJ in *Marleasing SA v La*

Comercial Internacional de Alimentación[1] mean that domestic legislation even pre-dating a European obligation must be construed in line with the European obligation. There is therefore a case at least for construing the ERA provision on transfer of businesses and undertakings in line with the Acquired Rights Directive and TUPE. In conclusion, then, the test of what is a transfer for the purposes of the ERA *should* be in line with TUPE. In any event, this is what the domestic courts have always tried to do in practice. Curiously, however, in *Green-Wheeler v Onyx (UK) Ltd*[2] the EAT held that it was not possible to construe what is now s 211(2) of the ERA in line with Directive 77/187. It is submitted that this is inconsistent with previous UK practice and also with remarks by the EAT in *Macer v Abafast Ltd*[3] and *Gibson v Motortune Ltd*,[4] discussed below.

1 [1992] 1 CMLR 305.
2 (30 July 1993, unreported), EAT 925/92.
3 [1990] ICR 234.
4 [1990] ICR 740. See also *A & G Tuck Ltd v Bartlett and A & G Tuck (Slough) Ltd* [1994] IRLR 162, EAT; *Justfern Ltd v D'Ingerthorpe* [1994] IRLR 164, EAT; *Smedvig v Wilce* (12 November 1992, unreported), (S)EAT 428/92. In *Green-Wheeler*, however, the EAT found for the employee on a different ground, ie that the accrued right to complain of unfair dismissal passed to a transferee under TUPE.

7.49 *Assuming* that the concept of a transfer under the ERA and the Directive and TUPE is largely the same there will probably, in the future, be less emphasis on the ERA as opposed to TUPE. If the contract of employment under TUPE is transferred then surely continuity of employment thereunder will also be transferred. Previously there existed a difference between the ERA and TUPE in that TUPE excluded non-commercial ventures from its ambit. Now that TUPE applies to both commercial and non-commercial ventures by virtue of the amendments made to TUPE by s 33 of TURERA, it is unlikely that there will be many different interpretations of the ERA compared with TUPE. However, it must be said that the ERA provisions are the primary source for calculating a statutory continuity of employment even though the question of continuity should be made academic if TUPE applies.

7.50 We have, in Chapter 8, discussed the application of *Litster* to cases where an employer tries to avoid the application of TUPE and the transfer of the contract of employment by dismissing individuals employed in the undertaking prior to the transfer ensuring that the employees concerned are not employed immediately before the transfer.

7.51 *Litster* of course was not concerned with the EP(C)A provisions now found in the ERA and there is, one might suppose, at least *some* question mark about whether an employer can get round the transfer of continuity of employment under the ERA by dismissing employees so that they are not, within the wording of the ERA, employed in the undertaking 'at the time of' the transfer. As previously stated, if TUPE swallows up the ERA and transfers continuity the argument is academic. In case not, however, the EAT has tackled this question too.

7.52 Previously, the leading authority was *Teeside Times Ltd v Drury*[1] where the Court of Appeal differed about what 'at the time of transfer' meant. Goff LJ thought an employee would have to be employed actually at the point of transfer although he thought that a technical interval of a couple of hours was irrelevant. Stephenson LJ construed 'time of transfer' as meaning the period of transfer and thought that an interval between employments could occur without breaking continuity provided that such interval came under and was saved by the various provisions of what was Sch 13 of the EP(C)A and are now ss 210 to 219 of the ERA. Eveleigh LJ thought that any break between employment was not material if connected with the mechanics of transfer and if 'the dismissal was a step towards the re-engagement'.

---

[1] [1980] ICR 338.

7.53 In two cases, *Macer v Abafast Ltd*[1] and *Gibson v Motortune Ltd*,[2] the EAT took a robust approach and decided to follow the approach of Eveleigh LJ in *Teeside Times*. Wood J said, in *Macer v Abafast Ltd*:

> 'In approaching the proper construction to be given to the words in the Act of 1978, the Court should lean in favour of that interpretation which best gives effect to the preservation of continuity of service and hence to the preservation of rights of the employee and to obviate and discourage a tactical manoeuvre which seeks to avoid the clear intention of Parliament.'

He decided that an interval between successive employments may be ignored if it is related to the machinery of the transfer. Of course if it were too long, it might not be viewed as an interval related to the machinery of transfer. He rejected the mechanistic approach of Stephenson LJ which was reliant upon the other rules in Sch 13 of the EP(C)A (now ss 210 to 219 of the ERA) and the existence of successive counting weeks. He said:

> '. . . it seems to us that to make an arbitrary rule that a gap of more than one week, eg that ten days, breaks the continuity of employment, but if that gap is less than one week does not, allows us manipulation of the situation and is contrary to the intentions of the legislation and the guidance in *Litster*'s case'.

In short, however, the EAT's approach in *Macer v Abafast Ltd* and *Gibson v Motortune Ltd* allows the issue of intervals between successive employments to be construed broadly in line with *Litster* (see Chapter 8, below).[3] *Macer v Abafast Ltd* has been applied by the EAT in three subsequent cases. In *A & G Tuck Ltd v Bartlett* and *A & G Tuck (Slough) Ltd*[4] an employee who remained in the employment of the transferor and who did not enter the employment of the transferee until two weeks after the moment of transfer was nonetheless entitled to preservation of continuity of employment under para 17(2) of Sch 13 to the EP(C)A (now s 218(2) of the ERA). The EAT held that the delay in joining the transferee was related to the machinery of transfer (following *Macer)*. In *Justfern Ltd v D'Ingerthorpe*[5] Mr D'Ingerthorpe was employed by Edwin Mendoza and Associates as a lecturer at their hotel and travel training college from 18 August 1986 to 10 October 1988 when the staff at the college were told that the business had closed down. One week after the closure he was contacted by another member of staff with a view to arranging a meeting to discuss the possibility of the college re-opening. The college was in fact subsequently purchased and re-opened on 24 October with Mr D'Ingerthorpe as one of five teachers re-employed. It was held that there was no break in continuity during the two week period Mr D'Ingerthorpe was not employed by the college. It was held that a wide interpretation had to be given to the words 'at the time of transfer' and it was held that Mr D'Ingerthorpe was employed at the time of transfer notwithstanding that he was in receipt of unemployment benefit during part of the period of his absence. According to the EAT the principle in *Macer v Abafast Ltd* was not limited to frustrating deliberate avoidance schemes. Schedule 13, para 17(2) of EP(C)A, now s 218(2) of the ERA, was capable of operating over a period of uncertainty as to whether or not an employee would be re-employed by the purchaser of a business. Receipt of unemployment benefit did no more than create such uncertainty.

Finally, in *Smedvig Ltd v Wilce*[6] an employee employed as a driller on a drilling rig enjoyed continuity of employment when the rig was sold even though there was a nine day break between the end of his contract with the vendor and the beginning of his contract with this new employer. The EAT again confirmed that it was correct for the industrial tribunal to follow *Macer* and construe para 17(2) in the same spirit as the House of Lords had construed TUPE in *Litster* in order to protect the rights of employees involved in transfer.

---

1 [1990] ICR 234.
2 [1990] ICR 740.
3 Contrast the slightly different approach of the EAT in *Green-Wheeler v Onyx (UK) Ltd* (30 July 1993, unreported), EAT 925/92 which dealt with the problem by treating an employee's accrued right to complain of unfair dismissal as a liability that can pass to a transferee under TUPE.
4 [1994] IRLR 162, EAT.
5 [1994] IRLR 164.
6 (12 November 1992, unreported), (S)EAT 428/92.

(B) Change of employer through Act of Parliament: ERA, s 218(3)

7.54 This paragraph provides that if, under direction of Parliament, the contract of employment between any body corporate and an employee is modified to substitute another body corporate as the employer the resultant change of employer will not break the continuity of employment of the employee concerned.

(C) Death of an employer and transfer to personal representatives: ERA, s 218(4)

7.55 This paragraph provides that if, upon the death of an employer, an employee is taken into the employment of the personal representatives or trustees of the deceased employer the employee will enjoy continuity of employment notwithstanding the change of employer that has occurred.

7.56 The operation of this provision is illustrated well by *Rowley Holmes & Co v Barber*.[1] Here, the employer of an employee died and left his practice as a solicitor to the employee who was an unqualified clerk. By the employer's will that same employee was also appointed executor and trustee. Being unqualified, the clerk was not able to run the practice and so subsequently the practice was sold by the clerk *qua* executor and trustee to another solicitor. It was held that throughout the changes of employer, the employee's employment was continuous. His employment had been transferred first to the personal representative, thence to the purchaser of the business. The fact that the transfer to the personal representative was to the employee himself *qua* personal representative was irrelevant. He could wear two hats, one *qua* employee and one *qua* executor. The provision applied.

[1] [1977] 1 All ER 801, [1977] 1 WLR 371, EAT.

(D) Change in the composition of a partnership and trustees and personal representatives: ERA, s 218(5)

7.57 If there is a change in composition of a partnership or personal representatives or trustees who employ an employee, such change in partners, personal representatives or trustees will not break continuity of employment and any period of employment with a previously constituted partnership, body of personal representatives or trustees will count towards employment with a newly constituted partnership, personal representatives or trustees as the case may be.[1]

[1] For the effect of dissolution of a partnership at common law see *Briggs v Oates* [1990] IRLR 472.

7.58 The provision clearly covers the case of retirement or expulsion or removal of an individual from a partnership, or as a personal representative or trustee and employment of an employee thereafter by the remaining partners, personal representatives or trustees. One problem in practice, however, is the emphasis in s 218(5) on partners, personal representatives or trustees in the *plural*. So, for example, in the case of a partnership, if a partnership of a number of individuals ceases to be carried on by those individuals and continues to be run by only one in the future or, alternatively, where a sole trader ceases to carry on as such and carries on thereafter in partnership with others, would the provision apply? It seems likely that it will not.[1] This is very odd and, as a result, the (somewhat strained) decision in two cases was that in such circumstances there was, on the facts, a transfer of a business on the dissolution of a partnership and subsequent takeover by a former partner as sole proprietor under s 218(2) so as to avoid this problem of interpretation under s 218(5).[2] This was so even though in one of the cases a doctor's partnership was involved and there was a prohibition on the sale of goodwill under the relevant legislation, a factor which, ordinarily, would have cast some doubt on the application of s 218(2) (as goodwill is normally part and parcel of a sale of a business).[3] It would be much better if the law were that s 218(5) applied both to transfers between a partner (or personal representative or trustee) or partners (or personal representatives or trustees) inter se, ie both singular and plural. But this does not yet seem to be the position.[4]

[1] *Harold Fielding Ltd v Mansi* [1974] 1 All ER 1035; *Wynne v Hair Control* [1978] ICR 870, EAT.

[2] *Allen & Son v Coventry* [1980] ICR 9, [1979] IRLR 399, EAT; *Jeetle v Elster* [1985] ICR 389, [1985] IRLR 227, EAT.

[3] *Jeetle v Elster*; National Health Services Act 1977. On the other hand, under TUPE, this would now probably be a transfer given how TUPE has been recently interpreted in the light of European Court decisions. The case of *Spijkers v Gebroeders Benedik Abbatoir CV* [1986] 2 CMLR 296, ECJ emphasises that no one fact (eg the absence of goodwill transfer, as in *Jeetle*) is conclusive.

[4] See McMullen, *Business Transfers and Employee Rights* pp 21–23.

(E) Associated employers: ERA, s 218(6)

7.59 Where an employee of an employer is taken into the employment of another employer who at the time when the employee enters his employment is an associated employer of the first employer, continuity of employment of the employee transferred is preserved.[1]

[1] *Binns v Versil Ltd* [1975] IRLR 273, IT.

7.60 A vital part of this paragraph is the meaning of an 'associated employer'. This is defined in s 231 of the ERA, where it is provided that 'any two employers are to be treated as associated if one is a company of which the other (directly or indirectly) has control, or if both are companies of which a third person (directly or indirectly) has control'. 'Control' means control by a numerical majority of shares in the general meeting of a limited company rather than 'de facto' control.[1] In a leading case on the subject, *Payne v Secretary of State for Employment*[2] the Court of Appeal confirmed that voting control was the usual test under s 153(4) of the EP(C)A, now s 231 of the ERA. But it had to consider the facts of a case where the employee transferred from a company the shareholders of which were a Mr and Mrs Chapman, who had just one share each, to employment with Mr Chapman himself. The court held that the register of shares of a company might not be conclusive on the issue of voting control as a shareholder might be a nominee for another. The court upheld the tribunal's finding in this case that Mrs Chapman was a nominee for Mr Chapman notwithstanding there was no formal agreement about this. Accordingly, the employee was transferred between two associated employers, Mr Chapman's company and Mr Chapman himself. The court (*obiter*) also suggested that *de facto* control might be relevant for the purposes of s 153(4), in spite of previous comments in case law to the contrary. A definitive pronouncement on that issue is awaited. A related question is whether control by a third person can mean control by a common group of third persons if the group acts in concert. However in *South West Launderettes Ltd v Laidler*[3] the Court of Appeal thought, even if so, there would have to be uniformity in the composition of a group of individuals whom it was alleged exercised such control in relation to all allegedly associated companies (which was not the case in *Laidler*).[4] However Mustill LJ in *Laidler* queried whether s 153(4) of the ERA admitted of any interpretation that plurality of control was possible and this doubt was voiced again (*obiter*) in the later Employment Appeal Tribunal case of *Strudwick v IBL*.[5]

[1] *Secretary of State for Employment v Newbold* [1981] IRLR 305, EAT; *Washington Arts Association Ltd v Forster* [1983] ICR 346, EAT; *Hair Colour Consultants Ltd v Mena* [1984] ICR

671, EAT; *Umar v Pliastar Ltd* [1981] ICR 727; *South West Launderettes Ltd v Laidler* [1986] ICR 455, [1986] IRLR 305, CA; *Strudwick v IBL* [1988] ICR 796, [1988] IRLR 457, EAT. See also *Minetti v DVK Executive Hotels Ltd*, CA, 22.11.88, *IDS Brief* 389/January 1989.

[2] [1989] IRLR 352, CA.

[3] [1986] ICR 455, [1986] IRLR 305, CA.

[4] Also *Poparm Ltd v Weekes* [1984] IRLR 388; *Cann v Fairfield-Rowan Ltd* (1966) 1 KIR 510; *Strudwick v IBL* [1988] ICR 796, [1988] IRLR 457, EAT. Compare *Harford v Swiftrim Ltd* [1987] ICR 439, [1987] IRLR 360, EAT.

[5] [1988] ICR 796, [1988] IRLR 457, EAT, also doubting *Harford v Swiftrim Ltd* [1987] ICR 439, [1987] IRLR 360, EAT (n 4, above).

7.61 It has been held that the definition of 'company' in s 153(4) of the EP(C)A and now s 231 of the ERA is exhaustive and that the word 'company' means 'limited company' and does not include incorporated associations, partnerships, local authorities, health authorities or the like.[1] On the other hand, two more recent cases illustrate a more robust approach to this definition. In *Pinkney v Sandpiper Drilling Ltd*[2] it was held that para 18 of Sch 13 of the EP(C)A, now replaced by s 218(6) of the ERA, applied upon a transfer of an employee from a company to a partnership or joint venture of three companies of which a third person, namely a group, had control. Taking a broad view, the EAT thought it would be wrong if employee rights in this context could be defeated simply because the employer's trading form happened to be slightly unusual and comprised a joint venture or partnership as opposed to a limited company in the strict sense.[3] This seems to conflict with the Court of Appeal decision in *Merton London Borough Council v Gardiner*[4] and for that reason should be treated with caution until further judicial comment is available; but the broad employee orientated view in this case is commendable. In *Hancill v Marcon Engineering Ltd*[5] it was held that an overseas (American) company should be regarded as a 'company' for the purposes of s 231 of the ERA. Thus when an employee worked for an American company, Marcon Engineering Inc, and thereafter transferred to an English limited company, Marcon Engineering Ltd, and both companies were controlled by a Dutch company, Marcon Beheermaatschappij BV, it was held that there had been a transfer between associated employers. In this case Wood J argued that a broad interpretation must be applied to the principle of transfer of continuity of employment on change of employer. Again this approach is welcome, albeit expressly inspired by the decision in *Litster v Forth Dry Dock & Engineering Co Ltd*, a case on TUPE and not on the provision here under discussion.[6]

[1] *Merton London Borough Council v Gardiner* [1981] QB 269, CA; *Southern Electricity Board v Collins* [1970] 1 QB 83; *Southwood Hostel Management Committee v Taylor* [1979] ICR 813, EAT; *Hillingdon Area Health Authority v Kauders* [1979] ICR 472, EAT; *Bell v Lothian Health Board* EAT 36/91.

[2] [1989] ICR 389, [1989] IRLR 425, EAT 3; cf *Wynne v Hair Control* [1978] ICR 870, EAT.

[3] [1981] ICR 186.

[4] [1990] ICR 186.

[5] [1989] ICR 103, EAT.

[6] [1989] ICR 341. As will be seen, in *Litster*, a purposive interpretation was applied to TUPE to make the regulations conform to the aims of the Acquired Rights Directive, ie to safeguard employee rights in a broad way. On the face of it, it may be questionable whether that entitles a tribunal or court to adopt such an approach under the ERA, s 211(6) which is not concerned with transfers of undertakings at all. It is of course at least arguable that ERA, s 218(2) may be so interpreted (see *Macer v Abafast Ltd* [1990] ICR 234, EAT and *Marleasing SA v La Comercial Internacional de Alimentación* [1992] 1 CMLR 305, ECJ). See also para 7.48.

(F) Local Education Authority Schools: ERA, s 218(7)

7.62 Transfers between a Local Education Authority and Governors of Schools and *vice versa* will not cause a break in continuity of employment of the employee transferred and periods of employment with one employer will count towards employment with the second employer.

(G) Transfers within the Health Service: ERA, s 218(8)

7.63 If a person employed in relevant employment by a health service employer is taken into relevant employment by another health service employer, the period of employment at the time of change counts as a period of employment with the second employer and the change does not break continuity of employment.[1]

---

[1] This provision was inserted by the Health Authorities Act 1995. 'Relevant employment' is employment of a description in which persons are engaged while undergoing professional training which involves their being employed successively by a number of different held service employers and which is specified in an order made by the Secretary of State. By virtue of ERA, s 218(10) the following are designated health service employers for this purpose: health authorities established under s 8 of the National Health Service Act 1977; special health authorities established under s 11 of the National Health Service Act 1977; national health service trusts established under Part I of the National Health Service and Community Care Act 1990; the Dental Practice Board and the Public Health Laboratory Service Board. The Employment Protection (National Health Service) Order 1996, SI 1996 638 specified the descriptions of employment in respect of which continuity is preserved namely: employment as a registered medical practitioner or registered dental practitioner in the grade of registrar, senior registrar or specialist registrar; employment in the grade of clinical scientist trainee or clinical psychology trainee; and employment in the grade of general management training scheme trainee or financial management training scheme trainee.

8 Transfer of undertakings

John McMullen

1 INTRODUCTION

8.01 The UK statutory source is the Transfer of Undertakings (Protection of Employment) Regulations 1981 (TUPE).[1] These Regulations were introduced to implement the EC Council Directive of 14 February 1977 on the approximation of the laws of member states relating to the safeguarding of employees' rights in the event of transfers of undertakings, businesses or parts of businesses (the 'Acquired Rights' Directive).[2] The legislative history of the Regulations is traced in detail elsewhere.[3] Some important changes to TUPE were made by the Trade Union Reform and Employment Rights Act 1993 (TURERA) partly in response to infringement proceedings brought against the UK by the EC Commission for defective transposition of the Directive. These proceedings culminated in the case of *EC Commission v United Kingdom*,[4] which is important reading.[5]

[1] SI 1981/1794. For a treatment of the entire subject, see McMullen, *Business Transfers and Employee Rights* (Butterworths, 2nd edn, 1992); see also Hepple and O'Higgins, *Encyclopedia of Labour Relations Law* para 1B 501–516 and the bibliography in *Business Transfers and Employee Rights*, op cit, pp 359–362.

[2] EC Council Directive 77/187. See the useful article by T Kerr on 'Implementation of Directive 77/187 into Irish Law and Case Law of the Court of Justice' in *Acquired Rights of Employees* (Irish Centre for European Law, 1988). See too, Hepple (1976) 5 ILJ 197, (1977) 6 ILJ 106. See also *EC Commission Report to the Council on progress with regard to the implementation of Directive 77/187 EEC relating to the safeguarding of employees' rights in the event of transfers of undertakings, businesses or parts of businesses*, June 1993. The Commission of the EC also commissioned reports on the Directive particularly as it affects contracting out which make interesting reading. See eg reports by Paul Davies (Oxford University) on the UK, Ireland and Denmark, Professor Rolf Birk (University of Trier) on Belgium, Germany, France, Luxembourg and the Netherlands, Constantin Iliopoulos on Greece and Eduardo Gonzalez Biedma on Spain, Portugal and Italy. The Directive is now in the course of revision and a new version has been adopted by the Commission of the EC. Its progress onwards, however, has not been smooth. At the moment any proposed change to modify the effect of the Directive in relation to contracting out has been abandoned. It is briefly referred to in para 8.101.

[3] McMullen, *Business Transfers and Employee Rights* ch 6.

[4] C-382/92 [1994] ICR 664, ECJ.

[5] A significant complaint by the EC against the UK was *not* dealt with by TURERA. This was that the right to be informed/consulted about a transfer under TUPE applied *only* in favour of recognised trade union representatives. This led to the UK's unsuccessful defence by *EC Commission v United Kingdom* C-382/92 [1994] ICR 664, [1994] IRLR 392, ECJ on this point and to the changes brought in by the Collective Redundancies and Transfer of Undertakings (Protection of Employment) (Amendment) Regulations 1995 (SI 1995/2587) referred to at para 8.85.

8.02 The chief aim of the Acquired Rights Directive is to 'provide for the protection of employees in the event of a change of employer, in particular, to ensure their rights are safeguarded'. The House of Lords in *Litster v Forth Dry Dock and Engineering Co Ltd*[1] and previously in a different context (equal pay) in *Pickstone v Freemans plc*[2] has accepted that a purposive approach should be applied to the construction of UK legislation intended to give effect to European obligations. The terms of the Directive and European Court of Justice decisions thereon are therefore vital to the construction of TUPE which in particular should be looked at in the light of the aim above quoted. On the other hand, the principle has its limitations. The 'purposive' approach cannot be used if to do so would be to distort express contradictory language. So stated the House of Lords in *Webb v EMO Air Cargo (UK) Ltd*.[3] A good example is the express inclusion (now repealed by TURERA) of the requirement in TUPE as originally drawn that an undertaking has to be commercial in nature, in breach of the Directive.[4] It is doubtful whether the purposive approach could have solved that particular problem.[5]

1 [1989] IRLR 161, HL. See also *Marleasing SA v La Comercial Internacional de Alimentación*: C-106/89 [1992] 1 CMLR 305, ECJ.

2 [1989] AC 66, HL.

3 [1993] IRLR 27, HL.

4 See *Dr Sophie Redmond Stichting v Bartol*: C-29/91 [1992] IRLR 366, ECJ. Although the ECJ's decision in *Dr Sophie* made it clear that the Directive covered non-commercial ventures, the position was confirmed by the court's ruling in *EC Commission v United Kingdom* (Case 382/92) [1994] ICR 664, ECJ that the UK had been in breach of the Directive on this point.

5 This is implicit in the approach of Wood J in the EAT in *Wren v Eastbourne Borough Council* [1993] IRLR 425 when he said 'it falls therefore to industrial tribunals and to this tribunal to construe the phrase "the nature of a commercial venture" in accordance with UK law'. (At the time of this EAT case, TURERA had removed the commercial venture requirement in response to the ECJ decision in *Dr Sophie Redmond Stichting v Bartol*: C-29/91 [1992] IRLR 366, ECJ which indicated that the Directive contained no such limitation. But the transfer in *Wren* took place before TURERA. As it later transpired, however, an industrial tribunal rehearing *Wren* on remit from the EAT (*Wren v Eastbourne Borough Council (No 2)*, Case No 28732/90 (6 May 1994, unreported and affirmed in *UK Waste Control Ltd v Wren and Eastbourne Borough Council* [1995] ICR 974, EAT, decided, in any event that because of the requirements imposed in relation to compulsory competitive tendering by local government legislation, the activity the subject of that case (contracting out of refuse disposal by a local authority to a private contractor) *was* in the nature of a commercial venture.

8.03 The importance of the Directive to the public sector cannot, however, be underestimated. Directives have so called vertical effect only, ie in contrast to Treaty provisions (such as Art 119 on equal pay) they are binding on the member state of the Union as an obligation to implement the legislation into domestic law. They can only be enforced by an *individual* against the state or an emanation of the state as employer and then, too, only if the Directive concerned is unconditional and also the provision of the Directive concerned is sufficiently precise.[1] A state employer or emanation of the state, according to *Foster v British Gas plc*: C-188/89[2] and *Doughty v Rolls-Royce plc*[3] means a body which (1) has been made responsible pursuant to statute for providing a public service (2) under the control of the state and (3) has for that purpose special powers over and above what is the norm. All of these conditions must be fulfilled.

1 See, in Directive 75/129 (redundancies), *Griffin v South West Water Services Ltd* [1995] IRLR 15.

2 C-188/89; [1991] ICR 84, ECJ.

3 [1992] IRLR 126, CA.

8.04 It is more or less common ground that government departments, local authorities, health authorities, further education corporations and NHS Trusts are likely to be emanations of the state.[1] Such public employees may therefore rely on the Directive itself if more favourable than TUPE. The scope of 'emanation of the State' was potentially considerably widened by the High Court decision in *Griffin v South West Water Services Ltd*[2] where a privatised utility (a wholly owned subsidiary of Southwest Water plc the share capital of which following privatisation was owned by institutional and private investors) was held to be an emanation of the State. Blackburne J held that the three conditions for this characterisation (see para 8.03) were satisfied. He also held, first, that the question is not whether the *body* is under the control of the State, but whether the *public service* in question is under the control of the State, secondly, that the legal form of the body is irrelevant; thirdly that the fact that the body is a commercial one is also irrelevant; fourthly that it does not matter that the body does not carry out any of the traditional functions of the State and is not an agent of the State or, finally that the State does not possess day-to-day control over the activities of the body.

[1] For health authorities see *Marshall v Southampton and South West Hampshire Area Health Authority (Teaching)*: 152/84 [1986] ICR 335, ECJ. The issue of whether an employer was an emanation of the state was conceded in relation to further education corporations in *R v Secretary of State for Employment, ex p National Association of Teachers in Further and Higher Education* (5 October 1992, unreported), in relation to an NHS Trust in *Porter and Nanyakkara v Queen's Medical Centre* [1993] IRLR 486 and in relation to a further education corporation in *Kenny v South Manchester College* [1993] IRLR 265.

[2] [1995] IRLR 15.

8.05 That of course leaves (subject to the purposive approach above mentioned) private sector employees in a twilight world of less favourable treatment. However, the interesting possibility now arises that a private sector employee may, if harmed by non-implementation of a Directive, sue the member state responsible for non-implementation for any damage sustained.[1]

[1] See *Francovich and Bonifaci v Italy*: C-6, 9/90 [1992] IRLR 84, ECJ. The conditions under which such a claim can be brought were clarified by *Brasserie du Pêcheur SA v Federal Republic of Germany* and *R v Secretary of State for Transport, ex p Factortame Ltd* [1996] IRLR 267. But the conditions laid down in those judgments may not make an action by an individual against a member state on the grounds of defective transposition quite so easy as might otherwise have been thought. The effect of the decision is that where a member state acts in a field where it has a wide discretion, Community law does cover a right on individuals to obtain redress for loss or damage caused by breach attributable to a member state provided that the rule of law infringed must be intended to confer rights on an individual; the breach must be sufficiently serious; and there must be a direct causal link between the breach of the obligation resting on the state and the damage sustained by the injured party. The decisive test for finding that a breach of Community law was sufficiently serious was whether the member state manifestly and gravely disregarded the limits on its discretion. The factors which the competent court might take into consideration included the clarity and precision of the rule breached; the measure of discretion left by that rule to the national authorities; whether the infringement and the damage caused by was intentional or involuntary; whether any error of law was excusable or inexcusable; the fact that the position taken by a Community institution may have contributed towards the omission and the adoption or retention of national measures or practices contrary to Community law. Although, for example, in relation to the Acquired Rights Directive, the Minister introducing the Regulations reported to the House of Commons that he was introducing them with 'a remarkable lack of enthusiasm' (Mr David Waddington, *Hansard* HC Deb, 7 December 1981, col 680) it is perhaps doubtful in relation to some significant areas that a claim could be brought particularly in view of lack of clarity in relation for example to whether commercial or non-commercial ventures were covered by the Directive.

8.06 The sum of this discussion is that there is no doubt that European law will become increasingly important in this area (see also para 8.101).

8.07 It is to be noted that the provisions of TUPE are additional to, and not in substitution for, the provisions about statutory continuity of employment on business transfers in the ERA under s 218(2) of the ERA.[1] But the provisions of s 218(2) deal only with bridging of continuity on change of employer—*not* the wholesale transfer of employment terms. And they assume that an employee of the transferor is voluntarily re-engaged by a transferee. Nothing in s 218(2) *obliges* a transferee so to do. The TUPE Regulations go further and provide for an automatic transfer of contracts of employment along with the rights, obligations and duties in relation thereto, thus negativing the common law rule in *Nokes v Doncaster Amalgamated Collieries Ltd*[2] that a contract of employment may not be transferred without the consent of the employee.[3] As the Regulations transfer the contract itself to a transferee, this will ordinarily involve transfer also of accrued statutory continuous employment. Thus it can be argued that when the Regulations apply s 218(2) is rendered otiose.[4]

1 See Chapter 7, above.

2 [1940] AC 1014, [1940] 3 All ER 549, HL.

3 Subject to the right of the employee to object to the transfer of his contract without further claim: *Katsikas v Konstantinidis*: C-132, 138, 139/91 [1993] IRLR 179, ECJ; TUPE, reg 5(4)(A) (as inserted by TURERA, s 33(4)).

4 Before the changes made by TURERA, TUPE excluded non-commercial ventures from its scope (see TUPE, reg 2(1)). The Directive has no equivalent limitation. It was therefore argued that para 17(2) of Sch 13 of the EP(C)A, now replaced by s 218(2) of the ERA, might have an importance of its own for employees (for continuity only) in the case of transfers of non-commercial undertakings (see McMullen, *Business Transfers and Employee Rights* ch 5). Now that TUPE applies to both commercial and non-commercial ventures, s 218(2) is likely in practice to be subsumed by TUPE.

8.08 Strictly, the ERA still provides the statutory basis for calculating continuity of employment and if continuity of employment were preserved by virtue of the provisions of the ERA it would not be necessary to look to TUPE for further assistance on that point alone. However, now that TUPE has been amended by TURERA to cover both commercial and non-commercial ventures (see below), it can be argued that a TUPE transfer (transferring the contract and all rights in connection with it) should include a transfer of accrued statutory continuous employment.[1]

1 Cf the view of the EAT in *Green-Wheeler v Onyx (UK) Ltd* (30 July 1993, unreported), EAT 925/92.

8.09 Another provision of the EP(C)A, s 94, used to contain rules about redundancy liability upon a business transfer.[1] It provided, broadly, that when there was a change in the ownership of a business, if the new owner made an offer to continue the employment of an employee prior to the ending of the old contract with the original owner, and this was accepted, the dismissal which would occur at common law upon sale of the business was deemed not to have happened for redundancy purposes and there would be no claim for a redundancy payment against the original owner. Accrued service for the purposes of a future claim against the transferee of the business was preserved by virtue of the EP(C)A.[2] There was, however, no need to use s 94 in a case where TUPE applied, for, in that case, the contract is transferred to the new owner automatically and there will be no dismissal arising out of a change of employer on sale of the business. However, s 94 had some residual importance, where for example, there was a transfer of a non-commercial venture, when TUPE did not apply (see para 8.18). Once it was decided that commercial ventures should be covered by TUPE (by virtue of the provisions of TURERA—see para 8.21) s 94 became otiose, and was repealed by TURERA.[3] Another criticism of s 94 was that it referred to a change in *ownership* of a business. As will be seen below, no change of ownership is necessary under European law in order for a transfer of an undertaking to take place.

1 See Chapter 20, below.
2 EP(C)A, Sch 13, para 11 now amended by s 213 of the ERA.
3 TURERA, Sch 10.

8.10 In addition to transferring the contract of employment from the transferor to the transferee, TUPE has other protective functions. Thus, transfer-connected dismissals are automatically unfair unless for an economic, technical or organisation reason entailing changes in the workforce.[1] TUPE also provides for the transfer to a transferee of recognition of trade unions and of collective agreements.[2] And TUPE imposes on employers obligations to inform and consult with recognised trade unions prior to a transfer.[3]

1 Regulation 8.
2 Regulations 9 and 6 respectively.
3 Regulation 10.

2 APPLICABILITY

8.11 TUPE has certain limitations and exclusions:

(1) The Regulations do not apply to sales of assets alone. Only an economic entity retaining its identity after the transfer will be covered by TUPE and the Directive (see below).[1]
(2) The Regulations cover only employees and not workers engaged under contracts for services.[2]
(3) Regulations 8, 10 and 11 do not apply to employees ordinarily working outside the UK.[3]
(4) The Regulations do not apply to employees on board a ship registered in the UK if the employment is wholly outside the UK or if the employee is not ordinarily resident in the UK.[4]
(5) Regulations 5 and 6 (automatic transfer of contracts of employment and collective agreements) are expressed not to apply to occupational pension schemes, by reg 7, which excludes transfer of rights thereunder from the transferor to the transferee whether under the contract of employment or under the collective agreement. Until recently the scope or even validity of this exclusion was highly controversial and even now to an extent remains so. As explained below, the EAT in *Warrener v Walden Engineering Ltd*[5] and the High Court in *Adams v* (1) *Lancashire County Council* (2) *BET Catering Services Ltd* [1996] IRLR 154 have created some certainty by emphasising this exclusion. But those contracting to perform services to the private sector in market testing arrangements (see

below) may find *commercial* pressure to provide comparable pension terms for transferring employees (see in general, para 8.46). TURERA also removed from the exclusion in reg 7 any provisions of an occupational pension scheme which do not relate to benefits for old age, invalidity or survivors (thus potentially allowing transfer of, for example, redundancy enhancements contained in a pension scheme).

(6) Regulation 9 (transfer of recognition of trade union from transferor to transferee) does not apply unless the undertaking or part of the undertaking transferred maintains an identity distinct from the remainder of the transferee's undertaking.[6]

(7) Regulation 5 of the Regulations does not transfer any liability of any person to be prosecuted for, convicted of and sentenced for any criminal offence.[7]

(8) The Regulations do not apply to an employee who is not employed in the undertaking or part of the undertaking transferred.[8] Here, references to a person employed in the undertaking or part thereof before the transfer mean *immediately before* the transfer.[9] This issue is a question of fact.[10] In the House of Lords' decision in *Litster v Forth Dry Dock and Engineering Co Ltd*[11] it was held that it was necessary to deem included among those employed in the undertaking or part transferred, those employees who would have been employed therein immediately before the transfer had they not been automatically unfairly dismissed within the meaning of reg 8 of the Regulations (see below).

(9) The Regulations do not apply to employees who do not meet the normal qualifying conditions for unfair dismissal protection. Hence, employees with less than two years qualifying service have no right to complain about a transfer connected unfair dismissal.[12]

---

1 *Kenmir Ltd v Frizzell* [1968] 1 All ER 414, [1968] 1 WLR 329; *Spijkers v Gebroeders Benedik Abattoir CV*: 24/85 [1986] 2 CMLR 296, ECJ; *Dr Sophie Redmond Stichting v Bartol*: C-29/91 [1992] IRLR 366, ECJ; *Rask and Christensen v ISS Kantineservice AS*: C-209/91 [1993] IRLR 133, ECJ. See the discussion later in this chapter.

2 Regulation 2(1). Although there is an extended definition of employee, 'employee' here means any individual who works for another person whether under a contract of service or apprenticeship *or otherwise* but does not include anyone who provides services under a contract for services. It is thought that this might catch some workers traditionally excluded from the usual definition of employee, but whom, it is not yet clear. It does not cover an equity partner in a firm, even if he provided services as a managing partner: *Cowell v Quilter Goodison & Co Ltd* [1989] IRLR 392, CA. The ECJ has held, in *Mikkelsen v Danmols Inventar A/S* [1986] 1 CMLR 316 that it is for the member states to determine who is an employee for the purposes of the Directive. At the time of writing, extension of the Directive to a wider range of employment relationships is proposed. An amended version of the Directive seeks to provide:

> '. . . Member States shall not exclude from the scope of this Directive, contracts of employment or employment relationships solely because:
>
> (i) of the number of working hours performed or to be performed; or
> (ii) that they are employment relationships governed by a fixed duration contract of employment within the meaning of Article 1(1) of Council Directive 91/383/EEC; or
> (iii) that they are temporary employment relationships within the meaning of Article 1(1) of Council Directive 91/383/EEC.'

3 Regulation 13(1).

4 Regulation 13(2).

5 [1993] IRLR 420.

6 Regulation 9(1).

7 Regulation 5(4), eg under the Health and Safety at Work etc Act 1974 or the Factories Acts.

8 Regulation 5(1).

9 Regulation 5(3).

[10] For an industrial tribunal case see *Anderson v Kluwer* (1987) COIT 1697/249. For the European Court test see *Botzen v Rotterdamsche Droogdok Maatschappij BV*: 186/83 [1986] 2 CMLR 50, ECJ – was the employee *'assigned'* to the business or part transferred? For more recent UK case law see also *Duncan Webb Offset (Maidstone) Ltd v Cooper* [1995] IRLR 633. *Securicor Guarding Ltd v Fraser Security Services Ltd*, EAT 350/95; *Michael Peters Ltd v* (1) *Farnfield* (2) *Michael Peters Group plc* [1995] IRLR 190; *Sunley Turift Holdings Ltd v Thomson* [1995] IRLR 184.

[11] [1989] IRLR 161.

[12] Regulation 8(5) as inserted by the Collective Redundancies and Transfer of Undertakings (Protection of Employment) (Amendment) Regulations 1995, SI 1995/2587. The Regulations specifically address the decision of the EAT in *Milligan v Securicor Cleaning Ltd* [1995] IRLR 288 in which the EAT interpreted Regulation 8 as giving the right to claim unfair dismissal to employees who had not served the normal two year qualifying period. Article 4(1) of the Acquired Rights Directive provides that protection against dismissal 'shall not apply to certain specific categories of employees who are not covered by the laws or practice of the Member States in respect of protection against dismissal'. The EAT reasoned that because Regulation 8 did not specifically exclude employees with less than two years service from the right not to be unfairly dismissed, such employees impliedly qualified for protection within Regulation 8(1). The 1995 Regulations therefore amend TUPE by specifically excluding from the protection of Regulation 8 all employees who do not meet the normal qualifying conditions for unfair dismissal. A legal challenge to the validity of the new Reg 8(5) by a consortium of trade unions later failed (*R v Secretary of State for Trade and Industry, ex p Unison, GMB and NASUWT* (High Court, [1996] IRLR 438).

3 REGULATION 3 AND A 'RELEVANT TRANSFER'

8.12 The TUPE Regulations only apply to a relevant transfer under reg 3, which means a transfer from one person to another of an undertaking or part of an undertaking situated immediately before the transfer in the United Kingdom or a part of one which is so situated.[1] The first point to note is that because of the requirement of a transfer 'from one person to another' the Transfer Regulations do not apply to a takeover by way of change in the ownership of share capital of a limited company.

[1] Regulation 3(1). On a share disposal there is no change in the identity of the legal 'person' employing the employee. Obviously, then, no change to the contract can occur without agreement. However, a TUPE transfer is *more* advantageous to employees in two ways. First, reg 8 of TUPE makes transfer connected dismissals automatically unfair (subject to reg 8(2)). Secondly, before a TUPE transfer, worker representatives have the right to information, and, possibly, consultation under reg 10. These employee rights do not of course apply on a share sale takeover. See McMullen, *Business Transfers and Employee Rights* ch 1.

8.13 Much of the previous case law on this subject was generated by para 17(2) of Sch 13 to the EP(C)A (now found in s 218(2) of the ERA) and s 94 of the EP(C)A now repealed by TURERA. The leading case under those provisions was *Kenmir Ltd v Frizzell*[1] where Widgery J said: 'The vital consideration is whether the effect of the transaction [is] to put the transferee in possession of a going concern, the activities of which he [can] carry on without interruption'. This test is a little limited, but was nonetheless adopted (albeit amplified) in relation to the Directive by the Advocate General of the European Court, Slynn, AG in the European Court in *Spijkers v Gebroeders Benedik Abbatoir CV*: 24/85[2] in a case on the Acquired Rights Directive.

[1] [1968] 1 All ER 414, [1968] 1 WLR 329.

[2] [1986] 2 CMLR 296, ECJ.

8.14 What is a transfer of an undertaking, as far as UK law is concerned, is a question of fact. But it is clear that a mere asset sale, without more, does not amount to a transfer of an undertaking. When there is such an asset sale the Regulations will not apply.[1] Whether there is a transfer of an undertaking as opposed to an asset only sale is a question of fact for an industrial tribunal.[2] An industrial tribunal is, under UK law, entitled to look at substance rather than form.[3] Although it is purely a question of fact, material considerations in cases under the EP(C)A on whether there has been a business transfer have included whether items other than mere assets are sold, whether work in progress is transferred, whether goodwill has been transferred, whether customers have been adopted (particularly where the transferor assists in the carrying over of these customers) whether there is an agreement by the transferor not to compete with the transferee, whether there has been a transfer of a transferor's trading name and so forth.[4] As is implicit above, it is also relevant to consider whether the same economic activities are carried on after, compared with before, the transfer.[5] If the activities are different, this may point to an asset sale;[6] conversely, if the activities remain the same, it may indicate there has been a business transfer.[7]

1 *Woodhouse v Peter Brotherhood Ltd* [1972] 2 QB 520, [1972] 3 All ER 91, CA; *Melon v Hector Powe Ltd* [1981] 1 All ER 313, HL (not cases on TUPE, but equally applicable), cf *Modiwear Ltd v Wallis Fashion Group Ltd* (1980) EAT 535/80.

2 *Melon v Hector Powe Ltd* [1981] 1 All ER 313, HL; *Manin Management Services Ltd v Ward* (1989) Times, 9 February, CA.

3 *Rencoule (Joiners and Shopfitters) Ltd v Hunt* (1967) 2 ITR 475.

4 *Kenmir Ltd v Frizzell* [1968] 1 All ER 414, [1968] 1 WLR 329; *Modiwear Ltd v Wallis Fashion Group Ltd* (1980) EAT 535/80; *Ward v Haines Watts* [1983] ICR 231, EAT; *Rencoule (Joiners and Shopfitters) Ltd v Hunt* (1967) 2 ITR 475; *Ault v Gregory* (1967) 2 ITR 301; *Bonser v Patara Ltd* (1966) 2 KIR 23; *Spijkers v Gebroeders Benedik Abattoir CV*: 24/85 [1986] 2 CMLR 296, ECJ; *Thompsons Soft Drinks Ltd v Quayle* EAT 12/81.

5 *Spijkers v Gebroeders Benedik Abattoir CV*: 24/85 [1986] 2 CMLR 296, ECJ.

6 *Woodhouse v Peter Brotherhood Ltd* [1972] 2 QB 520, CA; *Woodhouse, Applebee v Joseph Allnatt Centres* EAT 292/80.

7 *Modiwear Ltd v Wallis Fashion Group Ltd* (1980) EAT 535/80.

8.15 However, many of the above considerations derive from case law prior to recent definitive European Court decisions. Generally there should now be reference instead to the tests in the European Court cases ranging in particular from *Spijkers v Gebroeders Benedik Abattoir CV*: 24/85[1] to for example *Dr Sophie Redmond Stitching v Bartol*: C-29/91[2] (see below) above all else. This should apply whether the case is one under s 218(2) of the ERA or under TUPE.[3] Generally a health warning should be sounded about UK case law on the test of a transfer decided before cases such as *Dr Sophie Redmond*. Whether or not the end result in such cases would today be correct on the facts, the reasoning will certainly often be out of date.

1 [1986] 2 CMLR 296, ECJ.

2 [1992] IRLR 366, ECJ.

3 In *Marleasing SA v La Comercial Internacional de Alimentación SA*: C-106/89 [1992] 1 CMLR 305 the European Court stated:

> '. . . the obligation of member states under a Directive is to achieve its objects, and their duty by virtue of Art 5 of the Treaty to take all necessary steps to ensure the fulfilment of that obligation binds all authorities of member states including national courts within their jurisdiction. It follows that in applying national law, whether the provisions concerned *pre-date or post-date*

> *the Directive*, the national court asked to interpret national law is bound to do so in every way possible in the light of the text and aim of the Directive to achieve the results achieved by it and thus to comply with Art 189(3) of the Treaty.'

Thus it is perfectly arguable, under *Marleasing*, that the provisions of the ERA derived from the EP(C)A, even though they pre-date the Acquired Rights Directive, should be interpreted in line with the Directive. Even if this argument, although a compelling one, is not accepted by UK courts, UK courts have traditionally been inclined to marry up the approach under the EP(C)A with TUPE in order that a consistent pattern can emerge. (Cf *Green-Wheeler v Onyx (UK) Ltd* (30 July 1993, unreported), EAT 925/92.)

European law

8.16 There are various tests and guidelines that may be gleaned from European Court of Justice cases on the Acquired Rights Directive and from UK decisions applying them.

Economic entity retaining its identity

8.17 As stated, most of the previous case law should be looked at in the light of more recent European Court decisions, a good example of which is *Dr Sophie Redmond Stichting v Bartol*: C-29/91,[1] in which the test was stated as follows:

> '. . . the decisive criterion for establishing whether there is a transfer within the meaning of the Directive is whether the business retains its identity, as would be indicated, in particular by the fact that its operation was either continued or resumed. On the other hand, in order to determine whether those conditions are fulfilled, it is necessary to consider all the factual circumstances characterising the transaction in question, including the type of undertaking or business concern, whether the business's tangible assets, such as buildings and movable property are transferred, the value of its intangible assets at the time of the transfer, whether or not the majority of its employees are taken over by the new employer, whether or not its customers are transferred and the degree of similarity between activities carried on before and after the transfer and the period, if any, for which those activities are suspended. It should be noted however that all those circumstances are merely single factors in the overall assessment which must be made and cannot therefore be considered in isolation.'

---

[1] [1992] IRLR 366, ECJ.

TUPE and the Directive apply to non-commercial ventures

8.18 Previously, TUPE restricted the definition of a transfer of an undertaking to the transfer of a commercial venture.[1] This caused considerable problems in the application of the Regulations to charitable activities, non-profit making concerns, public sector transfers and to cases of contracting out where, prior to the contracting out, it may well have been the case, whether in the public or private sector, that the activity contracted out was not being run in the nature of a commercial venture prior to contracting out.[2]

---

[1] See TUPE, reg 2(1) (as originally drawn). See also *Woodcock v Committee for the Time Being of the Friends' School, Wigton & Genwise Ltd* [1987] IRLR 98, CA.

[2] See *Woodcock*, where a Quaker School of charitable status was held to be an undertaking which

was not in the nature of a commercial venture for the purposes of the Transfer Regulations. See also *Expro Services Ltd v Smith* [1991] IRLR 156, EAT; *Stirling v Dietsmann Management Systems Ltd* [1991] IRLR 368, EAT. See also *UK Waste Control Ltd v Wren and Eastbourne Borough Council* [1995] ICR 974.

8.19 It had always been argued that the Directive was not confined to commercial ventures.[1] The position under TUPE, however, became untenable after the delivery of the European Court decision in *Dr Sophie Redmond Stichting v Bartol*: C-29/91.[2]

---

[1] See McMullen, *Business Transfers and Employee Rights* ch 4. The draft revised version of the Directive approved by the Commission in September 1994 would specifically provide that it applies 'to public or private undertakings engaged in economic activities whether or not they are operated for gain' (Art 1(3)).

[2] [1992] IRLR 366, ECJ.

8.20 The facts in this case were that the Dr Sophie Redmond Foundation was a foundation providing assistance to drug addicts. It was funded by grants from the local authority. The local authority decided to terminate its subsidy to the foundation and to switch it to the Sigma Foundation. Certain employees transferred. The question was whether there was a transfer of an undertaking so as to protect transferred employees' rights. The European Court of Justice held:

> 'In accordance with the approach of the Court to give a sufficiently broad interpretation to the concept of legal transfer in Article 1(1) of EC Directive 77/187 so as to give effect to the purpose of the Directive there is a legal transfer where a public body decides to terminate a subsidy paid to one legal person as a result of which the activities of that person are terminated and transferred to another legal person with similar aims.
>
> The Directive applies wherever, in the context of contractual relations, there is a change in the legal or natural person responsible for carrying on the business and who incurs the obligations of the employer towards employees of the undertaking.
>
> Transactions arising out of the grant of subsidies or to foundations or associations whose services are not remunerated are not excluded from the scope of Directive 77/187. The Directive applies to all employees who are covered by a protection against dismissal under national law, even if it be limited.'

It became clear as a result of this decision that TUPE was in breach of the Directive. Whilst employees in the public sector might immediately rely upon *Dr Sophie Redmond* as against a public employer, it was obviously necessary to bring UK law expressly into line with the Directive for the purposes of all employees.

8.21 TURERA (s 33) therefore amended the Regulations by abolishing the exclusion of non-commercial ventures. Accordingly, the argument, particularly in the context of contracting out and market testing, that the activity has not, previously to contracting out, been run in the nature of a commercial venture is no longer available. This also enlarges the possibility that the transfer of activities from the public sector to the private sector generally, and indeed transfers within the public sector, involve transfers under the Directive and/or TUPE (see also the discussion at para 8.28 on contracting out and market testing). Finally, confirmation that the provisions of TUPE on this point did not comply with the Directive was given by the ECJ in *EC Commission v United Kingdom*.[1]

[1] Case No 382/92 [1994] ICR 664.

A broad view encompassing atypical transfers

8.22 It is important to recognise that the Regulations deal not only with the sale and purchase of recognisable businesses as traditionally defined, but also with atypical transfers generally. A broad, and not simply traditional, approach is required. In short, European law requires an 'employment' definition of a transfer as opposed to a 'conveyancing' definition.[1]

[1] A phrase coined by Hepple and O'Higgins in *Encyclopedia of Employment Law* para 1B 501–516.

No transfer of absolute ownership needed

8.23 There is no need for there to be a transfer of absolute ownership of assets, goodwill etc (the grant of leases, licences and contracts, for example, frequently does not involve a transfer of absolute ownership but simply a contract to manage, but given appropriate circumstances there can still be a transfer of undertaking). A good example is *Foreningen af Arbejdsledere i Danmark v Daddy's Dance Hall A/S*: 324/86.[1]

[1] [1988] IRLR 315, ECJ.

8.24 In this case, Irma Catering had a lease with Palads Teatret which was determined on 28 January 1983 with effect from 25 February 1983. Mr Tellerup was an employee of the business operated by Irma Catering and was dismissed with notice expiring on 30 April 1983. On 25 February 1983 a new lease was granted by Palads Teatret to Daddy's Dance Hall. Mr Tellerup was re-engaged by Daddy's Dance Hall. He was later dismissed by Daddy's Dance Hall on 26 April 1983. A dispute arose about the terms of his employment which existed on the date of termination on the length of his notice to which he was entitled from Daddy's Dance Hall.

8.25 It was held that the Directive applied to a situation where, after the termination of a lease, the owner of the undertaking leases it to a new lessee who continues to run the business and 'it is of no importance to know whether the ownership of the undertaking has been transferred'.

Change of management

8.26 Rather than any question of a transfer of ownership, as above discussed, the European law test is concerned with a *change of management*. Thus, in *Daddy's Dance Hall*,[1] it was stated:

> 'the Directive . . . applies as soon as there is a change resulting from a conventional sale or from a merger of the natural or legal person responsible for operating the undertaking who consequently enters into obligations as an employer towards the employees working in the undertaking . . .'.

The impact on the above for atypical transfers, such as in the context of contracting out and market testing, is enormous.[2]

[1] See also *Berg and Busschers v IMI Besselsen*: 144, 145/87 [1990] ICR 396, ECJ; *Landsorganisationen i Danmark v Ny Molle Kro*: 287/86 [1989] ICR 330, ECJ; *P Bork International A/S v Forenigen af Arbejsledere i Danmark*: 101/87 [1990] 3 CMLR 701, ECJ.

[2] See the volume of discussion in *Municipal Journal* and *Local Government Chronicle* from 1992 onwards.

Bipartite and tripartite transfers

8.27 Certain types of change of employer such as changeovers of lessees, licensees, franchisees and contractors involve three parties, instead of the traditional two. Thus the ultimate owner of the undertaking may have licensed management of the enterprise or activity to a licensee. At the end of the period of licence, the licensee may be replaced by a third party, namely a second licensee. The question is whether, upon such a changeover, there can be a direct transfer from outgoing licensee to incoming licensee. The answer should be, in principle, that there is a direct transfer. For example, the facts of *Daddy's Dance Hall* (see para 8.24 above) suggest a direct transfer from Irma Catering to Daddy's Dance Hall. In *Dr Sophie Redmond Stichting v Bartol* (see para 8.20) there seems to have been no dispute that there was a direct transfer from outgoing charitable foundation to incoming charitable foundation and, in short, there seems no reason why, in principle, the replacement of the franchisee, licensee or contractor by another franchisee, licensee or contractor should not result in a direct transfer between outgoing contractor and incoming contractor. Of course the position may be different where the intervention of the ultimate owner amounts to more than simply a mechanism for replacing the contractors and where the ultimate owner takes back the actual management of the enterprise for more than a *de minimis* period.[1] In the EAT in *Dines v (1) Initial Health Care Services and (2) Pall Mall Services Group Ltd*[2] discussed at para 8.34 it was suggested that it could be more difficult for there to be a transfer between outgoing and incoming contractors, *sed quaere*. Nonetheless the learned Judge in that case did accept that *in principle* there could be a transfer between two such parties. And reg 3(4) of TUPE, as amended by TURERA, states that a transfer may take place 'whether or not any property is transferred to the transferee by the transferor'. Finally, the position seems beyond much doubt after the Court of Appeal in *Dines*[3] robustly held that a transfer can (following *Daddy's Dance Hall*) take place in two phases. Thus a changeover of contractors supplying services to Orsett Hospital resulted in a transfer between outgoing contractor and incoming contractor.[4] That there can be a direct transfer between outgoing contractor and incoming contractor is also made easier by the principle that no contractual link is necessary between transferor and transferee. This was confirmed by the European Court recently *Albert Merckx and Patrick Neuhuys v Ford Motors Co Belgium SA*[5] and prior to the ruling of the court in that regard, this had also been the view of the Advocate General Lenz in *Merckx* and also Advocate General Cosmas in *Ole Rygaard v Strø Mølle Akustik A/S*.[6]

[1] UK case law on business transfers prior to recent European Court cases was certainly consistent with the possibility of a direct transfer between outgoing managers and incoming managers. Good examples are *Cartwright v Norton* EAT 91/82, unreported; *Norris (t/a Little Brickhill Service Station) v Bedwell* EAT 875/83 and *LMC Drains Ltd v Waugh* [1991] 3 CMLR 172, EAT and *Metro Rod Services Ltd v Waugh* EAT, 5.6.91 182/90. Even more persuasive, as mentioned in the text, are the more recent ECJ cases which imply this approach.

[2] [1993] IRLR 521, EAT.

[3] [1994] IRLR 336, CA.

[4] See also *Porter v Queen's Medical Centre* [1993] IRLR 486 (transfer when two district health authorities terminated contract with general hospital to provide paediatric services and granted new contract with NHS Trust) and *Kenny v South Manchester College* [1993] IRLR 265 transfer when arrangement to provide prison education services switched from local authority to further education college. One industrial tribunal case casts doubt on the contractor to contractor transfer theory, ie *Unison v* (1) *Leeds City Council* (2) *City of Leeds College of Music* COIT 17611/94. The tribunal decided there were actually *two* transfers, outgoing contractor to customer and customer to contractor, *sed quaere*. Of course, our analysis that there is a direct changeover from outgoing service provider to incoming service provider without going through the customer is dependent on a direct changeover of management between outgoing contractor and incoming contractor. If, for example, during the changeover process, the customer became involved in management it *would* in fact become a transferee before re-letting the contract to the incoming contractor (at that stage being of course a transferor). Such was the case in the recent, unreported case of *Vaux Breweries Ltd v Tutty* (EAT/33/95, 18 April 1996). On the facts, it involved two transfers. Tutty was employed as steward of the River Wear Social Club (employer, River Wear Social Club Limited). When the club got into financial difficulty the Vaux Brewery gave financial assistance to the pub in view of its contractual arrangements concerning sale of products, leading to a mortgage of the club's premises to the brewery and eventually, participation by the sales manager of the brewery in management of the club. Eventually the club was sold to Messrs Jones and Howarth. But before then, in December 1993, Mr Tutty was asked to leave the club and the club continued to trade, managed in effect by the brewery until February 1994 when contracts were exchanged with Messrs Jones and Howarth, completion taking place on 11 March. Instead of their being a transfer directly between River Wear Social Club Limited and Jones and Howarth there was, in the meantime, a transfer back to the facilitator of the eventual sale, Vaux, in view of the assumption of active management of the club between December and February by the brewery. Accordingly, liability for Mr Tutty's claim rested with the brewery. But the result is entirely consistent with the analysis above. The third party (Vaux) became involved in management and so was a transferee.

[5] Case Numbers C-171/94 and C-172/94, [1996] IRLR 467.

[6] [1996] IRLR 51.

8.28 The matter is a little complicated by the requirement in the Directive that there must be a transfer resulting from 'a conventional sale or from a merger'. How can such a 'legal' transfer or merger take place between, say, an outgoing and incoming contractor where there is no legal nexus between them? The requirement was skilfully and purposively clarified in the case of *Dr Sophie Redmond Stichting v Bartol*: C-29/91.[1] In this case it will be remembered that a local authority decided to terminate its subsidy to one charitable foundation and to switch it to another charitable foundation. It was held that there was a transfer of an undertaking between these respective charitable foundations even though there was no contract (in the sense understood in English law) or legal transfer between them.

[1] [1992] IRLR 366, ECJ.

8.29 Advocate General Van Gerven reasoned as follows:

> '. . . the court effectively accords a great deal of significance to the concept of a "legal transfer". It suffices that the transfer "occurs on the basis of a contract", even if, according to the Court . . . from the judgment in *Berg*, a transfer in a case where the business is restored to the former employer, follows a termination "resulting from an agreement between the contracting parties or a unilateral declaration by one of them or indeed a judicial decision". According to the judgments in *Daddy's Dance Hall* and *Bork*, it is not even necessary that there should be an agreement between the transferor and the ultimate transferee.

> Was the transfer of Sophie Redmond to Sigma effected (broadly) on the basis of a contract?
>
> On this point I would like to draw a parallel with the case of the law of the court on competition law. As is well known, the court interprets the concept of "agreement" within the meaning of Article 85(1) of the Treaty very broadly so as to render *as effective as possible* the prohibition or practices which restrict competition set out in that provision. Consequently, "gentleman's agreements" have also been considered constituting agreements within the meaning of Article 85(1) given that such agreements constitute a faithful expression of the common intent of the parties to the agreement with respect to their conduct in the common market. It follows that for Article 85(1) to apply it suffices that there be consensus between the parties (oral or in writing, express or implied) to enter into a reciprocal arrangement to restrict their freedom of movement in the market with a view to restricting competition.
>
> It seems to me that, in order to render the rules set out in the Directive as effective as possible, the element of consensus between the parties also plays a decisive role in the assessment of the requirement for a "contract" within the meaning of the Directive in question. If it seems that agreements exist between the parties relating to the transfer of the undertaking in question or, where appropriate, of the business or part of the business, in my opinion, the Directive does apply even if, as in the judgment of *Berg* . . . this transfer specifically follows unilateral declarations by one of the parties or the act of a third party (in that case a judicial decision). As appears from the judgment in *Bork* it is of decisive importance that the undertaking is finally restored to a transferee who continues to operate it, even if there is no agreement between the transferee and the initial owner of the undertaking'.

It is also material to note that the court itself in that case also said:

> 'Nor is the Directive prevented from applying by the fact that the relevant decision is taken unilaterally by the public body rather than agreement with the body subsidised. There is equally a unilateral decision where an owner decides to change a lessee, a situation which the court has held before within the scope of the Directive'.[1]

[1] In any event, in the revised Directive (adopted by the Commission in September 1994), the prerequisite of a legal transfer or merger is dropped. The Directive is expressed to apply to 'the transfer of an undertaking, business or part of a business to another employer effected by contract or by some other disposition or operation of law, judicial decision or administrative measure'.

Implication for contracting out, market testing, facilities management and other atypical transfers

8.30 Contracting out and market testing has become a major commercial issue in recent times. Contracting out has taken place in the past of course. Private sector organisations have, always, considered contracting out in the areas for example of catering, cleaning, maintenance and such like. In the case law in relation to contracting out in such areas however the trend was, on the whole, against there being a transfer of an undertaking.[1] The high water mark of this is always said to have been *Port Talbot Engineering Co Ltd v Passmore and Evans*.[2] But contracting out could always *in theory* have fallen within the definition of a business transfer. A good example here is *Rastill v Automatic Refreshment Services Ltd*.[3]

[1] See eg cases discussed in McMullen, *Business Transfers and Employee Rights* ch 4; *Robert Seligman Corpn v Baker* [1983] ICR 770, EAT; *Curling v Securicor Ltd* [1992] IRLR 549, EAT.
[2] [1975] ICR 234.
[3] [1978] ICR 289, EAT.

8.31 Now there are new areas where contracting out/market testing is occurring. These include local government,[1] central government[2] and the National Health Service,[3] as well as in the private sector where, in the latter case there is increasing concentration on the core business and outsourcing of ancillary functions.

[1] See compulsory competitive tendering under the Local Government Planning and Land Act 1980 and the Local Government Act 1988 and the Local Government Act 1992. See Deregulation and Contracting Out Bill 1994. See also *The Role of Competitive Tendering in the Efficient Provision of Local Services (Local and Regional Authorities in Europe, No 49)*, Council of Europe, 1993. At the time of writing, a research paper published by the Equal Opportunities Commission, *The Gender Impact of CCT in Local Government* by K E Scott and D Whitfield (EOC, 1995) is exciting some interest.
[2] See the *Government's Guide to Market Testing*, HMSO 1993; *The Citizen's Charter*; 2nd Report 1994.
[3] See White Paper, 'Competing for Quality: Better Public Services' (CM 1730). There is also extensive discussion of the issues of contracting out in the *Financial Times* and *The Times* since 1992/93 and the references to specific contracting out issues and government departments involved are too numerous to mention in this footnote.

8.32 Against the backdrop of increasing externalisation of service functions, the law has radically changed. In short it has swung completely in the opposite direction towards a likelihood of a transfer of an undertaking in such cases. Thus in the European Court case of *Rask and Christensen v ISS Kantineservice AS*: C-209/91,[1] a private company (Phillips) decided to contract out the management of a canteen facility to a private contractor for a fee. It was held by the European Court that such a transaction could amount to a transfer of an undertaking. In particular, in the opinion of the European Court it did not matter whether the service was performed exclusively for the owner of the undertaking; the owner of the undertaking continued to own assets; or the owner of the undertaking was under some obligation (whether statutory or contractual (eg to employees)) to provide the service concerned.[2]

[1] [1993] IRLR 133, ECJ.
[2] Nor did it matter that a degree of control was retained by the transferor (see also *Birch v* (1) *Nuneaton and Bedworth Borough Council* (2) *Sports and Leisure Management Ltd* [1995] IRLR 518, EAT).

8.33 The principal test was whether there was a transfer of an economic entity retaining its identity after the transfer compared with the activities carried on before.

8.34 This broad approach was followed in subsequent cases both in the ECJ and the UK Courts.

8.35 In *Kenny v South Manchester College*[1] the High Court held in an Order 14A (of the RSC) hearing that the wide construction of the Directive in *Rask* meant that a 'realistic and robust' view must be taken in favour of employees. The High Court therefore had no hesitation in holding that the transfer of prison education services from a local education authority to a further education corporation following competitive tendering was a transfer of an undertaking.

1 [1993] IRLR 265.

8.36 In *Porter and Nanyakkara v Queen's Medical Centre*[1] the issue arose out of the unfortunate matter of Beverley Allitt, a nurse employed at the Grantham and Kesteven General Hospital who was charged with the murder of a number of babies. After an enquiry the regional health authority asked the two relevant district health authorities to provide an alternative provider of paediatric and neo-natal services. Accordingly the authorities terminated their arrangements with Grantham and Kesteven General Hospital and instead entered into an NHS contract with the Queen's Medical Centre (an NHS Trust) for the further provision of paediatric services. It was held, applying the test in *Dr Sophie Redmond* and *Rask*, that there was a transfer of an undertaking between respective providers of the services. The undertaking providing these services had retained its identity through the change of provider and thus had satisfied the criteria set down by the ECJ. In this case, it seemed immaterial that there was no contractual nexus between outgoing provider and incoming provider. There was a relevant transfer under the Directive (the employees lost, in the event, on the interpretation of another aspect of the Directive).

1 [1993] IRLR 486.

8.37 In both *Kenny* and *Porter* there was a transfer even though there was no legal relationship between the outgoing and incoming contractor and it was accepted that there could be a transfer even though the services provided by the contractor following the transfer were performed in a slightly different manner. But as long as there was the transfer of an economic entity retaining (in substance) its identity the Directive would apply.

8.38 Meanwhile, in the EAT, in *Dines v (1) Initial Health Care Services Ltd (2) Pall Mall Services Group Ltd*[1] the case of a changeover of cleaning contractors providing services to Orsett Hospital came to be decided. One of the key arguments which influenced the EAT was the notion that there had to be a nexus of some sort between outgoing contractor and incoming contractor. We have already dealt with this point at para 8.27 above. We have argued that such a nexus was not essential. This view has recently been vindicated by the European Court in *Merckx* (see para 8.27). A second point was that there was between this particular transferor (outgoing contractor) and transferee (incoming contractor) a lack of assets transfer. This in the view of the EAT was a particularly important point against the transfer of an undertaking. Accordingly, the EAT decided that there was no transfer. Shortly afterwards, however, the referral to the European Court in *Christel Schmidt v Spar und Leihkasse der früheren Ämter Bordesholm, Kiel und Cronshagen*: C-392/92[2] was decided. In this case, the European court considered the outsourcing by a bank of the cleaning of one of its branches. Only one part-time cleaner was involved in cleaning a branch on behalf of the bank before it decided to outsource the cleaning of the branch to a private contractor. Mrs Christel Schmidt asserted rights under the Acquired

Rights Directive against the cleaning contractor when the contractor took over. It was held that there could be a transfer of an undertaking in such a circumstance. It was first, immaterial that there was only one person engaged in the undertaking providing the services concerned and secondly, the Court confirmed that the contracting out of a cleaning function was certainly within the meaning of the Directive. The Court was faced with strong arguments that as no assets had been transferred from transferor (the bank) to the transferee (the contractor) this was a powerful argument against a transfer of an undertaking. But the Court replied as follows:

> 'The arguments of the Government of the Federal Republic of Germany and of the United Kingdom based on the absence of any transfer of tangible assets cannot be accepted . . . The fact that in its case law, the Court includes a transfer of such assets among the various factors to be taken into account by a national court to enable it, when assessing a complex transaction as a whole, to decide whether an undertaking has in fact been transferred does not support the conclusion that the absence of these factors precludes the existence of a transfer. The safeguarding of employees' rights, which constitutes the subject matter of the Directive as is clear from its actual title, cannot depend exclusively on consideration of a factor which the Court has in any event already held not to be decisive on its own (judgment in case 24/85: *Spijkers v Benedik* [1986] ECR 1119, at paragraph 12).
>
> According to the case law of the Court (see the judgment in *Spijkers* cited above at paragraph 11, and the judgment in case C-29/91 *Dr Sophie Redmond Stichting v Bartol*) . . . the decisive criterion for establishing whether there is a transfer for the purposes of the Directive is whether the business in question retains its identity. According to that case law, retention of that identity is indicated inter alia by the actual continuation or assumption by the new employer of the same or similar activities. Thus, in this case, where all the relevant information is contained in the order for reference, the similarity in the cleaning work performed before and after the transfer, which is reflected, moreover, in the offer to re-engage the employee in question, is typical of an operation which comes within the scope of the Directive and which gives the employee whose activity has been transferred the protection afforded to him by that Directive'.

There are perhaps two significant points to note about *Christel Schmidt*. First, the emphasis is on whether there was a continuation of identity rather than any other single factor (see the factors set out in *Dr Sophie Redmond Stichting v Bartol* at para 8.17). This considerably enlarges the possibility of a transfer of services, without more, falling under the Directive and therefore TUPE. Secondly, unlike other European Court cases where the Court is concerned to state matters of principle, leaving the application of the principles to the facts to the domestic court, in *Christel Schmidt*, the court decided that the facts were sufficiently set out in the reference to it and therefore it was enabled, in effect, to decide that on facts such as occurred in *Christel Schmidt*, there would be a transfer. In both these respects, the decision in *Christel Schmidt* is a little controversial. In particular, in relation to the question whether the transfer of an activity or function alone can amount to a transfer of an undertaking without more, there seems to be a significant difference between the judgment of the court and the opinion of the Advocate General. The Advocate General offered a more cautious approach. His view was that the issue was 'whether a particular case involves a transfer of an economic unit, that is to say an organised whole consisting of persons and (tangible and/or intangible) assets by means of which an economic activity is carried out having a specific, even ancillary objective of its own'.[3] Finally, in *Dines v (1) Initial Health Care Services Ltd and (2) Pall Mall Services Group Ltd*[4] the Court of Appeal, fortified by recent European Court decisions, including *Christel Schmidt* had no difficulty in finding that the changeover of cleaning contractors at Orsett Hospital *was* a transfer of an undertaking. The Court of Appeal, similarly, as in *Schmidt,* disposed of the argument that there was no transfer of assets. This was not a crucial factor. The power factor was the identity of the activity after the transfer compared with before. The court pointed out that certain ancillary functions such as cleaning, could not by their very nature be performed very differently following outsourcing compared with before. Therefore there was a transfer of an undertaking. Furthermore the transfer was between outgoing and incoming contractor even though it was effected 'in two phases'. As we have mentioned at para 8.27 it is now beyond doubt following the ECJ's decision in *Merckx* that *no* contractual link is necessary between transferor and transferee, contrary to what the EAT in *Dines* had erroneously thought.

1 [1993] IRLR 521, EAT.

2 [1994] IRLR 302, ECJ.

3 This idea that some level of minimum organisational framework is necessary for a transfer to occur was also taken up by two other Advocate Generals elsewhere. See Advocate General Cosmas in *Ole Rygaard v Strø Mølle Akustik A/S* [1996] IRLR 51 when he stated 'it will be for the national court to determine inter alia whether the activity transferred in the given case is autonomous from an organisational point of view in the sense that persons and possibly materials have been allocated for its completion and Advocate General Lenz in *Merckx* "... the court recognise[s] in the terms 'undertaking/business and part of the business' an underlying notion of economic entity"'. At present, the idea seems confined to Advocate General level. The revised version of the Directive approved by the Commission of the EU in September 1994 (see para 8.101) sought to change the definition of a transfer to the following (Art 1(1)): '... The transfer of an activity which is accompanied by the transfer of an economic entity which retains its identity shall be deemed to be a transfer within the meaning of this Directive. The transfer of only an activity of an undertaking, business or part of a business, whenever or not it was previously carried out directly, does not in itself constitute or transfer within the meaning of the Directive. This parallels more the Advocate General's opinion in *Christel Schmidt*, rather than the decision of the Court. But even so the distinction between activity on the one hand and activity and economic entity on the other is very difficult. The combined Legal and Social Affairs Committee of the European Parliament rejected the new definition and it has now been dropped from the proposal.

4 [1994] IRLR 336, CA.

8.39 *Christel Schmidt* has been applied with enthusiasm in the Employment Appeal Tribunal. In *Isles of Scilly Council v* (1) *Brintel Helicopters Ltd* (2) *R Ellis*[1] Morison J decided that a transfer took place following a 'contracting in'. The Isles of Scilly Council (IOSC) owns St Mary's Airport. Between 1986 and 1990, IOSC contracted out the management of the airport, including the air traffic control function. This was to a company called Brintel International Helicopters Limited (BIH). In 1990, IOSC sought competitive tenders for the management contract and a company called Airwork Limited won the tender and took over the management and air traffic control functions formerly undertaken by BIH. After the management contract was awarded to Airwork, Airwork took over all of the operations of BIH except for the fire-fighting and baggage handling which BIH continued to perform. BIH therefore continued to employ the five employees who brought the case. BIH (subsequently changing its name to

Brintell Helicopters Limited) went into administration and IOSC terminated the arrangements between it and BIH, and IOSC took the activity back in-house. Morison J held that there had been a transfer of an economic entity or the transfer back in-house (a 'contracting in'!), and he applied and synthesised recent European Court decisions. He thought that three points had to be kept in mind:

(1) 'An economic entity may well just comprise activities and employees. In the service industry tangible assets may be unimportant or, possibly non-existent. Thus for example the economic entity may consist of the provision of services where the real asset may be goodwill or possibly just the right to provide the service in question. To apply a "tangible asset test" would be wrong. Thus the contracting out of the provision of a canteen service to an outside contractor may fall within the Directive even if the contractor provided the services from the transferor's premises to the transferor's employees at prices dictated by the transferor: *Rask*. The economic entity is the provision of a canteen service at the company's premises, carried on by and through the employment of canteen staff. When the company contracted out that service the economy entity survived and was transferred to the third party so that those who did the work before were entitled to follow their work after the contracting out. This would be so even where there was only one employee of the transferor engaged on the business which was contracted out: *Schmidt*.

(2) The economic entity does not have to be the same before and after the transfer in the sense that the business had been taken over and run by the transferee. The fact that there is no goodwill transferred because the old economic entity has come to an end and the alleged transferee started up an identical new business will not of itself prevent the application of the Directive. In *Spijkers* the transferor's activities, owning and running a slaughterhouse, had entirely ceased and there was no longer any goodwill in the business. The premises and certain goods were transferred and the transferee started up a new slaughterhouse business having taken over none of the transferor's customers but all his employees bar Mr Spijkers. It was held that the fact there was a break in time between the old business ceasing and the new one starting and the lack of a transfer of goodwill did not thereby prevent the application of the Directive [or the Regulations]. The slaughterhouse business [the economic entity] was identifiably in existence after the alleged transfer in the sense that its operation was actually being continued or had been taken over by the new employer with the same or similar activities.

(3) Industrial tribunals should not be persuaded that there is one factor which is common to all cases where a transfer to which the Regulations apply has occurred. It is common for advocates to find that a particular feature was regarded as important in one case and seek to persuade another tribunal that its absence in another case is crucial. Such an approach is logically fallacious and is to be avoided. There could be no statement that in every transfer X will occur so that in the absence of X there can be no transfer.'

Morison J thought another way of putting it was 'is the job previously done by the employee still in existence?'[2]

The conclusion is that the trend in recent case law is to emphasise the question of whether the identity of the operation is similar (in broad terms) after the transfer compared with before.[3] Unless the service provider contracting with the customer for the provision of services in a contracting out, market testing or outsourcing exercise can show that the service being provided after the transfer is fundamentally different from that provided before, there is, at present, likely to be a transfer of an undertaking. This will no doubt lead to increased activity between contracting parties to apportion liabilities by way of commercial agreements.

As will be seen from the discussion in *Brintel*, above, the decision in *Christel Schmidt* has led many to interpret the law as meaning that as long as identity is preserved, an activity alone together with employees amounts to an economic entity and therefore an undertaking. This approach does at least have the benefit of certainty. At the time of writing, though, there is a body of opinion which holds that the definition should be restricted and the position prior to *Christel Schmidt* returned to. As an attempt to alter the Acquired Rights Directive in this regard failed[4] it is possible that the European Court itself could always clarify its thinking in *Christel Schmidt*.

In C-48/94: *Ole Rygaard v Strø Mølle Akustik A/S*,[5] Mr Rygaard was employed by a firm of carpenters, Svend Pedersen A/S which had a contract with SAS Service Partner A/S for the construction of a canteen. Svend Pedersen then informed its customer that it wanted another contractor to finish off the contract. The new contractor, Strø Mølle submitted a tender which was then accepted. On 31 January 1992 Svend Pedersen sent Mr Rygaard a letter giving him notice that he would be dismissed on 31 January 1992. In the letter the employer gave notice of its intention to wind up the firm and informed him that the outstanding works under the contract would be taken over by Strø Mølle. It went on to state that with effect from 1 February 1992 Mr Rygaard would be transferred to the sub-contracting firm which would continue to pay him until the end of the employment relationship.

On 10 February 1992 Strø Mølle took over the work. Mr Rygaard continued to work for Strø Mølle until 26 May 1992 when he was given notice taking effect on 30 June 1992. He claimed damages for wrongful dismissal against Strø Mølle and claimed the application of the Acquired Rights Directive. The local court formulated the following question for the ECJ:

> 'Is Council Directive 77/187/EEC applicable when contractor B, pursuant to an agreement with contractor A, continues part of building works begun by contractor A and (i) an agreement is made between contractor A and contractor B under which some of contractor A's workers are to continue working for contractor B and contractor B is to take over materials on the building site in order to complete the contracted work and (ii) after the taking over there is a period in which contractor A and contractor B are both working on the building works at the same time?
>
> Does it make any difference that the agreement on the completion of the works is entered into between the awarder of the main building contract and contractor B with contractor A's consent?'

The court cited the usual factors in *Spijkers*. Mr Rygaard contended that the conditions in *Spijkers* were satisfied and also that the identity of the activity on which he was previously employed had remained the same in Stø Mølle's hands. However, the court ruled that this was not enough. The authorities relied upon by Mr Rygaard pre-supposed that the transfer related to a 'stable economic entity' whose activity was not limited to performing one specific works contract. Therefore there was no transfer within the meaning of the Directive.

Some commentators argue that this is a radical reversal of the approach in *Christel Schmidt* but it is to be noted that there were specific facts and that the putative transfer in this case concerned the handing over of outstanding work under a specific single project as opposed to an ongoing activity of the customer.[6]

---

[1] [1995] IRLR 6.

[2] A similarly broad approach was taken also by Morison J in *Workman Birchley v Service Systems Ltd* (EAT, unreported) and by Mummery J in *Kelman v* (1) *Care Contract Services Ltd* (2) *Grampian Regional Council* [1995] ICR 260, EAT. See also *Charlton and Charlton v* (1) *Charlton Thermosystems (Romsey) Ltd* (2) *Ellis* [1995] IRLR 79, EAT; *Birch v* (1) *Nuneaton and Bedworth Borough Council* (2) *Sports and Leisure Management Ltd* [1995] IRLR 518, EAT and *UK Waste Control Ltd v* (1) *Wren* (2) *Eastbourne Borough Council* (25 May 1995, unreported), EAT.

[3] For an example of change of identity defeating a TUPE transfer see (1) *Mathiesan* (2) *Cheyne v United News Shops Ltd* (25 January 1995, unreported), EAT. But the revised version of the Directive (if effected) (see n 3, above) may herald a return to the approach in the Advocate General's opinion in *Christel Schmidt* where a number of factors are relevant. At the time of writing the proposal (particularly with regard to the definition of transfer) has been rejected (19 July 1995) by the Joint Affairs/Legal Affairs Committee of the European Parliament and subsequently abandoned by the Commission.

[4] See n 3 above.

[5] [1996] IRLR 57.

[6] In the EAT, Mummery J, in *BSG Property Services v Tuck* indeed sought to confine it to its own facts, ie to activities under a 'short term on-off contract' (see also *Campion-Leall v* (1) *Wail* (2) *Gardner Merchant Ltd* EAT 1112/94; *Bagoban and Portugal v* (1) *West Berkshire Priority Care (NHS Trust) Services* (2) *Sense*, EAT 595/94).

8.39A And the most recent case in the European Court namely *Albert Merckx and Patrick Neuhuys v Ford Motor Co Belgium SA*[1] adopted the traditional holistic approach in *Spijkers* citing, in reliance, *Dr Sophie Redmond Stichting v Bartol* and approving, for example, once more, the statement in *Christel Schmidt* that no asset transfer is needed for a transfer to take place.

---

[1] Cases C-171/94, C-172/94 [1996] IRLR 467 (6th Chamber).

8.39B On the traditional approach, it must have been fairly easy for the Court to come to the conclusion that a transfer existed in *Merckx*. Basically, the facts were that Merckx and Neuhuys were salesmen with a Ford dealer, Anfo Motors. Ford was also its main shareholder. In October 1987 Anfo informed Merckx and Neuhuys that it was going to discontinue its activities in December and that with effect from November Ford would be working with another, independent dealer, Novarobel, covering the same municipalities covered by the Anfo dealership. Novarobel was going to take 14 of the 64 employees of Anfo. Anfo sent a letter to customers to inform them of the discontinuance of its activities and to recommend the new dealer, Novarobel. The dealership was going to be situated in another place and certain different working conditions were going to apply without any guarantee as to whether the client base would be retained or a particular turnover achieved. For this reason, Merckx and Neuhuys refused to transfer. They ran two arguments. The first was that they were entitled to refuse to transfer on account of a significant change in expected levels of remuneration (see para 8.49). They also ran the argument that there was no transfer in the first place. It is this aspect that we deal with here.

8.39C The Court re-stated its test that whether there is a transfer depends on whether the entity in question retains its identity as indicated inter alia by the fact that its operation is actually continued or is resumed. Also, the factors as set out in *Spijkers* and *Dr Sophie Redmond Stichting v Bartol* were matters legitimately to be taken into account.

8.39D In the light of those principles it was concluded that the economic risk associated with the business was transferred to another employer and Novarobel carried on the activity performed by Anfo without interruption in the same sector subject to similar conditions and it took on part of the staff and was finally recommended to customers in order to ensure continuity in the operation of the dealership. Those factors taken as a whole supported the view that the transfer of the dealership was capable of falling within the scope of the Directive. In making this finding, the court considered and rejected some propositions on behalf of Merckx and Neuhuys thus:—

- It was not relevant that there was no transfer of tangible or intangible assets.
- It was not fatal that the principal place of business was different from Anfo:

  'The purpose of an exclusive dealership for the sale of motor vehicles of a particular make in a certain sector remains the same even if it is carried on under a different name, from different premises and from different facilities. It is also irrelevant that the principal place of business is situated in a different area of the same conurbation provided that the contract territory remains the same.'

- Merckx and Neuhuys were wrong in suggesting that simply because the first undertaking ceased trading and was put into liquidation, the economic entity had ceased to exist and could not retain its identity. The aim of the Directive could not be undermined simply because the transferor discontinued its activities when the transfer was made and was then put into liquidation. If the business of that undertaking was carried on by another undertaking those facts tended to confirm rather that there had been a transfer for the purposes of the Directive.
- Merckx and Neuhuys pointed out that the majority of staff were dismissed on the transfer of the dealership. However, that again, was not fatal. Those dismissals might have been economic, technical or organisational dismissals under Article 4 (see para 8.69 below) and in any event, failure to comply with Article 4 could not affect the existence of a transfer for the purposes of the Directive.
- Finally, it was not necessary for there to be a contractual link between transferor and transferee (see para 8.27 above).[1]

[1] Further guidance may come from current referrals to the ECJ in the area of the transfer definition namely *Ayse Süzen v Zehnacker Gebäudereinigung GmbH Krankenhausservice* (Case No C-13/95) and *Simone Moll v Berhane Megshena* (Case No C-229/95). The latest referral to the ECJ on the subject of the transfer definition is *Bulut v Deutsche Bundespost* (Case No C-121/96). Also, cases are being referred to the EFTA Court on similar issues (see *Eilert Eidesund v Stavanger Catering A/S* (Case C-2/95).

The time of the transfer

8.40 It is important to know when the transfer takes place for various reasons, including whether an employee is employed 'immediately before' so to pass under reg 5 (but see the importance of *Litster* (para 8.52 for this concept), for the purpose of the allocation by the parties of their respective rights from a certain date and also for reg 10 (below) (information and consultation before transfer).

8.41 The question of date of the transfer will be a question of fact.[1] If the transaction is muddled or piecemeal or takes place in several fragmented steps, there is also a possibility that the whole transaction may be regarded as one, ie is a linked transaction under reg 3(4). Regulation 3(4) states:

'It is hereby declared that a transfer of an undertaking or part of one . . . may be effected by a series of two or more transactions . . . .'

[1] See *Mohammed v Delaney* (12 December 1986, unreported), EAT 606/86.

8.42 Many (though, of course, not all) sales of business take place by exchange of contracts after which there follows a period whereafter completion takes place. What is the point of transfer in that case? Is it exchange or completion? Some cases suggest exchange, or alternatively, regard the transfer as taking place over a period of time embracing exchange and completion.[1] But the overwhelming balance of authority favours the interpretation that *completion* is the point of transfer.[2]

[1] *Kestongate Ltd v Miller* [1986] ICR 672, EAT; *Kennedy Brookes Hotel Catering Ltd v Reilly and Cook* EAT 53/82; *Wright v A W Smith (Gosport) Ltd* COIT 17923/86.

[2] *Batchelor v Premier Motors Ltd* COIT 17295/82/LN; *Dickinson v Bryant* EAT 73/84; *Field v Henry Barnett* EAT 761/84; *Secretary of State for Employment v Spence* [1987] QB 179, CA; *Wheeler v Patel* [1987] ICR 631, [1987] IRLR 211, EAT; *Secretary of State for Employment v Galbraith* EAT 107/87; *Brook Lane Finance Co Ltd v Bradley* [1988] ICR 423, [1988] IRLR 283, EAT. And the EAT in *Wheeler v Patel* also rejected the idea that reg 3(4) (see para 8.41) could be used to link exchange and completion.

8.43 However, as explained above, a transfer, under European law, takes place on change of *management*. If this is at a different time than that timetabled by the parties, a *de facto* transfer will prevail. Thus, for example, implementation of the transaction before completion of the legal formalities is not without its complications. The Court of Appeal has held in *Dabell v Vale Industrial Services (Nottingham) Ltd*[1] that there can be a transfer of a business notwithstanding that a proposed merger is subsequently called off. Whether or not there has been a transfer of a business must be judged as at the date when the act of which the employee complains occurred, said the Court of Appeal. In this case Mr Dabell was employed by Vale Industrial Services. Vale became technically insolvent. It received an offer for the purchase of its business from Nofotec. An agreement in principle was reached and orders, machines and other items and materials transferred together with a list of Vale's debtors. Three employees of Vale, including Mr Dabell, were sent to a site under the control of Nofotec where they started work. Shortly thereafter Mr Dabell claimed constructive and unfair dismissal. Sometime afterwards negotiations between Vale and Nofotec foundered and the merger did not actually take place. It was held that at the time of the resignation Vale had closed its premises and everything had been handed over to Nofotec, including machines, customer connection, goodwill, existing contracts and employees. So there was a transfer of a business (here for EP(C)A purposes) within the ordinary meaning of the words and Nofotec had to answer the claim. This case pre-dates the European Court cases discussed earlier in the text, but is entirely consistent with them.

[1] [1988] IRLR 439, CA.

4 REGULATION 5

8.44 Regulation 5 of the Transfer Regulations provides that a relevant transfer shall not operate so as to terminate the contract of employment of an employee employed by a transferor in the undertaking or part transferred. It further provides that any contract which would otherwise have been terminated by the transfer (ie at common law) shall have effect after the transfer as if originally made between the employee and the transferee.[1] Additionally, all of the transferor's rights, powers, duties and liabilities under or in connection with a contract of employment are transferred to the transferee[2] and anything done before the transfer is completed by or in relation to the transferor in respect of the contract of employment is deemed to have been done by or in relation to the transferee.[3] The automatic substitution of the transferee for transferor in the employment relationship is consistent with the intent of Art 3(1) of the Directive. Thus in *Berg and Busschers v Besselsen*: 144, 145/87[4] the European Court said: '. . . Article 3(1) of Directive 77/187 of 14 February 1977 must be interpreted as meaning that after the date of transfer, and by virtue of the transfer alone, the transferor is discharged from his obligations arising from the contract of employment or the employment relationship . . . subject however to the power of the member states to determine that the transferor and transferee should be severally liable after the transfer'.[5] References to a person employed in the undertaking or part transferred are to be construed as meaning references to a person employed in the undertaking (or part) 'immediately before' the transfer[6] or a person who would have been so employed had he not been unfairly dismissed within the meaning of reg 8 (see below).[7]

1 Regulation 5(1).
2 Regulation 5(2)(a).
3 Regulation 5(2)(b).
4 [1990] ICR 396, ECJ.
5 The UK did *not* include joint or several liability or in TUPE. A revised version of the Directive makes joint liability mandatory in certain circumstances. The Scottish EAT held in *Allan v Stirling District Council* [1994] IRLR 208 that the transferor was jointly liable with the transferee. But this was doubted in *Ibex Trading Co Ltd v Walton* [1994] IRLR 564 and overturned by the Court of Session [1995] IRLR 301.
6 Regulation 5(3).
7 Regulation 5(3) as supplemented by words implied by the House of Lords in *Litster v Forth Dry Dock and Engineering Co Ltd* [1989] IRLR 161, HL in order to interpret the Transfer Regulations in accordance with the terms of the Acquired Rights Directive as explained by the European Court in *P Bork International A/S v Foreningen af Arbejdsledere i Danmark*: 101/87 [1989] IRLR 41, ECJ (see below).

8.45 Under these provisions the following are likely to be transferred under reg 5 to a transferee when a relevant transfer has taken place:

(1) All contractual liabilities in relation to employees.[1]
(2) Statutory employment rights, eg redundancy seniority, continuity of employment, the right to claim unfair dismissal and other statutory rights such as the right to return to work after maternity leave that depend upon continuous service.[2] This is because, if the contract is transferred, continuity will be preserved on transfer and continuity previously recognised. The Transfer Regulations therefore probably duplicate protection about preservation of continuity on business transfers existing in the ERA.[3]
(3) Very possibly, liability to an employee in tort.[4]
(4) *Semble* liability to an employee on complaint by him of non-payment of a protective award obtained by a trade union under the Employment Protection Act 1975, s 100.[5]

[1] Regulation 5(2).

[2] For example unfair dismissal and redundancy payments seniority: *Apex Leisure Hire v Barratt* [1984] ICR 452, EAT; and race and sex discrimination: HL Official Report (5th series) col 1497 (10 December 1981). See, recently *Green-Wheeler v Onyx UK Ltd* EAT 925/92.

[3] Above, and see ERA, s 218(2).

[4] Arising out of obiter comments in *Secretary of State for Employment v Spence* [1987] QB 179, [1986] ICR 651, CA. Thus the wording of the Transfer Regulations and the Directive could allow for a transfer of a personal injury claim in tort, or under the implied term in the employment contract regarding employee safety (*Wilson v West Cumbrian Health Care National Health Service Trust*, Newcastle County Court (3 August 1994, unreported).

[5] Arising out of obiter comments in *Angus Jowett & Co Ltd v National Union of Tailors and Garment Workers* [1985] ICR 646, EAT.

8.46 However, the following are not transferred to the transferee, ie:

(1) An industrial training board levy.[1]

(2) A protective award in favour of a recognised trade union under s 189 of TULR(C)A.[2]

(3) Rights under or in connection with an occupational pension scheme (reg 7)[3]. Although this is the case, TURERA amended reg 7 by stipulating that provisions of occupational pension schemes which do not relate to benefits for old age, invalidity or survivors' benefits are not to be treated as being part of an occupational pension scheme and are therefore not excluded from the operation of Reg 5. Finally, under this heading those potential transferees tendering for contracts in relation to Government, local authority, and NHS market tests have been met with requests to honour transferring employees' pension rights notwithstanding reg 7. The legal basis for this request is probably slender. The argument is that if pension rights are left behind with the transferor, there may be a residual claim for constructive dismissal against the transferor, which he should therefore seek to avoid by asking a transferee to adopt the pension responsibilities. This has never been tested, and, with respect, may be wrong. But it is set out in the *Government's Guide to Market Testing*. Commercially, of course, there may be other pressures on a bidder to make available respectable pension rights to transferring employees.

(4) Criminal liability.[4]

Transfer of certain other rights enjoyed during employment can also cause logistical problems. This is particularly so in the case of rights tailored to the transferor's identity, such as commission schemes (eg those dependent on a transferor company's profits (or even those of a group company)), restrictive covenants, stock options and job titles.[5]

[1] *Plastics Processing Industry Training Board v Norsk Hydro Polymers* (3 December 1984, unreported), QBD.

[2] *Angus Jowett & Co Ltd v National Union of Tailors and Germent Workers* [1985] ICR 646, EAT.

[3] Some controversy was for a while generated by the saga of *Walden Engineering Co Ltd v Warrener* (industrial tribunal) [1993] 3 CMLR 179, [1993] ICR 967, EAT. In the original industrial tribunal case the facts were that the transferor ran a contracted out occupational pension scheme. It then transferred its business. The transferee did not continue the occupational pension scheme. A notice was issued to all employees transferred to the effect that they would be contracted back into the State Earnings Related Pension Scheme (SERPS) following the transfer. The employee brought a claim under s 11 of the EP(C)A asking for a declaration as to what his terms and conditions of employment were because he was concerned that the new employer was not meeting the level of benefits previously enjoyed under the transferor's occupational pension scheme. Prima facie of course reg 7 excludes these matters from transfer.

But the applicant argued that whatever reg 7 said, it was necessary to construe the Regulations in the light of the Acquired Rights Directive and in particular Art 3(3) which states as follows:

> 'Paragraphs 1 and 2 shall not cover employees' rights to entitlements to old age invalidity or survivors benefits under supplementary company or inter-company pension schemes outside the statutory social security schemes in member states. Member states shall adopt the measures necessary to protect the interests of employees and of persons no longer employed in the transferor's business at the time of the transfer within the meaning of article 1(1) in respect of rights conferring on them immediate or prospective entitlement to old age benefits, including survivors benefits, under supplementary schemes referred to in the firm paragraph.'

Looking at this, the applicant argued that a purposive interpretation of reg 7, while not requiring the transferee to cause the individual to remain a member of the same pension scheme prior to the transfer, did require the transferee to provide the same or equivalent pension benefit terms as previously enjoyed. He also argued that the transferor's pension scheme was not a supplementary scheme. Rather, it stood in substitution for the state scheme. This was because it was contracted out of SERPS. The Tribunal accepted the submissions and held that the contracted out pension scheme of the transferor was not a supplementary scheme and therefore the applicant was entitled after the transfer to pension benefits no less favourable than those which he had enjoyed as a member of the transferor's scheme. This was followed by the Bristol Industrial Tribunal in *Perry v Intec Colleges Ltd* [1993] IRLR 56 (where more persuasive reasoning was applied).

However, the EAT decided in *Warrener* [1993] IRLR 420 that the industrial tribunal decision should be reversed. The EAT therefore ruled that pension rights do not transfer to a transferee.

The precise reasoning of the EAT was as follows:

(1) A contracted out occupational pension scheme is a supplementary pension scheme within the meaning of Art 3(3) of the Acquired Rights Directive and therefore the exclusion of occupational pension schemes from TUPE under reg 7 is in line with European law.

(2) The EAT also said that the troublesome wording of Art 3(3) of the Acquired Rights Directive which does appear to require member states to take measures to 'protect the interests of employees and persons no longer employed in the transferor's business at the time of the transfer within the meaning of Art 1(1) in respect of rights conferred on them in respect of immediate or prospective entitlement to old age benefits including survivors' benefits under supplementary schemes referred to in the first sub-paragraph' simply means member states must protect any pension scheme rights which crystallise at the time of transfer and the true meaning of Art 3(3) is that this creates no liability for the transferor or transferee. In this respect, *Perry v Intec Colleges Ltd* was disapproved.

In *Adams v (1) Lancashire County Council (2) BET Catering Services Ltd* [1996] IRLR 154 it was even more convincingly decided in the High Court that pension rights were validly excluded by Reg 7 (although an appeal was lodged).

[4] Regulation 5(4).

[5] There are many issues here. Transfer of a stock option, for example, is in practice extremely problematic anyway since the shares over which the option arises will exist in the transferor company (or even its parent) and they could not in fact be exercised against the transferee. Presumably as with profit-sharing schemes (see below) the transferee would have to introduce a similar scheme or compensate for the breach of contract arising from non-provision of the benefit. The wording of the scheme will, however, often ensure the right is not transferred to a new employer. It is arguable that a collateral contract arises to carry the stock option rights; not the contract of employment. And reg 5 may not transfer the collateral contract, only the contract of employment (although cf the Directive which is wider, covering rights under the employment *relationship*). This follows from *Chapman and Elkin v CPS Computer Group plc* [1987] IRLR 462, CA where in fact the employees were not prejudiced because, notwithstanding the business transfer, the employees were able to exercise rights against the transferor. They were contained in a collateral contract which was to exercise rights against the transferor. They were contained in a collateral contract which was not transferred. The scheme allowed exercise of the rights on 'redundancy'. Although a business transfer had taken place, negativing redundancy dismissals, this did not affect rights under the scheme; consider the position, too, if the scheme provides for lapse on disposal of a company or business (*Thompson v ASDA-MFI Group plc* [1988] Ch 241, [1988] IRLR 340). However, the decision in *Chapman* was aimed at preserving the option rights the employees wanted to trigger against their old employer. If an employee wanted to assert transfer of such rights to a transferee the writer is not at all sure that they would not be considered rights under or in connection with the employment contract.

What happens, also, to a profit-sharing scheme? This is likely to be in the contract of employment. But the scheme obviously cannot be transferred—it relates to the transferor's profits. Is, again, the transferee obliged to set up a similar scheme? Presumably so.

Restrictive covenants pose the same sort of problem. There seems no doubt why in principle they should not transfer but there may be problems with their working if they do. To be noted is the practical approach taken by the Court of Appeal in *Morris Angel & Son Ltd v Hollande* [1993] IRLR 169 (restrictive covenant enforceable by plaintiff transferee to prevent defendant employee from doing business with persons who had in the previous year done business with transferred *undertaking*, rather than with the transfer itself).

8.47 In addition, the transferee can acquire dismissal liability. First, if the Regulation applies, and the transferor has done nothing to terminate the contract of employment before the point of transfer and a transferee refuses to engage the employees, he will have dismissed them, probably constructively, and so he will be liable for all potential claims arising out of any dismissal. Secondly, the transferee could be liable for pre-transfer dismissal liability where the dismissal is effected by the transferor probably, this time, under reg 5(2)(b).[1] Whether this will happen will depend on whether either the employee is employed in the undertaking 'immediately before' the transfer (which will usually not be the case) or whether, if not, the pre-transfer dismissal falls foul of reg 8. If so, liability will be transferred (see *Litster v Forth Dry Dock and Engineering Co Ltd*,[2] below). If not, the transfer of liability will depend on the employee being employed at the point of (or immediately before the) transfer under the rule in *Secretary of State for Employment v Spence*[3] (see below). The EAT in Scotland did at one time suggest, in *Allan v Stirling District Council*[4] that liability for an automatically unfair dismissal under reg 8 could also attach to a *transferor*. While reg 5(2)(a) says employment obligations *shall* be transferred to the transferee, reg 5(2)(b) is worded differently. It says things done by a transferor shall be *deemed* to have been done by a transferee. It did not mean that this was to the *exclusion* of the transferor's liability. *Berg and Busschers* (see above), said the EAT was only expressly concerned with the type of liability under reg 5(2)(a). This ambitious interpretation was overruled by the Court of Session and the liability on transfer stays firmly with the transferee.[5]

---

1 Regulation 5(2)(b) provides that the transferee inherits liability for acts of the transferor. It could also cover matters such as breaches of contract or grievances. A recent example of this is to be found in *DJM International Ltd v Nicholas* [1996] IRLR 76 where a transferee was held liable for a complaint of discrimination which arose against a transferor even though this was not under the current contract of employment of the transferring employee but under a contract of employment which preceded it. As Regulation 5 transfers not only contractual liabilities but also liability for acts done by a transferor in relation to an employee it does not matter that this may not be under a current employment contract.

2 [1989] IRLR 161, HL.

3 [1987] QB 179, [1986] ICR 651, CA.

4 [1994] ICR 434, EAT.

5 [1995] IRLR 301.

8.48 Can an employee object to transfer? If so, what are his rights? The European Court of Justice in *Katsikas v Konstantinidis*: C-132, 138, 139/91[1] held that it was not inconsistent with the Directive for member states to provide for a right of objection to the transfer of the employment contract on the part of the individual. However, the European Court left it to member states to determine under national law what was the fate of the employment contract on such an occasion. By TURERA[2] it was made clear that in the event of an employee objection to the employment with the transferee such objection shall operate so as to terminate the contract of employment with the individual but he shall not be treated for any purpose as having been dismissed by the transferor. It therefore follows that employees may object but if they do, they lose all dismissal rights and cannot therefore claim terminal payments from the transferee or transferor.

1 [1993] IRLR 179, ECJ.
2 TUPE, reg 5(4A) as inserted by TURERA, s 33(4).

8.49 Finally, reg 5(5) allows an employee to resign from the employment of a transferee if there is a 'substantial change in his working conditions to his detriment'. Certainly, if an employee has been constructively dismissed under the definition in the EPCA 1978 (ie he is faced with a fundamental breach of contract on the employer's part) he may trigger his rights under reg 5. The question remains whether reg 5(5), referring to change of 'working conditions' is more widely drawn than the traditional definition of constructive dismissal. In *Dabell v Nofotec Ltd*[1] the EAT thought that the test in reg 5(5) was independent of the domestic law of constructive dismissal. Regulation 5(5) followed European law and therefore *enlarged* employee rights rather than was simply descriptive of employee rights. It is submitted that this is correct.

1 EAT 22/92, unreported. See recently *Merckx v Ford Motors Co Belgium SA* (Cases 171/94, C-172/94 [1996] IRLR 467, ECJ).

8.50 The identity of the transferee per se will not ground such a claim (unless, under reg 5(5), the change is significant and to the employee's detriment). As, after TURERA, the employee exercising his right to object to a transfer will lose all rights against the transferor and transferee (his objection will not be deemed to have been a dismissal) more attention may be paid by employees to reg 5(5).

Liabilities passing to a transferee, including liability for pre-transfer dismissals

8.51 As has been seen, the effect of reg 5 is to pass all liabilities in relation to transferred employees to the transferee. What often happened in practice in the early days of TUPE though, is that the transferor and transferee contrived that the employees were not covered by reg 5 by trying to make sure that the employees were not employed in the undertaking immediately before the transfer because of a pre-transfer dismissal. This was done with the aim that they would not be transferred under reg 5 and the employees might be re-engaged by the transferee without the transferee having to adopt existing contracts of employment. If this scheme were to work, any liability for a pre-transfer dismissal would in those circumstances also lie with the transferor from whom the employee would also be expected to claim all termination payments, viz accrued wages, holiday pay, sick pay, notice payments, redundancy payments and unfair dismissal compensation (if any) from the transferor.

8.52 This blatant attempt to undermine TUPE was halted by the decision of the House of Lords in *Litster v Forth Dry Dock and Engineering Co Ltd*.[1] The effect of this case is that a transferee may be liable for pre-transfer dismissals even if the employees are not employed in the undertaking immediately before the transfer. This will be in a case where the dismissals are automatically unfair under reg 8 (see below), that is to say, they are in connection with the transfer and are not for an economic, technical or organisational reason entailing changes in the workforce. As collusive dismissals will generally fall foul of reg 8 (see below), liability for such dismissals will pass to the transferee. The reason why a collusive dismissal may fall foul of reg 8 is this. There will be a transfer connected dismissal because the dismissal would not have taken place but for the transfer. But there may be difficulties in satisfying the employer's defence that there is an economic, technical or organisational reason entailing changes in the workforce where the dismissal has taken place simply to break continuity of employment, or to ensure that a sale takes place, or to ensure that the business is more attractive to the transferee, or to obtain a better price for the business. This is especially so where there is a specific transferee in mind (see para 8.65).

1 [1989] IRLR 161, HL.

8.53 An economic, technical or organisational reason has to be one entailing changes in the workforce and it has been held (see below on our discussion of reg 8) that the necessity for the dismissal must be related to the operational needs of the business and not simply to effect the sale or obtain a better price or to break continuity. Where employees are re-engaged after the transfer or where new labour is engaged by the transferee at lower rates of pay then, patently, there seems to have been no need, in terms of the requirements of the business, to effect the dismissals, and the dismissals should be automatically unfair. If so, liability will be transferred to the transferee. In other cases, that is to say, where there has been a dismissal prior to the transfer and although a transfer connected dismissal, it is for an economic, technical or organisational reason entailing changes in the workforce (because, perhaps, prior to the transfer there has been no direction from the transferee to dismiss and there is a genuine redundancy or inability to pay wages or such like), the question of whether liability for employees is transferred to the transferee depends on the rule in *Secretary of State for Employment v Spence*[1] which provides that in such cases only employees employed in the business up to the point of (or immediately before the) transfer will be transferred under reg 5. In such cases of pre-transfer dismissal that are for an economic, technical or organisational reason entailing changes in the workforce, all liabilities will therefore stay with the transferor. Likewise, dismissals unconnected with the transfer are also governed by *Spence*.

1 [1986] ICR 651, CA.

8.54 *Litster* is best understood by looking at the issues historically. From the very beginning the tribunals were uneasy about employers being able to avoid the regulations by effecting termination of employment slightly before the transfer with a view to avoiding the effect of reg 5. So earlier cases concentrated on the words 'immediately before' in reg 5 and gave it a broad interpretation. In the view of some of these tribunals 'immediately before' did not mean a precise instance of time but could mean a period of time before the transfer.[1]

1 *Alphafield Ltd v Barratt* [1984] 3 All ER 795, EAT; *Ellison v R & J K Pullman (Retail) Ltd* COIT 10988/83; *Kestongate Ltd v Miller* [1986] ICR 672, EAT; *Dickinson v Bryant* EAT 73/84; *Bullard v Marchant* [1986] ICR 389.

8.55 However, this broad interpretation was rejected in *Secretary of State for Employment v Spence*[1] where the Court of Appeal decided that an employee had to be employed in the business right up to the point of transfer for his contract to be transferred under reg 5. The facts of that case were that in November 1983 the employer went into receivership. At 11.00 am on Monday, 28 November the workforce was dismissed and at 2.00 pm on the same day the business was sold to a company which subsequently re-engaged the dismissed workforce. The applicants claimed a redundancy payment from the transferor. As the transferor was insolvent a claim for reimbursement was made to the Secretary of State. He would not pay as he thought any liability had been transferred to the transferee in that the employees had been employed in the business, in his view, immediately before the transfer. The industrial tribunal found in favour of the employees and that the transferor was liable and therefore the Secretary of State had to reimburse. The Court of Appeal confirmed that the employees had been dismissed prior to the transfer and were no longer employed at the point of transfer consistent with the Directive (which requires employment at the 'date' of transfer) and the view of the European Court[2] and, in the view of the Court of Appeal, by a proper construction of TUPE. So it became clear from this case that employees had to be employed actually at the point or moment of transfer to be covered by reg 5 and those dismissed beforehand, however soon, were not transferred to the transferee. The Secretary of State therefore had to reimburse.

1 [1986] ICR 651, CA.
2 *Mikkelsen v Danmols Inventar A/S*: 105/84 [1986] 1 CMLR 316, ECJ; *Wendelboe v LJ Music ApS*: 19/83 [1986] 1 CMLR 476, ECJ.

8.56 It was thought that this authoritatively settled the question. Further, the Court of Session in Scotland in *Forth Estuary Engineering Ltd v Litster*[1] approved *Secretary of State for Employment v Spence* and held expressly that it made no difference that the pre-transfer dismissal was colluded at by the transferor and transferee to get round the Transfer Regulations. It still meant that the employee was not transferred to the transferee. Any interval between the pre-transfer dismissal and transfer was fatal to the application of reg 5.

1 [1988] IRLR 289.

8.57 This approach was, however, completely out of line with European law. This was expressly exposed by the European Court in *P Bork International A/S v Foreningen af Arbejdsledere i Danmark*: 101/87.[1] In this case lessees 'B' of a business were served with notice of termination of the lease by the lessor 'A'. The lessor (A) temporarily took the business back and thereafter leased it to a third party, 'C'. The employees in the business ceased to be employed before the surrender of the original lease by B. About half were re-engaged by C. A lapse of time took place between termination of cmployment by B and re-engagement by C. It was held that there could be a transfer of an undertaking under Art 1(1) of the Acquired Rights Directive in these circumstances. The problem was whether the re-engaged workers could invoke the Acquired Rights Directive to transfer their rights from B to C. This was because it was accepted that, ordinarily, only workers who have a current contract of employment at the date of transfer may invoke the Directive. This follows from the discussion about *Spence* above.[2]

---

1 [1989] IRLR 41, ECJ.
2 And from the European Court cases cited at n 2, para 8.55.

8.58 However, the European Court of Justice held that this was subject to the mandatory provisions of Art 4(1) (see reg 8 of TUPE) of the Acquired Rights Directive which provides that 'the transfer of an undertaking . . . shall not in itself constitute grounds for dismissal by the transferor or transferee'. This meant that an employee unlawfully dismissed under Art 4(1) (ie in connection with a transfer but where there was no economic technical or organisational reason for dismissal entailing changes in the workforce ('eto')—a defence not made out here because the workers were re-engaged) must be considered as still employed by the undertaking at the date of transfer. This meant, in effect, that employment obligations in relation to them were effectively transferred from transferor to transferee notwithstanding the interval between successive employments.

8.59 This obviously appeared to qualify the *Spence* case in the area of liability for employment obligations relating to employees who have been automatically unfairly dismissed in connection with a transfer if, indeed, it were applied to English law for the purposes of interpreting TUPE. The mandatory effect of Art 4 had not been dealt with in the English cases to date and had certainly been overlooked in *Spence*.

8.60 But because of the wording of TUPE (which differs from the Acquired Rights Directive) it was not at all certain whether the Transfer Regulations could be construed to give effect to the *Bork* decision. The basis of Art 4(1) is that it prohibits transfer connected dismissals where there is no eto and says, in effect, that they ought not to have happened. Hence, employees can be deemed still to be in employment at the point of transfer notwithstanding that unlawful dismissal. However, in TUPE there is no concept of prohibiting the dismissal. It is simply stated, in reg 8(1), that it is unfair. It is certainly not a natural reading of TUPE that this means the dismissals were deemed not to have taken effect. Quite the contrary. The natural reading is that such a dismissal has taken effect but it has to be compensated. So in view of that and in view of the Court of Appeal decision in *Spence*, some doubt was expressed as to whether the *Bork* decision would be applied in the UK to interpret the Transfer Regulations. If that were the case, that would have meant that the TUPE Regulations as drafted were in breach of the Directive as interpreted by the European Court.

8.61 Definitively, however, in the House of Lords case of *Litster v Forth Dry Dock and Engineering Co Ltd (in receivership)*[1] their Lordships held TUPE had to be construed to give effect to our obligations under the Directive, as interpreted by the European Court, and had to be read to the effect that liabilities and responsibilities for an employee who is dismissed in connection with an impending transfer where the dismissal is unfair under reg 8(1) are automatically transferred to the transferee whether or not there was an interval between dismissal and transfer.

[1] [1989] IRLR 161, HL.

8.62 The facts were that Forth Dry Dock and Engineering Co Ltd went into receivership in September 1983. Forth Estuary Engineering Limited was incorporated with a view to acquiring the business of Forth Dry Dock. At 3.30 pm on 6 February 1984 the entire workforce of Forth Dry Dock was dismissed with immediate effect. The transfer was executed at 4.30 pm. Within 48 hours of the dismissals it was learnt that Forth Estuary Engineering Ltd was recruiting employees. A number of former employees applied for these jobs but only three were engaged. It later materialised that the new company was recruiting at lower wages and ended up with a similar sized workforce to that employed by the transferor, which was now in receivership. As will be seen to be very relevant, it is unlikely on those facts that this transfer connected dismissal was for an eto entailing changes in the workforce. It looks collusive. In the industrial tribunal the proceedings were prior to *Secretary of State for Employment v Spence* and although there had been a small interval between dismissal and transfer, the industrial tribunal held nonetheless that the employees had been employed immediately before the transfer. This issue was not canvassed fully before the Employment Appeal Tribunal but, by the time the case got to the Court of Session, the Court of Session had the benefit of reading *Spence*, decided to follow *Spence* and held that as the dismissal had occurred before the transfer, even though only an hour before, the employees were not employed near enough to the point of transfer to be transferred to the transferee.

8.63 The House of Lords, however, heard argument about the *Bork* case and concluded that unless the *Bork* case was applied, TUPE would be in breach of the Directive, a consequence that should be avoided if at all possible. But it was doubtful, as has been stated, if, on a literal reading of the Regulations, it was possible to give effect to the decision in the *Bork* case. However, an earlier decision of the House of Lords in *Pickstone v Freemans plc*[1] had held that a purposive construction had to be given to the United Kingdom legislation that was intended to give effect to European legislation. So the way the House of Lords dealt with the situation was this. One solution was to say that the words 'immediately before' the transfer could be given a broad and flexible approach so that where there was a pre-transfer dismissal, the employee was employed immediately before the transfer. But that was not perfect and would lead to vagueness and uncertainty. Accordingly, reg 5(1), which refers to a person being employed immediately before the transfer, should now be read as if there were inserted immediately after those words, words to the effect 'or would have been so employed if he had not been unfairly dismissed in the circumstances described in reg 8(1)'. For these purposes employment was deemed statutorily to continue to the point of transfer.

[1] [1989] AC 66, [1987] 3 All ER 756, CA.

8.64 So, as previously discussed, this means that a pre-transfer dismissal, however long before the transfer, which is automatically unfair under reg 8, will result in liability passing to the transferee. Only if the dismissal is unconnected with the transfer, or (presumably) if connected, and an eto exists, will *Secretary of State for Employment v Spence* still apply. The House of Lords held (a little unconvincingly perhaps) that there was no conflict between the findings in *Litster* and the facts of *Secretary of State for Employment v Spence* because on the facts of *Spence* the workforce had been dismissed before an actual deal had been agreed and there was every possibility of the business not being sold at all. The receiver was under pressure from the Bank to stop paying wages in any event and for that reason the pre-transfer dismissals took place. As it happened, a deal was concluded very shortly after the dismissals, but it had not been certain to happen. Therefore, presumably, there was an eto applying to the facts on the pre-transfer dismissal in *Spence* (or alternatively, of course, it was unconnected with the transfer).

8.65 The immediate questions that now have to be asked in relation to reg 5 are as follows:

(1) Was the time between the dismissal and the transfer of so short a duration that the employee was employed immediately before the transfer? In effect, was the employee employed actually at the point of transfer or were dismissal and tranfer '. . . so closely connected in point of time that it is, for practical purposes, impossible, realistically, to say that they are not precisely contemporaneous' (per Lord Oliver)? If so, the contract of employment will be transferred to the transferee under reg 5.[1]
(2) If the answer to the above is 'no', that is to say there is a pre-transfer dismissal which means there is some interval between dismissal and the transfer, the next question to ask is: was there a dismissal which was connected with the transfer so as to invoke reg 8 which makes such a dismissal prima facie automatically unfair? If reg 8 is invoked, does reg 8(2) apply, which says that the dismissal shall not be automatically unfair if there is an economic, technical or organisational reason for the dismissal entailing changes in the workforce ('eto')? If there is no such eto, then liability for the pre-transfer dismissal will pass to the transferee.
(3) If there is a connected pre-transfer dismissal but it is for an eto (or if there is an unconnected dismissal), then, provided that the employee was not employed in the business immediately before the transfer (see (1)), liabilities will remain with the transferor and *Secretary of State for Employment v Spence* will apply.[2]

The concept of dismissal for an eto is more fully discussed below in relation to reg 8.[3]

---

[1] There are two points here. First, there are suggestions in *Litster v Forth Dry Dock and Engineering Co Ltd* [1989] IRLR 161, HL that de minimis intervals can be ignored in looking at whether the employee was employed 'immediately before' the transfer (yet the House of Lords accepted the result of *Secretary of State for Employment v Spence* [1987] QB 179, CA on its facts (ie eto dismissal before transfer, employment obligations not transferred)) where the interval was just three hours. So what amounts to a *de minimis* interval?

Secondly, *Spence* assumes employees have to be employed at the time of transfer rather than the date of transfer to be employed immediately before. 'Date' of transfer, though, could mean any time on the same day. And the Acquired Rights Directive refers to 'date' not time. The Court of Appeal followed the Advocate General Sir Gordon Slynn's advice in *Wendelboe v LJ Music ApS*: 19/83 [1985] ECR 457, ECJ that the 'time' of transfer was the rule; yet in the judgment of the ECJ itself in that case, 'date' of transfer is referred to. So it is not yet settled that dismissals which are not automatically unfair under reg 8 will not be passed to a transferee if they occur on the same day as the transfer. See Kerr, op cit, *Acquired Rights of Employees*.

[2] One interesting point that arises is this. Do employees have to qualify for unfair dismissal (ie have two years' employment) to fall under *Litster*? Probably so, but we will have to wait for litigation to settle the issue. The question is that the deemed existence of employees who have been dismissed prior to the transfer is dependent on the concept of them having been dismissed automatically unfairly under reg 8. But unfair dismissal requires a qualifying period, as stated. It would seem unfair that those who are short of the qualifying period and who are sacked prior to the transfer for the purpose of avoiding reg 5 should be excluded from the deemed *Litster* transfer of employment. On the other hand, Art 4(1) of the Directive allows member states to provide that '[the prohibition against transfer connected dismissals] shall not apply to certain specific categories of employees who are not covered by the rules or practice of the member states in respect of protection against dismissal'. It could therefore be argued that this unfortunately legitimises exclusion from *Litster* of those employees with short service.

[3] The question arises of course whether, to fall foul of reg 8, a dismissal has to be in connection with 'the' transfer that actually takes place or with 'a' transfer that may or may not take place. See *Harrison Bowden Ltd v Bowden* [1994] ICR 186, EAT and other cases discussed at para 8.75.

8.65A As will be discussed below, the question arises whether employees have to qualify for unfair dismissal (ie have two years' employment) to fall under *Litster*. If an employee would have been automatically unfairly dismissed contrary to Regulation 8 in relation to a pre-transfer dismissal, the employment should transfer. Of course, in relation to any *claim* against a transferee, the qualifying period would then be relevant. So a short-serving worker deemed to be transferred under *Litster* would be able to exercise any claim against the transferee not requiring a qualifying period (eg if re-engaged and offered less pay, a claim under the ERA, Part II, Protection of Wages) but if, for example, unfairly dismissed, would have to have served for two years. At least so it seemed until the EAT decision in *Milligan v Securicor Cleaning Ltd*[1] which held that the right not to be unfairly dismissed under Regulation 8 as presently drafted was free standing. The reasoning was this. Article 4(1) of the Directive allows member states to provide that '[the prohibition against transfer connected dismissals] shall not apply to certain specific categories of employees who are not covered by the rules or practice of the member states in respect of protection against dismissal'. In *Milligan* the employer argued that this legitimised the exclusion of employees from the right to claim under Regulation 8 if they had short service. But the EAT held that in order to take advantage of the potential exclusion under Article 4(1) the exclusion would have to be apparent from TUPE itself, not from simply the general unfair dismissal legislation to which it cross-referred. In TUPE there is no express exclusion of short serving workers; it is merely implicit from the fact that in general unfair dismissal law a two year qualifying period has to be served. The upshot of *Milligan* was that any employee dismissed contrary to Regulation 8 could claim unfair dismissal irrespective of length of service. However, the Government has since reversed *Milligan* by amending Regulation 8[2] to expressly exclude employees who do not meet the normal qualifying conditions for unfair dismissal.

[1] [1995] IRLR 288.

[2] Regulation 8(5) as inserted by the Collective Redundancies and Transfer of Undertakings (Protection of Employment) (Amendment) Regulation 1995, SI 1995/2587.

5 REGULATION 4 AND HIVING DOWN

8.66 There are special provisions in relation to hiving down under reg 4. Hiving down is a practice followed (in the past at least) by receivers and also by administrators of insolvent companies to facilitate the sale of an insolvent company's undertaking or part thereof. For example, in the case of an administrative receivership or administration under the Insolvency Act 1986 the following might occur. This, of course, is by way of example and is not an exhaustive survey of this practice. The receiver or administrator (hereafter receiver) of the insolvent company, A, might create a wholly owned subsidiary, B, to which the business to be sold is transferred. The employees necessary to continue the business as a going concern are retained by the insolvent company A and lent out to B in order to perform the work required by the business. In due course a purchaser, C, either acquires the share capital of B or takes a transfer of the business (from B). B of course has no employees as they remained the employees of parent A. Shortly before the acquisition of B or its business by C the receiver will have dismissed those employees. Part or all of that workforce may in due course be offered fresh employment with C but they go to C, it is planned, having suffered a break in employment rights. They make their claims for notice payments, redundancy payments, arrears of wages and so forth against the insolvent parent A. That company is unable to pay and reimbursement of those debts is made by the Secretary of State under s 182 of the ERA.

8.67 The Transfer Regulations at first glance might have inhibited this process. There might have no longer been any point in hiving down the business from A to B because under the present reg 5, employees would automatically follow the business transfer and be transferred to B. In response to insolvency practitioners' representations at the time of introduction of TUPE, reg 4 was introduced. This postpones the effect of reg 5 and a relevant transfer is deemed not to have taken place until either the wholly owned subsidiary, B, leaves the control of the parent, A, or the business is disposed of by the subsidiary, B. However, if the receiver dismisses the employees before the disposition of the business to the purchaser, C, at the behest of the purchaser or otherwise simply to ensure the sale takes place or to get a better price for the business it is likely liability for such dismissals will pass to the purchaser under the principle in *Litster v Forth Dry Dock and Engineering Co Ltd* (see above).

8.68 In practical terms there would therefore seem no point whatsoever (from an employment law point of view) in hiving down in order to side step the Regulations. Regulation 4 is therefore somewhat of a dinosaur provision.

6 UNFAIR DISMISSALS AND THE TRANSFER REGULATIONS: PROBLEMS AND PITFALLS

Introduction

8.69 Regulation 8 of the Transfer Regulations provides for automatic unfair dismissal liability in cases of transfer connected dismissals. It is based on the mandatory rule against such dismissals in Art 4 of the Directive. Its intention is to stop employers using a business transfer as an excuse for dismissals and to provide extra protection over and above the ordinary law of unfair dismissal. It is very important to note that liability for a dismissal which falls foul of reg 8 and which is effected by the transferor prior to the transfer may pass to the transferee under the interpretation of reg 5 in *Litster v Forth Dry Dock & Engineering Co Ltd* (see para 8.61). Because of this alone the question of the scope of reg 8, which was no more than obliquely dealt with by the House of Lords in *Litster*, is likely to continue to excite interest.

Finally, we should note the interesting EAT decision of *Milligan v Securicor Cleaning Ltd*[1] which decided that notwithstanding the normal qualifying period for unfair dismissal of two years, an employee dismissed contrary to Regulation 8, ie in connection with a transfer but where there is no economic, technical or organisational reason entailing changes in the workforce, could claim irrespective of his length of service. The argument went that although Article 4(1) of the Directive appears to legitimise exclusion by member states of certain specified categories of workers, if an exclusion is to be relied upon it must be express in TUPE itself. There is no express exclusion of short serving workers in TUPE itself. The unfair dismissal provisions formerly in the EP(C)A and now in the ERA which allow for the exclusion are indirectly and not directly referred to. The upshot of *Milligan* was that all workers automatically unfairly dismissed under Regulation 8 could claim, irrespective of service. However, the Government has since reversed the effects of *Milligan* by including within Regulation 8[2] an express exclusion from protection of employees who do not meet the normal qualifying conditions for unfair dismissal.

1 [1995] IRLR 288.
2 Regulation 8(5) as inserted by the Collective Redundancies and Transfer of Undertakings (Protection of Employment) (Amendment) Regulation 1995, SI 1995/2587.

8.70 If there is a dismissal in connection with the transfer either by the transferor or transferee before or after the transfer (and there is no limitation in time) the dismissal is treated as automatically unfair.[1] However, where there is an economic, technical or organisational reason entailing changes in the workforce a dismissal is not automatically unfair.[2] The reason for the dismissal is then deemed, for unfair dismissal purposes, to be for some other substantial reason under s 98(1) of the ERA, whether or not it is fair depends upon the usual principles under s 98(4) of the ERA.[3]

1 Regulation 8(1).
2 Regulation 8(2). Redundancy would certainly fall under this umbrella: *Meikle v McPhail (Charleston Arms)* [1983] IRLR 351.
3 Regulation 8(2)(b). See *Shipp v D J Catering IDS Brief* 245 (January 1983).

8.71 The provisions of the Regulation apply whether or not the employee in question is employed in the undertaking or part of the undertaking transferred or to be transferred. Thus, for example, it could cover dismissals by a transferee of employees employed in his existing workforce to make way for employees he acquires in the business which he has just bought.[1]

1 Regulation 8(3).

8.72 Regulation 8 appears to apply both to constructive and express dismissals[1] even though it is not apparent from the face of reg 8 that constructive dismissals are covered. There seems no reason why constructive dismissals should not be covered, however, as the concept of dismissal seems to interface with the concept of dismissal under the ERA which includes constructive dismissals (see Chapter 19, below).

[1] *Wheeler v Patel* [1987] ICR 631, [1987] IRLR 211, EAT (express dismissals); *Berriman v Delabole Slate Ltd* [1985] ICR 546, CA (constructive dismissals).

8.73 In many cases transfer connected dismissals will not be automatically unfair because they are for an economic, technical or organisational reason entailing changes in the workforce, eg redundancy. We now propose to look at areas where there is risk that the 'eto' defence does not apply.

Transfer connected dismissals and *Litster*

8.74 Sometimes dismissals are effected by a transferor at the request of a transferee for the purpose solely of severing continuity of employment in order that employees can be re-engaged free of previous continuous service (although such obvious tactics to avoid TUPE are less common these days). Alternatively, a transferor may dismiss at the request of the transferee in order to meet the transferee's perception of what level of staff is needed following the transfer. Such dismissals will, it is suggested, inevitably be automatically unfair and caught by *Litster*. It is true that there are two EAT decisions that would say the opposite. For example, in *Anderson v Dalkeith Engineering Ltd*[1] the transferor dismissed employees at the behest of the purchaser. Prima facie this was an automatic unfair dismissal. But the EAT held that there was an economic, technical or organisational reason for dismissal and the dismissal was, in the end, not automatically unfair. The question of fairness was to be decided under s 57(3) of the EP(C)A now amended by s 98(4) of the ERA and in the circumstances the dismissal was not unfair. The vendor's compliance with the purchaser's request was not unfair unless there was an additional oblique motive. By contrast, in *Forth Estuary Engineering Co Ltd v Litster*[2] a transferor dismissed employees prior to the transfer without an express request by the purchaser that this should occur. It was held that there was an economic, technical or organisational reason for the dismissals but they were unfair under s 57(3) because there was insufficient consideration as to the need for the dismissals bearing in mind the absence of a stipulation by the purchaser that dismissals should occur. After these cases it became attractive for purchasers to stipulate (perhaps in the vending agreement itself) for dismissals to occur prior to the transfer. This was to seek to ensure that such dismissals might be fair, as in the case of *Anderson v Dalkeith Engineering Ltd*, as opposed to the result in *Forth Estuary Engineering Co Ltd v Litster*. However, that practice is questionable and from what follows it will be seen that this is highly likely to make the dismissal automatically unfair and lead to the dismissal liability being passed to the transferee under *Litster*.

[1] [1985] ICR 66, [1984] IRLR 429, EAT.
[2] [1986] IRLR 59, EAT—see now the House of Lords' decision [1989] IRLR 161.

8.75 The important point about *Anderson v Dalkeith Engineering Ltd* and *Forth Estuary Engineering Co Ltd v Litster* is that it is assumed in those cases that the pre-transfer dismissals concerned were for an economic, technical or organisational reason entailing changes in the workforce thus leaving the dismissals to be examined solely under s 57(3) (now s 98(4) of the ERA). But, as stated, it is surely the case that those sort of dismissals would not fail at the first hurdle and be automatically unfair under reg 8(1). So held the EAT in *Wheeler v Patel.*[1] This was another case where the transferor dismissed the employee prior to the transfer to comply with the purchaser's wishes. However, the EAT held that the dismissals were prima facie automatically unfair and the economic, technical or organisational reason defence did not apply. This is because the word 'economic' in the phrase 'economic, technical or organisational' had to be construed ejusdem generis with the words 'technical' and 'organisational' and the word economic had to be given a limited meaning relating to the conduct of the business. It did not include broader economic reasons for dismissal such as the achievement of an agreement for sale. If the economic reasons were no more than a desire to obtain an enhanced price or achieve the sale it would not be a reason which related to the conduct of the business. This case has been followed in Scotland in *Gateway Hotels Ltd v Stewart.*[2] It is suggested that these two cases correctly represent the law on this point.[3] Undoubtedly *Wheeler v Patel* and *Gateway* are very important cases in practice. There is, on occasion, collusion between vendor and purchaser that employees are dismissed before the sale. But it is important to reiterate that such collusive dismissals will, because of this approach to reg 8, result in pre-transfer dismissal liability being passed to the transferee under the principle in *Litster v Forth Dry Dock & Engineering Co Ltd.* On the other hand, a genuine redundancy dismissal before the transfer should be for an eto entailing changes in the workforce and therefore not automatically unfair and should therefore not involve the transferee in liability. The question arises of how dangerous it is for a transferee to get involved in pre-transfer dismissals even if they are part of a genuine down-sizing exercise (and hence a genuine redundancy programme). In one case, *Harrison Bowden Ltd v Bowden*[4] it was held that reg 8 might be offended in relation to a pre-transfer dismissal even where no single prospective transferee had been identified (although a transfer was in the mind of the receiver dismissing the employees concerned). The ultimate transferee was liable. Subsequent cases such as *Longden v Ferrari Ltd and Kennedy International Ltd*[5] and *Ibex Trading Co Ltd v Walton*[6] stand for a less rigid approach, the latter, for example, holding that there was no automatic unfair dismissal of employees (and so no liability on a transferee) in respect of dismissals that took place months before the transfer, when the transfer was 'a mere twinkle in the eye' and *ex hypothesi* no specific transferee had been identified.[7] The practical advice should be that if a transferee has been identified he gets involved in pre-transfer dismissals at his own risk. In other cases if dismissals occurred well before the transfer was in mind, the risk will be less. He should nonetheless take an indemnity from the transferor if he can.

---

1 [1987] ICR 631, [1987] IRLR 211, EAT.
2 [1988] IRLR 287, EAT.
3 And it seems their approach is implicitly approved by the House of Lords in *Litster v Forth Dry Dock and Engineering Co Ltd* [1989] IRLR 161 (where it was assumed no eto applied) and by *P Bork International A/S v Foreningen af Arbjedsledere i Danmark*: 101/87 [1989] IRLR 41, ECJ.
4 [1994] ICR 186, EAT.
5 [1994] IRLR 157, EAT.
6 [1994] IRLR 564, EAT.
7 See also *Swinnock v Governor of Chester (Automotives) Ltd*, EAT 189/93.

Transfer connected dismissals and reorganisations

8.76 The problem of reg 8 dismissals is very pronounced in relation to harmonisation of terms and conditions imposed on employees by a transferee after those employees have been transferred to the transferee under reg 5. A transferee may willingly honour employment terms that may be transferred to him under reg 5. But he may have existing employees and existing terms and conditions which differ from those of the employees he has acquired. Understandably, perhaps, he may seek to harmonise terms and conditions of the transferred employees. An employer who expressly or constructively dismisses employees who decline to go along with change may, however, encounter difficulty with reg 8. Such was the case in *Berriman v Delabole Slate Ltd.*[1] Here an employee went over to a transferee under reg 5. He was then offered fresh terms by his new employer which differed from his old terms. He objected to these, but the employer insisted. This was a breach of contract. Regulation 5(5) preserves the right of an employee to terminate his contract of employment without notice if a substantial change is made in his working conditions to his detriment, apparently allowing a claim of constructive dismissal. The applicant exercised this right.[2]

1 [1985] ICR 546, CA.

2 As discussed at para 8.49, reg 5(5) appears to be *wider* than the usual definition of constructive dismissal in allowing a claim where there is a change in working *conditions* (whether fundamental contractual terms or not). As it is based on Art 4(2) of the Directive there is good ground for such a view (see *Dabell v Nofotec*, para 8.49).

8.77 The Court of Appeal held that the dismissal was prima facie automatically unfair under reg 8(1). Further, it was not for an economic, technical or organisational reason entailing changes in the workforce. For a change in the workforce within the meaning of reg 8(2) there had to be a change in the composition (or, *semble*, function, see below) of the workforce. This did not happen in the present case. There was a change merely in the terms and conditions enjoyed by the workforce and not the composition thereof. It is true, up to a point, that the composition of the workforce changed (by one) when the applicant resigned. But the Court of Appeal said that any change in the workforce must be part of the motive of the dismissal as opposed merely to a consequence of it. *Berriman* is a constructive dismissal case but the principle applies equally, of course, to express dismissals.

8.78 Nonetheless, the Court of Appeal in *Berriman* did say that where there was a change in the job *function* of the workforce this might entail a change in the workforce itself. So this might mean that where more drastic changes in terms occur (presumably where there is an issue of a completely new job description to employees) this may entail a change in the workforce because of a change in function. This has been followed in at least one industrial tribunal decision.[1] The difficulty in practice is that it may be difficult to draw the line between a job change that does not involve an entire change of job function and one that does. And of course it does seem anomalous that an employee exposed to a more drastic change of terms (because his whole job function may be different) is less protected than an employee faced with a more minor change in his terms. In conclusion, however, this discussion indicates how powerful reg 8 can be in restraining an employer's freedom to harmonise terms and conditions of his workforce in the context of transfers of undertakings. This, of course, accords with the spirit of the Acquired Rights Directive on which the Transfer Regulations are based.[2]

[1] *Lane v Dyno-rod plc* COIT 17833/85.
[2] For further examples, see *Servicepoint Ltd v Clynes and Wigfalls plc* EAT 154/88, IDS Brief 5.9.89, p 4; *Crawford v Swinton Insurance Brokers Ltd* [1990] ICR 85, EAT. See McMullen, *Business Transfers and Employee Rights*, op cit, for a fuller discussion of reg 8 and, in particular, an employer's options in attempting to introduce change.

Establishing an eto – an overview

8.79 It remains to summarise what scope there is for an employer either to argue that a dismissal is not in connection with a transfer or, if it is, that it is for economic, technical or organisational reason entailing changes in the workforce.

(1) We have already considered pre-transfer dismissals. If these are collusive, they are liable to attract the principle in *Litster v Forth Dry Dock and Engineering Co Ltd* and be automatically unfair under Reg 8 (see para 8.75).
(2) If there is a dismissal for economic or redundancy reasons prior to the transfer then arguably even if in connection with the transfer, it may be for an economic, technical or organisational reason entailing change(s) in the workforce. A workforce reduction must satisfy the requirement 'entailing changes in the workforce'.
(3) However, we have discussed that if a transferee has been identified there is a distinct risk that such dismissal will fall under reg 8 and rebound on the transferee. There is some suggestion that this could be the case even if no prospective transferee has been identified at all (thus leaving the ultimate transferee with the problem of an inherited reg 8 dismissal). But there is growing case law to counter that proposition. In any event, any transferee would be wise to take an indemnity against any possible liability for a pre-transfer dismissal from a transferor.
(4) Most transfer dismissals which do not entail a change in the workforce, ie no workforce reduction nor change in job functions of the workforce will probably be automatically unfair under reg 8 (see para 8.78).
(5) Post-transfer dismissals on the ground of genuine redundancy should be justifiable as being for an economic, technical or organisational reason entailing changes in the workforce, even if connected with the transfer. The opinion of Advocate General Walter Van Gerven in *d'Urso v Ercole Marelli Elettromeccanica Generale SpA*: C-362/89[1] would suggest otherwise. For he was of the opinion that transfer connected dismissals can never be justified. He stated:

> 'I do not share [the view] according to which the Directive permits any dismissal for economic, technical or organisational reasons. In fact, the Directive expressly prohibits such dismissals when they are the result of the transfer of the undertaking. Only dismissals which would have been made in any case, for example if a decision was taken before there was any question of transferring the undertaking, fall within the exclusion. Article 4 of the Directive cannot therefore be relied upon as support for an argument for dismissing some of the employees because the undertaking has been transferred.'

This obviously is a very strict view of Art 4 of the Directive (see reg 8). However, it ignores the express implied defence in Art 4 mirrored by reg 8(2) to the effect that transfer connected dismissals *can* be justified if there is an economic, technical or organisational reason entailing changes in the workforce. Also, the court itself did not seem to follow this line of reasoning. It stated:

> '. . . it must be recalled that Art 4(1) of the Directive forbids in terms the use of the transfer itself as a reason for dismissal by the transferor and by the transferee but that, on the other hand, the Directive shall not stand in the way of dismissals which may take place for economic, technical or organisational reasons entailing changes in the workforce'.

However, the case of a post-transfer workforce reduction came for consideration before the EAT in *Trafford v Sharpe & Fisher (Building Supplies) Ltd.*[2] It was held that such an exercise gave rise to redundancy dismissals. Whether or not connected with a transfer, such dismissals would be for an economic, technical or organisational reason entailing changes in the workforce. They were therefore not automatically unfair. In *Trafford* the EAT specifically dealt with the troublesome opinion of the Advocate General in *Marelli*. The EAT pointed out that to say that transfer connected dismissals can never be justified was to ignore the express wording in Art 4 concerning economic, technical or organisational reasons. Also, it was unaware of any decision of the European Court which gave the same construction to Art 4 as that suggested by the Advocate General in *Marelli*. As the EAT said:

> 'This tribunal agrees that a purposive approach should be adopted to the construction of Regulation 8 and that the purpose of the Directive is a social one, aiming at the safeguarding of the rights of workers in the event of a change of employer. Such an approach does not however always mean that words should be inserted to enable an employee to succeed in a claim. The rights of workers must be safeguarded "so far as possible". It is not always possible to safeguard the rights of workers. As is recognised in the second sentence of Article 4(1) the rights of workers not to be dismissed on the transfer of an undertaking must not stand in the way of dismissals which take place for economic reasons entailing changes in the workforce. In such cases the rights of workers may be outweighed by the economic reasons'.[3]

Thus genuine post-transfer redundancies *should* fall under Reg 8(2) and be justifiable as being for an economic, technical or organisational reason entailing changes in the workforce. (Such dismissals must of course be demonstrated to be fair before an industrial tribunal for the purposes of the EP(C)A).

There is no doubt that a transferee should obtain an indemnity from a transferor in respect of any pre-transfer dismissal. And if he cannot obtain such an indemnity, he involves himself in pre-transfer dismissals at his own risk. Particularly with regard to the EAT decision in *Trafford*, he may be advised, if he perceives the business to be over-manned, to take the business with its overmanning and to implement the redundancies himself. He may wish to ask, in the commercial agreement with the transferor, for a contribution towards the redundancy costs arising.

[1] [1992] IRLR 136, ECJ.
[2] [1994] IRLR 325.
[3] Other employer-oriented decisions may be found in *Sewell v DMG Realisations* (February 1990, unreported), IT and *Porter and Nanyakkara v Queen's Medical Centre (Nottingham University Hospital)* [1993] IRLR 486.

7 LEGAL CONTROLS ON AN EMPLOYER'S RIGHT TO AGREE CHANGES IN TERMS AND CONDITIONS IN THE CONTEXT OF A TUPE TRANSFER

8.79A Some of the discussion above concentrates on how difficult it is for employers to *impose* variations of contract in connection with a transfer. For if dismissals result, *Berriman v Delabole Slate* suggests that resultant dismissals will be automatically unfair unless the dismissals are not only for an economic, technical or organisational reason but *also* entail a change in the workforce or their functions (in other words, satisfy the definition of redundancy). But if the staff are still needed (and are not redundant), but in reality are needed to work on different terms and conditions, often to their detriment, any resultant dismissals will be automatically unfair.

8.79B However, it has always been assumed that an employer may *agree* a change with an employee. Perhaps one of the most significant recent developments in relation to TUPE has been the case of *Wilson v St Helens Borough Council*[1] which suggests otherwise. In this case, a community home was controlled by the Lancashire County Council. The trustees invited St Helen's Borough Council to take it over. It agreed but only if there was no adverse impact on its resources. 76 employees were offered jobs by St Helen's Borough Council under new terms and conditions. The effective date of the new contracts was 1 October 1992. On 2 March 1993 one of the applicant's unions (Unison) asked for a restoration of the County Council's terms and conditions. Thereafter, between December 1993 and June 1994 the applicants started proceedings in the industrial tribunal complaining of deductions from wages under the Wages Act (now Part II of the ERA). They claimed that the variation was ineffective and that there had been a deduction from ages under the County Council terms and conditions. The industrial tribunal held in effect that there had been no deduction contrary to the Wages Act because the employees had worked on in the face of unilateral variation and by their conduct, had affirmed their contracts. The contracts had effectively been changed and therefore there was no deduction from the wages due.

[1] [1996] IRLR 320.

8.79C The EAT rejected this, relying upon the case of *Foreningen af Arbejdsledere i Danmark v Daddy's Dance Hall.*[1] In that case it was held that whether an employee may waive rights conferred by the Acquired Rights Directive depended upon whether the reason for the waiver was the transfer. *Daddy's Dance Hall* concerned a transfer of an undertaking following which the new management altered terms and conditions. The question was whether these new terms and conditions could validly be accepted by an employee notwithstanding the mandatory effect of the Directive in preserving employee rights following a transfer. The court stated that the Directive meant that an employee could not waive the rights conferred on him by the Directive even if the disadvantages resulting from this waiver were offset by such benefits that, taking the matter as a whole, he was not placed in a worse position. In theory the new employer could make an agreement with the employee to alter the employment relationship but:

> '. . . [the employment] relationship may be altered with regard to the transferee to the same extent as it could have been with regard to the transferor provided that the transfer of the undertaking itself may never constitute the reason for that amendment.'

Notwithstanding English law principles about variation of contracts, under the *Daddy's Dance Hall* principle, if the reason for the variation was the transfer itself, it would be ineffective in so far as employees were worse off. The employees' claims in *Wilson* could therefore succeed.

8.79D The implications of *Wilson* have yet to be worked out but are undoubtedly serious. For *Wilson* seems to apply to:

— A variation apparently effected under English law by imposed change followed by affirmation.
— A consensual variation.
— A consensual variation with significant consideration.

And there is an apparent retrospective in effect of *Wilson* in that breach of contract claims may be brought within six years of the breach and claims under Part II of the ERA are not subject to the normal three month time limit for claims where there is a series of deductions. In such a case, the three month limit runs from the last in such a series of deductions.

1 [1988] IRLR 315.

8.79E Clearly, considerable attention will be paid in the courts in the near future to the possibility of arguing that any variation of contract post-transfer is not by reason of the transfer but is by reason of some external cause.[1] In the meantime, the decision is being appealed, and there will no doubt be considerable attempts to distinguish it.

1 The EFTA Court has also been asked to give an advisory opinion on whether in these circumstances an employee may legally agree to a disadvantageous amendment to his employment contract: *Langeland v Norske Fabricom A/S*, Case No C-3/95.

8 COLLECTIVE ISSUES

Collective agreements

8.80 Regulation 6 of the Transfer Regulations provides that a collective agreement made between a transferor and a recognised trade union is, on a relevant transfer, transferred to a transferee. However, a collective agreement in English law is generally unenforceable unless the parties have expressly indicated in writing that it is to be enforceable and this rarely happens.[1] This provision may therefore be of limited importance in practice at least if it is taken on face value.[2]

[1] Trade Union and Labour Relations (Consolidation) Act 1992, s 179; *National Coal Board v National Union of Mineworkers* [1986] ICR 736, [1986] IRLR 439; *Monterosso Shipping Co Ltd v International Transport Workers' Federation, The Rosso* [1982] 3 All ER 841, [1982] ICR 675, CA.

[2] An interesting conflict arises between reg 6 and its equivalent in the Directive, Art 3(2), which states that . . . 'the transferee shall continue to observe the terms and conditions agreed in any collective agreement on the same terms and conditions applicable to the transferor under that agreement, until the date of termination or expiry of the collective agreement, or the entry into force or application of another collective agreement. Member states may limit the period for observing such terms and conditions, with the proviso that it shall not be less than one year'. Is UK law consistent with this provision? See also *Bail v BET Catering* (Case No 67073/95) (IT, unreported).

8.81 When it does apply, reg 6 only transfers the collective agreement 'in its application in relation to [an] employee . . . whose contract of employment is preserved by reg 5(1)', ie not in its application to other employees referred to or covered by the agreement. This interpretation of the Acquired Rights Directive by the Transfer Regulations is supported by the European Court of Justice case of *Landsorganisationen i Danmark v Ny Molle Kro*: 287/86[1] which held that Art 3(2) of the Directive (which provides that the transferee shall continue to observe the terms and conditions agreed in any collective agreement on the same terms applicable to the transferor under that agreement) does not require a transferee to observe the provisions of a collective agreement in relation to workers not employed at the date of transfer.

[1] [1989] IRLR 37, ECJ.

Recognition

8.82 Regulation 9 of TUPE provides that where a trade union is recognised by a transferor then following a relevant transfer the transferee is deemed to recognise the same trade union to the same extent. This provision could be said to be subject to the same criticism as reg 6. For, following the Employment Act 1980 and the repeal of ss 11–16 of the Employment Protection Act 1975 (which allowed ACAS to recommend recognition against an employer's wishes), there is no legal duty to recognise or continue to recognise a trade union and again, following a transfer, recognition of a trade union could unilaterally be rescinded by a transferee.[1] It is this very point which caused the European Court to find against the UK in infraction proceedings brought by the Commission of the EC on the ground that designation in the UK of recognised trade union representatives as employees' representatives for the purpose of information and consultation rights (see para 8.89) was a defective implementation of the Directive.[2]

[1] See Employment Act 1980, s 19. Regulation 9(2)(b) implicitly acknowledges this state of affairs when it says 'any agreement for recognition may be varied or rescinded accordingly'. One theory, though, is that this means *by agreement*, so held an industrial tribunal in *GMB v Initial Cleaning* (1994) unreported. Although undoubtedly in accordance with the spirit of the Directive this conflicts with the voluntary nature of recognition in the UK.

[2] See *EC Commission v United Kingdom* [1994] ICR 664, ECJ (Case No 382/92) discussed below. It therefore needs amending by legislation so that other worker representative rights are protected (see below).

8.83 Finally, reg 9(1) provides that recognition is only transferred where the undertaking or part transferred maintains an identity distinct from the remainder of the transferee's undertaking.

Information and consultation

8.84 More important in the collective field is reg 10, which creates information and consultation obligations with appropriate representatives in the context of a transfer of an undertaking. All of the discussion which follows must however be read in the light of the decision of the European Court in *EC Commission v United Kingdom*[1] which decided that Art 6 of the Directive (on information and consultation obligations in favour of employees' representatives (within the meaning of Art 2(c)) had not been correctly transposed by TUPE in that TUPE originally confine these rights to recognised trade union representatives. Amending legislation has followed in the UK enlarging the rights accordingly as the point had not been dealt with in the revisions to TUPE in TURERA (see below). It is also arguable that even before such legislation non-union employee representatives or, alternatively, non-recognised trade union representatives need to be informed and consulted where recognition does not exist and the employer is an 'emanation of the State' (see above). For the Directive can be directly applicable in such circumstances. It would, however, have to be established that the obligations were unconditional and sufficiently precise to be so enforced.[2] References to recognised trade union representatives in the discussion which follows must therefore be subject to the above changes potential or actual.

---

1 [1994] ICR 664, ECJ.

2 The High Court ruled that similar obligations in Directive 75/129 (redundancies) were, however, not so unconditional and sufficiently precise (*Griffin v South West Water Services Ltd* [1995] IRLR 15.

8.85 We have already hinted (para 8.87 and para 8.84) at why *Commission v the United Kingdom* went against the UK government. The deregulation in TUPE of recognised trade union representatives as the sole employee representative was in line with other UK employment protection law (eg s 188 of the Trade Union and Labour Relations (Consolidation) Act 1992 in relation to redundancy consultation). However, the information and consultation obligations under Art 6 of the Directive provide for information/consultation with employee representatives, not confined to the UK concept of recognised trade union representatives. This was a plank of the Commission's case in its infraction proceedings launched against the UK in October 1992 and is one that was not, curiously, addressed by TURERA. The UK's position was that the concept of representatives of employees is defined in Art 2(c) of the Directive as meaning 'the representatives of the employees provided for by the laws or practice of the member states . . .'. Laws and practice of UK labour law is for consultation to take place with representatives of recognised trade unions only. But as recognition is voluntary, how could there be an effective system of worker representation? As the ECJ pointed out:

> 'The interpretation proposed by the UK could allow member states to determine the cases in which employee representatives can be informed

> and consulted, since they can be informed and consulted only in undertakings where national law provides for the designation of employee representatives . . . in those circumstances, UK law, which allows an employer to frustrate the protection provided for employees by Article 6(1) and 6(2) of the . . . Directive must be regarded as contrary to Article 6 thereof.'

The changes to UK labour law, as suggested above, that will arise from this decision, are profound. In response to the ruling of the ECJ, the UK Government responded with the Collective Redundancies and Transfer of Undertakings (Protection of Employment) (Amendment) Regulations 1995[1] which substantially amend Regulation 10 by providing for consultation of employees' representatives in line with the Acquired Rights Directive. In summary, the Regulations provide as follows:

(1) Employers are required to consult *either* a recognised independent trade union *or* elected representatives of affected employees under the TUPE Regulations. However, where there is a class of employees in respect of which class a union is not recognised, the employer *must* invite the employees to elect representatives.
(2) Employers may be allowed to use existing consultative machinery which could reasonably have such consultation as one of its purposes and which is based on an elective principle.
(3) Employers will not have to make standing arrangements for elected representatives. Because business transfers are infrequent, ad hoc arrangements will be permissible as long as they are effective.
(4) The Regulations do not specify any means of election, nor do they restrict the choice of who may be elected.
(5) Representatives must be employees themselves.
(6) Representatives must be allowed access to the affected employees and such accommodation and other facilities as may be appropriate.
(7) Elected representatives acquire similar rights as are enjoyed by health and safety representatives, ie the right not to be subjected to a detriment or to be dismissed on the ground that they are representatives and the right to reasonable time off without pay for these purposes.
(8) It will not be open to either a trade union or an elected representative to argue that they should have been consulted in place of the other.

Bearing in mind the representative to be informed and possibly consulted may either be a trade union representative or other elected representative, the neutral word 'representative' is used below.

[1] SI 1995/2587. The Regulations came into force on 26 October 1995 but did not apply to transfers taking place before 1 March 1996. On 15 May 1996 the High Court rejected a challenge by a consortium of unions to the validity of the Regulations (*R v Secretary of State for Trade and Industry, ex p Unison, GMB and NASUWT* [1996] IRLR 438). The arguments raised by the unions were that arrangements for selection of representatives are inadequate; organisers of an election are not protected; there is inadequate provision for facilities such as manpower, information or financial resources for representatives; no time off is allowed for organisers of the election and nor are facilities for the election of representatives guaranteed; there is no adequate provision for complaint. None of these arguments succeeded.

8.86 Regulation 10 states that long enough before a relevant transfer to enable consultation to take place between an employer of any 'affected employees' and representatives, the employer has to inform representatives of:

(1) the fact that the relevant transfer is to take place, when approximately it is to take place and the reasons for it; and
(2) the legal, economic and social implications of the transfer for the affected employees; and
(3) the measures which he envisages he will, in connection with the transfer, take in relation to those employees or if the envisages that no such measure will be taken, that fact; and
(4) if the employer is the transferor the measures which the transferee envisages that he will, in connection with the transfer, take in relation to such of those employees as by virtue of reg 5 become employees of the transferee after the transfer or if he envisages that no measures will be so taken, that fact.[1]

[1] Regulation 10(2). See also the model letter in the Appendix.

8.87 'Affected employee' means any employee of the transferor or transferee (whether or not employed in the undertaking transferred) who may be affected by the transfer or measures taken in relation to it.[1]

[1] Regulation 10(1).

8.88 There is no minimum period of time over which these obligations must take place. Information has to be provided 'long enough' before the transfer to enable consultations to take place. This contrasts with the minimum periods (up to 90 days in larger redundancies) involved in consultation in mass redundancies under s 188 of TULR(C)A.

8.89 The transferee has to give the transferor such information at such time as will enable the transferor to perform his duties under reg 10(2)(d) (see above), ie the duty to give information about what measures the transferee envisages he will take in connection with the transfer.[1]

[1] Regulation 10(3).

8.90 The information which is to be given to the representatives has to be delivered to them or sent by post to an address notified by them to the employer in the case of elected representatives or sent by post to the union at the address of its head or main office.[1] The regulation does not say that the information has to be in writing but this is implicit.

[1] Regulation 10(4).

8.91 Where measures are envisaged by an employer he has to enter into consultation with representatives.[1] If no measures are proposed then no consultation need take place. In *Institution of Professional Civil Servants v Secretary of State for Defence*[2] Millett J expressed some opinion on the meaning of the words 'measures' and 'envisages'. He thought 'measures' was a word of widest import which included any action, step or arrangement and that 'envisage' simply meant visualises or foresees. He thought that manpower projections were not measures but that positive steps to implement those manpower projections, eg by reductions in manpower levels, would be. In the course of any required consultations the employer has to consider any representations made by (presently) the trade union and reply to those representations and if he rejects any of those representations, state his reasons.[3] There is a special circumstances defence whereby if there are special circumstances which render it not reasonably practicable for an employer to perform a duty imposed on him under the regulation he has to take all such steps towards performing that duty as are reasonably practicable in the circumstances in lieu of strict compliance with the regulation.[4] This parallels the provisions of s 188 of the TULR(C)A where there is a special circumstances defence for non-compliance with the strict requirements of s 188 in the context of consultation about mass redundancies. In the context of TULR(C)A 'special circumstances' has been very narrowly construed against employers who have relied upon it.[5] It is reasonable to suppose that the provision in TUPE will be similarly narrowly construed, especially as it may be argued that the inclusion of the defence is in breach of the Directive. In the case of business transfers it may be attractive for employers to argue that they cannot fully comply with their obligations to inform and consult because of the speed that attends the sale of undertakings. This was accepted as a possibility given suitable facts in one industrial tribunal case.[6] But, as stated, in view of the suggested infringement of European law, the 'defence' should be narrowly applied until removed by amending legislation.

1 Regulation 10(5); *Nattke v Rank Leisure Ltd* IT case No 29431/82/LC, a position criticised by Millet J in *Institution of Professional Civil Servants v Secretary of State for Defence* [1987] IRLR 373.

2 [1987] IRLR 373.

3 Regulation 10(6).

4 Regulation 10(7). Although this is *not* to be seen in the Directive.

5 *Clarkes of Hove v Bakers' Union* [1978] ICR 1076, CA.

6 *Nattke v Rank Leisure Ltd* IT case No 29431/82/LC.

8.92 An important change brought about by TURERA is that only consultation under reg 10 has to be 'with a view to seeking [employee representatives'] agreement to measures to be taken'. Although this has always been European law[1] the overdue translation into domestic law will bring great change.

1 See Directive 77/187, Art 6(2). The long-running breach of European law before TURERA was enacted culminated in the breach forming part of the EC Commission's pleaded case against the UK for infraction of the Acquired Rights Directive it was one of the points on which the ECJ ruled against the UK in *EC Commission v United Kingdom* [1994] ICR 664 (although by that time TURERA had been enacted).

8.93 The remedy for failure to inform and consult is a complaint presented to an industrial tribunal in the case of a failure relating to employee representatives, by any of the employee representatives to whom the failure related; or in the case of a failure relating to representatives of a trade union, by the trade union; or in any other case by any of the employees who are affected employees.[1] In such tribunal proceedings it is expressly provided that it is for the employer to seek to show there were special circumstances, as discussed above, which rendered it not reasonably practicable for him to perform the duty imposed on him and that if so he took all such steps towards its performance as were reasonably practicable in those circumstances.[2] This 'defence' is of course subject to the criticisms made above. Also if the complaint against the transferor is that he has failed to reveal any measures which the transferee envisages he will, in connection with the transfer, take in relation to employees, the transferor may seek to show that it was not reasonably practicable for him to perform the duty in question on the ground that the transferee had failed to give him the requisite information at the requisite time.[3] In such a case, though, he must give the transferee notice of intention to show that fact and the giving of notice makes the transferee a party to the proceedings.

1 Regulation 11(1).
2 Regulation 11(2).
3 Regulation 11(3).

8.94 If the complaint by the representatives or affected employees is well founded the tribunal has to make a declaration to that effect. Further, it may order the employer to pay compensation to such descriptions of affected employees as may be specified in its award. If the transferee has been joined in the proceedings it may also order the transferee to pay appropriate compensation.[1] The compensation concerned is now a maximum of four weeks' pay (replacing the original limit of just two (sic) weeks pay) for each employee in question as the tribunal considers just and equitable having regard to the seriousness of the failure of the employer to comply with his duty.[2] No longer does any compensation awarded to an employee under reg 11 reduce any compensation entitlement under s 190 of TULR(C)A (redundancy consultation). And no longer does any remuneration payable under a protective award under TULR(C)A and any payment made to the employee by the employer by way of damages for breach of contract (such as payment in lieu of notice) in respect of a period falling within the protection period under TULR(C)A reduce the amount of any compensation which may subsequently be awarded under reg 11.[3] All of the changes above mentioned, made by s 33 of TURERA, were in response to the infraction proceedings brought by the EC Commission against the UK government on the ground that TUPE was in breach of the Acquired Rights Directive. As is well known, European law requires an effective remedy for breach, under the principle in *Von Colson and Kamann v Land Nordrhein-Westfalen*: 14/83.[4] There was, it is submitted, hardly any doubt that the previous maximum award available of two weeks, together with the employer's right of set-off, was a state of affairs in breach of the principle. It remains to be seen whether the changes go far enough to satisfy the rule in *Von Colson*, however. *Quaere* whether any arbitrary limit is in accordance with the rule.[5] (In the end (after TURERA had been enacted) the ECJ in *EC Commission v United Kingdom*[6] simply ruled that the previous unit of two weeks pay *was* in breach of the Directive, without passing comment on whether the new limit of four was adequate.) An employee may complain to an industrial tribunal that he has not been paid compensation in pursuance of the order in favour of the trade union.[7] Complaints under reg 11 and by an employee to enforce an order in favour of the trade union for compensation payable to an employee have to be presented within three months of the date on which the relevant transfer is completed in the case of the former or the date of the tribunal's order in favour of the trade union in the case of the latter, or, in either case, within such further period as the tribunal considers reasonable in a case where it is satisfied that it was not reasonably practicable for the complaint to be presented before the end of the period of three months.[8]

1 Regulation 11(4).
2 Regulation 11(11) (as amended by TURERA).
3 Regulation 11(7) (as amended by TURERA).
4 [1986] 2 CMLR 430, ECJ. And see now *Marshall v Southampton & South West Hampshire Area Health Authority (No 2)*: C-271/91 [1993] IRLR 445, ECJ.
5 Regulation 11(5) (as amended by TURERA).
6 [1994] ICR 664, ECJ.
7 Regulation 11(8).
8 See *Marshall (No 2)*.

9 CONTRACTING OUT

8.95 The Transfer Regulations contain restrictions on contracting out. Any provision of any agreement whether in a contract of employment or not is void in so far as it purports to exclude or limit the operation of regs 5, 8 or 10 or to preclude any person from presenting a complaint to an industrial tribunal under reg 11.[1]

1 Regulation 12.

10 EUROPEAN LAW AND THE ACQUIRED RIGHTS DIRECTIVE – FUTURE DIRECTIONS

8.96 There is no doubt that previous UK infraction of the Acquired Rights Directive has led to unnecessary controversy and ultimate defeat in the European Court in *EC Commission v United Kingdom*[1] on a number of points. The main complaints before the European Court in respect of the UK's alleged infraction of the Acquired Rights Directive were as follows:

(1) Its failure to provide measures enabling workers' representatives to be designated with a view to the application of the Directive in cases where an employer is not prepared voluntarily to recognise such representatives.
(2) Its limitation of the scope of its legislation designed to implement the Directive to situations in which the business transferred is owned by the transferor.
(3) Its exclusion of certain undertakings from the scope of the Directive.
(4) Its failure to require a transferor or transferee who envisages measures in relation to his employees and is under an obligation to consult the representatives of his employees to do so with a view to reaching agreement.
(5) Its failure to provide for sufficiently effective and deterrent sanctions in the case of failure by an employer to inform and consult workers' representative as required by the Directive.

In *EC Commission v United Kingdom*[1] the court found against the UK save in respect of complaint (2). By then, however, the UK had, in TURERA dealt with all of the complaints save for the complaint in paragraph (1). After *EC Commission v United Kingdom* the outstanding issue, namely the direct designation of worker representatives has also led to (as discussed above) amending legislation. As to the future, a revised Directive has now been produced by the Commission of the EU. Some principal features are as follows:

(1) A revised definition of the transfer of an undertaking.[2]
(2) A new community wide definition of the employment relationship so as to define which type of workers fall under the Directives.[3]

(3) Provision for joint liability of transferor and transferee.[4]
(4) Relaxation of the provisions of the Directive in respect of insolvency situations.[5]
(5) Improvement of workers representatives' rights in respect of transnational transfers.[6]

Whether through the continued interpretation of the existing law on transfer of undertakings or whether by introduction of new provisions, there is no doubt that the subject will be of vital and continuing interest.

1 [1994] ICR 664, ECJ.
2 See n 3, para 8.39; Art 1(1). Though this was subsequently dropped.
3 Article 2(2).
4 Article 3(1).
5 Article 3(3), Article 4(3).
6 Article 6(4).

9 Statutory sick pay

Ian Smith

The background and the scheme

9.01 Prior to 6 April 1983, an employee who was unable to work due to sickness could claim sickness benefit from the state; those unable to work due to an industrial accident were eligible instead for industrial injury benefit which was marginally more generous than ordinary sickness benefit. In addition, however, by 1983 the large majority of employees were covered by private contractual sick pay schemes under their contracts of employment[1] which normally operated by 'topping up' the state benefit to a higher level (eg to basic weekly wage, 80% of basic wage, or some other figure). The government considered this to a wasteful duplication of administrative effort[2] and so instituted as from 6 April 1983 the Statutory Sick Pay (SSP) scheme, under Part I of the Social Security and Housing Benefits Act 1982 (SSHBA). The essence of this scheme is that the employer is obliged to pay out to his sick employee a (flat rate) amount of SSP that represents what the state used to pay.[3] Under the scheme from 1983 to 1994, the employer then recouped all or most of the amounts paid out as SSP from his NI contributions, so that ultimately he paid *out* SSP, but did not pay it. Now, however, that right to recoupment has been abolished in most cases, and so it is the employer who foots the bill[4]. The employer then discharges any contractual sick pay obligation by topping up the amount of SSP to the amount payable under the contract.

---

[1] Normally, of course, any such right will be expressly set out and quantified in the contract. Difficulties have been encountered where this is not so, but where the employee tries to sue on an implied term covering sick pay; earlier case law suggested that there might be a presumption in favour of the payment of wages during sickness (*Marrison v Bell* [1939] 2 KB 187, [1939] 1 All ER 745, CA; *Petrie v MacFisheries Ltd* [1940] 1 KB 258, [1939] 4 All ER 281, CA; *O'Grady v M Saper Ltd* [1940] 2 KB 469, [1940] 3 All ER 527, CA; *Orman v Saville Sportswear Ltd* [1960] 3 All ER 105 [1960] 1 WLR 1055), but this was disapproved in *Mears v Safecar Security Ltd* [1982] ICR 626, [1982] IRLR 183, CA where it was held that there is no such presumption but that a court or tribunal must consider each case on its facts to determine the correct inference (see also *Howman & Son v Blyth* [1983] ICR 416, [1983] IRLR 139, EAT, on the quantification of an implied term). Note that by virtue of the ERA, s 1(4)(d)(ii) any term as to sick pay should be included in the written particulars of terms of employment to be given to a new employee (see Chapter 5, above).

[2] Income during initial sickness (Cmnd 7864, 1980).

[3] For the SSP scheme generally, see *Harvey* Div H; the provisions of (now) the SSCBA are supplemented by regulations, in particular the Statutory Sick Pay (General) Regulations 1982, SI 1982/894, *Harvey* Div R.

[4] Statutory Sick Pay Act 1994.

9.02 Administration of what used to be state sickness benefit is thus given over to employers. The old state benefit is now only payable to (i) non-employees who qualify, and (ii) employees who for some reason are excluded from the SSP system (see below). One other major reform in 1983 was the abolition of the separate industrial injury benefit; there is thus now no 'industrial preference' which has the advantage for the employer that there is only one applicable rate of SSP whether the absence is caused by an industrial accident, or some other accident or sickness–the employer does not have to enquire into the cause of the absence in order to operate the system.

9.03 The scheme was considered such a success by the government that it was radically extended by the Social Security Act 1985, as from 6 April 1986. As originally enacted, the scheme required the employer to pay up to eight weeks SSP in a tax year (after which an employee who was still sick had to claim benefit from the state); however, the 1985 Act extended this maximum period to 28 weeks and put it on to a rolling basis, so that it can span tax years. The net result is that the employer now administers all short-term income-maintaining sickness pay—if the employee is still off sick after 28 weeks, he must then claim from the state, but his claim will now be for the long-term incapacity benefit. Since then, the scheme has been subject to two further changes. First, with the overall consolidation of the social security legislation in 1992, all the relevant provisions are now to be found in Part XI (ss 151–163) of the Social Security Contributions and Benefits Act 1992 (the 'SSCBA'). Secondly, as seen above, the Statutory Sick Pay Act 1994 has removed the employer's right to recoup the amounts paid out from his NI contributions (unless his payments of SSP in any particular period exceed a prescribed amount).

9.04 A useful source of reference on SSP (particularly for the details of the scheme and worked examples) is the Employer's Guide to SSP (NI 227), obtainable from the DSS.

Who qualifies for SSP?

9.05 SSP is payable to an employee who on a particular day 'is, or is deemed in accordance with regulations to be, incapable by reason of some specific disease or bodily or mental disablement of doing work which he can reasonably be expected to do under [his] contract'.[1] There are three qualifying conditions, each with its own jargon.

[1] SSCBA, s 151(4). The SSP (General) Regulations 1982, reg 2 (*Harvey* Div R) covers those convalescing, infectious or on shift work; in the case of the latter, see also s 26(6) which covers shifts spanning midnights. For the qualifying conditions generally, see *Harvey* Div H.

9.06 (i) The day in question must form part of a *period of incapacity for work* (a 'PIW').[1] This means a period of four or more consecutive days (on a calendar basis); this preserves the rule, common to social security claims, that there are three waiting days before SSP is payable. This works simply in the case of one long illness, but could be harsh in the case of several periods of illness within a short period of time (though possibly due to the same cause); to prevent the three-waiting-days rule applying to each occasion, there is (again in common with other social security claims) a 'linking rule', ie that any two PIWs (of four days or more) which are separated by not more than eight weeks are treated as a single PIW[2] so that the three-waiting-days rule applies only once. A series of PIWs may be linked in this way, provided that there is no more than eight weeks between any two (though subject to an absolute maximum of three years for any one PIW).

---

[1] SSCBA, s 152.
[2] Ibid, s 152(3).

9.07 (ii) The PIW must fall within a period of entitlement (as between the employee and his employer).[1] This is basically a drafting device, serving two purposes. The first is to introduce the rules on when entitlement begins and ends. Thus, a period of entitlement begins with the commencement of the PIW and ends with whichever of the following occurs first:

—the end of the PIW (with, if necessary, the application of the linking rule);
—the expiry of the maximum 28-week payment period;
—the termination of the contract of employment;[2]
—a pregnant employee reaches the sixth week before confinement;
—the employee is imprisoned or otherwise legally detained;
—the employee goes outside the EC (other than as a seaman, airman or employee on the continental shelf).

---

[1] SSCBA, s 153, as supplemented by reg 3 of the General Regulations and the SSP (Mariners, Airmen and Persons Abroad) Regulation 1982, SI 1982/1349, *Harvey* Div R.
[2] Unless the contract was terminated 'solely or mainly for the purpose of avoiding liability for SSP'; reg 4 of the General Regulations.

9.08 The second purpose is to introduce certain exclusions from SSP altogether, by deeming a period of entitlement never to arise in this case: these exclusions are largely found in Sch 11 to the Act[1] and cover principally (in addition to those affected by the above rules):

—pensioners;
—temporary employees, employed for a specified period of three months or less;[2]
—employees whose pay is so low that they do not pay NI contributions (thus preserving the contributory nature of the scheme); in the tax year 1996/97 this figure is set at £61 per week;
—those receiving state benefits (incapacity benefit or the old maternity allowance) within eight weeks prior to the new PIW; in such a case the employee's proper course is to return to the DSS, not to claim from the employer; such an employee will have been given a 'linking letter' by the DSS when 'signed off' by them which will tell the employer when the relevant eight-week period elapses, after which the employer must resume paying SSP if the employee falls ill again;
—new employees who have not yet started work;
—an employee affected by a trade union dispute at his workplace, unless he proves that he was not directly interested in the dispute.[3]

---

[1] Sch 11, para 2.

2 This is particularly important in the case of genuinely seasonal workers, and others on short-term contracts. If, however, the period of employment exceeds three months, then the employee does become eligible for SSP if sick: Sch 11, para 4.

3 This is akin to the rule depriving those affected by a trade dispute of unemployment benefit or jobseeker's allowance; see Smith & Wood, *Industrial Law* (6th edn, 1996) ch 9 head 3. On the meaning of 'directly interested', see *Presho v Insurance Officer* [1984] ICR 463, [1984] IRLR 74, HL.

9.09 The administrative details for dealing with the above are as follows. If the sick employee's maximum period of entitlement (28 weeks normally) runs out (or is likely to within a fortnight), the employer serves on him form SSP 1(T) (the 'transfer form') which states that fact and contains details on making a claim then from the DSS for whatever state benefit is payable to take over from SSP. If the employer considers that no SSP is payable at all because the employee falls into one of the excluded categories, he serves on the employee form SSP 1(E) (the 'exclusion form') which states so, giving reasons.

9.10 (iii) The day in question must be a *qualifying day*;[1] it is left principally to employer and employee (or union) to decide which are to be qualifying days and these will normally (though not necessarily) reflect the employee's normal working days. The purpose of this requirement is to try to ensure that SSP is only payable in relation to days that the employee would in fact have worked had he been fit, though by leaving the matter to agreement (subject to residual provisions in the absence of any agreement) the scheme leaves some room for flexibility and the simplification of entitlement, eg in the case of shift work or irregular work patterns. However, one form of agreement has been banned—an employer and employee cannot agree that a qualifying day shall simply be any day on which the employee happens to be ill ('maximising').[2]

1 SSCBA, s 154.

2 Regulation 5(3) of the General Regulations.

9.11 In order to be eligible for SSP, an employee who satisfies the above qualifying conditions must notify the employer of his incapacity. The form and timing of the notification is left principally to the employer, subject to residual provisions in regulations.[1] Self certification applies for the first seven days of incapacity, after which the employer may require medical certificates, the form of which is prescribed by regulations.[2]

1 Regulation 7; for the procedure for claiming SSP, see *Harvey* Div H.

2 SSP (Medical Evidence) Regulations 1985, SI 1985/1604; *Harvey* Div R. If an employer considers that an employee is abusing the self certification system he may (instead of proceeding directly to his own disciplinary procedures) seek the help of the DSS who may investigate a case where there have been four self certificated illnesses (not progressing into a second week, and so not being medically certified) within the space of a year; see the Employers' Guide (NI 227).

9.12 One case covered by special provisions arises where an employee changes employment between bouts of incapacity. Originally, a new employee began employment with a clean slate, so that the new employer did not have to bother about any SSP entitlement with the previous employer. However, when the scheme was extended in 1986 (above) this changed. The present provisions are slightly complicated:

(i) the employee may *not* link a PIW with his previous employer with a PIW with his new employer (even if they are within eight weeks of each other); thus, he must always serve the three waiting days with the new employer;

(ii) however, the new employer may link a PIW with the previous employer if it is within eight weeks of a new PIW with him; thus, the amount of time covered by that previous PIW counts towards the maximum 28 week's entitlement vis-à-vis the new employer.[1]

[1] Regulation 3A of the General Regulations.

9.13 How does the new employer know whether there was a PIW with the previous employer that might come within the linking rule? The answer is yet another form—if an employee has a PIW ending within eight weeks of leaving employment, that employer must provide him with a 'leaver's statement' (form SSP 1(L)); this must be disclosed to a new employer by the employee if the latter is sick during the first eight weeks of the new employment and the new employer will be able to see from it whether the linking rule applies. In fact, it might be a useful practice for an employer to adopt to ask any new employee whether he has a form SSP 1(L) (or a 'linking letter' from the DSS (above), in the case of someone who has had to have recourse to state benefits towards the end of his previous employment).

What is payable?

9.14 The rate of SSP is fixed by regulations which periodically amend the SSCBA, s 157. Originally there were three rates (dependent on normal weekly earnings); this was pared down to two, but then the upper rate was pegged for several years so that the two rates converged, and finally this was altered so that there is now only one rate, which since April 1996 is £54.55.

9.15 Payment is to be made through the employer's normal payment system;[1] it may not be made in kind; any attempt to contract out of the SSP system is void.[2] SSP is taxable and subject to NI contributions.

[1] Regulations 8–11 of the General Regulations. Note that the Secretary of State may pay SSP outstanding because of the employer's insolvency.

[2] SSCBA, s 151(2).

9.16 As already seen, the large majority of employees will also be covered by a contractual sick pay scheme, whose terms depend upon the contract. Having paid out SSP, the employer under such a scheme will then top the SSP up to the amount stipulated in the contract for the day or week in question. This is a private matter between the employer and employee; any complaint would have to be taken to the common law courts, usually the county court, as an ordinary breach of contract action, or to an industrial tribunal if outstanding on termination of employment.

Reimbursement, records and remedies

9.17 As the scheme (as originally conceived) was that the employer should *administer* SSP payments (not actually foot the bill for them), there had to be a mechanism whereby the employer was reimbursed. This was done by allowing the employer to deduct an amount representing SSP from the National Insurance contributions that he was liable to pay for the period in question; if they were not large enough, there was provision for the Secretary to State to refund directly. However, as seen above, the Statutory Sick Pay Act 1994 abolished most employers' rights to recoup the amount paid out.

9.18 There remains, however, an exceptional case in which SSP can still be recouped. Originally this applied to small employers, but since April 1995 it has been altered to apply to any employer (of whatever size), who, in any particular tax month, pays out as SSP more than 13% of his liability to pay NI contributions for that month; in such a case the employer is entitled to recoup the excess.[1]

1 Statutory Sick Pay Percentage Threshold Order 1995, SI 1995/512.

9.19 The employer must keep records;[1] there is a legal obligation to keep them for three years after the end of the tax year to which they relate. Otherwise, however, they may be kept in any way thought appropriate by the employer, provided that they show the prescribed information. The DSS have a form that can be used if required and there are various privately produced packages (some computerised) available on the market.

1 Social Security Administration Act 1992, s 129(4); reg 13 of the General Regulations.

9.20 An employee has a right to require the employer to give him certain information on what the employer says is his entitlement to SSP.[1] An employee who considers that he has not been paid SSP properly may refer the matter to an adjudication officer of the DSS;[2] if the adjudication officer's decision is adverse, there is a right to appeal in the normal way to a Social Security Appeal Tribunal[3] (and then again, on a point of law, to a Social Security Commissioner). In such a case, the employer is not a party; at the end of the day, the determination will be issued to him, stating the employee's correct entitlement.

1 Regulation 15 of the General Regulations.
2 Social Security Administration Act 1992, s 20; there is a six-month time limit, flowing from the beginning of the disputed SSP period: Social Security (Adjudication) Regulations 1995, SI 1995/1801, reg 20. Note, however, that certain listed questions must be submitted to the Secretary of State (for example, whether the claimant is or is not an 'employee'): Social Security Administration Act 1992, s 17(1)(g); in the case of these questions, there is no appeal to a SSAT from the Secretary of State's decision.
3 Social Security Administration Act 1992, s 22; procedure is governed by the Social Security (Adjudication) Regulations 1995, SI 1995/1801.

10 Maternity

Barry Mordsley and Ian Smith

1 STATUTORY MATERNITY PAY

The background and the scheme

10.01 The present government have shown considerable interest in making certain social security payments through the employer, on the model of statutory sick pay, which is considered above. When the 1986 Social Security Bill was first published, it was intended to make the new Family Credit (replacing FIS) payable through the employer; this proposal was eventually dropped, but the Act as eventually passed did reform the whole area of maternity pay, producing the present system of Statutory Maternity Pay (SMP). As with SSP, the area was ripe for reconsideration with, from the government's point of view, wasteful duplication of administrative effort. The old system was that the state (DSS) paid maternity allowance to those who qualified; in addition, if the employee had been employed for at least two years the employer had to pay maternity pay (under the EP(C)A), *but* (a) the amount of state maternity allowance had to be deducted and (b) the amount paid by the employer as maternity pay was recoverable by him from the state-run Maternity Pay Fund. In addition, many employments were covered by more generous contractual maternity schemes, topping up these minimum amounts to higher levels.

10.02 This scheme, effective from 6 April 1987 and now (pursuant to the consolidation of the social security legislation in 1992) contained in Part XII (ss 164–171) of the Social Security Contributions and Benefits Act 1992 (the 'SSCBA'), repealed the previous law (including the Maternity Pay Fund) and replaced it with rights to receive SMP through the employer, who recoups the relevant amounts from NI contributions. The net result is similar to the previous scheme, but administratively simpler, and with new terminology.[1] The system was subject to further change (from October 1994) by the Trade Union Reform and Employment Rights Act 1993 in order to fit in with the EU Pregnant Workers Directive and to be consistent with the other major changes made to maternity rights generally as from the same date.

[1] For the SMP scheme generally, see *Harvey* Div J; the scheme is principally contained in the SSCBA, and the SMP (General) Regulations 1986, SI 1986/1960, *Harvey* Div R.

10.03 Under the amended scheme, a woman who qualifies (below) is entitled to SMP at the higher rate for the first six weeks of the maternity pay period (MPP) and at the lower rate for the remainder (usually twelve weeks). The higher rate is 9/10ths of her normal weekly pay; the lower rate is fixed by regulations, currently at £54.55, and must not be lower than the current rate (or lowest rate) for SSP.

Any further contractual obligations (by way of topping up) are a matter between the employer and the employee.

10.04 As with SSP, a useful source of reference on SMP (with the detailed rules and working examples) is the *Employer's Guide to SMP* (NI 257), obtainable from the DSS.

Who qualifies for SMP?

10.05 To qualify for SMP, the woman must earn more than the lower earnings limit for paying NI contributions (£61 per week in the tax year 1996/97) and must have been continuously employed[1] by the employer for at least 26 weeks by the *fifteenth* week before the expected week of confinement (that fifteenth week before being known as the 'qualifying week'); she must have been still pregnant by the eleventh week before the expected week of confinement (or have been confined by then) and must have ceased work wholly or partly because of the pregnancy or confinement.[2] Note that receipt of SMP is *not* conditional on the employee remaining in employment or intending to return to work after confinement.

[1] The General Regulations, regs 11–16 contain provisions safeguarding continuity of employment, modelled on the general continuity provisions now to be found in the ERA, Part XIV (see Chapter 7, above) including (i) temporary cessation of work, (ii) stoppages of work, and (iii) changes of employer. Particularly notable among the last is the incorporation of the concept of 'associated employers' (see Chapter 1, above).

[2] SSCBA, s 164(2).

10.06 The employee must give evidence of the expected date of confinement[1] (from which the employer can work out the expected week), and must give the employer notice (in writing if the employer so requires) of her intended absence at least 21 days before it begins (unless it is not reasonably practicable to do so).[2]

[1] SMP (Medical Evidence) Regulations 1987, SI 1987/235; *Harvey* Div R.

[2] SSCBA, s 164(4).

10.07 Any attempt to contract out of the SMP scheme is void;[1] if the employee is dismissed before the qualifying week because it was physically or legally impossible for her to continue, she is deemed still eligible for SMP.[2]

[1] SSCBA, s 164(6).

[2] Regulation 4 of the General Regulations; reg 3 provides that termination of a contract of employment solely or mainly for the purpose of avoiding SMP is ineffective for that purpose.

What is payable?

10.08 The amount of lower level SMP is fixed by regulations,[1] currently (1996/7) at £54.55 per week. The amount of higher level SMP depends on the employee's earnings, being 9/10ths of her 'normal weekly earnings' over the period for eight weeks up to the qualifying week.[2] As with SSP, normal weekly earnings approximate to the gross figures used for PAYE and NI purposes.[3]

1 Regulation 6 of the General Regulations.
2 SSCBA, s 166(2).
3 Regulation 21 of the General Regulations.

10.09 The maximum maternity pay period (MPP) is 18 weeks,[1] 6 weeks at the higher level, then 12 weeks at the lower level. It may start at the 11th week before the expected week of confinement, but the employee may delay the start (ie carry on working) until the time of confinement (*unless* before that time, and after the sixth week before, she is absent from work wholly or partly because of the pregnancy; in which case the MPP is triggered automatically). As under the old maternity pay scheme, an employee can (if it is physically possible) work right up to the confinement (drawing full wages) and then leave and claim full maternity rights.[2]

1 SSCBA, s 165(1). On the MPP generally, see *Harvey* Div J.
2 *ILEA v Nash* [1979] ICR 229, [1979] IRLR 29, EAT.

10.10 In addition to certain exceptions where no SMP is payable (eg where the employee is imprisoned or abroad),[1] an employee will begin to lose the maximum 18-week entitlement if (i) she works for her employer for any part of a week during her MPP (since that disentitles her for the whole of that week),[2] or (ii) she starts work for another employer after confinement but during her MPP.[3] If an employer considers that he is not liable to pay SMP to an employee who has claimed it, he served upon her form SMP 1 (similar to SSP 1(E)) which states his reasons.

1 Regulation 9 of the General Regulations; SMP (Persons Abroad and Mariners) Regulations 1987, SI 19877/418, *Harvey* Div R.
2 SSCBA, s 165(4).
3 Ibid, s 165(6); reg 8 of the General Regulations.

10.11 SMP is to be paid through the employer's normal payment system and may not be paid in kind,[1] but is treated as pay and so is liable to PAYE and NI contributions.

1 Regulations 27 and 29 of the General Regulations. Note that under reg 7 the Secretary of State may pay amounts of SMP outstanding on an employer's insolvency.

10.12 As with contractual sick pay, any contractual obligation to top up SMP to a higher level (or, eg, for a longer period) is a matter of agreement between the parties, enforceable if necessary in the ordinary courts.

Reimbursement, records and remedies

10.13 The system for reimbursement of the employer for amounts paid out as SMP is similar to that which used to apply generally to SSP, ie by deduction of those amounts from NI contributions payable by the employer in respect of the period in question (with powers for the Secretay of State to refund directly any shortfall if those contributions are not large enough to cover the amount deductible).[1] Unlike the position now with SSP where reimbursement has been stopped for most employers,[2] reimbursement of SMP has only been reduced by the recent legislation. Thus an employer can recoup 90% of the amount paid out. However, there is also a 'small employer's relief', in that a small employer (defined as an employer whose contributions payments do not exceed £20,000) (a) may recoup the whole amount, and (b) may also recover a further 5½ of that amount, representing the extra NI contributions payable on it.

1 SMP (Compensation of Employers) Regulations 1994, SI 1994/1882, *Harvey* Div R.
2 See para 9.18, above.

10.14 The employer must keep records for a period of three years after the tax year in which the MPP ended.[1] Again, these may be kept in any way thought appropriate by the employer, provided that they show the prescribed information. The DSS have a form (SMP 2) which may be used if required.

1 Regulation 26 of the General Regulations.

10.15 An employee has a right to require the employer to give her certain information on what the employer says is her entitlement to SMP.[1]

1 Social Security Administration Act 1992, s 15(2).

10.16 An employee who considers that she has not been paid SMP properly may refer the matter to an adjudication officer of the DSS;[1] if the adjudication officer's decision is adverse, there is a right of appeal in the normal way to a Social Security Appeal Tribunal[2] (and then again, on a point of law, to a Social Security Commissioner). In such a case, the employer is not a party; at the end of the day, the determination will be issued to him, stating the employee's correct entitlement.

1 Social Security Administration Act 1992, s 20; there is a six-month time limit, flowing from the beginning of the disputed SMP period: Social Security (Adjudication) Regulations 1995, SI 1995/1801, reg 20. Note, however, that certain listed questions must be submitted to the Secretary of State: Social Security Administration Act 1992, s 17(1)(h); in the case of one of these questions, there is no appeal to a SSAT from the Secretary of State's decision.
2 Social Security Administration Act 1992, s 22; procedure is governed by the Social Security (Adjudication) Regulations 1995, SI 1995/1801.

2 THE RIGHT TO RETURN TO WORK AND THE RIGHT TO MATERNITY LEAVE

General rights to maternity leave

10.17 Following alterations made in TURERA 1993 there are now two parallel sets of provisions for pregnant employees. All employees are now given certain rights which are considered first.[1] Employees with two years' service have further rights which are effectively superimposed on the first set of provisions and are often referred to as extended maternity leave rights. An employee who is absent from work at any time during her maternity leave period is entitled to the benefit of the terms and conditions of employment, which would have been applicable to her if she had not been absent (and had not been pregnant or given birth to her child).[2] However, this does not confer any entitlement to remuneration during the MLP.[3] The cases will have to determine what is 'remuneration'. Pension contributions should continue to be paid[4] but the position on pure benefits such as a car is less clear.

---

1 The provision as to maternity leave below was introduced in October 1994. These changes were made to comply with the Pregnant Workers Directive 92/85.

2 ERA, s 71.

3 ERA, s 71.

4 This is now inserted in the Social Security Act 1989 (Commencement No 5) Order 1994, SI 1994/1661.

10.18 A problem might also arise in relation to bonuses payable during the MLP. This whole area is a legal minefield. Thus if the bonus was payable during the MLP but it covered a longer period it should be reduced proportionally rather than not paid. Similar requirements could be applied to commissions but they usually cover a shorter period. Then there is the cash value of benefits taken up such as cheap mortgages. They could be classified as non-remuneration. The use of a car would seem to be a benefit and therefore not remuneration. Holiday entitlement will probably accrue during such leave and this should be contrasted with extended maternity leave where such rights are a matter of contract. A definition of 'remuneration' would have been most helpful. The *Gillespie*[1] case has decided that although payments made by the employer to the employee during maternity absence are 'pay' neither Article 119 nor the Equal Treatment Directive requires women to receive full pay during maternity leave.[2]

---

1 It becomes even muddier if one is paid a cash equivalent of a benefit.

2 [1996] IRLR 214, ECJ.

Maternity leave period commencement

10.19 An employee's maternity leave period begins with the date she notifies her employer as the date on which she intends her absence to commence or, if earlier the first day on which she is absent from work for pregnancy or childbirth,[1] provided that it is after the beginning of the sixth week before the expected week of childbirth. However, where childbirth occurs before the day with which the maternity leave period would have otherwise commenced then it is the date of childbirth when the period begins.[2]

---

[1] Defined in the ERA, s 235(1) as the birth of a living child or the birth of a child whether living or dead after 24 weeks of pregnancy.
[2] ERA, s 72.

Duration of maternity leave period

10.20 The period lasts for 14 weeks from its commencement but where there is a statutory requirement prohibiting the employee from being employed after the 14 weeks has expired then the MLP lasts until the restriction ends. If the birth is later than the expiry of the 14 weeks the period lasts until the birth. If the employee is dismissed before the MLP would have ended then the period ends at the time of the dismissal.[1] In no circumstances may any woman work in the two weeks following childbirth even if she may want to do so.[2] Any breach of this provision is a criminal offence enforceable under the Health and Safety at Work Act.

---

[1] ERA, s 73.
[2] The Maternity (Compulsory Leave) Regulations 1994, SI 1994/2479. They implement the Pregnant Workers' Directive.

Conditions of obtaining the right

10.21 To obtain the right to the benefit of terms and conditions given during the MLP she must:[1]

(a) notify her employer of the date on which she intends her absence to begin not less than 21 days before that date or if that is not reasonably practicable as soon as is reasonably practicable. The date notified cannot be before the beginning of the eleventh week before the expected week of childbirth;
(b) where she is first absent or partly because of pregnancy or childbirth before the notified leave date or before she had notified such a date and after the beginning of the sixth week before the expected week of childbirth she notifies her employer as soon as reasonably practicable that she is absent for that reason; or
(c) where childbirth takes place before the notified leave date or notification of such date she notifies her employer that she has given birth as soon as is reasonably practicable after the birth.

The employer can require any of these notices to be in writing.

---

[1] ERA, s 74.

Requirement to inform employer of pregnancy

10.22 An employee must inform her employer in writing at least 21 days before her maternity leave period commences or, if that is not reasonably practicable, as soon as is reasonably practicable:

(a) that she is pregnant; and
(b) the expected week of childbirth or, if the childbirth has occurred, the date on which it occurred. She must also produce on request a certificate from a doctor or midwife stating the expected week of childbirth.[1] These conditions must be fulfilled in order to obtain the benefits of the terms and conditions during the MLP.

[1] ERA, s 75.

Requirement to inform employer of return during maternity leave

10.23 An employee who intends to return to work earlier than the end of her maternity leave period must give her employer not less than seven days' notice of the date of her intended return.

10.24 An employee who returns to work early without notifying her employer or giving notice has no right to return and the employer can send her home and require seven days' notice. There is no contractual obligation to pay any remuneration during this period. When the 14 weeks expires the employee can simply return without any need to give notice.[1]

[1] ERA, s 76.

Redundancy during maternity leave period

10.25 If the employer decides that it is not practicable by reason of redundancy to continue to employ her under her existing contract during her maternity leave period she must, where there is a suitable available vacancy, be offered, before the ending of her original contract, alternative employment with her employer or his successor or an associated employer. This must be under a new contract which must take effect immediately upon the ending of her previous contract. Furthermore, the new contract must be both suitable and appropriate for her and the provisions as to capacity and place and other terms and conditions must not be substantially less favourable to her.[1] Thus, the employer must establish that redundancy is the reason for dismissal but an employee is not entitled to a new job but only to be offered one if there is a suitable available vacancy. The terms of the new job do not need to be the same as the old and indeed may be less favourable but not substantially so. If the employer fails to offer a suitable vacancy this is treated as an automatically unfair dismissal.[2]

[1] ERA, s 77. If the original contract provided that changes could be made then such changes would not constitute a redundancy. The terms 'suitable', 'appropriate' and 'substantially less favourable' are considered elsewhere.
[2] ERA, s 99 and see unfair dismissal below.

10.26 As there is an express reference to capacity and place one would assume that any substantial change of location or status would make the alternative substantially less favourable.

Contractual rights

10.27 Where an employee has a corresponding right in her contract of employment she may take advantage of whichever right is in any particular respect the more favourable when comparing it with the statutory right.[1]

[1] ERA, s 78.

The right to return to work[1]

10.28 The basic right of the employee is to return to work with her original employer, or his successor, in the *job* in which she was employed under the *original contract of employment* and on terms and conditions not less favourable than those which would have been applicable to her if she had not been so absent.[1] This right to return is the original provision and is only applicable to employees with two years' service.[2]

[1] Section 79 which preserves seniority, pension rights and similar rights.
[2] See more details below. Note that the conditions applicable to the MLP apply to the right to return.

10.29 This basic right involves further definition but it should be noted at the outset that the right is subject to a number of conditions and qualifications and the procedure for claiming is complex.[1] As we shall note, a failure to comply entails a loss of rights and this has been strictly enforced although a more liberal approach may now be commencing.[2]

[1] See eg comments in *Lavery v Plessey Telecommunications Ltd* [1982] ICR 373, [1983] IRLR 180.
[2] See eg *Hilton International Hotels (UK) Ltd v Kaissi* [1994] IRLR 270, EAT.

10.30 'Job' is defined as 'the nature of the work she is employed to do in accordance with her contract and the capacity and place in which she is so employed'.[1]

[1] ERA, s 234.

10.31 The 'job' test is contractual, namely what was she employed to do rather than what was she actually doing.[1] However, a recent decision in another area of employment law if allowed might lead to a change in this approach.[2] Minor administrative changes are of no consequence.[3]

[1] This applies in other areas of employment law, eg *Runnals' v Richards and Osborne Ltd* [1973] IRLR 124.
[2] See *Bass Leisure Ltd v Thomas* [1994] IRLR 104 where the EAT refused to apply the contractual approach to a geographical mobility clause.
[3] *Edgell v Lloyd's Register of Shipping* [1977] IRLR 463.

10.32 'Capacity' has been equated with status, its only meaningful equivalent. The place of work must be alterable in the contract to justify a change in location unless it would be within a reasonable daily reach of her home.[1] Also it is what the contract says, not what has actually happened under it, that counts. Thus the fact that an employee has worked in one place throughout her employment does not in any way negate the employer's contractual rights regarding mobility. That has always been the approach but it must be read in the light of the comments made in the previous paragraph on the *Bass Leisure* case. If that case is followed then the contractual approach may disappear. It is too early to say that this is the position based on one case.

[1] For example *Courtaulds Northern Spinning Ltd v Sibson* [1988] ICR 451, [1988] IRLR 305, CA.

10.33 The right to return is to return on terms and conditions not less favourable than before. However, if changes were made to all employees' contracts in her grade or position during her absence then she should not be able to complain about that. As regards seniority, pension rights and other similar rights, the absence does not break continuity but indeed counts towards it.[1] However, it appears that she does not acquire any additional rights such as holiday entitlement or holiday pay.[2] It is very surprising that this issue has not been authoritatively decided after so many years on the statute book.

[1] ERA, s 79.
[2] *Hirjee v Sidal Aluminim* EAT 285/80.

10.34 When a clerk who had an established grade and who was transferred to an unestablished grade which, *inter alia*, rendered her more vulnerable to redundancy, it was held to be a non-compliance with the employee's statutory right and the tribunal ordered her reinstatement.[1]

[1] *McFadden v Greater Glasgow Passenger Transport Executive* [1977] IRLR 327.

3 QUALIFICATION AND CONDITIONS FOR THE RIGHT

10.35 A woman's statutory right is to return to her old job provided it is not later than 29 weeks after the beginning of the week in which childbirth occurs. However, there are a number of hurdles the employee has to surmount before she can claim this right:

(a) she must, at the beginning of the 11th week before the expected week of childbirth, have at least two years' continuous employment;[1]
(b) she must have informed her employer in writing at least 21 days before her maternity leave period commences or, if that is not reasonably practicable, as soon as is reasonably practicable—
    (i) that she is pregnant; and
    (ii) of the expected week of childbirth or, if the childbirth has occurred, the date on which it occurred;[2]
    (iii) that she intends to exercise her right to return to work.[3]
(c) where her employer has requested, not earlier than 21 days before the

end of her maternity leave period, her written confirmation of intention to return she must have replied within 14 days of receiving the request, or if that is not reasonably practicable as soon as is reasonably practicable;[4]

(d) she must have produced a certificate from a doctor or midwife of the expected week of confinement, if her employer has requested it;[5]

(e) she must have notified her employer in writing at least 21 days in advance of the date on which she intends to return to work.[6]

All of these provisions are construed strictly—see, for example, *Institute of the Motor Industry v Harvey*.[7]

1 ERA, s 79.
2 ERA, s 75(1).
3 ERA, s 80.
4 ERA, s 80.
5 ERA, s 75(2).
6 ERA, s 82(1).
7 [1992] IRLR 343. This date is referred to as the 'notified day of return'.

10.36 The 'expected week of childbirth means the week beginning with midnight between Saturday and Sunday in which it is expected that childbirth will occur.[1] 'Childbirth' means the birth of a living child or the birth of a child whether living or dead after 24 weeks of pregnancy.[2] This is a complicated provision and the EAT has ruled in *Secretary of State for Employment v A Ford & Son (Sacks) Ltd*[3] that you cannot simply subtract 11 weeks from the day the baby is due. It is necessary to go though the procedure of working out the week which means a week ending on Saturday[4] and then counting back eleven Sundays from the Sunday of the expected week. In the case in question, this meant that the employee did not satisfy the two years' requirement on that date, even though she did on the 'expected date' basis. So much for labour law being comprehensible to the lay person!

1 ERA, s 235(1).
2 ERA, s 235(1).
3 [1986] ICR 882.
4 ERA, s 235(1).

10.37 The concept of 'continuous employment' is dealt with in the section on continuity.

4 NOTICE TO EMPLOYER

10.38 We have already noted that an employee must have given 21 days' written notice before her maternity leave period begins of the pregnancy, the expected week of her childbirth, and her intention to exercise her right to return. If she fails to state her intention to return, then the notice is insufficient.[1] She must comply strictly with these criteria and a conditional notice has been held inadequate.[2]

1 *F W Woolworths plc v Smith* [1990] ICR 45, EAT.
2 *Osborne v Thomas Bolton* COIT 794/248.

10.39 The notice of absence must be of 21 days' duration but if that is not reasonably practicable such notice as is reasonably practicable.[1] This requirement is applied quite strictly and does not protect the employee who cannot make up her mind. Thus in *Nu-Swift International Ltd v Mallinson*[2] the employee who was 38, and had not had a baby for 16 years, was uncertain whether she would return after the birth. This was because of fears for the baby's health. She had told her employer she would probably not return but when she was told the baby would be fine she told her employers she would return, but she did not give the requisite 21 days' notice before she left. When she was not re-engaged she claimed unfair dismissal and the tribunal held it was not reasonably practicable to have given the notice because of her anxiety. However, the EAT reversed and said the relevant question was whether the employee knew of her rights. She did and could have given her notice. The Act was not intended to protect those who were uncertain. The simple lesson is that an employee must give a notice, even if she is not sure she will be returning.

1 See below in 'Unfair Dismissal' for a full explanation of this phrase.
2 [1979] ICR 157, [1979] IRLR 537.

10.40 If an employee had to leave suddenly because of unexpected complications such as a premature birth one assumes that this would be a situation where it was not reasonably practicable to give the requisite notice. If an employee could show she was ignorant of her rights and the conditions the tribunal might well, as a matter of fact, decide in her favour. This is an unlikely scenario today.

5 CONFIRMATION, NOTIFICATION AND POSTPONEMENT OF RETURN

Confirmation

10.41 As employees often give notice of intention to return when they have no such intention if all is well, an employer can ask the employer to confirm in writing that she will be returning. The request must be made in writing not earlier than 21 days before the end of her maternity leave period. The employee must reply within 14 days of receiving the request or if that is not reasonably practicable as soon as is reasonably practicable.[1] The employer must, at the same time as the request, state that a failure to reply will extinguish the right to return.[2]

1 ERA, s 80.
2 ERA, s 80.

Notification

10.42 The employee must give written notice to the employer at least 21 days before the day on which she proposes to return. This day is known as the notified day of return and must be before the end of 29 weeks after the beginning of the week in which childbirth occurs.[1] The difference between the actual and expected date can be very significant, as shown in *Lavery v Plessey Telecommunications Ltd.*[2] It is vital that the actual date is given.

[1] ERA, ss 82(1) and 79(1).
[2] [1982] ICR 373; affd on other grounds in [1983] ICR 534, CA.

10.43 In *Lavery* the baby was expected on 2 April and the employer was notified of this. The baby was born on 20 April, unknown to the employer. The 29 weeks from the later date expired on 8 November, whereas from the earlier date it was 27 October. Ms Lavery gave five days' notice[1] of her return on 22 October. The employer, believing her notice to be inadequate, immediately rejected her claim and was held entitled to do so. Although she had plenty of time to give another notice, the fact remained that she had given inadequate notice.

[1] It was then seven days that were required, not 21.

Postponement

10.44 Both employer and employee have rights to postpone the return. The provisions, like all of those in this area, are complicated.

10.45 The employee can postpone her return by up to four weeks from the notified date of return or, if this has not been provided, from the end of the 29-week period on medical grounds. She must give her employer a doctor's certificate stating her incapacity which must be because of disease or bodily or mental disablement which need have nothing to do with the pregnancy or confinement. The certificate must be handed over before the notified date or the expiry of the 29 weeks. Any failure to comply with this means that the right to return is lost.[1] A postponement on medical grounds is only allowed once.[2]

[1] ERA, s 82(3) and note also *Kelly v Liverpool* (see para 10.55 below) where the employee was genuinely off sick but four weeks only were permitted.
[2] ERA, s 82(4).

10.46 If she has notified a day of return but there is an interruption of work for whatever reason which renders it unreasonable to expect her to return on the notified day she may instead return when work resumes or as soon as reasonably practicable afterwards.[1] If no day of return has been notified as a result of the interruption she can still exercise her right to return provided she returns before 28 days have elapsed since the interruption ended even though this is beyond the 29 week period.[2]

[1] ERA, s 82.
[2] ERA, s 82(6).

10.47 The employer may postpone the return by up to four weeks from her notified date for 'specified reasons' which are not stated in the statute. Provided the employer specifies the reason he is apparently protected.[1]

[1] ERA, s 82(2).

6 EXCEPTIONS AND QUALIFICATIONS TO THE RIGHT TO RETURN

Suitable available vacancy

10.48 We have already identified the employee's basic right to return to the same job as she was employed in under the original contract of employment. However, there are some situations where the right may be lost. We have noted that the employee must comply with certain qualifying criteria and must follow the complex procedure strictly. However, if the employer can show it is not practicable by reason of redundancy to allow her to return the employee will either get a redundancy payment or, where there is a suitable available vacancy, she is entitled to be offered alternative employment.[1] This can be with the employer or his successor or an associated employer.[2] The new contract must be of work which is both suitable for the employee and appropriate for her to do in the circumstances and the new terms and conditions, including capacity and place, must not be substantially less favourable than if she had returned under the original contract. Where there is a suitable vacancy which the employer does not offer then this failure renders the employee's 'dismissal'[3] automatically unfair[4] – the question of reasonableness does not arise. The strictness of this provision was shown in *Community Task Force v Rimmer*.[5]

1 ERA, s 81.
2 Defined in ERA, s 231.
3 See below in unfair dismissal.
4 The equivalent provision for the maternity leave period is contained in ERA, s 99. ERA, s 99(4).
5 [1986] ICR 491, [1986] IRLR 203, EAT.

10.49 In *Rimmer* the employers were funded mainly by the Manpower Services Commission (MSC). During Ms Rimmer's maternity leave the employer decided to redeploy her as her job had become redundant. However, the MSC would not permit this because it was against their policy. The employer, which would have had its funding cut had it retained the employee, did not offer her the job. It was held that this was an automatically unfair dismissal irrespective of whether it was economic or reasonable–it was a suitable available vacancy. Appointing someone in the same job as the employee a few weeks before her return was unfair.[1] In the case it was stated that the right to return is established as soon as the woman gives notice of her intention to return and does not need to be crystallised by the later notice of intention to actually return. The duty to make an offer of a suitable vacancy arises immediately she goes on leave.

1 *Philip Hodges & Co v Kell* [1994] ICR 656.

10.50 There remain the questions of what is 'suitable' and 'appropriate' and not 'substantially less favourable' and these are very similar to the tests for 'suitable' employment in redundancy, although there is a dearth of authority in relation to maternity leave. The redundancy case authorities will eventually be regarded as applicable to maternity and vice versa, one assumes.

10.51 Where there is a genuine redundancy and no suitable vacancy a redundancy payment is made but if the employer can show that the employee would have been dismissed for redundancy during her period of maternity leave then that earlier date is the date for calculating the redundancy payment.[1]

[1] ERA, s 137(2).

Refusal of reinstatement

10.52 Where the employer does not permit a return to work then the employee is treated as having been employed until the notified day of return and dismissed from that date.[1] These statutory provisions do not lead automatically to a remedy but at least the employee gets over the burden of proving she has been dismissed. In fact in many cases there will be an automatically unfair dismissal and in most cases the dismissal will be unfair.

[1] ERA, s 96(1) (unfair dismissal) and ERA, s 137 (redundancy).

Non-redundancy reason for dismissal

10.53 We have already noted the redundancy reason for dismissal but the employer may refuse to reinstate for a reason other than redundancy. This is most likely because of a business reorganisation the engagement of a permanent replacement will have to be proved by the employer to be a necessary step but if it is it will probably constitute a defence. In this situation if the employer or associated employer offers employment where the work is suitable and appropriate and the terms of the contract are not substantially less favourable, there is no dismissal where the employee accepts or unreasonably refuses that offer.[1] The redundancy analogy is once again apt.

[1] ERA, s 96(3) and (4).

Small employers

10.54 Where the employer employs five or less employees (including her and any of an associated employer) then the employee is excluded from claiming if the employer can show it was not reasonably practicable for any reason to allow her to return and it was not reasonably practicable to offer her alternative employment.[1] This does not exclude a redundancy payment.

[1] ERA, s 96(2).

10.55 These provisions are replete with uncertainty. Allowing any reason to exclude the right is very broad although it has to be reasonably practicable. It is difficult to understand what it might envisage beyond a business reorganisation.

10.56 The burden of proof regarding non-redundancy reasons and the small employer exception is fixed clearly on the employer.[1]

[1] ERA, s 96(5).

Redundancy dismissals

10.57 Where redundancy is given as the reason for dismissal then there is still the possibility of there being an unfair dismissal for redundancy and the Act[1] provides that in determining reasonableness the tribunal must decide the question as if she had not been absent from work. Therefore it is not merely whether there has been a genuine redundancy but also whether there has been an unfair selection or procedure.

[1] ERA 1978, s 137(2)(a).

7 SUITABLE ALTERNATIVE EMPLOYMENT[1]

Contractual rights

10.58 Employers often provide rights regarding maternity as a matter of contract. If these rights are not as generous as the statutory rights then the latter apply but if they are more generous the employee is entitled to take advantage of them. However, she is not entitled to exercise a contractual right and a statutory right separately but may 'take advantage of whichever right is, in any particular respect, the more favourable'. The Act's provisions are then modified to give effect to any more favourable contractual terms and they are then known as a composite right.[2] The right to return can be under the 'contract of employment or otherwise'. The last two words were probably inserted as a matter of caution to cover arrangements made which were not inserted in any contract and could possibly be said not to be contractual.

[1] See section on Redundancy.
[1] ERA, s 93.

10.59 Occasionally the employee has no statutory rights and is relying on an agreement with the employer. This was held to be enforceable in the interesting case of *Lucas v Norton of London Ltd.*[1] Ms Lucas had informed her employer that she was pregnant and in a discussion they had reached a 'nebulous agreement' that she might return. However, she did not give a notice of absence and thereby lost her statutory right. Subsequently she telephoned to ascertain the position regarding return but was told that her job no longer existed. She was given two weeks' pay in lieu of notice and this was of crucial importance because the EAT held that this amounted to a recognition of the existence of the contract. Therefore the failure to permit her return was an ordinary dismissal not a statutory dismissal.[2] There must be some basis for establishing that the contract is subsisting. Therefore had the employer not paid the money in lieu of notice the decision may have been different.[3]

1 [1984] IRLR 86, EAT.
2 Under ERA, s 91(1). See also *Institute of the Motor Industry v Harvey* [1992] IRLR 343, EAT.
3 See eg *McKnight v Adlestones (Jewellers) Ltd* [1984] IRLR 453.

10.60 It is thus clear that the failure to comply with the maternity leave procedure does not terminate the contract even though the statutory right to return is lost. Whether or not the contract comes to an end depends on the agreement and action of the parties and on the Common Law. If there is an express or implied agreement to continue the contract then this will mean the contract continues but there is no presumption that it continues[1] if the employer merely consents to the employee leaving work and remuneration ceases. The appropriate inference is that there has been an agreed termination. If SMP is paid then the contract continues until the payment ends. Thus a long-serving employee who did not give written confirmation of her intention to return despite being requested to do so was unfairly dismissed when she was off sick and the employers had not investigated her position.[2] Although she had no contractual statutory right to return she retained her right not to be unfairly dismissed although the employer might be justified in not permitting the employee to return if she is dismissed in the course of attempting to return to work. However, the fact that she was on sick leave throughout was an issue distinguishing this case from most others.[3]

1 *Crouch v Kidsons Impey* (1996) IRLR 79, EAT.
2 *Hilton International Hotels (UK) Ltd v Kaissi* [1994] IRLR 270, EAT.
3 *Crouch v Kidsons Impey* (1996) IRLR 79, EAT.

10.61 Where there is a composite right it is important to note that the statutory provisions will apply where they have not been modified. Further, any notice provisions, whether statutory or contractual, must be complied with. In *Lavery* (above) the employee failed to give sufficient notice of intention to return and that extinguished her statutory rights. She claimed she had contractual rights which the court was prepared to accept in principle. However, the contract did not amend the notice requirement regarding return and therefore this applied to the contractual right which meant that she could not claim the right to return. Ironically, had she not given any notice at all she might have been able to succeed given the reasoning in *Lucas* (above). It seems it is better to do nothing than to do it wrong.

10.62 If the employer agrees to extend the notified day of return, as a matter of contract, that does not mean that the employee thereby becomes subject to the ordinary law of unfair dismissal as opposed to the special maternity provisions. In *Dowuona v John Lewis plc*[1] it was agreed that the employee could have one week's holiday at the end of her maternity leave. Before she returned she sent in a sick note postponing her date of return for four weeks in accordance with her statutory rights. However, she did not return on that date because she was unwell and the employers subsequently refused to take her back. She argued that she had failed to return after the holiday rather than from maternity leave so that she could claim that it was an ordinary dismissal case. The Court of Appeal did not accept this and said that with the additional week for holiday she was exercising a contractual right to return as permitted by what is now

ERA, s 95. Therefore it was a dismissal occurring in the course of her attempting to return after maternity leave and it was the statutory maternity provisions which were relevant. These had not been complied with and therefore there was no right to return.

---

[1] [1987] IRLR 310.

10.63 If an employer fails to respond to medical certificates sent in after a four-week postponement has already been given, this does not mean that the employer has agreed that the employment should continue. Accordingly, when the employee subsequently wished to return and the employer refused this was not treated as a dismissal in *Kelly v Liverpool Maritime Terminals Ltd.*[1] The statutory procedure was not followed but the employer agreed to allow a return. However, she was not fit to return and sent a Doctor's certificate for four weeks with a covering letter. Three further certificates were sent. No response was made by the company to any of the certificates but when the last one was received the company wrote to say that her right to return had ceased and that she would not be able to return. Mrs Kelly claimed this was a dismissal; she said she was requesting sick leave and the company's failure to respond was an implied agreement to this or, alternatively, they were estopped from denying that they had agreed. The Court of Appeal rejected these arguments and confirmed the lower courts. They said that the employer's silence did not constitute an agreement and estoppel did not arise in the circumstances.

---

[1] [1988] IRLR 310.

10.64 An employer might permit a return on different terms and conditions but the employee cannot claim to combine the contractual and statutory rights as shown in *Bovey v Board of Governors of the Hospital for Sick Children.*[1] Ms Bovey was a full-time physiotherapist on Grade 1. She wanted to return on a part-time basis but this was on a basic grade. She accepted but later claimed she had the right to return on a part-time basis on Grade 1. The EAT said that the right to return part-time was covered by s 85 but although she had a statutory right to return full-time in Grade 1 and a contractual right to return part-time in the basic grade, she could not select the best parts of both to give her a job the employer did not have.

---

[1] [1978] ICR 934, [1978] IRLR 241.

---

8 CONTINUITY

10.65 The detailed provisions on continuity are contained elsewhere. However, some basic points relating to maternity leave should be made. Continuity is preserved where an employee returns in accordance with the statutory scheme.[1] If the contract subsists during the absence there is no need to use this provision and it would seem that it does.[2] In the *Harvey* case Ms Harvey took maternity leave serving the proper notice. Her post became redundant during her maternity leave. A debate ensued over when she would return because her job duties were not agreed, the employer saying he could not provide them until he knew when she was returning. She said she wanted to know about the job and eventually this led to the employer suspending her pension payments and asking for the return of the company car. Ultimately she resigned claiming a breakdown in trust and confidence having never sent a notice of intention to return. The EAT held that as no notice had been sent there could be no dismissal under what is now ERA s 96 which dealt with a failure to permit a return to work when a notice had been served. However, it was held that where the first notice had been served her contract would continue unless it was terminated by agreement, resignation or dismissal. These events had not occurred and therefore the employee was entitled to claim constructive dismissal. However, she was unable to rely on any breach in relation to any obligation regarding her return to work as no notice had been served.[3]

1 ERA, s 212(2).
2 *Institute of the Motor Industry v Harvey* [1992] IRLR 343.
3 See also discussion of ERA, s 84 – there are some issues which need clarification.

10.66 Where there is no contract of employment and the absence is for pregnancy or confinement then weeks of absence to a maximum of 26 count.[1]

1 ERA, s 212(4).

10.67 This provision is rendered superfluous by the fact that the statutory return does not break continuity so is only relevant where there is no right to return. If there is a return within 26 weeks then continuity is preserved.[1]

1 See *Mitchell v Royal British Legion Club* [1981] ICR 18, [1980] IRLR 425, EAT.

9 REMEDIES

10.68 Under the Act[1] the employee whose rights have been refused can claim she has been dismissed and the normal remedies for unfair dismissal and redundancy obtain.

1 ERA, ss 137(1) and 96(1).

10.69 If the employee is dismissed before she begins the process of exercising her right to return, then any case proceeds as an ordinary unfair dismissal case. If the dismissal occurs after that process begins, then it is the special maternity provisions which apply and she is deemed dismissed on the notified day of return.[1] An employee who pursues a redundancy payment or unfair dismissal and obtains compensation must give credit for it in a subsequent right to return claim.[2]

1 See *Lavery, Duowana* above and *Harvey*.
2 ERA s 84(2).

10.70 Where a return is prevented the employer must show the reason why he refused permission to return and then reasonableness is assessed.[1]

[1] ERA, s 99.

10 EXCLUSIONS

10.71 The following are excluded from the right to return:

(a) those employed in the police service;[1]
(b) those who ordinarily work outside Great Britain.[2]

[1] ERA, s 200.
[2] ERA, s 196.

Link with dismissals for pregnancy or childbirth

10.72 It is noted below that while it has always been unfair to dismiss for pregnancy this has been substantially extended by TURERA 1993 and most importantly there is no qualifying period needed to make an unfair dismissal claim. The main extension grounds relate to the maternity leave period so that if there is a dismissal during the maternity leave period and the reason or principal reason is that: (i) she has given birth or any other reason connected with her having given birth to a child, or (ii) if the reason was that she took the benefits of maternity leave or (iii) she is redundant and ERA, s 77 has not been complied with, then there is an automatically unfair dismissal.[1]

[1] ERA, s 99.

Remedy

10.73 An employee denied benefits during her maternity leave period can claim a breach of contract in either the county court or the industrial tribunal now that jurisdiction has been granted for contract claims.

Rights on suspension on maternity grounds

10.74 An employee is regarded as suspended on maternity grounds where because of any statutory requirement or any recommendation in any relevant provision of a code of practice issued under the Health and Safety At Work Act she is suspended from work on the ground that she is pregnant, has recently given birth or is breastfeeding a child. Before a suspension occurs the employee has a right to be offered any available suitable alternative work. 'Suitable' means work which is of a kind which is both suitable and appropriate for her in the circumstance and where the terms and conditions are not substantially less favourable than her existing terms. If the employer fails to offer such work the employee can complain to the industrial tribunal which can award compensation to the employee provided she claims within the three month time limit or within such further period as was reasonable where it was not reasonably practicable to have presented the complaint. The amount of compensation payable is what amount the tribunal considers just and equitable having regard to the infringement of the complainant's right by the employer's failure and to any loss sustained by the employee.[1]

---

[1] ERA, s 70(7).

Right to remuneration on suspension

10.75 An employee who is suspended on maternity grounds shall be entitled to be paid remuneration by her employer while she is so suspended. No remuneration is payable where the employer has provided work which is suitable alternative work and the employee has unreasonably refused to perform such work. If there is a failure to make payment of remuneration the employee can complain to the industrial tribunal within the same time limit as stated in the previous paragraph. The amount of the remuneration is one week's pay for each week of suspension and part of a week is reduced proportionately.[1]

---

[1] ERA, s 69 and see Chapter 12 below.

Pregnancy and safety

10.76 Although health and safety falls outside the scope of this book and suspension on maternity grounds has been discussed above this topic will be considered only briefly here.

Employers are faced with difficult problems when they believe that a pregnant employee can no longer do her job in safety because of her condition. Assuming there is no alternative job the employer considering dismissing will almost certainly find he has committed an act of sex discrimination and unfair dismissal. If he retains the employee he may find that he may be prosecuted or sued on health and safety grounds. The Management of Health and Safety At Work Regulations require employers to determine and assess any risks to their workers. Regulations[1] came into force at the end of 1994 which specifically implement the Pregnant Workers' Directive.[2]

The Regulations refer to three categories:

(a) those who are pregnant;
(b) those breastfeeding; and
(c) those who have given birth in the last six months.

The employer must assess the special risks that such women face in the workplace and take measures to avoid those risks. Where it is not possible to prevent or reduce the risk sufficiently then her working conditions or hours of work must be altered. If this is not reasonable or would not avoid the risk the employee must be offered suitable alternative work or if none is available suspend her from work on full pay (which is referred to above). There will be disputes over many of these issues and it will be interesting to see whether the Health and Safety Executive take a more pro-active line in this area than in other areas of health and safety. It is likely that there will be considerable pressure brought on them to enforce the law both by individuals and bodies like the EOC.

These developments raise doubts about the correctness of a decision of the EAT[3] in 1994 where it was held not to be sex-discriminatory to dismiss a pregnant woman who worked as a trainee veterinary nurse who might be exposed to x-rays and infections from various animals. The EAT said she was not dismissed for pregnancy but because of the real health and safety concerns caused by the pregnancy. As a comparable man would have been dismissed there was no discrimination. Legal developments[4] since then would lead to the view that the case would be decided differently today. The regulations do not directly impact on this decision but are an important backdrop to the situation.

1 Management of Health & Safety At Work (Amendment) Regulations 1994, SI 1994/2865.
2 92/85 EEC.
3 *Hopkins v Shepherd & Partners* [1994] ICR 39, EAT.
4 *Webb v EMO Air Cargo (UK) Ltd* [1994] IRLR 482, ECJ.

Maternity leave and pensions

10.77 A woman can now receive full pension rights for periods of paid leave.[1] She can continue in membership of the pension scheme or join if she would otherwise have become eligible. She must be credited with the same pension benefits she would have received had she been working normally and receiving her normal remuneration. She also gets the benefit of any improvements gained in the period contributions must be made on the pay received. These rights accrue irrespective of whether the woman returns to work after maternity leave. Throughout the maternity leave period pension provision must be maintained.

1 Social Security Act 1989.

11 Guarantee payments

Barry Mordsley

1 INTRODUCTION

11.01 Situations frequently arise where employers wish to lay-off their workers; the reasons for this are numerous. The most obvious is that there has been a decline in demand for the employer's products on a temporary basis—if it were permanent one assumes the employees would be made redundant. This assumption may become less justifiable in the future. We are already seeing a move to the concept of 'core' and 'peripheral' workers and it might be that the peripherals will simply be laid-off with their names being retained in the anticipation of an increase in demand. This is a common phenomenon in the USA and may become so here. It may create problems regarding the concept of continuity but here is not the place to consider that question.

11.02 Other reasons for lay-off could be the stoppage of vital spare parts to the employer because of a dispute at another factory, or a shortage of raw materials. There have been cases where there have been lay-offs because of foot and mouth disease[1] and the death of a monarch.[2] One could go on. When there is a lay-off the question then arises as to whether there is a right to be paid. As this section is dealing with guarantee payments this matter can only be dealt with briefly. First, it is important to consider what the contract says. If there is no contractual right to lay-off then the employer would, it is suggested, be in breach of contract in refusing to pay. Despite some contrary authority[3] there is no implied term which permits an employer not to pay wages simply because he cannot provide work. Even where there is a contractual right to lay-off without pay then it is arguable that this can only be exercised for a reasonable period of time,[4] although this is contentious as there is also a decision which states that the proper approach is to apply for a redundancy payment under the statutory provisions.[5]

1 *Jones v Sherman* (1979) 14 ITR 63.
2 *Minnevitch v Café de Paris (Londres) Ltd* [1936] 1 All ER 884.
3 *Browning v Crumlin Valley Collieries* [1926] 1 KB 522.
4 *Dakri & Co Ltd v Tiffen* [1981] ICR 256, [1981] IRLR 57, EAT.
5 ERA, s 148 et seq and see *Kenneth MacRae & Co Ltd v Dawson* [1984] IRLR 5, EAT.

11.03 Many employers will have negotiated lay-off arrangements with the recognised unions and provide guaranteed week agreements. For such employees the provisions on guarantee payments are virtually superfluous and we shall see that they may be excluded from the provisions.[1] However, guarantee payments will be relevant whether or not the employer has a contractual right to lay-off. The payment is not conditional on this nor does it provide the right to lay-off.

[1] ERA, s 35 see below.

2 THE RIGHT TO A GUARANTEE PAYMENT

11.04 The basic right provided to an employee is to be given a guarantee payment in respect of any day in which he has not been provided with work and on which he was required to work for any part of that day. The payment is only made where the reason for there being no work is a diminution in the requirements of the employer's business for work of the kind which the employee is employed to do or any other occurrence affecting the normal working of the employer's business in relation to work of the kind which the employee is employed to do. The day is known as a 'workless day' and is a midnight-to-midnight calculation. Where work straddles midnight then the day on which the longer period of work is done is treated as the relevant day.[1] Thus a nightworker losing one shift can only claim for one day.

[1] ERA, s 28 generally for all of the above.

11.05 The 'workless day' must therefore be a day on which the employee is normally required to work. This apparently simple concept is not quite so simple as it appears. The position of casual workers is not clear in this context although the lack of clarity relates to the general uncertainty as to their status.[1] If 'casuals' are really casual in that they are called in on a very haphazard basis then it is hardly consistent with their being normally required to work on any particular day. There is no normality in their working relationship and it is difficult to see how they could be entitled to a payment. If they are 'regular casuals'[2] then the argument becomes much weaker because one can discern a pattern of work. An example of a regular casual homeworker being treated as an employee is the case of *Airfix Footwear Ltd v Cope*[3] because the court regarded the employee as working on a fairly regular basis. However, an earlier decision[4] takes a contrary view. The employee was a part-time worker who was called upon as and when needed and who did not have to work if she did not want to. She had worked on average more than 16 hours a week for two and a half years but was then told that no more work was available. She claimed a guarantee payment. The EAT held that there was no written contract of employment nor was there any implied contract which required the employee to work and therefore she was not entitled to a payment.

[1] See earlier section.
[2] See *O'Kelly v Trusthouse Forte plc* [1984] QB 90, [1983] IRLR 369, CA.
[3] *Airfix Footwear Ltd v Cope* [1978] IRLR 396, EAT.
[4] *Mailway (Southern) Ltd v Willsher* [1978] ICR 511, EAT.

11.06 When the employer closes the factory for non-business reasons there is no entitlement because the employee is not required to be there. The same applies to statutory holidays. Accordingly, when the employers decided to allow employees in on a limited basis during the shutdown, they could not complain when the employers decided there was insufficient work for them to do.[1] This was not a day when employees would normally be required to work.

[1] *York and Reynolds v Colledge Hosiery Co Ltd* [1978] IRLR 53.

11.07 Normal requirements have to be considered in the light of the contract of employment in existence when the guarantee payment is claimed. Thus if an employer has prevailed upon an employee to reduce her days of work and she subsequently complains about it she will be unable to claim a payment because she has acquiesced in the variation and is no longer normally required to work on those days.[1] It might be thought that this was the purpose of a guarantee payment but there will always remain the problem of determining when the original contract is superseded and it will be a matter of degree as to the period of time which has elapsed.

[1] *Clemens v Peter Richards Ltd* [1977] IRLR 332, EAT.

11.08 The employee must then show the reason for his lay-off and it can only be for the specified reasons, either a diminution in the employer's business or anything else affecting the normal working of the employer's business, both of which impact on the employee's work. The fact that the employer finds he needs fewer employees to do the work is not a ground for making the payment—that would be a redundancy. This is a very narrow distinction and much too fine a one for an ordinary mortal to appreciate.

11.09 A voluntary closure does not fall within the permitted reasons. In *North v Pavleigh Ltd*[1] the firm closed for two days for Jewish holidays. Although the employee was normally required to work on those days, the lay-off did not arise because of 'an occurrence affecting the normal working of the employer's business'. The tribunal distinguished between natural disasters such as fire, flood or failure of the power supply and voluntary closures for personal reasons. Although one can perceive this difference it is a harsh one and it is preferable to adopt decisions which take a contrary view.[2] A voluntary closure could well lead to an action for wages due under the contract in any event.

[1] *North v Pavleigh* [1977] IRLR 461, IT.

[2] Eg entitlement in *Newbrooks and Sweet v Saigal* COIT 689/154 when the employer fell ill suddenly.

11.10 Weather conditions which require a closure entitle an employee to a payment but not if the factory remains open but the weather prevents the employee from arriving.

3 EXCLUSIONS FROM, AND ENTITLEMENTS TO, A GUARANTEE PAYMENT

11.11 The basic requirement is continuous employment[1] of at least one month.[2] An employee who is employed under a contract for a fixed term of three months or less, or under a contract made in contemplation of the performance of a specific task which is not expected to last for more than three months, is not entitled to a payment unless he has already attained three months' employment when he claims. If an employee is recruited without mention of there being a fixed term then the employer may still be able to show a custom to the effect that a fixed term was what was contemplated.[3]

[1] See above.
[2] ERA, s 29(1).
[3] See eg *Vanson v Osborne* COIT 674/153 where a potato picker was laid-off after eight weeks and was held not entitled because pickers always know they are employed to pick a particular crop.

11.12 Some categories of employees are excluded from claiming. These are those working outside Great Britain, share fishermen and those in the police service.

11.13 Furthermore it is possible to contract out of the provisions.[1] The Secretary of State has to give approval and the procedure applies where there is a collective agreement or wages order[2] under which the employees have a right to guaranteed remuneration. The parties apply and the Secretary of State will approve only where the agreement provides a procedure whereby the employee can go to arbitration or adjudication to enforce his rights or to an industrial tribunal. There is no need for the agreement to provide as favourable terms as the statutory scheme provided there is a procedure. A number of exemption orders have been made although they may be varied or revoked on application by some or all of the parties or on the Secretary of State's own initiative.[3]

[1] ERA, s 35.
[2] ERA, s 35(2).
[3] ERA, s 35(6).

4 LIMITATIONS ON RIGHTS TO A GUARANTEE PAYMENT

11.14 There are three ways in which the right may be lost:

- (i) industrial action of other employees;
- (ii) unreasonable refusal of suitable alternative work;
- (iii) where the employee does not comply with reasonable requirements to ensure his services are available.

(i) Industrial action

11.15 If the failure to provide work occurs in consequence of a strike, lock-out or other industrial action involving any employee of the employer or of an associated employer[1] there is no right to a guarantee payment. Industrial action includes behaviour which is not necessarily in breach of contract.[2] Industrial action need not be the sole cause of the lay-off provided it is a factor and the immediate cause of the lay-off.[3] A refusal to cross picket lines of another group of workers who have a separate dispute is enough to fall within the exception and disqualify the employees who are laid off.[4]

[1] Defined in ERA, s 231.
[2] *Faust v Power Packing Casemakers* [1983] IRLR 117, CA, an overtime ban.

[3] *Thomson v Priest (Lindley) Ltd* [1978] IRLR 99.
[4] *Garvey v J and J Maybank (Oldham) Ltd* [1979] IRLR 408.

(ii) Suitable alternative work

11.16 Where the employer has offered to provide alternative work for the day which is suitable in all the circumstances, whther or not the work could be required under the contract, and the employee has unreasonably refused that offer there is no right to a payment. These tests are discussed fully under the redundancy section. However, as the work is only very temporary and can fall outside the contractual obligations it will be very difficult for the employee to succeed once the alternative is offered, unless he can show that he has a particular problem with the alternative work, such as an allergy to a particular chemical.

(iii) Employer's reasonable requirements

11.17 To cope with the problem the employer faces he may have to impose emergency arrangements and if the employee unreasonably refuses to comply he loses his right to a payment. Thus in *Meadows v Faithful Overalls Ltd*[1] a factory ran out of oil for central heating and as the temperature was below the statutory minimum the workers were asked to wait in the canteen. They were told supplies were due to arrive by 9.45 am but when they did not arrive the workers went home despite being told the supplies would soon arrive. The payment was refused, and rightly said the tribunal. It was reasonable to ask them to remain at 9.45 am.

[1] *Meadows v Faithful Overalls Ltd* [1977] IRLR 330, IT.

5 CALCULATION OF PAYMENT

11.18 The maximum entitlement, which will apply to most employees, because the rates are not very high, is £14.50 per day[1] with a maximum of five days in any three-month period.[2] Subject to these limits, to which we shall return, the amount of payment is the number of normal working hours multiplied by the guaranteed hourly rate. If there are no normal working hours for the day in question, then there is no entitlement to a payment. Employees who work under flexible hours contracts could be faced with a problem. The guaranteed hourly rate is calculated by different methods. A week's pay must be calculated[3] and then if the normal hours do not differ you simply divide the week's pay by normal hours. The latter are taken as those in force on the workless day unless the employee was then on short time when the hours are taken as those under the original contract.[4] Where the normal hours do differ from week to week then the rate is a week's pay divided by the average normal hours over the last 12 weeks, or where the employee has not been employed for long enough to enable average hours to be calculated then the hours are assessed by the employee's reasonable expectations and the experience of comparable employees.[5]

[1] Reviewable annually, ERA, s 31(7) and s 208.
[2] ERA, s 31.
[3] ERA, ss 221–229.

[4] This is not easily reconcilable with *Clemens v Peter Richards*—see footnote 1 to para 11.07 above.

[5] ERA, s 30(2)–(4).

11.19 The maximum of five days every three months is scaled down proportionately when the employee works less than five days a week, even when they are long days or nights.[1]

[1] See *Trevethan v Sterling Metals* [1977] IRLR 416.

11.20 *Set off.* The right to a guarantee payment does not affect the right of an employee to his contractual remuneration. However, there is to be no double payment so a payment under either will be set-off against the other.

11.21 Where an employee received contractual payments for five workless days these not only discharged any obligation to pay guarantee pay but were also to be taken into account in calculating the maximum number of days in a three-month period.[1]

[1] *Cartwright v Clancey Ltd* [1983] IRLR 355.

6 REMEDIES

11.22 The employee brings his claim to an industrial tribunal where there has been a total or partial failure to pay the guarantee payment.

11.23 The limitation period is three months from the workless day although there is provision to extend this period when it was not reasonably practicable to present the claim.[1]

[1] See meaning of this in the section on unfair dismissal.

11.24 The tribunal can award payment of the appropriate sum as calculated above which means a present maximum of £72.50.[1]

[1] ERA, s 34.

12 Medical suspension

Barry Mordsley

1 RIGHTS TO PAY WHILE SUSPENDED ON MEDICAL GROUNDS

12.01 An employee who is suspended from work by his employer on medical grounds in consequence of certain specified provisions is entitled, subject to certain conditions and limitations, to be paid remuneration while suspended for up to 26 weeks. It is clear that the employee must be fit for work because the Act[1] provides that he is not entitled to pay for any period when he is physically or mentally incapable of work.

[1] ERA, s 65(3).

12.02 An employee is treated as suspended only when he continues in employment but is not provided with work or does not perform the work he normally performed before the suspension. Thus even if he continues working but carrying out different tasks he is regarded as suspended. If he is being paid his usual wage then providing the right appears to be superfluous.

12.03 To be able to claim the employer must be required by statute or statutory instrument or be recommended by a Code of Practice under s 16 of the Health and Safety etc Act 1974 to suspend the employee and the relevant provision must be listed in ERA, s 64(3). This list may be, and has been, revised and covers those working with lead, dangerous chemical processes or radiation.

2 QUALIFICATIONS AND EXCLUSIONS

12.04 The employee must have one month's continuous employment when the suspension begins.[1]

[1] ERA, s 65(1).

12.05 Those excluded are those who work abroad, share fishermen and those in police service. Those who are employed on a fixed term contract of three months or less cannot claim unless they have already worked for three months when the suspension begins.[1] A similar exclusion applies to those employed on a specific task which is not expected to last for more than three months unless this three months' employment has already been completed.[2]

1 ERA, s 65(2)(a).
2 ERA, s 65(2)(h).

12.06 As stated earlier, the employee must be fit for work so if the unsafe environment actually causes harm to the employee's health he is then disentitled!

12.07 The employee loses his right to remuneration if his employer offers him suitable alternative work which he unreasonably refused even though he is not obliged to do it under his contract. He also loses his right where he does not comply with reasonable requirements imposed on him to ensure his services are avilable.[1]

1 On the meaning of these phrases, see section on guarantee payments.

3 RIGHTS AND REMEDY

12.08 The amount an employee can recover is a week's pay[1] for each week of suspension. Any payment made to the employee under his contract during the period of suspension is set off against medical suspension remuneration and vice versa.

1 ERA, ss 221–228.

12.09 The remedy for the employer's failure to pay is a complaint to an industrial tribunal.[1] The complaint must be made within three months beginning with any day for which payment is claimed but the tribunal can extend the time if it was not reasonably practicable to comply.[2]

1 ERA, s 70(1).
2 See section on unfair dismissal for the meaning of this phrase.

12.10 Finally, provisions regarding unfair dismissal relating to medical suspension are discussed later.[1] The sections provide that where an employee is dismissed because of the need to carry out a medical suspension there is a special qualifying period of one month.

Where a replacement is recruited for an employee who has been suspended on medical grounds and the replacement is subsequently dismissed to make way for the original employee's return then this is a valid ground for dismissal subject to the test of reasonableness.

1 ERA, s 106(3) dismissal of replacement and s108(2) – qualifying period of one month.

4 SUSPENSION FROM WORK ON MATERNITY GROUNDS

12.11 Section 67 of the ERA provides the right to an employee who has been suspended on maternity grounds for health and safety to be provided with suitable alternative work if it is available. The suspension will have occurred because she is pregnant or has recently given birth or is breastfeeding. There is a suspension where the contract subsists and the employee is not provided with work or her normal work. New regulations[1] require the suspension of:

(a) an employee of child bearing age where she is engaged in work posing a health risk to a new or expectant mother or her baby from any processes, condition or agents and it is not reasonable 'to alter her working conditions or it would not avoid such risk';
(b) a new or expectant mother working at night where a certificate from a doctor or mid-wife shows this is necessary for her health and safety that she not be at work for any period specified in the certificate.

The right to complain arises where the employee is suspended before being offered the suitable alternative work. There is a three-month time limit, with the reasonably practicable extension, and compensation can be awarded based on the loss suffered.

Where the employee is suspended on maternity grounds she is entitled to be paid remuneration while the suspension lasts; namely a week's pay for each week of suspension, unless she has been offered suitable alternative work which has been unreasonably refused.

Any contractual right to remuneration is set off against any tribunal award and vice versa, which therefore means that there is a right to claim it in the tribunal with a three month time limit.

---

[1] The Suspension From Work (on Maternity Grounds) Order 1994, SI 1994/2930 which came into effect on 1 December 1994.

13 Rights in relation to trade union membership and health and safety

Barry Mordsley

1 INTRODUCTION

13.01 Employees have rights to join unions and take part in their activities and these are rights which generally may be enforced against the union itself,[1] as well as against their employers. ILO conventions recognise workers' rights to freedom of association and to organise and bargain collectively. Although employees are free to join a union of their choice, in practice it may not be so easy and further there is very little in UK law which requires employers to bargain with unions.[2] There has for many years been a duty to effectively bargain with recognised trade unions over redundancies and on transfers of undertakings. The ECJ held[3] that this legislation was not a compliance with the relevant Directives which require consultation with workers' representatives because there is no compliance when there is no recognised union. The Government has now introduced legislation[4] so as to comply with this judgment which requires more consultation on these issues with either a recognised trade union or representatives of the employees. Such individuals must not, in any way, suffer any detriment as a result of such activity.[5] Further, there is no positive statutory statement of rights to join the union and take part in its activities, as opposed to the 'negative' right described below, which can have an influence on courts' interpretation. There is now statutory protection for employees who are denied employment because of their union membership or non-membership.[6] No mention is made of union activities of employment applicants.[7] However, the EAT has recently held that if an individual was refused employment because of his union activities it was open to the tribunal to conclude that he had been refused employment because of his union membership.[8] This is a considerable development.

---

[1] This is outside the scope of this section. All references to the sections on trade union membership and activities are references to the Trade Union and Labour Relations (Consolidation) Act 1992 unless otherwise indicated.

[2] Some special exceptions exist for the dwindling band of nationalised industries.

[3] *EC Commission v United Kingdom* [1994] IRLR 392 and 412.

[4] The Collective Redundancies and Transfer of Undertakings (Protection of Employment) (Amendment) Regulations 1995, SI 1995/2587.

[5] ERA, s 47. The protection extends to candidates for election.

[6] TULR(C)A 1992, ss 137ff.

[7] See below.

[8] *Harrison v Kent County Council* [1995] ICR 434, EAT.

2 THE RIGHT NOT TO BE REFUSED EMPLOYMENT ON GROUNDS OF UNION MEMBERSHIP

Introduction

13.02 Since the mid-1970s it has been unlawful to refuse to employ somebody on the basis of their sex or race and indeed in the Industrial Relations Act 1971 it was unlawful also on the basis of union membership. The Industrial Relations Act was repealed in 1974 but the Employment Act of 1990 reintroduced the right for a person not to be denied employment on grounds of union membership. This has now been re-enacted in the Trade Union and Labour Relations (Consolidation) Act 1992[1] and all references in this particular section are to that Act unless otherwise indicated.

[1] Section 137 ff.

13.03 The legislation originally introduced the right to those who were refused employment on the grounds of non-membership but this was realised to be inequitable and was extended to both membership and non-membership. It was originally aimed at eradicating the 'closed shop' or 'union membership agreement'.

The rights

13.04 It is unlawful to refuse a person employment because he is or is not a member of a trade union or because he is unwilling to accept a requirement:

(a) to take steps to become one or cease to be, or to remain or not to become, a member of a trade union; or
(b) to make payments or suffer deductions in the event of his not being a member of a trade union.[1]

[1] Section 137(1).

13.05 Unlike the rights obtaining when one is in employment, the right in relation to recruitment only gives protection in relation to union membership which means that an individual's union activities in a previous employment can be relied upon by an employer as justifying not recruiting the individual. Although it now seems to be clear that past union activities can be held to be the basis of a fear of proposed union activities with an employer, that appears to be restricted to the question of activities and does not extend to membership.[1] There are certain to be arguments as to whether the real reason for rejecting an individual is based on his union membership or activities. Arguments will be raised that union activities are a necessary incident of union membership and indeed it is difficult to separate these elements.

However, the recent EAT ruling in *Harrison* throws some doubt on this proposition and further development will be awaited with interest.

[1] *Fitzpatrick v British Railways Board* [1991] IRLR 376, CA.

Advertisements

13.06 Refusal of employment on union grounds is conclusively presumed to have been the reason for a refusal in relation to certain advertisements placed by employers and is unlawful.[1] Thus, where an advertisement is published which indicates or might reasonably be understood as indicating:

(a) the employment to which the advertisement relates is open only to a person who is, or who is not, a member of a trade union; or
(b) that any such requirement to become or cease to be a member of a union, or to make payments or suffer such deductions as mentioned above where a person does not satisfy that condition or is unwilling to accept that requirement;

then the conclusive presumption applies.[2] An 'advertisement' includes any form of advertisement or notice whether it is public or not and references to publishing an advertisement are so construed.[3] One assumes it would apply to an internal notice on the notice board. Where there is an arrangement or practice under which employment is only offered to persons put forward by a trade union and the union only puts forward members, any non-member refused employment pursuant to this arrangement shall be taken to have been refused employment because he is not a member of the union.[4]

1 Section 137(1).
2 Section 137(3).
3 Section 143(1).
4 Section 137(4).

13.07 Unlike race and sex discrimination legislation, advertisements which might found an action by an individual are not in themselves actionable at the suit of an external body like the CRE or EOC.

Refusal of employment

13.08 This apparently deceptively simple concept is carefully defined.[1] There is a refusal of employment if the 'employer':

(a) refuses or deliberately omits to entertain and process his application or enquiry; or
(b) causes him to withdraw or cease to pursue his application or enquiry; or
(c) refuses or deliberately omits to offer him employment of that description; or
(d) makes him an offer of such employment, the terms of which are such as no reasonable employer who wishes to fill the post would offer and which is not accepted; or
(e) makes him an offer of such employment but withdraws it or causes him not to accept it.

The care which has been taken over this drafting suggests that it will be difficult for an employer to out-flank this legislation.

1 Section 137(5).

13.09 Where there is an offer of employment on terms which include a requirement that he is to be or not to be a member of a trade union or that he must become or cease to become a member of a trade union or make payments or suffer deductions if he does not become a member of a trade union and he does not accept the offer for those reasons he shall be treated as having been refused employment for that reason.[1]

[1] Section 137(6).

Employment agencies

13.10 It is unlawful for an employment agency to refuse a person any of its services:

(a) because he is, or is not, a member of a trade union; or
(b) because he is unwilling to accept a requirement to take steps to become or cease to be or to remain or not to become, a member of a trade union.[1]

[1] Section 138(1).

13.11 Where an advertisement is published which indicates or might reasonably have been understood as indicating:

(a) that any service of an employment agency is available only to a person who is, or is not, a member of a trade union; or
(b) that any such requirement as is mentioned above, will be imposed in relation to a service to which the advertisement relates, a person who does not satisfy that condition, or as the case may be is unwilling to accept that requirement, and who seeks to avail himself of and is refused that service, shall be conclusively presumed to have been refused it for that reason.[1]

[1] Section 138(3).

13.12 A person shall be taken to be refused a service if he seeks to use it but the agency:

(a) refuses or deliberately omits to make the service available to him; or
(b) causes him not to avail himself of the service or to cease to avail himself of it; or
(c) does not provide the same service, on the same terms, as is provided to others.[1]

[1] Section 138(4).

13.13 Where a person is offered a service on terms which include a requirement that he is or is not a member of a trade union, or any such requirement as is mentioned above, and he does not accept the offer as he does not satisfy or as the case may be is unwilling to accept that requirement, he shall be treated as having been refused a service for that reason.[1]

[1] Section 138(5).

13.14 Under these provisions, 'employment' means employment under a contract of employment and 'employment agency' means a person who, whether for profit or not, provides services for the purposes of finding employment for workers or supplying employers with workers, but a trade union should not be regarded as an employment agency by reason of services provided by it only for, or in relation to, its members.[1] The definition of 'employment agency' as including non-profit making organisations will ensure that it is made very difficult to avoid the law via this route.

[1] Sections 143(1) and 143(2).

Enforcement of the right

13.15 A person who is unlawfully refused employment by an 'employer' or refused a service of any employment agency can complain to an industrial tribunal.[1] There is a three-month time limit which begins from the date of the conduct to which the complaint relates or where the tribunal is satisfied that it is not reasonably practicable for the complaint to have been presented before that period within such further period as the tribunal considers reasonable. As the concept of a refusal of employment is sophisticated so must the date of the conduct complained about be in relation to time limits. Where there is an actual refusal, this is the date of the refusal. Where there was a deliberate omission to entertain and process the complainant's application or enquiry or to offer employment, then the date would be the end of the period in which it was reasonable to expect an employer to act. There is considerable room for disagreement over this particular issue and it will be interesting to see whether the tribunals will fix a date for the end of the period and then determine whether it was reasonably practicable to complain in time where the employee genuinely believed that the matter may have taken longer. It is quite clear that the employee's belief may well enable him to bring himself within an extended period which may be granted beyond the three months. Where the complainant withdraws his application as a result of the 'employer's' conduct, it will be the date of the conduct. Where the offer was withdrawn it will be the date when it was withdrawn and when an offer was made but was not accepted, it will be the date upon which the offer was made. Similar provisions apply to the date of conduct in relation to employment agencies.[2]

[1] Sections 137(2) and 138(2).
[2] Section 139.

The proper defendant

13.16 Where a person has a right to complain against a prospective employer and against an employment agency arising out of the same facts, he may sue either or both and, if he sued one only, he can subsequently request the other party to be joined as can the first respondent. The request will automatically be granted if it is made before the hearing of the complaint[1] but may be refused if it is made after that time and no request will be permitted after the tribunal has made its decision. Where the complaint succeeds against both parties, the tribunal may order that compensation shall be paid by one party or the other or partly by one and partly by the other as the tribunal may consider just and equitable in the circumstances.[2]

1 There will be no problem in relation to time limits.
2 Section 141.

Action against third parties

13.17 Where the complainant or the respondent complains that the respondent was induced to act by pressure which a trade union or other person exercised on him by calling, organising, procuring or financing a strike or other industrial action, or by threatening to do so, the union or person may be joined as a party to the proceedings. Once again, the request will be granted for joinder before the hearing of the complaint but may be refused after that time and no request will be permitted after the tribunal has made its decision. Once again compensation can be paid wholly or partly by the person joined.[1]

1 Section 142.

Remedies

13.18 Where the complaint succeeds, a tribunal must make a declaration to that effect and may make such of the following as it considers just and equitable:

(a) an order requiring the respondent to pay compensation to the complainant of such amount as the tribunal may determine; or
(b) a recommendation that the respondent take, within a specified period, action appearing to the tribunal to be practicable for the purpose of obviating or reducing the adverse effect on the complainant of any conduct to which the complaint relates. Compensation is to be assessed on the same basis as damages for breaches of statutory duty and specifically permits compensation for injury to feelings to be awarded. If the respondent fails to comply with the recommendations without reasonable justification the tribunal can increase its award of compensation but it must not exceed the statutory maximum limit as exists for unfair dismissal which is presently (1996/7) set at £11,300.[1]

1 Section 140.

Exclusions

13.19 The usual exclusions apply so that members of the armed forces cannot exercise this right, neither can individuals where there is a certificate in relation to national security, those employed in the police service, those who ordinarily work outside Great Britain, share fishermen and those working on ships registered outside Great Britain.[1]

1 See Part VII of the Act. Section 273ff.

3 THE RIGHT TO TRADE UNION MEMBERSHIP AND ACTIVITIES

13.20 There are four basic rights: these are not to have action (short of dismissal) taken against him as an individual by his employer for the purpose of:

(a) preventing or deterring him from being or seeking to become a member of an independent trade union or penalising him for so doing; or
(b) preventing or deterring him from taking part in the activities of an independent trade union at any appropriate time or penalising him for so doing; or
(c) compelling him to be or become a member of any trade union or of a particular trade union or one of a number of particular trade unions; or
(d) enforcing a requirement (whether or not imposed by his contract of employment or in writing) that in the event of his failure to become or his ceasing to remain a member of any trade union or of a particular trade union or of one of a number of particular trade unions he must make one or more payments[1] or suffer deductions from his remuneration. There is no qualifying period of employment or minimum number of hours per week in order to claim the right.

1 TULR(C)A 1992, s 146.

13.21 There is some authority on the above rights which will be considered below but it is clear that action against the employee is unlawful only if its purpose is to infringe the employee's rights. It shall be for the employer to show the purpose for which action was taken against the complainant and in this context pressure of industrial action or the threat of it must be ignored.[1] It is vital to distinguish between 'purpose' and 'effect'[2] a matter which is discussed below.

1 Section 148.
2 *Gallacher v Department of Transport* [1994] IRLR 231, CA.

13.22 Where the tribunal finds that the employer had two or more purposes, one of which was to further a change in his relationship with all or any class[1] of his employees and another one which fell within one of the proscribed grounds, then the tribunal must disregard the latter purpose unless they consider that the action of the employer was such as no reasonable employer would take having regard to the purpose of altering employment relationships as stated above.[2]

1 See definition below.
2 Section 148(3) inserted by TURERA, s 13.

13.23 It is quite apparent that this very late amendment to the TURERA was aimed at nullifying the decisions which had just been made by the Court of Appeal[1] which held that it was unlawful for an employer to offer a financial inducement to employees who accepted personal contracts and would not permit the union to act on their behalf. The Court held that this inducement had the effect of deterring employees from being members. Nothing in these provisions or decisions prevented an employer from de-recognising a union which is regarded as a collective issue. It is the impact on the individual employee that matters. This rapid amendment was very much a 'knee-jerk' reaction to the court decision. It is extremely unusual, to say the least, to state that even if an action was taken mainly for a particular purpose that that purpose can be disregarded. It is almost making a mockery of the substantive right of trade union membership. However, this legislative change has become less important since the House of Lords reversed the Court of Appeal decision in the *Wilson*[2] case. It held, by a majority, that the failure to accord a pay rise to those who refused to sign new contracts was not an action taken against employees and further was not taken with the purpose of deterring union membership.

1 *Association Newspapers Ltd v Wilson* and *Associated British Port v Palmer* [1993] IRLR 336, CA.
2 [1995] IRLR 258, HL.

13.24 A 'class' means 'those employed at a particular place of work, those employees of a particular grade, category or description or those of a particular grade, category or description employed at a particular place of work'.[1] It is difficult to know how these categories or descriptions will be interpreted but it will be argued that it will cover those who are prepared not to be union members. If that is the case then all will turn on what action would 'no reasonable employer' take. It is possible that one factor might be the differential between the terms offered to members and non-members. However, it could be argued that this analysis somewhat begs the question in that the class is being defined after the action had been proposed. That is, when a proposal has been accepted. These are difficult and complex issues.

1 Section 148(5).

13.25 What is 'action short of dismissal'? 'Action' is defined[1] as including an omission, but a failure to accord an employee a benefit accorded to other employees was held to be lawful in the *Wilson* case,[2] overruling the *Ridgway*[3] decision.

1 Section 298.
2 [1995] IRLR 258, HL.
3 *National Coal Board v Ridgway* [1987] ICR 641, CA.

13.26 It has also been held that the refusal of a parking permit and the denial of representation by an official of one's own union constitutes 'taking action' against the employee.[1] However, the *Wilson* case is so far-reaching in relation to the definition of 'action' that these cases must have some doubt cast upon them. While 'action' is defined to include an omission, the House of Lords has effectively nullified this aspect of the definition.

1 See *Carlson v Post Office* [1981] ICR 343, EAT and *Cheall v Vauxhall Motors Ltd* [1979] IRLR 253 – see below. Reprimanding a shop steward for talking to the press and warning of disciplinary action if it was repeated was included: *British Airways Engine Overhaul Ltd v Francis* [1981] ICR 278, EAT.

13.27 Does 'taking action' include the threatening of action? Under a strict interpretation it would appear that it does not, yet a threat is some kind of action and in a broad sense one can see that it would have a very definite effect. We have no authoritative decision. In one case[1] the employer threatened to close his business to prevent union recognition. The tribunal said this was action but the EAT, without the benefit of argument on this, doubted if this was right. A tribunal felt bound by this decision that threats were included and thus a threat to report firemen for holding a union meeting on the premises without permission was held to fall within the subsection.[2] In contrast, in another area of labour law a threat of industrial action has been held not to constitute the taking of industrial action.[3] *Harvey* agrees with this view in the present context but then suggests that if, as a result of the threat, the employees do not proceed with their proposed behaviour this should be treated as 'taking action'. With respect, this is not altogether an easy path to follow and it would be simpler to say that threats either fall within or outside the subsection. One should judge by what the 'defendant' has done, not by how the 'plaintiff' reacts.

1 *Brassington v Cauldon Wholesale Ltd* [1978] ICR 405, [1977] IRLR 479, EAT.
2 *Carter v Wiltshire County Council* [1979] IRLR 331, IT.
3 *Midland Plastics v Till* [1983] ICR 118, [1983] IRLR 9, EAT; but note *Lewis and Britton v E Mason & Sons* [1994] IRLR 4, EAT.

13.28 The action must be taken against the employee 'as an individual'. The purpose of these words is to ensure that action taken against an employee's trade union is not to be treated as action against the individual. This is an easier distinction to state than to apply in practice. It arises as a result of the problems that arose under the Industrial Relations Act of 1971 in a number of cases. The distinction, in any sense, is a very artificial one because discrimination against one's trade union is certain to have some impact on the individual employee. We have already mentioned the *Ridgway* case in which this question arose. The pay differential arose because the NCB was, in essence, favouring the UDM over the NUM. However, the Court of Appeal was quite sure that the amount of pay an individual receives must impact on him as an individual even if it is affected by negotiations between the employer and the union.

13.29 Different treatment of unions by employers does not necessarily lead to discrimination against individuals. For example, the act of recognition is not in itself discriminatory although its effects may be. Acts which relate to recognition or negotiation do not necessarily lead to a finding of unlawfulness.

13.30 Thus, in *Carlson v Post Office*[1] Slynn J stated 'Many agreements between an employer and recognised unions must confer benefits on those unions and their members which may lead in fact to disadvantages being suffered by those who are members of other, non-recognised unions. That itself is not a breach of the Act'. What is required is to consider the employer's purpose and he would, presumably, be able to argue that the differential treatment is as a result of recognising one but not another union. As this case related to the denial of a car parking facility which is very much an individual matter, one wonders at the comments made in relation to the *Ridgway* case mentioned earlier. The waters are indeed muddy.

1 [1981] ICR 343, [1981] IRLR 158, EAT.

13.31 The famous case of *Post Office v Union of Post Office Workers and Crouch*[1] distinguished between organisational activities of unions in which discrimination against members would be inferred and negotiating activities in which it would not. But if an employee is permitted representation by his union, say, at a disciplinary hearing, that should surely be classified as an individual right.[2] It has been held that where an individual employee used her trade union official to help clarify and negotiate the terms and conditions of her employment this was an important incident of union membership and when she was dismissed following her enlisting his help this was held to be a dismissal for union membership. One had to consider the consequences of membership as part of the membership rights.[3] However, in the *Wilson* and *Palmer* cases the majority of their Lordships thought that the two should not be equated. This is a far reaching proposition and has been questioned by the EAT which has suggested that *Armitage* was correct on its own facts and that tribunals can still find action being taken on grounds of union membership when one is obtaining assistance from the union.[4]

1 [1974] 1 All ER 229, [1974] ICR 378, HL.
2 See the Industrial Relations Act case of *Howle v GEC Power Engineering* [1974] ICR 13.
3 *Discount Tobacco and Confectionery Ltd v Armitage* [1990] IRLR 15, EAT.
4 *Speciality Care plc v Pachela* [1996] IRLR 248 but not support for *Wilson* in *NACODS v Gluchowski* [1996] IRLR 252.

13.32 In *Cheall v Vauxhall Motors Ltd*[1] the employer refused to allow Cheall's Union, APEX, to make representations about a shift allowance. The employer did not want to upset a rival union and it was held that Cheall had been penalised by his employer for his union membership.

1 [1979] IRLR 253.

13.33 The action against the employee must be taken for the purpose of preventing him from being a member or taking part in its activities. We have already noted that it is for the employer to show the purpose for which the action was taken and the onus is therefore clearly on him. However, all of the above cases must be considered in the light of the statutory alteration made in 1993. We must await judicial interpretation. Further, he is not entitled to take into account any pressure exercised on him by threats of industrial action.[1]

1 Section 148.

13.34 As we have already seen in the *Carlson* case (above) it was not enough that the employee suffered by being denied a parking permit – it had to be with the purpose of preventing etc. If the employer could show another purpose for his action, for example, to avoid multi-unionism, he is protected. Therefore one does not look at the effect of the employer's behaviour but at its purpose.[1] Thus where although the effect of the employer's action might have been to force membership of a particular union that was not its intention and therefore the employer had not acted unlawfully. We have already noted the dual-purpose provision inserted by TURERA 1993.

[1] *Gallacher v Department of Transport* [1994] IRLR 231, CA.

13.35 Finally, let us briefly consider the words preventing, deterring, penalising and compelling. There is very little discussion of these phrases in the cases. In an Industrial Relations Act case[1] the employer pointed out to the employee the 'dangers or troubles' of leaving the union. This was held not to have prevented or deterred him from exercising his right to be a non-member as the matters mentioned were outside the employer's control and the employer made it quite clear that the decision was the employee's. This fine distinction is very similar to the distinction between 'information' and inducing breach of contract; a distinction which has exercised many fine minds to date.

[1] *McWilliam v Collins, Sons & Co* [1974] ICR 226.

13.36 However, where an employee was moved from work he preferred to other work to reduce his contact with colleagues so as to stop him talking about union membership it was held that this action was taken to prevent or deter him from exercising his union activity rights. However, the action was not taken to penalise him which is an interesting interpretation given that it was work which he enjoyed less.[1]

[1] *Robb v Leon Motor Services Ltd* [1978] ICR 506, [1978] IRLR 26, EAT.

13.37 In *Carlson*'s case (above) where the employee was denied a parking permit the EAT remitted the case to the tribunal but said this refusal could be a penalty. A penalty was not to be limited to a positive punishment or a financial penalty but could be any situation where an employee was subject to a disadvantage.[1]

[1] Shades of discrimination law here see *Jeremiah v Ministry of Defence* [1979] IRLR 436, CA on the definition of 'detriment'.

4 THE RIGHTS–SPECIFICALLY

(i) To join an independent trade union

13.38 An 'independent' trade union is one not under the domination or control of an employer and not liable to interference by an employer tending towards such control.[1] This may be as a result of financial or material support or by other means whatsoever. The definition extends to cover groups of employers or employers' associations. It will therefore exclude associations which are at a very early stage of development and are therefore dependent on the employer and associations which continue very much under the employer's aegis.[2]

[1] Section 5.
[2] See eg *Squibb UK Staff Association v Certification Officer* [1979] 2 All ER 452, [1979] IRLR 75, CA.

13.39 The precise meaning of this right was examined in the *Ridgway* case (above) where the NCB had argued that their action in not paying a pay rise to NUM members was not illegal because they had not prevented employees from joining a trade union. If there was a penalty it was because of their membership of the NUM not simply because they belonged to a union. This argument succeeded at the EAT but in the Court of Appeal it was held that employees had the right to join the union of their choice and were not to be penalised for doing so. Thus, the subsection covered the case where the employer's purpose is to prevent an employee from being a member of a particular union as well as one where that purpose is to prevent him from being a member of any union whatsoever. It is submitted that the new 1993 provision regarding purpose could well lead to this case being decided differently today unless a robust approach is taken to this unusual drafting. In any event the House of Lords in *Wilson*[1] held that *Ridgway* was wrongly decided and thus the general proposition in the text must be open to considerable doubt.

1 See para 13.25 above.

(ii) A right to take part in the activities of the union

13.40 Union activities are not defined. But like elephants, people know what they are when seen or described. Furthermore, the activity need not be sufficiently precise to be identifiable. One should approach the protection purposively.[1] Attendance at union meetings would clearly be covered but it is difficult to accept that industrial action can constitute union activities. Of course, in one respect, it clearly is, but the existence of a statutory provision relating to dismissal of strikers and the fact that industrial action almost by definition will only take place at an 'inappropriate time' means that it cannot be covered.[2] However, participating in the preliminary planning and organising of industrial action can amount to taking part in union activities.[3]

1 *Fitzpatrick v British Railways Board* [1991] IRLR 376, CA.
2 See *Drew v St Edmundsbury Borough Council* [1980] ICR 513, [1980] IRLR 459, EAT.
3 *Britool Ltd v Roberts* [1993] IRLR 481.

13.41 The courts have been restrictive in their interpretation of union activities. It has been held that there is a distinction between the activities of an independent trade union and the activities of an individual independent trade unionist. Thus, where individual employees complained about health and safety although the subject-matter could constitute union activities, it was held to be the activities of individuals even though the unions had been involved to some extent.[1] This is a very narrow interpretation. A dismissal case involving union activities shows that narrowness even further.[2] In *Therm A Stor Ltd v Atkins*[3] the employer dismissed a number of employees following a letter from their union's district secretary to him asking for recognition. The Court of Appeal said the dismissal was an 'indefensible reaction' but it was not a dismissal for union activities. It was an employer's reaction to a trade union's activities not a reaction to an individual employee's activities in a trade union context. Where an employee's activities fall within the phrase 'the activities of an independent trade union' must be judged objectively.[4] From these authorities it is difficult to see where the area of protection lies—at its highest it is an extremely narrow area.

1 *Chant v Aquaboats Ltd* [1978] 3 All ER 102, [1978] ICR 643, EAT and *Drew* (see footnote 1 to para 13.20 above).
2 The provisions are in s 152 and are identical to s 146 – see below.
3 [1983] IRLR 78.
4 *Port of London Authority v Payne* [1992] IRLR 447, EAT.

13.42 The distinction between 'purpose' and 'effect' has already been alluded to. The words 'for the purpose of' connote an object which the employer desires or seeks to achieve. Thus when a full-time union official was rejected for a promotion for a higher civil service grade on the basis that he needed to take a job to show his managerial skills this was not unlawful even though the only way he could take the job was to reduce his union duties. The tribunal considered that the employer's recommendation was intended to deter him from spending so much time on union work even though it accepted that the recommendation was both in his best interests and understandable. The EAT and the Court of Appeal did not agree. The employer's purpose it was stated, was to ensure that only those with sufficient management experience were fit for promotion. It was not to deter the employee.[1]

While this decision appears correct it is apparent that there will be cases which are less clear and tribunals and courts will have to be astute to ensure that certain requirements or recommendations are not used as a smokescreen to hide a general deterrence to union activities. The problem is that there is an understandable reluctance to interfere with managerial prerogative as to these matters and that this argument might be too easily acceded by tribunals and courts. However, with their experience it is to be hoped that genuine cases will be perceived by them.

1 *Gallacher v Department of Transport* [1994] IRLR 231, CA.

13.43 It is thus much more likely that a union official will be protected. Thus in *British Airways Engine Overhaul Ltd v Francis*[1] a reprimand by an employer for failing to get clearance for a press release was held to relate to the union activities of Mrs Francis, a shop steward who was criticising the union for its attitude to equal pay.

1 [1981] ICR 278, [1981] IRLR 9, EAT.

13.44 However, protection is not limited to union officials so if an employee were dismissed because he sought the advice of a union representative and then sought to apply it, he is likely to be protected.[1] Activities of recruitment and formation of a branch seeking recognition will qualify irrespective of the employee's status.[2] A manager who made disparaging remarks about his employer at an induction course for trainee managers when he was speaking on behalf of the union and who was demoted for this had been treated on the basis of his taking part in union activities.[3]

1 *Brennan v Ellward (Lancs) Ltd* [1976] IRLR 378, EAT and *Dixon v West Ella Developments Ltd* [1978] ICR 856, [1978] IRLR 151, EAT; *Discount Tobacco v Armitage* [1990] IRLR 15, EAT.
2 *Lyon v St James Press Ltd* [1976] ICR 413, [1976] IRLR 215, EAT.
3 *Bass Taverns Ltd v Burgess* [1995] IRLR 596, CA.

13.45 In the *Lyon* case the employer complained of the secretive way in which the union recruitment had taken place which, he said, had created disruption and dissension within the workforce. The EAT rejected this and said if he had been open about his activities they would never have developed. However, it did say that wholly unreasonable, extraneous or malicious acts done in support of union activities might render the dismissal fair. Such actions would be very unusual and unlikely to apply in many cases. Over-enthusiastic attempts to get employees to join the union constitute taking part in union activities and cannot be used as a ground to justify dismissal according to the case of *Robb v Leon* (above).

At an appropriate time

13.46 The union activities must take place at an appropriate time which means:

(a) outside his working hours (meaning when he is required to be at work); or
(b) within working hours but at a time at which, in accordance with arrangements agreed with, or consent given by, his employer it is permissible to take part in those activities.[1]

[1] Section 146(2).

13.47 Working hours raises the question of hours when the employee is required to be at work but not actually working. In the *Post Office v Crouch* case (above) it was said that such periods could be treated as outside working hours and could therefore be an appropriate time. These would include tea breaks and periods before and after actual work.

13.48 Activities can take place on the employer's premises—this is the inference that one must draw from the previous paragraph and in fact it was stated expressly in the *Post Office* case. However, the employer is not required to 'incur expense or submit to substantial inconvenience'. Activities can take place provided they do not cause such substantial inconvenience either to their employer or their non-union colleagues. Employers must tolerate minor infringements of their strict legal rights which do them no real harm. A one-hour stoppage was held to be more than a minor inconvenience in one case.[1]

[1] *Marley Tile Co Ltd v Shaw* [1980] ICR 72, [1980] IRLR 25, CA – see below.

13.49 Employers may make arrangements for, or give consent to, the carrying on of activities during working hours. Originally, it was thought that this consent had to be express[1] but the Court of Appeal has held that in a proper case consent can be implied.[2] However, in that case the court very severely limited the situations in which consent could be implied. It said that it could be inferred from custom and practice but not silence. However, in that case the circumstances were such that there were opportunities for implication which were not taken. The EAT has said that if employees are allowed to talk at work they should not be prevented from talking about union affairs so long as it does not interfere with their work or cause disruption.[3]

1 *Robb v Leon* above.
2 *Marley Tile* above.
3 *Zucker v Astrid Jewels Ltd* [1978] ICR 1088, [1978] IRLR 385.

13.50 The fact that activities must take place during work hours appears to mean that it is not possible to argue that you have been dismissed for union activities when they relate to a period prior to engagement. However, the position is not so clear. In *City of Birmingham District Council v Beyer*[1] a well-known union militant knew he would not obtain a job with an employer because of his reputation. He gave a false name, was discovered and was dismissed. A year later he found another job with the same employer, gave his true name but was almost immediately discovered and dismissed. The employer said, and this was accepted by the EAT, that he had been dismissed for his gross deceit a year earlier and not for union activities. In any event the EAT said that activities could not possibly refer to those outside and before the employment began. Accordingly, there was no protection, even though he had to resort to deceit to hide his union links. The more recent *Fitzpatrick*[2] decision provides the opportunity for the employee to argue that he was dismissed for his proposed union activities based on his past activities with a previous employer. Although s 146 makes no reference to proposed activities, nevertheless if action were taken against an individual based on previous actions which created suspicion in the employer's mind a tribunal or court could rely on *Fitzpatrick* and find this to be the purpose for which action was taken. If the employer dismisses or penalises the employee because of his deceit then this falls outside the protection granted to employees. *Fitzpatrick* does decide that what happened in previous employment can be relevant to action taken by a subsequent employer. This is supported by the *Port of London Authority v Payne*[3] case where shop stewards were selected for redundancy because the employer believed they would engage in disruptive activities. That belief was based on their previous activities which were trade union activities and therefore the dismissals were automatically unfair. Clearly this principle would apply to membership rights also. A further extension of this line occurred in the *Harrison* case referred to above.

1 [1978] 1 All ER 910, [1977] IRLR 211.
2 [1991] IRLR 376, CA.
3 [1992] IRLR 447, EAT.

(iii) The right not to join

13.51 No employee can be compelled to be or become a member of any trade union or of a particular trade union or of one of a number of particular trade unions.

13.52 This general right is no longer subject to any closed shop situations which in essence were deprived of any protection by the Employment Act 1988.

13.53 The statutory words are plain and need no further comment. Prior to the effective abolition of the closed shop in 1988 this was hardly the case.

(iv) A right not to contribute

13.54 This provision should cease to be of much concern with the effective abolition of the closed shop. However, the closed shop or union membership agreement has not actually been outlawed but been stripped of protection and therefore this provision may still be relevant to closed shops.

13.55 Closed shop agreements almost always provide that certain employees can be excluded on certain grounds, usually of conscientious objection. However, they usually have to pay to the union or a charity to avoid the 'free rider' argument. The Act[1] provides that there is to be no victimisation for refusing to make such payments. The closed shop exception was repealed in 1988. The employer is not permitted to make a deduction from the employee's pay based on this payment because this is also prohibited.

1 Section 146(3) and (4).

5 EXCLUSIONS AND QUALIFICATIONS

13.56 Those who work abroad, the armed forces, share fishermen and those in the police service cannot claim the right not to be victimised. There is no minimum period to qualify for the rights but you have to begin employment.[1]

1 See *Beyer* above.

6 THE REMEDY

13.57 A complaint goes to a tribunal[1] and must be presented within three months beginning with the date of the act or last act of alleged victimisation. There is an escape clause allowing for a longer period where it was not reasonably practicable[2] to have brought the claim. In one case[3] the EAT did not use unfair dismissal law as an analogy and treated the date of dismissal of the appeal or its communication as the date from which the period ran. The employees appealed against a reprimand and this appeal was dismissed and communicated to them. The EAT, affirming the tribunal, said time should run from the date that the appeal result was communicated to them. This is probably fairer than the unfair dismissal rule which relates the period back to the original dismissal.

1 Section 147.
2 For a full discussion of this phrase see the section on unfair dismissal.
3 *British Airways Board v Clark* [1982] IRLR 238.

13.58 The EAT was less liberal in *Adlam v Salisbury and Wells Theological College*[1] where four employees complained that they were being paid on a different basis from others. They said that they did not appreciate they were suffering a detriment until well after the basis was changed. Under s 147(a) where the action is part of a series of similar actions the time limit can run from the last of the actions. The employers argued that each weekly pay packet was a separate breach and time could run from the last pay packet. The EAT thought otherwise and held that each weekly payment was simply a continuation of the original action which was the change and which had occurred a year earlier. Accordingly, the claim was well out of time and the EAT adverted to the possibility of claims being brought very late which would be absurd. Given developments in the discrimination field this is unlikely to be followed.[2]

1 [1985] ICR 786.
2 See the section on discrimination below.

13.59 The burden of proof is on the employee to prove the act of alleged victimisation.[1] Then it is for the employer to prove the purpose of the act.[2]

1 This may be difficult if an unfair dismissal analogy is used — see *Smith v Hayle Town Council* [1978] ICR 996, [1978] IRLR 413, CA which places a very onerous task on the employee.
2 Section 148.

13.60 It is suggested that it cannot be a good defence to a victimisation claim that it was carried out to avoid industrial action by other workers. Where the industrial action has been called or threatened in order to induce the victimisation the employer or employee is entitled to join the person(s) or union which organised the industrial action provided the request is made before the hearing. After that time the tribunal has a discretion to refuse but it can never join the third party after it has made its finding.[1]

1 Section 149.

13.61 Those involved in the actual or threatened industrial action will have to be judged by whether they could reasonably foresee the likelihood of victimisation as a consequence of their action.[1] This does not avoid liability to the complainant—it is simply a question of whether the employer or union should pay the compensation or if it is to be shared, in what proportion.

1 See *Ford Motor Co Ltd v Hudson* [1978] 3 All ER 23, [1978] IRLR 66, EAT and *Colwyn Borough Council v Dutton* [1980] IRLR 420, EAT.

13.62 If the employee succeeds, the tribunal makes a declaration to that effect and can award compensation which is of an amount as is considered just and equitable having regard to the infringement of the complainant's rights and the loss suffered. The loss includes any expenses incurred and loss of any benefit which he might have received. The compensation is subject to the duty to mitigate and there is the possibility of contributory fault.[1] Although the remedy is not penal the seriousness of the default is relevant and allows compensation for injury to body, reputation, feelings or health as well as financial loss. The leading authority on this is *Brassington v Cauldon Wholesale Ltd*.[2] In this case the employer said he would rather close down than recognise the union. The EAT said loss was more than financial and could include loss for injury to feelings or where stress had been engendered or where the employee's sincere wish to join a union had been frustrated. This allows awards to be more than merely minimal and in *Ridgway*'s case[3] the Court of Appeal said compensation could be given for the frustration and stress occasioned by having to work alongside others who were being paid more for doing the same work. These claims were not to be regarded as de minimis.[4]

1 See s 149 generally and on contributory fault and mitigation see the unfair dismissal section.
2 [1978] ICR 405, [1977] IRLR 479 (and see above).
3 See above.
4 May LJ dissented on this point and said *Brassington* was wrongly decided.

7 EMPLOYMENT PROTECTION IN HEALTH AND SAFETY CASES

Introduction

13.63 The provisions below were introduced in the Trade Union Reform and Employment Rights Act 1993.

13.64 The 1993 Act provided a new right to employees against being dismissed where the reason relates to health and safety[1] and also being subjected to a detriment in health and safety cases. These provisions are now contained in ss 44, 48 and 49 of the ERA.

1 See Chapter 19.

Basic provisions

13.65 Every employee has a right not to be subjected to any detriment by any act or deliberate failure to act by his employer done on the ground that:

(a) Having been designated by the employer to carry out activities in connection with preventing or reducing risks to the health or safety of employees at work, he carried out, or proposed to carry out, any such activities.
(b) Being a representative of employees on matters of health and safety at work, or a member of a safety committee—
    (i) in accordance with arrangements established under or by virtue of any enactment; or
    (ii) by reason of being acknowledged as such by the employer;

    he performed or proposed to perform, any functions as such a representative or a member of such a committee.
(c) Being an employee at a place where—
    (i) there was no such representative or safety committee; or
    (ii) there was such a representative or safety committee but it was not reasonably practicable for the employee to raise the matter by those means;

    he brought to his employer's attention, by reasonable means, circumstances connected with his work which he reasonably believed were harmful or potentially harmful to health or safety.
(d) In circumstances of danger which he reasonably believed to be serious and imminent and which he could not reasonably have been expected to avert, he left, or proposed to leave, his place of work or any dangerous part of his place of work; or refused to return while the danger persisted.
(e) In circumstances of danger which he reasonably believed to be serious

and imminent, he took, or proposed to take, appropriate steps to protect himself or other persons from the danger.

The appropriateness of the steps taken are to be judged by reference to all the circumstances, including his knowledge of the facilities and advice available to him at the time. An employee is not to be regarded as having been subjected to any detriment in relation to (e) above if the employer shows that it was or would have been so negligent for the employee to take the steps which he took or proposed to take that a reasonable employer might have treated him as the employer did.[1]

[1] ERA, s 44.

Enforcement of the right

13.66 An employee can complain to the industrial tribunal that he has been subjected to a detriment in contravention of the above provisions and it will then be for the employer to show the ground upon which any act or deliberate failure to act was done. There is a three months' time limit with the normal extension if it was not reasonably practicable for the complaint to have been presented and it is stated that if there had been a number of actions or omissions at the time the limit runs from the last such action or ommission, and where the action is extended over a period it means the last day of the period. Where there is an omission it shall be treated as having been done when it was decided upon.[1]

[1] ERA, s 48.

Remedies

13.67 If the tribunal finds that the complaint is well-founded it must make a declaration to that effect and may make an award or compensation which should reflect the amount which the tribunal considers just and equitable in all the circumstances having regard to the infringement complained of and to any loss which is attributable to the act or failure which infringed the employee's right.[1] The loss includes any expenses reasonably incurred and loss of any benefits which might reasonably be expected to have been obtained. The compensation will be reduced by any contributory fault and there is a duty to mitigate loss. The fact that there is mention of the complaint regarding the infringement means that compensation will be payable if the tribunal considers it suitable over and above the loss suffered. It is unlikely that very serious injury to feelings will have been suffered but it all depends on the circumstances and it may well be that the tribunal will feel inclined to make awards on that basis. Comments on these provisions have been made in the chapter on unfair dismissal as there have been corresponding rights introduced in relation to unfair dismissal but it is quite clear that there will be some issues which will need to be clarified by the tribunals and courts which will obviously have to set out guidelines in due course.

[1] ERA, s 49.

14 Time off work

Barry Mordsley

1 INTRODUCTION

14.01 The employee has a fundamental duty to be ready and available for work and a failure to be so is a clear breach of contract. However, in an emergency, almost all employers would allow time off and the law would almost certainly protect an employee against any disciplinary measures taken because of an absence in such circumstances.[1]

[1] Note, however, *Warner v Barbers Stores* [1978] IRLR 109.

14.02 In practice many employers, particularly larger employers, have been permitting time off for a wide variety of reasons for quite some time. These would include compassionate leave and study leave and for trade union duties. More recently some employers have conceded the right to some paternity leave. The European Community is at present considering a draft Directive on parental leave on which the UK is clearly its greatest opponent. So far as trade union duties are concerned the Code of Practice issued in 1971 recommended that shop stewards be allowed paid time off to carry out their industrial relations functions and be trained. However, no statute provided this right although some employers might have conceded the right contractually, either expressly or impliedly, by custom and practice. The position now is very different. Statutes have provided a right to time off, sometimes with pay, in a number of situations which we consider below. Briefly, they are:

- (a) for union officials and safety representatives to carry out their duties and undergo training;
- (b) for members to take part in union activities;
- (c) for employees to carry out public duties;
- (d) for employees being made redundant to look for new jobs;
- (e) for ante-natal care.
- (f) for employee representatives.

14.03 These rights have led, in many cases, to careful negotiation over the extent of time off. As it is always 'reasonable' time off that is permitted it is preferable for the parties to agree on these issues rather than to litigate about them. Accordingly, in recent times there has been a decline in the number of cases over these matters although the courts have laid down some guidelines and principles in the cases and this may have led to a decline as there is some guidance to help to understand the legal position. The cases relate mainly to time off for union duties to which we now turn.

2 TIME OFF FOR TRADE UNION DUTIES[1]

(a) Exclusions and qualifications

14.04 Those who work abroad (share fishermen) and those in the police service are excluded from all rights to time off. There are no longer restrictions on part-timers.[2]

1 All references in this section are to the Trade Union and Labour Relations (Consolidation) Act 1992 unless otherwise stated.
2 Employment Protection (Part Time Employees) Regulations 1995, SI 1995/31.

(b) The basic rights

(i) General definitions

14.05 An employee who is an official of an independent trade union recognised by his employer has the right to take time off during his working hours for the purpose of carrying out any duties of his, or such an official, concerned with:

(a) negotiations with the employer related to or connected with collective bargaining matters (s 178(2)) in relation to which the trade union is recognised by the employer; or
(b) the performance on behalf of employees of the employer of functions related to or connected with matters falling within that provision which the employer has agreed may be so performed by the trade union.[1]

It should be noted that as employers have total discretion as to whether to recognise or de-recognise a trade union these rights are completely subject to that decision. Paid time off is also permitted for the purpose of undergoing training in aspects of industrial relations:

(a) relevant to the carrying out of such duties mentioned in (a) above; and
(b) approved by the TUC or his own union.[2]

These rights have been extended to employee representatives elected for the purposes of consultation over collective redundancies or a transfer of undertaking and also to candidates for such elections. The right is to paid time off.[3]

1 TULR(C)A 1992, s 168(1).
2 Ibid, s 168(2).
3 ERA, s 61.

14.06 The amount of time off, the purposes for which, the occasions on which and any conditions applicable, are those that are reasonable in all the circumstances, having regard to the provisions of a Code of Practice issued by ACAS.[1]

1 TULR(C)A 1992, s 168(3).

14.07 'Official' is defined[1] to include the shop steward or workplace representative. An 'independent' union is one not under the control or possible control of an employer.[2] A 'recognised' union is one recognised for collective bargaining purposes[3] which covers a wide range of matters.[4]

[1] TULR(C)A 1992, s 119.
[2] Ibid, s 5.
[3] TULR(C)A 1992, s 178(3).
[4] Ibid, s 178(2) and see *National Union of Gold, Silver and Allied Trades v Albury Bros Ltd* [1978] ICR 62, [1977] IRLR 173, EAT.

14.08 'Official' covers all officers and others elected or appointed in accordance with the union rules. Unions have to be careful to ensure that officials are properly elected or appointed because any challenge by the employer on this will be scrutinised by the tribunal. In *Doyle*'s case[1] the equality officer of the NUJ had taken time off to attend a training course organised by the union. The employer challenged whether she had been elected in accordance with the rules and was, ultimately, unsuccessful, but the EAT did consider the matter very carefully.

[1] See eg *Doyle v Westminster Press Ltd* EAT 201/83.

(ii) Duties connected with collective bargaining

14.09 These have been referred to above and the matters contained in the statute[1] are quite comprehensive covering such matters as terms and conditions of employment, physical conditions, termination or suspension of employment, allocation of work, discipline, union membership, union officials' facilities and the machinery for negotiation or consultation and recognition.

There needs to be a link between the duty for which leave is sought and collective bargaining as defined. A meeting of union officials in order to prepare for negotiations falls within the definition provided the other criteria are satisfied. It does not matter that other unions are also recognised nor does the other side to the bargaining have to be present.[2]

[1] Section 178(2).
[2] *London Ambulance Service v Charlton* [1992] IRLR 510, EAT.

(iii) The Code

14.10 Some assistance can be derived from the Code of Practice[1] which, as previously mentioned, is alluded to in the statutory provisions. Paragraph 13 includes:

(a) collective bargaining with the appropriate level of management;
(b) informing constituents about negotiations or consultations with management;
(c) meetings with other lay officials or with full-time union officers on matters which are concerned with industrial relations between his or her employer and any associated employer and their employees;

(d) interviews with and on behalf of constituents on grievance and discipline matters concerning them and their employer;
(e) appearing on behalf of constituents before an outside official body, such as an industrial tribunal, which is dealing with an industrial relations matter concerning the employer; and
(f) explanations to new employees whom he or she will represent of the role of the union in the workplace industrial relations structure.

[1] Time off for trade union duties and activities, ACAS Code of Practice 3—1977.

14.11 This is not an exhaustive list and each case will turn on its own facts. It would cover a meeting of representatives who want to discuss a possible claim against the employer. In *Beal v Beecham*[1] ASTMS sought paid time off for their representatives to attend a meeting of the ASTMS National Advisory Committee (NAC) for the Beecham group. The meeting was called to discuss matters of an industrial relations nature and to plan a co-ordinated industrial relations strategy. The company would not pay because collective bargaining was dealt with at a different level from the NAC. It was held that the duties extended beyond collective bargaining and they could embrace preparatory and explanatory work provided it had direct relevance to an industrial relations matter. Attending a meeting to exchange information would not qualify, but formulating a national policy could. Here the agenda and minutes showed at least some of the policies were concerned with industrial relations matters, which were to go into the 1979 wage claim, and accordingly the meeting fell within the statutory provisions. However, it should be noted that this case was decided before the law changed in 1989. The formulation of a national policy and the furtherance of industrial relations might well lead to this case being decided differently today because it does not directly relate to the collective bargaining with that employer.

[1] In *Beal v Beecham Group Ltd* [1982] 3 All ER 280, [1982] IRLR 192, CA.

14.12 However, where a committee's main function is to exchange information and experience and it has no powers to negotiate or represent, it will probably mean that no paid time off will be given.[1] Sood was an ASTMS official who wanted to attend the Product Advisory Committee (PAC) meeting. The EAT held that attendance was not required to enable him to carry out his duties even though his attendance would be beneficial to him and to the union. The EAT made it clear that the planning of strategy could fall within the statutory definition. Once again this would have to be directed to the employer in question.

[1] *Sood v GEC Elliott Process Automation Ltd* [1980] ICR 1, [1979] IRLR 416, EAT.

14.13 The repeal of legislation which will have an impact on terms and conditions was held to be sufficiently proximate to industrial relations between an employer and his employees to justify paid time off. In *British Bakeries (Northern) Ltd v Adlington*[1] the employees were officials of the union which had organised a meeting concerning the repeal of an Act relating to hours of work and mounting opposition to the repeal. The Court of Appeal, reversing the EAT and restoring the tribunal decision, held that whether any particular preparatory or advisory committee was sufficiently proximate to the actual negotiations with the employer so as to constitute 'industrial relations' was a matter of degree and therefore a question of fact for the tribunal. The tribunal had applied the law correctly and its decision should not be interfered with. A different view was taken when the advice of a committee was held to be too remote from the actual negotiations conducted between the union and management.[2]

[1] [1989] IRLR 218, CA. Although the decision related to industrial relations it would probably be decided the same way because it was a situation which clearly related to the employer in question.

[2] *Ashley v Ministry of Defence* [1984] ICR 298, [1984] IRLR 57, EAT.

14.14 There may be problems in the public sector although this is a diminishing area, for example, there may be opposition to a government's pay policy or its privatisation policy. In *British Gas Corpn v Wignall*[1] NALGO was concerned that a Parliamentary Bill was a threat to the jobs and the terms of employment of their members. A request was made relating to a meeting to discuss how to deal with the Bill. The tribunal decided that the government was the employer but the EAT said it was not the employer in nationalised industries. The case was remitted to determine whether the meeting could affect the relationship between the corporation and its employees. In the *Adlington* case it was suggested that the consequences of privatisation would be too diffuse or general to justify paid time off.[2]

[1] EAT 36/83.

[2] Per Kerr CJ.

14.15 Employees attending unofficial union meetings will not be given paid time off because it is necessary to show that a meeting is for official union duties.[1] This is not altogether easy to follow as unofficial meetings may well fall within the statutory definition but it is defensible on the ground that it might open the floodgates. If, however, the meeting's purpose is to deal with collective bargaining matters with the employer, it is not altogether logical.

[1] See *Ashley v Ministry of Defence*, above.

(iv) Training

14.16 With regard to training in industrial relations the Code of Practice[1] lays down certain principles which essentially reiterate the statute. The training must be relevant to the official's duties and therefore will vary. Initial and further training is mentioned. The union should inform management what training it has approved for the purpose and, if requested, should supply a syllabus with the contents of the course. A few weeks' notice should be given.

1 Paras 14–20.

14.17 In *Young v Carr Fasteners*[1] the company introduced a pension scheme in which there was no prospect of employee participation. The official claimed time off with pay to attend a union course on 'Pensions and Participation'. The EAT held that advising members about pensions was as much a part of industrial relations as advising about wages and therefore it was training relevant to her duties. This is a not ungenerous decision to the official, bearing in mind there was no prospect of participation and with the statutory changes made in 1989 it is a decision which is not likely to be followed. General training is not permitted but must be carefully targeted on matters which the union negotiates with the employer on. Thus, in *Menzies v Smith and McLaurin*[2] the company was negotiating a redundancy agreement with the union. The official sought paid leave for a course which was mainly about job security but covered a number of other topics. The EAT held that the course was too general and further, that he had failed to establish that anything he had learned on the course was of assistance to him in negotiating with the company over redundancy.

1 [1979] ICR 844, [1979] IRLR 420, EAT.
2 [1980] IRLR 180, EAT.

(v) Mixed purpose meetings

14.18 Sometimes a meeting or training course will cover some matters which are concerned with collective bargaining matters and some which are not, as in the *Menzies*[1] case. The *Beal v Beecham* case[2] has held that provided one of the purposes is connected with industrial relations then that is sufficient to qualify as a duty and it is not necessary to ascertain the predominant purpose of the meeting. Nevertheless, in *RHP Bearings v Brookes*[3] the EAT said that the tribunal should consider the activities of the meeting in some detail and ask how much of it fell within the statute and how much without. The employer would then be able to calculate how much time off should be given (a proportion of the total time) and then this proportion should be compensated at full pay. The *Beal* case would obviously need to be viewed in the light of the statutory alteration and collective bargaining matters would replace industrial relations.

1 [1980] IRLR 180, EAT.
2 See above.
3 [1979] IRLR 452.

(vi) Amount of time off

14.19 This is subject to the test of reasonableness and the Code is relevant.[1] It refers to the employer's need to keep the premises open and to minimise the effects on production or service or safety standards.

1 See paras 23–30.

14.20 There is uncertainty regarding the standard to be applied to reasonableness. The case of *Ministry of Defence v Crook and Irving*[1] is the standard authority to suggest that you consider the matter from the employer's viewpoint, that is, it is a subjective rather than an objective test. This would require the tribunal to ask if the employer's behaviour was within the range of reasonable conduct.[2] This is not what s 168 says and the test should be an objective one. However, despite the general comments made in the *Crook and Irving* case it could be that they were made because the employer was not given all the information that he should have received. The EAT said that the standard is whether the employer acted reasonably but they were obviously affected by the employer's lack of knowledge. It would be unfair on an employer to attribute to him knowledge which he did not have and which he had no reasonable means of acquiring. One can try to limit the effect of the decision on this factual basis but the authority nevertheless remains.

1 [1982] IRLR 488, EAT.
2 See *Depledge v Pye Telecommunications Ltd* [1981] ICR 82, [1980] IRLR 390, EAT.

14.21 If there is an existing procedure agreement which governs the matters for which paid time off is being sought, the employer is not required to pay.[1] Furthermore, it is likely that where there is an agreement regarding time off which lays down the purposes for which paid time off will be provided, the employer will not be unreasonable in refusing to provide pay for other purposes. Similarly, if an agreement provides rates for the time off the tribunal will not undermine the agreement by providing a different rate through the statutory provisions.

1 See *Ashley v Ministry of Defence*, above.

3 HOW MUCH PAY?

14.22 Once it is established that the duties an official is carrying out are within s 168 and that time off is reasonable, there is an automatic right to paid time off. If the tribunal thinks time off should be provided, but unpaid, then it must base its decision on reasonableness and refuse on that ground.

14.23 The provisions regarding pay are contained in s 169. An employee is entitled to be paid remuneration he would have received during the hours of absence. Where the remuneration does not vary he is paid his normal pay but where it does vary based on the work done the average hourly earnings are calculated.

14.24 Payment is made for working hours which means[1] when the employee is required to be at work. Overtime can only be included if it is obligatory on both sides and therefore payments for voluntary overtime will be excluded. Thus in *Davies and Alderton v Head, Wrightson Teesdale Ltd*,[2] where two hours overtime had been regularly worked, it was excluded on the basis that it had not become a contractual obligation. Working hours are defined restrictively. Thus where an employee was rostered to work between 3 pm and 11 pm, and attended a union course with permission from 9 am till 4 pm, attended work from 4.40 pm till 7 pm, the employer's refusal to pay him beyond 7 pm was upheld. He argued that he usually worked 8 hours and the course was in substitution for that and therefore he should receive his full pay. The EAT held that it could only order paid time off if the time off related to the time when he was required to be at work. This was not the case and accordingly the claim failed.[3]

However, this approach is almost certainly invalid given the European Court of Justice's decision in *Bötel*'s case.[4] A German part-time female employee went on a training course and was paid only for the hours on the course that were equivalent to her part-time hours. The ECJ held that was unlawful on the basis that it indirectly discriminated against her under Article 119 and the Equal Pay Directive unless it could be justified. The statutory provisions cannot be used as justification to override EC law and an employee would find it extremely difficult to justify the distinction. However, the ECJ has also held that Article 119 and the Equal Pay Directive are not breached by a refusal to pay overtime rates to a part-time employee until she has worked the same number of hours as a full-time employee.[5]

1 Section 173(1).
2 [1979] IRLR 170.
3 *Hairsine v Kingston upon Hull City Council* [1992] IRLR 211.
4 *Arbeiterwohlfarht der Stadt Berlin v Bötel* [1992] IRLR 423.
5 *Stadt Lengerich v Helmig* [1995] IRLR 216.

14.25 In determining the average hourly earnings of an employee if no fair estimate of his earnings can be made, then the average is that of comparable employees, or if there are no comparable employees a reasonable estimate is made.[1] There is no formula for assessing the average over any period of time and there is no reference to a 'week's pay'.

1 Section 169(3).

14.26 If there is a right to contractual remuneration the employee cannot recover both statutory and contractual remuneration—one discharges the other.[1]

1 Section 169(4).

4 THE REMEDY

14.27 A complaint may be made to a tribunal that an employer has failed to permit the employee to take time off or to pay him the whole or part of any amount required.[1] There is something of a contradiction here because s 169(1) refers to the right to statutory pay only where the employer has permitted the time off. Does this mean that the employee can only claim pay where time off has been granted, but on an unpaid basis, or does it mean that an employee who takes time off without permission and therefore without pay can then claim that he should have been paid? *Harvey* says he is only entitled to pay when he is absent with permission but it is surely arguable, using s 168(4) that the alternative view is correct. We await an authoritative decision. It has been held that an employer cannot fail to permit to allow time off unless a request was made, that it came to the appropriate person, and it was refused or ignored.[2]

[1] Section 169(5).
[2] *Ryford Ltd v Drinkwater* [1996] IRLR 16, EAT.

14.28 The complaint must be presented within three months of the employer's default but the usual extension may be permitted.[1]

[1] See s 171 and unfair dismissal section.

14.29 If the complaint succeeds the tribunal must make a declaration with a discretion to make an award of such amount as is just and equitable in the circumstances, taking into account the employer's default, the employee's loss and also any injury suffered by the employee.[1]

[1] See Compensation for Victimisation above.

14.30 To support the view that a complaint can be made that time off has been refused s 172(3) permits the tribunal to order payment of any sum due under s 68 when paid time has been refused.

A TIME OFF FOR SAFETY REPRESENTATIVES

1 INTRODUCTION

14.31 All independent recognised trade unions are entitled to appoint safety representatives who are entitled to paid leave as is necessary to perform their statutory functions.[1]

[1] See para 4(2), Safety Representatives and Safety Committee Regulations 1977, SI 1977/500 made under s 2(4) Health and Safety at Work etc Act 1974–hereinafter SR Regulations and HASWA.

14.32 There are various relevant statutory and extra-statutory provisions affecting this. Under s 2(4) of HASWA, provision is made for the Secretary of State to make regulations for the appointment by recognised trade unions of safety representatives from among the employees. These representatives represent the employees in consultation with the employers regarding safety arrangements and their efficacy. They are also given a wide range of functions under the Safety Representatives Regulations.[1] These include the investigation of potential hazards and dangerous occurrences, the cause of accidents, and complaints regarding health and safety as well as the attendance at safety committee meetings. The Health and Safety Commission has issued two relevant Codes of Practice. The general one provides[2] that representatives should take all reasonably practical steps to keep themselves informed of the legal requirements regarding the health and safety of employees, particularly the ones they represent and also of the hazards of the workplace and their employer's health and safety policy. There is also a Code regarding time off for the training of the representatives.[3] This will be considered below. There is no reason why safety representatives should not be able to argue that the general time off provisions relating to trade union duties should apply to them.[4] However, if there were a conflict the Safety Code would have priority.

1 Safety Representatives and Safety Committees (1978).
2 Paragraph 5.
3 Also issued in 1978.
4 TULR(C)A 1992, s 168.

2 WHO CAN BE A SAFETY REPRESENTATIVE?

14.33 They must be a member of an independent[1] recognised trade union.[2] Representation on a negotiating committee has been held sufficient.[3] They must, generally, have been employed with that employer for two years or have had two years' experience in similar employment.[4]

1 See elsewhere for definitions, TULR(C)A 1992, s 50.
2 Regulation 3(1). A recognised union is one recognised for the purposes of negotiations in relation to any matter that could form the subject-matter of a trade dispute (reg 2(1)).
3 *Hempstead v Cleveland County Council* COIT 9/172/58.
4 Regulation 3(4).

14.34 The union must notify the employer of the representatives' names and whom they represent.[1] There is no guide to the number who should be appointed. If there is no notification or the union is not recognised, any safety representatives are not formally appointed and have no statutory functions and therefore have no right to time off.

1 Regulation 3(2).

3 FUNCTIONS OF SAFETY REPRESENTATIVES AND TIME OFF

14.35 The main functions have already been mentioned; they include the right to make inspections in three different sets of circumstances. First, a three-monthly inspection is permitted on reasonable written notice. Where there has been a substantial change in the conditions of work a further inspection is permitted. Second, where there has been a notifiable accident or dangerous occurrence or where a notifiable disease has been contracted, an inspection can take place to establish the cause. Finally, an inspection of documents is permitted where the employer is required to keep them.[1]

1 Regulations 5–7.

14.36 To perform these functions the representative is entitled to such paid time off as is necessary. There is no statutory limitation of reasonableness as there is with ordinary trade union duties. There is always the question as to whether the activity is a safety representative function but subject to that it is very difficult to challenge the amount of time off that has been taken. There are no limitations with respect to the exigencies of the business or the amount of time off that has already been taken. Employers will not get a very sympathetic response when health and safety risks are an issue.

4 TRAINING AND TIME OFF

14.37 A representative is entitled to such paid leave as shall be necessary for undergoing such training in aspects of those functions as may be reasonable in all the circumstances having regard to the provisions of the Code of Practice.

14.38 The Code is quite specific–paid time off should be provided to attend basic training facilities approved by the TUC or the representative's own union. Further approved training should be undertaken where there are special responsibilities or changes in circumstances or the law.[1]

[1] Paragraph 3.

14.39 Representatives should have an understanding of the legal requirements, the nature and extent of workplace hazards and the measures necessary to eliminate them, and of their own health and safety policy.[1]

[1] Paragraph 4.

14.40 Unions should inform management of the courses approved and supply a copy of the syllabus if requested. A few weeks' notice of attendance should be provided. The number attending should be reasonable bearing in mind the availability of courses and the employer's operational requirements.[1] There is no 'rule of thumb' approach here and all the circumstances must be considered.[2]

[1] Paragraph 5.

[2] In *Waugh v London Borough of Sutton* COIT 1270/114 one course per union per year was held to be unreasonable and too rigid.

14.41 There is a distinction between the health and safety courses and other general training courses. Under the TULR(C)A the course must be approved by the TUC or the union, whereas for health and safety this 'requirement' is in the Code not in the statute or regulations. In *White v Pressed Steel Fisher*[1] the representative wanted to attend a union course but the employer wanted him to attend its own course in which the TUC had refused to participate. The tribunal, upheld by the EAT, held that the employer's course was as good as the union's except for the TUC input which was not the employer's fault. The EAT remitted the case to the tribunal for re-hearing on the question as to whether the lack of TUC input made it necessary for him to go to the union approved course.

[1] [1980] IRLR 176.

14.42 The fact that an employer believes that its own systems are beyond criticism is not a ground for refusing paid time off. In *Howard v Volex Accessories*[1] Ms Howard was a safety representative who applied for paid time off to attend a TUC course on chemical hazards. After discussion with others her superior refused permission but she attended taking it as two days' holiday. She and her colleagues worked with lead and she and others had occasionally suffered symptoms associated with lead and she felt there was a potential danger. The tribunal decided that she was entitled to feel that she should know more about the chemical and other hazards at the place of work. The TUC course would assist her in this and the company's argument that it was doing everything it could by investigating and checking for hazards was no defence, even though there were in-house training courses. The two days were accordingly reimbursed.

1 COIT unreported.

5 AMOUNT OF PAY

14.43 It is calculated in the same way as for ordinary trade union duties[1] and it is provided that there cannot be payment under both the TULR(C)A and the Safety Representative Regulations.[2] Safety representatives are treated as synonymous with trade union officials. However, bearing in mind that it is easier to establish a safety function because there is no need to show reasonableness it is likely that the claim will be made under the regulations rather than the TULR(C)A. The only exception to this is where the course may be challenged by an employer's course which is only possible under the safety regulations. Contractual pay is set off against the statutory payment and vice versa.[3]

1 See above section.
2 Paragraph 3(a) Schedule to SR Regulations.
3 Paragraph 3(b)–(c) Schedule to SR Regulations.

6 REMEDY

14.44 A representative can complain to an industrial tribunal that the employer has failed to allow paid time off or has paid the wrong sum.[1] The time limit is three months but the tribunal can extend the time where it was not reasonably practicable to have issued the complaint.[2] The tribunal can make a declaration if the complaint is well-founded and can award compensation as is just and equitable, having regard to the employer's default and the employee's loss.

1 Paragraph 11(1).
2 Paragraph 11(2) and see unfair dismissal section for meaning of this.

14.45 In *Diamond v Courtaulds Hosiery Ltd*[1] the employee, with permission, attended a ten-day course (one day a week for ten weeks). After two weeks all the employees were laid off because of a shortage of work and paid only the guaranteed fall-back pay. The employer paid Diamond this amount but the tribunal awarded him his full pay.[2]

1 [1979] IRLR 449, IT.

2 *Harvey* criticises this decision on the basis that the representative is entitled to time off during his working hours which means when he is required to be at work and the representative was not so required during this period and therefore should have been disentitled. Note *Hairsine v Kingston upon Hull City Council* [1992] IRLR 211, EAT discussed in the section above on trade union duties which would support *Harvey*'s views but also note *Bötel*'s case [1992] IRLR 423, ECJ where discrimination issues arose (see above).

B TIME OFF FOR UNION ACTIVITIES

1 THE BASIC RIGHT

14.46 Every employee who is a member of an independent trade union recognised by his employer can claim unpaid time off working hours to take part in union activities.[1] These are defined as any activities of his union and any other activities where the employee is acting as a representative of his union. Thus the activities need not be concerned with industrial relations with the employer but can stretch to any union activity including voting at union elections. It must still emanate from the union and not from individuals as a 'frolic of their own'. Representative activities would include attendance at joint union meetings, conferences or industrial training boards. The activities cannot include taking part in industrial action although a representative can claim for representing others taking such action provided he is not. When a teacher was refused unpaid leave to attend a lobby of Parliament under the aegis of the TUC in relation to the Education Reform Bill this refusal was upheld. The tribunal, upheld by the EAT, said that the lobby was intended to convey only political or ideological objections to legislation, it cannot be regarded as trade union activities even if the legislation was of vital concern to the union's members. There needed to be more of a direct link to the relationship with the employer.[2]

1 TULR(C)A 1992, s 170.

2 *Luce v Bexley London Borough Council* [1990] IRLR 422.

2 HOW MUCH TIME?

14.47 The amount of time is that which is reasonable in all the circumstances having regard to the Code of Practice.[1] There are a number of relevant factors including the amount of time which has already been permitted for union activities and/or duties. In one case[2] the employee was already allowed 12 weeks' leave, some paid, for his union duties and activities when he asked for ten more days to help in the preparation of a union magazine. The employer refused and this refusal was upheld by the tribunal and the EAT. His request was not reasonable in all the circumstances given that he already had 12 weeks' leave of absence. It was not the test that each activity should be considered separately but it had to be considered in the light of all the circumstances which included the amount of time that had already been taken off.

[1] See above.
[2] *Wignall v British Gas Corpn* [1984] ICR 716, [1984] IRLR 493, EAT.

14.48 The employee refused time off can go to an industrial tribunal[1] within three months of the date when the failure to permit time off occurred but it may be extended.[2]

[1] TULR(C)A 1992, s 170(4).
[2] If not reasonably practicable – see the unfair dismissal section. See TULR(C)A 1992, s 171.

14.49 The tribunal can make a declaration where the complaint succeeds and can award compensation as is just and equitable bearing in mind the employer's default and the employee's loss.[1]

[1] TULR(C)A 1992, s 172.

C TIME OFF FOR PUBLIC DUTIES

1 INTRODUCTION

14.50 Reasonable employers have, for many years, provided time off to their employees who wish to carry out public duties. Thus, the introduction of statutory rights did not create many problems for these employers and indeed although time off for public duties is unpaid many employers still make no deductions from normal pay. Most problems revolve around the amount of time off that is being requested. Most employers are usually keen to have employees involved in civic obligations but obviously an understanding has to be reached between the parties if the obligations become very time-consuming.

2 EXCLUSIONS

14.51 Those who ordinarily work outside Great Britain,[1] share fishermen[2] and merchant seamen,[3] are excluded. So also are crown employees whose contracts include a term restricting their right to engage in certain political activities or activities which conflict with their official functions if the public duty has some connection with these activities.[4] There does not appear to have been a case on this but one can consider GCHQ as a possible analogy.

[1] ERA, s 196(2).
[2] ERA, s 199(2).
[3] ERA, s 199(4).
[4] ERA, s 191(5).

3 WHAT DUTIES?

14.52 These are those carried out as:

- (a) A Justice of the Peace;
- (b) a member of a local authority;
- (c) a member of any statutory tribunal;
- (d) a member of a health authority or board;
- (e) a member of a managing or governing body of an educational establishment maintained by a local authority;
- (f) a member of the Environment Agency or the Scottish Environment Protection Agency.[1]

1 ERA, s 50(2).

14.53 The Secretary of State can add or remove an office or body to his list.[1] The duties of such members (not JPs) are attendance at meetings or doing anything to discharge the functions of such bodies[2] and the Secretary of State can modify these duties.[3]

1 ERA, s 50(10)(a).
2 ERA, s 50(3).
3 ERA, s 50(10)(b).

14.54 The Act does not suggest that the time off should be paid but as union duties have payment specifically provided, the only inference that can reasonably be drawn is that it is unpaid. However, it has been stated by the EAT[1] that where an employer imposes conditions on the time off, including those relating to pay, it could be said that the conditions amounted to a refusal to allow time off. This can be quite difficult because extensive time off may be permitted but if it is unpaid the employee may well, in the absence of payment by the body concerned, find it financially impossible. This is a complicated way of providing that such leave is to be paid.

1 In *Corner v Buckinghamshire County Council* [1978] ICR 836, [1978] IRLR 320.

4 HOW MUCH TIME OFF?

14.55 The amount of time off, the occasions and any conditions subject to which it may be taken are those which are reasonable in all the circumstances having regard, in particular, to the following:

- (a) how much time off is required for the performance of the duties of the office or as a member of the body in question and how much time is required for the performance of the particular duty;
- (b) how much time off the employee has already been permitted for union duties, training and activities;
- (c) the circumstances of the employer's business and the effect of the employee's absence on running the business.

The statute therefore makes clear that other factors, where appropriate, may be brought into the equation.

14.56 As regards the time off that is required to perform public duties there can be no real guidelines because it all depends on the body's workload and the quantity and quality of the employee's contribution. The employee needs to produce evidence from the body as to the requirements. Often the parties use the tribunals effectively to arbitrate as to what is a reasonable amount of time off. However, the tribunal only has power to deal with a failure to permit time off and cannot make a declaration as to the amount of days to be given in the future.[1] However, this can be circumvented, at least informally, by the tribunal making a recommendation for the future and the parties will usually be happy to accept this.

[1] See *Ratcliffe v Dorset County Council* [1978] IRLR 191, IT.

14.57 When time off has already been given for union duties and activities this is a factor to be considered. As an analogy one should note the case of *Wignall v British Gas Corpn*.

14.58 As regards the effects on the employer's business, the employer must show that he has taken reasonable steps to establish the effect of the absence on the particular department. It is not sufficient to have a blanket refusal.

14.59 Some of the factors that might be relevant would be the size of the unit in which the employee works—obviously the larger the unit the easier it is to cover for an absence. However, if it can be shown that the employee occupies a vital role and is difficult to replace, then the size of the unit will be of less importance. However, where the employer is a large organisation the tribunal will expect him to make some compromises himself.[1]

[1] See eg *Emmerson v IRC* [1977] IRLR 458, IT where it was held that the Revenue could have appointed an assistant from a nearby district without very much difficulty.

14.60 The employer's existing requirements may be such that it is very difficult to grant time off without disrupting his production and upsetting his customers. However, unless the employee occupies such a key role it will be difficult to show that he could not have made some alternative arrangements and where there are surplus staff the argument is really not maintainable.

14.61 Where an employee is given time off but is told that he must maintain his existing workload by rearranging his work this has been held to constitute a refusal of time off.[1] Key employees have been mentioned and their absence may cause disruption. If, however, they are, in effect, being penalised for being good workers the tribunal is likely to permit time off. It is not sufficient that the public duties for which the employee seeks time off are important—they usually are. What is vital is to consider the pattern and amount of absences, the needs of the employer and any relevant third party.[2]

[1] See *Ratcliffe v Dorset County Council*, above.

[2] *Borders Regional Council v Maule* [1993] IRLR 199, EAT where a school was held not to have unreasonably refused time off to a teacher for training for a Social Security Appeals Tribunal.

14.62 Thus in *Emmerson v IRC*[1] the employee was a member of Portsmouth Council and had been receiving 18 days' paid leave per year to carry out public duties. He was elected leader of the opposition which required greater work and more leave. He asked for additional unpaid leave which could be granted under the regulations and was refused. He sought a declaration that he had been refused reasonable time off but did not seek compensation. He was successful. It was necessary to balance the need to carry out his duties with the need of the employer to have his work done adequately. A reasonable period of extra time would be 12 days and although his duties would exceed the 30 days he was given he would have to compromise and give up some of his own time. Although he was the only training officer this was because he was good at his job and it would not be right to put him at a disadvantage because of this. The employer could make alternative arrangements without much difficulty.

[1] See footnote 1 to para 14.59.

5 THE REMEDY

14.63 A complaint of a refusal to allow time off goes to a tribunal[1] and must be presented within three months with the proviso that it may be extended.[2] The tribunal must make a declaration if it finds the case proved[3] and can award compensation based on the employer's default and the loss suffered by the employee.

[1] ERA, s 51(1).
[2] Where it was not reasonably practicable to have presented a complaint – see the unfair dismissal section.
[3] ERA, s 51(3).

14.64 The tribunals have decided that they cannot stipulate what time off would be reasonable in the circumstances although they can give indications as in *Emmerson* but not impose conditions as to payment.

D TIME OFF TO LOOK FOR ANOTHER JOB

1 THE BASIC RIGHT

14.65 The basic right is to paid time off work to look for new employment or to make arrangements for training in future employment when one has been given notice of dismissal for redundancy.[1]

[1] ERA, s 52(1).

2 EXCLUSIONS AND QUALIFICATIONS

14.66 Those excluded are those working abroad, share fishermen, merchant seamen, and those in police service.[1]

[1] ERA, ss 196, 199 and 200.

14.67 The employee must also show that he has been given his notice of dismissal and it is not enough that a long advance warning has been given.[1] It must be by reason of redundancy which has a technical meaning.[2] Thus a reorganisation may not be, but usually is, a redundancy. Finally, two years' service is required although oddly 16 hours' service per week was never a requirement.[3]

[1] See the sections on unfair dismissal and redundancy.
[2] See ERA, s 139 and the section on redundancy and note *Dutton v Hawker Siddeley Aviation Ltd* [1978] ICR 1057, [1978] IRLR 390 where the EAT opined that there was an entitlement to time off even though an offer of suitable alternative employment had been made. That was relevant to the question of whether an employee was entitled to a redundancy payment not whether he was entitled to time off.
[3] ERA, 52(2).

3 THE AMOUNT OF TIME OFF

14.68 The employee is entitled to reasonable time off with pay. There is nothing in the statute or in any case to determine what is 'reasonable'. It is fair to suggest that where the unemployment level is high it will be more difficult for an employer to argue that the employee is vital to his business given that he is being made redundant, but there might be circumstances which justify this argument such as the need to finish a particular job.

14.69 It is not unreasonable for an employer to ask that an employee gives advance notice of when he wants time off. However, the fact that an employee refuses to provide details of his appointments for jobs is not a ground for refusing time off, although it could be a factor in determining reasonableness.[1] Where there are multiple redundancies it would probably not be unreasonable for the employer to 'stagger' the dates when time off is required.

[1] *Dutton v Hawker Siddeley Aviation Ltd* [1978] ICR 1057, [1978] IRLR 390, EAT.

4 HOW MUCH PAY?

14.70 An employee allowed time off during working hours is entitled to be paid at the appropriate hourly rate.[1] This is calculated by dividing a week's pay by the number of normal working hours in a week or where such number differs from week to week the figure must be averaged out over the last 12 weeks.

[1] ERA, s 53(2) and (3) a week's pay is calculated by reference to ERA, ss 221–229.

14.71 However, the maximum liability of the employer is two-fifths of the employee's week's pay[1] although there may be separate contractual liability. Where there is a right to paid time off under the contract then the employee can select whichever provides better terms but he cannot get double payment.[2]

1 ERA, s 53(5).
2 ERA, s 53(7).

14.72 Where the employer refuses to allow time off, as contrasted with the situation where he allows it but unpaid, the employee can still claim on the same basis as above but again with a maximum of two-fifths of a week's pay. This will be in addition to what he has earned under the contract and will be paid as compensation.

5 THE REMEDY

14.73 An employee can go to a tribunal and complain that he has been refused time off unreasonably or that he has not been paid for the absence.[1] The complaint must be presented within three months from the day that the time off has been refused. Where the employer has refused to pay the time limit still seems to apply from the original day even though time off has been given. It would be more logical to run the period from the date of the refusal to pay in that situation. The time limit can be extended.[2]

1 ERA, s 54(1).
2 Where it was not reasonably practicable to have presented the complaint (see the section on unfair dismissal). Section 54(2).

14.74 If the tribunal finds the complaint succeeds it must make a declaration and award the amount of pay that is due.[1]

1 ERA, s 54(3).

E TIME OFF FOR ANTE-NATAL CARE

1 THE BASIC RIGHT

14.75 An employee who is pregnant and who has, on medical advice,[1] made an appointment for receiving ante-natal care has the right to paid time off to keep her appointment. The employer may refuse if it is reasonable to do so.[2] It may be reasonable to refuse where, for example, the employee can make an appointment outside working hours or at lunch-time, or, if she is part-time on a non-working day. Each case will turn on its own facts. It is not permissible to rearrange the working week to accommodate the employer. This right was introduced in the Employment Act 1980. Furthermore the Pregnant Workers Directive 92/85 requires member states to ensure that time off with pay is provided to attend ante-natal examinations if they have to take place during working hours.

[1] Registered medical practitioner, midwife or health visitor.
[2] ERA, s 55(1).

2 QUALIFICATIONS AND CONDITIONS

14.76 The right is not provided to those working outside Great Britain,[1] share fishermen[2] and those in police service,[3] but there is no qualifying period of employment.

[1] ERA, s 196.
[2] If there are any women! ERA, s 199.
[3] ERA, s 200.

14.77 The employee must be pregnant to claim the time off; if she has sought time off to confirm the pregnancy but it is ascertained that she is not pregnant she does not satisfy the Act's provisions. Although there has been criticism that this cannot have been Parliament's intention it is, and it is submitted, wholly in accordance with such intention because time off is given for ante-natal care which you cannot have if you are not pregnant!

14.78 An appointment for ante-natal care must have been made on medical advice. Without this the employee does not qualify and it raises the question as to the legal position if the employee does not make an appointment because she has not been provided time off. Strictly she is not entitled but in practice one assumes she must have made an appointment to be seeking the time off or a remedy for its refusal. One assumes a tribunal would not interpret this point in too literal a fashion.

14.79 Except on the first appointment an employee will not be permitted time off for an appointment unless, when requested, she produces both a medical certificate stating she is pregnant and an appointment card or some document showing the appointment has been made.

3 AMOUNT OF TIME OFF

14.80 There is no statement as to what is the proper amount that should be given. The employer must not unreasonably refuse time off so she can keep her appointment. Every appointment is, it is suggested, likely to be necessary and it would be almost impossible to challenge on the basis that it is not. However, it is possible that the number of appointments may appear excessive although the burden on the employer to show he was not unreasonable would be quite onerous. It might be possible to argue that an appointment could be changed where it was not absolutely necessary, medically. For example, the employer might have a particular busy period and ask the employee to postpone her appointment for a brief period. This may well be reasonable on the employer's part. Ante-natal care is not defined but it is presumed that it will cover all matters including relaxation classes to assist in the birth itself. Breast-feeding classes would be more borderline, but one would expect both employers and tribunals to be liberal in this regard.

4 HOW MUCH PAY?

14.81 The statute provides that the time off is paid at the appropriate hourly rate.[1] This is one week's pay divided by the number of normal weekly hours, or where the hours are variable by working out the average over the previous 12 weeks. If the employee has not been employed that long then the hours which fairly represent the number are assessed taking into account the average number the employee could expect in accordance with her contractual terms and the average number of other employees working in relevant comparable employment.[2]

[1] ERA, s 56(1).
[2] ERA, s 56(2)–(4).

5 THE REMEDY

14.82 A complaint may be made to an industrial tribunal that the employer has unreasonably refused time off or has failed to pay the sum under the statute.[1] The complaint has the usual three months' time limit with the usual possible extension.[2] If the complaint succeeds the tribunal must make a declaration and must also award compensation based on her financial loss. There is no discretion here, which is different from some other provisions. If an employee is dismissed for attempting to enforce her right to time off this would be construed as dismissal for assertion of a statutory right which would be automatically unfair without the need for any qualifying period of employment.[3]

[1] ERA, s 57(1).
[2] ERA, s 57(2).
[3] ERA, s 104.

F TIME OFF FOR EMPLOYEE REPRESENTATIVES[1]

1 THE BASIC RIGHT

14.83 As a consequence of the European Court of Justice decision that the United Kingdom had failed to comply with the requirements of the Collective Redundancies and the Acquired Rights Directive[2] regulations were introduced with effect from the 26 October 1995[3] requiring the provision of information to and consultation with employee representatives in circumstances where collective redundancies were proposed or a transfer of an undertaking intended where hitherto such obligations only applied in circumstances where there was a recognised trade union.

[1] See also chapters 8 and 20.
[2] *EC Commission v United Kingdom* [1994] ICR 664, [1994] IRLR 392, ECJ.
[3] The Collective Redundancies and Transfer of Undertakings (Protection of Employment) (Amendment) Regulations 1995.

14.84 The 1995 Regulations amended the EP(C)A by incorporating a provision now to be found in the ERA, s 61 entitling an elected employee representative to reasonable time off during the employee's working hours in order to perform the representative's functions as an employee representative or as a candidate for election.

2 QUALIFICATIONS AND CONDITIONS

14.85 The right is available to an employee representative for the purposes of Chapter II of Part IV of TULR(C)A and regulations 10 and 11 of the Transfer of Undertakings (Protection of Employment) Regulations 1981. In addition the right is also available to a candidate in an election in which any person elected will, on being elected, be an employee representative.[1]

[1] ERA, s 61(1)(b).

3 AMOUNT OF TIME OFF

14.86 The putative or elected employee representative is allowed 'reasonable time off' during the employee's working hours in order to perform his functions as an employee representative or candidate. As is the case for time off for ante-natal care. 'Reasonable time-off' is not defined by reference to any period.

4 HOW MUCH PAY?

14.87 Once again, as with time-off for ante-natal care, the employee is entitled to be paid remuneration by the employer for the period of absence at the 'appropriate hourly rate' (see para 14.81 above).

5 THE REMEDY

14.88 A complaint to an Industrial Tribunal may be made by an employee who is entitled to reasonable time-off as an actual or prospective employee representative on the basis that the employer has unreasonably refused the employee 'reasonable time-off' or has failed to pay the employee the whole or part of any amount to which the employee is entitled in respect of a period of time-off.

G MISCELLANEOUS MATTERS – IN BRIEF

1 UNFAIR DISMISSAL

14.89 If an employee takes unauthorised leave for any of the above and is dismissed for this the normal unfair dismissal provisions will apply and it is unlikely that a single act would be sufficient to justify dismissal but, as always, it depends on all the circumstances. It gets more tricky for employers where the dismissal relates to trade union activities because of the much higher compensation awardable. It is difficult to say whether a refusal would justify a constructive dismissal claim but an employee has to show a fundamental breach of contract. The right is statutory, not contractual and further it might be difficult to show a fundamental breach.[1]

[1] See generally unfair dismissal section.

2 RELIGIOUS ACTIVITIES

14.90 Time off for religious activities has not yet become a serious issue in British labour law. However, with the growth of ethnic minorities and some strong religious beliefs this may still exercise the judiciary. In fact in *Ahmed v Inner London Education Authority*,[1] it did. Ahmed was a devout Muslim and employed as a full-time teacher. He never told his employer that he would need to be absent for about one hour every Friday so that he could pray in a nearby mosque. Although the employer provided paid time off for entire days where there was a special religious obligation, there was no such provision for partial absence as here. The employer refused leave but the employee took it anyway. Other employees complained that it was unfair that he should be paid full time and the employer then said he would have to work for four-and-a-half days if he wanted to continue to pray. He resigned, claiming the right to time off without loss of pay. He relied on the Education Act and subsequently on the European Convention on Human Rights, guaranteeing the freedom of religion. The Court of Appeal, by a 2:1 majority, declared that his rights were subject to the employer's need for him to carry out his teaching duties. This issue has, it is suggested, some way to run yet.

[1] Under the Education Act 1944, s 8.

14.91 In more recent times, there have been some tribunal cases where racial discrimination has been claimed on the basis that such full-time attendance could be indirectly discriminatory in that the condition impacts more on some ethnic minorities. There are some problems here because the legislation does not prohibit religious discrimination and further, the employer is usually able to reorganise his working time to allow an employee to practise religious beliefs.[1] It is outside the scope of this section to discuss this matter fully.

[1] These matters are discussed in the section on discrimination.

3 GENERALLY

14.92 With all of the time off rights there will usually not be much doubt over whether the purpose falls within the statutory provision but the question of reasonableness will be very important. Employers can exercise a degree of control here by stipulating a procedure for time off requests, preferably agreed with the union.

14.93 Following the Codes' provisions, employers should be advised of the apopintment of officials, and, by analogy, of public appointments. The employer should be advised of the purpose of the time off and the expected period of absence and this includes training.

14.94 Production difficulties are matters which can be taken into account and this emphasises the importance of agreement in advance as to the principles applying.

15 Insolvency

Barry Mordsley

1 INTRODUCTION

15.01 Employees are given certain protection when their employer becomes insolvent. For many years, under company law provisions, employees have been accorded special status as 'preferential creditors.'.[1] The protection given to employees was extended by widening the concept of 'wages'.

[1] See now ss 175 and 386 and Sch 6, para 9 ff. Insolvency Act 1986 (EP(C)A 1978, s 121 repealed).

15.02 Furthermore, employees can claim payment of certain debts directly from the Government itself where the employer is unable to satisfy the claim because of insolvency. A redundancy or statutory maternity payment can also be claimed from the Government where the employer is insolvent. Finally, in some cases an employee who belongs to an occupational pension scheme may be able to claim against the relevant Government department where the employer has failed to pay his contributions to the pension scheme.[1]

[1] For more detailed coverage of the subject see *Harvey* I, 1. Note also *Francovich and Bonifaci v Italy* [1992] IRLR 84, ECJ on Enforceability of Insolvency Directive 80/987/EEC.

2 EXCLUSIONS AND QUALIFICATIONS

15.03 The right to recover certain debts is not provided to those who work abroad, although this exclusion does not extend to EEC workers[1] or to share fishermen. The same exclusions apply to the right to claim debts against the Government with the addition of share fishermen. Crown employees, House of Lords and House of Commons staff are also excluded.[2] There is no qualifying period of continuous employment.

[1] SI 1983/624. There must be no discrimination against nationals of EEC states.
[2] ERA, ss 191, 194 and 195.

15.04 None of the rights can be claimed unless the employer is 'insolvent'. This is defined[1] and means that:

(i) an individual employer is made bankrupt or has made a composition or arrangement with his creditors;

(ii) he has died and his estate is being administered as an insolvent one;
(iii) where the employer is a company:
  (a) a winding-up order or an administration order has been made;
  (b) a resolution for voluntary winding up has been passed;
  (c) a receiver or manager of its undertaking has been duly appointed or possession taken by or on behalf of debenture-holders secured by a floating charge of any property of the company comprised in or subject to the charge;[2] or
  (d) a voluntary arrangement proposed under the Insolvency Act 1986 has been approved.[3]

[1] ERA, s 183.
[2] *Secretary of State for Employment v Stone* (1994) ICR 761 where the EAT accepted the SOS's argument that the change was fixed not floating and therefore there was no insolvency.
[3] There are different definitions for Scotland.

15.05 The problem here is that an insolvency only comes about if some formal step is taken and the mere inability to pay debts is insufficient. Thus if no steps have been taken to wind up the company or make an individual bankrupt no rights accrue under the insolvency legislation. However, a redundancy payment can be claimed from the Secretary of State where an employee has taken all reasonable steps to recover the payment from the employer and the employer has not paid it. There is no need to show insolvency here.[1]

[1] See ERA, s 166(1)(a).

3 PREFERENTIAL DEBTS

15.06 The definition covers remuneration for the four months prior to the act of insolvency which includes commission, guarantee pay, remuneration for medical suspension and for suspension on maternity grounds (under s 66 of ERA), time-off payments and protective awards. Accrued holiday pay is included.[1] All these payments are treated as 'wages' so as to be given priority in a liquidation. They have priority over floating charges and unsecured debts but not over fixed charges. The maximum sum which an employee can claim in priority is fixed at £800, a figure which has remained as such for many years.

[1] See Insolvency Act 1986, Sch 6, paras 9–14.

4 GUARANTEED DEBTS

15.07 Certain debts[1] payable to the employee are guaranteed payment by the Secretary of State from the National Insurance Fund which, understandably, in recent times of high unemployment, has had a huge drain on its resources.

[1] Detailed below.

15.08 An employee must apply in writing to the Secretary of State who must be satisfied that the employer has become insolvent,[1] that the employment has been terminated and that on the relevant date[2] the employee was entitled to be paid the whole or part of any debt to which the section applies.[3]

[1] See above.
[2] See below.
[3] See s 182 of ERA.

15.09 The relevant date is either the date of the insolvency, the date of termination of employment or, where there is a basic award for unfair dismissal or a protective award, the date of that award.[1]

[1] Section 185 of ERA.

15.10 The debts which are covered are quite lengthy and will be considered singly below. Arrears of pay in respect of one or more but no more than eight weeks can be claimed. Pay is not defined as a week's pay for this purpose but there is a maximum of £210 (annually reviewable) per week.[1] Any sum payable under the contract, howsoever referred to, is recoverable.

[1] ERA, s 186(1) and see below.

15.11 For the purposes of this statutory provision, arrears of pay include a guarantee payment, pay during medical and maternity suspension, pay for time off for union duties, ante-natal care and while under notice of redundancy, and a protective award.[1]

[1] ERA, s 184(2).

15.12 Money which would have been earned in the statutory notice period is guaranteed. If the employee works out the period but is not paid for it no legal problem arises because the employee sues for a liquidated sum. If, however, the employee is dismissed without notice his claim is converted into one for damages for wrongful dismissal. This right to damages is always subject to mitigation. However, a strong argument has been made that this statutory minimum notice is a period for which wages are payable whatever an employee has earned, or should have earned, during the period. This argument has been rejected by the House of Lords[1] which said that the employer's failure is a breach of contract and thus is subject to the usual damages rules, including the duty to mitigate.

[1] See *Westwood v Secretary of State for Employment* [1985] AC 20, [1985] ICR 209, HL followed in *Secretary of State for Employment v Cooper* [1987] ICR 766, EAT. On the facts found in *Westwood* see now Social Security (General Benefit) (Amendment) Regulations 1984.

15.13 Up to six weeks' holiday pay in the twelve months prior to the insolvency can be claimed subject to the maximum of £210 per week.[1] Holiday pay means pay in respect of a holiday actually taken or any accrued holiday pay which, under the employee's contract, would in the ordinary course have become payable to him in respect of the period of a holiday if his employment with the employer had continued until he became entitled to a holiday.[2]

[1] ERA, s 186(1).
[2] ERA, s 184(3).

15.14 A basic award of compensation for unfair dismissal is also a guaranteed debt as is the reimbursement of any fee or premium paid by an apprentice or an articled clerk.[1]

[1] ERA, s 184(1). The reimbursement must be reasonable: see ERA, s 184(4).

15.15 The guaranteed debts are in the main, periodic payments and such payments shall not exceed £210[1] per week for any debt. The maximum is applied to the gross figure, that is before the deduction of income tax and national insurance.[2]

[1] Reviewable annually, see s 186(1) and (2) of the ERA.
[2] *Morris v Secretary of State for Employment* [1985] ICR 522, [1985] IRLR 297, EAT.

15.16 Sometimes there is a delay in payment from the Government. The Department should not pay until the relevant official, who will be the liquidator, for example,[1] sends to the Department a statement showing what is owing to the employee. However, if the Secretary of State is satisfied that he does not require such a statement in order to determine the amount of the debt, which remains unpaid, he may make a payment without a statement.[2]

[1] See full list in ERA, s 187(4).
[2] ERA, s 187(2).

5 THE REMEDY

15.17 An employee can complain to an industrial tribunal that the Department has not paid or not fully paid. The tribunal has the power to declare that the Secretary of State ought to make a certain payment.[1]

[1] ERA, s 188(3).

15.18 There is a time limit of three months from the date on which the Secretary of State's decision is communicated to him with a power to extend if it was not reasonably practicable to comply in time.[1] There is a lacuna in the provisions in that there is no power to complain that the Department has delayed unreasonably in deciding and one cannot complain until a decision has been made.

1 ERA, s 188(2).

15.19 Where the Secretary of State makes a payment to an employee of a guaranteed debt the employee's rights in respect of it are transferred to the Secretary of State who is entitled, therefore, to any priority of the employee including any preferential debt status.[1]

1 ERA, s 189.

15.20 The Secretary of State is entitled to receive information from the employer or any person handling the insolvent's debts. Any failure to provide information is a criminal offence.[1]

1 ERA, s 190.

6 REDUNDANCY PAY AND INSOLVENT EMPLOYERS

15.21 An employee entitled to a redundancy payment can apply to the Secretary of State where the employer is insolvent.[1]

1 ERA, s 166(1)(b).

15.22 The employee must show that the employer is liable to make the payment, that he has not yet been paid all or part of it and the employer is insolvent.[1]

1 Defined in ERA, s 166(5), (6) and (7) – the same as in s 183.

15.23 When an employer is insolvent in that he cannot pay his debts, a claim can be made on the grounds that the employee has taken all reasonable steps to recover the payment from the employer.[1]

1 ERA, s 166(1)(a).

15.24 If the Secretary of State makes a payment he can then take proceedings against the employer to recover the money and can require information from the employer. Failure to provide it without reasonable excuse or deliberately providing false information is an offence.[1]

1 ERA, ss 167 and 169.

7 PENSION CONTRIBUTIONS

15.25 The contributions due from the employer to an occupational pension scheme may, in insolvency, be paid by the Department of Employment out of the National Insurance Fund.[1] An occupational pension scheme means a scheme which can provide benefits to employees on the termination of their employment or on their death or retirement.[2]

[1] Section 124 of the Pensions Schemes Act 1993.
[2] Defined fully in s 123 of the Pension Schemes Act 1993.

15.26 A written application must be made by 'persons competent to act' for the scheme which means its trustees. The employee cannot apply himself. The Department must be satisfied that the employer is insolvent, that the contributions related to the employee and were overdue.[1]

[1] Section 124 of the Pensions Schemes Act 1993.

15.27 An application can be made for the payment of arrears of contributions. The Department must pay the employer's contributions up to a maximum sum, being the lowest of one of the following:

(a) arrears within the 12 months before insolvency;
(b) the amount needed to pay employees' benefits on dissolution of the scheme;
(c) 10% of the last 12 months' payroll for employees covered by the scheme. The payroll includes contractual remuneration and statutory payments, and holiday pay.[1]

[1] See s 124(4) of the Pension Schemes Act 1993.

15.28 The employee's contributions to the scheme are also payable by the Department where they are due from the employer who has already deducted them from the employee's pay.[1] The maximum payable is limited to what has been deducted from the employee's pay in the 12 months before insolvency.[2]

[1] Section 124 of the Pension Schemes Act 1993.
[2] See also s 125 of the Pension Schemes Act 1993 as regards relevant officials, applicable also to employer's contributions.

15.29 Where a relevant officer has been appointed then the arrears and remuneration must be certified by him and he must provide the Department with a statement showing the unpaid contribution. The Department is generally not liable to make any payment out of the Redundancy Fund until it has received such a statement and certificate but if the Secretary of State is satisfied that he does not require a statement in order to determine the amount of unpaid relevant contributions he may make a payment without obtaining a certificate.[1]

[1] Section 125(5) of the Pension Schemes Act 1993.

15.30 If the Department refuses the claim in whole or in part, the trustees of the scheme can complain to the industrial tribunal within three months, beginning with the date of the communication of the Department's decision on the application unless the time is extended because it was not reasonably practicable to comply.[1] There is no redress about delay in providing the certificate. The tribunal can make a declaration as to liability and amount.[2]

1 See Chapter 19 for the meaning of this phrase.
2 Section 126 of the Pension Schemes Act 1993.

15.30A Although insolvency protection was introduced in 1975, there is an Insolvency Directive 80/987. If there is an allegation of failure to implement the Directive under the *Francovich* principle this cannot be remedied in the industrial tribunal but must be dealt with by the High Court.[1]

1 *Secretary of State for Employment v Mann* [1996] IRLR 4, EAT.

8 LIABILITY OF RECEIVERS AND ADMINISTRATORS

General introduction

15.31 The Insolvency Act 1986[1] deals with the liability of an administrator or administrative receiver to employees when they take over the running of the business. The law in this area has been settled for some considerable time but recently the situation became very controversial when the House of Lords confirmed the Lower Court decisions to the effect that administrators were liable in a situation where they had never been hitherto. Under the 1986 Act[2] the administrator and administrative receiver are not taken to have adopted a contract of employment by reason of anything done or omitted to be done within 14 days of appointment. There is a standard practice whereby they write to employees stating expressly that while they will continue to pay salaries and benefits they would act as agents of the company and would not adopt or assume personal liability under the contract. This is exactly what happened in what as known as the *Paramount Airways* case.[3] The administrator there was unable to obtain a purchaser and as a consequence the employees were dismissed.

1 Sections 19 and 44 is amended by IA 1994.
2 Sections 19(5) and 44(2).
3 *Powdrill v Watson* [1995] IRLR 269.
1 *Secretary of State for Employment v Mann* [1996] IRLR 4, EAT.

15.32 In the *Paramount Airways* case[1] two employees claimed their contractual entitlement including payment in lieu of two months and holiday pay. Under the Act the administrator would be liable unless he had not adopted the contract. The administrators here had said in a letter to the employers that they were not adopting the contracts and were offering new contracts. However, they did continue to pay the same pay and benefits.

1 [1995] IRLR 269, HL.

15.33 It was held that there had been an adoption after 14 days despite the letter sent by the administrator. If the contract continued there was an implied adoption. The reality was that the old contracts continued. It would be necessary to negotiate completely new contracts.

The 1994 Act

15.34 What this meant was that the employees' rights had priority even over the administrator's remuneration and expenses. No wonder this caused consternation among receivers and administrators. So much so that legislation[1] has been passed with retrospective effect to limit the effects of this decision. The amendments are a little complicated but they have the effect of limiting liability arising from the adoption of a contract of employment to 'qualifying liabilities' which means the liability to pay wages, sick pay, holiday pay and pension contributions in respect of services rendered after the adoption of the contract. This does not include benefits.

1 Insolvency Act 1994.

15.35 Clearly the legislation would now exclude VAT payments such as arrears of wages and would include wages once the contract was adopted. However, the amendment says nothing about termination payments such as notice monies, unfair dismissal, redundancy or a protective award. It is unclear whether there would be liability for these matters and it may not have been Parliament's intention but the wording of the legislation is not that clear. One would assume the liability would transfer to the receiver.

15.36 No help is given whatsoever on the meaning of adoption and whether it is possible to contract out of the liability. In a recent case the EAT stated that it was not necessary for there to be a positive act and each case must be determined on its own facts.[1]

The Act applies to contracts adopted after 15 March 1994[2] and does not affect the position of employees dismissed more than 14 days after an appointment but prior to 15 March 1994.

1 *Doegar v Herbert Muller (In Receivership) and Secretary of State*, EAT 867/93.
2 The date of a Government announcement.

15.37 For the future given that contractual claims have a six year limitation period there must still be a significant number of people affected who can still bring claims. It should also be noted that while the *Paramount Airways* case related to administrators the principle has now been extended to administrative receivers.[1] Both groups are covered by the 1994 amendments. This area of law has a little way to run yet.

1 *Re Ferranti International plc* and *Re Leyland Daf Ltd* [1994] 4 All ER 300, Lightman J, Chancery Division, 26 July 1994.

16 A week's pay

Christopher Osman

16.01 The calculation of a week's pay is relevant for the purposes of a number of statutory rights including the calculation of redundancy payment entitlement,[1] guarantee payments,[2] payments made under the insolvency provisions of the ERA,[3] and the basic and additional awards of compensation for unfair dismissal.[4] The maximum amount of a week's pay in relation to the various statutory rights is subject to periodic (generally annual) revision by statutory instrument.

[1] See Chapter 20.
[2] See Chapter 11.
[3] See Chapter 15.
[4] See Chapter 19.

Schedule 14

16.02 The relevant provisions are now found in the ERA. Sections 221 to 229 apply to employments where there are normal working hours; in the case of s 221 to employees whose normal hours of work, whether by the hour or the week or other period, do not vary with the amount of work done,[1] and in the case of s 222 where there are normal working hours but the employee may be required to work those hours on days of the week or at times of the day which differ from week to week or over a longer period.[2] Section 223 contains further elaboration regarding the apportionment of remuneration to hours of work for the purposes of ss 221 and 222. Section 224 provides the method of calculation to be used in cases of employments with no normal working hours and ss 218 and 219 defines the 'Calculation Date' relevant to ss 221 and 223. Finally, ss 220 and 221 deal respectively with the maximum amount of a week's pay for various purposes and the method of calculation to be employed where the individual has not been employed for the purposes of ss 221, 223 and 224.

[1] Section 221(2) deals with the most straightforward situation – an employee working regular hours and paid at a flat rate – whilst s 221(3) relates to employees, again working regular hours, but who are paid a variable rate, eg those who are employed on piece work.
[2] In short, employees working rotating shifts.

16.03 Throughout the ERA, ss 221 to 229 there is reference to 'remuneration' in connection with the calculation of a week's pay but in fact the term is nowhere defined. The relevant case law has established that the term embraces wages and salaries and also extends to include 'expenses' where such payments are not actually reimbursement of expenses incurred in connection with the employment but are, by their nature, an additional payment to the employee. The expression does not extend to include a benefit in kind (eg company car) and generally excludes any payment made by someone other than the employer.[1] However, this series of general propositions deserves and requires more detailed consideration.

[1] *S and U Stores Ltd v Wilkes* [1974] 3 All ER 401, [1974] IRLR 283, NIRC.

Wages and salaries

16.04 First, it is the rate of pay which is in force at the relevant Calculation Date (see further below).[1] In the circumstances where the rate is expressed oddly (eg so many hours at £x per hour but where the employee does not in fact work that number of hours but receives a wage calculated as if he did) you look to the real rate of pay.[2] 'Wages and salaries' also includes bonuses and commission if the employee is contractually entitled to them.[3] In circumstances where such payments are made annually or in accordance with a timetable that does not coincide with the relevant 12 week calculation period (see below) applicable to an employee, the payment will be apportioned over the relevant period to arrive at the appropriate week's pay.[4]

[1] See *Valentine v Greater Lever Spinning Co* (1966) 1 ITR 71. There have been aberrations, see eg *Carrod v Pullman Spring Filled Co Ltd* (1967) 2 ITR 650, but cf *Leyland Vehicles Ltd v Reston* [1981] ICR 403, [1981] IRLR 19, EAT which is to be preferred.

[2] See *Ogden v Ardphalt Asphalt Ltd* [1977] 1 All ER 267, [1977] ICR 604, EAT.

[3] See *Amalgamated Asphalte Companies Ltd v Dockrill* (1972) 7 ITR 198 and *Weevsmay Ltd v Kings* [1977] ICR 244.

[4] *J & S Bickley Ltd v Washer* [1977] ICR 425, EAT.

Payments in kind

16.05 As indicated above these are not included. Perhaps the most common these days will be the company car but other examples would include free accommodation, interest-free season ticket loan, etc.[1]

[1] See eg *Skillen v Eastwoods Froy Ltd* (1966) 2 ITR 112; *Lyford v Turquand* (1966) 1 ITR 554.

Expenses

16.06 A simple reimbursement of expenses incurred by the employee in the course of his or her employment is not remuneration[1] but this may be contrasted with payments which, whilst characterised as expenses, do not in fact relate to a reimbursement of a payment made by the employee. Not infrequently such payments may steer close to the wind where the Inland Revenue are concerned[2] but this is not always the case. For example, allowances for entertainment of customers or clients which are not or only partially expended on their purpose are not uncommon and will normally be declared in the case of directors on form PIID.

[1] *S and S Stores Ltd v Wilkes,* above.
[2] *Cole v Fred Stacey Ltd* [1974] IRLR 73, but see also *S and U Stores Ltd v Lee* [1969] 2 All ER 417, [1969] 1 WLR 626.

Payments by third parties

16.07 Typically a waiter cannot include tips or gratuities for the purposes of calculating remuneration since the customer is not obligated to pay them and these are, in any event, not payable by the employer.[1] In contrast, a service charge may be included where the employer pays this into a bank or pool for distribution to the staff.[2] Here the customer is obligated to pay the service charge to the employer and the employee is obligated, under the terms of the pooling arrangement, to pass the payment on to the staff.

[1] *Palmanor Ltd (t/a Chaplins Night Club) v Cedron* [1978] ICR 1008, [1978] IRLR 303.
[2] *Tsoukka v Potomac Restaurants Ltd* (1968) 3 ITR 259; *Keywest Club Ltd v Choudhury* [1988] IRLR 51, EAT.

The calculation of a week's pay

16.08 Before considering the permutations covered by the ERA, ss 221 to 229 it should be noted that a week's pay means gross and not net pay.[1]

[1] *Secretary of State for Employment v John Woodrow & Sons (Builders) Ltd* [1983] ICR 582, [1983] IRLR 11, EAT.

The various permutations

16.09 See Diagram 16.09, p 302.

Case A

16.10 This is perhaps the simplest category (s 221). A week's pay equals the contractual remuneration (at the Calculation Date defined in ss 225 and 226) for a normal working week excluding overtime save in circumstances where overtime is *compulsory* and *guaranteed* as well. The normal hours of work may be at any time of the day or night and so, if a permanent night worker receives twice the hourly rate that a day worker does, it is the double rate which constitutes the normal remuneration.

Case B

16.11 Typically piece workers and those paid a variable amount dependent upon the amount of work they do fall into this category (ERA, s 221(3)).[1] In such cases a week's pay comprises the average weekly rate of pay multiplied by the normal working hours per week. For this purpose the average is calculated by reference to the previous 12 weeks. This comprises the 12 weeks ending with the relevant week where the Calculation Date is the last day of the week but otherwise ends with the last complete week.

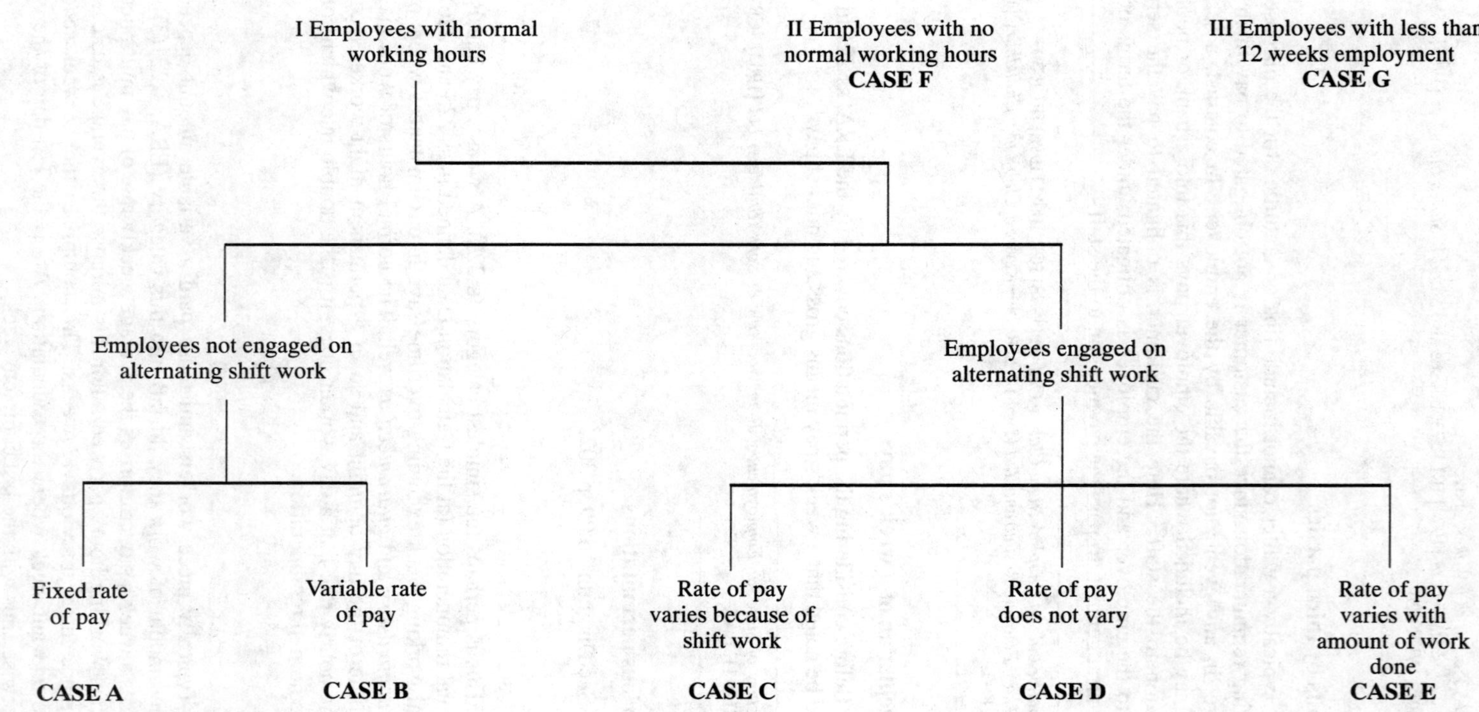
I Employees with normal working hours
II Employees with no normal working hours
CASE F
III Employees with less than 12 weeks employment
CASE G
Employees not engaged on alternating shift work
Employees engaged on alternating shift work
Fixed rate of pay
CASE A
Variable rate of pay
CASE B
Rate of pay varies because of shift work
CASE C
Rate of pay does not vary
CASE D
Rate of pay varies with amount of work done
CASE E

As far as the 12 calendar weeks are concerned, only those during which the employee would not be entitled to any pay for work at all are disregarded[2] extending the period backwards until there are 12 calendar weeks during which the employee was due payment for work (s 223(2)). Having identified the relevant 12 weeks the total number of hours actually worked (inclusive of overtime where compulsory and guaranteed) are arrived at (s 223(1)) and the total remuneration payable (but excluding overtime premia) is calculated. Although overtime premia is excluded (on the basis it is for working more than the normal hours of work) shift bonuses, which are referable to working unsocial hours, are not.

---

[1] *Stephenson v Vigers Stevens and Adams Ltd* (1966) 1 ITR 158; *Jones v Shellabear Price Ltd* (1967) 2 ITR 36.

[2] It must be a week during which (disregarding guaranteed minimum pay) the employee was due some pay for work done: *Adams v John Wright & Sons (Blackwall) Ltd* [1972] ICR 463, NIRC.

Case C

16.12 In this case (covered by s 222) a week's pay equals the average normal working hours per week multiplied by the average hourly rate (see Case B and ss 222(3) and 223). Section 222(3) provides that to calculate the average normal working hours you take a 12 week average. Having established the Calculation Date, it will be the 12 calendar weeks ending on the day in question and if this is not at the end of a week it will be the end of the last complete week before the Calculation Date (s 222(4)). Having ascertained the total number of hours falling in the period (including overtime only where compulsory and guaranteed) the average weekly hours of work are found by dividing by 12.

Case D

16.13 As for Case A.

Case E

16.14 As for Case B.

Case F

16.15 This is covered by s 224 and in such a case a week's pay equals the average weekly remuneration calculated over the relevant 12 week period. Having identified the Calculation Date the 12 weeks in question will be the 12 calendar weeks immediately preceding the Calculation Date. If the Calculation Date is not at the end of a week the relevant period will be the 12 weeks ending with the last complete week before the Calculation Date. If during any of the 12 weeks in question the employee is not entitled to any remuneration it is disregarded and an earlier week substituted until you have the last 12 calendar weeks in which the employee was due payment. The total remuneration received in respect of the 12 weeks is then divided by 12.

Case G

16.16 Unless a previous period of employment counts as continuous (in accordance with ss 210 to 219) so that 12 weeks (including weeks when the employee was employed by the predecessor) is available for calculation purposes the Industrial Tribunal must decide (applying the provisions of ss 221 to 229 that it considers appropriate as nearly as possible) what a week's pay amounts to. In doing so the Industrial Tribunal may have regard to a list of factors set out in s 228 which include reference to what other individuals in relevant comparable employment with the same or another employer receive.

16.17 Finally, it should be noted that whilst s 228(4) provides that the Secretary of State may by regulation prescribe the method of calculation of a week's pay in particular cases, at the time of writing no order has been made.

PART III
STATUTORY RIGHTS ARISING UPON THE TERMINATION OF EMPLOYMENT

17 The right to receive a written statement of reasons for dismissal

John McMullen

1 INTRODUCTION

17.01 An employer is not obliged, at common law, to give an employee any reasons for his dismissal, in writing or otherwise.[1] Indeed, as Freedland[2] points out, the common law even allows an employer subsequently to justify a summary dismissal by reasons he was unaware of at the time of dismissal.[3]

---

1 *Ridgway v Hungerford Market Co* (1835) 3 Ad & El 171 at 177, per Lord Denman CJ, cited by M R Freedland, *The Contract of Employment* (1976), p 221.

2 Op cit.

3 *Boston Deep Sea Fishing and Ice Co v Ansell* (1888) 39 Ch D 339, CA; cf, in unfair dismissal law, *W Devis & Sons Ltd v Atkins* [1977] AC 931, HL (cf also *Cyril Leonard & Co v Simo Securities Trust Ltd* [1972] 1 WLR 80, CA; *Freedland* (1972) 1 ILJ 100).

17.02 There is also no general duty on an employer at common law to give a departing employee a reference.[1] On the other hand, if he does, he should, as a matter of common sense at least, exercise care. It was originally held[2] that an employer who gave a reference might owe the employee concerned (and indeed the recipient of the reference) a *legal* duty to take reasonable care to ensure that the contents of the reference were accurate—so held the High Court in *Lawton v BOC Transhield Ltd*.[3] And in *Spring v Guardian Assurance plc*[4] the High Court again stated that a reference which included a negligent mis-statement amounted to a breach of the common law duty of care (although this was based on the particular facts of the case). However, the Court of Appeal in *Spring v Guardian Assurance plc*[5] overturned the ruling of the High Court in that case and also declared that *Lawton v BOC Transhield Ltd* was wrong. It held, that as a general proposition, the giver of a reference owed no duty in the law of negligence to the subject of the reference. His duty to the subject was governed by and lay in the tort of defamation only. If it were otherwise the defence of qualified privilege in an action for defamation where a reference was given, or the necessity for the plaintiff to prove malice in an action for malicious falsehood would be by-passed.[6] The House of Lords rejected these arguments. It held by a majority of 4 to 1 (Lord Keith dissenting) that there *was* a duty on an employer not to act unreasonably and carelessly in providing a reference about his employee or ex-employee. The duty was to avoid making untrue statements negligently or expressing unfounded opinions even if honestly believed to be true or honestly held. The fact that an employee could also sue for defamation or injurious falsehood did not prevent an action in negligence arising. The majority also held there was a duty implied into the contract of employment to take reasonable care in preparing a reference, in the circumstances set out in their Lordships' opinions.[7] Lord Slynn pointed out that employers might be able to disclaim liability for inaccurate references both to the employee and the future employer. But if there is an implied term in the contract of employment that a reference will be prepared accurately it would seem doubtful that a disclaimer given otherwise than when the term arose (ie on formation of contract) could be effective as far as the *employee* was concerned. And such a disclaimer might in any event be subject to the Unfair Contract Terms Act 1977. Employers must now be extremely careful in preparation of references and may be tempted to avoid difficult areas such as expression of opinion.

---

1 *Gallear v J F Watson & Son Ltd* [1979] IRLR 306. Although in *Spring v Guardian Assurance plc* [1994] IRLR 460, HL (House of Lords) Lord Woolf was prepared to imply a duty in the following circumstances: (i) the existence of a contract of employment or services; (ii) the fact that the contract relates to an engagement of a class where it is the normal practice to require a reference from a previous employer before employment is offered; (iii) the fact that the employee cannot be expected to enter into that class of employment except on the basis that his employer will, on the request of another prospective employer made not later than a reasonable time after the termination of a former employment, provide a full and frank reference as to the employee. Lord Slynn endorsed the general rule against a duty to supply but acknowledged that certain contracts may by implication carry that duty.

2 Under the principle in *Hedley Byrne & Co Ltd v Heller & Partners Ltd* [1964] AC 465, HL.

3 [1987] 2 All ER 608.

4 [1992] IRLR 173.

5 [1993] IRLR 122.

6 [1994] IRLR 460. It can also be a criminal offence under the Servants' Characters Act 1972 (still partially in force) to issue a false (in the manner defined by the Act) written testimonial about a servant.

7 See particularly Lords Goff, Slynn and Woolf.

---

2 THE STATUTORY RIGHT TO PARTICULARS OF REASONS FOR DISMISSAL

17.03 Now to the statute. Although it does not amount to an obligation to give a reference, s 92 of the ERA obliges an employer to supply an employee, on request, with a written statement containing particulars of reasons for the employee's dismissal. This has to be provided, if reasonably possible, within 14 days of the request. Special provisions apply (see below) in the case of a woman dismissed when pregnant or after childbirth in circumstances in which her maternity leave period ends by reason of the dismissal (the 'maternity provisions'). That section should be consulted first if the complaint occurs in such circumstances.

17.04 Section 92 of the ERA is a re-enactment of s 70 of the Employment Protection Act 1975 which introduced the right. The right only applies to employees as defined by ERA, s 230(1), ie to those working under a contract of service or apprenticeship, and not to self-employed workers. Apart from in a case where the maternity provisions apply (see below), to qualify for the right an employee must also have been continuously employed by the employer for a minimum period. The qualifying period was originally six months ending with the effective date of termination of employment[1]; but by the Employment Act 1989 the qualifying period for entitlement to a written statement was changed to two years and it was also provided that, for the future, further change might be effected by statutory instrument as with the case of unfair dismissal qualifying periods.[2]

[1] ERA, s 92(3). See Chapter 7, above, for continuous employment and Chapter 19, below, for definition of the effective date of termination of employment: ERA, s 97(1) to (4).

[2] As discussed in Chapter 19, the issue of qualifying periods for employment protection rights may be affected by the litigation concerning the possible discriminatory effect (contrary to the Equal Treatment Directive 76/207/EEC) of the two year qualifying period for unfair dismissal claims (see *R v Secretary of State for Employment, ex p Seymour-Smith and Perez* [1995] IRLR 464.

17.05 Those excluded from claiming include overseas employees,[1] share fishermen[2] and policemen.[3]

[1] ERA, s 196. Save for workers employed on the continental shelf in territorial waters: Employment Protection (Offshore Employment) Order 1976, SI 1976/766 (as amended).

[2] ERA, s 199(2).

[3] Ibid, s 200(1). Members of the naval, military and air forces, previously excluded by EP(C)A, s 138(3), are now covered, by virtue of s 192 of the ERA.

17.06 The right to request a written statement applies after a dismissal by an employer. This means dismissal by an employer with or without notice, or a deemed dismissal that arises by virtue of a non renewal of a fixed term contract.[1] But it does *not*, it seems, apply following a constructive dismissal.[2]

[1] ERA, s 92(1).

[2] *Broomsgrove v Eagle Alexander Ltd* [1981] IRLR 127, EAT. The precise wording of s 92(1) is as follows:

'An employee is entitled to be provided by his employer with a written statement giving particulars of the reasons for the employee's dismissal—

(a) if the employee is given by the employer notice of termination of his contract of employment;
(b) if the employee's contract of employment is terminated by his employer without notice; or
(c) if, the employee is employed under a contract for a fixed term and that term expires without being renewed under the same contract . . .'

There is a conspicuous absence of reference to employee-initiated termination: – hence the problem.

17.07 An employee may complain to an industrial tribunal if his employer has unreasonably failed,[1] on request, to supply a written statement to him within 14 days of the request, or at all, or on grounds that the particulars given in purported compliance with the section are inadequate or untrue.[2] A claim must be submitted within three months of the effective date of termination of employment.[3] There is a discretion on the part of the industrial tribunal to hear late claims provided that the tribunal considers it was not reasonably practicable for the complaint to be presented before the end of the period of three months following the effective date of termination.[4] As with unfair dismissal applications the complaint may also be presented before the employment is ended if the dismissal is with notice and the complaint is presented after notice is given.[5] It is implicit that an employee is only entitled to complain of a breach of s 92 if the employee has actually made a request for reasons (but cf the maternity provisions, discussed below). In *Catherine Haigh Harlequin Hair Design v Seed*[6] the employee, Miss Seed, was summarily dismissed by her employers who then gave her a letter setting out the reason for her dismissal, with which she disagreed. She made a complaint that the particulars given to her were untrue and the industrial tribunal upheld her complaint. However, it is important to note that she never requested the reasons for her dismissal but had been given them unilaterally, as commonly occurs. The Employment Appeal Tribunal confirmed that an industrial tribunal had no jurisdiction to entertain an employee's complaint that written particulars were untrue in circumstances where the employee had made no request for written particulars under s 92(2) but had simply based the complaint on the reasons contained in a letter given unilaterally to her when she was dismissed. In all cases then, whether the complaint under s 92 is about unreasonable failure or about whether the particulars given are inadequate or untrue, a request is necessary before the provisions of s 92 can come into effect. As explained below, however, s 92(4) does away with the need for a prior request in the context of maternity (as more fully described below).

[1] Originally the complaint had to be of 'refusal' (see below). Paragraph 11 of Sch 8 to TURERA changed this to 'failure', a change probably more favourable to employees as embracing sins of omission as well as commission.
[2] ERA, s 92(6).
[3] Ibid, s 93(3) (for definition of the 'effective date' see Chapter 19, below, and ERA, s 97(1) and (2) and 92(4)).
[4] Ibid, ss 93(3) and 111(2).
[5] Ibid, ss 93(3) and 111(4).
[6] [1990] IRLR 175, EAT.

17.08 Initially, the approach of the tribunals was legalistic and strict,[1] one case, for example, suggesting (wrongly, as it later transpired (see below)) that supply of reasons otherwise than within 14 days of the request was *per se* a breach of the section.[2] However, in subsequent cases it was recognised that the section was penal and not compensatory. This was partly because s 53 of the EP(C)A 1978 as originally drawn referred to an unreasonable '*refusal*'. It was a penalty upon an employer for a conscious and unreasonable refusal to supply written particulars of dismissal. Accordingly, the section was to be construed more loosely.[3] Failure to supply was not necessarily to be equated with an unreasonable *refusal* to supply.[4] Now, however, under s 93 of the ERA the complaint may be made of unreasonable '*failure*' (a word now substituted for 'refusal'). The law from now on will arguably be construed more tightly.

[1] *Keen v Dymo Ltd* [1977] IRLR 118; *Joines v B and S (Burknall) Ltd* [1977] IRLR 83; *Horsley Smith and Sherry Ltd v Dutton* [1977] ICR 594, [1977] IRLR 172, EAT.
[2] *Keen v Dymo Ltd* (above).
[3] *Charles Lang & Sons Ltd v Aubrey* [1978] ICR 168, [1977] IRLR 354, EAT.
[4] *Ladbroke Entertainments Ltd v Clark* [1987] ICR 585, EAT.

17.09 No particular form is required for supply of the statement, but, as the EAT stated in *Horsley Smith and Sherry Ltd v Dutton*,[1] 'the document must be of such a kind that the employee, or anyone to whom he may wish to show it, can know from reading the document itself why the employee has been dismissed'. And there is no doubt that the statement should be in *writing*. So confirmed the EAT in *McBrearty v Thomson (t/a Highfield Mini-Market)*,[2] Lord Mayfield emphasising that the purpose of the section was not simply to give information to the employee but to give written reasons that could be shown to a third party (eg an adviser) who wished to know why he or she had been dismissed.

[1] [1977] ICR 594, [1977] IRLR 172, EAT.
[2] 653/90, IDS Brief 450 (August 1991), p 15, EAT.

17.10 The obligation then breaks down into two parts, first, whether there has been an unreasonable failure to supply reasons, and second, whether the reasons, if supplied, are sufficient and/or accurate.

3 UNREASONABLE FAILURE

17.11 Section 53 of the EP(C)A was, until the enactment of TURERA, concerned with an unreasonable *refusal* to supply reasons. Schedule 8, para 11 of TURERA changed the text to unreasonable *failure* to supply reasons (see now s 93 of the ERA). The case law on unreasonable refusal may therefore be of historical value but it is set out here lest some principles may be of assistance in case the concept of unreasonable 'failure' is not construed dramatically differently from the expression unreasonable 'refusal'. As has been mentioned, reasoning applied in early cases on the concept of 'refusal' seemed to suggest that delay beyond the end of the 14 day period alone amounted to an unreasonable refusal. However, this was subsequently held not to be the case. As stated, the emphasis of the section was on *refusal*; not on failure to supply. Mere delay in supplying the reasons did not of itself amount to an unreasonable refusal.[1] It was necessary to look at the reasons behind the delay. However, there came a point at which excessive delay might of itself amount to unreasonable refusal, especially where there was no adequate explanation for the delay.[2] Nonetheless, it was possible for an employer, in exceptional circumstances, to escape liability even in a case where the particulars had not been supplied at all. Again, this is because failure to supply was not to be equated with an unreasonable refusal to supply. In *Ladbroke Entertainments Ltd v Clark*[3] an employee who had been dismissed for alleged gross misconduct requested a written statement of reasons for dismissal. The employers promised that this would be forthcoming but, through a genuine oversight, it was not sent. It was held by the EAT that in such circumstances the employer could not be said to have unreasonably refused to supply a written statement of reasons for dismissal.

[1] *Lowson v Percy Main and District Social Club and Institute Ltd* [1979] ICR 568, [1979] IRLR 227, EAT.
[2] *Charles Lang & Sons Ltd v Aubrey* [1978] ICR 168, [1977] IRLR 354, EAT. See also *Clements v Decent* (23 June 1983, unreported), EAT (long-standing failure to supply after clear request was implicit refusal).
[3] [1987] ICR 585, EAT.

17.12 Similarly, employers who delayed supplying a statement beyond the 14 day period because of a failure of communication with their solicitors[1] and, in another case, who had not realised, on reasonable gounds, because of the vagueness of the request, that the employee had asked for a written statement,[2] had not reasonably refused to supply a statement. Finally, it was held not unreasonable to refuse to provide a statutory statement when the employer and the employee had arranged that the ostensible reason was different from the true one so as to secure more favourable retirement terms for the employee.[3]

1 *Lowson v Percy Main and District Social Club and Institute Ltd* [1979] ICR 568, [1979] IRLR 227, EAT.
2 *HT Greenwood v Miller* (15 December 1987 unreported), EAT, IDS Brief (1987) 365, p 6.
3 *Petch v Department of Health and Social Security* (1987) 339 IRLIB 13, EAT.

17.13 One example of a case where the employer was held to have acted unreasonably by declining to supply a written statement is *Daynecourt Insurance Brokers Ltd v Iles.*[1] Here the employee had been dismissed because of alleged theft from the employer. The police were brought in, and they requested the employer not to communicate with the employee any further. The employee requested a written statement of reasons for dismissal and, in accordance with the police request, the employer failed to reply. In answer to the employee's complaint of non-supply the employer pleaded the police request in defence. However, the industrial tribunal considered that the employer had unreasonably refused to supply a written statement. The EAT declined to interfere with the tribunal's decision, confirming that deciding what was an unreasonable refusal to supply a written statement involved an objective test and the question was, what was expected of a reasonable employer? Here the employer had unreasonably acted on a blanket request not to communicate with the employee and had assumed without further enquiry, that the request extended to not complying with the duty to supply a written statement to the employee.

1 [1978] IRLR 335.

17.14 As stated, it remains to be seen whether the above cases will be helpful or not in construing the new wording which is now to be found in s 88 of the ERA to the effect that, in order to complain of non-supply, it must be shown that there was an unreasonable failure to supply rather than an unreasonable refusal to supply. It may be posited that the new wording under TURERA at least imagines that sins by omission as well as commission are covered. Certainly, the change in wording clearly tightens up the position but to what extent can only be seen from future case law. Some of the previous case law may, however, be useful in terms of defining the concept of 'unreasonableness' at least.

17.15 As has been stated, the right to request a written statement seems not to apply in favour of an employee who has been constructively dismissed. In such cases the employer will commonly deny there has been a dismissal at all. However, in cases of alleged constructive dismissal, or other cases where dismissal is denied, it is not the end of the matter if an employer simply says that there has been no dismissal and declines to supply the statement on that ground. An industrial tribunal is entitled to investigate whether or not there has been a dismissal and is not bound by the employer's bald statement that there is no dismissal. However, a genuine belief on the part of the employer that no dismissal had taken place may make the employer's failure to supply a statement reasonable.[1] The test in cases where dismissal is disputed was considered most recently in *Broomsgrove v Eagle Alexander Ltd*[2] in which the EAT considered, more stringently, that the issue was whether the employer both genuinely and *reasonably* believed that there was no dismissal.

[1] *Brown v Stuart Scott & Co Ltd* [1981] ICR 166, EAT.
[2] [1981] IRLR 127, EAT.

17.16 Many employers are asked for a written statement for dismissal after they have already orally communicated the reasons for dismissal, or after they have already issued a letter of dismissal setting out reasons for dismissal, or in circumstances where they are convinced that the employee is already well aware of the reasons for dismissal. It is not an answer, where a statement has not been supplied, simply to say that the employee was already aware of the reasons; this would be a *prima facie* breach of the section.[1] But what if the employer has, previous to the request, written a letter of dismissal which supplied reasons? It is dubious whether the mere existence of an earlier letter of dismissal (even if it has given reasons) justifies non-supply of a written statement in response to a later statutory request. It is likely that a failure to respond here would amount to a *prima facie* breach of the obligation to supply a written statement.[2] May an employer, however, in a reply to a request for a written statement, simply refer the employee to an earlier document which gives the reasons? Earlier cases indicated that this was not possible.[3] But in *Kent County Council v Gilham*[4] the Court of Appeal considered that it was possible for an employer to refer to an earlier document, for example, a letter of dismissal, giving full reasons for dismissal, provided that a copy of the earlier letter was included by the employer in the letter referring to it.[5]

[1] As the section requires a statement in writing, a failure (previously, refusal) is a *prima facie* breach; the tribunal must then consider whether this was unreasonable.
[2] *Joines v B and S (Burknall) Ltd* [1977] IRLR 83. Although some comments in this case *suggest* that it would not be an *unreasonable* refusal (now failure) to supply a written statement where the letter of dismissal had been very detailed indeed and where the employer genuinely regarded the request for a written statement thereafter as vexatious (*sed quaere*).
[3] *Horsley Smith and Sherry Ltd v Dutton* [1977] ICR 594, [1977] IRLR 172, EAT. Although in *Marchant v Earley Town Council* [1979] IRLR 311, [1979] ICR 891, EAT some doubt was expressed as to whether this would be an *unreasonable* refusal (now failure).
[4] [1985] ICR 227, CA.
[5] Note the requirement when relying on an earlier letter giving reasons to send a copy of the original letter with the reply to the statutory request. But the EAT found an omission to do so in *White v Youth Development Trust* (25 February 1985, unreported), EAT, IDS Brief (1985) 303, p 5 did not mean the employers had, in that case, *unreasonably* refused (as the test then was) to supply a statement.

17.17 An employer does not, it is submitted, comply with the section by providing reasons through an answer on industrial tribunal form IT3 (a notice of appearance to an employee's originating application claiming unfair dismissal). Section 92 assumes an independent response to the s 92 request direct to the employee.[1] The reasons have therefore to be given to the employee himself;[2] but it has been held that the reasons may be sent to a legal adviser appointed by the employee as agent for receiving reasons.[3]

[1] *Rowan v Machinery Installations (South Wales) Ltd* [1981] ICR 386, [1981] IRLR 122, EAT.
[2] Ibid.
[3] *Kent County Council v Gilham* [1985] ICR 227, CA.

4 SUFFICIENCY AND ACCURACY OF REASONS

17.18 An employee may complain if the particulars in purported compliance with the statute are inadequate or untrue. As is clear from the quotation from *Horsley Smith and Sherry Ltd v Dutton*[1] already referred to,[2] sufficient detail must be given to the employee to enable him to know why he has been dismissed and what type of dismissal claim he should bring, and, presumably, what sort of case the employer might have against him. It is submitted that it is doubtful whether an employer complies with the section, for example, by simply referring to one of the reasons for dismissal set out in s 98 of the ERA alone. Section 92 emphasises that *particulars* of the reasons for dismissal must be given. However, the standard may not be unrealistically high. One EAT decision has stated that an employer who indicated that the reason for dismissal was 'dishonesty' had satisfied the section and that the employee was not entitled to particulars of each act relied upon within the umbrella reason of dishonesty.[3] And a statement by an employer, who dismissed for alleged theft, that referred to the reason being 'gross industrial misconduct concerning the incidents that took place on Saturday 26th October 1985' was held sufficient in view of the reference to the 'incidents'.[4] However, an employer must bear in mind that the written statement is admissible in evidence in any proceedings[5] (eg in a subsequent unfair dismissal case before an industrial tribunal: see below) and he may therefore in practice be bound by the statements of fact that he makes in the written statement of particulars of reasons for dismissal. For that reason he may be reluctant to go into enormous detail. An employer who chooses, however, to be delphic may run the risk of breach of s 92. On the whole, therefore, it may be safer for an employer to provide *some* brief particulars and not to rely on the minimum.

---

1 [1977] ICR 594, [1977] IRLR 172, EAT.
2 See para 17.09.
3 *Earl v Valleyhorn Ltd* (3 September 1981, unreported), EAT. See, too, *Bonimart v Delemore* (26 September 1980) (1985) 275 IRLIB 6, EAT.
4 *Walls v City Bakeries* (24 February 1987, unreported), EAT, IDS Brief (1987) 348, p 6.
5 ERA, s 92(5).

17.19 Finally, there will be a breach of the section if the particulars supplied are untrue.[1] Thus, in *Watkins v Bennett*[2] the employer stated the reason for dismissal to be incompetence and inability to work unsupervised, but the industrial tribunal later found the dismissal to be on ground of suspected dishonesty. It was held that the claim under s 92 should succeed. Not all cases, however, where the reason for dismissal is disputed will result in a successful application under s 92 that the particulars supplied are untrue. In *Harvard Securities plc v Younghusband*[3] the facts were that during the time of the applicant's employment with his employer another employee had been arrested and charged with certain offences including taking clients' property. All of the staff were informed of the arrest and the charges involved and, according to the company, requested not to pass on that information to any third party. The applicant was dismissed because of a telephone conversation he had with another person who was believed to be an employee of a rival firm during which he discussed the arrest. The employers formed the view that the telephone conversation led to the matter being disclosed to the press. In response to a request for a written statement of reasons for dismissal the applicant was sent a letter which stated that:

> 'You improperly divulged to a third party confidential information relating to a business of the company. Your summary dismissal is in accordance with Clause 10.3 of the company's standard rules of employment.'

Mr Younghusband disputed the statement and brought a claim under s 88 claiming that the written reason was untrue because in his view the information in question could not in any sense be regarded as confidential. An industrial tribunal agreed with him. However, the Employment Appeal Tribunal held that it was wrong. According to the EAT, s 93 requires an employer to state truthfully the reason that he was relying on in dismissing the employee. Section 93 was concerned with the veracity of what the employer put forward as a reason for dismissal. It did not entail an examination of the justification for the dismissal. There is no need under s 93 to embark upon consideration of whether the reason was 'intrinsically a good, bad or indifferent one'. The purpose of s 93 was to commit the employer to the reason that he genuinely relied upon and to ensure the employee does not start a case (eg for unfair dismissal) with the disadvantage of not knowing what it was that the employer relied upon for dismissing him. Whether the employers in this case were correct in describing the information in question as confidential was irrelevant. They had identified a breach of confidentiality in their own minds and that was the reason clearly they had relied upon. There was no breach of s 93.[4]

---

1 *Oliver v MacDonald* (1981) COIT 3197/81.
2 *Watkins v Bennett* (COIT 1634/189), IT, IDS Brief (1985) 301, p 17.
3 [1990] IRLR 17, EAT.
4 In a sense this is consistent with the view of Cairns L J in *Abernethy v Mott, Hay and Anderson* [1974] ICR 323, CA that:

> 'a reason for the dismissal of an employee is a set of facts known to the employer or it may be of beliefs held by him which cause him to dismiss the employee'

is the test to be applied for examining the reason for dismissal put forward by the employer in unfair dismissal proceedings. (See also *Trust House Forte Leisure Ltd v Aquilar* [1976] IRLR 251; see a controversial application of this test to constructive dismissal cases in *Ely v YKK Fasteners (UK) Ltd* [1993] IRLR 500, CA.)

---

5 ENFORCEMENT

17.20 As discussed, the employee's remedy is by complaint to an industrial tribunal. The complaint may be of unreasonable failure to supply the written statement or that the statement, if given, contains untrue or inadequate particulars. It is possible to combine complaints. Thus, if a statement is supplied after the end of the 14 day period, an employee may complain that there has been an unreasonable failure to supply within the 14 day period and that the particulars therein are inadequate and/or untrue, if that is the case.[1] If the tribunal finds that the complaint is well founded it:

(i) may declare what the reasons for the dismissal were, and
(ii) may award the employee two weeks pay.[2]

---

1 *Arlett v A M K (Property Management) Ltd* EAT 475/81.
2 For the definition and calculation of a week's pay, see Chapter 16, above, and ERA, s 226(2).

6 EFFECT OF THE WRITTEN STATEMENT

17.21 As mentioned above, the written statement, once given by the employer, is admissible in evidence in any proceedings, eg for unfair dismissal. In a subsequent unfair dismissal case it may be difficult for an employer credibly to rely on different reasons from those originally supplied in response to a request for a written statement. Also, *semble*, where the tribunal makes a declaration of reasons for dismissal after default by an employer it will similarly be difficult for an employer to successfully adduce additional or different reasons for dismissal in any subsequent unfair dismissal proceedings. Additional care must therefore be taken by employers to ensure the adequacy and accuracy of a written statement of particulars of reasons for dismissal where the employee has presented or is intending to present a claim for unfair dismissal, as the consequences of inaccuracy may not only involve breach of s 93, but also cause problems in defending an unfair dismissal claim.

7 THE MATERNITY PROVISIONS INTRODUCED BY TURERA

17.22 The Trade Union Reform and Employment Rights Act 1993 made an important modification to s 53 of the EP(C)A 1978 (now s 88 of the ERA) in the context of an employee exercising maternity rights. Section 92(4) of the ERA now provides that an employee is entitled to be provided with a written statement giving particulars of the reasons for dismissal if she is dismissed:

(a) at any time while she is pregnant; or
(b) after childbirth in circumstances in which her maternity leave period ends by reason of the dismissal.

It is important to note that:

(a) such an employee does not have to make a request for a written statement;
(b) no qualifying period applies.

The general discussion of s 92 in this chapter should therefore be read in the light of these important exceptions. The drafting of s 92(4) is economical, to say the least. In some ways it appears alone within s 92 as a free-standing right, although much of the corpus of rules about the operation of the general s 92 right apply equally. To be noted, however, are the following additional points:

(1) A general s 92 statement has to be provided *within 14 days* of a *request*. Obviously no request is needed under s 92(4). Correspondingly, though, no time limit for the supply of reasons (eg from the date of dismissal) is set! This is surely sloppy drafting. It would have been easy to provide that the statement be provided within 14 days of dismissal.

(2) The general s 92 right is available after a request which follows three specific types of 'termination' of employment, ie:
   (a) when an employer has terminated by notice;
   (b) when an employer has terminated without notice;
   (c) when a fixed term contract has expired and is not renewed.

It is the absence here in s 92(1) of reference to *employee* initiated termination that has caused the courts to rule that constructive dismissals are not covered (see para 17.06). But s 87(4) simply refers to a right to receive written reasons following '*dismissal*'. Would this open the way to a right under s 92(4) to written reasons following a constructive dismissal even if the remainder of s 92 does not apply in such a case?

(3) The right to a statement under s 92(4) may mean an employee is entitled to a statement when neither employer nor employee appreciates that, at the time of dismissal, the employee is pregnant! Presumably a failure in those circumstances would not then be an unreasonable failure.

8 OTHER CHANGES MADE BY TURERA

17.23 We have already mentioned the change made by Sch 8, para 11, substituting unreasonable 'failure' to supply reasons in the place of unreasonable 'refusal' to supply, in s 53(4) of the EP(C)A, now s 93(1) of the ERA. In Sch 10 it is provided that the sentence formerly reading in s 53(4) of the EP(C)A 'A complaint may be presented to an industrial tribunal by an employee against his employer on the ground that . . .' now reads 'A complaint may be presented to an industrial tribunal by an employee on the ground that . . .'.

18 The right to statutory notice on termination of employment

John McMullen

1 INTRODUCTION

18.01 Under s 86 of the ERA an employee is entitled to statutory notice of termination of employment, the length of which is dependent on the employee's service. This operates as a statutorily implied term in the contract of employment and creates a minimum floor of protection for employees. In turn, the section requires a comparatively modest minimum period of notice from an employee to an employer to terminate the employment.

1 See also *Harvey* Div A8.

2 QUALIFICATION AND EXCLUSIONS

18.02 The right applies only to employees as defined by ERA, s 230(1), ie to those working under a contract of service or apprenticeship, and does not apply to self employed workers. To fall within the section an employee must have been continuously employed for a period of not less than one month, whether for the purposes of minimum notice to be given to him by the employer or from him to the employer.[1]

1 Section 86(1),(2). For continuous employment, see Chapter 7, above.

18.03 Certain types of workers are expressly excluded, namely overseas employees,[1] mariners,[2] Crown employees,[3] the armed forces[4] and Parliamentary staff.[5]

1 ERA, s 196.
2 Ibid, s 199(1).
3 Ibid, s 191 and see *Harvey* IA.
4 Ibid, s 192.
5 Ibid, ss 194 and 195.

18.04 Other individuals excluded from protection are those recruited for a specific task which is not expected to last for more than three months (unless the employment actually continues for more than three months),[1] and, of course, those whose employment terminates by reason of expiry of a fixed term.[2] However, in the latter case, if the employee has been recruited on a fixed term contract of one month or less and three months' or more employment has occurred, the contract takes effect thereafter as a contract for an indefinite period and is subject to s 86.[3]

[1] Section 86(5).
[2] As defined by *Dixon v BBC* [1978] QB 438, [1977] IRLR 337, EAT.
[3] Section 86(4).

18.05 It would seem that the common law itself provides other exclusions. For example, if the contract is to terminate on the occurrence of a particular event it could be argued that the contract comes to an end upon the occurrence of that event automatically without the need for action by either party. Thus in *Brown v Knowsley Borough Council*[1] a teacher was employed 'only as long as sufficient funds are provided either by the Manpower Services Commission or by other firms/sponsors to fund it'. When the funding ceased the job finished and it was held that the contract came to an end automatically, without the need for notice. The contract was discharged by performance.[2] This will occur, too, when the contract is for completion of a specific task; the contract will be discharged by performance on completion.[3] Also, a termination by mutual agreement does not amount to an attempt to give notice by either party and, in such a case, the provisions of s 86 should not be triggered.[4] Finally, if the contract of employment has been frustrated at common law prior to the purported giving of notice by the employer, s 86 will not apply and nor will the guaranteed payments during notice under s 87 (below) which are dependent thereon.[5]

[1] [1986] IRLR 102, EAT.
[2] See also *Wiltshire County Council v National Association of Teachers in Further and Higher Education* [1980] ICR 455, [1980] IRLR 198, CA.
[3] *Wiltshire; Ironmonger v Movefield Ltd (t/a Deering Appointments)* [1988] IRLR 461, EAT; *Ryan v Shipboard Maintenance Ltd* [1980] ICR 88, EAT. See also Chapter 1, above, and Chapter 19, below. But cf the specific treatment of fixed task contracts not expected to last for more than three months which run on thereafter, when the right to notice will apply (ERA, s 86(5) and para 18.04).
[4] *Sheffield v Oxford Controls Ltd* [1979] IRLR 133, EAT; *Logan Salton v Durham County Council* [1989] IRLR 99, EAT, criticised by the editor of the *Industrial Relations Law Reports* at [1989] IRLR 97. See also *Birch v University of Liverpool* [1985] ICR 470, CA; *Scott v Coalite Fuels and Chemicals Ltd* [1988] ICR 355, EAT (early retirement vs dismissal).
[5] *Notcutt v Universal Equipment Co (London) Ltd* [1986] 3 All ER 582, [1986] 1 WLR 641, CA. See also other cases on frustration, eg *Marshall v Harland and Wolff Ltd (No 2)* (Practice Note) [1972] ICR 97; *Egg Stores (Stamford Hill) Ltd v Leibovici* [1977] ICR 260, [1976] IRLR 376, EAT; *Hare v Murphy Bros Ltd* [1974] 3 All ER 940, [1974] IRLR 342, CA; *FC Shepherd & Co Ltd v Jerrom* [1985] ICR 552, [1985] IRLR 275, EAT; *Williams v Watsons Luxury Coaches Ltd* [1990] ICR 536, EAT.

3 THE CONTENT OF THE RIGHT

18.06 Under s 86(1) an employee is entitled to not less than one week's notice if his period of continuous employment is more than one month but less than two years and not less than one week's notice of termination of employment for each year of continuous employment if his period of continuous employment is two years or more but less than twelve years. If his period of continuous employment is twelve years or more he is entitled to not less than twelve weeks' notice.[1] In turn an employer is, under s 86(2), entitled to receive from an employee who has been continuously employed for one month or more not less than one week's notice of termination of employment.[2]

[1] Section 86(1).
[1] Section 86(2).

4 SOME FEATURES OF AND GENERAL RULES ABOUT NOTICE

18.07 There are a number of additional points to be noted, some of which are apparent from the section and some not.

18.08 The section creates a statutory *minimum* period of notice. It does not displace any more favourable period of notice *implied* by the common law where the contract is silent.[1] Nor can it displace any more generous *express* provision in the contract concerning notice. Where the implied or express term as to notice is more generous than the statutory minimum the contractual notice can of course be relied upon. This applies both in respect of notice an employee is entitled to expect from an employer and in respect of notice an employer is entitled to receive from an employee. Conversely, however, it is not possible to give shorter notice than the statutory minimum notwithstanding an express provision in the contract. If an employer or an employee gives shorter notice than the statutory minimum this could lead to an action for damages for breach of contract on the part of the recipient of short notice (see below).

[1] For example as in *Hill v CA Parsons & Co Ltd* [1972] Ch 305, [1971] 3 All ER 1345, CA. See also *Chitty on Contracts* vol 2, para 3491 and MR Freedland, *The Contract of Employment* pp 151–153.

18.09 Nothing in the section indicates that the notice has to be in writing.[1]

[1] At common law this is not necessary unless notice is contractually required to be in writing: *Chitty on Contracts* vol 2, para 3488; *Latchford Premier Cinema Ltd v Ennion* [1931] 2 Ch 409.

18.10 Nothing in the section prevents the parties from waiving their respective rights to notice or prevents an employee accepting a payment in lieu of notice.[1] A potential problem here occurs with s 97(2) (in the context of unfair dismissal) and s 145(5) (in the context of redundancy) which allow an employee dismissed without notice or with short notice to have his employment extended for certain statutory purposes by the extent of the statutory notice (or balance thereof as the case may be) which has not been given to him. Might this mean that if a payment in lieu of notice is given the employment cannot so be extended? It has been held, however, that acceptance of a payment in lieu of notice does not prejudice the right of an employee under s 145(5) to have his 'relevant date' of termination of employment extended for statutory redundancy payments purposes by the extent of statutory minimum notice under s 86.[2] The contractual aspect of the statutory waiver in s 86(3) was considered in *Trotter v Forth Ports Authority*.[3] In that case Mr Trotter, when made redundant, received £35,000 under a Government compensation scheme. The employer's understanding was that, thereby, Mr Trotter had waived his right to notice of termination. Mr Trotter disputed this and said he had not waived his right to his statutory minimum notice

(12 weeks). He brought a claim for damages. One of his arguments was that s 86(3) refers only to a waiver of the right to notice and that an employee cannot waive his right to a payment in lieu of notice even if he waives the right to a period of notice. However, this was rejected by the Court of Session. A payment in lieu of notice is not a consensual payment, but a claim for damages for breach of contract.[4] If the right to notice is waived, termination of the contract without notice is not a breach and no damages are due.[5]

[1] Section 86(3). See *Staffordshire County Council v Secretary of State for Employment* [1989] IRLR 117, CA.

[2] See *Staffordshire County Council v Secretary of State for Employment* [1989] IRLR 117, CA where the Court of Appeal overturned the EAT ([1988] IRLR 3) holding that the effect of s 86(3) was in contract only. The case was about an employer's claim for rebate, but is of wider application. The same principle should apply to s 97(2) (unfair dismissal) (s 97(4), which extends employment on a constructive dismissal for unfair dismissal purposes is less relevant as a payment in lieu of notice will usually not be made in such circumstances).

[3] [1991] IRLR 419.

[4] Entirely consistent with the ruling of the House of Lords in *Delaney v Staples* [1992] IRLR 191, HL. A more controversial aplication of s 86(3) may be found in *Marshall (Cambridge) Ltd v Hamblin* [1994] IRLR 260 where the EAT held that an employee who submitted three months' notice of termination of employment (and who was prepared to work it) was not dismissed by the action of the employer in refusing to allow him to work out his notice. There was provision in the contract for a payment in lieu of notice. The employer relied on this to pay off the employee and end the relationship forthwith. It was held that the terms of s 86(3) support the view that an employer has the right to waive a period of notice and, where it is specified in the contract, make a payment in lieu. With respect this is a novel approach. A contractual provision of this type is normally intended to allow an employer to make a payment in lieu of notice given by *him*. To apply it to foreshorten an *employee's* notice should have the effect of a dismissal and it is submitted that nothing in s 86(3) should have supported the employer's contrary argument.

[5] *Baldwin v British Coal Corporation* [1995] IRLR 139.

18.11 Notice of dismissal must be distinguished from a mere advance warning of dismissal. The former triggers s 86. The latter does not.[1]

[1] *International Computers Ltd v Kennedy* [1981] IRLR 28, EAT; *Morton Sundour Fabrics Ltd v Shaw* (1966) 2 ITR 84; *Haseltine Lake & Co v Dowler* [1981] ICR 222, [1981] IRLR 25, EAT. (Cf *Greenaway Harrison Ltd v Wiles* [1994] IRLR 380, EAT.)

18.12 A notice of dismissal (or resignation), once given, cannot be withdrawn, at least if the dismissal notice is lawful. However, it can be argued that if the notice is *unlawful* in some way (eg is of insufficient length) it can be withdrawn by the guilty party before it is accepted by the injured party and thus, the *status quo* may as a result be restored.[1] These are common law principles but there is no reason to suppose they do not apply here.

[1] *Riordan v War Office* [1959] 3 All ER 552, [1959] 1 WLR 1046; *Harris and Russell Ltd v Slingsby* [1973] 3 All ER 31, [1973] ICR 454. An unlawful notice, being a breach of contract, can be withdrawn by the guilty party before acceptance by the injured party. The elective theory of termination of contracts gives the guilty party the opportunity to repair his breach prior to acceptance thereof by the injured party. See, by analogy, *Harrison v Norwest Holst Group Administration Ltd* [1985] IRLR 240, CA. Also there are some cases, decided in the context of unfair dismissal, which appear to allow resignations or dismissals in the heat of the moment to be retracted: see Chapter 2, above.

18.13 When notice is given it is deemed to be exclusive of the day on which it is given.[1]

[1] *West v Kneels Ltd* [1987] ICR 146, [1986] IRLR 430, EAT.

18.14 A notice of dismissal when despatched, for example by post, is only effective when read by the recipient and not when despatched.[1]

[1] *Brown v Southall and Knight* [1980] ICR 617, [1980] IRLR 130, EAT, per Slynn J; *Hindle Gears Ltd v McGinty* [1985] ICR 111, [1984] IRLR 477, EAT. And delivery to an employee's union is not sufficient: *Morris v Bailey* [1969] 2 Lloyds Rep 215, CA.

18.15 In s 86(6) of the ERA it is stated that the section does not affect any right of either party to treat the contract as terminable without notice by reason of such conduct by the other party as would have enabled him to treat it as terminable prior to the passing of the Act. This means, for example, that an employee who could lawfully be summarily dismissed at common law, eg for gross misconduct, will not be entitled to statutory notice either. However, it has now been held that an employer will not escape liability to pay due notice under s 86 merely by labelling the dismissal as one for gross misconduct where the facts do not support that there has in fact been gross misconduct.[1]

[1] *Lanton Leisure Ltd v White and Gibson* [1987] IRLR 119, EAT.

5 ENFORCEMENT

18.16 The claim for monies due under the notice period laid down by s 86 is a claim in contract and not under statute.[1] In spite of the fact that the statutory minimum is contained in statute it has been held that it does not operate as a statutory right but merely implies, through statute, a minimum period of notice into the contract of employment. A claim for monies arising from failure to give notice is therefore a claim for damages for breach of contract. *Semble* it is therefore subject to the principles in relation to damages in contract law generally at common law, such as the duty on the injured party to mitigate loss.[2] It used therefore to follow that the right was enforceable only in the ordinary courts and *not* in the industrial tribunals. However, in 1994 the Secretary of State at long last exercised his power under s 131 of the EP(C)A (as amended by s 38 of TURERA) to confer jurisdiction on industrial tribunals in respect of contract claims. The Industrial Tribunals Extension of Jurisdiction (England and Wales) Order 1994[3] allows industrial tribunals to hear breach of contract claims. The types of claim covered are (a) a claim for damages for breach of a contract of employment or any other contract connected with employment; (b) a claim for a sum due under such a contract; (c) a claim for the recovery of a sum in pursuance of any enactment relating to the terms or performance of such a contract.[4] Certain exclusions apply which are not relevant to this chapter.[5] However, it is a condition of bringing a claim before an industrial tribunal that the claim arises or is outstanding on the termination of the employee's employment.[6] This demonstrates that a claim for damages arising from failure to give statutory notice is an ideal claim to bring under the new industrial tribunal jurisdiction, subject to the fact that the amount awarded by a tribunal cannot exceed £25,000.[7] On insolvency of an employer, the sums in question are guaranteed by the Secretary of State for Employment under s 182 of the ERA.[8]

[1] *Westwood v Secretary of State for Employment* [1985] AC 20, [1985] ICR 209, HL.

[2] Ibid; *Secretary of State for Employment v Wilson* [1978] 3 All ER 137, [1977] IRLR 483, EAT.

[3] SI 1994/1623. A similar order applies in Scotland. The orders are effective in respect of termination of employment on or after 12 July 1994.

[4] SI 1994/1623, art 3.

[5] See SI 1994/1623, arts 4 and 5.

[6] SI 1994/1623, art 3(c).

[7] SI 1994/1623, art 10.

[8] ERA, s 184(1).

6 GUARANTEED RIGHTS OF EMPLOYEES DURING STATUTORY NOTICE

18.17 Section 87 of the ERA and ss 87 to 91 to the ERA also provide for certain guaranteed rights during the statutory period of notice under s 86 even if these rights would not otherwise be available under the contract of employment. This applies both to notice given by an employer under s 86(1) or an employee under s 86(2). Thus where:

- (i) the employee is ready and willing to work but no work is provided for him by his employer;[1] or
- (ii) the employee is incapable of work because of sickness or injury;[2] or
- (iii) the employee is absent from work wholly or partly because of pregnancy or childbirth;[3]
- (iv) the employee is absent from work in accordance with the terms of his employment relating to holidays;[4]

the employee is entitled to be paid during the period of notice notwithstanding that his or her contract may provide for no payment or short payment (see below). However, this guaranteed right is not applicable:

- (a) where the employee asks for time off, including under any statutory rights provided for by ss 50, 52, 55 and 56 of the ERA and ss 168 and 170 of the Trade Union and Labour Relations (Consolidation) Act 1992,[5] in which case the employer is not obliged to pay during the period of agreed absence;
- (b) in a case where the *employee* has given notice and, where if after the notice is given and before the employment ends, the employee goes on strike in a strike of employees of the employer, in which case payment is excluded altogether;[6]
- (c) where, during the notice period, the employee repudiates the contract and the employer lawfully terminates for that reason, in which case there is no need to pay for the remainder of the notice period after acceptance of the repudiation.[7]

[1] ERA, s 88(1)(a).

[2] Ibid, s 88(1)(b).

[3] Ibid, s 88(1)(c).

[4] Ibid, s 88(1)(d).

[5] For example, time off for an employee to look for work during notice of redundancy: see Chapter 14, though in those cases payment may be guaranteed under the provisions of the ERA apart from s 87 (see the relevant provision accordingly).

[6] ERA, s 91(2); but it is interesting to note that the exclusion does not apply also to participation

in industrial action *short* of a strike, cf ss 237 to 239 of the TULR(C)A (Chapter 19, below). But *quaere* whether he would then be ready and willing to work. As stated, this blanket disqualification only applies where it is the employee who gave the notice. If the employer gave notice this rule does not apply though, *semble*, an employee would not be entitled to payment for the actual period on strike, as he would not be ready and willing to work.

7 ERA, s 91(4).

18.18 The employee is during such notice period entitled to be paid:

(a) where there are normal working hours, at an average hourly rate of remuneration produced by dividing a week's pay by the number of normal working hours;[1]

(b) where there are no normal working hours, a week's pay for each week of the period of notice;[2]

and as stated above, this is so whether the contract provides that no payment at all is to be made or whether it provides for payment less than the above minimum payments.

1 ERA, s 88. See Chapter 16, above, for the definition of a week's pay.

2 ERA, s 89.

18.19 Further points to note are:

(i) sick pay, statutory sick pay, maternity pay, statutory maternity pay and holiday pay and in some cases, sickness or industrial injuries benefit paid by the DSS, are to be taken into account in calculating payments due from the employer;[1]

(ii) if it is the employee who initiates termination, ie by giving notice to the employer, the employer's liability does not arise until the employee actually leaves the employer's service by virtue of the employee's notice.

1 ERA, ss 87(2), 89(4) and 90.

18.20 Where statutory notice has been given, the remedy for non-payment of monies due under s 86 is contractual and the monies are recoverable either in the ordinary courts or under the recently granted industrial tribunal jurisdiction over contract claims, if appropriate.[1]

1 *Westwood v Secretary of State for Employment* [1985] AC 20, [1985] ICR 209, HL; *Secretary of State for Employment v Wilson* [1978] 3 All ER 137, [1977] IRLR 483, EAT. On industrial tribunal contract claims see para 18.16.

18.21 Of course, the sums under s 87 apply only where statutory notice has been given. But if the employee has been dismissed without notice he may sue the employer for damages for breach of contract and the sums that the employee would otherwise have received under s 87 may, according to s 91, be taken into account in assessing those damages. There is a duty to mitigate loss.[1]

1 *Westwood v Secretary of State for Employment* [1985] AC 20, HL.

18.22 Whether or not notice has been given and whether or not a claim is brought under s 87 or s 86(5) respectively, sums payable under s 87 or s 91(5) are guaranteed by the Secretary of State under s 182 of the ERA on employer insolvency.

18.23 There is one major loophole to be borne in mind in considering this scheme. Section 87(4) of the ERA provides that s 87 and the guaranteed rights of an employee during notice shall not apply in relation to a notice given by an employer or an employee if the notice to be given by the employer under the contract to terminate the contract must be at least one week more than the notice required by s 86(1). Thus, if an employee is entitled to a more generous period of notice under his contract than that provided for by s 86(1), the guaranteed rights during notice do not apply.[1] And it is to be noted that this is an 'all or nothing' position. An employee who enjoys notice longer than the statutory minimum is not entitled even to the guaranteed rights under s 87 in relation to such part of his contractual notice as is equivalent to the statutory notice. He loses his rights altogether. It is hard to explain this anomaly.

---

1 And the view of *Chitty on Contracts* (vol 2, para 3494) is that this includes the situation where the obligation of the employer to give notice longer than the statutory minimum by one week or more arises by implication (ie where there is no express term as to notice and the court implies a reasonable period at common law).

19 Unfair dismissal

Barry Mordsley

1 INTRODUCTION

Contrast with wrongful dismissal and general introduction

19.01 Until 1965[1] an employee had only one basic right against his employer (which he still retains) if his employment was terminated. He was entitled to receive the proper period of notice to terminate employment. A failure to provide this notice is a breach of contract and the employer is obliged to pay damages for this breach. The employee's claim is that he has been wrongfully dismissed[2] and the proper period of notice is the one expressly agreed between the parties, subject to statutory minima. Where there is no express agreement the courts are free to imply a term as to what would be a reasonable period. The action for wrongful dismissal was always heard in the ordinary courts, not in the industrial tribunal, because it originates from the common law, not statute.[3] However, tribunals have now been given jurisdiction to deal with breach of contract claims with a limit of £25,000 compensation.[4]

1 When the Redundancy Payments Act was enacted. (See Chapter 20 for details.)
2 See Chapter 12 for details.
3 But note Part II of the ERA which provides a remedy for unlawful deductions in industrial tribunals.
4 Industrial Tribunals (Extension of Jurisdiction) (England and Wales) Order 1994, SI 1994 No 1623 – see elsewhere in the text.

19.02 The employer was entitled to terminate the contract by notice *for whatever reason.* However reprehensible his reason it was not challengeable unless the contract had some special clauses which allowed dismissal only where certain reasons obtained. In 1972 the right not to be unfairly dismissed was introduced.[1] This required the employer to show the reason for the dismissal, and that this fell within one of the permitted listed reasons. Having satisfied that requirement it was then for the tribunal to decide whether the employer had acted reasonably or not in all the circumstances in treating that reason as justifying dismissal. Some reasons were to be treated as automatically justifying a dismissal and some reasons had the opposite effect.[2]

1 By the Industrial Relations Act 1971 – the right is now contained in Part X of the ERA.
2 See below.

19.03 This was a fundamental change and a culture shock to many employers. In fact most of Europe had already introduced the right and some employers had sophisticated agreements with trade unions relating to disciplinary matters. These would provide rules so that employees would know what kind of behaviour was proscribed and what penalty would be meted out and a procedure for the implementation of any discipline. A note of any disciplinary rules and procedures is now required to be included in the statutory statement of particulars.[1] If a dispute cannot be resolved internally, the matter is sometimes referred to an arbitrator if there is a collective agreement. This is no longer necessary as the industrial tribunal performs this role but some collective agreements still retain this referral right.[2]

1 ERA, s 3.

2 At the very end of 1994 the Government issued a Green Paper 'Resolving Employment Rights Disputes – Options for Reform' (HMSO Cm 2707). Following this it is considering arbitration as a possible alternative to the industrial tribunal. The Government is concerned over the number of claims and the ensuing cost. A proposed Bill providing this option was produced by the Government in July 1996.

19.04 Thus, since 1972, the employer has to justify the dismissal and must have 'good cause' for his action. No longer can he act on a whim. This right has not superseded the wrongful dismissal claim but is superimposed on it. Thus, a dismissal can be both wrongful and unfair where the employer has no valid reason for dismissal and has not given notice to terminate. Where the employer has given proper notice the dismissal can still be unfair where there is no valid reason or the employer has not acted reasonably. Although the two claims can be litigated in different forums[1] a successful unfair dismissal claim will mean that compensation is awarded which will almost always cover the period of notice required to be given.[2] However, most breach of contract claims are below £25,000 and can therefore be heard in the tribunal. If there is a possibility of a duplication of compensation it will be important tactically to consider where a claim should be heard first because of the statutory maximum compensation for unfair dismissal. There is very little EC law on dismissals. The Commission is at present carrying out a detailed study on national rules and practices on individual dismissal. It is likely that a draft Directive will be put forward for discussion in 1997.

1 But see footnote 3 to para 19.01 above.

2 But see *O'Laoire v Jackel International Ltd (No 2)* [1991] IRLR 170, CA.

19.05 Wrongful dismissal claims will remain important for two major reasons: (i) there are many exclusions from the unfair dismissal right and (ii) there is a maximum sum awardable for unfair dismissal claims which is very low[1] and which will not be of very great assistance to those on higher incomes. For such individuals it is quite common for actions to be brought for both unfair and wrongful dismissal concurrently. However, this point is valid for many others today as there are long periods of unemployment with accompanying larger losses.

1 The method of assessing compensation will be considered later but the compensatory element of it is now set at £11,300. It is reviewable annually but it is not necessarily increased.

19.06 Furthermore, the common law remains very important, particularly for employees where there is a public law element, because the courts may be prepared to grant injunctions restraining dismissals where there has been a breach of procedure or where no substantive grounds justifying discipline exist.[1] No such power exists for industrial tribunals where there are such breaches. Even where there is a finding of unfair dismissal and a tribunal orders re-employment ultimately the employer can refuse to re-employ and can instead pay extra compensation. Thus, the common law remedy for employees remains important.

[1] See elsewhere but note that it is not a remedy often granted.

19.07 There are certain matters which are common to both wrongful and unfair dismissal. Conduct which would justify an employer dismissing summarily must necessarily justify a finding of fair dismissal, it is submitted, but the converse is not necessarily true because something less than gross misconduct may be enough. Another common issue is whether there has been a termination of the contract by the employer. Thus, if it is argued that the parties have agreed that the contract would terminate on the occurrence of certain events there is no dismissal and no claim whatsoever arises.

19.08 Some of the more important practical differences, apart from the question of jurisdiction and compensation already mentioned, include:

(a) there are no preliminary hurdles such as two years' service and age limits for wrongful dismissal;
(b) the limitation periods are three months for unfair and six years for wrongful dismissal;
(c) settlements are binding at common law but one cannot contract out of claiming unfair dismissal unless this is done through a conciliation officer or by a compromise agreement;[1]
(d) there is a concept of 'contributory fault' in unfair dismissal which reduces compensation but not in wrongful dismissal;
(e) the expiry of a fixed term contract constitutes a 'dismissal' for unfair dismissal purposes but not at common law;
(f) costs are awarded against the loser in wrongful dismissal cases but very rarely awarded in unfair dismissal;
(g) the concept of 'constructive dismissal' is not known at common law, only for unfair dismissal;[2]
(h) at common law an employer can rely on a reason unknown to him at the time of dismissal but discovered subsequently. This is not permitted for unfair dismissal although it can affect the compensation awarded;
(i) damages for wrongful dismissal are based on actual entitlement whereas compensation for unfair dismissal can include probable losses, not merely contractual entitlements.

The above are some of the differences but do not purport to be exhaustive and exclusive.

[1] See below for more details.
[2] It would constitute a repudiation which the employee could accept by terminating the contract and thus the distinction is more apparent than real.

Basic qualifications to claim

19.09 Below we find a number of specific exclusions and required qualifications for claiming unfair dismissal. Thus, for instance there is no right to claim where the employment is mainly overseas employment, where the employee is above the maximum age for claiming or where there is a contracting-out in relation to the expiry of a fixed-term contract.[1]

[1] See below at the end of this chapter.

(i) Contract of employment

19.10 The most important restriction on the right to claim is the need to show that you are employed under a contract of employment. Thus, the self-employed or the independent contractor is excluded although a contract of apprenticeship is included.[1] This major exclusion is discussed elsewhere in the text, but it should be noted that you do not need anything in writing to constitute a contract of employment. Neither is an express agreement required – an implied one is sufficient. With the growth in casual employment and the entirely new patterns of work emerging this exclusion could well be of considerable significance in the future. Some of the tests used to determine an individual's classification are whether he is under the employer's control, or integrated into the employer's business. The economic reality of the situation is also considered as is the question of whether the contract involves mutual obligations on both parties. It is vital to appreciate that the parties cannot by their own agreement determine the employment status.

[1] ERA, s 230(2). Note that those employed under training contracts are apparently excluded, see eg *Wiltshire Police Authority v Wynn* [1981] QB 95, CA.

(ii) Illegality

19.11 Another legalistic question which can preclude a claim proceedings is where the contract is an illegal contract. Again, this is considered elsewhere in the text, but an obvious example would be where there was a relationship whereby one party was carrying out burglaries for another and this was terminated. An arrangement regarding prostitution would also be illegal because it is contrary to public policy. The most frequent problem in this regard is where there is some element of tax evasion. If so, this is a contract tainted with illegality. Often it is discovered that the employee has been receiving part of his wages in cash in order to avoid paying tax or has been receiving reimbursement of expenses which have not been incurred. This information will lead to the tribunal declining to accept jurisdiction. Although in a recent case the EAT held that an occasional payment to an employee without deduction of tax does not necessarily render the contract unenforceable for illegality.[1] In an early case[2] it was argued that the right to claim unfair dismissal was a statutory right and should remain unaffected by any illegality. The EAT responded by saying that the statutory right was superimposed on the contract of employment and it was an essential pre-requisite that the contract was a legal contract. However, more recently the courts have been considering the relative blame to be attached to the parties and also do not want to discourage the disclosure of fraud.[3]

---

[1] *Annandale Engineering v Samson* [1994] IRLR 59, EAT.
[2] *Tomlinson v Dick Evans U Drive Ltd* [1978] ICR 639, EAT.
[3] *Hewcastle Catering Ltd v Ahmed and Elkamah* [1991] IRLR 473, CA; *Salvesen v Simons* [1994] IRLR 52, EAT.

19.12 It must be established that the employee knew of, and participated in, the illegality. Thus, if the employee can establish that he believed that the employer was paying the appropriate tax he can still proceed. Furthermore, it is that particular employee's state of knowledge that is relevant, not whether an employee ought to have known[1] although it will not be particularly easy to establish that the employee was not aware of what was happening.

---

[1] *Davidson v Pillay* [1979] IRLR 275, EAT.

19.13 Another issue which has exercised the judiciary is when the contract is essentially perfectly legal but it is performed illegally in part. In *Coral Leisure Group Ltd v Barnett*[1] the employee was employed as a public relations executive specialising in providing services to overseas visitors. He claimed that during his employment he was asked to obtain the services of prostitutes for the company's clients. Prostitution is not illegal but the company alleged it was immoral and contrary to public policy. The EAT held that the illegality argument did not succeed because he was not employed for that specific purpose. It was an improper mode of performing his contractual obligations which were aimed at preserving his employer's goodwill.

---

[1] [1981] ICR 503, EAT.

Insolvency and restrictions on proceedings

19.13A The right to claim unfair dismissal where the employer is insolvent is severely restricted. There are different kinds of insolvency. Once a bankruptcy petition has been presented the court may stay any proceedings or execution against the debtor.[1] Once a bankruptcy order has been made the consent of the court will be necessary to commence proceedings.[2] There is no definition of 'court' and whether this provision applies to industrial tribunals.

Company liquidations may be compulsory or voluntary. In compulsory liquidation after a petition is presented a stay of proceedings against the company may be sought.[3] Once an order has been made no action can be commenced or proceeded with against the company without the court's leave.[4] In a voluntary liquidation there is no automatic bar to proceedings but application can be made for an order for a stay of proceedings.[5]

Administrative receivership has no effect on the ability of an applicant to commence or pursue proceedings because the company effectively continues with the receiver effectively replacing the directors, albeit attempting to sell perhaps a major part of the business to recover the debt owing.[6]

An administration order is a concept introduced in 1985. Its aim is to achieve part-payment to creditors in satisfaction of their debts and to enable the company to carry on. Once a petition for an order has been presented no proceedings can be commenced or continued except with the consent of the administrator or the leave of court. It has been held[7] that applications to the tribunal fall within this but the court did say that it would be in rare cases only that it would be appropriate for consent to be refused for the bringing of proceedings for unfair dismissal in respect of redundancy.[8]

1 Section 285 of the Insolvency Act (IA) 1986.
2 Section 346 of the IA 1986.
3 Section 126 of the IA 1986.
4 Section 130 of the IA 1986.
5 Section 112 of the IA 1986.
6 Sections 10 to 11 of the IA 1986.
7 *Carr v British International Helicopters Ltd (in administration)* [1994] IRLR 212, EAT.
8 On insolvency debts (see elsewhere in the text).

(iii) Two years' employment

19.14 The concept of continuous employment has been considered elsewhere and is very elaborate. To make an unfair dismissal claim it is necessary, with some limited exceptions, to have two years' continuous employment at the effective date of termination.[1] The period of time required to claim has altered considerably since the right to claim was introduced. It began at two years, was reduced to 26 weeks, and then was increased to one year and is now set at two years. When these changes were made it had a significant impact on the unfair dismissal caseload. It would be fair to say that when the period was increased to two years most of those involved in the area believed it was unnecessary to extend the period beyond one year. The decision was more political than one based on industry's needs.

The qualifying period is necessary for an applicant to succeed in an unfair dismissal claim but it is not something which strikes at the tribunal's jurisdiction. Thus where an employer tried to raise the point at the EAT when it had not been raised earlier the EAT held that it was too late to do so and decided that it was not a jurisdiction issue which would render the tribunal award a nullity.[2] In a recent case[3] a challenge was made to the two year qualifying period by means of an application for judicial review of the Secretary of State's decision to increase the period from one to two years. The Divisional Court said the Order[4] was not void as there was power to make it. The allegation that the Order was disciminatory under the Equal Treatment Directive should have been made within three months of the Order coming into force and to quash it now would be likely to cause substantial hardship and if the applicants[5] were correct they could pursue their claim against the UK Government based on the *Francovich* case.[6] Although the applicants had locus standi to challenge by judicial review in any event they had no remedy under the directive directly as private employees. The Court of Appeal granted a declaration[7] that the two year qualifying period was indirectly discriminatory against women and was not objectively justifiable. The two individual appellants had started to bring proceedings for judicial review relying on the Equal Treatment Directive to challenge an Order[8] made in 1985 which increased the qualifying period from one to two years.

However, the Court refused to quash the 1985 Order as this would cause too many problems. The case has gone to the House of Lords whose decision is imminent. If it affirms the decision then the Government will have to consider abolition of the two year qualifying period as a minimum and it may well be that a very short or nil qualifying period will emerge.[9] It will, of course, have to apply to both sexes, otherwise there would be direct sex discrimination.

---

1 See below.
2 *Leicester University Students' Union v Mahomed* [1995] IRLR 292, EAT.
3 *R v Secretary of State for Employment, ex p Seymour-Smith and Perez* [1994] IRLR 448.
4 Unfair Dismissal (Variation of Qualifying Period) Order 1985.
5 The Applicants both had under two years' service.
6 See elsewhere in the text. In brief a claim can be made against the UK Government based on its failure to implement a Directive.
7 *R v Secretary of State for Employment, ex p Seymour-Smith and Perez* [1995] IRLR 464, CA.
8 Unfair Dismissal (Variation of Qualifying Period) Order 1985.
9 As is commonplace in Europe.

Special cases where no qualifying period required

19.15 Where an employee is dismissed for trade union reasons – either for his membership or non-membership of a trade union or his union activities – there is no qualifying period of employment.[1] An employee who is dismissed because of suspension of work on medical grounds need only have one month's employment. An employee dismissed for pregnancy or childbirth can bring an unfair dismissal claim at any time and there are special provisions discussed below.[2] There is no qualifying period where an employee is dismissed for health and safety reasons; for asserting a statutory right, for Sunday working refusal where there is protection. Dismissals unlawful under anti-discrimination legislation can be challenged under the relevant discrimination Act.

---

1 See below.
2 A claim under the anti-discrimination legislation can be made where the dismissal is alleged to be discriminatory.

General structure of unfair dismissal claim

19.16 In contemplating any claim for unfair dismissal a simple structure can be adopted. First, one should ascertain if the claimant is qualified to claim or disqualified from claiming. For example, the need to show an employment relationship of two years in most cases.

19.17 There are then a number of specific statutory exclusions to be considered. These are considered below and include the question of where the employee was working and whether he has made his claim within the limitation period.

19.18 Then one must see if the employee has actually been dismissed. This is a technical and difficult question despite its apparent simplicity.[1]

[1] See Chapter 2.

19.19 All the above matters are for the employee to establish so that the burden of proof is on him and he will almost always begin the case in the tribunal. In certain cases where continuous employment is in issue there is a presumption of continuity.[1] If these matters are not in contention so that the employer concedes that the employee is qualified and has been dismissed then the employer will begin the case because he has to show the reason for the dismissal. The statutory burden is clearly on him to show the reason and that it falls within one of the permitted persons. There are some reasons which make the dismissal automatically fair or unfair: thus a dismissal for trade union reasons is unfair as is a dismissal for pregnancy. Where the employee is dismissed for taking official industrial action then the tribunal has no jurisdiction unless there have been selective dismissals and has no jurisdiction whatsoever where there has been unofficial industrial action. Where the dismissal is for one of the normal reasons, such as conduct or capability, then the next stage is for the tribunal to ask whether the employer has acted reasonably or not in treating this reason as justifying dismissal in all the circumstances.

[1] ERA, s 210(5).

19.20 If the tribunal decides the dismissal is unfair it must then consider the appropriate remedy. The primary remedy is reinstatement or re-engagement and if not appropriate, compensation is awarded. The level of compensation involves a considerable degree of discretion, not merely, for example, as to the length of future loss but also whether the employee caused or contributed to his dismissal. If the employer does not comply with a re-employment order extra compensation is awarded.[1]

[1] Known as the 'additional award' or 'special award' in certain cases – see below.

19.21 An appeal can be instituted against the tribunal decision on a matter of law to the Employment Appeal Tribunal and thence to the Court of Appeal and the House of Lords with leave.

2 EXCLUSIONS

Upper age limit

19.22 Employees who have attained the normal retiring age where they work, or, where there is none, 65 when they are dismissed, cannot claim they have been unfairly dismissed. The statutory provision is that you cannot claim if 'in the undertaking in which he was employed there was a normal retiring age for an employee holding the position which he held and the age was the same whether the employee holding that position was a man or a woman' and the employee has attained that age and in 'any other case the age of 65'.[1]

[1] ERA, s 102(1).

19.23 This is a change from the original provision, implemented following the decision[1] of the European Court of Justice that differential retiring ages for men and women was unlawful discrimination under EEC law.[2] Thus if there is a normal retiring age then this will be applied provided that it is not discriminatory. It may be higher or lower than 65.

---

1 *Marshall*'s case [1986] ICR 335 (see elsewhere).
2 Equal Treatment Directive 76/207.

19.24 Originally it was held that an employee was disqualified where he had reached the normal retiring age or was 65 (60 for a woman) but then the House of Lords held that the alternative specific age only applied where there was no normal retiring age.[1] The change in the legislative wording now makes this interpretation clear beyond challenge.

---

1 *Nothman v Barnet London Borough* [1979] ICR 111.

19.25 The use of the word 'normal' indicates that there can be difficult questions of interpretation and these indications are correct. It was originally thought that it was the minimum age at which employees could be compelled to retire by contract but then in *Waite v Government Communication Headquarters*[1] the House of Lords gave an authoritative judgment on the question. First, if there is a contractual retiring age this creates a presumption that this is the normal retiring age. If it is shown that all or almost all employees do actually retire at that age then that is the normal age. However, where it is shown that they do not retire at that age the presumption is rebutted. If in practice the employees actually retire at another definite higher age then that age becomes the normal age but if they all retire at different times then there is no normal retiring age and you revert to 65.[2] This is so even though the age band may only be 62 to 63[3] or even where none of the varying ages are beyond 60.[4] Obviously statistics will be relevant in determining these issues but the presumption will not be easily rebuttable and in *Waite* itself the fact that just over one-quarter of the relevant group of officers were retained after they had attained 60 fell far short of showing that the contractual retiring age had been abandoned or departed from. It has been decided that the normal retirement age cannot go below the contractual retirement age.[5]

---

1 [1983] ICR 653. For a more recent reaffirmation of these principles see *Barclays Bank plc v O'Brien* [1994] IRLR 580, CA.
2 *Mauldon v British Telecommunications* [1987] ICR 450, EAT.
3 *Swaine v Health and Safety Executive* [1986] ICR 498, EAT.
4 *Secretary of State for Scotland v Meikle* [1986] IRLR 208, EAT.
5 *Bratko v Beloit Walmsley Ltd* [1995] IRLR 629. This attempts to nullify the contrary comments in *Barber v Thames Television* – see para 19.27, footnote 6.

19.26 The main factor in establishing a normal retiring age is the reasonable expectation of employees of all age groups holding the same position as the claimant at the effective date of termination of the claimant's contract. It has been confirmed[1] that it is his expectation when he is dismissed that is relevant, not his expectation when he was recruited or at some later time. The cases[2] show that an employer can unilaterally alter this reasonable expectation. The employer must, of course, comply with his obligations under the contract and he must also clearly communicate his change of policy to the employees. If the employee occupies a unique position there can be no normal retiring age at least for a group.[3]

[1] In *Hughes v Department of Health and Social Security* [1985] ICR 419, HL. *Brooks v British Telecommunications plc* [1992] IRLR 66, CA.

[2] Apart from *Hughes* see eg *Whittle v MSC* (1987) IRLR 441 and *Brooks v British Telecommunications plc* [1992] IRLR 66, CA where it was held that a notice in the British Telecom Gazette could constitute notice of a reaffirmation of a change in the normal retirement age.

[3] *Patel v Nagesan* [1995] IRLR 370, CA.

19.27 Another question which needs to be considered is the employee's 'position' defined[1] as the 'following matters taken as a whole that is to say his status as an employee, the nature of his work and his terms and conditions of employment'. This raises general questions as to who falls within the appropriate category but as a matter of principle it has been determined that you consider the position of the employee at the time of dismissal not at some earlier time when he might have belonged to a special group. Thus the employment history is disregarded.[2] In considering employees holding the same 'position' it has been stated that you should look at what the employee is doing not what his contract could require him to do.[3] Where there are no other employees holding the position which the claimant held there can be no normal age because it is not possible to make a comparison.[4] It is not permissible simply to include in the group those who are nearing the age of 60.[5] However, where an employer changes his retirement age policy and phases in the change it is permissible to take into account that particular term which fixes the retirement age in determining the 'position' held because the definition includes 'terms and conditions of employment'.[6] Whether it was intended to cover a term which actually refers to the retirement age is an interesting issue. It is also necessary to identify the undertaking which requires the tribunal to look at the nature and extent of control in each case. How the employee identifies the undertaking is a useful starting point.[7] Tribunals have been warned that they should not always treat the issue of normal retiring age as a separate matter from the rest of the case because the whole facts may be relevant.[8]

[1] ERA, s 235(1).

[2] *Brooks v British Telecommunications plc* [1991] IRLR 4, EAT.

[3] See *Hughes* (above) where a group of employees holding an equivalent position to Hughes had been transferred to the Civil Service in 1948 from local authority employment. This group had different expectations from the bulk of DHSS civil servants but their Lordships decided that they were simply Senior Executive Officers in the DHSS and had the same rights as this grade in the DHSS.

[4] *Age Concern Scotland v Hines* [1983] IRLR 477, EAT.

[5] See *Brooks v British Telecommunications plc* (above).

[6] *Barber v Thames Television plc* [1992] ICR 661, CA reverses EAT and restores IT decision.

[7] *Brooks v British Telecommunications plc* [1991] IRLR 4, EAT.

[8] *Secretary of State for Education v Birchall* [1994] IRLR 630, EAT.

19.28 Where the employee is dismissed for trade union reasons there is no upper age limit so dismissing a 90-year-old shop steward for trade union reasons is automatically an unfair dismissal! This is also true of dismissal of workers in relation to Sunday working[1] and also where the dismissal is for health and safety reasons, assertion of statutory rights and pregnancy although the latter reason may not be relevant in many cases.

1 ERA, s 109(2).

Working abroad

19.29 Employees are excluded from the right to claim unfair dismissal where under the contract of employment they ordinarily work outside Great Britain.[1] This has caused problems from the outset and there is still uncertainty as to the application of these provisions. Originally the courts, adopting a tax analysis, held that an employee could work ordinarily outside and inside Great Britain[2] but this has now been discredited. The problems arise because employees may be based in Great Britain but work mainly abroad or may be based abroad but work mainly in Great Britain. Also there can be difficulties where employees are sent abroad for specific jobs. It is clear that one does not judge the question by simply considering whether more time has been spent abroad than in Great Britain.

1 ERA, s 196(2) (3).
2 *Portec v Mogensen* [1976] ICR 396, EAT.

19.30 The leading case which established the modern test is *Wilson v Maynard*.[1] Wilson was a management consultant, who, when dismissed, had worked in Great Britain for about 40 weeks and in Italy for about 50 weeks. As is quite common there was no term relating to place of work but the court implied a term obliging him to move to any place where the employers had contracts. The EAT had held he could work both inside and outside Great Britain but the Court of Appeal rejected this and stated that the vital question was what the terms of the contract required. They said that it would be artificial to consider what had happened in practice because the contract had been cut short and therefore it was necessary to contemplate what would have happened had the contract run its course. Thus if an employee had a five-year contract, the first two years to be spent in France the remainder in Great Britain and he was dismissed after two years he could not have spent any time in Great Britain but the contract test would almost certainly give him protection. Without a specific provision the court will have to work out what might have happened.

1 [1978] ICR 376.

19.31 However, the contract test does not always provide an answer. The Court of Appeal appreciated that and said that where the contract test does not provide a clear answer then the test is to ascertain the employee's base. This does not mean that he spends all his time at the base but it is the place which would be regarded as his headquarters and where he starts and finishes his travels. Thus an oil rig worker would not be based on the rig but at the office from which his work is administered.[1] Other criteria which assist in determining the base are where the employee lives, where he is paid and in what currency and where he pays tax and national insurance. In a subsequent Court of Appeal case[2] one judge was doubtful whether the 'base' test was the one to apply and another said that often the evidence of the parties was of more relevance.

---

[1] Per Denning MR in *Todd v British Midland Airways Ltd* [1978] ICR 959 commenting on *Claisse v Hostetter* [1978] ICR 812, EAT.
[2] Ibid.

19.32 In the last major Court of Appeal case on this subject[1] one judge again cast some doubt on the base test but it appears from the facts that it was very relevant in determining the answer. The employee was recruited in Dacca, Bangladesh and was then sent to England for three years where he worked almost all that time except for a very short period in Brussels. He was recalled to Dacca but refused to return and was later dismissed. He had worked for a long time in Great Britain, had his home there, was paid in English currency and paid National Insurance contributions. This led the EAT to conclude that he could claim but the Court of Appeal reversed this decision. They said that throughout his contract he could be recalled to Dacca and this was clearly his base. In practice it is almost always the first question one would ask in determining the answer.

---

[1] *Janata Bank v Ahmed* [1981] ICR 791.

19.33 Where the employee is posted to a variety of places consecutively then he will probably be based in the place where he was originally recruited. This is likely to be the place from where his work is administered and where he reports between postings.[1] This is premissed on the right of the employer to send employees abroad—if there is no such right then it is highly arguable that there has been a variation of the contract and the employee will ordinarily work where he happens to be at the time of dismissal.

---

[1] *Grandmet v Graham*, EAT 677/78.

19.34 Thus the position is not entirely clear for employees who spend periods of time abroad but there have been several judicial comments to the effect that this exclusion should be interpreted narrowly and perhaps this is why there have not been a glut of cases. As regards continuity of employment it is preserved where the employee works abroad although the need to show you are not working outside Great Britain at the time of dismissal still obtains. However, where the employee has worked on a separate contract for his work abroad and then returns to a different 'British' contract it is only the latter contract that one looks at, that is to say the one subsisting at the time of the dismissal, that is relevant. Thus it would not matter if the employee worked only a matter of days under the British contract following the 'foreign' contract.[1]

---

[1] *Weston v Vega Space* [1989] IRLR 429, EAT.

19.35 There are special provisions regarding those who work on board a ship. If the ship is registered in the UK the employee is deemed to be ordinarily working in Great Britain, unless the employment is wholly outside Great Britain or he is not ordinarily resident in Great Britain. Thus, an employee, recruited in Great Britain, for a ship registered in the UK but working exclusively in the Caribbean, could not make his claim because he worked wholly outside Great Britain despite the fact that his employer paid for his travel to the Caribbean.[1]

1 *Wood v Cunard Line Ltd* [1990] IRLR 281, CA.

Some statutory exceptions to the right

19.36 There are various groups of workers who are specifically excluded from the right to claim. These include those employed in the police service;[1] those whom the Minister has certified should be exempted from protection for the purposes of safeguarding national security;[2] employees of a foreign state employed for non-commercial purposes[3] and those employees with less than two years' continuous employment.[4] It is no longer necessary to have a minimum number of hours worked per week.

1 ERA, s 200(1) which has been held to include those in the prison service: *Home Office v Robinson* (1982) ICR 31 but this has now been reversed by statute.

2 ERA, s 193(1) – recall the *GCHQ* case.

3 Eg diplomats – see details and further qualifications in State Immunity Act 1978.

4 ERA, s 108(1). Employees dismissed for certain reasons will not need two years' employment.

The need to claim in three months

19.37 To claim the unfair dismissal right a complaint must be presented to the tribunal within three months from the effective date of termination[1] or within such further period as the tribunal considers reasonable in a case where it is satisfied that it was not reasonably practicable for the complaint to have been presented before the three months expired.[2] If a claim has been made within the three months then an additional or substituted respondent can be named after the period has expired. This is a matter for the tribunal rules, not the jurisdiction.[3]

1 See below.

2 ERA, s 111(2).

3 *Drinkwater Sabey Ltd v Burnett* [1995] IRLR 238, EAT.

19.38 Thus there are three steps: (i) Was the complaint presented within the three months? (ii) If not, was there something which rendered it not reasonably practicable to do so? This is often referred to, erroneously, as being within the tribunal's discretion. There has to be a specific reason which satisfies the tribunal and it cannot extend time limits because it considers it fair or equitable to do so. (iii) If the tribunal is satisfied that there was a good reason for the late claim, for example, because of the employee's sickness, it will then have to determine how long to extend the period for claiming. That does involve a certain degree of discretion – for example, if an employee was physically unable to present within the three months this does not give him an unlimited period thereafter. Consideration will have to be given to when the employee was fit again and how long it should have taken to pursue the proceedings.

19.39 There have been many cases on this area since unfair dismissal was introduced but they are now diminishing as the limitation period becomes better known and the tribunals become stricter. Very good reasons have to be given by an applicant to show it was not reasonably practicable to claim within three months.

19.40 The complaint must be sent to the Central Office of Industrial Tribunals although an application sent to a regional office has been held valid.[1] The limitation is a jurisdictional matter and cannot be waived by the parties.[2] The period of three months begins from the day of dismissal which is therefore included in the calculation. Thus, a dismissal on 21 March, at whatever time of the day or night (before midnight) has an expiry date of 20 June.[3] The correct way of calculating the three months is to establish the effective date of termination, take the date before it and then go forward three months. If there is no corresponding day in the month the last day of the month is taken.[4]

1 *Bengey v North Devon District Council* [1977] ICR 15, EAT.
2 *Rogers v Bodfari (Transport) Ltd* [1973] ICR 325, NIRC.
3 See eg *Hammond v Haigh Castle & Co Ltd* [1973] ICR 148, NIRC.
4 *Pruden v Cunard Ellerman Ltd* [1993] IRLR 317, EAT.

19.41 A complaint must be presented to the tribunal, which means that it must be received by them. A claim is within the time limits even if delivered after office hours but before midnight on the last day of the limitation period.[1] The ordinary court rules regarding limitation do not apply to non-working days. There they do not count and one moves forward to the next working day. With the tribunal as there is no need to do anything with the application immediately on receipt everything turns on delivery.[2] However, if there is no letter-box or suitable receptacle for the delivery of mail the Court of Appeal has suggested that the applicant should be able to show it was not reasonably practicable to have presented the complaint within the relevant period.[3] This is not cast-iron but should avail the applicant. However, in *Ford v Stakis Hotels and Inns Ltd*[4] the EAT said that where there was no post-box the day should not count and one should move to the next day the tribunal was open. This needs to be clarified. It is perfectly permissible to fax an application.

1 *Post Office v Moore* [1981] ICR 623, EAT.
2 Applications can be made by fax.
3 *Hetton Victory Club Ltd v Swainston* [1983] ICR 341.
4 [1988] IRLR 46.

19.42 *Reasonably practicable.* The onus of proving it was not reasonably practicable to be 'in time' is on the applicant.[1] The Court of Appeal has stated that the issue is essentially a matter of fact and therefore tribunal rulings will be very difficult to overturn. The *Palmer*[2] case stated that the words lie somewhere between reasonable on the one hand and reasonably physically capable of being done on the other. Either interpretation could veer too far in one side's favour and practicable should be seen as equivalent to feasible. The tribunal should consider the substantial cause of the employee's failure – was it illness or some other valid reason. It will be relevant to know if the employee knew he could complain and whether the employer made any misrepresentation to the employee. It may be relevant to see if the employee was being advised and the extent of the adviser's knowledge and to determine whether the employee or his adviser were at fault in allowing the deadline to pass.[3]

1 *Porter v Bandridge Ltd* [1978] ICR 943.
2 *Palmer v Southend-on-Sea Borough Council* [1984] IRLR 119.
3 See *Dedman v British Building and Engineering Appliances Ltd* [1974] ICR 53, CA and see below.

19.43 The applicant's ignorance of his right to make a claim may allow him to proceed but the ignorance must itself be reasonable. It cannot be an abysmal level of ignorance and if it arises from the fault of the complainant in not making inquiries as he reasonably should have made in all the circumstances the claim will be disallowed.[1] Today, it will be unusual for a tribunal to be convinced that an applicant did not know of his rights, particularly when the test now is probably whether he ought to have known of his rights not simply whether he knew.[2] In the *Haywood Hicks* case[3] the EAT said that an intelligent, well-educated man ought to have investigated his rights within the time limit. The corollary to this is that the less well-educated and intelligent individual has more chance of claiming late. Where there is very little understanding of the language or the applicant is deficient this may well constitute grounds. Knowledge of the right to claim will normally mean that he will be deemed to know of the time limit.[4] It will certainly require the employee to use all available means to pursue his rights. Where the employee can show that he is ignorant of a fact which is fundamental to the right to complain then this may well persuade the tribunal to allow a late claim. Thus where an employee was dismissed for redundancy but then discovered that another employee had been re-engaged he claimed unfair dismissal but was three days beyond the time limit. The tribunal, affirmed by both the EAT and the Court of Appeal, held that he could proceed with his claim.[5] It said that the expression 'reasonably practicable' imports three stages. First, the applicant must show it was reasonable for him not to be aware of the factual basis on which he could claim within the three months. Secondly, there is an objective qualification of reasonableness in the circumstances to be applied to the subjective test of the applicant's state of mind. The applicant must establish that the knowledge which he gains has been reasonably gained by him in the circumstances and that this knowledge is crucial, fundamental or important to his change of belief on whether there are grounds to claim. Thirdly, the acquisition of this knowledge must be crucial to the decision to bring a claim.

1 *Walls Meat Co Ltd v Khan* [1979] ICR 52, CA – where the level of ignorance was held reasonable in the circumstances.
2 See *Porter v Bandridge*, above and *Avon County Council v Haywood-Hicks* [1978] ICR 646.
3 See *Porter v Bandridge* and *Avon County Council*, above.
4 *House of Clydesdale v Foy* [1976] IRLR 391, EAT.
5 *Machine Tool Industry Research Association v Simpson* [1988] ICR 558 approving *Churchill v Yeates & Sons Ltd* [1983] ICR 380.

19.44 Being unaware of vital facts is one thing but misunderstanding the true position goes beyond this. However, where several shipyard workers were dismissed for redundancy after their employer had gone into voluntary liquidation and claimed late, their applications were permitted to proceed because they initially believed that work would pick up and they would be re-employed. It was only later that they realised the shipyard was closing. It closed 15 weeks after they were dismissed and it was only then that they realised their dismissals were irreversible.[1] Once the applicant discovers the position he must act quickly, but there are no specific time limits as to what is a reasonable period.[2] Furthermore where a new ground for dismissal comes to light after the three month period has expired and the existing claim is amended within a reasonable period after discovering the relevant fact, the tribunal can consider it even though the initial ground put foward was time-barred.[3]

[1] *James W Cook & Co (Wivenhoe) Ltd v Tipper* [1990] IRLR 386, CA.
[2] *Marley (UK) Ltd v Anderson* [1996] IRLR 163 commenting on the *James W Cook* case.
[3] In *Marley (UK) Ltd v Anderson*, above.

19.45 The fact that an employee asks advisers to act for him and it is their fault that a claim is not made in time does not assist the employee; he must look to his advisers for a remedy.[1] However, there is no rule that bad advice from a third party will prevent the employee from being able to argue it was not reasonably practicable to present within the time limit. It does, however, depend on who this third party is and in two cases employees have been able to proceed where they relied on mistaken advice from an industrial tribunal employee.[2] In the *Sen* case the employee was being advised by a solicitor who also gave erroneous advice but the Court of Appeal said the employee could rely on the tribunal employee's advice.[3] If an employee goes to an adviser about some other matter related to his dismissal, for example a criminal charge, it is likely that the adviser would be at fault if the employee was not advised about the unfair dismissal time limits. This is a case clearly on the borderline.

[1] *Riley v Tesco Stores Ltd* [1980] IRLR 103, CA.
[2] *Jean Sorelle Ltd v Rybak* [1991] IRLR 153, EAT; *London International College v Sen* [1993] IRLR 333.
[3] The application was one day late – the common mistake being that the three months time limit expired on 9 October when the dismissal took place on 9 July. The correct last day is 8 October.

19.46 Postal delays are often used as an excuse. In one case[1] the EAT said that it was an extremely dangerous practice to leave it until the last minute. Certainly posting at Christmas is known as a hazardous exercise and last-minute applications may well not receive as much sympathy as they might at other times of the year. It is all very much a question of fact for the tribunal and virtually unappealable. However, we have now received much clearer guidance from the EAT in a case[2] where an application had to be received by Monday 22 May. It was posted on Friday 19 May and arrived on 23 May, one day late. The application was permitted to proceed when evidence was given by the applicant that usually letters posted would arrive in time when he wrote to his mother. The EAT said it is reasonable for tribunals to follow the guidance on the service of documents by post set out in the relevant Queen's Bench Division Practice Direction which provides that it will be taken that delivery in the ordinary course of post was effected two days or four days after posting for first and second class mail respectively. This does not appear to mean that one will never be able to argue when the application was sent one day before the time limit but it is getting extremely close to that position and it is respectfully submitted this will be established soon. Where an application is posted some time before the expiry date and the application is not received the applicant cannot simply rely on the fact of posting to allow the claim to proceed. Where a solicitor posted the application five weeks before the limit expired and the application was not received, it was held that the claim should not proceed because it is a matter of ordinary and prudent practice to employ some system of checking that replies which might reasonably have been expected have been received.[3] While this may be true for a solicitor or trade union and might be for a Law Centre or CAB it would surely be asking too much of an unrepresented applicant, it is suggested.

1 *Beanstalk Shelving Ltd v Horn* [1980] ICR 273.
2 *St Basil's Centre v McCrossan* [1991] IRLR 455.
3 *Capital Foods Retail Ltd v Corrigan* [1993] IRLR 430 reinforced by *Camden and Islington Community Services NHS Trust v Kennedy* (1996) IRLR 381.

19.47 Often there are internal or domestic appeals against dismissals which can be quite protracted. The position is that this is no excuse for not making a claim[1] however much it might be understandable for an employee to take the view that internal appeals have to be completed. The existence of criminal proceedings is also not an excuse for delaying tribunal proceedings even though the employee will obviously be preoccupied with the criminal proceedings.[2] Any solicitor involved in the criminal proceedings should be careful to advise regarding the unfair dismissal claim.[3]

1 *Bodha v Hampshire Area Health Authority* [1982] ICR 200, EAT.
2 See *Porter v Bandridge*, above.
3 *Trevelyans (Birmingham) Ltd v Norton* [1991] ICR 488, EAT.

19.48 Applications can be made before the effective date of termination provided they are made after notice has been given.[1] This includes notice given by an employee when he is claiming constructive dismissal[2] but not to the expiry of a fixed term contract which expires by effluxion of time not by notice.[3] There have been considerable developments in relation to the limits and EC law concerning equal pay and sex discrimination. These developments are still being worked through. It has been held[4] that a teacher who was dismissed in 1976 working less than the minimum hours requirement and who could not therefore claim, could not bring proceedings in 1994. It was, nevertheless, held that the time limits were not discriminatory. That of course is correct but a purposive approach to the question could still have led to a different result. The employee had no realistic opportunity to bring a claim until the law changed in her favour after the 1994 decision against the Secretary of State. However, the Court of Appeal stated that it was not impossible to bring an action as it was arguably unlawful at the time of the original dismissal. This is the most obvious case where the 'Floodgates' argument would apply and one can appreciate the reason for the decision.

1 ERA, s 111(3).
2 *Presley v Llanelli Borough Council* [1979] ICR 419, EAT.
3 *Throsby v Imperial College of Science and Technology* [1978] ICR 357, EAT.
4 *Biggs v Somerset County Council* [1996] IRLR 203, CA.

Effective date of termination

19.49 As we have already noted the time limit described above runs from the 'effective date of termination' which accordingly needs to be considered. It is also necessary to ascertain this date to establish whether an employee has sufficient continuous service to claim and it is also used in determining the basic award of compensation. It is defined in three ways:

(i) where the contract is terminated by notice it is the date the notice expires;
(ii) where the contract is terminated without notice it is the date the termination takes effect;
(iii) where the employee is employed under a contract for a fixed term it is the date that term expires.[1]

[1] See ERA, s 97(1).

19.50 There are no problems in determining the effective date where it is the expiry of a fixed term contract which is self-explanatory. The problems have mainly arisen when the employer asks the employee to leave immediately which would fall within (ii) above but then gives notice which is obviously not worked out and this would then fall within (i).

19.51 Where notice is given orally on a working day this day is excluded from the calculation of the period of notice which has been given and the period begins on the following day.[1] In principle, where the expiry date is not given in a letter, this should apply to any written communication giving a period of notice but there is no authority to this effect. It has been decided that the date on which a P45 is received or the date on the P45 does not determine the effective date.[2]

[1] *West v Kneels Ltd* [1986] IRLR 430, EAT.
[2] *Newham London Borough v Ward* [1985] IRLR 509, CA.

19.52 Where the employer dismisses by letter and actually gives notice in the letter the effective date is the date the notice expires even though the employee is asked to leave immediately.[1] The position is that notice has been given but the employee is not being required to work it out. If however the employer unambiguously dismisses with immediate effect but then gives pay in lieu of notice this takes effect as an immediate dismissal.[2] This sounds simple, but it has led to many problems which stem from the letters sent which usually, quite understandably, refer to the employee's entitlement to notice and then state that a payment will be made as notice. Even when the employee leaves immediately this scenario could possibly lead to a finding that the effective date is the expiry of the notice.[3] It is the employer's responsibility to make the letter clear by stating that termination of employment is immediate because any ambiguity will be construed against the employer.[4] The *Chapman* case establishes that it is all a matter of construction of the letter and the construction should not be a technical one but should reflect what an ordinary reasonable employee would understand by the words used in the light of the facts known to the employee when he received his letter. This last point is relevant to the principle that where an employee is dismissed orally and this is confirmed in writing it is necessary to consider both what was said and written.[5] Where the employee is summarily dismissed by letter the effective date will be the date when the employee reads the letter or has a reasonable opportunity of doing so.[6] The effective date has to be decided in a practical and common sense manner, having regard to what the party understood at the time and irrespective of whether there had been some constitutional procedural failure in the lead-up to the decision.[7]

1 *Adams v GKN Sankey Ltd* [1980] IRLR 416, EAT.
2 *Dedman v British Building and Engineering Appliances Ltd* [1974] ICR 53, CA.
3 *SCCL v Godwin*, EAT 247/88.
4 See eg *Chapman v Letheby and Christopher Ltd* [1981] IRLR 440, EAT.
5 *Leech v Preston Borough Council* [1985] ICR 192, EAT.
6 *Brown v Southall and Knight* [1980] IRLR 130, EAT.
7 *Newman v Polytechnic of Wales Students Union* [1995] IRLR 72, EAT.

19.53 *Changing the effective date.* Where notice has been given this date may be brought forward. This may be by agreement but the exact legal effect is uncertain. In one case it was held to substitute a new termination date but in another[1] it was held that the original date remained the effective date. In a more recent redundancy rebate case[2] the Court of Appeal has held that an employee who waived his rights to notice and accepted a payment in lieu of notice would not affect the effective date of termination as being the expiry of the notice. Where an employer asks an employee to work on beyond the original termination date but at a different site in the hope that a fresh contract will materialise on the original site a subsequent dismissal will still take place even when the employee later resigns when no contract materialises. Nothing can preclude the parties from reaching an agreement to alter the effective date of termination.[3]

1 *TBA Industrial Products Ltd v Morland* [1982] IRLR 331, CA.
2 *Staffordshire County Council v Secretary of State for Employment* [1989] IRLR 117.
3 *Mowlem Northern Ltd v Watson* [1990] IRLR 500, EAT.

19.54 Under statute[1] an employee given notice may serve a counter notice to expire before the employer's notice and this becomes the fresh effective date.[2] The reason for the dismissal remains the employer's reason for dismissing.

1 ERA, s 95.
2 *Thompson v GEC Avionics Ltd* [1991] IRLR 488, EAT.

19.55 Nothing prevents an employer from summarily dismissing an employee who is already under notice. In this situation the dismissal takes immediate effect and the original notice is superseded. However an unfair dismissal claim already submitted after the original notice was given remains valid.[1] For statutory purposes the common law problems as to whether a repudiation of contract needs to be accepted are irrelevant because the effective date is simply the date of the dismissal.[2] This has been held to apply even where the disciplinary procedure has not been complied with.[3] Thus although an appeal procedure appeared to defer the effective date the fact that the original letter of dismissal was stated to have immediate effect was enough to displace the disciplinary procedure. This is without prejudice to the employee's right to claim that there has been a breach of contract and it is possible that where this means that the employee is excluded from claiming unfair dismissal[4] a head of damages could cover the loss of a right to claim unfair dismissal.

[1] *Patel v Nagesan* [1995] IRLR 370, CA.
[2] *Cort & Son Ltd v Charman* [1981] ICR 816, EAT.
[3] *Batchelor v British Railways Board* [1987] IRLR 136, CA.
[4] Because he has not attained two years' employment.

19.56 *Internal appeals* It is usual for employers to provide a right of appeal against dismissal and for the procedure to state that dismissal has immediate effect, subject to appeal, and that if the appeal is successful the employee is reinstated from the original dismissal date. However, the procedure agreement may use ambiguous words. Thus in *Sainsbury Ltd v Savage*[1] the procedure stated that pending the decision of an appeal against dismissal the employee would be suspended without pay. The appeal was dismissed but the question of the effective date was in issue. The Court of Appeal held that despite the fact that there was a suspension, not a dismissal, the effective date was the original date. However, where the employee has remained on full pay from the original decision it must be strongly arguable that the effective date is when the appeal is dismissed.

[1] [1980] IRLR 109, CA.

19.57 *Statutory extension* The Act[1] provides that where dismissal is effected without the provision of the minimum statutory period of notice required to terminate the contract this minimum must be added on. This applies to cases of constructive dismissal as well.[2] However, this provision only applies for computing the two years' service, calculating the basic award and the amount of a week's pay where the limit has been altered. It does not apply for the purpose of deciding whether a claim has been presented in time. The employee can only add the statutory minimum – he cannot add any contractual notice.[3]

[1] ERA, s 97(2).
[2] Ibid, s 97(4).
[3] *Fox Maintenance Ltd v Jackson* [1978] ICR 110, EAT.

19.58 An employer's right to dismiss summarily cannot be removed by this statutory provision. However, a tribunal cannot simply accept the employer's argument that the conduct justified summary dismissal – it will have to examine this issue first.[1]

[1] *Lanton Leisure Ltd v White* [1987] IRLR 119, EAT.

19.58A *Constructive dismissal* It can easily be seen that establishing the effective date in a constructive dismissal case can be problematic. It could be the date the repudiatory conduct occurred, although if there is a course of conduct this is not easy to understand in itself or it could be that when such repudiation is accepted by means of a resignation. In one case[1] an employee was a director of two companies and also their chairman and Chief Executive under a service agreement. He was removed as a director from both boards on 11 and 12 March 1992 respectively which he learned about at the latest on 17 March. However, he was not certain how his removal as a director affected him as an employee until 18 March when he received a letter from the companies when he clearly accepted that he could not continue as an employee. He presented his claim on 17 June, the last day possible on the assumption that 18 March was the effective date. The Tribunal held that 18 March was the effective date, the EAT reversed, stating the question to be 'when did the termination take effect?' There is no universally applicable rule that it is only when acceptance occurs that termination take effect. Nor does it depend on what the employee understood. It depended on the legal relationship between the parties and the EAT said that removal of the directorships inevitably involved the termination of employment immediately.

While this analysis might be strictly legally correct, and this is arguable, it is not only a harsh application for employees but it would be difficult to operate in practice. There are many instances of repudiatory conduct which are not challenged by the injured party and which leave the contract subsisting. Furthermore the contractual rule is that repudiation requires acceptance before it can constitute a termination. There is a series of repudiatory actions – is it the first or last of such actions that counts? It will obviously be the last in the employee's mind if he resigns based on that but he may discover that the effective date was much earlier. It is admitted that it would be legally correct, fairer and easier to operate if the effective date ran from the date of the resignation or at least the unequivocal understanding by the employee of his position.

1 *BMK Ltd and BMK Holdings Ltd v Logue* [1993] IRLR 477.

Arguments precluding complaint and ACAS role

19.59 The general rule in relation to settlements of disputes is that the parties are bound by what they have agreed so that if X accepts £Y in full and final settlement of his claim against Z that concludes the matter. As regards statutory employment rights this is not the case. Under ERA, s 203 any provision in any agreement is void if it attempts to exclude or limit the operation of any provision of the Act or attempts to preclude anyone from complaining to the tribunal. Many employers fall foul of this provision. This provision does not cease to have effect even after liability has been determined by the tribunal because there remains the issue as to the remedy[1] which may mean compensation and the possibility of ACAS involvement.

1 *Courage Take Home Trade Ltd v Keys* [1986] IRLR 427, EAT.

19.60 However, the settlement may take the form of a tribunal decision in which the applicant withdraws and the proceedings are dismissed on the basis of an agreed payment which can be sued upon in the civil courts. If the tribunal proceedings are merely adjourned generally then the parties can return to the tribunal.

19.61 The main exception to the no settlement rule is that the settlement is valid when a Conciliation Officer has taken action and the employee has agreed to withdraw his complaint.[1] Under the Industrial Tribunals Act 1996 it is the officer's duty to endeavour to promote a settlement without its being determined by a tribunal. He is required to promote re-employment and if this is not possible to promote agreement on compensation.

[1] ERA, s 203(2)(e). See eg *Council of Engineering Institutions v Maddison* [1976] IRLR 389, EAT.

19.62 The officer need not do very much to constitute 'taking action' and he is under no duty to ensure that the settlement terms are just and equitable. He takes action by merely seeking to promote a settlement even though he takes no part in reaching it.[1] In the *Duport* case the parties had reached a settlement before the officer was called in and could even discuss re-employment. Even a telephone call is sufficient.[2]

[1] *Moore v Duport Furniture Products Ltd* [1982] ICR 84, HL. In practice, ACAS will sometimes not act if they have not been actively involved in reaching a settlement.
[2] *Whittaker v British Mail Order Corpn* [1973] IRLR 296.

19.63 The officer is not even under an obligation to explain the framework of the legislation and thus a failure to advise the applicant of his right to claim future earnings did not render the settlement void.[1] A failure to raise the issue of re-employment might be challengeable as it is the officer's primary duty. In the *Slack* case the EAT opined that a settlement could be set aside if an officer acted in bad faith, adopted unfair methods or was not impartial. This would be extremely difficult to establish.

[1] *Slack v Greenham (Plant Hire) Ltd* [1983] ICR 617.

19.64 Although settlements are recorded on the standard COT 3 form there is no need for the agreement to be reduced in writing provided it has been made through the Conciliation Officer. It is obviously better if it is reduced to writing.

19.65 The final possible challenge to the settlement is that the party never understood the agreement or agreed under duress. Economic duress can only avoid the contract if it amounted to a coercion of will vitiating consent. It would be very rare to encounter economic duress of this kind, particularly after a Conciliation Officer has been involved.[1]

[1] *Hennessy v Craigmyle & Co Ltd* [1986] ICR 461, EAT.

19.66 An officer can become involved by request of either party before a complaint has been presented or he may when proceedings have begun if he considers that there is a reasonable prospect of success.[1] This is interpreted to mean that ACAS will become involved if the employee has been dismissed or is under notice of dismissal but it is not necessary to show that he has even considered making a complaint.[2] In practice, however, ACAS will now only become involved once an originating application has been made which appears to be a breach of statutory duties under s 18 of the Industrial Tribunal Act 1996 which states that it is ACAS duty to endeavour to promote a settlement of a potential claim.[3]

1 Industrial Tribunals Act 1996, s 18.
2 See *Hennessey*, above.
3 ACAS initiated a policy change in July 1990.

19.67 When a representative reaches a settlement which is made under the auspices of a conciliation officer that settlement is binding on the client whether or not the representative had actual authority. Such a representative has an ostensible or implied authority and includes lawyers or CAB advisers.[1]

1 *Freeman v Sovereign Chicken Ltd* [1991] IRLR 408, EAT. A trade union representative or indeed anyone authorised to act on behalf of a party must have, at least, ostensible authority.

19.67A Since TURERA 1993 a new procedure (see ERA, s 203(3)) has been introduced whereby employees can enter into 'compromise agreements' obtaining advice from an independent lawyer which validly removes their rights to claim. This procedure and the role of ACAS will be considered more carefully at the end of this chapter.

19.68 An individual can validly contract out of unfair dismissal rights when he is employed under a fixed term contract which is of one year or more, which contract has not been renewed and the employee has agreed to the exclusion of rights in writing before the fixed term expires. Thus the exclusion need not be in the original contract.

19.69 Where one fixed term contract follows another the exclusion must be in the last contract which must be of one year or more. Thus an 18-month contract without a contracting out clause was followed by a seven-month contract with an exclusion clause. The EAT held that the two contracts could not be put together for the purposes of establishing that it was a sufficiently long period to allow contracting out.[1] However, this must be seen in the light of the *Mulrine*[2] case which decided that the final contract's length is not the only factor and that it is necessary to consider the fairness of the end result.

1 *Open University v Triesman* [1978] IRLR 114, CA. This topic is discussed more fully below.
2 *Mulrine v University of Ulster* [1993] IRLR 545.

19.69A Teachers in aided schools are protected where they are dismissed by the governors as a result of a local authority's requirements.[1] Crown employees can claim unfair dismissal. The only exception is where a Minister issues a certificate stating that the employment should not be given protection on the grounds of national security.[2] House of Commons staff have been able to claim for some time and now House of Lords' staff can bring unfair dismissal proceedings.[3] We have already discussed the position of seamen employed to work on ships registered in the UK in the section above.[4] The master and crew members of a fishing vessel remunerated only by shares in the profits of gross earnings of the vessel are not protected for unfair dismissal purposes.[5] Police officers cannot claim unfair dismissal as the Prison Act 1952 provides that every prison officer shall have the authority of a constable so prison officers are also excluded.[6] Following an amendment made in the 1993 TURERA, Armed Forces members can now bring unfair dismissal claims with very limited exceptions.[7] Employees working on off-shore installations within British Territorial waters are protected provided they do not ordinarily work outside either those waters or Great Britain. This applies to employees who are engaged on work connected with the exploration of the seabed or sub-soil and the exploitation of their natural resources.[8]

---

1 ERA, s 134(1).
2 ERA, s 193(1).
3 ERA, ss 194 and 195.
4 See paragraphs on 'Working Abroad'.
5 ERA, s 199(2).
6 ERA, s 200 and see *Home Office v Robinson and the Prison Officers Association* [1981] IRLR 524, EAT.
7 ERA, s 192.
8 See Employment Protection (Off-Shore Employment) Order 1976 (SI 1976/766) as amended by SI 1977/588, SI 1981/208 and SI 1984/1149.

OTHER MISCELLANEOUS EXCLUSIONS

Dismissal procedures agreement

19.70 The parties to a dismissal procedures agreement can apply to the Secretary of State for approval which, if given, is substituted for statutory unfair dismissal rights.

19.71 The Secretary of State must be satisfied that the trade unions are independent, that there is a procedure to be followed where unfair dismissal has been alleged, available to all employees covered in the agreement, that the remedies are on the whole as beneficial as the statutory remedies and that there is a procedure whereby any disputes can go to arbitration and adjudication and so forth.[1]

---

1 ERA, s 110.

19.72 The only agreement which has been designated is believed to be between the Electrical Contractors' Association and the EETPU.

Qualifying number of hours in order to claim unfair dismissal

19.72A Although Chapter 7 deals with the question of continuity of employment, in order to claim unfair dismissal protection it had always been necessary for the employee to have worked 16 hours or more per week or have worked under a contract which normally involved 16 hours per week unless he had worked for 5 years in which case the figure reduced to 8 hours.

In 1994 the House of Lords held that providing differential protection for employees who work for less than 16 hours a week relating to qualification for redundancy pay was incompatible with Article 119 of the Treaty of Rome and Council Directive 75/117. The House of Lords indicated that the thresholds could also be unlawful in relation to unfair dismissal.[1]

The issue turned on whether unfair dismissal compensation could constitute 'pay'. In a subsequent case[2] it was held that such compensation was pay within Article 119 which entitled the employee to rely upon Article 119 to bring a complaint of unfair dismissal. In particular the employee worked more than 8 but less than 16 hours a week but did not have 5 years' service. It was held that this did not preclude her from bringing a case of unfair dismissal and the same principle has since been applied in a further case.[3]

It is therefore safe now to say that there are no valid statutory requirements as to hours in order to claim unfair dismissal. Thus any employee who works for any amount of time for any employer provided he or she has two years' continuous employment is entitled to claim that he or she has been unfairly dismissed. It has been held that the doctrine of res judicata did not apply to the situation where an employee brought a claim under Article 119 when the previous proceedings made no reference to it and the earlier case was decided on the basis of the law's requirement.[4] Article 119 does not provide a right to claim unfair dismissal under its provisions.[5] Regulations now provide that there are no hours requirements.[6]

---

1 *R v Secretary of State for Employment, ex p Equal Opportunities Commission* [1994] IRLR 176.
2 *Mediguard Services Ltd v Thame* [1994] IRLR 504, EAT.
3 *Clifford v Devon County Council* [1994] IRLR 628, EAT.
4 *Methilhill Bowling Club v Hunter* [1995] IRLR 232, EAT but note *Setiya v East Yorkshire Health Authority* [1995] IRLR 348 where the EAT refused to allow a late appeal on the basis of the legal charge and was clearly concerned about the 'floodgates' effect.
5 *Barber v Staffordshire County Council* [1996] IRLR 209, CA.
6 SI 1995/31.

---

3 HAS THERE BEEN A DISMISSAL?

19.73 If the employee has managed to surmount the hurdles of showing he is qualified to claim, the next obstacle is to show that he has been dismissed.[1] The onus of proof is on the employee to show that he was dismissed and therefore if the tribunal cannot decide if there was a dismissal or a resignation it is permissible to rely on the burden of proof[2] although it will be very unusual that a tribunal is unable to reach a conclusion on this conflict.

---

1 See *Harvey* Div D 2, 3 and 4.
2 *Morris v London Iron and Steel Co Ltd* [1988] QB 493, [1987] ICR 855, CA.

19.74 The concept of 'dismissal' is given statutory recognition.[1] Thus the exclusive definition states that there is a dismissal where:

(a) the contract under which he is employed by the employer is terminated by the employer whether it is so terminated by notice or without notice, or
(b) where under that contract he is employed for a fixed term the term expires without being renewed under the same contract, or
(c) the employee terminates that contract, with or without notice, in circumstances such that he is entitled to terminate it without notice by reason of the employer's conduct.

Thus it covers employer or employee termination with or without notice, or the non-renewal of a fixed-term contract. The employee termination is known as 'constructive dismissal'.

---

1 By ERA, s 95.

19.75 This definition is exhaustive so anything that does not fall within it is excluded. However, there are many technicalities in this area so, for example a resignation, which is excluded, may be a forced one which would constitute a dismissal. A number of issues which relate to dismissal have already been covered[1] and these will be mentioned only briefly.

[1] See Chapter 2.

Maternity leave

19.76 When an employee has qualified for maternity rights she is entitled to return to work after confinement and if she is refused permission to return she is deemed to have been dismissed and is treated as having been employed until the date she gave for her return and dismissed on that date.[1] The conditions that have to be complied with to permit this return are both onerous and complex[2] and if they are not complied with the employee loses her statutory right to return and there is no deemed dismissal.[3]

[1] ERA, s 96(1).
[2] See Chapter 10 Maternity Rights for fuller discussion. Note that these provisions were amended and consolidated in TURERA 1993.
[3] See *Lavery v Plessey Telecommunications Ltd* [1983] IRLR 202, [1983] ICR 534, CA.

19.77 However, an employer may provide a maternity leave scheme which gives greater rights than the statutory scheme and the Act[1] permits an employee with such rights to take advantage of whichever right is, in any particular respect, the more favourable. However, if the employee is claiming this composite right[2] she still has to comply with all the other statutory requirements unaffected by the contract and a failure to do so means there is no statutory dismissal nor is there an ordinary dismissal.[3]

[1] ERA, s 85.
[2] See note 1 to para 19.73.
[3] See *Lavery v Plessey*, para 19.76 above.

19.78 Matters become more complicated where the employee is relying on a contractual right to return. If there is something which supports the view that there is a contractual arrangement a failure to allow the employee to return can be an ordinary dismissal where the contract subsisted during maternity leave[1] but where there is no evidence to suggest that the contract was subsisting she will be treated as having left the employment.[2] However, the position is not entirely clear as has already been discussed above[3] and the loss of the statutory right to return does not mean there can be no ordinary dismissal which will depend on what has been agreed and the common law.[4]

[1] *Lucas v Norton of London Ltd* [1984] IRLR 86, EAT; *Hilton International Hotels (UK) Ltd v Kaissi* [1994] IRLR 270, EAT.
[2] *McKnight v Adlestones (Jewellers) Ltd* [1984] IRLR 453.
[3] See ch 10.
[4] See *Crouch v Kidsons Impey* [1996] IRLR 79, EAT.

Self dismissal

19.79 Employers occasionally have written to employees, often in the situation where they are on strike, that they have 'dismissed themselves'. This concept of 'self dismissal' or 'constructive resignation' as it is occasionally called has already been referred to above,[1] but it is worth mentioning in this context. The proper approach is that the employee, by his conduct, will have repudiated the contract, and the employer terminates the contract by accepting the repudiation.[2] This is standard contractual doctrine and must be accepted as correct.

[1] See Chapter 2.
[2] *London Transport Executive v Clarke* [1981] ICR 355, [1981] IRLR 166, CA.

Automatic termination

19.80 This has also been considered[1] but, to reiterate, when the employee and employer have 'agreed' that the occurrence of certain circumstances such as the non-return to work on a particular day, will lead to an agreed termination of the contract or a mutual agreement, this will not be permitted because it will fall foul of s 203 of the ERA as being an attempt to oust the provisions of the Act and prevent an employee from pursuing his employment rights.[2]

[1] See Chapter 2.
[2] *Igbo v Johnson Matthey Chemical Ltd* [1986] ICR 505, [1986] IRLR 215, CA.

Agreed termination

19.81 However, where the court decides that the employee has given his consent freely to the termination, particularly if there is some reason why the employee may have done this, such as qualifying for an early retirement scheme, then this is not to be treated as a dismissal even where a notice of termination has been given.[1] This last proposition is very extreme but was justified on the basis that the employee had subsequently taken early retirement as a substitute for redundancy.[2] In the *Liverpool* case it was, however, stated that this would not prevent a volunteer for redundancy from being treated as dismissed.

[1] *Scott v Coalite Fuels and Chemicals Ltd* [1988] ICR 355, [1988] IRLR 131, EAT.
[2] See also *Birch v University of Liverpool* [1985] ICR 470, [1985] IRLR 165, CA.

19.82 Another common situation where a dismissal is considered to be by agreement is where the employee agrees to go after being induced by an offer of settlement. In such a situation there is no dismissal. If the employee is faced with an ultimatum 'resign or be dismissed' his resignation would be treated as a forced dismissal but, where, in due course, terms of a settlement emerge then the operative cause of any subsequent resignation is the monetary offer.[1] It has even been held that a resignation based on an understanding that it would avoid the hassle of disciplinary proceedings has also been held to be a voluntary resignation although this becomes more questionable.[2] What has to be determined is 'who really terminated the employment' and the *MBS* case is authority for the view that this is a question of fact for the tribunal. This view is also contentious because this issue contains many questions of law within it. Where the employee has been 'inveigled' into resigning this constitutes a dismissal.[3] However, the principle remains that if there is a valid agreement entered into freely and without duress and for a financial consideration this will be upheld and will not be void under ERA, s 203.[4]

[1] *Staffordshire County Council v Donovan* [1981] IRLR 108, EAT. The position of a 'take it or leave it' offer is uncertain but would probably be regarded as a settlement, not a dismissal, if it were accepted. The issue would be whether the employee really consented where he had no effective choice.
[2] *Martin v Glynwed Distribution Ltd (t/a MBS)* [1983] ICR 511, [1983] IRLR 198, CA.
[3] *Caledonian Mining Co Ltd v Bassett* [1987] ICR 425, [1987] IRLR 165, EAT.
[4] *Logan Salton v Durham County Council* [1989] IRLR 99, EAT.

Words used at termination

19.83 Ambiguous words may be used either by an employer or employee which can be uncertain in impact. Words may appear clear at face value but in the circumstances they can appear differently and it might be that they were spoken in the heat of the moment and not intended or they may have been uttered by an immature employee and the employer should realise that they may not have been intended.[1]

[1] *Sovereign House Security Services Ltd v Savage* [1989] IRLR 115, CA.

19.84 Thus when unambiguous words of dismissal are used in the heat of the moment and are withdrawn almost immediately there is no dismissal because the employer can recant them.[1] If unequivocal words of resignation are used in a normal case the employer is entitled to accept the resignation. The natural meaning of the words and the employer's understanding of them leave no room for what a reasonable employer might have understood.[2] However, there are exceptions, such as where the employee is immature, or where the words are said in the heat of the moment or where an employee has been jostled into the decision. Also idle words might be used under emotional stress and this is particularly so where the employee is of below average intelligence.[3] It has also been stated that where there is an exchange between the parties there may be something which could lead a tribunal to decide that there was no real resignation despite what might appear at first sight.[4] The courts are becoming more sophisticated in their approaches to this problem. Where the words used are ambiguous then it appears that the test to determine whether they are words of resignation or termination is an objective one. That is to say how would the words have been understood by the reasonable listener? It is also necessary to look at all the surrounding circumstances both before and after the words are uttered to decide how a reasonable employee or employer would have understood them.[5] Where there is a resignation, even in the heat of the moment, there is no onus on the employer to seek to recoup the situation and to investigate the employee's true intention. However, where the resignation occurs under special circumstances, such as bad temper, an employer should allow a reasonable period (a day or two) to elapse before accepting a resignation at its face value during which it may emerge that the resignation was not really intended.[6]

[1] *Martin v Yeomen Aggregates Ltd* [1983] ICR 314, [1983] IRLR 49, EAT.
[2] *Sothern v Franks Charlesly & Co* [1981] IRLR 278, CA.
[3] *Barclay v City of Glasgow District Council* [1983] IRLR 313, EAT.
[4] *Sovereign House Security Services Ltd v Savage* [1989] IRLR 115, CA.
[5] *J & J Stern v Simpson* [1983] IRLR 52: *Tanner v D T Kean Ltd* [1978] IRLR 110, EAT.
[6] *Kwik-Fit (GB) v Lineham* [1992] IRLR 156, EAT.

Dismissal and redundancy

19.85 The definition of dismissal for redundancy payment claims is almost identical to[1] that for unfair dismissal and the differences have been alluded to in the chapter on redundancy.[2]

---

[1] See ERA, ss 136 and 137.
[2] See Chapter 20 below.

Termination by employer

19.86 This may be with or without notice. There is not very much to discuss where the employee is dismissed with immediate effect although the problems in relation to repudiation and termination have already been mentioned.[1]

---

[1] See Chapter 2 above.

19.87 To constitute a notice of termination the notice must be specific and fix a definite date. It is not sufficient to give a long advance warning[1] nor is it sufficient that it should be some specific date or such earlier date as the employer or employee may select.[2] It is not sufficient for an employer to announce that a factory is to be closed down by a specific date and that the employees should find alternative employment as quickly as possible.[3] Two issues arise here: first, was this tantamount to a dismissal on the 'resign or be dismissed' principle? It was held that it was not. Secondly there is the issue of whether the specific date of the factory closure was adequate to terminate the employee's contract. The court said it was not because they were two separate matters and one could not definitively ascertain the employee's termination date. This very strict approach has been followed[4] and is worthy of some criticism. Surely the fact that the employee might leave earlier is of no consequence, as he can serve a counter notice if he wishes at any time, provided it is not a redundancy case where there are special rules (see Chapter 20 on Redundancy). It is true that factory closures will almost always be redundancy situations. Furthermore, if the employee were to terminate the contract earlier or even later, if that were possible, surely the original statement can still constitute a notice of termination even of the individual's contract of employment. A notice of termination can be supplanted by a summary dismissal for example.[5] Where there is a genuine resignation by the employee and he is working out his notice, the employer can terminate the contract earlier by paying money in lieu of notice (provided this is permitted in the contract) without this being treated as a dismissal.[6] The employer can waive the period of notice and make a payment in lieu. This was a strong case because the employee lost his right to earn commission during the notice period – the court told him that he could pursue a claim in the county court. It should also be noted that where an employee fails to comply with the statutory maternity procedure that does not necessarily mean that there can be no dismissal. The Act provides[8] that where the employee is entitled to return and has followed the statutory procedure then if she is not permitted to return she shall be treated as having been continuously employed until the notified day of return, and dismissed from that date. The *Kaissi* case shows that the contract can continue and whether it does depends on the agreement and the parties' actions. In a particular case there was nothing in the agreement and nothing done by the parties which terminated the contract. The court did say that the employer may be justified in not permitting a return if she is dismissed in the course of attempting to return to work but in this case, the employer took the initiative to terminate because they had received no written confirmation of intention to return.

[1] *Morton Sundour Fabrics Ltd v Shaw* (1966) 2 ITR 84.
[2] *Burton Group Ltd v Smith* [1977] IRLR 351, EAT.
[3] *International Computers v Kennedy* [1981] IRLR 28, EAT.
[4] *Doble v Firestone Tyre and Rubber Co Ltd* [1981] IRLR 300, EAT.
[5] *Stapp v Shaftesbury Society* [1982] IRLR 326, CA.
[6] *Marshall (Cambridge) Ltd v Hamblin* [1994] IRLR 260, EAT.
[7] *Hilton International Hotels (UK) Ltd v Kaissi* [1994] IRLR 270, EAT. See also *Crouch v Kidsons Impey* [1996] IRLR 79, EAT.
[8] ERA, s 96(1).

Counter notice

19.88 The Act provides that where an employer gives notice to terminate the contract then the employee can give notice to terminate the contract on an earlier date. If so then the employee is still taken to be dismissed and for the reasons given by the employer.[1] The effective date of termination is determined by the employee's counter notice.[2]

[1] Contrast stricter provisions where the dismissal is for redundancy.
[2] *Thompson v GEC Avionics* [1991] IRLR 488 – see para 19.52, above.

19.89 Although this is very helpful to an employee it still requires that there be a notice of termination by the employer in the first place and thus what has been stated above is very relevant.

19.90 The above exposition regarding employer termination and events falling outside the definition of 'dismissal' has been relatively brief, bearing in mind that it has been covered elsewhere.[1]

[1] Particularly Chapter 2.

Termination of fixed-term contracts without their renewal

19.91 It should first be explained why this situation should constitute a dismissal at all as it is arguable that there should be no rights occurring after a contract has come to an end. The principle involved is a recognition of the fact that there is no true freedom of contract and that employers may impose this form of contract on their employees. If this is so then employers could avoid the unfair dismissal and redundancy law by employing workers on one fixed-term contract followed by another, with a break in between or simply not renewing the contract and replacing one employee with another. This unfairness is prevented by such conduct being regarded as a dismissal although, as we shall see later,[1] it may not be an unfair dismissal if the employee is aware that the contract is of a short duration although this would not prevent it from being a redundancy provided the necessary two years' continuous employment was worked.[2]

[1] See 'some other substantial reason' under reasons for dismissal.
[2] See below.

19.92 The main question is whether the contract is one for a fixed term, a question which has caused a few problems. The first issue is whether a fixed term remains one if there is a provision in the contract whereby it can be terminated by notice. Logic would suggest that it could not be a fixed term contract because it can be unfixed by notice and that hardly appears to be a defined period. The Court of Appeal originally held this to be the legal position but in due course it was appreciated by employers that if they recruited employees on such contracts and did not renew their contracts this would not be the expiry of a fixed-term contract or an employer termination and employees would be unprotected as they would not be able to show that they had been dismissed which, as we have noted, is an essential prerequisite for claiming unfair dismissal. This loophole was blocked in *Dixon v BBC*[1] when it was held that a contract for a specified period could remain a fixed-term contract even where there was a notice clause in it.

1 [1979] QB 546, [1979] ICR 281.

19.93 A contract to perform a specific task which will end when the task is performed is not a fixed-term contract. The contract comes to an end when the task is fulfilled so that there is a discharge by performance. A fixed term needs a definite beginning and end.[1] It does not mean that the employee need be working throughout the period provided he is contractually obliged to be available. Thus a teacher employed to teach throughout an academic session is still employed under a fixed-term contract for that period even though the course came to an end earlier or because there were insufficient students to teach the course.[2]

1 *Wiltshire County Council v National Association of Teachers in Further and Higher Education* [1980] ICR 455, [1980] IRLR 198, CA.
2 Ibid.

19.94 It is also not possible to have a fixed-term contract by reference to some external event such as the life of an individual or the duration of a team's life in the Premier Division of the Football League. It cannot be a fixed term because there is no definite end date. This principle has been applied in rather contentious circumstances in *Brown v Knowsley Borough Council*[1] where the contract specified that the appointment would last only as long as sufficient funds were provided by sponsors. When these ran dry the contract came to an end. It was not a fixed-term contract because there was no specified end date. This was not an employer termination either but an automatic termination on the non-happening or happening of a future event. No action was required and there was no dismissal thereby depriving the employee of the opportunity of arguing regarding fairness. This decision is controversial because it appears to be very close to ousting ERA, s 203. It could be expanded to cover matters such as retaining the job provided there was a certain rate of profits. These are matters which are very much in the hands of the employers despite the obvious influence of external events and thus this development should be carefully controlled otherwise employee protection will be diminished.

1 [1986] IRLR 102, EAT.

19.95 The parties are free to contract out of their rights to claim unfair dismissal in a fixed-term contract of one year or more.[1]

[1] ERA, s 197, see below in relation to contracting-out.

Constructive dismissal – introductory comments

19.96 To claim a constructive dismissal the employee must show:

(a) that the employer has committed a fundamental breach of contract or shows an intention no longer to be bound by it;
(b) this was the reason he left;
(c) that he did not act too hastily, and
(d) that he did not delay too long.

19.97 After an early vigorous debate as to whether constructive dismissal depended on the employer's breach of contract rather than the unreasonableness of his behaviour the test is now clearly contractual. However, the development of implied terms has been such that there is not such a large difference as would be anticipated.

19.98 The leading case of *Western Excavating (ECC) Ltd v Sharp*[1] established the principles stated above and that the test was contractual. The Court of Appeal said that the words of the subsection are the language of contract. Thus 'whether an employee is "entitled" to terminate his contract of employment without notice by reason of employer's conduct and claim constructive dismissal must be determined in accordance with the law of contract'. Rather optimistically and certainly unrealistically it was said that 'sensible persons have no difficulty in recognising conduct by an employer which under law brings a contract of employment to an end'.[2] Since that statement there have been numerous sensible people who have tried to work out the parameters of permissible behaviour in employment contracts. The judge himself referred to 'persistent and unwanted amorous advances' as clearly conduct justifying resignation. It is unlikely anyone would wish to argue with that but it took a long time before sexual harassment was taken seriously.[3]

[1] [1978] QB 761, [1978] 1 All ER 713.
[2] Per Lawton LJ.
[3] For example, note *Bracebridge Engineering Ltd v Darby* [1990] IRLR 3, EAT, where it was held that a single act can constitute sexual harassment.

Examples of fundamental breach

19.99 The most important term in any contract is the pay or salary. If the employer interferes with this then this is likely to be fundamental. Originally, it was considered that the smallest of reductions would justify resignation but it now appears settled that any interference must be of a material amount.[1] What is a material amount is a matter of degree but it would not include a very small reduction. One issue which arises here is that this need for a material reduction might affect the lower paid adversely. Thus it might be arguable that a £5 reduction from £100 is not material but a 5% reduction on £1,000 per week would lead to a £50 decrease and might be regarded as material. In dealing with this problem the only fair way is to adopt a percentage basis but we have had too few cases to have developed such sophistication.

1 *Gillies v Richard Daniels & Co Ltd* [1979] IRLR 457, EAT.

19.100 Where an employer reduces wages, relying on a provision in the contract which entitles him so to do, this is not a breach of contract which can justify the employee's resignation.[1] It is the same principle which justifies a demotion after poor performance or conduct. There is no breach of contract if it is provided that such demotion can occur.

1 *White v Reflecting Roadstuds Ltd* [1991] IRLR 331, EAT.

19.101 The employer must pay the wages on the date that he is required although in practice a few days' delay would not normally result in any action nor would it be likely to lead to a successful claim. The circumstances of the case must be looked at[1] and when there has been a delay and it has been complained about on several occasions the employee is not obliged to give the employer what is in effect a final warning that he will resign.[2]

1 *Adams v Charles Zub Associates Ltd* [1978] IRLR 551, EAT.
2 *Stokes v Hampstead Wine Co Ltd* [1979] IRLR 298, EAT.

19.102 If the employer changes the formula or basis on which he will pay wages then he is obliged to explain to the employee what the effect of such a change will be. The change in the formula is not per se sufficient because one needs to know if there will be a material change and thus one needs to know the effect. The employer is required to explain to the employee the effect of the alteration and if he is unable to do so then this constitutes a repudiation justifying resignation.[1]

1 *Hill Ltd v Mooney* [1981] IRLR 258, EAT.

19.103 One issue which often creates problems is that of pay increases. Employees rarely have an express right to a pay increase but occasionally a right to a cost of living increase is included. Usually, however, a pay increase is expected annually and is given and when one is not forthcoming it creates dissension. The failure to give a pay increase would very rarely provide a cause of action to the employee because such a right will rarely be provided and it is highly unlikely that a tribunal would accept that it had become a custom and practice to provide one as an implied term of the contract. In fact it has been stated that it is impossible to imply that there will always be a pay rise[1] even though an employer must not treat his employees arbitrarily, capriciously or inequitably in matters of remuneration.[2]

1 *Murco Petroleum Ltd v Forge* [1987] ICR 282, [1987] IRLR 50, EAT.
2 *Gardner (FC) v Beresford* [1978] IRLR 63, EAT.

19.104 Where there are other benefits accruing in the employment these are treated as equivalent to pay for the purposes of constructive dismissal and therefore any withdrawal of such benefits would constitute conduct justifying resignation. The most important benefit would be a car and if this is withdrawn this would be a repudiation.[1] A minor change in the kind of car provided would probably not constitute a material change.

1 *Moore v Rowland Winn* [1975] IRLR 162.

19.105 The employee can complain if there is an important change in his job duties. The duties that can be required of an employee depend on the contract but where a sales manager finds that almost all his sales activities have been removed this is a repudiatory breach[1] and the same is true where an employee doing a number of different things finds that the interesting duties have been removed and he has been left with duties of a humdrum nature.[2] However, this was a very strong case and if an employee is employed to carry out general duties he cannot dictate which ones he is to carry out.[3] There is a little uncertainty as to the employer's powers to transfer an employee to different duties on a temporary basis. In one case[4] a transfer to suitable work without any loss of wages was held not necessarily to constitute a breach of contract but the period must be of limited duration. In a later case[5] a substantial alteration to the terms of the contract even on a temporary basis was held to be a repudiation. Both cases are at EAT level and it is difficult to reconcile them although the answer may lie in the fact that in the second case the alteration was substantial.

1 *Ford v Milthorn Toleman Ltd* [1980] IRLR 30, CA.
2 *Coleman v Baldwin* [1977] IRLR 342.
3 *Peter Carnie & Son Ltd v Paton* [1979] IRLR 260, EAT.
4 *Millbrook Furnishing Industries Ltd v McIntosh* [1981] IRLR 309.
5 *McNeill v Charles Crimm (Electrical Contractors) Ltd* [1984] IRLR 179.

19.106 The right of the employer to transfer the employee is dealt with more fully elsewhere[1] but it is vital to examine the contract. If there is an express right to move the employee then this is conclusive provided the employer exercises the right reasonably.[2] It is necessary to establish that a particular provision has become contractual. Acceptance of new terms cannot be implied from the fact that an employee does not object to new terms which have been sent to her and to which she had not objected.[3] Where, for example, an employer has a discretion under a mobility clause whether to make a relocation allowance this was subject to an implied term that it would be exercised in such a way as not to render it impossible for an employee to comply with his contractual obligation to move. The implied term cannot override the express term but it can qualify it in relation to the manner of its exercise.[4] However, the law does not go so far as to require that the express right be subject to an implied term that the right would be exercised in a reasonable way. What it does do is to require employers to reach their decisions responsibly. A purely capricious decision would not be protected.[5] This, however, is a long way from 'reasonably' and the express provision is once again given considerable weight. If there is no express term then a term will be implied that the employee must be prepared to travel to any place within reasonable daily travelling distance of his home.[6] If the employer goes beyond his powers then the employee can claim constructive dismissal.

1 See below.
2 *McAndrew v Prestwick Circuits Ltd* [1988] IRLR 514, EAT. This relates to the procedure adopted.
3 *Aparau v Iceland Frozen Foods plc* [1996] IRLR 119.
4 *United Bank Ltd v Akhtar* [1989] IRLR 507, EAT.
5 *White v Reflecting Roadstuds Ltd* [1991] IRLR 331, EAT.
6 *Courtaulds Northern Spinning Ltd v Sibson* [1988] ICR 451, [1988] IRLR 305, CA.

19.107 There are various other breaches which could justify a resignation such as suspending an employee without any contractual right or justification or excessive length of suspension even where there is a contractual right.[1] The employer is required to provide a healthy and safe working environment and any failure to provide this is a fundamental breach of contract.[2] A demotion or serious loss of status can also justify resignation particularly where this is accompanied by the loss of decent work conditions.[3] Where a large organisation refuses time off in an emergency this is probably a repudiation.[4] An employer is entitled to introduce a no-smoking policy and if an employee resigns in protest this will not entitle him to claim constructive dismissal.[5] It is also necessary that employees should be afforded a reasonable opportunity to obtain redress for a grievance promptly and failure to provide such an opportunity or a procedure is a fundamental breach of contract.[6]

1 *McLory v Post Office* [1992] ICR 758.
2 For example *British Aircraft Corpn v Austin* [1978] IRLR 332, EAT.
3 *Wadham Stringer v Brown* [1983] IRLR 46, EAT.
4 *Warner v Barbers Stores* [1978] IRLR 109.
5 *Dryden v Greater Glasgow Health Board* [1992] IRLR 469, EAT.
6 *WA Goold (Pearmak) Ltd v McConnell* [1995] IRLR 516, EAT.

Trust and confidence

19.108 The employer must treat his employees in a reasonable manner and must do nothing which is calculated or likely to destroy or seriously damage the relationship of confidence and trust between employer and employee.[1] This duty has been applied in many cases and in various situations. Before unfair dismissal law was introduced it had been decided that an employee must do nothing which would undermine the confidential relationship which existed between the parties.[2] In an early case a director had told a colleague in his secretary's presence that the secretary was 'an intolerable bitch on Monday mornings' and this comment had shattered the relationship and this was a constructive dismissal.[3] A similar result is achieved when an overseer is told that he cannot do his job when that was not a true expression of opinion[4] or when an employer persistently uses foul language which goes beyond the limits of the contract.[5] An unjustified warning or a series of warnings can justify a claim where it is argued that the warnings were given with a view to disheartening him and driving him out.[6]

1 *Woods v WM Car Services (Peterborough) Ltd* [1982] ICR 693, [1983] IRLR 413, CA.
2 *Sinclair v Neighbour* [1967] 2 QB 279, [1966] 3 All ER 988, CA.
3 *Isle of Wight Tourist Board v Coomb* [1976] IRLR 413.
4 *Courtaulds Northern Textiles Ltd v Andrew* [1979] IRLR 84, EAT.
5 *Palmanor Ltd v Cedron* [1978] ICR 1008, [1978] IRLR 303.
6 *Walker v Josiah Wedgwood & Sons Ltd* [1978] ICR 744, [1978] IRLR 105, EAT.

19.109 The employee is entitled to receive his employer's support when dealing with employees and any failure to provide this amounts to a constructive dismissal.[1] This also applies to a situation where an employee is being shunned by colleagues whom he supervises[2] or where his authority is undermined by the employer,[3] or where his behaviour is reported to the police before the employer has adequate justification to do so or without giving the employee the opportunity of explaining his conduct.[4] This may not always be required as in some exceptional cases it may be necessary to do so to protect others.[5] The obligation of good faith also applies to the employer's rights and powers under a pension scheme. Although the company's interests must be protected this must not operate in such a way that there is any breach of the obligation of good faith owed to employees.[6]

---

1 *Associated Tyre Specialists Ltd v Waterhouse* [1977] ICR 218, [1976] IRLR 386, EAT; *Whitbread plc v Gullyes* 1.7.94 EAT 478/92.

2 *Wigan Borough Council v Davies* [1979] ICR 411, [1979] IRLR 127, EAT.

3 *Wetherall (Bond Street W1) Ltd v Lynn* [1978] 1 WLR 200, [1978] ICR 205, EAT.

4 *Fyfe and McGrouther Ltd v Byrne* [1977] IRLR 29; and *Robinson v Crompton Parkinson Ltd* [1978] ICR 401, [1978] IRLR 61, EAT.

5 *Dumfries and Galloway Regional Council v Tindall* EAT 295/92 where the employee worked at a residential home for difficult young people and was accused of assaulting a resident, only days after a previous allegation had been made.

6 *Imperial Group Pension Trust Ltd v Imperial Tobacco Ltd* [1991] IRLR 66.

19.110 However, the law does not go as far as saying that there is a term that an employer will treat the employee in a reasonable manner. This would be too wide and uncertain[1] and would probably render the *Western Excavating* distinction between unreasonable conduct and breach of contract nugatory. In that case the employee resigned because his employer would not lend him some money and his resignation would allow him to obtain his accrued pay. The Court of Appeal held that the employer's behaviour may have been unreasonable but it could not be characterised as a breach of contract. This would almost certainly be decided in the same way today. In the *WM Car* case although there were a number of changes to the employee's contract they were not held to be a fundamental breach. The tribunal is required to look at the employer's conduct as a whole and determine whether it is such that its cumulative effect, judged reasonably and sensibly, is such that the employee cannot be expected to put up with it.[2]

---

1 *Post Office v Roberts* [1980] IRLR 347, EAT.

2 *Woods v W M Car Services*, at para 19.108.

19.111 The employee is entitled to take into account past breaches and add them to any final breach and claim that together they cumulatively amount to a breach of the implied obligation of trust and confidence.[1] This is often referred to as the 'last straw' and is equivalent to the employer's right to do the same when judging the employee's behaviour at work. There does not have to be any intention on the part of the employer to repudiate the contract nor does there have to be deliberate conduct or bad faith to destroy mutual trust and confidence.[2]

---

1 *Lewis v Motorworld Garages Ltd* [1986] ICR 157, [1985] IRLR 465, CA.

2 See *Woods v WM Car Services, P O v Roberts* and *Lewis v Motorworld*, above.

Duty to inform employees of terms and conditions

19.112 A relatively new development is an obligation on the employer to take reasonable steps to bring the terms of the contract to the employee's attention so that they may enjoy its benefits. Obviously this is not required where the terms have been negotiated with the individual employee but where there has been collective bargaining or a document is incorporated into the contract by reference and the employee might well be unaware of its contents. In the particular circumstances of this case[1] the employer was held to be in breach by failing to inform employees of their right to enhance their pension entitlement by the purchase of added years. It is not easy to predict which other terms this could apply to but one can see that a tribunal or court might consider that an employee should be made aware of a grievance procedure where this was incorporated by reference.

[1] *Scally v Southern Health and Social Services Board* [1991] IRLR 522, HL.

General principles

19.113 Where the employer imposes a punishment which is grossly out of proportion to the offence the employee has committed, this can constitute a repudiation of the contract.[1]

[1] *BBC v Beckett* [1983] IRLR 43, EAT.

19.114 Whether the facts constitute a repudiatory breach is very much a question of fact for the industrial tribunal as there is no rule of law for determining whether repudiatory conduct has occurred. This means that it will only be possible to interfere with the decision if the tribunal has misdirected itself or reached a perverse decision.[1]

[1] *Woods v WM Car Services*, at para 19.108. See also *British Telecommunications plc v Sheridan* [1990] IRLR 27, CA.

19.115 Although we have noted that the employer's intentions are not relevant to whether there has been repudiatory conduct one particular problem has arisen in relation to the interpretation of the contract of employment. It has been held that where a party takes a view of the contractual position and acts in accordance with that view this is not a repudiatory breach of contract even if it transpires that his view is erroneous. What has been said is that it has to be shown that he did not intend to be bound by the contract as properly construed.[1] Although there have been attempts to modify this position[2] and criticise the *Punch* decision, the later *Bridgen* case seems to affirm the position. The ramifications of this approach are quite dramatic because an employer may take a wholly erroneous view as to the contractual position and still be protected against a constructive dismissal claim unless he is acting in bad faith. This is one area where objectivity plays 'second fiddle' to subjectivity in relation to constructive dismissal. However, one expects tribunals will take a robust view in relation to this point. This principle does not extend to permitting an employer to rely on a genuine, though mistaken belief of fact. Thus where an employer appointed a replacement and told customers that an employee would not be returning this could constitute grounds to justify a constructive dismissal claim. If the employer acted genuinely mistakenly that would be taken into account overall in determining the issue.[3]

[1] *Bridgen v Lancashire County Council* [1987] IRLR 58, CA following *Frank Wright & Co (Holdings) Ltd v Punch* [1980] IRLR 217.
[2] Templeman LJ in *Financial Techniques (Planning Services) Ltd v Hughes* [1981] IRLR 32, CA.
[3] *Brown v JBD Engineering* [1993] IRLR 568, EAT.

19.116 It is not open to an employer to argue that the person mistreating the employee had no authority so to mistreat the employee. The simple test of vicarious liability for the employer's action is to be applied and thus when an employee was reprimanded by her supervisor in a humiliating, intimidating and degrading manner this was the employer's conduct and there could be no argument regarding the supervisor's authority.[1] It is no defence to an employer that a removal of the employee's duties was implemented through an invalid resolution.[2] It is permissible to have contributory fault even where there is a constructive dismissal.[3]

[1] *Hilton International Hotels (UK) Ltd v Protopapa* [1990] IRLR 316, EAT.
[2] *Warnes v Trustees of Cheriton Oddfellows Social Club* [1993] IRLR 58, EAT.
[3] See below.

Anticipatory breach

19.117 The last point made applies in relation to anticipatory breach so that where there is a genuine dispute about the contractual terms it is not an anticipatory breach for one party to do no more than argue his point of view, or even to insist on his view. This is a very long way from the situation where the employer states that he will not be bound by the contract in any circumstances.[1] However, this legal position does not help the employee very much when he feels strongly about a particular issue and it is not a very practical solution to suggest that the matter can be litigated quite easily in a separate action. It is also not very equitable where the tribunal or court decides that the employee's interpretation is undoubtedly correct as has happened in some of these cases.

[1] See *Financial Techniques v Hughes*, above.

19.118 Where the employer threatens to break the contract then the employer is able to withdraw his repudiatory conduct or threat before it is accepted. Thus when an employer informed the employee that he would lose his directorship in a fortnight, as the obligation was a future obligation it was in the nature of an anticipatory breach and the employer was entitled to withdraw the threat before it was put into practice.[1] This places the burden on the employee of either unequivocally accepting the threatened repudiation or trying to resolve the issue. In the above case there was no unequivocal acceptance of the repudiation and by the time there was the employer had withdrawn his threat. It is not an anticipatory breach to tell an employee that his employment would eventually be terminated because there was nothing to suggest that the employer would terminate without giving notice and act in breach of contract.[2] A proposal to vary contractual hours and to give due notice of termination if she did not agree amounted to an anticipatory breach of a fundamental term.[3] If the employer repudiates the contract an employee does not have to raise a grievance under the grievance procedure before accepting the repudiation although it is always a sensible step to take both practically and also it might have an influence on the tribunal.[4]

1 *Norwest Holst Group Administration Ltd v Harrison* [1985] ICR 668.
2 *Haseltine Lake & Co v Dowler* [1981] ICR 222, [1981] IRLR 25, EAT.
3 *Greenaway Harrison Ltd v Wiles* [1994] IRLR 380, EAT.
4 *Seligman and Latz Ltd v McHugh* [1979] IRLR 130, EAT.

Acceptance of repudiation

19.119 The employee must indicate in a clear unambiguous fashion that he is exercising his entitlement to claim constructive dismissal.[1] Although it is not strictly necessary to state the exact reason why he left there must be no doubt as to why the employee left.[2] The moral for employees is that they should state very expressly why they are leaving. If there is any doubt as to why they are leaving because there may be other reasons the employee may find that the employer defends the claim on the basis that he was not aware of why the employee had left.

1 *Logabax Ltd v Titherley* [1977] ICR 369, [1977] IRLR 97, EAT.
2 *Walker v Josiah Wedgwood*, see para 19.104 above.

19.120 We have already noted that it is necessary for the employee to unequivocally communicate his acceptance of the employer's repudiation and if this is not done then the employee will be deemed not to have accepted the repudiation.[1] An example of this would be where the employee was trying to negotiate a settlement based on the breach. Again, the employee will need to act very carefully in this situation. Ultimately the employee must be careful not to leave too soon – he must not pre-empt the situation and leave before any breach has occurred.

1 *Norwest Holst v Harrison*, see para 19.112 above.

19.121 A further difficulty is that the employee 'must make up his mind soon after the conduct of which he complains, for if he continues for any length of time without leaving, he will lose his right to treat himself as discharged. He will be regarded as having elected to affirm the contract'.[1] Thus delay will cause problems for the employee. However, it is not merely the passage of time that is important. One must consider the circumstances surrounding the delay and if the employee is absent from work this will be an important factor in contradicting affirmation. Thus where an employee delayed his resignation for ten weeks following a demotion this was not too long because he had been absent through sickness and furthermore he had protested against the demotion. If he had worked for that period without resigning, even under protest that might have been too long. It is difficult to say what period would be permitted in those circumstances but it is interesting to note that the redundancy provisions allow a four week trial period for any new job.[2] However, the comments contained in *Cox Toner v Crook*[3] seem to be more generous. An employee, who was also a director, was accused of serious misconduct which led to six months of correspondence between solicitors. Ultimately the employer refused to withdraw its allegations and one month later the employee resigned. It was held that there was affirmation of the contract. Although the employee had not accepted the position because he had protested there had been a seven month delay during which he had carried on working and been paid. Even if the six month period could be accepted the final month's delay after it was obvious that the employer was not withdrawing its allegations was fatal to the employee. Any delay could be an implied affirmation of the contract but an employee could reserve his rights to accept the repudiation or allow the employer to remedy the breach and then performance would not prejudice his position.

1 *Western Excavating (EEC) Ltd v Sharp* [1978] QB 761, [1978] ICR 221, CA.
2 ERA, s 131(3).
3 [1981] ICR 823, EAT.

19.122 Sometimes the employer gives the employee time to make up his mind and continues to pay the employee. In such a situation the employee will not be taken to have affirmed the contract but the period of delay must be reasonable in all the circumstances.[1]

1 *Bliss v South East Thames Regional Health Authority* [1987] ICR 700, [1988] IRLR 308, CA.

19.123 An employee cannot claim constructive dismissal where he continues to report for duty after issuing an originating application, since his behaviour is not consistent with his position that he had treated the contract as at an end by reason of the employer's conduct. An employee cannot go on acting as if he was employed when he is also saying he is not.[1] However, this apparently simple proposition is not quite as straightforward as it appears because the wording of the dismissal subsection refers to termination of the contract, not of the relationship. Thus in principle at least you can have your contract terminated and yet remain working and the cases[2] on employer dismissal seem to support that.

1 *Hunt v British Railways Board* [1979] IRLR 379, EAT.
2 *Alcan Extrusions v Yates* (1996) IRLR 327, applying *Hogg v Dover College* (1990) ICR 39.

19.124 Earlier we referred to the point that it is permissible for the employee to claim that past conduct of the employer can be used to justify a subsequent breach as being sufficient to resign (the 'last straw' argument).[1] This raises the point that such past breaches have not been complained about or have not led to a resignation and therefore there has been delay. In the *Lewis* case the Court of Appeal held that it was possible to look at a course of conduct and delay did not affect the employee's rights to claim in this situation.

1 *Lewis v Motorworld Garages Ltd* [1985] IRLR 465, CA.

Frustration

19.125 This concept has been covered elsewhere but it should be stated at this juncture that if the contract is frustrated there is no dismissal. It had been held that frustration did not apply to certain employment contracts but the doctrine is now alive and well even for periodic contracts determinable by relatively short notice. The doctrine can apply in a number of cases but its most obvious application in employment is related to sickness[1] and occasionally imprisonment.[2] The details of this are contained elsewhere in the book.[3]

1 See the principles in *Marshall v Harland and Wolff Ltd* [1972] 1 WLR 899, NIRC.
2 *FC Shepherd & Co Ltd v Jerrom* [1987] QB 301, [1986] 3 All ER 589, CA.
3 The doctrine is not well regarded by lay members of tribunals and the EAT and its development is likely to be non-existent. See *Williams v Watsons Luxury Coaches Ltd* [1990] IRLR 164, EAT.

4 REASONS FOR DISMISSAL

Reasons generally – an introduction

19.126 Once an employee can show he is qualified to claim he has been unfairly dismissed and has actually been dismissed, it is for the employer to show the reason for the dismissal. If there is more than one reason then he must show the principal reason for the dismissal.[1] This reason[2] must be one of the reasons as laid down in s 98(2) of the ERA or be some other substantial reason of a kind such as to justify the dismissal. These reasons are capability or qualifications, conduct, redundancy or contravention of an enactment. If the employer satisfies the tribunal that the reason is a permitted reason then the tribunal must determine whether the employer has acted reasonably in dismissing for that reason which is determined in accordance with equity and the substantial merits of the case.[3]

1 ERA, s 98(2).
2 See later for further consideration of this.
3 *Smith v Hayle Town Council* [1978] ICR 996, CA and see below where the concept of reasonableness is considered.

19.127 There are some reasons for dismissal which are not judged by the test of reasonableness. Thus, if it is established that the employee has been dismissed for trade union membership or activity this is an unfair dismissal. The same applies where the reason is the employee's non-membership and there are now no exceptions to this as the 'closed shop' or 'union membership agreement' protection is effectively abolished. Where the employee is dismissed for taking part in official industrial action then provided there is no selectivity the tribunal has no jurisdiction to determine whether the dismissal was unfair. Where the industrial action is unofficial there is no protection for employees whatsoever. Dismissal for carrying out the functions of an employee representative or candidate or of a pension trustee is also unfair.

19.128 Dismissals for pregnancy or childbirth are generally automatically unfair as are dismissals for 'spent' convictions and dismissals in breach of Part IV of the ERA. Dismissals for health and safety reasons and asserting a statutory right are also unfair automatically.[1]

1 ERA, ss 99, 100 and 101.

19.129 The employee may seek to show that the dismissal was for one of these reasons and the employer will then attempt to rebut this. The burden is always on the employer to show the reason but where the dismissal is for 'trade union' reasons and the employee does not have sufficient qualifying service to claim unfair dismissal then the burden will be on the employee to show that the dismissal was for a trade union reason.[1]

[1] This will apply to the new automatically unfair grounds referred to in note 1 in para 19.128 as it is the employee who is seeking the special protection.

Trade union reasons – membership and activities

19.130 It is an automatically unfair dismissal where the principal reason for the dismissal was that the employee: (a) was, or proposed to become a member of an independent trade union; (b) had taken part or proposed to take part, in the activities of an independent trade union at an appropriate time or (c) was not a member of any trade union or a particular trade union or one of a number of particular trade unions or had refused or proposed to refuse to join or remain in a trade union.[1]

[1] TULR(C)A 1992, s 152.

19.131 There is no qualifying period for claiming and the normal retirement age exclusion does not apply.[1]

[1] TULR(C)A 1992, s 154.

Membership

19.132 A proposal to join an independent union is enough even if the employee is unsure which one of several unions he wishes to join and past membership is covered.

19.133 It is only membership of 'independent' unions which is covered. This concept is defined to mean one not under the control or domination of the employer or a group of employers or of one or more employers' associations and is not liable to interference by any employer or any such group or association (arising out of the provision of financial or material support or by any means whatsoever) tending towards such control.[1] Trade unions usually obtain a certificate of independence from the Certification Officer but this is not an essential prerequisite. It is hardly likely that anyone would suggest that the TGWU was not independent. There is more of a problem with staff associations, particularly those recently established, which may well not have been weaned from the employer's influence and which may well depend financially on the employer. As the financial consequences of an unfair dismissal for union membership are quite severe the definition of 'independent' may well become more important in the future.

[1] TULR(C)A 1992, s 5.

19.134 The subsection does not refer to a right to join a particular trade union and in 1982 this position was confirmed.[1] However, the analogous provision relating to union membership rights where action short of dismissal is taken[2] has been interpreted[3] so that it would not be unlawful to discriminate against an employee for joining the union of his choice. In that case the employer had argued that provided an employee was free to join an independent trade union it did not matter if one particular union was discriminated against provided there was freedom to join another independent union and not be discriminated against. This argument was rejected. An employee was held to have the right to join a particular trade union and not be victimised for joining that particular union. The same conclusion it is submitted would obtain in relation to a dismissal.[4]

1 *Rath v Cruden Construction Ltd* [1982] ICR 60, EAT which would not be decided differently following legislative amendment in 1982.
2 See elsewhere for details, s 146 TULR(C)A 1992.
3 *National Coal Board v Ridgway* [1987] ICR 641, CA.
4 Ibid.

19.135 The concept of 'membership' is not very limited. Thus when a member asked her union official to clarify and negotiate her terms of employment and was dismissed very soon after this was held to be an important aspect of union membership and the consequences of union membership should fall within the statutory protection.[1] However, the House of Lords has recently held[2] that the *Armitage* case is not authority for the broad proposition that membership of the union and making use of its services are in some way to be equated. This can only lead to a widening of the distinction which is certainly not a purposive interpretation. However, the EAT has attempted to resurrect *Armitage* by suggesting that using the union's services can be equated to membership.[3]

1 *Discount Tobacco and Confectionery Ltd v Armitage* [1990] IRLR 15, EAT confirmed as being correct by the House of Lords in *Associated Newspapers Ltd v Wilson* [1995] IRLR 258, which said that invoking the union's assistance in relation to employment would be part of union membership.
2 In the *Wilson* case referred to in footnote 1.
3 See *Speciality Care plc v Pachela* [1996] IRLR 248 and para 13.31 above.

Union activities

19.136 It is an automatically unfair dismissal where the reason is the employee's participation or proposed participation in union activities.[1] The employee may be a union official and then there is much greater scope for activities. Representing members and discussing cases with them would be included as would be collecting subscriptions, recruiting and distributing union literature. Ordinary members will naturally have a narrower relevant range of activities[2] and these would include attendance at any union meeting or conference, voting and help in recruitment.[3] Taking part in industrial action has been held not to be union activities.[4] However, participating in the preliminary planning and organising of industrial action can amount to taking part in union activities.[5] It has been held that a shop steward's dismissal after he had made disparaging remarks about his employer at an induction course for trainee managers was for union activities and therefore unfair. The fact that he was part of the management team did not mean he was to be inhibited in his comments.[6]

1 What constitutes 'union activities' has already been discussed in more detail elsewhere in the book but a brief summary follows.

2 *Drew v St Edmundsbury Borough Council* [1980] IRLR 459, EAT.
3 Where union recruitment was carried out secretly and management claimed this was misconduct because of the conflict it had created and its secret nature the EAT held it was union activity. It said there should be proper protection in this situation – *Lyon v St James Press Ltd* [1976] ICR 413.
4 See *Drew*, above n 2.
5 *Britool Ltd v Roberts* [1993] IRLR 481.
6 *Bass Taverns Ltd v Burgess* [1995] IRLR 596.

19.137 However, the activities must be those of the union and not the activities of a union member acting independently. This very narrow distinction was highlighted in *Chant v Aquaboats Ltd*[1] where Chant was dismissed after organising and presenting a petition complaining about safety conditions. The union had approved the petition which had emanated from Chant. The employer claimed the reason for dismissal was the employee's poor work performance but the industrial tribunal found that the reason was that he had organised the petition. If the employee had worked for two years then it would have been unfair but lacking this period, he was unable to show he was dismissed for union activities. If the union had objected to the petition then this decision would be more understandable. As it stands it would appear that the petition would have to originate from the union to obtain protection. Nevertheless, an interview and a meeting of members in which the union was criticised for its attitude on equal pay were held to be union activities.[2] Yet when an employer dismissed employees as a direct result of the union's request for recognition this was held to be the action of the union and not of its individual members and the Court of Appeal refused to characterise this action against the union as action against individual members.[3] In the *Ridgway*[4] case discrimination on pay against the union was held to be action taken against union members but this case has recently been overruled and the House of Lords has held that it is permissible to pay individuals different amounts on the basis that one is prepared to forego the benefits of the collective bargaining procedure and accept a pay increase differential instead.[5] This case turned on the meaning of 'act and action'. They are defined[6] as including omissions but the Lords by a 3:2 majority surprisingly held that the withholding of a benefit to an employee which is conferred on another was not action taken against the employee. Their Lordships held 'action' was not apt to include an 'omission' the withholding of the benefit. They relied on both the grammar and the legislative history but it is suggested that their finding lacks industrial reality and common sense. On the facts it was also decided that there was insufficient evidence to establish the employer's purpose had been to deter the applicants from membership or to penalise them for it as opposed to deterring them from making use of certain services of the union or making membership of the union less attractive to them.

1 [1978] ICR 643, EAT.
2 *British Airways Engine Overhaul Ltd v Francis* [1981] IRLR 9, EAT.
3 *Carrington v Therm-A-Stor Ltd* [1983] ICR 208.
4 [1987] ICR 641.
5 *Associated Newspapers v Wilson* [1995] ICR 406.
6 See ERA, s 235(1).

Previous union activities

19.138 An employee cannot rely on union activities in a previous employment as constituting the reason for his dismissal by his current employer[1] but where it is apparent that the real reason for dismissal is the fear that these activities will be repeated in the present employment this is unlawful.[2] The Act does refer to 'proposed'[3] union activities as well as current ones. However, the Court of Appeal in *Fitzpatrick* makes it clear that the *Beyer* case is still valid on the basis that where the employee was dismissed for deceiving the employer when he applied for the job that is still a valid reason for dismissal. In the *Fitzpatrick* case the tribunal had found as a fact that the employer was concerned about the disruptive influence the employee might have and not with the fraudulent application. Nevertheless, it is open to a tribunal to conclude that an employee has been refused employment because of his union membership where an individual was refused employment because of his union activities.[4]

1 *City of Birmingham District Council v Beyer* [1977] IRLR 211, EAT.
2 *Fitzpatrick v British Railways Board* [1991] IRLR 376.
3 TULR(C)A 1992, s 152(1)(b).
4 *Harrison v Kent County Council* [1995] ICR 34.

19.139 This approach has been confirmed by the EAT in a recent case[1] where the selection of shop stewards for redundancy because they would engage in disruptive activities in the future was a dismissal on grounds of trade union activities. The employer's belief was based on their past activities and it was necessary to establish whether they were the activities of the union. They were and therefore the employer's belief in relation to their future activities related to trade union activities. When a tribunal held that it was irrelevant, in considering a claim that an employee had been dismissed for union activities, why he had not been selected for alternative employment it had misdirected itself. The tribunal had erroneously restricted the scope of its factual inquiry.[2]

1 *Port of London Authority v Payne* [1992] IRLR 447.
2 *Driver v Cleveland Structural Engineering Co Ltd* [1994] IRLR 636.

Appropriate time

19.140 To obtain special protection the union activities must take place at an appropriate time meaning outside working hours or inside them with the employer's consent or by arrangement with him.[1] Working hours means any time when the employee is required to be at work under his contract[2] but would not include breaks.[3] This would cover refreshment breaks but it is not clear whether it would include periods when the employee is strictly at work but has finished his shift. After working hours have been completed the employer would be expected to provide his premises for union meetings provided he was not seriously inconvenienced or put to expense. He must tolerate minor infringements of his property rights.[4]

1 See Chapter 13.
2 TULR(C)A 1992, s 152(2).
3 *Post Office v Union of Post Office Workers* [1974] ICR 378, HL.
4 Ibid.

19.141 During working hours it is necessary that the employer gives his consent but it has been held that consent can be implied in a proper case. It is more likely in a case where the union is recognised but it is by no means easy to establish.[1] It is permissible to talk to one's colleagues about union matters at work provided talking is generally permitted but this does not permit harassment of colleagues[2] or disruption of work. Evidence of a custom or practice allowing activities during work hours is important but all the circumstances of the case must be considered.[3]

1 See eg *Marley Tile Co Ltd v Shaw* [1980] IRLR 25, CA.
2 *Robb v Leon Motor Services Ltd* [1978] ICR 506, EAT.
3 See the *Marley Tile* case on this.

19.142 As the definition of 'appropriate time' refers to the employer who carried out the dismissal it is apparent that the provisions do not assist an employee who is relying on union activities in a previous employment. This was shown in *City of Birmingham District Council v Beyer*[1] where the employee was dismissed for giving a false name in a previous employment with the employer. He used a false name because he was a union activist and would not be able to obtain employment if he gave his real name. The EAT held that the reason for dismissal was the previous deceit which was not union activities but in any event these activities did not occur during this particular employment and could not be used by the employee.[2] However, the broader approach taken in the *Fitzpatrick* and *Payne* cases which deal with a concern as to future activities shows that an over-technical approach as to the meaning of 'appropriate time' is not being taken.[3]

1 [1977] IRLR 211.
2 See above.
3 See above.

Non-membership of a union

19.143 It is an automatically unfair dismissal when an employee is dismissed because he was not a member of any trade union or of a particular union or had refused or proposed to refuse to become or remain a member. This right of non-membership applies to any trade union, not just an independent one, as required with the right to membership. When an employee threatened to leave the union unless it changed some of its practices and was subsequently dismissed this was held to constitute a proposal to refuse to remain a member even though it was conditional. His employer's argument that the reason for dismissal was for dishonesty was rejected.[1]

1 *Crosville Motor Services Ltd v Ashfield* [1986] IRLR 475, EAT.

19.144 Until 1988 this right of non-membership was subject to statutory provision which rendered the dismissal fair where the employee had refused to join where there was a union membership agreement or closed shop. There was a substantial list of exceptions to this but all these provisions have now been repealed and the union membership agreement has been deprived of protection. Where there is a dispute as to the reason for dismissal the employer will seek to establish another reason for dismissal because he will no longer be able to use the union membership agreement as a defence. There will be struggles over this because of the high levels of compensation.[1]

1 See below.

Third party pressure

19.145 Where pressure has been exerted on an employer to dismiss an employee by means of industrial action, or threats of it, it is not permissible to take account of this factor in determining the reason for dismissal and whether it was reasonable to dismiss.[1] Thus, the fact that disruption may be caused at the workplace by the dissension between members of a union and any non-members is no justification for the employer to dismiss even though it might be in a non-union dispute situation.[2] However, in a non-union dispute situation it is unlikely to escalate into industrial action or threats of industrial action.

1 ERA, s 107.
2 See below 'some other substantial reason'.

19.146 Where pressure is exerted it is not necessary for those exerting pressure to aim specifically at one employee. It is enough that it could be foreseen that it would be likely to result in the dismissal of these employees in respect of whom the pressure was being brought.[1]

1 *Ford Motor Co Ltd v Hudson* [1978] IRLR 66, EAT.

Burden of proof

19.147 Where the employee has less than two years' service he has to establish that the reason for the dismissal is a trade union reason. This means that the onus is on him to establish this reason as he is seeking to overcome the normal disqualification. We have already noted the case of *Chant v Aquaboats Ltd*[1] where the employer's reason for dismissal was rejected but the employee was unable to show that the organising of a petition was a trade union activity and therefore could not succeed.[2]

1 [1978] ICR 643, EAT.
2 *See also Therm-A-Stor v Atkins*, above.

19.148 A number of cases have raised this issue, and the courts have not always been as searching as in some of the discrimination cases in seeking to establish the true cause of dismissal. Thus, in *Smith v Hayle Town Council*,[1] where a senior executive alleged he had been dismissed for his membership of NALGO, by a 2–1 majority the Court of Appeal held that union membership was not the reason for dismissal even though it had been referred to at his dismissal meeting. Had this been a race or sex discrimination case it is suggested that at the very least an inference would have been drawn for the employer to rebut. That was the approach of the dissenting judge Denning MR. It has also been held that tribunals should always hear evidence from the employer even where the employee's case appears weak.[2] There may be considerable evidence to hear in relation to the circumstances surrounding the dismissal. The test is to establish the state of mind of the employer to determine the reason for dismissal, it is not the right approach to simply say that the applicant would not have been dismissed if he had not been a union member.[3]

[1] [1978] ICR 996.
[2] *Goodwin Ltd v Fitzmaurice* [1977] IRLR 393.
[3] *CGB Publishing v Killey* [1993] IRLR 520, EAT.

19.149 Where the employee has two years' service the normal rules apply so that the employer must establish the reason for dismissal because the burden remains on him. Where he puts forward another reason it is for the employee to rebut this reason and it is a matter for the tribunal to decide.[1] If it rejects the employer's reason then the case must succeed.

[1] *Shannon v Michelin (Belfast) Ltd* [1981] IRLR 505, CA and *Maund v Penwith District Council* [1984] ICR 143, CA.

Refusal to make payments

19.150 Where the reason, or one of the reasons, for the dismissal was:

(a) the employee's refusal or proposed refusal to comply with a requirement, whether or not in the contract or in writing, that if he does not join a union, or a particular union, he must make a payment or payments; or
(b) his objection, or proposed objection (however expressed), to the operation of a provision (whether or not in his contract or in writing) under which if he does not join a union or a particular union his employer is entitled to deduct one or more sums from his remuneration;

then the reason is treated as a non-membership reason[1] and the dismissal is accordingly unfair.[2]

References to a trade union include references to a branch or section of the union.[3]

[1] TULR(C)A, s 152(1)(c).
[2] TULR(C)A, s 152(3).
[3] TULR(C)A, s 152(4).

Compensation and contributory fault

19.151 The remedies available to an employee dismissed for trade union reasons are considered below[1] but there are allied matters which are considered more appropriate to deal with at this stage. Wherever compensation is awarded the tribunal must consider whether the applicant has caused or contributed to the dismissal and, if he has, reduce compensation accordingly. Under the Act[2] the tribunal must disregard any conduct or action insofar as it constitutes a breach or proposed breach of a requirement whether in the contract or whether or not in writing:

(a) to be or become a member of any trade union or of a particular trade union;
(b) to cease to be, or refrain from becoming, a member of any trade union or of a particular trade union; or

(c) not to take part in the activities of any trade union or of a particular trade union.

The tribunal must also disregard the employee's refusal to make any payment in lieu of membership or allow a deduction instead of membership.

[1] See para 19.540 ff, below.
[2] TULR(C)A, s 155.

19.152 These provisions appear to be clear but nevertheless they have been considered by the EAT.[1] The employee was a secretary at the employer's regional office and she resigned from the TGWU, joining APEX. Her dismissal was held to be automatically unfair as it was because she refused to remain a member of the TGWU. A 20% reduction would have been appropriate, according to the tribunal, because her conduct in resigning without seeking prior discussion was 'confrontational and if not bloody minded was certainly unreasonable'. However, the tribunal said that the statute precluded any reduction whatsoever. The EAT reversed this, saying that contributory fault can be found in such a case and a distinction has to be drawn between what is done by the employee and the way in which it is done. If the employee's conduct prior to dismissal deserves criticism then a reduction can be made.[2]

[1] *Transport and General Workers' Union v Howard* [1992] IRLR 170.
[2] The case was remitted to determine what was the appropriate figure as the employee never dealt with these questions.

Interim relief

19.153 There is a special procedure which applies when the employee alleges that the dismissal was for trade union membership or activities, or non-union membership.[1] He can apply for an order that he be re-employed or at least paid his full wages until the case is finally determined so that the contract continues. The employee must comply with a strict application procedure to seek interim relief.

[1] TULR(C)A, ss 161–167.

19.154 The application must be presented within seven days from the effective date of termination[1] with a request for interim relief. The application should state that dismissal was for union membership or activities and that interim relief is being sought but it has been held that there is no need to provide details.[2] Indeed, the Act does not require them.

[1] See earlier in this chapter for the meaning of this.
[2] See *Barley v Amey Roadstone Corpn Ltd* [1977] ICR 546, EAT where a letter mentioning unfair dismissal and interim relief was held sufficient.

19.155 Except where the case is one of non-membership and within the same seven day period the applicant must present a certificate signed personally by an authorised official of the union stating that at the date of the dismissal the employee was, or had proposed to become, a member of the union and that there appear to be reasonable grounds for supposing that the reason for his dismissal was in relation to union reasons.[1]

[1] TULR(C)A, s 161(3).

19.156 An 'authorised official' means an official of the union authorised by the union to act for interim relief purposes[1] and a document purporting to be an authorisation of an official by a union to act for the purposes of the section and to be signed on behalf of the union shall be taken to be such an authorisation unless the contrary is proved.[2] Thus, where there is a signature it will be presumed valid but if it is challenged by the employer the union will have to produce the evidence of authorisation. Authority can be shown by some written special or general authorisation or by reference to the union rule-book. Implied authority might be possible but it is not usually sufficient to rely upon.[3]

[1] TULR(C)A, s 161(4).
[2] TULR(C)A, s 161(5).
[3] *Farmeary v Veterinary Drug Co Ltd* [1976] IRLR 322.

19.157 There is no provision permitting late application and certificates but in *Barley v Amey*[1] the court allowed the claim to proceed where the certificate had arrived late but the application had been presented in time. There are a number of technicalities in relation to the certificate but usually, provided there is substantial compliance with the requirements, it will be sufficient.[2] However, there are a number of cases which do not adopt such a tolerant attitude and therefore unions should not make mistakes. The official should certainly have considered the grounds for supposing that the individual has been dismissed for union reasons and state his reasons. It would not be sufficient to state that the dismissal was for union reasons.

[1] See above.
[2] *Bradley v Edward Ryde & Sons* [1979] ICR 488, EAT.

19.158 The application is then served on the employer who is given at least seven days' notice of the hearing which should take place as soon as practicable and should not be adjourned except in special circumstances.

19.159 Interim relief can be granted where the tribunal considers that the complaint is likely to succeed at the full hearing. The correct approach is to ask if the employee has established a 'pretty good' chance of succeeding at the full hearing. A real possibility of succeeding is insufficient.[1] The same questions that are relevant in determining whether there are union grounds for dismissal apply to interim relief proceedings but the employer faces greater difficulty because of the standard of proof required.

[1] *Taplin v Shippam Ltd* [1978] IRLR 450, EAT.

19.160 Where the complaint succeeds the tribunal must explain to the parties, if they are there, what powers it has and must ask the employer if he is willing to reinstate the employee, or, if not, re-engage him.[1] Reinstatement means putting the employee back in his former job with full back pay. Re-engagement means in another job on terms and conditions which must be specified. If the employee agrees to re-engagement then the tribunal makes a re-engagement order. If he refuses and it is a reasonable refusal a continuation of contract order[2] is made but if it is unreasonable no interim relief will be given.

1 These terms will be fully explained later in this chapter.
2 See below in this chapter.

19.161 If the employer refused to reinstate or re-engage or does not attend the hearing the tribunal makes a continuation order.[1] This means that the contract continues until the determination or settlement of the complaint and the employee receives his full pay, back pay, and receives all benefits he could have received had he been working. Whatever order the tribunal makes either the employer or employee may apply to it for the revocation or variation of the order because of the relevant change in circumstances.[2]

1 TULR(C)A, s 163(1).
2 TULR(C)A, s 165(1).

19.162 Where the employer does not comply with a reinstatement or re-engagement order the continuation order will be made together with an order for compensation as the tribunal considers just and equitable having regard to the infringement of the employee's rights, and to any loss he has suffered.[1]

1 TULR(C)A, s 166(1).

19.163 Where the employer does not comply with the terms of a continuation order then the tribunal must determine the amount of pay owed by the employer and compensation will be awarded in the usual way where the unfair dismissal case is heard on the same day. If not, compensation as is just and equitable having regard to the loss suffered by the employee is awarded.[1]

1 TULR(C)A, s 166(3)–(5).

19.164 The interim relief lasts until the substantive hearing but where there is an appeal against that decision the relief lasts until the appeal is dispensed with in the absence of an express revocation of the order at the tribunal hearing.[1]

1 *Zucker v Astrid Jewels Ltd* [1978] IRLR 385, EAT.

19.165 Where it is alleged that the employer was induced to dismiss the employee by pressure of industrial action or the threat of it and this pressure was exercised because the employee was not a member of any trade union, or particular union, or of one of a number of unions, then either the employee or the employer may request the tribunal to join the person or union which exercised the pressure as a party to the proceedings.[1] Before the hearing began the tribunal must grant the request but afterwards it has a discretion. After the remedy is granted joinder will not be permitted. Where the joinder takes place at the interim relief stage at least three days' notice must be given.[2] The tribunal, when awarding compensation can apportion it between the two parties and can award the total amount to be paid by one party.

1 Section 160(1).
2 Section 162(3).

19.165A Employee representatives or candidates in relation to collective redundancies and transfers of undertaking are unfairly dismissed if the reason for the dismissal relates to the performance or proposed performance of their functions.[1] The same protection applies to trustees of occupational pension schemes.[2]

1 ERA, s 103.
2 ERA, s 102.

Dismissal for pregnancy

General provisions

19.166 Following the adoption of the EEC Directive in October 1992 on the protection of pregnant women, legislation was introduced to implement the Directive. The Trade Union Reform and Employment Rights Act 1993 made very wide-ranging changes to the law on pregnancy dismissals. The section on pregnancy is rewritten. There is now an unfair dismissal if:[1]

(a) the reason or principal reason for the dismissal is that she is pregnant or any other reason connected with her pregnancy;
(b) her maternity leave period[2] is ended by the dismissal and the reason or principal reason for her dismissal is that she has given birth to a child or any other reason connected with her giving birth to a child;
(c) the reason or principal reason for her dismissal where her contract was terminated after the end of her maternity leave period is that she took or availed herself of the benefits of maternity leave;
(d) the reason or principal reason for her dismissal where:
  (i) before the end of her maternity leave period she gave her employer a certificate from a registered medical practitioner stating that by reason of disease or bodily or mental disablement she would be incapable of work after the end of that period; and
  (ii) her contract of employment was terminated within the four-week period following the end of her maternity leave period in circumstances where she continued to be incapable of work and the certificate relating to her incapability remained current

  is that she has given birth to a child or any other reason connected with her having given birth to a child;
(e) the reason or principal reason for the dismissal is a requirement or recommendation such as is referred to in ERA, s 66(1);[3] or
(f) her maternity leave period is ended by the dismissal and the reason or principal reason is that she is redundant and she has not been offered a suitable available vacancy.[4]

1 See s 94.
2 See Chapter 10 on maternity.
3 Suspension for health and safety reasons.
4 This is required by s 77.

19.167 A woman takes maternity leave if she is absent from work during her maternity leave period and she avails herself of the benefits of maternity leave if during that period she avails herself of the benefit of any of the terms and conditions of her employment preserved by ERA, s 71 during that period.[1]

[1] ERA, s 99 and see Chapter 10 on maternity rights.

19.168 It is further provided that where there is a redundancy dismissal and the selection was based on any of the grounds stated above, then that is an inadmissible reason and becomes automatically unfair. This statutory provision essentially enacts the previous House of Lords decision.[2]

[1] ERA, s 99.
[2] *Stockton-on-Tees Borough Council v Brown* [1988] ICR 410.

19.169 It is further provided[1] that an employee dismissed while pregnant or after childbirth where the maternity leave period ended by reason of the dismissal is entitled to a statement of written reasons for her dismissal without making any request. If she is dismissed when she is pregnant or after childbirth when her maternity leave period ends by reason of dismissal there is no qualifying period.[2]

[1] ERA, s 92(4).
[2] ERA, s 109(2).

19.170 The maternity leave period commences on the first day upon which the employee is absent from work because of pregnancy or childbirth but where that day is before the beginning of the eleventh week before the expected week of childbirth, maternity leave commences on the first day of which she is so absent after the beginning of that week. However, where childbirth occurs before the day her maternity leave period would otherwise commence, her leave period commences with the day upon which childbirth occurs. It lasts for 14 weeks unless there is some statutory prohibition on her being employed because of the recent birth in which case it continues until the expiry of the period in which she is so prohibited. If she is dismissed before her leave period would end, then it is deemed to end as at the date of dismissal.[1]

[1] See ERA, ss 71, 78, 92, 93, 99(1)–(3) and 108–109.

19.171 Where during her maternity leave period her contract ends through redundancy, she is entitled where there is a suitable vacancy to be offered immediate alternative employment with her employer or successor or an associated employer under a contract which provides work of a kind which is both suitable and appropriate for her, in the circumstances and where the terms and conditions are not substantially less favourable to her, including the capacity and place in which she is to be employed.[1]

[1] ERA, s 77.

Health and safety reasons

19.172 The requirements relating to health and safety referred to above[1] are those imposed by or under any enactment or any relevant provision of a code of practice issued or approved under s 16 of the Health and Safety at Work etc Act 1974.[2] Now it will become automatically unfair to dismiss for such health and safety reasons without any qualifying period. This causes serious doubt to be shed on the decision that it was not unlawful to dismiss a pregnant woman because of her fear for her own and her baby's safety.[3]

[1] ERA, s 99(1)(d).
[2] ERA, s 66.
[3] *Hopkins v Shepherd & Partners* [1994] ICR 39, EAT.

General

19.173 Some of the existing case law will be relevant to the new provisions. The Act provides that the dismissal will be unfair where the reason or principal reason is the pregnancy or any other reason connected with her pregnancy. Thus, if the employer is unaware of the pregnancy any dismissal cannot be unfair on this ground. The reason must be connected with the pregnancy and therefore if there is some reason such as a reorganisation as a result of the pregnancy which leads to the dismissal this would automatically be unfair. However, where there was a genuine reorganisation which led to the employee's dismissal whilst she was pregnant or on maternity leave, then this could still be protected action by the employer. However, it would be scrutinised carefully by the tribunal.

19.174 The fact that an employee is incapable of carrying out her job as a result of her pregnancy will no longer be a defence to an employer.

Burden of proof

19.175 The section is silent on this question and thus the tribunal must decide the question without any assistance on this. A dismissal for pregnancy will always be open to allegations of sex discrimination.[1] If the employer seeks to establish that there is another reason for dismissal the burden is on him to show this was the reason.

[1] See Chapter 24.

Pregnancy and pregnancy-connected reason

19.176 In accordance with the usual rules determining the employer's reason for dismissal, this is judged by what the employer knew at the time of the dismissal. Thus if he was unaware that the employee was pregnant at that time it cannot be a pregnancy dismissal. Accordingly when an employee had been warned on a number of occasions regarding her absences due to gastro-enteritis and was eventually dismissed this was not a pregnancy dismissal because the employer did not know or believe her to be pregnant.[1] This was a rather exceptional case because the employee was able to inform her employer that she was pregnant one day after the decision was made, but the employer still went ahead with the dismissal which had already been notified.

1 *Del Monte Foods Ltd v Mundon* [1980] ICR 694, EAT.

19.177 The corollary of this is that if the employer knew she was pregnant then dismissal for absences due to pregnancy are very likely to be treated as automatically unfair. In one case[1] an employee had received two written warnings about her sickness absence and a final warning for going to hospital for a gynaecological operation. She later told her manager that she was pregnant but had a miscarriage and was then dismissed. This was held to be a dismissal for the miscarriage which was a reason connected with her pregnancy and was an automatically unfair dismissal. However, if the absences are genuinely not connected with the pregnancy, the employer might be able to avoid the automatically unfair dismissal finding. If an employer dismisses an employee on maternity leave because he cannot obtain a temporary replacement but only a permanent one this is a dismissal connected with the pregnancy and automatically unfair. A wide view has to be taken and the background to the employer's decision was the employee's pregnancy.[2] Where the illness extends beyond the MLP then there is a four week period of absolute protection. It will be interesting to see how tribunals deal with absences beyond the four weeks. If the reason could be construed as connected to the taking of maternity leave then it will remain automatically unfair but if not then it does not fall within ERA, s 94 and the employee will have to fall back on ordinary dismissal rules and will need two years' service.

1 *George v Beecham Group* [1977] IRLR 43, IT.
2 *Clayton v Vigers* [1990] IRLR 177, EAT.

Dismissal of replacement

19.178 Where an employer engages an employee to replace an employee absent because of pregnancy or confinement and he informs the replacement in writing that her employment will be terminated when the other resumes, this is treated as a substantial reason for dismissal, although it is still subject to the test of reasonableness.[1] As the qualifying period for claiming unfair dismissal is now two years there is no relevance to this section in the present context. However, if the qualifying period were to be reduced to six months then it could once again be relevant.

1 ERA, s 99(2).

Refusal to allow a return to work

19.179 This matter has already been discussed[1] but at this juncture it is worthwhile reiterating that failure to permit a woman to return after extended maternity absence (2 years) is treated as a dismissal[2] with certain exceptions.[3] The notified date of return[4] being the effective date of termination. If the reason for dismissal falls outside ERA, s 94, which is quite likely then the ordinary rules apply with one modification to the standard reasonableness test.[5] The tribunal must determine the question as to reasonableness as if the employee had not been absent from work.

[1] See above and also chapter on Maternity Rights.
[2] ERA, s 91(1).
[3] ERA, s 91(2) to (5).
[4] See above.
[5] See below.

19.180 We have already noted[1] the strict approach taken when there is a failure to comply with the notice requirements.[2] You know the employee cannot use s 91(1). She cannot utilise the ordinary dismissal provision under s 90 unless the contract is continuing and she is relying on an agreement[3] or is dismissed during her maternity leave absence but not in the course of attempting to use the statutory procedures.[4]

[1] See Chapter on Maternity Rights.
[2] *Lavery v Plessey Communications* [1982] ICR 373, EAT and *Dowuona v John Lewis plc* [1987] ICR 788, CA.
[3] *Lucas v Norton of London Ltd* [1984] IRLR 86, EAT.
[4] *Hilton International Hotels (UK) Ltd v Kaissi* [1994] IRLR 270, EAT.

19.181 Where pregnancy is found to be the reason for dismissal then, as we have noted it is automatically unfair dismissal. It will, however, also be an act of sex discrimination. While there are limits to compensation for unfair dismissal[1] there are now no such limits for sex discrimination[2] and claims will obviously be made concurrently.[3]

[1] See below.
[2] See separate chapter on Discrimination.
[3] See for example *Ministry of Defence v Cannock* [1994] IRLR 509, EAT.

Transfer of undertaking

19.182 The Transfer of Undertakings Regulations 1981 have a considerable impact on the law relating to unfair dismissal. The regulations and their impact on dismissal have been considered elsewhere[1] and, accordingly, will only be mentioned very briefly here.

[1] See above, Chapter 8.

19.183 Regulation 8 provides that either before or after a relevant transfer any employee of the transferor or transferee shall be treated as unfairly dismissed if the transfer or a reason connected with it is the reason or the principal reason for the dismissal. This very wide-sweeping provision is immediately qualified because the regulations then provide that where an economic, technical or organisational reason entailing changes in the workforce of either the transferor or the transferee is the reason, or principal reason, for dismissing an employee, then the above provision is not to apply and the dismissal shall be treated as being for a substantial reason[1] which could justify the dismissal. However, it is still subject to the test of reasonableness. The action is against the transferee and the transferor is not jointly liable.[2] There is no obligation on the employee to transfer but if he refuses then there is no deemed dismissal by the transferor.[3]

1 Within ERA, s 93(1)(b).
2 *Stirling District Council v Allan* [1995] IRLR 301.
3 Regulation 5(4B).

19.184 These two provisions appear to be completely contradictory and the cases appear to indicate that this is the position. There is a very real need to establish a clear definition of the words 'economic, technical or organisational'. The conflict is obvious as a purchaser of a business may well wish to reduce staff to save costs. Without the benefit of legal analysis one can see how it is easy to see that this could be classified as an economic reason, but could also be a dismissal effected as a result of the transfer.[1] You cannot change terms and conditions of a workforce and claim the benefit of the regulations because this is not 'entailing changes in the workforce' but changes in the terms and conditions.[2] You can, however, have a change in the workforce if the same people are kept on but they are given entirely different jobs to do.[3]

1 See *Litster v Forth Dry Dock* [1989] ICR 341, HL, which very much establishes priority to the transfer-connected reason and also makes clear that the time of the dismissal is not the vital criterion. Chapter 8 contains a detailed analysis. However, this is a developing area on which see Chapter 8 for a fuller analysis.
2 *Delabole Slate (Ltd) v Berriman* [1985] IRLR 305, CA. See further Chapter 8.
3 *Crawford v Swinton Insurance Brokers Ltd* [1990] IRLR 42, EAT.

Compensation

19.185 There are, at the time of writing, TUPE published proposals to amend the Acquired Rights Directive which amendments may lead to a new directive in 1996. This is relevant in this context insofar as the scope of the directive is now wider than many people envisage which has created greater thought about the narrowness of the 'ETO' reason for dismissal. The directive is amended to reduce its scope. This might lead to less criticism of this ETO reason and less grounds to alter it. It is clear that it is in direct conflict with the main thrust of the directive which is to protect employees when a transfer occurs. A strong attempt was made to challenge the ETO defence on this basis by arguing that the defence was, effectively in breach of the directive. The EAT[1] rejected the argument so it is clear that the ETO defence can apply even where the transfer is the reason for this dismissal. Where there is a re-organisation which leads to the replacement of employees with different qualifications from the original employees, this can fall within the defence. The supply of paediatric and neonatal services were transferred from two different health authorities to an NHS Trust, a transfer under the transfer regulations. The consultant paedatricians were made redundant but four were appointed in their place who had different specialisms. This was held to be an ETO defence being a re-organisation.[2] However, the EAT has held that there should be a restricted interpretation of the Defence otherwise it will destroy the main protection given by the directive and regulations.[3] This area of the law is in need of some clarification!

1 *Trafford v Sharpe & Fisher (Building Supplies) Ltd* [1994] IRLR 325.
2 *Porter v Queen's Medical Centre* [1993] IRLR 486.

[3] *Wheeler v Patel* [1987] ICR 631 supported by *Gateway Hotels Ltd v Stewart* (1988) IRLR 287. Note also *Ibex Trading Co Ltd v Walton* [1994] IRLR 564.

Automatically unfair redundancy

General introduction

19.186 Employees who are dismissed for redundancy will, in almost all cases,[1] receive a redundancy payment but in addition they may be able to claim that they have been unfairly dismissed. There are certain principles or guidelines which should be followed in redundancy dismissals and which if not followed, may lead to a finding of unfair dismissal.[2] This would be based on the grounds of reasonableness[3] but there are also special situations which may lead to a finding of automatically unfair dismissal without the question of reasonableness being considered.[4]

[1] There are certain exclusions—see Chapter 20 on redundancy.
[2] These will be considered below.
[3] Under s 93(4) and (6).
[4] There are some minor amendments to this provision contained in Sch 7 of TURERA 1993.

19.187 Thus where the employee has been dismissed for redundancy but it is shown that the circumstances which constituted the redundancy applied equally to one or more other employees in the same undertaking who held positions similar to that held by him and who have not been dismissed and the reason or principal reason for his selection was an inadmissible reason then the dismissal is unfair.[1] 'Inadmissible'[2] means a dismissal in relation to health and safety matters,[3] pregnancy or maternity,[4] or assertion of a statutory right.[5] It is further provided[6] that where the reason relates to union membership or activities,[7] this is an unfair dismissal. A selection based on the employer's view that an employee is spending too much time on union duties falls within this category although there can be contributory fault in this case.[8]

[1] Section 98.
[2] ERA, s 98(2), (3) and (5).
[3] ERA, s 95.
[4] ERA, s 94(1) to (3).
[5] ERA, s 97.
[6] TULR(C)A 1992, s 153.
[7] Ibid, s 152.
[8] *Dundon v GPT Ltd* [1995] IRLR 403.

Redundant

19.188 The definition of redundancy[1] is dealt with elsewhere[2] – it is a technical definition but is understood in general terms to cover a closure of a business or a part of it and, of more relevance here, also where there is a reduction in the need for employees to carry out work of a particular kind. In this context it is for the employer to show that there is a redundancy situation and this was the reason for dismissal. This also covers closure of a particular place of business or a changing need in a particular place. There are interesting developments in relation to the contractual text.[3]

[1] ERA, s 132(1), (2).
[2] See Chapter 20.
[3] See *Johnson v Peabody Trust* (1996) IRLR 387.

Same undertaking

19.189 Somewhat surprisingly the legislation does not define 'undertaking'[1] which leaves the tribunals and courts to adopt a pragmatic attitude to the question. There have been very few cases which have considered this point. In perhaps the leading authority, albeit in a different context[2] it was stated that where there are separate activities it is not enough to show that these activities are similar and that the persons are connected. 'One would expect some evidence of organisational unity, for example common accounting, management purchasing arrangements, insurance and so on.'[3] 'Undertaking' is not necessarily synonymous with departments.[4] Where there were two factories close to each other with the same works manager, with flexibility of labour between them and producing the same goods, it was held that this was an undertaking.[5]

[1] The word 'establishment' is not defined in the consultation on redundancies procedure TULR(C)A 1992, s 188 or in TUPE Regulations 1981, reg 10.
[2] Of a provision now repealed.
[3] Per Phillips J in *Kapur v Shields* [1976] ICR 26.
[4] *Heathcote v North Western Electricity Board* [1974] IRLR 34.
[5] *Oxley v Tarmac Roadstone Holdings* [1975] IRLR 100.

Employees holding similar positions

19.190 'Position' is defined in the Act[1] and means 'the following matters taken as a whole: his status as an employee, the nature of his work and his terms and conditions of employment'. This requires a consideration of the department in which the redundancy situation has arisen, or of the category or description of jobs affected.[2] The more general, and the less skilled, the work, the more likely it is that the employees will be treated as holding similar positions. If an employee does highly specialised work then he will not hold a similar position to others doing less specialised work even though they may have similar job titles.[3] In considering 'position' where the dismissal selection is based on trade union reasons it is not permissible to treat a shop steward as occupying a special position simply because he is carrying out union activities.[4]

[1] By ERA, s 228(1).
[2] *Gargrave v Hotel and Catering Industry Training Board* [1974] IRLR 85, NIRC.
[3] *Simpson v Roneo* [1972] IRLR 5.
[4] *O'Dea v ISC Chemicals Ltd* (1995) IRLR 599.

19.191 Where employees often transfer freely from one department or unit to another then it is much more likely that they hold similar positions but this is not established simply because one employee can perform a colleague's job.[1] Flexibility must operate both ways.[2]

[1] *Dorrell and Ardis v Engineering Developments (Farnborough) Ltd* [1975] IRLR 234.
[2] *Powers v A Clarke & Co (Smethwick) Ltd* [1981] IRLR 483.

19.192 The inadmissible reasons are all discussed elsewhere in the text and need not be repeated here. It is worth noting that the provisions rendering a dismissal unfair when there was a selection in contravention of a customary arrangement or agreed procedure were repealed at the end of 1994.[1]

[1] Deregulation and Contracting Out Act 1994, s 360.

19.193 It is automatically unfair to select an employee for redundancy where there are other employees holding similar positions and the reason for selection related to the rights of the worker in relation to Sunday trading.[1]

[1] ERA, s 96.

Rehabilitation of Offenders Act 1974

19.194 In an attempt to help ex-prisoners shake off the stigma of past convictions and to obtain employment the 1974 Act entitles an employee to treat a 'spent' conviction as a non-event – in that he is not obliged to disclose it to an employer. When he is being recruited and is asked questions regarding previous convictions he is entitled to disregard any 'spent' convictions and the employee is not to be subjected to any liability or otherwise prejudiced in law by reason of any failure to acknowledge or disclose a spent conviction.[1] More specifically, it is provided that such failure to disclose shall not be a proper ground for dismissing or excluding a person from any office, profession, occupation or employment.[2]

[1] RHA 1974, s 4(2).
[2] Ibid, s 4(3)(b).

19.195 A conviction becomes 'spent' only after a certain period of time and any sentence which exceeds 30 months cannot become spent. Accordingly, for major offences the Act will not assist employees. There is a sliding scale for the periods of time for the conviction to become spent from six months for an absolute discharge, to seven years for a period in borstal, up to ten years where there is a sentence of six months to two-and-a-half years.

19.196 Furthermore, the Act provides[1] that the Secretary of State may by order make provision to exclude or modify the above requirements and make general exceptions. Certain professions and occupations have been excluded such as solicitors, barristers, teachers and social workers.[2] The Secretary of State can of course add to this list. The list relates to occupations where it is perceived that the general public interest overrides the individual's rights to be rehabilitated. The employer cannot decide that certain employments that he is involved with should be excluded.[3] In one case security guards were dismissed following the discovery of minor spent convictions and the dismissals were unfair.[4] If there has been a failure to disclose a conviction which is not spent the employer can dismiss because the confidence between employer and employee will have been dissipated by the employee's concealment.[5] This does not mean that an employee must disclose of his own accord – it means that he must not lie in response to a question. The only problem that arises here is how big this gap between recruitment and discovery can be. In *Torr* it was 16 months but in theory it could be longer.

1 RHA 1974, s 4(3)(b).

2 This exception applies to administrative positions.

3 *Property Guards Ltd v Taylor and Kershaw* [1982] IRLR 175, EAT.

4 It was not clear if the basis for dismissal was that the employer had not shown a valid reason or had not acted reasonably.

5 *Torr v British Railways Board* [1977] IRLR 184, EAT.

National security

19.197 Where a minister signs a certificate that dismissal was for the purpose of safeguarding national security then this is conclusive proof that the dismissal falls within the category.[1] This is a wide power but it is believed that it is sparingly used. However, in the famous GCHQ case a certificate was provided under what is now ERA, s 186 by the Minister certifying that employment of a certain description was required to be excepted from statutory protection for the purpose of safeguarding national security. A direction was given under the Civil Service Order in Council 1982 to amend the terms of employment so as to exclude a right to trade union membership. The House of Lords held, inter alia, that a mere assertion that questions of national security were involved was not enough. The government would have to produce evidence that the decision was based on grounds of national security – here there was evidence that the Prime Minister reasonably believed that prior consultation might result in disruption at GCHQ that would pose a threat to national security.[2]

1 Industrial Tribunals Act 1996, s 10.

2 *R v Secretary of State for Foreign and Commonwealth Affairs, ex p Council of Civil Service Unions* [1985] IRLR 28, HL.

Dismissal and assertion of statutory rights

19.198 Since TURERA 1993 where an employee has been dismissed because he brought proceedings against his employer to enforce a statutory employment protection right or alleges that there has been an infringement of such right then this dismissal becomes automatically unfair.[1] The same applies to the selection of an employee for redundancy on this ground. The right to claim applies irrespective of the length of service or hours of work or indeed age and applies to all rights conferred by the ERA which can be taken to an industrial tribunal, the right to the statutory minimum period of notice, and individual rights under the Trade Union and Labour Relations (Consolidation) Act 1992 which cover deductions from pay, union activities and time off. It has been extended to cover all rights of employees in relation to Sunday trading. The employee need not specify the right provided he made it reasonably clear to the employer what the right claimed to have been infringed was. Furthermore, like the anti-discrimination victimisation provisions, it is immaterial whether the employee has the right or not and whether it has been infringed or not but the claim to the right and of its infringement must have been made in good faith. This provision may have quite an impact on some employers' treatment of employees making claims for such rights. A claim for one or two weeks' wages is one thing, but a claim for unfair dismissal compensation is another thing altogether.[2] It has been held that dismissal for a refusal to give consent to a new contract which would infringe the Wages Act falls within the provision. It is not necessary for the right to be actually infringed.[3]

1 ERA, s 98(2), (3) and (5).
2 ERA, s 97.
3 *Mennell v Newell and Wright (Transport Contractors Ltd)* (1996) IRLR 384.

Dismissal and industrial action

General introduction

19.199 There is often mention of an employee's right to strike. There is no such right in the UK – obviously there is no constitutional right and the law has never provided a remedy to dismissed strikers. At common law they were and still are, in fundamental breach of contract in failing to be ready, able and willing to work and the statutory law of unfair dismissal continues in this vein. Provided the employer does not selectively dismiss only some of those who take part in industrial action the tribunal is deprived of jurisdiction. This provision even extends to the situation where the employer has locked-out his employees. As we shall see the merits of the dispute are irrelevant as all that has to be established is that there is some form of industrial action. Where there is a selective dismissal or re-engagement this does not mean that there is an unfair dismissal but the tribunal at least has jurisdiction to hear the case. The matter is then determined under the test of reasonableness, and the employer will usually claim that the employee's action was misconduct. If the action taken is unofficial, which means that it is not authorised or endorsed by the union, there is no right whatsoever to complain of unfair dismissal even if there are selective dismissals.[1]

1 For a general treatment of the topic see also *Harvey* Div D, part 13.

19.200 The Act provides that where at the date of the dismissal the employer was conducting or instituting a lock-out or the complainant was taking part in a strike or other industrial action then the tribunal cannot determine the issue of unfair dismissal unless a 'relevant employee' has not been dismissed or has been offered re-engagement within three months of the ending of his employment and the complainant has not been offered re-engagement.[1] Where the complaint relates to a failure to re-engage the provisions of the Act substitute the employer's reason for not offering re-engagement as the reason for dismissal. Where an employee is dismissed and the reason or principal reason for dismissal or selection for redundancy relates to the new health and safety rights[2] or maternity rights[3] these provisions do not apply.[4] This applies equally to unofficial industrial action.[5]

[1] TULR(C)A 1992, s 238.
[2] See below.
[3] See above.
[4] Section 237(1A).
[5] TULR(C)A, s 238(2A).

19.201 The date of dismissal is defined as the effective date of termination[1] except in the situation where the employer has terminated by notice when it is the date on which the notice was *given*.[2]

[1] ERA, s 92(1).
[2] TULR(C)A, s 238(5).

19.202 'Relevant employees' means, where there is a lock-out,[1] employees who were directly interested in the dispute and where there is a strike or other industrial action means those employees at the establishment who were taking part in the action at the complainant's date of dismissal.[2] The reference to 'establishment' is the one from which the employer works.

[1] TULR(C)A, s 238(3)(a).
[2] TULR(C)A, s 238(3)(b).

19.203 Finally, when considering re-engagement offers, this can include offers made by a successor to the original employer or an associated employer and they mean offers to be either in the job which he held immediately before the date of dismissal or in a different job which would be reasonably suitable in his case.[1]

[1] TULR(C)A, s 238(4).

19.204 Thus there are a number of definitions to consider but it is interesting that the section contains no definition of strike, lock-out or other industrial action. Where such action does occur then one should reiterate that all employees can be dismissed with impunity but after three months even 'relevant employees' can be re-engaged without fear of a claim.

Lock-outs

19.205 Although the sections do not provide a definition of lock-out there is one for the purposes of continuity. This states, to paraphrase, that it is the closing of a place of employment, or suspension, or the employer's refusal to continue employment in consequence of a dispute in order to compel employees to accept terms and conditions of employment.[1] It might not seem that important to distinguish between a lock-out and a strike but in fact there is a very significant distinction because 'relevant employees' are defined differently. In simple terms everyone with an interest is counted where it is a lock-out whereas it is only those still striking who count for industrial action purposes. Thus an employer will usually want to show that there is a strike rather than a lock-out because it limits the numbers of relevant employees who may provide a remedy to a complainant.

[1] ERA, s 228(4).

19.206 It is often very difficult to distinguish a lock-out from industrial action particularly when it has been held that the provisions are not affected by whether the employer's action was reasonable or blameworthy.[1] If employees strike, however provocative the employer's behaviour, they can be dismissed for participating in industrial action. However, if the employer believes that industrial action is to commence and gives notice of closure then this is treated as a lock-out even if, subsequently, he asks them to return.[2]

[1] *Thompson v Eaton Ltd* [1976] ICR 336, EAT. Where the employers installed new machinery without consultation with employees which led to industrial action. Although the court said the employers were partly at fault the employees wer dismissed for participating in industrial action.
[2] *Campey & Sons Ltd v Bellwood* [1987] ICR 311, EAT.

19.207 The Court of Appeal has now considered the issue very carefully in *Express and Star Ltd v Bunday*.[1] Following unsuccessful lengthy negotiations the management introduced 'single keying' for its newspaper. The union's response was to instruct its members not to work on material not set and composed by NGA members. The following day the employees were taken to one room, the rest of the premises being closed, and were asked if they would work without restriction otherwise they would be immediately suspended without pay. Subsequently over 50 employees were dismissed two months later and they complained of unfair dismissal. At the tribunal it was held to be industrial action rather than a lock-out. The EAT reversed this and said the test was not whether there was a breach of contract but who stopped work continuing. The Court of Appeal restored the tribunal and said the question is to be determined on the facts and merits of each case by the tribunal using its industrial relations expertise. It said that there was no definition of strike or lock-out deliberately because it is difficult if not impossible, to draft a definition which is going to fit every case. Furthermore the definition for continuity purposes was not to be used directly for determining questions under TULR(C)A, s 238 although it could give an indication of the sort of ingredients to be looked for. The Court also said that whether there had been a breach of contract would be a material consideration in a substantial number of cases in deciding whether there has been a lock-out, although it was not a necessary pre-requisite. One of the judges[2] said lock-out not only comprehended the act of the employer in refusing to allow employees to work but also the reason why he so refused. The tribunal was therefore entitled as a matter of law to consider whether the adoption of new technology involved a change in the terms and conditions of the employees' contracts of employment.

[1] [1987] IRLR 422.
[2] Glidewell LJ.

19.208 How far the above takes us in understanding whether something is a lock-out is questionable. It certainly lays down some guidelines and parameters but, with respect, it seems that the question that the EAT posed is much simpler and easier to apply.

Strike and industrial action

19.209 There is a definition of strike for continuity purposes which is 'the cessation of work by a body of persons acting in combination, or a concerted refusal or a refusal under a common understanding of any number of persons employed to continue to work for an employer in consequence of a dispute done as a means of compelling their employer . . . to accept . . . terms or conditions of . . . employment'.[1] This has been applied in several cases but the *Bunday* case has now said that this definition should not be applied although its ingredients were relevant. A strike has been judicially defined, not in a s 238 context, as 'a concerted stoppage of work by men done with a view to improving their wages and conditions . . .'.[2]

[1] ERA, s 228(5).
[2] Per Lord Denning in *Tramp Shipping Corpn v Greenwich Marine Inc* [1975] ICR 261, CA.

19.210 Industrial action comprises any behaviour which disrupts work and would include a go-slow, work-to-rule, overtime bans and picketing.[1] As with the definition of a strike and lock-out its definition is a question of fact not law, and the tribunal should use its experience in deciding its issue. More controversially, and more difficult to apply, is the proposition that the tribunal should consider the purpose and intention of the action and if it is intended to pressurise the employer it should be classified as industrial action.[2] It is much more uncertain to consider these subjective issues than it is to consider the impact of the action taken which can be assessed objectively but the Court of Appeal makes it clear that action taken with the objective of applying pressure on the employer or of disrupting his business is industrial action.[3] A better view might be that the intentions or purpose behind the action is a relevant factor but not as important as the effect of the industrial action.

[1] *Midland Plastics v Till* [1983] ICR 118, EAT and see *Thompson v Eaton*, above, where attempts to prevent the installation of new machinery were held to constitute industrial action.
[2] *Power Packing Casemakers v Faust* [1983] ICR 292, CA.
[3] As suggested in *Rasool v Hepworth Pipe Co Ltd* [1980] ICR 494, EAT.

19.211 The *Faust* case makes it clear that the industrial action taken does not have to be a breach of contract. The employees had agreed among themselves that they would refuse to work overtime which was not obligatory. The court said that industrial action was not in breach of contract but that was not necessary and the pressure on the employer converted it into industrial action.

19.212 A threat of industrial action at a future date is not industrial action because it does not actually comprise the taking of industrial action.[1] It is a stage of a negotiating process and is a display of power without actual participation in industrial action. This point is also connected with trade union activities. If a meeting is held in which a decision as to whether to take industrial action is to be decided this should not, logically, be treated as industrial action because it has not even been decided whether to take it. In the *Rasool* case[2] there was a further problem in that the employer had refused permission for the meeting which caused considerable disruption. The EAT affirmed the tribunal decision that this was union activity but in a subsequent case it was held that an immediate overtime ban decided upon at a meeting might or might not be industrial action.[3] This odd statement can be explained by the fact that the EAT held that it was reasonable to take either view and they should defer to the tribunal's finding of fact that this was not industrial action. This approach means that another tribunal could reasonably hold that the same activity constituted industrial action. This is highly unsatisfactory and bearing in mind that threats of industrial action probably do not constitute industrial action neither should meetings, even if unauthorised. It is stretching the concept of industrial action to suggest that a brief isolated stoppage, albeit unauthorised, should constitute such action, although there should be some limits on its duration and it is probably unreasonable to suggest there should be more than one meeting. However, when an employee on behalf of his colleagues, telephoned his employer to inform him that they would not come to work the following day unless his colleagues were re-instated, and they were all dismissed, the EAT said, affirming the tribunal, that this was industrial action. The EAT did say that further negotiations could not be expected as the communication was in the evening and work had already been allocated to the employees who were drivers. These were important points because the EAT is clearly saying, it would seem, that a threat would not be industrial action if there was an opportunity for the threat not to be carried out. In this particular case that was impossible.[4]

1 *Midland Plastics v Till*, above para 19.218.
2 See above.
3 *Naylor v Orton and Smith Ltd* [1983] IRLR 233.
4 *Lewis and Britton v E Mason & Sons* [1994] IRLR 4.

What constitutes participation in industrial action

19.213 It is obviously not possible for the employer to have the benefit of TULR(C)A, s 238 unless the complainant employee was actually taking industrial action. Furthermore, as we shall see later, the relevant employees must have been taking part[1] otherwise they are not 'relevant'.

1 But note the difference where there is a lock-out – see above.

19.214 As with the question of whether there is 'industrial action' the question of participation is one to be decided by the industrial tribunal as a question of fact.[1] It would be surprising if it could be held that an individual employee could participate in industrial action because, as we have already noted, it requires concerted action. There is also a problem in that there would be no 'relevant' employees for the employee to compare himself with and the legislation is premised on the basis that there is another relevant employee who has not been dismissed or re-engaged. Nevertheless when an employee told his employer he would only drive a particular vehicle if he was given an extra £5 for overnight subsistence, the EAT held, affirming the tribunal, that one person could take industrial action. The employee was refusing an instruction and was attempting to coerce his employer into improving the employee's terms and conditions.[2]

[1] *Coates v Modern Methods and Materials Ltd* [1982] ICR 763, CA.
[2] *Lewis and Britton v E Marsh & Sons* (1994) IRLR 4, EAT.

19.215 Once it is established that employees are participating in industrial action it does not matter that the employer has provoked or even 'engineered' the industrial action[1] and we have already noted that even where the employer is heavily to blame for the industrial action this is not relevant.[2] This is a direct result of the statutory provisions which ask simply whether or not there was industrial action and disregard the employer's behaviour and also his motives.[3]

[1] *Marsden v Fairey Stainless Ltd* [1979] IRLR 103, EAT.
[2] *Thompson v Eaton*, above.
[3] See *Faust*'s case, above.

Industrial action and redundancy

19.216 The link between strikes and redundancy is noted in the provisions relating to redundancy payments. In one case[1] employees refused to work overtime following a dispute over a bonus. They were warned it could lead to their dismissals which is what happened after further fruitless negotiations. the employees were never replaced after a decision by the employers to discontinue using direct dock labour. The employees claimed redundancy payments and unfair dismissal stating that the employers had conspired to deprive them of redundancy pay and manoeuvred them into industrial action. The tribunal agreed but the EAT reversed. The Court of Appeal by a 2/1 majority held that the dismissals were for industrial action and not redundancy. It said that if an employer dismisses strikers and engages either new employees or contract labour from another company the reason for dismissal is still the industrial action. The majority were so utterly convinced of the position that they dismissed the applications rather than remitting the case. Waite LJ dissenting, said it was important to determine if there was a redundancy situation at the time of dismissal and, if so, did that situation supply the reason for dismissal. He felt that the tribunal was entitled to infer from the timing of the employer's decision to continue using direct labour that there was a redundancy situation at the time of the dismissal and that was the reason for dismissal. He also said that the tribunal had carefully investigated the position and had in effect not reached the decision lightly and his decision should not be interfered with. This case shows the difficulty in looking behind the industrial action. In one sense this decision is entirely consistent with the other cases which show you must not consider why industrial action has taken place even if it has been engineered. However, if it is proper to determine the reason for the dismissal surely it is the correct approach to determine the factual position overall and not to look simplistically at the fact that industrial action has taken place. However, it shold be stated that the wording of the statutory provision does appear to preclude looking behind the industrial action.

[1] *Baxter v Limb Group of Companies* [1994] IRLR 572.

19.217 In the past there have been doubts as to whether participation in industrial action was to be judged by the employee's own attitude to it or by his mere absence. It is now clear that it is the employee's actions which determine the question.[1] In *Coates* it was said that participation is judged by what the employee does and not by what he thinks or why he does it. Therefore the employee who refused to cross the picket line because of fear of abuse could reasonably be regarded as participating in the strike even though he had gone to the factory on the first morning of the strike intending to work. The employee's support or otherwise of the strike, even if expressed to colleagues, must be made clear to the employer otherwise he might be deemed to have participated in the industrial action. Problems arise when the employee is not at work for some other reason such as holidays or illness. The employee is not then in breach of any contractual obligation but he could be held to be participating if he associated himself with the strike, or attended at the picket line, or took part in the other activities of the strikers with a view to furthering their aims.[2] In the *Bolton* case it was re-emphasised that one judges the question of participation by the employee's actions or omissions but the answer is not invalidated by the fact that the employer was unaware of his actions or omissions.[3] This could be problematic because the employer would point out an employee's absence and make an assumption that he was participating in the industrial action if he had not received any information to the contrary. However, he might simply be sick. In that situation the employer's assumption would probably prove to be a false one because it appears that it is not possible to treat someone absent as participating in industrial action unless he has associated himself with it. Once you have associated yourself with the action then you remain associated unless you indicate to the contrary. Thus even if you are sick on the day of dismissal your part association is enough to constitute participation[4] even though the burden remains on the employer to show that the employee is participating.[5] Thus it is insufficient to rely on an employee's failure to sign an undertaking confirming she had abandoned industrial action when she was off sick and had done nothing either to support or oppose the strike.[6] It is now very clear that whether an employee is participating in a strike is to be determined by what he actually did and not by what the employer honestly and reasonably believed.[7]

1 *Coates v Modern Methods*, above.
2 *Bolton Roadways Ltd v Edwards* [1987] IRLR 392, EAT.
3 Scott J disapproved of the contrary assertion as stated in *Hindle Gears Ltd v McGinty* [1984] IRLR 477, EAT.
4 *Williams v Western Mail and Echo Ltd* [1980] IRLR 222, EAT.
5 *Hindle*, above note 3.
6 *Rogers v Chloride Systems Ltd* [1992] ICR 198, EAT.
7 *Manifold Industries Ltd v Sims* [1991] ICR 504, EAT and *Jenkins v P & O European Ferries (Dover) Ltd* [1991] ICR 652, EAT.

19.218 Although a threat to take industrial action is not industrial action[1] an employee who informs his employer that he will join existing industrial action when he begins his next shift is taking part in industrial action from the time the employee informed the employer of his intention.[2]

1 See above.
2 *Winnett v Seamarks Bros Ltd* [1978] ICR 1240, EAT and see discussion in para 19.220, above.

Relevant employees

19.219 We have already noted the statutory definition and, where there is a lock-out, this means employees directly interested in the dispute in contemplation or furtherance of which the lock-out occurred. Therefore there is no need for an employee to have been locked-out to be a 'relevant' employee. He must simply have a direct interest and it has been held that this covers employees who had been involved at some stage in the dispute which led to the lock-out and they need not have a direct interest at the time of the complainants' dismissal.[1] This follows from the wording 'were directly interested' but it would, it is suggested, apply to any worker whether or not he had ever been locked-out provided some direct benefit is obtained. There is a wholly analogous position in relation to social security and disqualification from benefit where a worker has a direct interest in an industrial dispute. The House of Lords has held that a worker would be directly interested where the outcome of the dispute would be applied automatically to all employees and this would arise because of a collective agreement or an established custom and practice.[2] Thus a worker from a totally different group from the group locked-out may still be directly interested and a 'relevant' employee. Employers have to tread carefully. It does not matter if employees have returned to work following an ultimatum and lock-out by employers. They will remain relevant[3] and therefore will have to be dismissed if the employer wishes to take advantage of TULR(C)A, s 238.

1 *Fisher v York Trailer Co Ltd* [1979] ICR 834, EAT.
2 *Presho v Insurance Officer* [1984] AC 310.
3 See *Campey*'s case, above.

19.220 Where there is a strike or other industrial action there are more matters to consider. A relevant employee is one taking part in the action at the date of the complainant's dismissal and who is at the same establishment as the complainant. In this situation therefore a striker may change his mind and return to work and from that time he is no longer a relevant employee and therefore he can be retained by the employer without this giving jurisdiction to the tribunal.[1] Employers can use this inducement in their attempts to get employees to return. This principle can also apply where an employee may have been supporting the strike but then became involved in something else and could not support the strike. He therefore ceases to be a relevant employee despite past support.[2]

1 See eg *Hindle*, above.
2 *Atkins v Abraham Alloys* EAT 370/89 where the 'relevant employee' had been on the picket line but was on territorial army duties when the other employees were dismissed.

19.221 The relevant employees must be participating in the same industrial action as the complainant otherwise they will not be 'relevant'. This means that the relevant employee must act in concert with those taking the industrial action.[1]

1 *McCormick v Horsepower Ltd* [1981] ICR 535 where an engineer went on strike in sympathy with his colleagues, boilermakers, but he did not act in concert with them and therefore the Court of Appeal held he had not taken part in the same strike.

19.222 The 'establishment' means the one from which the complainant works. This will not usually create difficulties but where there are a number of sites it is arguable that they constitute one establishment. If there is a central base from which the separate workers are managed it might be that they constitute an establishment. If, however, the site operates independently it will probably be regarded as an establishment in its own right.[1]

[1] See *Barratt Developments (Bradford) v Union of Construction Allied Trades and Technicians* [1977] IRLR 403, EAT.

The date and timing of dismissal

19.223 The complainant's dismissal must take place during the lock-out or industrial action for the employer to take advantage of TULR(C)A, s 238, and as already seen, he must be participating in it if it is industrial action. Once the employee has notified the employer that he has ceased participating in the strike the employer cannot use the section.[1]

[1] *Heath v Longman (Meat Salesmen)* [1973] ICR 407, NIRC; *Glenrose Fish Merchants Ltd v Chapman* EAT 245/89.

19.224 The date of the dismissal is defined as the date on which any employer's notice was given, or where none was given the effective date of termination.[1] As in ordinary dismissal cases it is necessary to communicate the fact of dismissal to the employee or give him a reasonable opportunity to learn about it. Thus a notice of dismissal sent by post is not effective until it is received and if an employee returns to work before that date the employer cannot use TULR(C)A, s 238.

[1] See above for meaning of this.
[2] See *Hindle*, above.

Selective dismissal or re-engagement

19.225 Employers are free to dismiss all strikers with impunity but once they discriminate then it is open to those dismissed to bring a claim. The provisions are very favourable to employers in this regard because the employer is given the opportunity to remove the discrimination until the end of the tribunal hearing. Thus the employer can avoid the jurisdiction by dismissing any relevant employees long after the strike has ended as long as it happens by the end of the tribunal hearing.[1] Furthermore the dismissals can be for any reason and need have no connection with the dispute.[2] Thus whatever discrimination has occurred during the dispute can be cured prior to the tribunal hearing ending.

[1] *P&O European Ferries (Dover) Ltd v Byrne* [1989] IRLR 254, CA. This is a harsh ruling especially if the case has been lengthy and expensive and an employee finds that the potential fruits of his labour are suddenly removed.
[2] *McCormick*, above.

19.226 An easy way round the non-discrimination rule is to dismiss all employees on strike but then to re-engage only some. The law forbids this but employers have to wait for only three months from the re-engaged's employee's date of dismissal before re-engaging that employee with impunity. At one time there was in practice an overall ban.

19.227 Furthermore, the employer need not offer re-engagement at the same time to all the dismissed strikers provided that the offer is not made within three months of his dismissal. The period is to be treated as one where the parties try to settle their differences.[1] The fact that an employee has found another job is irrelevant because there is no need for acceptance. The employer is required to offer re-engagement only.

[1] *Highland Fabricators Ltd v McLaughlin* [1985] ICR 183, EAT.

19.228 The offer of the re-engagement must be made by the original employer or his successor or an associated employer and must be to re-engage either in the job the employee held immediately before the date of dismissal or in a different job which would be reasonably suitable in his case. There have not been many cases regarding this but it has been held that the definition of 'job' does not include the employee's disciplinary status or employment terms which do not relate to the nature of the work, capacity, or workplace. Thus an employee offered re-engagement on the basis that he would be treated as on the final warning stage of the disciplinary procedure was permissible even though other employees were offered re-engagement without such a condition.[1] A general advertising campaign offering employment to those who apply does not amount to an offer to any particular individual even though the opportunity to apply is well known.[2]

[1] *Williams v National Theatre Board Ltd* [1982] IRLR 377, CA.
[2] *Crosville Wales Ltd v Tracey* [1993] IRLR 60, EAT.

19.229 An offer of re-engagement need not be in writing although as a matter of evidence it is obviously preferable. Thus where an employee did not receive an offer in writing which had been sent to other strikers it was sufficient that he knew of the terms of the offer and understood that it applied to him.[1] An offer need not be expressly made to the employee provided the employee is aware of its availability.[2] Where an offer of employment is made to an employee who has recently been dismissed from another site for taking part in a strike, and he begins employment, only to be dismissed immediately the position is ascertained, he is still re-engaged and therefore a relevant employee for these purposes.[3] He disclosed that he had worked for the company before on a particular site, but not the one from which he was dismissed. Although there was a mistake it could have been avoided by a telephone call from the company. There was therefore jurisdiction as a relevant employee had been re-engaged.

[1] *Marsden v Fairey Stainless*, above.

[2] *Bolton Roadway v Edwards*, above.
[3] *Bigham and Keogh v GKN Kwikform Ltd* [1992] IRLR 4, EAT.

19.230 What is a suitable offer has received very little judicial comment and analogies should be considered in the maternity and redundancy areas.

Time limits

19.231 Where there is a claim based on selective re-engagement a special time limit is provided. It is six months from the complainant's date of dismissal[1] in contract to the usual three months. The provisions relating to extension of time apply. There is a special rule substituting the date of the employer's notice for the effective date of termination.[2]

[1] Section 239.
[2] Section 238(5).

Reasonableness of dismissal

19.232 Where s 238 does not apply the dismissal is not automatically unfair but has to be determined under the normal rules relating to reasonableness. Even though there may be difficulties surrounding the strike and feelings may be running high the employer's obligations to act fairly are not modified.[1]

[1] For example *McLaren v National Coal Board* [1988] IRLR 215, CA.

Pressure on employer by industrial action

19.233 It is provided[1] that in determining any question as to the reason for dismissal or whether it was reasonable no account must be taken of any pressure which, by calling organising procuring or financing a strike or other industrial action, or threatening to do so, was exercised on the employer to dismiss the employer and any such question must be determined as if no pressure had been exercised.

[1] By ERA, s 107.

19.234 Thus if the employer relies solely on the industrial pressure as the reason for dismissal it will be unfair because there is no valid reason for dismissal.[1] Pressure may not always fall within the exact wording of the section but dismissal need not be expressly demanded for the section to apply. The question is whether dismissal is a reasonably foreseeable consequence of the pressure extended on the employer.[2]

[1] *Hazells Offsets Ltd v Luckett* [1977] IRLR 430.
[2] *Ford Motor Co Ltd v Hudson* [1978] IRLR 66, EAT.

19.235 An employee cannot complain of unfair dismissal if at the time of dismissal he was taking part in an unofficial strike or other unofficial industrial action. The action is regarded as unofficial in relation to any particular employee unless he is a member of a trade union and the action has been authorised or endorsed by that union or where he is not a member he has colleagues who are taking part in the industrial action who are members of a union which has authorised or endorsed the action.[1]

---

[1] TULR(C)A, s 237(1).

19.236 An act has been authorised or endorsed by a trade union if it was done or authorised or endorsed:

(a) by any person empowered by the rules to authorise or endorse acts of the kind in question; or
(b) by the principal executive committee or the president or general secretary; or
(c) by any other committee of the union or any other official of the union (whether employed by it or not).

For the purposes of the last sub-paragraph (c):

(i) any group of persons constituted in accordance with the rules of the union is a committee of the union; and
(ii) an act shall be taken to have been done, authorised or endorsed by an official if it was done, authorised or endorsed by, or by any member of, any group of persons of which he was at the material time a member, the purposes of which included organising or co-ordinating industrial action. The above provisions apply whatever the rules of the union say or what any contract or rule of law says but they are subject to the provisions on repudiation discussed below.

Repudiation

19.237 An act shall not be taken to have been authorised or endorsed by a trade union if it was repudiated by the executive, president or general secretary as soon as reasonably practicable after coming to the knowledge of any of them. Where an act is repudiated, written notice of such repudiation must be given to the committee or official in question without delay and the union must do its best to give individual written notice of the fact and date of repudiation without delay to every member of the union who the union has reason to believe is taking part or otherwise taking part in industrial action as a result of the act and also to the employer of every such member.

19.238 The form of notice must contain the following statement:

> 'Your union has repudiated the call (or calls) for industrial action to which this notice relates and will give no support to unofficial industrial action taken in response to it (or them). If you are dismissed while taking

unofficial industrial action you will have no right to complain of unfair dismissal.'

19.239 If the above requirements are not complied with, the repudiation shall be treated as ineffective. Furthermore, an act shall not be treated as repudiated if at any time after the union concerned purported to repudiate it the executive, president or general secretary has behaved in a manner which is inconsistent with the purported repudiation.

19.240 The executive, president or general secretary shall be treated as so behaving if upon a request made to any of them within six months of the purported repudiation by the person who:

(a) is a party to a commercial contract whose performance has been or may be interfered with as a result of the act in question; and
(b) has not been given written notice by the unions of the repudiation;

it is not forthwith confirmed in writing that the act has been repudiated.[1]

[1] TULR(C)A, s 21.

19.241 The question whether industrial action is to be so taken in any case shall be determined by reference to the facts as at the time of dismissal providing that, where an act has been repudiated, industrial action shall not be treated as unofficial until the end of the following working day after the day upon which the repudiation takes place.[1]

[1] TULR(C)A, s 237(4).

19.242 For the purposes of this particular provision, the 'time of dismissal' means:

(a) where the employee's contract of employment is terminated by notice, when the notice is given;
(b) where the employee's contract is terminated without notice, when the termination takes effect; and
(c) where the employee is employed under a contract for a fixed term, when that term expires.[1]

[1] TULR(C)A, s 237(5).

19.243 An employer is thus given an opportunity to be as selective as he wishes in determining whom he thinks should be dismissed. It is, however, noteworthy that one cannot use this section if none of the participants in the strike are union members because the strike cannot then be regarded as unofficial. However, the normal provisions as to dismissal for industrial action would then apply. Employees who are trade union members when the action began are treated as union members throughout for the purposes of determining whether the action is unofficial even if they have ceased their membership.

19.244 We shall have to wait to see how these provisions are used and note whether possibly unscrupulous employers will attempt to use these provisions to rid themselves of troublemakers. It should be noted, however, that with the width of the provisions in relation to authorisation or endorsement it is quite likely that the action will not be unofficial and therefore one would not have to rely on the normal provisions as laid down in TULR(C)A, s 238. It is certain that the provisions on unofficial strikes may spawn a number of problems such as the one-day strike or the 'lightning' strike.

Dismissal for health and safety reasons

19.245 The Trade Union Reform and Employment Rights Act introduced new rights against dismissal in health and safety cases now contained in the ERA.[1]

[1] ERA, s 100.

19.246 It states that where the reason or principal reason for a dismissal is for one of the following reasons it should be treated as unfair and that means that it will be automatically unfair without the need to consider the question of reasonableness.

19.247 The reasons are as follows:[1]

'(1) . . . that the employee: –

(a) having been designated by the employer to carry out activities in connection with preventing or reducing risks to health and safety at work, carried out, or proposed to carry out, any such activities,

(b) being a representative of workers on matters of health and safety at work, or a member of a safety committee—

(i) in accordance with arrangements established under or by virtue of any enactment, or

(ii) by reason of being acknowledged as such by the employer,

performed or proposed to perform, any functions as such a representative or a member of such a committee,

(c) being an employee at a place where –

(i) there was no such representative or safety committee, or

(ii) there was such a representative or safety committee but it was not reasonably practicable for the employee to raise the matter by those means,

brought to his employer's attention, by reasonable means, circumstances connected with his work which he reasonably believed were harmful or potentially harmful to health or safety,

(d) in circumstances of danger which he reasonably believed to be serious and imminent and which he could not reasonably have been expected to avert, left, or proposed to leave, or (while the danger persisted) refused to return to his place of work or any dangerous part of his place of work, or

(e) in circumstances of danger which he reasonably believed to be serious and imminent, took, or proposed to take, appropriate steps to protect himself or other persons from the danger.

(2) For the purposes of sub-section (1)(e) whether steps which an

employee took, or proposed to take, were appropriate shall be judged by reference to all circumstances including, in particular, his knowledge and the facilities and advice available to him at the time.

(3) Where the reason (or, if more than one, the principal reason) for the dismissal of an employee was that specified in sub-section (1)(d) above, the dismissal should not be regarded as having been unfair if the employer shows that it was, or would have been, so negligent for the employee to take the steps which he took, or proposed to take, that a reasonable employer might have dismissed him for taking or proposing to take them.

1 ERA, s 100.

19.248 Of the consequential amendments to the substantive changes, the most important were:

(a) health and safety reasons as referred to above which are automatically unfair reasons are also treated as automatically unfair reasons for selection for redundancy;[1]

(b) there is no qualifying period for claiming unfair dismissal where this is the reason;[2]

(c) this reason justifies a special award and the minimum basic award and all that follows with that when the employee is a representative, therefore the penalty is heavy;[3]

(d) the provisions of interim relief will apply to health and safety dismissals of representatives.[4]

Some early tribunal cases have applied the provisions to employees where they were dismissed for refusing to drive vehicles which they believed to be unsafe.

1 Amending what is now s 105.
2 Amending ERA, ss 108 and 109.
3 Amending ERA, ss 117, 118, 119, 120, 121, 122, 124(3) and 125.
4 This is implemented by redrafting what is now ss 128 and 132.

19.249 There has been considerable discussion over protection of employees where health and safety matters are concerned and also in relation to the concept of 'whistle-blowing'. The latter has not been inserted into the new Act other than in relation to health and safety matters where an employee representative was carrying out his functions which presumably would include disclosure of a health and safety risk. However, a private Members' Bill was introduced into Parliament in 1995 to protect whistleblowers.

19.250 The provisions seem fairly self-explanatory although there will inevitably be some questions of interpretation. One assumes there will not be a problem in determining who is 'designated by the employer to carry out activities' although where there is some very informal designation, particularly in small businesses, this will obviously create difficulties. There will also be discussion as to what activities actually prevent or reduce risks to the health and safety of employees at work. There might be some debate as to what functions a safety representative actually has. There is likely to be disagreement over where there are circumstances of danger which were serious and imminent where the employee left his place of work or took employees away from work. The tribunals and courts will have to work out these problems in due course.

Offshore employees

19.251 The new provisions have a forerunner in the Offshore Safety (Protection against Victimisation) Act 1992 which make it an unfair dismissal when an offshore employee is dismissed for carrying out or proposing to carry out his functions which are those relating to his membership of a safety committee or in relation to his activities as a safety representative. The provisions in relation to union membership and activities, including remedies, are mirrored in these provisions.

Sunday working

19.252 The Sunday Trading Act 1994 came into force on 26 August 1994. Its provisions are now contained in Part IV of the ERA. These permit certain kinds of shops to open on Sundays. Basically small shops can open freely on Sunday but large shops may open for only six continuous hours between 10 am and 6 pm. The Act contains some detailed provisions regarding employment rights of shopworkers who are defined as those who are required to do shopwork which means working in or about a shop on a day on which the shop is open to serve customers. A shop in general terms covers any premises or any retail trade or business. The Act contains a careful definition of such shops. A shopworker would certainly include all those employed in the shop including supervisors and managers even if they are not directly involved in serving customers. The extended rights are applied whatever the age, length of service or hours of the employee. The Act provides that the shop worker shall have the right not to be dismissed, made redundant for that reason or be subjected to any other detrimental action for declining to work on Sundays. The only people who are not protected under the legislation are those who are employed to work only on Sundays.

19.253 Existing shop workers are known as protected shop workers and are absolutely protected. There is a further category known as opted-out shopworkers. They comprise workers who may be required to work on a Sunday but not exclusively on a Sunday and they have given their employer an opting-out notice in writing stating that they object to Sunday working. Essentially the employee becomes a protected shop worker once three months have expired from the date of the notice period.

19.254 If the employer fails to give the prescribed notice notifying the employee of his right to opt out within two months of the Agreement that he would work on Sundays then the period of notice is reduced to one month. The employee is entitled to change his mind about Sunday working so that he may opt in by expressly stating that he wishes to work on a Sunday but then change his mind later by opting-out.

19.255 It will be an automatically unfair dismissal to dismiss an employee if the reason or principal reason was that the shopworker refused or proposed to refuse to do shop work on Sunday or on a particular Sunday.[1] This will not apply to an opted out shopworker where he refused to work during the notice period of the opting out.[2] There will also be an automatically unfair dismissal if the reason was that the shopworker gave or proposed to give an opting-out notice to the employer. It is also automatically unfair to dismiss an employee in a redundancy situation where the principal reason is related to Sunday working. The Act is extended to apply protection to workers against the imposition of any penalties for refusing to do Sunday work.

[1] ERA, s 101(1).
[2] ERA, s 45.

19.256 In the midsummer of 1995 a private members' bill[1] was introduced, with all party support, which is intended to protect individuals from being penalised as a result of having disclosed or proposed to disclose, certain kinds of information in the public interest. This is the phenomenon known as 'whistle-blowing'. The information which is protected information is defined in the bill and the person disclosing must have raised it internally first, must not be acting in bad faith and must believe the information to be accurate and have reasonable grounds for that belief. The information must have been acquired, inter alia, in the course of his employment and be of such significance that its disclosure would be in the public interest. Anyone dismissed for this reason would be automatically unfairly dismissed and there would be no limit on compensation nor would there be a two year qualifying period or a restriction on those over normal retiring age. Interim relief would apply. We must of course, await with interest to see if this important proposal manages to become law.

[1] The Whistleblowers' Protection Bill 1995.

Reasons for dismissal

The statutory reasons

19.257 We have already considered the reasons for dismissal which are not linked with the test of reasonableness but which stand on their own as fair or unfair. We must now consider the more common situation where an employer produces a reason which can be described as one of the usual reasons. These reasons are contained in ERA, s 98(2) and if the employer establishes this reason it is for the tribunal to consider whether the employer has acted reasonably or unreasonably in treating that reason as justifying dismissal.

19.258 The ERA provides that it is for the employer to show what was the reason or principal reason for the dismissal. Then he must show it was a reason within s 98(2) or some other substantial reason of a kind such as to justify the dismissal of an employee holding the position which the employee held.[1]

[1] ERA, s 98(1).

19.259 The permitted reasons are:

(a) Those related to the capability or qualifications of the employee for performing work of the kind which he was employed to do. Capability relates to skill, aptitude, health or any other physical or mental quality, and qualifications means any degree, diploma or other academic, technical or professional qualification relevant to the position which the employee held.[1]
(b) Those related to the employee's conduct.
(c) That the employee was redundant.
(d) That the employee could not continue to work in the position he held without contravention (by him or his employer) of a duty or restriction imposed by or under a contract.

1 ERA, s 98(3).

19.260 One should finally mention 'some other substantial reason' because a body of case law has developed on this reason which has a wide coverage. Before considering the reasons individually there are some general comments which need to be made concerning reasons.

Need to show a reason

19.261 In producing the reason there is a little uncertainty regarding the need to show the substance of the reason at this stage. The section does say that it must be for a reason within s 98(2) 'or some other substantial reason' and this implies that the reason must be a substantial one. However, it appears that the 'substantial' test is deferred to the s 98(4), (6) standard and that the tribunals and courts are prepared to accept there is a valid reason without too much difficulty. Provided the reason was capable of justifying the dismissal then the employer will satisfy the test of showing a valid reason. This test 'is designed to deter employers from dismissing employees for some trivial or unworthy reason'.[1] Thus, if the reason could justify the dismissal then it can be a substantial reason.[2] In the *Gilham* case the Court of Appeal held that the employer's reason for dismissal, namely to implement economies imposed by government policy, was quite clearly a substantial reason.[3]

1 Per Griffiths LJ in *Gilham v Kent County Council (No 2)* [1985] ICR 233.

2 See above.

3 They agreed with the tribunal as to reasonableness and therefore the dismissal was held to be unfair.

The basis of the reason and multiple reasons

19.262 This is more complex than appears at first because there may be several factors which have an influence on the employer's decision. It is usually quite simple to determine the reason – the employee has been fighting on the premises, or been absent due to sickness or is not performing to a required standard. It becomes more complicated when there are different types of behaviour which fall within one of the permitted reasons, for example, disobedience and lateness which are examples of misconduct. An incident which, in isolation, might not result in dismissal, might do so after other unrelated incidents. The 'last straw' concept is well understood in courts and tribunals. However, it becomes even more complicated when the factual basis for dismissal is of a totally different kind from the previous incident justifying some form of disciplinary action. For example, an employee might be dismissed for absence after he has been previously warned about his work performance. The employer is required to state the reason for the dismissal and the tribunal must be notified as to the reason. Does the employer refer to the previous incident or incidents or warnings? In practice, he usually will and it has been stated that 'the reason' for dismissal is frequently made up of all sorts of reasons and sub-reasons. Therefore, the correct practice is to consider all the reasons which form part of 'the reason' for dismissal when determining whether the dismissal is fair or unfair'.[1]

1 *Patterson v Messrs Bracketts* [1977] IRLR 137, EAT.

19.263 This does show that the 'multiple reason' issue is to be determined at the 'fairness' stage although strictly it should be considered at the 'reason' stage, because 'a reason for dismissal is a set of facts known to the employer or beliefs held by him which cause him to dismiss the employee'.[1] As we shall see a genuine belief, certainly in relation to conduct or capability, will be enough. However, although the employer need not dissect the reason or reasons in excessive analytical detail,[2] if he gives two or more reasons for dismissal and it is not clear which was the prevailing reason the employer may fail because the principal reason has not been established.[3] What needs to be established is the factual basis for the dismissal. The legal classification usually follows quite easily. If the factual basis cannot be explained there is a real problem.

1 *Abernethy v Mott, Hay and Anderson* [1974] ICR 323, CA.
2 *Bates Farms v Scott* [1976] IRLR 214, EAT.
3 *Carlin v St Cuthbert's Co-operative Association Ltd* [1974] IRLR 188, NIRC.

19.264 Since 1987, it is almost certain that the employer will fail in this situation. In *Smith v City of Glasgow District Council*[1] the employer relied on three charges to justify dismissal. One charge, a particularly serious one, was not established at the industrial tribunal in that the tribunal found that the employer had no reasonable grounds for its belief. However, it found the dismissal fair, and was upheld by the EAT, on the basis that the other charges justified dismissal. The House of Lords affirming the Court of Session's reversal of this decision, held that the employer had failed to establish the principal reason for dismissal. As an important part of the reason for dismissal had collapsed the employer had failed to establish the reason and therefore the dismissal was unfair.

1 [1987] ICR 796.

19.265 If the employer could justify the dismissal of the employee on each of the charges in isolation the decision would almost certainly have been different.

19.266 It is up to the employer to show clearly what was the reason for dismissal. Even where there has been some wrongdoing which could be classified as misconduct the employer must explain the basis for its decision. Thus, where a worker negligently reversed a dustcart and killed a member of the public the employer said the reason was the employee's breach of the Council's procedure. This was found not to be the case and the EAT found that the employer had not satisfied the burden of showing the reason for dismissal.[1]

[1] *Adams v Derby City Council* [1986] IRLR 163.

19.267 The employer has to show why in fact he dismissed the employee, and that this falls within one or other of the five legal reasons. This is not an exercise in elaborate legal classification.[1] Once the employer produces evidence to the tribunal that appears to show the reason for the dismissal it is up to the employee to show that there is some doubt as to whether that was the true reason. This is an evidential not a legal burden but the onus of establishing the reason remains on the employer.[2]

[1] *Union of Construction Allied Trades and Technicians v Brain* [1981] ICR 542, CA.
[2] *Maund v Penwith District Council* [1984] ICR 143, CA.

Establishing the correct reason in law

19.268 The employer will know why he has dismissed the employee but may not always state the correct reason. This may be because he misunderstands the law or it may be an attempt to be charitable. There might be other reasons known only to the employer. An example of a misunderstanding would be where an employer tells an employee that he was dismissed for redundancy but the real reason was incompetence.[1] An example of the other kind would be where an employee was told he was being dismissed for incapability relating to stock losses when the real reason was a belief that the employee was dishonest.[2]

[1] *Abernethy*, above.
[2] For example *Hotson v Wisbech Conservative Club* [1984] ICR 859, EAT. Both this example and the one referred to in note 1 are not quite as simple as they appear. The *Abernethy* case could also be an example of a charitable employer not wanting to tell the employee he is incompetent. The *Hotson* case is one of many where the employer may believe that the employee is dishonest but may think he has insufficient evidence or wishes once again to be charitable by not characterising the behaviour as theft.

19.269 In the *Abernethy* case the employee refused to transfer from head office and was dismissed for redundancy. In his response to the employee's claim for unfair dismissal the employer said that the reason for dismissal was redundancy. The tribunal said there was no redundancy but that he was fairly dismissed for incapability. The Court of Appeal were faced with the argument that the employer had dismissed for redundancy and could not now claim it was incapability. Upholding the fairness of the dismissal the Court held that the factual basis was clear and it did not matter that the employer attached the wrong legal label. This case does not reconcile itself easily with cases such as *Adams v Derby City Council* above.

19.270 From this case it can be seen that the strict rules as to pleadings in the ordinary courts do not apply in the industrial tribunal. However, there are some limitations on this as can be seen from the examples below. Nevertheless, the courts are not entirely predictable in their approaches and the best view is that it is possible to decide a case based on any reason, provided it is either pleaded or 'expressly ventilated' at the hearing.[1] This is subject to the principle that ground cannot be shifted to suddenly impute criminal activity. Thus, in the *Hotson* case a club barmaid was dismissed for gross inefficiency in handling bar takings. At the hearing, on a suggestion by the Chairman, the employer's representative agreed that the dismissal was based on dishonesty and the tribunal found the dismissal was fair based on suspected dishonesty. The EAT allowed the appeal and said that the difference between inefficiency and dishonesty went beyond a change of label and should have been raised at the outset. It was sufficiently serious and grave to require the employee to have time to answer the charge.[2] As a matter of good industrial relations and practice and indeed common sense one could add that the dismissal procedure would have been handled differently.

1 *Murphy v Epsom College* [1980] ICR 80, CA.
2 See above.

19.271 Although an earlier case[1] said that it was vital to plead 'some other substantial reason' if one wanted to rely on it, this is probably no longer correct. In that case, the employer had throughout argued their case based on redundancy but at the last minute tried to claim 'some other substantial reason'. This was held not to be a purely technical point but in a later case the Court of Appeal indicated that it was permissible to use a different reason provided it had been raised at some stage in the tribunal.[2] This means that it would not even be necessary to state it as the grounds for dismissal nor even plead it in the employer's response. In a subsequent case the EAT held that it was permissible to hold that 'some other substantial reason' could be used by the tribunal in its decision when it had not even been argued by the employer.[3] The EAT said that this was a matter of labelling and the difference in grounds did not go to facts or substance and thus the tribunal decision was affirmed. The EAT said that if the employee could show he had suffered prejudice then the employer would have to show that the change made no difference. Given the narrowness of the distinction between a reorganisation and a redundancy as a matter of law and given that the factual basis would not alter the decision it is understandable but a later EAT decision throws severe doubt on it.[4] An employer pleaded and argued redundancy as the reason for dismissal but the tribunal found 'some other substantial reason' as the real reason. The EAT allowed the appeal on the basis that the employees had not had an opportunity to deal with the point. They also stated that it was desirable where there are no professional representatives to spell out the different labels during the argument at the hearing.[5]

1 *Nelson v BBC* [1977] ICR 649, CA.
2 *Murphy*, distinguishing *Nelson*, above.
3 *Hannan v TNT-IPEC (UK) Ltd* [1986] IRLR 165.
4 *Burkett v Pendletons (Sweets) Ltd* [1992] ICR 407.
5 See also *Gorman v London Computer Training Centre* [1978] ICR 394 and *McCrory v Magee* [1983] IRLR 414.

19.272 The same reasoning would apply to a dismissal based on misconduct or incapability. If the employee works carelessly, making too many mistakes this would usually be classified as conduct but it might be that the employee is inherently unable to take care for long periods and this would then fall within capability. Provided the factual basis is adhered to then the reason of conduct or capability would suffice and an employer would, and should, not be prejudiced by arguing the wrong reasons.[1] As a practical matter the employer should of course argue in the alternative. One example, in the writer's personal experience was where an employee was dismissed for, inter alia, failing to process credit cards correctly whereby the name of the customer was not properly impressed leading to the employer suffering losses as it was unable to recover on these transactions. Despite retraining the employee continued to make these mistakes. This could have been capability or conduct. It was incompetence but it was also carelessness which could constitute misconduct. It was argued on the grounds of capability and this was held to be justified. It may be important for an employer to categorise the behaviour at an early stage as he may have different procedures for dealing with capability as contrasted with conduct. In most cases, however, it will not be vital to distinguish.

---

1 See *Sutton and Gates (Luton) Ltd v Boxall* [1979] ICR 67, EAT where carelessness was distinguished from an inherent incapacity to function.

19.273 Where there is an internal appeal against dismissal the appeal may open up fresh facts which might justify dismissal for another reason. Although the appeal forms part of the dismissal process it has been stated that the employer cannot justify the dismissal by a reason that was not the original reason.[1] To reconcile these apparently contradictory views it is suggested that facts established at the appeal hearing can be used to justify or mitigate the original reason if it is related but where they are unrelated the employer would have to start again with a fresh ground for dismissal. Otherwise the employee will, in effect, be deprived of a right to appeal. There would only be one opportunity to deal with the issue. However, this is far from impeccable logic given the established position that defects in a disciplinary hearing can be remedied by having a comprehensive appeal which, in effect, means that only one proper substantive hearing is given.[2]

---

1 *Monie v Coral Racing Ltd* [1981] ICR 109, CA.
2 *Whitbread & Co plc v Mills* [1988] IRLR 501, EAT.

Capability

Definitions

19.274 As already stated a reason for dismissal related to the capability or qualifications of the employee for performing work of the kind which he was employed by the employer to do is a permitted reason for dismissal.[1] Capability is assessed by reference to skill, aptitude, health or any other physical or mental quality.[2] Examples of such incapacity include an employee's inflexibility and lack of adaptability which would fall under 'aptitude' or 'mental qualities',[3] an employee's refusal to co-operate and a constitutional incapacity to mend his ways,[4] and a lack of drive and adaptability.[5] A more obvious example is where the employee is unable to attain the standard of work his employers require of him. It appears from authority that employers can impose higher standards than equivalent employers in the industry and that they can raise such standards although this would have to be implemented fairly.

1 ERA, s 98(2)(a).
2 ERA, s 98(3).
3 *Abernethy v Mott, Hay and Anderson* [1974] ICR 323, CA.
4 *Dunning & Sons (Shopfitters) Ltd v Jacomb* [1973] ICR 448, NIRC.
5 *Brown v Hall Advertising Ltd* [1978] IRLR 246.

19.275 The onset of some physical disability may be a justifiable reason to dismiss. It could be a physical quality. Thus the loss of a limb or an eye may make it impossible to perform the job. The discovery that an employee is colour blind may make an employee unable to work properly as may drug addiction or a use of drugs.

19.276 'Qualification' means 'any degree, diploma or other technical or professional qualifications relevant to the position which the employee held'.[1] An obvious qualification that may be required is a driving licence.[2] Although it may be possible to carry on some jobs by using a chauffeur, such as a sales representative, this cannot be the case for a motor mechanic. Thus when such a person lost his licence the employers acted fairly in dismissing because holding of the licence was a continuing requirement even though it had not been stated as such in the contract, but it had been in the job advertisement.[3]

1 ERA, s 98(3).
2 Note case of breach of an enactment below.
3 *Tayside Regional Council v McIntosh* [1982] IRLR 272, EAT.

19.277 It has been held that employers can insist on their own in-house requirements as well as recognised external qualifications.[1] The employer can justify such requirements as aptitude tests because the EAT has interpreted 'qualifications' as including 'matters relating to aptitude and ability'.[2]

1 *Blackman v Post Office* [1974] ICR 151, NIRC.
2 *Blue Star Ship Management Ltd v Williams* [1978] ICR 770.

19.278 Usually the qualifications issue will arise at the recruitment stage and if the employee were to lie about his qualifications and to be found out subsequently, this would be classified as deceit and misconduct. If, however, the employee fails to obtain qualifications which were stated to be necessary, then he may be dismissed even though his work performance is satisfactory.[1]

1 See *Blackman*, above.

19.279 If an employer introduces fresh requirements regarding qualifications they must satisfy the test of relevance, but the few cases there have been on this issue support the right of management to make such changes if they are necessary for the business and the change is handled reasonably.[1]

[1] For an example where it was not, see *Evans v Bury Football Club* EAT 185/81 where a new football manager decided he needed a qualified physiotherapist. Evans had little experience and was unqualified but the dismissal was held to be unfair because the employee had been misled by his employer.

The standards required of the employee

19.280 In 1977 the EAT stated, in a capacity case, but applicable more generally, that 'the operation of unfair dismissal legislation should not impede employers unreasonably in the efficient management of their business'.[1] Although there is the qualification of the word 'unreasonably' this statement is nevertheless supportive of management's right to manage which, it is suggested, pervades the law of unfair dismissal. The classic case on incapacity standards requires that the employer honestly believes on reasonable grounds that the man is incapable or incompetent. Provided there are reasonable grounds for the belief it is not necessary for the employer to prove that he is in fact incapable or incompetent.[2] In this particular case an airline pilot had bounced his plane on landing causing considerable damage to it but not to any passengers. Although it was only one isolated incident the dismissal was justified because of the high degree of professional skill required and the potential consequences of a departure from those standards. In these circumstances the length of good service of the employee will probably be of less importance than in other situations.

[1] *Cook v Thomas Linnell & Sons Ltd* [1977] ICR 770.
[2] *Alidair Ltd v Taylor* [1978] ICR 445, CA.

19.281 The standards imposed by the employer are very much a matter for him to set and the tribunal cannot set its own standards in substitution for the employer's. However, the employers must produce some evidence to establish the reasonable grounds for their belief and also to show that this was the true reason for dismissal. This is not always easy to produce particularly with more senior employees because their qualities are not easy to assess. The employer's genuine belief in the employee's incapacity is some evidence of incompetence but that belief would need to be backed up by some harder evidence even if it is not particularly easy to verify. This might be shown up by poor figures or an unhappy staff atmosphere. Blue collar workers' standards are often easier to assess and verify; for example they might be producing less than the norm or than their previous levels or might be falling below certain targets which management regards as achievable.

Employers' obligations

19.282 Before dismissing, an employer should ensure he has done everything to assist the employee in attaining a reasonable standard of performance. Thus the employer should be sure that he has made clear the standards required of the employee and that they are realistic. There should have been support by providing the employee with proper training and support staff, where necessary under supervision. The employer should establish whether there are any reasons why the employee is not performing properly – these may be internal, for example difficult working conditions or external, such as in particularly difficult domestic circumstances. There needs to be proper monitoring of the employee's performance, and a promoted employee should be treated as a new employee in this regard. New employees are divided into probationers and there are several cases which require employers to have a special regard for them so that they have been properly appraised, and given advice or warning where appropriate.[1] If an employee does carry out the above it may well result in there not being any need for a dismissal whatsoever. If the employer has carried out these obligations he is some way to showing that he acted reasonably.

1 See *Post Office v Mughal* [1977] ICR 763 and *White v London Transport Executive* [1982] QB 489, EAT.

Proper procedures

19.283 All of the above matters will be relevant to the question of reasonableness and the way a dismissal is carried out will also have to satisfy the tribunal. Although there are general principles of procedures, which will be discussed below, there are some matters, mainly of common sense, which can be examined here. The Code of Practice 1977 does not deal specifically with dismissal for incapability but the ACAS handbook[1] does. It does not have the authority of the Code because its provisions are not admissible in the sense of it being mandatory to admit them. However, there is nothing to prevent its provisions being referred to in the tribunal. There is an entire chapter devoted to 'sub-standard' work in the handbook. *Inter alia*, this states that the standard of work should be explained and employees left in no doubt as to what is required of them and the consequences of any failure to meet the required standards. It continues by recommending training and supervision and the institution of an appraisal system. Before dismissing an employee should be asked for an explanation for his poor performance and this should be checked and alternative work be considered before dismissal. An opportunity to improve should be provided. It is vitally important that the employer adopts a fair procedure so that the employee knows what allegations are being made against him and has the opportunity to rebut them, or, as is more likely in performance cases, to give an explanation.

1 ACAS advisory handbook 'Discipline at Work' 1987.

Warnings

19.284 Warnings are necessary in almost all cases because it is impossible to assess what the employee is capable of until he knows his job is really in danger. Warnings are a matter of substance not procedure and where the tribunal is satisfied that a warning would make no difference because the employee wants to do things his way then it may be dispensed with.[1] However, this is not a step to be taken lightly because tribunals will want to be convinced that the employee is so inflexible.

[1] *Dunning & Sons (Shopfitters) Ltd v Jacomb* [1973] ICR 448, NIRC.

19.285 There have been some cases which have suggested that senior employees do not need warnings. It may be true that they are more likely to be aware of what is required of them but once again employers should be careful to ensure that this is really the case. If this can be established and it is certainly easier with senior employees then the employer will be able to avoid the need for a formal warning.[1] In another older case a failure to review an employee's salary was held to constitute a warning by implication.[2] Where there is gross incompetence the courts have been prepared to dispense with a warning.[3]

[1] *James v Waltham Holy Cross UDC* [1973] ICR 398.
[2] *Judge International v Moss* [1973] IRLR 208.
[3] See *James*, above.

19.286 The employee should be given a period of time to allow opportunity for improvement. The length of time will depend on matters like the employee's length of service, how good his performance has been over the period and how inadequate his present performance is.[1] Giving an employee a longer period to improve than originally stipulated is not unfair behaviour. It may be over generous but it is not unreasonable.[2]

[1] *Sibun v Modern Telephones* [1976] IRLR 81.
[2] *Kraft Foods Ltd v Fox* [1978] ICR 311.

Dismissal for ill-health

General

19.287 We have already noted that dismissal for ill-health or a physical quality falls within the reason of capability. As a body of case law on these matters has built up it is being considered separately. Dismissals following absence is given a separate chapter in the ACAS handbook which will be considered later. One must distinguish between dismissals following a single absence for a major illness or injury and one following a series of absences for what may be totally unconnected ailments. It is possible that these latter absences may be uncertificated and the employer might be suspicious about the absences. In this situation it is possible that the reason would be classified as misconduct and some cases have taken this line. For the purposes of this section we will treat the absences as certificated and not suspicious. The decision to dismiss must be supported by evidence showing the effect on the employer's business and there must be a fair procedure, especially since the *Polkey*[1] decision.

[1] [1988] ICR 142, HL.

Effects on the business and dismissal decision

19.288 Where the employee has been absent for sickness the basic question is whether in all the circumstances the employer can be expected to wait any longer and if so, how much longer. The matters to be taken into account are the nature of the illness, the likely length of the continuing absence, the need of the employers to have done the work which the employee was engaged to do and all the circumstances of the case.[1] Although employers must take into account the interests of the employee the interests of the business remain paramount. The criteria outlined above are very similar to those used in determining whether a contract has been 'frustrated' through sickness. After an uncertain period it now appears to be the case that the frustration doctrine is applicable to sickness absence in employment law[2] although its application may be very limited.[3] This is not the right place to dwell on this topic but it must be appreciated that if the frustration argument does succeed then there is no need to consider the reason for dismissal and its reasonableness because there would be no dismissal and the employee's case could not proceed. In what follows here we are obviously not working on that assumption but unfair dismissal law on this topic is very influenced by frustration cases.[4] Where an employee firefighter suffered a nervous breakdown as a result of the employer's accusations of race discrimination and harassment which proved to be without foundation he was dismissed on medical grounds. Although the proper procedure was followed the tribunal found this was an unfair dismissal because his illness was induced by his employers. The EAT reversed holding that the cause of the condition was irrelevant to the question of fairness and entered into areas which the tribunal should not intrude.[5]

1 *Spencer v Paragon Wallpapers Ltd* [1976] IRLR 373, EAT.
2 *Notcutt v Universal Equipment Co (London) Ltd* [1986] ICR 414, CA.
3 *Williams v Watsons Luxury Coaches Ltd* [1990] IRLR 164, EAT.
4 *Marshall v Harland and Wolff Ltd* [1972] 2 All ER 715, NIRC.
5 *London Fire and Civil Defence Authority v Betty* [1994] IRLR 384, EAT.

19.289 Factors which the employer should take into account include the employee's past service and its quality. The longer and better the more likely it is that the employee should retain his job.

19.290 A medical report should be obtained which must be carefully assessed to determine the nature and effect of the illness and how much longer the absence will continue. Although a dismissal decision is a management not a medical decision, it would be very unusual and unfair to make this decision without full medical information. The employer must be sufficiently well-informed to make a decision and this means that the employer should understand the nature of the illness and how long it is likely to last. If he is unaware of this basic information it is almost impossible to make any proper assessment. The effect of the ailment is also a critical piece of information because it may establish that the employee will not be able to work properly again, for example, after a heart attack.

19.291 The importance of the job is a very influential factor in considering the question. The higher up in the hierarchy an employee is the more likely it is that he will need replacement quickly. The corollary of this is that where the job is not a 'key' job the employer will be able to manage without needing to dismiss. The job could be carried out by colleagues who might be prepared to do some overtime. The possibility of obtaining a temporary replacement should always be considered before dismissing, even with a 'key' employee but this is usually much less feasible. The effect on other employees must also be considered and if the absence is lowering morale the employer is able to use this as a relevant factor.

19.292 Where sick pay is provided this is also a relevant factor in that it is less common to dismiss during the currency of sick pay. However, this is not a conclusive factor by any means. An obvious example is where a man has a stroke and will never be able to work properly again. The fact that he has a three-month sick pay entitlement does not mean that the employer has to wait till the three months expires. An employee with no sick pay entitlement cannot be fairly dismissed on that basis. One has to take account of all the other factors and this is one of them.

19.293 Sometimes the contract makes provision regarding sickness and general absence. In one case the contract provided that dismissal would occur after a number of absences in one year which meant almost an entire year of absence. It was an unusual contract! The EAT held that, despite this extreme provision, it did not preclude the employer from dismissing until the period expired.[1] In another case it was provided that any man absent from two shifts in a 14 day period would be classified as unsuitable. The employee worked on a North Sea oil platform and was dismissed in accordance with the clause. The Court of Session upheld the dismissal because of the special nature of the employment and the need to comply with deadlines.[2] It is suggested that this comes dangerously close to an attempt to contract out of the Act's provisions[3] in that it is dictating what is reasonable, but the court had no qualms concerning this.

1 *Smiths Industries v Brookes* [1986] IRLR 434.
2 *Leonard v Fergus and Haynes* [1979] IRLR 235.
3 ERA, s 203.

Access to Medical Reports Act 1988

19.294 As already stated the employers must make careful enquiries as to the employee's medical prognosis so as to 'inform themselves upon the true medical position'.[1] The employer should obtain a proper medical report so as to be properly informed. The natural place to begin is the employee's own doctor. The Access to Medical Reports Act 1988 provisions are of some importance here. The Act gives every individual a right of access to any medical reports relating to him which is to be, or has been, supplied by a medical practitioner for employment purposes.[2] 'Employment purposes' covers the situation both before and during employment. The medical practitioner is one who is or has been responsible for the 'clinical care' of the individual. Thus it would exclude the company doctor or independent medical adviser, unless the company doctor had assumed the clinical care of the employee which might be possible.

1 *East Lindsey District Council v Daubney* [1977] ICR 566, EAT.
2 Section 1.

19.295 Any employer who wants a medical report for employment purposes must notify the employee of his proposal to make the application and obtain his consent. The employer must inform the employee of his rights under the Act which include the right of an individual:

(a) to withhold his consent to the application;
(b) to access to the medical report before it is supplied to the employer or within six months after;
(c) to refuse consent to disclosure of the report to the employer;
(d) to amend details in the report which the employee thinks are incorrect or misleading.

The doctor need not disclose the report if he considers it would be likely to cause serious harm to the physical or mental health of the individual.

19.296 The employer will face problems when the employee refuses access to the doctor, and refuses to be examined by the company doctor or an independent doctor. The employer is required to discover the true medical position but is being prevented from doing so and should not be penalised for not doing something he was prevented from doing. However, he should make it clear to the employee that he will have to act on the information available to him and this might result in dismissal. If an employee has denied access to the employer it is submitted that the tribunal would take a serious view of this despite the individual's freedom of action.

19.297 Where there are two medical reports which are not wholly in agreement it is incumbent on the employer to ensure he has enough information on which to base his decision. The employer should try to resolve any ambiguity, after discussion with the employee. There is no absolute rule that it is necessary to consult a doctor although it is extremely unlikely that this step would be omitted and it would in most cases render the dismissal unfair.[1]

1 *Patterson v Messrs Bracketts* [1977] IRLR 137, EAT.

Consultation

19.298 Employers should take sensible steps according to the circumstances to consult the employee and to discuss the matter with him. Discussion and consultation will often bring to light facts and circumstances of which the employer was unaware and will throw new light on the problem. The employee may wish to seek medical advice on his own account and which if brought to the notice of the employer's medical advisers may cause them to change their opinion. If the employee is not consulted and given an opportunity to state his case, an injustice may be done.[1] There is not much one can add to this quote but *Polkey*'s[2] case has reinforced its importance. *Polkey* would simply find the dismissal unfair not by reference to any 'injustice' but to the employer's unfair procedure.

What is required of the employer is that he listens to the employee's version of events and has periodic discussions with him to establish whether there is any improvement and what the prognosis is. A tribunal must always determine as a matter of fact and judgment what consultation if any is necessary or desirable in the known circumstances of the particular case. It must then determine what consultation took place and whether it was adequate.[3] A failure to consult can be excused where the employers had a genuine concern to avoid giving the employee information about her health of which she did not appear to be aware.[4]

---

1 *Daubney*'s case – see above.
2 [1988] ICR 142, HL.
3 *A Links & Co Ltd v Rose* [1991] IRLR 353.
4 *Eclipse Blinds Ltd v Wright* [1992] IRLR 133 where the GP said the employee's ultimate prognosis was not good.

19.299 A warning is not appropriate because it suggests that the employee is being required to change or improve his conduct and you cannot do this in relation to sickness or disability.[1] Some cases have suggested that personal consultation is always required in a sickness case but, as the EAT has stated, consultation is for a specific purpose and 'if it is clear that the purpose cannot be achieved the need for consultation diminishes or even disappears'.[2] The *Polkey* case requires consultation in all cases unless it would be utterly useless or futile. If an employee has suffered a disabling injury or heart attack or stroke this may mean his normal employment is over but it is possible that an employee could do some part-time work in the future or some lighter work.

---

1 *Spencer v Paragon Wallpapers Ltd* [1976] IRLR 373. Contrast short-term absence below.
2 *Taylorplan Catering (Scotland) Ltd v McInally* [1980] IRLR 53.

19.300 Given medical developments there are far fewer illnesses today which would preclude any form of future employment.

19.301 Before dismissing the employer must consider whether there is alternative work which the employee can do. He is not under an obligation to offer it if he considers the employee is not capable of doing it but he should not refuse to offer it because it is at a lower level or wage. That is a matter for the employee to consider. There is no onus on the employer to create a special job for the employee where none exists[1] but he should try to accommodate the employee if this is not too difficult. The burden will be greater on a larger employer.[2] It is this possibility of reaching some compromise which makes the procedure of consultation and discussion so important.

---

1 *Merseyside and North Wales Electricity Board v Taylor* [1975] ICR 185.
2 *Garricks (Caterers) v Nolan* [1980] IRLR 259, EAT.

19.302 The ACAS handbook[1] lays down a comprehensive list of steps to take in dealing with long-term ill-health absence. It recommends:

(i) periodical contact (both ways);
(ii) that the employee should be kept fully informed if his employment is at risk;

(iii) the employee's doctor should be asked when a return to work is expected and what type of work the employee will be capable of;
(iv) consideration of alternative employment;
(v) that where there is reasonable doubt about the nature of the illness or injury the employee should be asked if he will agree to another examination;
(vi) that if the employee refuses a decision will be taken on the available evidence and that this might result in dismissal;
(vii) that where the employee's job can no longer be kept open and no alternative work is available the employee should be informed of the likelihood of dismissal.

1 Discipline at Work 1987.

Short-term absences

19.303 As already suggested it can be argued that this falls within conduct rather than capability. The dismissal could be said to be for absence which is a matter of conduct. Nevertheless we shall treat the absences as genuinely for ill-health and therefore within 'capability'. The better view is that it should be treated as a conduct ground for dismissal. However, the procedure is very different from long-term absence. The employer is entitled to look at the absence record and say that 'enough is enough' and dismiss the employee.[1] It should be stated that when an employer dismisses for persistent absences, even if they are genuine, they are still better classified as conduct.

1 *International Sports Co Ltd v Thomson* [1980] IRLR 340, EAT.

19.304 The employer acts upon what he considers to be an unacceptable level of absence. There seems to be no authority on what is 'unacceptable' and, following usual unfair dismissal principles, the tribunal will be reluctant to substitute its views for that of management unless they are wholly unreasonable. The employer needs to show he is fully aware of the absence record and the reasons for the absence. He will need to follow a fair procedure by giving the employee the opportunity to explain the absences and will also have to have given warnings. When the employee makes representations he will be able to explain his absences and if they are related to one another then the employer should probably treat it as a long-term absence and obtain a proper medical report before making disciplinary decisions. Where the absences are for unrelated illnesses this step must not be necessary because it would not provide any help to the employer in making its management decision. However, the employer should ensure that there is a common thread or link with the ailments. The EAT has said that where there was absence due to ill-health this was not a disciplinary situation and employers had to treat the employee with compassion, sympathy and understanding. Although the EAT implicitly rejected the concept of a warning in this situation it then said that the purpose of the system operated by an employer is to give a caution that the stage had been reached where, with the best will in the world, it becomes impossible to continue with the employment.[1] If this is not a warning it is difficult to see the distinction.

[1] *Lynock v Cereal Packaging Ltd* [1988] ICR 670.

19.305 In the *Lynock* case the EAT said that in cases of intermittent absences from work due to ill-health there was no obligation on an employer to obtain medical evidence, which indicates the equivocal attitude being shown as to whether it is a dismissal for capability or conduct. It also said that an employer should have regard to the whole history of the employment and to take account of a range of factors including the nature of the illness and the likelihood of its recurrence, the length of the absences compared with the intervals of good health, the employer's need for that particular employee, the impact of the absences on the work of the workforce and the extent to which the employee was made aware of his position.

19.306 Where absence is a result of drink or drugs this will usually be treated as a case of misconduct, but where this has become an intractable problem then this will probably fall within the area of incapability and the employer should carry out the full blown procedure in assessing the medical position, consulting and discussing. Disabled employees can be dismissed for incapacity but the employer should be prepared to tolerate higher levels of absence than normal and should give special consideration to such an employee.[1]

[1] *Seymour v British Airways Board* [1983] ICR 148, EAT.

19.307 The ACAS handbook[1] recommends that absences should be investigated promptly and the employee asked for an explanation. Where there is no medical advice to support frequent self-certified absences the employee should be asked to consult a doctor to establish whether medical treatment is necessary. If no good reason for the absences are shown the matter should be dealt with as a disciplinary matter. The employee should be told what improvement in attendance is expected and warned of the likely consequences if this does not happen. Before dismissing because there has been no improvement the employer should consider the employee's age, length of service, performance, the likelihood of a change in attendance, the availability of suitable alternative work and the effect of past and future absences on the business.

[1] See above.

Conduct

Introductory

19.308 Another permitted reason for dismissal is the employee's conduct which may justify dismissal. As with the reason of 'capability' there are procedural requirements which must be complied with so as to make the dismissal fair. It has never been authoritatively determined that these relate to the establishment of the reason as distinct from satisfying the requirement of reasonableness. Nevertheless if they are not followed the dismissal will be unfair under one or other and in practice the procedure is usually considered in relation to reasonableness. If one considers the main requirements imposed on the employer it would appear that they relate to the establishment of the reason rather than reasonableness and, furthermore, one would probably classify them as substantive rather than procedural requirements.

19.309 The main requirements were laid down in the oft-quoted case of *British Home Stores Ltd v Burchell*.[1] The EAT stated that the employer must show he genuinely believed that the employee committed the misconduct; that he had reasonable grounds on which to formulate that belief after a reasonable degree of investigation.[2] Although these matters will be examined more carefully when considering reasonableness they immediately show that the employer does not have to show he was correct in his belief provided he had a genuine belief at the time.[3] This leads to the position that even though the tribunal establishes the employee did not commit the misconduct the dismissal can still be fair provided the tests are satisfied. This does create considerable surprise to those learning of this rule for the first time. It is also clear that the burden of proof on the employer is the normal civil burden, namely a balance of probabilities. Finally, the investigation need not be of every possible matter that arises provided there has been a reasonable investigation in the circumstances. If some important matter is not pursued then it is not going to be a reasonable investigation.

---

[1] [1980] ICR 303n.
[2] These principles have been approved by the Court of Appeal in *Weddel & Co Ltd v Tepper* [1980] ICR 286.
[3] For example *Ferodo Ltd v Barnes* [1976] ICR 439.

Definition of conduct

19.310 There is none contained in the Act and if one considers the possible situations that might lead to a finding of misconduct it would prove impossible to provide an exhaustive definition. In fact some factual situations may well fall within other permitted reasons. We have already noted that poor performance at work may be a result of competence or capability or it may be more to do with carelessness which would fall within misconduct. Other examples are where an employee competes with his employer in some outside activity – this would be misconduct but it could also fall within fidelity and 'some other substantial reason' – similarly where a customer complains about an employee's behaviour. This could be one of these two legal reasons.[1] In practice, in the tribunal, it would be extremely unusual for much time to be spent in assigning the proper reason unless the question arose of whether there was a breach of disciplinary procedure if conduct were the proper reason.

---

[1] See later eg *Dobie v Burns International Security Services (UK) Ltd* [1984] ICR 812, CA.

19.311 There is no rule that the conduct which the employer relies on must be gross misconduct. Gross misconduct entitles the employer to dismiss without giving notice[1] or money in lieu of notice but the tribunal has to ask itself whether the misconduct justified the dismissal not whether the employer was entitled to dismiss without notice. Often an isolated act of serious misconduct will justify instant dismissal and hence will be fair but often it is less serious and may be the culmination of a series of incidents which may have led to warnings. Maybe there has been previous unconnected conduct and the final conduct which the employer relies on may be quite minor. This is often referred to as 'the last straw' dismissal. It is always important to look at all the circumstances because the employer may have a particularly difficult or, exceptional, or peculiar situation to cope with which may justify a sterner approach than normal. It might be that an employee is deliberately provoking the employer and the employer's reaction might be more understandable. Thus analogies with wrongful dismissal cases are not always helpful but there is more similarity than is sometimes suggested. For example, the circumstances of disobedience have to be taken into account of in wrongful dismissal cases.[2] There can still be gross misconduct even where the employer offers to consider re-employing in some other capacity.[3]

1 See Chapter 2.
3 *Laws v London Chronicle* [1959] 2 All ER 285, CA.
3 *Hamilton v Argyll and Clyde Health Board* [1993] IRLR 99, EAT.

19.312 Conduct has been defined helpfully as 'actions of such a nature, whether done in the course of employment or outside it, that reflect in some way upon the employer–employee relationship'.[1] Thus, as we shall see, conduct totally unconnected with work might justify dismissal if there could be some influence on the employment relationship. As an example, if an employee who has responsibility for the handling of money is convicted of theft outside work this might well justify dismissal. Below are considered some examples of misconduct but they are not intended to be exhaustive of the possible categories nor of the conduct falling within them. Where the employer is relying on the evidence of an informant who wishes to remain anonymous he must be careful to maintain a fair balance between the desirability of protecting informants who are genuinely in fear and providing a fair hearing of issues for employees who are accused of misconduct.[2] However, it is not necessary for an employer to produce third parties to provide evidence such as dissatisfied customers or passengers to an employee where it is alleged that he did not issue tickets to the value of the fares collected.[3] However, the allegations made must be clearly explained to the employee to give him a proper opportunity to explain his version of events, put forward any defence and challenge the allegations.

1 *Thomson v Alloa Motor Co* [1983] IRLR 403, EAT.
2 *Linfood Cash and Carry Ltd v Thomson* [1989] IRLR 235, EAT.
3 *Ulsterbus Ltd v Henderson* [1989] IRLR 251.

Fighting or violence

19.313 As a general proposition it is fair to dismiss for such behaviour at work because it is regarded as very serious misconduct whether or not the company's rules and procedures refer to it.[1] However, the employer must follow the *Burchell* principles. Furthermore where the fighting is only of a minor nature the failure to specify in the rules that fighting justified dismissal could help tip the balance.[2] However, this is only one of a number of factors that may be relevant.

Thus the employer should be consistent in his treatment of the protagonists although if he takes a view that one party was the aggressor having carried out a proper investigation, then almost certainly he will be able to differentiate in his treatment of the employees. He might also justify such discriminatory treatment on the basis of the employee's length of service and its quality. Thus even when the disciplinary rules provide that violence to a colleague would merit dismissal a failure to consider the quality and length of the employee's service led to an unfair dismissal finding in one EAT case.[3] The danger to other employees or to the employer's property are factors which can be taken into account.

[1] *Parsons & Co Ltd v McLoughlin* [1978] IRLR 65, EAT.
[2] See eg *Meyer Dunmore International v Rogers* [1978] IRLR 167, EAT.
[3] *Taylor v Parsons Peebles* [1981] IRLR 119.

19.314 An employer must carry out a proper investigation by interviewing the witnesses to the incident. If this leaves the employer unclear as to who instigated the violence or the witnesses are not in agreement then provided all the other relevant criteria are considered the employer will probably be able to dismiss both parties[1] because fighting is a serious offence. It becomes more serious when the incident occurs in the proximity of machinery and even minor incidents may be treated very seriously in these circumstances.

[1] Regarding multiple suspects; see below eg *Monie v Coral Racing Ltd* [1980] ICR 109, CA.

19.315 Where employers suddenly alter their approach to violence by dismissing when in the past they have only issued a warning then the dismissal is likely to be unfair despite the fact that it would fall within the range of reasonable responses. To make this change without warning is unfair and it would be inconsistent bearing in mind past behaviour.[1] However, this must not be taken too far because each case turns on its own facts and no two cases will be identical. Apart from the different service records there may be evidence of provocation and if this is substantial it may mean that the employer cannot dismiss fairly. The employer is not prevented from changing his policy unilaterally – it is just that he must not apply it without warning of the change of policy.

[1] See eg *Post Office v Fennell* [1981] IRLR 221, CA.

19.316 Although abusive language is not violence in the physical sense it may be of a threatening nature and if so it can be treated very seriously as it may have unfortunate consequences. If it is not threatening then it is necessary to consider the context and place in which it occurs. Thus if it can be shown that it was commonplace to use such language at the particular workplace the employer cannot act on it. If there is an isolated incident then the employer should not act hastily but give the employee the opportunity to cool down and apologise.[1] The employer should always investigate to see if there was provocation. If the language has had a severe impact on the recipient or it is aimed at a superior in the context of refusing a reasonable instruction it might be possible to justify dismissal but it must be considered whether the use of the language has made the continuation of the relationship impossible.[2] In two swearing gardeners' cases[3] this point was made clearly. In the *Pepper* case the swearing at the employer was much milder than in the *Wilson* case but the circumstances justified dismissal of Pepper but not Wilson because in the former case the gardener had repudiated the contract which was not the finding in the latter case.

[1] *Charles Letts & Co Ltd v Howard* [1976] IRLR 248, EAT.
[2] *Wilson v Racher* [1974] ICR 428, CA.
[3] *Wilson*, above and *Pepper v Webb* [1969] 1 WLR 514, CA.

Absenteeism

19.317 We have already discussed absenteeism due to long-term sickness and the fact that it may be caused by several different illnesses or not by illness at all. An isolated incident or a very small number of absences would not justify dismissal but would merit discipline of some kind. If the absence record is poor and provided the employer has given warnings and investigated the reason for the absences the employer is entitled to say that 'enough is enough'.[1] This would be the case even where the absences were backed up by medical certificates unless it would be shown that they have all related to one particular ailment which was persisting. It would then be arguable that the persistent absences were all part of a long-term sickness. In that situation it would appear that the absences should be treated as ill-health absences. Therefore one would need to follow the normal procedure in such cases.[2]

[1] *International Sports Co Ltd v Thomson* [1980] IRLR 340, EAT.
[2] Consultation, discussion, medical information and so forth.

19.318 When the absences are unconnected there is no point in having a medical examination because the illnesses will be short-lived and the doctor is unlikely to predict future behaviour. However, no harm can arise as a result of the examination and it may actually establish some underlying reason for the absences, but it is not necessary. The clearest explanation of this is laid down in the ACAS advisory handbook. This requires the employer to investigate the absences promptly and to ask the employee for an explanation. Where there is no medical advice to support frequent self-certified absences the employee should be asked to consult a doctor to establish whether medical treatment is necessary and whether the underlying reason for absence is work-related. If after investigation it appears that there were no good reasons for the absences they should be dealt with under the disciplinary procedure. If there are temporary domestic problems the employer should consider whether an improvement is likely before deciding what to do. The employee should be told what improvement in attendance is expected and warned of the likely consequences if this does not happen.

19.319 If there is no improvement the handbook says that the employee's age, length of service, performance, the likelihood of a change in attendance and the effect of the absences on the business should all be taken into account in determining what the employer should do.

19.320 The cases do not lay down any rules as to what is an unsatisfactory level of absence. Rules which stipulate such a level can be helpful in determining this question but tribunals are not bound to accept them as justifying dismissal. The employer must consider all the circumstances in the usual way. Where the employee is absent because he wants a holiday or has some pursuit to follow this is an absence like any other but as it is planned it seems to be treated more seriously. It is flouting the fundamental obligation of the employee to be ready, able and willing to work. The same could be said of extending an authorised holiday particularly where an extended leave has already been granted.

Disobedience

19.321 An employee must obey his employer's lawful and reasonable orders, which means that they must fall within the scope of the contract and must not expose the employee to danger. The circumstances of the disobedience must also be considered. Overall, however, managerial prerogative still reigns.

19.322 What the employee is required to do will be ascertained by looking at the contract which may incorporate a collective agreement and include works rules. These will usually cover matters such as the hours[1] and place of work, sickness and holiday entitlement but the statutory particulars[2] only refer to the job title and do not require a job description. Accordingly there may not be a clear statement of the job functions of the employee which may be needed in a case where the contractual obligations are not clear. In many cases it will not be clear what their precise ambit is and it will be for the tribunals and courts to imply a term and to construe the term as determined.[3] Employees are expected to adapt to new technology.[4]

---

[1] Where there are terms relating to hours of work they may be subject to the test of reasonableness. Note *Johnstone v Bloomsbury Health Authority* [1991] IRLR 118, CA where the three judges in the CA disagreed about this and on the question of the duty owed to the employee regarding his health and safety. There are also EEC developments regarding the maximum number of hours that can be worked over a period of time.

[2] ERA, s 1.

[3] See above for discussion of implied terms.

[4] *Cresswell v Board of Inland Revenue* [1984] 2 All ER 713.

19.323 Employees cannot be required to carry out a dishonest act such as the falsification of company records[1] and cannot be asked to do something which is either dangerous to themselves or to the public generally.[2]

---

[1] *Morrish v Henlys (Folkestone) Ltd* [1973] 2 All ER 137, NIRC.

[2] Note the provisions regarding dismissal for health and safety reasons in the ERA, s 100.

19.324 Even where there is a contractual right to require the employee to do something the employer should make this request in a reasonable fashion. Thus although the employer may be able to require the employee to transfer his place of work the employer must give the employee a reasonable period of notice to make this change.[1] Obviously a change of location creates more upheaval than would say a change in job function but nevertheless, one would expect an employer to act reasonably by giving reasonable notice of any change. This would apply particularly to any changes in the time that work is carried out or in the amount of overtime. Although, ultimately, such changes can be made even where there is no contractual right, if this has discernible business advantages, this should be carried out fairly.[2] Thus if the employer adopts a fair procedure he will be able to insist on an employee working overtime[3] or performing additional duties.[4]

[1] *McAndrew v Prestwick Circuits Ltd* [1988] IRLR 514, EAT – see discussion of this in the section on 'Constructive dismissal', above.

[2] See below 'some other substantial reason' for dismissal.

[3] *Horrigan v Lewisham London Borough Council* [1978] ICR 15, EAT.

[4] *Ellis v Brighton Co-operative Society* [1976] IRLR 419, EAT.

19.325 It is always necessary to consider all the circumstances of a case to decide if a dismissal is reasonable. Thus in a wrongful dismissal case where a secretary followed her 'boss' out of a room after being ordered to remain by the managing director and was dismissed it was held to be wrongful because she was placed in an impossible predicament and it was wrong to dismiss her for this one act.[1] Other reasons for refusal have already been mentioned such as exposing oneself to danger or criminality and it has also been held permissible to refuse to do something which might expose one to civil liability.[2] Provided this belief is a reasonable one that can justify the refusal. Company rules are there to be followed but a failure to follow them does not lead automatically to a finding of unfair dismissal even if the rule provides that dismissal will follow. It is still up to the tribunal or court to determine if dismissal is justified.[3]

[1] *Laws v London Chronicle* [1959] 1 WLR 698, CA.

[2] *Union of Construction Allied Trades and Technicians v Brain* [1981] ICR 542, CA.

[3] *Ladbroke Racing Ltd v Arnott* [1983] IRLR 154. This clearly is a general point applicable to the test of reasonableness.

Alcohol and drugs

19.326 As these matters seem to be increasing and as they can be so serious it is worthwhile discussing them briefly. The most important point is that alcoholism and drug addiction should be seen as a long-term sickness problem not as a misconduct problem. Therefore the employer should adopt the normal procedure for such sickness issues which requires investigation and assessment of the true medical position and so forth. Most cases, thankfully, are not ones of dependency, but employees who drink or take drugs at work will, in general, be in difficulties.

19.327 Nevertheless, as regards alcohol the cases show that it is a blue-collar worker who is in real danger of losing his job, not the white-collar worker. This is not simply a case of class discrimination because the cases usually show the importance of the dangers of working with machinery. If an employee is discovered in a drunken state in charge of a machine that would be gross misconduct justifying dismissal. Drinking while in charge of a machine that could be dangerous is also usually treated as gross misconduct because an employer has to give consideration to the safety of all his workers, including the employee who is drinking. Some employers have rules which forbid the possession of alcohol at work but in this extreme situation the employer must justify his policy.

19.328 If management has witnesses at a senior level in the company who were convinced about the employee's drunkenness that is usually sufficient despite the evidence of the employee's colleagues.[1] However, the employer is obliged to carry out the usual investigation and give the employee the opportunity of putting forward his case and explaining that there might be factors which explain his conduct. There is also authority which states that the employee should be given an opportunity to apologise for his behaviour and for his subsequent loss of temper.[2]

1 *Gray Dunn & Co Ltd v Edwards* [1980] IRLR 23.
2 *Charles Letts & Co Ltd v Howard* [1976] IRLR 248, EAT.

19.329 The use or possession of drugs at work will usually be regarded as gross misconduct and dismissal would accordingly be justified. Off-duty use and possession would generally not justify dismissal unless it would harm the employer's business, by injuring his reputation or harming his contacts or employees.[1] This would not be likely. However, in one case[2] a dental technician who returned late from lunch because he had been arrested for, and charged with, possession of cannabis, was held to be fairly dismissed. The employer said it was not appropriate to retain someone doing skilled work who was using drugs and who might influence younger staff. Although there had been no real attempt to discuss the matter with the employee who had over five years' service the EAT affirmed the tribunal in its view that the decision fell within the band of reasonable responses. However, where a security guard was charged with sex offences against children and dismissed because it was reasonable to believe he was guilty and it would affect the company's reputation, the dismissal was unfair because no consideration was given to any alternative course of action despite agreements with the union. Furthermore, the customer for whom the employee worked had not been contacted. It was necessary to obtain the truth of the matter and ascertain the customer's view.[3]

1 *Norfolk County Council v Bernard* [1979] IRLR 220.
2 *Mathewson v RB Wilson Dental Laboratory Ltd* [1988] IRLR 512.
3 *Securicor Guarding Ltd v R* [1994] IRLR 633, EAT.

19.330 Contact with children or vulnerable persons by the employee would be a factor which would militate against the employee and provide the employer with a stronger basis to justify dismissal.[1]

1 In the *Bernard* case, above, the teacher laid much emphasis on his lack of contact. The dismissal was held to be unfair. Sexual misconduct is a good analogy: *P v Nottinghamshire County Council* [1992] ICR 706, CA.

19.331 Both with alcohol and drugs the reputation of the employer is something he is entitled to defend and if the employer can establish that its image has been or might be tarnished by the retention of a person who has been convicted of a drugs or alcohol offence this will be of great value to the employer.

Fidelity

19.332 The employee owes a duty to his employer to be honest, loyal and not to do anything which would destroy the confidential relationship that exists between the parties. These duties have developed considerably in the common law and are still doing so in the context of clauses which prohibit the disclosure of confidential information or competition with the employer. In unfair dismissal much of this would fall under 'some other substantial reason' as well as conduct.

19.333 While the employee is working for the employer he must do nothing which would compete with him. Working for a rival is not necessarily wrong unless the employee has access to confidential information.[1] Where the employee has set up in business in competition with the employer this justifies dismissal because even though the competition and harm is slight the employer is entitled to say that he no longer has confidence in the employee and that the relationship of trust and confidence has been dissipated.[2] However, where the employee indicates that he intends to set up in competition or work for a rival in the future that is not sufficient to justify dismissal.[3] However, if one goes further and makes plans with a colleague to try to induce another colleague to join them and try to obtain the custom of the employer's best customer this would be unfair competition and justify dismissal, particularly where, as here, the individual and his colleague were the managing director and senior manager.[4] An employer is entitled to expect an employee not to compete for contracts with existing customers, which is different from indicating an intention to compete.[5] Where there is access to confidential information the position is less clear because there have been remarkably few authorities. In that situation the probability is that the employer will either send the employee home on 'garden leave' or will terminate the notice. Certainly a dismissal would not be justified unless it could be shown that confidential information was being passed over or that there was a very serious risk of this happening. However, it is arguable that a transfer to another suitable job on the same terms and conditions might not be unreasonable.

---

1 *Hivac Ltd v Park Royal Scientific Instruments Ltd* [1946] Ch 169, CA and *Nova Plastics Ltd v Frogatt* [1982] IRLR 146, EAT.
2 *Mansard Precision Engineering Co Ltd v Taylor* [1978] ICR 44, EAT.
3 *Laughton and Hawley v Bapp Industrial Supplies Ltd* [1986] ICR 634, EAT.
4 *Marshall v Industrial Systems* [1992] IRLR 294, EAT.
5 *Adamson v B & L Cleaning Services Ltd* [1995] IRLR 193, EAT.

19.334 It has been long established that an employee must not solicit his employer's customers for the benefit of his own or someone else's business, while he remains employed.[1] This is an obvious conflict of interest which would not need to be referred to in the contract of employment.

---

1 *Wessex Dairies Ltd v Smith* [1935] 2 KB 80, CA.

19.335 When an employee discloses confidential information to an outsider then this is a serious matter. What needs to be considered is whether the information is very confidential or is something much less important and whether it will cause harm to the employer's business and provide a benefit for the recipient. The risk of confidential information being disclosed in the future might, in some circumstances, justify a dismissal for example where a very close relative, such as a spouse, sets up in competition. Another example would be where an employee develops a personal relationship with a client/customer who is in competition with other clients and where it is possible that advantageous confidential information could be transmitted to that client to the disadvantage of other clients. Provided the employer investigates the position properly and is appraised of all the relevant facts, then it is unlikely that a tribunal would disagree with his assessment that there is a conflict of interest and potential damage could be caused to him.

19.336 The law governing the employee competing against his former employer is extremely complex and is dealt with elsewhere. It is not relevant in this context other than to consider the position where an employee refuses to sign a restrictive covenant. Where the employee is asked to sign at the commencement of employment there is no difficulty – either he signs and is employed or he does not and is not. If the employer decides to impose one during the employment then the situation is more difficult. In the leading case, it was held that the dismissal of the employee following his refusal to sign the new clause was fair. The reason was 'some other substantial reason' because the employee had not really committed any misconduct. The court did consider the extent of the covenant to see if it was for a reasonable period of time and covered a reasonable area.[1] Whether that is a fruitful approach is questionable given that these are very legalistic concepts and are the province of other courts. Furthermore, problems could arise: thus if the tribunal considers the covenant is too far-reaching does it then hold it is therefore unenforceable and it would not have affected the employee if he signed it? These are troubled waters.

---

1 *RS Components Ltd v Irwin* [1973] ICR 535, NIRC.

Dishonesty

19.337 It is quite common for employers to believe that they must prove dishonesty beyond a reasonable doubt and that if an employee is acquitted or criminal charges are not made the employee cannot be fairly dismissed. The test remains as was stated earlier, namely genuine belief on reasonable grounds after a reasonable investigation and the standard is that of a balance of probabilities. Nevertheless when the police get involved it does create complications.

19.338 If an employee is charged with theft this does not absolve the employer from making his own enquiries.[1] The employer should try to discuss the situation with the employee to give him an opportunity to explain his position.[2] However, the employee might refuse to take part in the investigation because understandably he might prejudice his position in relation to the criminal proceedings. This does not mean that the employer can do nothing because if the evidence produced is, in the absence of an explanation, sufficiently indicative of guilt then he can dismiss.[3] In the *Courage* case the evidence that the employer had otbained was quite strong but the employer might believe in the employee's guilt on a reasonable amount of evidence and this would probably be sufficient. In the absence of sufficient evidence the only safe course is to suspend but this may not be very practical given the delay that may occur in the criminal trial. Therefore an employer should do his best to obtain as much information as possible to see if he can reach a decision.

1 *Scottish Special Housing Association v Cooke* [1979] IRLR 264.
2 *Harris (Ipswich) Ltd v Harrison* [1978] IRLR 382, EAT.
3 *Harris v Courage (Eastern) Ltd* [1982] ICR 530, CA.

19.339 Offering the employee the opportunity of explaining his position is always a necessary part of the procedure but it also provides the employer with added strength if the employee declines the opportunity. This is because there have been cases[1] where the courts have criticised the employee for not protesting his innocence and stated that the employee should do this even where he has not been asked for his version of events.

1 See for example *Carr v Alexander Russell Ltd* [1979] ICR 469 and *Parker v Clifford Dunn Ltd* [1979] ICR 463, EAT.

19.340 A genuine belief in the employee's dishonesty is required in all situations bar one. That is where the employer suspects more than one employee of theft and cannot determine which is the guilty party. In this situation the law assists the employer by entitling him to dismiss on reasonable suspicion. He cannot actually believe X is guilty if Y and Z are equally suspected. This problem first arose in the Court of Appeal case of *Monie v Coral Racing Ltd*[1] where money was stolen in circumstances where there were two suspects but the employer could not tell which of them was guilty. The dismissal of both was held to be fair because the employer was certain it was one of them. In a more recent case[2] three suspects were dismissed who had worked in an off-licence where there had been serious stock losses for many years. Following meetings and warnings and moving the employees away to other branches so as to establish who was the culprit the employer dismissed all three, being unable to determine who was responsible. The industrial tribunal found the dismissal unfair because it felt that more transfers could have taken place and it was not a case of dishonesty. The EAT reversed this decision saying that the principle of multiple dismissal could apply to incompetence as well as dishonesty, provided certain conditions were satisfied. These conditions have been restated more recently by the EAT[3] in a case confirming the validity of group dismissals. They are:

(a) the act if committed by an individual would justify dismissal;
(b) the employer has made a reasonable – that is, a sufficiently thorough – investigation into the matter and with appropriate procedures;
(c) as a result of that investigation the employer reasonably believed that more than one person could have committed the act;
(d) the employer acted reasonably in identifying the group of employees who could have committed the act and each member of the group was individually capable of so doing;
(e) as between the members of the group the employer could not identify the individual perpetrator.

If these conditions are satisfied and provided the beliefs were based on solid and sensible grounds the employer can dismiss all[4] the members of the group. Where the employer genuinely believes one of the group to be innocent because she happens to be his daughter and has explained her position the employer can omit her from the group dismissed.[5] This principle might create problems in the future.

[1] [1981] ICR 109.
[2] *Whitbread & Co plc v Thomas* [1988] IRLR 43, EAT.
[3] *McPhie and McDermott v Wimpey Waste Management Ltd* [1981] IRLR 316 is a case where the employees were dismissed for gross misconduct but it could just as easily be characterised as incompetence.
[4] *Parr v Whitbread & Co plc* [1990] IRLR 39, EAT.
[5] *Frames Snooker Centre v Boyce* [1992] IRLR 472, EAT.

19.341 An employee might confess to the theft to his employer. If so the employer can act upon it and the criminal law is irrelevant in these circumstances. Thus in one case[1] the employer induced the employee to confess by indicating that he would then be fair to him. In fact the employer then dismissed the employee who claimed the benefit of the 'Judges' Rules' by saying that the confession had been improperly obtained. The EAT did not accept this and the dismissal was held to be fair. If the employer acts on a confession which is subsequently retracted his behaviour is reasonable although it is necessary to look at the facts of each case.[2]

[1] *Morleys' of Brixton Ltd v Minott* [1982] ICR 444, EAT.
[2] *University College at Buckingham v Phillips* [1982] ICR 318.

19.342 Confessions put a different light on the degree of investigation which is required. Once a confession is made then it cannot be expected that an employer should carry on further investigations even if the confession is made to the police.[1] Although it is not common for employees to be 'caught in the act' if that is the case then the employer is not required to carry out further investigations.[2] However, if there is any margin for doubt the employer should carry out an investigation to make sure he has acted reasonably. The rules concerning admissibility of evidence in criminal law are not relevant to unfair dismissal.

[1] See *Parker*'s case, above, para 19.339.
[2] *Scottish Special Housing Association v Linnen* [1979] IRLR 265.

19.343 Although it is not required for the employer to await the outcome of any criminal proceedings (because the standards are different), some employers in fact do so. The employee may carry on working as before although an employer might be wary about this and might face the argument that if the allegations are so serious then the employee should at least have been suspended. Unless the contract states otherwise suspension must be on full pay. One can only assume that employers are abiding by this principle because there have been no reported cases on a failure to make this payment. An alternative view is that employees are grateful that their employer is keeping the job open for them and they therefore refrain from taking action.

19.344 If the employee is ultimately convicted the employer will almost always be able to rely on this conviction as sufficient evidence without carrying out his own investigation.[1] Short of imprisonment the employer should still carry out an investigation despite a guilty plea. This is the effect of a Court of Appeal decision in 1988[2] in the aftermath of the miners' strike. The employee pleaded guilty to assaulting another miner and although there were internal hearings the employer failed to make reasonable enquiries. The tribunal held that the special circumstances of the strike absolved the employee but the EAT, affirmed by the Court of Appeal said that the opportunity to explain was required in all cases. There might be a specific reason why this had not taken place which a tribunal should investigate but the standards were not different. This echoes what was said above about the need to follow a fair procedure.

1 *Kingston v British Railways Board* [1984] ICR 871.
2 *McLaren v National Coal Board* [1988] ICR 370.

19.345 However, the cases in the 1990s have resiled from this requirement somewhat even though it is always preferable to have some degree of investigation. Where an employee pleaded guilty in a criminal trial to theft from his employers and then at a disciplinary hearing argued that he had been pressured to plead guilty the employer had acted fairly based on the guilty plea. Although the employer had not carried out a very full investigation it was entitled to rely on the guilty plea without having to ask the solicitor for an account of the relevant circumstances.[1] When a prison officer was convicted of embezzlement this, together with the fact that there had been some enquiries made, was enough to justify a finding of fair dismissal.[2] It was made clear that not every conviction would justify dismissal – it would depend on the nature of the offence. Where a groundsman pleaded guilty to indecently assaulting his daughter his employer dismissed him after a disciplinary hearing because of the risk to other children. The tribunal decided the dismissal was unfair because there had been inadequate investigation of the offences and therefore the employer could not assess the risk properly. This was reversed by the EAT who were affirmed by the Court of Appeal[3] who placed considerable weight on the guilty plea. The Court of Appeal also made the point, which is relevant to all the reasons for dismissal, and indeed reasonableness, that where an employer considers alternative employment he may take this step after notice has been given provided it has not yet been effected.

1 *British Gas plc v McCarrick* [1991] IRLR 305, CA.
2 *Secretary of State for Scotland v Campbell* [1992] IRLR 263, EAT.
3 *P v Nottinghamshire County Council* [1992] IRLR 362.

19.346 Even where the employee is acquitted there may be evidence adduced which the employer can rely on to justify the dismissal. If this is the case the evidence should be put to the employee to give him an opportunity to comment on it. If the employer undertakes not to dismiss until after the criminal trial if he changes his mind he must inform the employee and give him an opportunity to make representations at that stage.

19.347 Whenever a false time sheet is submitted or there is false clocking this is theft for unfair dismissal purposes and the employer can accordingly treat these matters as gross misconduct justifying dismissal.[1] Cheating on expenses claims are usually treated in the same way but if they are very minimal the employer should take all the circumstances into account when carrying out his investigation and making his decision. However, in all these kinds of situations the employee is required to do nothing to undermine the confidence of the employer and where money is concerned this can happen very easily.[2]

1 *Stewart v Western SMT Co Ltd* [1976] IRLR 553, EAT.

2 In *Sinclair v Neighbour* [1967] 2 QB 279, CA, a wrongful dismissal case, the employee put an IOU in the till and replaced the money. This was held to justify summary dismissal on the basis of undermining the employer's confidence particularly when he was aware his employer would disapprove.

19.348 Theft at work from a colleague is not so serious according to one authority which has not been challenged[1] even though the theft was from the employee's supervisor. Where the theft occurs outside the workplace the employer is still entitled to act upon it if it could affect the employee in his work.[2] The original ACAS Code of Practice provides that the offences should be examined in relation to the duties of the employee to see whether they make him unsuitable for his work or unacceptable to other employees. Thus a bus conductor was justifiably dismissed after theft because his work involved taking money from the public[3] as was a senior meat inspector who had taken money from his rugby club. This latter dismissal was based on the fact that he was employed by a local authority and occupied a position where integrity was of considerable importance. The employer will always have to consider the nature of the offence, the relationship with his colleagues, possible contact with the public as well as its own reputation.

1 *Johnson Matthey Metals Ltd v Harding* [1978] IRLR 248, EAT. Dismissal would not be outside a range of reasonable responses it is suggested.

2 *Singh v London County Bus Services Ltd* [1976] IRLR 176. Where a bus conductor had been found guilty of an offence involving his Building Society account.

3 Ibid.

19.349 Dishonesty is clearly misconduct but some actions may fall short of being dishonest yet lead to serious misgivings and dismissal. Poor stock control in places like an off-licence or by a barperson at a club or public-house are often regarded seriously. The same applies to a failure to follow the correct procedure for ringing up money on a till. Thus where an employee who had fourteen years' unblemished service failed to follow the proper procedure in relation to a small amount in a test purchase this justified her dismissal.[1]

1 *Scottish Midland Co-operative Society Ltd v Cullion* [1991] IRLR 261.

19.350 A serious view is also taken of any misuse of a computer so if an unauthorised password is used to enter a computer where confidential information is contained this is classified as gross misconduct without any need to find out why access was sought.[1] However, this should always be investigated in practice.

[1] *Denco Ltd v Joinson* [1991] IRLR 63, EAT.

Concluding remarks on conduct

19.351 The above categories of conduct are not intended to be exclusive or exhaustive – they are intended to cover what are seen as the most important examples of misconduct. Other areas which have not been mentioned, or only peripherally or briefly include personality conflicts and sexual relationships,[1] smoking[2] and breach of company rules. The main principles have, hopefully, been mentioned, and further general principles will be covered in the sections on reasonableness and 'some other substantial reason' and include those contained in the ACAS Disciplinary Code and the ACAS Handbook.

[1] But see below 'some other substantial reason'.
[2] This is an issue for the nineties and it seems that employers will be permitted to introduce no-smoking areas and probably complete bans provided they carry this out reasonably and on reasonable notice.

Redundancy

19.352 We have already considered automatically unfair redundancy dismissals. However, redundancy can be a valid reason for dismissal, as we shall see, provided it is carried out reasonably. It would seem that if the employer is dismissing for redundancy it should not be unfair and when the legislation was introduced this was the view taken by some. However, a considerable body of case law has developed in this area and there are many cases where a redundancy dismissal has been carried out unfairly.

19.353 When a union is recognised the leading case is that of *Williams v Compair Maxam Ltd*[1] which laid down some principles which would usually apply. They are as follows:

(a) the employer will seek to give as much warning as possible of impending redundancies so as to enable the union and employees who may be affected to take early steps to inform themselves of the relevant facts, consider possible alternative solutions and if necessary find alternative employment in the undertaking or elsewhere;
(b) the employer will consult the union as to the best means by which the desired management result can be achieved fairly and with as little hardship to the employees as possible. In particular the employer will seek to agree with the union the criteria to be applied in selecting the employees to be made redundant. After the selection the employer will consider with the union whether the selection has followed the criteria;
(c) the employer will seek to establish criteria which do not depend solely on the selector's opinion but can be checked objectively such as attendance record, efficiency, experience or length of service;
(d) the employer will seek to ensure a fair selection is made in accordance

with the criteria and will consider any representations the union may make;

(e) the employer will try to find alternative employment before dismissal.[2]

[1] [1982] ICR 156, EAT.

[2] These principles should be adapted when no union is recognised.

19.354 In a nutshell therefore what is required is warning and consultation, fair selection criteria, properly applied and a consideration of alternative employment. The principles are not rules of law but are guidelines to be adapted for smaller non-unionised employers. The procedures are very important and a failure to follow them will lead to an unfair dismissal finding unless the employer can show that it would have been an utterly futile exercise.[1] However, where the employer can show that it was likely that the procedure would have made no difference to the result the compensation would be severely limited.[2] In practice the tribunal will calculate the percentage, the result will be the same if the proper procedure were followed.

[1] *Polkey v Dayton Services Ltd* [1988] ICR 142, HL.

[2] *Mining Supplies (Longwall) Ltd v Baker* [1988] ICR 676, EAT. Two weeks' pay is the norm according to this case.

19.355 On the standard of proof required the tribunal has to be satisfied that it was reasonable to dismiss each of the applicants selected. It is not enough to show that it was reasonable to dismiss an employee – it must be the particular employee who must be selected fairly and treated fairly.[1] There is not to be an investigation into the reasons for creating redundancies or into the rights and wrongs of the declared redundancy.[2] It has also been suggested that it is impermissible to consider whether there was a genuine redundancy situation[3] but surely the employee can adduce evidence that it was not the true reason for dismissal and this would have to be considered.

[1] See *Compair Maxam* case, para 19.353 above.

[2] *Moon v Homeworthy Furniture (Northern) Ltd* [1976] IRLR 298, EAT.

[3] *Redland Roof Tiles Ltd v Eveleigh* [1979] IRLR 11, EAT.

Selection

19.356 The employer must establish the unit of selection (the group of employees to be considered for redundancy) but provided he has considered the issue the tribunal will uphold his selection unless his decision is unreasonable.[1] If there is an agreed procedure then of course the employer must follow this. If the union has agreed the unit of selection this also assists the employer in showing he has acted reasonably.[2] Where a group of workers regularly transfer departments so that there are interchanges then the unit of selection should not be artificially small so as to exclude one group. The unit must be a reflection of what actually happens.

[1] *Thomas and Betts Manufacturing Ltd v Harding* [1980] IRLR 255, CA.

[2] *Huddersfield Parcels Ltd v Sykes* [1981] IRLR 115, EAT.

19.357 The criteria for selection must be capable of objective assessment so that purely subjective criteria would not be acceptable. Occasionally, however, some criteria which do not appear to be very easily capable of objective assessment seem to slip through the net.

19.358 The most common criterion used is length of service which is simple to operate, particularly in a small organisation. However, in sophisticated operations, particularly where skilled workers are required, it is increasingly becoming inadequate for employers who may need to retain individuals with certain skills. Perhaps the leading case to attack 'last in first out' successfully was *BL Cars Ltd v Lewis*[1] where the criteria were 'length of service, occupation and skills, but these factors will be considered within the overall objective of retaining a balanced workforce'. The employee was chosen despite having longer service than most in his unit but the EAT, reversing the tribunal, said length of service could not override other factors such as criticisms of his work. However, there is a need to show clear criteria such as capability or suitability to override seniority – other nebulous criteria would not suffice. Seniority is based on the continuous employment of employees not the total amount of separate periods.[2]

1 [1983] IRLR 58.
2 *International Paint Co Ltd v Cameron* [1979] ICR 429.

19.359 The need for a balanced workforce is perfectly understandable but it needs to be explained otherwise there is a danger that it may be incapable of objective assessment. In one case[1] the employer succeeded where the criteria were 'quality of work, efficiency in carrying it out and the attitude of the persons evaluated to their work'. The employee had been selected because of his lack of co-operation and bad language.[2] Absenteeism is another reasonable criteria and like any other factors which can be used to criticise the employee do not have to be of such a poor quality as to justify a prior warning. The employer should ensure that the absence record is accurate and check there was absence.[3] Flexibility as to travel and hours of work have been held justifiable as criteria and so have the health records of employees. We have already discovered that selection based on pregnancy is automatically unfair dismissal.[4] The disabled need to have special consideration given to them but their disability does not become a factor in the selection criteria process. The employer surmounts this hurdle at a later stage when considering individual hardship.

1 *Graham v ABF Ltd* [1986] IRLR 90, EAT.
2 The employer's case failed on warning and consultation but the criteria were held valid.
3 *Paine and Moore v Grundy (Teddington) Ltd* [1981] IRLR 267, EAT.
4 *Brown v Stockton-on-Tees Borough Council* [1988] ICR 410, HL. See ERA, s 98.

19.360 Having selected the criteria it is incumbent on the employer to apply them fairly to all those in the unit of selection. If the employer acts arbitrarily in this regard he will be found to have acted unfairly.

19.361 The employer's main obligation is to show his method of selection was fair in general terms and that it was applied reasonably in the case of the employee. Witnesses of some seniority should explain the circumstances of the dismissal.[1] However, a senior manager is entitled to rely on assessments of employees made by those having direct knowledge of their work.[2] The tribunal must not substitute its decision on selection for that of the employer[3] but must ask whether the selection was one which a reasonable employer could have made.[4] It is not permissible for the employer to effectively allow the employee to choose whether he should be made redundant at the expense of another employee. It is unfair to put the onus on the employee where this is part of the employer's responsibility to manage the business.[5]

1 *Buchanan v Tilcon Ltd* [1983] IRLR 417.
2 *Eaton Ltd v King* [1996] IRLR 199, Ct of Session, where the senior manager giving evidence at the tribunal had not carried out assessments and could not explain marks that had been awarded. All the employer has to do is to prove the method of selection was fair in general terms. However, it was held that the dismissals were unfair because there had been no fair and proper consultation with the employees or their representatives.
3 *Watling & Co Ltd v Richardson* [1978] ICR 1049, EAT.
4 *BL Cars Ltd v Lewis* [1983] IRLR 58.
5 *Boulton & Paul Ltd v Arnold* [1994] IRLR 532, EAT.

19.362 In a very recent decision[1] the Court of Appeal has taken a very restrictive view as to challenges to an employer's selection process, albeit at the interlocutory stage of discovery. 530 employed out of a total of 7000 were made redundant. The workforce was divided into categories and all the employees were assessed on the basis of six criteria and the lowest scorers in each category were selected. Nearly half of those selected complained of unfair dismissal and they wanted to see the assessments of the employees retained. The tribunal's order of discovery was qualified by the EAT and the Court of Appeal which said that the question for the tribunal was whether the applicant was unfairly dismissed not whether some other employee could have been fairly dismissed. However, this is precisely the question for the tribunal. Where it is accepted that there should not be an over-minute analysis it is crucial to be able to make comparisons. Obviously there were concerns that the tribunal hearing might become 'hopelessly protracted' but discovery prior to tribunal hearings might encourage more settlements or withdrawals. The EAT has ordered discovery in a subsequent case which dealt with the dismissal of one employee from amongst a group of eight. Several criteria were agreed with the union which included length of service. The applicant claimed that an employee with much shorter service was retained and the EAT affirmed the order for discovery and particulars relating to the other employees. The EAT implied that the *Green* case had probably gone too far, but in the *Eaton*[2] case the Court of Session preferred the *Green* approach.

1 *British Aerospace plc v Green* [1995] IRLR 433.
2 See para 19.361, n 2.

Warnings and consultation

19.363 The importance of these steps has already been mentioned following the *Polkey* decision. There is a statutory procedure for recognised trade unions which Browne-Wilkinson J referred to in the leading case of *Compair Maxam*.[1] These steps should not be seen as required simply because the possibilities of alternative employment need to be considered. There is a possibility that the employee could persuade the employer to adopt different solutions to avoid redundancies and the employee is at least given some time to make plans for the future. For example, the selected employee might be able to show that another employee was hoping to be made redundant. This would not oblige the employer to select that individual but it should at least be considered. A warning of redundancies and a statement of selection criteria is insufficient to constitute consultation which must be fair and genuine and should give employees a fair and proper opportunity to understand the position and express their views. The obligation to consult is separate from the obligation to warn.[2]

[1] See para 19.353 above.
[2] *Powell v Hubbard Group Services Ltd* [1995] IRLR 195.

19.364 It is extremely difficult for an employer to establish that there were exceptional circumstances which justified a failure to consult and the fact that immediate decisions had to be made and that the employee was the only one who could be dismissed was not a justification.[1] A very important qualification to the *Polkey* case is that it has been decided that where the employer fails to consult and consultation would have served no useful purpose it is not necessary for the employer to have deliberately decided at the time of the dismissal that consultation would be useless.[2] The Tribunal can make the decision, based on the facts known to the employeer at the time of the dismissal, by reference to what it thinks is reasonable.[3] The Tribunal, must, where there has been a breach of procedure, calculate what percentage chance there is that the employee would have been dismissed in any event.[4] This is a reduction based on what is just and equitable to award as compensation. However, where it is considered that there should be no compensation this should be confined to situations where there are merely procedural and not substantive failings.[5]

[1] *Heron v City Link–Nottingham* [1993] IRLR 372, EAT.
[2] *Duffy v Yeoman & Partners Ltd* [1994] IRLR 642, CA.
[3] This is re-establishing the *British Labour Pump* principle which was supposedly eradicated by *Polkey* [1988] ICR 142, HL.
[4] *Campbell v Dunoon and Cowal Housing Association* [1993] IRLR 496.
[5] *Steel Stockholders (Birmingham) Ltd v Kirkwood* [1993] IRLR 515, EAT.

Alternative work

19.365 The employer is obliged to look for alternative work and this is not limited to considering the section in which the employee worked, even if this means dismissing someone else.[1] The employer must look carefully and even offer a job which entails a demotion which is a matter for the employee to consider.[2] However, there is no need to make an offer which could be construed as insulting to the employee. The employee must be given sufficient information about the new job to enable him to make a sensible decision.[3] Where the employee is offered an alternative position he is entitled to a trial period and if this is refused the dismissal will be unfair if the refusal is unreasonable[4] which, it is submitted, it will be in almost all cases.

[1] *Thomas v Betts*, above. This was a comment made in 1980 and if it means that one must 'bump' another employee from another section altogether and dismiss him it is certainly not the current

practice and it is respectfully submitted, cannot follow logically otherwise all other employees jobs would be at risk in this situation and this cannot have been intended.

2 *Avonmouth Construction Co Ltd v Shipway* [1973] IRLR 14.

3 *Modern Injection Moulds Ltd v Price* [1976] ICR 370.

4 *Elliott v Richard Stump Ltd* [1987] ICR 579.

19.366 If the employer has given notice of dismissal but the dismissal has not yet taken effect and a sudden change means that the employer requires employees he should offer the vacancies to the employees who have been given notice before he fills the vacancies with newly-recruited employees.[1]

1 *Stacey v Babcock Power Ltd* [1986] QB 308, EAT.

19.367 Furthermore, the employer must give the redundant employee reasonable consideration for vacancies. Where an employee on a one-year fixed term contract did not have her contract of employment renewed after a new post had been created her application failed, because, said the Court of Appeal, she was never fairly considered for it. Thus the way in which she had been treated in relation to this new application was relevant in determining the reasonableness of the employer's dismissal decision.[1] However, a long-serving employee would not be entitled to claim he should have priority for any new position created against other applicants. A job can be advertised and he will have to compete.[2]

1 *Labour Party v Oakley* [1988] ICR 403. In 1989 ACAS produced a very useful advisory booklet 'Redundancy Handling' which details the points that have been examined above. It gives guidance on forward planning so as to avoid redundancies and also how to establish a redundancy procedure and what to put in it. It also emphasises the importance of consultation, the need for objective selection criteria and the requirement of looking for alternative jobs. Other useful information is contained in the booklet.

2 *Rennie v Grampian Regional Council* EAT 475/90.

Statutory restrictions

19.368 A permitted reason for dismissal is that the employee 'could not continue to work in the position which he held without contravention (either on his part or on the part of his employer) of a duty or restriction imposed by or under an enactment'.[1] Although it would not be very surprising if this were to be treated as an automatically fair dismissal it is, in fact, still subject to the test of reasonableness. In fact, there are very few cases which arise under this reason, the most obvious type being where an employee loses his driving licence and he is employed to drive or requires to drive to carry on his job.

1 ERA, s 98(2)(d).

Loss of driving licence

19.369 Where the employee loses his licence the employer must consider whether the job can be carried on without a licence because it is possible that this can be effected without undue inconvenience to the employer. If the employee is employed as a driver then it is rather difficult to see how a dismissal could be unfair but it might be that the employee could ask his spouse or friend to drive him. If that were possible any suggestion by the employee should be considered by the employer to see if this is practicable.

19.370 If the employee drives for the purpose of simply transporting him from place to place it must first be asked whether this is possible on public transport which is relatively efficient in the UK. This may not be very easy if the employee usually carries a large amount of stock or tools. The employee might be able to get someone to drive him, and if he is reasonably well paid he might even be able to afford a chauffeur, although this is very unlikely. It might be that the driving required is not very extensive and that colleagues could cover for him. This will depend very much on the size of the organisation, the larger one being able to cover more easily, or being able to accommodate him in other work.[1]

---

1 See *Appleyard v FM Smith (Hull) Ltd* [1972] IRLR 19.

19.371 The above matters show how critical it is that there should be consultation and discussion with the employee because he might be able to offer suggestions which the employer had not appreciated were possible. Thus when an employee had engaged a chauffeur and arranged to pay an extra insurance premium on his company car but was dismissed before these arrangements could be implemented the dismissal was unfair.[1] This is not to suggest that the employer must abide by the employee's arrangements although the ones just mentioned do not seem problematic. The employer must at least give the employee the opportunity of putting forward his suggestions and they should be considered seriously by the employer. The employer should also give a reasonable opportunity to the employee to make arrangements and should not act too hastily by dismissing immediately after a positive breath test. Sometimes charges are withdrawn or dismissed and the employee is not banned until convicted. The employer should also consider the possibility of alternative employment.

---

1 *Mathieson v WJ Noble* [1972] IRLR 76.

Other grounds

19.372 It must first be pointed out that the employer has no margin for error when relying on this reason – on the wording of the sub-section either the reason exists or it does not. Thus where the employer genuinely believes that there would be contravention of an enactment this does not provide him with a valid reason, unlike the situations where the reason is conduct or capability. There the statutory wording permits a genuine belief. The leading case is *Bouchaala v Trusthouse Forte Hotels Ltd*[1] where the employer was actually advised by the Department of Employment that the continued employment of Mr Bouchaala would be illegal. The employee was dismissed but 11 days later the Home Office wrote to the employer stating that he did not require a work permit. The tribunal rejected the complaint of unfair dismissal on the grounds of the employer's genuine belief that continued employment would be illegal but the

EAT rejected this argument saying there was no basis for permitting genuine belief to operate under ERA, s 98(2)(d). However, they affirmed the decision on the grounds that the employer's belief constituted 'some other substantial reason'. There can be no questions asked about the merits of the statutory ban – if it exists that is the end of the matter.

1 [1980] ICR 721, EAT.

19.373 In determining whether the employer has acted reasonably in dismissing the employee the employer should establish whether the employee can carry on with part of his work and consider whether he could do some alternative work. He will need to see if the ban is going to last for a long time and if it is related to a medical condition he will need to establish the precise medical position and prognosis. Thus, if it is not permitted to employ a person with a particular condition on certain processes the employer should establish if this condition is likely to continue. If not, the employer should consider whether it is possible to continue employment in some other capacity for a temporary period.

19.374 There are many jobs which require specific qualifications, some more obscure than others. In one quite well known case[1] the employee was a trainee hearing aid dispenser who had failed his examinations on three occasions. Having completed five years' employment his name was removed from the register of hearing aid dispensers under the Hearing Aid Council Act of 1968 because he had not passed the examinations. His continued employment would have been a criminal offence with a maximum fine of £100 per day. He was dismissed but subsequently he applied for an extension to resit the examinations. The EAT held the dismissal unfair because the breach of statute did not make it fair – it was necessary to consider all the circumstances. The employer could have sought an extension and it was not likely that proceedings would have been taken against the employers.

1 *Sutcliffe and Eaton Ltd v Pinney* [1977] IRLR 349.

19.375 This case shows how carefully employers must act when they are faced with what is, apparently, a valid reason for dismissal. It is not sufficient to rely purely on the technical wording of the statute because it might be that it is never enforced, or is easily waived. The employer must check the position and the longer and better the service of the employee the greater degree of investigation that is required.

Some other substantial reason

Introductory

19.376 So far we have discussed reasons which are clearly understandable to anyone although they all have considerable refinements as a result of the case law. There is a sweeping-up reason which does not fall within any of the other categories which is 'some other substantial reason of a kind such as to justify the dismissal of an employee holding the position which that employee held'.[1]

Although it has been held[2] that the sub-section is not to be construed ejusdem generis with the other reasons so that it can cover anything there is, nevertheless, a certain degree of overlap with other reasons in some situations. For example, where the employee has committed a breach of fidelity this could be classified as conduct or some other substantial reason and one's sexual orientation could be classified under both these reasons. A very common overlap is where there is reorganisation which could constitute a redundancy or some other substantial reason.

[1] ERA, s 98(1)(b).
[2] *RS Components Ltd v Irwin* [1973] ICR 535, NIRC.

Establishing a 'substantial' reason

19.377 What the sub-section does is to require the tribunal to 'consider the reason established by the employer and to decide whether it falls within the category of reasons which could justify the dismissal of an employee – not that employee but an employee – holding the position which that employee held'.[1] Thus it depends on the kind of job the employee does as different reasons will justify the dismissal depending on the job.

[1] *Dobie v Burns International Security Services (UK) Ltd* [1984] ICR 812, CA.

19.378 An allied point relates to the standard required of an employee in establishing this reason. The use of the word 'substantial' implies that there should be some substance in establishing the reason which is not the test in relation to other reasons although it is arguable that it could be, bearing in mind the use of the word 'other'. In fact, the same standard is applied to this reason. Thus it has been held that the burden of showing a substantial reason is designed to deter employers from dismissing for some trivial or unworthy reason. Once it is shown that the reason could justify the dismissal then it is sufficient and the question of reasonableness must then be considered.[1] A less strict approach[2] is to see if the employer considered the reason to be substantial and of a kind such as to justify dismissal. This more subjective approach could not avail the employer if the reason was whimsical or capricious which no person of ordinary sense would entertain but beyond that if it is genuine it is sufficient.[3]

[1] *Gilham v Kent County Council (No 2)* [1985] ICR 233, CA. The same discussion has been entered into regarding *British Home Stores Ltd v Burchell* [1978] IRLR 379.
[2] If the above can be regarded as strict.
[3] *Saunders v Scottish National Camps Association Ltd* [1981] IRLR 277 and *Harper v National Coal Board* [1980] IRLR 260, EAT.

19.379 There are two specific situations which in the legislation are designed to be substantial reasons for dismissal; they are when a replacement is employed for an employee absent on maternity leave or because of medical suspension[1] and who is then dismissed to make way for the employee's return. These are substantial reasons which must, however, still satisfy the test of reasonableness. However, as the employee requires two years' service to claim unfair dismissal which will not be obtained it is superfluous to discuss this further.

1 See earlier sections on this and ERA, s 106.

19.380 We have already discussed the question of pleading the proper reason and this problem arises with the possible overlap of reasons mentioned briefly above. The right practical answer for the employer is that he should plead in the alternative if he is uncertain which is the correct reason. Despite an earlier case[1] which required precise pleading where the dismissal was for redundancy/some other substantial reason it is suggested that this is no longer necessary and that the better view is that provided there is no change in the factual basis relied on by the employer and the different grounds are really different labels and nothing more, the late introduction of a reason even without mentioning it in the written pleadings is valid. The Court of Appeal decision[2] which states that the ground should be expressly ventilated in the tribunal so that both parties can have a full and proper opportunity to deploy their cases on that matter has now been affirmed by a more recent decision.[3] It is suggested that if the tribunal intends to use that reason as justifying dismissal where it has not been expressly pleaded or argued it is incumbent on the tribunal to inform the parties of this before the proceedings and to give them an opportunity to comment on it. We shall return to this point to consider it as a matter of substance below.

1 *Nelson v BBC* [1977] ICR 649, CA.
2 *Murphy v Epsom College* [1985] ICR 80.
3 *Burkett v Pendletons (Sweets) Ltd* [1992] ICR 407, EAT.

Reorganisation

19.381 Perhaps the most important development in unfair dismissal and certainly the most advantageous to employers since the 1980s has been the support the law has given to them when they have wanted to carry out business reorganisations. Thus even though any unilateral material alteration to an employee's contract is a repudiatory breach the employer may be able to defend any unfair dismissal claim where he can show the business advantage attaching to such alteration. This was not a very prevalent development in the 1970s and if there is support for the view that law reflects and follows economic developments in society this is certainly a very good example.

19.382 In earlier cases of redundancy it had been held that reorganisation of working hours was not a redundancy situation provided the work remained the same.[1] The classic statement was that of Lord Denning '. . . nothing should be done to impair the ability of employers to reorganise their workforce and their terms and conditions of work so as to improve efficiency'.[2] This extremely wide statement is the flag-bearer for the development of 'some other substantial reason'.

1 For example *Lesney Products & Co Ltd v Nolan* [1977] ICR 235, CA.
2 See *Lesney*, above.

19.383 As there is indubitably a breach of contract the employer must give proper notice to terminate the contract and offer a new contract on the new terms, if he is going to alter the terms. An attempt to vary the contract by other methods will lead to difficulties for the employer.[1]

[1] See elsewhere eg *Rigby v Ferodo Ltd* [1988] ICR 29, HL.

19.384 The standard required of the employer is not as high as to require him to show the re-organisation is necessary but that there is a sound good business reason for the change, and the only sensible way of dealing with it is to offer the employees reasonable new contracts.[1] If the employee refuses then a substantial reason for dismissal exists.[2]

[1] *Hollister v National Farmers' Union* [1979] ICR 542, CA.
[2] For example *Bowater Containers Ltd v McCormack* [1980] IRLR 50, EAT and *Hollister*, above.

19.385 The employer must also show what his business reasons were and that they were substantial and therefore must produce some evidence to show that there was a reorganisation or that there was some need for economy and it is material for the tribunal to know whether the company was making profits or losses.[1] Furthermore, if the employer has decided on a new policy he has to provide evidence of its advantages and the importance of it. Thus, when a part-time doctor was dismissed following the resignation of his fellow part-timer because the employer wanted to appoint one full-timer this was held unfair as the employer had provided no evidence to support its policy.[2] This is not to suggest that this places a high onus on the employer because this might be seen as encroaching on managerial prerogative. It does require the employer to explain the reason for his actions.

[1] *Ladbroke Courage Holidays Ltd v Asten* [1981] IRLR 59, EAT.
[2] *Banerjee v City and East London Area Health Authority* [1979] IRLR 147, ECJ.

19.386 As in all other reasons it is necessary for the employer to have consulted with the employee about the changes. In many cases there will be a number of employees affected and an individual will find it harder to justify his refusal to change where the union has agreed to the alteration[1] or the vast majority of the employees have agreed.[2] However, the consultation with the union is not a substitute for consultation with individual employees who should always be consulted.[3] Although individuals may have personal reasons why the changes should not be foisted on them this is not the vital criterion because the test is whether the employer has acted reasonably in making the changes, not whether it creates an injustice or disadvantage for employees.[4] Thus even if the changes impact unreasonably upon the employee it is the employer's behaviour that counts and this point is considerably strengthened, if not totally fortified by the *Polkey*[5] decision.

[1] *Bowater*, above.
[2] *Horrigan v Lewisham London Borough Council* [1978] ICR 15, EAT.
[3] *Martin v Automobile Proprietary Ltd* [1979] IRLR 64, EAT.
[4] *Chubb Fire Security Ltd v Harper* [1983] IRLR 311, EAT and *Richmond Precision Engineering Ltd v Pearce* [1985] IRLR 179, EAT.
[5] [1988] ICR 142, HL.

19.387 Furthermore, ultimately, if there is insufficient consultation or negotiation this does not render the dismissal unfair because there is no requirement that there must always be consultation – it is only one of the factors which has to be taken into account when looking at the circumstances of the case.[1] The EAT in the *Hollister* case had held that the lack of consultation and negotiation had rendered the dismissal unfair but the Court of Appeal said that this was putting a gloss on the statute and reversed the decision.

[1] *Hollister*, para 19.384 above.

19.388 The right of the employer to make contractual changes is a powerful one and is the most important aspect of this particular reason. There are many other areas where the reason has been used successfully by the employer, some coinciding with other reasons, some operating only within this reason. Some of the areas are outlined below.

Fixed-term contracts

19.389 We have already noted that the expiry of a fixed-term contract without its being renewed operates as a dismissal but that does not mean it is an unfair dismissal. However, the mere expiry without more does not constitute a substantial reason for dismissal.[1] This is natural as the whole purpose of deeming the expiry of a fixed-term contract to be a dismissal is to guard against employers using this device to avoid unfair dismissal protection. However, the expiry of the contract may be a substantial reason where the employee knows he has been employed for a particular period or a particular job on a temporary basis. It is up to the tribunal to balance the need for employers who have a genuine need for fixed-term employment, which is known not to be ongoing, to be protected against the employee's need for protection against being deprived of their rights by an artificiality.[2] The *Terry* case and its approach was expressly approved by the Court of Appeal in the *Fay* case[3] where the temporary employee found he was replaced by a permanent employee. The Court held that the employee was well aware that the job was a temporary one and for a specific purpose.

[1] *Terry v East Sussex County Council* [1976] ICR 536, EAT.
[2] See *Terry*, above.
[3] *North Yorkshire County Council v Fay* [1985] IRLR 247.

19.390 If the employee was not appointed to fulfil a specific short-term requirement but was merely appointed a temporary employee without knowing whether his contract will be renewed, the tribunal must consider the situation carefully. If there was an assurance of continuation the employer will be in difficulties, but if nothing was said it will be necessary for the tribunal to work out what was understood at the time the contract was made and then it will have to apply the principles from *Terry* as mentioned above. A temporary employee's application for any new post should be given proper consideration.[1]

[1] *Labour Party v Oakley* [1988] ICR 403, CA.

Third-party pressure

19.391 A customer's pressure or any third party pressure on an employer to dismiss an employee may justify dismissal for some other substantial reason. The customer may have developed a particular dislike for an employee and may base his demand on that. The fairness of the dismissal does not depend on the employee's misconduct. Thus when the US navy wrote to the employer stating that an employee was no longer acceptable for any work for the US government the ultimatum justified the dismissal even though there was no misconduct established. The US Government's work constituted over 80% of the employer's business and the ultimatum justified the dismissal.[1] The EAT suggested that this was sufficient even though the third party's motives might have been suspect.

[1] *Scott Packing and Warehousing Ltd v Paterson* [1989] IRLR 166.

19.392 In a subsequent major case the Court of Appeal resiled somewhat from this extreme position by stating that to justify dismissal at the behest of the third party the employee should have been told when he made the contract that he could be dismissed in these circumstances. If so then it cannot be contrary to equity and the substantial merits of the case.[1] In the *Dobie* case the County Council had the right to approve the employment or continued employment of security staff at Liverpool Airport. It is uncertain how much weight should be attached to the comment in this case about injustices to the employer being important given the *Polkey*'s approach to the reasonableness of the employee's behaviour. However, one can categorise the behaviour within the employer's actions – he should have notified the employee.

[1] *Dobie v Burns International Security Services (UK) Ltd* [1984] ICR 812 – it might still be inequitable in some cases but this is what the Court said.

19.393 The existence of the consultation is not sufficient to justify the dismissal because the tribunal must consider whether the employer has made proper efforts to obtain a change of mind by the third party and will need to be satisfied that there has been an actual threat to withdraw business.[1] It will not be enough to take a view that a customer/client will be unhappy to have an employee working for them who has been charged with sex offences against children without asking the customer.[2] Finally the employer should have made an attempt to find other work for the employee as it may be possible to switch work around with other employees.

[1] *Grootcon (UK) Ltd v Keld* [1984] IRLR 302, EAT.
[2] *Securicor Guarding v R* [1994] IRLR 633, EAT. The employee was a security guard.

19.394 Where a third party withdraws funding from the work which the employee is doing it is incumbent on the employer to ascertain the reason for the withdrawal and to explain this to the employee. Withdrawal of funding is not conclusive and if the employer does not act properly the dismissal will be unfair.[1]

[1] As it was in *Pillinger v Manchester Area Health Authority* [1979] IRLR 430.

Staff disruption

19.395 Where there are difficulties between staff an employee's behaviour might constitute misconduct but is more likely to fall within 'some other substantial reason' on the basis that it is damaging the business where employees are arguing with each other. In one case a woman constantly upset her female colleagues by talking about her sexual activities and boasting about them and was fairly dismissed.[1] However, the employer must take steps to improve the position and should not dismiss until it is clear that there will be no improvement.[2] Staff disruption may also be caused by disapproval of staff who have been convicted of certain sexual offences such as child abuse, molestation or rape, where they obviously did not receive custodial sentences. The disharmony might constitute grounds for dismissal but it must be remembered that if pressure by industrial action is threatened or taken this must be disregarded.[3]

[1] *Treganowan v Knee & Co Ltd* [1975] ICR 405.
[2] *Turner v Vesterric Ltd* [1980] ICR 528, EAT.
[3] ERA, s 100.

Unorthodox behaviour

19.396 The law is very supportive of employers in any prejudice they may have against what might be classified as non-conventional behavior. Some might say the law was too supportive. Thus is has been held fair to dismiss a homosexual man after he was involved in an incident outside work because he worked in a camp with young children. Although the evidence established he was uninterested in young children the EAT justified the dismissal on the basis that a considerable proportion of employers would take a similar view.[1] A pandering to prejudice! The same result obtained for a man convicted of indecency in a public lavatory.[2] An employee who suddenly began having epileptic fits and attacking employees was fairly dismissed for some other substantial reason or capability.[3] A failure to disclose a past history of mental illness constituted a composite 'some other substantial reason' namely the fact that there had been mental illness and the failure to disclose it.[4] A prison sentence of three months could be some other substantial reason.[5]

[1] *Saunders v Scottish National Camps Association Ltd* [1981] IRLR 277.
[2] *Wiseman v Salford City Council* [1981] IRLR 202.
[3] *Harper v National Coal Board* [1980] IRLR 260, EAT.
[4] *O'Brien v Prudential Assurance Co Ltd* [1979] IRLR 140.
[5] *Kingston v British Railways Board* [1984] ICR 781, CA.

AIDS

19.397 There has been very little debate and no authoritative case law regarding the position of AIDS sufferers. There is certainly no specific statutory reference to AIDS. Thus the position would be governed by ordinary principles of unfair dismissal.[1]

[1] There may be sex discrimination issues.

19.398 If someone is suffering from AIDS that in itself is not a ground for dismissal but if it leads to an inability to work or to considerable absence this can be dealt with under the reason of capability. The more contentious question is whether a dismissal could fall within 'some other substantial reason' where other employees or customers object. One assumes that an employer would not risk dismissing an AIDS sufferer just for that very reason as there would then be no valid reason within ERA, s 98(2).

19.399 The cases so far are not very illuminating but are certainly not very supportive of AIDS sufferers. In one case a cinema projectionist was convicted of gross indecency in a public lavatory and as a consequence his colleagues pressured the employer into dismissing him because of their fears of becoming HIV positive. There was no proof that he even had AIDS.[1] The tribunal found the dismissal fair but the EAT reversed the decision,[1] saying that an incorrect procedure had been adopted. The EAT did not, however, criticise the employer for their substantive decision. An industrial tribunal has held[2] that where a cook was selected for redundancy based on his inability to fit in with colleagues the fact that this emanated from the belief he had AIDS did not render the selection unfair. The tribunal did say that a good employer must act promptly to allay suspicions of HIV infection. In due course this issue will need to be discussed properly. The Government has issued a booklet making it quite clear that dismissal because of HIV infection would not be justified. Surely when the pressure comes from colleagues a dismissal could not be justified even though this may cause internal disruption. What, however, of the client/customer who insists on the individual's dismissal? We have already seen that third party pressure provides a sound defence provided that certain procedures are followed. Surely the tribunals and courts will not permit a third party to insist on an individual's dismissal unless there are sound business reasons for doing so which are not linked with AIDS.

[1] *Buck v Letchworth Palace* (1987) 36488/86.
[2] *Cormack v TNT Sealion* 1825/126.

Restrictive covenants and competition

19.400 We have already discussed unilateral alterations to contracts. Perhaps the first major case on some other substantial reason concerned the imposition of a restrictive covenant. The employer was facing the situation where employees were leaving, competing and soliciting his customers. The employer decided to impose the covenant in the face of a decline in profits and commission for staff. Nearly all the staff signed but some did not and were dismissed. It was held that the dismissal was fair because the employer had a substantial reason for dismissal and had acted fairly.[1]

[1] *RS Components Ltd v Irwin* [1973] ICR 535, NIRC.

19.401 A not uncommon situation is where an employee has a spouse or close relative or friend working for a competitor.[1] The employer may be nervous about the possibility of confidential information being passed over and the problem of unfair competition. If there is a serious risk of damage to the employer's business, the dismissal is likely to be upheld but the situation needs to be handled carefully. The nature of the possible conflict should be ascertained as well as the exact nature of the relationship before discussing it with the employee. If there is little chance of confidential information or unfair competition ensuing the employer is unlikely to be able to lawfully dismiss.

1 This has already been mentioned under fidelity in 'conduct' discussions.

Further miscellany

19.402 A genuine but erroneous belief that an employee could not be legally employed was held to justify a dismissal[1] as was a genuine but mistaken belief in an employee's non-membership of a union.[2] When an employee was dismissed to make way for the employer's son this was held to be fair but it should be noted that the employee was aware from an early stage of his employment that this was likely to occur.[3] It is also fair to dismiss a spouse when the other spouse has been dismissed and they are employed as a married couple.[4] It must be the case that the two rise or fall together as there may be situations where husband and wife are employed by the same employer but their employment is not linked. If that is the case the employer cannot fairly dismiss a spouse if the other has been dismissed even if it has been for dishonesty. There is no guilt by association. If there is evidence to the contrary then of course the employer can act upon it. In one case[5] an employee advised his employer that he intended to resign to take up a job in Australia. The impression the employer obtained was that this would happen quickly but no written notice of termination nor any notifications of the actual date he would be leaving was given. Two months later the employer explained a replacement was being sought and they wanted an exact date and if not it would be assumed to be 21 December. On that date the employee stated he was staying. His subsequent dismissal was held to be fair on the basis of the late notification that the employee was changing his mind about resigning which could constitute 'some other substantial reason' despite the fact that it had not been pleaded and the employee had relied on there being no dismissal. This reason for dismissal is certainly versatile.

1 *Bouchaala v Trusthouse Forte Hotels Ltd* [1980] ICR 721, EAT.
2 *Leyland Vehicles Ltd v Jones* [1981] ICR 428, EAT.
3 *Priddle v Dibble* [1978] ICR 149.
4 *Kelman v Oram* [1983] IRLR 432, EAT.
5 *Ely v YKK Fasteners (UK)* [1993] IRLR 500, CA.

Transfer of undertakings

19.403 These have already been discussed[1] but it should be noted here that where there is an economic, technical or organisational reason for dismissals this is to be treated as a substantial reason for dismissal although this is still subject to reasonableness.[2]

[1] See Chapter 8 and this Chapter.
[2] Regulation 8(2) of the Transfer of Undertakings (Protection of Employment) Regulations 1981.

5 REASONABLENESS

Introduction

19.404 We have now considered the different reasons for dismissal, those that are automatically fair or unfair and those which, when established, need to satisfy the test of reasonableness.[1] We have also mentioned the problems relating to arguing the right reasons for dismissal and multiple reasons for dismissal. We must now move on to the stage after the employer has established the reason, namely whether he acted reasonably. The tribunal must decide whether 'in the circumstances (including the size and administrative resources of the employer's undertaking) the employer acted reasonably or unreasonably in treating it as a sufficient reason for dismissing the employee, and that question shall be determined in accordance with equity and the substantial merits of the case'.[2] As might be expected there is a wealth of case law on this sub-section which will be examined below. Although the employer must act reasonably in the procedural manner of dismissal much of what can be classed as procedure could just as easily be regarded as substantive. A simple example is the need for an employer to carry out a proper investigation into the circumstances of a dismissal. Many would describe this as a procedural requirement but it is vital in determining whether the employer had good grounds for dismissing which must be regarded as substance. Although below we do refer to some matters as procedural or substantive these should not be regarded as absolute categorisations in many cases. What is most important is to determine whether the employer acted reasonably and not to be over concerned as to whether it is substance or procedure. That is not to suggest that the distinction is not important as it often is. Lord Donaldson MR, when he was President of the National Industrial Relations Court, stated that unfair dismissal is not a common sense concept. That is true of some parts but not of all as the reader can decide having looked at the matter as a whole but the judicial comment shows that there is a certain amount of technicality.

[1] See also *Harvey* Div D, Part 7.
[2] ERA, s 98(4), 'it' refers to the reason used by the employer.

Information discovered after dismissal

19.405 At common law where a claim is made for wrongful dismissal the employer can defend the claim for breach of contract by relying on anything he learns about the employee even though he learns about this after the dismissal occurs.[1] Unfair dismissal law is very different and turns on the wording of the statutory provisions. Thus one can only consider fairness by looking at the reason for dismissal and whether treating that reason as justifying dismissal was reasonable. After-acquired information cannot affect the question of liability. In the well-known case of *Devis & Sons Ltd v Atkins*[2] the employee was dismissed for incapability but was later discovered to have been stealing from his employer. The House of Lords and the employer could not rely on this information to justify the dismissal. However, as was also stated, it can have a significant impact on compensation as this must be what the tribunal considers to be a just and equitable amount and in that case virtually no compensation was ordered. As we shall see there is a further element of compensation, the basic award, and even though two weeks' pay had to be provided under the statute in that case,[3] this is no longer necessary.[4]

1 *Boston Deep Sea Fishing and Ice Co v Ansell* (1888) 39 Ch D 339, CA.
2 [1977] AC 931, [1977] 3 All ER 40.
3 Known as the 'rogue's charter'.
4 ERA, s 122(2), see below.

19.406 Some modifications of the rule have been established. The first and most serious problem arising is that relating to the position of appeals. An appeal, or the lack of one, occurs after the date of dismissal because, as we have already noted the effective date of termination relates to the date of dismissal and is unaffected by any appeal.[1] For example time limits run from the date of dismissal not from the date of the appeal. However, for the purpose of considering fairness, the appeal procedure is now very relevant. Thus if the employer does not permit the employee to exercise his contractual right of appeal this in itself becomes an unfair dismissal.[2] Given the well understood industrial relations practice to allow appeals against dismissal in almost all circumstances it is submitted that a failure to allow one even where it was non-contractual should be treated as unfair, particularly in larger organisations.

1 Some agreed procedures may retain the employee in employment until the appeal decision.
2 *West Midland Co-operative Society Ltd v Tipton* [1986] AC 536, [1986] 1 All ER 513, HL.

19.407 Connected with this, but nevertheless separate, is the question of evidence adduced at the appeal hearing. Following *Devis* strictly such evidence should not be admissible in determining fairness. However, in *Tipton*, the House of Lords, following comments in earlier cases,[1] held that it was artificial to exclude what was discovered in the appeal process from the decision as to reasonableness. Such discoveries might help or hinder the employee in his claim. Thus it might be discovered at the appeal hearing that the employee had a good reason for his misconduct or lack of capability[2] which might make a dismissal unfair. Alternatively further evidence may be produced which will justify the employer's decision. If the appeal establishes that the original reason cannot be supported but another reason emerges it is up to the employer to consider whether he wishes to initiate a fresh dismissal process but he should not act on the new reason simply based on the appeal.[3] Finally, on appeal in *Tipton* it was stated that an employer could reasonably refuse to grant an appeal where an employee has pleaded guilty to a serious offence of dishonesty and where an appeal could not affect the outcome. This comment should be treated with caution by employers who should be careful to follow a fair procedure in all circumstances.[4]

1 For example, see *National Heart and Chest Hospitals Board of Governors v Nambiar* [1981] ICR 441, [1981] IRLR 196, EAT and *Greenall Whitley plc v Carr* [1985] ICR 451, [1985] IRLR 289, EAT.

[2] As in *Nambiar* (above) where the employee's medication explained his behaviour. The dismissal ultimately was held to be fair because there was no job for the employee to return to.
[3] See *Nambiar* n 1 above, and *Monie v Coral Racing Ltd* [1981] ICR 109, [1980] IRLR 464, CA.
[4] See discussion above regarding guilty pleas in the section on conduct. If the appeal related to penalty there can be no reason to exclude the right to appeal.

19.408 Sometimes circumstances alter or new information is discovered after a dismissal decision has been taken but before it has been implemented. A tribunal is entitled to have regard to the conduct of the employer after the decision has been taken but before dismissal is put into effect.[1] Thus when an employer gave an employee three months' notice of redundancy but during the notice period obtained new work and took on new employees but did not keep the employee on that this was an unfair dismissal. The EAT said that *Devis*'s case did not mean that you could not take into account matters that occurred before the dismissal actually took effect even though the decision had already been made.[2] By analogy the duty to consider alternative employment can be carried out after notice has been given but before it is effected.[3]

[1] *ILEA v Lloyd* [1981] IRLR 394, CA.
[2] *Stacey v Babcock Power Ltd* [1986] QB 308, [1986] 2 WLR 207.
[3] *P v Nottinghamshire County Council* [1992] ICR 706, CA.

Burden of proof

19.409 When unfair dismissal rights were introduced there was no onus of proof – it was neutral. Then the law was changed so that the employer had to show that he acted reasonably. In 1980 the law was changed back to a neutral stance on reasonableness so that the tribunal has to decide if the employer acted reasonably or unreasonably and this is still the position. The employer still has to show the reason for dismissal and that it was a permitted reason. We have already noted that if a reason, at least in respect of an important part, is neither established in fact nor believed to be true on reasonable grounds the employer will fail. Thus if this factual basis collapses so does the case.[1]

[1] *Smith v City of Glasgow District Council* [1987] ICR 796, [1987] IRLR 326, HL.

19.410 The amendment made in 1980 was a response to employers who believed that they were guilty until they proved their innocence of having carried out an unfair dismissal. On the whole it is only a cosmetic change and 'simply affects which way round the tribunal has to look at its problem at the time of the hearing'.[1] Occasionally, however, it is relevant. Thus in a selection for redundancy case[2] the employee's argument that a certain case should be followed was not accepted because that case was decided when the onus was on the employer to show that he acted reasonably.[3] It does seem rather narrow to make decisions on that basis as principles of fairness should be established irrespective of the burden of proof and it is submitted that it would be highly unusual for that kind of reasoning to be adopted today. It has, however, been a decisive factor in one case on whether there had been a dismissal.[4]

[1] *Abbott and Standley v Wesson-Glynwed Steels Ltd* [1982] IRLR 51, EAT.
[2] *Green v Fraser* [1985] IRLR 55, EAT.
[3] See also *Merseyside and North Wales Electricity Board v Taylor* [1975] ICR 185, [1975] IRLR 60.
[4] *Morris v London Iron and Steel Co Ltd* [1988] QB 493, [1987] IRLR 182, CA. It is unlikely that cases will be determined on the burden of proof.

Constructive dismissal

19.411 If the employer has committed a fundamental breach of contract so as to constitute a constructive dismissal then it is highly likely that the dismissal will be unfair. If behaviour is so unreasonable that it breaks the contract then it does not convert into reasonable behaviour for the purpose of considering the test of reasonableness.[1] However, there are situations where a fundamental breach of contract may still be a fair dismissal. We have already noted that dismissal can be for 'some other substantial reason' and that this can embrace fundamental unilateral alterations which can be justified by the need for a business re-organisation. If an employee resigns in protest against the change this will clearly be a constructive dismissal but not unfair if the employer can produce his business reason and has acted reasonably.[2] If the employer only argues that there has been no constructive dismissal but does not mention fairness the tribunal does not have to consider it of its own motion.[3]

[1] *Cawley v South Wales Electricity Board* [1985] IRLR 89, EAT.
[2] See *Savoia v Chiltern Herb Farms Ltd* [1982] IRLR 166, CA.
[3] *Hill Ltd v Mooney* [1981] IRLR 258, EAT.

Wrongful dismissal

19.412 An action for wrongful dismissal is one where the employee claims he has not been given proper notice to terminate the contract. This right may run concurrently with the unfair dismissal right which relates to the reason for dismissal. Sometimes the two rights are not understood as separate rights and confusion reigns. They do have effect on each other with regard to compensation but as regards liability this is limited.

19.413 A tribunal has no power to make a finding of unfair dismissal merely because the employer has failed to give a proper period of notice. Thus where there are grounds for dismissal but the employer dismisses without notice that cannot render the dismissal unfair.[1] It is, however, possible to consider the fact that it was a summary dismissal in the context of whether it was reasonable to dismiss at all and it might be a factor, albeit a relatively minor one, to tip the balance. However, if a decision to dismiss has been made and it has been made on reasonable grounds and in a fair manner, it is the employer's decision whether to dismiss with notice.[2]

[1] *Treganowan v Robert Knee & Co Ltd* [1975] ICR 405, [1975] IRLR 247 and *BSC Sports and Social Club v Morgan* [1987] IRLR 391, EAT.
[2] See *BSC Sports*, above.

The standard of reasonableness

19.414 One can do no better than quote verbatim from the EAT decision of *Iceland Frozen Foods Ltd v Jones*[1] when considering the appropriate standard to determine whether the employer has acted reasonably or not. 'The correct approach for an industrial tribunal to adopt in answering the question posed by ERA, s 98(4) is as follows:

(1) the starting point should always be the words of s 98(4) themselves;
(2) in applying the section an industrial tribunal must consider the reasonableness of the employer's conduct not simply whether they (the members of the industrial tribunal) consider the dismissal to be fair;
(3) in judging the reasonableness of the employer's conduct an industrial tribunal must not substitute its decision as to what was the right course to adopt for that of the employer;
(4) in many (though not all) cases there is a band of reasonable responses to the employee's conduct within which one employer might reasonably take one view another quite reasonably take another;
(5) the function of the industrial tribunal as an industrial jury, is to determine whether in the particular circumstances of each case the decision to dismiss the employee fell within the band of reasonable responses which a reasonable employer might have adopted. If the dismissal falls within the band the dismissal is fair, if the dismissal falls outside the band it is unfair'.

1 [1983] ICR 17, [1982] IRLR 439.

19.415 The first thing that one notices about this approach is that there is considerable latitude given to employers. Applying the words of the statute the approach is therefore to consider the employer's behaviour[1] and not to consider the matter afresh and decide what it, the tribunal, would have done. The role of the tribunal is almost an administrative law standard of reviewing the employer's decision to consider if he acted reasonably but it is not quite so extreme. If it were, then a decision of unfairness would only arise if the employer had acted wholly unreasonably. Nevertheless, it gets very close particularly when considering the 'range of responses' approach.

1 Reinforced in *Polkey*'s case (see below).

19.416 This approach has been alluded to in an earlier case[1] relating to an employee's absence record. It was stated there that in a given set of circumstances it is possible for two perfectly reasonable employers to take different courses of action. Frequently there would be a range of responses ranging from summary dismissal to a mere informal warning which could be reasonable and this is why the tribunal must not substitute its decision for the employers.[2] Thus the range is enormous and it is so large that one could argue that it emasculates the role of the tribunal in determining what is a reasonable reaction. It is perfectly natural for a tribunal to say that certain behaviour merits a warning but not a dismissal but that is precisely what this test states is impermissible. In this respect it is submitted that this test goes too far – the whole purpose of tribunals in unfair dismissal is to decide if employers act reasonably in dismissing and surely they should be able to say it is unreasonable if only a warning is merited. They are after all an industrial jury with a certain degree of expertise. However, one suspects that the test is not always applied as strictly as would appear and provided the tribunal does not fall into the error of saying what it would have done its decision is unlikely to be upset on appeal. This is because the question is one of fact and is therefore virtually unappealable.[3] It is not necessary for a tribunal to pose the question of whether the behaviour fell within the range of reasonable responses because it is not an error of law to fail to do so.[4] Furthermore, as was stated in the *Iceland Frozen* case the band of reasonable responses applies in many, not all, cases.

1 *Rolls Royce Ltd v Walpole* [1980] IRLR 343.

2 The Court of Appeal has also used the test in *British Leyland (UK) Ltd v Swift* [1981] IRLR 91.

3 *Union of Construction Allied Trades and Technicians v Brain* [1981] ICR 542, [1981] IRLR 224 on appeals see below.

4 *Murray Mackinnon v Forno* [1983] IRLR 7, EAT.

19.417 The range of responses test is extremely close to the requirement that tribunals must not substitute their decision for that of the employer. However, it is very difficult not to stray into the 'no substitution' requirement because by saying that the employer acted unreasonably or outside the range of reasonable responses the tribunal is in reality saying that it would not have dismissed in those circumstances.[1]

1 See *Conlin v United Distillers* [1994] IRLR 169 where the tribunal falls into this error and is corrected by the EAT. The tribunal also must not substitute its own evaluation of the witnesses for that of the employers and if they do so that is an error of law: see *Morgan v Electrolux Ltd* [1991] IRLR 89, CA. If a witness is rejected by the tribunal it must be based on logical and substantial grounds: *Linfood Cash and Carry Ltd v Thomson* [1989] IRLR 235, EAT.

19.418 The probability is that this depends almost entirely on the choice of wording in the tribunal decision. Provided the range of responses test is accepted then the decision is likely to be upheld but if it is not then the contrary result will follow.[1] The tribunal must consider how the employer behaved and if it fell within a reasonable range of responses or within the band of reasonableness. As was stated in the UCATT case the right question to ask is 'would a reasonable employer in those circumstances dismiss'? It is sufficient that a reasonable employer would regard the circumstances as a sufficient reason for dismissing – it is not necessary that all reasonable employers would dismiss in those circumstances. Where an internal appeal panel establishes that one employee is more at fault than another in an incident this decision can only be attacked on the basis that the decision was so irrational that no employee could reasonably have accepted it.[2] It must be understood that the test does not mean that such a high degree of unreasonableness must be shown that nothing short of a perverse decision to dismiss can be held to be unfair.[3] It is essential that it should be apparent from the tribunal's decision that the correct test has been identified and applied. Unless the tribunal refers to the sub-section or at least summarises the wording then it is difficult to conclude that the tribunal applied its mind to the statutory requirements. It is also proper for the tribunal to refer to the range of responses to s 98(4) otherwise it might be thought there was an error of law.[4]

---

[1] Note the *Iceland Frozen* case for a good example of the tribunal trying to reformulate the test and being reversed (see above).
[2] *Securicor Ltd v Smith* [1989] IRLR 356.
[3] *Rentokil Ltd v Mackin* [1989] IRLR 286, EAT.
[4] *Conlin v United Distillers* [1994] IRLR 169.

Other matters relevant to reasonableness

19.419 The most important question is that relating to procedure and if the employer adopts an unfair procedure in dismissing this will probably render the dismissal unfair unless it is a very minor breach of procedure. This will be considered more carefully below.

19.420 The tribunal must consider the size and administrative resources of the employer's undertaking in assessing reasonableness but before this became a statutory requirement it was a factor which tribunals took into account in any event. Thus it has been held that the failure to provide an appeal was excusable in a small organisation.[1] Where a doctor's receptionist was dismissed after complaints by patients the dismissal was held to be fair despite certain procedural defects.[2] Another situation where a small organisation will obviously get preferential treatment is where the employer has to consider alternative employment.[3] However, even though the employer is small this does not absolve him from carrying out the basic procedures such as investigation[4] and this point is reinforced by the *Polkey* decision, which emphasises the importance of proper procedures. Even the smallest of employers will not find it onerous to comply with the basic tenets of natural justice. The corollary of the statutory change is that larger organisations should ensure that they have proper procedures, and such organisations find tribunals are less forgiving to them for procedural breaches.

---

[1] See *Royal Naval School v Hughes* [1979] IRLR 383 and *Tiptools Ltd v Curtis* [1973] IRLR 276, NIRC.
[2] *MacKellar v Bolton* [1979] IRLR 59.
[3] *Bevan Harris Ltd v Gair* [1981] IRLR 520.
[4] *Henderson v Granville Tours Ltd* [1982] IRLR 494, EAT.

19.421 'Equity and substantial merits' are also contained in the sub-section but they are not matters which have a developed jurisprudence. Although one might think that this has something to do with justice the position is that justice in the general sense ranks very low behind the employer's need for reasonable procedures.[1] What is required is that the employer behaves consistently so that he does not suddenly change his policy regarding certain behaviour, dismissing when in the past he has not done so. That does not mean that an employer is precluded from dismissing in these circumstances. What is required here is that employees are made aware that the previous situation has altered and that certain behaviour is no longer to be tolerated. Although it could be argued that where the previous sanction has been a warning that dismissal falls within a reasonable range of responses it would seem that the need to be consistent would probably override that. There is also a need to be consistent among employees who are involved in a similar or the same incident otherwise it would be open to attack. However, where an employee is guilty of serious dishonesty it is a 'very, very strong thing to say that an employer has acted irrationally' in dismissing. If the employer decides that he can trust one employee in the future, but not another, it is his decision not the tribunal's.[2]

[1] See later and note some other substantial reason above, eg *Chubb Fire Security Ltd v Harper* [1983] IRLR 311, EAT. *Polkey* also reinforces the emphasis on the employer's behaviour.
[2] *Post Office v Gould and Grakem* 11.5.94 EAT 587/92.

19.422 In perhaps the leading case on this[1] an employee was dismissed for hitting a colleague, usually regarded as gross misconduct.[2] However, the employer had always been lax and the employee managed to persuade the tribunal that because the employer had acted differently in the past the dismissal was unfair. The Court of Appeal agreed and said that equity in the phrase 'equity and substantial merits' 'comprehends the concept that employees who behave in much the same way should have meted out to them much the same punishment'. If that is not done then the employer may not act reasonably. There are, however, considerable qualifications to this principle as can be seen below.

[1] *Post Office v Fennell* [1981] IRLR 221.
[2] See above.

19.423 The employer will always have to consider the exact circumstances of any relevant incident and also the records of each individual concerned. Thus in a fight, for example, one should be aware of whether one party is the aggressor and of the respective service records of the protagonists which may justify differential treatment. This more individualistic approach was taken in another leading case[1] where the EAT said that consistency of treatment would only be relevant in three sets of circumstances. 'First, it may be relevant if there is evidence that employees have been led by an employer to believe that certain categories of conduct will be either overlooked or at least will not be dealt with by the sanction of dismissal. Secondly, there may be cases where evidence in relation to other cases supports an inference that the purported reason stated by the employee is not the real or genuine reason for dismissal. Thirdly, evidence as to decisions made by an employer in truly parallel circumstances may be sufficient to support an argument in a particular case, that it was not reasonable on the part of the employer to visit the particular employee's conduct with the penalty of dismissal and that some lesser penalty would have been appropriate in the circumstances. Industrial tribunals should scrutinise arguments based upon disparity with particular care and there will not be many cases in which the evidence supports the proposition that there are other cases which are truly similar or sufficiently similar to afford an adequate basis for argument. It is of the highest importance that flexibility should be retained and employers and tribunals should not be encouraged to think that a tariff approach to industrial misconduct is appropriate.' This approach has been confirmed and the requirement to act consistently means that before reaching a decision to dismiss an employer should consider truly comparable cases of which he knew or ought reasonably to have known.[2] The courts are reluctant to find that cases are truly comparable.[3] If a distinction is made then the question is whether it was so irrational that the employer should not have made it.[4] Thus disciplinary records and mitigating factors should be taken into account and it will be difficult to challenge an employers' decision.

[1] *Hadjioannous v Coral Casinos Ltd* [1981] IRLR 352.
[2] *Procter v British Gypsum Ltd* [1992] IRLR 7.
[3] *Paul v East Surrey District Health Authority* [1995] IRLR 305, CA.
[4] *Harrow London Borough v Cunningham* [1996] IRLR 256.

19.424 Although this appears to reduce the importance of consistency of treatment the above statement permits arguments about consistency to be raised and although flexibility is most important consistency is still important and where it is not applied dismissal will probably be unfair. An employer is not permitted to justify inconsistency on the basis that different individuals handled the dismissal. The consistency principle must be applied to the institution as a whole.[1]

[1] *Cain v Leeds Western Health Authority* [1990] IRLR 168, EAT.

Disciplinary rules

19.425 The legal position in relation to disciplinary rules is often misunderstood. Where the rules provide that certain offences will lead to dismissal this is not conclusive because the employer cannot arrogate to itself the right to determine what is reasonable. The statutory test of fairness must be superimposed on the rules so that all the circumstances including the breach of the rule, must be considered.[1] An employer who simply applies the rules without further consideration will not act reasonably. Conversely the fact that the rules do not indicate that a breach will lead to dismissal does not mean that the employer cannot dismiss. Once again, all the circumstances including the rules, must be considered.[2] Where there is a breach of the rule the question for the tribunal is whether it was reasonable for the employer to find that the employee intended to break the rule not whether the employers were justified in treating the employee as being in actual infringement of the rule.

[1] *Ladbroke Racing Ltd v Arnott* [1983] IRLR 154.
[2] *Elliott Bros (London) Ltd v Colverd* [1979] IRLR 92 – rules will be considered below. Note also *Post Office v Marney* [1990] IRLR 170, EAT.

Appeal against tribunal decisions

19.426 This part is not intended to deal with the procedure of appealing to the EAT but to explain on what basis an appeal might be made successfully against a tribunal decision. A decision on reasonableness is invariably based on findings of fact and an appeal can only be made on a question of law. An appeal would probably be successful where one could say of the tribunal decision 'My goodness that was certainly wrong'[1] but tribunal decisions will not be tampered with lightly because they are usually based on findings of fact in which tribunals have an expertise and discretion.[2] Furthermore the EAT is not to assume that a failure by the tribunal to refer to some point means that it has overlooked it and is not to 'search around with a fine toothcomb for some point of law'.[3]

[1] *Neale v Hereford and Worcester County Council* [1986] ICR 471, CA.
[2] *Union of Construction Allied Workers and Technicians v Brain*, para 19.416 above.
[3] *Retarded Children's Aid Society Ltd v Day* [1978] 1 WLR 763, [1978] ICR 437, CA.

19.427 The grounds of interference were laid down in the oddly named case of *Spook Erection v Thackray*.[1] The tribunal would have to have either misdirected itself in law, entertained the wrong issue, or proceeded upon a misapprehension or misconstruction of the evidence or taken into account matters which were irrelevant to its decision, or reached a decision so extravagant that no reasonable tribunal properly directing itself on the law could have arrived at. An example of a misdirection of law is where the tribunal has substituted its decision for the employer's or has stated the wrong burden of proof or misallocated the onus of proof. A perverse decision is one which is obviously so wrong that it cannot stand and as regards facts if the tribunal ignores important ones or misconstrues them then the decision can be attacked. However, this approach has subsequently been modified to some extent. Thus in 1990 the Court of Appeal ruled that the EAT could interfere with the tribunal decision if they were satisfied that the tribunal had misdirected itself as to applicable law, or if there was no evidence to support a particular finding of fact or if the decision was perverse ('my goodness that was certainly wrong'). Misunderstanding or misapplication of the facts is not a separate basis for allowing an appeal.[2] The Court of Appeal cut back on 'perversity' in *Piggott Bros & Co Ltd v Jackson*[3] by saying a decision could only be perverse if it was not a permissible option. This would almost always involve identifying a finding of fact unsupported by any evidence or a clear self-misdirection in law by the tribunal. If that cannot be done then it may well not be perverse and the EAT should re-examine with the greatest care its preliminary conclusion that the decision was not a permissible option.

1 [1984] IRLR 116.
2 *British Telecommunications plc v Sheridan* [1990] IRLR 27.
3 [1991] IRLR 309.

19.428 These principles were applied in a gross misconduct case where a finding of unfair dismissal was set aside by the EAT[1] and a finding of fair dismissal substituted. The EAT said it could find a decision perverse even where there was no error of law on the face of it or finding of fact unsupported by evidence. It could find a decision not to be a permissible option or so clearly wrong in the light of its own experience and sound practices in the industrial field.

1 *East Berkshire Health Authority v Matadeen* [1992] ICR 723.

19.429 Where a misdirection is found the EAT must then ask whether in any event the decision is plainly and unarguably right. If it is, then the decision stands, otherwise it must be remitted.[1] If it is plainly wrong and the facts do not require further investigation the EAT is bound to substitute its own conclusions as to what those findings require in law.[2] The Court of Appeal has ruled that where the EAT finds the tribunal has erred in law in finding unfair dismissal the EAT must remit to the tribunal unless no tribunal, properly directing themselves, could have come to the conclusion that the employee was not unfairly dismissed.[3]

1 *Dobie v Burns International Security Services (UK) Ltd* [1984] 3 All ER 333, [1984] ICR 812.
2 *McLeod v Hellyer Bros* [1987] ICR 526.
3 *Morgan v Electrolux Ltd* [1991] IRLR 89.

19.430 The higher courts have generally attempted to lighten the burden on tribunals and the EAT by discouraging reference to case law[1] and guidelines[2] and not requiring a detailed summary of the facts[3] although where they are in conflict findings should be made. The intention is that there should be as little legalism as possible so that laypersons should not be discouraged from going to the tribunal. However, the disapproval of guidelines or principles is not something which has been generally welcomed either by both sides of industry or representatives at tribunals as everyone would like to know what the basic principles of good industrial relations practice are.

1 *Anandarajah v Lord Chancellor's Department* [1984] IRLR 131.
2 *Bailey v BP Oil (Kent Refinery) Ltd* [1980] ICR 642, [1980] IRLR 287, CA.
3 *Kearney v Varndell* [1983] IRLR 335, CA.

Managerial prerogative and immoral, irresponsible and unacceptable behaviour

19.431 Where an employee behaves in a manner which is a little different from the norm the law provides the employer with a considerable degree of support in protecting him from unfair dismissal claims. Thus when a homosexual employed as a maintenance handyman at a children's camp was involved in an incident outside work with other homosexuals he was dismissed fairly.[1] The EAT said that the tribunal was entitled to take the view that a considerable proportion of employers would wish to restrict the employment of a homosexual particularly when he was required to work close to young children. The EAT conceded that this attitude could not be supported by scientific evidence but that was not the point. Provided the employer had approached the matter fairly and properly he could not be faulted for doing what he thought proper.

1 *Saunders v Scottish National Camps Association Ltd* [1981] IRLR 277.

19.432 This view is over-supportive of employer's possible prejudices where there was no danger involved in employing the employee – it was a decision based purely on prejudice. A similar decision on a similar basis was reached where an employee was convicted of gross indecency.[1]

1 *Wiseman v Salford City Council* [1981] IRLR 202, EAT.

19.433 A heroin addict who failed to disclose his addiction was held to be fairly dismissed in *Walton v TAC Construction Materials*.[1] Although it was held to be fair because he had obtained employment by deception the EAT also held as a separate issue that the employer was entitled to refuse to employ a drug addict and that investigation of the situation was accordingly unnecessary.

1 [1981] IRLR 357.

19.434 In one decision[1] a dental technician who was convicted and fined for possessing cannabis during a lunch hour outside work was held fairly dismissed because of the possible influence he might have on the other members of staff and the unsuitability of continuing to employ him in his particular job. The EAT said the response was a reasonable one. It is a little difficult to understand how the kind of job he was doing could be affected by cannabis use and the influence on other employees would be minimal bearing in mind that not much public opprobium attaches to the smoking of cannabis. It has been held fair to dismiss an insurance agent who would visit the public when he had a long history of mental illness, a decision which is more understandable although such practice should be assessed carefully to ensure there is no unnecessary discrimination.[2]

[1] *Mathewson v R B Dental Laboratory Ltd* [1988] IRLR 512.
[2] *O'Brien v Prudential Assurance Co Ltd* [1979] IRLR 140.

19.435 The thread which seems to run through these cases is that the tribunals and courts will be very reluctant to interfere with an employer's views on matters which relate to an employee's private life, even when these will have only a marginal impact, if any, on the employer. The law seems to defer to management views over such matters without any objective justification which does place those employees not conforming to the norm in an extremely vulnerable position.

Some principles pervading reasonableness

19.436 There are some cases which have established principles which, while they relate to a specific reason, have been extended to others. In the main this has applied to conduct and capability which often stand together as do some other substantial reason and redundancy. Some of the principles below could be classified as procedural but they are so important, when relevant, that they go to the heart of whether the employer acted reasonably. However, a disclaimer must be issued in that there are vital principles within the procedure section below which also go to the heart of reasonableness. No claim is made that these are less important because of their location in this chapter because reasonableness is not to be tested by breaking down the categories into substance and procedure. However, one can make some distinctions which are just about defensible. For example, if there is a breach of natural justice because a manager is judge and jury where he has also investigated this is a serious matter but it is quite likely to be a breach which may not lead to a different result, although it is not something which in any way should be condoned. If, however, the employer fails to carry out a proper investigation then he may not have all the information on which to base his decision. The first defect might lead to unfairness[1] but the second defect must lead to an unfairness finding other than in the most extreme of circumstances. One must not exaggerate this distinction because in some circumstances a breach of natural justice per se might justify a finding of unfair dismissal.[2]

[1] Possibly more likely since *Polkey* (see below).
[2] For example contrast *Slater v Leicestershire Health Authority* [1989] IRLR 16, CA with *Moyes v Hylton Castle Working Men's Social Club and Institute Ltd* [1986] IRLR 482, EAT.

19.437 An employer's general loss of confidence in his employee's ability to do his job properly is enough to justify dismissal provided there are reasonable grounds for the employer's belief because unfair dismissal legislation should not impede employers unreasonably in the efficient management of their business.[1] In the particular case the employee was a manager and the EAT said that the quality of management was imponderable and difficult to assess precisely, and therefore his superiors' subjective opinion about him carried some weight. This is a case which is supportive of management in an understandable situation but it is capable of abuse and must be watched carefully.

1 *Cook v Linnell & Sons Ltd* [1977] ICR 770, [1977] IRLR 132.

19.438 The most commonly quoted case in industrial tribunals must be *British Home Stores Ltd v Burchell*.[1] It deals with the issue of misconduct but its precepts have been applied in capability cases and are often regarded as procedural. However, they are so fundamental that they should be regarded as of critical importance. The case concerned allegations of dishonest acts regarding staff purchases. The EAT, reversing the tribunal, and holding the dismissal to be fair, said that the employer had to have a reasonable suspicion amounting to a belief in the employee's guilt. There were three elements:

(1) the employer had to show that he did believe in the guilt;
(2) the employer would have to establish that he had reasonable grounds on which to sustain that belief;
(3) when the employer formed the belief on those grounds he must have carried out as much investigation as was reasonable in the circumstances of the case.

1 [1980] ICR 303, [1979] IRLR 379 and see *Boys and Girls Welfare Society v McDonald* [1996] IRLR 129.

19.439 This case has been cited with approval in numerous cases and was approved by the Court of Appeal not long after it was given.[1] The Court made it clear that equity demanded that the employee be given a fair opportunity of explaining before dismissal and that the employer should not jump to conclusions before reaching his decision. It is not usually a problem for an employer to establish that he genuinely believed in the employee's misconduct or incapability unless it is a purely fictional reason but reasonable grounds and investigation oblige the employer to show that he took some real care over the dismissal. His investigation, which will have to involve discussing the matter with the employee, should clothe him with the reasonable grounds for the belief.

1 *Weddel & Co Ltd v Tepper* [1980] ICR 286, [1980] IRLR 96.

19.440 It is very important to note that he must have reasonable grounds but it is not necessary to establish his belief beyond reasonable doubt. The test is a balance of probabilities, no more. Thus even if it is established at the tribunal that the employee did not commit the act of misconduct this does not mean that the employer has unfairly dismissed because it is the *British Home Stores* test which needs to be satisfied. Thus when an employee was dismissed for an act of vandalism at work but this was shown not to have been committed by him when the case was heard the EAT said that the test was whether the employer had reasonable grounds for his belief, not whether he had in fact committed the offence.[1] This may appear extremely odd and harsh because it does not appear very equitable for an employee to be dismissed for something he has not done but, as has been previously stated, it is the employer's procedures which are to be judged not the injustice to the employee.[2] Of course in almost every case a reasonable investigation should lead to the correct answer and therefore there should be no injustice but this is certainly not guaranteed. A recent decision[3] has given something of an updating to the *BHS* principles and has modified them. The EAT has suggested that acting reasonably involves consideration of four subsidiary questions, they are:

(1) Has the employer shown that he has complied with the pre-dismissal procedures which a reasonable employer could and should have applied in the circumstances of this case?
(2) Where there is a contractual appeal process has the employer carried it out in its essentials?
(3) Where conduct is the main reason has the employer proved that at the time of dismissal he has a reasonable suspicion amounting to belief in the guilt of the employee and if necessary has complied with the principles in *British Home Stores v Burchell*?
(4) Has the employer dealt fairly with the employee during the disciplinary hearings and the appeal process?

1 *Ferodo Ltd v Barnes* [1976] ICR 439, [1976] IRLR 302.
2 This is reinforced by *Polkey*.
3 *Whitbread & Co plc v Mills* [1988] IRLR 501.

19.441 The *British Home Stores* principles have also been modified again by the former EAT President Wood J.[1] They require the employer to prove on the balance of probabilities:

(a) that he believed again on the balance of probabilities (not beyond reasonable doubt) – that the employee was guilty of the misconduct, and
(b) that in all the circumstances based upon knowledge of and after consideration of sufficient relevant facts and factors he could reasonably do so.

In applying *British Home Stores v Burchell* it is the subjective belief of the employer that counts after his investigation. It does not matter if the tribunal members are not convinced of the employee's guilt.[2] The tribunal must not reopen the factual issues on the basis of which the employers reached their conclusion.[3] In determining whether the employer carried out reasonable investigations, a tribunal should consider the nature of the material which was before the employer when the decision to dismiss was taken. It would not be unfair if material first emerged at the tribunal hearing.[4] It is submitted that it is necessary to take care with this argument because it must directly be arguable that a reasonable investigation should have included certain factors.

1 *ILEA v Gravett* [1988] IRLR 497.
2 *Scottish Midland Co-operative Society Ltd v Cullion* [1991] IRLR 261.
3 *British Gas plc v McCarrick* [1991] IRLR 305, CA.
4 *Dick v Glasgow University* [1993] IRLR 581.

19.442 An issue related to the above is where the employer faces a problem but cannot identify which employee is at fault. In this situation an employer cannot genuinely believe X is guilty if he is unsure whether it is X, Y or Z who is the offending party. In one case money had been stolen from a safe and after investigation it was established that it could only be the manager or his assistant who could have removed it. The employer could not ascertain which of them was guilty or if both were and he therefore dismissed both. The Court of Appeal affirmed the lower courts decision and said the dismissal was fair.[1] It was also said that in a situation like this the *British Home Stores* principles could be modified so that reasonable suspicion was sufficient. The *British Home Stores* principles were not intended to be of universal application and there were solid and sensible grounds for the employer's decision.

[1] *Monie v Coral Racing Ltd* [1981] ICR 109, [1980] IRLR 464, CA.

19.443 Subsequently this principle was extended to a case of incompetence where two motor mechanics had signed a report stating that a vehicle had sufficient oil which was not correct and the vehicle seized up. The employer could not satisfy himself which of the two was guilty and dismissed them both. The dismissal was upheld but the EAT said that the *Monie v Coral* principle should not be pushed too far.[1]

[1] *McPhie and McDermott v Wimpey Waste Management Ltd* [1981] IRLR 316.

19.444 Nevertheless it was used to justify the dismissal of three employees who worked in an off-licence which had suffered serious stock losses for many years. The employer had made great efforts to identify the cause of the losses and the culprits. The employees had been given warnings and had been transferred to separate places of work but when they returned the stock losses continued. The EAT reversed the tribunal and held that the dismissals were fair and that the *Monie v Coral* principle was capable of being applied to a case of capability or conduct not involving dishonesty although such a case would be exceptional. 'Blanket' dismissals of a group were permitted even where it is possible, or indeed probable, that not all were guilty of the act. It was necessary to satisfy three conditions to permit this. First, the act must be such that if committed by an identified individual would justify the dismissal of that individual. Secondly, the tribunal must be satisfied that the act was committed by one or more of the group all of whom can be shown to be individually capable of having committed the act complained of. Thirdly, the tribunal must be satisfied that there has been a proper investigation by the employer to identify the person or persons responsible for the act. The EAT said it would be rare that on a proper investigation, it would be impossible to determine the culprit and unlikely that more than a mere handful would be left under suspicion.[1]

[1] These principles have been modified in subsequent cases which are discussed above in para 19.395. The most important case is *Parr v Whitbread & Co plc* [1990] IRLR 39.

19.445 This wide berth given to the employer once again concentrated on the employer's behaviour not on any injustice to the employee and this fits in with the way unfair dismissal law has developed. It should be noted that a 'mere handful' could presumably cover five employees and the way the EAT expressed itself the employer could dismiss a larger number. Also the EAT could be optimistic in suggesting that an investigation would only rarely fail to identify the culprit. Thus the decision really opens up the possibility of multiple dismissals.[1]

1 *Whitbread & Co plc v Thomas* [1988] ICR 135, [1988] IRLR 43.

Miscellaneous general principles relating to reasonableness

19.446 A number of principles have emerged in relation to ERA, s 98(4) which do not easily slot into other parts of this chapter. There is no thread to these principles and therefore it is not possible to categorise them in any way because they are discrete.

19.447 We know that a breach of rules which states that this will lead to dismissal is not conclusive[1] but furthermore where the employee was aware that his conduct could probably result in dismissal this is a relevant factor. What the tribunal must look at is the employer's behaviour and whether he acted reasonably.[2] However, as part of the overall requirement to act fairly, the employer should always give credit to the employee's length of service and its quality. If the employee's behaviour is a serious breach of his duties then length of service will not be of very much assistance to him.[3]

1 See *Ladbroke Racing Ltd v Arnott* [1983] IRLR 154 and note *Post Office v Marney* [1990] IRLR 170, EAT.
2 *Trusthouse Forte (Catering) Ltd v Adonis* [1984] IRLR 382, EAT.
3 *AEI Cables Ltd v McLay* [1980] IRLR 84.

19.448 An employee's reaction when confronted with his alleged wrongdoing is a factor which can be taken into account by the employer in determining whether to dismiss. Although it was not the basis on which the employer was planning to dismiss it is, nevertheless, conduct prior to the dismissal and can therefore be relied upon. However, one must be cautious about taking this too far because an employee might behave oddly in that situation. If he concocts a series of lies to explain this position then that is a breach of trust which the employer can rely on.[1] A breach of trust is also more easily established when the work relationship is a close one, for instance when there is a small office[2] or where the relationship is between an employee and his secretary.[3] We have already noted that a breach of trust may occur when an employee seeks to work for a competitor and there are reasonably solid grounds for supposing that he is doing so in order to abuse his confidential position and disclose confidential information.[4] The same applies to an attempt to obtain the employer's main customer and induce his employees to leave.[5]

1 *British Leyland (UK) Ltd v Swift* [1981] IRLR 91, CA.
2 And note some other substantial reason and work relationships in this context.
3 *Brown v Hall Advertising Ltd* [1978] IRLR 246.
4 *Harris and Russell Ltd v Slingsby* [1973] 3 All ER 31, [1978] IRLR 221.
5 *Marshall v Industrial Systems and Control Ltd* [1992] IRLR 294, EAT.

Procedural reasonableness

Generally

19.449 An employer will not have acted reasonably if he has not adopted a fair procedure. From its inception there was always a debate as to whether it was necessary to adopt a fair procedure when it would have made no real difference to the outcome. In the early days the debate took place mainly in the redundancy context – was there any point in consultation and discussion when there was no way of avoiding redundancies? Some cases held that there was no unfair dismissal because the procedure was pointless whereas others decided that there was an unfair dismissal with limited compensation.[1] Then in 1979 we had a very definitive view, albeit only in the EAT, which was that it was only unfair if the procedural defect would have made any difference to the outcome.[2] This approach was criticised by many, including some judges, but it held firm until 1987. The *Labour Pump* approach was criticised mainly on two fronts: first because it condoned poor industrial relations by not penalising the failure to carry out a proper procedure which a good employer should comply with and second on a legal basis. The legal basis was that permitting this approach was in conflict with the rule in *Devis & Sons Ltd v Atkins*[3] which forbade the admissibility of any matter arising after the dismissal. The *Labour Pump* approach required the tribunal to predict at the hearing what the effect of having a proper procedure would have been. In *Polkey v Dayton Services Ltd*,[4] the House of Lords held that the reasonableness of the dismissal could only be decided by looking at what the employer knew when he dismissed and it was not permissible to consider facts which arose after the dismissal or whether the employee had in fact suffered any injustice.[5] The ramifications of this vitally important decision will be considered at the end of this section when we have examined the different stages in the procedure. It should be noted that this victory may in many cases be a pyrrhic one because the effect of the procedural breach must still be taken into account in assessing compensation and if it would have made very little difference this is reflected in the compensation which may, accordingly, be minimal. Compensation is not to penalise the employer, even when he has unfair procedures, it is to compensate the employee for the loss he has suffered. Despite this, procedural correctness is now very much top of the agenda when it comes to unfair dismissal. Different procedures apply for the different reasons for dismissal. Thus when an employee is dismissed for redundancy there is no need for investigation but there is a need to consult and discuss the situation with the employee. For ill-health warnings are inappropriate. These are just two examples of the many differences obtaining.

---

1 This was the approach adopted in *Clarkson International Tools Ltd v Short* [1973] ICR 191, [1973] IRLR 90, NIRC which considered the whole issue.
2 *British Labour Pump Co Ltd v Byrne* [1979] ICR 347, [1979] IRLR 94.
3 [1977] AC 931, [1977] 2 All ER 321, CA.
4 [1988] AC 344, [1987] 3 All ER 974, HL.
5 Note the inroads into this by *Duffy v Yeomans* (1994) considered above.

Good procedure – an overview

19.450 The employer should have disciplinary rules and procedures[1] because they are 'necessary for promoting fairness and order in the treatment of individuals and in the conduct of industrial relations'. Employees need to know what is expected of them, or what is not expected of them and the procedures obtaining if they do something wrong. It is also desirable that they know what the sanction for breach is.

[1] See ACAS Code of Practice 1 1977 Disciplinary Practice and Procedures and ACAS Handbook 1987 Discipline at Work and ERA, s 1.

19.451 Before dismissing for most reasons it will be necessary to have warned the employee that his behaviour is such as to justify dismissal if, for example, his performance does not improve or he commits an act of misconduct.

19.452 Prior to any dismissal the employer must carry out a proper investigation and inquiry. He should investigate before he decides to instigate any disciplinary hearing to ensure that there is something which justifies discipline. If the matter relates to serious misconduct it is likely that the employee would be suspended and indeed should be in most cases. This will usually involve discussing the matter with the employee at that stage but he must certainly be given the opportunity of putting his views forward at the disciplinary hearing. At this hearing the persons present should be identified to the employee. He should be given notice of the charges that will be made against him and be given the opportunity to be represented either by a union official or a colleague. The person deciding should not be judge and jury in his own cause which means that he should not have carried out the investigation as well as making the decision.[1]

[1] In *Clark v Civil Aviation Authority* [1991] IRLR 412 the EAT said it would be appropriate to suspend on full pay if investigation was required and laid down what a proper procedure should be, explaining that natural justice principles would have to be followed. They would require identification of the allegation, indicate whether the evidence would be in statement form or by witnesses. The employee and representative should be allowed to ask questions and call witnesses, explain and argue the case. They should be asked if there is anything further they wish to add and mitigation should be considered.

19.453 If dismissal does occur then an opportunity to appeal should be given. As we have already seen a failure to allow a contractual right of appeal is unreasonable.[1] The opportunity to use the grievance procedure is not a substitute for allowing the employee to put forward his explanation at a disciplinary hearing.[2] Where there is a contractual right of appeal with a panel constituted in a particular way a defect in the composition of the appeal body (two instead of three members present) is a significant contractual and jurisdictional failure not simply a procedural error. However, this failure does not lead automatically to a finding of unfairness and the matter must be considered in the usual way taking this factor into account.[3]

[1] See *Tipton*'s case, above.
[2] *Clarke v Trimoco Motor Group Ltd* [1993] IRLR 148, EAT.
[3] *Westminster City Council v Cabaj* [1996] IRLR 349, CA.

Rules and procedures

19.454 As stated these are necessary to promote fairness by setting standards of conduct at work and having a fair method of dealing with any breach of rules. However, rules cannot cover all the circumstances that may occur and they have to vary according to the size of the employer and the nature of his business. However, they should cover matters such as gross misconduct offences, absenteeism and lateness, poor performance and health and safety. It is obvious that the employees should be provided with a copy of the rules or have easy access to them and they should be explained particularly to employees with limited English.

19.455 The disciplinary procedure should indicate the disciplinary action which may be taken and state who has authority to take disciplinary action, the right of the individual to have notice of charges, to have a representative and the right to an appeal.

19.456 We have already noted that the existence of rules and a procedure which imposes a penalty for breach of them are not conclusive in determining the reasonableness of dismissal which must still be decided by the tribunal.[1] If the rules do not refer to the offence being complained about or appear to treat a breach more lightly than appears to be the case, the employer has the added problem of showing he acted reasonably in this regard. However, the absence of a clear rule explaining the consequences of breach is not by any means fatal to the employer's case.[2] If the employee has committed an act of gross misconduct he is almost invariably going to be aware of how serious this is, for example fighting[3] or gross insubordination. Thus the absence of a rule is a factor militating against the employer but in many circumstances it may not be very significant. If, however, the employer has a stricter attitude than most to certain activities, for example, accepting small gifts from clients, this should be something spelt out in the rules and procedures. The technical differences between the consequences of a breach of a rule rendering the employee 'liable to dismissal' or 'will lead to dismissal' are very unlikely to be significant.[4]

1 See *Ladbroke*'s case, para 19.447 above.
2 *Elliot Bros (London) Ltd v Colverd* [1979] IRLR 92.
3 *Parsons & Co Ltd v McLoughlin* [1978] IRLR 65, EAT.
4 *Distillers Co (Bottling Services) Ltd v Gardner* [1982] IRLR 47, EAT. Note also *Procter v British Gypsum Ltd* [1992] IRLR 7, EAT which confirms this view.

19.457 The rules are not meant to be exhaustive and usually this is stated expressly or cannot really be in practice. Thus an offence which falls outside a list can still merit dismissal.[1] The employee's knowledge that the misconduct would justify summary dismissal will assist the employer but not if such offences have not led to dismissal in the past.

1 *Alidair Ltd v Taylor* [1978] ICR 445, CA.

Warnings

19.458 The norm is that a warning is necessary in most cases but this is not an absolute rule. A simple example is where the employee has committed an act of gross misconduct where a single incident justifies dismissal. This applies also where there is evidence of a very seriously defective performance such as crash landing an aeroplane.[1] Warnings are a matter of substance, not procedure. Thus there is no absolute rule about them and if an employee is so set in his ways that the employer is convinced that a warning will not alter them and the tribunal is itself convinced that the employer genuinely believed this on reasonable grounds then the fact that there has been no warning will not make the dismissal unfair.[2] The same argument applies to an employee who is 'determined to go his own way'.[3] Despite these cases and even where the behaviour is not very acceptable it is surely arguable that an employee might actually change his mind and his behaviour if he knew that any similar behaviour would lead to a dismissal. However, the House of Lords in *Polkey* held that dismissal without warning may not be unfair if the employer could reasonably have concluded that a warning would be utterly useless.

1 *Brooks & Son v Skinner* [1984] IRLR 379, EAT.
2 *Dunning v Jacomb* [1973] ICR 448, [1973] IRLR 206, NIRC where the employee had an unbending and unco-operative nature and an inability to get on with clients.
3 *Retarded Children's Aid Society v Day* [1978] IRLR 128, CA.

19.459 Where the dismissal is for poor performance it is almost invariably necessary to give a warning because the employee is usually able to improve if he is given an inducement to do so.[1] The employer should make clear the consequences of a failure to improve. Where there is gross incompetence which is considered to be irredeemable then warnings may be dispensed with although usually this is connected with some other factor. Thus in *Grant v Ampex*[2] the EAT said that sometimes inadequacy is so great that no warning is necessary. The other factor there was that the employee was never prepared to admit any of the shortcomings that were drawn to his attention. Other cases have reached the same result.[3] However, they should be seen as exceptions to the general rule that a warning is necessary.

1 *Winterhalter Gastronom Ltd v Webb* [1973] ICR 245, [1973] IRLR 120, NIRC – no-one knows he is capable of jumping the gate until the bull is right behind him.
2 [1980] IRLR 461.
3 *Littlewoods Organisation Ltd v Egenti* [1976] ICR 516, [1976] IRLR 334.

19.460 In the *Egenti* case no explicit warning had been given that dismissal was being considered but the employee's work had been unfavourably assessed. This was held sufficient to constitute a warning as was a failure to review an employee's salary.[1] The position should usually be clear and this is usually more so the higher the status of the employee. An oral warning can be just as valuable as a written warning but it requires to be proved. As has been stated 'There is no special magic about the written warning. To an intelligent man a verbal warning should be just as effective'.[2]

1 *Judge International v Moss* [1973] IRLR 208.
2 *McCall v Castleton Crafts* [1979] IRLR 218.

19.461 Employees should be given a reasonable opportunity to improve and this means a reasonable period of time with appropriate support. The determination of a reasonable period depends on the length of service, its quality, the extent of the employee's under-performance and the needs of the business.

Employees should be monitored during this period and given assistance in areas which should have been identified when the warning was given. When the employee has been given a period in which to improve but the employer allows a longer period to see if there is any improvement the over-generosity of the employer cannot be classified as being unreasonable.[1]

[1] *Kraft Foods Ltd v Fox* [1978] ICR 311, [1977] IRLR 431.

19.462 It is not the function of a tribunal to determine whether a warning should have been issued but if it can be established that it was not given in good faith and there were no prima facie grounds for giving it then the tribunal can take this factor into account.[1] An alternative way of expressing it is to say that it must be given on adequate evidence and not for any oblique or improper motive.[2] The warning need not relate directly to the incident for which the applicant was dismissed. Thus it was an error of law for a tribunal to decide otherwise.[3] In that case all the incidents related to conduct. The matter is not so easy when the warning relates to a different *legal* reason. Thus if a warning was given for poor performance and the dismissal was for misconduct it would be a matter of balance and of doing what was fair in the circumstances.

[1] *Stein v Associated Dairies Ltd* [1982] IRLR 447.
[2] *Tower Hamlets Health Authority v Anthony* [1989] IRLR 394, CA. See also *CRS Ltd v Luces* 15.11.93 EAT 145/93.
[3] *Auguste Noel Ltd v Curtis* [1990] IRLR 326, EAT.

19.463 The *Stein* case also stated that there is no rule of law that where a final warning for a previous offence is under appeal there is an obligation on the employer not to dismiss for a subsequent offence until that appeal has been decided. This has been confirmed by a recent decision of the Court of Appeal[1] which says that reasonableness should also be judged by the length of time which will elapse until an appeal is heard.

[1] *Tower Hamlets Health Authority v Anthony* [1989] IRLR 394, CA.

19.464 Warnings are not appropriate in long-term ill-health cases, but they are required where there is persistent short-term absenteeism for different ailments. Even where there is a genuine certified illness during short-term absences although they are not truly disciplinary situations the EAT has suggested that employers should give a caution that the stage had been reached where with the best will in the world, continued employment would become impossible. All the circumstances of the employment would be taken into account.[1]

[1] *Lynock v Cereal Packaging Ltd* [1988] ICR 670, [1988] IRLR 510.

19.465 Both the 1977 Code of Practice and the 1987 handbook published by ACAS lay down a recommended warnings procedure. The Handbook refers to three warnings, oral, first written and final written but it states that a stage or stages can be omitted. The employer who adopts a warning procedure in his contracts thereby creates individual rights enforceable as a matter of contract.

We have already noted the importance of employers complying with a proper procedure and this is reinforced where there is a contractual procedure. Where a warning is given and is stipulated to last for a given period then that period is strictly construed against the employer and any ambiguity will be interpreted in favour of the employee.[1]

1 *Bevan Ashford v Malin* [1995] IRLR 360, EAT.

19.466 In redundancy cases a warning is replaced by the need for consultation which is a necessary step unless the employer reasonably considers that it would be utterly useless.[1] The forerunner of *Polkey* was *Freud v Bentalls Ltd*[2] where it was stated that 'Good industrial relations practice requires that, unless there are special circumstances which render such consultation impossible or unnecessary, a fair employer will consult with the employee before dismissing him'. The EAT said that consultation was one of the foundation stones of modern industrial relations practice and only a special reason would excuse non-consultation. It is not merely discourteous not to consult but it deprives the employee of the opportunity of exploring the possibility of alternative employment.[3] Consultation cannot be dispensed with on the basis that the employers decided not to consult because on a previous redundancy the workforce had said they preferred not to have any consultation.[4] Although the size of the company can determine the degree of consultation it cannot excuse a total lack of consultation.[5] In a redundancy selection case where an employee is selected based on a criterion related to conduct or capability there is no need to have warned the employee about that failing prior to redundancy selection.[6]

1 *Polkey v Dayton Services Ltd* [1988] AC 344, [1987] 3 All ER 974, HL. It is the norm that there should be consultation.
2 [1983] ICR 77, [1982] IRLR 443.
3 See *Abbotts and Stanley v Wesson-Glynwed*, above and *Holden v Bradville Ltd* [1985] IRLR 483.
4 *Ferguson v Prestwick Circuits Ltd* [1992] IRLR 266.
5 *De Grasse v Stockwell Tools Ltd* [1992] IRLR 269.
6 *Gray v Shetland Norse Preserving Co Ltd* [1985] IRLR 53.

Investigation

19.467 Much of the law regarding investigation has already been discussed. The *British Home Stores v Burchell*[1] case requires as much investigation as is reasonable in all the circumstances and this has been modified[2] so the employer believes in the misconduct based on the knowledge of and after consideration of sufficient relevant factors that he could obtain.

1 [1980] ICR 303, [1979] IRLR 379.
2 *ILEA v Gravett* [1988] IRLR 497, EAT.

19.468 In the *Gravett* case the EAT reiterated that the degree of inquiry and investigation will vary from case to case. There will be cases where the employee is virtually caught in the act and at the other extreme there will be situations where the issue is one of pure inference. For the latter the amount of inquiry required, including questioning of the employee, will increase. The employer must face the employee with the information which he has either in an investigation prior to the disciplinary hearing or in the hearing itself. It may be that after hearing the employee's version of the events the employer should carry out further investigation. The test is whether a reasonable employer could have reached the conclusion to dismiss on the available relevant evidence.

19.469 The employer is not required to be certain of the employee's wrongdoing. He must have reasonable grounds for his belief based on the balance of probabilities.[1] This is based on what the employer knew at the time he dismissed and it is not open to the employer to say that any further investigation after the dismissal would have supported his decision.[2] The *Henderson* case was one where a written complaint was made about a coach driver's driving. This was a six page letter and the employer had effectively decided to dismiss unless the driver had a reasonable excuse. The employee was called in to a meeting, handed the letter and asked for his comments. He denied the allegations but was then dismissed. It was held to be unfair dismissal because he had not been given a real chance to rebut the allegations. He should have been given time to consider his response, to reconstruct the journey and the employer could possibly have carried out further investigations.

1 *AEI Cables* and *Ferodo*, paras 19.447 and 19.440 above.
2 *Henderson v Granville Tours*, para 19.420 above.

19.470 This is an extreme example and the law places limits on the degree of investigation required on an employer who possesses information which points strongly towards the commission of a dismissable offence.[1] In the *Gray Dunn* case three senior employees were convinced that the employee was intoxicated at work and the manager refused to allow colleagues of the employee to give evidence to the contrary. The employer's action was upheld because the evidence was sufficiently strong and the employee admitted he had been drinking but it should not be regarded as good practice.

1 *Gray Dunn & Co Ltd v Edwards* [1980] IRLR 23.

19.471 Where the employee admits dishonesty there is very little scope, if any, for investigation of the kind suggested in *British Home Stores v Burchell*.[1] The whole exercise would seem to be superfluous when the employee is suspected of dishonesty at work although investigations should occur immediately and the employee should be asked for an explanation before his memory fades. However, this should not be pursued at a time when the employee is in emotional distress after having been accused of dishonesty. Some time should be allowed to elapse.[2] We have already noted that an employer can act on a confession, howsoever obtained,[3] and also on evidence adduced at a criminal trial but it is improper to interview an employee in the presence of police officers.[4]

1 *Royal Society for the Protection of Birds v Croucher* [1984] ICR 604, [1984] IRLR 425, EAT.
2 *Tesco (Holdings) Ltd v Hill* [1977] IRLR 63.
3 *Morleys' of Brixton Ltd v Minott* [1982] ICR 444, [1982] IRLR 270, EAT.
4 *Read v Phoenix Preservation Ltd* [1985] ICR 164, [1985] IRLR 93, EAT.

19.472 Criminal charges are not a ground for absolving the employer from investigation[1] but there are conflicting authorities on the question whether a proper investigation need be made after an employee has been convicted of a criminal offence.[2] Following *Polkey*, it is probably always desirable for the employer to carry out some degree of investigation and allow the employee to state his case. Where the employee is actually caught red-handed some older cases[3] have suggested there is no need for an investigation but this policy should be adopted with considerable caution, if at all. Such an investigation would probably be brief.

1 *Scottish Special Housing Association v Cooke* [1979] IRLR 264.
2 In *Dillett v National Coal Board* [1988] ICR 218, CA the procedural defect of no original disciplinary hearing (there was an appeal) and delay did not render the dismissal unfair but in *McLaren v National Coal Board* [1988] ICR 370, [1988] IRLR 215, CA the failure to allow the employee to state his case after he admitted assaulting a colleague and was convicted was an unfair dismissal. These cases and many others arose out of the miners' strike in the mid-1980s. Note also the previous discussion of this and other more recent cases which place greater emphasis on the plea of guilty and limit the need for investigation in these circumstances. There should still be a disciplinary hearing.
3 *Carr v Alexander Russell Ltd* [1979] ICR 469n, [1976] IRLR 220 and *Scottish Special Housing Association v Linnen* [1979] IRLR 265.

The right to state one's case and a fair hearing

19.473 The right to state one's case is closely connected if not inextricably intertwined with the need for the employer to carry out a proper investigation as there will not be the latter if the employee has been deprived of the opportunity to explain the position. He should have been given reasonable notice of the charges, be given the right to be represented and the opportunity to state his case. In most cases he should be able to ask questions against his accusers but where the manager making the decision is relying on witnesses' statements he may have to rely on challenging the manager or on the manager's understanding of the position. It is, however, preferable that witnesses should be there so that the employee can ask them questions. This is not a legal requirement. However, there is no need to bring along to a disciplinary hearing any individuals who are not fellow-employees. For example, where the employee has been dismissed following complaints by customers, he is not entitled to demand that the customers be present at the hearing and answer his questions.

19.474 The principles applicable are lifted directly from the 'natural justice' doctrine. They are that:

(a) the person should know the nature of the accusation against him;
(b) he should be given an opportunity to state his case;
(c) the domestic tribunal should act in good faith.[1]

1 *Khanum v Mid-Glamorgan Area Health Authority* [1979] ICR 40, [1978] IRLR 215, EAT.

19.475 He should have a chance to state his case in detail and must know sufficiently what is being said against him so that he can properly put forward his case. There is no requirement that the charges be stated in writing – it may be sufficient if the allegations are made orally – the point is that there is no particular form of procedure and it is all a question of degree.[1] It will always depend on the circumstances. Thus, for example, if there are a number of detailed allegations against the employee it would be undesirable to do this orally because otherwise the employee would find it difficult to respond coherently. He would need time to consider the allegations and a proper opportunity to construct a response.[2] If the employer deliberately decides not to disclose the details of the nature and seriousness of the allegations before a disciplinary hearing this is unfair.[3] Where the essence of the case against an employee is contained in written statements by witnesses and the employee is not shown copies of such statements this is unfair. It is insufficient to provide a broad general outline of what the statements contained.[4] However, this procedural failure must be considered in the light of all the circumstances and it may not necessarily make the dismissal unfair. Thus if it could be established that the detail in the statements was fully explained and understood by the employee and he was able to comment on it it is probable there is nothing unfair. Where the detail is understood and the employee knows exactly what is being alleged although there is a defective procedure in not disclosing the witnesses' statements this must be seen in the context of what occurred. The vital question is whether there was a fair process. A dismissal will be unfair where there was a defect of such seriousness that the procedure itself was unfair or where the results of the defect taken overall were unfair. The position does not alter because the procedural defect was based on a policy adopted by the employers, namely not disclosing the witnesses' statements.[5] Thus one must take a broad-brush approach in determining fairness in this context.

1 *Bentley Engineering Co Ltd v Mistry* [1979] ICR 47, [1978] IRLR 437.
2 See *Hendersons*' case, para 19.469 above.
3 *Spink v Express Foods Group Ltd* [1992] IRLR 320, EAT.
4 Louies v Coventry Hood and Seating Co Ltd [1990] IRLR 324, EAT.
5 Fuller v Lloyds Bank plc [1991] IRLR 336, EAT.

19.476 There are many cases which deal with specific natural justice failures but it is all a question of degree and it is only where there has been a total breach of the principle that a finding of unfairness will be made. Usually the breach is less significant and it will be taken into account in assessing reasonableness in general. However, in one case[1] a dismissal was held to be unfair based on the fact that the two witnesses to the alleged sexual harassment by the employee took part in the decision to dismiss. The employer was a working men's social club and the witnesses were the club's chairman and assistant secretary. They comprised two of the five who sat on a sub-committee which investigated the incident and they also participated in the full committee's decision to dismiss. The EAT reversing the tribunal said this was unfair. It did recognise that there would inevitably be cases where a witness to an incident will be the person who has to take the decision to dismiss but in this case it was entirely unnecessary. It was impossible for them to disassociate their role as witnesses from that of judge and it put the others involved in the decision in an impossible position. This is quite a robust decision protecting employees and even more so when one notes that it was prior to the *Polkey* decision.

1 *Moyes v Hylton Castle Working Men's Social Club and Institute Ltd* [1986] IRLR 482.

19.477 A more traditional and conservative approach to natural justice occurred in *Slater v Leicestershire Health Authority*.[1] There the manager who inspected a patient's buttocks following an allegation that the employee had slapped the patient also carried out the disciplinary hearing. The employee claimed this was a breach of natural justice but the Court of Appeal affirmed that the dismissal was fair and that a person who had conducted the investigation was able to conduct a fair inquiry. The Court recognised that the person holding the inquiry must be seen to be impartial but also stated that the rules of natural justice do not form an independent ground on which a decision to dismiss may be attacked although a breach will clearly be an important matter in determining reasonableness. Given the importance of *Polkey* it is surprising that a breach of natural justice is not regarded as unfair per se but maybe the Court was nervous about over-stating the position given that there are possible exceptions. Nevertheless employers should be careful to ensure that justice appears to be done. Thus where an employee appealed against a decision made at a disciplinary hearing the person hearing the appeal had a private discussion with the person who chaired the disciplinary hearing at the conclusion of the appeal. This was a serious breach of natural justice said the Court of Appeal.[2]

1 [1989] IRLR 16.
2 *Campion v Hamworthy Engineering Ltd* [1987] ICR 966.

19.478 The ACAS Code and Handbook, especially the latter, lay down very carefully the procedures to be adopted in dealing with disciplinary matters. The Handbook has a separate chapter on the conduct of disciplinary interviews and how to avoid disciplinary action by timely and positive discussion with the employee which is entitled, positively, as 'counselling'. The details are too lengthy to include here but the provisions are a very useful guide to employers on how to conduct good industrial relations.

Curing a defective disciplinary hearing

19.479 It is now clear that where there are procedural defects in the original disciplinary hearing these can be cured by a full appeal hearing where there is a comprehensive review.[1] Thus where an employee did not receive detailed particulars of the charge against her prior to the disciplinary hearing this was put right by a rehearing on appeal where she was fully aware of the charge.[2] However, where the appeal is heard by a person who was heavily involved in the original investigation and in bringing the charges this is not a proper appeal process so as to cure any original defect. It was emphasised that for any appeal process to put right any original defect it must stand on its own merits as providing all the rights the employee would have had at the original hearing such as proper notice of the complaint and a full opportunity of stating one's case.[3] Although this may ultimately obtain a fair result it could be argued that where there is an unfair disciplinary hearing and the proper appeal substitutes for this hearing then the employee has effectively been deprived of one bite of the cherry in that he has had only one effective hearing. This is particularly so where there is a contractual right to an appeal. However, this strict approach would probably not endear itself to a court or tribunal which is supposed to eschew legalism in these matters.[4] Once again the ACAS Code and Handbook refer to the need to have fair and proper appeal procedures.

[1] *Whitbread & Co plc v Mills* [1988] IRLR 501, EAT and *Clark v Civil Aviation Authority* [1991] IRLR 412, EAT.
[2] *Sartor v P & O European Ferries (Felixstowe) Ltd* [1992] IRLR 271, CA.
[3] *Byrne v BOC Ltd* [1992] IRLR 505, EAT.
[4] Even though this is impossible to attain.

The opportunity to appeal

19.480 We have already noted that if an employer refuses to allow an appeal to which the employee has a contractual right this may well be an unfair dismissal.[1] This extends to the situation where an appeal is allowed but only deals with the question of sentence contrary to the contractual disciplinary procedure which provided there should be an appeal against both liability and sentence.[2] Where a contractual disciplinary procedure is interpreted by an employer as precluding any consideration of the appropriate sentence because the employee was the subject of 'suspended dismissal' following a previous offence this did not render the dismissal unfair.[3] This somewhat surprising decision was based on the EAT's view that there was an overall fair procedure and the fundamental question was whether the dismissal was unfair. It is submitted that the EAT, which reversed the tribunal, adopted a somewhat flawed argument and did not consider *Tipton* sufficiently. In fact, it is suggested, the EAT attempted to circumvent *Tipton* by saying not every breach of an employee's contractual right of appeal necessarily renders a dismissal unfair. This could be said, it is suggested, in relation to a minor breach but not where the penalty is not considered. This decision gives undue support to the employer's own contractual procedure ousting general principles of unfair dismissal law. The *Tipton* case has also decided that what is ascertained at an appeal must be considered by the employer in deciding whether to dismiss. Logically the employee denied a right of appeal could also say this was unfair procedure but *Polkey* concentrates on following the agreed procedure and if nothing is agreed then there is nothing to bite on. However, it is good practice to allow an appeal but it has been held that the absence of an appeal does not of itself make the dismissal unfair. It is a factor to be considered.[4] Where the dismissal is for redundancy and the company handbook provides no right of appeal against a redundancy dismissal which it did for gross misconduct a failure to provide an appeal does not render the dismissal unfair.[5] There is nothing in the Code of Practice which suggests there should be an appeal in such circumstances.

[1] *West Midland Co-operative Society Ltd v Tipton* [1986] AC 536, [1986] 1 All ER 513, HL.
[2] *Stocker v Lancashire County Council* [1992] IRLR 75, CA.
[3] *Post Office v Marney* [1990] IRLR 170.
[4] *Shannon v Michelin (Belfast) Ltd* [1981] IRLR 505, CA.
[5] *Robinson v Ulster Carpet Mills Ltd* [1991] IRLR 348, NICA.

19.481 It is ideal that a person who conducted the disciplinary hearing should not be involved in the appeal other than to present the findings of the hearing. The EAT has, nevertheless, said that it is impossible to have total disconnection in many cases and rules about separation cannot be applied in all cases. It has even been said that it 'must be difficult to show that the rules of natural justice have been infringed if the person hearing the appeal in fact took the decision'[1] provided that the employee has had his say. This perhaps goes a little to far because the vast majority of employers are able to provide a person to hear the appeal who is different from the person chairing the disciplinary hearing. However, the purpose of the EAT's comment is to ensure that employers do not become trapped in over-regulated procedures.

1 *Rowe v Radio Rentals Ltd* [1982] IRLR 177.

19.482 Where an employee fails to appeal this does not mean that he has acquiesced in his dismissal[1] although it may be something which a tribunal will take into account.

1 *Chrystie v Rolls-Royce (1971) Ltd* [1976] IRLR 336.

Polkey v Dayton *and thereafter*

19.483 This case has been referred to so many times that one cannot end this section without a final reference to it. The case concerned the dismissal of a van driver who was handed a redundancy letter and immediately sent home and dismissed. The House of Lords, reversing the lower courts, held that the failure to consult or warn the employee would normally render a dismissal unfair and remitted the case to the tribunal to determine reasonableness on the basis of facts known to the employer when he dismissed and on the basis that the lack of consultation and warning would normally render a dismissal unfair.

19.484 The House of Lords has made it clear beyond peradventure that it is no longer permissible to ask if the procedural breach has made any difference to the end result. The test is what the employer knew at the time of dismissal.

19.485 It will now generally be unfair to dismiss where there has been a failure to take any of the necessary procedural steps which have been outlined above. Once again the law concentrates on what the employer has done, not on the question of injustice or otherwise to the employee. However, there is an important exception which will be argued about for many years. Where the normal procedural steps would be regarded as 'utterly useless' or 'futile' then the breach of procedure can be excused. The court intended that these situations would be exceptional and an employer should tread warily before trying to argue that it was utterly futile. It is impossible to list examples but it might be arguable that an employer who was closing his business completely and making all the employees redundant would see no point in consulting and warning employees.[1] Even there one can see why it is good practice to give notice to employees so that they can make alternative arrangements and there is usually no good reason why an employer cannot notify his employees in advance. Being caught red-handed might be another situation where procedural requirements can be waived but again even there there might be something the employee can say in mitigation and there should still be a hearing.

[1] This is unlikely to succeed.

19.486 However, the change is not wholly beneficial for the employee. Where the remedy is compensation the tribunal can still consider the procedural flaw in the light of whether it would have made any difference as regards the level of compensation. If the tribunal considers that the step was purely procedural and has had no effect on substance, employees may find their victory rather hollow. Thus a failure to consult over redundancy may lead to an award of only two weeks' pay.[1] In a capability case it is arguable that a warning would not have led to an improvement and therefore compensation could be limited to the period before dismissal. This has yet to be worked out. However, employees may be re-employed if tribunals begin to award this remedy. Furthermore, the tribunal must consider on a percentage basis what difference it would have made had the procedure been followed properly.[2]

[1] *Mining Supplies (Longwall) Ltd v Baker* [1988] ICR 676, [1988] IRLR 417, EAT.
[2] See below in section on compensation.

19.487 The new approach can also assist employers to the detriment of employees by concentrating on the reasonableness of the employer's behaviour rather than on any injustices to the employee. This was a principle already developed in 'some other substantial reason'[1] but it has now developed in conduct such as the 'blanket dismissal' case[2] where three employees were fairly dismissed even though the employer was unsure who was the guilty party. However, there have been cases where procedural breaches have led to unfair dismissal findings[3] and overall one must welcome the new approach because it will improve the position of employees by encouraging employers to adopt proper procedures and to abide by them and also to improve industrial relations.

[1] For example *Chubb Fire Security Ltd v Harper* [1983] IRLR 311, EAT.
[2] *Whitbread & Co plc v Thomas* [1988] ICR 135, [1988] IRLR 43, EAT.
[3] For example *McLaren v National Coal Board*, para 19.472 above.

6 REMEDIES

Re-employment – introductory remarks

19.488 If the employee succeeds in his complaint of unfair dismissal the tribunal must consider what remedy to provide. It must first consider whether the employer should be reinstated, then, if not, whether he should be re-engaged and then, if not, what compensation should be awarded. It is possible for the tribunal to find a dismissal unfair but award nil compensation. An example of this would be the *Devis & Sons Ltd v Atkins*[1] situation (where misconduct discovered after the dismissal made it unjust to award compensation). Following the *Polkey*[2] decision there will be more findings of unfair dismissal but in some cases the compensation will not be at a high level. This will reflect the fact that some procedural failings will not necessarily mean that the employee has suffered much loss. The tribunal may also order interim relief where a trade union official has been dismissed for trade union reasons.[3] However, special awards may be made where dismissal is for trade union, maternity, and health and safety reasons and these are considered below.

1 [1977] AC 931, [1977] 2 All ER 321, CA.
2 [1987] 1 All ER 984, [1987] ICR 301, CA.
3 TULR(C)A, s 161.

19.489 Reinstatement means putting the employee back in his job without suffering any loss. Re-engagement means that the employee is re-employed in a job comparable to the old job by the employer, or his successor or an associated employer. Although the primary remedy is re-employment the number of employees who have been ordered to be re-employed has remained extremely low since the inception of unfair dismissal rights. It is at present about 2% of those that succeed in their claims which is extremely low. As a percentage of all claims made it would be minute, bearing in mind the settlement/withdrawal rate of about two-thirds and the success rate of those that proceed (about one-third). Why this is so is not easy to pinpoint. Many applicants do not seek re-employment because they feel that the relationship has soured and they do not seek their job back. Many employers feel the same even where the employee wants to return and they fiercely resist re-employment. Although the employee's wishes are obviously a prerequisite to any order for re-employment the employer's objections do not prevent an order but have to be taken into account in determining the practicability of making an order. It may be that tribunals accept these objections too readily and this helps to explain the low rate but in the writer's experience it is rarely sought. The lack of re-employment is common throughout most of Europe but not in North America where it is the normal remedy provided by arbitrators under collective bargaining agreements.

19.490 The tribunal can 'order' re-employment but it must be understood that this is not an order in the usual judicial sense. Thus a failure to comply with it does not lead to a finding of contempt as the employment relationship is considered to be a voluntary one[1] and neither party can force themselves on the other. If the employer is ordered to re-employ but fails to do so then the employee is entitled to return to the tribunal where compensation will be assessed and will include an 'additional award' for the failure to re-employ. The ultimate remedy is financial. The low level of re-employment is seen by some as a major failing of the legislation and criticism is levelled at tribunals for this but it is at present impossible to assess precisely the reasons for the low level and it may be much more to do with the parties' feelings as to the breakdown of confidence between them.

1 TULR(C)A 1992, s 236.

19.491 Where a complaint succeeds the tribunal must explain to the employee that orders for reinstatement and re-employment can be made, and the circumstances in which they can be made and must ask the employee if he wishes to return.[1] If he so wishes the tribunal must consider the remedy but if there is no order compensation must be ordered.[2] Thus the tribunal is obliged to explain the remedies as soon as the decision of unfairness is reached. The employee is not bound by what he has written or not written on his originating application. The wording is mandatory and it has been held that the tribunal must follow this duty even where the employee is professionally represented.[3] However, in certain circumstances it has been held that where this would only be a formality there is no such duty. In general, however, tribunals should perform this duty. A failure to ascertain the applicant's wishes regarding re-employment does not render a tribunal decision a nullity.[4]

---

1 A failure to explain the remedies does not render the tribunal decision a nullity: *Cowley v Manson Timber Ltd* [1995] IRLR 153, CA.

2 ERA, s 112.

3 *Pirelli General Cable Works Ltd v Murray* [1979] IRLR 190, EAT.

4 *Cowley v Manson Timber Ltd* [1994] ICR 252, EAT where the applicant was approaching retirement age, had been professionally represented and had not sought re-employment.

Reinstatement

19.492 Such an order requires the employer to treat the employee in all respects as if he had not been dismissed and on making such an order the tribunal must specify:

(a) any amount payable by the employer in respect of any benefit which the employee might reasonably be expected to have had but for the dismissal, including arrears of pay, for the period between the date of termination of employment and the date of reinstatement;
(b) any rights and privileges, including seniority and pension rights which must be 'restored to the employee';
(c) the date by which the order must be complied with.[1]

---

1 ERA, s 114(2).

19.493 If the employee would have benefited from an improvement in his terms and conditions of employment had he not been dismissed this improvement must be included in the order but this is without prejudice to the generality stated above.[1]

---

1 ERA, s 114(3).

19.494 The above are statutory requirements and the tribunal has no discretion to vary them. As we shall see below there are statutory limits on compensation and it is sometimes considered that the limit applies to back pay in a reinstatement order. It does not, and there is no limit – the tribunal must simply put the employee back in the position that he would have been in had he remained employed. Usually this will not be too complex but if there have been fluctuations in the employer's business which might have led to changes in the employee's earnings or the employee had been sick these matters must be investigated.

19.495 The tribunal, in exercising its discretion to reinstate must take into account the following:

(a) whether the employee wishes to be reinstated;
(b) whether it is practicable for the employer to comply with an order for reinstatement;
(c) where the complainant cause or contributed to some extent to the dismissal, whether it would be just to order his reinstatement.[1]

1 ERA, s 116(1).

19.496 It is somewhat odd to place the complainant's wishes together with the other two factors because it must surely be the case that the tribunal would not reinstate where the employee did not wish to return and this should be an essential prerequisite rather than one of the relevant factors.

Practicability

19.497 The practicability of reinstatement has been considered less often than it has been in re-engagement cases but the principles adopted must be applicable to reinstatement and therefore the cases on both forms of re-employment will be considered together here. First, there is a statutory question to consider. The employer may have engaged a permanent replacement for a dismissed employee but this fact must not be taken into account in determining the practicability of reinstatement or re-engagement. This would be a very simple method of avoiding re-employment. However, the employer is then provided with important exceptions to this rule. If he can show that it was not practicable to arrange for the dismissed employee's work to be done without engaging a permanent replacement then this is a factor which can be brought into the equation. One could reasonably conclude that it would be almost a conclusive factor against re-employment. Whether it was practicable to engage a temporary replacement will presumably depend on the nature of the business and more importantly, the nature of the work. A chief accountant is not easy to replace on a temporary basis but a typing assistant would be. The second exception is where the employer engaged the replacement after the lapse of a reasonable period without having heard from the dismissed employee that he wished to be re-employed and that when the replacement was engaged it was no longer reasonable to arrange for the work to be done except by a permanent replacement. Thus here the employer must still show the need for a permanent replacement but the standard is relaxed from 'practicable' to 'reasonable'. This is a significant relaxation and in many cases the employer's arguments will be difficult to rebut. What is a 'reasonable period' for the purpose of waiting to hear from the employee is difficult to assess. An originating application must be submitted within three months and if that contains a request for re-employment one would assume that a reasonable period would not have lapsed.[1]

1 See ERA, s 116(5), (6).

19.498 In one case[1] an employee was held to have been unfairly dismissed and the tribunal ordered reinstatement on the basis that his replacement was not permanent and it was practicable to reinstate. The employer did not comply, claiming there was insufficient work but the tribunal retained the order saying that if there were to be a redundancy the applicant would have to take his chance with the others. The EAT set aside the order saying it was not practicable because it would result in a redundancy process or in significant overmanning and that this was against the spirit of the legislation and common sense and justice. Logic is somewhat lacking here because once it has been decided that there was no need for a permanent replacement surely the order should stand and the replacement employee be dismissed. That is the whole purpose of the quite sophisticated statutory provision regarding replacements. Further support for management has been given in a recent case[2] where a re-engagement order was set aside which had been granted because the employer had not invited applications for voluntary redundancy from the existing workforce. While stating that the fact there are no vacancies does not per se render it impracticable to reinstate it was stated that it is not the function of the tribunal to tell the employer how to run its own business. The employer is required to explain why there are no vacancies and he can explain how the best interests of the business can be served. The tribunal should carefully scrutinise the reasons advanced by the employer, due weight should be given to the commercial judgment of the management and the standard must not be set too high. An employer cannot be expected to explore every avenue.

1 *Cold Drawn Tubes Ltd v Middleton* [1992] ICR 318, EAT.
2 *Port of London Authority v Payne* [1994] IRLR 9, CA.

19.499 There have been a number of cases dealing with 'practicable'. Where re-employment might lead to industrial conflict it will not be regarded as practicable to re-employ. Thus if re-engagement would inevitably lead to serious industrial strife it would not be practicable or in accordance with equity that the employee should be re-engaged.[1] The tribunal must consider the realities of the situation and if the evidence points overwhelmingly to the conclusion that the consequences of any attempt to re-engage the employee will result in serious industrial strife it will be neither practicable nor in accordance with equity to make such an order.[2] Both of these cases make it clear that 'practicable' does not mean 'possible' but means that it is capable of being carried into effect with success. However, a more recent case[3] has rejected this as the test and said the word 'practicable' does not mean 'capable' or 'possible'. The EAT said the tribunal must use their experience and common sense, look at what has happened and what is likely to happen, in making its decision.

1 *Coleman v Magnet Joinery Ltd* [1975] ICR 46, [1974] IRLR 343, CA.
2 *Bateman v British Leyland UK Ltd* [1974] ICR 403, [1974] IRLR 101, NIRC.
3 *Rao v Civil Aviation Authority* [1992] ICR 503 affirmed on other grounds by CA in [1994] IRLR 240; see also *Meridian Ltd v Gomersall* [1977] ICR 597.

19.500 It will not be considered practicable to re-employ where there is friction or animosity between the employer and employee, although the possibility of moving departments and location must be considered. However, if confidence has been broken between the parties re-employment is unlikely to be practicable. This is particularly likely where the employer is a small employer. There will be no re-employment order where there is a redundancy situation or the employee is unfit to work. Where an employee believed she was the victim of a conspiracy by her employers then she was not likely to be a satisfactory employee if re-employed and the Court of Appeal stated that the legislation is not intended to vindicate an employee's reputation.[1] It has also been held that where there must exist a close personal relationship reinstatement can only be appropriate in exceptional circumstances and should not be pursued unless there was powerful evidence that it would succeed.[2]

[1] *Nothman v Barnet London Borough (No 2)* [1980] IRLR 65.
[2] *Enessey Co SA v Minoprio* [1978] IRLR 489, EAT.

19.501 If there is no suitable slot for the employee then it is not practicable to comply with any re-engagement order and the order does not place a duty on the employer to search for and find a vacancy for the employee.[1]

[1] *Freemans plc v Flynn* [1984] ICR 874, [1984] IRLR 486, EAT.

19.502 It is important to note that when the tribunal makes a reinstatement order under s 107 or indeed a re-engagement order this in itself does not lead to the additional award when the employer does not comply with the order. There is a need for another hearing and then under s 117 the employer has to satisfy the tribunal that it was not practicable to comply with the order[1] which means the onus is on him to show this. The question of practicability is dealt with substantively at the second stage (s 117).[2] This was considered very comprehensively by the Court of Appeal recently[3] which reversed the EAT and held that the order made at the first stage is of necessity provisional. The conclusion as to practicability is made when the employer finds whether he is able to comply with the order in the prescribed period. The onus is heavily on him.

[1] ERA, s 117(4)(a).
[2] *Timex Corpn v Thomson* [1981] IRLR 522, EAT and the same point was made in *Freemans* case, para 19.501 above.
[3] *Port of London Authority v Payne* [1994] IRLR 9, CA.

19.503 In calculating the amount payable by the employer when reinstating or re-employing, the employer is entitled to deduct any wages in lieu of notice or ex gratia payments paid by the employer and any remuneration paid by another employer.[1] The employee is not entitled to profit from the exercise and this provision is entirely equitable.

[1] ERA, s 114(4).

19.504 In determining whether to order reinstatement the question of whether it is expedient to order it, in the sense of fulfilling some objective is not a relevant or proper consideration. The tribunal must confine itself to the three statutory criteria.[1]

[1] *Qualcast (Wolverhampton) Ltd v Ross* [1979] ICR 386, [1979] IRLR 98, EAT.

Re-engagement

19.505 The tribunal is bound to consider whether to order reinstatement before re-engagement but if this is not ordered it must consider re-engagement. An order for re-engagement is an order that the employee be engaged by the employer, or by a successor of the employer or by an associated employer, in employment comparable to that from which he was dismissed or other suitable employment. On making such an order the tribunal shall specify the terms on which re-engagement is to take place including:

(a) the identity of the employer;
(b) the nature of the employment;
(c) the remuneration for the employment;
(d) any amount payable by the employer in respect of any benefit which the complainant might reasonably be expected to have had but for the dismissal, including arrears of pay, for the period between the date of termination and re-engagement;
(e) any rights and privileges, including seniority and pension rights, which must be restored to the employee, and
(f) the date by which the order must be complied with.[1]

1 ERA, s 115(2).

19.506 Accordingly it can be seen that the tribunal has a considerable degree of discretion in determining the re-engagement terms and in doing so it must take into account any wish expressed by the employee as to the nature of the order to be made.[1] In deciding whether to make an order at all the practicability of compliance must be taken into account and so must the employee's contributory fault if there is any.[2] In the latter situation the tribunal must consider whether it is just to order re-engagement. The same points made above in relation to the engagement of a permanent employee apply equally to a case of re-engagement as indeed do the provisions relating to deductions to be made from arrears of pay.[3] Where the tribunal does order re-engagement it must be done on terms which are, so far as is reasonably practicable, as favourable as an order for reinstatement.[4]

1 ERA, s 116(3)(a).
2 ERA, s 116(3)(b) and (c).
3 ERA, s 115(3).
4 ERA, s 116(4).

19.507 An employer is associated with another if one is a company of which the other (directly or indirectly) has control, or if both are companies of which a third person (directly or indirectly) has control.[1] This definition is considered more fully elsewhere. A subsidiary and holding company are clearly associated.

1 ERA, s 231.

19.508 The tribunal discretion exists because the new employment need not be the same but comparable or suitable. The statutory requirement is that it should be, if possible, as favourable as a reinstatement order. Generally this is complied with, particularly as regards pay. Where an order is made despite a contributory fault finding the tribunal will sometimes use its discretion to provide different terms, either in relation to pay or sometimes as to arrears of pay. If the tribunal decides that there is no contributory fault when considering substantive liability it should not re-open the question for the purposes of deciding whether to make a re-engagement order.[1] Where the contributory fault was high an order for re-engagement should not have been made.[2]

1 *Boots Co plc v Lees-Collier* [1986] ICR 728, [1986] IRLR 485, EAT.
2 *Nairne v Highland and Islands Fire Brigade* [1989] IRLR 366.

19.509 A tribunal is required to specify the terms of the re-engagement order. It is insufficient to order re-engagement without stipulating its terms,[1] although it is generally undesirable to order re-engagement in respect of a specific job, as distinct from identifying the nature of the proposed employment.[2] It has also been stated by the EAT that tribunals should not make 'offer directions' whereby the employer was ordered to make an offer on certain specified terms within a certain period. It was better to make the order in the required statutory form and 'offer directions' were probably not permitted.[3] Where the order covers arrears of pay, which it must do, the arrears should be specified by rates of pay rather than a lump sum since it is possible that reinstatement might take place earlier than the stipulated date.[4] There is no duty to mitigate in relation to the period between the dismissal and the date of the order for re-employment. This applies to the entire period and the employee could not be criticised for failing to mitigate by not bringing his unfair dismissal application immediately.

1 *Pirelli*'s case, para 19.491 above.
2 *Rank Xerox v Stryczek* [1995] IRLR 568, EAT.
3 *Lilley Construction v Dunn* [1984] IRLR 483.
4 *O'Laoire v Jackel International Ltd* [1990] IRLR 70, CA.

19.510 Where re-engagement is ordered at a lower rate of pay and arrears of pay are awarded the arrears must be based on the original higher rate, not the new lower rate.[1] In *Electronic Data Processing Ltd v Wright* the old rate was £8,000 and the new rate was £5,000 and this was acceptable but such a reduction would very rarely be seen as comparable or suitable employment. In the same case the order did not state the location of the work because the tribunal did not know that the employer operated in more than one location. The EAT held it was permissible for the tribunal to add this to its original order. The Act provides[2] that when a person is re-employed the order should include any improvement that the employee would have received had he remained in employment but these should be restricted to contractual rights according to the Court of Appeal.[3] Rather oddly the wording of the statute in relation to re-engagement is more liberal and might allow a non-contractual benefit to be provided. As a matter of law a tribunal cannot order re-engagement on significantly more favourable terms than the original job.[4]

1 *Electronic Data Processing Ltd v Wright* [1986] ICR 76, [1986] IRLR 8, EAT.
2 ERA, s 114(3) reinstatement, s 108(2)(d) re-engagement.
3 *O'Laoire v Jackel International Ltd* [1991] IRLR 70.
4 *Rank Xerox v Stryczek* [1995] IRLR 568.

Enforcement of re-employment orders and additional awards

19.511 If a re-employment order is made but the employer does not comply with it the tribunal will make an additional award unless the employer satisfies the tribunal that it was not practicable to comply with the order, or where the dismissal was for union reasons in which case a 'special award' is made.[1] If a re-employment order is made and the employee is re-employed but the terms of the order are not fully complied with the tribunal has power to make an award of extra compensation having regard to the loss sustained by the employee because of the employer's failure to comply fully with the order.[2] The extra sum is added to the sum which would have otherwise been awarded and there is no statutory maximum to be applied following a change made by TURERA 1993.[3] This appears to have reversed the effect of a Court of Appeal decision in 1990.[4] Thus if the employee is reinstated on less favourable terms this is treated as a total failure to comply with a reinstatement order within s 117(3) rather than a partial compliance under s 117(1). The latter refers to a failure by the employer to comply with ancillary matters which may be in the order and not to the terms of the order for reinstatement as such.[5] In this case the additional award was accordingly made and the statutory maximum was not applied. It has already been noted that it is not a compliance with the re-engagement order to re-employ the employee in a different place from his original location.[6]

1 See below – to be extended for health and safety and maternity dismissals.
2 ERA, s 117(1).
3 Section 30 inserting a new provision now to be found in s 124(4), ERA.
4 *O'Laoire v Jackel International Ltd* [1990] IRLR 70.
5 *Artisan Press Ltd v Srawley* [1986] ICR 328, [1986] IRLR 126, EAT.
6 *Electronic Data Processing Ltd*, para 19.510 above.

19.512 Where the additional award is made then it is for between 13–26 weeks' pay unless the dismissal was a breach of the sex or race discrimination legislation in which case it is for between 26–52 weeks' pay. A week's pay is subject to a statutory ceiling annually reviewable.[1] It will be considered more fully below.[2] The discretion for the tribunal is quite wide and the exercise of such discretion should be explained. Some form of proper assessment and balancing must take place. Factors to be taken into account include the employer's conduct in refusing to comply with the order and the extent to which the compensatory award has met the loss suffered. Thus if the employee has another job the amount will probably be reduced and where the employer is a large one and there will be no real objection to reinstatement it will be larger.[3] However, the award is not intended to be a precisely calculated reflection of financial loss.[4] It is permissible to take into account an employer's genuine objection to reinstatement in assessing the award[5] and so can a failure to mitigate loss be considered where it goes to the merits of the case.[6]

1 At present (1996/7) £210 per week.
2 In the basic award section.
3 *Morganite Electrical Carbon Ltd v Donne* [1988] ICR 18, [1987] IRLR 363, EAT.
4 *Mabirizi v National Hospital for Nervous Diseases* [1990] IRLR 133, EAT.
5 *Mabirizi* (above).
6 *Mabirizi* (above).

19.513 Although compensatory and basic awards are subject to deduction for any contributory fault where an additional award is made in these circumstances, which will not be common, this latter award is not subject to deductions. Where there is an act of indirect race or sex discrimination no compensation can be awarded unless the discrimination is intentional. However, if it is an unfair dismissal then the tribunal can award reinstatement and a failure to reinstate can lead to an additional award being made.

19.514 Where a re-employment order specifies arrears of pay and other monetary sums the follow-up to any failure by an employer to pay is a further hearing of the tribunal under s 117. This is the only remedy available as the monetary provisions of a reinstatement order do not create a cause of action enforceable in the county court.[1] Any sum payable in pursuance of a tribunal decision can be recovered through the county court but the two options are mutually exclusive.[2] Thus the employee cannot enforce part of an award and then return to claim unfair dismissal compensation. This is not altogether easy to follow because the monetary award for arrears is a totally separate issue from the other awards which reflect other losses. The monetary sum recoverable in the county court is not subject to the statutory maximum limit. This sum will be used to offset against any compensatory award but cannot be used in this way for basic and additional awards. The fact that the employee chooses to proceed in the county court for arrears should not preclude him from seeking extra compensation for the failure of the employer to reinstate.

1 *O'Laoire v Jackel International Ltd* [1990] IRLR 70, CA.
2 Industrial Tribunals Act 1996, s 15.

Compensation – general statutory structure

19.515 Compensation comprises a basic award and a compensatory award. Additional awards have already been mentioned and special awards will be considered below. The basic award is a payment based on past service and its calculation is laid down in the statute, subject to deductions. The compensatory award is, as its name implies, to compensate the employee for loss suffered, and is also subject to deductions.

Basic award

19.516 This is intended to compensate the employee for the loss of job security and is a form of reward for past service and to compensate for the fact that he will have to build up his period of continuous employment after dismissal.

19.517 Subject to the deductions stated below the basic award is calculated by reference to the period of continuous employment ending with the effective date of termination[1] by starting at the end of the employment and reckoning backwards the number of years of employment and allowing one and a half weeks' pay for each year on which the employee was not below the age of 41, one week's pay for each year he was not below the age of 22 and half a week's pay for any years before that. There is a maximum of 20 years that can count and there is a limit to the amount of a week's pay which is at present (1996/7) £210 (reviewable annually). The present maximum basic award is therefore £6,300 based on a maximum of 20 years' service × £210 (maximum weekly earnings) × one and a half (maximum multiple – based on age). Unlike the redundancy provision any years of employment over the age of 16 count. There is an upper age limit of 65, irrespective of whether there is a high normal retiring age and as from 64 there is a reduction of 1/12 for each complete month worked.[2]

[1] ERA, s 97(1) – see above and note s 97(2) which adds the statutory minimum notice where this is not given.
[2] See s 119 generally.

19.518 The concept of a week's pay is defined in Part XIV, Chapter II of the ERA.[1] It is very complicated[2] and what follows is a brief summary of its main provisions. In effect it is the contractual remuneration for the normal working hours and if there are none it is the average weekly contractual remuneration. Overtime hours and pay do not count unless they are obligatory on both sides, that is, the employer is obliged to provide it and the employee to work it.[3]

[1] Section 220.
[2] See Chapter 16.
[3] *Tarmac Roadstone Holdings Ltd v Peacock* [1973] 2 All ER 485, [1973] ICR 273, CA.

19.519 There is no definition of pay or remuneration but it means contractual monetary payments for the work. It obviously includes wages or salary and any other form of monetary contractual entitlement such as a bonus, allowances or commission. Expenses do not count unless they represent a profit element in which case they should not be classified as expenses and the contract will be illegal! Tips are not included because they are not obligations on the employer. However, a fixed obligatory service charge which is distributed to employees does count.

19.520 A week's pay for basic award purposes is the gross amount and is the amount an employee receives for working his normal hours. If he is a piece worker then his average hourly rate of remuneration will be calculated by taking the average for the last 12 weeks. This applies to commission also. The formula is very complex[1] and there are also provisions for workers with no normal working hours.[2]

[1] See ERA, s 221.
[2] See ERA, s 224.

19.521 There is a minimum basic award where the employee is dismissed for trade union reasons, namely the employee's actual or proposed union membership and activities or his refusal or proposed refusal to belong to a union or where his selection for redundancy was for a trade union reason. In this case the minimum is £2,770.[1] The award is worked out in the usual way subject to this minimum but deductions for contributory fault can be made from this figure.[2]

[1] Also reviewable annually (TULR(C)A 1992, s 156(1)). TURERA 1993 extended this minimum basic award to health and safety dismissals (see now ERA, s 120(1)).
[2] TULR(C)A 1992, s 156(2) but see para 19.525, above.

Reductions in the basic award

(a) Redundancy

19.522 Where an employee has been dismissed for redundancy because he has unreasonably refused an offer of suitable alternative employment or has unreasonably terminated a trial period in a new job then he receives two weeks' pay as a basic award.[1] This will occur very rarely.

[1] ERA, s 121.

(b) Refusal of reinstatement

19.523 Where the employee has unreasonably refused an offer which would have had the effect of reinstating him in all respects as if he had not been dismissed the tribunal shall reduce or further reduce the amount of the basic award to such extent as it considers just and equitable having regard to its finding.[1] This does not cover re-engagement and there must be a complete reinstatement. It is intriguing to postulate on what might be a reasonable refusal. The tribunal has a discretion concerning its reduction but it must make some reduction.

[1] ERA, s 122(1).

(c) Conduct

19.524 Where the tribunal considers that any conduct of the employee before the dismissal or before any dismissal notice was given was such that it would be just and equitable to reduce or further reduce the amount of the basic award to any extent, the tribunal shall do so.[1] This subsection deals with the 'rogues' charter' as mentioned in *Devis & Sons Ltd v Atkins*[2] so that an employee who is discovered to have been guilty of misconduct after the dismissal can have a nil basic award. The amount of the deduction is in the tribunal's discretion but the deduction should be the same for both basic and compensatory awards.[3]

[1] ERA, s 122(2).
[2] [1977] AC 931, [1977] 2 All ER 321, CA.
[3] *Royal Society for the Prevention of Cruelty to Animals v Cruden* [1986] ICR 205, [1986] IRLR 83, EAT. This question is dealt with below.

19.525 There are two other statutory provisions which involve reductions and they are both related to union reasons. Where the employee was selected for redundancy for union reasons there is a minimum basic award but in that case it is only the amount by which this minimum figure exceeds the normal basic award which can be reduced. If it exceeds the minimum then there can be no reduction.[1] The other provision is that the tribunal must disregard any conduct leading to dismissal that was a breach of a contractual term relating to union membership or activities or any refusal to make payments to a third party in lieu of union membership.[2] Both situations are unlikely to occur because contributory fault is not very likely in union dismissal cases.

[1] Section 122(3).
[2] TULR(C)A, s 155.

(d) Redundancy payment

19.526 Where an employee receives a redundancy payment this extinguishes the basic award[1] because they are almost invariably the same, the only difference being when the employee began work at the age of 16 from when the basic award begins to run, unlike the redundancy situation. This would cover a contractual redundancy scheme and, as we shall note, where any contractual scheme pays more than the statutory scheme the excess is set off against the compensatory award. However, where the employer makes an ex gratia payment which is stated to include the statutory redundancy payment and the reason is not in fact, redundancy then no deduction is made.[2]

[1] ERA, s 122(4).
[2] *Boorman v Allmakes Ltd* [1995] IRLR 553.

Ex gratia payments

19.527 Such payments can certainly be set off against the compensatory award which is intended to reflect loss.[1] However, whether it can be set against the basic award is far less clear. It depends on the nature of the payment. If an employer concedes that he has dismissed unfairly and pays an amount specifically referable to the basic award then the employer is entitled to say he has paid such an award. This applies also where the employer does not admit liability. However, where a general payment is made then it is a question of construction in each case to see if the basic award is covered.[2] In the *Chelsea* case the employee was given a cheque with a letter describing it as 'ex gratia compensation . . . as a result of the termination of your employment'. The EAT held that the words used amounted to an offer to compensate the employee for any employment protection rights including the basic award for unfair dismissal and therefore no basic award was payable. Thus it all turns on the wording.

[1] *Rushton v Harcros Timber and Building Supplies Ltd* [1993] IRLR 254, EAT.
[2] *Chelsea Football and Athletic Co Ltd v Heath* [1981] ICR 323, [1981] IRLR 73. In *Darr v LRC Products Ltd* [1993] IRLR 257, the EAT said it was open to the employer to provide that any severance payment could even be set off against any additional award that might be made.

Compensatory awards – general introduction and general principles

19.528 This is intended to cover the employee's actual loss, no more no less. It is not intended to be punitive or to express disapproval of the employer's policies. The amount of the award is to be such amount as the tribunal consider just and equitable in all the circumstances having regard to the loss suffered in consequence of the dismissal insofar as that loss is attributable to the employer's action.[1] The loss includes expenses incurred as a consequence of the dismissal and loss of any benefit which he might reasonably be expected to have had but for the dismissal.[2] Further provisions relate mainly to deductions which will be considered later. The maximum amount of compensation that can be awarded as a compensatory award is £11,300, a figure which is reviewed annually. The issue of awarding 'just and equitable' compensation is not contained in the provisions of the basic award. Thus procedural defects which have caused the employee no loss cannot lead to any reduction in the basic award whereas they can be deducted from the compensatory award. The basic award can only have deductions based on the employee's conduct.[3]

1 ERA, s 123(1).
2 ERA, s 123(2).
3 See *Charles Robertson v White* [1995] ICR 349, EAT for a good explanation of the difference.

19.529 The leading early case is *Norton Tool Co Ltd v Tewson*[1] which laid down principles which are still the guiding principles. They are that the purpose of compensation is to compensate fully but not to award a bonus and that the amount is to be determined by what is just and equitable in all the circumstances having regard to the complainant's loss. Loss does not include injury to feelings. The burden of establishing the loss is on the employee. The tribunal must set out its reasoning in sufficient detail to show how it operated. The award should include the following:

(a) immediate loss of wages (meaning up to the final hearing);
(b) future loss of wages (as from the hearing);
(c) loss arising from the manner of dismissal (very rarely provided);
(d) loss of protection in respect of unfair dismissal (£100–£200 range).

1 [1973] 1 All ER 183, [1972] ICR 501, NIRC.

19.530 All of the above emanate from the *Norton Tool* case. Thus where an employer has an appallingly unfair procedure but this creates no loss there can be no compensatory award. However, it is unusual for there to be a nil compensatory award. Furthermore, when the procedure is very bad this is a factor which can be taken into consideration because once the actual loss is ascertained in deciding what is just and equitable the tribunal must look at all the circumstances. This includes asking the question 'How unfair was the unfair dismissal?'[1] In practice the tribunals use a broad brush approach and their assessments are not that precise. This has been recognised by the EAT who understand that compensation has to be assessed quickly in a somewhat rough and ready way.[2] If the employer chooses one reason for dismissal, abandoning another reason which would have been valid grounds for dismissal, it is still just and equitable to award compensation in the full amount.[3]

1 *Townson v Northgate Group Ltd* [1981] IRLR 382, EAT.
2 *Fougére v Phoenix Motor Co Ltd* [1977] 1 All ER 237, [1976] ICR 495.
3 *Trico-Folberth Ltd v Devonshire* [1989] IRLR 396, CA.

19.531 Although the burden of proof is on the applicant to prove his loss nevertheless the tribunal must itself raise the categories of compensatory award to which must be added to the above the loss of pension rights.[1] It must inquire into the various heads of damage although the employee must still prove his loss. This can be problematic when pensions are involved and tribunals can make employees aware of their rights to apply for disclosure of relevant documents.[2] A rather undeveloped potential head of loss is that relating to the employer's national insurance contributions. This benefit is lost as a direct result of the dismissal. Where the dismissal led to depression and consequent invalidity benefit the fact that the employee thereby was unable to work did not prevent him from recovering compensation during that period and this was attributable to the employer's action.[3] In this case invalidity benefit was held to be deductible from the compensation as it was more akin to insurance payments than anything else. But it has now been said that this is wrong and will not be followed.[4] The same principle applies where the employee becomes unfit for work because of anxiety and reactive depression as a result of the dismissal.[5]

1 *Tidman v Aveling Marshall Ltd* [1977] ICR 506, [1977] IRLR 218, EAT.
2 *Copson and Trahearn v Eversure Accessories Ltd* [1974] ICR 636, [1974] IRLR 247, NIRC.
3 *Hilton International Hotels (UK) Ltd v Faraji* [1994] IRLR 267, EAT.
4 *Puglia v C James & Sons* [1996] IRLR 70, EAT.
5 *Devine v Designer Flowers Wholesale Florist Sundries Ltd* [1993] IRLR 517, EAT.

Immediate loss

19.532 This means loss to the date of the hearing at which compensation is assessed so if there is a separate hearing for compensation it is that hearing which counts. The figure is calculated net but fringe benefits can be included and so can all payments that were likely to be received – it is not necessary to show a contractual entitlement.[1] Thus where there is a reasonable expectation of overtime this is included[2] as are expected pay increases[3] and tips.[4] All fringe benefits can be counted. The obvious one is the company car and the private use is what must be compensated. There are various methods of calculating the loss and the AA or RAC tables are quite a useful guide. Accommodation provided by the employer is another important benefit in kind and a market value can be put on this. Other benefits include medical insurance, low interest loans and free or subsidised meals. Each individual may have separate rights but can claim actual loss.

1 Contrast wrongful dismissal.
2 *Mullet v Brush Electrical Machines* [1977] ICR 829.
3 *York Trailer Co Ltd v Sparkes* [1973] ICR 518, NIRC.
4 *Palmanor Ltd v Cedron* [1978] ICR 1008, [1978] IRLR 303.

19.533 The position regarding notice pay has caused a few problems. If the employer dismisses without notice or pay in lieu of notice there is a right to claim net pay for the period of notice. The *Norton Tool v Tewson* case[1] established that. However, if the employee finds other work during this period he suffers less than the full notice pay amount. The cases have never established a clear answer as to whether credit must be given. The better view is that during the notice period no credit need be given for such earnings because there is a right to this notice. Thus the *Norton Tool* principle 'secures . . . save in exceptional circumstances the opportunity to earn during the notice period without giving credit for earnings from another employer against wages due during the period of notice'.[2] In the *Babcock* case the court did state that when an employee was entitled to long notice and was getting a new job quickly it might be possible to make deductions from the net wages. The above case only refers to the period of statutory notice and when there is a contractual notice period in excess of the statutory minimum any earnings are set off for this excess period.[3]

1 [1972] IRLR 86, NIRC.
2 *Addison v Babcock FATA Ltd* [1988] QB 280, [1987] ICR 805, CA.
3 *Vaughan v Weighpack Ltd* [1974] ICR 261, [1974] IRLR 105, NIRC.

19.534 This principle, in effect, reiterates that compensation is not to provide a bonus and this point has been shown where a fixed term contract was terminated with 29 weeks to run. Immediately after dismissal the employee set up his own business and during the 29 weeks received £10,000 more in gross earnings than if he had remained an employee. The EAT held that *Norton Tool* could not be applied in these circumstances so as to provide the employee with his earnings during the 29 week period. Good industrial practice could not override the point that compensation was there to compensate for loss not to provide a windfall.[1] If the basis is good industrial practice it might be possible to argue that no credit should be given during the entire contractual period of notice, not just the statutory period, but this will still meet the argument that compensation is for loss suffered. Clarification is needed!

1 *Isleworth Studios Ltd v Rickard* [1988] QB 882, [1988] IRLR 137.

19.535 If the employer has paid money in lieu of notice then he is entitled to deduct this sum from the compensatory award to prevent double remuneration.[1]

1 See *Babcock*, para 19.533 above.

19.536 An ex gratia payment is also offset against the compensatory award[1] as is any redundancy payment insofar as it exceeds the basic award.[2] Thus any generous contractual scheme will allow the employer to use this in any unfair dismissal case. The ex gratia payment will not be deducted if the tribunal considers it would have been paid in any event.[3]

1 *Horizon Holidays Ltd v Grassi* [1987] ICR 851, [1987] IRLR 371, EAT.
2 ERA, s 116(7).
3 *Roadchef Ltd v Hastings* [1988] IRLR 142, EAT.

19.537 If the employee obtains other employment the earnings from it are deducted, as we have noted. If the employee finds apparently permanent employment but loses this prior to the hearing it is arguable that his subsequent dismissal was the cause of his loss from that date until the hearing.[1] In the *Moosa* case this argument was premissed on the basis that the employee had acquired the right not to be unfairly dismissed by his new employer. If one confines this case on this basis then the two year qualifying rule will render this decision superfluous. It will be virtually unthinkable that an employee will have two years' service and then pursue his original claim. Therefore this case should be limited in application and the normal rules should apply. However, the tribunal is at least entitled to consider why the employee has not retained the new job. This might go to mitigation. The tribunal must assess compensation until the date of the hearing. If the employee has obtained new employment the loss will be calculated to that date but what if the employee obtains a much higher salary/wage in the new job? The dismissing employer is not permitted to set off this higher figure against the loss suffered prior to obtaining the new job. Although compensation is to reflect loss the EAT felt it was going too far to permit credit in these circumstances.[2]

1 *Courtaulds Northern Spinning Ltd v Moosa* [1984] ICR 218, [1984] IRLR 43, EAT.
2 *Fentiman v Fluid Engineering Ltd* [1991] ICR 570.

19.538 If an employee claims that he has been paid less than he was entitled to, the tribunal, in assessing compensation, must investigate the position to ascertain his entitlement so as to obtain an accurate figure.[1]

1 *Kinzley v Minories Finance Ltd* [1988] ICR 113, [1987] IRLR 490, EAT.

Future loss

19.539 Where the employee has found another job at a higher wage or salary then this creates no problem because there is no future loss, subject to the pension position. If the new job is at a lower wage the tribunal will still assess future loss based on this difference over a period of time which is within its discretion. If the employee has not obtained a new job the tribunal has to estimate when he will get one and what level of earnings he will obtain. This is a very imprecise operation and the tribunal is required to compare the employee's salary prospects for the future in each job and see as best it can how long it will take the employee to reach in his new job the equivalent salary to that he would have reached had he remained with his old employers. The amount of shortfall, measured by reference to difference in net take home pay during the period before he reaches parity, is his future loss.[1]

1 *Tradewinds Airways Ltd v Fletcher* [1981] IRLR 272, EAT.

19.540 The length of time to assess future loss is to be estimated by the tribunal on the basis of its members' collective knowledge of industrial relations in its own area.[1] They may also have local knowledge which they can act upon. There is no maximum period for assessing future loss which can be very lengthy in some circumstances.[2] Tribunals can take into account the personal characteristics of the employee such as his age or poor health in assessing compensation.[3] This has also been applied in a case with an employee suffering from defective eyesight.[4] Where an employer is near retirement and might be excluded from claiming unfair dismissal that is not per se a ground for limiting compensation. The tribunal must assess whether the employee would have continued in employment and if so the compensation can extend beyond the normal retiring age.[5] There is no norm in assessing compensation but in today's economic climate the periods of unemployment are longer and compensatory awards are increasing, albeit still only slowly. As they increase and the compensatory award begins to look low in comparison to actual wages[6] deductions for contributory fault begin to be less relevant.

---

[1] *Bateman v British Leyland UK Ltd* [1974] ICR 403, [1974] IRLR 101, NIRC.
[2] *Morganite Electrical Carbon Ltd v Donne* [1988] ICR 18, [1987] IRLR 363, EAT.
[3] *Fougère v Phoenix Motor Co Ltd* [1977] 1 All ER 237, [1976] ICR 495, EAT.
[4] *Brittains Arborfield Ltd v Van Uden* [1977] ICR 211, EAT.
[5] *Barrel Plating and Phosphating Co Ltd v Danks* [1976] 3 All ER 652, [1976] ICR 503, EAT.
[6] The Law Society's Employment Law Committee has calculated the maximum award should be £30,000 based on inflation figures since 1975. The basic award should be approximately £450 (August 1992).

19.541 As the Government has encouraged self-employment those losing their jobs have often taken this route. Assuming this is a reasonable course of action so as to mitigate loss which is very likely these days,[1] then the tribunal must carry out its usual task and work out earnings but must also take account of money spent on setting up the business[2] such as interest on capital borrowed. An employee will not receive compensation if he goes on a training course because he has taken himself out of the labour market.[3] It has been held that the loss of tax rebate is recoverable.[4]

---

[1] But only if it is unlikely that the employee will be unable to find another job.
[2] *Lee v IPC Business Press Ltd* [1984] ICR 306, EAT and *Gardiner-Hill v Roland Beiger Technics Ltd* [1982] IRLR 498.
[3] *Holroyd v Gravure Cylinders Ltd* [1984] IRLR 259, EAT. In today's economic climate it might well be perfectly reasonable to attend a short course.
[4] *Lucas v Lawrence Scott Electromotors Ltd* [1983] ICR 309, [1983] IRLR 61, EAT.

19.542 Where there is an unfair dismissal because the employer has not carried out a fair procedure the compensation could well be limited if the procedural flaw was technical. Thus if an employee is unfairly dismissed for redundancy the level of compensation will depend on whether the tribunal finds that he would have been made redundant fairly at a later date.[1] In *Polkey*, which was an unfair redundancy case, in discussing procedural failures the 'likely effect on the situation had those steps been taken should be considered at the stage of assessing compensation'.[2] In a post-*Polkey* decision a failure to carry out proper consultation led to an unfair dismissal finding but the EAT reduced a six weeks' award to two weeks and said that a nil award was possible.[3] Whenever a redundancy dismissal is unfair because of the failure to follow a fair procedure a two-stage process has to be followed in assessing compensation: (i) if the proper procedure had been followed would the employee have remained in employment? (ii) if so, what would that employment have been and what wage would have been paid?[4] It is now permissible to ask the question as to what might have happened had the employer considered the question even if he had not done so.[5] In an ill-health case where there was contributory fault the EAT said it was perfectly proper for there to be a deduction for contributory fault and also an assessment of the percentage chance of the employee remaining in employment had there been a fair procedure. In this case it was held there was a 20% chance he would have remained in employment. There was no double penalty. The compensation should be assessed as to what was just and equitable and then a deduction for contributory fault should be made.[6]

---

[1] *Delanair Ltd v Mead* [1976] ICR 522, [1976] IRLR 340, EAT.

[2] *Polkey v Dayton Services Ltd* [1987] 1 All ER 984, [1987] ICR 301, CA. See also *Campbell v Dunoon and Cowal Housing Association Ltd* [1993] IRLR 496.

[3] *Mining Supplies Longwall Ltd v Baker* [1988] ICR 676, [1988] IRLR 417.

[4] *Red Bank Manufacturing Co Ltd v Meadows* [1992] IRLR 209.

[5] *Duffy v Yeoman & Partners Ltd* [1994] IRLR 642, CA.

[6] *Rao v Civil Aviation Authority* [1994] IRLR 240, CA.

19.543 The procedural failing in not giving a warning regarding incompetence is more difficult to work out. In an early case[1] where the employee was not warned of the risk of dismissal the court said that compensation should be assessed on the basis of deciding what would have been a fair period to give the employee to improve his conduct or performance after a warning. That would be the period of compensation. However, surely this can only apply in a case of gross incompetence where the employee cannot change his ways. Otherwise, what is the point of warnings? If it has the effect of an improved performance it has fulfilled its role. The tribunal should not be asked to assess what might have happened after the warning because it is too much of an imponderable question.

---

[1] *Winterhalter Gastronom Ltd v Webb* [1973] ICR 245, [1973] IRLR 120, NIRC.

19.544 In assessing future loss a 5–10% discount for accelerated payment may be applied where the period is quite lengthy, but this is becoming less common.

Loss of statutory rights

19.545 When an employee is dismissed he loses his period of continuous employment upon which his rights to claim employment protection may depend. For example he needs two years to claim unfair dismissal and redundancy and he has to start again. The EAT has suggested that an employee should be awarded £100 for this with a review of this figure every few years.[1]

---

[1] *Muffett Ltd v Head* [1987] ICR 1, [1986] IRLR 488. It is now thought that £200 might be more appropriate but the figure is a matter for each tribunal to consider in all the circumstances.

19.546 There is a separate claim for the loss of a right to claim statutory notice. Every employee with at least 12 years' service is entitled to 12 weeks' notice and it will be 12 years before he attains the same position. It has been suggested that the employee should receive half of his statutory rights in this situation. It is a claim for loss of an intangible benefit.[1] It has not been pursued much in recent times.

---

[1] *Daley v A E Dorsett (Almar Dolls) Ltd* [1982] ICR 1, [1981] IRLR 385, EAT. See also *Arthur Guinness Son & Co (Great Britain) Ltd v Green* [1989] IRLR 288, EAT.

19.547 If the employee decides to become self employed or is unlikely ever to work again then the two awards mentioned above are inappropriate and are not made.

Expenses

19.548 These are expressly included as a head of claim and the tribunals are quite generous in awarding them. Thus the expenses of looking for a new job, such as the cost of attending interviews, telephone and postage costs are recoverable. So are all the costs involved in any necessary change in home location such as estate agents' and solicitors' fees and removal expenses. The legal cost of an unfair dismissal claim cannot be recovered.[1]

1 *Nohar v Granitstone (Galloway) Ltd* [1974] ICR 273, EAT.

Pension loss

19.549 This creates many problems but the situation has improved since guidelines prepared by a committee of chairmen of industrial tribunals, in consultation with the Government Actuary's Department were published.[1] They will be used widely but it is not an error of law for a tribunal to refuse to adhere to them.[2] In each case it is a question of evaluating the factors on either side to see whether adjustment should be made or whether the guidelines are a safe guide at all. If there is a senior employee with fairly long service then it may well be that the pension alone will exceed the statutory maximum figure.

1 *Industrial Tribunals Compensation for Loss of Pension Rights* 1991, 2nd edn.
2 *Bingham v Hobourn Engineering Ltd* [1992] IRLR 298, EAT.

19.550 As stated earlier it is up to the employee to prove his loss but the tribunal must consider the categories of loss and should tell the employee that he is entitled to apply for an order for inspection of documents.[1] The tribunal is accordingly required to inquire into pension loss. First, it must be established that the benefit of an occupational pension scheme has been lost and then it must be quantified. Even where it is clear that the loss exceeds the maximum the tribunal must estimate the loss for the purpose of obtaining the right amount of the 'prescribed element'.

1 *Copson and Trahearn v Eversure Accessories Ltd* [1974] ICR 636, [1974] IRLR 247, NIRC.

19.551 There are two types of pension loss:

(1) loss for past service is the loss of a pension position that has been earned at the date of dismissal. Thus a woman of 40 who is dismissed after 10 years' service has obtained 10 years' service towards a pension payable in 25 years time when she is 65;
(2) future loss is the loss of future pension opportunity, namely to improve her pension position until her retirement. This can be complicated because it depends on what happens after the dismissal. The guidelines categorise the heads of loss as:

(a) loss of pension rights from the dismissal to the hearing;
(b) loss of future pension rights;
(c) loss of enhancement of accrued pension rights.

19.552 There are two main methods of assessing loss of pension rights after unfair dismissal. They are:

(1) the contribution method which totals the contributions made by the employer and employee during the employment;
(2) the actuarial method which assesses the benefits accruing to the employee from the pension scheme. There are various actuarial methods but the guidelines provide a basis for assessment. That is because they make allowance for factors which can reduce pension loss. An employee might well not stay with his employer until retirement age unless he is near it. The employee will receive a deferred pension if he has two years' service and must give credit for this as well as for the fact that he would have made contributions to the pension scheme if he had remained in employment (unless it is a non-contributory scheme). Any payment received as compensation must reflect the fact that it is an accelerated payment and accordingly must be discounted.

19.553 With loss of pension position the contributions method calculates the contributions paid by both parties during the employment. The rates of contribution at the date of dismissal are multiplied by the years of service. The guidelines recommend that this method should only be used when the employee has under five years' service.

19.554 The actuarial method of assessing benefit is more accurate and more difficult. An easier alternative is to calculate the cost of purchasing an annuity which would provide the same pension at retirement. This approach is not suitable where the employee is many years from retirement because the pension is calculated on final salary and it will be impossible in most cases to predict accurately what this will be.

19.555 The guidelines provide a solid basis for valuation and they operate by means of a table which takes the accrued pension benefit and multiplies it by an appropriate figure. This provides for the employee's age and sex, the possibility of a salary increase, inflation, and the taking of a deferred pension.

19.556 It has been stated that the assessment of pension loss should not require the employee to produce elaborate statistical evidence and that a rough and ready approach is acceptable.[1] It has also been stated that the value of the accrued benefit must be taken as at the date of termination but the figure for the deferred pension must be adjusted for revaluation.[2] This may be sensible but it will not be seen as that 'rough and ready'.

---

1 *Manpower Ltd v Hearne* [1983] ICR 567, [1983] IRLR 281, EAT.
2 *Mono Pumps Ltd v Froggatt and Radford* [1987] IRLR 368, EAT.

19.557 The 'withdrawal factor' mentioned above must be considered by the tribunal and is mentioned in the guidelines. This possibility of early leaving must be considered by the tribunal but it is up to the tribunal to assess the actual percentage to apply. It may decide that an employee is very likely or unlikely to remain and can adjust the figure accordingly. Thus it can take account of the probability that the employee would have been fairly dismissed for his performance before retirement.[1] The withdrawal factor should be applied to the combined value of the net loss of pension rights for past service, for the period of unemployment, and if applicable, for lack of occupational pension rights in new employment.[2]

1 *TBA Industrial Products Ltd v Locke* [1984] ICR 228, [1984] IRLR 48, EAT.
2 *Manpower v Hearne*, para 19.556 above.

19.558 After dismissal pension loss continues. At the hearing date the employee may still be unemployed or he may have a new job with or without an occupational pension scheme. For any period of unemployment the loss of the employer's contributions is the recommended method. The tribunal must assess any period of future unemployment if there is no new job available. For older employees there may not be one and in that situation it might be sensible for this period of unemployment to be added on to the employee's past pensionable service although tribunals often retain the contributions method for any period of unemployment.

19.559 If the employee has found a new job without a pension scheme the employer will be contracted in to the state scheme and the guidelines recommend that the new employer's contributions should be credited so that the loss of the previous employer's contributions should be reduced by three per cent. It is for the tribunal to assess how long it will be before he finds another job with a pension scheme.

19.560 This is unrealistic because it will be assumed that he will remain in the new job. The only way to reduce this loss is for the employer to argue that in the new job his salary will increase to compensate for the pension loss. If it is held reasonable for an employee to become self employed the tribunal must assess how his earnings will progress and calculate his loss accordingly.

19.561 Where the employee has found a new job with a pension scheme which is inferior then the tribunal must attempt to ascertain the loss on an annual basis and then multiply it for the number of years the employee is likely to remain in the job.

Interest

19.562 Since April 1990 interest is payable at the judgment rates (as at June 1996 this was 8%) 42 days after the decision is sent to the parties. Any sum which is subject to recoupment is exempt from interest. If an appeal is lodged interest still accrues. Where a decision is sent with summary reasons and an application is made for full reasons the time runs from the sending of the summary reasons.

Deductions from compensation

19.563 We have now considered the heads of compensation apart from any loss arising from the manner of dismissal referred to in *Norton Tool.* The employee has to prove that the manner of the dismissal was such that it has created problems for him in obtaining new work. This is virtually impossible to prove and accordingly, it has never developed as a separate head of compensation. It must be appreciated that this is totally different from injury to feelings as a result of the way a dismissal is carried out. No one has ever suggested that this can be compensated for per se; it is necessary to affect the opportunities to get new work. The concept of actual loss again reigns.

Just and equitable

19.564 The Act[1] provides that the amount of compensation to be accorded shall be such amount as the tribunal considers just and equitable in all the circumstances having regard to the loss suffered. It can include benefits lost and expenses. This should be contrasted with contributory fault where the employee's conduct has led or partially led to the dismissal.[2] However, it has recently been decided that post-dismissal conduct (not pre-dismissal conduct discovered after the dismissal relating to the employment) should be disregarded.[3] Otherwise it could lead to too much uncertainty later.

1 ERA, s 123(1).
2 ERA, s 123(6).
3 *Soros v Davison and Davison* [1994] IRLR 264, EAT – where the employees sold information about the employer to a national newspaper.

19.565 The main point to note is that the tribunal, apart altogether from the question of contributory fault, has total freedom to award nil compensation if it considers it just and equitable to do so. Thus if the employers have carried out an improper procedure but the employee was wholly responsible for his dismissal a nil award was justified.[1] A large reduction was justified where an employee was incapable of working but there had been a defective procedure.[2] Reductions for procedural errors are now made regularly and they operate entirely separately from contributory fault.[3]

1 *Chaplin v H J Rawlinson Ltd* [1991] ICR 553, EAT and note *Devis v Atkins* [1977] ICR 662, HL.
2 *Slaughter v Brewer & Sons Ltd* [1990] IRLR 426, EAT and note *Tele-Trading Ltd v Jenkins* [1990] IRLR 430, CA.
3 *Rao v Civil Aviation Authority* (1994) IRLR 240, CA.

19.566 We have already noted that deductions have to be made for money earned from new employers, for monies paid in lieu, ex gratia payments, and for generous contractual redundancy schemes. No deductions can be made by the employer as a result of his suffering pressure of industrial action or the threatening of such action for the purpose of dismissing the employee.[1] There are two main grounds for reducing the award, namely the employee's contributory fault[2] and his failure to mitigate his loss.[3] No deduction is made for the receipt of invalidity benefit.[4]

1 ERA, s 123(5).
2 ERA, s 123(6).

3 ERA, s 123(4).
4 *Hilton International Hotels (UK) Ltd v Faraji* [1994] IRLR 267, EAT.

Contributory fault

19.567 There is a specific provision which allows a deduction from compensation where the dismissal 'was to any extent caused or contributed to by any action of the (employee). (The tribunal) shall reduce the amount of the compensatory award by such proportion as it considers just and equitable'.[1] This requires a deduction if contributory fault is established but it will be recalled that, in any event, the tribunal has a discretion to award compensation as it considers just and equitable in all the circumstances.[2] Where dismissal is unfair because of a procedural irregularity a high degree of contributory fault may be established.[3]

1 ERA, s 123(6).
2 ERA, s 123(1). In the *Slaughter* and *Tele-Trading* cases (referred to above in para 19.565) the relationship between s 123(1) and 123(6) is discussed.
3 *Nairne v Highland and Islands Fire Brigade* [1989] IRLR 366.

19.568 The wording of s 123(6) makes it clear that it can only be used where the conduct of the employee was known before the dismissal because otherwise it could not have contributed to the dismissal. Conduct discovered after dismissal can be dealt with under s 123(1) which has already been considered.[1]

1 See *Tele-Trading Ltd v Jenkins* [1990] IRLR 430, CA. In *Slaughter v Brewer & Sons Ltd* [1990] IRLR 426 the employee was dismissed for ill-health but the tribunal deducted 80% for contributory fault. The EAT said contributory fault would rarely apply in ill-health cases except, for example, where the employee refused to attend for medical examination or did not get medical reports when requested. However, a case such as this where the employee really was incapable could lead to a drastic reduction in compensation under the just and equitable ground.

19.569 The tribunal in deciding whether to make a reduction for contribution must take a broad, common-sense view of the situation, to decide what part if any the employee's own conduct played in causing or contributing to the dismissal and then to decide what, if any, reduction should be made in the assessment of the employee's loss.[1] In the *Hollier* case the Court of Appeal stated that this assessment is so obviously a matter of impression, opinion and discretion that there will be no interference with the tribunal's decision unless there is either a plain error of law or the conclusion is one which no reasonable tribunal could have reached on the evidence.

1 *Hollier v Plysu Ltd* [1983] IRLR 260.

19.570 In an earlier case[1] the Court of Appeal stated that the tribunal should make three findings:

(1) there was culpable conduct by the employee in relation to his unfair dismissal because it cannot be just and equitable to reduce compensation without such blame. Such conduct is not limited to conduct which

is either a breach of contract or tort but includes conduct which is perverse, foolish, bloodyminded, or unreasonable. However, not all unreasonable conduct is blameworthy and it depends on the degree of unreasonableness involved.

(2) The unfair dismissal must have, to some extent, been caused or contributed to by the employee's conduct. The conduct can consist of doing nothing or in declining or being unwilling to do something.

(3) It is just and equitable to reduce the compensation by a specific extent.

1 *Nelson v BBC (No 2)* [1980] ICR 110, [1979] IRLR 346.

19.571 The subsection refers to the conduct of the employee and accordingly it cannot be used to reduce compensation where the employee's performance at work is not satisfactory. In any event it would be wrong to describe such behaviour as blameworthy. Contributory fault refers to something over which the employee has control such as misbehaviour or lack of effort. If he is doing his best and this is not good enough it is wrong to say he has contributed to his dismissal.[1] However, there are often very fine lines between performance and conduct and it is very difficult to categorise and to determine whether it is under the employee's control or not.[2]

1 *Kraft Foods Ltd v Fox* [1978] ICR 311, [1977] IRLR 431.
2 *Moncur v International Paint Co Ltd* [1978] IRLR 223, EAT.

19.572 It is necessary for the conduct to have been an operative cause of the dismissal and it is insufficient for there to be some misconduct unconnected to the dismissal.[1] However, the tribunal should not be over-technical in allocating the reason for dismissal and must realistically see if there has been contributory conduct[2] which has somewhat contentiously been extended to include the conduct of his solicitors or any agents.[3] We have already noted above that a payment in lieu of notice (and indeed any other payment made by the employer) is deductible from compensation. Any contributory fault deduction should be made before any payments made by the employer are deducted.[4] This can make a considerable difference to the outcome and was stated by the EAT to be both logical and fair.

1 *Hutchinson v Enfield Rolling Mills Ltd* [1981] IRLR 318, EAT.
2 *Maris v Rotherham Corpn* [1974] 2 All ER 776, [1974] ICR 435, NIRC.
3 *Allen v Hammett* [1982] ICR 227, [1982] IRLR 89, EAT.
4 *Derwent Coachworks v Kirby* [1994] IRLR 639, EAT.

19.573 When there has been a constructive dismissal the employer has committed a breach of contract and accordingly it would be less likely to find a case of contributory fault. Nevertheless, it is perfectly possible to make such a deduction and this is not confined to exceptional circumstances.[1] However, an early case[2] has suggested that where the constructive dismissal comprises a number of separate small incidents it is permissible to look at the employee's conduct broadly over the whole period. If one is to take a broad, common-sense view then this approach appears eminently sensible. It has been held that a reduction can be made even where no direct causal connection between the employee's conduct and the dismissal was established. A workman performed his work very defectively and as a result the employer wrongly withheld his overtime payments. The employee resigned and the EAT confirmed the tribunal decision that this was an unfair dismissal but held that a one-third reduction in compensation was appropriate to reflect the employee's contribution because the non-payment arose as a direct result of the employee's poor workmanship.[3] The case establishes that contributory fault can arise in a constructive dismissal case and there is no legal requirement that there be exceptional circumstances nor that the contributory fault is the sole or principal cause of the dismissal.

1 *Morrison v Amalgamated Transport and General Workers Union* [1989] IRLR 361 commenting on *Holroyd v Gravure Cylinders Ltd* [1984] IRLR 259, EAT.
2 *Garner v Grange Furnishings Ltd* [1977] IRLR 206.
3 *Polentarutti v Autokraft Ltd* [1991] IRLR 457, EAT.

19.574 Participating in industrial action cannot constitute contributory fault and indeed cannot be taken into account in determining what amount of compensation is just and equitable.[1] A failure to disclose a spent conviction[2] is not contributory fault as there is no duty to do so. Where an employee is convicted of a criminal offence and this was why he was dismissed this is grounds for a 100% reduction.[3] We have already noted that any reduction in the compensatory award should be equal to the reduction in the basic award.[4] Where there is more than one employee involved in an incident such as a fight it is not permissible to consider how the other employee was treated in determining the extent of the contributory fault. Thus where the other person was suspended for two weeks this was an irrelevant factor – one had to consider the employee's own contribution.[5]

1 *Crosville Wales Ltd v Tracey (No 2)* [1996] IRLR 91, CA, reversing EAT.
2 *Property Guards Ltd v Taylor and Kershaw* [1982] IRLR 175, EAT.
3 *Ladup Ltd v Barnes* [1982] ICR 107, [1982] IRLR 7, EAT.
4 *Royal Society for the Prevention of Cruelty to Animals v Cruden* [1986] ICR 205, EAT.
5 *Parker Foundry Ltd v Slack* [1992] IRLR 11, CA.

Mitigation

19.575 The employee is obliged to mitigate his loss in the same way as at common law.[1] This obligation only applies to the compensatory award, although, as we have seen, the basic award can be reduced where the employee unreasonably refuses an offer of reinstatement.

1 ERA, s 123(4).

19.576 The tribunal is obliged to consider the question whether or not it is raised because the statute requires it.[1] The traditional answer as to the burden of proof in dealing with mitigation is that if the employer claims there has been a failure to mitigate it is for him to prove it.[2] This has been affirmed by the EAT in *Fyfe v Scientific Furnishings Ltd*[3] which stated that an earlier decision[4] was wrong.

[1] *Morganite Electrical v Donne*, above.
[2] *Bessenden Properties Ltd v Corness* [1977] ICR 821, [1974] IRLR 338, CA.
[3] [1989] IRLR 331.
[4] *Scottish and Newcastle Breweries plc v Halliday* [1986] ICR 577, [1986] IRLR 291.

19.577 The duty to mitigate only arises after the dismissal so there is no failure to mitigate if an alternative job offer is refused before dismissal[1] although this may have an impact on the fairness of the dismissal. Where the employer offers reinstatement or re-engagement after dismissal a refusal will probably be a failure to mitigate unless the employer's treatment of the employee has been such that his refusal is reasonable.[2]

[1] *Savoia v Chiltern Herb Farms Ltd* [1982] IRLR 166, CA; *Prestwick Circuits Ltd v McAndrew* [1990] IRLR 191.
[2] *Artisan Press Ltd v Srawley* [1986] ICR 328, [1986] IRLR 126, EAT.

19.578 The method of assessing compensation when there has been a failure to mitigate is to assess when the employee should have been able to obtain fresh employment. It has to be shown that if the employee had taken a particular step, after a particular time then, on a balance of probabilities he would have gained employment. From that date the loss is extinguished or reduced by the income from the other source. Therefore the tribunal must identify what step the employee should have taken, the date on which that step would have produced an alternative income and thereafter to reduce compensation by alternative income which would have been earned.[1] It is entirely wrong to deal with a failure to mitigate on the basis of a percentage reduction.[2]

[1] *Gardiner-Hill v Roland Beiger Technics Ltd* [1982] IRLR 498.
[2] *Peara v Enderlin Ltd* [1979] ICR 804, EAT.

19.579 Mitigation is all about reasonableness and it will be difficult to challenge a tribunal's findings in this regard as they will be findings of fact. An employee should not accept immediately an offer which is well below his previous salary but if he has had a longish period where he has not been able to obtain a job then he must be prepared to accept a reduction.[1] A useful test is for the tribunal to ask itself whether, if the employee had no hope of recovering compensation from anybody else and if he had consulted merely his own interests, and acted reasonably in all the circumstances, he would have accepted the new job in mitigation of the loss he had suffered. If the answer is yes then he should have taken the job and there has been a failure to mitigate.[2]

[1] See generally *Gallear v J F Watson & Son Ltd* [1979] IRLR 306, EAT and *A G Bracey v Iles* [1973] IRLR 210.
[2] *Bessenden Properties*, para 19.576 above.

19.580 If an employee sets up his own business rather than seek fresh employment this may be a perfectly reasonable step and arguably, given today's economic climate and encouragement of self-employment it is more likely to be reasonable than in previous times. In the *Gardiner-Hill* case[1] a senior employee aged 55 with

16 years' specialised experience had acted reasonably in setting up his own business. An employee must try to reduce his losses and this was not an unreasonable way of doing so. He must, however, try to obtain a job if this is achievable.

[1] See para 19.578 above.

19.581 It has been decided that there was no failure to mitigate loss of pension rights when an employee chose to take a refund of contributions rather than a deferred pension.[1] However, it is submitted that where this leads to a considerable diminution of rights then it must be arguable that there has been a failure to mitigate.

[1] *Sturdy Finance Ltd v Bardsley* [1979] ICR 249, [1979] IRLR 65, EAT.

19.582 Where an employee has been constructively dismissed there is no obligation on him to process a claim through the company's grievance procedure and there is no failure to mitigate loss.[1] A similar view obtains where an employee fails to appeal against dismissal under the internal appeal procedure because it is impossible to assess what would have happened.[2] Nevertheless, with the growing importance of appeals in relation to fairness this view may need re-consideration.

[1] *Seligman and Latz Ltd v McHugh* [1979] IRLR 130, EAT.
[2] *William Muir (Bond 9) Ltd v Lamb* [1985] IRLR 95, EAT and *Lock v Connell Estate Agents* [1994] ICR 983, EAT.

Limits on compensation

19.583 Section 124 prescribes an upper limit of compensatory award, which is reviewed annually and is at present £11,300. We have noted above how compensation is assessed and how deductions are made. There is a very important subsection[1] which ensures that this maximum figure is to be applied after all the deductions have been made. This can be extremely important for higher paid employees and is relevant to all payments made by employers to employees and contributory fault for example. Thus let us say that an employee has a loss of £40,000 in the tribunal's calculations and that he has been held 50% to blame for his dismissal. Deducting this from the £40,000 would leave £20,000 and the maximum award of £11,300 would then be made. If, however, one went straight down to the maximum award before applying the deduction the employee would receive only half of £11,300. Under s 124(5) it is stated that '. . . the limit applies to the amount which the Industrial Tribunal would, apart from this section, otherwise award in respect of the subject-matter of the complaint after taking into account any payment made by the (employer) to the (employee) in respect of that matter and any reduction in the amount of the award required by any enactment or rule of law'.[2] Therefore the higher figure is payable.

[1] ERA, s 124(5).
[2] For an example relating to this see *UBAF Bank Ltd v Davis* [1978] IRLR 442 and *Walter Bruund (London) Ltd v Murray* [1991] ICR 327, EAT.

Recoupment

19.584 Where the tribunal makes a compensatory award it must establish whether the employee has received unemployment or income benefit. If so then the amount that is awarded for immediate loss which is the amount up till the date of the hearing[1] is subject to recoupment. This means that this figure is not paid directly to the employee but the state is entitled to receive from the employer the amount that represents the benefits received by the employee. The balance is then paid to the employee.[2] The idea is that the employee should not get double compensation and that the state recovers some of the benefit which should not go into the employer's hands either. The figure assessed is known as the 'prescribed element' and it is subject to deductions for contributory fault in the same way that the compensatory award is reduced.

---

[1] When the compensation is fixed see *Mason v Wimpey Waste Management Ltd* [1982] IRLR 454.
[2] Employment Protection (Recoupment of Unemployment Benefit and Supplementary Benefit) Regulations 1977.

Compensation and damages for wrongful dismissal

19.585 There is a basic simple principle that there must not be double recovery for the same loss so that the respondent (defendant) is entitled to claim a set-off of one claim against another. It must, however, be clear that the claims are truly the same. In *O'Laoire v Jackel International Ltd (No 2)*[1] the employee was unfairly and wrongfully dismissed. The tribunal assessed the employee's loss in excess of £100,000 but could award the then maximum sum of £8,000. In his wrongful dismissal claim the employer claimed set-off of the £8,000 but this was refused. It was for the employer to prove there was a double recovery but he was unable to do so because it was impossible to allocate the £8,000 to any one of the particular parts in the £100,000 loss. Therefore it could not be attributed to the loss of earnings during the notice period and could not be set off. However, this is only a problem when the loss exceeds the statutory maximum because there will be specific allocations of the compensation in other cases. In practice this makes it important to draft termination payments agreement carefully.

---

[1] [1991] IRLR 170, CA.

Special awards

19.586 Whenever an employee is dismissed because:

(1) of his membership or proposed membership of an independent trade union;
(2) he took part or proposed to do so in an independent trade union's activities; or
(3) he was not a member of any union or a particular union or refused or proposed to refuse to join or remain in a union;[1] or
(4) he was selected for redundancy because of his membership, non-membership or union activities;[2]
(5) he is carrying out health and safety activities as a designated representative;
(6) he is carrying out his functions as a trustee of a pension scheme or as

an employee representative for redundancy or transfer situations or is a candidate for such functions;

then there is an automatically unfair dismissal and special compensation is payable.

1 TULR(C)A 1992, s 152 and note s 152(3) for its interpretation.
2 TULR(C)A 1992, s 153.

19.587 Following an unfair dismissal finding where re-employment is not sought he will receive the normal compensatory award. The basic award is also calculated normally but is subject to a minimum sum of £2,770.[1]

1 All the figures are reviewable annually.

19.588 Where re-employment is sought but no order is made by the tribunal then the basic and compensatory awards are as above but in addition there is a special award of 104 weeks' pay without any upper limit of pay subject to a minimum of £13,775 and a maximum of £27,500.[1] To obtain this award the employees must specifically request it.[2]

1 Section 158(1).
2 Section 157.

19.589 Where re-employment is ordered and is complied with the employer must make good any loss suffered between the date of dismissal and re-employment.

19.590 Where re-employment is ordered but not complied with then the basic and compensatory awards are as above but the special award is 156 weeks' pay, without any upper limit, subject to a minimum of £20,600 unless the employer can show that it was not practicable for him to comply with the order in which case it will be 104 weeks' pay.[1]

1 Section 158(2).

19.591 Where the order to re-employ is made the employer might re-employ but on different terms. We have noted that where the terms of an order are not fully complied with then the maximum figure of £11,300 may be all that is available if the employer's actions are construed as a partial rather than a total failure to comply. In the *Artisan Press*[1] case security staff were re-employed as cleaners with minor security functions which was a very different job. They complained that the employer had failed to comply with the order but the employer said there had been only a partial failure to comply. It was held that there had been a total failure to comply and the higher award could be made. It was only ancillary matters that would make it into a partial compliance.

1 See para 19.577 above.

19.592 A special award can be reduced where the employee is over 64 so that for each complete month worked it is reduced by one-twelfth and disappears at

65.[1] It can also be reduced where the employer's conduct before dismissal or before notice was given makes it just and equitable to reduce it.[2] Finally it can be reduced where the employee has unreasonably prevented a re-employment order from being complied with or has unreasonably refused an offer by the employer which would have the effect of reinstating him.[3] The amount of the reduction is a matter for the tribunal's discretion and it must decide on the basis of what is 'just and equitable'. An employee may not act unreasonably in refusing an offer if he genuinely and reasonably believes that the employer will be hostile to him because of the previous treatment suffered.

1 Section 158(3).
2 Section 158(4).
3 Section 158(5).

19.593 In determining whether it is practicable for the employer to comply with any re-employment order the engagement of a permanent replacement must not be taken into account in determining practicability unless the employer can show it was not practicable for him to arrange for the employee's work to be done without engaging a permanent replacement.[1]

1 Section 158(6). The above provisions are mirrored in ERA, s 125 for health and safety dismissals. The figures for the special award are the same as stated here for trade union reasons. They do not appear to have been introduced for pregnancy/maternity related dismissals.

19.594 Where the employer has suffered pressure from a third party in calling a strike or industrial action or threatening to do so and the pressure was exercised because the employee was not a member of any trade union or a particular union then either the employer or employee can join the third party who can be ordered to pay all or some of the compensation.[1]

1 Section 160.

Compensation where there is an act of sex and/or race discrimination

19.595 Where a dismissal is held unfair it may also be an act of sex discrimination or race discrimination or both. That is to say it may be a racially motivated dismissal and as such compensation can be awarded under the Race Relations Act 1976. The Act provides[1] that even if an unfair dismissal is an act of sex and race discrimination the same act cannot lead to an award of compensation higher than the present compensatory award limit laid down in ERA, s 117 for unfair dismissal purposes. Of course there is now no limit to the compensation awardable under the anti-discrimination legislation (see separate chapter on discrimination). If reinstatement or re-engagement is ordered and not complied with then the additional award is higher for acts of sex or race discrimination.[2]

1 ERA, s 126.
2 See above and ERA, s 117(3).

7 SETTLEMENTS, CONCILIATIONS AND CONTRACTING OUT

General introduction

19.596 It is very common for an employer and employee to reach an agreement concerning the employee's leaving the employment involuntarily. The employee may resign, under pressure, which would be classified as a dismissal and may do so without any financial inducement. If there is any form of financial inducement then any resignation will be deemed to stem from that rather than any original pressure and there will be no dismissal.[1] If there has been a dismissal it may be that, subsequently, the employer pays off the employee's claims 'in full and final settlement' of all claims. They will almost certainly be valid to dispense with common law claims but it will not dispense with statutory claims, including unfair dismissal. This is not because of any claim of duress but because the Act[2] provides as such.

---

[1] See section on 'Dismissal'.
[2] ERA, s 203(1).

Contracting-out

19.597 Under s 203(1) any provision in any agreement shall be void in so far as it purports:

(a) to exclude or limit the operation of any provision of this Act, or
(b) to preclude any person from presenting a complaint to, or bringing any proceedings under this Act before an industrial tribunal.

19.598 The intention is that employees should not be forced to relinquish their rights by any agreement which might be foisted upon them. Although it may be a genuine agreement there is a danger that employees, commonly with unequal bargaining power and less expertise and knowledge than employers, will give up more than they should do. However, the position is not really that gloomy for employers, because if they use the services of a conciliation officer they will be able to preclude proceedings.

19.599 Furthermore, even if they do not, any sum they pay to the employee will in almost all circumstances be set off against any compensation that may be awarded. One assumes that an employee who has agreed a settlement is unlikely to be reinstated. The set-off of payments may not be so valuable in the case of a highly-paid employee who may have suffered considerable loss. This is a result of ERA, s 124 which states that the maximum compensatory award must be applied only after all deductions have been made. Thus let us assume an employee was earning £30,000 net and his employer paid him £10,000 on termination. Ignoring the basic award and any other claim let us assume that the employee remains unemployed for six months. His loss would be £15,000 and although the employer could deduct the £10,000 paid which is more than the maximum sum awardable, there is still £5,000 that can be awarded as well as any basic award.

Compromise agreements

19.600 The TURERA 1993 has introduced provisions whereby it is permissible to contract out of the provisions of the unfair dismissal legislation provided that the employee has received independent legal advice from a qualified lawyer.[1]

[1] Now contained in the ERA, s 203(2) and 203(3).

19.601 This is therefore an important qualification to the basic restriction on contracting-out. The contracting-out will be applicable to an agreement to refrain from instituting or continuing any proceedings.

19.602 The conditions regulating compromise agreements so as to render an agreement valid are:

(a) the agreement must be in writing;
(b) it must relate to the particular complaint;
(c) the employer must have received independent legal advice from a qualified lawyer as to the terms and effect of the proposed agreement and in particular its effect on his ability to pursue his rights before an industrial tribunal;
(d) there must be in force when the adviser gives the advice a policy of insurance covering the risk of a claim by the employee in respect of loss arising in consequence of the advice;
(e) the agreement must identify the adviser; and
(f) the agreement must state the conditions regulating Compromise Agreements under this Act are satisfied. A qualified lawyer is defined as meaning a 'barrister' (advocate in Scotland) whether in practice as such or employed to give legal advice or solicitor with a practising certificate. 'Independent' means advice given by a lawyer who is not acting for the employer or an associated employer. There are equivalent rights to make Compromise Agreements in relation to sex discrimination and race relations claims, and the Trade Union and Labour Relations (Consolidation) Act 1992.

These provisions do not seem unduly onerous but it will be important that the independent legal advice for evidential purposes is either in writing or a note given of the exact advice. Problems have arisen as to whether solicitors have a 'policy of insurance' because they are covered under indemnity agreements with the Law Society. It is extremely unlikely that this will create a problem and the Government is planning to eradicate the problem. The meaning of 'independence' has been questioned. The fact that an employer pays the local fee to the employee's solicitor should not compromise his independence. Can the lawyer be independent of his acts for the employee in other matters or has he acted for him previously? If each transaction is separate it would appear that there should be no difficulty.

Fixed-term contract

19.603 The other exception is that it is permissible to contract-out of unfair dismissal rights where there is a fixed-term contract of one year or more and the dismissal consists only of the expiry of that term without its being renewed. The exclusion of the claim has to be in writing but it need not be in the actual contract, although it is likely to be.[1] The contracting out must take place before the fixed term expires. It does not prevent a claim for a breach of contract if the contract does not run its full term and if the employee has sufficient qualifying service he can bring an unfair dismissal case although his compensation would be limited until the end of the fixed-term. It is not permissible to contract out where the dismissal relates to Sunday working.[2]

1 ERA, s 197(1).
2 ERA, s 203.

19.604 Where the employee is employed on a fixed-term contract which has followed a previous fixed-term contract the final contract must be of at least one year or more if there is to be a valid exclusion in it. Thus where an 18 month fixed-term contract without any exclusion clause was extended in a further seven month contract which did contain an exclusion clause it was held[1] that it was not permissible to put the contracts together to obtain the requisite two year fixed-term period. However, in *Mulrine v University of Ulster*[2] an employee had entered a two-year fixed term contract with an exclusion clause. Having obtained an extension of EEC funding the contract was extended for a further four months on the same terms. The previous cases had stated that the final contract had to be one year or more but the extension was only four months here. It was held that the earlier authorities should not be applied if it would produce an unfair result, which it did here. They said that the four months was simply an extension or renewal of the original contract and not a new contract. Therefore the exclusion still applied. This is still consistent with *Triesman* in that the original contract there did not have an exclusion clause and the extension did.

1 *Open University v Triesman* [1978] ICR 524, [1978] IRLR 114, CA and *BBC v Ioannou* [1975] QB 781, [1976] ICR 267, CA.
2 [1993] IRLR 545.

The width of s 196

19.605 It is clear beyond peradventure that any agreement to abandon the right to complain of unfair dismissal in consideration of a sum of money is void unless a conciliation officer has taken action under s 18 of the Industrial Tribunals Act 1996[1] or a compromise contract has been entered into. Often a tribunal determines that there has been an unfair dismissal but leaves it to the parties to settle the level of compensation. The section continues to take effect where the parties agree compensation at this stage[2] and only ceases to operate when the tribunal has given its decision on both liability and remedy. The conciliation officer's duties also continue until this time.

1 *Council of Engineering Institutions v Maddison* [1977] ICR 30, [1976] IRLR 389, EAT.
2 *Courage Take Home Trade Ltd v Keys* [1986] ICR 874, [1986] IRLR 427, EAT.

ACAS involvement

19.606 The agreement which an employer and employee reach will be valid and s 203(1) does not apply where a conciliation officer has 'taken action' under s 18 of the Industrial Tribunals Act 1996. A conciliation officer can become involved before a complaint has been presented to the tribunal or after its presentation.[1]

[1] Industrial Tribunals Act 1996, s 18.

19.607 Before a complaint is presented either employer or employee can seek the officer's services and his duty is to endeavour to promote a settlement of the proposed complaint without it being determined by an industrial tribunal. After the complaint has been presented the conciliation officer can initiate an attempt to settle the complaint. It is not necessary that the employee should even have reached the stage of considering presenting a complaint for the officer to intervene. All that is required is that the potential claimant should be alleging action that would enable him to present an unfair dismissal complaint.[1]

[1] *Hennessey v Craigmyle & Co Ltd* [1986] ICR 461, [1986] IRLR 300, CA.

19.608 The taking of action by the conciliation officer does not require that he take a positive initiative. If the parties accept that re-employment, which is the prime remedy for the officer to obtain, is not practicable, and the officer believes that this is right, he still takes action when the parties have agreed the level of compensation. He then has to ascertain that the parties had truly agreed and then put this agreement on the standard form COT 3 for signature.[1] This case is also authority for the view that the officer is under no duty to ensure that a settlement is fair to both parties. He is not obliged to follow any specific formula and the nature of his function must depend on the particular circumstances of the case. He is not even under a statutory duty to give a brief description to the employee of the relevant framework of his statutory rights. The EAT did say that a conciliated settlement could be set aside if a conciliation officer acted in bad faith, adopted unfair methods, or was not impartial.[2] A representation of a party will have ostensible authority to bind that party in signing a COT 3 agreement.[3]

[1] *Moore v Duport Furniture Products Ltd* [1982] ICR 84, [1982] IRLR 31, HL.
[2] *Slack v Greenham (Plant Hire) Ltd* [1983] ICR 617, [1983] IRLR 271.
[3] *Freeman v Sovereign Chicken Ltd* [1991] IRLR 408.

19.609 Although reference has been made to recording an agreement on the standard COT 3 form this is not an essential prerequisite for the taking of action by a conciliation officer. Some involvement albeit minor is sufficient. The agreement need not even be in writing provided there is clear evidence of an oral agreement between the parties in which the officer has been involved. This will be sufficient to prevent a claim.[1] A typical COT 3 settlement form of wording appears in the Appendix.

[1] *Gilbert v Kembridge Fibres Ltd* [1984] ICR 188, [1984] IRLR 52, EAT.

19.610 The possibility of arguing that there has been economic duress is not very strong but it was argued in the *Hennessey* case.[1] The Court of Appeal said that the duress would have to amount to a coercion of will vitiating consent and that the payment made or contract entered into was an involuntary act. It would be very rare to encounter such economic duress and it would be even more remote where the agreement was reached after the employee received independent advice and assistance from a skilled conciliation officer. Although the officer did provide advice in this case we can see from the previous cases cited that he does not need to do much to constitute 'taking action'. Further, he does not even need to explain to an employee what his rights are. In such a situation albeit an extreme one, one could find a ludicrous settlement which the officer had merely confirmed. If this could not be set aside and it appears that this is the case some conciliation officers might be a little disturbed by the activity or inactivity of some of their colleagues.

[1] *Hennessey v Craigmyle & Co Ltd* [1986] ICR 461, [1986] IRLR 300.

ACAS since 1990

19.611 Despite all that has been written above ACAS has changed its policy since July 1990 and generally will only intervene when an originating application (ITI) has been issued. ACAS will not want to get involved prior to that action.

19.612 Furthermore, ACAS will not be prepared to provide a COT 3 form to parties who have already reached an agreement. ACAS considers that it must take part itself in the settlement otherwise it considers it is not fulfilling its statutory duty. It would appear that there is a statutory duty on ACAS to promote a settlement without the matter being determined by the tribunal.[1] This aspect of the legislation appears to have been ignored by ACAS, which is regrettable.

[1] Industrial Tribunals Act 1996, s 18.

Tribunal settlements

19.613 The tribunal itself may be faced with the parties agreeing a settlement either at the outset of proceedings or during them. The employee may withdraw his complaint and then the tribunal can make an order dismissing the complaint. The tribunal might be asked to record a decision as to the agreed terms. This makes it directly enforceable but the sum is subject to recoupment. A record of a settlement is, however, not a decision and cannot be sued on in the county court, and it is arguable that it is of no effect. The position is unclear. If the proceedings are adjourned generally on agreed terms then, if the money is not paid, the employee can return to the tribunal and can even add a new respondent to the proceedings at that stage.[1]

[1] *Milestone School of English v Leakey* [1982] IRLR 3, EAT.

20 Redundancy

John McMullen

A REDUNDANCY PAYMENTS

1 INTRODUCTION

20.01 The right to a redundancy payment on termination of employment by reason of redundancy was first created by the Redundancy Payments Act 1965. Re-enacted it now appears in Part XI of the ERA.

20.02 An often quoted dictum of Lord Denning MR in *Lloyd v Brassey*[1] gives us some insight into the question of what the legislation is supposed to achieve.

> 'As I read the Act, a worker of long standing is now recognised as having an accrued right in his job and his right gains in value with the years. So much so that if the job is shut down, he is entitled to compensation for loss of the job . . . it is not unemployment pay. I repeat "not". Even if he gets another job straightaway, he is nevertheless entitled to full redundancy payment. It is, in a real sense, compensation for long service.'

1 [1969] 2 QB 98 at 102, CA.

20.03 More recently, the Northern Ireland Court of Appeal stated, in *McCrea v Cullen & Davison*[1] that:

> 'the [legislation] was passed at a time when it was generally recognised that if British industry was to recover its competitive position in world markets the widespread practice of overmanning had to be reduced, and the provision of redundancy payments for those who were to lose their jobs in consequence was designed to make the implementation of the policy more acceptable to trade unions'.

1 [1988] IRLR 30.

20.04 Whether there can be one single aim which is consistent as a labour policy over 30 years of changing circumstances and economic conditions is questionable. Indeed, views about what the legislation achieves have always been varied. Fryer,[1] in his leading article in 1973, identified six, as he put it, 'myths' of the redundancy legislation, namely that it provides an element of employment security; that it gives some sort of job property right to workers; that by regulating redundancy it restricts managerial discretion; that it compensates workers for loss of their jobs; that redundancy payments act as a disincentive to find alternative work; and that it affords minimum cover to all who lose their job because of redundancy.[1] Although a commentary influenced by a debate running over 20 years ago, Fryer's evaluation of these so-called 'myths' is instructive, even today. And it is interesting that he concluded that there was need for a considerable strengthening of the protection afforded to workers threatened by redundancy – for this is a concern, particularly in relation to financial limits of redundancy pay, that has been voiced over a number of years.

[1] Fryer, 'The Myths of the Redundancy Payments Act' (1973) 2 ILJ 1. See also, Parker, Thomas Ellis and McCarthy, 'Effects of the Redundancy Payments Act' (HMSO, 1981) and Grunfeld, *The Law of Redundancy* (3rd edn) pp 1-4; Bourn, *Redundancy Law and Practice* ch 1; and *Harvey* III.

20.05 It is not hard to see why the redundancy payments available under the scheme have largely lost their value with inflation over the years: the current maximum redundancy payment of £6,300 is now almost derisory.[1] There is a strong case for revision of the system on that ground alone. Another curious development has been recent governmental attitudes to the now defunct redundancy rebate. It used to be the case that an employer received a rebate of a percentage of the redundancy payment he had to make. By the Wages Act 1986 redundancy rebates (then 35% of the statutory redundancy payment) were limited to employers with nine or fewer employees and the Employment Act 1989 abolished the employer's rebate in all cases. Although redundancy payments are not what they should be, the cumulative costs of implementing redundancy without the rebate for small employers, or even large employers engaged in mass redundancies, could be significant. It is now possible that the removal of the rebate may encourage corresponding resistance by employers of redundancy payments liability thus bringing the area back into the forefront of employment case law. It has been noted that, in the main, before 1972, employers tended to contest claims for redundancy whereas, after the introduction of unfair dismissal protection, this employer resistance appeared to lessen. After all, making a redundancy payment (particularly with rebate applicable) to sweeten the pill of dismissal was cheaper than having to pay unfair dismissal compensation. It would be interesting to speculate whether, now that the rebate has been finally abolished, we are seeing increased case law about the substance of the law of redundancy because of more disputes about liability.[2]

[1] See also Marsh, (1985) *Law Society's Gazette*, 15 December. In August 1992, the Law Society calculated that the then current amount of a week's pay (£205) should have been either £445.73 (uprated by movement in earnings) or £334.73 (uprated by movement in prices). That would have given maximum redundancy payments of £13,371.90 or £10,031.70 respectively. The failure effectively to uprate payment levels over the years is a major criticism. The payment is based on multiples of a week's pay (subject to a statutory cap) – see para 20.92. This is usually increased annually. At the time of writing, the latest increase took place with effect from 27 September 1995 (SI 1995/1953) and is just £210.

[2] Lewis, *Twenty Years of Statutory Redundancy Payments in Great Britain* (1985). The total number of registered industrial tribunal cases concerning redundancy payments was 5,022 in 1990–1991, 5,234 in 1991–1992, 7,084 in 1992–1993 and 8,567 in 1993–1994 (Source: *Employment Gazette*, October 1994). Equally, though, any rise may be attributable to economic factors.

20.06 Finally, it is argued that the statutory scheme may have been effectively supplemented or even supplanted by private contractual schemes. This may be so in certain industry sectors. But such schemes are far from universal. For many if not most employees, the statutory scheme is all there is.

2 PRELIMINARY CONSIDERATIONS

(A) Qualifications and exclusions

20.07 The right to a redundancy payment is afforded to an employee who works under a contract of employment (which means a contract of service or of apprenticeship).[1] This is in common with the right to enjoy most other statutory employment rights and it is to be noted that self-employed workers may not claim a redundancy payment. The employee must have been employed for at least two years continuously ending with the 'relevant date'.[2]

---

[1] ERA, s 230(1).

[2] ERA, s 155. For continuous employment see Chapter 7, above. The relevant date is, broadly, the date of termination of employment. The detailed rules about the 'relevant date' are discussed at para 20.83. The qualifying period of two years applies to all employees regardless of hours worked per week (the Employment Protection (Part-Time Employees) Regulations 1995, SI 1995/31 – see Chapter 7, above). These Regulations were passed in response to the House of Lords decision in *R v Secretary of State for Employment, ex p Equal Opportunities Commission* [1994] ICR 317. Prior to the Regulations, the structure of the EP(C)A was such as to require at least 16 hours service per week for two years before an employee qualified for a redundancy payment. Those working less than 16 hours but more than 8 hours effectively qualified after 5 years employment. The House of Lords determined that this differential hours' requirement discriminated against part-time workers and was ruled contrary to European sex discrimination law. Accordingly, the Regulations were introduced with the effect that all employees, regardless of hours worked per week, qualify for a statutory redundancy payment upon two years continuous employment. Qualifying periods for employment rights are of course, at the time of writing under scrutiny following the decision in *R v Secretary of State for Employment, ex p Seymour-Smith* [1995] IRLR 464, discussed in Chapter 19.

20.08 Certain employees are excluded altogether, for example overseas employees,[1] share fishermen,[2] public servants,[3] those employed by overseas governments,[4] some domestic servants (ie where their employer is the father, mother, grandfather, grandmother, stepfather, stepmother, son, daughter, grandson, granddaughter, stepdaughter, stepson, brother, sister, half brother or half sister of the employee),[5] those who are aged under 18[6] or who have attained the age of 65,[7] those covered by an exemption order in force in respect of a particular employment covered by a collective agreement approved by the Secretary of State[8] and, finally, employees who have contracted out of the right to receive a redundancy payment under ERA, s 190 (ie those having agreed to waiver clauses in fixed term contracts of two years or more excluding the right to payment that arises on non-renewal of a fixed term contract).[9]

---

[1] ERA, s 196.

[2] ERA, s 199(2).

[3] ERA, ss 159 and 191 (also see *Harvey* Div B).

[4] ERA, s 160(1).

[5] ERA, s 161.

[6] ERA, s 211.

[7] ERA, s 156(1). Until the Employment Act 1989 there were differential ages beyond which payments did not apply, for men (65) and women (60). The Act took effect from 16 January 1990.

[8] ERA, s 157. For an example, see Redundancy Payments (Exemption) Order 1980, SI 1980/1052 (some employees of Lancashire County Council).

[9] ERA, s 197.

20.09 If, on redundancy, an employer offers suitable alternative employment which is unreasonably refused, the redundant employee may lose his right to a redundancy payment that would otherwise be applicable.[1]

[1] ERA, s 141 and see below.

20.10 There are other cases where exclusions apply. An employee may be dis-entitled to a redundancy payment if there is misconduct or strike action.[1] A redundancy payment may be reduced or abrogated by receipt of a pension by an employee.[2] And he must make his claim following the relevant date of termination within six months or within such further period not exceeding six months at the discretion of an industrial tribunal.[3] Finally, another qualifying matter is the prerequisite of a dismissal and although the concept of dismissal has been discussed elsewhere in this book[4] the subject is given a brief treatment below in relation to the particular context of redundancy.

[1] ERA, ss 150 and 140 and see below.
[2] ERA, s 158 and see below.
[3] ERA, s 164 and see below.
[4] See Chapter 2, above.

(B) The requirement of dismissal

20.11 The right to a redundancy payment cannot be exercised unless the employee has been dismissed. A dismissal is defined in s 136 of the ERA as occurring when the contract is terminated by the employer with or without notice (ie an employer-initiated termination);[1] where a fixed term contract is allowed to expire without its being renewed;[2] and where the employee terminates his contract of employment with or without notice in circumstances such that he is entitled to terminate it without notice by reason of the employer's conduct (ie an employee-initiated termination in response to a serious breach of contract, or, as it is commonly known, a 'constructive' dismissal).[3]

[1] ERA, s 136(1)(a).
[2] ERA, s 136(1)(b).
[3] ERA, s 136(1)(c). A termination by operation of law, eg through frustration, is not a dismissal, save only where s 136(5) (see para 20.65) applies and the event affects the employer (eg the employer's death). See *Marshall v Harland and Wolff Ltd* [1972] ICR 101; *Egg Stores (Stamford Hill) Ltd v Leibovici* [1977] ICR 260, [1976] IRLR 376, EAT; *FC Shepherd & Co Ltd v Jerrom* [1987] QB 301, [1986] ICR 802, CA; *Notcutt v Universal Equipment Co (London) Ltd* [1986] ICR 414, CA. Also, on a different point, although expiry of a fixed term is covered, if the appointment is for a specific task and the contract expires on completion thereof, there will be a discharge of the contract by performance and no dismissal takes place then: *Wiltshire County Council v National Association of Teachers in Further and Higher Education* [1980] ICR 455, [1980] IRLR 198, CA; *Ironmonger v Movefield Ltd (t/a Deering Appointments)* [1988] IRLR 461, EAT. And the same applied where a contract of employment was expressed to last only so long as funds were provided by the MSC or other sources. The contract came to an end automatically on the occurrence of this event (ie failure of funds) and there was then no dismissal (*Brown v Knowsley Borough Council* [1986] IRLR 102, EAT).

20.12 It is important to note that an employer's warning of impending redundancy may not be a dismissal. The reason why such a warning may sometimes not amount to a dismissal or even a notice of dismissal is because a notice of dismissal must give the employee information precisely as to when the employment will end; many warnings do not do this. Thus, in *Morton Sundour Fabrics Ltd v Shaw*[1] an employee was warned by his employer that the department in which he was employed would close down at some date in the future. As a result, the employee decided to seek alternative employment and anticipate the termination of his employment. He was successful in his efforts and gave notice to his employer of resignation and left. But as stated, in order to terminate the contract of employment the notice given to an employee must specify the date or contain material from which the date of termination is ascertainable. Here there was none and so it was held there was no dismissal and that the employee had resigned. As the employee had resigned, he lost his rights. This principle has been upheld in a number of other cases[2] and it is equally applicable to unfair dismissal law as well as to redundancy. In all of these cases an employer's warning of a future dismissal was held not to be an express dismissal. Nor, it seems, will such an advance warning of dismissal amount to a constructive dismissal, at least if the length of the employer's warning of impending dismissal is long enough to allow the employer, within that period, to serve a valid notice of dismissal of the appropriate length.[3]

1 (1967) 2 ITR 84.

2 *Burton Group Ltd v Smith* [1977] IRLR 351, EAT; *International Computers v Kennedy* [1981] IRLR 28, EAT; *Pritchard-Rhodes Ltd v Boon and Milton* [1979] IRLR 19, EAT; *Haseltine Lake & Co Ltd v Dowler* [1981] ICR 222, [1981] IRLR 25, EAT; *Secretary of State for Employment v Greenfield*, EAT 147/89. See also *Ingersoll-Dresser Pumps (UK) Ltd v Taylor*, EAT 391/94.

3 *Devon County Council v Cook* [1977] IRLR 188; *Haseltine Lake & Co Ltd v Dowler* [1981] ICR 222, EAT. A contrasting case in this area where, on the facts, an employer's threat to dismiss on notice was held to give rise to a constructive dismissal is *Greenaway Harrison Ltd v Wiles* [1994] IRLR 380, EAT. However, there were particular features to the case perhaps not applicable to the discussion here and see criticism by McMullen, *In House Lawyer* September 1994, p 39.

20.13 If the employer has given a valid notice of dismissal it is possible for an employee to anticipate the expiry of that notice and leave early, although this, too, is not without its pitfalls. First, it is possible for an employee and an employer to agree, during the period of notice served upon the employee, to foreshorten that period of notice in order to allow an employee to leave early. In such circumstances the courts may be prepared to say that all that has happened is that the employer and employee had agreed consensually to change the date of expiry of the notice without taking away the essential character of the dismissal by reason of redundancy.[1] An alternative interpetation is that the employer and employee have superimposed upon the original dismissal a termination of employment by mutual agreement; and a termination by agreement is not a dismissal within the meaning of the statute. Such an arrangement would therefore be disastrous for an employee. However, it is submitted that the courts would, on the whole, be reluctant to find a termination by mutual agreement in a case where a redundancy dismissal notice has already been served. It is probably more likely that they would construe the agreement as one simply altering the date on which the employee leaves as a result of his earlier notice of dismissal.[2]

1 *McAlwane v Boughton Estates Ltd* [1973] ICR 470. Or alternatively there is no reason why the termination date cannot, by agreement, be postponed: *Mowlem Northern Ltd v Watson* [1990] IRLR 500, EAT.

2 But cf the case of *Scott v Coalite Fuels and Chemicals Ltd* [1988] ICR 355, [1988] IRLR 131, EAT referred to at n 3, para 20.18.

20.14 Apart from cases of altering the date of leaving by agreement it may be possible for an employee unilaterally to anticipate the expiry of the employer's notice and still preserve his rights. By virtue of s 142 of the ERA it is provided that where the employer has given notice to an employee to terminate the contract of employment, and, at a time within the 'obligatory period' of that notice, the employee gives notice in writing to the employer to terminate the contract of employment on a date earlier than the date on which the employer's notice is due to expire, the employee shall, notwithstanding his counter notice, still be taken to be dismissed by his employer.[1] However the main pitfall for employees here is that the employee's notice must be given during the 'obligatory period' of the employer's notice. The obligatory period is a period equal to the minimum period which is required to be given by an employer to terminate the contract of employment either by virtue of s 86 of the ERA or under the contract of employment, whichever is the greater, worked back from the date of expiry of the period of notice that the employer has actually given.[2] Now, in most cases, this will cause few problems because the period of notice that the employer has given will be equal to the obligatory period, ie will be equal to the period of notice he is required by law to give. But suppose an employer gives notice more generous than the minimum which he is required to give, and suppose, too, the employee gives his counter notice to the employer outside (ie before the commencement of) the obligatory period. In this case the employee's rights are lost entirely and he will be deemed to have resigned and will have lost his redundancy payment.[3] Of course, if the employee's action was with the agreement of the employer, a mutual agreement to vary the date of termination might have been struck along the lines discussed above.[4] But if the employee unilaterally attempts to anticipate the expiry of the employer's notice outside the obligatory period he will lose his rights.

1 ERA, s 142(1)(a).
2 ERA, s 136(4).
3 *Pritchard-Rhodes Ltd v Boon and Milton* [1979] IRLR 19, EAT.
4 See *CPS Recruitment Ltd v Bowen* [1982] IRLR 54, distinguishing *Pritchard-Rhodes*, on this ground, on the facts.

20.15 If the employee's notice is given at the appropriate time, ie within the obligatory period of the employer's notice, it is not clear what amount of notice has to be given to the employer. Section 86 of the ERA says that the minimum period of notice to be given by an employee to an employer under statute (in the contract it may be greater) is one week (see Chapter 18, above). However, it has been held in *Ready Case Ltd v Jackson*[1] that notice given by the employee for present purposes may be less than that which is required by law and still be effective. Nonetheless, it has also been held that there must be some notice, at least, which is sufficient to indicate to an employer that there is an intention to anticipate the expiry of the employer's notice.[2] And s 142 does, of course, require an employee to give notice in writing of his intention to anticipate the expiry of the employer's notice.

1 [1981] IRLR 312, EAT.
2 *Walker v Cotswold Chine Holme School* (1977) 12 ITR 342, EAT.

20.16 Assuming the employee has given a valid counter notice the employer may, before the employee's counter notice is due to expire, give him a counter counter notice (again in writing) requiring him to withdraw his counter notice and to continue in employment until the date on which the employer's original notice was due to expire.[1] The employer's counter counter notice must also state that unless he does so, the employer will contest any liability to make a redundancy payment to the employee in respect of the termination of the contract of employment.[2] If the employer does serve this notice and if the employee does not comply with it the employee will be disentitled to the redundancy payment that would otherwise be due except to the extent that it appears to the industrial tribunal, having regard both to the reason for which the employee seeks to leave the employment and those for which the employer requires him to continue in it, to be 'just and equitable'.[3] This therefore gives the industrial tribunal a discretion to order payment of the entire redundancy payment or such part of it as the tribunal thinks fit notwithstanding the employer's counter counter notice and the employee's failure to comply with it.[4]

1 ERA, s 142(1).
2 ERA, s 142(2).
3 ERA, s 142(3) and (4).
4 ERA, s 142(3) and (4).

20.17 As has been mentioned above, a termination by mutual agreement will not be a dismissal for the purposes of s 136 of the ERA. In the context of redundancy, however, it is common for volunteers to be solicited and voluntary redundancies have some similarities with consensual termination. Does an employee run the risk of disentitlement merely because he has volunteered for redundancy? Not necessarily, is the answer.

20.18 There are two common situations. One is where there is a genuine mutual agreement between the employer and employee, where no pressure is applied by the employer for termination of employment to take place. The other is a termination which results from the initiative of the employer notwithstanding that it is accepted or even invited by the employee. In the former case there will be no redundancy dismissal; in the latter case there will. Thus, in *Burton Allton and Johnson Ltd v Peck*[1] it was held that when an individual volunteered for redundancy, the employer having already declared that redundancies would have to be implemented, there was a dismissal within the meaning of s 136 and therefore a right to a redundancy payment. However, in *Birch v University of Liverpool*[2] it was held no redundancy payments were due. Here the employees applied for retirement under the Universities Retirement Compensation Scheme. Their applications to be retired happened after the University had announced to its staff that there had been a reduction in funds and that there would have to be a reduction in the number of staff employed. It was held in this case that there was a genuine consensual termination and therefore no dismissal. The dividing line is very fine indeed in some cases.[3]

1 [1975] ICR 193, [1975] IRLR 87. See also *Morley v CT Morley Ltd* [1985] CR 499, EAT.
2 [1986] ICR 470, [1985] IRLR 165, CA.
3 Another controversial case is *Scott v Coalite Fuels and Chemicals Ltd* [1988] ICR 355, [1988] IRLR 131, EAT where an employee already under notice of dismissal for redundancy was given the option of early retirement so as to trigger pension benefits. Held: that he had come to an agreement to end his employment and he had not been dismissed. See also (in a different context) *Sheffield v Oxford Controls Ltd* [1979] ICR 396, EAT and *Logan Salton v Durham County Council* [1989] IRLR 99, EAT. For two more recent cases with contrasting outcomes see *Gateshead Metropolitan Borough Council v Mills* (EAT 610/92) and *Renfrew District Council v Lorrie* (Court of Session, 23.6.95).

3 THE DEFINITION OF REDUNDANCY

20.19 It is tempting to use some sort of shorthand for the legal definition of redundancy, such as, for example, 'a redundancy situation'. But this can lead to misunderstanding as the Court of Appeal in *Lesney Products & Co Ltd v Nolan*[1] pointed out. The statutory wording must be examined in each case. Section 128 of the ERA states that an employee is entitled to a redundancy payment either on dismissal by reason of redundancy[2] or when he is laid off or kept on short time within the meaning of s 135 (discussed below).[3] The definition of redundancy in connection with dismissal is in s 139(1) which states as follows:

> '(1) For the purposes of this Act an employee who is dismissed shall be taken to be dismissed by reason of redundancy if the dismissal is attributable wholly or mainly to:
>
> (a) the fact that his employer has ceased or intends to cease:
> (i) to carry on the business for the purposes of which the employee was employed by him or
> (ii) to carry on that business in the place where the employee was so employed, or
>
> (b) the fact that the requirements of that business:
> (i) for employees to carry out work of a particular kind, or
> (ii) for employees to carry out work of a particular kind in the place where the employee was employed by the employer, have ceased or diminished or are expected to cease or diminish.'[4]

1 [1977] ICR 235, [1977] IRLR 77, CA.
2 ERA, s 136(1)(a).
3 ERA, s 136(1)(b).
4 But a different definition applies for consultation on mass redundancies with employee representatives under s 188 of TULR(C)A: see para 20.97.

20.20 Sub-paragraph (a) covers the case of closure of the business as a whole, or, if not as a whole, at the workplace where the employee was employed. Sub-paragraph (b) covers the case where the business may be continuing but there is a general cessation or falling off in the requirement of the business for employees to carry out work of a particular kind. It is expressly provided that the requirements of the business can include the business of the employer or of an associated employer so that, in effect, if, within a group of associated employers there is a need to reduce labour on account of a diminution of work, each associated company within the group can be looked at for the purposes of selecting employees for redundancy notwithstanding that one associated company may be less affected (or indeed not affected at all) by a downturn in the business. Both sub-paragraphs refer to the 'place' where the employee was employed, which has generated much case law on exactly when an employee may claim a payment on change of work location. For the sake of simplicity we have subdivided the redundancy cases into two limbs. Limb A deals with closure of the business and movement of work location and Limb B with diminishing requirements. The test is not as straightforward as it looks and it is necessary very closely to examine both Limb A and Limb B having regard to the case law that they have each given rise to.

The presumption of redundancy

20.21 Before doing this it should be remembered that the starting point is s 163(2) of the ERA which provides that there is a presumption of redundancy. That is to say, an employee is presumed to have been dismissed by reason of redundancy unless the employer is able to establish the contrary.[1] This presumption applies to a claim under Part XI of the ERA, ie to a claim for a redundancy payment and does not apply to Part X of the ERA, ie to a claim for unfair dismissal. Therefore, if an employer alleges that a redundancy dismissal is fair for the purposes of Part X (unfair dismissal) the presumption of redundancy does not apply so that the employer has to prove the redundancy reason for dismissal and if he cannot do so, the dismissal will be unfair. This distinction is neatly illustrated by the often cited case of *Midland Foot Comfort Centre Ltd v Moppett*[2] where Mrs Moppett brought a case before the tribunal which combined a claim for a redundancy payment and unfair dismissal compensation. Mrs Moppett was, for the purposes of her redundancy claim, entitled to the benefit of the presumption of redundancy. The employer was unable to rebut this and so the redundancy payment was awarded. The employer then sought to rely upon redundancy as the reason for dismissal in unfair dismissal law. However the presumption of redundancy did not apply for this purpose and the employer had to prove to the industrial tribunal that redundancy was the real reason for dismissal. On the facts the employer was unable to do so and the claim for unfair dismissal compensation succeeded.

1 *Willcox v Hastings* [1987] IRLR 298, CA. The presumption of redundancy also applies in the case of s 188 of TULR(C)A (information and consultation obligations to worker representatives): see para 20.97 and TULR(C)A, s 195(2).

2 [1973] IRLR 141.

Limb A: Closure of the business or movement of location

20.22 The business may generally close down or activities may simply cease at the place where the employee is employed. Either case may satisfy the definition of redundancy under Limb A. A closure can be permanent or temporary since it is provided, in s 139(6), that 'cease' means to cease either permanently or temporarily and from whatever cause and 'diminish' is construed similarly. As the subsection covers a cessation arising 'from whatsoever cause' this means, generally, the industrial tribunal will not inquire about the reason for the redundancy.[1] It is the employer's prerogative to declare a redundancy, unless of course it is a sham and, in reality, there is no redundancy in truth at all.

1 *Moon v Homeworthy Furniture (Northern) Ltd* [1977] ICR 117, [1976] IRLR 298, EAT; *Goodwin Ltd v Fitzmaurice* [1977] IRLR 393.

20.23 As stated, Limb A applies also to a case where an employer ceases to carry on business at the place where the employee is employed or moves the workplace. Thus, if an employee is employed at location A and the employer desires to move his business or the employee's work place to location B the employee will, on the face of it, be entitled to a redundancy payment if dismissal occurs. He may however lose that redundancy payment if the offer of a job at location B amounts to an offer of suitable alternative employment which is unreasonably refused by the employee (see below).

20.24 But it is not quite as simple as that. Whether there has been a cessation of the business at the place where the employee has been employed or whether the employer is entitled to change the work place must be answered by looking at the employee's contract. The reasoning in a large number of cases boils down to a proposition that the words 'in the place where the employee was so employed' in s 139(1)(a)(ii) and s 139(1)(b)(ii) (see above) have to be read as meaning 'in the place where the employee was so employed *or where he could be required to work under his contract of employment*'. Therefore if there is a term in the employee's contract that he will be geographically mobile, either within a limited radius or, indeed, generally, and the employer has asked the employee to move within the scope of that term to do other work, there will be no redundancy falling under Limb A. This is because there is no redundancy at the place where the employee is required to work for the employer under the contract. So an express mobility clause will generally mean there will be no redundancy entitlement on an imposed change of location or work, depending, of course, on the terms of the mobility clause. And if there is no express dismissal and the employee resigns in protest at the change claiming a payment through the means of constructive dismissal, he will fail at the first hurdle of dismissal, as the employer will not have been in breach of contract (upon which constructive dismissal depends).[1] There are a number of cases on the point. In *United Kingdom Atomic Energy Authority v Claydon*[2] Claydon was employed under a contract which required him to work at any of his employer's establishments in the United Kingdom. The employer closed the unit where he worked in Suffolk and asked him to transfer to Berkshire. He refused and was dismissed. It was held that the place where the employee was employed meant any place where he could be required to work under his contract of employment, that is to say, at any of the employer's establishments. Accordingly, the employee was not redundant. Similarly, too, in *Sutcliffe v Hawker Siddeley Aviation Ltd*[3] Sutcliffe was employed under a contract which required him to be geographically mobile anywhere in the United Kingdom. He was employed at RAF Marham but this unit was closed by the employer and he was asked to move to RAF Kinloss. He refused and was dismissed. It was held he was not entitled to a redundancy payment upon the dismissal because the place where he was employed was anywhere where he could lawfully be required to work under his contract.[4]

---

[1] On the other hand, if an employer wants to rely on a mobility clause, he must do so at the time. An employer who does not invoke a mobility clause cannot say that its mere existence entitles him to claim, after he has closed down the workplace where the employees were employed, that he *might* have required them to work elsewhere (even though he did not) so disentitling the employees from redundancy payments. So held the EAT in *Curling v Securicor Ltd* [1992] IRLR 549. As Knox J said:

> 'The employer can invoke the mobility clause in the contract and require the employee to go to a new location or job, if the clause entitles him to do so, whereupon no question of redundancy will arise. Alternatively, the employer can decide not to invoke the mobility clause and rely instead on alternative suitable offers of employment as a defence to claims to a redundancy payment. In the former example, the original employment continues, in the latter it ceases but is replaced in circumstances which, unless the employee reasonably refuses the offer of suitable alternative employment, provide the employee with continuity of employment but relieve the employer of liability to make a redundancy payment. What the employers cannot do is

dodge between the two attitudes and hope to be able to adopt the most profitable at the end of the day'.

2 [1974] ICR 128, [1974] IRLR 6.

3 [1973] ICR 560, [1973] IRLR 304.

4 See also the case of *Anglia Regional Co-operative Society v O'Donnell*, EAT 27.05.94 (655/91) in which it was held that an employee was unfairly dismissed for redundancy for refusing to transfer to a new location on the ground that the mobility clause on which the employers tried to rely was not part of her contract of employment. The employer had recently issued new terms and conditions which contained an extended mobility clause. However, the employee did nothing to indicate acceptance of the new terms and conditions. When the employer attempted to rely upon the new mobility clause in order to require the employee to relocate from Beccles to Lowestoft, the employee refused and was dismissed. The EAT upheld the industrial tribunal's decision that the dismissal was unfair. The employee's original contract contained a mobility clause which covered the Beccles area only and the employer was not entitled to rely upon this to move the employee as far as Lowestoft. However, the EAT did find that the offer of a transfer to Lowestoft had been an offer of suitable alternative employment which the employee had unreasonably refused. Hence, the employer was under no obligation to make a statutory redundancy payment and the basic award in the tribunal was reduced to nil. For other cases on express mobility terms, see *Parry v Holst & Co Ltd* (1968) 3 ITR 317; *Rank Xerox Ltd v Churchill* [1988] IRLR 280. See also *Meade-Hill and National Union of Civil and Public Servants v British Council* [1995] IRLR 478 in which the Court of Appeal struck out a mobility clause on the grounds that it indirectly discriminated against female employees. See Sex Discrimination Act 1975, s 77.

20.25 If there is no express mobility term it may be possible to imply one. But this possibility has to be treated with some caution. In *Stevenson v Teesside Bridge and Engineering Ltd*[1] the employee was a steel erector working at one particular site. Work finished at that site and the employee was asked to move to another site. He refused and was dismissed. It was held that it was customary for steel erectors to move from site to site without objection and therefore it was implied by custom and practice in the industry that he could be required to work at any site at the employer's request. However, it seems that the courts will not readily imply a mobility term into every type of contract of employment; it all depends on the facts. Some of the cases, for example, in which an implied term was found concern so-called 'travelling men', the distinction being between an employee who customarily moves from site to site and a local employee who is employed either to work on one site or at one location.[2]

1 [1971] 1 All ER 296, 6 ITR 44.

2 *McCaffrey v E E Jeavons & Co Ltd* (1967) 2 ITR 636.

20.26 In *Courtaulds Northern Spinning Ltd v Sibson*[1] the employee was employed as a lorry driver working out of one transport depot in Greengate, Lancashire. His contract contained no express mobility clause. At his depot all employees belonged to one trade union but he then resigned from the union. In order to head off industrial action in protest by other employees the employer stipulated that the employee must either rejoin the union or transfer to another depot at Chadderton, only one mile away. The employee refused either to rejoin or transfer and resigned, claiming constructive dismissal. Although the claim he submitted was for unfair dismissal, the issue in this case is equally relevant for the present discussion, ie whether there was a contractual right to transfer him to Chadderton. It was held there was an implied term in the contract entitling the employer to transfer the employee to work at any place within reasonable daily reach of his home. So, in this case, there was no breach of contract.

[1] [1988] ICR 451, [1988] IRLR 305, CA.

20.27 The Court of Appeal approved a statement of Browne-Wilkinson J in *Jones v Associated Tunnelling Co Ltd*[1] on the question of implying mobility terms that:

> 'The term to be implied must depend on the circumstances of each case. The authorities show that it may be relevant to consider the nature of the employer's business, whether or not the employee has in fact been moved during the employment, what the employee was told when he was employed, and whether there is any provision made to cover the employee's expenses when working away from daily reach of his home.'

[1] [1981] IRLR 477.

20.28 But this is not an exhaustive list of considerations. Relevant in the present case was the fact that Greengate was in reality just a start and finish point for the work to be done and that the employee was, for much of the time, 'on the road'. The position was different from, say, a shop assistant who would always work at one locality each and every day. It was therefore appropriate to imply into this contract a term that the employee was mobile to the extent that he would be required to work out of any location within reasonable daily reach of his home. In a different context it was held that an office manageress working in High Holborn could be asked to move to Regent Street. The employee, a commuter, could be required by implication to work anywhere in central London.[1] And often, depending on the circumstances, it will be possible to ask a court to imply a term that an employee may be asked to be mobile over comparatively short distances. Unless the circumstances are unusual, though, it will be much harder to imply mobility to a significant extent. One exceptional case is *Little v Charterhouse Magna Assurance Co Ltd*[2] where a general manager employed under a contract and initially based in Uxbridge was asked to move to Bletchely. It was held that it was possible to imply a UK-wide mobility obligation having regard to the status of the individual in all the circumstances of the case.

[1] *Managers (Holborn) Ltd v Hohne* [1977] IRLR 230, EAT.
[2] [1980] IRLR 19.

20.29 One case where the court declined to imply a mobility clause though, and which may be more typical, is *O'Brien v Associated Fire Alarms Ltd.*[1] Here an employee was employed by a company which supplied and installed fire and burglar alarms in the United Kingdom. The country was divided into two areas each controlled from an area office. O'Brien worked in the north western area and lived in Liverpool from which the north western area was controlled. He had always worked in and around Liverpool and parts of the north west within commuting distance of Liverpool. He was then directed to work in Barrow-in-Furness which was 120 miles from Liverpool. It was held that while there was an implied term that employees would be mobile to places within daily travelling distance from their homes, Barrow-in-Furness was too far and therefore, when dismissed, O'Brien was entitled to a redundancy payment.

[1] (1968) 3 ITR 182, CA.

20.30 Obviously employers wishing to maximise flexibility and to avoid redundancy claims arising should consider wide express mobility clauses. But some caution should be exercised in applying mobility clauses arbitrarily. If there is a mobility term it may cause hardship if this is unreasonably applied by the employer. The EAT adapted the implied term to this possibility in *McAndrew v Prestwick Circuits Ltd*[1] by holding that, in that particular case, it was an implied term that the employee would not be transferred to another location except on reasonable notice. This was arguably taken a step further in *United Bank Ltd v Akhtar*[2] where the EAT also held that an express mobility clause could be overridden by the employer's implied obligation to maintain trust and respect. Another division of the EAT in *White v Reflecting Roadstuds Ltd*[3] refused to accept a proposition that this meant that it was now implied that all express terms had to be exercised reasonably. But it supports the view that an arbitrary or capricious exercise of a power, such as in the case of a mobility clause, may breach the implied term of trust and respect.

[1] [1988] IRLR 514.
[2] [1989] IRLR 507,
[3] [1991] ICR 733.

20.31 *Harvey*[1] considers that the cases on implied terms do not support the reasoning in *United Kingdom Atomic Energy Authority v Claydon* that it is the contract which determines the place at which the employee is employed. The learned editors consider that the correct exercise under Limb A (and Limb B, where the place where the employee is employed is concerned) is to ask where the employee *actually* works under his contract of employment rather than where he *might be required to work* under his contract of employment. If there is a move of location from where he actually works he should be considered redundant even if, under the contract, he could be required to work at a new location, or, indeed, elsewhere. There is no ground, they say, for introducing a gloss on the statutory wording requiring a tribunal to look at the contract of employment. In the case of travelling employees, like Mr Stevenson and Mr Sibson, the place where they actually worked, or drove from, as the case may be, was either one particular site or a site within a reasonable commuting distance, and this explains why they failed to recover a redundancy payment or succeeded in showing constructive dismissal, as the case may be. In spite of the results in *Stevenson* and *Sibson* this approach would have, overall, the effect of entitling more employees to a redundancy payment.

[1] Div E4.

20.32 The view in *Harvey* is certainly an alternative interpretation of the statutory wording. But it is not supported by a number of authorities which found it relevant to see whether an employee was *contractually* mobile. It is therefore submitted that the test which is likely to continue to be applied by the court is the 'contract' test, that is to say, the place where the employee is employed for the purposes of Limb A (or Limb B where that wording appears) is where he actually works or where he might be required to work at the lawful request of the employer. In many cases, such as *Stevenson* and *O'Brien*, the result would be the same on either test. But in others not. For example, on the test proposed by Harvey the employee in *United Kingdom Atomic Energy Authority v Claydon* would have succeeded in his claim for a redundancy payment. Under the contract test, though, he was not redundant.[1]

[1] However a more recent case, *Bass Leisure Ltd v Thomas* [1994] IRLR 104, EAT, supports, to a certain extent, the approach in *Harvey*. In this case Mrs Thomas was employed by Bass as a collector collecting takings from pub fruit machines. She had worked for Bass for more than ten years from its Coventry depot which was about 10 minutes drive from her home. This was especially convenient for her. Bass decided to close its Coventry depot and offered Mrs Thomas relocation in Erdington, some 20 miles west of Coventry. Mrs Thomas agreed to give the change a try but subsequently terminated her employment and sought a redundancy payment. Bass sought to defend Mrs Thomas's claim on the basis of a mobility clause which purported to give the company a right to transfer employees to an alternative place of work subject to certain conditions. Her dismissal arose because Bass had breached the mobility clause by not complying with the conditions contained within the clause. This entitled Mrs Thomas to claim constructive dismissal. Nonetheless, of course, it was still necessary to consider the employer's power, under the mobility clause, to deploy her to another geographical location. The EAT, however, held that an employee's place of work for redundancy purposes is a question of *fact*, taking into account the employee's fixed or changing place of work and any contractual terms which provide (simply) evidence of the place of work. It remains to be seen whether *Bass* indicates a shift away from the contractual approach (see also the approach in *Curling v Securicor Ltd* [1992] IRLR 549, EAT discussed at para 20.24, n 1). Guidance from the Court of Appeal would be useful.

Limb B: Cessation or diminution in requirement for employees in the business

20.33 Cases under Limb B can cause even more difficulty than cases under Limb A. Limb B covers the case, for example, where there is a need to shed labour simply because there is less work; or alternatively where the work is rationalised and made more efficient so that there is a need for fewer employees to do the work; and, finally, where the requirement for work of a particular kind itself disappears, for example where a job disappears entirely, or where work done previously by one particular type of job holder is required to be done in the future by an entirely different type of job holder.

20.34 One of the simpler forms of redundancy under Limb B is where fewer employees are needed to do the work in the business either because of a reduced order book, technological change or increased efficiency. Thus in *Sutton v Revlon Overseas Corpn Ltd*[1] the employer dismissed a chief accountant and reallocated the work previously done by him among three of his colleagues. The work was still required to be done but fewer employees (three instead of four) were needed to do it. The dismissed employee was entitled to a redundancy payment. In *Carry All Motors Ltd v Pennington*[2] there were employed at a transport depot both a transport clerk and a depot manager. The company considered that the two posts could be merged and the work carried out by one employee alone. Accordingly the transport clerk was dismissed. It was held that the transport clerk was entitled to a redundancy payment. In *McCrae v Cullen & Davison Ltd*[3] a company in which Mr McCrae was the general manager was taken over. The new owner appointed himself managing director and the general manager was required to work alongside the managing director. After a while the managing director found that he could perform both the functions of the managing director and the general manager and accordingly dismissed the general manager. It was held that the general manager had been dismissed by reason of redundancy and was entitled to a payment.[4] A redundancy would also arise under these principles in cases where jobs are lost, say, through automation.[5]

---

[1] [1973] IRLR 173. See also *Loudon v Crimpy Crisps* (1966) 1 ITR 307.

[2] [1980] ICR 806, [1980] IRLR 455, EAT.

[3] [1988] IRLR 30. See also *Dolton Transport Ltd v Saunders*, EAT 593/88; *British Midland Airways Ltd v Kynnersley*, EAT 512/85.

[4] A contrary view to these cases was taken by the EAT in *Frame it v Brown*, EAT 177/93, 13.12.93 where it was held that a reduction of workers from four to three with reallocation of the dismissed employee's work among the remaining three was not a redundancy. This must be wrong.

[5] It also used to be self-evident that replacement of direct labour with self-employed workers or by an outside contractor firm would also mean that the direct labour dismissed to make way would be dismissed by reason of redundancy. Ex hypothesi there would be a cessation of the requirement for *employees* to do work of a particular kind. See *Lang v Briton Ferry Working Mens' Club and Institute* (1967) 2 ITR 35; *Bromby & Hoare Ltd v Evans* [1972] ICR 113; *Amos v Max-Arc Ltd* [1973] ICR 46, [1973] IRLR 285. This is very much subject now, however, to whether such contracting out would now attract the provisions of the Transfer of Undertakings (Protection of Employment) Regulations 1981 – see Chapter 8, above. Previously, the cessation of management of an activity and contracting out the function to contractors would often lead to a redundancy dismissal of those employed in the activity as the original employer would cease to have any work available for the employees, who would become employees of the contractor. Since the European Court decisions in *Rask v ISS Kantineservice A/S* [1993] IRLR 133 and *Dr Sophie Redmond Stitching v Bartol* [1992] IRLR 366 and many cases subsequently it is much more likely now that contracting out would attract the provisions of the Transfer of Undertakings (Protection of Employment) Regulations 1981. If so, employment contracts are then not terminated by the transfer, but, rather, transferred to the contractor and no dismissal (still less a redundancy dismissal) arises – see Chapter 8, above.

20.35 Sometimes an employer reacts to a reduced order book not by dismissing employees, but by reducing hours. That might result in a constructive dismissal which should lead to a redundancy payment as there has been a diminution in the requirement of work of a particular kind to be done by employees. Thus in *Hanson v Wood (Abington Process Engravers)*[1] the employing company suffered a temporary recession. Instead of laying off or expressly dismissing individual workers the employer decided to reduce the hours of all of the workers. It was held that this might amount to a constructive dismissal which would be by reason of redundancy for the reasons stated above.

---

[1] (1967) 3 ITR 46.

20.36 In some case law attention has been focused on the concept of the wording 'requirements of [the] business for employees to carry out work of a particular kind' which now appears in ERA, s 139(1)(b)(ii). Suppose an employer has dismissed employees because he can no longer afford to keep them; but if he could afford to, he would have kept them, because the business could certainly accommodate them by allocating work to them. Does this mean that the requirements of the business for employees have not really ceased or diminished, so that there is no redundancy entitlement? In *Delanair Ltd v Mead*,[1] Delanair, which made heaters for the car industry, depended heavily on a contract with Ford. Ford reduced the order book considerably and as a result made Mr Mead redundant. His work was absorbed by other existing members of staff. But they needed to do overtime to cover the additional duties allocated to them which had been previously performed by Mr Mead. The employer argued that there was no redundancy because there was no diminution in the output of the department. The industrial tribunal agreed and found that no redundancy payment was due because there was no overall diminution in work. The EAT said however that the industrial tribunal had erred by applying the wrong test. The statute requires attention to be paid to the requirements of the business for employees to do the work rather than to whether there is an overall diminution in work. The dismissals were therefore by reason of redundancy. However, the EAT did not remove all doubt from the area. It went on to suggest that if an employer had not carried out a proper appraisal of whether there was the need to dispense with the services of an individual, a dismissal on the ground of economy without regard to the requirements of the business for employees to carry out the particular type of work might not be a redundancy dismissal. So despite the result in *Delanair* it could be possible for an employer to seek to escape redundancy payments liability by pleading that economic necessity alone brought about the dismissal and the overall requirements of the business were still for the employee to do the work concerned. However, this possibility has not been taken up in other EAT cases. For example, in *Association of University Teachers v University of Newcastle-upon-Tyne*,[2] due to failure of outside funding the University was obliged to discontinue a course for which there was still student demand. A lecturer was consequently dismissed and his union claimed the employer had not consulted with the union as required by s 99 of the Employment Protection Act 1975 (now s 188 of TULR(C)A). The case therefore turned on the definition of redundancy in the EPA under EPA, s 125(6), (7) then the same as the ERA definition (but see now TULR(C)A, s 195). It was argued that there was no redundancy dismissal because the overall need for the course had not ceased or diminished. The University simply could no longer afford to run the course. It was held that although, in an ideal world, the services of the lecturer were required, in practical terms the University had made a decision to shed labour and discontinue the course. Fewer employees were therefore required by the employer. The correct approach was to focus on the cause of the dismissal and not the cause of the redundancy which gave rise to it; therefore, as the services of the lecturer were not required, his dismissal was by reason of redundancy. And in *Halfords v Roche*[3] the employer dismissed a telephonist as part of a cost-efficiency exercise. Her work was absorbed by, and distributed among, other employees. Despite the fact that the dismissal arose out of economic grounds, it was by reason of redundancy. There had been an appraisal of staffing requirements and a decision made that one employee was surplus and the work could be redistributed. There was a diminution in the requirement for employees to do work of a particular kind. This is not to say that all economic dismissals will be by reason of redundancy. Some most definitely will not, simply because there is no cessation or diminution in the requirement for employees to do the work. The case of *Chapman v Goonvean and Rostowrack China Clay Co Ltd*,[4] discussed below, is an excellent example of such a case.

---

1 [1976] ICR 522, [1976] IRLR 340, EAT.

2 [1987] ICR 317, [1988] IRLR 10, EAT; *Carry All Motors Ltd v Pennington* [1980] ICR 806, [1980] IRLR 455, EAT; *Ladbroke Courage Holidays Ltd v Asten* [1981] IRLR 59, EAT.

3 *IDS Brief* 396, 1 May 1989, p 2.

4 [1973] 2 All ER 1063, [1973] 1 WLR 678, CA. See, too, *Smith v Grampian Regional Council*, EAT 243/90 (Council decision, in the context of competitive tendering under the Local Government Act 1988, to maintain number of employees but reduce hours to be worked in order to reduce the

pay bill and improve competitiveness of the Council's Direct Service Organisation. Held: no redundancy arose). Contrast *McCafferty v Rankin Park Club*, EAT 205/90. See also *Dacorum Borough Council v Eldridge and Townsend*, EAT 608/89, where in circumstances not dissimilar to those in *Smith* (above), redundancy payments were applicable. The result in *Dacorum* may however have turned on the employer's failure to rebut the statutory presumption of redundancy.

20.37 A redundancy can also occur where the employee's job changes so much through a reorganisation or redefinition that the job, as it emerges, is an entirely new job. The old job, being work of a particular kind, has disappeared and the employer's requirement for employees to do it has ceased. Whether the reorganisation or redefinition is significant enough for this to happen is a question of fact and degree in each case. In *Robinson v British Island Airways Ltd*[1] the posts of flight operations manager and general manager operations and traffic were both discontinued at the instance of the employer and a new job of operations manager was created. Robinson, who failed to get the job of operations manager, was redundant as the new job was very much different from his old, disappeared, job. In *Murphy v Epsom College*[2] a plumber was dismissed and replaced by a heating technician. It was held that the plumber had been dismissed by reason of redundancy because the new job was substantially different from the old job. In *Hall v Farrington Data Processing Ltd*[3] the job of a salesman with managerial functions was sufficiently different from that of a salesman without managerial functions so as to cause a redundancy when the requirement for a mere salesman ceased. Similarly in *Denton v Neepsend Ltd*[4] an employee worked on a cold saw. His employers wanted to introduce an abrasive cutting machine. It was held that the job of using the new machine required different skills and techniques and was more demanding and therefore a redundancy arose when the job was changed. The test in general is that contained in *Amos v Max-Arc Ltd*[5] where the National Industrial Relations Court said 'work of a particular kind . . . means work which is distinguished from other work of the same general kind by requiring special aptitudes, skills or knowledge'.

---

1 [1978] ICR 304, [1977] IRLR 477, EAT.
2 [1985] ICR 80, [1984] IRLR 271, CA.
3 (1969) 4 ITR 230.
4 [1976] IRLR 164.
5 [1973] ICR 46, [1973] IRLR 285.

20.38 It is not however possible to find a redundancy dismissal when the reason for dismissal was that the employer required different personal attributes or qualifications from an employee but the work required from employees was basically the same. In *Vaux and Associated Breweries Ltd v Ward (No 2)*[1] the unfortunate Mrs Ward, who was aged 57, was dismissed from her post as a barmaid when her employers wished to turn the pub in which she worked into a modern roadhouse with a younger and 'more glamorous' barmaid. It was held that there was still work of a particular kind required to be done (ie that of a barmaid) and therefore Mrs Ward was not entitled to a redundancy payment. Similarly, too, in *Pillinger v Manchester Area Health Authority*[2] the employee, Pillinger, was a research officer paid on Grade II. He was then promoted to Grade IIS. The employer decided that the work only justified it being done by a Grade II officer. It was held that as the work required was just the same after as before the dismissal there was no redundancy upon the decision to dismiss the Grade IIS employee and replace him with a Grade II employee.

[1] (1970) 5 ITR 62.
[2] [1979] IRLR 430. See, too, *Kleboe v Ayr County Council* (1 May 1972, unreported) NICR.

20.39 Although we have stated that a reorganisation which changes the very nature of the job may mean a redundancy arises, reorganisational change per se is not necessarily redundancy. An employer may impose reorganisational change and dictate different requirements as to how the work is to be performed but this may not mean that the work as previously performed has disappeared. As stated in *North Riding Garages Ltd v Butterwick*[1]

> 'for the purposes of the [ERA] an employee who remains in the same kind of work is expected to adapt himself to new methods and techniques and cannot complain if his employer insists on higher standards of efficiency than those previously required; but if new methods alter the nature of the work to be done it may follow that no requirement remains for employees to do work of the particular kind which has been superseded and they are truly redundant. Thus if a motor manufacturer decides to use plastic instead of wood in the body work of his cars and dismisses the wood workers they may well be entitled to redundancy payments'.

[1] [1967] 2 QB 56, [1967] 1 All ER 644.

20.40 In *Chapman v Goonvean and Rostowrack China Clay Co Ltd*[1] the arrangements made by the employer included the provision of transport to and from work. Ten workers were involved and eventually three were made redundant. The employer then decided that it was no longer economic to provide transport for the seven remaining employees and so the employer ceased the provision of free transport. This was a serious breach of contract and therefore led to a constructive dismissal. But it was held that it was not by reason of redundancy. The requirements of the business for employees had not diminished beyond the need to reduce the work force by three and notwithstanding the withdrawal of free transport the seven remaining members were still employed to do the work that they were previously employed to do. In *Johnson v Nottinghamshire Combined Police Authority*[2] the employer decided to alter the time of day at which the work was to be performed. The two employees concerned worked five days a week 9.30 to 5.00 or 5.30. The employer decided to change the hours to two shifts of 8.00 to 3.00 and 1.00 to 8.00 six days a week alternate weeks. But the work that the employees were doing remained exactly the same after as before. It was held that there was no redundancy entitlement. It was held that work of a particular kind refers to the work that is being done and mere alteration of the time of day at which it is to be done does not result in redundancy. In *Lesney Products & Co Ltd v Nolan*[3] the employer decided to reorganise the day shift by splitting up one single day shift into two. The existing hours were Mondays to Thursdays 8.00 to 5.00 and Fridays 8.00 to 2.30. After the change the employees were required to work 7.30 to 3.30 or 2.00 until 10.00 Mondays to Fridays. Those who refused to go along with the change were dismissed but it was held that they were not entitled to redundancy payments. There was no diminution in the requirement of work of a particular kind to be done but simply an alteration of the times of day at which the work was to be done.

[1] [1973] 2 All ER 1063, CA. See *Smith v Grampian Regional Council*, EAT 243/90.
[2] [1974] 1 All ER 1082, [1974] IRLR 20, CA.
[3] [1977] ICR 235, [1977] IRLR 77, CA.

20.41 It could well be argued that working at different times of the day can involve different skills, attributes, stamina and preferences and in some cases the job may appear, in practical terms, very different. For example, it could be argued that night shift work is different from day shift work. The EAT considered as much in *MacFisheries v Findlay*, confirming that a redundancy payment was due.[1] However, this idea is arguably in conflict with *Johnson* and *Lesney* and should be treated with some caution. Similarly, can part-time work be different from full-time work? The cases are divided. There are indications in *Johnson* that part-time work is not a different kind of work from full-time work.[2] But of course if there is a movement from part-time working to full-time working it could be argued that there is a requirement for fewer employees to perform the work of a particular kind for the business thereby resulting in a redundancy as defined by statute.

[1] [1985] ICR 160. See also *Little Chef Ltd v Harvey* (21 December 1978, unreported), EAT (weekend working held to be different work from weekday working; but cf *Johnson*). Cf also *Maher v PhotoTrade Processing Ltd*, EAT 451/83 – night shift abolished – move to day shift not change amounting to redundancy.
[2] *Rosie v Watt* (1966) 1 ITR 201; *Pollock v Victor Vale (Holdings) Ltd* (1966) 1 ITR 368. Compare *Brown v Dunlop Textiles Ltd* (1967) 2 ITR 531. Compare, too, *Ellis v G A Property Services Ltd* (industrial tribunal) COIT 2095/158.

20.42 At the end of the day, some reorganisations will result in the applicability of redundancy payments; some will not. As the EAT stated in *Campsmount Farm Estate v Kozyra*:[1] 'In truth a reorganisation may or may not end in redundancy; it all depends on the nature and effect of the reorganisation'. The statutory definition of redundancy in s 139(1) of the ERA should be carefully applied to the facts of each case.

[1] EAT 499/85, per Hutchinson J. See, too, *Mayne v AB Electronic Components Ltd*, EAT 1/80; *Trusthouse Forte Hotels Ltd v Jones*, EAT 82/82; (1) *McGibbon* (2) *McCoy v OIL Ltd*, EAT 11.11.94 (537/94) (refusal to accept new terms and conditions offered in the context of business reorganisation held not to amount to dismissal by reason of redundancy).

20.43 There are two further grey areas which might cause problems for employees trying to claim a redundancy payment that apparently seems due to them. The first is this. Suppose that when the employee applies for employment it is appreciated that the job will disappear in due course as the employee is taken on in anticipation of a diminishing need. Can the employer argue, when the employee's employment is eventually terminated, that because a cessation or diminution of a requirement of work of a particular kind was anticipated at the outset, a redundancy payment is not applicable? This would be a remarkable interpretation of the legislation but it was one that found favour with the EAT in *Lee v Nottinghamshire County Council*.[1] In this case the employee was invited to become a lecturer at a teachers' training college and it was understood that it was a temporary job for one or two years at the most. The reason why it was temporary was because the fall in birth rate meant a reduced demand for teachers and hence those who were employed to teach them. Upon the termination of the employee's contract the industrial tribunal awarded a redundancy payment. But the EAT reversed the industrial tribunal, holding that as the cessation or diminution had already been anticipated prior to the commencement of the employment, the Act did not apply. However, the Court of Appeal reversed the EAT, holding that the legislation must be given its plain meaning. As a matter of fact, during the course of the employee's employment there had been a cessation or diminution of a requirement of work of a particular kind to be performed. Therefore the redundancy payment was due.

[1] [1980] IRLR 284, CA.

20.44 The second point is that earlier we referred to the 'contract test' when discussing the interpretation of Limb A. That is to say, in looking at the question of what is the place where the employee is employed, if an employee can, under the terms of his contract, be required to work at any other location at the request of the employer there may be no redundancy payment due in connection with any dismissal that arises from an imposed change of location. A similar question arises in interpreting Limb B in deciding whether an employee is redundant because his job has disappeared. The question therefore arises, what is his job? Is it what he is actually doing or what he is doing and what he might be required to do under his contract? Thus, if the description of duties in the contract of employment is sufficiently wide so that the employee can be required to perform job functions other than the one that has disappeared, the need for which still exists in the employer's business, can he be said to be redundant?

20.45 There are two schools of thought on the way Limb B ought to be interpreted. One, the 'job function' school, says that you do not look at the contract but, instead, you must look to see what job the employee was actually performing and see whether that function has disappeared. If so, he will be entitled to a redundancy payment. The other, the 'contract test' school, says that, if, under the terms of the contract of employment, the employee may be required to perform jobs other than the one that has disappeared in the prima facie redundancy situation that has arisen, then he is not genuinely redundant and, therefore, semble, he should not be entitled to a redundancy payment. Now, in many situations (as with the similar dilemma in construing Limb A), the job function test will not produce any different result from the contract test, because the employee may be both employed to do one specific thing and may actually be performing that job and nothing else. If so, when the job function disappears so does the job as defined by the employee's contract. A redundancy payment is due whichever test is applied. However, a different result might be possible where the employee's contract of employment contains a very wide job description listing other tasks to be performed if required and which goes beyond the specific job that is being undertaken at present. Here, if the job function test is applied the redundancy payment will be due. If the contract test is applied, it will not.

20.46 The point first arose, not in a redundancy claim proper, but from some unfair dismissal cases in which the employee sought to dispute that there had been a valid reason for dismissal falling under the heading of redundancy under s 98(2) of the ERA (see Chapter 19, above). In *Nelson v BBC*[1] Nelson was employed as a producer in the BBC Caribbean service. Under his contract he was required to be mobile and move to any department at the request of the BBC. Ultimately the Caribbean service was closed down, and the BBC offered Nelson alternative work. He refused to accept this and was dismissed. He claimed unfair dismissal. The BBC sought to resist the claim for unfair dismissal on the basis that there was a redundancy because he was employed only in the Caribbean service and, therefore, when this was closed down this was a genuine redundancy and therefore a fair dismissal for that reason. The Court of Appeal held that as under the contract Nelson was obliged to work elsewhere outside the Caribbean service at the request of the employer the dismissal was not by reason of redundancy. So it was unfair as the employer had no alternative permitted reason apart from redundancy to offer ('some other substantial reason' under s 98(1) of the ERA (see Chapter 19, above) might have applied but it had not been pleaded). The case came before the Court of Appeal a second time, in *Nelson v BBC (No 2)*,[2] on the issue of compensation for unfair dismissal. As the case is concerned with compensation, the merits were not discussed in detail. But there are comments supportive of the court's decision in *Nelson (No 1)* that Nelson had been found not to be redundant.

1 [1977] ICR 649, [1977] IRLR 148, CA.
2 [1980] ICR 110, [1979] IRLR 346, CA.

20.47 In *Cowen v Haden Ltd*[1] Mr Cowen was employed as a regional surveyor. After a heart attack he was made a divisional contracts surveyor with a view to making his life easier. Under his contract, he had, also, if required, to undertake other duties which reasonably fell within his capabilities. Later, the company found that it could do without a divisional contracts surveyor and he was dismissed. The company defended the claim on the basis that there was a genuine redundancy and therefore the dismissal was fair. The EAT felt obliged to follow what it saw as the contract test applied in the *Nelson* case and held that Mr Cowen was not redundant because there was other work available under the terms of his contract as divisional contracts surveyor. In the Court of Appeal, it was held, on the facts of the case, that the position of divisional contracts surveyor was a special one and could be differentiated from the post of any other surveyor and, therefore, when the need for a divisional contracts surveyor ceased, Mr Cowen was redundant. In this particular case the clause in his contract requiring him to do other work falling within his capabilities had to be construed in a way which meant that he was required to do other work within his capabilities as a divisional contracts surveyor. The work of any other surveyor was outside the clause. Therefore there was, on this finding, no other work he could be required to do under his contract when the post of divisional contracts surveyor was dispensed with. Obiter, however, the Court of Appeal stated that, nonetheless, the ratio decidendi of *Nelson v BBC (No 1)* was that the test of redundancy was whether there had been a cessation or diminution of the requirement under the contract for employees to perform the kind of work that Nelson was employed to do. In other words, the contract test was supported, obiter as it turned out. The debate between the virtues of the contract test on the one hand and the job function test on the other, continues. But when it arose recently in *Pink v White and White & Co (Earls Barton) Ltd*[2] the contract test was emphatically applied.

In the latest case on the subject, *Johnson v Peabody Trust*[3] the EAT confirmed, once more, that whether a redundancy arose should be determined in accordance with the contract test. However, it was not to be applied in an over-technical or legalistic way, but should be looked at in a common sense manner in order to ascertain the basic task which the employee was contracted to perform. Thus the appellant, who was employed as a roofer, was dismissed by reason of redundancy when the employer's requirement for roofers diminished, notwithstanding a flexibility clause in his contract which required him to carry out multi-trade operations where possible. The obligation to work on multi-trade operations was very much a subsidiary obligation introduced to provide a degree of flexibility within the workforce in times of increasing economic difficulty faced by employers.

---

1 [1983] ICR 1, [1982] IRLR 314, CA.
2 [1985] IRLR 489, EAT. See also *Haines v Metropole Casinos (UK) Ltd* EAT 666/81; *Hyat v Stowe School Ltd* EAT 2/84; *Perkins Engine Group Ltd v Overend* EAT 479/88.
3 [1996] IRLR 387.

20.48 As has been stated, the difference between the job function and contract test is immaterial when the job function performed by the employee is the same as the job description in the contract of employment. Where, however, the contract of employment contains an extremely wide job description, theoretically embracing duties other than those actually performed by the employee, the result of the contract test may be to deny an employee a redundancy payment (although the contract test is to the advantage of the employee in unfair dismissal cases like *Nelson* because if there was no redundancy and the employer pleads no other reason for dismissal, the dismissal will be unfair).[1] The predominant view in case law at present seems to favour the contract test; but until the House of Lords pronounces upon the matter, there will continue to be debate.

---

1 The issue of the contract became quite important to Mr Tipper, in the case of *Tipper v Roofdec (No 2)* EAT 478/89. He was an HGV driver (although it was understood he could be called on to do other duties) who lost his driving licence. He was given alternative work, but this then came to an end. It was held he was not redundant. The reason for termination was that he could no longer work as a driver (plus ancillary duties) through loss of his licence. His job was still there and needed to be filled; that was his contractual work. He had not entered into a *new* contract to do the alternative work exclusively. (See also *Runnals v Richards Osborne Ltd* [1973] ICR 225.)

'Bumping' or 'transferred' redundancies

20.49 'Bumping' occurs as follows. An employee may be redundant but, perhaps because of his long service, it may be thought to be desirable to retain his services and to give him another employee's job. The employee whose job is given to the redundant employee may have to be dismissed to make way. That employee who is 'bumped' out will be entitled to a redundancy payment. Thus in *Gimber & Sons Ltd v Spurrett*[1] a warehouse manager was dismissed because his job was given to a sales representative who had lost his own job through redundancy. It was held that when there is a reduction in the requirements for employees in one area of an employer's business and an employee who, as a consequence, is redundant is transferred to another area, an employee who is displaced by the transfer of the first employee and dismissed by reason of the transfer is dismissed by reason of redundancy. The principle was restricted, however, in *Babar Indian Restaurant v Rawat*[2] to bumping within one business only. It was held there that when the employer closed down one of its businesses and dismissed an employee in another business to make way for an employee who had been made redundant from the shut-down business the dismissal of the employee eventually shunted out to make way was not by reason of redundancy. This perhaps shows the unwillingness of the courts to take the principle too far.[3] It has also been argued that if the contract test is the correct test for a redundancy, bumping does not sit easily alongside it. For in bumping cases there is no cessation or diminution of the work for which the bumped employee was employed to do under his contract. The job in his contract still exists. As authority for bumping predates the case law about the contract test, this is said to cast doubt upon the contract test.[4]

---

1 (1967) 2 ITR 308.
2 [1985] IRLR 57.
3 Although it is submitted the decision may be questionable because s 139 of the ERA expressly provides that businesses of associated employers are deemed to be one business for determining whether there is a cessation or diminution of a requirement for work of a particular kind to be done by employees in a business (see above).
4 *IDS Handbook on Employment Law* 37, p 32; *Harvey* Div E5.

---

4 RE-EMPLOYMENT

20.50 Under s 138(1) of the ERA, if the employee's contract of employment is renewed or he is re-engaged under a new contract of employment in pursuance of an offer, whether in writing or not, made by his employer before the ending of his employment under the previous contract and the renewal and re-engagement takes place either immediately on the ending of the old employment or within four weeks thereafter, the employee is deemed not to have been dismissed by his employer by reason of redundancy. This is often called the 'vanishing' or 'disappearing' dismissal.[1] As a result there is no liability to make a redundancy payment to the employee. But continuous employment is preserved by virtue of s 206(2) of the ERA and the employee's seniority for the purposes of any future redundancy dismissal is thereby preserved. However, if such an offer is made and either if the new terms and conditions of employment do not differ from the previous terms and conditions of employment or, if they do, if the new offer constitutes an offer of suitable alternative employment in relation to the employee and, in either case, the employee unreasonably refuses the offer he will remain dismissed but he will not be entitled to a redundancy payment by reason of the dismissal.[2]

---

1 *Harvey* Div E3. See also *EBAC Ltd v Wymer* [1995] ICR 466.
2 ERA, s 146(1).

20.51 To protect an employee it is provided in s 138 of the ERA, in relation to the offer of employment, that if the capacity and place in which the employee is employed or the other terms and conditions of the employment differ wholly or in part from the corresponding provisions of the previous contract, there is a trial period in relation to the contract as renewed.[1] This trial period begins with the ending of the employee's employment under the previous contract and ends with the expiration of a period of four weeks beginning with the date on which the employee starts work under the new contract.[2]

1 ERA, s 138(2).
2 ERA, s 138(3). It has been held by the Court of Appeal that 'four weeks' means four calendar weeks, not four full working weeks during which the employee has had the opportunity of working. This seems harsh, but the Court said that it would not read into the Act words that were not there. Thus, in *Benton v Sanderson Kayser Ltd* [1989] ICR 136, [1989] IRLR 19, CA an employee whose employment terminated on 21.12.86 and whose trial period started forthwith did not have the right to say the seven day Christmas closure could be excluded from the trial period. His trial period ended on 18.1.87 even though this meant he had, in reality, only three weeks in which to try out the new job. He lost his right to a redundancy payment when he resigned on 19.1.87, one day late.

20.52 Exceptionally, the four week trial may be extended by agreement between the employer and the employee. But such agreement has to be made between the employer and the employee or the employee's representative before the employee starts work under the new contract; has to be for the purpose of retraining the employee for employment under the new contract; has to be in writing; has to specify the end of the trial period; and has to specify the terms and conditions of employment which will apply in the employee's case after the end of the period.[1] These detailed conditions have to be followed in full for an extension to apply.

1 ERA, s 138(6).

20.53 If, during the trial period, the employee terminates the contract or gives notice to terminate it, or if the employer, for a reason connected with or arising out of the change to a renewed or new employment, terminates the contract or gives notice to terminate it, the employee is treated as having been dismissed on the date on which his employment under the previous contract (or, if there has been more than one trial period, the original contract) ended. The dismissal is treated as being the reason for which he was originally dismissed (ie redundancy) and his right to a redundancy payment is preserved.[1] However, if prima facie the terms of the new contract are suitable and the employee unreasonably terminates the contract or unreasonably gives notice to terminate it during the trial period he is disentitled to a redundancy payment by reason of the dismissal from employment under the previous contract.[2]

1 ERA, s 138(4), (5).
2 ERA, s 141(4).

20.54 For these provisions to apply the offer of re-employment need not be in writing but it must be precise enough to amount to an offer in law and give the employee sufficient information to show how, basically, the new contract is different from the old.[1]

1 *Havenhand v Thomas Black Ltd* (1968) 3 ITR 271; *McKindley v William Hill (Scotland) Ltd* [1985] IRLR 492, EAT; *McCreadie v Thomson & MacIntyre (Pattern Makers) Ltd* (1971) 6 ITR 177.

20.55 The four week statutory trial period is rigid and the employee will be deemed to have accepted the new employment if he carries on working beyond the four week period. The only statutory exception to this is where the trial period is extended by agreement, as mentioned above, for the purposes of retraining. But, as stated, all of the conditions described above for the extension to apply must be met. If they are absent, an employee who leaves after the end of four weeks during what he believes to be an extended trial period will lose his right to a redundancy payment. For the purposes of statute he will be deemed to have resigned.

20.56 It is possible that, in such circumstances, if the employer has made a promise to extend the trial period which does not meet the statutory conditions this will still be binding on the employer. But this would be at common law and not under statute and a contractual claim would have to be made for a payment equivalent to the statutory payment, and not for the statutory payment itself. There is no reported instance of this happening but it seems a sound proposition on first principles. Success would, however, depend on the terms of the promise made by the employer, eg whether they are precise enough to amount to an unequivocal promise to make a payment in any event.

20.57 There is another instance whereby a trial period may be longer than four weeks, although this is not, in truth, an exception to the four week trial period, but a case which involves a separate trial period additional to the statutory trial period. For it has been recognised that at common law an employee may be entitled to a common law trial period in addition to a statutory trial period in certain circumstances. This applies in the case of constructive dismissals by reason of redundancy but not to express dismissals. The reasoning behind the existence of the common law trial period in constructive dismissal cases is this. The statutory trial period runs from the ending of the old contract. Therefore, if the employee has been expressly dismissed with notice or a payment in lieu of notice, his contract will end at the time stated by the employer and the statutory trial period will start running from the ending of the old employment and cannot last more than four weeks from the commencement of the new employment (unless extended for retraining under statute). Suppose, however, the employee is not expressly dismissed but is the victim of a repudiatory breach short of dismissal. This might arise, for example, where the employer unilaterally requires the employee to change location or job duties in circumstances where the contract does not oblige the employee to work at the changed location or to perform the new job duties. The employer's ultimatum may, in effect, constitute an offer of re-employment. May the employee try out the new conditions? If so, does he only have four weeks under the new regime to make up his mind to accept the new conditions or reject them? The answer is that, here, the overall period of trial may be longer than four weeks. This is because the employer's actions have not amounted to an express dismissal. Instead, they were a repudiatory breach of contract. A repudiatory breach of contract, however drastic, does not of itself end the contract of employment.[1] It needs an acceptance by the injured party to bring it to an end.[2] Particularly if the employee indicates his reservations or otherwise says that he is testing the water or working under protest under the new conditions[3] then, merely by working under the new conditions, the employee will not be deemed to have accepted the new employment and thereby have treated his old employment as at an end. He will be allowed a reasonable period at common law in which to make up his mind and in which to make his election to treat the employment as at an end. This period could, at common law, be longer than four weeks in appropriate cases.

[1] *Gunton v Richmond-Upon-Thames London Borough Council* [1981] Ch 448, CA. There are opposing views, but the majority of case law supports the proposition in the text.
[2] *Gunton*; *McMullen* (1982) CLJ 110.
[3] *Marriott v Oxford and District Co-operative Society (No 2)* [1970] 1 QB 186, [1969] 3 All ER 1126, CA.

20.58 This is well illustrated by two cases on the subject. Thus, in *Air Canada v Lee*[1] the employee was employed as a switchboard operator. The employer moved its business to new premises where the switchboard was located in the basement of the building. The employee found this very unsatifactory and uncongenial but tried out the new conditions for a while, ie about two months. After this period the employee resigned and claimed constructive dismissal and a redundancy payment. This was after a period obviously more than the length of the statutory trial period. However, it was held that she was nonetheless entitled to a redundancy payment. Following the employer's repudiation of the original contract the employee had a reasonable time at common law in which to decide whether or not to accept the breach as terminating the contract or to affirm the contract. In these circumstances two months was not an unreasonable time and the statutory trial period only came into play once the old contract had been terminated.

[1] [1978] ICR 1202, [1978] IRLR 392, EAT.

20.59 So, too, in *Turvey v CW Cheyney & Sons Ltd*[1] the employee was employed as a polisher but work diminished and he was offered employment in a different department of the employer's business. This was a breach of his contract. But he agreed to try out the new employment and he stayed on for a little over four weeks. Then he resigned. It was held that he was not disentitled to a redundancy payment. This was not an express dismissal but a case of employer repudiation which was not effective until the employee treated the employment as at an end after a reasonable period during which the employee was able to make up his mind as to whether he wanted to accept the breach as terminating, or affirm the new contract without losing his rights. Again the statutory trial period was not relevant until the old employment had come to an end and this did not happen until the constructive dismissal. Both these cases seem to be based on the fact that the employee was able to resign during the common law trial period and the ratio is that the statutory trial period had not bitten at all. Theoretically, it may further be supposed that an employee may work on for a longer period than the ending of the common law trial period as long as he resigns during a four week period thereafter although in practice it may be nearly impossible to decide when the common law period ends and the new employment starts.

[1] [1979] ICR 341, [1979] IRLR 105, EAT. See also *Bevan v CTC Coaches Ltd* EAT 107/88, (1989) IRLIB 21 March 1989, p 10; *Coopind (UK) Ltd v Buckland* EAT 403/89; *Kentish Bus and Coach Co Ltd v Quarry*, EAT 16.05.94 (287/92).

20.60 Next, as stated, the right to a redundancy payment will be lost if the new employment is the same as the old employment or, if not, was suitable in relation to the employee and, secondly, in either case, the employee's refusal of the offer of new employment or his resignation during the trial period if applicable is unreasonable. Much case law has been generated on what is 'suitable' employment and what may be an 'unreasonable' refusal thereof.

20.61 In practice, when presenting or defending an industrial tribunal claim on the point it is often hard to separate the two concepts of suitability and unreasonableness.[1] However, it seems that whether the job is 'suitable' in relation to the employee involves an objectively based approach including job comparison (for example comparing the new conditions with the old such as pay, status, location of work and so on). 'Unreasonableness', on the other hand, may allow more subjectively based factors to be taken into account including an employee's personal circumstances.[2] For example, suppose an employee is employed as an engineering foreman at location A. Suppose also that a redundancy arises because the employer wishes to change the place of work to location B (we assume, in this example, for the sake of argument, that there is no mobility term express or implied (see above)). It is to be assumed that the employer is happy to offer the employee a job as an engineering foreman at the different location. The offer made to the employee is likely to be suitable. However, whether the employee's refusal of that job is reasonable or unreasonable may involve personal considerations. For example, it might be reasonable for an employee to refuse the suitable alternative employment on grounds that the travelling time to work is much greater than in the case of the old employment and that factor might affect employees differently. Some employees may have difficulties with public transport; some may have problems with getting children to school and some, for example, might have other health or domestic considerations which make the new conditions unsatisfactory and their rejection reasonable.

[1] *Spencer and Griffin v Gloucestershire County Council* [1985] IRLR 393, CA; *Thomas Wragg & Sons v Wood* [1976] ICR 313, EAT; cf *Knott v Southampton and South-West Hampshire Health Authority* [1991] ICR 480, EAT.

[2] See *Cambridge & District Co-operative Society Ltd v Ruse* [1993] IRLR 156, where the EAT said: 'We consider that, as a matter of law, it is possible for the employee reasonably to refuse an objectively suitable offer on the ground of his personal perception of the employment offered'.

20.62 It is important to stress that these issues involve questions of fact in each case and it is not particularly helpful to set out too many examples lest they be (wrongly) taken as precedents. But it has been held that the following issues, namely status,[1] location,[2] fringe benefits,[3] hours of work[4] and pay[5] have been relevant in determining whether an offer of employment is 'suitable'. And factors that have been thought relevant on the question of reasonableness of the employee's refusal include the lateness or vagueness of the offer,[6] housing and schooling considerations,[7] domestic problems,[8] medical reasons[9] and financial uncertainty of the employer.[10] The burden of proof in showing that the employment was suitable and the refusal was unreasonable is on the employer.

[1] *Miller v Nettle Accessories Ltd* (1966) 1 ITR 328; *Taylor v Kent County Council* [1969] 2 QB 560, [1969] 2 All ER 1080; *Kane v Raine and Co Ltd* [1974] ICR 300. See, too, *National Carriers Contract Services v Urey*, EAT 233/89; *Hutchinson v British Railways Board* (industrial tribunal) COIT 2059/44. But see *Cambridge and District Co-operative Society Ltd v Ruse* [1993] IRLR 156, EAT (discussed at n 1, para 20.61) where an offer of a job was considered suitable, but the employee's perception of a drop in status made it reasonable for him to refuse it.

[2] *Gotch & Partners v Guest* (1966) 1 ITR 65; *Anglia Regional Co-operative Society v O'Donnell*, EAT 27.05.94 (655/91).

[3] *Carron Co v Robertson* (1967) 2 ITR 484.

[4] *Kykot v Smith Hartley Ltd* [1975] IRLR 372; *Morrison & Poole v Cramic Engineering Co Ltd* (1966) 1 ITR 404.

[5] *Tocher v General Motors Scotland Ltd* [1981] IRLR 55, EAT; *Kennedy v Werneth Ring Mills Ltd* [1977] ICR 206, EAT.

[6] *Bryan v George Wimpey & Co Ltd* (1967) 3 ITR 28; *Roberts v Essoldo Circuit (Control) Ltd* (1967) 2 ITR 351.

[7] *Bainbridge v Westinghouse Brake and Signal Co Ltd* (1966) 1 ITR 55.

[8] *Rose v Shelley & Partners* (1966) 1 ITR 169.

[9] *Williamson v National Coal Board* (1969) 4 ITR 43. It has also been held (predictably) that making a number of insufficiently specific offers is no adequate substitute for a single offer of suitable alternative employment (*Curling v Securicor Ltd* [1992] IRLR 549, EAT).

[10] *G D Systems Ltd v Woods* EAT 26.3.93 C470/91.

20.63 There used to be special provisions about re-employment after a business was transferred. Section 94 of the EP(C)A used to provide that where there was a change in the ownership of a business for the purposes of which an employee was employed similar rules, *mutatis mutandis* to those now contained in s 141 or 138 of the ERA (discussed above), applied. Thus if the new owner made an offer of renewal or re-engagement to the employee prior to the ending of the old contract, s 138 applied *mutatis mutandis* as if the offer had been made by the original owner. If the offer was of employment on the same conditions or otherwise, the offer was suitable and the employee refused it unreasonably, the right to a redundancy payment would be lost. And if the employee accepted the new employment and commenced within four weeks of the termination of the old employment, dismissal by the transferor was deemed not to have taken place and seniority accrued for the purposes of any future claim against the transferee. A trial period also applied.

20.64 These provisions were overtaken by TUPE (discussed in Chapter 8, above). Where there is a transfer of an undertaking, after TUPE, there will be no dismissal by reason of redundancy. In practical terms therefore, s 94 became otiose. However, there was, until the changes effected by TURERA (see Chapter 8, above), some doubt about whether TUPE would apply in all situations of transfers of undertakings. Particularly, TUPE was expressed to apply only to transfers of commercial ventures and not non-commercial ventures. There was a possibility that s 94 would apply to both commercial and non-commercial ventures. Once TUPE included non-commercial ventures within the definition of a transfer of an undertaking, there was no need whatsoever for s 94 and it was repealed by TURERA with effect from 30 August 1993.

5 DEATH OF AN EMPLOYER OR EMPLOYEE

20.65 The death of a party to a contract of personal service might be regarded as a frustrating event at common law. Frustration involves a termination of the contract by operation of law and is not a dismissal.[1] The basic rule is that a redundancy payment only arises following a dismissal. But s 136(5) of the ERA deems the death of the employer to be a dismissal of an employee by reason of redundancy. A redundancy payment is then due. (Section 136(3) also applies to any other termination of the employee's contract by operation of law where this is as a result of an act on the part of the employer or any event affecting an employer. But, in practice, the most common case under this section will be the death of an individual employer (although the dissolution or winding up of an employer – if not otherwise a dismissal – would also be covered).)

[1] On frustration by employer's death, see *Farrow v Wilson* (1869) LR 4 CP 744. For other cases of frustration (albeit affecting an employee) which have caused termination by operation of law see *Marshall v Harland and Wolff Ltd (No 2)* [1972] ICR 97; *Egg Stores (Stamford Hill) Ltd v Leibovici* [1977] ICR 260, [1976] IRLR 376, EAT; *FC Shepherd & Co Ltd v Jerrom* [1986] ICR 802, [1986] IRLR 358, CA; *Notcutt v Universal Equipment Co (London) Ltd* [1986] 3 All ER 582, [1986] ICR 414, CA. A frustrating event affecting an employee is not covered by s 129 (but see para 20.67), so that will cause the contract to end by operation of law with no dismissal at all.

20.66 However, if the employee is taken on by the deceased employer's personal representatives the legal position is covered by s 167 of the ERA which mirrors the operation of ss 134 and 131 (discussed above upon change of employer, but with some differences). Principally, it is permissible for the new employment to commence as late as eight weeks after the ending of the old employment (contrast four weeks in the case of ss 141 and 138 of the ERA) and, second, it is not specifically provided (as a matter of common sense!) that the offer from the personal representatives of the new employment has to be made before the ending of the old contract (contrast ss 141 and 138(1) of the ERA). Subject to those points, rules similar to ss 141 and 138 apply. That is to say, the employee may reject the new employment on the point of offer if it is different from the old and not suitable, or during the trial period of four weeks if it is not suitable or, if suitable, it is reasonable so to do. A redundancy payment is due in the above circumstances but will be lost if the employment was held to be suitable or the rejection or termination unreasonable.

20.67 Certain statutory provisions cover the case of death of an employee. These provisions involve a considerable amount of speculation as to what would have happened had the employee survived. First, if the employer has given notice to an employee to terminate the contract of employment for redundancy and before that notice expires the employee dies, then for the purposes of the redundancy provisions, the contract is deemed to have been duly terminated by the employer by notice expiring on the date of the employee's death.[1] Second, where an employer has given notice to an employee to terminate the contract of employment and has offered to renew the contract of employment or re-engage under a new contract then if the employee dies without having either accepted or refused the offer and the offer has not been withdrawn before his death, the entitlement of the deceased employee's estate to the redundancy payment depends on whether it would have been unreasonable on the part of the employee (had he lived) to have refused the offer.[2] Third, where an employee's contract of employment has been renewed or he has been re-engaged under a new contract of employment and during the trial period the employee dies without having terminated or having given notice to terminate the contract, the entitlement of the employee's estate to a redundancy payment will depend on whether it would have been reasonable for the employee, had he lived, to have terminated the employment during the trial period.[3] Fourth, if an employee gives notice to terminate his employment during the trial period but dies before the expiry of that notice his notice is deemed to have expired upon his death and the entitlement of his estate to a redundancy payment depends on whether it would have been reasonable for the employee, had he lived during the trial period, to have terminated the contract.[4] There are also rules about lay-off and short-time situations and other matters.

[1] ERA, s 176(1), (2).

[2] ERA, s 176(3).
[3] ERA, s 176(4).
[4] ERA, s 176(4).

6 LAY-OFFS AND SHORT-TIME AND REDUNDANCY ENTITLEMENT

20.68 As can be seen from the above, the right to a redundancy payment depends ordinarily upon the employee having been dismissed, either expressly, constructively or through non-renewal of an expired fixed term contract. The ERA provides, however, in s 148, that an employee who is laid off or put on short-time working may in certain circumstances be entitled to a redundancy payment.

20.69 First though, there is, at common law, no right to lay off an employee through lack of work or otherwise unless this is contained in the contract via either an express term or by implication.[1] Therefore, in the absence of an enabling provision in the contract, express or implied, an employer who lays an employee off may be faced with a constructive dismissal claim and if the lay-off is because there is no work for the employee to do, this may give rise to a redundancy payment under the normal rules. Similarly, too, at common law there is no right to put an employee on short-time working unless the contract permits this expressly or by implication[2] and, again, if this happens without an enabling term of the contract the employee may resign and claim constructive dismissal and again if the reason for the short-time working is because there is insufficient work for the employee to do, this should also give rise to a redundancy payment under the normal rules.

[1] *Jones v Harry Sherman Ltd* (1969) 4 ITR 63; *Waine v R Oliver (Plant Hire) Ltd* [1977] IRLR 434, EAT.
[2] *Miller v Hamworthy Engineering Ltd* [1986] ICR 846, [1986] IRLR 461, CA.

20.70 Subject to the discussion at para 20.69, the statutory definition of lay-off is where an employee is employed under a contract on such terms and conditions that his remuneration thereunder depends upon his being provided by the employer with work of the kind which he is employed to do. Such an employee is treated as laid-off during any week in respect of which he is not provided with work and as a result he is not contractually entitled to remuneration.[1]

[1] ERA, s 147(1).

20.71 Short-time working under statute occurs where there is a diminution in the work provided for an employee under the contract and as a result the employee's remuneration for any week is less than half a week's pay.[1]

[1] ERA, s 147(2).

20.72 Redundancy liability on lay-off or short-time occurs under the following extremely complicated rules. First, the employee has to be laid off or kept on short-time for four or more consecutive weeks or a series of six or more weeks (of which not more than three were consecutive) within a period of 13 weeks. Secondly, the employee must serve a notice to his employer of his intention to claim a redundancy payment in respect of the lay-off or short-time. The notice must be in writing and must be given within four weeks of the last of the weeks of lay-off or short-time that the employee seeks to rely upon.[1]

1 ERA, s 148.

20.73 However, an employee is not entitled to a redundancy payment if the employer gives a counter notice under s 149 of the ERA. This notice must be in writing and given within seven days of the service on the employer of the employee's notice of intention to claim. The notice must state that the employer will resist any liability to make a redundancy payment in pursuance of the employee's notice of intention to claim. And it must be established that, on the date of service of the employee's notice of intention to claim, it was reasonably to be expected that the employee, if he continued to be employed by the same employer, would not, later than four weeks after the date of the employee's notice, enter upon a period of employment of not less than 13 weeks during which he would not be laid off or kept on short-time for any week.[1] If, however, during the next four weeks after the date of service of the employee's notice of intention to claim, the employee is laid off or kept on short time for each of those weeks, it is conclusively presumed that it cannot reasonably be expected that the employee will not be laid off or kept on short time for the 13 week period mentioned above.[2] Here if the employer gives a counter notice within seven days after the service of the employee's notice of intention to claim and does not withdraw the counter notice by a subsequent notice in writing to the employee, the employee is not entitled to a redundancy payment except in accordance with a decision of the industrial tribunal.[3]

1 ERA, s 152(1).
2 ERA, s 152(2).
3 ERA, s 149.

20.74 The final additional hurdle that the employee must surmount to be entitled to his redundancy payment in pursuance of his notice of intention to claim is that he must terminate his contract of employment by at least one week's notice whether given before, or after, or at the same time as, the notice of intention to claim, or by such period of minimum notice required to be given by an employee to terminate his contract under his contract of employment if longer.[1] That notice of termination of employment must be given within certain periods in differing circumstances. First, if the employer fails to give a counter notice within seven days after the service of the employee's notice of intention to claim the period is three weeks after the end of those seven days.[2] Second, if the employer has given a counter notice within those seven days but withdraws it by a subsequent notice in writing, the period is three weeks after the service of notice of withdrawal.[3] Third, if the employer does give a counter notice within seven days and does not withdraw it and the question of the employee's right to a redundancy payment in pursuance of the notice of intention to claim is referred to an industrial tribunal, the period is three weeks after the industrial tribunal has notified the employee of its decision about that reference.[4]

[1] ERA, s 150. In *Walmsley v C & R Ferguson Ltd* [1989] IRLR 112 it was held that no particular terms of art are required to indicate the necessary notice of termination of employment. So when an employee, having referred to the fact he had been laid off for the requisite number of weeks, said in writing to the employer '... I am left with no option but to resign and instigate industrial tribunal proceedings against you. I look forward to hearing from you within seven days', the Court of Session held the letter was capable of bearing the meaning that the empoyee had duly served the one week's notice required of him.

[2] ERA, s 150(3)(a).

[3] ERA, s 150(3)(b).

[4] ERA, s 150(3)(c).

20.75 Finally, no account can be taken of any week during which an employee is laid off or kept on short-time working where the lay-off or short-time is wholly or mainly attributable to a strike or a lock-out, whether the strike or lock-out is in the trade or industry in which the employee is employed or not and whether it is in Great Britain or elsewhere.[1]

[1] ERA, s 149. For 'strike' and 'lock-out' see s 235(4) and (5) of the ERA. It is important to note that other forms of industrial action short of a strike, eg a go slow or a work to rule, are not covered and their existence need not be taken into account if the employee is laid off or put on short-time working as a result.

7 STRIKES AND MISCONDUCT

20.76 Subject to the ERA, s 140 (see below), under s 140(1) of the ERA an employee may be disentitled to a redundancy payment where the employer is entitled to terminate the contract of employment by reason of the employee's conduct without notice and the employer actually terminates the contract of employment either without notice; or by giving shorter notice than that which in the absence of such conduct the employer would be required to give to terminate the contract; or by giving full notice which is accompanied by a statement in writing that the employer would by reason of the employee's conduct have been entitled to terminate the contract without notice.[1]

[1] ERA, s 140(1)(a) to (c).

20.77 At first glance, it is hard to see why this provision is included in the legislation at all. For, in effect, it says that if the employer is entitled to dismiss by reason of misconduct (in effect because of a repudiatory breach of contract on the part of the employee) there is no right to a redundancy payment. One would have supposed that such a dismissal was not by reason of redundancy in any event, but a dismissal for conduct, thus raising no question about entitlement to a redundancy payment in the first place. However, it is thought that the section is meant to catch cases where, for example, the employee is dismissed by reason of redundancy but there are also other grounds which would have entitled the employer to dismiss summarily for misconduct where, but for s 140(1), the employee would still be entitled to the redundancy payment because of the presumption of redundancy.[1] It might also apply where the dismissal is by reason of redundancy and the employer is unaware at the time of dismissal that there is misconduct which would have entitled the employer to dismiss without notice on that ground. This will usually not be where the dismissal is with full notice as the employer, being unaware of the misconduct, will not have included the obligatory written statement to the effect that the employer would have been entitled to dismiss with no notice (see above). But it might include a case of a summary dismissal ostensibly on the ground of redundancy which occurs prior to an employer's knowledge of actual misconduct. Thus, in *X v Y Ltd*[2] an employee dismissed summarily by reason of apparent redundancy was disentitled to a redundancy payment because of his employer's subsequent discovery of misconduct which then entitled him to rely upon s 140(1).

1 ERA, s 163(2).
2 *X v Y Ltd* (1969) 4 ITR 204.

20.78 It has been held in *Simmons v Hoover Ltd*[1] that conduct entitling the employer summarily to dismiss for the purposes of s 140(1) includes strike action which (contrary to some previous case law indications) was in that case held to be repudiatory of the contract of employment and therefore misconduct within the terms of the section.[2]

1 [1977] QB 284, [1976] IRLR 266, EAT.
2 There has always been controversy about whether a strike with notice amounts to a breach of contract: *Morgan v Fry* [1968] 2 QB 710, [1968] 3 All ER 452, CA. In *Simmons v Hoover Ltd* [1977] ICR 61 it was suggested that the effect of a strike notice would simply be notice of an intended breach of contract. But it seems the better view is that it depends on the wording of a strike notice; if appropriately worded it could be construed as a lawful notice of termination (*Boxfoldia Ltd v National Graphical Association* [1988] ICR 752, [1988] IRLR 383) in which case there would, of course, be no breach of contract (but a resignation would not entitle the employee to statutory rights).

20.79 There are exceptions to disentitlement to a redundancy payment in the case of misconduct or strike action if the misconduct or strike action occurs during the notice period which follows an earlier dismissal by reason of redundancy. First, under s 140 of the ERA, if an employee has been given notice of dismissal by reason of redundancy but subsequently takes part in a strike and is, for that reason, dismissed with short notice then, if the second dismissal takes place during the obligatory period (see para 20.14) of the employer's notice the strike will not affect entitlement to the redundancy payment.[1] Secondly, if during notice of a dismissal an employee commits an act of misconduct (other than going on strike) and the dismissal occurs during the obligatory period of the employer's notice the employee is prima facie disentitled to the redundancy payment but an industrial tribunal may at its discretion, in so far as it is just and equitable to do so, award all or part of the redundancy payment notwithstanding the misconduct.[2]

1 ERA, s 140(2).
2 ERA, s 140(3), (4).

20.80 It is important that there must be two dismissals for s 140 to apply, the first for redundancy and the second during the notice, the second being on account of strike action, or, alternatively, for misconduct. Thus, in *Simmons v Hoover Ltd*[1] employees went on strike. During this strike the employer sent letters of dismissal giving the employees one week's notice of termination on grounds that it was necessary to reduce the labour force. The employee in question had an entitlement to six weeks' notice of termination of employment and was therefore dismissed with short notice for the purposes of s 140. He claimed a redundancy payment. It was held that the employee was disentitled to a redundancy payment and could not rely upon s 140 which required a second dismissal on account of an ensuing strike. Here there was only one dismissal, ostensibly on ground of redundancy, after the strike had started. Section 140 also applies to cases under s 147, ie to lay-off and short-time working, so that if an employee has served notice of intention to claim a redundancy payment through lay-off or short-time and thereafter is dismissed by reason of strike action, or misconduct, the above provisions apply, *mutatis mutandis*.[2]

1 [1977] QB 284, [1976] IRLR 266, EAT.
2 See *Harvey* Div E3.

20.81 It can be seen from the above that in the case of dismissal subsequent to an original dismissal for redundancy on account of strike or other misconduct, employees dismissed on account of a strike are more favourably treated (ie they have an absolute right to the redundancy payment) than employees dismissed by reason of misconduct (where the payment is discretionary).[1] However, by virtue of s 143 of the ERA, an employer may have some additional redress in practical terms in the case of strikes. Where, during the notice of dismissal by reason of redundancy, the employee begins to take part in the strike, the employer may serve on the employee a notice in writing requesting him to agree to extend the contract of employment beyond the time of expiry of the notice in writing by an additional period comprising the number of days lost by striking. The notice has to indicate the reasons for making the request and has to stress also that unless either the employee complies with the request, or the employer is satisfied that in consequence of sickness, injury or otherwise the employee is unable to comply with it, the employer will contest any liability to pay the redundancy payment in respect of the original dismissal.[2] An employee is taken to comply with the request in the notice of extension if on each available day within the proposed period of extension he attends at work and is ready and willing to work.[3] It is then provided that the notice period is deemed to be extended to the last day on which the employee attends ready and willing to work within the period of extension.[4] If the employee does not comply with the request and does not attend for work during all of the available days during the proposed extension he is disentitled to a redundancy payment unless the employer agrees to make such a payment notwithstanding the failure to comply. However, an industrial tribunal may award part or all of the redundancy payment as seems appropriate if it is considered reasonable for the employee not to have complied with the request.[5]

1 *Lignacite Products Ltd v Krollman* [1979] IRLR 22.
2 ERA, s 143(1) and (2).
3 ERA, s 144(1).
4 ERA, s 143(7) and (8).
5 ERA, s 143(5) and (6).

8 ADMINISTRATIVE PROVISIONS – PUTTING THE CLAIM IN ON TIME – QUANTUM AND OTHER MATTERS

Time limits

20.82 A redundancy payment is not payable unless before the end of six months beginning with the 'relevant date' (see below) either the payment has been agreed and paid; or the employee has made a claim for the payment by notice in writing given to the employer; or a question as to the right of the employee to the payment or as to the amount of the payment has been referred to an industrial tribunal; or an unfair dismissal complaint has been presented by an employee to an industrial tribunal. If the employee fails to ensure any of these steps is taken, but within an additional period of six months, either makes a claim by notice in writing given to the employer; or refers the issue of a redundancy payment to an industrial tribunal; or makes an unfair dismissal complaint; and it appears to the tribunal to be just and equitable that the employee should receive a redundancy payment having regard to the reasons shown by the employee for his failure to take any of the relevant steps within the first six months and to all the other relevant circumstances, then a redundancy payment may be payable nonetheless.[1]

[1] ERA, s 164. It has been held, however, that where there is a dispute about a contractual redundancy payment in respect of civil servants of the type mentioned in what is now s 171(3) of the ERA and where there is a reference to an industrial tribunal under s 170 allowed by the contract of employment, no six month time limit applies. The time limit is the contractual limitation period of six years: *Greenwich Health Authority v Skinner and Ward* [1989] ICR 220, EAT. Presumably, any other claim for a contractual redundancy payment is also governed by the contractual limitation period.

The 'relevant date'

20.83 The 'relevant date' triggers the start of the limitation period for submitting a claim. It fixes the end of employment for the purposes of deciding whether an employee was employed for at least two years before termination (ie whether the employee qualifies to make a claim) and it also fixes the end of employment for the purposes of determining how long the employee's employment lasted when calculating the size of the redundancy payment. Although the question of size of payment is discussed later, the concept of 'relevant date' is discussed here.

20.84 When the employee's contract of employment is terminated by notice, whether given by the employer or by the employee, the relevant date is the date on which the notice expires.[1] When the contract of employment is terminated without notice it is the date on which the termination takes effect.[2] When the employee is employed under a contract for a fixed term and that term expires it is the date on which the term expires.[3]

[1] ERA, s 145(2)(a).
[2] ERA, s 145(2)(b).
[3] ERA, s 145(2)(c).

20.85 In a re-employment case under s 138, where there is a reasonable termination by an employee during a trial period and, as a result, the employee is treated as having been dismissed on the termination of his employment under the previous contract, the relevant date is the relevant date as defined above in relation to the renewed or new contract for the purposes of time limits for putting in a claim for a redundancy payment. But for any other purposes (such as, for example, calculating the length of continuous employment for the purposes of calculating the size of the redundancy payment) the date is the relevant date as defined above in relation to the previous contract.[1]

[1] ERA, s 145(4).

20.86 Where an employee is taken to be dismissed by virtue of s 136(3) (para 20.14) (employee anticipating expiry of employer's notice) the relevant date is the date on which the employee's notice to terminate the contract of employment expires.[1]

[1] ERA, s 145(3).

20.87 In a case where there has been a lay-off or short-time working and an employee puts in a notice of intention to claim a redundancy payment the relevant date in a case falling under s 148(1)(a) (right to put in a notice of intention to claim following lay-off or short-time working for four or more consecutive weeks) is the date on which the last of the four or more consecutive weeks before the service of the notice came to an end. In a case falling within s 148(1)(b) (right to submit a notice of intention to claim as a result of lay-off or short-time working for a series of six or more weeks within a period of 13 weeks) it is the date on which the last series of six or more weeks before the service of the notice came to an end.[1]

[1] ERA, s 153.

20.88 In cases of summary dismissals with or without a payment in lieu of notice s 145(5) allows the relevant date to be postponed by the amount of statutory minimum notice to which the employee was entitled under s 86(1) of the ERA (see Chapter 18, above). However, this is only for limited purposes, that is to say for calculating the two year qualifying period under s 155; for calculating the length of service to arrive at the amount of the redundancy payment (s 162(1)); and for calculating a week's pay to arrive at the redundancy payment amount (s 227(4)), for example to give the employee the benefit of any increase in the amount of a week's pay that can be taken into account that may have occurred between the date of the summary dismissal and the date of the notional expiry of the statutory minimum period of notice (see also Chapter 18, above).

20.89 There is a difference between the rules for redundancy payments and unfair dismissal here. In unfair dismissal, employment can be extended by a period equivalent to statutory notice on a constructive dismissal without notice as well as an employer-initiated dismissal (ERA, s 97(4)). This is not the case under s 145(5).

20.90 Section 86(3) of the ERA says that nothing in s 86 is to be taken as preventing a party from waiving his right to notice or from accepting a payment in lieu. If a payment in lieu is accepted, does this mean that s 145(5) does not apply? The EAT in *Secretary of State for Employment v Staffordshire County Council*[1] held that acceptance of a payment in lieu of notice indeed meant that s 145(5) could not extend the employment to a later 'relevant' date. However, this decision was reversed by the Court of Appeal where it was held that even if a party had waived all or part of his statutory notice or accepted a payment in lieu, s 145(5) still operated to extend the 'relevant date'.[2]

---

1 [1987] ICR 956, [1988] IRLR 3.
2 [1989] ICR 664. See also the discussion on statutory notice in Chapter 18, above.

20.91 Where the employee dies during the period of notice of dismissal the contract is deemed duly terminated by the employer by notice expiring on the employee's death.[1] Where the employee dies after the termination of the contract but before the date on which it ought to have terminated if proper notice under s 86 had been given then, for the purposes of the three cases mentioned in s 145(5) (see above), the relevant date is taken to be the date of death.[2]

---

1 ERA, s 176(1).
2 ERA, s 176(2).

Amount

20.92 The amount of a redundancy payment is calculated under the rules in ERA, s 162. The employee is entitled to one and a half weeks pay for every year during which he was 41 years of age or over. He is entitled to one week's pay for every year during which he was aged 22 years or over but less than 41. And he is entitled to half a week's pay for every year during which he was under 22 and 18 or over. Weeks under 18 years of age do not count. The amount of a week's pay is dealt with in Chapter 16.[1] The maximum amount of a week's pay that can be taken into account is usually altered periodically by statutory instrument and is presently £210.[2] A maximum of 20 years' service worked back from the relevant date can be taken into account for the purposes of calculating the redundancy payment (thus yielding a maximum payment at the time of writing of £6,300). This means that this is the present maximum redundancy payment under statute. The EP(C)A as originally drawn provided that employees who reached the state pensionable age of 65 for men and 60 for women ceased altogether to have the right to a redundancy payment.[3] However, this discrimination was removed by the Employment Act 1989 which provided that where there is a normal retiring age of less than 65 and the age is the same whether the employee holding that position is a man or a woman, a redundancy payment cannot be claimed beyond normal retiring age. In any other case (that is to say, where there is no normal retiring age) a redundancy payment cannot be claimed beyond the age of 65 whether the claimant is a man or a woman.[4] Originally the EP(C)A also provided that a redundancy payment was scaled down monthly by 1/12th per month in the year before employees reached the state pensionable age, that is to say, under the EP(C)A in a man's 64th year and in a woman's 59th year.[5] The discrimination involved here was also removed by the Employment Act 1989 and in a woman's case scaling down does not apply now until her 64th year, as with the case of a man.[6]

[1] And see also *British Coal Corpn v Cheesbrough* [1990] IRLR 148.
[2] The convention until recently has been that the level of a week's pay has been raised annually. At the time of writing, the latest increase was effective from 27 September 1995. The maximum amount of a week's pay rose from £205 to £210, yielding an increase in the maximum payment from £6,150 to £6,300. Prior to this, there had been no increase since 1992.
[3] EP(C)A, s 82(1).
[4] Employment Act 1989, s 16.
[5] See now ERA, s 156.
[6] Employment Act 1989, s 16. See now ERA, s 162(4), (5).

20.93 An employee is entitled to a written statement from an employer indicating how a redundancy payment is calculated unless an industrial tribunal has already fixed the amount of a redundancy payment by a decision of the tribunal.[1] If the employer fails to comply with this obligation without reasonable excuse he commits a criminal offence.[2] Further, the employee may demand a statement if not already supplied with one, giving the employer at least one week to comply therewith. If the employer fails to comply with this request without reasonable excuse he may commit a further criminal offence.[3] If an employer fails to give a written statement or indeed any sort of voluntary statement indicating how the redundancy payment is calculated he runs the risk, in cases where he makes a general ex gratia payment to an employee on termination of employment which exceeds the amount of the statutory payment, of the employee later asserting that it was not intended that the ex gratia payment should include the statutory redundancy payment. This might allow the employee a fresh opportunity to claim a redundancy payment in addition to the ex gratia payment even if, all along, the employer may have intended the ex gratia payment to include the redundancy payment.[4]

[1] ERA, s 165(1).
[2] ERA, s 165(2).
[3] ERA, s 165(3).
[4] *Collin v Flexiform Ltd* (1966) 1 ITR 253; *Galloway v Export Packing Services Ltd* [1975] IRLR 306.

Exclusion or reduction of redundancy payment on account of pension rights

20.94 There are complicated provisions which may allow an employer to reduce or extinguish any redundancy payment entitlement due to accrual by an employee of a pension on or soon after the dismissal by redundancy. It is not proposed here to cover these rules in detail which are dealt with excellently in *Harvey*. However, this brief mention is a reminder that the provisions should always be considered if an employee's pension rights on a redundancy dismissal are triggered thereby.[1]

[1] ERA, s 158; Redundancy Payments Pensions Regulations (SI 1965/1932). *British Telecommunications plc v Burwell* [1986] ICR 35, EAT (but see the discussion on *Burwell* in *Harvey*). In *Royal Ordnance plc v Pilkington* [1988] ICR 606, [1988] IRLR 466, EAT, it was held that where continuity of employment is not broken by a transfer of an undertaking to another, the transferee is, when eventually making an employee redundant, entitled to offset against the redundancy payment not only the value of pension benefits accrued with the transferee, but also with the transferor. The Court of Appeal agreed with this principle but on the facts reversed the EAT because the transferor (Civil Service) pension was payable prior to the time of dismissal so the Regulations did not apply and no offset operated.

The National Insurance Fund, the old Redundancy Fund and the (defunct) Redundancy Rebate

20.95 Until the Employment Act 1989 an employer was, under what was then s 104 of the EP(C)A, entitled to a rebate on redundancy payments paid by him out of what was previously known as the Redundancy Fund. Since 1985 the rate of rebate has been 35%. But the Wages Act 1986 denied the right to claim rebate to employers who had more than nine employees. The Employment Act 1989 abolished the right to rebate altogether.[1]

1 Employment Act 1989, s 17. See the discussion on the effects of this change at para 20.05.

20.96 The Redundancy Fund was replaced by the National Insurance Fund with effect from 1 February 1991.[1] Under s 167 of the ERA, where an employee claims that his employer is liable to pay him a redundancy payment and the employee has either taken all reasonable steps (other than legal proceedings) to recover the payment from the employer and the employer has refused or failed to pay it or has paid part of it and has refused or failed to pay the balance or the employer is insolvent and the whole or part of the payment remains unpaid, then the employee may apply to the Secretary of State for a payment under ERA, s 166.[2] When a payment is made by the Secretary of State to an employee all rights and remedies of an employee in respect of the payment reimbursed by the Secretary of State are transferred to the Secretary of State who may then recover from the employer.[3] Any dispute with the Secretary of State about liability of an employer or the amount of the sum payable may be referred to an industrial tribunal.[4]

1 Employment Act 1990, s 13.
2 Section 166(1), 167(1).
3 ERA, s 170(3).
4 ERA, s 170(2).

B CONSULTATION ON MASS REDUNDANCIES

9 OBLIGATIONS TO INFORM AND CONSULT WORKER REPRESENTATIVES

20.97 TULR(C)A as originally drawn required an employer to inform and consult with representatives of a recognised trade union before implementation of redundancies.[1] These provisions were intended to implement the EEC Council Directive 75/129 of 17 February 1975 (the 'Collective Redundancies Directive').[2] However, a fundamental change in this area has been triggered by the case of *EC Commission v United Kingdom*[3] in which the UK was held to be in breach of the Directive by confining these rights to recognised trade union representatives. The Directive applies to workers' representatives. For reasons explained in detail below the restriction of worker representative to recognised trade union representative was held to be contrary to European law. Amending legislation by virtue of the Collective Redundancies and Transfer of Undertakings (Protection of Employment) (Amendment) Regulations 1995[4] has now been implemented and, while trade unions may still play a part in the consultation process, they no longer enjoy exclusivity and an employer is now required to consult either elected representatives of the employees or representatives of a recognised trade union where it is proposed to dismiss as redundant 20 or more employees at one establishment within a period of 90 days or less. Another important change brought about by

TURERA was to enlarge the definition of redundancy for these provisions alone. Section 195 of TULR(C)A states now:

> 'In this chapter reference to dismissals as redundant are references to dismissal for a reason not related to the individual concerned or for a number of reasons all of which are not so related.'

Previously, the definition for the purposes of TULR(C)A was exactly the same as the definition of redundancy for the purposes of the ERA and individual redundancy payment entitlement (see above). But for the purposes of information and consultation the definition is wider. It is suggested that within s 195 now are any dismissals for an economic or reorganisational reason as well as for traditional redundancy reasons. Dismissals, therefore, to effect change in contracts of employment for economic or organisational reasons clearly fall under s 195, triggering the consultation obligations, even if such reorganisational dismissals would not ordinarily fall under the definition of redundancy in what is now the ERA (see para 20.19). The change to s 195 does not affect the traditional definition of redundancy for redundancy payments liability which remains, as before, limited.

---

1 TULR(C)A, s 188.

2 See Freedland (1976) ILJ 24, for comment.

3 [1994] IRLR 412, ECJ.

4 SI 1995/2587. The regulations came into force on 26 October 1995 but did not apply to dismissals taking effect before 1 March 1996.

The impact of European law on the information/consultation obligations

20.98 It is important to note that the source of the collective obligation to inform/consult is European law, principally Directive 75/129 and also Directive 92/56 which had to be implemented by Member States by 23 June 1994. As with the area of transfer of undertakings (see Chapter 8, above) there was always a long-running controversy about the interaction between UK law and European law in that the provisions of s 188 as originally drawn (formerly in the Employment Protection Act 1975, s 99 onwards) always fell short of what is required in the 1975 Directive.

20.99 On 21 October 1992 the Commission of the European Communities brought infringement proceedings against the UK for breach of Directive 75/129. The complaints were that domestic legislation was in breach by:

(1) failing to provide for the designation of employee representatives where this does not occur voluntarily in practice;
(2) limiting the scope of its legislation designed to implement the Directive to a less wide range of dismissal situations than that foreseen by the Directive;
(3) failing to require an employer who is contemplating collective redundancies to consult workers' representatives with a view to reaching an agreement and in relation to the matters specified in the Directive; and
(4) failing to provide for effective sanctions in the case of failure to consult workers' representatives as required by the Directive.

Some of these matters were addressed by the changes to TULR(C)A made by TURERA (see above and below), but not all. The principal matter outstanding was the failure to provide for effective designation of employee representatives. In *EC Commission v United Kingdom*,[1] in infringement proceedings brought by the EC Commission against the UK for breach of the Directive, all of these complaints were upheld. As mentioned, TURERA had addressed all complaints prior to this ruling save for the worker representative part. As recognition of trade unions in the UK is voluntary, the ECJ ruled there was no effective transposition by the UK of the obligation to make employers consult with worker representatives, if this was confined to consultation with recognised trade union representatives. Amending legislation has therefore followed (see below).

1 [1994] IRLR 412, ECJ.

20.100 As discussed, the disparity between the terms of the Directive and UK law is lessened by TURERA and the Collective Redundancies and Transfer of Undertakings (Protection of Employment) (Amendment) Regulations 1995.[1] But there are even other significant areas of divergence remaining. These include the inclusion of a special circumstances defence to non-consultation in TULR(C)A, whereas this does not appear in the Directive, and a possible difference of interpretation between how soon consultation has to begin, UK law triggering the obligation when a proposal is formed, European law triggering the obligation when redundancies are contemplated (an earlier point in time).[2]

1 SI 1995/2587.
2 See para 20.102 below and n 1.

20.101 Public sector employees can in any event rely upon the Directive direct if employed by the state or an emanation of the state as defined in *Foster v British Gas*[1] at least where the Directive is unconditional and sufficiently precise.[2] Private sector workers may not rely upon the Directive direct. A Directive has a purely vertical effect in this regard. However it is possible for a private sector employee to ask a court or tribunal in the UK to interpret the provisions of TULR(C)A purposively, ie in line with the provisions of the Directive.[3] This is not possible, however, where to do so would be to distort the meaning of the UK legislation, for example where the UK legislation contains express contradictory language.[4] The question of public sector workers' rights became immediate once the ECJ had ruled that the information/consultation requirements of the Directive had been inadequately transposed (and TURERA had failed to deal with the issue).[5] However, in *Griffin v SouthWest Water Services Ltd*[6] the High Court held that the information/consultation provisions were not unconditional and sufficiently precise so as to be horizontally effective as above discussed.

1 [1990] IRLR 353, ECJ, [1991] IRLR 268, HL. See also *Doughty v Rolls-Royce plc* [1992] IRLR 126, CA.
2 *Van Duyn v Home Office (No 2)* [1974] ECR 1337, ECJ; *Becker v Finanzamt Münster-Innenstadt* [1982] 1 CMLR 499, ECJ.
3 *Pickstone v Freemans plc* [1990] ICR 697, HL; *Litster v Forth Dry Dock & Engineering Co Ltd* [1989] IRLR 161, HL.
4 *Duke v GEC Reliance Ltd* [1988] ICR 339, HL; *Finnegan v Clowney Youth Training Programme Ltd* [1990] ICR 462, HL; *Wren v Eastbourne Borough Council* [1993] IRLR 425, EAT.
5 *EC Commission v United Kingdom* [1994] IRLR 412, ECJ.
6 High Court, [1995] IRLR 15.

20.102 Under s 188 of TULR(C)A as amended an employer proposing[1] to dismiss as redundant 20 or more employees at one establishment within a period of 90 days or less must consult about the dismissals with the appropriate representatives of any of the employees affected. For the purposes of s 188, the appropriate representatives of the affected employees are employee representatives elected by the affected employees or, if the employees are of a description in respect of which an independent trade union is recognised by the employer, representatives of the trade union.[2] In the case of employees who both elect employee representatives and are represented by a recognised trade union, the employer may choose whether to consult with the elected employee representatives or representatives of the trade union. However, if either there is no recognised trade union or if there are workers of a description not covered by a recognised agreement, he *must* invite employees to elect employee representatives.

---

1 Proposal to dismiss means something approaching a decision to dismiss. This narrow view of 'proposal' means that consultation does not have to begin until a fairly advanced stage of the exercise; see *Harvey* III [1366]. See also *National and Local Government Officers' Association v National Travel (Midlands) Ltd* [1978] ICR 598, EAT; *Association of Patternmakers and Allied Craftsmen v Kirvin Ltd* [1978] IRLR 318, EAT; *National Union of Public Employees v General Cleaning Contractors* [1976] IRLR 362; *Union of Shop, Distributive and Allied Workers v Leancut Bacon Ltd* [1981] IRLR 295, EAT. The EC 'Collective Redundancies' Directive 75/129, which s 188 implements, refers to a duty to consult employee representatives arising when collective redundancies are *contemplated* (Art 2). This contrasts with the duty to inform the public authorities of *projected* redundancies (Art 3). A view taken in the European Court in *Dansk Metalarbejderforbund and Spenialarbejderforbund i Danmark v Neilson & MaskinFabrik A/S (in liquidation)*: 284/83 [1986] 1 CMLR 91 seems to indicate the duty under Art 2 arises at an earlier stage than it has been interpreted as arising in domestic law under s 188 because it arises when redundancies are contemplated. The EAT in *Hough v Leyland DAF Ltd* [1991] IRLR 194 concluded that there was no conflict between UK law and European law on this point. Similarly, in *Re Hartlebury Printers Ltd (in liquidation)* [1993] IRLR 516 the High Court held that since 'proposed' equates to 'having in view or expecting', 'contemplating' in Art 2(1) of the Directive can be construed in a sense equivalent to 'proposing'. Therefore, in the opinion of Morritt J s 99 of the EPA 1975 (as it then was) *could* be assumed to comply with the UK's obligations under the Directive. However the Court of Appeal in *R v British Coal Corpn and Secretary of State for Industry, ex p Vardy* [1993] IRLR 104, ruled that there was a difference between the UK legislation and the Directive. However, because of the clear divergence in wording between UK law and European law, it was not possible to give effect to the wider European wording. Although the courts are supposed to interpret domestic legislation in line with European legislation whenever possible (*Pickstone v Freemans plc* [1989] AC 66, CA; *Litster v Forth Dry Dock & Engineering Co Ltd* [1989] 1 All ER 1134, HL) it is not possible to do so in the light of clear contradictory wording (see *Webb v EMO Air Cargo Ltd* [1993] IRLR 27, HL). Cf however the contrasting approach in *Griffin v SouthWest Water Services Ltd*, for the question of when consultation must begin.

2 TULR(C)A, s 188(1B).

Employee representatives

20.102A Under s 188 of TULR(C)A as amended, the employer may choose whether to consult representatives of recognised trade unions or elected employee representatives. An employer who recognises a trade union for collective bargaining purposes is not therefore obliged to consult with it about collective redundancies and may instead opt to consult elected employee representatives. Where an employer does recognise a trade union and chooses to consult with it, the employer must in addition still consult with employee representatives elected by employees who are not of a description covered by the recognition agreement.[1] An employer who does not recognise any trade unions for collective bargaining purposes can, of course, only consult through elected employee representatives. However, TULR(C)A contains no guidance on the matters to be considered by the employer when inviting the election of employee representatives. The representatives must, however, be employees of the company.[2] The employer is not required to elect permanent or standing representatives and the employer need only invite employees to elect representatives on an ad hoc basis as and when the employer proposes to declare 20 or more redundancies. TULR(C)A does not specify any method of election nor does it specify how many representatives must be elected. However, the employer can consult via existing consultative machinery, the members of which have been elected by employees (whether before or after dismissals have been proposed by the employer) otherwise than for the specific purpose of consultation, provided that it is appropriate for the employer to consult with them about the dismissals having regard to the purpose for which they were originally elected. Hence, employee bodies such as staff committees or Works Councils may be consulted by the employer provided that the body has an elected membership covering the affected employees and has consultation on dismissals as one of its roles.[3] Employee representatives must be afforded access to the employees whom it is proposed to dismiss, together with such other accommodation and facilities as may be appropriate.[4]

---

1 The question of whether non-members of a trade union are employees of a description in respect of which a trade union is recognised by the employer has been addressed by the Court of Appeal in Northern Ireland in the case of *Northern Ireland Hotel and Catering College (Governing Body) and North Eastern Education and Library Board v National Association of Teachers in Further and Higher Education* [1995] IRLR 83. The Court decided that the statutory obligation on an employer to consult a trade union (in accordance with Article 49(1) of the Industrial Relations (Northern Ireland) Order 1976) relates to an employee of a description or category in respect of which the union is recognised, whether or not that employee is a member of that particular union. On the facts, the respondent union was recognised by the employers in respect of the relevant category of employees, in this case college lecturers, and the Court held that the union should have been consulted with regard to the proposed redundancies of two lecturers who were not members of the respondent union. The union should have been consulted because it was recognised by the employers in respect of employees 'of a description' whom it proposed to dismiss, ie college lecturers (cf *Makro Self Service Wholesalers Ltd v Union Shop, Distributive and Allied Workers* EAT, 25.07.94 (828/93) in which the EAT held that the insertion into a staff handbook of a clause about trade union membership did not amount to an extension of the recognition agreement to cover managerial staff).

2 TULR(C)A, s 196(1).

3 TULR(C)A, s 196(1).

4 TULR(C)A, s 188(5A).

20.103 Consultation has to begin in good time[1] and in any event within a minimum specified period. Thus if the employer proposes to dismiss as redundant 100 or more employees at one establishment within a period of 90 days or less the consultation period must begin at least 90 days before the first of those dismissals takes effect. Where an employer proposes to dismiss as redundant 20 or more employees at one establishment within a period of 90 days or less the period of consultation must commence at least 30 days before the first of those dismissals takes effect.[2]

---

1 Previously consultation had to begin at the earliest opportunity. The Government took the opportunity, when enacting the Collective Redundancies and Transfer of Undertakings (Protection of Employment) (Amendment) Regulations 1995, to substitute 'in good time', the actual words used by the Collective Redundancies Directive.

2 TULR(C)A, s 188(1A). In *R v British Coal Corpn and Secretary of State for Trade and Industry, ex p Price* [1994] IRLR 72 (a non-TULR(C)A case) the divisional court gave guidance on

the nature of fair consultation generally. This was a case arising out of the closure of a large number of collieries. The Secretary of State had promised that closures would not take place until after consultation had been completed. The NUM brought an action for judicial review challenging whether adequate consultation had taken place. The court concluded that it had but went on to give valuable guidance as to the nature of fair consultation generally. In the words of Glidewell LJ:

> 'It is axiomatic that the process of consultation is not one in which the consultor is obliged to adopt any or all of the views expressed by the person or body whom he is consulting. I would respectfully adopt the tests as proposed by Hodgson J in *R v Gwent County Council, ex p Bryant* reported, as far as I know, only at [1988] COD 19, when he said:
>
> "Fair consultation means:
>
> (a) consultation when the proposals are still at a formative stage;
> (b) adequate information on which to respond;
> (c) adequate time in which to respond;
> (d) conscientious consideration by an authority of the response to consultation".
>
> Another way of putting the point more shortly is that a fair consultation involves giving the body consulted a fair and proper opportunity to understand fully the matters about which it is being consulted and to express its views on those subjects, with the consultor thereafter considering those views properly and genuinely.'

See now however the specific change to the concept of consultation in the context of TULR(C)A, in requiring consultation *with a view to reaching agreement* (discussed below).

20.104 For the purposes of consultation required by TULR(C)A the employer has to disclose in writing to appropriate representatives the following information:

(1) the reason for his proposals;
(2) the numbers and descriptions of employees whom it is proposed to dismiss as redundant;
(3) the total number of employees of any such description employed by the employer at the establishment in question;
(4) the proposed method of selecting the employees who may be dismissed;
(5) the proposed method of carrying out the dismissals with due regard to any agreed procedure including the period over which the dismissals are to take effect; and
(6) the proposed method of calculating the amount of any redundancy payments to be made (otherwise than in compliance with an obligation imposed by or by virtue of any enactment) to employees who may be dismissed.[1]

This information has to be given to each of the appropriate representatives by delivery to them or sent by post to an address notified by them to the employer or, in the case of representatives of a trade union, sent by post to the union at the address of its head or main office.[2]

---

1 TULR(C)A, s 188(4) as amended by s 33 of TURERA.

2 Section 188(5). In *National and Local Government Officers' Association v London Borough of Bromley* EAT 11.1.93 (671/91), *IDS Brief* 497/July 1993 p 15, it was argued by the union that consultation did not begin until the information had reached the relevant official, notwithstanding that it had hitherto been delivered to a person at the union's offices. This was rejected by the EAT which held that delivery to a person at the offices with apparent authority to receive was enough. The question of whether information is adequate to enable proper consultation to begin is a question of fact (*Spillers-French (Holdings) Ltd v Union of Shop, Distributive and Allied Workers* [1979] IRLR 339, EAT). In *GEC Ferranti Defence Systems Ltd v MSF* [1993] IRLR 101, EAT and *MSF v GEC Ferranti (Defence Systems) Ltd (No 2)* [1994] IRLR 113, EAT it was held, on the facts, that the information requirement was not satisfied by the employer giving to the union a copy of form HRI (notification to the Department of Employment, see para 20.118) and thus it was doubtful whether meaningful consultation could begin.

20.105 It is important to note that the provisions of TURERA considerably improved the consultation obligations. This was to require conformity with European law. For example, previously, s 188(6) only required the employer during the course of consultation to consider any representations made by the union and to reply to those representations and, if he rejected any of those representations, to state the reasons. This was replaced by TURERA and the requirement during the course of consultation is now to be consultation about ways of:

(1) avoiding dismissals;
(2) reducing the number of employees to be dismissed; and
(3) mitigating the consequencs of the dismissals.[1]

Furthermore, to underpin this, s 188 provides that consultation has to be 'undertaken by the employer with a view to reaching agreement with the appropriate representatives'. Again this was inserted by TURERA (as amended by the 1995 Regulations) to make TULR(C)A comply with the terms of the Directive which always did require an employer to consult with a view to reaching an agreement.

[1] TULR(C)A, s 188(2).

20.106 If there are 'special circumstances' which render it not reasonably practicable for the employer to comply with any of the requirements of suppy of information and consultation the employer has to take all such steps towards compliance with that requirement as are reasonably practicable in the circumstances. It is for the employer to prove in any tribunal proceedings complaining of infringements of the section that there were such 'special circumstances' which rendered it not reasonably practicable for him to comply with any requirement of s 188, and, also, that he took all such steps towards compliance with that requirement as were reasonably practicable in these circumstances. If the industrial tribunal is satisfied that there were special circumstances and that steps as described above were taken it may find there was no infringement of the provisions by the employer. But special circumstances are not easy to establish and it should not be assumed that this defence will easily be satisfied.[1] Where the employer has invited the election of employee representatives, and the invitation was issued long enough before the time when consultation is required to begin, the employer is treated as complying with the requirements if he begins consultation as soon as is reasonably practicable after the election of representatives.[2]

[1] TULR(C)A, s 188(7). See *Clarkes of Hove v Bakers' Union* [1978] ICR 1076, CA and the discussion at para 20.115.
[2] TULR(C)A, s 188(7A).

20.107 In one sense the 'special circumstances' defence is controversial: it has no parallel in the Directive and, therefore, arguably for this reason, s 188 is in breach of the Directive. One change here has however been made by TURERA in compliance with Directive 92/56. It is provided that where the decision leading to the proposed dismissal is that of a person controlling the employer (directly or indirectly), failure on the part of that person to provide information to the employer shall not constitute special circumstances rendering it not reasonably practicable for the employer to comply with such a requirement.

20.108 In the event of infringement of the consultation and information obligations a complaint may be presented to an industrial tribunal. Where the employer has failed to consult employee representatives, any of the employee representatives to whom the failure related may present a complaint. Similarly, the appropriate trade union may present a complaint in the case of a failure relating to trade union representatives. However, in any other case, any of the employees who have been or may be dismissed as redundant are entitled to bring a claim.[1] If the complaint is well founded the tribunal makes a declaration to that effect and it may also make a protective award.[2] This is an award covering such employees as may be specified in the award being employees who have been dismissed or whom it is proposed to dismiss as redundant and in respect of whose dismissal or proposed dismissal the employer has failed to comply with s 188.[3] It is an order for a payment of remuneration to these employees for a protected period.[4] The protected period is a period not exceeding 90 days in a case where the minimum period of consultation was to be 90 days and 30 days where the minimum period of consultation was to be 30 days.[5] These are maxima and it is possible that a smaller (or nil) award may be made by the tribunal even though the employer has breached the provisions. This will depend on what the tribunal determines to be just and equitable in all the circumstances having regard to the seriousness of the employer's default in complying with the requirements of the provisions.[6] Thus, in *Sovereign Distribution Services Ltd v Transport and General Workers' Union*[7] it was stressed that the purpose of s 188 was to ensure consultation took place even where an employer thought it would serve no purpose. So where an employer sent out dismissal notices on the same day redundancies were first notified and where no written information was given pursuant to s 188, a significant award was made.

---

[1] TULR(C)A, s 189(1).
[2] TULR(C)A, s 189(2).
[3] TULR(C)A, s 189(3).
[4] TULR(C)A, s 189(4).
[5] TULR(C)A, s 189(4).
[6] TULR(C)A, s 189(4)(b). For a full discussion on the considerations to be taken into account, on the issue of what is 'just and equitable', see *Harvey* Div E 16.
[7] [1990] ICR 31, EAT.

20.109 There has been some confusion as to when the protected period (and hence payment under the award) commences.[1] The better view seems to be that it commences on the date on which the first dismissal to which the complaint related was proposed to take effect, not when it actually occurred or, in the case of proposed dismissals that have not yet been implemented, the date of the industrial tribunal award.[2]

---

[1] *E Green & Sons (Castings) Ltd v Association of Scientific, Technical and Managerial Staffs* [1984] ICR 352, [1984] IRLR 135, EAT. Compare *GKN Sankey Ltd v National Society of Metal Mechanics* [1980] ICR 148, [1980] IRLR 8, EAT. See also *General and Municipal Workers' Union (Managerial, Administrative, Technical and Supervisory Association Section) v British Uralite* [1979] IRLR 413; *National Union of Teachers v Avon County Council* [1978] ICR 626, [1978] IRLR 55, EAT; *Transport and General Workers' Union v RA Litster & Co Ltd* (1986) IRLIB 21 May 1989, p 11, EAT.
[2] *Harvey* Div E 16; *Transport and General Workers' Union v Ledbury Preserves (1928) Ltd* [1986] ICR 855, [1985] IRLR 492, EAT, preferring *E Green & Sons (Castings) Ltd v Association of Scientific, Technical and Managerial Staffs* over *GKN Sankey Ltd v National Society of Metal*

Mechanics. However, this is a matter of some controversy and there are arguments in favour of the commencement date being after the first dismissal actually took place; *Harvey* Div E 16.

20.110 Under s 190 of TULR(C)A, if the industrial tribunal has made a protective award under s 189 the employee included in the description of employees to which the award relates is then entitled to be paid remuneration by the employer for the protected period as specified in the award.[1] The rate of remuneration payable under the award is a week's pay (see Chapter 16, above) for each week of the protected period and, if remuneration has to be calculated for less than one week, the amount of a week's pay is reduced proportionately.[2] It used to be the case that an employer could reduce his liability under the protective award by setting off any payments made to an employee under his contract of employment or by way of damages for breach of that contract in respect of the period falling within the protected period. In other words, for example, he could set off wages or a payment in lieu of notice. One of the complaints of the EC Commission about our implementation of the Directive was the failure to provide an adequate remedy. Under the principle in *Von Colson and Kamann v Land Nordrhein-Westfalen*[1] a remedy must be effective. TURERA therefore abolished the right of the employer to set off payments under the contract or damages for breach of contract falling under the protected period and s 190(3) of TULR(C)A was therefore repealed.

---

1 [1984] ECR 1891, ECJ. After *Marshall v South West Hampshire Area Health Authority (No 2)* [1993] IRLR 445, ECJ it remains to be seen whether the provisions of TULR(C)A, retaining as they do an overall cap on compensation, are in compliance with European law. This point was not specifically addressed by the European Court in *EC Commission v United Kingdom* [1994] IRLR 412, ECJ (see above).

20.111 There are provisions for reduction of the protective award. For example, an employee ceases to be entitled to remuneration under the award when he is fairly dismissed by his employer during the period of the protective award for a reason other than redundancy,[1] or in a case where the employee unreasonably terminates his contract of employment over this period.[2] Also, in dismissal cases, the employer may make the employee an offer before the ending of his employment under the old contract to renew his contract or to re-engage under a new contract so that the renewal or re-engagement will take effect before or during the protected period. If the terms and conditions of the new contract do not differ from the old contract or, if they do, the offer constitutes an offer of suitable employment in relation to the employee,[3] then, if the employee unreasonably refuses the offer, he is not entitled to any remuneration under a protective award in respect of any period during which, but for the refusal, he would have been employed. This latter point is subject to the enjoyment of a trial period on the part of the employee and the provisions concerning the trial period here mirror the provisions concerning a trial period in the redundancy payments provisions of the ERA (see above).[4]

---

1 TULR(C)A, s 191(1)(a).
2 TULR(C)A, s 191(1)(b).
3 TULR(C)A, s 191(2).
4 TULR(C)A, s 191(3)–(7).

20.112 An employee who is not paid remuneration under a protective award may complain to an industrial tribunal. If successful he is entitled to an order that the employer pays him the amount of remuneration which the industrial tribunal finds is due under the award.[1]

[1] TULR(C)A, s 192.

The concept of 'establishment'

20.113 Information and consultation under TULR(C)A has to take place in respect of redundancies proposed at the same establishment. What is an 'establishment' seems to be a question of fact for the industrial tribunal. Until recently (see below) guidance included the view that an establishment must denote some degree of permanence perhaps of buildings, administration, centralisation of records and tools and equipment.[1] However, for the first time, the European Court has looked at the concept of 'establishment' for the purposes of Directive 75/129. Therefore 'establishment' for the purposes of TULR(C)A must be considered in the same way. In *Rockfon A/S Specialarbejderforbundet i Danmark*[2] the facts were that Rockfon is part of the multi-national group Rockwool International which comprises, in total, four companies. The group has a centralised personnel department in a company called Rockwool A/S.

[1] See *Barley v Amey Roadstone Corpn Lrd* [1977] ICR 546, [1977] IRLR 299, EAT; *Barratt Developments (Bradford) v Union of Construction, Allied Trades and Technicians* [1978] ICR 319, [1977] IRLR 403, EAT; *Clarkes of Hove Ltd v Bakers' Union* [1979] 1 All ER 152, [1978] ICR 1076, CA; *Harvey* Div E; *E Green & Sons (Castings) Ltd v Association of Scientific, Technical and Managerial Staffs* [1984] ICR 352, [1984] IRLR 135, EAT.

[2] [1996] IRLR 168.

20.113A Rockfon dismissed 24 workers out of its workforce of 162. For determining when the consultation provisions were triggered, Denmark adopted the scheme in the Directive which provided that if dismissals occurred over a period of 30 days (as was the case in Rockfon) consultation provisions applied where workers to be dismissed were:

— At least 10 in establishments normally employing more than 20 and less than 100 workers.
— At least 10% of the number of workers in establishments normally employing at least 100 but less than 300 workers.
— At least 30 in establishments normally employing 300 workers or more.

20.113B If Rockfon A/S was itself an establishment clearly, the consultation provisions were triggered because the redundancies exceeded 10%. Rockfon contended however that it was the Rockwool *group* which constituted the establishment and, since the group employed more than 300 workers, consultation would only have been required if in excess of *30* workers were to be dismissed.

Danish law defines an establishment as a unit which, inter alia, has a management and which can independently effect large scale dismissals. The district court held that Rockfon was an establishment because the joint personnel department had only a consultative role and Rockfon itself had the power to carry out dismissals. The matter was referred to the European Court. The European Court held that Article 1(1)(a) of the Directive did not preclude two or more interrclated undertakings in a group neither or none of which has a decisive inference over the other or others from establishing a joint recruitment and dismissal department so that dismissals on ground of redundancy in one of the undertakings could take place only with that department's approval. For 'establishment' for the purposes of the Collective Redundancies Directive must be understood as designating the unit to which the workers made redundant are 'assigned' to carry out their duties. It was not necessary to construe establishment as meaning a unit endowed with a management which could independently effect collective redundancies. That would be incompatible with the aim of the Directive because it would allow companies belonging to the same group to try and make it more difficult for the Directive to apply to them by conferring the power to take decisions concerning redundancies on a separate decision making body.

20.113C By analogy with the law on whether an employee is employed in an undertaking for the purposes of the Acquired Rights Directive 77/187 the European Court held:

> 'An employment relationship is essentially characterised by the link existing between the employee and the part of the undertaking or business to which he is assigned to carry out his duties. Therefore "establishment" in Article 1(1)(a) must be interpreted as meaning "depending on the circumstances" the unit to which the workers made redundant are assigned to carry out their duties'.

20.113D In the UK, the Employment Protection Act 1975, s 99, subsequently consolidated into s 188 of the Trade Union and Labour Relations (Consolidation) Act 1992 provided for minimum periods of consultation, of 30 days where between 10 and 100 workers were to be made redundant in any establishment and 90 days where the numbers in any establishment were 100 or more. However, s 188, as originally drawn, provided for consultation where even a *single* redundancy were to be effected in any establishment. The Collective Redundancies and Transfer of Undertakings (Protection of Employment) (Amendment) Regulations 1991 altered the redundancy consultation regime in s 188 by raising the minimum threshold for redundancies to 20 or more redundancies in any period of 90 days. Therefore, the effect of the *Rockfon* decision, although well intentioned, is to make it more difficult for worker representatives to establish that consultation requirements should be triggered. If 'establishment' is to be defined narrowly as a unit to which the employee is 'assigned' this is likely to be much smaller in practice than an establishment as previously interpreted by UK tribunals and courts. The irony of *Rockfon* then is that while the decision may be helpful in member states which use a percentage test for employee thresholds triggering consultation, it rebounds to the disadvantage of employees in the UK, and will assist employers in some cases especially as the 1995 Regulations have lifted the threshold for establishments to a minimum of 20 employees.

20.113E Finally, the provisions of the Act apply only to one employer. So, if a number of associated employers genuinely operate at the same establishment, each separate employer's redundancy programme has to be considered separately and the number of redundancies proposed as a whole by separate (even though associated) employers at this establishment cannot be aggregated for the purpose of enlarging the consultation period.[1]

---

[1] *Transport and General Workers' Union v Nationwide Haulage Ltd* [1978] IRLR 143, IT; *Harvey* Div E.

20.114 An employer might be tempted artificially to stagger his redundancy programme in order that he might implement redundancies in small consecutive groups thus in each case attracting less onerous information and consultation periods in respect of each group of dismissals. It is submitted that if this is plainly a sham the industrial tribunal could look behind this arrangement and decide that the redundancy programme was connected. But the statutory scheme is regrettably not entirely safe from possible abuse by unscrupulous employers and from dubious fragmentation exercises.

'Special circumstances'

20.115 As has already been discussed, there is a 'special circumstances' defence for the employer. It is unwise to generalise about the sort of facts which might give rise to special circumstances such as insolvency (eg receivership), sudden reduction of the order book and so forth. The circumstances must be special in each case. In other words either an insolvency or perhaps a sudden falling off of orders might be a special circumstance in one case but not in another. A case commonly cited to illustrate the narrowness of the special circumstances defence is *Clarkes of Hove Ltd v Bakers' Union*.[1] In that case the company had been in financial difficulty for some time and had long been seeking assistance. Eventually all avenues proved to be impossible and, meanwhile, the company underwent serious losses. It was decided that the company should cease trading immediately and 300 employees were summarily dismissed. A receiver was appointed very shortly thereafter. It was held that while it was not reasonably practicable to comply fully with the information and consultation provisions since the proposal to dismiss and the actual dismissals were simultaneous there were no special circumstances absolving the company totally from the duty to inform and consult. In the view of the industrial tribunal special circumstances were 'something out of the ordinary run of events'.[2] These might include, according to the industrial tribunal, the destruction of the plant, a general trading boycott or a sudden withdrawal of supplies from the main supplier.[3] The industrial tribunal decided that insolvency of itself was not a special circumstance. This decision was approved by the Court of Appeal and has considerable weight.[4] This principle is underpinned by two more recent cases. In *Re Hartlebury Printers Ltd (in liquidation)*[5] it was held that there was no principle that s 188 does not apply to a case where the employer is a company in administration and the administrator proposes the dismissals. In addition, an administration order does not of itself render it impracticable for an employer to comply with the consultation requirements. Therefore that a company is in administration is not of itself a 'special circumstance' within the meaning of s 188(8) rendering it not reasonably practicable for the employer to comply with those consultation requirements. Further, in *GMB v Rankin and Harrison*[6] it was held that the shedding of employees in order to make a sale of a business more attractive (the company was in receivership) is not something special to a particular case but is a common fact in any form of receivership or insolvency. Similarly that the business could not be sold and that there were no orders are again common features of insolvencies and not special circumstances. However, exceptionally, if there is a genuine uncertainty as to whether, for example, the employer might lose a vital contract, or when a contract might end and so there is a genuine difficulty in predicting when redundancies might have to be proposed, this could amount to special circumstances if inaction over the period of uncertainty postponed the start of consultation and thereby caused a breach of TULR(C)A.[7] We have already noted (at para 20.107) one modification to the availability of the special circumstances defence made by TURERA.

[1] [1979] 1 All ER 152, [1978] ICR 1076, CA.
[2] Ibid.
[3] Ibid.
[4] Further illustrations of the courts' approach can be found in *Association of Pattern Makers and Allied Craftsmen v Kirvin Ltd* [1978] IRLR 318, EAT; *Union of Shop, Distributive and Allied Workers v Leancut Bacon Ltd* [1981] IRLR 295, EAT; *Armour v Association of Scientific, Technical and Managerial Staffs* [1979] IRLR 24, EAT.
[5] [1992] IRLR 516.
[6] [1992] IRLR 514, EAT.
[7] See the circumstances in *Hartlebury Printers Ltd (in liquidation)* [1993] IRLR 516. See also *Union of Textile Workers v FA Morris Ltd (in liquidation)* EAT 484/91.

'Recognition'

20.116 As stated, the rights under s 188 as amended apply both to elected employee representatives and recognised independent trade unions as the case may be. The question of recognition is therefore still relevant. Recognition can arise in several ways. It can arise from a collective agreement (but in that case it does not of course matter whether the agreement itself is legally enforceable).[1] It can arise informally and it can even be implied from a previous course of dealing.[2] According to the cases the question is a mixed one of fact and law.[3]

[1] *Amalgamated Society of Boiler Makers, Shipwrights, Blacksmiths and Structural Workers v George Wimpey & Co Ltd* [1977] IRLR 95, EAT.
[2] *National Union of Gold, Silver and Allied Trades v Albery Bros Ltd* [1978] ICR 62, [1977] IRLR 173; affd [1979] ICR 84, [1978] IRLR 504, CA.
[3] *National Union of Tailors and Garment Workers v Charles Ingram & Co Ltd* [1978] 1 All ER 1271, [1977] ICR 530, EAT; cf *Transport and General Workers' Union v Dyer* [1977] IRLR 93, EAT.

20.117 Recognition has to be recognition 'for the purpose of collective bargaining', ie in relation to one or more of the matters specified in s 244 of TULR(C)A.[1] It has been held that for the purposes of recognition this must be recognition of negotiating rights as opposed to merely representational or consultation rights. However, it seems that the grant of partial negotiation rights to a trade union would be sufficient to count as recognition.[2] Recognition has to be 'to any extent' and therefore if there is a partial recognition covering say one or two only of the matters set out in s 244 this will count for the purposes of the rights to consultation and notification over redundancies.

[1] TULR(C)A, s 178(3).
[2] *National Union of Gold, Silver and Allied Trades v Albery Bros Ltd* [1978] ICR 62, [1977] IRLR 173; affd [1979] ICR 84, [1978] IRLR 504, CA (on different grounds).

Notification to the Department of Trade and Industry

20.118 Until 1984, an employer intending to dismiss any employee by reason of redundancy had to give advance information of that dismissal to the Department of Employment under the Redundancy Rebate Regulations. The Redundancy Rebate Regulations 1984[1] then abolished that requirement and thereafter the sole advance notification provisions to a government department[2] are presently those under s 193 of TULR(C)A.

[1] SI 1984/1066.
[2] Following the abolition of the Department of Employment on 5 July 1996 the employer is now obliged to notify the Department of Trade and Industry.

20.119 Under s 193 of TULR(C)A as amended the duty to notify the Department arises where 100 or more employees are to be made redundant within a period of 90 days or less or where 20 or more employees at one establishment are to be made redundant within such a period. The period of notification to the Department is respectively 90 days and 30 days.[1] A copy of the notice under s 193 of TULR(C)A has to be given to the appropriate representatives.[2] A special circumstances defence similar to that under s 188 may apply.[3] If there is default under the section it is provided by the EPA that the Department of Employment may take criminal proceedings.[4] The duty to notify under s 193 applies *whether or not* the employer has recognised any trade union and *whether or not* there are other employee representatives.

1 TULR(C)A, s 193(1), (2).
2 TULR(C)A, s 193(6).
3 TULR(C)A, s 193(7) (as amended by TURERA).
4 TULR(C)A, s 194.

Inter-relationship between collective obligations to inform and consult and liability to individual employees for unfair dismissal

20.120 The reader is referred to Chapter 19, above, on unfair dismissal. It is stressed that failure to inform and consult with employees or their representatives may, in the case of redundancy dismissals, result in unfair dismissal liability.[1]

1 *Polkey v A E Dayton Services Ltd* [1988] AC 344, [1987] ICR 142, HL; *Williams v Compair Maxam Ltd* [1982] ICR 156, [1982] IRLR 83, EAT; *Holden v Bradville Ltd* [1985] IRLR 483, EAT; *Graham v ABF Ltd* [1986] IRLR 90, EAT; *Lafferty Construction Ltd v Duthie* [1985] IRLR 487; *Huddersfield Parcels Ltd v Sykes* [1981] IRLR 115, EAT; *Grundy (Teddington) Ltd v Plummer* [1983] ICR 367, [1983] IRLR 98, EAT. *Dyke v Hereford and Worcester County Council* [1989] ICR 800, EAT; *Pink v White and White Co (Earls Barton) Ltd* [1985] IRLR 489, EAT; *Walls Meat Co Ltd v Selby* [1989] ICR 601, CA.

C MISCELLANEOUS

10 TIME OFF DURING NOTICE OF REDUNDANCY TO LOOK FOR OTHER WORK

20.121 Under s 52(1) of the ERA an employee who has two years service (including the length of his notice or statutory notice under s 86(1)) who has been given notice of redundancy may be entitled to reasonable time off to look for new employment or to make arrangements for training and future employment. During such time off he is entitled to be paid the amount of a week's pay divided by the number of normal hours in a week times the number of hours taken.[1]

1 For the definition of a 'week's pay' see Chapter 16, above.

20.122 Complaint that an employee has been unreasonably refused the time off is made to an industrial tribunal which may make an award limited to two-fifths of a week's pay. This subject is also dealt with elsewhere, in more detail, in Chapter 14, above.[1]

1 See *Dutton v Hawker Siddeley Aviation Ltd* [1978] IRLR 390, EAT.

PART IV
EQUAL PAY AND DISCRIMINATION

21 Discrimination – the EU dimension

Brian Napier

1 INTRODUCTION

21.01 The present domestic law concerned with the promotion of equality between the sexes and the elimination of racial discrimination in employment matters is mainly contained in four statutes: the Equal Pay Act 1970, the Sex Discrimination Act 1975, the Race Relations Act 1976 and the Sex Discrimination Act 1986 (all as amended).[1] Discrimination on grounds of sex is contrary to various standards which have been promulgated over the years by many different international bodies, including the International Labour Organisation, the United Nations, and the Council of Europe. In the framing of the United Kingdom's legislation against discrimination, American experience of equal rights legislation during the 1960s was a formative influence. But it is the standards of the European Union which, because of their binding legal effect under the European Communities Act 1972, have exercised and continue to exercise the greatest influence on English law. Community action in relation to discrimination dates from the adoption of the Social Action Programme in 1973, when the Community accepted that it would take action in fields other than those narrowly defined by economic considerations. The most recent proposals for new measures are to be found in the Fourth Equality Action Programme, adopted by the Council in December 1995. The Social Protocol of the Maastricht Treaty envisaged further extension of Community measures in relation to the principle of equal pay for equal work,[2] but the UK is excluded from its scope.

[1] For discrimination on the grounds of trade union membership or in respect of participation in industrial action see Chapter 13, above.
[2] Article 6.

21.02 Racial discrimination as such falls outside the direct scope of the Treaty of Rome, but Community discrimination law is important here too. This is because the structure and content of the Race Relations Act 1976, insofar as it applies to employment, is modelled closely on the Sex Discrimination Act 1975, and the interpretation of the latter, as we shall see, is much affected by Community requirements. Additionally, Art 48 of the EEC Treaty guarantees free movement of labour within the Community for nationals of Member States. This Article has direct effect, in the sense of giving enforceable rights to individuals against all employers, whether public or private.

21.03 The interaction between domestic law and the standards of Community law has already given rise to many problems in the English courts, as well as being the cause of several amendments to our domestic legislation. Many questions –

including some which raise fundamental issues of constitutional law and Parliamentary sovereignty – are still unresolved. The relationship between English and Community law will continue to be an area of keen legal debate for the foreseeable future. Accordingly, the first section of this chapter is devoted to an account of how Community law works. Strictly speaking, of course, Community law is not something separate from domestic law – it forms part of English law itself and has to be applied by the courts of the United Kingdom[1] – but it is nevertheless convenient to use the concept to denote a body of standards and procedures which has grown up independently of the legislature and courts of the United Kingdom, and which can be used, in different ways, to test domestic legislation and the interpretations of that legislation in our courts.[2] In view of the fact that typically Community law is held up as representing a standard which our domestic law does not meet, it is as well to make it clear that there is no reason why domestic law should not go further than Community law in granting protection against discrimination.[3] Community law is available to parties in all courts, including the industrial tribunals,[4] and national courts are bound to set aside any rule of domestic law which stands in the way of remedies protecting directly applicable Treaty rights.[5] There is, however, no right to invoke Community law when domestic law provides a sufficient remedy.[6]

1 *HP Bulmer Ltd v J Bollinger SA* [1974] Ch 401, CA, per Lord Denning MR at 418–19. European Communities Act 1972, s 2(1).
2 For example *Garland v British Rail Engineering Ltd*: 12/81 [1983] 2 AC 751, [1982] IRLR 111, ECJ.
3 The leading example is *Jenkins v Kingsgate (Clothing Productions) Ltd*: 96/80 [1981] 1 WLR 972, [1981] IRLR 228, ECJ.
4 *Secretary of State for Scotland v Wright and Hannah* [1991] IRLR 187, EAT.
5 *Factortame Ltd v Secretary of State for Transport (No 2)*: C-213/89 [1991] 1 All ER 70, ECJ; *Equal Opportunities Commission v Secretary of State for Employment* [1994] 1 All ER 910, HL.
6 *Blaik v Post Office* [1994] IRLR 280, EAT.

2 SOURCES OF COMMUNITY LAW

21.04 What is loosely referred to as 'European discrimination law' comprises three main elements: (a) the provisions of the EC Treaty relevant to discrimination, (b) the Directives concerning discrimination issued in terms of Art 189 of the EC Treaty, and (c) the interpretation of the Treaty and the Directives to be found in the jurisprudence of the European Court of Justice. We shall examine each in turn.

EC Treaty

21.05 Article 119 of the EC Treaty establishes the principle of 'equal pay for equal work'. This is an objective which finds its justification both in economic terms – the standardization of labour costs in different Member States, and in terms of social progress – the pursuit of pay equality being considered as a legitimate aim in itself. The Article prohibits paying lower wages on the ground of sex not only where a worker of one sex is engaged in work of equal value to the work of a worker of the opposite sex, but also where the higher paid worker is engaged in work of a lower value.[1] Equality, of course, may be achieved either by increasing or decreasing the pay of the worker of the opposite sex. The

ECJ has ruled that in principle equality may be achieved by reducing the advantages of the favoured sex.[2]

[1] *Murphy v Bord Telecom Eireann*: 157/86 [1988] ICR 445, [1988] IRLR 267, ECJ.
[2] *Smith v Avdel Systems Ltd*: C-408/92 [1994] IRLR 602, ECJ.

21.06 The legal status of Art 119 is that although, as part of the Treaty, it is directed at Member States, it is accepted that it has direct effect in the Member States of the Community[1] and thus may be relied on by individuals (whether or not they work in the public sector) as a basis for claims which fall within its scope, even when such claims are apparently blocked by the provisions of domestic legislation. Its impact in the past has been limited by the restricted judicial interpretation given to Art 119 by the ECJ, but now, both in that court and in the English courts, it would appear that this will be given a much wider interpretation.[2] It may be used, where appropriate, to challenge indirect as well as direct discrimination.[3] Exceptionally, the retrospective impact of successful claims under Art 119 may be limited because of the very large financial and practical consequences such claims have.[4]

[1] *Defrenne v Sabena*: 43/75 [1976] ICR 547, ECJ.
[2] *Bilka-Kaufhaus v Weber von Hartz*: 170/84 [1987] ICR 110, [1986] IRLR 317, ECJ; *Pickstone v Freemans plc* [1989] AC 66, [1987] IRLR 218, CA; *Hammersmith and Queen Charlotte's Special Health Authority v Cato* [1988] 1 CMLR 3, [1987] IRLR 483, EAT.
[3] *Bilka-Kaufhaus* above; *Rinner-Kühn v FWW Spezial-Gebäudereinigung GmbH I Co KG*: 171/88 [1989] IRLR 493, ECJ; *Equal Opportunities Commission v Secretary of State for Employment* [1994] 1 All ER 910, HL.
[4] *Barber v Guardian Royal Exchange Assurance Group*: C-262/88 [1990] 2 All ER 660, ECJ; *Vroege v NCIV Instituut voor Volkshuisvesting BV, Stichting Pensionfonds NCIV*: C-57/93 [1994] IRLR 651, ECJ.

Directives

21.07 Although Art 119 is the main source of Community standards, it does not by itself explain the achievements of Community law in combating discrimination. Article 119 is complemented by various Directives which expand and extend the principle of equal pay and equal treatment. Directives of the Council are binding as to result, but leave to national authorities the choice of form and methods.[1] There are six main Directives:

(1) Directive 75/117/EEC.[2] This, inter alia, requires the elimination of all discrimination on grounds of sex with regard to remuneration where work is the same or of equal value.
(2) Directive 76/207/EEC.[3] This is mainly concerned with elaborating the scope of equal opportunities in employment (excluding social security matters) and the specific means by which absence of discrimination in employment is to be effected. Broadly, it extends the principle of equal pay to make it apply to conditions of work as well as to remuneration.
(3) Directive 79/7/EEC.[4] This applies the principle of equal treatment to social security schemes and to social assistance schemes which provide protection against sickness, old age, work accidents and other risks. It does not apply to occupational schemes, as opposed to statutory ones.

(4) Directive 86/378/EEC.[5] This specifically deals with the principle of equal treatment in relation to occupational pension schemes.
(5) Directive 86/613/EEC.[6] This applies the principle of equal treatment to the self-employed and is concerned with the protection of self-employed women during pregnancy and motherhood.
(6) Directive 92/85/EEC.[7] This gives protection to pregnant women in respect of maternity leave, allowances and job security.

1 EEC Treaty, Art 189.
2 Council Directive of 19 February 1975
3 Council Directive of 9 February 1976.
4 Council Directive of 19 December 1978.
5 Council Directive of 24 July 1986.
6 Council Directive of 11 December 1986.
7 Council Directive of 19 October 1992.

21.08 The Equal Pay Act 1970 and the Sex Discrimination Act 1975 (both as amended) purport to implement Directives 75/117/EEC, 76/207/EEC, 79/7/EEC and 86/378/EEC in English law. Under Art 189 of the EC Treaty, all Directives share the characteristic of being directed at Member States, leaving to such states the decision as to how their content is to be implemented by legislation in the national legal system. It has been held, for example, that the Equal Treatment Directive does not require a Member State to penalise sex discrimination relating to access to employment by a sanction which takes the form of requiring the erring employer to enter into a contract of employment with the victim.[1] Although the primary remedy for failure on the part of a Member State to implement a Directive is infringement proceedings before the ECJ at the instance of the European Commission, the jurisprudence of the ECJ has established that in some circumstances an individual who as a result of his government's failure has suffered loss may be able to recover damages from the state.[2] Additionally, in circumstances where it is possible to identify an employer as an 'emanation of the State', it may be possible to rely directly on a Directive in proceedings taken against that employer. What entities qualify for such a description is, however, often uncertain.[3] It should also be noted that before any part of a Directive can have direct effect it must be clear and precise in its terms and be capable of having effect without intervention on the part of national authorities.[4]

1 *Von Colson and Kamann v Land Nordrhein-Westfalen*: 14/83 [1984] ECR 1891, [1986] 2 CMLR 430, ECJ.
2 *Francovich and Bonifaci v Italy*: C-6, 9/90 [1992] IRLR 84, ECJ. But note that such a claim may not be brought in an industrial tribunal: *Secretary of State for Employment v Mann* [1996] IRLR 4, EAT.
3 See, eg, *Griffin v South West Water Services Ltd* [1995] IRLR 15, Ch D; *Fidge v Governing Body of St Mary's Church of England Aided Junior School* (1994) Times, 9 November, EAT.
4 *Van Duyn v Home Office (No 2)*: 41/74 [1975] 3 All ER 190, ECJ.

21.09 Directives are important in discrimination law in different ways. First, they restate and clarify the principle of equal treatment contained in Art 119, allowing for the identification of types of discrimination which fall outside the 'direct and overt discrimination' which is caught by Art 119. Secondly, in carrying out such a function they provide a standard against which the adequacy of the domestic legislation in the Member States may be judged. On two occasions where discrimination has been concerned the United Kingdom has been the subject of infringement proceedings initiated by the European Commission, and has been found by the European Court of Justice to have fallen short of the standards required by the Equal Pay (75/117) and Equal Treatment (76/207) Directives.[1] This has led, on both occasions, to amendment of the domestic legislation of the United Kingdom. A Directive may also affect the interpretation to be given to a domestic statute.[2]

---

[1] *EC Commission v United Kingdom*: 61/81 [1982] ICR 578, [1982] IRLR 333, ECJ; *EC Commission v United Kingdom*: 165/82 [1984] 1 All ER 353, [1984] IRLR 29, ECJ.
[2] *Duke v GEC Reliance* [1988] AC 618, [1988] IRLR 118, HL. Compare *Garland v British Rail Engineering Ltd*: 12/81 [1983] IRLR 257, HL; *Litster v Forth Dry Dock and Engineering Co Ltd* [1989] 1 All ER 1134, [1989] ICR 341, HL.

Judicial interpretation

21.10 The European Court of Justice (ECJ) has the task of interpreting the scope and effect of the Treaty of Rome, and of the Directives made under the powers contained in Art 189 of the Treaty. While the courts of a Member State are also expected to interpret and apply Community law, in the final analysis it is the ruling of the ECJ which takes priority. Article 177 of the Treaty enables references to be made to the ECJ by national courts in order to decide questions of Community law relating to the Treaty or instruments made under it. The rulings of the ECJ thus have a key impact on the relationship between Community law and the domestic law of the United Kingdom. One of the best-known illustrations of this influence is the decision in *Barber v Guardian Royal Exchange Assurance Group*[1] which, by bringing occupational pension benefits within the scope of the equality required by Art 119, has had the effect of greatly enlarging the coverage of equal pay law. Because of the supremacy of Community law, judges may in effect hold that domestic statutes are invalid if they identify a conflict between the requirements of national and Community law. It is not necessary for a reference to be made to Luxembourg for this to occur. Most famously, the House of Lords[2] ruled that the threshhold requirements in UK legislation, which worked to the detriment of part-time workers, offended against Art 119. In due course, the legislation was amended by Parliament, but the offending provisions were legally ineffective even before they were removed from the statute book.

---

[1] C-262/88 [1990] IRLR 240, ECJ.
[2] *R v Secretary of State for Employment, ex p Equal Opportunities Commission* [1994] IRLR 176, HL. And see now *R v Secretary of Employment, ex p Seymour-Smith* [1995] IRLR 464, CA.

---

3 EQUAL TREATMENT AND EUROPEAN UNION STANDARDS

Article 119

21.11 The main problems that have arisen with Art 119 centre on the definition of its terms and on the extent to which discrimination which is unintentional is contrary to it. The right of individuals to rely directly on Art 119 before their national courts has been established as a principle of Community law since 1976.[1]

[1] *Defrenne v Société Anonyme Belge de Navigation Aerienne*: 43/75 [1976] ICR 547, ECJ.

21.12 The Article states that absence of discrimination based on sex means that pay for the same work at piece rates shall be calculated on the basis of the same unit of measurement, and that pay for work at time rates shall be the same for the same job. 'Pay' is defined within the article as meaning the ordinary basic or minimum wage or salary and any other consideration whether in cash or in kind and whether received directly or indirectly by the worker from his employer in respect of employment.

21.13 The meaning of 'pay' has frequently been a cause of difficulty in the interpretation of Art 119, and even the guidance given in a series of ECJ decisions[1] now makes it clear that a broad approach is appropriate, there is still a degree of uncertainty associated with the concept. It has been held that Art 119 will apply to severance payments made under the terms of a collective agreement[2] and also to payments on redundancy, whether these are statutory or contractual in nature.[3]

It makes no difference whether payment is made during employment or after this has ended, provided that it can be said that it is made 'in respect of employment'.[4]

Although, after *Barber*, occupational pension payments are correctly to be seen as 'pay' and thus falling within the scope of Art 119, there is earlier ECJ authority[5] to the effect that a deduction made by an employer from gross pay to cover an employee's contributions to an occupational pension scheme falls outside it. It has been held that the compensation awarded for unfair dismissal is also 'pay' within the meaning of Art 119, with the result that an individual excluded from claiming unfair dismissal under domestic law because of the number of hours she worked might pursue a remedy in discrimination law.[6] A more recent decision of the CA, however, has raised a doubt whether this is in fact the correct legal analysis.[7]

[1] *Barber v Guardian Royal Exchange Assurance Group*: C-262/88 [1990] 2 All ER 660, ECJ; and, also, *Arbeiterwohlfahrt der Stadt Berlin e V v Bötel*: C-360/90 [1992] IRLR 423, ECJ.

[2] *Kowalska v Freie und Hansestadt Hamburg*: C-33/89 [1990] IRLR 447, ECJ.

[3] *Hammersmith and Queen Charlotte's Special Hospital Authority v Cato* [1987] IRLR 483, EAT; *McKechnie v UBM Building Supplies (Southern) Ltd* [1991] IRLR 283, EAT.

[4] *Garland v British Rail Engineering Ltd*: 12/81 [1982] IRLR 257, HL.

[5] *Newstead v Department of Transport and HM Treasury*: 192/85 [1988] IRLR 66, ECJ. See too *Neath v Hugh Steeper Ltd*: C-152/91 [1994] IRLR 91, ECJ.

[6] *Mediguard Services Ltd v Thame* [1994] IRLR 504, EAT.

[7] *R v Secretary of State for Employment, ex p Seymour-Smith* [1995] IRLR 464, CA.

21.14 For some time it was thought that Art 119 did not apply to discrimination that was 'indirect', the sense of resulting from the determination of pay by apparently objective criteria which in fact had the consequence of lower remuneration for workers of one sex.[1] But this doubt has now been resolved in favour of a broader construction of Art 119; a scheme of payment which works to the detriment of part-time workers compared with full-time workers (where significantly more women are part-timers) will amount to an infringment of Art 119, unless the employer can show that such a practice can be explained by objectively justified factors unrelated to sex. An absence of intention to discriminate is not by itself enough to avoid an infringement of Art 119.[2] In a decision of fundamental constitutional importance,[3] the House of Lords has ruled that legislation that excluded part-time workers from certain benefits could be challenged by reference to Art 119 and the prohibition therein contained on 'indirect' discrimination.

[1] *Jenkins v Kingsgate (Clothing Productions) Ltd*: 96/80 [1981] 1 WLR 972, [1981] ICR 592, ECJ.

[2] *Bilka-Kaufhaus v Weber von Hartz*: 170/84 [1986] IRLR 317, ECJ.

[3] *Equal Opportunities Commission v Secretary of State for Employment* [1994] 1 All ER 910 HL. See too *Rinner-Kühn v FWW Spezial-Gebäudereinigung GmbH, CoKG*: 171/88 [1989] IRLR 493, ECJ.

21.15 It is no requirement of a claim under Art 119 that the worker with whom comparison is made is contemporaneously employed doing equal work with the same employer.[1] On the other hand, Art 119 may only be used to combat discrimination that is 'direct and overt'. This limitation excludes such discrimination as is hidden, although in such circumstances a remedy may arise under one or more Directives. For the avoidance of doubt it is worth repeating that Art 119 is capable of being used to challenge 'indirect' discrimination in pay or in access to occupational pension schemes.

[1] *Macarthys Ltd v Smith*: 129/79 [1981] QB 180, [1980] ECR 1275, ECJ.

21.16 It has been held that Art 119 can be relied upon by an applicant able to show that she is paid less in a job which is of equal value to another, where the job she is in is carried out almost exclusively by women and the other predominantly by men. In such circumstances there is a prima facie case of discrimination, and the employer is required to show that the difference in pay is based on objectively justified factors unrelated to any discrimination on grounds of sex. Such justification may be provided by economic arguments (such as the state of the employment market) but it will not be enough simply to show that the different pay rates have been set by the operation of collective bargaining.[1]

[1] *Enderby v Frenchay Health Authority and Secretary of State for Health*: C-127/92 [1993] IRLR 591, ECJ.

Directives

21.17 The two principal Directives on Equal Pay and Equal Treatment have very substantially widened the practical impact of Art 119, and are thus crucial to a proper understanding of Community law. This is so despite the ECJ's assertion (in 1981) that Art 1 of the Equal Pay Directive merely restates the principle of equal pay set out in Art 119 and in no way alters the content or scope of the principle.[1] Thus, it has been held that the conditions of access to a voluntary redundancy scheme operated by an employer may be challenged by reference to the Equal Treatment Directive, taken together with Art 119.[2] The same Directive (again read in conjunction with Art 119) led to the ruling that the imposition of a retirement age that was different for men and women doing the same job was unlawful under Community law.[3]

[1] *Jenkins v Kingsgate (Clothing Productions) Ltd*: 96/80 [1981] 1 WLR 972, [1981] IRLR 228, ECJ.

[2] *Burton v British Railways Board*: 19/81 [1982] QB 1080, [1982] ICR 329, ECJ.

[3] *Marshall v Southampton and South-West Hampshire Area Health Authority (Teaching)*: 152/84 [1986] QB 401, [1986] IRLR 140, ECJ.

21.18 As far as the Equal Pay Directive is concerned, the European Court of Justice has not precisely defined the relationship this has to Art 119. Despite dicta to the effect that it merely restates the principle contained in Art 119 and is concerned with the practical application of the principle of equal pay, it does apparently impose a wider range of obligations on employers than Art 119 alone. It was by reference to this Directive that the first infringement case against the United Kingdom was brought. The failure of the Equal Pay Act 1970 to allow a claim for equal pay on the part of a person of the opposite sex doing work of equal value where no job evaluation has been carried out led to the finding that the United Kingdom had not properly implemented its duties to eliminate sex discrimination with regard to remuneration.

21.19 Whether or not, in a given case, a Directive may be used by an individual to support a claim before an English court, depends on whether the situation is one where the doctrine of 'direct effect' (below) applies. Both the Equal Pay and Equal Treatment Directives are instruments which have 'direct effect' at least in part.

4 THE IMPLEMENTATION OF EUROPEAN STANDARDS IN ENGLISH LAW

Article 169

21.20 Mention has already been made of the use of Art 169 of the Treaty. This allows the Commission to take proceedings against a Member State on the ground that it has failed properly to implement its treaty obligations. In the field of equality legislation, this procedure has twice been invoked by the EC Commission against the United Kingdom.[1]

[1] *EC Commission v United Kingdom*: 61/81 [1982] ICR 578, [1982] IRLR 333, ECJ; *EC Commission v United Kingdom*: 165/82 [1984] 1 All ER 353, [1984] IRLR 29, ECJ.

European Communities Act 1972

21.21 As a consequence of the European Communities Act 1972, Community law may provide an independent and superior source of law, overruling any provision of English law with which it is in conflict. Alternatively, it may simply provide a guide to the proper interpretation of a United Kingdom statute. The House of Lords has made it clear that it is unwilling to construe a domestic statute so as to produce an inconsistency between domestic and Community law.[1] In some cases it will even go so far as to insert words into the domestic statute in order to prevent an inconsistency from arising.[2]

1 *Pickstone v Freemans plc* [1988] AC 66, [1988] IRLR 357, HL; *Litster v Forth Dry Dock and Engineering Co Ltd* [1989] 1 All ER 1134, [1989] IRLR 161, HL; *Webb v EMO Air Cargo (UK) Ltd* [1993] IRLR 27, HL and [1995] IRLR 645, HL.
2 See, eg *Litster*, above.

21.22 By s 2(1) of the ECA 1972, directly effective or directly applicable Community law is made binding in the UK, but this section gives no guidance in deciding what parts of Community law are directly effective or directly applicable. Such a question is, in the final analysis, a matter of Community law itself, but domestic courts will also be called upon to make such judgments, subject, of course, to correction by the ECJ.[1]

1 European Communities Act 1972, s 3(1); *Equal Opportunities Commission v Secretary of State for Employment* [1994] 1 All ER 910, HL; *R v Secretary of State for Employment, ex p Seymour-Smith* [1995] IRLR 464, CA; *Milligan v Securicor Cleaning Ltd* [1995] IRLR 288, EAT.

21.23 Where Art 119 operates to overrule a provision in a domestic statute it may do so by amending the offending provision in the domestic statute to bring it into conformity with European law (the 'monist' view),[1] or it may confer a right to bring proceedings independently of the domestic statute (the 'dualist' view). The former would appear to give a result which is easier to apply in a practical sense, and is the best explanation of the decision in *Macarthys Ltd v Smith*.[2] Both the Court of Appeal and the House of Lords have in the past adopted an approach that is distinctly dualist in character.[3] In these decisions the analysis of the Court of Appeal (in *Pickstone*) and the House of Lords (in *Duke*) was that there should be no distortion of the meaning of a United Kingdom statute in order to achieve conformity between it and the standards required by Community law. In both cases, the courts decided that persons excluded from making a claim by the natural meaning of the British statutory provisions had to pursue an independent claim based on Community law. But the dualist approach (and the associated idea of 'free-standing' rights under Community law) causes many problems when it comes to considering procedural rules and other aspects of adjectival law. It is perhaps for that reason that the EAT and the CA have recently firmly come out in favour of a monist analysis.[4]

1 See *Pickstone v Freemans plc* [1987] IRLR 218, CA, per Purchas LJ at 229.
2 129/79 [1979] 3 All ER 325, [1979] ICR 785, ECJ.
3 *Pickstone v Freemans plc* [1987] IRLR 218, CA; *Duke v GEC Reliance Ltd* [1988] AC 618, [1988] IRLR 118, HL.
4 *Biggs v Somerset County Council* [1995] IRLR 452, EAT; [1996] IRLR 203, CA.

21.24 Section 2(4) of the European Communities Act 1972 requires that a court or tribunal must construe any enactment passed or to be passed in the UK so as to be consistent with Community law. The same point has also been made by the ECJ.[1]

[1] *Marleasing SA v La Comercial Internacional di Alimentación*: C-106/89, [1992] 1 CMLR 305, ECJ.

21.25 It is a rule of Community law that a national court must interpret and apply the legislation adopted for the implementation of a Directive in conformity with the requirements of Community law, insofar as it is given discretion to do so under national law.[1] In general, as mentioned above, an English court will seek to interpret a UK statute in a way which makes for conformity with the relevant Community standards it purports to implement[2] but there are definite limits to this rule. It does not permit a court to distort the construction of an Act of Parliament which was not drafted to give effect to a Directive and which is not capable by its terms of complying with the meaning sought to be imposed upon it in order to bring it into line with the Directive.[3] This has the important result that the Equal Treatment Directive (76/207/EEC) may not be used to produce a distorted reading of the words of the Sex Discrimination Act 1975.

[1] *Von Colson and Kamann v Land Nordrhein-Westfalen*: 14/83 [1984] ECR 1891, ECJ.

[2] *Delabole Slate Ltd v Berriman* [1985] IRLR 305, CA; *Garland v British Rail Engineering Ltd*: 12/81 [1983] 2 AC 751, [1982] IRLR 257, HL: *Pickstone v Freeman plc* [1989] AC 66, [1988] IRLR 357, HL; *Litster v Forth Dry Dock & Engineering Co Ltd*, above.

[3] *Duke v GEC Reliance Ltd* [1988] AC 618, [1988] IRLR 118, HL. Contrary to the views expressed by Lord Diplock in *Garland v British Rail Engineering Ltd*: 12/81 [1982] IRLR 257, HL, s 6(4) of the Sex Discrimination Act 1975 should not be construed so as to bring it into conformity with the Equal Treatment Directive. See also *Finnegan v Clowney Youth Training Programme Ltd* [1990] IRLR 299, HL.

The concept of direct effect

21.26 In *Macarthys Ltd v Smith*[1] the ECJ held that a woman whose claim for equal pay under the Equal Pay Act 1970 failed because she could not show a man contemporaneously employed on like work in the same employment (as the UK statute then required), was nevertheless entitled to receive equral pay under Art 119. This is a clear example of the superiority of a directly applicable provision of Community law over anything contrary in domestic law. The same decision, however, emphasised that Art 119 could only be invoked in the event of 'direct and overt discrimination which may be identified solely with the criteria of equal work and equal pay referred to in the Article.' This qualification, together with the restrictions on the meaning of 'pay' within Art 119[2] limits the utility of Art 119 as a means of giving a direct remedy to individuals.[3] Nevertheless, it has been established that Art 119 may be used to challenge the kind of 'hidden' discrimination that arises when an apparently sex-neutral condition operates to the detriment of women.[4]

[1] 129/79 [1981] QB 180, [1980] ICR 672, ECJ.

[2] See para 21.14, above.

[3] Compare *Leverton v Clwyd County Council* [1989] AC 706, [1988] IRLR 239, CA.

[4] *Enderby v Frenchay Health Authority*: C-127/92 [1993] IRLR 591, ECJ.

21.27 On the other hand, the Equal Pay Directive (which is said to restate the principle of equal value contained in Art 119) allows identification of a broader range of discriminatory practices. However, this Directive is not directly applicable in domestic courts in the same way as Art 119. As a Directive, it may not be used to bring a claim against an employer or prospective employer outside the public sector.

21.28 If the equality Directives can be relied upon as giving rights to individual claimants, then there is considerable potential for extending the impact of anti-discrimination law.' Many of the qualifications and exclusions which are found in the British legislation have no counterpart in the Community instruments. In *Marshall v Southampton and South-West Hampshire Area Heath Authority (Teaching)*[1] the ECJ was prepared to give such direct effect to Art 5(1) of the Equal Treatment Directive (76/207), with the result that a female employee dismissed in pursuance of a scheme which fixed differential retirement ages for men and women was held entitled to succeed in a claim under the Sex Discrimination Act 1975 (s 6(4)). This decision led to the passing of the Sex Discrimination Act 1986, which amended the British law on retirement ages so as to bring it into line with the ECJ's ruling. The general significance of the *Marshall* decision is, however, restricted by two important considerations. The ECJ addressed itself only to Art 5(1) of the Equal Treatment Directive, and based its decision on a finding that this provision was 'unconditional and sufficiently precise'. It does not follow, therefore, that other Directives, or even other provisions of the Equal Treatment Directive, will be seen as having the same direct effect, although the ECJ has subsequently indicated that Arts 3(1) and 4(1) of the Equal Treatment Directive should be similarly construed.[2] In the second *Marshall* case[3] it was held that Art 6 of the Directive (which requires there to be an adequate remedy for discrimination) could be used by an individual to set aside domestic legislation imposing limits on the amount of compensation recoverable. The limits successfully challenged have now been removed by legislation.

---

1 152/84 [1986] QB 401, [1986] IRLR 140, ECJ.

2 *Johnston v Chief Constable of the Royal Ulster Constabulary*: 222/84 [1987] QB 129, [1986] IRLR 263, ECJ.

3 *Marshall v Southampton and South-West Hampshire Area Health Authority (No 2)*: C-271/91 [1993] IRLR 445, ECJ.

21.29 A second and separate point is that the *Marshall* case was concerned with action taken by an employee who was in the employment of the State. The principle of direct effect does not support the bringing of a claim by someone who is not in the employment of the State (see above para 21.08). Whether a particular employer is 'an emanation of the State' is a difficult question. It would appear that, as far as English law is concerned, merely being in the public sector is not enough. Probably such a body must also be classed as exercising governmental powers in the sense of being responsible for providing a public service under the control of the State and having for that purpose special powers.[1] The reason why the State is singled out for special treatment in this way is that it is the Member State which has failed in its duty to implement the Directive in its domestic law. The question of classification is one which falls to the English courts to decide.[2]

[1] *Foster v British Gas plc*: C–188/89 [1991] IRLR 268 at 270, HL, per Lord Templeman; *Doughty v Rolls-Royce plc* [1992] IRLR 126, CA.

[2] For the general considerations which have to be satisfied before a Directive may be relied upon by an individual, see *Van Duyn v Home Office (No 2)*: 41/74 [1975] Ch 358, [1975] 3 All ER 190, ECJ.

Jurisdiction of industrial tribunals

21.30 Where an applicant asserts an entitlement to a right derived from Community law – either under Art 119 or a Directive which has direct application – then he may address such a claim to an industrial tribunal, and need not go to the ordinary courts. Although tribunals have not been specifically given such jurisdiction, it has been held as a matter of interpretation that they have it.[1] It is still a moot point, however, whether in exercising this jurisdiction they are exercising a power which they enjoy directly under Art 119, or whether they are still operating under the statutory powers given them by national law. The most recent authority suggests that it is the second interpretation which is to be followed[2] but the matter is not yet free from doubt. The time limits and other procedural rules which apply to claims made under such jurisdiction will be fixed by the domestic courts, by analogy with the nearest comparable remedy available under domestic law.[3] Where a claim is brought on the basis of a Directive and it is established that the Directive has not been properly implemented in domestic law, then any time limit will only run from (and not before) the date when full and proper implementation takes place.[4] By contrast, where a claim relies on Art 119 itself (and relates to a situation where Art 119 can be seen as having direct effect) there is no obvious reason to delay the start of any time limit until the introduction of amending legislation. There may, however, be a discretion on the part of a tribunal to allow a claim which is apparently made out of time.

[1] *Secretary of State for Scotland v Wright and Hannah* [1991] IRLR 187, EAT.

[2] *Biggs v Somerset County Council* [1995] IRLR 452, EAT; [1996] IRLR 203, CA.

[3] *Cannon v Barnsley Metropolitan Borough Council* [1992] IRLR 474, EAT.

[4] *Emmott v Minister for Social Welfare and A-G*: C-208/90 [1991] IRLR 387, ECJ; *Rankin v British Coal Corpn* [1993] IRLR 69, EAT.

22 The framework of equal opportunities law in Britain

Brian Napier

1 INTRODUCTION

22.01 The domestic legislation on sex equality in employment matters consists of two principal statutes – the Equal Pay Act 1970 (the EqPA), and the Sex Discrimination Act 1975 (the SDA). Both have been in force since 29 December 1975. The Race Relations Act 1976 (the RRA) deals with racial discrimination in employment. These statutes have been amended in several respects since their enactment, with particularly important changes taking place in 1983, when the Equal Pay (Amendment) Regulations 1983 incorporated the principle of equal pay into the EqPA, and in 1986, when the Sex Discrimination (Amendment) Act made changes in both the SDA and the EqPA. There has been no upper limit on the amount of compensation recoverable for an act of sex discrimination in employment since 1993; in racial discrimination cases the limit was removed in 1994. Proposals for the repeal of the existing legislation on sex discrimination and the enactment of a new single measure, incorporating the requirements of Community law, have been discussed for some time but so far to no avail.[1]

[1] *Equal Pay for Men and Women, Strengthening the Acts*, EOC, November 1990.

22.02 The difference between the SDA and the EqPA is that the SDA is concerned with discrimination in relation to non-contractual benefits at work, as well as covering practices and procedures relating to recruitment, training, promotion and dismissal. It also covers discrimination in contractual benefits, provided this does not consist in the payment of money under a contract of employment. Under the EqPA, an individual is entitled to be treated not less favourably than a person of the opposite sex who works for the same employer as regards pay and other terms of the contract of employment, in three distinct situations: (a) where they are employed on like work (ie the same work or work which is broadly similar); (b) where they are employed on work which has been rated as equivalent under a job evaluation scheme, or (c) where they are employed on work which is of equal value.

22.03 Under the SDA, discrimination on marital grounds, and by way of victimisation, is also prohibited. These matters are examined below.[1]

[1] See paras 24.41 and 24.42, below.

22.04 In relation to discrimination on racial grounds, the Race Relations Act 1976 prohibits discrimination on the grounds of colour, race, nationality and ethnic or national origins. This applies, generally, to all work-related discriminatory practices, including the arrangements for hiring and dismissal.

2 EQUAL OPPORTUNITIES COMMISSION

22.05 The Equal Opportunities Commission is the statutory body which oversees the working of the anti-discrimination legislation and is charged with the duty of working towards the elimination of discrimination, the promotion of equality of opportunity between men and women, and keeping under review the operation of the legislation.[1]

[1] Sex Discrimination Act 1975, s 53(1)(a)–(c).

22.06 In terms and composition, powers and general characteristics, the EOC is the twin of the Commission for Racial Equality (CRE), which has parallel responsibility for the elimination of discrimination on racial grounds. The differences between the two commissions are noted below. So far, the CRE, unlike its twin, has had little cause to refer to EC law in its implementation of its duties; subject to these differences, the duties and powers of the two bodies are substantially the same.

22.07 The EOC is controlled by commissioners who are appointed by the Secretary of State, but it is not itself part of the Crown although it is financed by public funds. Its functions are not confined to discrimination in employment matters – it also has powers in relation to discrimination in education and in the provision of goods and services – but only the employment aspects of its operations are considered here. In order to carry out its duties, it is empowered to act in various ways. It may assist applicants in the bringing of complaints of discrimination if the case raises a question of principle or it is unreasonable to expect the complainant to deal with the case unaided, for example due to the complexity of the matter, or, if any other special consideration applies. Many of the major cases which have established key interpretations of the legislative provisions on discrimination have featured applicants financially supported by the EOC. Secondly, it may conduct formal investigations for any purpose connected with the carrying out of its duties, and this may lead to the issue of a non-discrimination notice to put a stop to particular discriminatory practices.[1] Thus, for example, the EOC in 1987 investigated the discriminatory practices of an airline which had a policy of only employing women as cabin staff on its aeroplanes.[2] The EOC also has powers which allow it to undertake or assist research or education activities necessary or expedient for the furtherance of its objects[3] and to issue Codes of Practice.[4]

[1] Sex Discrimination Act 1975, ss 67–71.
[2] Equal Opportunities Commission, *Formal Investigation Report: DAN-AIR*, January 1987.
[3] Sex Discrimination Act 1975, s 54.
[4] See para 22.10, below.

22.08 There is also the possibility of the EOC intervening in discriminatory practices in more direct ways by bringing legal proceedings against named individuals. It can do this (a) before an industrial tribunal in respect of unlawful discriminatory advertisements, instructions to discriminate or pressure to discriminate;[1] (b) before an industrial tribunal in respect of an act done by a person allegedly in contravention of the employment provisions of the SDA or the EqPA, where the proceedings are brought with a view to making an application for persistent sex discrimination under the immediately following provision,[2] and (c) before a county court where it appears to the Commission necessary to restrain by injunction a person likely to commit discriminatory acts.[3] The standing of the EOC to challenge, by means of judicial review, decisions of the Secretary of State regarding thc introduction of legislation productive of discrimination has been confirmed by a leading decision of the House of Lords.[4]

1 Sex Discrimination Act 1975, s 72. No such complaint may be made by an individual. No compensation may be awarded by the tribunal under such proceedings.

2 Sex Discrimination Act 1975, s 73(1). No compensation may be awarded by the tribunal under such proceedings.

3 Sex Discrimination Act 1975, s 71(1). This power exists only where the person against whom the injunction is sought has, within a period of five years, had a non-discrimination notice served on him, or has, within such period, been found by an industrial tribunal to have committed a breach of the employment provisions of the equality legislation.

4 *Equal Opportunities Commission v Secretary of State for Employment* [1994] 1 All ER 910, HL.

22.09 There are detailed provisions regulating the procedure to be followed when the EOC undertakes a formal investigation under s 57 powers. These are designed to give proper protection to individuals and to ensure observation of the principles of natural justice, but in practice they are so complicated that they arguably frustrate the effective operation of the law. Speaking of the analogous controls on the investigative powers of the Commission for Racial Equality, Lord Denning described the regulations as 'a spider's web spun by Parliament'[1] and commented that the legislative machinery was so elaborate and cumbersome that it was in danger of grinding to a halt. Similar reservations have been expressed by Sir Nicholas Browne-Wilkinson in a non-judicial capacity.[2] The Equal Opportunities Commission has itself maintained that the procedural limitations are unnecessarily restrictive of its functions, and that they should, in part, be repealed.[3]

1 *Commission for Racial Equality v Amari Plastics Ltd* [1982] ICR 304, at 313, CA, per Lord Denning MR.

2 Sir N Browne-Wilkinson, 'Racial Discrimination: the Role of the Civil Law', The Kapila Fellowship Lecture 1986, Council of Legal Education.

3 Equal Opportunities Commission, *Legislating for Change?* (1986) pp 25–26.

Codes of Practice

22.10 The EOC has a specific power to issue Codes of Practice which, though not *per se* constitutive of any legally enforceable obligations, are admissible in any proceedings under the SDA before an industrial tribunal. A tribunal is required to take into account, so far as it is relevant to any question arising in the proceedings, the provisions of such Codes.[1] A Code of Practice on Equal Opportunity Policies, Procedures and Practices in Employment came into force on 30 April 1985. In April 1995 the Commission published a draft of a new proposed Code of Practice on equal pay.

[1] Sex Discrimination Act 1975, s 56A(10).

3 COMMISSION FOR RACIAL EQUALITY

22.11 The powers and composition of the Commission for Racial Equality (CRE) are broadly similar to those of the EOC, although its objectives are somewhat differently defined. The CRE has the duties of (a) working towards the elimination of discrimination; (b) promoting equality of opportunity and good relations between persons of different racial grounds generally; and (c) keeping under review the working of the Race Relations Act 1976 (RRA) and, when required by the Secretary of State or when it otherwise thinks it necessary, to draw up and submit to the Secretary of State proposals for amending it. Like the EOC, the CRE may conduct investigations, support research and education relevant to its objectives, and it also has powers to give financial or other assistance to appropriate organisations.[1] The CRE may issue Codes of Practice, and has done so, in like manner to the EOC.[2]

[1] Race Relations Act 1976, s 44.
[2] CRE, *Code of Practice for the Elimination of Racial Discrimination and the Promotion of Equality of Opportunity in Employment*, 1983.

4 ADJUDICATION OF COMPLAINTS

22.12 Complaints by individuals, relating to alleged discrimination in employment, arising under the EqPA, SDA and RRA, are brought before Industrial Tribunals. Concilation, through the offices of the Advisory, Conciliation and Arbitration Service, is a precursor of tribunal hearings taking place. Appeal on questions of law from the decisions of an Industrial Tribunal lies to the Employment Appeal Tribunal.[1] The Industrial Tribunal also itself acts as an appellate body in respect of appeals against non-discrimination notices issued under the SDA and RRA. Procedure before Industrial Tribunals in such matters is in general governed according to the ordinary rules of procedure, but there is a special complementary procedure for equal pay claims based on equal value.[2] There has been some simplification of the procedure to be followed in the making of an equal value claim, as a result of amendment in 1994.[3]

[1] Employment Protection (Consolidation) Act 1978, s 136(1).
[2] Industrial Tribunals (Constitution and Rules of Procedure) Regulations 1993 (SI 1993/2687).
[3] Industrial Tribunals (Constitution and Rules of Procedure) (Amendment) Regulations 1994 (SI 1994/536).

5 DISABLED PERSONS

22.13 The law on disability in employment, meaning the 'quota' system as set out in the Disabled Persons (Employment) Act 1944 has been, for many years, largely ignored in practice. The 'quota' system, under which employers are obliged to employ a certain percentage of the registered disabled, is now operated by only a small minority of employers, and for many years there has been little, if any, attempt to enforce this law by official agencies.

22.14 New legislation[1] envisages the introduction of a new approach towards promoting the rights of disabled people in employment. The legislation has many similarities with the existing legal framework applicable to discrimination on grounds of sex, although the rights it proposes to give to the victims of disability discrimination are less substantial in several respects. It introduces a general duty on employers to make 'reasonable adjustments' to working conditions or the workplace in order to accommodate the special needs of the disabled. This applies to all employers who employ more than 20 employees. Individuals who consider they have suffered discrimination have a right of access to industrial tribunals. But it will not be an easy matter to establish a winning case. There will be many arguments open to an employer who seeks to show that he has done all that he could reasonably be expected to in a given case. There will also be several specific exemptions to cover, for example, an employer's obligation to comply with building regulations and situations where the employer is ignorant of the condition which constitutes the disability. The definition of disability is 'a physical or mental impairment which has a substantial and long-term adverse effect on [a person's] ability to carry out normal day-to-day activities.'[2]

---

1 Disability Discrimination Act 1995.
2 Section 1(1).

23 Equal pay

Brian Napier

1 EQUAL PAY ACT 1970

23.01 The basic structure of the EqPA depends on the compulsory insertion, by statute, of an 'equality clause' into every contract under which a woman[1] is employed at an establishment in Great Britain, unless her contract already contains such a term. An equality clause relates to terms (whether concerned with pay or not) under which a woman is employed, and 'employed' here means employed under a contract of service, or apprenticeship, or a contract personally to execute any work or labour. The effect of the equality clause is to modify automatically any term of her contract which is less favourable than a term of a similar kind in a contract under which a man is employed in the same employment, so that the woman's term becomes no less favourable. Such modification takes place in the following circumstances:

(1) Where the woman is employed on like work with the man with whom comparison is made.
(2) Where the woman is employed on work rated as equivalent with that of the man.
(3) Where the woman is employed on work which, not being work in relation to which head (1) or (2) applies, is in terms of the demands made upon her (for instance under such headings as effort, skill and decision) of equal value to that of the man.

[1] Under the equality legislation, discrimination against men is generally prohibited to the same extent as discrimination against women; hence references to 'woman' should be taken to include 'man' unless the contrary is indicated.

23.02 The burden of showing that she comes within one of these three sets of circumstances falls on the woman, and the satisfying of this burden of proof has been one of the major obstacles facing those who have sought to make use of the EqPA. The burden, however, falls on the employer where the pay system being questioned is characterised by a lack of 'transparency'.[1] It is also a requirement of success under the EqPA that the woman can find a male comparator in the same employment. The choice of comparator is for her to make, though she should take care to ensure that she selects someone who is representative of the class to which he belongs.[2] The important early decision of the ECJ in *Macarthys Ltd v Smith*[3] established that a woman was not obliged to make comparison with a man contemporaneously employed with her. A woman may make comparison with a man who was recently employed in the same employment. But no claim can be made on the basis of what the woman alleges she would get were she a man. The concept of the 'hypothetical male' is not accepted as valid for the purposes of the EqPA.

---

[1] *Handels-og Kontorfunktionaerernes Forbund i Danmark v Dansk Arbejdsgiverforening* ('*Danfoss*'): 109/88 [1989] IRLR 532, ECJ.
[2] *British Coal Corpn v Smith* [1994] IRLR 342, CA.
[3] 129/79 [1981] QB 180, [1980] ICR 672, ECJ.

23.03 The operation of the equality clause is also subject to the availability of a defence allowed to the employer by s 1(3) of the EqPA; if the employer can prove (a) that he did not directly or indirectly discriminate against the woman, and (b) that the difference between the woman's contract and the man's is genuinely due to a material factor which is also (or, in some circumstances, may be) a material difference between the woman's case and the man's, then the equality clause will not operate to produce a change in the contract. The limits of this defence are vital to an understanding of the practical effects of the equal pay legislation. There is no literal equivalent to s 1(3) in the body of Art 119, but the ECJ, in *Enderby v Frenchay Health Authority and Secretary of State for Health*[1] has ruled that an employer is obliged to show an objective reason for a difference in pay between jobs of equal value if there is a prima facie case of discrimination. Such a prima facie case arises, in particular, if one of the jobs is done by a woman where almost all members of the profession are female, and the other is done by a man, where the profession is predominantly male. Because the EqPA has to be construed in the light of relevant EC law, the same principle must be seen as governing the s 1(3) defence. This means that even in the absence of any gender-specific criterion or condition governing entrance to the higher-paid job, and even in the absence of proof of any intention to discriminate, the employer is obliged to rebut the allegation of indirect discrimination by showing justification for the rule in question. A more detailed consideration of the section 1(3) defence will be found below.[2]

---

[1] C-127/92 [1993] IRLR 591, ECJ. And see also *British Coal Corpn v Smith; North Yorkshire County Council v Ratcliffe* [1994] IRLR 342, CA.
[2] See paras 23.14ff.

23.03A It would appear, after *Enderby* that the technical requirements of indirect discrimination under the SDA (see Chapter 24, para 14) may not always be required in order to succeed in a claim of non-intentional discrimination brought under the EqPA. Indeed, according to the views expressed by Lord Slynn in a recent decision of the House of Lords[1] there may be no need to make the distinction between direct and indirect discrimination at all in applying the 1970 Act. That distinction nowhere appears in the EqPA itself. It may therefore be easier to establish a claim based on unintentional discrimination when equal pay is in issue rather than equal treatment, but the authorities on this important point are still somewhat divided.[2]

---

[1] *Ratcliffe v North Yorkshire County Council* [1995] IRLR 439, HL.
[2] Cf, eg, *Staffordshire County Council v Black* [1995] IRLR 234, EAT.

---

2 LIKE WORK

23.04 The meaning of 'like work' given by s 1(4) is work which is 'of the same or broadly similar nature'. Furthermore, the differences (if any) between the things she does and the things the comparator does must not be of practical importance in relation to terms and conditions of employment, and accordingly in any comparison regard is to be had to the frequency with which any such differences occur in practice, as well as to the nature and extent of the difference. Comparison must be made with a man in the same employment.

23.05 The interpretation of the phrase 'like work' by the courts has resulted in the evolution of certain broad principles. In deciding whether differences between the man's work and the woman's work are of practical importance, a tribunal should take a broad view, and ask the question whether the differences are such that in the real world they are likely to be reflected in the terms and conditions of employment.[1] The time at which work is performed is, prima facie, not likely to be sufficient to prevent work which would otherwise be termed 'like work' from being such,[2] and it will often be appropriate to remunerate someone who has to work unsocial hours by way of a separate premium, rather than through an amendment of basic rates of pay. In deciding whether differences are of practical importance, it is not sufficient to look at what could be required of workers under their contracts of employment – a tribunal must look to see what actually happens in practice rather than what might theoretically be demanded of the parties under their contracts.[3] On the other hand, a difference in responsibility between the man's work and the woman's work has been accepted as capable of amounting to a difference of practical importance.[4] Where a woman is paid less than a man for doing a job which, though broadly similar in content, carries more responsibility she may fail in a claim made under s 1(4)[5] although in such a situation she may be able to argue that her claim succeeds on the basis of equal value – either under s 1(2)(c) of the EqPA or under Art 119 of the EC Treaty.[6]

1 *Capper Pass Ltd v Lawton* [1977] QB 852, [1976] IRLR 366, EAT.
2 *Dugdale v Kraft Foods Ltd* [1977] 1 All ER 454, [1977] IRLR 368, EAT.
3 *Electrolux Ltd v Hutchinson* [1977] ICR 252, [1976] IRLR 410, EAT; *Thomas v National Coal Board* [1987] ICR 757, [1987] IRLR 451, EAT.
4 *Eaton Ltd v Nuttall* [1977] 3 All ER 1131, [1977] ICR 272, EAT.
5 *Waddington v Leicester Council for Voluntary Services* [1977] 2 All ER 633, [1977] ICR 266, EAT.
6 *Murphy v Bord Telecom Eirann*: 157/86 [1988] ICR 445, [1988] IRLR 267, ECJ; para 21.05, above.

3 WORK RATED AS EQUIVALENT

23.06 Section 1(5) defines 'work rated as equivalent' as the situation where a woman's job and that of a man in the same employment have been given an equal value, in terms of the different demands made under various headings (such as effort, skill, decision, etc) under a properly conducted job evaluation study. Such a study must, it would appear,[1] be 'analytical', in the sense that the valuation of the jobs should have been undertaken in a way that takes account of the demands made on the employees under different headings. An evaluation conducted on other grounds (eg looking at the jobs 'as a whole', or the acceptability of the end result to the workforce as a whole – the so-called 'felt fair' approach) will not be good enough. The job evaluation study must be completed and accepted as valid by the parties before it can be relied on by the employee, but it is not a prerequisite of effectiveness that the employer has agreed to implement such a completed report.[2]

1 *Bromley v H & J Quick Ltd* [1988] 2 CMLR 468, [1988] IRLR 249, CA.
2 *O'Brien v Sim-Chem Ltd* [1980] 3 All ER 132, [1980] ICR 573, HL.

23.07 In the modern law the importance of job evaluation studies lies not so much in their potential for employees as a mechanism for achieving equal pay, but rather in their potential for employers as a means of resisting a claim brought under the heading of equal value.[1] The defensive aspect of job evaluation schemes is further considered in the immediately following section.

1 See *Leverton v Clwyd County Council* [1989] IRLR 28 at 34, HL, per Lord Bridge.

4 WORK OF EQUAL VALUE

23.08 It was because of the absence under the EqPA of any generalised right for employees to insist on pay comparability by reference to equal value that the United Kingdom was in 1982 found to be in breach of Community law. The outcome was an amendment of the EqPA in 1984. The present situation is that, in circumstances where a woman is employed on work which is neither like work nor work rated as equivalent she can claim equal pay in respect of work of equal value. Comparison must be made with a man in the same employment,[1] and the work must be of equal value, judged in terms of the demands made by the two jobs under such headings as effort, skill and decision. The procedure for adjudicating on such a claim is substantially different to that applicable to claims brought under the 'like work' or 'rated as equivalent' provisions.[2] There can be no doubt that the prospect of securing equal pay for work of equal value breathed new life into the EqPA in the 1980s, though the initial optimism with which the new procedure was greeted turned out to be short-lived. Many individuals presented cases to tribunals relying on this new heading, even though applications were allowed only on a residual basis, ie where the headings of 'like work' or 'work rated as equivalent' were not applicable. But only a small number of these complaints have been successful. This has been due to the complexity of the law and the extremely convoluted nature of the adjudicatory process. An employer, for example, may plead as a preliminary matter a 'material factor' defence. As a result it may be many months (and often years) before a final decision is reached by a tribunal on the question of substance. In relation to equal value claims two fundamentally important principles have been laid down by the House of Lords:

(1) Where comparison is made with a man who is paid more than the woman, and the claim is made with a view to obtaining an increase for the woman, then (assuming the jobs are found to be of

equal value) the effect of the equality clause is that the terms of employment in the two jobs will be looked at strictly on a paired basis. This means, in particular, that the woman receiving less money as a result of a difference in basic rates of pay or overtime rates is entitled to receive an increase to bring herself into line with the money received by the man.[3]

(2) A claim for equal value may be brought even though a man (other than the comparator chosen by the woman) in the same employment is employed on work which is like work or work rated as equivalent to the work done by the woman.[4]

---

1 As defined by EqPA, s 1(6)(b). This allows claims, in some circumstances, to be made on the basis of comparisons with employees (of the same employer) working in other establishments. See *British Coal Corpn v Smith* [1994] IRLR 342, CA.

2 EqPA, s 1(2)(c).

3 *Hayward v Cammell Laird Shipbuilders Ltd* [1988] AC 894, [1988] IRLR 257, HL.

4 *Pickstone v Freemans plc* [1989] AC 66, [1988] IRLR 357, HL. The contrary view, that such a claim was not permitted, was adopted by the Court of Appeal ([1987] IRLR 218) and led that court to a controversial interpretation of the effect of Art 119 of the EEC Treaty on English law. This controversy was avoided by the analysis of the House of Lords, which recognised that unless the claim could succeed there would be a serious conflict between the EqPA and EEC law.

---

5 EQUAL REMUNERATION

23.09 The Equal Pay Act operates to bring into line any contractual term that is different between a woman and her male comparator, but in practice it is the term or terms relating to remuneration which have proved to be the most contested by far. Where there is a prima facie inequality in pay, can the employer seek to justify the difference by showing that the woman who receives less pay than the man is compensated for the difference by other conditions of employment? This, in essence, was the question raised in *Hayward v Cammell Laird Shipbuilders Ltd*[1] and answered in the negative. In technical terms, the woman is entitled, under s 1(2)(c)(i) to have rectified a term less favourable than a term of a similar kind in the man's contract, and the House of Lords decided that this meant the woman's pay or overtime rates should be directly compared with the rates paid to her comparator. It was not permissible for the employer to argue that, judged in terms of an overall 'package' taking into account such matters as holiday entitlements and sickness benefits, she was not worse off. The main argument against such an interpretation was the fear of 'leapfrogging' – the woman having achieved equality of pay, the man might then seek an improvement in his position by pointing to the inequality between him and the woman by reference to the other components of the package. It remains, however, to be decided to what extent such a claim might be defeated by other provisions of the Equal Pay Act – notably s 1(3), which is further considered below. Where an employer can show that differences between contracts are the product of non-discriminatory pay structures and are objectively justified, he will be able to resist a claim for equal value which otherwise would succeed.[2] It may even be that a mistake which is not objectively justified can provide a good defence (provided it does not involve a material factor tainted by sex). Such was the decision of the EAT in *Yorkshire Blood Transfusion Service v Plaskitt*[3] where the additional payment to the man was attributable to a genuine mistake on the employer's part. The Court drew a distinction between alleged indirect discrimination (where objective justification was required for an employer's defence) and direct discrimination (in issue in *Plaskitt*) where it held this was not so. Where indirect discrimination is alleged, however, it is certain that the burden of showing justification, whatever the standard, falls on the employer.[4]

[1] [1988] AC 894, [1988] IRLR 257, HL.
[2] *Equal Opportunities Comm v Secretary of State for Employment* [1994] 1 All ER 910, HL.
[3] [1994] ICR 74, EAT.
[4] *British Coal Corpn v Smith* [1994] IRLR 342, CA.

23.09A The meaning of 'pay' itself has been clarified following decisions of the ECJ on the interpretation of Article 119 (see above, para 21.13). But the decisions of domestic courts have also been important here. Redundancy payments were held to be within 'pay' by the *Barber*[1] decision. But whether compensation for unfair dismissal also so qualifies has been a question keenly debated for some time. Although it is a payment which comes from the employer, can it be said that it is made in respect of the employee's employment – which is the crucial test? In *R v Secretary of State for Employment, ex p Equal Opportunities Commission*[2] Lord Keith saw 'much to be said in favour' of the view that it was, but left the issue open. Subsequently the EAT acted on the basis that Art 119 did cover unfair dismissal compensation[3] but more recently the Court of Appeal[4] has again raised a doubt. The CA has held that this analysis was not *acte clair*, thus inviting further litigation on the point. The issue is of profound importance for women who, not being qualified to pursue claims of unfair dismissal, must seek to challenge dismissals by reference to equality law.

[1] *Barber v Guardian Royal Exchange Assurance Group Ltd*: C-262/88 [1990] IRLR 240, ECJ.
[2] [1994] IRLR 176, HL.
[3] *Mediguard Services Ltd v Thame* [1994] IRLR 504, EAT; *Methilhill Bowling Club v Hunter* [1995] IRLR 323, EAT.
[4] *R v Secretary of State for Employment, ex p Seymour-Smith* [1995] IRLR 464, CA.

6 THE MAKING OF THE COMPARISON

23.10 In order to benefit from an equality clause, the woman must be able to point to a man (the comparator) who is employed on like work, work rated as equivalent or work of equal value in the same employment. In consequence of *Macarthys Ltd v Smith*[1] and the overriding effect of Art 119, such a comparator need not be contemporaneously employed with the woman, though such is the natural meaning of the statutory wording. It is now established law that the comparator may be someone who was previously engaged in such work, though it is not clear how far back in time such comparisons may be made. It is not, however, possible to make use of comparison on the basis of how an employer *would* treat a man, for the concept of the 'hypothetical male' forms no part of the Equal Pay Act. When comparison is made it must be with someone in the 'same employment', and this is defined (s 1(6)) as meaning 'employed by an employer or associated employer at the same establishment or at establishments in Great Britain which include that one at which common terms and conditions of employment are observed either generally or for employees of the relevant classes'. Many problems can arise when comparison is made with someone in another establishment who does not work under identical conditions of employment. The House of Lords has indicated that in such a situation a valid comparison can be made if it can be said that, in a broad sense, the terms of the applicant and the comparator are common, either for employees generally or for employees of the relevant classes.[2] The actual level of remuneration and other benefits received may, however, vary from place to place as a result of local-level bargaining supplementing national agreements without this necessarily precluding a finding that two establishments are observing common terms.[3] Where a man is chosen as a comparator from a different establishment it must be shown not only that he has the same employer but also that the terms and conditions of employment of men of the relevant class at his establishment are common with, meaning the same as, the terms and conditions of men of the relevant class employed at the women's establishment. But it is not necessary that the terms and conditions of employment for women employees are the same at both establishments in order for a cross-establishment claim to be made.[4]

1 129/79 [1981] QB 180, [1980] IRLR 210, ECJ, para 23.02, above.

2 *Leverton v Clwyd County Council* [1989] 1 All ER 78, [1989] IRLR 28, HL. See too *Barclays Bank plc v James* [1990] IRLR 90, EAT; *British Coal Corpn v Smith* [1994] IRLR 342, CA.

3 *Thomas v National Coal Board* [1987] IRLR 451, EAT.

4 *British Coal Corpn v Smith*, above.

7 EXCLUSIONS

Pensions and retirement

23.11 The equality clause does not (subject to qualifications to ensure equal access to certain occupational pension schemes and to non-discrimination in relation to treatment in connection with retirement) operate in respect of any terms of a contract relating to death or retirement (s 6(1A)). But the identification of such a term is often not a simple matter. In the light of *Barber v Guardian Royal Exchange Assurance Group*,[1] and subsequent cases, it is clear that financial benefits received under occupational pension schemes are to be seen now as 'pay' and so be caught by the general provisions of the Act. The ECJ have also now held that the exclusion of part-timers from company pension schemes is discriminatory and the right to join falls within the scope of Art 119 of the European Treaty.[2] The Social Security Act 1989 also restricts the scope of the exemption contained in s 6(1A), by extending the scope of the equality clause to cover membership conditions imposed by certain employment-related benefit schemes. So too it is established law that access to occupational pension schemes is protected by Art 119(3), so that s 6(1)(a) must be read as subject to that qualification.[3]

1 C-262/88 [1990] IRLR 240, ECJ.

2 *Vroege v NCIV Instituut voor Volkshuisvesting BV, Stichting Pensionfonds NCIV* [1994] Case C-57/93, ECJ [1994] IRLR 651, ECJ.

3 *Bilka-Kaufhaus GmbH v Weber von Hartz*: 170/84 [1986] IRLR 317, ECJ.

Pregnancy and childbirth

23.12 An exclusion is granted under s 6(1)(b) in respect of terms of employment giving special treatment to women in connection with pregnancy or childbirth. This allows an employer to, eg, provide maternity leave without thereby being open to challenge by reference to the equality clause by his male employees. The Trade Union Reform and Employment Rights Act 1993[1] provides for improved statutory rights in respect of maternity leave for female employees. These provisions are discussed separately (see Chapter 10), together with the new rules on maternity pay which were introduced in 1994.

1 See now Part VIII of the ERA.

Compliance with existing law

23.13 Under the Act an exemption exists to allow for compliance with existing law (s 6(1)(a)). The significance of this exemption has now been very much narrowed as a consequence of the repeals of discriminatory industrial safety provisions by the Sex Discrimination Act 1986 and the Employment Act 1989. In addition, it may be noted that the Employment Act 1989 (s 1) provides that legislation prior to the Sex Discrimination Act 1975 is generally of no effect insofar as it imposes a requirement to do something which would be unlawful discrimination under the Sex Discrimination Act. There are very limited exceptions to cover certain situations where the action in question is done for the protection of women.

8 THE EMPLOYER'S DEFENCES

23.14 Where a woman has succeeded in showing that she is qualified to make a claim under the Equal Pay Act, and that she is engaged on work with a male comparator which is like work, work rated as equivalent or work of equal value, she has come a long way in achieving success. But there is one final stage of great importance; if the employer is able to show that the difference between the woman and the male comparator falls within the statutory defence permitted him by s 1(3), the claim will not succeed. This defence is generally known as the 'material factor defence' and it varies in its formulation, according to whether it arises in connection with a claim for equal value or under one of the other possible headings. The defence in itself raises complicated issues of substance, but it also is important to know at precisely what stage or stages in the proceedings it may be introduced, and with what effect. No accurate assessment of the impact made by the equality legislation can be given without taking into account how far the material factor defence limits the reach of the basic concepts which have been explained above.

The 'material factor' defence

23.15 It is provided that an equality clause shall not operate to cancel a variation between a man's contract and a woman's, when the employer (the burden lies on him) proves that the variation is genuinely due to a material factor which is not the difference of sex. Where the claim is made on the basis of like work or work rated as equivalent, the factor *must* be a material difference between the woman's case and the man's; where the claim is made on the basis of equal value, the factor *may* be a material difference. The distinction between the two forms the defence may take is explained by the wish of the government to give a wider scope to the defence in equal value claims, and thus to minimise what were seen as the unwelcome and inflationary consequences of the reform of 1984.[1] Judicial interpretation of s 1(3) in relation to a 'like work' claim has meant, however, that the difference in wording between the two formulations of the defence is unimportant. The scope of the defence in relation to 'like work' and 'work rated as equivalent' has been widened so as broadly to bring it into line with the situation the government was seeking to achieve in relation to equal value claims. The s 1(3) defence will not provide an escape route for an employer when the circumstances which once justified such an argument have disappeared.[2]

[1] See, eg, *McGregor v General Municipal Boilermakers and Allied Trades Union* [1987] ICR 505 at 513, EAT, per Wood J.

[2] *Benveniste v University of Southampton* [1989] IRLR 122, CA.

Objective difference

23.16 The employer who seeks to rely on s 1(3) has to show, on a balance of probabilities,[1] that there is good reason for the difference between the woman's contract and the man's. Such a difference might exist where, for example, the comparator, though engaged on like work or work of equal value, was receiving more pay because of working longer hours. So too different levels of remuneration may be justified by showing that the higher paid employee has longer service, better qualifications, or better productivity. A difference between the man's conditions and those of the woman may not be sufficient to prevent a finding that the work is, within the meaning of the Act, 'like work', but it may nonetheless provide the basis for a s 1(3) defence.[2] One commonly found such basis is the so-called 'red circle' cases, where a worker is transferred from a higher paid job to a lower paid one, but retains his old rate of pay subsequent to the transfer. If a fellow employee of the opposite sex in the new job claims equal pay with the transferee, that claim may be defeated by the employer showing the special reasons just mentioned. A similar situation may arise following a re-grading exercise carried out by an employer, where the protection of the wages of employees already in post is regarded as standard good industrial relations practice.[3] But there is no automatic rule that a 'red circle' argument will always satisfy the conditions of s 1(3), and each case will be considered on its merits. In particular, a 'red circle' will not last forever, and an employer will not be able to rely upon it when the special circumstances which produced it have lapsed with the passage of time.[4] Neither will such a defence be allowed under s 1(3) when there is a finding that the differential which the 'red circle' preserves had its origin in past sexual discrimination.[5] Indeed, as a matter of general principle, the s 1(3) defence cannot be made out when the factor relied upon is one which discriminates, directly or indirectly, against women. An example might be where extra pay was awarded on the basis of length of service. It follows from this that where a factor does have disparate impact, it is for the employer to show that it is objectively justifiable for him to rely upon it, and if he fails to do so he may not rely upon it as a basis for a s1(3) defence. This point was accepted in the *Danfoss* case as a matter of Community law,[6] and in *Enderby*[7] this important point was reiterated. In the later case the court expressed the view that non-discriminatory collective bargaining arrangements would not, of themselves, provide the necessary objective justification for pay differentials. On the other hand, the state of the employment market might be sufficient. Although these observations were made in relation to Art 119, there is no doubt that they apply equally to the interpretation of s 1(3).

[1] *National Vulcan Engineering Insurance Group Ltd v Wade* [1979] QB 132, [1978] IRLR 225, CA.
[2] *National Coal Board v Sherwin* [1978] ICR 700, [1978] IRLR 122, EAT.
[3] *Charles Early and Marriott (Whitney) Ltd v Smith* [1978] QB 11, [1977] ICR 700, EAT.
[4] *United Biscuits Ltd v Young* [1978] IRLR 15, EAT; *Outlook Supplies Ltd v Parry* [1978] 2 All ER 707, [1978] IRLR 12, EAT.
[5] *Snoxell v Vauxhall Motors Ltd* [1978] QB 11, [1977] ICR 700, EAT.
[6] *Handels-og Kontorfunktionaerernes Forbund i Danmark v Dansk Arbejdsgiverforening*: 109/88 [1989] IRLR 532, ECJ.
[7] *Enderby v Frenchay Health Authority and Secretary of State for Health*: C-127/92 [1993] IRLR 591, ECJ.

23.16A In order to show indirect discrimination in a claim brought under the Sex Discrimination Act, an applicant has to show the presence of a requirement or condition which is such that a considerably smaller proportion of women (compared to men) are able to comply with it.[1] In an equal pay context, an employer who is faced with a claim of indirect discrimination does not necessarily have a defence simply by showing the absence of such a condition or requirement. This was the gist of the ECJ's decision in *Enderby v Frenchay Health Authority and Secretary of State for Health*[2] in relation to Art 119; it was confirmed as relevant also to the proper interpretation of s 1(3) by the CA in *British Coal Corpn v Smith*.[3] In the words of Balcombe LJ:

> 'It may well be that indirect discrimination which was not justified and therefore was unlawful under s 1(1)(b) could never provide a "material factor" defence under s 1(3). But it does not follow that s 1(3) is limited to cases covered by s 1(1)(b).'

This tells us what will not satisfy s 1(3). More positively, what is required is that the employer can show genuine need and that the means chosen to meet that need are both suitable and necessary for the purpose.[4] A response which is not proportionate to the problem faced will not pass this test.

[1] Sex Discrimination Act 1975, s 1(1)(b).
[2] C-127/92 [1993] IRLR 591, ECJ.
[3] [1994] IRLR 342, CA.
[4] *Bilka-Kaufhaus GmbH v Weber von Hartz*: 170/84 [1986] IRLR 317, ECJ.

23.17 While it is impossible to give any comprehensive account of the kind of arguments that may be successful under s 1(3), it is worth quoting the words of Lord Keith in the *Rainey* case,[1] the facts of which are more fully considered below:

> 'The difference must be "material", which I would construe as meaning "significant and relevant", and it must be between "her case and his".

Consideration of a person's case must necessarily involve consideration of all the circumstances of that case. These may well go beyond what is not very happily described as "the personal equation", ie the personal qualities by way of skill, experience or training which the individual brings to the job. Some circumstances may on examination prove to be not significant or not relevant, but others may do so, though not relating to the personal qualities of the employer. In particular, where there is no question of intentional sex discrimination whether direct or indirect . . . a difference which is connected with economic factors affecting the efficient carrying on of the employer's business or other activity may well be relevant.'

[1] *Rainey v Greater Glasgow Health Board* [1987] IRLR 26 at 29, HL.

23.18 In the *Rainey* decision the House of Lords accepted the view expressed by the European Court of Justice[1] that an employer would not be in infringement of Art 119 if he could show a difference in conditions was based on objectively justified economic grounds as applicable also to a defence raised under s 1(3). But their Lordships also went significantly further than the ECJ by recognising that a defence under s 1(3) could be made out even in the absence of *economic* grounds, provided they were objectively justified. 'Administrative efficiency' in a non-commercial organisation was given as an example of such a possibility. However, in any case where s 1(3) is invoked, it is not enough for the employer to believe that such ends would be achieved; there is an obligation for him to show that *in fact* the differential was reasonably necessary in order to achieve the particular objective.[2] Neither is it enough for justification to be based on generalised and untestable assumptions about different categories of workers; the criteria adopted must be based on objective standards.[3]

[1] That is in *Bilka-Kaufhaus v Weber von Hartz*: 170/84 [1987] ICR 110, [1986] IRLR 317, ECJ; para 21.15, above.

[2] *Jenkins v Kingsgate (Clothing Productions) Ltd (No 2)* [1981] ICR 715, [1981] IRLR 388.

[3] *Rinner-Kühn v FWW Spezial-Gebäudereinigung GmbH, Co KG*: 171/88 [1989] IRLR 493 at 496, ECJ.

Collective agreements as justification

23.19 Following *Enderby* it is now clear that the fact that wages are fixed by apparently non-discriminatory collective bargaining will not, of itself, provide the justification necessary to defeat a prima facie case of indirect discrimination. Nevertheless, the ECJ did not go so far as to deny that such collective bargaining arrangements could be relied upon by an employer, and they will continue to be relevant for s 1(3) purposes.[1] But they will be persuasive evidence of justification only insofar as (a) they are themselves free of indirect discrimination, and (b) they justify all of the difference between the woman's pay and her comparators. The payment of higher wage rates to full-timers as against part-timers is *prima facie* indirect discrimination against women, given that far more women than men work part-time.[2] It has been held by the EAT[3] that it is not enough to show that a difference in pay is caused by a factor that is free from sex discrimination; what is necessary is proof that the variation is genuinely due to a material factor other than sex.

[1] *Reed Packaging Ltd v Boozer* [1988] ICR 391, [1988] IRLR 333, EAT.
[2] *Equal Opportunities Commission v Secretary of State for Employment* [1994] 1 All ER 910, HL.
[3] *Barber v NCR (Manufacturing) Ltd* [1993] IRLR 95, EAT.

Market forces

23.20 One aspect of s 1(3) merits attention because of the practical significance it has for the scope of the defence. An employer may seek to justify a difference in contractual conditions between a man and a woman by arguing that he had to offer more advantageous terms to the male comparator in order to recruit him. The validity of such an argument has for long been controversial. As originally interpreted, s 1(3) was held to be restricted to matters such as qualifications for characteristics which fell within the employee's 'personal equation'.[1] In the words of Lord Denning MR in *Clay Cross*,[1] if the law were to allow the admission of extrinsic forces under s 1(3) 'the door would be wide open. Every employer who wished to avoid the statute would walk straight through it'. It was indeed because of this line of authority that the government chose to amend the wording of s 1(3) in 1984 at the time of the introduction of the new equal value procedure. The government – which on policy grounds certainly did not welcome the change to British law made necessary by European law – was determined that its impact should be confined as much as possible. One way of achieving this was to ensure that here at least 'market forces' should be capable of providing a defence. The potential gap between s 1(3) as it applies to equal value claims as opposed to all others has never really developed, because of a change in judicial interpretation. The EAT has confirmed[2] that the change in wording that has taken place in s 1(3) since 1984 is 'all important' and that earlier authorities on the meaning of the provision are not necessarily of great assistance in an equal value context. Nevertheless, the operation of market forces should not be seen as permitting pay differences which are tainted by sex discrimination. In *Ratcliffe v North Yorkshire County Council*[3] the House of Lords refused to allow a pay differential between men and women doing work rated as equivalent where the differential was attributable to a 'market forces' argument. In that case the women (who worked as school dinner ladies) suffered a reduction in pay in order to allow their local authority employer to compete in a local market in which the pay of women was unfairly suppressed. The industrial tribunal had held that the employers were unable, in these circumstances, to show a defence based on s 1(3), and their Lordships ruled that they were entitled to reach that decision.

[1] *Clay Cross (Quarry Services) Ltd v Fletcher* [1979] 1 All ER 474, [1979] ICR 1, CA.
[2] *McGregor v General Municipal Boilermakers and Allied Trades Union* [1987] ICR 505, EAT.
[3] [1995] IRLR 439, HL.

23.21 If there is no discrimination, however, the position is significantly different. Until the decision of the ECJ in *Enderby* the main authority, was *Rainey v Greater Glasgow Health Board*[1] in which it was held that s 1(3) was capable of justifying a difference in pay between men and women doing the same job within the National Health Service. The men had been recruited into the NHS from private practice where they had been carrying on business as prostheticians, and in order to attract them it had been necessary to pay a higher level of remuneration than that paid to personnel already working in the NHS engaged in the same profession. A claim for equal treatment to bring the remuneration of the two groups into line was unsuccessful, because of a s 1(3) defence. The House of Lords accepted that the circumstances justified the pay differential. It was accepted that the NHS service would not have been possible without the recruitment of experienced staff from the private sector, and this meant offering such recruits terms of employment no less favourable than they were already receiving in their jobs. This interpretation of s 1(3) was seen as in line with the approach taken to Art 119 by the ECJ in *Bilka-Kaufhaus v Weber von Hartz*[2] and also the earlier interpretation of s 1(3) given by the EAT in *Jenkins v Kingsgate (Clothing Productions) Ltd (No 2)*.[3] The 'market forces' argument that lay at the heart of the employer's case was classed as falling within the 'economic or other reasons' which *Jenkins* had established was acceptable as a possible base for the statutory defence.

1 [1987] AC 224, [1987] IRLR 26, HL.
2 170/84 [1987] ICR 110, [1986] IRLR 317, ECJ.
3 [1981] ICR 715, [1981] IRLR 388.

23.22 Although *Rainey* was a claim for equal pay based on 'like work', it can scarcely be doubted that a similar result would follow if it had been made under the heading of 'equal value', given the less demanding (from the employer's point of view) wording of s 1(3) in such cases.

Legislative authority

23.23 It is not enough, to show a defence under s 1(3), to point to differences in pay which are based on a scheme which has statutory authority. The test of objective justification will not necessarily be satisfied by showing this explanation for the payment of a particular wage. The Divisional Court took this view in the early stages of the *Enderby* litigation[1] and in the decision in *R v Secretary of State for Employment, ex p Equal Opportunities Commission*[2] this approach was confirmed by the House of Lords. The principle is clear: the obligation to comply with the principle of equality, as expressed in Art 119, is something which takes priority over any provision of domestic law. Statute is no more a basis for a valid s 1(3) defence than is a collective agreement; both can be challenged on the basis that they incorporate indirect discrimination.

1 *R v Secretary of State for Social Services, ex p Clarke* [1988] 1 CMLR 279, [1988] IRLR 22, DC.
2 [1994] 1 All ER 910, HL.

9 EQUAL VALUE CLAIMS

23.24 Apart from s 1(3), an employer faced with a claim for equal value may rely on a job evaluation study to justify a difference in pay or other terms. A claim for equal value will fail if the employer can establish that there are 'no reasonable grounds for determining that the work is of equal value' (EqPA, s 2A(1)). It is specified that one situation where there are no such grounds is where a job evaluation study within the meaning of s 1(5) has been carried out, and there are no reasonable grounds for determining that the evaluation was made on a system which discriminates on the grounds of sex (s 2A(2)). For a job evaluation study to be used in this way, however, it must be 'analytical' in the sense of evaluating the work of the man and woman in terms of the demands made under different headings.[1]

[1] *Bromley v H & J Quick Ltd* [1988] 2 CMLR 468, [1988] IRLR 249, CA (see para 23.06, above).

10 ENFORCEMENT

23.25 Claims to enforce the right to equal treatment must be made by employees to an industrial tribunal. If a claim is successful, arrears of remuneration for a period of up to two years prior to the date on which proceedings were instituted may be recovered.[1] An equal pay claims must be lodged within six months of leaving employment, under s 2 (4) of the EqPA.[2] Where the employee remains in employment, there is no time limit on the bringing of proceedings.

[1] EqPA, s 2(5).
[2] *Etherson v Strathclyde Regional Council* [1992] IRLR 392, EAT.

23.26 Since the effect of the equality clause is to amend the terms of the contract of employment, it would in principle be possible for a claim to be brought before the ordinary common law courts in reliance upon it. But powers are given to courts to strike out such claims if they find that they could more conveniently be decided by an industrial tribunal.[1]

[1] EqPA, s 2(3).

11 RETROSPECTIVE CLAIMS

23.26A A question of some difficulty is whether an individual who has been excluded from a statutory right under the provisions of UK law, and who becomes aware that such exclusion was not warranted uner Community law, can challenge, by reference to Community law, acts which were prejudicial but which took place many years ago. The matter is particularly important in relation to part-time workers. Until the law changed in February 1995, such employees were subject to different and more restrictive statutory qualifying conditions in respect of a range of statutory rights, including unfair dismissal and redundancy, than full-time employees. Following the ruling in *R v Secretary of State for Employment, ex p Equal Opportunities Commission*[1] attempts were made to re-open dismissals of part-timers which had taken place many years previously. Although the matter is not yet free from doubt,[2] it would appear that success for such applicants is unlikely. In *Biggs v Somerset County Council*[3] it was held that a claim in respect of a dismissal that was 18 years old was out of time. The standard time limit for bringing an unfair dismissal (or redundancy) claim was held also to govern claims in which reliance on Community law was an essential element. In part, the basis for this ruling is the argument that a part-time worker could have challenged the legality of the UK restrictions before the *EOC* decision; therefore the time limits of the UK statute could be held to run against such an applicant from the moment of her dismissal. The controversy which attaches to this issue is a reflection of the difficulties encountered in balancing justice to the individual against the need to recognise legal certainty and an end to litigation.

1 [1994] IRLR 176, HL.
2 Cf *Rankin v British Coal Corpn* [1993] IRLR 69, EAT.
3 [1995] IRLR 452, EAT. Confirmed by the CA: [1996] IRLR 203.

12 TRIBUNAL PROCEEDINGS

23.27 Failing a conciliated settlement or the withdrawal of the claim, an industrial tribunal will hear the claim. The proceedings which take place, however, differ substantially according to whether the basis of the claim is (a) like work or work rated as equivalent, or (b) equal value. The difference is best explained by referring to the regulations governing both types of claim,[1] where there are in effect two different schemes, contained in Schs 1 and 2, which apply according to whether or not the claim for equal treatment is one based on equal value.

1 Industrial Tribunal (Constitution and Procedure) Regulations 1993, SI 1993/2687, as amended.

23.28 Where a claim is made in respect of 'like work' or 'work rated as equivalent' it is dealt with by the tribunal according to the standard procedures, as set out in Sch 1 to the Regulations. As such claims are covered by the standard procedure, it is not necessary to examine them further here.[1] It may be noted, however, that jobs are to be seen as 'rated as equivalent' (s 1(5)) when, although allocated a different number of points on a job evaluation scheme, both are placed in the same grade according to the rules of the scheme.[2]

1 For an outline of the general procedure followed by industrial tribunals, see para 24.21 ff.
2 *Springboard Sunderland Trust v Robson* [1992] ICR 554, EAT.

Equal value claims

23.29 On the other hand, an equal value claim is governed by procedure which is unique, once the claim has reached the stage of the hearing. The special nature of the proceedings centres round the role of the 'independent expert' who may be appointed by the court to investigate the factual basis of the claim and to report to the court. Such an expert will be chosen from a panel appointed for this purpose by the Advisory, Conciliation and Arbitration Service, and he will, in effect, carry out a job evaluation to decide the question. The task of the expert is to take account of all information supplied to him (and representations received) and to seek to reach a conclusion as to whether the work in question is work of equal value. His report should contain a summary of the findings on which it is based, together with his conclusions, if any, regarding the question of equal value.[1] Pending the carrying out of this task, the hearing before the tribunal is adjourned, to be resumed when the report is submitted. While the expert does not in law have the power to decide authoritatively the question of equal value – that is something only the tribunal can do – in practice his findings are likely to be decisive, if for no other reason than that the tribunal will often have no other evidence before it on which to base its decision.[2] For this reason there are various safeguards designed to ensure that the expert properly performs his duties. The tribunal may refuse to admit a submitted report on various grounds detailed in the regulations,[3] such as failure to act fairly, or that the conclusion it contains is one which, taking account of the facts before him, could not reasonably have been reached by the expert. In such circumstances a fresh report will be commissioned. Furthermore, the expert may be required to attend the resumed hearing of the tribunal and may be cross-examined on his report.[4] On the other hand, the clear intention of the regulations is that, save in special circumstances, the expert's report is to provide the factual evidence on which the tribunal makes up its mind. In general, the parties are not permitted to give evidence on factual matters.[5] A party who so wishes is entitled to bring one expert witness of his own to give expert evidence on the question of equal value, and this witness too may be cross-examined at the hearing.[6]

1 Schedule 2, r 8A(3)(c).
2 Compare *Tennants Textile Colours Ltd v Todd* [1989] IRLR 3, NICA.
3 Schedule 2, r 8A(13)(c).
4 Schedule 2, r 9(2A).
5 Schedule 2, r 9(2C), (2D). There are two main exceptions, set out in r 9(2D): (a) when the matter of fact is raised in connection with a s 1(3) defence, and (b) when the expert's report contains no conclusion as to whether the work is of equal value and the tribunal is satisfied that this is because of the refusal or deliberate omission of a person to comply with a direction by the tribunal to furnish information or produce documents.
6 Schedule 2, r 9(2B).

23.30 While the appointment of an expert may be seen as standard procedure in equal value claims, it is by no means inevitable. In the first place, the tribunal is given power to determine a question of equal value without the need of an expert's report in circumstances where it is satisfied that 'there are no reasonable grounds for determining that the work is of equal value'.[1] In other words a tribunal may dismiss a claim which it sees as completely far-fetched or hopeless at the outset. Secondly, as mentioned earlier, the existence of a non-discriminatory job evaluation scheme giving different values to the woman's work and the man's will give the tribunal the right to dismiss the claim without the appointment of an expert.[2]

1 EqPA, s 2A(1)(a).
2 EqPA, s 2A(2).

23.31 The other main circumstances which can lead to the dismissal of a claim at a preliminary stage is where the tribunal has decided it would be appropriate to hear evidence and argument on the availability of the s 1(3) defence, and, having done so, has decided that the defence is made out.[1] There is no obligation on a tribunal to decide to hear the s 1(3) issue at a preliminary stage, but it has been held that a tribunal which does not dismiss a claim after having done so and reaching a conclusion that the defence is made out, would be in breach of its duties.[2] Where the s 1(3) defence is raised as a preliminary issue, the employer is no longer (since an amendment to the law introduced in 1984) entitled to have it considered later, at the stage when the tribunal has before it the expert's report. The situation where s 1(3) is being considered by the tribunal at the full hearing is one of the exceptional situations where the parties are permitted to adduce evidence on factual matters upon which a conclusion in the expert's report is based.[3] There is no difference in the content of the s 1(3) defence, whether it is raised as a preliminary issue, before the case is sent to an expert, or after a finding by the expert that there is work of equal value.[4]

---

1 Schedule 2, r 9(2E).
2 *Reed Packaging Ltd v Boozer* [1988] ICR 391, [1988] IRLR 333, EAT.
3 Schedule 2, r 9(2D)(a).
4 *McGregor v General Municipal Boilermakers and Allied Trades Union* [1987] ICR 505, EAT.

---

13 COLLECTIVE AGREEMENTS

23.32 Until its repeal by the SDA 1986, s 3 of the EqPA allowed for the referral of discriminatory collective agreements to the Central Arbitration Committee, and gave powers to that body to modify them. That procedure has now disappeared from the law, and is replaced by a wholly different method of controlling discriminatory agreements. Section 77 of the SDA 1975 was extended so as to apply to collective agreements[1] and has the result that all discriminatory terms in collective agreements are rendered void. This is an unusual sanction, given that unless the contrary is stated, there is a presumption that collective agreements are not legally enforceable contracts.[2] The rules made by an employer for his workers, and the rules of a trade union, employers organisation or professional bodies are also brought within the scope of s 77, and will similarly be void and unenforceable if discriminatory within the meaning of that section. A new right[3] for individuals affected by discriminatory collective agreements allows an application to be made to an industrial tribunal for a declaration that a term which contravenes the principle of equal treatment is void. A discriminatory term in a collective agreement or other document may be relied upon by the person discriminated against insofar as this confers rights upon him.[4]

---

1 SDA 1986, s 6.
2 Trade Union and Labour Relations Act 1974, s 18(1).
3 Sex Discrimination Act 1975, s 6(4A); introduced by the Trade Union Reform and Employment Rights Act 1993, s 32.
4 Sex Discrimination Act 1986, s 6(5).

---

24 Discrimination

Brian Napier

1 INTRODUCTION

24.01 Although Parliament first specifically legislated on discrimination in 1919[1] the present law on discrimination is contained in two principal statutes, the Sex Discrimination Act 1975 (SDA) and the Race Relations Act 1976 (RRA). In 1986 a second, amending Sex Discrimination Act was enacted; there have also been changes made to the two parent Acts by other legislation. These statutes apply also to discrimination outside the workplace, but only employment discrimination is considered here. Sex and race are the two forms of discrimination which have been primarily targeted by statute, but other types of discrimination are also proscribed – both in the statutes mentioned and elsewhere. Discrimination against the disabled is now governed by the Disability Discrimination Act 1995, not fully in force at the time of writing.[2] Discrimination against persons in employment because of their membership of or participation in the affairs of a trade union is subject to separate statutory regulation.[3] Discrimination in respect of marital status and victimisation, is, however, prohibited under the two main acts. Discrimination by trade unions towards members or prospective members on grounds of sex or race is also contrary to these statutes,[4] as is discrimination by vocational training bodies,[5] and partnerships.[6] An important reform, introduced by the Trade Union Reform and Employment Relations Act 1993,[7] makes dismissal for the assertion of certain statutory rights automatically unfair; dismissal for the exercise of rights given under either of the main discrimination statutes is not covered by this new right, but it is difficult to imagine circumstances in which a dismissal involving an act of sex or racial discrimination could be classified as fair.

1 Sex Discrimination (Removal) Act 1919. This Act is now of little importance.
2 See ch 25, below.
3 Trade Union on Labour Relations (Consolidation) Act 1992, ss 146, 152.
4 SDA, s 12; RRA, s 11.
5 SDA, s 14; RRA, s 13.
6 SDA, s 11; RRA, s 10.
7 Section 29.

24.02 The general scope of the discrimination legislation is considered immediately below, together with certain concepts of substance and procedure important in understanding how British domestic law attempts to combat the different forms of discrimination encountered. The details of the law relating to the regulation of different particular types of unlawful discrimination are considered after an exploration of the general ambit of statutory discrimination law.[1]

1 See *Harvey* Div L for a detailed review of the SDA and RRA.

24.03 The SDA and RRA are very similar and share many of the basic concepts used to identify and prohibit discrimination in the employment field. Where concepts and terminology are common, there is judicial authority[1] as well as common sense to support the view that they should be similarly interpreted. On the other hand, the linkage with Community law which exists in relation to sex discrimination law can be the basis for an interpretative approach which is broader than that which would be appropriate in purely domestic matters.

[1] *Hampson v Department of Education and Science* [1988] IRLR 87 at 94, EAT, per Popplewell J.

2 SCOPE OF THE LEGISLATION

24.04 There are many types of discrimination in employment which escape legal regulation under English law. Discrimination on the grounds of religion or age, for example, is not *per se* unlawful, and no one may complain of an infringement of rights if he or she is refused employment, disadvantaged in or dismissed from employment on such grounds. Such discrimination may of course, quite independently of the discrimination legislation, be the basis for an unfair dismissal claim, constitute the infringement of some other statutory right, or may amount to some act in breach of the contract of employment. On the other hand, an act which disadvantages someone and is for a reason proscribed under the discrimination legislation will produce an infringement of statutory rights which permits a complaint to be made to an industrial tribunal, provided the relevant conditions are met. If successful, this complaint can lead to the making of an award of compensation or other remedy in favour of the aggrieved individual. There is no upper limit on the amounts which can be awarded under this heading. As mentioned earlier, the Equal Pay Act 1970 and the Sex Discrimination Act 1975 are to be interpreted as providing an interlocking code dealing with employment discrimination on grounds of sex. There is thus no overlap between them, and a valid claim must fall under one or other of the two headings; it cannot fall under both. Excluded from the scope of the SDA are, in particular, claims which relate to the payment of money under a contract of employment. Such claims can only be regulated under the EqPA, under the conditions which have been considered above as applicable to such claims. As there is no equivalent to the Equal Pay Act in relation to racial discrimination, all claims, whether or not concerned with the payment of money, relating to such discrimination must be made under the RRA.

24.05 The statutory rules governing discrimination in employment apply to all who work or seek to work under a contract of employment or apprenticeship, or a contract personally to execute any work or labour.[1] Thus the law applies not only to employees but also to the self-employed. Crown employees (ie civil servants) are also protected as, since 1995, they are members of the armed forces. Persons undergoing training, however, are probably excluded from the main system of protection of the Acts,[2] as are persons who suffer discrimination under business contracts.[3] Coverage, however, extends to all workers irrespective of their length of service, or the number of hours they work each week. The rules regarding discrimination against women apply equally, with a few narrow exceptions which are considered below, to discrimination against men.

Similarly, a few statutory exceptions to the general rules make allowance for lawful discrimination on grounds of racial grouping.

1 SDA, s 82(1); RRA, s 78(1).
2 *Daley v Allied Suppliers Ltd* [1983] ICR 90, [1983] IRLR 14, EAT.
3 *Mirror Group Newspapers Ltd v Gunning* [1986] 1 WLR 546, [1986] IRLR 27, CA.

Unlawful acts and prospective employees

24.06 It is unlawful for an employer to discriminate in the arrangements he makes for the purpose of determining who should be offered employment, in the terms on which employment is offered, or in refusing or deliberately omitting to offer employment.[1] In relation to sex discrimination, an offer of employment on terms which, were they to be accepted, would be modified by operation of the equality clause read into every contract of employment by s 1 of the EqPA 1970 is expressly stated to be unlawful.[2] But, on the other hand, there will be no contravention of the statute when the equality clause would not come into play because of the employer's defence under s 1(3) of the EqPA.[3]

1 SDA, ss 6(1)(a)(b)(c); RRA, s 4(1)(a)(b)(c).
2 SDA, s 8(3).
3 SDA, s 8(4).

24.07 Where there exists a 'genuine occupational qualification' (discussed below, para 24.35) a defence may be available to the employer. But in the absence of such a defence or one based on objective justification it will be unlawful for an employer, for example, to advertise vacancies in ways which discriminate against members of one sex or racial group.[1] A simple absence of intention to discriminate is not a defence, but may limit the employer's or would-be employer's liability to pay compensation.[2]

1 *Brindley v Tayside Health Board* [1976] IRLR 364, IT.
2 See below, para 24.13.

24.08 Quite apart from the question whether by placing an advertisement for a job vacancy an employer is making 'arrangements . . . for the purpose of determining who should be offered employment' (and as such is open to actions on the part of aggrieved individuals), it is unlawful to publish or to cause to be published certain advertisements which indicates an intention to do an act which is discriminatory on a proscribed ground.[1] But only the EOC or CRE may bring proceedings in respect of any such unlawful advertisement.

1 SDA, s 38(1); RRA, s 29.

Unlawful acts when employment has commenced

24.09 An employer must not discriminate against someone in his employment on any proscribed ground in the way he affords that person access to opportunities for promotion, transfer or training, or to any other benefits, facilities or services, or by refusing or deliberately omitting to afford access to them, or by dismissing the person or subjecting him or her to any other detriment.[1]

[1] SDA, s 6(2)(a)(b); RRA, s 4(2)(b)(c).

24.10 In relation to discrimination on grounds of race, it is also unlawful to discriminate in the terms of employment afforded to the person employed.[1] Under the SDA, this is also true, but there is an express exclusion in respect of benefits consisting of the payment of money when the provision of those benefits is regulated by the contract of employment; in such cases, only the EqPA can provide a remedy.[2]

[1] RRA, s 4(2)(a).
[2] SDA, s 6(6).

3 DISCRIMINATION AND THIRD PARTIES

24.11 Under the legislation, an employer will be liable for a wrongful act done by an employee in the course of his employment.[1] But an employer will not be liable for an act which is clearly outside what the employee is authorised to do.[2] Moreover, where an attempt is made under the legislation to hold an employer vicariously liable, the employer has the defence that he took such steps as were reasonably practicable to prevent the doing of the act.[3] It is unlawful for a person to induce a discriminatory act in the employment field, and a person who knowingly gives assistance to the doing of an unlawful discriminatory act is himself liable.[4] Case law has also made it clear that unlawful discrimination arises not just where a person suffers less favourable treatment because of his own characteristics, but also where the reason is the characteristics of some other person, where these fall within one of the proscribed reasons.[5]

[1] SDA, s 41; RRA, s 32.
[2] *Irving and Irving v Post Office* [1987] IRLR 289, CA. See now *Tower Boot Co Ltd v Jones* [1995] IRLR 529, EAT.
[3] SDA, s 41(3); RRA, s 32(3); *Balgobin v Tower Hamlets London Borough Council* [1987] ICR 829, [1987] IRLR 401, EAT.
[4] SDA, ss 40, 42; RRA, ss 31, 33.
[5] *Showboat Entertainment Centre Ltd v Owens* [1984] 1 All ER 836, [1984] IRLR 7, EAT.

4 DIRECT DISCRIMINATION

24.12 Direct discrimination in employment occurs where a person is treated less favourably than another person whose circumstances are similar, because of one of the proscribed reasons.[1] The motive behind such treatment does not matter, in the sense that even a good motive will not excuse treatment otherwise directly discriminatory.[2] In the leading case[3] it has been said that where direct discrimination is in issue, the key question is whether 'but for' his or her sex, the applicant would have been treated differently. Although this 'but for' test is not to be seen as universally applicable[4] it has the considerable advantage of being easily comprehensible and simple to operate. Usually where direct discrimination arises the discriminator will intend the result, in that it will be his purpose to treat the victim less favourably and his conduct will be motivated by a particular proscribed ground. But it has been held that where a woman is subjected to conduct amounting to sexual harassment at work, the person who is responsible cannot put forward a defence based on the argument that a man would have been treated in an equally disagreeable way, ie that there was no sex-based objective to the campaign.[5] It is also direct discrimination on grounds of sex to treat a person less favourably because of a sex-based assumption that women in general have a less important economic role within the family.[6] Direct discrimination has to be proved by the complainant, on the balance of probabilities, and it may be proved both by means of direct evidence and by inferences drawn from primary facts.[7] There is no question of direct discrimination being shown to be justified by an employer, but, conversely, what may appear to be direct discrimination will not in law be such in the absence of a gender-related factor.[8] It will not be enough for a woman to say that she sees a particular treatment as disadvantageous to her. That is a question for the tribunal to decide. Thus, in *Burrett v West Birmingham Health Authority*[9] a woman nurse complained of having to wear a cap as part of her working uniform. Her application failed not only because male nurses also had to wear uniform (albeit different) but also because the tribunal found that the rule in question did not amount to 'less favourable treatment'.

---

1 SDA, ss 1(1)(a), 3(1)(a); RRA, s 1(1)(a).

2 *Peake v Automotive Products Ltd* [1978] QB 233, [1977] ICR 968, CA, as later explained in *Ministry of Defence v Jeremiah* [1980] QB 87, [1980] ICR 13, CA; *Din v Carrington Viyella Ltd* [1982] ICR 256, [1982] IRLR 281, EAT.

3 *James v Eastleigh Borough Council* [1990] 2 AC 751, HL, following *Birmingham City Council v Equal Opportunities Commission* [1989] AC 1155.

4 In *Webb v EMO Air Cargo (UK) Ltd* [1992] 4 All ER 929, HL, it was held that it should not be applied where the woman was complaining of direct discrimination by reference to the treatment which would be accorded to a hypothetical man.

5 *Strathclyde Regional Council v Porcelli* [1986] IRLR 134.

6 *Skyrail Oceanic Ltd v Coleman* [1981] ICR 864, CA. Cf *Ratcliffe v North Yorkshire County Council* [1995] IRLR 439, HL.

7 *Noone v North West Thames Regional Health Authority* [1988] IRLR 195, CA.

8 *Bullock v Alice Ottley School* [1992] IRLR 564, CA.

9 [1994] IRLR 7, EAT.

---

5 INDIRECT DISCRIMINATION

24.13 The concept of indirect discrimination, which has been considered above in relation to equal pay, forms a central part of the framework of anti-discrimination law. The definition of indirect discrimination, found, *mutatis mutandis*, in s 1(1)(b) of both Acts, comprises three elements: (1) the application of a particular requirement or condition which is apparently neutral in its effect from the point of view of sex or race, (2) an outcome which shows that the proportion of women (members of a racial group) who can comply with it is considerably smaller than the proportion of men (non-members of that racial group) able to comply, and (3) a demonstration that the person who complains of indirect discrimination has suffered a detriment because of inability to comply with the requirement or condition. One of the reasons why indirect discrimination is so far-reaching a concept is that it can arise in the absence of any intention to discriminate – indeed this will usually be the case. An absence of intention is, however, important at a later stage, when it comes to a consideration of remedies. An employer who can show that he never intended by the imposition of the requirement or condition to discriminate on the ground of the proscribed reason will not be subject to an award of damages in respect of the discrimination that has been proved against him.[1]

[1] SDA, s 66(3); RRA, s 57(3).

24.14 Once the three elements mentioned above have been shown to exist, a prima facie case of indirect discrimination is made out; this done, the burden of proof shifts to the respondent employer, who may show that the requirement or condition was justifiable, irrespective of the sex or racial group of the person who has suffered detriment. Such justification, if achieved, will defeat the allegation of indirect discrimination.[1]

[1] The courts have acknowledged the difficulties which attend proof of discrimination and therefore the appropriateness of placing a burden of proof on the alleged discriminator to give an innocent explanation for what may be unlawful behaviour: *Baker v Cornwall County Council* [1990] IRLR 194 at 198, CA, per Neill LJ.

Requirement or condition

24.15 The requirement or condition which has to be shown as a first step in demonstrating indirect discrimination can take many forms. One illustration, in relation to sex discrimination, is the requirement that an employee be engaged in full-time employment. Because of the high proportion of women who combine paid employment with domestic responsibilities, and for other reasons, the proportion of women who work part-time is far higher than the proportion of men. Thus the use of the part-time/full-time distinction as a criterion for allocating advantages or disadvantages in employment will amount (in the absence of justification) to indirect discrimination. In what is now the leading case[1] it was held that the exclusion of part-time workers from a range of statutory rights amounted to unlawful discrimination against women. Their Lordships had no difficulty in rejecting the argument put forward by the Government, to the effect that such exclusion was objectively justified by reason of the cost reduction it brought to employers. As was observed, cost reduction might also be achieved by paying part-time workers less, pro-rata, than full-timers, and such a practice was clearly discriminatory. The selection of part-timers for dismissal on redundancy grounds is another example of behaviour which, in the absence of justification, is clearly unlawful indirect discrimination.[2] The imposition of age limits for job applications may also amount to indirect discrimination on grounds of sex.[3] In race relations cases, the imposition of dress requirements or education qualifications for access to jobs may be similarly construed.[4] It may even be indirect discrimination for an employer to insert a mobility clause in terms of employment.[5]

1 *R v Secretary of State for Employment, ex p Equal Opportunities Commission* [1994] IRLR 176, HL.
2 *Clarke v Eley (IMI) Kynoch Ltd* [1983] ICR 165, EAT.
3 *Price v Civil Service Commission* [1978] 1 All ER 1228, [1977] IRLR 291, EAT.
4 *Panesar v Nestlé Co* [1980] IRLR 64, CA.
5 *Meade-Hill v British Council* [1995] IRLR 478, CA.

24.16 The Court of Appeal has, however, held that where an employer expresses a preference – as opposed to an outright requirement – for a quality, which is such that a considerably smaller proportion of persons drawn from a particular racial group can comply with it, this will not give rise to indirect discrimination.[1] This decision has reduced the impact which indirect discrimination has had in practice. The ruling on this point by the court has been described as a development which 'risks undercutting the entire indirect discrimination concept'.[2] The EOC has itself proposed that a practice or policy having an adverse impact upon one sex as opposed to the other or upon married persons as opposed to single should be sufficient for the establishing of indirect discrimination.[3] An attempt has been made to argue that, by reason of developments in Community law in the area of indirect discrimination in pay,[4] the scope of the Sex Discrimination Act should not be limited by the requirement to show a 'requirement or condition'. So far, however, this argument has failed to convince our courts.[5] This narrow definition of indirect discrimination, however, may well not apply to claims under the Equal Pay Act.[6]

1 *Perera v Civil Service Commission* [1983] ICR 428, [1983] IRLR 166, CA.
2 A Byre, *Indirect Discrimination,* EOC, January 1987, p 25.
3 EOC, *Equal Treatment for Men and Women: Strengthening the Acts,* 1988, p 9. See too *Meer v Tower Hamlets London Borough Council* [1988] IRLR 399 at 403, CA, per Balcombe LJ.
4 *Enderby v Frenchay Health Authority and Secretary of State for Health*: C–127/92 [1993] IRLR 591, ECJ.
5 *Bhudi v IMI Refiners Ltd* [1994] IRLR 204, EAT.
6 *Enderby*, above. But cf *Staffordshire County Council v Black* [1995] IRLR 234, EAT.

24.17 What may appear to be a 'requirement' for the doing of a job may turn out to be something different, with negative consequences for the woman complaining of discrimination. Thus in *Clymo v Wandsworth London Borough Council*[1] an employer's insistence that a senior librarian's job be filled by a full-time employee was said not to be a 'requirement' but rather something that was part of the nature of the job itself. This meant that no issue of indirect discrimination arose. It seems, from observations made in the case, that the higher the status associated with the job, the more likely it is that a rule requiring full-time work will be seen as part of the job definition.

1 [1989] IRLR 241, EAT. Cf *Briggs v North Eastern Education and Library Board* [1990] IRLR 181, NICA.

Smaller proportion can comply

24.18 The test whether persons 'can comply' with a requirement or condition set has been interpreted as meaning 'can comply in practice', and not merely in theory. Thus, although Sikhs (a 'racial group' within the meaning of the RRA) could in theory abandon the wearing of turbans, a rule which excluded a child from school unless he removed his turban was classed as indirectly discriminatory against them as a group.[1] By way of contrast, the Court of Appeal has by a majority held that a single divorced parent who had no intention of marrying was nonetheless not in a situation where she 'could not comply' with a requirement that she be married in order to participate in certain work-related benefits.[2] The point in time at which the applicant's ability to comply is to be assessed is the time when the alleged detriment occurs – not some earlier date.[3] Where it is alleged that a smaller proportion of women or black people can comply with a particular requirement or condition, it is often difficult to know what proportion is required to establish indirect discrimination, and on what basis a comparison is to be made between the different groups. The courts give no firm answer to the former question, except in a negative sense. The EAT has indicated that elaborate statistical evidence is not necessary in all cases,[4] and this has usually been taken as giving a large measure of discretion and scope for 'general knowledge' to the industrial tribunals which hear complaints at first instance. Some surprising decisions have been upheld on appeal, notably a finding that the proportion of women who regularly undertake a child-caring role precluding full-time employment is not considerably smaller than the proportion of men so placed.[5] It has also been held that a provision requiring the general closure of shops on Sunday (Shops Act 1950, s 47) did not amount to indirect discrimination against women, although there are far more female shop workers than male.[6] Probably the best approach is to ask if the proportion of women otherwise qualified who can comply is 'considerably smaller' than the proportion of men in a similar position.[7] Of course, it will often be difficult to know the basis on which comparison falls to be made between the particular groupings. In the *Kidd* decision the Industrial Tribunal was held entitled to compare the position of men and women regarding availability for full-time work in the context of households where there were young children to be looked after. Given this limitation, it is somewhat less surprising that the tribunal reached the decision it did, although it is still a finding that most commentators have criticised as being out of touch with common sense. The problem is often described as being the choice of the appropriate 'pool' for comparison purposes, and perhaps the main impact of the *Kidd* decision is that under it the tribunal is given considerable discretion over the composition of the relevant groups.[8] But that discretion is not without its limits. A superior court may correct a tribunal's definition of the 'pool' when it is too restrictive, and thereby produces an unwarranted finding of indirect discrimination.[9] By statute (SDA, s 5(3); RRA, s 3(4)) it is provided that the relevant circumstances between the cases being compared should be the same. No guidance is given in the statutes, but the judges have indicated that a fairly wide interpretation of the words is in order.[10]

According to Mustill LJ (in *Jones v Chief Adjudication Officer*)[11] the general approach to follow in dealing with indirect discrimination requires seven stages:

- identify the criterion for selection;
- identify the relevant population, comprising all those who satisfy all the other criteria for selection;
- divide the relevant population into grounds representing those who satisfy the criterion and those who do not;
- predict statistically what proportion of each group should consist of women;
- ascertain what are the actual male/female balances in the two groups;

– compare the actual with the predicted balances;
– if women are found to be under-represented in the first group and over-represented in the second, it is proved that the criterion is discriminatory.

Mutatis mutandis, the same rules apply when what is in issue is indirect discrimination on grounds of race, rather than sex.

---

1 *Mandla v Dowell Lee* [1983] 2 AC 548, [1983] IRLR 209, HL.
2 *Turner v Labour Party Superannuation Society* [1987] IRLR 101, CA.
3 *Clarke v Eley (IMI) Kynoch Ltd* [1983] ICR 165, [1982] IRLR 482, EAT.
4 *Price v Civil Service Commission* [1978] 1 All ER 1228, [1977] IRLR 291, EAT. And see *McCausland v Dungannon District Council* [1993] IRLR 583, NICA.
5 *Kidd v DRG (UK) Ltd* [1985] ICR 405, [1985] IRLR 190, EAT.
6 *Chisholm v Kirklees Metropolitan Borough Council* [1993] ICR 826.
7 *Bilka-Kaufhaus GmbH v Weber von Hartz*: 170/84 [1986] IRLR 317, ECJ.
8 See also *Pearse v City of Bradford Metropolitan Council* [1988] IRLR 379, EAT; *Greencroft Social Club and Institute v Mullen* [1985] ICR 796, EAT.
9 *Jones v University of Manchester* [1993] ICR 474, CA; *London Underground Ltd v Edwards* [1995] IRLR 355, EAT.
10 Cf *Webb v EMO Air Cargo (UK) Ltd* [1992] 4 All ER 929, HL.
11 [1990] IRLR 533 at 537, CA.

Detriment

24.19 It is not enough for a woman or black person to show a condition or requirement that has a disproportionate impact – in addition she must show that it was to her detriment that she could not comply with it.[1] The meaning of 'detriment' has been considered by the courts on several occasions, and it is possible to be specific about certain requirements. In the first place, it is not an answer to an alleged detriment to show that the complainant is in fact receiving extra pay or benefits if the other conditions for complaint are met: 'An employer cannot buy a right to discriminate by making an extra payment to the men. If he could, it would drive a gaping hole in the statute'.[2] On the other hand, mere deprivation of choice is not by itself a sufficient 'detriment'. A balance has to be struck between the discriminatory effect of a condition and the reasonable needs of the person imposing the condition. All the circumstances of the case have to be taken into account, and the test is objective – would or might a reasonable worker take the view that a detriment existed, making allowances for trivial differences which would be disregarded?[3] The test appears to turn on whether such a worker would complain about the working condition or environment – it is not necessary that he or she be so distressed that continued working is rendered impossible.[4] Another limitation is that it is no detriment to refuse someone an advantage (like job sharing) where no-one else of her grade enjoys such a benefit.[5] The notion of detriment arises both in the definition of indirect discrimination and in the definition of discrimination by employers in the two Acts.[6] It would appear that the word has the same meaning in both locations, and, further, that a requirement which constitutes a detriment for the purpose of showing indirect discrimination can also constitute a detriment for the purpose of showing that discrimination in employment has taken place.[7]

---

1 SDA, s 1(1)(b)(iii); RRA, s 1(1)(b)(iii).
2 *Ministry of Defence v Jeremiah* [1980] QB 87, [1980] ICR 13 at 24, CA, per Lord Denning MR.

[3] Ibid, per Brightman LJ at 30.
[4] *De Souza v Automobile Association* [1986] ICR 514, [1986] IRLR 103, CA.
[5] *Clymo v Wandsworth London Borough Council* [1989] IRLR 241, EAT.
[6] SDA, s 6(2)(b); RRA, s 4(2)(c).
[7] *Home Office v Holmes* [1984] 3 All ER 549, [1984] IRLR 299, EAT.

Absence of justification

24.20 Where a complaint of indirect discrimination is made, and all the above requirements met, the employer will still avoid liability if he can show that the requirement or condition in question was 'justifiable' irrespective of the sex or racial characteristics of the person complaining. For this reason, it will usually be to the advantage of an applicant to show that he or she was a victim of direct discrimination, for as we have seen here no possibility of justification arises. Thus, for example, while it is potentially indirectly discriminatory on racial grounds to insist that workers do not wear beards, an employer in the food industry may be able to show that hygiene requirements justify such a rule.[1] Justification is for the employer to prove, on a balance of probabilities. In order to do so, he must show that the condition or requirement corresponds to a real need on the part of the undertaking which is appropriate with a view to achieving the object in question.[2] This test incorporates the notion of proportionality. It is not enough to show objective justification for the employer to show the absence of a requirement or condition having disproportionate impact, nor to establish a reason for acting which is itself tainted by gender.[3] Following the ruling of the House of Lords in the *Rainey* decision, it would appear that in deciding on the question of 'justifiability' a tribunal should take essentially the same approach that would be appropriate in evaluating a defence raised by an employer under s 1(3) of the EqPA 1970. This in turn is to be decided basically on the same approach as is appropriate in the interpretation of an employer's defence arising under Art 119 of the European Treaty.[4] The CA has confirmed[5] that an employee who seeks to show justification must so do on objective grounds. It is also clear that it is wrong, in examining the employer's defence, to place too much importance on a detriment suffered by an applicant because of his or her own peculiar personal circumstances.[6]

[1] SDA, s 1(1)(b)(ii); RRA, s 1(1)(b)(ii).
[2] *Singh v Rowntree Mackintosh Ltd* [1979] ICR 554, [1979] IRLR 199, EAT.
[3] *British Coal Corpn v Smith* [1994] IRLR 342, CA.
[4] *Rainey v Greater Glasgow Health Board* [1987] AC 224, [1987] IRLR 26, HL.
[5] *Hampson v Department of Education and Science* [1989] ICR 179, [1989] IRLR 69, CA.
[6] *University of Manchester v Jones* [1992] ICR 52 at 65, EAT, per Ian Kennedy J.

24.21 Thus in a situation where an employer required a woman health visitor to return to a five-day working week (full or part-time), the employer had insisted upon a condition which was such that the proportion of women who could comply was considerably smaller than the proportion of men. This was apparently indirectly discriminatory, but at the end of the day there was no unlawful discrimination, because it was found that the employer had demonstrated that the five-day working week was needed in order to provide an efficient service.[1] The extent to which justification may be provided by non-economic factors (such as administrative efficiency) remains controversial but there is little doubt that the thrust of recent leading decisions (notably *R v Secretary of State for Employment, ex p Equal Opportunities Commission*[2]) is to make the task facing the employer more substantial.

[1] *Greater Glasgow Health Board v Carey* [1987] IRLR 484, EAT.
[2] [1994] IRLR 176, HL.

6 TRIBUNAL PROCEEDINGS

24.22 Complaints of discrimination by aggrieved individuals under the SDA or RRA are brought before industrial tribunals, and are governed by the standard rules of procedure under the Industrial Tribunals (Constitution and Rules of Procedure) Regulations 1993, Sch 1. In addition, both the EOC and the CRE can take action before tribunals to combat discriminatory advertisements, instructions to discriminate or the bringing of pressure on a person to commit a discriminatory act.[1] The Commissions may also go to an industrial tribunal in order to obtain a finding that an individual has committed an act of discrimination within the tribunal's jurisdiction, preparatory to taking action to combat persistent discrimination in employment matters.[2] Among the most important of the general rules applicable to claims by individuals are the following: the requirement that claims be brought within three months of the act concerning which the complaint is made,[3] the provision made for conciliation through the offices of the Advisory, Conciliation and Arbitration Service,[4] and the rule that the decisions of industrial tribunals are subject to appeal on law only.[5] The success rate in sex discrimination cases has been low. So-called 'free-standing' rights, resulting from the application of Community law, are also properly heard by such bodies, despite the absence of express statutory authority to this effect.[6]

[1] SDA, s 72; RRA, s 63.
[2] SDA, s 73; RRA, s 64.
[3] SDA, s 76(1); RRA s 68(1). Provision is made for the bringing of claims out of time, where it would be just and equitable to do so.
[4] SDA, s 64; RRA, s 55.
[5] ERA, s 21(1).
[6] *Secretary of State for Scotland v Hannah* [1991] IRLR 187, EAT. *Biggs v Somerset County Council* [1995] IRLR 452, EAT.

24.23 Determining the time limits applicable to a claim which relies on a directly-effective provision of Community law is not always easy. The legislative instruments of the EU make no reference to such procedural matters, and in principle the rules here are to be taken from domestic (ie national) law.[1] Where domestic law has never properly implemented Community law, there is an argument that no time limit (whatever the duration) has started to run. This is particularly strong when the employer can be said to qualify as the State or an emanation thereof, and where the failure takes the form of the inadequate implementation of a Directive.[2] But public interest requires that there be an end to litigation and it seems likely that this will prove a powerful consideration. It would appear that an employer may be able to block claims which seek to bring to a tribunal old acts of discrimination by the argument that these claims could and should have been investigated at the time, with the applicant relying on directly-effective provisions of Community law to support his case. In other words, the direct effect of Community law may (from an employer's point of view) be seen as a shield of defence as well as a weapon wielded by the other side.[3]

[1] *Rewe-Zentralfinanz v Landwirtschaftskammer für Saarland*: 33/76 [1976] ECR 1989, ECJ.
[2] *Emmott v Minister for Social Welfare and A-G*: C-208/90 [1991] IRLR 387, ECJ.
[3] *Biggs v Somerset County Council* [1995] IRLR 452, EAT; affd [1996] IRLR 203, CA.

Burden of proof

24.24 The burden of proof in discrimination cases is on the applicant, and it is widely acknowledged that the operation in practice of this rule has proved a substantial limitation on the effectiveness of the legislation. In part the problem of proof is eased by the existence of special procedures (discussed immediately below) which facilitate the task by giving to applicants the right to gain access to information held by the alleged discriminator, but the complexity of the factual situations that can arise, taken together with the absence of legal aid for applicants, mean that many applicants still fall at this hurdle. In part the problem of proof is also eased by judge-made rules concerning the permissible inferences that may be drawn from particular fact situations and the right approach towards deciding who proves what. The Court of Appeal has on several occasions expressed the view that if there is a finding of discrimination and of difference of race and then an inadequate or unsatisfactory explanation by the employer for the discrimination, usually the legitimate inference will be that the discrimination was on racial grounds.[1] A recent authoritative review of the relevant cases concluded that:

> 'if discrimination takes place in circumstances which are consistent with the treatment being based on grounds of sex or race the industrial tribunal should be prepared to draw the inference that the discrimination was on such grounds unless the alleged discriminator can satisfy the tribunal that there was some other innocent explanation'.[2]

This way of expressing the law makes a considerable inroad on the principle that, given the absence of statutory guidance, it is for the applicant to prove her case – though it is still going too far to say that the burden of proof in discrimination matters is placed on the shoulders of the employer.[3]

[1] *Noone v North West Thames Regional Health Authority* [1988] IRLR 195, CA; *Bass Inns and Taverns Ltd v Joseph* (19 April 1994, unreported), CA.
[2] *Baker v Cornwall County Council* [1990] IRLR 194 at 198, CA, per Neill LJ.
[3] *Barking and Dagenham London Borough v Camara* [1988] IRLR 373, EAT; *King v Great Britain – China Centre* [1991] IRLR 513, CA.

24.25 Just after the introduction of the legislation of 1975 and 1976, it was predicted that the effectiveness of anti-discrimination law would depend critically on whether the legal principles and procedures developed to govern proof of discrimination were not unduly restrictive.[1] The relatively limited impact which the legislation has had in preventing indirect discrimination in employment matters would seem at least partially explicable by the difficulties of showing that discrimination has actually taken place. It is thus particularly important to note that the CA has accepted (in the *King* case) that a decision which is not ill-intentioned but based on an assumption that an applicant 'would not fit in' may provide the basis for a finding of discrimination.

1 L Lustgarten, 'Problems of Proof in Employment Discrimination Cases' [1977] 6 ILJ 212.

Questionnaires and discovery

24.26 The difficulties of proof referred to above are recognised in, and to a limited extent alleviated by, the existence of specific statutory provisions. There are two main possibilities: discovery of documents and use of interrogatories. Taking discovery first, the position is that an industrial tribunal has the same powers to order discovery or inspection of documents as is available to a county court hearing a case.[1] Where confidentiality is raised as a reason why there should not be discovery, a tribunal will certainly take it into account in coming to its decision, but such a plea will not *per se* be as decisive of the outcome. The correct approach will be for the tribunal to decide whether the documents concerned were necessary for the fair disposal of the case, and, if so, to see whether there are other procedures which might be adopted in the circumstances to gain access to the information contained therein. In the final analysis, the tribunal itself will examine the documents of which discovery is sought and decide which, if any, should be disclosed.[2]

1 Industrial Tribunal (Constitution and Rules of Procedure) Regulations 1993, SI 1993/2687, Sch 1, r 4(1)(b).
2 *Science Research Council v Nassé* [1980] AC 1028, [1979] ICR 921, HL.

24.27 Discovery may be resisted on the grounds that the request is oppressive, and in deciding on such an argument an industrial tribunal has considerable discretion. Examples of oppression can occur when the provision of the material sought, though relevant, would cause the party ordered great difficulty and expense, or when the effect of discovery would be to add unreasonably to the length and cost of the hearing.[1] Despite this qualification, however, there is no doubt that discovery has become more significant as a weapon in the hands of an applicant in the light of the ruling[2] that it is permissible to seek out statistical information by the use of discovery. In the *Singh* case, the complainant (who alleged he had been discriminated against on grounds of race by not being selected for promotion) was held entitled to discovery showing the number of white and non-white promoted workers over a two-year period. Once an application has established that an employer is operating a policy which discriminates against a particular group, then, unless the employer can put forward a satisfactory explanation connected with the complainant's particular case, it is reasonable to infer that the complainant who is a member of that group has been treated less favourably because of his membership, and not for some extraneous reason.

1 *West Midlands Passenger Transport Executive v Singh* [1988] 1 WLR 730, [1988] IRLR 186, CA.
2 Ibid.

24.28 In addition to the powers of discovery, statute[1] also envisages the use of questionnaires by applicants or potential applicants. This procedure is available not only to facilitate proof of discrimination, but also prior to the start of proceedings to help discover whether there is sufficient basis for an allegation of sex or race discrimination to be made. The details concerning time-limits and the format of the questionnaire are set by statutory order. A claimant or potential claimant may address what questions he likes to the alleged discriminator, and an industrial tribunal is directed that the answers, if any, made by the respondent to such questioning, are admissible in evidence before it. A respondent who fails to reply or who gives an answer which is seen as evasive may be faced with an inference that discrimination has taken place.[2] An applicant or respondent may also seek further particulars of the opponent's case, by making used procedures provided under the Industrial Tribunal rules.[3]

1 SDA, s 74; RRA, s 65.
2 *Virdee v EEC Quarries Ltd* [1978] IRLR 295.
3 Industrial Tribunals (Constitution and Rules of Procedure) Regulations 1993, SI 1993/2687, Sch 3, r 4.

Powers of tribunals

24.29 Where discrimination is held established, an industrial tribunal must make one or more of the following orders or recommendations: (1) an order declaratory of the rights of the parties; (2) an order requiring the payment of compensation; (3) a recommendation that the respondent take certain action to obviate or reduce discrimination.[1]

1 SDA, s 65; RRA, s 56.

24.30 Where compensation is the outcome, an applicant can claim for any pecuniary loss properly attributable to an unlawful act of discrimination. The amount will be assessed as though an ordinary court were calculating the recovery of damages in tort, with no upper limit on the amount recoverable. Until 1993 there was an upper limit of £11,000, but following the decision of the ECJ in *Marshall v Southampton and South West Hampshire Area Health Authority (No 2)*[1] (which held that such an upper limit was contrary to Community law because it did not provide the adequate remedy required by Art 6 of the Equal Treatment Directive) the financial ceiling was removed. Awards as high as £80,000 have been recorded.

1 C-271/91 [1993] IRLR 445, ECJ.

24.31 Compensation is a matter primarily regulated by the discretion of the industrial tribunal, and a decision on this matter should be set aside on appeal only where the tribunal 'is so out of the normal run that it can properly be described as a wholly erroneous estimate of the damage suffered'.[1] Damages may include in respect of injury to feelings; in appropriate cases this may justify a sum amounting to tens or hundreds of thousands of pounds. The large sums recovered by servicewomen who were dismissed on becoming pregnant provide a well-known example.[2] Settled cases, of course, bear witness to the payment of large sums; a female bricklayer who suffered sexual harassment at work received a settlement of £15,000 from her employers, after initiating tribunal proceedings.[3] It is to be noted that once a tribunal has decided in its discretion to make an order for compensation it must proceed in assessing quantum according to the usual rules for the assessment of damages; it is not permissible for it to award compensation on the general basis of what it sees as 'just and equitable' in the circumstances.[4] Contrary to earlier authority,[5] it now seems that an industrial tribunal is unlikely to be able to make an award of exemplary damages.[6]

1 *Noone v North West Thames Regional Health Authority* [1988] IRLR 195, CA per May LJ at 199.
2 *Ministry of Defence v Cannock* [1994] IRLR 509, EAT.
3 See article in The Independent, 7 January 1993.
4 *Hurley v Mustoe (No 2)* [1983] ICR 422, EAT.
5 *Bradford City Metropolitan Council v Arora* [1991] IRLR 165, CA.
6 *Deane v Ealing London Borough Council* [1993] IRLR 209, EAT.

24.32 The rule that no financial compensation will be awarded in the event of indirect discrimination, in the absence of a finding that the respondent intended to discriminate on a proscribed ground is removed with reference to sex discrimination, from 31 July 1996.[1]

1 The Sex Discrimination and Equal Pay (Miscellaneous Amendments) Regulations 1996, SI 1996/438, reg 2.

24.33 Where a recommendation is made by the tribunal for the taking of action to end discrimination, this may not be combined with a recommendation concerning the payment of wages at a particular level. In making a recommendation a tribunal should not propose the payment of financial compensation, as this is a matter which falls outside the proper scope of such orders.[1] It will also be wrong for a tribunal to make a recommendation for the taking of action which would assist a wronged applicant but at the cost of departure from general statutory obligations regarding selection of candidates for employment.[2]

1 *Prestcold Ltd v Irvine* [1981] ICR 777, [1981] IRLR 281, CA.
2 *Noone v North West Thames Regional Health Authority (No 2)* [1988] IRLR 530, CA.

7 COMPLIANCE WITH STATUTORY REQUIREMENTS

24.34 Under both statutes[1] it is provided that an act which is done in pursuance of statutory authority is not to be regarded as unlawful discrimination. In the case of the Sex Discrimination Act it is only existing statutory authority which concerns the protection of women which has this effect. The interpretation of this provision is that it excuses an act which would otherwise be unlawful only where both the act and the way it was carried out were reasonably necessary in order to comply with the requirements of legislation; the EAT has specifically rejected the view that the existence of statutory authority automatically gives an exemption from all discrimination law, on the ground that this would give an exemption that was too wide.[2] On the other hand, it has been held that an employer may rely on the duty imposed by s 2 of the Health and Safety at Work Act 1974 to justify his decision to exclude a female worker from work which would bring her into contact with a chemical potentially dangerous to women of childbearing age.[3]

[1] SDA, s 51(1); RRA, s 41(1)(a).
[2] *General Medical Council v Goba* [1988] ICR 885, [1988] IRLR 425, EAT.
[3] *Page v Freight Hire (Tank Haulage) Ltd* [1981] 1 All ER 394, [1981] ICR 299, EAT.

24.35 Women have for long been subject to restrictions under a variety of statutory provisions with regard to their hours and conditions of work. Important changes have, however, been made in the direction of repeal. The Sex Discrimination Act 1986 made several specific repeals[1] and, the Employment Act 1989 takes this process further by amending the 1975 Act. The position is complicated, but in essence the existence of legislation no longer provides automatic authority for the doing of acts which would otherwise constitute unlawful sex discrimination. Statutes which pre-date the SDA and impose a requirement that is discriminatory are to be read as amended by the SDA. Only where the acts done are necessary for the protection of women in limited areas is statute-based discrimination permitted.[2] And where the discrimination alleged is of the indirect variety, the employer is bound to provide justification for the condition or requirement imposed – even though the source is statutory.[3]

[1] Section 7.
[2] Employment Act 1989, s 1; Sex Discrimination Act 1975, s 51.
[3] Employment Act 1989, s 1(3).

8 SEX DISCRIMINATION

24.36 Under this heading we shall consider certain aspects of discrimination law which are found under the SDA but are not mirrored in the RRA. One point has already been made. There is no provision regarding discrimination in terms afforded to existing workers (as opposed to discrimination in terms offered to prospective workers) under the SDA; discrimination in this area is left to the regulation of the Equal Pay Act through the compulsory-implied equality clause. This means that, on occasions, a complaint of sex discrimination regarding terms observed will fail, because there is no corresponding male with whom comparison can be made, as required by the Equal Pay Act.

Genuine occupational qualification

24.37 Although the concept of genuine occupation qualification ('goq') is found in both main statutes, its content, naturally, varies according to whether the essential criterion is 'being a man (or woman)' or 'membership of a particular racial group'. The underlying idea is, however, the same in both locations: the need to make provision for a limited range of exceptional situations where wider considerations of public policy or utility justify action by an employer which would otherwise be unlawful. The behaviour in question would, without the statutory exception, institute intentional (and direct) discrimination. Where a goq is made out, an act done in relation to recruitment, or in relation to the provision of opportunities for promotion or transfer or training, which would otherwise be unlawful, is excused.

24.38 An employer will not be entitled to rely on a goq as a defence to alleged discrimination under either statute where the issue arises in relation to the filling of a vacancy and the employer already has in his employment persons of the sex or racial group in question. Further requirements are that such employees are (a) capable of carrying out the duties prescribed, (b) persons whom it would be reasonable to employ on such duties, and (c) of sufficient number to meet the employer's likely requirements in respect of those duties without undue inconvenience.[1]

[1] SDA, s 7(4)(a)(b)(c); RRA, s 5(3). See *Etam plc v Rowan* [1989] IRLR 150, EAT.

24.39 A further complication, which applies to sex discrimination alone, is the compatability of the various excluded categories with the coverage of Community law, in the shape of the Equal Treatment Directive (76/207). The United Kingdom was, in 1983, found to be in breach of this standard by reason of the general exclusion under the law then in force which permitted discrimination in a private household or by a small employer.[1]

[1] *EC Commission v United Kingdom*: 165/82 [1984] 1 All ER 353, [1984] ICR 192, ECJ. The law has now been amended accordingly: the previous exception for small employers has been dropped. For the position concerning private households, see the SDA, s 7(2)(ba).

24.40 The situations in which a goq is recognised under the SDA are set out in s 7 of the Act. They cover, broadly, three different types of situation – where there are physical, functional and social differences between the sexes which are regarded as justifying a measure of continuing discrimination. The goq exceptions apply equally to women and men.[1] It is to be noted that, in addition to the goq provisions, the statute also contains a number of detailed rules allowing discrimination in particular trades or professions, such as the police or ministers of religion.[2]

[1] See D Pannick, *Sex Discrimination Law* (OUP, 1985) ch 9.
[2] SDA, ss 17(3), 19.

24.41 In summary the following situations are classed as giving rise to a goq:

(1) Where the essential nature of the job calls for a man for reasons of physiology or, in dramatic performances or other entertainment, for reasons of authenticity, so that the essential nature of the job would be materially different if carried out by a person of the opposite sex.[1]
(2) Where the job needs to be done by a man in order to preserve decency or privacy because – (a) it is likely to involve physical contact with men in circumstances where they might reasonably object to its being carried out by a woman, or (b) the holder of the job is likely to do his work in circumstances where men might reasonably object to the presence of a woman because they are in a state of undress or are using sanitary facilities.[2]

(3) Where the job is likely to involve the holder doing his work, or living, in a private home and needs to be held by a man because objection might reasonably be taken to allowing a woman (a) the degree of physical or social contact with a person living in the home, or (b) the knowledge of intimate details of such a person's life, which is likely, because of the nature of the circumstances of the job or the home, to be allowed to or available to the holder of the job.[3]

(4) The nature or location of the establishment makes it impracticable for the holder of the job to live elsewhere than in premises provided by the employer, and – (a) the only such premises which are available for persons holding that kind of job are lived in, or normally lived in, by men and not equipped with separate sleeping accommodation for women and sanitary facilities which could be used by women in privacy from men, *and* (b) it is not reasonable to expect the employer either to equip those premises with such accommodation or provide other premises for women.[4]

(5) Where the job is carried out in a hospital, prison or other establishment for persons requiring special care, supervision or attention, and these persons are all men (disregarding any woman whose presence is exceptional), and it is reasonable, having regard to the essential character of the establishment, that the job should not be held by a woman.[5]

(6) Where the holder of the job provides individuals with personal services promoting their welfare or education, or similar personal services, and these services can most effectively be provided by a man.[6]

(7) Where the job needs to be held by a man because of restrictions imposed by laws regulating the employment of women.[7]

(8) Where the job needs to be held by a man because it is likely to involve work outside the United Kingdom in a country whose laws or customs are such that the duties could not, or could not effectively, be performed by a woman.[8]

(9) Where the job is one of two to be held by a married couple.[9]

---

1 SDA, s 7(2)(a). The EOC has proposed (*Legislating for Change?* 1986, p 18) that 'physiology' be replaced by 'anatomy' or other word that would be more appropriate to allow for instances where by reason of biology or anatomy no man could carry out the job.

2 SDA, s 7(2)(b). This provision is designed to avoid the causing of offence in situations where the presence of a man might be seen as objectionable.

3 SDA, s 7(2)(ba). This replaces a wider exemption which was held incompatible with the Equal Treatment Directive by the ECJ.

4 SDA, s 7(2)(c). This provision is designed to cover jobs in mobile or remote establishments, such as ships or oil-rigs.

5 SDA, s 7(2)(d). The EOC (op cit, p 19) have drawn attention to the possibility that these exceptions may be incompatible with Community law, and have recommended the repeal of this clause.

6 SDA, s 7(2)(e). Cf *Tottenham Green Under Five's Centre v Marshall (No 2)* [1991] IRLR 162, EAT.

7 SDA, s 7(2)(f). It is likely that this provision will shortly be repealed because of its perceived incompatability with Community law.

8 SDA, s 7(2)(g). This clause was designed to enable UK employers to recruit men for jobs in countries where women are not acceptable to business. It would not apply, of course, to disenfranchise any woman seeking employment in a member state of the European Community, for any such discrimination would be unlawful under the Equal Treatment Directive.

9 SDA, s 7(2)(h).

24.42 The relatively lengthy and detailed provision made for goq in statute has not been matched by the number of recorded decisions giving interpretations of the definitions.

Marital status

24.43 By s 3 of the SDA, discrimination on the grounds of marital status is rendered unlawful. Both direct and indirect discrimination in employment is covered, but no protection is given to unmarried persons who are treated less favourably than married persons. Only married persons are protected under this heading. An employer whose policy is not to employ women with young children is someone who potentially commits an act of indirect discrimination against married persons, but it should always be remembered that such an employer may be able to show justification (within the meaning of the term, considered above) for such an act. It will not be enough, however, to show that the action in question is convenient for the employer[1] – 'justification requires something which lies between that which is necessary on the one hand and that which is merely convenient on the other'.[2]

[1] *Hurley v Mustoe* [1981] IRLR 208, EAT.
[2] *University of Manchester v Jones* [1992] ICR 52 at 64, per Ian Kennedy J, EAT.

Collective agreements

24.44 The Sex Discrimination Act 1986 amended the law relating to collective agreements containing provisions in contravention of the principle of equal treatment, as developed under Community law. This has been achieved by the extension of s 77 of the SDA, which in its original form rendered void any contractual term which contravened the SDA. Because collective agreements are not generally understood to be legally binding agreements according to legislation and industrial relations theory[1] the section did not in its original form apply to such agreements. In 1983, the ECJ ruled that this amounted to a lacuna in the coverage of the United Kingdom's sex discrimination law[2] and the SDA was amended in a way that has been described in an earlier section.[3]

[1] Trade Union and Labour Relations Act 1974, s 18(1).
[2] *EC Commission v United Kingdom*: 165/82 [1984] 1 All ER 353, [1984] IRLR 29, ECJ.
[3] Para 24.37, above.

Pregnancy

24.45 A vexed question which has long troubled courts and tribunals is whether it is unlawful to treat a woman less favourably in employment because of pregnancy. Since men cannot become pregnant, one argument is that, however regrettable such behaviour may be, it will not constitute discrimination, the essence of which is treating like cases differently. After some considerable hesitation, however, that position was rejected by the English courts.[1] A second analysis, which was favoured by the House of Lords,[2] was to say that a pregnant woman was comparable to a sick man, in the sense that action taken against her would only be seen as sex discrimination if such a man would have been differently treated.

That analysis too is no longer tenable in the light of the ruling of the ECJ in *Webb v EMO Air Cargo (UK) Ltd*.[3] It is now clear that detrimental action taken against a woman on the ground of her pregnancy will generally amount to unlawful direct discrimination on the ground of sex, without any need to consider what treatment might have been accorded by the employer to a man in the same employment suffering some incapacity. It is still unclear, however, to what extent (if any) such discrimination may be justified by exceptional circumstances. It may be, for example, that dismissal on the ground of pregnancy can be justified if the woman was expressly recruited on a fixed-term contract to provide services for the period of time in respect of which she was not able to be at work because of her pregnancy. The increased protection available under equal treatment law for pregnant women is complemented by the extended rights in respect of unfair dismissal protection introduced with effect from October 1994 and now available under the ERA.[4]

1 *Hayes v Malleable Working Men's Club and Institute* [1985] ICR 703, EAT.
2 *Webb v EMO Air Cargo (UK) Ltd* [1992] 4 All ER 929, HL and [1995] IRLR 645, HL.
3 Case C-32/93 [1994] IRLR 482, ECJ.
4 See *Harvey* Div J.

9 RACIAL DISCRIMINATION

24.46 The RRA follows the pattern and coverage of the SDA, and prohibits discrimination in employment both in respect of prospective and actual employees. Its principal purpose, according to Balcombe LJ,[1] is to make acts of racial discrimination unlawful – it is not intended to benefit particular racial groups, and its interpretation will not be stretched in order to serve such a purpose. Unlike the SDA, however, the RRA specifically extends to cover discrimination in the contractual terms afforded to an employee.[2] Another difference is that the segregation of persons on racial grounds is expressly deemed to be less favourable treatment.[3] Although both Acts define direct discrimination in terms of less favourable treatment, it may be that the word has acquired a particular significance under the RRA. It has been held that a 'racial insult' can amount to unlawful discrimination, provided that it is of sufficient gravity to cause a reasonable worker to view it as a disadvantage to him in his working conditions.[4] But the same case in which this important point was established, also decided that the applicant had not been 'treated' less favourably in the sense required by the statute where the insult had not been intended to be heard by the person to whom the derogatory reference was made.

1 *Lambeth London Borough Council v Commission for Racial Equality* [1990] IRLR 231 at 234, CA.
2 RRA, s 4(2)(a).
3 RRA, s 1(2).
4 *De Souza v Automobile Association* [1986] ICR 514, [1986] IRLR 103, CA. Words or acts of discouragement may perhaps amount to less favourable treatment: *Simon v Brimham Associates* [1987] ICR 596, [1987] IRLR 307 at 309, CA, per Bingham LJ.

24.47 Two special features of the RRA, compared with the SDA, concern the concept of racial group and that of goq.

Racial group

24.48 The essence of the Act is discrimination on 'racial grounds', and these are defined, along with the phrase 'racial group'[1] in terms of 'colour, race, nationality or ethnic or national origins'. It is the concept of 'ethnic origins' which has caused most trouble in interpreting the statute: Sikhs, it has been held[2] constitute a 'racial group' because they are a distinct community, identified by certain characteristics. These characteristics are: (a) a long shared history, (b) a separate cultural tradition, (c) a common geographical origin or descent from a small number of common ancestors, (d) a common language and literature, the latter peculiar to the group, (e) a common and distinct religion, and (f) being a minority or being an oppressed or dominant group within a larger community.[3]

[1] RRA, s 3.
[2] *Mandla v Dowell Lee* [1983] 2 AC 548, [1983] IRLR 209, HL.
[3] Per Lord Fraser of Tullybelton at 211.

24.49 Gipsies (in the sense of members of a travelling race of people) have been held to constitute a racial group under this test,[1] but those who are gipsies merely in the sense of persons with no fixed abode are not so protected. Where less favourable treatment is accorded simply to 'travellers' then there may be indirect discrimination against gipsies as a racial group, but of course it is open for the alleged discriminator to justify any such action taken. It is to be remembered that such justification must be shown to satisfy the relatively stringent tests now imposed by the courts.[2] Where only some of the criteria referred to in *Mandla v Lee* are found to be present, it does not follow that there will be sufficient grounds to constitute a racial group: Welsh speakers, for example, are not recognised as such a group[3] and neither are Rastafarians.[4]

[1] *Commission for Racial Equality v Dutton* [1989] 1 All ER 306, [1989] IRLR 8, CA.
[2] *Hampson v Department of Education and Science* [1989] IRLR 69, CA; *Briggs v North Eastern Education and Library Board* [1990] IRLR 181, NICA.
[3] *Gwynedd County Council v Jones* [1986] ICR 833, EAT.
[4] *Crown Suppliers (Property Services Agency) Ltd v Dawkins* [1993] ICR 517, CA.

Genuine occupation qualification

24.50 The definition of goq under the RRA extends to the following situations:

(1) the job involves participation in a dramatic performance or other entertainment in a capacity for which a person of that racial group is required for authenticity;[1]
(2) the job involves participation as an artist's or photographic model in the production of a work of art or visual image for which a person of that racial group is required for authenticity;[2]
(3) the job involves working in a place where food or drink is provided to and consumed by members of the public in a particular setting for which a member of that racial group is required for authenticity;[3]

(4) the holder of the job provides members of that racial group with personal services promoting their welfare, and those services can most effectively be provided by a person of that racial group.[4]

[1] RRA, s 5(2)(a).
[2] RRA, s 5(2)(b).
[3] RRA, s 5(2)(c).
[4] RRA, s 5(2)(d). See *Tottenham Green Under Five's Centre v Marshall* [1989] ICR 214, [1989] IRLR 147, EAT.

Exclusions

24.51 The exemption allowed in relation to employment for the purposes of a private household is significantly wider than that available under the SDA (as amended). There is no remedy under the Act for racial discrimination here in relation to the offer of employment or the actual terms, access to opportunities, or dismissal.[1] It has also been held[2] that to require proof by an Indian citizen of his right to work in Britain does not amount to unlawful discrimination on racial grounds. The statutory work permit scheme was seen as the basis for this important limitation on the scope of the legislation.

[1] RRA, s 4(3).
[2] *Dhatt v McDonald's Hamburgers* [1991] IRLR 130, CA.

24.52 Other details include exemptions in relation to the training of foreign workers,[1] workers employed overseas,[2] and the recruitment of seamen overseas.[3] Certain organisations, by virtue of their international status, may also be exempted from the legislation.[4]

[1] RRA, s 6.
[2] RRA, s 8.
[3] RRA, s 9.
[4] *Mukoro v European Bank for Reconstruction and Development* [1994] ICR 897, EAT.

10 POSITIVE DISCRIMINATION

24.53 The SDA, as amended,[1] allows for the running of training programmes which would otherwise be discriminatory under the legislation in circumstances where there are few or comparatively few persons of one sex doing a particular job, and the training is intended to open up opportunities to persons of the opposite sex. So too a person may offer special training facilities for persons (who will predominantly be women) returning to work after an absence due to family or domestic commitments.[2] But Community Law imposes important limitations on any schemes which give women automatic priority in access to benefits or promotion.[3]

[1] Section 47, as amended by s 4 of the SDA 1986.
[2] SDA, s 47(3).
[3] *Kalanke v Freie Hansestadt Bremen* C-450/93 [1995] IRLR 660, ECJ.

11 VICTIMISATION

24.54 The law gives protection to persons who bring complaints under the EqPA, SDA, or RRA by providing that it is unlawful to treat anyone less favourably than another by reason that he or she has brought proceedings against the discriminator under the legislation, done any one of a number of related actions, or has 'done anything under or by reference to' the Act in question.[1] The victimisation must relate to acts done when the employment relationship is existing; thus it will not be an act capable of amounting to unlawful victimisation if an employer writes a bad reference about someone who has left his employment.[2] The question is often put in terms of whether the alleged victim has done what is referred to as a 'protected act'. An important qualification here is that there will be no protection under this heading where an allegation which leads to adverse treatment is both false and not made in good faith.[3] It has been explicity recognised that the purpose of these provisions is to give protection to persons who seek to rely on the discrimination legislation or to promote its operation by word or deed,[4] and a person may be said to have acted 'by reference to' the discrimination legislation even when his behaviour was not carried out with the idea of making a complaint with any particular statutory provision in mind. Thus action taken against a taxi driver who had secretly tape-recorded comments about him that were allegedly discriminatory on racial grounds was in a broad but nevertheless sufficient sense action taken by reference to the RRA in relation to the alleged victimisers.[5] The comparison that has to be made is with the treatment that has been or would be accorded to persons who have not committed the behaviour which the legislation seeks to protect.[6] But at the end of the day there is a burden on the applicant to establish a causal link between the doing of the protected act and the unfavourable treatment received; what is apparently an act of victimisation will not be unlawful if in fact the unfavourable treatment was motivated by some extraneous consideration on the part of the respondent employer – such as an alleged breach of trust on the part of the employee. It is to be noted that, in the special context of sex discrimination, Community law requires the taking of necessary measures to protect employees against dismissal as a consequence of taking action to indicate her legal rights.[7]

---

1 SDA, s 4(1); RRA, s 2(1).
2 *Nagarajan v Agnew* [1994] IRLR 61, EAT.
3 SDA, s 4(2); RRA, s 2(2).
4 *Cornelius v University College of Swansea* [1987] IRLR 141, CA.
5 *Aziz v Trinity Street Taxis Ltd* [1988] 2 All ER 860, [1988] IRLR 204, CA.
6 Ibid.
7 Equal Treatment Directive 76/207/EEC, Art 7.

25 Disability

Brian Napier

1 INTRODUCTION

25.01 Disability legislation in Britain dates back to 1944. But the law has taken on a new importance with the passing of the Disability Discrimination Act 1995. This Act, introduces a new regime for controlling discrimination against disabled employees and persons seeking work.[1] Although in some respects the new law follows the pattern of the two other discrimination statutes, it is weaker than either the SDA or RRA in relation to enforcement, and there are also important differences in the concepts used to define discrimination. A full appreciation of the DDA must, however, await not only the statutory codes of practice and guidances which are promised but not yet available at the time of writing but also the processes of judicial interpretation.

[1] The Act also applies to discrimination in relation to goods and services, property, education and public transport. These aspects of the law are not covered here.

25.02 The DDA applies, in relation to employment, only to employers who employ not less than 20 employees – an important exclusion which has no counterpart in either the SDA or RRA. Like the RRA (but unlike the SDA) the DDA has no significant basis in Community law. This means that, when the time comes to interpret its provisions in the courts, it will not be possible to argue for particular interpretations on the ground that such a reading is required to produce conformity between UK and EU law. It may also mean that some of the interpretations of common statutory provisions, found in authorities dealing with the SDA, are not binding when it comes to interpreting the DDA.

25.03 Compared with the 1944 Act (which relied on imposing obligations on employers to reserve certain occupations for the disabled, and to ensure that a certain proportion of their jobs were made available to the disabled, under the 'quota' system) the new law favours the giving of enforceable rights to the disabled as individuals. In the employment field, these rights are exercisable before industrial tribunals, and are sanctioned by, inter alia, the award of (unlimited) compensation. The circumstances in which compensation may be awarded are, however, restricted not only by the express requirements of the legislation but also by the concepts of disability which are fundamental to its operation.

2 PRINCIPAL CONCEPTS AND DEFINITIONS

Who is disabled?

25.04 A disabled person is one who:

> 'has a physical or mental impairment which has a substantial and long-term adverse impact on his ability to carry out normal day to day activities.'[1]

[1] DDA, s 1. Note that the prohibition on discrimination applies equally to someone who has had a disability in the past.

25.05 Employees who were on the disabled register provided in terms of the 1944 Act are conclusively assumed, without need for further examination or investigation, to satisfy the above definition. For those not so categorised, however, matters are less simple.

25.06 A number of key terms in the above master definition are either left undefined or are only partly explained in the primary legislation. For example, an 'impairment', if mental, will include only impairment resulting from or consisting in clinically well-recognised illnesses. A 'long-term effect' is generally one which has lasted or is likely to last for 12 months or more, or for the rest of the life of the person affected.[1] The meaning of 'normal day-to-day activities' is partially defined.[2] The impairment must affect certain individually identified bodily or mental functions (mobility, memory, perception etc). What is meant by 'substantial adverse effects' is left to be determined by Regulation.[3]

[1] Schedule 1, para 2
[2] Schedule 1, para 4.
[3] Schedule 1, para 5.

25.07 The effect of medical treatment on impairment is discounted; an impairment can still be said to have a substantial adverse effect on ability even though measures are being taken to treat or correct it.[1]

[1] Schedule 1, para 6.

3 DISCRIMINATION IN EMPLOYMENT

25.08 Discrimination in employment extends to those seeking employment as well as to those who have a job. It also applies only to employment at an establishment in Great Britain.[1] Those who work wholly or mainly outside Great Britain are excluded, even if some work is done at an establishment in Great Britain.[2]

[1] Section 4(6).
[2] Section 68(2).

25.09 The scope of the protection offered is broadly the same as that offered in respect of sex and race discrimination. That is to say, it extends to discrimination in relation to the offering of work, the terms on which employment is offered, opportunities during employment and dismissal or the subjecting of an individual to any other detriment.[1] Advertisements which discriminate against the disabled are not in themselves unlawful, but may, in somewhat limited circumstances, provide a basis for a finding by a tribunal that an employer refused employment on unlawful grounds.[2]

1 Section 4.
2 Section 11.

Direct and indirect discrimination

25.10 The discrimination which is prohibited is direct discrimination. The indirect variety is not expressly addressed by the legislation, in contrast with sex and race legislation, though it may be that practices or procedures which make difficulties for the disabled fall within the scope of particular prohibited activities. This at least would appear to be the view of the government, expressed in Parliament.[1] If, for example, mobility is required of a job applicant this may (indirectly) discriminate against a disabled person. It may amount to behaviour prohibited by s 4(1)(b), as discrimination in the terms on which employment is offered. It must be shown by a complainant that an employer 'for a reason related to the disabled person's disability' has treated the disabled person less favourably.[2] The scope of the phrase 'for a reason related to' will be of crucial importance – it might, for example, cover the refusal of employment to someone on the ground of a personality found unacceptable, where that personality was itself seen as linked with a disability.

1 HC Deb Standing Committee E, col 142.
2 Section 5(1).

25.11 The definition of discrimination is specifically extended to cover the situation where an employer, without justification, has failed to make reasonable adjustments as required by s 6 of the Act. The employer's duty is to make reasonable adjustments to arrangements which determine who is to be offered employment, and who is to receive benefits once in employment. The extent of the duty is to take 'such steps as it is reasonable, in all the circumstances of the case, for him to have to take.'

Defence of justification

25.12 The employer has a defence of justification, something which is not available to him where there is direct discrimination on grounds of race or sex. Justification has to be both material to the circumstances of the particular case and substantial.[1] Examples are given of the type of behaviour which may be required, although whether and to what extent such behaviour will be appropriate in any given case must obviously depend on particular facts. Further guidance is likely to be forthcoming from the Code of Practice which the Government plans to publish. Indications of the considerations which go to 'reasonableness' for the purposes of s 6(1) are also found in the legislation.[2]

[1] Section 5(3), (4).
[2] Section 4(4).

Other forms of discrimination

25.13 In addition to prohibiting discrimination in employment, protection is given against discrimination by bodies classed as 'trade organisations'[1] and discrimination against 'contract workers' is also declared unlawful.[2]

[1] Section 13. An example of a trade organisation is a trade union, but other organisations are covered too, where the members carry on a particular trade or profession for the purposes of which the organisation exists (s 13(4)).
[2] Section 12.

Vicarious and secondary liability

25.14 The employer is held liable for the unlawful acts of an employee done in the course of employment,[1] though this is subject to a defence based on the taking of reasonable steps. The employer will avoid liability if he can show he took such steps as were reasonably practicable either to prevent the employee from doing the act complained of, or doing, in the course of employment, acts of that description.[2] That means, presumably, that in some circumstances the training of staff in how to recognise and avoid disability discrimination may be a defence. There is also liability imposed on one who knowingly aids another to do an unlawful act[3] and an employee for whose act an employer is held liable is deemed to have aided the employer.[4]

[1] Section 58(1).
[2] Section 58(5).
[3] Section 57(1).
[4] Section 57(2).

Contractual terms

25.15 The legislation provides that any attempt by contract to require action in contravention of the Act is void.[1] So too is any attempt to contract out of the application of the Act, or to prevent the making of a complaint to an industrial tribunal, although allowance is made for the valid settlement of complaints under the auspices of ACAS or by means of a 'compromise agreement' supported by independent legal advice.[2]

[1] Section 9(1).
[2] Section 9(2), (3). Cf ERA, s 203.

4 ENFORCEMENT

25.16 Individuals may complain to an industrial tribunal by way of originating application, which must be presented within three months of the date of the alleged discrimination. A discretion to allow claims out of time is given to the tribunal, subject to its view that it would be just and equitable to do so.[1]

[1] Schedule 3, para 3(1).

25.17 Conciliation through the intervention of the Advisory Conciliation and Arbitration Service (ACAS) applies, as in relation to complaints of sex or race discrimination.

25.18 An industrial tribunal may, if it finds the complaint well-founded, take such of the following steps as it considers just and equitable:

(a) a declaration of rights;
(b) an order to the respondent to pay compensation to the complainant;
(c) a recommendation that, within a specified period, action be taken for the purpose of obviating or reducing the adverse effect on the complainant of any matter to which the complaint relates.[1]

[1] Section 8(2).

25.19 There is no provision for institutional enforcement by the National Disability Council, the supervisory body established to advise the Secretary of State on various matters relating to discrimination and the working of the DDA. Unlike the EOC or CRE, the NDC will not operate to give support (either financial or in the form of advice) to complaints brought by individual disabled persons.

APPENDICES

INTRODUCTION

These Appendices contain check lists, explanatory notes, sample forms and precedent models. The organisation of the Appendices largely reflects the main text so that the various items are grouped under the following headings:

- (a) the contract of employment/statement of terms and conditions;
- (b) transfer of an undertaking;
- (c) maternity;
- (d) statutory sick pay;
- (e) unfair dismissal;
- (f) settlement of unfair dismissal claims;
- (g) redundancy;
- (h) discrimination;
- (i) list of statutory rights and relevant qualifying periods/time limits for claim.

(A) The contract of employment/ statement of terms and conditions

INTRODUCTION

There is no prescribed form for a written contract of employment (indeed no requirement to have one at all) although, as explained in the text, there is a requirement to provide a statement of terms and conditions after the first two months of employment.

Notwithstanding the absence of a legal requirement for a written contract of employment, there is much to be said for reducing the essential terms of the employment to writing at the commencement of the employment, for the avoidance of doubt, and to do so through the medium of a formal contract of employment, letter of appointment or by delivering a statement of particulars of terms and conditions earlier than required by s 1 of the ERA (perhaps amending the statement of particulars to a contractually binding document by selecting the appropriate language—see below).

Employee Handbooks can also be a useful adjunct to contracts of employment/statement of particulars of terms and conditions, providing a repository for terms and policies which are generally applicable to the employer's workforce, eg disciplinary rules and procedures. The following is a fairly standard statement of particulars of terms and conditions of employment.

STATEMENT OF PARTICULARS OF EMPLOYMENT
given pursuant to the Employment Rights Act 1996, s 1[1]

From: [ ] (*Employer*) of (*address*)
To: [ ] (*Employee*) of (*address*)
(*date*)

1 INTRODUCTION

1.1 This statement sets out particulars of your employment with (*Employer*) as at (*date*)[2] which are required to be given to you under the Employment Rights

[1] This statement must be given to the employee not later than two months after the beginning of the employee's employment with the employer: ERA, s 1(1) and (2). As to the obligation to provide a statement see (ch 5, above). There is no obligation upon the employer to make the disciplinary and grievance procedures terms of the contract, and if such procedures become terms of the contract, the employer may be liable in damages for failure to comply with them: see *Gunton v Richmond-on-Thames London Borough Council* [1980] IRLR 321, [1980] ICR 755, CA, and *Dietman v London Borough of Brent* [1987] IRLR 259, [1987] ICR 737, CA.

[2] The date must not be more than seven days before the statement is given: ERA, s 1(4).

Act 1996. Your employment commenced on (*date*). [No employment with a previous employer counts as part of your period of continuous employment.] *or* [Your period of employment with (*name of previous employer*) counts as part of your period of continuous employment which accordingly began on (*date*).][3]

1.2 [The Collective Agreement(s) between (*specify*) and (*specify*) contain(s) (*specify details of terms and conditions covered by the agreement(s) which are relevant to your employment*).][4]

2 TERMS OF EMPLOYMENT

2.1 Job title[5]

The title of the job which you are employed to do is (*insert job title*). [The duties which this job entails are set out in the job description attached to this statement.] [The job description may from time to time be amended by the *Employer* and in addition to the duties set out in it you may [at any time *or* from time to time] be required to undertake additional or other duties as necessary to meet the needs of the business.]

2.2 Place of work[6]

Your usual place of work is (*specify*) (but you may be required to work at (*specify other locations etc*)) *and/or*
[You will [also] be required to work in (*specify country/location*) outside the United Kingdom] for (*specify period*).

2.3 Remuneration[7]

Your remuneration is £(*specify*) per [week *or* month *or* year] payable by (*state method of payment*) at [weekly *or* monthly] intervals on the (*day*) of each [week *or* month].
[During the period you will be working in (*specify country/location outside the United Kingdom*) your [*salary*] or [*wages*] will be paid in (*specify currency*) and you will be entitled to (*specify any additional remuneration/benefits applicable during this period*) and, upon your return to the United Kingdom (*specify any terms and conditions relating to the employee's return to the United Kingdom*).]

[3] See ibid, s 1(3)(c).

[4] See ibid, s 1(4)(j) which requires any collective agreements which directly affect the terms and conditions including (where the employer is not a party) the persons by whom they were made to be particularised.

[5] See ibid, s 1(4)(f).

[6] See ibid, s 1(4)(h) and (k)(i) which requires the employer to stipulate the place of work or, where the employee is required or permitted to work at various places, to give an indication of that and of the address of the employer (s 1(4)(h)) and, where the employee is required to work outside the UK for more than one month, the period for which he is to do so (s 1(4)(k)(i)).

[7] See ibid, s 1(4)(a), (b) and (k)(ii), (iii) and (iv) (which require the employer to stipulate the currency in which remuneration is to be paid while the employee is working outside the UK, any additional remuneration and benefits payable during this period and any terms and conditions relating to the employee's return to the UK).

2.4 Hours of work[8]

Your normal hours of work are from (*time*) to (*time*) [Monday to Friday inclusive]. A [1] hour [unpaid] break may be taken for lunch [at (*time*) or between (*time*) and (*time*)]. You will not be required to work overtime and any overtime which you do work at (*Employer's*) request will be paid at the rate of £(*specify*) *or* you will be required to work overtime if and when (*Employer*) deems this to be necessary and [you will not be paid for such overtime] *or* [you will be paid for such overtime at the rate of (*state the rate to be paid*)].

2.5 Holidays[9]

You are entitled, in addition to the normal public holidays [and (*Employers*) annual holiday of (*number*) days in (*state month*) each year], to take (*number*) working days in each holiday year which runs from (*date*) to (*date*) [and you will be paid your normal basic remuneration during such holidays].

[2.5.1 You are required to retain a sufficient number of holidays from your annual entitlement to cover (*Employers*) [Christmas or annual] shut-down period. You will be notified by [(*Employer*) individually] *or* [by way of a general notice] no later than (*date*) in each year of the number of days' holiday you are required to retain for this purpose].

2.5.2 If your employment commenced or terminates part way through the holiday year, your entitlement to holidays during that year will be assessed on a pro rata basis. Deductions from final salary due to you on termination of employment will be made in respect of any holidays taken in excess of entitlement.[10]

2.5.3 Holidays must be taken at times convenient to (*Employer*) and sufficient notice of intention to take holiday must be given to [your supervisor].

[2.5.4 Not more than (*state number*) of days' holidays may be taken at any one time unless permission is given by [your supervisor].]

[2.5.5 Holiday entitlement unused at the end of the holiday year cannot be carried over into the next holiday year.]

[2.5.6 [You will not be entitled to be paid in respect of holidays accrued due but untaken as at the date of termination of employment] *or* [you will be entitled to payment in lieu of holidays accrued but untaken as at the date of termination of employment].]

[2.5.7 A day's holiday pay for the purpose of this clause is (*state amount*).]

2.6 Sickness absence[11]

2.6.1 If you are absent from work on account of sickness or injury, you or someone on your behalf, should inform (*Employer*) of the reason for your absence as soon as possible but no later than the end of the working day on which absence first occurs.

[8] See ibid, s 1(4)(c).
[9] See ibid, s 1(4)(d).
[10] Any deduction must be made in accordance with Part II of the ERA, see Chapter 6, above.
[11] See ibid, s 1(4)(d)(ii). As to the Statutory Sick Pay scheme generally, see Chapter 9, above.

2.6.2 In respect of absence lasting [7 or fewer] calendar days, you need not produce a medical certificate unless you are specifically requested to do so. You must, however, complete (*Employer's*) self-certification form immediately you return to work after such absence.

2.6.3 In respect of absence lasting more than [7] calendar days, you must on the [8th] calendar day of absence provide a medical certificate stating the reason for absence and thereafter provide a like certificate [each week] to cover any subsequent period of absence.

[2.6.4 (*Employer*) reserves the right to ask you at any stage of absence to produce a medical certificate and/or undergo a medical examination.]

2.6.5 You will be paid your normal basic remuneration [less the amount of any Statutory Sick Pay or social security sickness benefit to which you may be entitled] for (*number*) working days in total in any one sick pay year which runs from (*date*) to (*date*).[12]

2.6.6 Entitlement to payment is subject to notification of absence and production of medical certificates as required above.

2.6.7 (*Employer*) operates the Statutory Sick Pay scheme and you are required to co-operate in the maintenance of necessary records. For the purposes of calculating your entitlement to Statutory Sick Pay 'qualifying days' are [those days on which you are normally required to work].[13] Payments made to you by (*Employer*) under its sick pay provisions in satisfaction of any other contractual entitlement will go towards discharging (*Employer's*) liability to make payment to you under the Statutory Sick Pay scheme.

2.7 Pension[14]

[(*Employer*) does not operate a pension scheme applicable to your employment] *or* [(*Employer*) operates a contributory pension scheme which you will be eligible to join on (*date*)] *or* [A non-contributory pension scheme is provided and you are entitled to membership of that scheme]. [Full particulars of the pension scheme are set out in a booklet which [has been *or* will be] given to you *or* which can be obtained from (*state where the booklet may be obtained*)]. A contracting-out certificate under the Social Securities Pension Act 1975 is [not] in force in respect of this employment.

2.8 Notice of termination of employment[15]

[The length of notice which you are obliged to give (*Employer*) to terminate your employment is [one week].]
The length of notice which you are entitled to receive from (*Employer*) to terminate your employment is [one week] until you have been continuously

[12] If any part of a sick pay year is worked, a pro rata entitlement may be provided for.

[13] As to qualifying days generally, see Chapter 9, above. They must be agreed in advance between employer and employee.

[14] The statement must include particulars of pension or pension schemes if any, or a statement that there is none, and state whether or not a contracting-out certificate is in force: ibid, ss 1(4)(d)(iii), 3(5).

[15] See ibid, s 1(4)(e). No notice is required to terminate a fixed term contract but the date of expiry must be stated: ibid, s 1(4)(g). The notice periods given are the minimum periods required by the ERA, s 86. Longer periods may be stated.

employed for [two years] and thereafter notice entitlement will be [one week for each year of continuous employment until you have completed 12 years of continuous employement after which time you will be entitled to 12 weeks' notice] *or*
[Your employment is on a temporary basis and is currently expected to continue only until *(date)*. Your temporary employment is subject to termination by either party giving to the other *(specify number)* [days] *or* [weeks] notice in writing of termination of employment] *or*
[Your employment is for a fixed term and will terminate on (date)]. [It may be terminated at any time before its expiry by either party giving to the other party *(specify number)* [days] *or* [weeks] notice in writing of termination of employment.]

2.9 Grievances and discipline[16]

2.9.1 *Grievance procedure*
[If you have a grievance regarding your employment] you should, in the first instance, speak to [your supervisor]. If the grievance is not resolved to your satisfaction, you should then refer it [to *(specify)* whose decision will be final] *or* [you should refer to the grievance procedure which [is attached] *or* [may be obtained on application to *(specify)*)].]

2.9.2 *Disciplinary rules and procedure*
The disciplinary rules applicable to you are [attached to this statement] *or* [to be found in *(specify place)*)]. If you are dissatisfied with any disciplinary decision taken in relation to you, you should refer to the disciplinary procedure which may be obtained on application to *(state from whom the disciplinary procedure may be obtained)*.

3 ACKNOWLEDGEMENT

Please acknowledge receipt[17] of this statement by completing the tear-off slip below and returning it to *(state to whom the slip should be returned)*.

(Signature of Employee)
I, *(Employee)*, acknowledge that I have received a statement of the particulars of my employment as required by the Employment Rights Act [and confirm my agreement that these constitute my contract of employment with *(Employer)*].

Signed:
Dated:

[16] These provisions are required by ibid, s 3. The grievance procedure and disciplinary rules and procedure may be fully stated here or, for convenience, set out in a separate document. The statutory obligation to provide particulars is satisfied by specifying the person to whom complaint should be made in the first instance and by making it known where the relevant procedures may be found: ibid, s 3(1)(a), (b) and (c). These provisions do not apply to rules, disciplinary decisions, grievances or procedures relating to health or safety at work: ibid, s 3(2).

[17] Acknowledgement of receipt of a copy of the statement does not without more render the statement a contractual document. See Chapter 5, above. The inclusion of words in square brackets is intended to transform the statement into a contract of employment.

CHECK LIST FOR THE PREPARATION OF A CONTRACT OF EMPLOYMENT/STATEMENT OF TERMS AND CONDITIONS

(a) The employer should consider the best way to record the terms and conditions of employment, eg formal contract, statement of particulars of terms and conditions of employment in accordance with s 1 of the ERA, with or without cross-referred documents such as an Employee Handbook.

(b) The employer should consider whether the employment is to be subject to a probationary period during which time the employee does not become entitled to all the benefits of a permanent member of staff and during, or at the end of which the employment may be terminated by either party giving to the other a shorter period of notice than would be required after the satisfactory completion of the probationary period. In the past, probationary periods have, to some extent, served the function of reminding the parties of the need to review an employee's performance before the employee became qualified, by virtue of his or her length of service, for protection against unfair dismissal. Now that the qualifying period is two years, this is perhaps less important since most probationary periods will be less than 12 months in duration, but the economics of disengagement can be minimised by the prudent use of a short notice period applicable during a probationary period.

(c) In selecting a notice period, there is inevitably a balance to be struck between financial implications to the employer of a relatively long period of notice and the desirability, particularly where a key employee is concerned, of ensuring that reasonable notice is received so that arrangements for a replacement can be made before the employee leaves. Correspondingly, from the employee's standpoint, he or she will be seeking the security of a reasonably long period of notice where it is the employer who wishes to terminate the employment but the freedom to disengage reasonably quickly in other circumstances. In many cases the statutory minimum period of notice under s 86 of the ERA will be sufficient but, equally, the more senior or the more critical the employee is to the overall operation the longer the notice period which may be required. There may be instances where a fixed term contract might be useful although the recent trend seems to be away from fixed term appointments for very senior personnel, eg directors, and towards 'evergreen' service agreements where the term of the agreement is automatically extended at intervals, or 'rolling' contracts with reasonably long notice periods. Where there is a danger of competition by a departing employee, additional protection over and above the inclusion of any restrictive covenant in that employee's contract may be secured by a strategically chosen period of notice (see further below).

(d) The following comments may be helpful in formulating a contract/statement of terms and conditions (and see also the footnotes to the model statement of particulars of terms and conditions of employment):

 (i) *Appointment and duties*—there is a requirement under s 1 of the ERA that the job title of an employee should be set out in a statement of particulars. In setting this out, it will usually be of assistance to give a general description of duties which is sufficiently broad to avoid later dispute as to whether or not a particular function lies within the scope of work that the employee may be required to carry out. Flexibility is the key and this may also extend to making it clear that the employee's physical place of work (if this is appropriate) can be changed as required by the employer.

(ii) *Remuneration*—at the same time as stipulating the employee's salary, it is useful to include a clear and unambiguous reference to the payment (or otherwise) of overtime. If an employee is required to work outside the normal hours of work but this is taken account of in the salary paid with no additional overtime payment, it is important to note this. Care should also be taken in choosing the language to describe any bonus entitlement. If it is intended to be discretionary, this should be made clear. If not, the mechanism for calculating 'a' or 'any' bonus should be carefully set out.

(iii) *Holidays*—it should be clearly stated what the employer's holiday year is, the entitlement during that year (with public holidays separately particularised—again with an eye to satisfying s 1 of the ERA), what provisions are to apply with regard to the carrying over of unused holiday entitlement from one year to another and the payment of salary in lieu of holiday not taken or recoupment of payment in respect of holidays taken in excess of entitlement in the event of an employee leaving during a holiday year.

(iv) *Incapacity for work and sick pay*—here again clarity is important particularly in relation to the interaction between SSP entitlement and contractual sick pay. Consideration should also be given to setting out the employee's entitlement to private medical insurance (if any) and any requirements which the employer may seek to impose on the employee concerning a medical examination. An express contractual right to have an employee medically examined may also prove useful to an employer. Note the Access to Medical Records Act 1988.

(v) *Confidentiality*—whilst not appropriate for all types of employment, there will be some where it is useful to remind an employee, through the inclusion of a specific provision, that he or she owes, at common law, certain duties of confidentiality to the employer. This is the case irrespective of the inclusion of an express term in the contract of employment, for the common law implies such a term, but the cosmetics may be important and such a provision can usefully extend to include specific obligations, eg to return papers and other property belonging to the employer which it may be anticipated will come into the employee's possession during the course of the employment immediately upon termination of it.

(vi) *Exclusive services*—again particularly where key employees are concerned, it may be useful to include in any contract of employment an express obligation on the part of the employee to refrain from working for any other party either on the basis that to do so might lead to possible competition or conflict of interest or, for example, through tiredness, make the employee less valuable to the employer during the normal working day.

(vii) *Competition*—for key employees, consideration might be given to the inclusion of restrictive covenants. This subject is discussed in some detail in the main text. Suffice it to say, for present purposes, that an employer should resist the temptation to include such provisions indiscriminately. To include such provisions in every contract from the cleaner to the Managing Director devalues and renders them less likely to be enforced in the event of a challenge in contrast to a provision which is clearly reasonable when applied to the particular individual and which has demonstrably been tailored to the particular circumstances surrounding, and the nature of, the employee's work for the employee. The judicious use of a reasonably long notice period in conjunction with the inclusion of a covenant may also afford an employer slightly greater protection than might otherwise be the case. It is always possible for an employer, faced with a key employee who is proposing to terminate the contract without giving proper notice, to seek an injunction preventing the employee breaching the contract of employment, assuming that the employer is otherwise prepared to keep the contract 'alive' for the balance of the notice period and to perform the employer's obligations under it (see the main text). Additionally, a 'gardening clause' might be included in the contract of employment providing the employer with a contractual right to send the employee home during the notice period but in the process keeping alive other obligations on the part of the employor which would be incompatible with the employee taking up new employment before the expiry of the notice period. In this way an employee in a sensitive position may be retained during the period of garden leave or notice without the risk of a breach of contract on the part of the employer if the employee is given no work to do or transferred to a sinecure for the duration of the notice period. This avoids the problem presented by keeping the employee in his or her existing post with the inevitable loss of impetus while working out a notice period and the acquisition of further confidential information which might be useful to a competitor. However, it should be noted that the consequences of the enforceability of these various provisions may not necessarily be predictable where the courts are concerned.

(viii) *Disciplinary rules and procedures*—having a good set of disciplinary rules and procedures is a useful form of insurance against procedural unfairness leading to a finding of unfair dismissal. In devising the form for these, regard should be had to the ACAS Code of Practice on Disciplinary Practice and Procedures in Employment.

(ix) *Inventions*—the need to include such a provision would obviously be confined to those employees and/or those categories of employee who may in the ordinary course engage in work likely to give rise to invention. In the case of inventions on or after 1 June 1978, s 39(1) of the Patents Act 1977 provides that where made in the course of an employee's normal duties or alternatively duties specifically assigned to him and, in either case, the circumstances are such that an invention might reasonably be expected to result, an invention will, subject to the provisions of the Act, belong to the employer. In addition, if an invention is made in the course of the employee's duties, and the employee has a special obligation to further the interests of the employer's undertaking because of the particular responsibilities arising from the nature of his or her duties in such circumstances the employer may be entitled to the invention. Whilst the Act applies irrespective of any provision inserted in the contract of employment; special care in framing any contractual description of the duties and responsibilities of the employee may assist in bringing a particular situation within the regime of the Act. Arguably the employee's duty of confidentiality in relation to the employer's business may well limit the employee's scope in seeking to exploit an invention which arguably does not fall within the regime of s 39 of the Act. A related topic is that of copyright where the Copyright, Designs and Patents Act 1988 is applicable and provides an exception to the general rule that ownership of copyright in a work vests in the author where employees are concerned, and the work is 'in the course of [the employee's] employment'. In such circumstances, copyright belongs to the employer subject to any agreement to the contrary. Here again one can see that careful framing of the duties and responsibilities, not to say an express reference to the position with regard to copyright, may prove of assistance. By way of a general postscript on the subject of confidential information, inventions and copyright, there may be cases where key employees engaged in technical and secret work for an employer should be the subject of a collateral secrecy agreement. The advantages are that such a document can be tailored to a particular category of employee or even a particular employee; the agreement may extend to include all provisions relating to or arising out of the confidential nature of the employee's work, and include restrictions intended to operate when the employment terminates. The collateral agreement, being separate from the main body of terms and conditions of employment, will probably impress on the employee the importance of the provisions within it in contrast to burying these in the middle of a lengthy contract of employment.

(x) *Wages Act*—having regard to the provisions of Part II of the ERA any employer wishing to make deductions other than those required by a statutory provision should ensure the inclusion of a provision in the contract which, when signed, will constitute a written agreement on the part of the employee to make the deduction. It is submitted that inclusion of such a provision in the statement of particulars of terms and conditions of employment in accordance with the ERA will not, of itself, be sufficient where the employee merely signs an acknowledgement of receipt of the statement and, in such circumstances, the alternative form of words shown on the model above transforming the statement into a contractual document is to be preferred.

(B) Transfer of an undertaking

There are several strands running through the Transfer of Undertakings (Protection of Employment) Regulations 1981 ('TUPE') the relative importance of which depend upon whether you are an employer or an employee (or a trade union representing affected employees).

From the employer's standpoint, one can list the matters which need to be considered in determining whether the regulations apply and, if so, what the implications are:

(a) *What is being transferred*? Is it simply shares in the company which owns the 'undertaking'? If so, the regulations will not apply. If it is the economic entity (with or even without the assets used in the operation) which is transferring it probably is an 'undertaking' and TUPE applies.

(b) If it appears to be an undertaking, or part of it, which is being transferred, *does it actually satisfy the definition in the regulations*? The requirement in TUPE that the undertaking must be in the nature of a commercial venture to fall within TUPE was held to be contrary to the EC Acquired Rights Directive and removed by the TURERA 1993.

(c) *What does the undertaking comprise*? is it only assets that are being transferred or is the undertaking being transferred a business or economic entity (ie a going concern)? The line can sometimes be a difficult one to draw with 'franchise' type businesses falling directly on it with consequent difficulties in predicting how TUPE will apply in practice. An express or implied transfer of goodwill will generally be a relevant factor. It does not matter that the cosmetics of any transfer agreement appear to reflect a state of affairs consistent purely with a transfer of assets, if the underlying reality is obviously different.

(d) Having established the applicability of the regulations, *what consequences need to be considered*? Transferors and Transferees were always required to inform and consult with recognised trade unions in advance of a transfer taking place but in relation to transfers on or after 1 March 1996 this obligation extended to a requirement to inform and consult employee representatives where there was no recognised trade union. See Chapter 8.

(e) The key provision as far as an employer is concerned will be reg 5 of TUPE which transfers the contracts of employment to those employed in the undertaking or part being transferred to the new party. It is clear there is very limited scope for preventing the automatic transfer of contracts of employment and the rights and liabilities (save for criminal ones) attaching.

(f) If the employees are working in the undertaking at the time of transfer, the process is automatic. If the transferor (for whatever reason) dismisses employees for a reason directly or indirectly connected with the transfer, a dismissal is, to the extent of the liabilities arising from it, without effect and the transferee acquires the liabilities consequent upon the action taken.

(g) A dismissal which is directly or indirectly related to the transfer will be automatically unfair (reg 8).

(h) However, where there is an *economic*, *technical* or *organisational* ('ETO') reason which entails changes to be made in the workforce, it may be possible to avoid the consequences of an unfair dismissal but the escape route is a narrow one. Redundancy would appear to fall within this Euro jargon, but;

(i) both transferor and transferee must be careful to avoid seeking to vary contracts in circumstances where to do so could give rise to a constructive dismissal claim on the part of the employee(s) affected. In such an event, the reg 8 escape route is not available. For the transferee, the implications could be potentially serious. There may be strong commercial reasons why the transferee finds it imperative to change terms and conditions (perhaps they are just too generous and/or they are quite inconsistent with the terms and conditions enjoyed by the transferee's existing workforce). Notwithstanding, negotiation and agreement provides the only safe route for a transferee to take in such circumstances.

(j) For the employer there is a duty to *inform* and *consult* either a recognised trade union or employee representatives.

(k) As regards *informing* the model letter below covers the framework of information required by reg 10. Facts required to be stated (when, how many etc) are relatively easy to deal with but again the vagueness of the (European) language intervenes to obscure what the employer needs to do in satisfying the obligation to inform (eg the requirement to stipulate the social implications of the proposed transfer). There may be circumstances where forecasts, opinions and assessments need to be included in order to satisfy the obligation under reg 10. In such a case (for example, information regarding future manning levels) it would appear the employer does not have to go so far as to explain or hold up for scrutiny the *reasoning* behind, merely the *results* of, the employer's deliberations in this regard.

(l) *Consultation* is different. It is only required where the employer (and in this regard it could mean both the transferor or the transferee since the affected employees need not be in the undertaking being transferred) considers taking *measures* in relation to the affected employees but must now (since the changes made to TUPE by TURERA) be carried out with a view to seeking the recognised trade union's agreement to the proposed measures.

(m) *Timing* is difficult. TUPE provides that the information required must be provided *long enough* before the relevant transfer to allow for consultation to take place. If there is nothing to consult about, the period can arguably be short to the point of being non-existent (although industrial relations considerations often dictate that it would be a fairly rash employer who sprang important news on representatives of the workforce), but otherwise the period has to be tailored to the subject matter about which consultation is required. It has been suggested that an employer could do worse than apply, by analogy, the consultation periods required pursuant to s 188 of the Trade Union and Labour Relations (Consolidation) Act 1992 in relation to redundancy consultation but this appears incorrect. Regulation 10 does not lay down a fixed period. The very purpose of the regulation, it is submitted, is to leave the consultation timetable flexible.

From the employee's standpoint, many of the comments made above are equally relevant. However, once again the key provision is reg 5, and the safeguard that a dismissal for a reason connected directly or indirectly to the transfer will be unfair. If it takes place before the transfer, the consequences will visit themselves on the transferee who will become liable for them unless for an ETO reason.

For the employee, it is likely that one area of concern will be that relating to the employee's pension position. Regulation 7 precludes the transfer of pension rights and it requires ingenious (and ultimately unconvincing) interpretations to be placed on this provision in the regulations to require the transferor to replicate pension rights lost by employees at the time of transfer. The transferring employee is vulnerable in this area and, in practice, in the absence of industrial or commercial pressure, there is little that an employee, faced with less satisfactory arrangements regarding pension entitlement following a transfer, may do, save possibly to look for other employment.

LETTER PROVIDING INFORMATION TO TRADE UNIONS AND INVITING CONSULTATION ON THE TRANSFER OF AN UNDERTAKING IN ACCORDANCE WITH THE TRANSFER OF UNDERTAKINGS (PROTECTION OF EMPLOYMENT) REGULATIONS 1982[1]

(*Date*)

To: (*local full-time official of recognised trade union or elected employee representative*)

Dear

I am writing to you in accordance with reg 10 of the Transfer of Undertakings (Protection of Employment) Regulations 1981 ('The Regulations') to inform you of our proposal to transfer (*specify undertaking*) to (*specify*).

It is proposed that the transfer of (*specify undertaking*) will take place on [or about] (*specify date*). The reasons for the transfer are (*specify*).[2]

The proposed transfer will affect (*identify number and description of employees*) who are presently employed in the undertaking. From a legal standpoint, the affected employees will, by virtue of the operation of the Regulations, transfer on their existing terms and conditions of employment and with continuity of employment for statutory and contractual purposes. As there will be no changes to existing terms and conditions of employment [(save in respect of pension—see further below)], it is not envisaged that there will be any economic implications arising from the transfer nor are there any social implications except in relation to pension arrangements as detailed below.[3] It is [not] envisaged that (*transferor*) will be taking [any] measures in connection with the transfer in relation to those employees who will be affected by the transfer[4] [or (*specify measures*)].

[Although in all other respects the terms and conditions of employment of those employees who will be transferring with the undertaking will be unaffected by the transfer of the undertaking, it will be necessary for their existing pension arrangements to be changed, since they will be unable to continue as members of the (*specify*) scheme following the transfer. Arrangements will be

[1] TUPE as amended provides (reg 10) that the recognised trade union in respect of affected employees or their employee representatives are entitled to be *informed* about the transfer of an undertaking and consulted about measures proposed to be taken in relation to affected employees by the transferor or transferee. Regulation 10(2) lists the information to be provided and stipulates that this is to be provided long enough before a relevant transfer to enable consultations to take place between the employer of any affected employees and the appropriate representatives. However, consultation is only required (reg 10(5)) where the employer of any affected employees envisages taking measures in relation to affected employees. In such circumstances, the employer is required (reg 10(6)) in the course of the consultations to consider any representations made by the trade union or employee representatives and reply to these representations stating reasons if any of the representations are rejected. By virtue of TURERA 1993, reg 10(5) has been amended to provide that consultation is to be carried out with a view to seeking the appropriate representatives's agreement to the measures to be taken. See further Ch 8, above and *Institution of Professional Civil Servants v Secretary of State for Defence* [1987] IRLR 373, 3 CMLR 35.

[2] Ibid, reg 10(2)(a).

[3] Ibid, reg 10(2)(b).

[4] Ibid, reg 10(2)(c).

implemented in relation to employees who are members of the (*specify*) scheme to enable them to become members of the (*specify*) pension scheme upon the transfer of their employment to (*transferee*). The (*transferee*) pensions scheme offers the same benefits as (*transferors*) pension scheme.][5]

(*Transferee*) has advised us that it does [not] envisage taking any other measures in relation to employees who transfer with the undertaking[6] [or (*specify measures*)].

I would be pleased to meet with you on (*specify*) to discuss the proposed transfer of (*specify*) and to consult with you regarding (*specify any measures it is envisaged will be taken in connection with the transfer*)[7] and to consider and reply to any representations which you wish to make on the subject of these measures.[8]

(*Specify any arrangements for representatives of the Transferee to meet with trade union or employee representatives.*)

5 By virtue of reg 7 rights, powers, duties or liabilities in relation to an occupational pension scheme within the meaning of the Social Security Pensions Act 1975 [the current definition is however to be found in s 1 of the Pensions Schemes Act 1993].

6 Ibid, reg 10(2)(d).

7 Ibid, reg 10(5).

8 Ibid, reg 10(5) as amended by TURERA 1993.

(C) Maternity

The twin rights of the pregnant woman ought, in theory and in practice, to be straightforward in their application but are anything but. The position has become more complicated by the introduction of a separate, though in many respects parallel, right to paid maternity leave for women who have less than the requisite two years' continuous employment as a consequence of TURERA 1993. The new right came into force on 23 June 1994 and applies to women expecting a baby on or after 16 October 1994. The following check list may be of assistance to employer and employee alike.

MATERNITY LEAVE: MORE THAN TWO YEARS' SERVICE

(a) The employee must have completed two years' continuous employment by the beginning of the eleventh week before the expected week of childbirth (EWC). It is immaterial that the employee does not actually work until then, as long as the contract of employment subsists until that time. An exception is made where the employee is dismissed because it was physically or legally impossible for her to continue.

(b) The employee must give her employer at least 21 days' *written* notice of her intention to take maternity leave (where reasonably practical). She must advise the employer both that she will be temporarily absent because of pregnancy and that she is going to return.

(c) A mechanism exists whereby an employer may ask the employee to confirm that she does intend to return. The employer's request for such confirmation may not be sought earlier than 49 days after the notified week of confinement and the request for confirmation must be in writing whilst, at the same time, the employer must take care to warn the employee, again in writing, that if she does not reply in writing, within 14 days or as soon as reasonably practicable thereafter, she will lose her right to return.

(d) The right to return must be exercised, in normal circumstances, not more than 28 weeks after the birth of the employee's baby. In passing, it may be noted that if the employee has a contractual right to return to work, she may claim a composite right consisting of the best parts of both the contractual and the statutory regime applicable to her. Statutory rights are, in this respect, a minimum.

(e) The right to return is exercised by the employee giving at least 21 days' notice in writing specifying the day upon which she proposes to return. This 'notified day of return' must, in normal circumstances, be no later than the last day of the 29th week after the childbirth. The 29 weeks are from and including the week of *actual* childbirth, not the expected week of childbirth previously notified to the employer.

(f) There are two instances where an employee may notify a day which is later than the 29-week period:

  (i) Where the employee is, for health reasons, incapable of returning to work she may extend the 29-week period by up to four further weeks. If she wishes to do so, it is necessary for her to produce a medical certificate as to her disability before the end of the 29 weeks. *However*, it should be noted the employee may not use this right and, in addition, postpone her right to return on medical grounds as described in paragraph (g) below.

  (ii) The employee may, where there is an 'interruption of work' due to industrial action or 'some other reason' at about the time the employee was due to return, give notice to return up to 28 days after the end of the interruption of work. It does not matter how long this interruption is for.

(g) There are three circumstances in which the employee's return may be postponed:

  (i) An employer may, for any good reason (and this must be explained to the employee), postpone her return for up to four weeks after the day chosen by the employee for her return. There is no obligation to pay salary during this period.

  (ii) The employee may postpone her return, on medical grounds, up to four weeks from to the day she was originally due to return. She must give her employer a medical certificate before the day she chose to return originally, and she is only entitled to one 'medical' postponement. As indicated above, this right cannot be invoked in addition to the right to delay service of notice of intention to return on medical grounds.

  (iii) The employee's return may be delayed as a consequence of an 'interruption of work' (see above).

MATERNITY LEAVE: LESS THAN TWO YEARS' SERVICE

(h) By virtue of s 73 of the ERA, a pregnant woman is entitled, irrespective of the length of service, to 14 weeks' maternity leave.

(i) The 14-week maternity leave period will begin on the date she notifies her employer that she wishes to leave to commence the period of maternity leave or, alternatively if earlier, on the first day the absence occurs wholly or partly because of pregnancy or childbirth after the beginning of the sixth week before the EWC.

(j) As with maternity leave available in the case where a woman has been employed for longer than two years, the employee must give 21 days' written notice before her maternity leave period is due to commence and the notice must state that she is pregnant and specify the date of EWC. The employee must produce, if requested to do so by the employer, a certificate from a doctor or midwife (a MAT B1 Form) specifying the EWC.

STATUTORY MATERNITY PAY: MORE THAN TWO YEARS' SERVICE

(k) For SMP an employee:
 (i) must be continuously employed for at least 26 weeks ending with the week immediately preceding the 14th week before her baby is due (this is known as the Qualifying Week);
 (ii) must have average weekly earnings which are not below the lower earnings limit for the payment of National Insurance Contributions;
 (iii) must still be pregnant at the 11th week before her EWC, or have given birth by then; and
 (iv) must have ceased working for the employer.

(l) To claim SMP, the employee must normally give 21 days' notice for intention to be absent but this does not have to be in writing unless the employer requests it. It is unnecessary for the employee to say other than that she will be away because of her pregnancy. There is no need to notify the employer when she proposes to return. Arguably, if she does not, she may not be 'an employee who is absent from work' for the purposes of SMP. However, although the employee may have resolved not to return to work, the regime for SMP assumes, in effect, she remains 'on the books' for the period necessary for her to claim SMP.

(m) For those above the lower earnings limit (£61 a week as at April 1996) SMP is 90% of average weekly earnings for six weeks followed by lower rate SMP (£54.55 as at April 1996) for a maximum of 12 weeks' leave.

(n) In two instances, notice need not be given. First, where the employee leaves for a reason unconnected with pregnancy after the beginning of the 15th week but before the EWC. Second, where the employee has her employment terminated (not unfairly) as a consequence of her being physically or legally unable to continue in employment.

(o) The maternity pay period may start any time after the 11th week before EWC up to the date the employee commences maternity leave (see para (l) above.

(p) The Statutory Maternity Pay (General) Regulations 1986 require the employee to supply a Maternity Certificate (in the form prescribed by the Statutory Maternity Pay (Medical Evidence) Regulations 1987) to the employer and, where entitlement depends upon the fact of confinement, evidence (a copy of the birth certificate will do) of childbirth within three weeks of the maternity pay period commencing, although this may be delayed for good cause for a period up to the end of the 13th week of the maternity pay period.

STATUTORY MATERNITY PAY: LESS THAN TWO YEARS' SERVICES

(q) For employees with less than 26 weeks' continuous employment at the qualifying week the state maternity allowance of £54.55 (as at April 1996) a week for a maximum of 18 weeks is payable provided they have worked and paid NI contributions in at least 26 of the 66 weeks before the EWC. For those with more than 26 weeks' continuous employment the rate is as for those with two years' service (see above).

The form reproduced below, SMP1, is that which an employer can use to notify an employee of the reason(s) for refusal to pay SMP.

SMP 1

Statutory Maternity Pay (SMP)

Your surname

Other names

Address

Postcode

National Insurance (NI) number

Works or clock number

Why I cannot pay you SMP

I have ticked the box that applies to you.

☐ I cannot pay you SMP.
I have ticked one of the boxes on the next page of this letter to tell you why.

☐ I cannot pay you any more SMP after the week which ends on Saturday / / . You are entitled to weeks SMP from me until then.
I have ticked one of the boxes on the next page of this letter to tell you why I cannot carry on paying you after this date.

What to do if you disagree

If you disagree with this decision, please get in touch with me. My name, address and phone number are at the bottom of this page. If you still disagree, you can ask your social security office for advice. You can find their phone number and address on the advert in the business numbers section of the phone book. Look under **Benefits Agency**. You may be able to ask for an adjudication officer's decision. You can get leaflet **NI 17A** *A guide to Maternity Benefits* from your social security office for more information about this.

Maternity Allowance

You may be able to get Maternity Allowance from your social security office. Ask your ante-natal clinic or social security office for a *Maternity Allowance claim pack.*

How to claim Maternity Allowance

Fill in the claim form **MA 1** which is in the pack and send it to your social security office with your *Maternity Certificate* **Mat B1** and this letter. If you gave me your **Mat B1**, I have sent it back to you with this letter. If you want to ask me anything about this letter, please get in touch with me.

Employer's signature

Employer's name and address

Postcode

Phone number

Date / /

Why I cannot pay you SMP - continued

I have ticked one of the boxes to tell you why I cannot pay you Statutory Maternity Pay (SMP).

☐	**You were not employed by me for long enough**	To get SMP you must be employed by me for at least 26 weeks in a row into the 15th week before your baby is due, even if your baby is born early. You would not have been employed by me for long enough even if your baby had not been born early. This is because you still would not have worked for me 26 weeks in a row into the 15th week.
☐	**Your earnings were too low**	To get SMP your average earnings must be enough to pay National Insurance (NI) contributions on.
☐	**You did not tell me soon enough that you would be away from work**	To get SMP you must give me at least 3 weeks notice that you will be away from work because you are pregnant. You did not have a good reason for giving me less notice than this.
☐	**You did not give me medical evidence soon enough**	To get SMP you must give me your *Maternity Certificate* **Mat B1**, or other acceptable evidence, within 3 weeks of the start of your Maternity Pay Period. If you had a good reason for taking longer than this, I could only allow you up to 13 weeks to give me this evidence.
☐	**You did not tell me soon enough that your baby had been born**	To get SMP you must tell me about your baby within 3 weeks of the date your baby is born. If you had a good reason for taking longer than this, I could only allow you up to 13 weeks to tell me.
☐	**You were out of the European Economic Area**	You cannot get SMP if you are out of the European Economic Area at the beginning of your Maternity Pay Period. If you have been getting SMP, you stop getting it when you leave the European Economic Area. If your baby is due on or after 18 August 1996 see the **note below**.
☐	**You were in legal custody**	You cannot get SMP if you are in legal custody at the beginning of your Maternity Pay Period. If you have been getting SMP, you stop getting it when you go into legal custody.

Some important dates that affect your claim for SMP

• **The week your baby is due**	The first day of that week is	/ /
• **The week that is 15 weeks before the week your baby is due**	The first day of that week is	/ /
• **Your Maternity Pay Period**	Your Maternity Pay Period is the period during which you could get SMP. Your Maternity Pay Period starts or would have started on	/ /

If your baby is due on or after 18 August 1996

If your baby is due on or after 18 August 1996 and you qualify for SMP, you can get SMP even if you are outside the European Economic Area.

If you are employed by a Great Britain employer but you work outside the European Economic Area you may still get SMP in certain circumstances.

SOCIAL SECURITY

benefits ba agency

An Executive Agency of the Department of Social Security

Printed for BPASS by Prudential Business Services / Print. 1840F 3/96

(D) Statutory sick pay

Reproduced below are Forms SSP1 and SSP1(L). The relative complexities of SSP are such that aside from the text, both employer and employee might, as an initial step in clarifying any doubt or uncertainty, find it beneficial to read The Employer's Guide to Statutory Sick Pay N270 produced by the Department of Health and Social Security.

SSP 1 (Apr 96)

Claim form

Statutory Sick Pay (SSP) and Incapacity Benefit

About this form

There are **4** sections in this form.

Section 1
is for the employer to give information about Statutory Sick Pay (SSP). Notes for the employer about when to fill in this form are on **page 2** of this form.

Sections 2, **3** and **4**
are for the employee to claim Incapacity Benefit.

Statutory Sick Pay is money paid by employers to employees who are away from work for 4 days or more in a row because they are sick.

Incapacity Benefit is a social security benefit you may be able to get if you are still sick when your SSP ends or if you cannot get SSP.

Section 1

About SSP and your employee

About your employee

Please tell us about your employee

Surname [ ]

Other names [ ]

National Insurance (NI) number Letters [ ][ ] Numbers [ ][ ] [ ][ ] [ ][ ] Letter [ ]

Clock or payroll number [ ]

Tax reference number [ ]

Notes to the employer

When to fill in this form

If you cannot pay any SSP to this employee
fill in **Section 1** of this form as soon as they have been sick for 4 days in a row. Count weekends, holidays and other days that the employee would not normally work.

If you have been paying SSP to this employee but you will soon have to stop paying SSP to them even though they are still sick
fill in **Section 1** of this form
- when you have been paying SSP for 23 weeks. This will let the employee know that their SSP will soon stop, or
- 2 weeks before you will stop paying SSP, if you know that this will be before they have had SSP for 23 weeks, or
- as soon as you can, if you have to stop paying SSP suddenly.

By law you must give this form to your employee
- no later than 7 days after you knew that the employee was sick for 4 days in a row, or if this is not possible
- no later than the first payday in the tax month, after you knew that the employee was sick for 4 days in a row.

If you use a computer

Instead of filling in **Section 1** you can attach a computer print out of the information we need. But please make sure the print out
- is in a format which is easy to understand
- contains all the information we ask for
- contains all the details in the employer's declaration on page 7, and
- has been signed.

If you are not sure if your print out will be suitable, send a copy to your social security office and they will advise you. You can find their phone number and address on the advert in the business numbers section of the phone book. Look under **Benefits Agency.**

If you want more information

For more information about SSP, please read leaflets
- **CA 27** *The Quick Reference Cards* for general information
- **CA 30** *The Employer's Manual* for detailed technical information.

You can get these leaflets from any social security office.

Ring the Social Security Advice Line for Employers – the phone call is free.
The number is **0800 393 539.**

Why you cannot get Statutory Sick Pay

I am filling in this form because

☐ I cannot pay you SSP

☐ I cannot pay you SSP after [/ /]

I have ticked a box to tell you why you cannot get SSP. The notes on **pages 4** and **5** explain the reasons in more detail.

I cannot pay you SSP because

A ☐ **You may be able to get Incapacity Benefit instead of SSP.**

B ☐ **Your contract of employment has expired.**

C ☐ **Your contract of employment has been brought to an end.**

D ☐ **You will soon have been getting SSP for 28 weeks or you have already had SSP for 28 weeks.**

E ☐ **You have not earned enough money.**

F ☐ **You are only going to work for me for 3 months or less.**

G ☐ **You are aged 65 or over.**

H ☐ **You are expecting a baby soon or you have just had a baby.**

J ☐ **You have already been sick on and off for 3 years.**

K ☐ **You were away from work because of a trade dispute on the first day you were sick.**

L ☐ **You were in legal custody or you were serving a term of imprisonment when you became sick.**
Or you are now in legal custody or sentenced to a term of imprisonment.

M ☐ **You were not in the European Economic Area (EEA) on the first day you were sick or you are not in the EEA now. But if you are sick on or after 6 April 1996 see page 5** ***Changes to SSP from 6 April 1996 – outside the EEA.***

N ☐ **You have not started working for me yet.**

Reasons why you cannot get SSP

A You cannot get SSP if you claimed Incapacity Benefit, Severe Disablement Allowance or Maternity Allowance during the last 8 weeks.

B You cannot normally get SSP after you stop working for your employer.

C You cannot normally get SSP after you stop working for your employer. Your employer will have to pay you SSP if they ended your contract of employment solely or mainly to avoid paying SSP.

D You cannot get SSP after you have had SSP for 28 weeks in a row or for periods of sickness that are 8 weeks or less apart and that add up to 28 weeks. SSP paid by another employer may be counted.

E You cannot get SSP if your average weekly earnings for the last 8 weeks before you went sick are less than the earnings that people pay National Insurance (NI) contributions on. All earnings before things like tax are taken off are counted.

F You cannot get SSP if you have a contract to work for an employer for 3 months or less.

G You cannot get SSP if on the first day you became sick you are aged 65 or over.

H You cannot get SSP for at least 18 weeks starting on one of the following dates

- the beginning of the week you are first entitled to Statutory Maternity Pay (SMP)
- the beginning of the week you are first entitled to Maternity Allowance (MA)

or

- if you already get SSP but cannot get SMP or MA, the earlier of
  - the day after your baby is born, or
  - the day after the day you are first away from work because of your pregnancy if this is after the start of the 6th week before the week your baby is expected

or

- if you do not already get SSP and you cannot get SMP or MA, the earlier of
  - the Sunday of the week your baby is born, or
  - the Sunday of the week you are first away from work because of your pregnancy if this is on or after the start of the 6th week before the week your baby is expected.

Statutory Maternity Pay (SMP) is money paid by the employer to women who are away from work because they are pregnant.
Maternity Allowance (MA) is a social security benefit you may be able to get if you are pregnant and cannot get SMP.

Reasons why you cannot get SSP – continued

J You cannot get SSP if during the last 3 years
- you have been sick on and off for 4 days or more in a row, and
- you have never been back at work for more than 8 weeks before going sick again.

K You cannot get SSP if you were away from work because of a trade dispute on the first day you were sick.
We use *trade dispute* to mean
- a strike
- a walkout
- a lockout
- another dispute about work.

L You cannot get SSP if you were
- in legal custody or sentenced to a term of imprisonment on the day you became sick, or
- your SSP will stop if you are now in legal custody or sentenced to a term of imprisonment.

M You cannot get SSP if you were in a country outside the EEA on the day you first became sick. Your SSP will stop if you go to a country outside the EEA. But if you are sick on or after 6 April 1996 see below *Changes to SSP from 6 April 1996 – outside the EEA*.

The European Economic Area is – England, Scotland, Wales, Northern Ireland, Austria, Belgium, Denmark, Finland, France, Germany, Gibraltar, Greece, Iceland, Italy, Liechtenstein, Luxembourg, the Netherlands (Holland), Norway, Portugal, Republic of Ireland, Spain and Sweden.

It does not include the Isle of Man or the Channel Islands.

N You cannot get SSP until you start working for your employer.

Changes to SSP from 6 April 1996 – outside the EEA

If you are sick
- on or after 6 April 1996, **and**
- there is more than 8 weeks between this period of sickness and an earlier period which started before 6 April 1996, **and**
- you are outside the EEA, **and**
- your employer is liable to pay Class 1 National Insurance contributions

you may be able to get SSP provided the other conditions for entitlement are met.

If you are sick
- before 6 April 1996, **or**
- after 6 April 1996 but there is 8 weeks or less between this period of sickness and an earlier period which started before 6 April 1996, **and**
- you are outside the EEA

you will not be entitled to SSP.

More information we need

The employee's first day of sickness

To work out this date you will need to check

- your sick records for this employee, and
- any form **SSP 1(L)** *Leaver's statement of SSP* from a previous employer.

If your employee has a form **SSP 1(L)** from a previous employer and has been off work sick for 4 days or more within 8 weeks and one day of **date 2** on their **SSP 1(L)**, the first day of sickness is **date 1** on form **SSP 1(L)**.

If your employee has had 2 or more spells of sickness of 4 days or more in a row which were 8 weeks or less apart, the first day of sickness is the first day they were off work sick at the beginning of these spells of sickness.

For all other employees who have been off work sick for 4 days or more in a row, the first day of sickness is the first day they were off work sick.

The first day of sickness is / /

About the SSP you have paid

How many weeks and days of SSP have been paid to this employee?
Count from the first day you have paid SSP.
If you are including any SSP paid by a previous employer, count from **date 1** on their form **SSP 1(L)**.

weeks days

How many qualifying days are there in the last week that SSP is due?
Count the number of qualifying days in the full week, not just the number of days they can get SSP for.
Remember, for most employees qualifying days are the days of the week that they normally work.

days

Employer's declaration

I declare
that the information I have given is correct and complete.

I understand
that if this employee has been getting SSP, I must continue to pay SSP until the date I have written on **page 3** of this form.

Employer's name

Signature

Date / /

Position in firm

Phone number and extension extension

Fax number

Address

Postcode

Business stamp

What to do next

Please send this form to your employee with any medical certificates that cover a period you cannot pay SSP for. *Medical certificates* are also called sick notes or doctor's statements.

Section 2

Your claim for Incapacity Benefit

Please read through Section 1 of this form. Your employer has filled in Section 1 to tell you why you cannot get Statutory Sick Pay (SSP).
Statutory Sick Pay (SSP) is money paid by employers to employees who are away from work for 4 days or more in a row because they are sick.

If you disagree with the decision, ask your employer to explain it to you.

If you still disagree, get in touch with your social security office and ask for an adjudication officer's decision. Leaflet **NI 244** *Statutory Sick Pay – check your rights* tells you more about this. You can get this leaflet from any social security office.

Please fill in the rest of this form if you want to claim Incapacity Benefit.

If you need help filling in this form, get in touch with your social security office. If you cannot fill in this form yourself, you can ask someone else to fill it in for you.

Part 1 **About you**

Please tell us about yourself

Surname	
Other names	
Any other surnames you have had	
Title	Mr/Mrs/Miss/Ms
Address	
	Postcode
Daytime phone number	Code Number
Date of birth	/ /

Marital status

married ☐ widow or widower ☐ separated ☐

single ☐ divorced ☐

Part 2 **About your work**

What is your usual occupation? [ ]

Have you been employed for more than 8 weeks in the 21 weeks before this period of sickness began?
Include periods of leave, career breaks, training.
No [ ]
Yes [ ]

Please tell us about the employer who sent you this form.
If you have more than one job with this employer, tell us what your main job is.

Job title [ ]

What are the main activities of the job? [ ]

Period of employment From / / To / /

Hours worked each week hours

Did you work for any other employers in the 21 weeks before this period of sickness began?
No [ ]
Yes [ ] Please tell us about any other employers in **Part 18**.

Do you have any other job?
No [ ]
Yes [ ] How many other jobs do you have? [ ]

Please send us form **SSP 1** for each of the jobs you have.
Section 1 must be filled in by the employer. But you do not have to fill in **Sections 2, 3** and **4** on each form.
If you cannot send us form **SSP 1** for each job, we will write to you to tell you what to do. But please fill in the rest of this form and send it back to us as soon as you can.

Do you also work as a self-employed person?
No [ ] Please go to **Part 3**.
Yes [ ]

What type of work do you do? [ ]

Are you still working as a self-employed person?
No [ ] What date did you last work as a self-employed person? / /
Yes [ ]

Part 3 About your sickness

When this period of sickness began

What date do you want to claim Incapacity Benefit from? / /

What was the last date
- **you worked for an employer, or**
- **you worked as a self-employed person?**

/ /

Did you work a night shift which included midnight on the date you last worked?

No ☐

Yes ☐ What time did you start the shift? am/pm

What time did you finish the shift? am/pm

Details of your sickness

Please give brief details of your sickness.
We need to know what your doctor says is wrong with you and how this stops you from working.

Have you been into hospital as an in-patient since you became sick?

No ☐ Please go to **page 11.**

Yes ☐ Please tell us about this.

Name and address of the hospital

Postcode

Date you went into hospital / /

Have you come out of hospital?

No ☐

Yes ☐ Date you came out of hospital / /

Do you have any special medical treatment?
By special medical treatment we mean
- dialysis
- radiotherapy
- chemotherapy
- plasmapheresis
- total parenteral nutrition for gross impairment of enteric function.

No ☐

Yes ☐

Part 3 **About your sickness** – continued

Please tell us how long you have been sick.
Tick the box that applies.

More than 7 days ☐ Please send us a medical certificate from your doctor with this claim form.
Medical certificates are also called sick notes or doctor's statements.

If your doctor has not given you a medical certificate yet, send this form to us straight away.

7 days or less ☐ You do not need to send us a medical certificate from your doctor with this claim form. But you will need to send us a medical certificate if you are sick for more than 7 days.
Medical certificates are also called sick notes or doctor's statements.

Please tell us the name and address of the doctor who is signing your medical certificates.

Postcode

Are you expecting a baby? **No** ☐

Yes ☐ What date is your baby expected? | / / |

Have you had a baby in the 18 weeks before the date you are claiming Incapacity Benefit from? **No** ☐

Yes ☐ What date was your baby born? | / / |

Do you think you are sick because of an accident at work while working for an employer? **No** ☐

Yes ☐ You may be able to get Industrial Injuries Disablement Benefit. We will send you leaflet **NI 6** *Industrial Injuries Disablement Benefit*. This will tell you about the benefit and how to claim it.

Do you think you are sick because of an industrial disease caused by conditions at work while working for an employer? If you are not sure whether the disease you have is an industrial disease, tick **Yes**. **No** ☐

Yes ☐ You may be able to get Industrial Injuries Disablement Benefit. We will send you leaflet **NI 6** *Industrial Injuries Disablement Benefit*. This will tell you about the benefit and how to claim it.
We will also send you leaflet **NI 2** *If you have an industrial disease* which will tell you about prescribed diseases.

Part 3 **About your sickness** – continued

Going back to work

Do you know when you will be well enough to work again? **No** ☐ Please go to **Part 4**. **Yes** ☐

What date will you go back to work? [/ /]

Will you go back to work on a night shift which includes midnight? **No** ☐ **Yes** ☐ What time will you start the shift? [am/pm] What time will you finish the shift? [am/pm]

If you do not have a job to go back to, tell us when you will be well enough to work. [/ /]

Part 4 **About the 8 weeks before you became sick**

Please fill in this part of the form if your employer cannot pay you any SSP.

This is because what you were doing in the 8 weeks before you became sick may affect when you start to get Incapacity Benefit.

Please tick any of these 3 statements that apply to you.

1 You cannot get any SSP at all. ☐

2 You were off work sick for 4 days or more in a row during the 8 weeks before this period of sickness began. ☐

3 You were working for a different employer during the 8 weeks before the date you became sick. ☐ Please tell us about the employer you worked for during that period

Employer's name and address

Postcode

Phone number

Code Number

Part 5 About any time you have spent abroad

We need to know about any time you have spent abroad.

We use *abroad* to mean any country outside the United Kingdom (UK). The UK is England, Scotland, Wales and Northern Ireland, including territorial waters next to the UK. But the UK does not include the Isle of Man or the Channel Islands.

Have you been abroad at any time during the 4 years before the date you are claiming Incapacity Benefit from? Tick **No**, if you went abroad for a holiday.

No ☐ Please go to **Part 6**.

Yes ☐ Which countries did you go to?

☐

☐

☐

Tick the description that applies to your time abroad

I worked for an overseas employer ☐

I worked for a UK employer ☐

I was self-employed ☐

I was getting money from a social security scheme of the country I was staying in ☐

None of these ☐

Part 6 **About other benefits**

Are you getting any other benefits? No ☐ Yes ☐

Tick **Yes**, if you are waiting to hear about a benefit.

For example,

- Income Support
- Retirement Pension
- Widow's Benefit
- War Widow's Pension
- Unemployability Supplement
- Invalid Care Allowance
- Training Allowance
- Business Start-Up Allowance

Tick **No**, if you just get Child Benefit. We will ask you about this later in the form.

Please tell us about the benefits below.

Name of benefit

Reference number, if known

Name of benefit

Reference number, if known

Name of benefit

Reference number, if known

Have you been paid any Statutory Maternity Pay (SMP) by an employer? No ☐ Yes ☐

If this has now stopped, please give the date of the last payment.

/ /

Have you been paid Disability Working Allowance during the 2 years before the date you became sick? No ☐ Yes ☐

Tick **Yes**, if you are not sure of the dates.

Are you getting the highest rate care component of Disability Living Allowance? No ☐ Yes ☐

Part 6 **About other benefits** – continued

Is anyone getting extra money added on to their social security benefit for you?
Tick **Yes**, if anyone is waiting to hear about getting extra money added on to their social security benefit for you.

No ☐

Yes ☐ Please tell us about the person who is getting, or waiting to hear about getting, this extra money.

Their surname

Other names

Address

Postcode

National Insurance (NI) number

Letters Numbers Letter

Please tell us which benefits they are getting or waiting to hear about.

Part 7 **More information**

Have you been on a training course in the 2 years before the date you became sick?
For example, Training for Work (TFW), Youth Training (YT), or an Employment Rehabilitation Course.

No ☐

Yes ☐ Please send us any papers that show when you did the training and how much training allowance you were paid. This could be the certificate you were given at the end of the training.
We may write to you about your training allowance. Please fill in the rest of this form.

Are you registered blind with a local authority?

No ☐

Yes ☐ Please tell us the name of the local authority.

Part 7 **More information** – continued

If you are entitled to Incapacity Benefit, this may affect the amount of income tax that you have to pay.

Please read leaflet **IR 144** *Income Tax and Incapacity Benefit* that comes with this claim pack before you fill in this part of the form. **Your answers will not affect your entitlement to Incapacity Benefit.** But it will help us to make sure that, as far as possible, you are given the right tax code and you pay the correct amount of tax.

If you do not answer these questions, you might pay more tax than you need to.

Will your employer continue to pay you while you are off sick after your SSP stops?

No ☐

Yes ☐ Please tell us the name and address of the employer.

Postcode

Will you get any occupational pension payments while you are sick?

No ☐

Yes ☐ Please tell us the name and address of the pension payer.

Postcode

Tax district and tax reference number

You will find this above your NI number on tax forms from the Inland Revenue. Or you can ask your employer or your pension payer. If you do not know your tax reference number, do not delay sending back this form.

Please send us form P45, if you have one.

Please tick to tell us if you want to claim any of these tax allowances.

Married couple's allowance ☐

Tick this box if you are a married man and you want to claim the full amount of the married couple's allowance.

To claim this you must be

- legally married and be living with your wife, and
- your wife must not have already claimed any of the allowance herself.

Blind person's allowance ☐

Tick this box if you are registered blind and you want to claim this allowance.

Section 3

Claiming extra Incapacity Benefit for another adult or children

Fill in **Section 3** of this form if you want to claim extra Incapacity Benefit for an adult or any children.

Claiming extra Incapacity Benefit for an adult

If you have any children living with you
You may be able to get extra Incapacity Benefit for
- your husband or wife, or
- someone who looks after children for you.

We will need some information about the children before we can pay extra money for an adult.

If you do not have any children
You may be able to get extra Incapacity Benefit for your husband or wife if they are aged 60 or over.

Claiming extra Incapacity Benefit for children

You may be able to get extra Incapacity Benefit for any children living with you if
- you have been sick for 28 weeks or more, or
- you are a woman aged 60 or over, or
- you are a man aged 65 or over.

Do you want to claim extra Incapacity Benefit for another adult or children?

No ☐ Please go to **Part 16**.

Yes ☐ Please tell us about your husband or your wife or the person who looks after children for you.

Their surname	
Their other names	
Their title	Mr/Mrs/Miss/Ms
Their date of birth	/ /
Their National Insurance (NI) number	Letters ☐☐ Numbers ☐☐ ☐☐ ☐☐ Letter ☐

What to do now

If you are a lone parent or a guardian and you only want to claim extra money for children, please go to **Part 14**.

If you want to claim extra money for someone who does not live with you and you employ to look after children for you, please go to **Part 13**.

Everyone else should go to **Part 8**.

Part 8 Claiming extra money for your husband or wife or a person who looks after children for you

Do you want to claim extra Incapacity Benefit for
- your husband, or
- your wife, or
- a person who looks after children for you?

No ☐ Please go to Part 9.
Yes ☐

Is the person in hospital at the moment?

No ☐
Yes ☐ Please tell us about this.

Name and address of the hospital

Postcode

Date they went into hospital

/ /

Do they normally live at a different address to you?

No ☐
Yes ☐ Please tell us about this.

Their address

Postcode

Do you send any money to this person?

No ☐
Yes ☐ How much do you send each week?

£

What date did you start making these payments?

/ /

Part 8 **Claiming extra money for your husband or wife or a person who looks after children for you** – continued

If you are claiming for your husband or wife

We need to see

- **your marriage certificate, and**
- **the birth certificate of your husband or wife.**

Please send the certificates to us with this form, if you have them. We will send them back to you as soon as we can. If you do not have the certificates, we will write to tell you what to do. But do not delay sending us this form.

If you want, you can bring the certificates to our office. We will give the certificates straight back to you after we have seen them.

Remember, we need to see the real certificates, not photocopies.

Are you sending your marriage certificate with this form? **No** ☐ **Yes** ☐

Are you sending the birth certificate of your husband or wife with this form? **No** ☐ **Yes** ☐

If you have ticked No to either of these questions, please say why you cannot let us see the certificate or certificates.

Part 9 If your husband or wife or the person who looks after children for you works for an employer

Is your husband or wife, or the person who looks after children for you, living with you now? **No** ☐ **Yes** ☐

Is your husband or wife, or the person who looks after children for you, working for an employer?
No ☐ Please go to **Part 10**.
Yes ☐ Please tell us about each employer.

Employer 1

Employer's name and address
Postcode

Payroll, staff or other reference number

What are their weekly earnings before income tax is taken off? £ a week — Please send us the latest payslip.

Include

- earnings or fees as a director
- maternity pay
- holiday pay
- bonus payments
- regular tips
- sick pay.

What are their weekly National Insurance (NI) contributions? £ a week

Please tell us about any items or services the employer provides, for example, meal vouchers.

Please give details of the weekly amount of any expenses connected with their work.

Do their earnings vary from week to week?
No ☐
Yes ☐ Please send their last 3 payslips with this form, if you have them.

Part 9 If your husband or wife or the person who looks after children for you works for an employer – continued

Employer 2

Employer's name and address

Postcode

Payroll, staff or other reference number

What are their weekly earnings before income tax is taken off? Include
- earnings or fees as a director
- maternity pay
- holiday pay
- bonus payments
- regular tips
- sick pay.

£ a week

Please send us the latest payslip.

What are their weekly National Insurance (NI) contributions?

£ a week

Please tell us about any items or services the employer provides, for example, meal vouchers.

Please give details of the weekly amount of any expenses connected with their work.

Do their earnings vary from week to week?

No

Yes Please send their last 3 payslips with this form, if you have them.

If you need to tell us about more than 2 employers, use the space in **Part 18**.

Is your husband or wife, or the person who looks after children for you, off work because of sickness, maternity leave or a trade dispute?

No Please go to **Part 10**.

Yes What date did they last work? / /

Are they getting any payments from their employer while they are off work? Include
- maternity pay
- Statutory Sick Pay (SSP)
- Statutory Maternity Pay (SMP).

No

Yes How much are they getting each week?

£ a week

Part 10 If your husband or wife or the person who looks after children for you is self-employed

Is your husband or wife, or the person who looks after children for you, self-employed?
Tick **Yes,** if they own a business or they have a share in a business.
This includes your business, if you have one.

No ☐ Please go to **Part 11**.

Yes ☐ Please tell us about this.

What is the name and address of the business?

Postcode

How much profit has the business made for the last complete business year?
By *profit*, we mean any profit, gain or other emoluments that have been agreed for income tax purposes.

£ ______

Does your husband or wife, or someone who looks after children for you, help in your business, if you are self-employed?

No ☐

Yes ☐ Please tell us about this.

Do you pay your husband or wife, or someone who looks after children for you, a wage?

No ☐

Yes ☐ What are their weekly earnings?

£ ______ a week

Is a charge made for their services against the profits from your business for income tax purposes?

No ☐

Yes ☐ What is the weekly charge?

£ ______ a week

Part 11 About other money coming in

Does your husband or wife, or the person who looks after children for you, have any other money coming in?
Do not tell us about Child Benefit. We will ask you about this later in this form.

No ☐ Please go to **Part 12**.

Yes ☐ What is this money?

How much do they get each week?
Please tell us the average weekly amount if the money is not the same each week.

£

Who pays the money?

What is their address?

Postcode

Does your husband or wife, or the person who looks after children for you, have any boarders or lodgers?

No ☐

Yes ☐ How much does each boarder or lodger pay each week?

Boarder 1 £ a week

Boarder 2 £ a week

Boarder 3 £ a week

If you need to tell us about more than 3 boarders, use the space in **Part 18**.

Part 12 About occupational and personal pensions

Does your husband or wife, or the person who looks after children for you, get an occupational pension or a personal pension?

No ☐ Please go to **Part 14.**

Yes ☐ Please tell us about each pension.

Pension 1

Type of pension

- Pension from an employer ☐
- Pension from a self-employed pension scheme ☐
- Personal pension ☐

Name and address of the pension payer

Postcode

Phone number of the pension payer — Code Number

What is the pension reference number?

How much pension do they get before income tax is taken off? £

How often is the pension paid?

Pension 2

Type of pension

- Pension from an employer ☐
- Pension from a self-employed pension scheme ☐
- Personal pension ☐

Name and address of the pension payer

Postcode

Phone number of the pension payer — Code Number

What is the pension reference number?

How much pension do they get before income tax is taken off? £

How often is the pension paid?

If you need to tell us about more than 2 pensions, use the space in **Part 18**.

Part 13 Claiming extra money for someone who does not live with you and you employ to look after children for you

Do you want to claim extra Incapacity Benefit for someone who does not live with you and you employ to look after children for you?

No ☐ Please go to **Part 14**.

Yes ☐

How much do you pay the person who looks after children for you each week? £

Please give details of any expenses you have in connection with the care of your children

Part 14 About children

If you do not want to claim extra Incapacity Benefit for any children and your husband or wife is aged 60 or over, please go to Part 15.

Everyone else must fill in this part.

We need to know more about children before we can pay extra money for your husband or wife, or the person who looks after children for you.

Remember, you cannot get extra money for children until you have been sick for 28 weeks or you are a woman aged 60 or over, or you are a man aged 65 or over. But please fill in the rest of this part now.

Tell us about each child on **pages 27** to **29**. If you need to tell us about more than 3 children, use the space in **Part 18**.

Are you or anyone who lives with you getting Child Benefit?

No ☐

Yes ☐ Please tell us about this.

Amount each week	Reference number
£	
£	

You will find the reference number on the front cover of your order book. If you have more than one book, please tell us both the reference numbers.

If your Child Benefit is paid straight into a bank account, the reference number will be on letters we have sent you about Child Benefit.

Part 14 **About children** – continued

Please tell us about any changes there are likely to be in the next 2 months that might make a difference to the amount of Child Benefit that is being paid.
For example, if a child is leaving school.

The changes you must tell us about are listed in
- the coloured pages of a Child Benefit order book
- the notes we sent to you if your Child Benefit is paid straight into a bank or building society account.

Are you, or your husband or your wife, getting a family benefit from another country for a child? **No** ☐ **Yes** ☐

Do you want to claim extra Incapacity Benefit for any children? **No** ☐ **Yes** ☐

Do you have a husband or wife, or another person living with you as husband or wife, who is not the person you are claiming for on page 17? **No** ☐ **Yes** ☐

Part 14 **About children** – continued

Child 1

Child's surname [ ]

Child's other names [ ]

Child's date of birth [/ /]

Are you this child's parent?
- **No** [ ]
- **Yes** [ ]

Does this child have a parent who lives with you but is not your husband or wife?
- **No** [ ]
- **Yes** [ ] Please tell us the parent's full name.

Mr/Mrs/Miss/Ms

Please tell us who is getting Child Benefit for this child
- You [ ]
- Your husband or wife who lives with you [ ]
- Your husband or wife who does not live with you [ ]
- Your ex-husband or ex-wife [ ]
- Someone who looks after children for you [ ]
- Not known [ ]

Does the child live at a different address to you?
- **No** [ ] Please go to **Part 15.**
- **Yes** [ ] Please tick where they are
  - in hospital [ ]
  - in care [ ]
  - living with another person [ ]

Please tell us the name and address of the place where they are living

Postcode

Part 14 **About children** – continued

Child 2

Child's surname ☐

Child's other names ☐

Child's date of birth / /

Are you this child's parent?
No ☐
Yes ☐

Does this child have a parent who lives with you but is not your husband or wife?
No ☐
Yes ☐ Please tell us the parent's full name.

Mr/Mrs/Miss/Ms

Please tell us who is getting Child Benefit for this child

- You ☐
- Your husband or wife who lives with you ☐
- Your husband or wife who does not live with you ☐
- Your ex-husband or ex-wife ☐
- Someone who looks after children for you ☐
- Not known ☐

Does the child live at a different address to you?
No ☐ Please go to **Part 15.**
Yes ☐ Please tick where they are.

- in hospital ☐
- in care ☐
- living with another person ☐

Please tell us the name and address of the place where they are living

Postcode

Part 14 **About children** – continued

Child 3

Child's surname

Child's other names

Child's date of birth / /

Are you this child's parent? **No** ☐ **Yes** ☐

Does this child have a parent who lives with you but is not your husband or wife? **No** ☐ **Yes** ☐ Please tell us the parent's full name.

Mr/Mrs/Miss/Ms

Please tell us who is getting Child Benefit for this child

- You ☐
- Your husband or wife who lives with you ☐
- Your husband or wife who does not live with you ☐
- Your ex-husband or ex-wife ☐
- Someone who looks after children for you ☐
- Not known ☐

Does the child live at a different address to you? **No** ☐ Please go to **Part 15.** **Yes** ☐ Please tick where they are.

- in hospital ☐
- in care ☐
- living with another person ☐

Please tell us the name and address of the place where they are living

Postcode

If you need to tell us about more than 3 children, use the space in **Part 18**.

Part 15 **About benefits and state pensions**

Any money paid by the Department of Social Security or any other government department to
- your husband or wife, or
- a person who looks after children for you, or
- any children you have

may affect the amount of the extra Incapacity Benefit that you can get.

And money paid to another person for you or anyone you are claiming for may also affect the amount of the extra Incapacity Benefit that you can get.

Please tell us about this money below. Include benefits, state pensions or allowances from the Department of Social Security or any other government department. But do not include any Child Benefit you have already told us about on this form.

Benefit 1

Name of benefit

Who is the benefit paid to?

Benefit reference number
This is on the front of the order book or letters about the benefit.

How much is paid each week? £

Which office deals with the benefit?

Benefit 2

Name of benefit

Who is the benefit paid to?

Benefit reference number
This is on the front of the order book or letters about the benefit.

How much is paid each week? £

Which office deals with the benefit?

If you need to tell us about more than 2 benefits, use the space in **Part 18.**

Section 4

More information we need

Part 16 Where you want to be paid – you can choose

Please read **pages 3** and **4** of the *Notes about Incapacity Benefit* that comes with this claim pack before you fill in this part of the form.

1 Payment straight into a bank account or building society account

Do you want your Incapacity Benefit paid straight into an account?

No ☐ Please go to **page 32**.

Yes ☐

How often do you want your Incapacity Benefit to be paid? Every 2 weeks ☐ Every 4 weeks ☐ Every 13 weeks ☐

What name or names is the account in?

Please tick what type of account it is

☐ Bank cheque account or deposit account or building society cheque account – NOT a mortgage account

Name of bank or building society

Branch name

Sorting code

Account number

Type of account deposit, current.

☐ Girobank account

Account number

☐ Building society savings account – NOT a cheque account or mortgage account

Name of building society

Account number

☐ National Savings Bank investment account – NOT an ordinary account

Account number

Part 16 Where you want to be paid – you can choose – continued

2 Payment at a post office

• **Payment straight into a Girobank or National Savings Bank account**

Getting your money in this way has many advantages and is the way we recommend.

Do you want your Incapacity Benefit paid straight into an account? **No** ☐ **Yes** ☐ Please fill in the details on **page 31**.

• **Payment by order book**

Do you want to be paid by order book at a post office? **No** ☐ **Yes** ☐ Please tell us about this.

Name and address of the post office where you want to get your money.
If you are not sure of the address, you can ask the post office to stamp the form here.

Do you want someone to go to the post office for you regularly? **No** ☐ **Yes** ☐ Please tell us their name and address.

Postcode

Part 17 **Special Rules**

Please read the *Notes about Incapacity Benefit* that come with this claim pack before you fill in this part of the form.

Please tick this box if you think the Special Rules apply to you The Special Rules are explained on **page 5** of the *Notes about Incapacity Benefit*.	☐	Ask your doctor or specialist for a **DS 1500 Report**. This is a report about your medical condition. You will not have to pay for it. You can ask the doctor's receptionist, or nurse or a social worker to arrange this for you. You do not have to see the doctor. You should be given the **DS 1500 Report** straight away. Ask for the report in a sealed envelope if you do not want anyone to see it. If you cannot get your **DS 1500 Report** in time, send us your claim form straight away. Send the **DS 1500 Report** as soon as you can.
Have you claimed Disability Living Allowance under the Special Rules which apply to that benefit but have not yet heard if you will get it?	**No** ☐ **Yes** ☐	If you have asked for a **DS 1500 Report** for your claim to Disability Living Allowance, you do not need to get another. Send the **DS 1500 Report** with your Disability Living Allowance claim if you are claiming Disability Living Allowance and Incapacity Benefit at the same time.

Part 18 **Other information**

You can use this space to tell us anything else you think we might need to know.

Part 19 **For people signing this form for someone else**

Please tell us why you are signing this form

Please tell us about yourself

Your full name

Your address

Postcode

Daytime phone number Code Number

Relationship, if any

Part 20 **Declaration**

- **I understand** that if I give information that is incorrect or incomplete, action may be taken against me.
- **I declare** that the information I have given on this form is correct and complete.
- **I declare** that if I have said that I want my benefit paid straight into an account, that I have read and understood the conditions applying to payment of benefit into a bank or other account. These conditions are summarised in the *Notes about Incapacity Benefit* that came with this form.
- **I agree** that the Department of Social Security, and any doctor advising the Department may ask
  - any doctor who has treated me
  - any hospital or place like that where I have been treated
  - anyone else who has given me treatment such as a physiotherapist

  for any information which is needed to deal with
  - this claim for benefit
  - any request for this claim to be looked at again

  and that the information may be given to that doctor or to the Department.
- **I also understand** that the Department may use the information which it has now or may get in the future to decide whether I am entitled to
  - the benefit I am claiming
  - any other benefit I have claimed
  - any other benefit I may claim in the future.

This is my claim for Incapacity Benefit

Signature

Date / /

Part 21 What to do now

Please make sure that

- **you have answered all the questions on this form that apply to you**
- **you have signed and dated this form.**

Send this form and any papers we have asked you for to your social security office. You can get an envelope that does not need a stamp from any post office.

Do not delay or you could lose money.

Part 22 What happens next

If you can get Incapacity Benefit
we will write and tell you

- how much you can get
- more about the benefit.

If you cannot get Incapacity Benefit
we will write and tell you the reason.

Part 23 Where to get help and advice

For information about your own claim, get in touch with your social security office. You can find the phone number and address on the advert in the business numbers section of the phone book. Look under **Benefits Agency**.
For more information about social security benefits generally

- ring Freeline Social Security on **0800 666 555**.
  The phone call is free. The person taking your call will not be able to see your papers or put you through to your social security office. But they have been specially trained to answer questions and give advice about all social security benefits.

- ring the Special Freeline if you want advice in these languages
  – Chinese **0800 252 451**
  – Punjabi **0800 521 360**
  – Urdu **0800 289 188**
  – Welsh **0800 289 011**.
  The phone calls are free.

- ring the Benefit Enquiry Line for people with disabilities – the phone call is free. The number is **0800 88 22 00**.
  If you have problems with hearing or speaking and use a textphone, ring **0800 24 33 55**. The phone call is free. If you do not have a textphone system they are available in some libraries or Citizens Advice Bureau offices.

- get in touch with an advice centre like the Citizens Advice Bureau.

For official use

Date of marriage	
Spouse's maiden name	
Spouse's date of birth	
Nature of evidence	
Verified by	
Checked by	
Certificate(s) returned by	
on (date)	

Printed in the U.K. by St. Ives Direct, St. Ives plc.
001931F 4/96 300,000.

SSP 1 (Apr 96) *Notes*

Notes about Incapacity Benefit

What is Incapacity Benefit?

Incapacity Benefit is a social security benefit for people who are sick.

You may be able to get Incapacity Benefit if you are sick and

- you have been getting Statutory Sick Pay (SSP) and this has now stopped, or
- you work for an employer but you cannot get SSP.

Statutory Sick Pay (SSP) is money paid by employers to employees who are away from work for 4 days or more in a row because they are sick.

You can find out more about Incapacity Benefit in leaflets **IB 202** *Incapacity Benefit* or **FB 28** *Sick or disabled?* You can get these leaflets from any social security office.

Who you can claim extra Incapacity Benefit for

Claiming extra Incapacity Benefit for an adult

If you have any children living with you
You may be able to get extra Incapacity Benefit for

- your husband or wife, or
- someone who looks after children for you.

If you do not have any children
You may be able to get extra Incapacity Benefit for your husband or wife if they are aged 60 or over.

Claiming extra Incapacity Benefit for children

You may be able to get extra Incapacity Benefit for any children living with you if

- you have been sick for 28 weeks or more, or
- you are a woman aged 60 or over, or
- you are a man aged 65 or over.

How to claim

There is a claim form in this pack.

Your employer will fill in **Section 1**.
You should fill in **Sections 2, 3** and **4**.

Do not delay sending in your claim form. If you wait, you could lose money. If you have been sick for more than 7 days, please send a medical certificate with the claim form. If your employer has given your medical certificate back to you, please send it with your claim form.
Medical certificates are also called sick notes or doctor's statements.

Other help

Disability Living Allowance
This is a social security benefit for people with an illness or disability who need

- help with getting around, or
- help with personal care, or
- help with both of these.

If you want to find out more about this, get leaflet **DS 704** *Disability Living Allowance – you could benefit* from any social security office.

Severe Disablement Allowance
This is a social security benefit for people with an illness or disability who

- cannot work because of their illness or disability, and
- have not paid enough National Insurance contributions to get Incapacity Benefit.

If you want to find out more about this, get leaflet **NI 252** *Severe Disablement Allowance* from any social security office.

Industrial Injuries Disablement Benefit
This is a social security benefit for people who are disabled because of

- an accident at work, or
- an industrial disease.

If you want to find out more about this, get leaflet **NI 6** *Industrial Injuries Disablement Benefit* from any social security office.

Disability Working Allowance
This is a tax-free, income-related benefit for people aged 16 or over who are working 16 hours or more a week but have an illness or disability that limits their earning capacity.

If you want to find out more about this benefit, get leaflet **DS 703** *The cash benefit for disabled people in work* from your social security office.

Income Support
This is a social security benefit for people who do not have enough money to live on.

NHS charges
You may be able to get help with paying for things like NHS prescriptions and NHS dental treatment.

Housing Benefit
Housing Benefit is paid by local councils to people who need help to pay their rent. Housing Benefit is **not** paid to help with the cost of mortgage interest payments.

Council Tax Benefit
You may be able to get Council Tax Benefit from your local council to help with paying your council tax.

You can find out more about these benefits in leaflet **FB 2** *Which Benefit?* You can get this leaflet from any post office or social security office.

Where you want to be paid – you can choose

You can choose where you want your Incapacity Benefit to be paid. We can arrange to pay your money straight into a bank or building society account.
Or we can arrange for you to get your money at the post office, either by payment straight into a Girobank account or a National Savings Bank account or by order book.

1 Payment straight into a bank account or a building society account

Getting your money paid in this way has many advantages.
We recommend you get your money in this way because

- it is safe – you do not have to carry cash around or risk your order book being lost or stolen
- it saves trouble – you could continue to have regular bills paid direct
- it is convenient – money can be paid into most bank or building society accounts, including Girobank and National Savings Bank, and withdrawn from any convenient branch or from a post office for a Girobank and National Savings Bank account
- it is also less expensive for us to arrange, which saves taxpayers' money.

The account can be

- in your name, or in your husband or wife's name
- a joint account in your name and someone else's name
- an account of a trustee, solicitor or accountant.

You can choose to be paid every 2 weeks, every 4 weeks or every 13 weeks

If you choose to be paid every 2 weeks
The money will be paid into an account for you on the last bank working day in each 2-week period.

If you choose to be paid every 4 weeks
The money will be paid into an account for you on the last bank working day in each 4-week period. Your first payment might cover a period of 2 to 5 weeks, but after this all payments will cover a 4-week period.

If you choose to be paid every 13 weeks
The money will be paid into an account for you on the last bank working day in each 13-week period. Your first payment might cover a period of 2 to 14 weeks, but after this all payments will cover a 13-week period.

Finding out how much is paid into the account
We will tell you when the first payment will be made, and how much it is for. After that please check with your bank or building society to find out how much is paid into your account. Get in touch with the office that deals with your Incapacity Benefit if you think you have not been paid the right amount of money.

If not enough money has been paid into the account, we will make a special payment or we will add the money we owe you onto your next payment. We will write to tell you what we are going to do.

If too much money is paid into the account because of the way the transfer credit system works, you will have to pay the extra money back. For example, if you give us some information which means you are entitled to less money, but we do not have time to change the amount paid, you will have to pay back any money you are not entitled to.

Where you want to be paid – you can choose – continued

2 Payment at a post office

Payment straight into a Girobank or a National Savings Bank account

Getting your money in this way has many advantages and is the way we recommend. We tell you why on **page 3** of these notes.

Payment by order book

Getting your money from a post office
We will send you an order book. Each order will be for 2 weeks. You can get your money on your Incapacity Benefit payday from your local post office. You can cash your order book at a different post office on 2 occasions, but after that you will need to fill in a form to change to another post office.

If your order book is lost or stolen
You will have to report this to your social security office, sign a declaration about how the book was lost or stolen and wait for a new order book.

If you want someone to go to the post office for you occasionally
Fill in the back of the order each time to say that they can get your money for you.

If you want someone to go to the post office for you regularly
Fill in their name and address in **Part 16** of your claim form. They can get your money for you on 2 occasions. You do not have to fill in the back of the order each time they get the money for you. So please make sure that you tell us about someone you can trust.

How your money is worked out

If you are entitled to Incapacity Benefit for less than a whole week, the amount that you get for each day will be the weekly amount divided by 7.

When we work out your Incapacity Benefit we round the amounts to the nearest penny.

You will not normally get any Incapacity Benefit for the first 3 days when you cannot work because you are sick. We call these *waiting days*.

You may get Incapacity Benefit for these 3 days if

- you have been getting Incapacity Benefit or Statutory Sick Pay within 8 weeks of your present claim, **or**
- you have been getting Disability Working Allowance and it is 2 years or less since you last claimed Incapacity Benefit, Sickness Benefit or Invalidity Benefit, **or**
- you have attended a recognised training course and it is 2 years or less since you last claimed Incapacity Benefit, Sickness Benefit or Invalidity Benefit.

Special Rules

Sadly, some people suffer from a terminal illness. The Special Rules apply to people who are not expected to live longer than 6 months because of an illness. But it is, of course, impossible to say exactly how long a person will live. Getting Incapacity Benefit under the Special Rules means that you will get the long-term rate of Incapacity Benefit when you have been sick for 28 weeks. This is not normally payable until a person has been sick for 52 weeks.

Tell us if you think the Special Rules apply to you. Please fill in **Part 17** of the claim form.

If you think you qualify for Incapacity Benefit under the Special Rules, you can also claim Disability Living Allowance if you have not already done so.

For people who are getting Disability Living Allowance
People who are getting the highest rate care component of Disability Living Allowance can get the long-term rate of Incapacity Benefit which would normally be payable after 52 weeks when they have been sick for 28 weeks.

Where to get help and advice

For information about your own claim, get in touch with your social security office. You can find the phone number and address on the advert in the business numbers section of the phone book. Look under **Benefits Agency**.
For more information about social security benefits generally

- ring Freeline Social Security on **0800 666 555**.
  The phone call is free. The person taking your call will not be able to see your papers or put you through to your social security office. But they have been specially trained to answer questions and give advice about all social security benefits.

- ring the Special Freeline if you want advice in these languages
  – Chinese **0800 252 451**
  – Punjabi **0800 521 360**
  – Urdu **0800 289 188**
  – Welsh **0800 289 011**.
  The phone calls are free.

- ring the Benefit Enquiry Line for people with disabilities – the phone call is free. The number is **0800 88 22 00**.
  If you have problems with hearing or speaking and use a textphone, ring **0800 24 33 55**. The phone call is free. If you do not have a textphone system they are available in some libraries or Citizens Advice Bureau offices.

- get in touch with an advice centre like the Citizens Advice Bureau.

SSP 1(L)

Leaver's statement of Statutory Sick Pay (SSP)

About this form

There are **2** sections in this form.
Section 1 is for the employer to give information about Statutory Sick Pay (SSP) and their employee.
Section 2 contains information for the employee.

Section 1

Notes to the employer

Who to use this form for

Use this form for anyone who

- asks for the form, and
- is not going to work for you any more or who has already finished working for you, and
- has been paid SSP in the last 8 weeks that they worked for you, and
- has been paid SSP for one week or more. Remember odd days can be rounded up, see **About SSP** on the **next page**.

About your employee

Please tell us about your employee

Surname

Other names

Letters Numbers Letter

National Insurance (NI) number

Clock or payroll number

An Executive Agency of the Department of Social Security

Notes to the employer – continued

First day of sickness for SSP purposes

This date will be

- the first day of your employee's period of incapacity for work with you, or
- **date 1** from **form SSP 1(L)** *Leaver's statement of Statutory Sick Pay (SSP)*, if you have taken sickness with a previous employer into account.

By a *period of incapacity for work* we mean, a period of sickness of 4 days or more in a row. All days of sickness are counted including Saturday and Sundays. Remember, periods of incapacity for work that are 8 weeks or less apart will link together and count as one period of incapacity.

The first day of sickness that has been taken into account for SSP is ____ / ____ / ____ **Date 1**

About SSP

The last date that you have to pay SSP for is ____ / ____ / ____ **Date 2**

The number of weeks of SSP that your employee will get altogether ____ weeks

This is the total number of weeks of SSP between **Date 1** and **Date 2**. Count the weeks that include **Date 1** and **Date 2** in this total.

Express odd days as a decimal fraction of a week by

1 dividing the number of days of SSP payable by the number of qualifying days in that week, **and**

2 multiplying by 7.

SSP of more than 3 days is rounded up to a whole week. SSP of 3 days or less do not count.

Employer's signature

Signature ____

Date ____ / ____ / ____

Position in firm ____

Business stamp ____

Phone number and extension ____ extension ____

Fax number ____

Please give this form to your employee

Section 2

Notes to the employee

What to do with this form

- **If you work for a new employer**
  Give this form to your employer in the first week that you are sick. It will help them to make sure you will get the right amount of Statutory Sick Pay (SSP).
- **If you do not work for an employer**
  You may be able to get Incapacity Benefit if you are sick for at least 4 days in a row. This form will help your social security office to make sure you get the right amount of Incapacity Benefit.

  Incapacity Benefit
  is a social security benefit for people with an illness or disability.
  You may be able to get Incapacity Benefit if
  – you are unemployed, or
  – you are self-employed, or
  – you work for an employer but you cannot get SSP.

  If you want to claim Incapacity Benefit, fill in form **SC 1** and send it with this form to your social security office. You can get form **SC 1** from
  – any social security office
  – your doctor's surgery or health centre
  – a hospital.

Where to get help and advice

For more information about social security benefits generally

- ring Freeline Social Security on **0800 666 555.**
  The phone call is free. The person taking your call will not be able to see your papers or put you through to your social security office. But they have been specially trained to answer questions and give advice about all social security benefits.
- ring the Special Freeline if you want advice in these languages
  – Chinese **0800 252 451**
  – Punjabi **0800 521 360**
  – Urdu **0800 289 188**
  – Welsh **0800 289 011.**
  The phone call is free.
- ring the Benefit Enquiry Line for people with disabilities – the phone call is free. The number is **0800 88 22 00.**

  If you have problems with hearing or speaking and use a textphone, ring **0800 24 33 55.** The phone call is free. If you do not have a textphone system they are available in some libraries or Citizens Advice Bureau offices.
- get in touch with your social security office. You can find the phone number and address on the advert in the business numbers section of the phone book. Look under **Benefits Agency**.
- get in touch with an advice centre like the Citizens Advice Bureau.

(E) Unfair dismissal

Reproduced below are Forms IT1 (an Application to the Industrial Tribunal) and IT3 (Notice of Appearance by Respondent). A checklist of points to be considered in relation to any actual or potential unfair dismissal claim (and relevant to both employer and employee) is set out below.

CHECKLIST

QUALIFICATION TO BRING A CLAIM

(a) For both employer and employee, it is important to establish in the context of any dismissal whether the employee is actually qualified to bring an unfair dismissal claim.

(b) The obvious starting point is the issue of whether the employee really is an employee. This is to be determined in accordance with the tests referred to in the text.

(c) Taking this as established, the next question is whether the employee has been dismissed. A mutually agreed termination does not constitute a dismissal but care needs to be exercised where a mutually agreed termination reveals itself, upon closer examination, to be a contrived 'self dismissal' or a constructive dismissal. In theory (but this is seldom applied in practice in employment cases) a contract may be frustrated by an intervening event, eg serious illness or imprisonment with the consequence that there may not in fact be a dismissal. Otherwise a resignation (prompted by pressure from the employer or consequent upon the employer's conduct) will constitute a dismissal, as will the expiry of a fixed term contract without its being renewed. However, a fixed term contract of one year or more with a provision excluding the employee's right to claim unfair dismissal will be effective to remove that dismissal from the legislative regime and preclude a claim.

(d) The next point to consider is whether the employee has the requisite two years' continuous employment in order to qualify for the right not to be unfairly dismissed. Care must be taken to add on the statutory minimum period of notice (one week) in circumstances where an employee is dismissed without notice when calculating this period. There is no qualifying period where the dismissal is for a reason relating to trade union activities or on grounds of pregnancy or in relation to the taking of maternity leave and a one month period only where the dismissal is on medical grounds in compliance with any law, regulation or code of practice provided for under the Health and Safety at Work etc Act 1974.

(e) Has the employee passed the normal retiring age? if so, a claim may not be brought. If there are discriminatory retirement ages or no normal retirement age, 65 will apply to all employees whatever their sex.

ISSUES RELEVANT TO BRINGING OR DEFENDING A CLAIM

(f) Where the employee is qualified for protection, it is necessary to determine the reason for dismissal. Potentially fair reasons for dismissal are categorised in ERA as follows:
   (i) incapability or qualification;
   (ii) conduct;
   (iii) redundancy;
   (iv) contravention of a statutory duty or enactment;
   (v) some other substantial reason.

(g) It should be remembered that there are both automatically fair and unfair reasons. As regards the former, any dismissal 'for the purpose of safeguarding national security' is automatically fair. As regards the latter, dismissal of an employee for spent conviction within the definition of the Rehabilitation of Offenders Act 1974, dismissal of a woman because she is pregnant or for a reason connected with her pregnancy, dismissal for union membership or participation in union activities, dismissal in circumstances where there is a transfer of an undertaking for a reason connected with that transfer, dismissal of health and safety representatives and employee representatives (in the context of TUPE and collective redundancies) for carrying out their duties and dismissal for asserting a statutory right under s 104 of the ERA may all result in an automatically unfair dismissal.

(h) Turning to the categorisation of reasons for dismissal, the following points may be noted.

CAPABILITY

(i)

Save in circumstances of gross incompetence or unsuitability, much will depend upon not only the underlying facts which have to be proved to the satisfaction of the industrial tribunal, but also the procedural fairness of any prelude to dismissal. In practice, warnings of an appropriate nature will have to be given (with a reasonable amount of time and opportunity to improve after they are given) before dismissal. An employer's disciplinary procedures should, ideally, be based upon the recommendations of the Advisory Conciliation and Arbitration Service in this regard (see the Code of Disciplinary Practice and Procedures in Employment Divs, *Harvey*). Where dismissal is consequent upon an employee's absence for reason of illness the usefulness, indeed the need, for warnings is much less apparent but, correspondingly, industrial tribunals will look to see that the employer has acted reasonably by taking into account all reasonably available medical evidence in determining whether or not to terminate employment. In cases of absenteeism, a mixture of medical evidence and warnings may be appropriate, but otherwise the employer will be unwise to dismiss without first carefully considering the medical evidence reasonably available both in terms of diagnosis and prognosis.

MISCONDUCT

(j) Gross misconduct may justify dismissal without the need for warning (theft, serious violence, etc) but, in most cases, warnings should be administered before dismissal and again the employer would do well to ensure that the disciplinary rules and procedures which the employer adopts reflect the recommendations of the Advisory Conciliation and Arbitration Service.

REDUNDANCY

(k) Complications in this area abound. First there may be an issue as to whether or not an employee is actually redundant. More than any other reason, redundancy is often euphemistically applied as a label by an employer who is dismissing for another reason. The dismissal will be automatically unfair if selection for redundancy is by reason of the employee belonging to or not belonging to a trade union or for taking part in union activities at an appropriate time (TULR(C)A, s 153). Additionally, selection for redundancy, contrary to agreed procedures and customary arrangements, will be automatically unfair. These matters aside, the standards guiding tribunals as to whether a dismissal for redundancy is fair will be found in *Williams v Compair Maxim Ltd* [1982] IRLR 83, [1982] ICR 156, EAT. In brief, the issues which will be focused upon will be whether the employer gave adequate warning of possible impending redundancies, consulted as required (collectively with any recognised trade union and individually with the affected employee) and considered possible alternative solutions and, as appropriate, alternative employment in the undertaking or elsewhere. In the event of this failing to avoid redundancy, selection must be seen to be fair using, so far as possible, objective criteria.

SOME OTHER SUBSTANTIAL REASON

(l) This 'catch all' category may include such circumstances as the imprisonment of the employee, personality clashes, termination at the end of engagements which were agreed and understood to be temporary, etc.

(m) The identification of the reason for the dismissal as falling within the categorisation of reasons contained in the ERA is of course part only of the exercise. There is the question of the reasonableness of the decision to dismiss. This is reviewed in detail in the text but procedural aspects are important in this regard.

REASONABLENESS/PROCEDURAL PROPRIETIES

(n) When it comes to the issue of reasonableness, an important aspect will be whether, from a procedural standpoint, the employer has approached the matter reasonably having regard, inter alia, to the size and administrative resources of the employer's undertaking. From an employers' standpoint (and for that matter from the employee's), the following are matters which ought to be borne in mind in formulating/applying disciplinary procedures to a particular given set of circumstances:

(i) Clear and unambiguous warnings should be given to an employee and suitably recorded. Even an oral warning (if it is intended to be formal) is best recorded in writing in the file of an employee.

(ii) Wherever possible, written warnings should contain not only an indication of what is wrong but also what improvements the employer wishes to see and over what period. Sensibly, a review should take place at the end of the period and the matter discussed.

(iii) Any final written warning administered by an employer should leave the employee under no misapprehension as to the consequences of a failure to improve or a repetition of the conduct to which the warning relates. The employer should avoid the natural temptation to beat around the bush. 'Will be dismissed', whilst it is blunt, is better than 'may render you liable to further disciplinary action' when spelling out the consequences to an employee. The employee knows where he or she stands if plain words are used and if the employer has reached the final warning stage, the time for 'fudging' language and consequences has passed.

(iv) Whatever the circumstances (even in the 'open and shut' case) the employee must be allowed a reasonable opportunity to know the case he or she has to meet and to say whatever can be said in defence. An employer should be scrupulous to arrange a disciplinary hearing to allow the employee to be accompanied by a friend/trade union representative or other representative (as appropriate). It is sensible for the employer to ensure that any disciplinary hearing is conducted by two representatives of the employer to minimise any dispute later as to what transpired in the course of the hearing and a careful note should ideally be taken.

(o) Wherever possible, there should be a right of appeal against dismissal and this should be drawn to the employee's attention. A fair appeal procedure may prevent successful reliance on procedural or other irregularities at an earlier hearing when it comes to making an unfair dismissal claim.

(p) In practice, if the recommendations of the Advisory Conciliation and Arbitration Service in relation to disciplinary matters are followed, this will satisfy an industrial tribunal. The temptation for an employer to dismiss when it is believed the grounds for dismissal are cast iron is quite clearly dangerous since, whatever the facts, procedural unfairness alone may result in a finding of unfair dismissal. Correspondingly, after acquired knowledge confirming the correctness of a decision taken in the heat of the moment, will not save the employer from a finding of unfair dismissal although, in both these cases, it may have some bearing on the level of compensation awarded. Set out on pp. 000–000 is a table summarising the compensation which an industrial tribunal can award (as at 30 September 1994) in unfair dismissal cases.

NOTE:

It should be noted that the awards of compensation above can be reduced, even below the minimum levels referred to, where (a) an industrial tribunal considers that the employee's conduct prior to dismissal was such that it would be just and equitable to make a reduction in compensation, or (b) when an industrial tribunal finds that the employee has unreasonably prevented compliance with the reinstatement order or has unreasonably refused an earlier offer of reinstatement made otherwise than in compliance with such an order; but there are certain qualifications to this where dismissal is for a reason relating to trade union membership, non-membership or activity and dismissal for some health and safety reasons in the form of an irreducible minimum for the basic award and the exclusion of certain conduct when it comes to considering any reduction (EA 1982, s 6). See text.

TABLE OF COMPENSATION LIMITS FOR UNFAIR DISMISSAL

Award	*ERA Provision*	*Maximum*
Basic award	s 119, s 227(1)(a)	£6,300 [30 weeks' pay at £210 per week]
Compensatory award	s 124(1)	£11,300
Additional award	s 117 & s 227(1)(b)	But *note* that in cases of dismissal on grounds of sex or race there is no limit on compensation (Sex Discrimination and Equal Pay (Remedies) Regulations 1993, SI 1993/2798 and the Race Relations (Remedies) Act 1994). Also *note* that the limit of £11,300 may be raised by the amount necessary for it to reflect the amount lost between the date of dismissal and the date when the employee should have been re-engaged pursuant to an order of the Tribunal. Not less than 13 weeks' pay (a week's pay is subject to the ceiling of £210 given a maximum of £2,730) and not more than 26 weeks' pay (£5,460).
Dismissal because of trade union membership or activities or non-membership of a trade union:		
(a) Where reinstatement or re-engagement is not sought by the applicant.	As above	Basic and compensatory award as above
(b) Where reinstatement or re-engagement is sought but no order made by the industrial tribunal.	s 125	In addition to a basic award and compensatory award as above, a special award of 104 weeks' pay (which is not subject to the £210 per week maximum referred to above) will be made subject to a minimum of £13,775 and a maximum of £27,500).
(c) Where reinstatement or re-engagement is ordered by the industrial tribunal and the employer fails to comply and is not able to satisfy an industrial tribunal that it was not reasonably practicable to comply.	s 125	156 weeks' pay (again not subject to the £210 per week maximum) subject to a minimum of £20,600.
Dismissal of employee for plaining of health and safety problems, etc.	s 100, s 105	Minimum basic award of £2,770. Compensatory award as above in relation to dismissal for trade union membership or activities, etc.

Application to an Industrial Tribunal in England and Wales

For proceedings in Scotland use IT1(Scot)

Guidance Notes

If you think you have a case for an Industrial Tribunal:

- Read booklet ITL1(E/W). It tells you about:

  what types of complaint they can consider;

  the Industrial Tribunal procedure;

  which booklet describes your complaint more fully.

- Read the Employment booklet which describes your complaint. It tells you about:

  who to contact if you need advice or representation;

  qualifying periods – how long do you have to work for an employer before you can apply for a Tribunal;

  time limits – you must send us your application form within the time allowed for your complaint.

You can get the booklets free from any Employment Service Jobcentre.

If we do not receive your application within the time-limit stipulated for your type of complaint, we may not be able to deal with it. If you are in doubt, please contact the Advisory Conciliation and Arbitration Service (ACAS) (Booklet ITL1(E/W) gives addresses and telephone numbers) or contact your local Employment Service Jobcentre.

If you need advice or help to complete your application, you can seek help from for example, your Trade Union or local Citizens Advice Bureau.

You can present the case yourself or have a representative to act for you. If you name a representative, all further communications will be sent to them and not to you. Please arrange for them to keep you informed of the progress of the case.

If your complaint concerns equal pay or sex discrimination you may wish to contact the Equal Opportunities Commission for advice about representation. If your complaint concerns race discrimination you may wish to contact the Commission for Racial Equality.

If you have a disability and need any special arrangements when visiting the Industrial Tribunal, please inform the staff at the office dealing with your case in advance. They do all they can to help you.

If you have a question about the Industrial Tribunal procedure and cannot find the answer in the booklets, please ring the Industrial Tribunal Enquiry line on 0345 959775. (All calls are charged at local rate).

Please answer all the questions on the application that apply to your complaint.

When you have completed the form detach and retain these notes and send the application form to the relevant Tribunal Office.

Applications can be faxed, delivered by hand or posted. If you fax your application do not post a copy as well. If you post the application take a copy for your records.

Guidance on where to send your application is overleaf.

Industrial Tribunal Offices in England and Wales

Ashford – Tufton House, Tufton Street, Ashford, Kent TN23 1RJ, *Fax: 01233 624423*

Bedford – 8-10 Howard Street, Bedford MK40 3HS, *Fax: 01234 352315*

Birmingham – Phoenix House, 1-3 Newhall Street, Birmingham B3 3NH, *Fax: 0121 236 6029*

Bury St Edmunds – 100 Southgate Street, Bury St Edmunds IP33 2AQ, *Fax: 01284 706064*

Bristol – The Crescent Centre, Temple Back, Bristol BS1 6EZ, *Fax: 0117 925 3452*

Cardiff – Caradog House, 1-6 St Andrews Place, Cardiff CF1 3BE, *Fax: 01222 225906*

Exeter – Renslade House, Bonhay Road, Exeter EX4 3BX, *Fax: 01392 430063*

Leeds – Albion Tower, 11 Albion Street, Leeds LS1 5ES, *Fax: 01132 428843*

Leicester – 5A New Walk, Leicester LE1 6TE, *Fax: 01162 255 6099*

Liverpool – Union Court, Cook Street, Liverpool L2 4UJ, *Fax: 0151 231 1484*

London South – Registration Section, Montagu Court, 101 London Road, West Croydon CR0 2RF, *Fax: 0181 649 9470*

London North – 19-29 Woburn Place, London WC1H 0LU, *Fax: 0171 273 8686*

Manchester – Applications Dept., PO Box 210, Manchester M60 3BW, *Fax: 0161 907 2048*

Newcastle – Quayside House, 110 Quayside, Newcastle Upon Tyne NE1 3DX, *Fax: 0191 222 1680*

Nottingham – 3rd Floor, Byron House, 2A Maid Marian Way, Nottingham NG1 6HS, *Fax: 01159 507612*

Reading – 5th Floor, 30-31 Friar Street, Reading RG1 1DY, *Fax: 01734 568066*

Sheffield – 14 East Parade, Sheffield S1 2ET, *Fax: 0114 276 2551*

Shrewsbury – Prospect House, Belle Vue Road, Shrewsbury SY3 7NR, *Fax: 01743 244186*

Southampton – 3rd Floor, Dukes Keep, Marsh Lane, Southampton SO1 1EX, *Fax: 01703 635506*

Stratford – 44 The Broadway, Stratford, London E15 1XH, *Fax: 0181 221 0398*

Where to send your application

- You will need to know the postcode for the place where you worked. If you have never worked for the employer use the postcode for the place where the matter which you are complaining about occurred.
- Refer to the chart below and send it to the tribunal office listed against the code e.g. PE10, 11 or 12 should go to Nottingham Office. (The full address of each office is on the reverse of these notes).
- Sending your application to the wrong office may cause delay. If you are in doubt where to send it, call the Industrial Tribunal Enquiry line on **0345 959775.**

Post Code Area	Tribunal Office	Post Code Area	Tribunal Office	Post Code Area	Tribunal Office	Post Code Area	Tribunal Office
AL	Bedford	GU1-10	London South	PE1-6	Leicester	SW1-2	London South
B	Birmingham	GU11-14	Southampton	PE7	Bury St Eds	SW3	London North
BA1-16	Bristol	GU15-16	London South	PE8	Bedford	SW4	London South
BA20-22	Exeter	GU17	Reading	PE9	Leicester	SW5-7	London North
BB	Manchester	GU18-25	London South	PE10-12	Nottingham	SW8-9	London South
BD	Leeds	GU26-35	Southampton	PE13-19	Bury St Eds	SW10	London North
BH	Southampton	HA	London North	PE20-25	Nottingham	SW11-20	London South
BL	Manchester	HD	Leeds	PE30-38	Bury St Eds	SY1-22	Shrewsbury
BN	Southampton	HG	Leeds	PL	Exeter	SY23-25	Cardiff
BR	Ashford	HP1-5	London North	PO	Southampton	TA1-5	Exeter
BS	Bristol	HP6-22	Reading	PR1-7	Manchester	TA6-9	Bristol
CA	Newcastle	HP23	London North	PR8-9	Liverpool	TA10-24	Exeter
CB	Bury St Eds	HP27	Reading	RG1-13	Reading	TD****	Newcastle
CF	Cardiff	HR	Cardiff	RG14-15	Southampton	TF	Shrewsbury
CH1-3	Liverpool	HU	Leeds	RG16-20	Reading	TN1-4	Ashford
CH4-8	Shrewsbury	HX	Leeds	RG21-28	Southampton	TN5-7	London South
CM	Stratford	IG	Stratford	RG29-45	Reading	TN8-18	Ashford
CO	Bury St Eds	IP	Bury St Eds	RH1-14	London South	TN19-22	Southampton
CR	London South	KT	London South	RH15-17	Southampton	TN23-31	Ashford
CT	Ashford	L	Liverpool	RH18-20	London South	TN32-33	Southampton
CV	Birmingham	LA1-6	Manchester	RM	Stratford	TN34-38	Ashford
CW1-5	Shrewsbury	LA7-23	Newcastle	S1-62	Sheffield	TN39-40	Southampton
CW6-10	Liverpool	LD	Cardiff	S63-64	Leeds	TQ	Exeter
CW11-12	Shrewsbury	LE	Leicester	S65-66	Sheffield	TR	Exeter
DA	Ashford	LL	Shrewsbury	S70-75	Leeds	TS	Newcastle
DE1-7	Nottingham	LN	Nottingham	S80-81	Sheffield	TW	London South
DE11-15	Leicester	LS	Leeds	SA	Cardiff	UB	London North
DE21-75	Nottingham	LU	Bedford	SE	London South	W	London North
DH	Newcastle	M	Manchester	SG1-7	Bedford	WA1-2	Liverpool
DL	Newcastle	ME	Ashford	SG8-14	Bury St Eds	WA3	Manchester
DN1-20	Leeds	MK	Bedford	SG15-19	Bedford	WA4-13	Liverpool
DN21	Nottingham	N	London North	SK	Manchester	WA14-16	Manchester
DN22	Sheffield	NE	Newcastle	SL	Reading	WC	London North
DN31-40	Leeds	NG	Nottingham	SM	London South	WD	London North
DT1-5	Southampton	NN1-13	Bedford	SN1-6	Bristol	WF	Leeds
DT6-8	Exeter	NN14-18	Leicester	SN7	Reading	WN1-7	Manchester
DT9-11	Southampton	NN29	Bedford	SN8-16	Bristol	WN8	Liverpool
DY	Birmingham	NP	Cardiff	SO	Southampton	WR	Birmingham
E	Stratford	NR	Bury St Eds	SP	Southampton	WS	Birmingham
EC	Stratford	NW	London North	SR	Newcastle	WV	Birmingham
EN	Stratford	OL1-13	Manchester	SS	Stratford	YO1-18	Leeds
EX	Exeter	OL14	Leeds	ST1-13	Shrewsbury	YO21-22	Newcastle
FY	Manchester	OL15-16	Manchester	ST14	Leicester	YO25	Leeds
GL	Bristol	OX	Reading	ST15-21	Birmingham	****TD post code area - English locations only. Scotland has its own tribunals	

INDUSTRIAL TRIBUNAL SERVICE

Received at ITO

FOR OFFICE USE

Case Number

Code

Initials ROIT

Applications to an Industrial Tribunal

- This form has to be photocopied. If possible please use BLACK INK and CAPITAL letters.
- Where there are tick boxes, please tick the one that applies.

1 Please give the type of complaint you want the tribunal to decide (for example: unfair dismissal, equal pay). A full list is given in Booklet ITL1. If you have more than one complaint list them all.

2 Please give your details

Mr ☐ Mrs ☐ Miss ☐ Ms ☐

First names

Surname

Date of birth

Address

Postcode

Telephone

Daytime Telephone

Please give an address to which we should send documents if different from above

Postcode

3 If a representative is acting for you please give details

Name

Address

Postcode

Telephone

Reference

4 Please give the dates of your employment

From To

5 Please give the name and address of the employer, other organisation or person against whom this complaint is being brought

Name of the employer, organisation or person

Address

Postcode

Telephone

Please give the place where you worked or applied to work if different from above

Address

Postcode

6 Please say what job you did for the employer (or what job you applied for). If this does not apply, Please say what your connection was with the employer

IT1(E/W)

7 **Please give the number of normal basic hours worked each week**

Hours per week

9 **If your complaint is NOT about dismissal, please give the date when the matter you are complaining about took place**

8 **Please give your earning details**

Basic wage/salary

£ : per

Average take home pay

£ : per

Other bonuses/benefits

£ : per

10 **Unfair dismissal applicants only**

Please indicate what you are seeking at this stage, if you win your case.

☐ Reinstatement: to carry on working in your old job as before (An order for reinstatement normally includes an award of compensation for loss of earnings.)

☐ Re-engagement: to start another job or new contract with your old employer: (An order for re-engagement normally includes an award of compensation for loss of earnings.)

☐ Compensation only: to get an award of money

11 **Please give details of your complaint**

If there is not enough space for your answer, please continue on a separate sheet and attach it to this form.

12 **Please sign and date this form, then send it to the address given on page 1.**

Signed

Date

IT1(E/W) Printed on recycled paper DTI/Pub 2400/80k/9/96/AR

THE INDUSTRIAL TRIBUNALS
NOTICE OF APPEARANCE BY RESPONDENT

In the application of

Case Number ./1996
(please quote in all correspondence)

* This form has to be photocopied, if possible please use Black Ink and Capital letters
* If there is not enough space for your answer, please continue on a separate sheet and attach it to this form

1. Full name and address of the Respondent:

Post Code:

Telephone number:

2. If you require documents and notices to be sent to a representative or any other address in the United Kingdom please give details:

Post Code:

Reference:

Telephone number:

3. Do you intend to resist the application? (Tick appropriate box)

YES ☐ NO ☐

4. Was the applicant dismissed? (Tick appropriate box)

YES ☐ (Please give reason below) NO ☐

Reason for dismissal:

5. Are the dates of employment given by the applicant correct? (Tick appropriate box)

YES ☐ NO ☐ (please give correct dates below)

Began on

Ended on

6. Are the details given by the applicant about wages/salary, take home or other bonuses correct? (Tick appropriate box)

YES ☐ NO ☐ (Please give correct details below)

Basic Wages/Salary	£	per
Average Take Home Pay	£	per
Other Bonuses/Benefits	£	per

PLEASE TURN OVER

for office use only
Date of receipt Initials

Form IT3 E&W - 1/95

7. Give particulars of the grounds on which you intend to resist the application.

8. Please sign and date the form.

Signed Dated

DATA PROTECTION ACT 1984
We may put some of the information you give on this form on to a computer. This helps us to monitor progress and produce statistics. We may also give information to:
* the other party in the case
* other parts of the Employment Department Group and organisations such as ACAS (Advisory Conciliation and Arbitration Service), the Equal Opportunities Commission or the Commission for Racial Equality.

Please post or fax this form to : The Regional Secretary 44 Broadway, Stratford, London, E15 1XH.

* IF YOU FAX THE FORM, DO NOT POST A COPY AS WELL
* IF YOU POST THE FORM, TAKE A COPY FOR YOUR RECORDS

Form IT3 E&W - 1/95

(F) Settlement of unfair dismissal claims

As explained in the text, s 203(1) of the ERA renders void any agreement which purports to exclude an employee from presenting a complaint to an industrial tribunal. Settlements under the auspices of a conciliation officer of the Advisory Conciliation and Arbitration Service are an exception to this where such settlements arise from action taken by a conciliation officer in accordance with s 18 of the Industrial Tribunals Act 1996. So also are settlements which comply with the requirements of s 203(3) of the ERA (basically where the employee is legally represented and a compromise agreement satisfying the somewhat complicated requirements imposed is concluded). Set out below is the standard form of a conciliation agreement (COT3) which is used to record the terms of settlement agreement in the case of an actual or threatened claim. In the case of the former the document will bear the industrial tribunal case number and, in the case of the latter, a unique reference number given to the settlement by ACAS.

In addition, some model wording for settlement of an unfair dismissal claim is reproduced below, although there are no particular requirements as to the form of words used and it will generally be the case (because, for example, there are a number of terms agreed between the parties) that the wording endorsed on the COT3 forms will cross-refer an attached schedule recording those terms in more detail. Model wording to be included in a settlement agreement intended to satisfy the conditions regulating compromise agreements under s 203(3) of the ERA is also reproduced below.

Advisory, Conciliation and Arbitration Service

ITRO No.	Tribunal No.

AGREEMENT FOLLOWING CONCILIATION ON A CLAIM MADE BY THE APPLICANT TO THE ADVISORY CONCILIATION AND ARBITRATION SERVICE (No application made to Tribunal at time of agreement) THAT ACTION HAD BEEN TAKEN BY THE RESPONDENT IN RESPECT OF WHICH A COMPLAINT COULD BE MADE TO AN INDUSTRIAL TRIBUNAL

Applicant	Respondent
Name Address	Name Address

Settlement reached as a result of conciliation action.

We the undersigned have agreed:

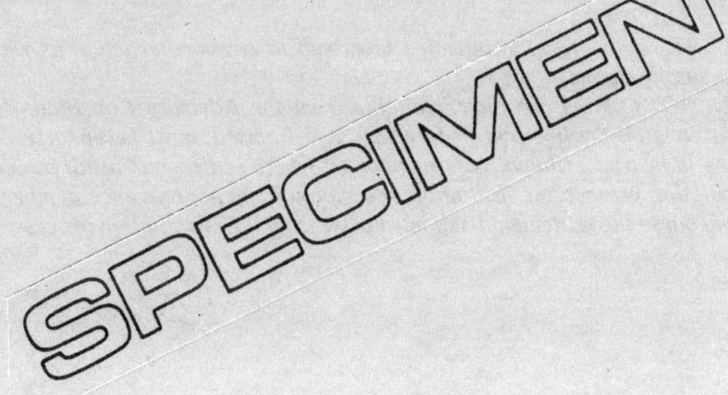

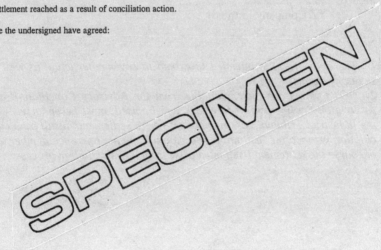

Applicant .... Date ....

COT3 NON (IT1) Respondent .... Date ....

UNFAIR DISMISSAL

Text of model wording for COT3 Settlement Agreement

We the undersigned have agreed as follows:

That XYZ Company Limited ('the Company') shall pay to and Mr A shall accept the sum of £[*specify*] in full and final settlement of all claims (whether at common law, under statute or European Community law) which Mr A may have against the Company arising under his contract of employment or directly or indirectly from the termination of his employment including (for the avoidance of doubt) any complaints under sections 23 and 111 of the Employment Rights Act 1996, section 63 of the Sex Discrimination Act 1975 and section 54 of the Race Relations Act 1976 or under Part II of the Employment Rights Act 1996 and any claim relating to wrongful dismissal.

Signed ....
(Mr A)

Signed ....
(XYZ Company Limited)

Notes:

1 The above form is intended to extend to cover contractual as well as statutory claims.
2 COT3 forms are only available from the Advisory Conciliation and Arbitration Service and, before they can be used, must be endorsed with the Industrial Tribunal case number or, where settlements result from conciliation prior to the institution of a claim, a unique reference number and of course the settlement itself must arise from the conciliation process.

MODEL WORDING FOR INCLUSION IN SECTION 203 COMPROMISE AGREEMENT

A. You acknowledge that prior to accepting the terms of this Agreement you have received independent legal advice from a qualified solicitor (the 'Qualified Solicitor') (whom you will request to complete the certificate included in this Agreement) as to the terms and effects of this Agreement and in particular on your ability to pursue your rights before an Industrial Tribunal or any of the complaints referred to in [*specify relevant paragraph in the Agreement*].

B. You confirm that you have been advised by the Qualified Solicitor that there is in force and was at the time you received the advice referred to above a (policy of insurance covering/cover under the Solicitors' Indemnity Fund for)* the risk of the claim by you in respect of a loss arising in consequence of that advice.

C. The parties hereto agree and acknowledge that the conditions regulating compromise agreements contained in s 203(2)(f) and (3) of the Employment Rights Act 1996 Sub-section 77(4)(A) of the Sex Discrimination Act 1995 and sub-s 72(4)(A) of the Race Relations Act 1976.

D. I, [ ] of [ ] confirm that I have given independent legal advice to [*specify*] of [*specify*] as to the terms and effects of the above letter and in particular its effect on [*specify*] ability to pursue his rights before an Industrial Tribunal.

E. I confirm that I am a solicitor of the Supreme Court holding a current practising certificate and that there is and was at the time that I gave the advice referred to above in force a (policy of insurance covering/cover under the Solicitors' Indemnity Fund for)* the risk of a claim by [*specify*] in respect of any loss arising in consequence of that advice.

Signed ....

Dated ....

*delete as appropriate

(G) Redundancy

Reproduced below is form HR1, employers' notification of proposed redundancies under s 188 of the Trade Union and Labour Relations (Consolidation) Act 1992, the requirements of which are referred to in the text. Additionally, a ready reckoner for calculating redundancy payments is also included, together with explanatory notes.

Department of Trade and Industry — Trade Union and Labour Relations (Consolidation) Act 1992

Advance notification of redundancies

0390/1

What you are required to do

As an employer, you are required by law to notify **a proposal to make redundant 20 or more employees within a 90 day period.**

- If 20 to 99 redundancies may occur at one establishment, ***you must notify us at least 30 days before the first dismissal.***
- If 100 or more redundancies may occur at one establishment, ***you must notify us at least 90 days before the first dismissal.***
- The date on which we receive your completed form is ***the date of notification.***

How to complete this form

- Use a separate form for each establishment where 20 or more redundancies may occur within a 90 day period.
- Write your answers in CAPITALS, as this will make it easier for us to read
- Where tick boxes appear, please tick those that apply.
- If there is not enough space for your answers, please use a separate sheet of paper and attach it to this form.
- Please return the completed form to:
  Department of Trade and Industry
  Redundancy Payments Office
  Hagley House
  83-85 Hagley Road
  Birmingham B16 8QG
- You must send a copy of this notification to the representatives of the employees being consulted.
- If the circumstances outlined in this form change, please notify us immediately.

Data Protection Act 1984

We will store the information you give us in a computer system, which will help us deal with it more efficiently.

- We may give it to selected government agencies and Training and Enterprise Councils/Local Enterprise Companies and Careers Services, who may offer to help you deal with proposed redundancies.
- We will *not* give it to any other agencies or organisations without first obtaining your consent.

Further information

- A more detailed explanation of this subject can be found in our leaflet PL833 "Redundancy consultation and notification".
- You can get leaflet PL833 from any Jobcentre or Unemployment Benefit Office.

1 Employer's details

Name

Address

Post code

Telephone number

2 Employer's contact

Name

Address *(if different to that given at 1)*

Post code

Telephone number *(if different to that given at 1)*

3 Establishment where redundancies proposed

Address given at 1 ☐

Address given at 2 ☐

Address different to that given at 1 or 2 ☐ ▶ *please give address below*

Post code

Nature of main business

HR1 (Rev) — **over ▶**

4 Reasons for redundancies

Please tick one or more boxes to show the main reason(s) for the proposed redundancies:

- lower demand for products or services ☐ A
- completion of all or part of contract ☐ B
- transfer of work to another site or employer ☐ C
- introduction of new technology/plant/machinery ☐ D
- changes in work methods or organisation ☐ E
- another reason ▶ ***please give brief details below*** ☐ F

5 Staff numbers/redundancies at this establishment

Occupational group	Number of employees	Number of possible redundancies
Manual		
Clerical		
Professional		
Managerial/technical		
Other		
Totals		
Number of long-term trainees included in above who may be made redundant		
Number of long-term trainees under 20 years of age included in above who may be made redundant		

6 Closure of establishment

Do you propose to close the establishment?

Yes ☐

No ☐

7 Timing of redundancies

Date of first proposed redundancy

Date of last proposed redundancy

8 Method of selection for redundancy

Please give brief details of how you will choose the employees to be made redundant.

9 Consultation

Are any of the groups of employees, who may be made redundant, represented by a recognised trade union?

Yes ☐ ▶ ***Please list these trade unions below***

No ☐

Have you consulted any of the trade unions listed above?

Yes ☐ ▶ ***Date consultation started***

No ☐

Have you consulted elected representatives of the employees?

Yes ☐ ▶ ***Date consultation started***

No ☐

Declaration

I certify that the information given on this form is, so far as I know, correct and complete.

Signed

Date

Position held

For our use

HMSO Print FMEDR 11/95 T103565 30K

READY RECKONER FOR CALCULATING REDUNDANCY PAYMENTS

SERVICE (years)		2	3	4	5	6	7	8	9	10	11	12	13	14	15	16	17	18	19	20
AGE (years)	20	1	1	1	1	—														
	21	1	1½	1½	1½	1½	—													
	22	1	1½	2	2	2	2	—												
	23	1½	2	2½	3	3	3	3												
	24	2	2½	3	3½	4	4	4	4	—										
	25	2	3	3½	4	4½	5	5	5	5	—									
	26	2	3	4	4½	5	5½	6	6	6	6	—								
	27	2	3	4	5	5½	6	6½	7	7	7	7	—							
	28	2	3	4	5	6	6½	7	7½	8	8	8	8	—						
	29	2	3	4	5	6	7	7½	8	8½	9	9	9	9	—					
	30	2	3	4	5	6	7	8	8½	9	9½	10	10	10	10	—				
	31	2	3	4	5	6	7	8	9	9½	10	10½	11	11	11	11	—			
	32	2	3	4	5	6	7	8	9	10	10½	11	11½	12	12	12	12	—		
	33	2	3	4	5	6	7	8	9	10	11	11½	12	12½	13	13	13	13	—	
	34	2	3	4	5	6	7	8	9	10	11	12	12½	13	13½	14	14	14	14	—
	35	2	3	4	5	6	7	8	9	10	11	12	13	13½	14	14½	15	15	15	15
	36	2	3	4	5	6	7	8	9	10	11	12	13	14	14½	15	15½	16	16	16
	37	2	3	4	5	6	7	8	9	10	11	12	13	14	15	15½	16	16½	17	17
	38	2	3	4	5	6	7	8	9	10	11	12	13	14	15	16	16½	17	17½	18
	39	2	3	4	5	6	7	8	9	10	11	12	13	14	15	16	17	17½	18	18½
	40	2	3	4	5	6	7	8	9	10	11	12	13	14	15	16	17	18	18½	19
	41	2	3	4	5	6	7	8	9	10	11	12	13	14	15	16	17	18	19	19½
	42	2½	3½	4½	5½	6½	7½	8½	9½	10½	11½	12½	13½	14½	15½	16½	17½	18½	19½	20½
	43	3	4	5	6	7	8	9	10	11	12	13	14	15	16	17	18	19	20	21
	44	3	4½	5½	6½	7½	8½	9½	10½	11½	12½	13½	14½	15½	16½	17½	18½	19½	20½	21½
	45	3	4½	6	7	8	9	10	11	12	13	14	15	16	17	18	19	20	21	22
	46	3	4½	6	7½	8½	9½	10½	11½	12½	13½	14½	15½	16½	17½	18½	19½	20½	21½	22½
	47	3	4½	6	7½	9	10	11	12	13	14	15	16	17	18	19	20	21	22	23
	48	3	4½	6	7½	9	10½	11½	12½	13½	14½	15½	16½	17½	18½	19½	20½	21½	22½	23½
	49	3	4½	6	7½	9	10½	12	13	14	15	16	17	18	19	20	21	22	23	24
	50	3	4½	6	7½	9	10½	12	13½	14½	15½	16½	17½	18½	19½	20½	21½	22½	23½	24½
	51	3	4½	6	7½	9	10½	12	13½	15	16	17	18	19	20	21	22	23	24	25
	52	3	4½	6	7½	9	10½	12	13½	15	16½	17½	18½	19½	20½	21½	22½	23½	24½	25½
	53	3	4½	6	7½	9	10½	12	13½	15	16½	18	19	20	21	22	23	24	25	26
	54	3	4½	6	7½	9	10½	12	13½	15	16½	18	19½	20½	21½	22½	23½	24½	25½	26½
	55	3	4½	6	7½	9	10½	12	13½	15	16½	18	19½	21	22	23	24	25	26	27
	56	3	4½	6	7½	9	10½	12	13½	15	16½	18	19½	21	22½	23½	24½	25½	26½	27½
	57	3	4½	6	7½	9	10½	12	13½	15	16½	18	19½	21	22½	24	25	26	27	28
	58	3	4½	6	7½	9	10½	12	13½	15	16½	18	19½	21	22½	24	25½	26½	27½	28½
	59	3	4½	6	7½	9	10½	12	13½	15	16½	18	19½	21	22½	24	25½	27	28	29
	60	3	4½	6	7½	9	10½	12	13½	15	16½	18	19½	21	22½	24	25½	27	28½	29½
	61	3	4½	6	7½	9	10½	12	13½	15	16½	18	19½	21	22½	24	25½	27	28½	30
	62	3	4½	6	7½	9	10½	12	13½	15	16½	18	19½	21	22½	24	25½	27	28½	30
	63	3	4½	6	7½	9	10½	12	13½	15	16½	18	19½	21	22½	24	25½	27	28½	30
	64	3	4½	6	7½	9	10½	12	13½	15	16½	18	19½	21	22½	24	25½	27	28½	30
SERVICE (years)		2	3	4	5	6	7	8	9	10	11	12	13	14	15	16	17	18	19	20

NOTES:

1 The employee's age and length of service give the number of 'weeks' pay' which the employee will be entitled to by way of a redundancy payment. Note the amount of 'a week's pay' for this purpose tends to be increased annually by statutory instrument.

(H) Discrimination

Reproduced below are the questionnaires prescribed for questions and replies under the Sex Discrimination (Questions and Replies) Order 1975 (SI 1975/2048, as amended by SI 1977/844) and the Race Relations (Questions and Replies) Order 1977 (SI 1977/842).

SD 74

SEX DISCRIMINATION ACT 1975

THE QUESTIONS PROCEDURE

CONTENTS

A complainant should obtain TWO copies of this booklet, one to send to the respondent and the other to keep.
Before completing the questionnaire or the reply form (as appropriate), the complainant and the respondent should read Part I of the guidance and (again as appropriate) Part II or III.

Issued by The Home Office and
The Department of Employment

SEX DISCRIMINATION ACT 1975 – GUIDANCE ON THE QUESTIONS PROCEDURE

PART I – INTRODUCTION

1 The purpose of this guidance is to explain the questions procedure under section 74 of the Sex Discrimination Act 1975•. The procedure is intended to help a person (referred to in this guidance as the **complainant**) who thinks she (or he) has been discriminated against by another (the **respondent**) to obtain information from that person about the treatment in question in order to –

(a) decide whether or not to bring legal proceedings, and

(b) if proceedings are brought, to present her complaint in the most effective way.

A questionnaire has been devised which the complainant can send to the respondent and there is also a matching reply form for use by the respondent (both are included in this booklet). The questionnaire and the reply form have been designed to assist the complainant and respondent to identify information which is relevant to the complaint. It is not, however, obligatory for the questionnaire or the reply form to be used: the exchange of questions and replies may be conducted, for example, by letter.

2 This guidance is intended to assist both the complainant and the respondent. Guidance for the complainant on the preparation of the questionnaire is set out in Part II; and guidance for the respondent on the use of the reply form is set out in Part III. The main provisions of the Sex Discrimination Act are referred to in the appendix to this guidance. Further information about the Act will be found in the various leaflets published by the Equal Opportunities Commission and also in the detailed Guide to the Sex Discrimination Act 1975. The leaflets and the Guide may be obtained, free of charge, from the Equal Opportunities Commission at –

Overseas House
Quay Street
Manchester M3 3HN
Telephone: 061–833–9244

The Guide and the EOC's leaflets on the employment provisions of the Act may also be obtained, free of charge, from any employment office or jobcentre of the Employment Service Agency of from any unemployment benefit office of the Department of Employment. The EOC's leaflets may also be obtained from Citizens Advice Bureaux.

How the questions procedure can benefit both parties

3 The procedure can benefit both the complainant and the respondent in the following ways: –

(1) If the respondent's answers satisfy the complainant that the treatment was not unlawful discrimination, there will be no need for legal proceedings.

(2) Even if the respondent's answers do not satisfy the complainant, they should help to identify what is agreed and what is in dispute between the parties. For example, the answers should reveal whether the parties disagree on the facts of the case, or, if they agree on the facts, whether they disagree on how the Act applies. In some cases, this may lead to a settlement of the grievance, again making legal proceedings unnecessary.

(3) If it turns out that the complainant institutes proceedings against the respondent, the proceedings should be that much simpler because the matters in dispute will have been identified in advance.

What happens if the respondent does not reply or replies evasively.

4 The respondent cannot be compelled to reply to the complainant's questions. However, if the respondent deliberately, and without reasonable excuse, does not reply within a reasonable period, or replies in an evasive or **ambiguous** way, his position may be adversely affected should the complainant bring proceedings against him. The respondent's attention is drawn to these possible consequences in the note at the end of the questionnaire.

Period within which questionnaire must be served on the respondent

5 There are different time limits within which a questionnaire must be served in order to be admissible under the questions procedure in any ensuing legal proceedings. Which time limit applies depends on whether the complaint would be under the employment, training and related provisions of the Act (in which case the proceedings would be before an industrial tribunal) or whether it would be under the education, goods, facilities and services or premises provisions (in which case proceedings would be before a county court or, in Scotland, a sheriff court).

Industrial tribunal cases

6 In order to be admissible under the questions procedure in any ensuing industrial tribunal proceedings, the complainant's questionnaire must be served on the respondent either:

(a) before a complaint about the treatment concerned is made to an industrial tribunal, but not more than 3 months after the treatment in question; or

(b) if a complaint has already been made to a tribunal, within 21 days beginning when the complaint was received by the tribunal.

However, where the complainant has made a complaint to a tribunal and the period of 21 days has expired, a questionnaire may still be served provided the leave of the tribunal is obtained. This may be done by sending to the Secretary of the Tribunal a written application, which must state the names of the complainant and the respondent and set out the grounds of the application. However, every effort should be made to serve the questionnaire within the period of 21 days as the leave of the tribunal to serve the questionnaire after the expiry of that period will not necessarily be obtained.

Court cases

7 In order to be admissible under the questions procedure in any ensuing county or sheriff court proceedings, the complainant's questionnaire must be served on the respondent before proceedings in respect of the treatment

•The prescribed forms, time limits for serving questions and manner of service of questions and replies under section 74 are specified in The Sex Discrimination (Questions and Replies) Order 1975 (SI 1975 No. 2048).

concerned are brought, but not more than 6 months after the treatment*. However, where proceedings have been brought, a questionnaire may still be served provided the leave of the court has been obtained. In the case of county court proceedings, this may be done by obtaining form Ex 23 from the county court office, and completing it and sending it to the Registrar and the respondent, or by applying to the Registrar at the pre-trial review. In the case of sheriff court proceedings, this may be done by making an application to a sheriff.

PART II – GUIDANCE FOR THE COMPLAINANT

NOTES ON PREPARING THE QUESTIONNAIRE

8 Before filling in the questionnaire, you are advised to prepare what you want to say on a separate piece of paper. If you have insufficient room on the questionnaire for what you want to say, you should continue on an additional piece of paper, which should be sent with the questionnaire to the respondent.

Paragraph 2

9 You should give, in the space provided in paragraph 2, as much relevant factual information as you can about the treatment you think may have been unlawful discrimination, and about the circumstances leading up to that treatment. You should also give the date, and if possible and if relevant, the place and approximate time of the treatment. You should bear in mind that in paragraph 4 of the questionnaire you will be asking the respondent whether he agrees with what you say in paragraph 2.

Paragraph 3

10 In paragraph 3 you are telling the respondent that you think the treatment you have described in paragraph 2 may have been unlawful discrimination by him against you. It will help to identify whether there are any legal issues between you and the respondent if you explain in the space provided **why** you think the treatment may have been unlawful discrimination. However, you do not **have** to complete paragraph 3; if you do not wish or are unable to do so, you should delete the word "because". If you wish to complete the paragraph, but feel you need more information about the Sex Discrimination Act before doing so, you should look to the appendix to this guidance.

11 If you decide to complete paragraph 3, you may find it useful to indicate—

(a) what **kind** of discrimination you think the treatment may have been ie whether it was
 direct sex discrimination,
 indirect sex discrimination,
 direct discrimination against a married person,
 indirect discrimination against a married person,
 or
 victimisation.

(b) which provision of the Act you think may make unlawful the kind of discrimination you think you may have suffered. (For an indication of the provisions of the Act which make the various kinds of discrimination unlawful, see paragraph 2 of the appendix).

(For further information about the different kinds of discrimination see paragraph 1 of the appendix).

Paragraph 6

12 You should insert here any other question which you think may help you to obtain relevant information. (For example, if you think you have been discriminated against by having been refused a job, you may want to know what were the qualifications of the person who did get the job and why that person got the job).

13 Paragraph 5 contains questions which are especially important if you think you may have suffered direct sex discrimination, or direct discrimination against a married person, because they ask the respondent whether your sex or marital status had anything to do with your treatment. Paragraph 5 does not, however, ask specific questions relating to indirect sex discrimination, indirect discrimination against a married person or victimisation. If you think you may have suffered indirect sex discrimination (or indirect discrimination against a married person) you may find it helpful to include the following question in the space provided in paragraph 6:

"Was the reason for my treatment the fact that I could not comply with a condition or requirement which is applied equally to men and women (married and unmarried persons)?
If so—
(a) what was the condition or requirement?
(b) why was it applied?"

14 If you think you may have been victimised you may find it helpful to include the following question in the space provided in paragraph 6:

"Was the reason for my treatment the fact that I had done, or intended to do, or that you suspected I had done or intended to do, any of the following:
(a) brought proceedings under the Sex Discrimination Act or the Equal Pay Act; or
(b) gave evidence or information in connection with proceedings under either Act; or
(c) did something else under or by reference to either Act; or
(d) made an allegation that someone acted unlawfully under either Act?"

Signature

15 The questionnaire must be signed and dated. If it is to be signed on behalf of (rather than by) the complainant **the person signing** should

(a) describe himself (eg "solicitor acting for (*name of complainant*))", and
(b) give his business (or home, if appropriate) address.

WHAT PAPERS TO SERVE ON THE PERSON TO BE QUESTIONED

16 You should send the person to be questioned the whole of this document (ie the guidance, the questionnaire and the reply forms), with the questionnaire completed by you. You **are strongly advised to retain, and keep in a safe place, a copy of the completed questionnaire** (and you might also find it useful to retain a copy of the guidance and the uncompleted reply form).

**Where the respondent is a body in charge of a public sector educational establishment, the six month period begins when the complaint has been referred to the appropriate Education Minister and 2 months have elapsed or, if this is earlier, the Minister has informed the complainant that he requires no more time to consider the matter.*

HOW TO SERVE THE PAPERS

17 You can either deliver the papers in person or send them by post. If you decide to send them by post you are advised to use the recorded delivery service, so that, if necessary, you can produce evidence that they were delivered.

WHERE TO SEND THE PAPERS

18 You can send the papers to the person to be questioned at his usual or last known residence or place of business. If you know he is acting through a solicitor you shoud send them to him at his solicitor's address. If you wish to question a limited company or other corporate body or a trade union or employers' association, you should send the papers to the secretary or clerk at the registered or principal office of the company, etc. You should be able to find out where its registered or principal office is by enquiring at a public library. If you are unable to do so, however, you will have to send the papers to the place where you think it is most likely they will reach the secretary or clerk (eg, at, or c/o, the company's local office). If is your responsibility, however, to see that the secretary or clerk receives the papers.

USE OF THE QUESTIONS AND REPLIES IN INDUSTRIAL TRIBUNAL PROCEEDINGS

19 If you decide to make (or already have made) a complaint to an industrial tribunal about the treatment concerned and if you intend to use your questions and the reply (if any) as evidence in the proceedings, you are advised to send copies of your questions and any reply to the Secretary of the Tribunals before the date of the hearing. This should be done as soon as the documents are available; if they are available at the time you submit your complaint to a tribunal, you should send the copies with your complaint to the Secretary of the Tribunals.

PART III – GUIDANCE FOR THE RESPONDENT

NOTES ON COMPLETING THE REPLY FORM

20 Before completing the reply form, you are advised to prepare what you want to say on a separate piece of paper. If you have insufficient room on the reply form for what you want to say, you should continue on an additional piece of paper, which should be attached to the reply form sent to the complainant.

Paragraph 2

21 Here you are answering the question in paragraph 4 of the questionnaire. If you **agree** that the complainant's statement in paragraph 2 of the questionnaire is an accurate description of what happened, you should delete the second sentence.

22 If you **disagree** in any way that the statement is an accurate description of what happened, you should explain in the space provided in what respects you disagree, or your version of what happened, or both.

Paragraph 3

23 Here you are answering the question in paragraph 5 of the questionnaire. If, in answer to paragraph 4 of the questionnaire, you have agreed with the complainant's description of her treatment, you will be answering paragraph 5 on the basis of the facts in her description. If, however, you have disagreed with that description, you should answer paragraph 5 on the basis of **your** version of the facts. To answer paragraph 5, you are advised to look at the appendix to this guidance and also the relevant parts of the **Guide to the Sex Discrimination Act 1975**. You need to know:—

(a) how the Act defines discrimination – see paragraph 1 of the appendix;

(b) in what situation the Act makes discrimination unlawful – see paragraph 2 of the appendix; and

(c) what exceptions the Act provides – see paragraph 3 of the appendix.

24 If you think that an exception (eg the exception for employment where a person's sex is a genuine occupational qualification) applies to the treatment described in paragraph 2 of the complainant's questionnaire, you should mention this in paragraph 3a of the reply form and explain why you think the exception applies.

Signature

25 The reply form should be signed and dated. If it is to be signed on behalf of (rather than by) the respondent, the person signing should–

(a) describe himself (eg "solicitor acting for (*name of respondent*)" or "personnel manager of (*name of firm*)"), and

(b) give his business (or home, if appropriate) address.

SERVING THE REPLY FORM ON THE COMPLAINANT

26 If you wish to reply to the questionnaire you are strongly advised to do so without delay. **You should retain, and keep in a safe place, the questionnaire sent to you and a copy of your reply.**

27 You can serve the reply either by delivering it in person to the complainant or by sending it by post. If you decide to send it by post you are advised to use the recorded delivery service, so that, if necessary, you can produce evidence that it was delivered.

28 You should send the reply form to the address indicated in paragraph 7 of the complainant's questionnaire.

THE SEX DISCRIMINATION ACT 1975 SECTION 74(1)(a)

QUESTIONNAIRE OF PERSON AGGRIEVED (THE COMPLAINANT)

Name of person to be questioned (the respondent)	To ....
Address	of ....
	....
Name of complainant	1. I ....
Address	of ....
	....
	consider that you may have discriminated against me contrary to the Sex Discrimination Act 1975.
Give date, approximate time, place and factual description of the treatment received and of the circumstances leading up to the treatment (see paragraph 9 of the guidance)	2. On
Complete if you wish to give reasons, otherwise delete the word "because" (see paragraphs 10 and 11 of the guidance)	3. I consider that this treatment may have been unlawful because

SD 74(a)

This is the first of your questions to the respondent. You are advised not to alter it	4. Do you agree that the statement in paragraph 2 is an accurate description of what happened? If not in what respect do you disagree or what is your version of what happened?
This is the second of your questions to the respondent. You are advised not to alter it	5. Do you accept that your treatment of me was unlawful discrimination by you against me? If not a why not? b for what reason did I receive the treatment accorded to me? c how far did my sex or marital status affect your treatment of me?
Enter here any other questions you wish to ask (see paragraphs 12–14 of the guidance)	6.
* Delete as appropriate If you delete the first alternative, insert the address to which you want the reply to be sent	7. My address for any reply you may wish to give to the questions raised above is *that set out in paragraph 1 above/the following address
See paragraph 15 of the guidance	Signature of complainant .... Date ....

NB *By virtue of section 74 of the Act, this questionnaire and any reply are (subject to the provisions of the section) admissible in proceedings under the Act and a court or tribunal may draw any such inference as is just and equitable from a failure without reasonable excuse to reply within a reasonable period, or from an evasive or equivocal reply, including an inference that the person questioned has discriminated unlawfully.*

THE SEX DISCRIMINATION ACT 1975 SECTION 74(1)(b)

REPLY BY RESPONDENT

Name of complainant	To ....
Address	of ....
	....
Name of respondent	1. I ....
Address	of ....
	....
Complete as appropriate	hereby acknowledge receipt of the questionnaire signed by you and dated
	.... which was served on me on (date) ....
* Delete as appropriate	2. I ***agree/disagree** that the statement in paragraph 2 of the questionnaire is an accurate description of what happened.
If you agree that the statement in paragraph 2 of the questionnaire is accurate, delete this sentence. If you disagree complete this sentence (see paragraphs 21 and 22 of the guidance)	I disagree with the statement in paragraph 2 of the questionnaire in that
* Delete as appropriate	3. I ***accept/dispute** that my treatment of you was unlawful discrimination by me against you.
If you accept the complainant's assertion of unlawful discrimination in paragraph 3 of the questionnaire delete the sentences at a, b, and c. Unless completed a sentence should be deleted (see paragraphs 23 and 24 of the guidance)	a My reasons for so disputing are

SD 74(b)

b The reason why you received the treatment accorded to you is

c Your sex or marital status affected my treatment of you to the following extent:–

Replies to questions in paragraph 6 of the questionnaire should be entered here

4.

Delete the whole of this sentence if you have answered all the questions in the questionnaire. If you have not answered all the questions, delete "unable" or "unwilling" as appropriate and give your reasons for not answering

5. I have deleted (in whole or in part) the paragraph(s) numbered .... above, since I am **unable/unwilling** to reply to the relevant questions of the questionnaire for the following reasons:–

See paragraph 25 of the guidance

Signature of respondent ....

Date ....

THE SEX DISCRIMINATION ACT 1975 SECTION 74(1)(b)

REPLY BY RESPONDENT

Name of complainant	To ....
Address	of ....
	....
Name of respondent	1. I ....
Address	of ....
	....
Complete as appropriate	hereby acknowledge receipt of the questionnaire signed by you and dated
	.... which was served on me on (date) ....
* Delete as appropriate	2. I ***agree/disagree** that the statement in paragraph 2 of the questionnaire is an accurate description of what happened.
If you agree that the statement in paragraph 2 of the questionnaire is accurate, delete this sentence. If you disagree complete this sentence (see paragraphs 21 and 22 of the guidance)	I disagree with the statement in paragraph 2 of the questionnaire in that
* Delete as appropriate	3. I ***accept/dispute** that my treatment of you was unlawful discrimination by me against you.
If you accept the complainant's assertion of unlawful discrimination in paragraph 3 of the questionnaire delete the sentences at a, b, and c. Unless completed a sentence should be deleted (see paragraphs 23 and 24 of the guidance)	a My reasons for so disputing are

SD 74(b)

b The reason why you received the treatment accorded to you is

c Your sex or marital status affected my treatment of you to the following extent:–

Replies to questions in paragraph 6 of the questionnaire should be entered here

4.

* Delete the whole of this sentence if you have answered all the questions in the questionnaire. If you have not answered all the questions, delete "unable" or "unwilling" as appropriate and give your reasons for not answering.

5. I have deleted (in whole or in part) the paragraph(s) numbered .... above, since I am **unable/unwilling** to reply to the relevant questions of the questionnaire for the following reasons:–

See paragraph 25 of the guidance

Signature of respondent ....

Date ....

APPENDIX

NOTES ON THE SCOPE OF THE SEX DISCRIMINATION ACT 1975

Definitions of discrimination

1 The different kinds of discrimination covered by the Act are summarised below (the references in the margin are to the relevant paragraphs in the **Guide to the Sex Discrimination Act 1975**). Some of the explanations have been written in terms of discrimination against a woman, but the Act applies equally to discrimination against men.

2.4 **Direct sex discrimination** arises where a woman is
to treated less favourably than a man is (or would be)
2.8 treated **because of her sex**

Indirect sex discrimination arises where a woman is treated unfavourably because she cannot comply with a condition or requirement which

(a) is (or would be) applied to men and women equally, **and**
(b) is such that the proportion of women who can comply with it is considerably smaller than the proportion of men who can comply with it, **and**
(c) is to the detriment of the woman in question because she cannot comply with it, **and**
(d) is such that the person applying it cannot show that it is justifiable, regardless of the sex of the person to whom it is applied.

2.9 **Direct discrimination against married persons in the**
to **employment field** arises where a married person is
2.12 treated, in a situation covered by the employment
provisions of the Act (ie those summarised under Group A in the table on the next page), less favourably than an unmarried person of the same sex is (or would be) treated **because she or he is married.**

Indirect discrimination against married persons in the employment field arises where a married person is treated, in a situation covered by the employment provisions of the Act, unfavourably because she or he cannot comply with a condition or requirement which

(a) is (or would be) applied to married and unmarried persons equally, **and**
(b) is such that the proportion of married persons who can comply with it is considerably smaller than the proportion of unmarried persons of the same sex who can comply with it, **and**
(c) is to the detriment of the married person in question because she or he cannot comply with it, **and**
(d) is such that the person applying it cannot show it to be justifiable irrespective of the marital status of the person to whom it is applied.

2.13 **Victimisation** arises where a person is treated less
to favourably than other persons (of either sex) are (or
2.14 would be) treated because that person has done
(or intends to do or is suspected of having done or itnending to do) any of the following:–

(a) brought proceedings under the Act or the Equal Pay Act; or
(b) given evidence or information in connection with proceedings brought under either Act; or
(c) done anything else by reference to either Act (eg given information to the Equal Opportunities Commission); or
(d) made an allegation that someone acted unlawfully under either Act.

Victimisation does **not**, however, occur where the reason for the less favourably treatment is an allegation which was false and not made in good faith.

Unlawful discrimination

2 The provisions of the Act which make discrimination unlawful are indicated in the table on the next page. Those in Group A are the employment provisions, for the purposes of which discrimination means direct sex discrimination, indirect sex discrimination, direct discrimination against married persons, indirect discrimination against married persons, and victimisation. Complaints about discrimination which is unlawful under these provisions must be made to an industrial tribunal. For detailed information about these provisions see chapter 3 of the **Guide**. For the purposes of the provisions in Group B, discrimination means direct sex discrimination, indirect sex discrimination and victimisation, but not direct or indirect discrimination against married persons. Complaints about discrimination which is unlawful under these provisions must be made to a county court or, in Scotland, a sheriff court. For detailed information about these provisions see chapters 4 and 5 of the **Guide**.

Exceptions

3 Details of exceptions to the requirements of the Act not to discriminate may be found in the **Guide**. The exceptions applying only to the employment field are described in chapter 3; those applying only to the educational field, in chapter 4; and those applying only to the provision of goods, facilities and services and premises, in chapter 5. General exceptions are described in chapter 7.

PROVISIONS OF THE SEX DISCRIMINATION ACT WHICH MAKE DISCRIMINATION UNLAWFUL

	Section of Act	Paragraphs of Guide
GROUP A		
Discrimination by employers of six or more employees in recruitment and treatment of employees	6	3.3–3.18
Discrimination against contract workers	9	3.19
Discrimination against partners	11	3.20
Discrimination by trade unions, employers' associations etc	12	3.21, 3.22
Discrimination by bodies which confer qualifications or authorisations needed for particular kinds of jobs	13	3.23–3.25
Discrimination in the provision of training by industrial training boards, the Manpower Services Commission, the Employment Service Agency, the Training Services Agency and certain other vocational training bodies	14	3.27, 3.28
Discrimination by employment agencies	15	3.29–3.31
Discrimination by the Manpower Services Commission, the Employment Service Agency and the Training Services Agency other than in vocational training or employment agency services	16	3.32
GROUP B		
Discrimination by bodies in charge of educational establishments	22	4.2–4.6, 4.11–4.15
Discrimination (other than that covered by section 22) by local education authorities	23	4.7, 4.8, 4.14, 4.15
Discrimination in the provision of goods, facilities or services to the public or a section of the public	29	5.2–5.9, 5.13–5.16
Discrimination in the disposal of premises	30	5.10–5.16
Discrimination by landlords against prospective assignees or sublessees	31	5.17

RR 65

RACE RELATIONS ACT 1976

THE QUESTIONS PROCEDURE

CONTENTS

A complainant should obtain TWO copies of this booklet, one to send to the respondent and the other to keep.
Before completing the questionnaire or the reply form (as appropriate), the complainant and the respondent should read Part I of the guidance and (again as appropriate) Part II or III.

Issued by The Home Office and
The Department of Employment

RACE RELATIONS ACT 1976
GUIDANCE ON THE QUESTIONS PROCEDURE

PART I – INTRODUCTION

1 The purpose of this guidance is to explain the questions procedure under section 65 of the Race Relations Act 1976•. The procedure is intended to help a person (referred to in this guidance as the **complainant**) who thinks he has been discriminated against by another (the **respondent**) to obtain information from that person about the treatment in question in order to –

(a) decide whether or not to bring legal proceedings, and
(b) if proceedings are brought, to present her complaint in the most effective way.

A questionnaire has been devised which the complainant can send to the respondent and there is also a matching reply form for use by the respondent (both are included in this booklet). The questionnaire and the reply form have been designed to assist the complainant and respondent to identify information which is relevant to the complaint. It is not, however, obligatory for the questionnaire or the reply form to be used: the exchange of questions and replies may be conducted, for example, by letter.

2 This guidance is intended to assist both the complainant and the respondent. Guidance for the complainant on the preparation of the questionnaire is set out in Part II; and guidance for the respondent on the use of the reply form is set out in Part III. The main provisions of the Race Relations Act are referred to in the appendix to this guidance. Further information about the Act will be found in the various leaflets published by the Commission for Racial Equality and also in the detailed **Guide to the Race Relations Act 1976**. The leaflets and the **Guide** may be obtained, free of charge, from the Commission for Racial Equality at –

Elliot House
10/12 Allington Street
London SW1E 5EH

The **Guide** and the CRE's leaflets on the employment provisions of the Act may also be obtained, free of charge, from any employment office or jobcentre of the Employment Service Agency of from any unemployment benefit office of the Department of Employment. The CRE's leaflets may also be obtained from local community relations councils.

How the questions procedure can benefit both parties

3 The procedure can benefit both the complainant and the respondent in the following ways: –

(1) If the respondent's answers satisfy the complainant that the treatment was not unlawful discrimination, there will be no need for legal proceedings.
(2) Even if the respondent's answers do not satisfy the complainant, they should help to identify what is agreed and what is in dispute between the parties. For example, the answers should reveal whether the parties disagree on the facts of the case, or, if they agree on the facts, whether they disagree on how the Act applies. In some cases, this may lead to a settlement of the grievance, again making legal proceedings unnecessary.
(3) If it turns out that the complainant institutes proceedings against the respondent, the proceedings should be that much simpler because the matters in dispute will have been identified in advance.

What happens if the respondent does not reply or replies evasively.

4 The respondent cannot be compelled to reply to the complainant's questions. However, if the respondent deliberately, and without reasonable excuse, does not reply within a reasonable period, or replies in an evasive or **ambiguous** way, his position may be adversely affected should the complainant bring proceedings against him. The respondent's attention is drawn to these possible consequences in the note at the end of the questionnaire.

Period within which questionnaire must be served on the respondent

5 There are different time limits within which a questionnaire must be served in order to be admissible under the questions procedure in any ensuing legal proceedings. Which time limit applies depends on whether the complaint would be under the employment, training and related provisions of the Act (in which case the proceedings would be before an industrial tribunal) or whether it would be under the education, goods, facilities and services or premises provisions (in which case proceedings would be before a county court or, in Scotland, a sheriff court).

Industrial tribunal cases

6 In order to be admissible under the questions procedure in any ensuing industrial tribunal proceedings, the complainant's questionnaire must be served on the respondent either:

(a) before a complaint about the treatment concerned is made to an industrial tribunal, but not more than 3 months after the treatment in question; or
(b) if a complaint has already been made to a tribunal, within 21 days beginning when the complaint was received by the tribunal.

However, where the complainant has made a complaint to a tribunal and the period of 21 days has expired, a questionnaire may still be served provided the leave of the tribunal is obtained. This may be done by sending to the Secretary of the Tribunal a written application, which must state the names of the complainant and the respondent and set out the grounds of the application. However, every effort should be made to serve the questionnaire within the period of 21 days as the leave of the tribunal to serve the questionnaire after the expiry of that period will not necessarily be obtained.

Court cases

7 In order to be admissible under the questions procedure in any ensuing county or sheriff court proceedings, the complainant's questionnaire must be served on the respondent before proceedings in respect of the treatment

•The prescribed forms, time limits for serving questions and manner of service of questions and replies under section 65 are specified in The Race Relations (Questions and Replies) Order 1975 (SI 1977 No. 842).

THE RACE RELATIONS ACT 1976 SECTION 65(1)(a)

QUESTIONNAIRE OF PERSON AGGRIEVED (THE COMPLAINANT)

Name of person to be questioned (the respondent)	To ....
Address	of ....
	....
Name of complainant	1. I ....
Address	of ....
	....
	consider that you may have discriminated against me contrary to the Race Relations Act 1976.
Give date, approximate time, place and factual description of the treatment received and of the circumstances leading up to the treatment (see paragraph 9 of the guidance)	2. On
Complete if you wish to give reasons, otherwise delete the word "because" (see paragraphs 10 and 11 of the guidance)	3. I consider that this treatment may have been unlawful because
RR 65(a)	

This is the first of your questions to the respondent. You are advised not to alter it	4. Do you agree that the statement in paragraph 2 is an accurate description of what happened? If not in what respect do you disagree or what is your version of what happened?
This is the second of your questions to the respondent. You are advised not to alter it	5. Do you accept that your treatment of me was unlawful discrimination by you against me? If not a why not? b for what reason did I receive the treatment accorded to me? c how far did considerations of colour, race, nationality (including citizenship) or ethnic or national origins affect your treatment of me?
Enter here any other questions you wish to ask (see paragraphs 12–14 of the guidance)	6.
* Delete as appropriate If you delete the first alternative, insert the address to which you want the reply to be sent	7. My address for any reply you may wish to give to the questions raised above is *that set out in paragraph 1 above/the following address
See paragraph 15 of the guidance	Signature of complainant .... Date ....

NB *By virtue of section 65 of the Act, this questionnaire and any reply are (subject to the provisions of the section) admissible in proceedings under the Act and a court or tribunal may draw any such inference as is just and equitable from a failure without reasonable excuse to reply within a reasonable period, or from an evasive or equivocal reply, including an inference that the person questioned has discriminated unlawfully.*

concerned are brought, but not more than 6 months after the treatment*. However, where proceedings have been brought, a questionnaire may still be served provided the leave of the court has been obtained. In the case of county court proceedings, this may be done by obtaining form Ex 23 from the county court office, and completing it and sending it to the Registrar and the respondent, or by applying to the Registrar at the pre-trial review. In the case of sheriff court proceedings, this may be done by making an application to a sheriff.

PART II – GUIDANCE FOR THE COMPLAINANT

NOTES ON PREPARING THE QUESTIONNAIRE

8 Before filling in the questionnaire, you are advised to prepare what you want to say on a separate piece of paper. If you have insufficient room on the questionnaire for what you want to say, you should continue on an additional piece of paper, which should be sent with the questionnaire to the respondent.

Paragraph 2

9 You should give, in the space provided in paragraph 2, as much relevant factual information as you can about the treatment you think may have been unlawful discrimination, and about the circumstances leading up to that treatment. You should also give the date, and if possible and if relevant, the place and approximate time of the treatment. You should bear in mind that in paragraph 4 of the questionnaire you will be asking the respondent whether he agrees with what you say in paragraph 2.

Paragraph 3

10 In paragraph 3 you are telling the respondent that you think the treatment you have described in paragraph 2 may have been unlawful discrimination by him against you. It will help to identify whether there are any legal issues between you and the respondent if you explain in the space provided **why** you think the treatment may have been unlawful discrimination. However, you do not **have** to complete paragraph 3; if you do not wish or are unable to do so, you should delete the word "because". If you wish to complete the paragraph, but feel you need more information about the Race Relations Act before doing so, you should look to the appendix to this guidance.

11 If you decide to complete paragraph 3, you may find it useful to indicate—

(a) what **kind** of discrimination you think the treatment may have been ie whether it was
 direct discrimination,
 indirect discrimination, or
 victimisation.

(b) which provision of the Act you think may make unlawful the kind of discrimination you think you may have suffered. (For an indication of the provisions of the Act which make the various kinds of discrimination unlawful, see paragraph 2 of the appendix).

(For further information about the different kinds of discrimination see paragraph 1 of the appendix).

Paragraph 6

12 You should insert here any other question which you think may help you to obtain relevant information. (For example, if you think you have been discriminated against by having been refused a job, you may want to know what were the qualifications of the person who did get the job and why that person got the job).

13 Paragraph 5 contains questions which are especially important if you think you may have suffered direct discrimination because they ask the respondent whether racial considerations had anything to do with your treatment. Paragraph 5 does not, however, ask specific questions relating to indirect discrimination or victimisation. If you think you may have suffered indirect discrimination you may find it helpful to include the following question in the space provided in paragraph 6:
paragraph 6:

"Was the reason for my treatment the fact that I could not comply with a condition or requirement which is applied equally to people regardless of their racial group?
If so—
(a) what was the condition or requirement?
(b) why was it applied?"

14 If you think you may have been victimised you may find it helpful to include the following question in the space provided in paragraph 6:

"Was the reason for my treatment the fact that I had done, or intended to do, or that you suspected I had done or intended to do, any of the following:
(a) brought proceedings under the Race Relations Act; or
(b) gave evidence or information in connection with proceedings under the Act; or
(c) did something else under or by reference to the Act; or
(d) made an allegation that someone acted unlawfully under the Act?"

Signature

15 The questionnaire must be signed and dated. If it is to be signed on behalf of (rather than by) the complainant, the person signing should–

(a) describe himself (eg "solicitor acting for (*name of complainant*))", and
(b) give his business (or home, if appropriate) address.

WHAT PAPERS TO SERVE ON THE PERSON TO BE QUESTIONED

16 You should send the person to be questioned the whole of this document (ie the guidance, the questionnaire and the reply forms), with the questionnaire completed by you. **You are strongly advised to retain, and keep in a safe place, a copy of the completed questionnaire** (and you might also find it useful to retain a copy of the guidance and the uncompleted reply form).

**Where a person has applied in writing to the CRE for assistance in respect of his case, the time limit of 6 months (or 8 months in respect of public sector education complaints) is extended by 2 months. It is open to the CRE to extend the period by a further month.*

HOW TO SERVE THE PAPERS

17 You can either deliver the papers in person or send them by post. If you decide to send them by post you are advised to use the recorded delivery service, so that, if necessary, you can produce evidence that they were delivered.

WHERE TO SEND THE PAPERS

18 You can send the papers to the person to be questioned at his usual or last known residence or place of business. If you know he is acting through a solicitor you shoud send them to him at his solicitor's address. If you wish to question a limited company or other corporate body or a trade union or employers' association, you should send the papers to the secretary or clerk at the registered or principal office of the company, etc. You should be able to find out where its registered or principal office is by enquiring at a public library. If you are unable to do so, however, you will have to send the papers to the place where you think it is most likely they will reach the secretary or clerk (eg, at, or c/o, the company's local office). It is your responsibility, however, to see that the secretary or clerk receives the papers.

USE OF THE QUESTIONS AND REPLIES IN INDUSTRIAL TRIBUNAL PROCEEDINGS

19 If you decide to make (or already have made) a complaint to an industrial tribunal about the treatment concerned and if you intend to use your questions and the reply (if any) as evidence in the proceedings, you are advised to send copies of your questions and any reply to the Secretary of the Tribunals before the date of the hearing. This should be done as soon as the documents are available; if they are available at the time you submit your complaint to a tribunal, you should send the copies with your complaint to the Secretary of the Tribunals.

PART III – GUIDANCE FOR THE RESPONDENT

NOTES ON COMPLETING THE REPLY FORM

20 Before completing the reply form, you are advised to prepare what you want to say on a separate piece of paper. If you have insufficient room on the reply form for what you want to say, you should continue on an additional piece of paper, which should be attached to the reply form sent to the complainant.

Paragraph 2

21 Here you are answering the question in paragraph 4 of the questionnaire. If you **agree** that the complainant's statement in paragraph 2 of the questionnaire is an accurate description of what happened, you should delete the second sentence.

22 If you **disagree** in any way that the statement is an accurate description of what happened, you should explain in the space provided in what respects you disagree, or your version of what happened, or both.

Paragraph 3

23 Here you are answering the question in paragraph 5 of the questionnaire. If, in answer to paragraph 4 of the questionnaire, you have agreed with the complainant's description of his treatment, you will be answering paragraph 5 on the basis of the facts in his description. If, however, you have disagreed with that description, you should answer paragraph 5 on the basis of **your** version of the facts. To answer paragraph 5, you are advised to look at the appendix to this guidance and also the relevant parts of the **Guide to the Race Relations Act 1976**. You need to know:—

(a) how the Act defines discrimination – see paragraph 1 of the appendix;

(b) in what situation the Act makes discrimination unlawful – see paragraph 2 of the appendix; and

(c) what exceptions the Act provides – see paragraph 3 of the appendix.

24 If you think that an exception (eg the exception for employment where being of a particular racial group is a genuine occupational qualification) applies to the treatment described in paragraph 2 of the complainant's questionnaire, you should mention this in paragraph 3a of the reply form and explain why you think the exception applies.

Signature

25 The reply form should be signed and dated. If it is to be signed on behalf of (rather than by) the respondent, the person signing should–

(a) describe himself (eg "solicitor acting for (*name of respondent*)" or "personnel manager of (*name of firm*)"), and

(b) give his business (or home, if appropriate) address.

SERVING THE REPLY FORM ON THE COMPLAINANT

26 If you wish to reply to the questionnaire you are strongly advised to do so without delay. **You should retain, and keep in a safe place, the questionnaire sent to you and a copy of your reply.**

27 You can serve the reply either by delivering it in person to the complainant or by sending it by post. If you decide to send it by post you are advised to use the recorded delivery service, so that, if necessary, you can produce evidence that it was delivered.

28 You should send the reply form to the address indicated in paragraph 7 of the complainant's questionnaire.

THE RACE RELATIONS ACT 1976 SECTION 65(1)(b)

REPLY BY RESPONDENT

Name of complainant	To ....
Address	of ....
	....
Name of respondent	1. I ....
Address	of ....
	....
Complete as appropriate	hereby acknowledge receipt of the questionnaire signed by you and dated
	.... which was served on me on (date) ....
* Delete as appropriate	2. I ***agree/disagree** that the statement in paragraph 2 of the questionnaire is an accurate description of what happened.
If you agree that the statement in paragraph 2 of the questionnaire is accurate, delete this sentence. If you disagree complete this sentence (see paragraphs 21 and 22 of the guidance)	I disagree with the statement in paragraph 2 of the questionnaire in that
* Delete as appropriate	3. I ***accept/dispute** that my treatment of you was unlawful discrimination by me against you.
If you accept the complainant's assertion of unlawful discrimination in paragraph 3 of the questionnaire delete the sentences at a, b, and c. Unless completed a sentence should be deleted (see paragraphs 23 and 24 of the guidance)	a My reasons for so disputing are

RR 65(b)

b The reason why you received the treatment accorded to you is

c Consideration of colour, race, nationality (including citizenship) or ethnic or national origins affected my treatment of you to the following extent:–

Replies to questions in paragraph 6 of the questionnaire should be entered here

4.

Delete the whole of this sentence if you have answered all the questions in the questionnaire. If you have not answered all the questions, delete "unable" or "unwilling" as appropriate and give your reasons for not answering

5. I have deleted (in whole or in part) the paragraph(s) numbered .... above, since I am **unable/unwilling** to reply to the relevant questions of the questionnaire for the following reasons:–

See paragraph 25 of the guidance

Signature of respondent ....

Date ....

THE RACE RELATIONS ACT 1976 SECTION 65(1)(b)

REPLY BY RESPONDENT

Name of complainant	To ....
Address	of ....
	....
Name of respondent	1. I ....
Address	of ....
	....
Complete as appropriate	hereby acknowledge receipt of the questionnaire signed by you and dated
	.... which was served on me on (date) ....
* Delete as appropriate	2. I ***agree/disagree** that the statement in paragraph 2 of the questionnaire is an accurate description of what happened.
If you agree that the statement in paragraph 2 of the questionnaire is accurate, delete this sentence. If you disagree complete this sentence (see paragraphs 21 and 22 of the guidance)	I disagree with the statement in paragraph 2 of the questionnaire in that
* Delete as appropriate	3. I ***accept/dispute** that my treatment of you was unlawful discrimination by me against you.
If you accept the complainant's assertion of unlawful discrimination in paragraph 3 of the questionnaire delete the sentences at a, b, and c. Unless completed a sentence should be deleted (see paragraphs 23 and 24 of the guidance)	a My reasons for so disputing are
RR 65(b)	

b The reason why you received the treatment accorded to you is

c Considerations of colour, race, nationality (including citizenship) or ethnic or national origins affected my treatment of you to the following extent:–

Replies to questions in paragraph 6 of the questionnaire should be entered here

4.

* Delete the whole of this sentence if you have answered all the questions in the questionnaire. If you have not answered all the questions, delete "unable" or "unwilling" as appropriate and give your reasons for not answering.

5. I have deleted (in whole or in part) the paragraph(s) numbered .... above, since I am **unable/unwilling** to reply to the relevant questions of the questionnaire for the following reasons:–

See paragraph 25 of the guidance

Signature of respondent ....

Date ....

APPENDIX

NOTES ON THE SCOPE OF THE RACE RELATIONS ACT 1976

Definitions of discrimination

1 The different kinds of discrimination covered by the Act are summarised below (the references in the margin are to the relevant paragraphs in the **Guide to the Race Relations Act 1976**).

2.3 Direct discrimination arises where a person is treated
to less favourably than another is (or would be) treated
2.7 because of his (or someone else's) colour, race, nationality (including citizenship) or ethnic or national origins.

Indirect discrimination arises where a person is treated unfavourably because he cannot comply with a condition or requirement which

(a) is (or would be) applied regardless of colour, race, nationality (including citizenship) or ethnic or national origins, and

(b) is such that the proportion of persons of a particular racial group (ie one defined by reference to colour, race, nationality (including citizenship) or ethnic or national origins) who can comply with it is considerably smaller than the proportion of persons not of that group who can comply with it, and

(c) is to the detriment of the person in question because he cannot comply with it, and

(d) is such that the person applying it cannot show that it is justifiable, regardless of the colour, race, nationality (including citizenship) or ethnic or national origins of the person to whom it is applied.

2.8 **Victimisation** arises where a person is treated less
and favourably than other persons are (or would be) treated
2.9 because that person has done (or intends to do or is suspected of having done or itnending to do) any of the following:–

(a) brought proceedings under the Act; or

(b) given evidence or information in connection with proceedings brought under the Act; or

(c) done anything else by reference to the Act (eg given information to the Commission for Racial Equality); or

(d) made an allegation that someone acted unlawfully under the Act.

Victimisation does not, however, occur where the reason for the less favourable treatment is an allegation which was false and not made in good faith.

Unlawful discrimination

2 The provisions of the Act which make discrimination unlawful are indicated in the table on the next page. Complaints about discrimination which is unlawful under the provisions in Group A (the employment provisions) must be made to an industrial tribunal. For detailed information about these provisions see chapter 3 of the Guide. Complaints about discrimination which is unlawful under the provisions in Group B must be made to a county court or, in Scotland, a sheriff court. For detailed information about these provisions see chapters 4 and 5 of the Guide.

Exceptions

3 Details of exceptions to the requirements of the Act not to discriminate may be found in the **Guide**. The exceptions applying only to the employment field are described in chapter 3; those applying only to the educational field, in chapter 4; and those applying only to the provision of goods, facilities and services and premises, in chapter 5. General exceptions are described in chapter 7.

PROVISIONS OF THE SEX DISCRIMINATION ACT WHICH MAKE DISCRIMINATION UNLAWFUL

	Section of Act	Paragraphs of Guide
GROUP A		
Discrimination by employers in recruitment and treatment of employees	4	3.4–3.16
Discrimination against contract workers	7	3.17
Discrimination against partners	10	3.20
Discrimination by trade unions, employers' associations etc	11	3.21
Discrimination by bodies which confer qualifications or authorisations needed for particular kinds of jobs	12	3.22
Discrimination in the provision of training by industrial training boards, the Manpower Services Commission, the Employment Service Agency, the Training Services Agency and certain other vocational training bodies	13	3.24, 3.25
Discrimination by employment agencies	14	3.26
Discrimination by the Manpower Services Commission, the Employment Service Agency and the Training Services Agency other than in vocational training or employment agency services	15	3.29
GROUP B		
Discrimination by bodies in charge of educational establishments	17	4.2–4.5
Discrimination (other than that covered by section 22) by local education authorities	18	4.6–4.7
Discrimination in the provision of goods, facilities or services to the public or a section of the public	20	5.2–5.5, 5.8–5.10
Discrimination in the disposal of premises	21	5.4–5.6
Discrimination by landlords against prospective assignees or sublessees	24	5.7
Discrimination by clubs or associations with 25 or more members (other than clubs or associations covered by sections 11 or 20).	25	5.11–5.13

(I) List of statutory rights and relevant qualifying periods/time limits for claim

Statutory right/claim	*Qualifying period*	*Relevant time limit for industrial tribunal complaint*
Unfair dismissal		
1 Unfair dismissal. ERA, Part X	2 years (A)	3 months from the effective date of termination of employment.
2 Unfair dismissal arising from failure to offer re-engagement in circumstances where dismissal is connected with industrial action. (TULR(C)A, s 239(2))	2 years (A)	6 months from the date of the employee's dismissal.
3 Unfair dismissal for a reason connected with medical suspension. (ERA, s 108(2))	1 month (A)	3 months from the effective date of termination of employment.
Written reasons for dismissal		
4 Written reasons for dismissal. (ERA, s 92)	2 years (B)	3 months from the effective date of termination of employment.

NOTE:

(A) In case of all these time limits for complaint, an industrial tribunal may extend the time limit where it considers it was not 'reasonably practicable' to present the claim within the time limit.
(B) There is no qualifying period where the dismissal takes place whilst the employee is pregnant or taking maternity leave.

Statutory right/claim	*Qualifying period*	*Relevant time limit for industrial tribunal complaint*
TRANSFER OF UNDERTAKINGS		
1 Failure to inform or con sult regarding transfer in accordance with reg 11 of the Transfer of Undertakings (Protection of Employment) Regulations 1981.	None	3 months from the date of the relevant transfer is completed.
2 Unfair dismissal arising from the transfer of the undertaking (reg 8 of the Transfer of Undertakings (Protection of Employment) Regulations 1981).	2 years	3 months from the effective date of termination of employment.

NOTE:

(A) The 3 month period in relation to unfair dismissal may be extended by an industrial tribunal if it considers it was not 'reasonably practicable' to present the claim within the time limit.
(B) Where an employer fails to pay compensation ordered by an industrial tribunal pursuant to reg 11 as a consequence of the employer failing to inform/consult with a recognised trade union or an employee representative, an individual employee has 3 months from the date of the industrial tribunal's order in which to lodge a complaint.

ERA, PART II		
Unlawful deduction from wages. (ss 13 to 26)	None	3 months from the date of deduction of the date payment received by employer.

NOTE:

An industrial tribunal can extend this time limit where they consider it was not 'reasonably practicable' to present the claim within the time limit.

STATUTORY SICK PAY		
Any question arising entitling an employee to SSP.	N/A	Reference by an employee to the adjudication officer should normally be made within 6 months of the earliest day in respect of which there is a dispute.

Statutory right/claim	*Qualifying period*	*Relevant time limit for industrial tribunal complaint*
MATERNITY		
1 Right to return to work. (ERA, Part VIII)	2 years	3 months from the notified day of return.
2 Time off for ante-natal care. (ERA, ss 55 to 57)	N/A	3 months from the date of the relevant appointment.
3 Unfair dismissal by reason of pregnancy or taking maternity leave. (ERA, s 99)	None	3 months from the effective date of terminaton of the employment.

NOTE:

For 2 and 3, an industrial tribunal can extend the time limit where they consider that it was not 'reasonably practicable' to present the claim within the time limit.

GUARANTEE PAYMENTS		
Guarantee pay. (ERA, ss 28 to 35)	1 month	3 months from the date in respect of which payment is claimed.

NOTE:

An industrial tribunal can extend the time limit where they consider it was not 'reasonably practicable' to present the claim within the time limit.

MEDICAL SUSPENSION		
Medical suspension pay. (ERA, ss 64, 65)	1 month	3 months from the date for which remuneration is claimed.

NOTE:

An industrial tribunal can extend the time limit where they consider it was not 'reasonably practicable' to present the claim within the time limit.

TIME OFF FOR TRADE UNION REASONS		
1 Time off for trade union duties. (TULR(C)A, s 168)	None	3 months from the date of the employers' failure to give time off or to pay remuneration.
2 Time off for union activities. (TULR(C)A, s 170)	None	3 months from date of failure to grant time off.

Statutory right/claim	*Qualifying period*	*Relevant time limit for industrial tribunal complaint*

NOTE:

An industrial tribunal can extend the time limit where they consider it was not 'reasonably practicable' to present the claim within the time limit.

TIME OFF FOR PUBLIC DUTIES

Time off for attending to public duties. (ERA, ss 50, 51)	None	3 months from the date of the employers' failure to give time off or to pay remuneration.

NOTE:

An industrial tribunal can extend the time limit where they consider it was not 'reasonably practicable' to present the claim within the time limit.

INSOLVENCY

Claims on insolvency of employer. (ERA, Part XII)	None although extensive rights dependent upon length of employment	3 months from the date on which employment terminated.

VICTIMISATION AND UNION MEMBERSHIP

1 Unfair dismissal for 'trade union' reason. (TULR(C)A, s 152)	None	3 months from the effective date of termination of employment.
2 Action short of dismissal. (TULR(C)A, ss 146–154)	None	3 months from the date of the last action which is the subject of the claim.
3 Unreasonable exclusion/expulsion from the trade union. (TULR(C)A, s 175)	None	6 months from the date of exclusion or expulsion.

NOTE:

(A) In the case of 1, 2 and 3, the industrial tribunal can extend the time limit where they consider it was not 'reasonably practicable' to present the claim within the time limit.

(B) In the case of 1, interim relief may be claimed under TULR(C)A, s 161, and the time limit here is 7 days from the effective date of termination of employment. In the case of 3, application for compensation after a successful claim may be made not less than 4 weeks but not more than 6 months from the date of the industrial tribunal's decision and the same period applies in the case of a successful claim in respect of unjustifiable discipline by a trade union.

Statutory right/claim	*Qualifying period*	*Relevant time limit for industrial tribunal complaint*
REDUNDANCY		
1 Redundancy payment. (ERA, Part XI)	2 years (although note no service before the age of 18 counts)	6 months from the 'relevant date' although the industrial tribunal may extend this where considered 'just and equitable'.
2 Consultation with recognised trade union(s) regarding proposed redundancies (TULR(C)A, Part IV, Chapter II)	N/A	Prior to dismissal or within 3 months from the date on which the dismissal is effective.
3 Failure by the employer to pay remuneration pursuant to protective award. (TULR(C)A, Part IV, Chapter II)	None	3 months from the last date in respect of which a complaint was made.
4 Time off to look for alternative work. (ERA, ss 52, 53)	2 years (counted up to the expiry of the notice period in respect of the redundancy)	3 months commencing with the day in respect of which time off is refused.
5 Dismissal on ground of redundancy which is automatically unfair. (ERA, s 105 and TULR(C)A, s 153)	2 years	3 months commencing with the effective date of termination of employment.

NOTE:

(A) With the exception of 1, an industrial tribunal can extend the time limit where they consider it was not 'reasonably practicable' to present the complaint in time.
(B) Civil servants and others to whom the separate arrangements in respect of redundancy apply (ss 159 and 164 of the ERA) may bring a claim before an industrial tribunal under s 177 and in such circumstances the normal 6 month limitation period for redundancy claims does not apply leaving the reference subject only to the ordinary limitation period of 6 years.

Statutory right/claim	*Qualifying period*	*Relevant time limit for industrial tribunal complaint*
DISCRIMINATION		
1 Sex discrimination claim. (SDA, Parts I, II and VII)	None	3 months from the date of the act complained of although an industrial tribunal may extend the time limit where they consider it 'just and equitable' and the nature of the complaint may be that it is, in effect, a continuing discriminatory act.
2 Sex discrimination claim pursuant to EEC legislation. (Equal Treatment Directive 76/207, Art 5)	None	None.
3 Race discrimination claim. (RRA, Parts I, II and VIII)	None	3 months from the date of the act complained of although an industrial tribunal may extend the time limit where they consider it 'just and equitable' and the nature of the complaint may be that it is in effect a continuing discriminatory act.
4 Equal pay claim. (EqPA)	None	At any time during employment or 6 months commencing with the date on which the employment terminated, per EAT in *Etherson v Strathclyde Regional Council* [1992] IRLR 392 to be preferred to *British Railways Board v Poole* [1988] IRLR 20, EAT which stated there was no time limit.
5 Equal pay/value claim under EEC legislation. (Treaty of Rome, Art 119 and Equal Pay Directive 75/117, Art 1)	None	None.

Statutory right/claim	*Qualifying period*	*Relevant time limit for industrial tribunal complaint*
ITEMISED PAY STATEMENT		
Failure to provide itemised pay statement. (ERA, ss 8 to 12)	None	At any time during employment or 3 months commencing with the date on which employment terminated.

NOTE:

In order to qualify, the employee must have worked at least 8 hours per week save where less than 20 are employed in which event the employee must work 16 hours per week or more than 8 but less than 16 hours per week for 5 years. An industrial tribunal can extend the time limit where it was not 'reasonably practicable' for the claim to be presented within the 3 month time limit.

Statutory right/claim	*Qualifying period*	*Relevant time limit for industrial tribunal complaint*
WRITTEN PARTICULARS OF EMPLOYMENT		
Failure to provide written particulars of employment. (ERA, ss 1 to 7)	1 month	At any time during employment or 3 months from the date on which employment terminates.

NOTE:

An industrial tribunal can extend the time limit where it was not 'reasonably practicable' for the claim to be presented within the time limit.

Statutory right/claim	*Qualifying period*	*Relevant time limit for industrial tribunal complaint*
EMPLOYMENT PROTECTION IN HEALTH AND SAFETY CASES		
1 Right not to be subjected to detriment on grounds of activities in connection with preventing or reducing risks to health and safety at work or performing functions of a health and safety representative or safety committee member (ERA, s 44).	None	3 months from the date of the act complained of.
2 Right not to be dismissed or selected for redundancy in relation to 1 above (ERA, s 100, s 105)	None	3 months.

Statutory right/claim	*Qualifying period*	*Relevant time limit for industrial tribunal complaint*
3 Right not to have action (including dismissal) taken against the employee for bringing circumstances believed to be harmful to health and safety to the employer's attention, leaving the place of work in the face of serious and imminent danger or taking steps to protect him or herself or others in such circumstances (ERA, s 44, s 100)	None	3 months from the date of the act complained of or dismissal.

NOTE:

An industrial tribunal can extend the time limit where it was not 'reasonably practicable' for the claim to be presented within the time limit.

DISMISSAL FOR ASSERTING A STATUTORY RIGHT

Dismissal for asserting statutory rights conferred by the ERA or where the remedy is by means of an application to the industrial tribunal; the right to minimum notice under ERA, s 86 and rights under TULR(C)A, ss 68, 86, 146, 168, 189 and 170 (individual rights related to trade unions—deductions from pay, union activities and time off).	None	3 months from the date of dismissal.

NOTE:

An industrial tribunal can extend the time limit where it was not 'reasonably practicable' for the claim to be presented within the time limit.

Index